OXFORD DICTIONARY OF
Phrase, Saying, and Quotation

OXFORD DICTIONARY OF

Phrase, Saying, and Quotation

THIRD EDITION

Edited by Susan Ratcliffe

OXFORD
UNIVERSITY PRESS

OXFORD
UNIVERSITY PRESS

Great Clarendon Street, Oxford OX2 6DP

Oxford University Press is a department of the University of Oxford.

It furthers the University's objective of excellence in research, scholarship,
and education by publishing worldwide in

Oxford New York

Auckland Bangkok Dar es Salaam Hong Kong Karachi
Kuala Lumpur Madrid Melbourne Mexico City Nairobi
New Delhi Shanghai Taipei Toronto

With offices in

Argentina Austria Brazil Chile Czech Republic France Greece
Guatemala Hungary Italy Japan Poland Portugal Singapore
South Korea Switzerland Thailand Turkey Ukraine Vietnam

First edition published 1997
Second edition published 2002
Third edition published 2006

British Library Cataloguing in Publication Data
Data available

Library of Congress Cataloging in Publication Data
Data available

Typeset in Stone and Rococo
by Interactive Sciences Ltd
Printed in Great Britain by
Clays Ltd, St Ives plc

ISBN 0–19–280650–5   ISBN 978–019–280650–5

1 3 5 7 9 10 8 6 4 2

Contents

⤙ Preface to the Third Edition ⤚

THE *Oxford Dictionary of Phrase, Saying, and Quotation* is a unique reference book which explores the links between quotations, which are essentially the words of a single individual, and those sayings and phrases which have become part of the common wisdom. Many new items have been added to this third edition, some newly minted, and others older but still current.

With the increasingly international nature of the *global village* (see **The Earth**), it is no longer the case that English-speakers refer only to proverbs or sayings of English origin. We have therefore used the Oxford English Corpus, a database of examples of English speech and writing, to identify proverbs originating from other languages and cultures which are being quoted in English today. Sometimes these proverbs have an obvious English parallel, such as the Japanese proverb *Poke a bush, a snake comes out*, which has clear affinities with *Let sleeping dogs lie*. The Indian saying *One who cannot dance blames the uneven floor* echoes the English proverb *A bad workman blames his tools*. In these cases the non-English version may simply be used to add colour or variety. But in other instances, such as another Japanese proverb *The nail that sticks up is certain to be hammered down*, there may be no close equivalent in English, and the borrowed expression is filling a real gap in the language. Indeed, there may even be a temptation to extend the concept: in the *New York Times* of 4 November 2005 we find 'There is a techie adage that goes like this: In China or Japan the nail that stands up gets hammered, while in Silicon Valley the nail that stands up drives a Ferrari and has stock options'.

Sometimes similar thoughts are borrowed from more than one culture. Thus we find both the African proverb *When spider webs unite, they can tie up a lion*, and the Maori saying *With your food basket, and with my food basket, the guest will have enough* at **Cooperation**. Likewise, the modern English saying *History is written by the victors* expresses a similar idea to the African proverb *Until the lions produce their own historian, the story of the hunt will glorify the hunter*. More recent sayings may also be borrowed, such as the Russian maxims *We pretend to work, and they pretend to pay us*, and *The less you know, the better you sleep*, which date from the Soviet era.

As in previous editions, one of the major themes of this book is the link between the phrases, sayings, and quotations. Thus, one widely quoted saying, *May you live in interesting times*, is said to derive from a traditional Chinese curse, but it has so far proved impossible to trace any original. However, an early reference to it is found in the 'ripple of hope' speech by the American politician Robert Kennedy, and a cross reference directs to this. Another quote from the same speech, referring to the 'ripple of hope', is to be found at **Idealism**. The early twentieth-century labour movement slogan *bread and roses*, summarizing the right to food for both mind and body, links to a contemporary song at **Human Rights**, and to a Middle Eastern proverb *If you have two coins, use one to buy bread, the other to buy hyacinths* at **Lifestyles**. The Russian proverb *Test before you trust* was taken up by Ronald Reagan in the form 'Trust but verify', and both are to be found under **Trust and Treachery**. Indeed, the whole area of politics is particularly fruitful in giving currency to new sayings. Thus, the Kurdish proverb *We have no friends but the mountains* has become widely quoted since the invasion of Iraq.

Regions which today are thought of as English-speaking have also contributed their share of local sayings. Some, such as the Australian *You have two chances, Buckley's and none* or *Rooster today, feather duster tomorrow* derive from the immigrant culture, while others, such as the Maori *The kumara does not speak of its own sweetness* have been inherited from the original inhabitants. Sometimes a change of focus is needed: to an English outlook, the Welsh proverb *More than one yew bow in Chester*, meaning that you may escape danger once, but not a second time, may appear opaque. But the reflection that Cheshire was once noted for its archers, and that in this instance Chester represents a natural enemy makes all clear. Sayings said to be of native American origin are particularly prominent in environmental contexts, summed up by *We do not inherit the earth from our parents, we borrow it from our children.*

New phrases include some arising directly from current events, such as *coalition of the willing*, and others which, while brought into prominence today, have a much longer history, such as *win hearts and minds* at **Opinion**, currently being applied to Iraq, but referred to by Theodore Roosevelt in 1906 under **Speeches**, and ultimately deriving, like so many others, from the Bible, at **Peace**. The phrase *throw someone to the lions* also has a long story: the saying *The Christians to the lions* is reported by Tertullian as early as the second century AD. Other phrases dating back many years include *road to Damascus* and *smell of the lamp*. Recent newcomers range from **Fashion** (*the new black*) and **Technology** (*grey goo*) to **Warfare** (*shock and awe*) and **Achievement** (*low-hanging fruit*).

The quotations included under each theme have been revised and updated, taking advantage of the Oxford Quotations reading programme, which continuously monitors current usage. Classic writers such as Robert Louis Stevenson 'If your morals make you dreary, depend upon it, they are wrong' and Euripides 'Mere cleverness is not wisdom' appear alongside modern scientists such as Alan Kay 'The best way to predict the future is to invent it'. Sometimes the most improbable combinations can be found: it was a delight to verify Martin Luther's picturesque view of the resurrection 'There will be little dogs, with golden hair, shining like precious stones'. And quotations can be found unexpectedly: a reference in a sermon by the politician Tony Benn in New College Chapel led to the discovery of Lao Tzu on **Leadership** '. . . when the work is done the people say "We did it ourselves"'.

As in all dictionaries of quotations, many and varied voices crowd around. Here you can find Jacques Chirac's unfavourable opinion of British cuisine, Mother Teresa on yesterday, tomorrow, and today, and the philosopher Bertrand Russell on **Gossip**: 'No one gossips about other people's secret virtues'. The writer J. K. Rowling compares **Poverty** to childbirth, the actress Halle Berry reflects on **Beauty**, and Aristophanes points out that 'You will never make a crab walk straight'. Whether phrase, saying, or quotation, here indeed is the place to find 'What oft was said, but ne'er so well expressed'.

Acknowledgements

I should like to thank all those involved in the preparation of this new edition, particularly Ralph Bates for library research, Jean Harker and Verity Mason for contributions to the Quotations reading programme, and Susanne Charlett for data capture. Particular thanks are due to James McCracken, Project Manager, English Dictionaries, for adapting the Oxford English Corpus software to search for international proverbs, and to the following who answered some of our endless queries on them: Ahmed Al-Shahi, Dianne Bardsley, Patience Chou, Richard Harms, Yuki Kissick, Yung-keung Lau, John Macalister, Bruce Moore, Shu-Ching Naughton, Natalia Pierce, Terence Ranger, and Jameela Siddiqi. I should also like to thank Elizabeth Knowles, Publishing Manager of Oxford Quotations Dictionaries and editor of the first edition of this book, who has been an invaluable source of advice and ideas at all times.

SUSAN RATCLIFFE

Oxford 2005

Preface to the Second Edition

As EDMUND BURKE tells us, 'Nothing in progression can rest in its original plan. We may as well think of rocking a grown man in the cradle of an infant'. The *Oxford Dictionary of Phrase, Saying, and Quotation* is a unique reference book which provides a means of access to aspects of our language more commonly separated, emphasising the links between individual remarks and fixed phrases and sayings. In this second edition we have focused more particularly on those links, adding new material and in many instances giving more detailed information on existing items.

Where sufficient fresh material has been available, new themes have been added. Topics such as **Computers and the Internet** ('The PC is the LSD of the '90's'), **Farming**, **Health and Fitness** ('Exercise is bunk'), **Management**, **The Paranormal** (*It's life, Jim, but not as we know it*), and **Photography** ('a moment of embarrassment and a lifetime of pleasure') make an appearance. In all themes, the order of the sections now reflects the importance of the phrases and sayings which distinguish this book from more conventional dictionaries of quotations.

Proverbs and sayings, which now appear at the beginning of each theme, have been enhanced by the introduction of many more modern sayings which have passed into the language, including advertising slogans such as . . .*But I know a man who can*, television catchphrases (*The truth is out there*), political sayings (*Don't ask, don't tell*), and even video games (*All your base are belong to us*). At the same time, more traditional sayings which still have a modern resonance have been added: *It is easier to build two chimneys than to maintain one* seems as true today as in the 16th century. Some modern sayings which sound ancient can indeed be traced back to much earlier forms: *I cried because I had no shoes, until I met a man who had no feet* derives from the 13th century Persian poet Sadi.

The information given on the proverbs and sayings has been greatly expanded. Glosses have been added to all but the clearest, explaining archaic or unusual usages or words, and indicating the circumstances in which the saying may be used. The historical aspect of the dictionary has been enhanced by adding an approximate date of first record for the proverbs (mid 17th century, early 19th century), though the reader should bear in mind that the proverb may well have been current long before, and indeed in many cases this first written appearance is of the form 'as has often been said'.

The phrase sections have been more closely linked to the rest of the book, by concentrating on phrases related to sayings or quotations, or with a history of some kind, and removing transparent idioms. So *like as two peas* has no story behind it, and has been removed, but *true blue* and *the Red Queen hypothesis*, which have interesting origins and links to quotations, have been added. We have been able to draw on the results of the reading programme for the *Oxford English Dictionary*, and this has brought to light many new items: modern sayings such as *Three strikes and you're out*, and older ones such as *Who goes home?*, old phrases such as *a poisoned chalice*, new ones such as *the triple-witching hour*, and others from all over the English-speaking world: *Buckley's chance* and *stolen generation* from Australia, *Big Blue Machine* from Canada, *watchful waiting* and *bully pulpit* from the United States, and *Jedburgh justice* from Scotland.

The quotations sections have been extensively revised. The ongoing reading programme of Oxford Quotations Dictionaries has been of great assistance here, monitoring the arrival of new quotations and the re-emergence of old ones. Thus non-Western cultures are more widely represented: in **Education** Confucius tells us 'In education there should be no class distinction', and in **Duty and Responsibility** the Bhagavadgita says 'And do thy duty, even if it be humble, rather than another's, even if it be great. To die in one's duty is life: to live in another's is death'. More material of historical interest has been included (for example the Declaration of Arbroath under **Scotland**, James Cook's views of the inhabitants of **Australia**, and Lord Reith's 1926 view of standards in **Broadcasting**), and there are still many new quotations from the past to re-discover. Recent wars have revived Helmuth von Moltke's 'No plan survives first contact with the enemy' (and the medieval concept of a *just war*), while modern science is still unsure whether to agree with Plato that 'God is always doing geometry', and a recent Chancellor of the Exchequer has quoted Colbert, Louis XIV's Finance Minister, on **Taxes**: 'The art of taxation consists in so plucking the goose as to obtain the largest possible amount of feathers with the smallest possible amount of hissing'. More recent quotations include the science-fiction writer Arthur C. Clarke on the millennium at **Festivals and Celebrations**, actress Julia Roberts on **Fame**, and US politician Donald Rumsfeld's advice on **Advice**.

The new additions range from the traditional maxim to the current soundbite, from the flippant to the philosophical, and from the moral to the subversive. So **Murder** now includes James Bond's *licensed to kill*, the Koran's 'Whoso slays a soul not to retaliate for a soul slain, nor for corruption done in the land, shall be as if he had slain mankind altogether', and the poisoner Thomas Griffiths Wainewright's justification for his crime 'She had very thick ankles'. **Excellence and Mediocrity** begins with the sixteenth century Latin saying *Corruptio optimi pessima* [*Corruption of the best becomes the worst*], and ends with George W. Bush's encouraging words 'And to the C students, I say you, too, can be president of the United States'. In **Quantities and Qualities**, the astronomer Patrick Moore considers infinity, while the theologian St Augustine discusses the number six, and the traditional saying *The whole is more than the sum of the parts* is related to Aristotle's thoughts on the subject in **Causes and Consequences**.

While more than 20% of this second edition is new, and extensive material has been added to the existing sayings and phrases, any such book must inevitably depend very heavily on all the work done for the previous edition, and I should like to acknowledge that. Likewise, I am grateful to the many people who have contributed to the current text in various ways. In particular, my thanks go to Elizabeth Knowles, editor of the first edition and Managing Editor of Oxford Quotations Dictionaries, for her practical assistance in matters lexical and her manifold ideas and encouragement while editing this book. Working on such a varied and wide-ranging text has been fascinating and enlightening, and I hope the reader will find it equally interesting.

SUSAN RATCLIFFE

Oxford, 2002

⤍ Introduction to First Edition ⤏

THE *Oxford Dictionary of Phrase, Saying, and Quotation* opens up an overall view of the central stock of our figurative language, by bringing together over 10,000 quotations, proverbs, and phrases, in a structure which at once allows access to individual items, and expresses the essential relationship between them.

Traditionally, dictionaries covering this aspect of the language have focused on the difference between the given categories. A dictionary of quotations, for example, is likely to establish its selection criteria on the definition of a quotation as 'a passage or remark quoted'; that is, a reference to something said by a particular person at a particular time. Such a definition by implication excludes the proverb, which we may define as 'a short pithy saying . . . held to embody a general truth', and the phrase 'a group of words (not a sentence) with a particular meaning'. However, even as we describe these categories, we are likely to think of exceptions to the rule. The most established proverbs, after all, come from the Old Testament book of *Proverbs*, and may thus be regarded as forming part of the wide range of biblical quotations. To take one verse as an example:

> Hope deferred maketh the heart sick: but when the desire cometh it is a tree of life.

This is a quotation; we derive from it the saying *Hope deferred makes the heart sick*, to set with other proverbial expressions about hope. One of these, recorded from the eighteenth century, is the comment (now often used ironically) *Hope springs eternal*, the source of which is a quotation from Pope's *Essay on Man*:

> Hope springs eternal in the human breast.
> Man never Is, but always To be blest.

The essential difference between a quotation and a proverb or saying is that a quotation is seen as something traceable back to a single utterance at a given instance (whether or not the precise time and place can now be identified); a proverb or saying embodies an essential truth, and as such is by implication capable of being coined by different people at different times. But it is also clear from these examples that there is a considerable degree of overlap, and that one can derive from the other.

It might be thought easier to make the case for confining phrases to a separate dictionary, but as soon as we begin looking at examples, the connection with the other two categories becomes clear. If we compare an unbreakable rule to *the law of the Medes and the Persians*, or say of an ominous sign that it is *the writing on the wall*, we are quoting directly from the biblical story in the Old Testament book of *Daniel* of Belshazzar's feast and the fall of Babylon. If we express the utter completeness of a loss in the words *at one fell swoop*, we are quoting Shakespeare, and if a cat catches a bird and we exclaim *Nature red in tooth and claw*, we are quoting Tennyson. The phrase deriving from the quotation is likely to have become so familiar that knowledge of its origin is submerged, but the links are there, and in this dictionary they can be seen. The links between proverbs and phrases can be even clearer, as in the relationship between *It is the last straw that breaks the camel's back* and *the final straw*.

With material brought together in this way, the reader need not feel that the item about which information is wanted has been excluded because of how it is regarded. You do not need to know whether *Dogs bark, but the caravan moves on* is a quotation or a proverb before looking for it here. Someone wanting an explanation of the term *weasel words* will be led by the keyword index to Theodore Roosevelt's explanation of the term in the quotations for **Language**. Approaching from another angle, someone looking for an apt or pithy association associated with a particular topic can turn to a specific section in search of *winged words*.

The interrelation between quotations, sayings, and phrases is best seen when considering items dealing with the same subject, and so this dictionary is arranged by theme. From **Absence** and **Achievement**, through **Broadcasting**, **Chance and Luck**, **Festivals and Celebrations**, **Government**, **Human Nature**, **Science**, **The Seasons**, and **Towns and Cities**, to **Youth**, the theme titles have been chosen to reflect as wide a range of subjects as possible, while most accurately representing the actual evidence. Classification of items is by subject rather than keyword; Montaigne's 'When I play with my cat, who knows whether she isn't amusing herself with me more than I am with her' (*Essais*, 1580) and the proverbial *A cat has nine lives* are properly found at **Cats**, but *A cat may look at a king* can be used in many contexts, and illustrates **Equality**.

Themes may bring together apparently disparate aspects of a single topic. **Winning and Losing** offers views of competition in a variety of fields. 'One more such victory and we are lost', said Pyrrhus of his costly defeat of the Romans at Asculum in 279 BC, a comment which gives us the phrase *Pyrrhic victory*. 'What is our aim? . . . Victory, victory at all costs . . . for without victory there is no survival', asserted Winston Churchill in 1940. 'What's lost upon the roundabouts we pulls up on the swings', said Patrick Chalmers in 1912, using the fairground metaphor expressed in the proverb *What you lose on the swings you gain on the roundabouts*. The world of sport offers different perspectives on the same theme. 'When in doubt, win the trick' is advice attributed to Edmond Hoyle; Pierre de Coubertin, establishing the modern Olympic Games, put forward the view that 'The important thing in life is not the victory but the contest; the essential thing is not to have won but to have fought well.' This statement of the ideals of amateurism can be set against the golfer Nick Faldo's 1996 assessment of the situation when leading a championship field in wet weather, 'Of course I want to win it . . . I'm not here to have a good time, nor to keep warm and dry.'

Quotations are the heart of the book, as they are at the centre of this overview of language: the standard movement is from quotation to proverb and phrase. (Although at times a quotation may make deliberate allusion to a known saying. *Don't put all your eggs in one basket* is traditional advice—modified by Mark Twain in *Pudd'nhead Wilson* (1894) to 'Put all your eggs in the one basket, and—WATCH THAT BASKET.') Each section, therefore, opens with quotations which are chronologically arranged, a pattern which allows us to hear the different voices speak over the centuries. 'A venal city ripe to perish, if a buyer can be found' said Sallust of Rome in the first century BC. 'All these men have their price', said Robert Walpole, of fellow-parliamentarians in the eighteenth century. 'Youth's a stuff will not endure', said William Shakespeare in 1601. Nearly 400 years later, we have Mary Quant's comment on the early stages of life, 'Being young is greatly overestimated . . . Any failure seems so total. Later on you realize you can have another go.'

Quotations for each theme are supported and enhanced by two further sections, for the best-known and most interesting proverbs and phrases associated with that theme. (For ease of use, and as specific dates are less significant in these groups, items are arranged alphabetically: for further details, see the notes on How to Use the Dictionary.) Coverage is intentionally selective: items have been chosen for their intrinsic interest, with the aim of illuminating the stock of figurative language for a given subject.

Proverbial sayings can come from any area of life. *Evil communications corrupt good manners* was originally a warning from St Paul to the Corinthians about their unsatisfactory mode of life. *April showers bring forth May flowers* and *Rain before seven, shine before eleven* are among the traditional sayings of calendar and weather lore. *Your King and Country need you* comes from a World War I recruiting poster. Modern advertising has proved a fertile ground, with such items as *Go to work on an egg* and more recently the Victoria and Albert's controversial *An ace caff with quite a nice museum attached.* Catch-phrases also make their contribution, in a range including Monty Python's *And now for something completely different* and the Nixon administration's political assessment *It'll play in Peoria.*

As with quotations, it is possible to hear a variety of voices in the 'general truths' which the proverbs express. Conflicting advice, centuries apart, is offered at **Advertising**: if we accept that *Good wine needs no bush*, we are unlikely to believe that *It pays to advertise.* At **Appearance**, the traditional view *The cowl does not make the monk* can be set against the assertion from the world of computing, *What you see is what you get* (the origin of the term *wysiwyg*). On the other hand, at **Causes and Consequences**, the old and new speak with one voice, as *Good seed makes a good crop* is matched with the terse assessment, *Garbage in, garbage out.*

Phrases, like proverbs, come from many sources, from the most traditional to brand-new: we have already seen examples from the Bible and Shakespeare. Classical references include *apple of discord, a sop to Cerberus, sow dragons' teeth*, and *Trojan horse.* If we describe someone as behaving like a *dog in a manger* we are making an allusion to one of Aesop's fables; the expression *Open Sesame* for an apparently magical solution to an insoluble problem takes us back to the *Arabian Nights* and the story of Ali Baba and the Forty Thieves. Modern politics has given us *clear blue water* and *fudge and mudge.* Sometimes it is possible to guess that a phrase may be emerging. The source-note to Norman Lamont's upbeat statement 'The green shoots of economic spring are appearing once again' points out that this is often quoted as 'The green shoots of recovery'; it seems probable that *green shoots of revovery* will become an established allusive phrase.

Different allusions to the same story may take us far from the original. One of the phrases at **Sleep** is the punning *the land of Nod*, a reference to the desolate land, 'east of Eden', given to Cain after the murder of Abel. 'I am rather inclined to believe that this is the land God gave to Cain,' said the sixteenth century explorer Jacques Cartier, on discovering the bleak northern shore of Labrador (see **Canada**). At **Order and Chaos**, we find the expression *raise Cain.*

It is, however, the interrelation between so many of the individual items which gives this book its particular identity. We may take as one example, the assessment made by Lord Randolph Churchill of the Irish political situation in 1886: 'I decided some time ago that if the G.O.M. [Gladstone] went for Home Rule, the Orange card would be the one to play.' *Play the —card*, deriving from this, has long been an established phrase, but both quotation and phrase were given a new twist by Robert Shapiro's assessment of the defence's conduct of the O. J. Simpson trial in 1995: 'Not only did we play the race card, we played it from the bottom of the deck.' These three items, quotation, phrase, and quotation, are included respectively at their appropriate themes; cross-references allow the reader to follow up the links between them.

Allusions are part of our linguistic stock-in-trade, and this dictionary allows the reader to find examples of both modification and source. ' "The question is," said Humpty-Dumpty, "whish is to be master—that's all." ' This passage from Lewis Carroll's *Through the Looking-Glass* (1872) was quoted by the Labour politician Hartley Shawcross in a speech in the House of Commons in 1946, often summarized in the statement, 'We are the masters now'. The theme for **Power** finds room for both these items, and gives the reader explicit links between them.

It has been an object to provide explanations where these are helpful, and where the further material will be of interest to the reader. As the source-notes for quotations provide background information where this is illuminating, the source-notes for proverbs and phrases clarify words and references which may now be obscure or misleading; for example, the original meaning of *Do not spoil the ship for a ha'porth of tar*, and the comparison originally drawn in the phrase *like the clappers*.

'Figurative language' is a broad term, and inevitably some exclusions have been made. We have not treated direct allusions, although allusive references are properly here: there is no entry for *Judas*, but his identity is explained in the source-note for *Judas kiss*. We have avoided the strictly encyclopedic, although again the information is given where needed: the source-note to the phrase *eighth wonder of the world* explains the reference to the Seven Wonders of the ancient world. Slang as a category is regarded as generally outside the remit of this book, although there are exceptions: *couch potato* was felt to claim a place. We have sought to be consistent rather than rigid, while believing that the nature of the material makes some inconsistency inevitable. It is also inevitable that the creation of this text will render apparent gaps which were invisible before the book existed. We look forward to adding to the stock of material that we have brought together; meanwhile we hope that the text in its current state will allow the reader to share our pleasure and interest in watching the interplay of quotations, proverbs, and phrases.

ELIZABETH KNOWLES

Oxford, January 1997

⤞ How to Use the Dictionary ⤝

THE sequence of entries is by alphabetical order of themes, from **Ability** and **Absence** to **Writing** and **Youth**. Theme titles have been chosen to reflect as wide a range of subjects as possible, and related topics may be covered by a single theme, for example **Apology and Excuses** and **Ways and Means**. Linked opposites may also be grouped in a single antithetical theme, such as **Heaven and Hell**, **Trust and Treachery**, and **Winning and Losing**. A cross-reference from the second element of the pair, for example '**Losing** *see* Winning and Losing', appears in its appropriate place in the alphabetic sequence both in the main text and in the **List of Themes**.

Where themes are closely related, 'see also' references are given immediately following the theme title. The heading **Belief** is thus followed by the direction 'see also **Certainty and Doubt, Faith**', and **Danger** by 'see also **Caution, Courage**'.

Each theme may have up to three subdivisions: PROVERBS AND SAYINGS, PHRASES, and QUOTATIONS. In each of the first two of these items are ordered alphabetically, but with initial 'A' and 'The' ignored. Each saying appears in bold. Where the saying is proverbial, a note of the area of origin is given, and for English proverbs the period when first found in written form (late 15th century, mid 18th century) is added. Where the saying has a more precise origin, such as an advertising slogan or a television catchphrase, a more exact date may be given. Where helpful a gloss is provided to explain the origin and usage of the saying. Phrases also appear in bold, followed by a brief definition text, as in '**crowning glory** a woman's hair'. In most cases, a note on the origin (for example an explanation of *Herod* for the phrase **out-Herod Herod**') follows the definition.

The quotations are given in chronological order within each theme. Where possible, quotations are precisely dated, either by the composition date of a letter or diary or the publication of a book published in the author's lifetime, or by external circumstances, such as a contemporary comment on a specific event. When the date is uncertain or unknown, and the quotation cannot be related to a particular event, the author's date of death has been used to date the quotation. Each quotation is accompanied by the name of the author to whom it is attributed; dates of birth and death (where known) are also given. In general, the authors' names are given in the form by which they are best known, so that we have 'Saki' rather than 'H. H. Munro'. Bibliographical information as to the source from which the quotation is taken follows the author's name; titles and dates of publication are given, but full finding references are not. 'Attributed' is used to indicate that the attribution is generally accepted, but that a specific reference has not been traced.

Sayings, phrases, and quotations are numbered in a single sequence throughout each theme.

Cross-references are made between items in the same theme and to and from specific items in other themes. Cross-references between items in the same theme are expressed in the form 'see **12** above' or 'see **34** below'. Cross-references to specific items in other themes use a similar style, but identify the target theme: 'see **Excess 6**' or 'see **Marriage 38**'.

Index

The index provides the facility for finding individual sayings, phrases, and quotations by key word. Both the keywords and the entries following each keyword, including those in foreign languages, are in strict alphabetical order. Singular and plural nouns (with their possessive forms) are grouped separately.

References show the theme name, sometimes in a shortened form (**Festivals** for **Festivals and Celebrations**; **Seasons** for **The Seasons**) followed by the number of the item within the theme: **Science 7** therefore means the seventh item within the theme **Science**.

⇸⇸ List of themes ⇷⇷

A
⇸⇷⇷

Ability
Absence
Achievement
Acting
Action and Inaction
Administration
Adversity
Advertising
Advice
Africa
Alcohol
Ambition
America
American Cities and States
Anger
Animals
Apology and Excuses
Appearance
Architecture
Argument
The Armed Forces
The Arts
Arts and Sciences
Australia

B
⇸⇷⇷

Beauty
Beginning
Behaviour
Belief
The Bible
Biography
Birds
Birth *see Pregnancy and Birth*
The Body
Books
Boredom
Borrowing *see Debt and Borrowing*
Britain
British Towns and Regions

Broadcasting
Business
Buying and Selling

C
⇸⇷⇷

Canada
Capitalism and Communism
Cats
Causes and Consequences
Caution
Celebrations *see Festivals and Celebrations*
Censorship
Certainty and Doubt
Chance and Luck
Change
Chaos *see Order and Chaos*
Character
Charity
Child Care
Children
Choice
The Christian Church
Christmas
The Cinema
Circumstance and Situation
Cities *see Towns and Cities*
Civilization *see Culture and Civilization*
Class
Clergy
Communism *see Capitalism and Communism*
Computers and the Internet
Conformity
Conscience
Consequences *see Causes and Consequences*
Consolation *see Sympathy and Consolation*
Constancy and Inconstancy

Conversation
Cooking and Eating
Cooperation
Corruption
Countries and Peoples
The Country and the Town
Courage
Courtship
Creativity
Cricket
Crime and Punishment
Crises
Criticism
Cruelty
Culture and Civilization
Custom and Habit
Cynicism *see Disillusion and Cynicism*

D
⇸⇷⇷

Dance
Danger
Day and Night
Death
Debt and Borrowing
Deception
Deeds *see Words and Deeds*
Defiance
Delay *see Haste and Delay*
Democracy
Despair
Determination and Perseverance
Difference *see Similarity and Difference*
Diplomacy
Discontent *see Satisfaction and Discontent*
Discoveries *see Inventions and Discoveries*
Disillusion and Cynicism
Dislikes *see Likes and Dislikes*
Dogs

⤻ Ability ⤸

PROVERBS AND SAYINGS

1 . . . But I know a man who can.
advertising slogan for the Automobile Association

2 Horses for courses.
originally (in horse-racing) meaning that different horses are suited to different race-courses; now used more generally to mean that different people are suited to different roles; English proverb, late 19th century

3 If you can talk, you can sing, and if you can walk, you can dance.
African proverb (Shona)

4 Inside the forest there are many birds.
people are of many different kinds and abilities ('many birds' = 'birds of many kinds'); Chinese proverb

5 In the country of the blind the one eyed man is king.
someone of moderate ability will dominate those with none; English proverb, early 16th century

6 A sow may whistle, though it has an ill mouth for it.
someone not naturally suited to a task will perform it badly; English proverb, early 19th century

PHRASES

7 all-singing all dancing
with every possible attribute, able to perform any necessary function; a phrase applied particularly in the area of computer technology, but originally coming from descriptions of show business acts. The term may derive ultimately from a series of posters produced in 1929 to promote the new sound cinema such as that advertising the Hollywood musical *Broadway Melody*, which proclaimed the words *All talking All singing All dancing*

8 jack of all trades
a person who can do many different kinds of work; see **Excellence** 3

QUOTATIONS

9 *Non omnia possumus omnes.*
We can't all do everything.
Virgil 70–19 BC: *Eclogues*

10 Natural abilities are like natural plants, that need pruning by study.
Francis Bacon 1561–1626: *Essays* (1625) 'Of Studies'

11 If a man write a better book, preach a better sermon, or make a better mouse-trap than his neighbour, tho' he build his house in the woods, the world will make a beaten path to his door.
Ralph Waldo Emerson 1803–82: attributed to Emerson in Sarah S. B. Yule *Borrowings* (1889); Mrs Yule states in *The Docket* February 1912 that she copied this in her handbook from a lecture delivered by Emerson; the quotation was the occasion of a long controversy owing to Elbert Hubbard's claim to its authorship

12 This very remarkable man
Commends a most practical plan:
You can do what you want
If you don't think you can't,
So don't think you can't think you can.
Charles Inge 1868–1957: 'On Monsieur Coué' (1928); see **Medicine** 24

13 BETTER DROWNED THAN DUFFERS IF NOT DUFFERS WONT DROWN.
Arthur Ransome 1884–1967: *Swallows and Amazons* (1930)

14 Intelligence is quickness to apprehend as distinct from ability, which is capacity to act wisely on the thing apprehended.
Alfred North Whitehead 1861–1947: *Dialogues* (1954) 15 December 1939

15 I could have had class. I could have been a contender.
Budd Schulberg 1914– : *On the Waterfront* (1954 film); spoken by Marlon Brando

16 I'm usually called a jack of all trades by people who are scarcely jacks of one.
Jonathan Miller 1934– : in *Daily Telegraph* 24 December 1988; see **Excellence** 3

➤➤ Absence ◄◄

see also **Meeting and Parting**

PROVERBS AND SAYINGS

1 Absence is the mother of disillusion.
American proverb, mid 20th century

2 Absence makes the heart grow fonder.
affection for a person is strengthened by missing
them; English proverb, mid 19th century, 1st century
BC in Latin

**3 He who is absent is always in the
wrong.**
someone who is not present cannot defend
themselves from blame; English proverb, mid 15th
century

4 A little absence does much good.
American proverb, mid 20th century

5 Out of sight, out of mind.
someone who is not present is easily forgotten; see
10 below; English proverb, mid 13th century

6 Where were you in '62?
advertising slogan for the film *American Graffiti*
(1973)

PHRASES

7 gone with the wind
gone completely, disappeared without trace, from
Ernest Dowson (see **Memory** 15); subsequently
popularized by the title of Margaret Mitchell's novel
(1936) on the American Civil War

8 Hamlet without the Prince
a performance or event taking place without the
principal actor or central figure, from an account

given in the *Morning Post*, September 1775, of a
theatrical company in which the actor who was to
play the hero ran off with the innkeeper's daughter;
when the play was announced, the audience was
told 'the part of Hamlet to be left out, for that night'

QUOTATIONS

9 The Lord watch between me and thee, when
we are absent one from another.
Bible: Genesis

10 Today the man is here; tomorrow he is gone.
And when he is 'out of sight', quickly also is
he out of mind.
Thomas à Kempis 1380–1471: *De Imitatione
Christi*; see 5 above

11 Absence diminishes commonplace passions
and increases great ones, as the wind
extinguishes candles and kindles fire.
Duc de la Rochefoucauld 1613–80: *Maximes*
(1678)

12 I wish you could invent some means to
make me at all happy without you. Every
hour I am more and more concentrated in
you; every thing else tastes like chaff in my
mouth.
John Keats 1795–1821: letter to Fanny Brawne,
August 1820

13 *Partir c'est mourir un peu,
C'est mourir à ce qu'on aime:
On laisse un peu de soi-même
En toute heure et dans tout lieu.*

To go away is to die a little, it is to die to that
which one loves: everywhere and always,
one leaves behind a part of oneself.
Edmond Haraucourt 1856–1941: 'Rondel de
l'Adieu' (1891)

14 The more he looked inside the more Piglet
wasn't there.
A. A. Milne 1882–1956: *The House at Pooh Corner*
(1928)

15 The heart may think it knows better: the
senses know that absence blots people out.
We have really no absent friends.
Elizabeth Bowen 1899–1973: *Death of the Heart*
(1938)

16 When I came back to Dublin, I was
courtmartialled in my absence and
sentenced to death in my absence, so I said
they could shoot me in my absence.
Brendan Behan 1923–64: *Hostage* (1958)

17 Most of what matters in your life takes place
in your absence.
Salman Rushdie 1947– : *Midnight's Children*
(1981)

18 I wasn't even in the index.
on the omission of their affair from John Major's
autobiography
Edwina Currie 1946– :in *The Times* 28
September 2002

⤞ Achievement ⤝

see also **Ambition, Effort, Problems and Solutions, Success and Failure**

PROVERBS AND SAYINGS

1 Didn't she [*or* he *or* they] do well?
catchphrase used by Bruce Forsyth in 'The
Generation Game' on BBC Television, 1973 onwards

**2 The difficult is done at once, the
impossible takes a little longer.**
slogan of the US Armed Forces; recorded earlier as a
quotation by Charles Alexandre de Calonne
(1734–1802) in the form 'Madam, if a thing is
possible, consider it done; the impossible?—that will
be done'

**3 The hand will not reach for what the
heart does not long for.**
desire is essential for achievement; Welsh proverb

4 Palmam qui meruit, ferat.
Latin, *Let him who has won it bear the palm*, adopted
by Lord Nelson (1758–1805) as his motto, from John
Jortin *Lusus Poetici* (3rd ed., 1748) 'Ad Ventos'

5 Per ardua ad astra.
Latin, *through struggle to the stars*, motto of the
Mulvany family, quoted and translated by Rider
Haggard in *The People of the Mist* (1894), and still in
use as motto of the RAF, having been approved by
King George V in 1913

**6 Seriously, though, he's doing a
grand job!**
catchphrase used by David Frost in 'That Was The
Week That Was', on BBC Television, 1962–3

7 Seekers are finders.
success is the result of effort; Persian proverb; see
Action 11

8 Still achieving, still pursuing.
American proverb, mid 20th century; from
Longfellow: see **Determination** 38

9 Whatever man has done, man may do.
anything that has been achieved once can be
achieved again; English proverb, mid 19th century;
see 26 below

**10 While the grass grows, the steed
starves.**
by the time hopes or expectations can be satisfied, it
may be too late; English proverb, mid 14th century

11 You cannot have your cake and eat it.
you cannot have things both ways; English proverb,
mid 16th century

PHRASES

12 bite off more than one can chew
take on a commitment one cannot fulfil

13 low-hanging fruit
something easily achieved or overcome; the
expression dates from the late 20th century, and the

image may be associated with the idea in *cherry-pick*:
choose selectively (as the most beneficial or
profitable items or opportunities) from what is
available

QUOTATIONS

14 The desire accomplished is sweet to the soul.
Bible: Proverbs

15 I have fought a good fight, I have finished
my course, I have kept the faith.
Bible: II Timothy

16 None climbs so high as he who knows not
whither he is going.
Oliver Cromwell 1599–1658: attributed

17 The General [Wolfe] . . . repeated nearly the
whole of Gray's Elegy . . . adding, as he
concluded, that he would prefer being the

author of that poem to the glory of beating
the French to-morrow.
James Wolfe 1727–59: J. Playfair *Biographical
Account of J. Robinson* (1815)

18 The distance is nothing; it is only the first
step that is difficult.
commenting on the legend that St Denis, carrying
his head in his hands, walked two leagues
Mme Du Deffand 1697–1780: letter to Jean Le
Rond d'Alembert, 7 July 1763; see **Beginning** 6

19 He has, indeed, done it very well; but it is a foolish thing well done.
on Goldsmith's apology in the *London Chronicle* for physically assaulting Thomas Evans, who had published a letter mocking Goldsmith
Samuel Johnson 1709–84: James Boswell *Life of Johnson* (1791) 3 April 1773

20 Now, gentlemen, let us do something today which the world may talk of hereafter.
Admiral Collingwood 1748–1810: before the Battle of Trafalgar, 21 October 1805; G. L. Newnham Collingwood (ed.) *A Selection from the Correspondence of Lord Collingwood* (1828)

21 *J'ai vécu.*
I survived.
when asked what he had done during the French Revolution
Emmanuel Joseph Sieyès 1748–1836: F. A. M. Mignet *Notice historique sur la vie et les travaux de M. le Comte de Sieyès* (1836)

22 That low man seeks a little thing to do,
Sees it and does it:
This high man, with a great thing to pursue,
Dies ere he knows it.
That low man goes on adding one to one,
His hundred's soon hit:
This high man, aiming at a million,
Misses an unit.
Robert Browning 1812–89: 'A Grammarian's Funeral' (1855)

23 I struggled for forty-seven years, I distinguished myself in every way I possibly could. I never had a compliment nor a 'Thank you', nor a single farthing. I translated a doubtful book in my old age, and I immediately made sixteen thousand guineas.
Richard Burton 1821–90: Arthur Symons *Dramatis Personae* (1923)

24 So little done, so much to do.
Cecil Rhodes 1853–1902: said on the day of his death; Lewis Michell *Life of Rhodes* (1910)

25 There are two tragedies in life. One is not to get your heart's desire. The other is to get it.
George Bernard Shaw 1856–1950: *Man and Superman* (1903)

26 What one man can invent another can discover.
Arthur Conan Doyle 1859–1930: *The Return of Sherlock Holmes* (1905) 'The Dancing Men'; see 9 above

27 Because it's there.
on being asked why he wanted to climb Mount Everest
George Leigh Mallory 1886–1924: in *New York Times* 18 March 1923

28 Give us the tools and we will finish the job.
Winston Churchill 1874–1965: radio broadcast, 9 February 1941

29 That's one small step for man, one giant leap for mankind.
Neil Armstrong 1930– : in *New York Times* 21 July 1969; interference in the transmission obliterated 'a' between 'for' and 'man'

30 Where there is no risk there can be no pride in achievement and consequently no happiness.
Ray Kroc 1902–84: *Grinding It Out* (1977)

31 At the end of your life you will never regret not having passed one more test, winning one more verdict or not closing one more deal. You will regret time not spent with a husband, a child, a friend or a parent.
Barbara Bush 1925– : in *Washington Post* 2 June 1990

32 When people are put into positions slightly above what they would expect, they're apt to excel.
Richard Branson 1950– : in *Success* November 1992; compare **Management** 4

33 Kids want to be famous. They don't want to be good at anything any more.
Ronan Keating 1977– : in *The Times* 5 April 2003

⇢⇢ Acting ⇠⇠

see also **The Cinema, The Theatre**

PROVERBS AND SAYINGS

1 **Anyone for tennis?**
a typical entrance or exit line given to a young man in a superficial drawing-room comedy

PHRASES

2 the Jersey Lily

the actress Lillie Langtry, (1853–1929); born in
Jersey, she was noted for her beauty and became
known as 'the Jersey Lily' from the title of a portrait
of her painted by Millais

QUOTATIONS

4 Suit the action to the word, the word to the
action; with this special observance, that
you o'erstep not the modesty of nature; for
anything so overdone is from the purpose of
playing, whose end, both at the first and
now, was and is, to hold, as 'twere, the
mirror up to nature.
William Shakespeare 1564–1616: *Hamlet* (1601)

5 He was a critic upon operas, too
And knew all niceties of sock and buskin.
Lord Byron 1788–1824: *Beppo* (1817); see 3 above

6 To see him act, is like reading Shakespeare
by flashes of lightning.
on Edmund Kean
Samuel Taylor Coleridge 1772–1834: *Table Talk*
(1835) 27 April 1823

7 She ran the whole gamut of the emotions
from A to B.
of Katharine Hepburn at a Broadway first night, 1933
Dorothy Parker 1893–1967: attributed

8 Don't put your daughter on the stage, Mrs
Worthington,
Don't put your daughter on the stage.
Noël Coward 1899–1973: 'Mrs Worthington' (1935
song)

9 Actors are cattle.
Alfred Hitchcock 1899–1980: in *Saturday Evening
Post* 22 May 1943

3 sock and buskin

comedy and tragedy: the *sock* was a light shoe worn
by comic actors on the Greek and Roman stage, and
the *buskin* a thick-soled laced boot worn by Athenian
tragic actors; see 5 below, **Theatre 8**

10 Shakespeare is so tiring. You never get a
chance to sit down unless you're a king.
Josephine Hull 1886–1957: in *Time* 16
November 1953

11 Just say the lines and don't trip over the
furniture.
advice on acting
Noël Coward 1899–1973: D. Richards *The Wit of
Noël Coward* (1968)

12 To grasp the full significance of life is the
actor's duty, to interpret it is his problem,
and to express it his dedication.
Marlon Brando 1924–2004: David Shipman
Marlon Brando (1974)

13 Acting is a masochistic form of
exhibitionism. It is not quite the occupation
of an adult.
Laurence Olivier 1907–89: in *Time* 3 July 1978

14 When I read 'Be real, don't get caught
acting,' I thought, 'How the hell do you do
that?'
Billy Connolly 1942– : John Miller *Judi Dench: With
a Crack in Her Voice* (1998)

Action and Inaction

see also **Idleness, Words and Deeds**

PROVERBS AND SAYINGS

1 Action is worry's worst enemy.

advocating the control of fruitless worry by taking a
decision and acting upon it; American proverb, mid
20th century

2 Action this day.

annotation as used by Winston Churchill at the
Admiralty in 1940

**3 Action without thought is like
shooting without aim.**

American proverb, mid 20th century

4 A barking dog never bites.

noisy threats often do not presage real danger;
English proverb, 16th century, 13th century in
French

**5 Better to light one candle than to
curse the darkness.**

motto of the American Christopher Society, founded
1945; see **Human Rights 19**

6 If it ain't broke, don't fix it.

warning against interference with something that is
working satisfactorily, late 20th century saying

7 If you want something done, ask a busy person.
implying that a busy person is most likely to have learned how to manage their time efficiently, late 20th century saying

8 It is as cheap sitting as standing.
often used literally; English proverb, mid 17th century

9 Lookers-on see most of the game.
those who are not participating are able to take an overall view; English proverb, early 16th century

PHRASES

13 have many (or other) irons in the fire
have a range of options or courses of action available, or be involved in many activities or commitments at the same time

14 the line of least resistance
an option avoiding difficulty or unpleasantness; the easiest course of action; see 28 below

QUOTATIONS

16 Nowher so bisy a man as he ther nas,
And yet he semed bisier than he was.
Geoffrey Chaucer 1343–1400: *The Canterbury Tales* 'The General Prologue'

17 Iron rusts from disuse; stagnant water loses its purity and in cold weather becomes frozen; even so does inaction sap the vigour of the mind.
Leonardo da Vinci 1452–1519: Edward McCurdy (ed. and trans.) *Leonardo da Vinci's Notebooks* (1906)

18 But men must know, that in this theatre of man's life it is reserved only for God and angels to be lookers on.
Francis Bacon 1561–1626: *The Advancement of Learning* (1605)

19 If it were done when 'tis done, then 'twere well
It were done quickly.
William Shakespeare 1564–1616: *Macbeth* (1606)

20 A first impulse was never a crime.
Pierre Corneille 1606–84: *Horace* (1640)

21 You have sat too long here for any good you have been doing. Depart, I say, and let us have done with you. In the name of God, go!
addressing the Rump Parliament, 20 April 1653; quoted by Leo Amery to Neville Chamberlain in the House of Commons, 7 May 1940. Chamberlain resigned three days later
Oliver Cromwell 1599–1658: oral tradition

22 We have left undone those things which we ought to have done; And we have done those things which we ought not to have done; And there is no health in us.
The Book of Common Prayer 1662: *Morning Prayer* General Confession

10 The road to hell is paved with good intentions.
English proverb, late 16th century; earlier forms omit the first three words

11 Seek and ye shall find.
an active search for something wanted is likely to be rewarded; English proverb, mid 16th century; see **Achievement 7, Prayer 7**

12 When in doubt, do nowt.
advising against taking action when one is unsure of one's ground; English proverb, mid 19th century

15 no peace for the wicked
no rest or tranquillity for the speaker; incessant activity, responsibility, or work; from the Bible (Isaiah), see **Good and Evil 14**

23 They also serve who only stand and wait.
John Milton 1608–74: 'When I consider how my light is spent' (1673)

24 He who desires but acts not, breeds pestilence.
William Blake 1757–1827: *The Marriage of Heaven and Hell* (1790–3) 'Proverbs of Hell'

25 Think nothing done while aught remains to do.
Samuel Rogers 1763–1855: 'Human Life' (1819)

26 It is vain to say that human beings ought to be satisfied with tranquillity: they must have action; and they will make it if they cannot find it.
Charlotte Brontë 1816–55: *Jane Eyre* (1847)

27 Action is consolatory. It is the enemy of thought and the friend of flattering illusions.
Joseph Conrad 1857–1924: *Nostromo* (1904)

28 For twenty years he has held a season-ticket on the line of least resistance and has gone wherever the train of events has carried him, lucidly justifying his position at whatever point he has happened to find himself.
of H. H. Asquith
Leo Amery 1873–1955: in *Quarterly Review* July 1914; see **14 above**

29 Waiting is still an occupation. It's having nothing to wait for that is terrible.
Cesare Pavese 1908–50: *Il Mestiere di vivere* (1952, translated as The Burning Brand, 1961) 15 September 1946

30 Under conditions of tyranny it is far easier to act than to think.
Hannah Arendt 1906–75: W. H. Auden *A Certain World* (1970)

31 The world can only be grasped by action, not by contemplation . . . The hand is the cutting edge of the mind.
Jacob Bronowski 1908–74: *The Ascent of Man* (1973)

32 I grew up in the Thirties with our unemployed father. He did not riot, he got on his bike and looked for work.
Norman Tebbit 1931– : speech at Conservative Party Conference, 15 October 1981

33 Let's go to work.
Quentin Tarantino 1963– : *Reservoir Dogs* (1992 film); spoken by Lawrence Tierney

34 I do nothing, granted. But I see the hours pass—which is better than trying to fill them.
E. M. Cioran 1911–95: in *Guardian* 11 May 1993

35 Inertia can develop its own momentum.
Douglas Hurd 1930– : in *Mail on Sunday* 27 May 2001

⤞ Administration ⤝

see also **Management**

PROVERBS AND SAYINGS

1 **A committee is a group of the unwilling, chosen from the unfit, to do the unnecessary.**
20th century saying

PHRASES

2 **men in suits**
bureaucrats, faceless administrators, regarded as representatives of an organization rather than creative individuals; probably related to *suit* = a man who wears a business suit at work, a business executive

3 **red tape**
excessive bureaucracy or adherence to rules and formalities, especially in public business; the expression refers to the reddish-pink tape which is commonly used for securing legal and official documents; see 5 below

QUOTATIONS

4 For forms of government let fools contest; Whate'er is best administered is best.
Alexander Pope 1688–1744: *An Essay on Man* Epistle 3 (1733)

5 Let Wilmington, with grave, contracted brow,
Red tape and wisdom at the council show.
Lord Hervey 1696–1743: 'To the Queen' (1736); see 3 above

6 I have in general no very exalted opinion of the virtue of paper government.
Edmund Burke 1729–97: *On Conciliation with America* (1775)

7 If any man will draw up his case, and put his name at the foot of the first page, I will give him an immediate reply. Where he compels me to turn over the sheet, he must wait my leisure.
on appeals made by officers to the Navy Board
Lord Sandwich 1718–92: N. W. Wraxall *Memoirs* (1884) vol. 1

8 Whatever was required to be done, the Circumlocution Office was beforehand with all the public departments in the art of perceiving—HOW NOT TO DO IT.
Charles Dickens 1812–70: *Little Dorrit* (1857)

9 A place for everything and everything in its place.
Mrs Beeton 1836–65: *The Book of Household Management* (1861); often attributed to Samuel Smiles; see Order 3

10 It is an inevitable defect, that bureaucrats will care more for routine than for results.
Walter Bagehot 1826–77: *The English Constitution* (1867) 'On Changes of Ministry'

11 Sack the lot!
on overmanning and overspending within government departments
John Arbuthnot Fisher 1841–1920: letter to *The Times*, 2 September 1919

12 Where there is officialism every human
relationship suffers.
E. M. Forster 1879–1970: *A Passage to India* (1924)

13 Official dignity tends to increase in inverse
ratio to the importance of the country in
which the office is held.
Aldous Huxley 1894–1963: *Beyond the Mexique
Bay* (1934)

14 This island is made mainly of coal and
surrounded by fish. Only an organizing
genius could produce a shortage of coal and
fish at the same time.
Aneurin Bevan 1897–1960: speech at Blackpool 24
May 1945

15 By the time the civil service has finished
drafting a document to give effect to a
principle, there may be little of the principle
left.
Lord Reith 1889–1971: *Into the Wind* (1949)

16 Meetings are held because men seek
companionship or, at a minimum, wish to
escape the tedium of solitary duties.
J. K. Galbraith 1908– : *The Great Crash 1929*
(1954)

17 Committee—a group of men who
individually can do nothing but as a group
decide that nothing can be done.
Fred Allen 1894–1956: attributed

18 Time spent on any item of the agenda will
be in inverse proportion to the sum
involved.
C. Northcote Parkinson 1909–93: *Parkinson's
Law* (1958)

19 In a hierarchy every employee tends to rise
to his level of incompetence.
Laurence J. Peter 1919–90: *The Peter Principle*
(1969); see **Management 4**

20 Guidelines for bureaucrats: (1) When in
charge, ponder. (2) When in trouble,
delegate. (3) When in doubt, mumble.
James H. Boren 1925– : in *New York Times* 8
November 1970

21 A memorandum is written not to inform the
reader but to protect the writer.
Dean Acheson 1893–1971: in *Wall Street Journal* 8
September 1977

22 Back in the East you can't do much without
the right papers, but *with* the right papers
you can do *anything*. They *believe* in papers.
Papers are power.
Tom Stoppard 1937– : *Neutral Ground* (1983)

23 A camel is a horse designed by a committee.
Alec Issigonis 1906–88: attributed; in *Guardian* 14
January 1991 'Notes and Queries'

⇢► Adversity ◄⇠

see also **Misfortunes, Suffering**

PROVERBS AND SAYINGS

1 Adversity makes strange bedfellows.
shared difficulties may bring together very different
people; see **Misfortunes 19**; English proverb, mid
19th century

2 After hardship comes relief.
African proverb (Swahili)

**3 A dose of adversity is often as needful
as a dose of medicine.**
American proverb, mid 20th century

**4 If life hands you lemons, make
lemonade.**
an adjuration to make the best of difficult
circumstances; late 20th century saying

PHRASES

5 gall and wormwood
a source of bitter mortification or vexation, originally
with allusion to the Bible (Genesis) 'lest there should
be among you a root that beareth gall and
wormwood'; *gall* = bile, the secretion of the liver,
wormwood = an aromatic plant with a bitter taste;
taken together as the type of something causing
bitterness and grief

6 the iron entered into his soul
he became deeply and permanently affected by
captivity or ill treatment; from the Bible (Psalms),

from Latin mistranslation of Hebrew for 'his person
entered into the iron', i.e. fetters

7 light at the end of the tunnel
a long-awaited sign that a period of hardship or
adversity is nearing an end; see **Optimism 37**

8 locust years
years of poverty and hardship; coined by Winston
Churchill in his *History of the Second World War*
(1948) to describe Britain in the 1930s; from the
Bible (Joel) 'I will restore to you the years that the
locust hath eaten'

9 school of hard knocks
the experience of a life of hardship, considered as a means of instruction; originally US

10 a thorn in one's side
a constant annoyance or problem, a source of continual trouble or annoyance; from the Bible

QUOTATIONS

12 He hath cast me into the mire, and I am become like dust and ashes.
Bible: Job; see **Death 44, Disillusion 3**

13 No stranger to trouble myself I am learning to care for the unhappy.
Virgil 70–19 BC: *Aeneid*

14 Sweet are the uses of adversity,
Which like the toad, ugly and venomous,
Wears yet a precious jewel in his head.
William Shakespeare 1564–1616: *As You Like It* (1599)

15 Prosperity doth best discover vice, but adversity doth best discover virtue.
Francis Bacon 1561–1626: *Essays* (1625) 'Of Adversity'

16 Adversity is sometimes hard upon a man; but for one man who can stand prosperity, there are a hundred that will stand adversity.
Thomas Carlyle 1795–1881: *On Heroes, Hero-Worship, and the Heroic* (1841)

17 When fortune empties her chamberpot on your head, smile—and say 'we are going to have a summer shower'.
John A. Macdonald 1815–91: spoken *c.* 1875 when Leader of the Opposition

(Numbers) 'those which ye let remain of them shall be . . . thorns in your sides'

11 under the harrow
in distress; *harrow* = a heavy frame set with iron teeth or tines, drawn over ploughed land to break up clods and root up weeds; see **Suffering 24**

18 But there, everything has its drawbacks, as the man said when his mother-in-law died, and they came down upon him for the funeral expenses.
Jerome K. Jerome 1859–1927: *Three Men in a Boat* (1889)

19 By trying we can easily learn to endure adversity. Another man's, I mean.
Mark Twain 1835–1910: *Following the Equator* (1897)

20 Adversity, if a man is set down to it by degrees, is more supportable with equanimity by most people than any great prosperity arrived at in a single lifetime.
Samuel Butler 1835–1902: *Way of All Flesh* (1903)

21 The heart *prefers* to move against the grain of circumstance; perversity is the soul's very life.
John Updike 1932– : *Assorted Prose* (1965) 'More Love in the Western World'

22 Life is not meant to be easy.
Malcolm Fraser 1930– : 5th Alfred Deakin lecture, 20 July 1971

23 A woman is like a teabag—only in hot water do you realise how strong she is.
Nancy Reagan 1923– : in *Observer* 29 March 1981

Advertising

PROVERBS AND SAYINGS

1 Any publicity is good publicity.
it is always preferable to have attention focused on a name than to be unnoticed; see **Fame 25**; English proverb, early 20th century

2 Don't advertise what you can't fulfil.
American proverb, mid 20th century

3 Good wine needs no bush.
there is no need to advertise or boast about something of good quality as people will always discover its merits; a bunch of ivy was formerly the

PHRASES

6 proclaim from the housetops
announce publicly, announce loudly; from the Bible (Luke) 'that which ye have spoken in the ear in closets shall be proclaimed upon the housetops'

sign of a vintner's shop; English proverb, early 15th century; see **16 below**

4 It pays to advertise.
American proverb, mid 20th century

5 Let's run it up the flagpole and see if anyone salutes it.
recorded as an established expression in the 1960s, suggesting the testing of a new idea or product

QUOTATIONS

7 Promise, large promise, is the soul of an advertisement.
Samuel Johnson 1709–84: in *The Idler* 20 January 1759

8 It is far easier to write ten passably effective sonnets, good enough to take in the not too enquiring critic, than one effective advertisement that will take in a few thousand of the uncritical buying public.
Aldous Huxley 1894–1963: *On the Margin* (1923) 'Advertisement'

9 Advertising may be described as the science of arresting human intelligence long enough to get money from it.
Stephen Leacock 1869–1944: *Garden of Folly* (1924) 'The Perfect Salesman'

10 Half the money I spend on advertising is wasted, and the trouble is I don't know which half.
Lord Leverhulme 1851–1925: David Ogilvy *Confessions of an Advertising Man* (1963)

11 Advertising is the rattling of a stick inside a swill bucket.
George Orwell 1903–50: *Keep the Aspidistra Flying* (1936)

12 It is not necessary to advertise food to hungry people, fuel to cold people, or houses to the homeless.
J. K. Galbraith 1908– : *American Capitalism* (1952)

13 The hidden persuaders.
Vance Packard 1914–97: title of a study of the advertising industry (1957)

14 The consumer isn't a moron; she is your wife.
David Ogilvy 1911–99: *Confessions of an Advertising Man* (1963)

15 A good poster is a visual telegram.
A. M. Cassandre 1901–68: attributed

16 Good wine needs no bush,
And perhaps products that people really want need no hard-sell or soft-sell TV push.
Why not?
Look at pot.
Ogden Nash 1902–71: 'Most Doctors Recommend or Yours For Fast, Fast, Fast Relief' (1972); see 3 above

17 Advertising is the greatest art form of the twentieth century.
Marshall McLuhan 1911–80: in *Advertising Age* 3 September 1976

18 Society drives people crazy with lust and calls it advertising.
John Lahr 1941– : in *Guardian* 2 August 1989

19 A great ad campaign will make a bad product fail faster. It will get more people to know it's bad.
Bill Bernbach 1911–82: *Bill Bernbach said* (1989)

⤞ Advice ⤝

PROVERBS AND SAYINGS

1 **Ask advice, but use your common sense.**
American proverb, mid 20th century

2 **Don't teach your grandmother to suck eggs.**
a caution against offering advice to the wise and experienced; English proverb, early 18th century

3 **A fool may give a wise man counsel.**
sometimes used as a warning against overconfidence in one's judgement; English proverb, mid 14th century

4 **Night brings counsel.**
sometimes used as a warning against taking a hasty action or decision; English proverb, late 16th century

5 **A nod's as good as a wink to a blind horse.**
the slightest hint is enough to convey one's meaning in a particular case; English proverb, late 18th century

6 **A word to the wise is enough.**
only a very brief warning is necessary to an intelligent person; English proverb, early 16th century; earlier in Latin *'verbum sat sapienti* [a word is sufficient to a wise man]': see 10 below

PHRASES

7 counsel of perfection
advice designed to guide one towards moral
perfection, often seen as ideal but impracticable;
sometimes with reference to the Bible (Matthew), 'If
thou wilt be perfect, go and sell all that thou hast,
and give to the poor'

8 Delphic oracle
the oracle of Apollo at Delphi in classical antiquity,
where a priestess, the Pythia, acted as a medium
through whom advice or prophecy was sought from
the gods. The characteristic riddling responses have
given rise to the use of *Delphic* to mean deliberately
obscure or ambiguous

9 Miss Lonelyhearts
a journalist who gives advice in a newspaper or
magazine to people who are lonely or in difficulties;
see 21 below

10 a word to the wise
used to imply that further explanation of or
comment on a statement or situation is unnecessary;
from the proverb: see 6 above

QUOTATIONS

11 A word spoken in due season, how good
is it!
Bible: Proverbs

12 Books will speak plain when counsellors
blanch.
Francis Bacon 1561–1626: *Essays* (1625) 'Of
Counsel'

13 Advice is seldom welcome; and those who
want it the most always like it the least.
Lord Chesterfield 1694–1773: *Letters to his Son*
(1774) 29 January 1748

14 Fools need advice most, but wise men only
are the better for it.
Benjamin Franklin 1706–90: *Poor Richard's
Almanac* (1758) January

15 It was, perhaps, one of those cases in which
advice is good or bad only as the event
decides.
Jane Austen 1775–1817: *Persuasion* (1818)

16 Of all the horrid, hideous notes of woe,
Sadder than owl-songs or the midnight
blast,
Is that portentous phrase, 'I told you so.'
Lord Byron 1788–1824: *Don Juan* (1819–24)

17 Get the advice of everybody whose advice is
worth having—they are very few—and then
do what you think best yourself.
Charles Stewart Parnell 1846–91: Conor Cruise
O'Brien *Parnell* (1957)

18 I always pass on good advice. It is the only
thing to do with it. It is never of any use to
oneself.
Oscar Wilde 1854–1900: *An Ideal Husband* (1895)

19 It's the worst thing that can ever happen to
you in all your life, and you've got to mind it
. . . They'll come saying, 'Bear up—trust to
time.' No, no; they're wrong. Mind it.
E. M. Forster 1879–1970: *The Longest Journey*
(1907)

20 Well, if you knows of a better 'ole, go to it.
caption to a cartoon of Old Bill and a friend in a
shellhole under fire
Bruce Bairnsfather 1888–1959: *Fragments from
France* (1915)

21 The Miss Lonelyhearts are the priests of
twentieth-century America.
Nathaniel West 1903–40: *Miss Lonelyhearts*
(1933); see 9 above

22 After all, when you seek advice from
someone it's certainly not because you want
them to give it. You just want them to be
there while you talk to yourself.
Terry Pratchett 1948– : *Jingo* (1997)

⤞ Africa ⤛

PROVERBS AND SAYINGS

1 **Always something new out of Africa.**
from Pliny: see 7 below; English proverb, mid 16th
century

PHRASES

2 African Eve
the hypothesis (based on study of mitochondrial
DNA) that modern humans have a common female
ancestor who lived in Africa around 200,000
years ago

3 the Dark Continent
Africa, referring to the time before it was fully
explored by Europeans, first recorded in H. M.
Stanley *Through the Dark Continent* (1878)

4 the Gold Coast
a former name (until 1957) for Ghana, so called
because it was an important source of gold

5 the Slave Coast
part of the west coast of Africa, between the Volta
River and Mount Cameroon, an area from which
slaves were exported in the 16th–19th centuries

6 the white man's grave
equatorial West Africa, traditionally considered as
being particularly unhealthy for whites

QUOTATIONS

7 *Semper aliquid novi Africam adferre.*
Africa always brings [us] something new.
originally referring to hybridization of African
animals
Pliny the Elder AD 23–79: *Historia Naturalis*; see 1
above

8 We are . . . a nation of dancers, singers and
poets.
of the Ibo people
Olaudah Equiano c.1745–c.97: *Narrative of the Life
of Olaudah Equiano* (1789)

9 Are you there . . . Africa of the millions of
royal slaves, deported Africa, drifting
continent, are you there? Slowly you vanish,
you withdraw into the past, into the tales of
castaways, colonial museums, the works of
scholars.
Jean Genet 1910–86: *The Blacks* (1959)

10 The wind of change is blowing through this
continent.
Harold Macmillan 1894–1986: speech at Cape
Town, 3 February 1960

11 The shape of Africa resembles a revolver, and
the Congo is the trigger.
Frantz Fanon 1925–61: attributed

12 I who have cursed
The drunken officer of British rule, how
choose
Between this Africa and the English tongue I
love?
Derek Walcott 1930– : 'A Far Cry From Africa'
(1962)

13 I have dedicated my life to this struggle of
the African people. I have fought against
white domination, and I have fought against
black domination. I have cherished the ideal
of a democratic and free society in which all
persons live together in harmony with equal
opportunities. It is an ideal which I hope to
live for, and to achieve. But my lord, if needs
be, it is an ideal for which I am prepared
to die.
Nelson Mandela 1918– : speech at his trial in
Pretoria, 20 April 1964, which he quoted on his
release in Cape Town, 11 February 1990

14 Hopeless doomed continent! Only lies
flourished here. Africa was swaddled in
lies—the lies of an aborted European
civilisation; the lies of liberation. Nothing
but lies.
Shiva Naipaul 1945–85: *North of South* (1978)

15 I am a woman and a woman of Africa. I am a
daughter of Nigeria and if she is in shame, I
shall stay and mourn with her in shame.
Buchi Emecheta 1944– : *Destination Biafra* (1982)

16 Westerners have aggressive problem-solving
minds; Africans experience people.
Kenneth Kaunda 1924– : attributed, 1990

17 The state of Africa is a scar on the
conscience of the world.
Tony Blair 1953– : speech to Labour Party
Conference, 2 October 2001

⇥ Alcohol ⇤

see also **Drunkenness**

PROVERBS AND SAYINGS

1 **Alcohol will preserve anything but a secret.**
American proverb, mid 20th century

2 **Don't ask a man to drink and drive.**
British road safety slogan, from 1964

3 **Guinness is good for you.**
reply universally given to researchers asking people why they drank Guinness; advertising slogan for Guinness, from c.1929

4 **Heineken refreshes the parts other beers cannot reach.**
slogan for Heineken lager, from 1975 onwards

5 **I'm only here for the beer.**
slogan for Double Diamond beer, 1971 onwards

6 **Let's get out of these wet clothes and into a dry Martini.**
line coined in the 1920s by Robert Benchley's press agent and adopted by Mae West in *Every Day's a Holiday* (1937 film)

7 **Vodka is an aunt of wine.**
Russian proverb

PHRASES

8 **shaken, not stirred**
popular summary of the directions for making the perfect martini given by James Bond, from Fleming; see 28 below

QUOTATIONS

9 Wine is a mocker, strong drink is raging.
Bible: Proverbs

10 No verse can give pleasure for long, nor last, that is written by drinkers of water.
Horace 65–8 BC: *Epistles*

11 Use a little wine for thy stomach's sake.
Bible: I Timothy

12 Claret is the liquor for boys; port, for men; but he who aspires to be a hero (smiling) must drink brandy.
Samuel Johnson 1709–84: James Boswell *Life of Johnson* (1791) 7 April 1779

13 Freedom and Whisky gang thegither!
Robert Burns 1759–96: 'The Author's Earnest Cry and Prayer' (1786)

14 O for a beaker full of the warm South,
Full of the true, the blushful Hippocrene,
With beaded bubbles winking at the brim,
And purple-stainèd mouth.
John Keats 1795–1821: 'Ode to a Nightingale' (1820)

15 Man wants but little drink below,
But wants that little strong.
Oliver Wendell Holmes 1809–94: 'A Song of other Days' (1848); see **Life** 26

16 Your lips, on my own, when they printed 'Farewell',
Had never been soiled by the 'beverage of hell';
But they come to me now with the bacchanal sign,
And the lips that touch liquor must never touch mine.
George W. Young 1846–1919: 'The Lips That Touch Liquor Must Never Touch Mine' (c. 1870); also attributed, in a different form, to Harriet A. Glazebrook, 1874

17 Wine may well be considered the most healthful and most hygienic of beverages.
Louis Pasteur 1822–95: *Études sur le vin* (1873)

18 Fifteen men on the dead man's chest
Yo-ho-ho, and a bottle of rum!
Drink and the devil had done for the rest—
Yo-ho-ho, and a bottle of rum!
Robert Louis Stevenson 1850–94: *Treasure Island* (1883)

19 We drink one another's healths, and spoil our own.
Jerome K. Jerome 1859–1927: *Idle Thoughts of an Idle Fellow* (1886)

20 And malt does more than Milton can
To justify God's ways to man.
Ale, man, ale's the stuff to drink
For fellows whom it hurts to think.
A. E. Housman 1859–1936: *A Shropshire Lad* (1896); see **Writing** 17

21 I'm only a beer teetotaller, not a champagne teetotaller.
George Bernard Shaw 1856–1950: *Candida* (1898)

22 Gin was mother's milk to her.
George Bernard Shaw 1856–1950: *Pygmalion* (1916); see **Likes** 7

23 Our country has deliberately undertaken a great social and economic experiment, noble in motive and far-reaching in purpose.
on the Eighteenth Amendment enacting Prohibition
Herbert Hoover 1874–1964: letter to Senator W. H. Borah, 23 February 1928

24 Prohibition makes you want to cry into your beer and denies you the beer to cry into.
Don Marquis 1878–1937: *Sun Dial Time* (1936)

25 It's a naïve domestic Burgundy without any breeding, but I think you'll be amused by its presumption.
James Thurber 1894–1961: cartoon caption in *New Yorker* 27 March 1937

26 Some weasel took the cork out of my lunch.
W. C. Fields 1880–1946: *You Can't Cheat an Honest Man* (1939 film)

27 A good general rule is to state that the bouquet is better than the taste, and vice versa.
on wine-tasting
Stephen Potter 1900–69: *One-Upmanship* (1952)

28 A medium Vodka dry Martini—with a slice of lemon peel. Shaken and not stirred.
Ian Fleming 1908–64: *Dr No* (1958); see 8 above

29 One reason why I don't drink is because I wish to know when I am having a good time.
Nancy Astor 1879–1964: in *Christian Herald* June 1960

30 A man shouldn't fool with booze until he's fifty; then he's a damn fool if he doesn't.
William Faulkner 1897–1962: James M. Webb and A. Wigfall Green *William Faulkner of Oxford* (1965)

31 I have taken more out of alcohol than alcohol has taken out of me.
Winston Churchill 1874–1965: Quentin Reynolds *By Quentin Reynolds* (1964)

32 I'd hate to be a teetotaller. Imagine getting up in the morning and knowing that's as good as you're going to feel all day.
Dean Martin 1917– : attributed; also attributed to Jimmy Durante

33 Wine is for drinking and enjoying, talking about it is deadly dull.
Jancis Robinson 1950– : in *Daily Mail* 19 October 1995

⤗ Ambition ⤖

see also **Achievement, Success and Failure**

PROVERBS AND SAYINGS

1 **Hasty climbers have sudden falls.**
the over-ambitious often fail to take necessary precautions; English proverb, mid 15th century

2 **The higher the monkey climbs the more he shows his tail.**
the further an unsuitable person is advanced, the more their inadequacies are apparent; English proverb, late 14th century

3 **It's ill waiting for dead men's shoes.**
often used of a situation in which one is hoping for a position currently occupied by another; English proverb, mid 16th century; see **Possessions** 8

4 **Many go out for wool and come home shorn.**
many who seek to better themselves or make themselves rich, end by losing what they already have; English proverb, late 16th century

5 **There is always room at the top.**
as a response to being advised against joining the overcrowded legal profession, it is also attributed to the American politician and lawyer Daniel Webster (1782–1852); English proverb, early 20th century; see **Opportunity** 22

QUOTATIONS

6 [I] had rather be first in a village than second at Rome.
Julius Caesar 100–44 BC: Francis Bacon *The Advancement of Learning*; based on Plutarch *Parallel Lives*

7 *Aut Caesar, aut nihil.*
Caesar or nothing.
Cesare Borgia 1476–1507: motto inscribed on his sword; John Leslie Garner *Caesar Borgia* (1912)

8 Who shoots at the mid-day sun, though he be sure he shall never hit the mark; yet as sure he is he shall shoot higher than who aims but at a bush.
Philip Sidney 1554–86: *Arcadia* ('New Arcadia', 1590)

9 When that the poor have cried, Caesar hath wept;
Ambition should be made of sterner stuff.
William Shakespeare 1564–1616: *Julius Caesar* (1599)

10 WALTER RALEGH: Fain would I climb, yet fear I to fall.
ELIZABETH: If thy heart fails thee, climb not at all.
Elizabeth I 1533–1603: lines written on a window-pane; Thomas Fuller *Worthies of England* (1662)

11 Cromwell, I charge thee, fling away ambition:
By that sin fell the angels.
William Shakespeare 1564–1616: *Henry VIII* (1613)

12 Better to reign in hell, than serve in heaven.
John Milton 1608–74: *Paradise Lost* (1667)

13 Well is it known that ambition can creep as well as soar.
Edmund Burke 1729–97: *Third Letter . . . on the Proposals for Peace with the Regicide Directory* (1797)

14 Before this time to-morrow I shall have gained a peerage, or Westminster Abbey.
Horatio, Lord Nelson 1758–1805: before the battle of the Nile, 1798; Robert Southey *Life of Nelson* (1813)

15 Remember that there is not one of you who does not carry in his cartridge-pouch the marshal's baton of the duke of Reggio; it is up to you to bring it forth.
Louis XVIII 1755–1824: speech to Saint-Cyr cadets, 9 August 1819

16 I had rather be right than be President.
Henry Clay 1777–1852: to Senator Preston of South Carolina, 1839; S. W. McCall *Life of Thomas Brackett Reed* (1914)

17 Ah, but a man's reach should exceed his grasp,
Or what's a heaven for?
Robert Browning 1812–89: 'Andrea del Sarto' (1855)

18 All ambitions are lawful except those which climb upwards on the miseries or credulities of mankind.
Joseph Conrad 1857–1924: *Some Reminiscences* (1912)

19 He is loyal to his own career but only incidentally to anything or anyone else.
of Richard Crossman
Hugh Dalton 1887–1962: diary, 17 September 1941

20 Do you sincerely want to be rich?
stock question to salesmen
Bernard Cornfeld 1927– : Charles Raw et al. *Do You Sincerely Want to be Rich?* (1971)

21 Yo I'll tell you what I want, what I really really want
so tell me what you want, what you really really want.
The Spice Girls: 'Wannabe' (1996 song, with Matthew Rowbottom and Richard Stannard)

⤕ America ⤔

see also **American Cities and States**

PROVERBS AND SAYINGS

1 **America is a tune. It must be sung together.**
American proverb, mid 20th century

2 **Good Americans when they die go to Paris.**
coinage attributed to Thomas Gold Appleton (1812–84); American proverb, mid 19th century

3 **It is a striking coincidence that the word American ends in can.**
American proverb, mid 20th century

PHRASES

4 **the American dream**
the ideal of a democratic and prosperous society which is the traditional aim of the American people; American social or material values in general; see **Idealism 19**

5 **the Bird of Freedom**
the emblematic bald eagle of the US

6 founding father

an American statesman at the time of the Revolution, especially a member of the Federal Constitutional Convention of 1787; see 29 below

7 Land of the Free

the United States of America, from 'The Star-Spangled Banner': see 15 below

8 Old Glory

the national flag of the United States; attributed to Captain William Driver (1803–86), who is reported to have said, 'I name thee Old Glory!', when saluting a new flag flown on his ship in 1831

9 the Stars and Bars

the flag of the Confederate States of America; it had three bars, and a circle of eleven stars for the eleven states of the Confederacy

10 the Stars and Stripes

the national flag of the United States; when first adopted in 1777 it contained 13 stripes and 13 stars, representing the 13 states of the Union; it now has 13 stripes and 50 stars

QUOTATIONS

11 We must consider that we shall be a city upon a hill, the eyes of all people are on us; so that if we shall deal falsely with our God in this work we have undertaken, and so cause Him to withdraw His present help from us, we shall be made a story and a byword through the world.
John Winthrop 1588–1649: *Christian Charity, A Model Hereof* (sermon, 1630)

12 Then join hand in hand, brave Americans all,—
By uniting we stand, by dividing we fall.
John Dickinson 1732–1808: 'The Liberty Song' (1768); see **Cooperation** 19

13 We the people of the United States, in order to form a more perfect Union, establish justice, insure domestic tranquillity, provide for the common defense, promote the general welfare, and secure the blessings of liberty to ourselves and our posterity do ordain and establish this Constitution for the United States of America.
Constitution of the United States 1787: preamble; see also **Race** 32

14 Where today are the Pequot? Where are the Narragansett, the Mohican, the Pokanoket, and many other once powerful tribes of our people? They have vanished before the avarice and oppression of the white man, as snow before the summer sun.
Tecumseh 1768–1813: Dee Brown *Bury My Heart at Wounded Knee* (1970)

15 'Tis the star-spangled banner; O long may it wave
O'er the land of the free, and the home of the brave!
Francis Scott Key 1779–1843: 'The Star-Spangled Banner' (1814); see 7 above

16 But this momentous question [the Missouri Compromise], like a firebell in the night awakened and filled me with terror. I considered it the knell of the Union.
Thomas Jefferson 1743–1826: letter to John Holmes, 22 April 1820; see **Danger** 15

17 I called the New World into existence, to redress the balance of the Old.
George Canning 1770–1827: speech on the affairs of Portugal, House of Commons, 12 December 1826

18 I have heard something said about allegiance to the South. I know no South, no North, no East, no West, to which I owe any allegiance . . . The Union, sir, is my country.
Henry Clay 1777–1852: speech in the US Senate, 1848

19 I was born an American; I will live an American; I shall die an American.
Daniel Webster 1782–1852: speech in the Senate on 'The Compromise Bill', 17 July 1850

20 Go West, young man, and grow up with the country.
Horace Greeley 1811–72: *Hints toward Reforms* (1850); see **Exploration** 7

21 The United States themselves are essentially the greatest poem.
Walt Whitman 1819–92: *Leaves of Grass* (1855)

22 A Star for every State, and a State for every Star.
Robert Charles Winthrop 1809–94: speech on Boston Common, 27 August 1862

23 What law have I broken? Is it wrong for me to love my own? Is it wicked for me because my skin is red? Because I am Sioux; because I was born where my fathers lived; because I would die for my people and my country?
Sitting Bull (Tatanka Iyotake) 1831–90: to Major Brotherton, recorded July 1881; Gary C. Anderson *Sitting Bull* (1996)

24 Give me your tired, your poor,
Your huddled masses yearning to breathe free.
inscription on the Statue of Liberty, New York
Emma Lazarus 1849–87: 'The New Colossus' (1883)

25 Isn't this a billion dollar country?
responding to a Democratic gibe about a 'million dollar Congress'
Charles Foster 1828–1904: at the 51st Congress, in *North American Review* March 1892; also attributed to Thomas B. Reed

26 America! America!
God shed His grace on thee
And crown thy good with brotherhood
From sea to shining sea!
Katherine Lee Bates 1859–1929: 'America the Beautiful' (1893)

27 I'm a Yankee Doodle Dandy,
A Yankee Doodle, do or die;
A real live nephew of my Uncle Sam's,
Born on the fourth of July.
George M. Cohan 1878–1942: 'Yankee Doodle Boy' (1904 song)

28 America is God's Crucible, the great Melting-Pot where all the races of Europe are melting and re-forming!
Israel Zangwill 1864–1926: *The Melting Pot* (1908)

29 I must utter my belief in the divine inspiration of the founding fathers.
Warren G. Harding 1865–1923: inaugural address, 4 March 1921; see 6 above

30 The chief business of the American people is business.
Calvin Coolidge 1872–1933: speech in Washington, 17 January 1925

31 The American system of rugged individualism.
Herbert Hoover 1874–1964: speech in New York City, 22 October 1928

32 I pledge you, I pledge myself, to a new deal for the American people.
Franklin D. Roosevelt 1882–1945: speech to the Democratic Convention in Chicago, 2 July 1932, accepting the presidential nomination

33 In the United States there is more space where nobody is than where anybody is. That is what makes America what it is.
Gertrude Stein 1874–1946: *The Geographical History of America* (1936)

34 God bless America,
Land that I love,

Stand beside her and guide her
Thru the night with a light from above.
Irving Berlin 1888–1989: 'God Bless America' (1939 song)

35 Yes, America is gigantic, but a gigantic mistake.
Sigmund Freud 1856–1939: Peter Gay *Freud: A Life for Our Time* (1988)

36 This land is your land, this land is my land,
From California to the New York Island.
From the redwood forest to the Gulf Stream waters
This land was made for you and me.
Woody Guthrie 1912–67: 'This Land is Your Land' (1956 song)

37 I like to be in America!
O.K. by me in America!
Ev'rything free in America
For a small fee in America!
Stephen Sondheim 1930– : 'America' (1957 song)

38 The weakness of American civilization, and perhaps the chief reason why it creates so much discontent, is that it is so curiously abstract. It is a bloodless extrapolation of a satisfying life . . . You dine off the advertisers 'sizzling' and not the meat of the steak.
J. B. Priestley 1894–1984: in *New Statesman* 10 December 1971

39 America is a vast conspiracy to make you happy.
John Updike 1932– : *Problems* (1980) 'How to love America and Leave it at the Same Time'

40 The microwave, the waste disposal, the orgasmic elasticity of the carpets, this soft resort-style civilization irresistibly evokes the end of the world.
Jean Baudrillard 1929– : *America* (1986)

41 God, guts and paranoia made America great.
Tom Holt 1961– : *Who's Afraid of Beowulf?* (1988)

⤞ American Cities and States ⤝

PHRASES

1 **the Aloha State**
Hawaii; *aloha* = Hawaiian word used when greeting or parting from someone

2 **the Bay State**
Massachusetts; the original colony was sited around Massachusetts Bay

3 **the Bear State**
Arkansas

4 **the Big Apple**
New York City

5 **the Big Easy**
New Orleans

6 **the Buckeye State**
Ohio, where buckeye trees are abundant

7 **the Centennial State**
Colorado, admitted as a state in 1876, the centennial year of the United States

8 **City of the Angels**
Los Angeles, California

9 City of Elms
New Haven, Connecticut

10 City of Magnificent Distances
Washington, DC

11 the Crescent City
New Orleans: the city is built on a curve of the Mississippi

12 the Diamond State
Delaware, said to be so named because it was seen as small in size but of great importance

13 the Empire City
New York

14 the Empire State
New York State

15 the Empire State of the South
Georgia

16 the Equality State
Wyoming, the first state to give women the vote

17 the Forest City
Cleveland, Ohio

18 the Garden State
New Jersey

19 the Golden State
California

20 the Gopher State
Minnesota

21 the Granite State
New Hampshire

22 the Great White Way
Broadway in New York City, referring to the brilliant street illumination

23 the Hawkeye State
Iowa

24 the Keystone State
Pennsylvania, the seventh or central one of the original thirteen States

25 Land of Enchantment
an informal name for New Mexico

26 the Lone Star State
Texas

27 the Magnolia State
Mississippi; the state's emblem is the magnolia flower

28 the Monumental City
the city of Baltimore, Maryland, named after the Washington Monument

29 Mother of Presidents
informal name for the state of Virginia and (later) Ohio; Virginia was the birthplace of Washington,

Jefferson, and Monroe, and Ohio the birthplace of Garfield and Taft

30 the North Star State
Minnesota; *North Star* the polestar

31 the Nutmeg State
the inhabitants of Connecticut reputedly passed off as the spice nutmeg-shaped pieces of wood; see **Deception** 12

32 the Old Dominion
Virginia

33 the Palmetto State
South Carolina

34 the Pelican State
Louisiana

35 the Prairie State
Illinois

36 the Prairie States
Illinois, Wisconsin, Iowa, Minnesota, and other states to the south

37 Quaker City
Philadelphia, founded by the Quaker William Penn in 1681

38 the Quaker State
Pennsylvania

39 Queen of the West
Cincinnati, Ohio

40 the Silver State
Nevada, referring to its silver mines

41 Soul City
the Harlem area of New York city, referring to the prevalence of soul music

42 the Sunflower State
Kansas; the sunflower is the state flower

43 the Tarheel State
North Carolina, with allusion to tar as a principal product of that state

44 the Treasure State
Montana, noted for its gold, silver, copper, and coal mines

45 the Turpentine State
North Carolina, from the quantity of turpentine obtained from its pine forests

46 the Volunteer State
Tennessee, from which large numbers volunteered for the Mexican War of 1847

47 the Windy City
Chicago

48 the Wolverine State
Michigan, where wolverines are found

QUOTATIONS

49 A very Italy, without its art.
of California
Oscar Wilde 1854–1900: letter to Norman Forbes-Robertson, 27 March 1882

50 A Boston man is the east wind made flesh.
Thomas Gold Appleton 1812–84: attributed

51 And this is good old Boston,
The home of the bean and the cod,
Where the Lowells talk to the Cabots
And the Cabots talk only to God.
John Collins Bossidy 1860–1928: verse spoken at Holy Cross College alumni dinner in Boston, Massachusetts, 1910

52 Hog Butcher for the World,
Tool Maker, Stacker of Wheat,
Player with Railroads and the Nation's
    Freight Handler;
Stormy, husky, brawling,
City of the Big Shoulders.
Carl Sandburg 1878–1967: 'Chicago' (1916)

53 California is a fine place to live—if you happen to be an orange.
Fred Allen 1894–1956: *American Magazine* December 1945

54 New York, New York,—a helluva town,
The Bronx is up but the Battery's down.
Betty Comden 1919– and **Adolph Green** 1915– : 'New York, New York' (1945 song)

55 The state with the prettiest name,
the state that floats in brackish water,
held together by mangrove roots.
Elizabeth Bishop 1911–79: 'Florida' (1946)

56 Last week, I went to Philadelphia, but it was closed.
W. C. Fields 1880–1946: Richard J. Anobile *Godfrey Daniels* (1975)

57 A hundred times I have thought: New York is a catastrophe, and fifty times: it is a beautiful catastrophe.
Le Corbusier 1887–1965: *When the Cathedrals were White* (1947) 'The Fairy Catastrophe'

58 A big hard-boiled city with no more personality than a paper cup.
of Los Angeles
Raymond Chandler 1888–1959: *The Little Sister* (1949)

59 Hollywood is a place where people from Iowa mistake each other for stars.
Fred Allen 1894–1956: Maurice Zolotow *No People like Show People* (1951)

60 I left my heart in San Francisco
High on a hill it calls to me.
Douglas Cross: 'I Left My Heart in San Francisco' (1954 song)

61 This is Red Hook, not Sicily . . . This is the gullet of New York swallowing the tonnage of the world.
Arthur Miller 1915–2005: *A View from the Bridge* (1955)

62 Washington is a city of southern efficiency and northern charm.
John F. Kennedy 1917–63: Arthur M. Schlesinger Jr. *A Thousand Days* (1965)

63 New York makes one think of the collapse of civilization, about Sodom and Gomorrah, the end of the world. The end wouldn't come as a surprise here. Many people already bank on it.
Saul Bellow 1915–2005: *Mr Sammler's Planet* (1970)

64 I had forgotten just how flat and empty it [middle America] is. Stand on two phone books almost anywhere in Iowa and you get a view.
Bill Bryson 1951– : *The Lost Continent* (1989)

⊷ Anger ⊶

PROVERBS AND SAYINGS

1 **Anger improves nothing but the arch of a cat's back.**
American proverb, mid 20th century

2 **A little pot is soon hot.**
a small person quickly becomes angry or passionate; English proverb, mid 16th century

3 **When angry count a hundred.**
advising against precipitate response (the number proposed varies, and sometimes the advice is ' . . . recite the alphabet'); English proverb, late 16th century; see 13, 16, 18 below

PHRASES

4 look back in anger
reflect on the past with indignation and resentment; with allusion to John Osborne's play *Look Back in Anger*: see **Generation Gap** 2

5 make someone's blood boil
infuriate someone

6 red rag to a bull
an object, utterance, or act which is certain to provoke someone, from the traditional belief (recorded from the late 16th century) that this colour is particularly irritating to the animal

QUOTATIONS

7 A soft answer turneth away wrath.
Bible: Proverbs; see **Diplomacy** 1

8 *Ira furor brevis est.*
Anger is a short madness.
Horace 65–8 BC: *Epistles*

9 Be ye angry and sin not: let not the sun go down upon your wrath.
Bible: Ephesians; see **Forgiveness** 4

10 Anger makes dull men witty, but it keeps them poor.
Francis Bacon 1561–1626: 'Baconiana' (1859); often attributed to Queen Elizabeth I from a misreading of the text

11 Anger is never without an argument, but seldom with a good one.
Lord Halifax 1633–95: *Political, Moral, and Miscellaneous Thoughts and Reflections* (1750)

12 The tygers of wrath are wiser than the horses of instruction.
William Blake 1757–1827: *The Marriage of Heaven and Hell* (1790–3) 'Proverbs of Hell'

13 When angry, count ten before you speak; if very angry a hundred.
Thomas Jefferson 1743–1826: letter to Thomas Jefferson Smith, 21 February 1825; see 3 above, 16, 18 below

14 Anger in its time and place
May assume a kind of grace.
It must have some reason in it
And not last beyond a minute.
Charles Lamb 1775–1834: 'Anger'

15 We boil at different degrees.
Ralph Waldo Emerson 1803–82: *Society and Solitude* (1870)

16 When angry, count four; when very angry, swear.
Mark Twain 1835–1910: *Pudd'nhead Wilson* (1894); see 3, 13 above, 18 below

17 It's my rule never to lose me temper till it would be dethrimental to keep it.
Sean O'Casey 1880–1964: *The Plough and the Stars* (1926)

18 When you get angry, they tell you, count to five before you reply. Why should I count to five? It's what happens *before* you count to five which makes life interesting.
David Hare 1947– : *The Secret Rapture* (1988); see 3, 16, 18 above

➤➤ Animals ◄◄

see also **Birds, Cats, Dogs**

PROVERBS AND SAYINGS

1 Feed a dog for three days and he will remember your kindness for three years. Feed a cat for three years and she will forget your kindness in three days.
Japanese proverb

2 From beavers, bees should learn to mend their ways.
A bee works; a beaver works and plays.
American proverb, mid 20th century

3 A howlin' coyote ain't stealin' no chickens.
American proverb, mid 20th century

4 If you want to live and thrive, let the spider run alive.
it was traditionally unlucky to harm a spider or a spider's web; English proverb, mid 19th century

5 No foot, no horse.
relating to horse care, and recorded in North America as 'no hoof, no horse'; English proverb, mid 18th century

6 **One white foot, buy him; two white feet, try him; three white feet, look well about him; four white feet, go without him.**
on horse-dealing, categorizing features in a horse which are believed to be unlucky; English proverb, recorded in various forms from the 15th century

7 **Three things are not to be trusted; a cow's horn, a dog's tooth, and a horse's hoof.**
one may be gored, bitten, or kicked without warning; English proverb, late 14th century

PHRASES

8 **the king of beasts**
the lion

9 **the lion's provider**
the jackal

10 **the little gentleman in black velvet**
the mole, in a Jacobite toast, from the belief that the death of William III was caused by his horse's stumbling over a molehill

11 **the ship of the desert**
the camel

QUOTATIONS

12 There went in two and two unto Noah into the Ark, the male and the female.
Bible: Genesis

13 A righteous man regardeth the life of his beast: but the tender mercies of the wicked are cruel.
Bible: Proverbs; see **Sympathy** 10

14 All breathing, existing, living, sentient creatures should not be slain, nor treated with violence, nor abused, nor tormented, nor driven away.
This is the pure, unchangeable, eternal law.
Jaina Sutras 6th century BC: *Ācārāṅga Sutra*

15 Nature's great masterpiece, an elephant,
The only harmless great thing.
John Donne 1572–1631: 'The Progress of the Soul' (1601)

16 The serpent subtlest beast of all the field.
John Milton 1608–74: *Paradise Lost* (1667)

17 Old pond,
leap-splash—
a frog.
Matsuo Basho 1644–94: translated by Lucien Stryk

18 The question is not, Can they reason? nor, Can they talk? but, Can they suffer?
Jeremy Bentham 1748–1832: *Principles of Morals and Legislation* (1789)

19 Tyger Tyger, burning bright,
In the forests of the night;
What immortal hand or eye,
Could frame thy fearful symmetry?
William Blake 1757–1827: *Songs of Experience* (1794) 'The Tiger'

20 Animals, whom we have made our slaves, we do not like to consider our equal.
Charles Darwin 1809–82: Notebook B (1837–8)

21 All things bright and beautiful,
All creatures great and small,
All things wise and wonderful,
The Lord God made them all.
Cecil Frances Alexander 1818–95: 'All Things Bright and Beautiful' (1848)

22 I think I could turn and live with animals,
they are so placid and self-contained,
I stand and look at them long and long.
They do not sweat and whine about their condition,
They do not lie awake in the dark and weep for their sins,
They do not make me sick discussing their duty to God,
Not one is dissatisfied, not one is demented with the mania of owning things.
Walt Whitman 1819–92: 'Song of Myself' (written 1855)

23 But I freely admit that the best of my fun
I owe it to horse and hound.
George John Whyte-Melville 1821–78: 'The Good Grey Mare' (1933)

24 When people call this beast to mind,
They marvel more and more
At such a little tail behind,
So large a trunk before.
Hilaire Belloc 1870–1953: *A Bad Child's Book of Beasts* (1896) 'The Elephant'

25 All animals, except man, know that the principal business of life is to enjoy it—and they do enjoy it as much as man and other circumstances will allow.
Samuel Butler 1835–1902: *The Way of All Flesh* (1903)

26 'Twould ring the bells of Heaven
The wildest peal for years,
If Parson lost his senses
And people came to theirs,
And he and they together
Knelt down with angry prayers
For tamed and shabby tigers
And dancing dogs and bears,
And wretched, blind, pit ponies,

And little hunted hares.
Ralph Hodgson 1871–1962: 'Bells of Heaven'
(1917)

27 God in His wisdom made the fly
And then forgot to tell us why.
Ogden Nash 1902–71: 'The Fly' (1942)

28 A four-legged friend, a four-legged friend,
He'll never let you down.
sung by Roy Rogers about his horse Trigger
J. Brooks: 'A Four Legged Friend' (1952 song)

29 Where in this wide world can man find
nobility without pride,
Friendship without envy, or beauty without
vanity?
Ronald Duncan 1914–82: 'In Praise of the Horse'
(1962)

30 I am fond of pigs. Dogs look up to us. Cats
look down on us. Pigs treat us as equals.
Winston Churchill 1874–1965: attributed; M.
Gilbert *Never Despair* (1988)

31 I hate a word like 'pets': it sounds so much
Like something with no living of its own.
Elizabeth Jennings 1926–2001: 'My Animals'
(1966)

32 I'm not over-fond of animals. I am merely
astounded by them.
David Attenborough 1926– : in *Independent* 14
January 1995

33 It is part of the pathos of a pet, that it always
stands on the edge of the moral dialogue,
staring from beyond an impassable barrier at
the life which is now everything to it, and
which yet it cannot comprehend.
Roger Scruton 1944– : *Animal Rights and Wrongs*
(1996)

⤙ Apology and Excuses ⤚

PROVERBS AND SAYINGS

1 **Apology is only egoism wrong
side out.**
American proverb, mid 20th century

2 **A bad excuse is better than none.**
it is better to attempt to give some kind of
explanation, even a weak one; English proverb, mid
16th century

3 **A bad workman blames his tools.**
often used as a comment on someone's excuses for
their lack of success; English proverb, early 17th
century, late 13th century in French; see 7 below

4 **Don't make excuses, make good.**
American proverb, early 20th century

5 **He who excuses, accuses himself.**
often used to mean that attempts to excuse oneself
show a guilty conscience; English proverb, early 17th
century

6 **It is easy to find a stick to beat a dog.**
it is easy to find reasons to criticize someone who is
vulnerable; English proverb, mid 16th century; see
Argument 21

7 **One who cannot dance blames the
uneven floor.**
Indian proverb; see 3 above

8 **When you are in a hole, stop digging.**
complicated explanations and attempts to exculpate
oneself often make a bad situation worse; late 20th
century saying, often associated with the British
Labour politician Denis Healey; see **Circumstance** 13

PHRASES

9 **eat humble pie**
make a humble apology and accept humiliation.
Humble pie is from a pun based on *umbles* 'offal',
considered as inferior food

10 **mea culpa**
an acknowledgement of one's guilt or responsibility
for an error; Latin, literally '(through) my own fault':
from the prayer of confession in the Latin liturgy of
the Church

11 **a sop to Cerberus**
something offered in propitiation; *Cerberus* = the
three-headed watchdog of classical mythology
which guarded the entrance of Hades; in the *Aeneid*,
Aeneas was able to pass him safely by drugging him
with a specially prepared cake

QUOTATIONS

12 Never make a defence or apology before you be accused.
Charles I 1600–49: letter to Lord Wentworth, 3 September 1636

13 A man should never be ashamed to own he has been in the wrong, which is but saying, in other words, that he is wiser to-day than he was yesterday.
Alexander Pope 1688–1744: *Miscellanies* (1727) vol. 2 'Thoughts on Various Subjects'

14 Never complain and never explain.
Benjamin Disraeli 1804–81: J. Morley *Life of William Ewart Gladstone* (1903); see 16 below

15 I have invented an invaluable permanent invalid called Bunbury, in order that I may be able to go down into the country whenever I choose.
Oscar Wilde 1854–1900: *The Importance of Being Earnest* (1899)

16 Never explain—your friends do not need it and your enemies will not believe you anyway.
Elbert Hubbard 1859–1915: *The Motto Book* (1907); see 14 above

17 As I waited I thought that there's nothing like a confession to make one look mad; and that of all confessions a written one is the most detrimental all round. Never confess! Never, never!
Joseph Conrad 1857–1924: *Chance* (1913)

18 It is a good rule in life never to apologize. The right sort of people do not want apologies, and the wrong sort take a mean advantage of them.
P. G. Wodehouse 1881–1975: *The Man Upstairs* (1914)

19 Very sorry can't come. Lie follows by post.
telegraphed message to the Prince of Wales, on being summoned to dine at the eleventh hour
Lord Charles Beresford 1846–1919: Ralph Nevill *The World of Fashion 1837–1922* (1923)

20 Several excuses are always less convincing than one.
Aldous Huxley 1894–1963: *Point Counter Point* (1928)

21 This is the only country in the world where you step on somebody's foot and he apologises.
Keith Waterhouse 1929– : in *Independent* 1 April 2000

22 I hope in my heart that one day the Prime Minister will be able to say sorry, that one day he will say sorry to the families of the bereaved.
the father of a soldier killed in Iraq, in a speech after losing to Tony Blair in the 2005 general election
Reg Keys 1952– : in *Mail on Sunday* 8 May 2005

⤜ Appearance ⤛

see also **The Body**

PROVERBS AND SAYINGS

1 Appearances are deceptive.
the outward form of something may not be a true guide to its real nature; English proverb, mid 17th century

2 A blind man's wife needs no paint.
there is no point in making efforts that cannot be appreciated; English proverb, mid 17th century

3 A carpenter is known by his chips.
the nature of a person's occupation or interest is demonstrated by the traces left behind; English proverb, mid 16th century

4 The cowl does not make the monk.
warning against judging nature and moral character by appearance; English proverb, late 14th century

5 Distance lends enchantment to the view.
English proverb, late 18th century, from Campbell: see **The Country and the Town** 11

6 A good horse cannot be of a bad colour.
colour is not an indicator of a horse's quality; English proverb, early 17th century

7 Keep that schoolgirl complexion.
advertising slogan for Palmolive soap, from 1917

8 Merit in appearance is more often rewarded than merit itself.
American proverb, mid 20th century

9 Never choose your women or linen by candlelight.
warning against being deceived by apparent attractions seen in a poor light; English proverb, late 16th century

10 What you see is what you get.
a late 20th century computing expression, from which the acronym *wysiwyg* derives. The expression is used generally to mean that the function and

value of something can be deduced from its outward appearance; there are no hidden drawbacks or advantages

PHRASES

12 the cut of someone's jib
the appearance or look of someone. Originally a nautical expression suggested by the prominence and characteristic form of the jib (a triangular sail set forward of the foremast) as the identifying characteristic of a ship

QUOTATIONS

13 A merry heart maketh a cheerful countenance.
Bible: Proverbs

14 There's no art
To find the mind's construction in the face;
William Shakespeare 1564–1616: *Macbeth* (1606)

15 He was one of a lean body and visage, as if his eager soul, biting for anger at the clog of his body, desired to fret a passage through it.
Thomas Fuller 1608–61: *The Holy State and the Profane State* (1642) 'Life of the Duke of Alva'

16 Had Cleopatra's nose been shorter, the whole face of the world would have changed.
Blaise Pascal 1623–62: *Pensées* (1670)

17 Has he not a rogue's face? . . . a hanging-look to me . . . has a damned Tyburn-face, without the benefit o' the Clergy.
William Congreve 1670–1729: *Love for Love* (1695); see **Clergy** 6

18 An unforgiving eye, and a damned disinheriting countenance!
Richard Brinsley Sheridan 1751–1816: *The School for Scandal* (1777)

19 Like the silver plate on a coffin.
describing Robert Peel's smile
John Philpot Curran 1750–1817: quoted by Daniel O'Connell, House of Commons, 26 February 1835

20 The Lord prefers common-looking people. That is why he makes so many of them.
Abraham Lincoln 1809–65: attributed; James Morgan *Our Presidents* (1928)

21 It's as large as life, and twice as natural!
Lewis Carroll 1832–98: *Through the Looking-Glass* (1872)

22 She may very well pass for forty-three
In the dusk with a light behind her!
W. S. Gilbert 1836–1911: *Trial by Jury* (1875)

23 Most women are not so young as they are painted.
Max Beerbohm 1872–1956: *The Yellow Book* (1894)

24 The photograph is not quite true to my own notion of my gentleness and sweetness of nature, but neither perhaps is my external appearance.
A. E. Housman 1859–1936: letter 12 June 1922

11 You can't tell a book by its cover.
outward appearance is not a guide to a person's real nature; English proverb, early 20th century

25 In England and America a beard usually means that its owner would rather be considered venerable than virile; on the continent of Europe it often means that its owner makes a special claim to virility.
Rebecca West 1892–1983: *The Thinking Reed* (1936)

26 Men seldom make passes
At girls who wear glasses.
Dorothy Parker 1893–1967: 'News Item' (1937)

27 Sure, deck your lower limbs in pants;
Yours are the limbs, my sweeting.
You look divine as you advance—
Have you seen yourself retreating?
Ogden Nash 1902–71: 'What's the Use?' (1940)

28 At 50, everyone has the face he deserves.
George Orwell 1903–50: last words in his notebook, 17 April 1949

29 My face looks like a wedding cake left out in the rain.
W. H. Auden 1907–73: Humphrey Carpenter *W. H. Auden* (1981)

30 No power on earth, however, can abolish the merciless class distinction between those who are physically desirable and the lonely, pallid, spotted, silent, unfancied majority.
John Mortimer 1923– : *Clinging to the Wreckage* (1982)

31 You can never be too rich or too thin.
Duchess of Windsor 1896–1986: attributed

32 I think your whole life shows in your face and you should be proud of that.
Lauren Bacall 1924– : in *Daily Telegraph* 2 March 1988

33 Being blonde is definitely a different state of mind. I can't really put my finger on it, but the artifice of being blonde has some incredible sort of sexual connotation.
Madonna 1958– : in *Rolling Stone* 23 March 1989

34 It costs a lot of money to look this cheap.
Dolly Parton 1946– : attributed, perhaps apocryphal

35 Anything which says it can magically take away your wrinkles is a scandalous lie.
Anita Roddick 1942– : in *Daily Telegraph* 19 October 2000

Architecture

PROVERBS AND SAYINGS

1 **In settling an island, the first building erected by a Spaniard will be a church; by a Frenchman, a fort; by a Dutchman, a warehouse; and by an Englishman, an alehouse.**
English proverb, late 18th century

2 **It is easier to build two chimneys than to maintain one.**
the cost of using and maintaining a building may be much greater than the cost of building it; English proverb, mid 16th century

3 **No good building without a good foundation.**
English proverb, late 15th century

4 **Si monumentum requiris, circumspice.**
Latin, *If you seek a monument, gaze around*, inscription in St Paul's Cathedral, London, attributed to the son of Sir Christopher Wren, its architect

PHRASES

5 **the Seven Wonders of the World**
the seven most spectacular man-made structures of the ancient world: traditionally they comprised the pyramids of Egypt, the Hanging Gardens of Babylon, the Mausoleum of Halicarnassus, the temple of Artemis at Ephesus in Asia Minor, the Colossus of Rhodes, the huge ivory and gold statue of Zeus at Olympia in the Peloponnese, and the Pharos of Alexandria (or in some lists, the walls of Babylon); see **Excellence 6**

QUOTATIONS

6 Well building hath three conditions. Commodity, firmness, and delight.
Henry Wotton 1568–1639: *Elements of Architecture* (1624)

7 Houses are built to live in and not to look on; therefore let use be preferred before uniformity, except where both may be had.
Francis Bacon 1561–1626: *Essays* (1625) 'Of Building'

8 Light (God's eldest daughter) is a principal beauty in building.
Thomas Fuller 1608–61: *The Holy State and the Profane State* (1642)

9 Architecture in general is frozen music.
Friedrich von Schelling 1775–1854: *Philosophie der Kunst* (1809)

10 Some people drink to forget their unhappiness; I do not drink, I build.
William Beckford 1759–1844: *Life at Fonthill* (1957) 17 August 1812

11 Form follows function.
Louis Henri Sullivan 1856–1924: *The Tall Office Building Artistically Considered* (1896); see **Beauty 36**

12 Remember that it is the glory of Gothic architecture that it can do *anything*.
John Ruskin 1819–1900: J. Mordaunt Crook *Dilemma of Style* (1987)

13 A house is a machine for living in.
Le Corbusier 1887–1965: *Vers une architecture* (1923)

14 Architecture, of all the arts, is the one which acts the most slowly, but the most surely, on the soul.
Ernest Dimnet: *What We Live By* (1932)

15 We shape our buildings, and afterwards our buildings shape us.
Winston Churchill 1874–1965: in the House of Commons, 28 October 1943

16 A bicycle shed is a building; Lincoln Cathedral is a piece of architecture. Nearly everything that encloses space on a scale sufficient for a human being to move in is a building; the term architecture applies only to buildings designed with a view to aesthetic appeal.
Nikolaus Pevsner 1902–83: *An Outline of European Architecture* (1943)

17 Less is more.
Ludwig Mies van der Rohe 1886–1969: P. Johnson *Mies van der Rohe* (1947); see **Excess 8**

18 The physician can bury his mistakes, but the architect can only advise his client to plant vines—so they should go as far as possible from home to build their first buildings.
Frank Lloyd Wright 1867–1959: in *New York Times* 4 October 1953; see **Medicine 17**

19 Architecture is the art of how to waste space.
Philip Johnson 1906– : in *New York Times* 27 December 1964

20 God is in the details.
Ludwig Mies van der Rohe 1886–1969:
attributed, in *New York Times* 19 August 1969; see
Order 1

21 A monstrous carbuncle on the face of a
much-loved and elegant friend.
on the proposed extension to the National Gallery,
London
Prince Charles 1948– : speech to the Royal
Institute of British Architects, 30 May 1984

22 People ask me if I'm an artist or an architect.
But I think they're the same.
Frank Gehry 1929– : in *Toronto Star* 4
September 1987

23 You should be able to read a building. It
should be what it does.
Richard Rogers 1933– : lecture, London,
March 1990

24 There is an ancient Egyptian saying that
'Man fears time, and time fears the
pyramids,' but this is no longer true. The
pyramids must fear time, too.
Zahi Hawass 1947– : in *New York Times* 10 August
1997; see **Time** 3

25 Skyscrapers are as much a reality as
urbanization itself . . . What do we do if we
don't build high? Give up and live in
bunkers? And then what, fret about death
by nerve gas or germ warfare?
Norman Foster 1935– : in *Guardian* 15
September 2001

⤳ Argument ⤝

see also **Opinion**

PROVERBS AND SAYINGS

1 Birds in their little nests agree.
used as a direction that young children should not
argue among themselves; a nursery proverb from
Isaac Watts *Divine Songs* (1715)

2 It takes two to make a quarrel.
some responsibility for a disagreement rests with
each party to it; English proverb, early 18th century;
see 20 below

**3 The more arguments you win, the less
friends you will have.**
American proverb, mid 20th century

PHRASES

6 apple of discord
a subject of dissension, from the golden apple
inscribed 'for the fairest' contended for by Hera,
Athene, and Aphrodite; the result of Paris's awarding
the apple to Aphrodite was that Hera through
jealousy brought about the Trojan War

7 bone of contention
a subject or issue over which there is continuing
disagreement; from a bone thrown between two

QUOTATIONS

9 It is better to dwell in a corner of the
housetop, than with a brawling woman in a
wide house.
Bible: Proverbs

**4 The only thing a heated argument
ever produced is coolness.**
American proverb, mid 20th century

**5 While two dogs are fighting for a
bone, a third runs away with it.**
while the attention of the disputants is on their
quarrel, both may lose possession of what they are
fighting over to a third party; English proverb, late
14th century; see 7 below

dogs as the type of something which causes a
quarrel; see 5 above

8 man of straw
originally, a dummy or image made of straw; from
this, a person compared to a straw image, a sham; a
sham argument set up to be defeated

10 Give you a reason on compulsion! if reasons
were as plentiful as blackberries I would give
no man a reason upon compulsion, I.
William Shakespeare 1564–1616: *Henry IV, Part 1*
(1597)

11 Our disputants put me in mind of the skuttle fish, that when he is unable to extricate himself, blackens all the water about him, till he becomes invisible.
Joseph Addison 1672–1719: in *The Spectator* 5 September 1712

12 My uncle Toby would never offer to answer this by any other kind of argument, than that of whistling half a dozen bars of Lillabullero.
Laurence Sterne 1713–68: *Tristram Shandy* (1759–67)

13 There is no arguing with Johnson; for when his pistol misses fire, he knocks you down with the butt end of it.
Oliver Goldsmith 1728–74: James Boswell *Life of Johnson* (1791) 26 October 1769

14 Every human benefit, every virtue and every prudent act, is founded on compromise.
Edmund Burke 1729–97: *On Conciliation with America* (1775)

15 I hate a fellow whom pride, or cowardice, or laziness drives into a corner, and who does nothing when he is there but sit and *growl*; let him come out as I do, and *bark*.
Samuel Johnson 1709–84: James Boswell *Life of Johnson* 10 October 1782

16 Who can refute a sneer?
William Paley 1743–1805: *Principles of Moral and Political Philosophy* (1785)

17 Persuasion is the resource of the feeble; and the feeble can seldom persuade.
Edward Gibbon 1737–94: *The Decline and Fall of the Roman Empire* (1776–88)

18 He never wants anything but what's right and fair; only when you come to settle what's right and fair, it's everything that he wants and nothing that you want. And that's his idea of a compromise. Give me the Brown compromise when I'm on his side.
Thomas Hughes 1822–96: *Tom Brown's Schooldays* (1857)

19 There is no good in arguing with the inevitable. The only argument available with an east wind is to put on your overcoat.
James Russell Lowell 1819–91: *Democracy and other Addresses* (1887)

20 It takes in reality only one to make a quarrel. It is useless for the sheep to pass resolutions in favour of vegetarianism, while the wolf remains of a different opinion.
William Ralph Inge 1860–1954: *Outspoken Essays: First Series* (1919) 'Patriotism'; see 2 above

21 Any stigma, as the old saying is, will serve to beat a dogma.
Philip Guedalla 1889–1944: *Masters and Men* (1923); see **Apology 6**

22 The argument of the broken window pane is the most valuable argument in modern politics.
Emmeline Pankhurst 1858–1928: George Dangerfield *The Strange Death of Liberal England* (1936)

23 Making noise is an effective means of opposition.
Joseph Goebbels 1897–1945: Ernest K. Bramsted *Goebbels and National Socialist Propaganda 1925–45* (1965)

24 The Catholic and the Communist are alike in assuming that an opponent cannot be both honest and intelligent.
George Orwell 1903–50: in *Polemic* January 1946

25 For your own good is a persuasive argument that will eventually make a man agree to his own destruction.
Janet Frame 1924–2004: *Faces in the Water* (1961)

26 Get your tanks off my lawn, Hughie.
to the trade union leader Hugh Scanlon, at Chequers in June 1969
Harold Wilson 1916–95: Peter Jenkins *The Battle of Downing Street* (1970)

27 That happy sense of purpose people have when they are standing up for a principle they haven't really been knocked down for yet.
P. J. O'Rourke 1947– : *Give War a Chance* (1992)

28 Conflicts, like living organisms, had a natural lifespan. The trick was to know when to let them die.
Ian McEwan 1948– : *Enduring Love* (1998)

➤➤ The Armed Forces ◄◄

see also **Warfare, Wars, World War I, World War II**

PROVERBS AND SAYINGS

1 **The army knows how to gain a victory but not how to make proper use of it.**
American proverb, mid 20th century

2 **A bloody war and a sickly season.**
naval toast in the time of Nelson, when an increased death rate meant more rapid promotion

3 **Daddy, what did you do in the Great War?**
daughter to father in First World War recruiting poster

4 **The first duty of a soldier is obedience.**
English proverb, mid 19th century

5 **If it moves, salute it; if it doesn't move, pick it up; and if you can't pick it up, paint it.**
1940s saying

6 **Old soldiers never die.**
English proverb, early 20th century; see 41 below

7 **One of our aircraft is missing.**
title of film (1941), an alteration of the customary formula used by BBC news in the Second World War, 'One of our aircraft failed to return'

8 **Providence is always on the side of the big battalions.**
English proverb, early 19th century; see **God** 20, **Strength** 19, **Warfare** 20

9 **A singing army and a singing people can't be defeated.**
American proverb, mid 20th century

10 **A soldier of the Great War known unto God.**
adopted by the War Graves Commission as the standard epitaph for the unidentified dead of World War One

11 **A willing foe and sea room.**
naval toast in the time of Nelson

12 **Your King and Country need you.**
1914 recruiting advertisement, showing Lord Kitchener with pointing finger

13 **Your soul may belong to God, but your ass belongs to the army.**
American saying to new recruits, mid 20th century

PHRASES

14 **the awkward squad**
a squad composed of recruits and soldiers who need further training; shortly before his death Robert Burns (1759–96) said, 'don't let the awkward squad fire over my grave'

15 **take the king's (or queen's) shilling**
enlist in the army. The reference is to the *shilling* formerly given to a recruit on enlistment

16 **the thin red line**
the British army; William Howard Russell said of the Russians charging the British at Balaclava, 'They dashed on towards that thin red line tipped with steel'; Russell's original dispatch to *The Times*, 14 November 1854, reads 'That thin red streak topped with a line of steel'; see **The Law** 13

17 **the wooden walls**
ships or shipping as a defensive force; the Athenian statesman Themistocles interpreted the Delphic oracle's reference to 'safety promised in a wooden wall' as referring to the Greek ships with which the decisive victory over the Persian fleet at Salamis was achieved; see **The Sea** 12

QUOTATIONS

18 For a city consists in men, and not in walls nor in ships empty of men.
speech to the defeated Athenian army at Syracuse, 413 BC
Nicias c.470–413 BC: Thucydides *History of the Peloponnesian Wars*

19 Then a soldier,
Full of strange oaths, and bearded like the pard,
Jealous in honour, sudden and quick in quarrel,
Seeking the bubble reputation
Even in the cannon's mouth.
William Shakespeare 1564–1616: *As You Like It* (1599)

20 I would rather have a plain russet-coated captain that knows what he fights for, and loves what he knows, than that which you call 'a gentleman' and is nothing else.
Oliver Cromwell 1599–1658: letter to Sir William Spring, September 1643

21 It is upon the navy under the good
Providence of God that the safety, honour,
and welfare of this realm do chiefly depend.
Charles II 1630–85: 'Articles of War' preamble; Sir
Geoffrey Callender *The Naval Side of British History*
(1952); probably a modern paraphrase

22 Rascals, would you live for ever?
to hesitant Guards at Kolin, 18 June 1757
Frederick the Great 1712–86: attributed

23 Heart of oak are our ships,
Heart of oak are our men:
We always are ready;
Steady, boys, steady;
We'll fight and we'll conquer again and
again.
David Garrick 1717–79: 'Heart of Oak' (1759
song); see **Character** 24

24 Discipline is the soul of an army. It makes
small numbers formidable; procures success
to the weak and esteem to all.
George Washington 1732–99: letter to the
captains of the Virginia Regiments, July 1759

25 Every man thinks meanly of himself for not
having been a soldier, or not having been
at sea.
Samuel Johnson 1709–84: James Boswell *Life of
Samuel Johnson* (1791) 10 April 1778

26 Who is the happy Warrior? Who is he
Whom every man in arms should wish
to be?
William Wordsworth 1770–1850: 'Character of
the Happy Warrior' (1807); see **39** below

27 As Lord Chesterfield said of the generals of
his day, 'I only hope that when the enemy
reads the list of their names, he trembles as
I do.'
usually quoted as 'I don't know what effect these
men will have upon the enemy, but, by God, they
frighten me'
Duke of Wellington 1769–1852: letter, 29
August 1810

28 *La Garde meurt, mais ne se rend pas.*
The Guards die but do not surrender.
when called upon to surrender at Waterloo, 1815
Pierre, Baron de Cambronne 1770–1842:
attributed to Cambronne, but later denied by him;
H. Houssaye *La Garde meurt et ne se rend pas* (1907)

29 An army marches on its stomach.
Napoleon I 1769–1821: attributed, but probably
condensed from a long passage in E. A. de Las Cases
Mémorial de Ste-Hélène (1823) vol. 4, 14 November
1816; also attributed to Frederick the Great

30 Ours [our army] is composed of the scum of
the earth—the mere scum of the earth.
Duke of Wellington 1769–1852: Philip Henry
Stanhope *Notes of Conversations with the Duke of
Wellington* (1888) 4 November 1831

31 *C'est magnifique, mais ce n'est pas la guerre.*
It is magnificent, but it is not war.
on the charge of the Light Brigade at Balaclava, 25
October 1854
Pierre Bosquet 1810–61: Cecil Woodham-Smith
The Reason Why (1953)

32 Theirs not to make reply,
Theirs not to reason why,
Theirs but to do and die:
Into the valley of Death
Rode the six hundred.
Alfred, Lord Tennyson 1809–92: 'The Charge of
the Light Brigade' (1854)

33 There is only one way for a young man to
get on in the army. He must try and get
killed in every way he possibly can!
Garnet Wolseley 1833–1913: in *Strand Magazine*
May 1892; see **Satisfaction** 10

34 The 'eathen in 'is blindness must end where
'e began.
But the backbone of the Army is the non-
commissioned man!
Rudyard Kipling 1865–1936: 'The 'Eathen'
(1896); see **Religion** 18

35 You can always tell an old soldier by the
inside of his holsters and cartridge boxes.
The young ones carry pistols and cartridges;
the old ones, grub.
George Bernard Shaw 1856–1950: *Arms and the
Man* (1898)

36 We're foot—slog—slog—slog—sloggin' over
Africa!—
Foot—foot—foot—foot—sloggin' over
Africa—
(Boots—boots—boots—boots—movin' up
and down again!)
There's no discharge in the war!
Rudyard Kipling 1865–1936: 'Boots' (1903); the
final line is from the Bible (Ecclesiastes)

37 They shall grow not old, as we that are left
grow old.
Age shall not weary them, nor the years
condemn.
At the going down of the sun and in the
morning
We will remember them.
particularly associated with Remembrance Day
services
Laurence Binyon 1869–1943: 'For the Fallen'
(1914)

38 When you go home, tell them of us and say,
'For your tomorrows these gave their today.'
particularly associated with the dead of the Burma
campaign of the Second World War, in the form 'For
your tomorrow we gave our today'
John Maxwell Edmonds 1875–1958: *Inscriptions
Suggested for War Memorials* (1919)

39 I saw him stab
And stab again

A well-killed Boche.
This is the happy warrior,
This is he . . .
Herbert Read 1893–1968: 'The Happy Warrior'
(1919); see 26 above

40 Nor law, nor duty bade me fight,
Nor public men, nor cheering crowds,
A lonely impulse of delight
Drove to this tumult in the clouds.
W. B. Yeats 1865–1939: 'An Irish Airman Foresees
his Death' (1919)

41 Old soldiers never die,
They simply fade away.
J. Foley 1906–70: 'Old Soldiers Never Die' (1920
song); possibly a 'folk-song' from the First World
War; see 6 above

42 I divide my officers into four classes as
follows: the clever, the industrious, the lazy,
and the stupid. Each officer always possesses
two of these qualities. Those who are clever
and industrious I appoint to the General
Staff. Use can under certain circumstances
be made of those who are stupid and lazy.
The man who is clever and lazy qualifies for
the highest leadership posts. He has the
requisite and the mental clarity for difficult
decisions. But whoever is stupid and
industrious must be got rid of, for he is too
dangerous.
Kurt von Hammerstein-Equord 1878–1943:
attributed, c.1933; possibly apocryphal

43 Wars may be fought with weapons, but they
are won by men.
George S. Patton 1885–1945: in *Cavalry Journal*
September 1933

44 You'll get no promotion this side of the
ocean,
So cheer up, my lads, Bless 'em all!
Bless 'em all! Bless 'em all! The long and the
short and the tall.
Jimmy Hughes and **Frank Lake**: 'Bless 'Em All'
(1940 song)

45 Naval tradition? Monstrous. Nothing but
rum, sodomy, prayers, and the lash.
often quoted as, 'rum, sodomy, and the lash', as in
Peter Gretton *Former Naval Person* (1968)
Winston Churchill 1874–1965: Harold Nicolson
diary 17 August 1950

46 To save your world you asked this man
to die:
Would this man, could he see you now,
ask why?
W. H. Auden 1907–73: 'Epitaph for the Unknown
Soldier' (1955)

47 In bombers named for girls, we burned
The cities we had learned about in school—
Till our lives wore out; our bodies lay among
The people we had killed and never seen.
When we lasted long enough they gave us
medals;
When we died they said, 'Our casualties
were low.'
Randall Jarrell 1914–65: 'Losses' (1963)

48 The sergeant is the army.
Dwight D. Eisenhower 1890–1969: attributed; see
34 above

49 How do you ask a man to be the last man to
die in Vietnam? How do you ask a man to be
the last man to die for a mistake?
John Kerry 1943– : speech to Senate Committee,
23 April 1971

50 When I was in the military, they gave me a
medal for killing two men and a discharge
for loving one.
Leonard Matlovich d. 1988: attributed

51 I expect you to rock their world. Wipe them
out if that is what they choose. But if you
are ferocious in battle remember to be
magnanimous in victory.
Tim Collins 1960– : speech to the men under his
command on arrival in Iraq, 20 March 2003

52 My son was just a piece of meat to them,
just a number.
on the politicians who sent her son to his death
in Iraq
Rose Gentle: in *Mail on Sunday* 4 July 2003

➤➤ The Arts ◄◄

see also **Acting, Arts and Sciences, Music, Painting and Drawing, Photography, Sculpture, Writing**

PROVERBS AND SAYINGS

1 **All arts are brothers; each is a light to
the other.**
American proverb, mid 19th century

2 **Art is long and life is short.**
originally from Hippocrates (see **Medicine 9**),
comparing the difficulties encountered in learning
the art of medicine or healing with the shortness of
human life ('Art' is now commonly understood in

the proverb in a less specific sense); English proverb, late 14th century; see also **Education** 17

3 Art is power.
American proverb, mid 19th century; see
Knowledge 4

PHRASES

4 ars gratia artis
art for art's sake; Latin, taken as the motto of Metro-Goldwyn-Mayer film studios, and apparently intended to say 'Art is beholden to the artists'; see 9 below

5 art for art's sake
used to convey the idea that the chief or only aim of a work of art is the self-expression of the individual

QUOTATIONS

6 Painting is silent poetry, poetry is eloquent painting.
Simonides *c.*556–468 BC: Plutarch *Moralia*

7 The poet ranks far below the painter in the representation of visible things, and far below the musician in that of invisible things.
Leonardo da Vinci 1452–1519: Irma A. Richter (ed.) *Selections from the Notebooks of Leonardo da Vinci* (1952)

8 In art the best is good enough.
Johann Wolfgang von Goethe 1749–1832: *Italienische Reise* (1816–17) 3 March 1787

9 Art for art's sake, with no purpose, for any purpose perverts art. But art achieves a purpose which is not its own.
Benjamin Constant 1767–1834: diary 11 February 1804; see 4, 5 above, 14, 21 below

10 God help the Minister that meddles with art!
Lord Melbourne 1779–1848: Lord David Cecil *Lord M* (1954)

11 I believe the right question to ask, respecting all ornament, is simply this: Was it done with enjoyment—was the carver happy while he was about it?
John Ruskin 1819–1900: *Seven Lamps of Architecture* (1849)

12 The artist must be in his work as God is in creation, invisible and all-powerful; one must sense him everywhere but never see him.
Gustave Flaubert 1821–80: letter to Mademoiselle Leroyer de Chantepie, 18 March 1857

13 Art is a jealous mistress.
Ralph Waldo Emerson 1803–82: *The Conduct of Life* (1860)

artist who creates it, and associated with the Aesthetic movement of the 1880s; see 9 below, **Writers** 1

14 Art for art's sake is an empty phrase. Art for the sake of the true, art for the sake of the good and the beautiful, that is the faith I am searching for.
George Sand 1804–76: letter to Alexandre Saint-Jean, 1872; see 9 above

15 Then a sentimental passion of a vegetable fashion must excite your languid spleen,
An attachment à la Plato for a bashful young potato, or a not too French French bean!
Though the Philistines may jostle, you will rank as an apostle in the high aesthetic band,
If you walk down Piccadilly with a poppy or a lily in your medieval hand.
W. S. Gilbert 1836–1911: *Patience* (1881); see **Writers** 1

16 All that I desire to point out is the general principle that Life imitates Art far more than Art imitates Life.
Oscar Wilde 1854–1900: *Intentions* (1891)

17 The Devil whoops, as he whooped of old:
'It's clever, but is it Art?'
Rudyard Kipling 1865–1936: 'The Conundrum of the Workshops' (1892)

18 We work in the dark—we do what we can—we give what we have. Our doubt is our passion and our passion is our task. The rest is the madness of art.
Henry James 1843–1916: 'The Middle Years' (short story, 1893)

19 I always said God was against art and I still believe it.
Edward Elgar 1857–1934: letter to A. J. Jaeger, 9 October 1900

20 The history of art is the history of revivals.
Samuel Butler 1835–1902: *Notebooks* (1912)

21 Art for Art's sake. Why not?
Art for Life's sake. Why not?
Art for Pleasure's sake. Why not?

What does it matter, as long as it is Art?
Paul Gauguin 1848–1903: formula for his work: Herbert Read *The Meaning of Art* (3rd ed., 1951); see 9 above

22 The true artist will let his wife starve, his children go barefoot, his mother drudge for his living at seventy, sooner than work at anything but his art.
George Bernard Shaw 1856–1950: *Man and Superman* (1903)

23 Art is vice. You don't marry it legitimately, you rape it.
Edgar Degas 1834–1917: Paul Lafond *Degas* (1918)

24 Another unsettling element in modern art is that common symptom of immaturity, the dread of doing what has been done before.
Edith Wharton 1862–1937: *The Writing of Fiction* (1925)

25 The artist is not a special kind of man, but every man is a special kind of artist.
Ananda Coomaraswamy 1877–1947: *Transformation of Nature in Art* (1934)

26 The proletarian state must bring up thousands of excellent 'mechanics of culture', 'engineers of the soul'.
Maxim Gorky 1868–1936: speech at the Writers' Congress 1934; see 29 below

27 I suppose art is the only thing that can go on mattering once it has stopped hurting.
Elizabeth Bowen 1899–1973: *Heat of the Day* (1949)

28 Art is born of humiliation.
W. H. Auden 1907–73: Stephen Spender *World Within World* (1951)

29 In free society art is not a weapon . . . Artists are not engineers of the soul.
John F. Kennedy 1917–63: speech at Amherst College, Mass., 26 October 1963; see 26 above

30 We all know that Art is not truth. Art is a lie that makes us realize truth.
Pablo Picasso 1881–1973: Dore Ashton *Picasso on Art* (1972)

31 An artist is someone who produces things that people don't need to have but that he — for *some reason* — thinks it would be a good idea to give them.
Andy Warhol 1927–87: *Philosophy of Andy Warhol (From A to B and Back Again)* (1975)

32 Filling a space in a beautiful way. That's what art means to me.
Georgia O'Keefe 1887–1986: in *Art News* December 1977

33 Art has to move you and design does not, unless it's a good design for a bus.
David Hockney 1937– : in *Guardian* 26 October 1988

34 All art, permanent or temporary, has a life in the immediate experience, but then has a life in the imagination.
Anish Kapoor 1954– : in *Sunday Times* 11 July 1999

Arts and Sciences

PHRASES

1 **the nine Muses**
in classical mythology the nine goddesses, daughters of Zeus and Mnemosyne, who preside over the arts and sciences

2 **the two cultures**
the arts and the sciences, from C. P. Snow *The Two Cultures and the Scientific Revolution* (1959)

QUOTATIONS

3 Histories make men wise; poets, witty; the mathematics, subtile; natural philosophy, deep; moral, grave; logic and rhetoric, able to contend.
Francis Bacon 1561–1626: *Essays* (1625) 'Of Studies'

4 Newton *was* a great man, but you must excuse me if I think that it would take many Newtons to make one Milton.
Samuel Taylor Coleridge 1772–1834: *Table Talk* (1835)

5 In science, read, by preference, the newest works; in literature, the oldest.
Edward Bulwer-Lytton 1803–73: *Caxtoniana* (1863) 'Hints on Mental Culture'

6 A contemporary poet has characterized this sense of the personality of art and of the impersonality of science in these words—'Art is myself; science is ourselves'
Claude Bernard 1813–78: *Introduction à l'Étude de la Médecin Experiméntale* (1865)

7 Don't talk to me of your Archimedes' lever. He was an absent-minded person with a mathematical imagination. Mathematics

commands all my respect, but I have no use for engines. Give me the right word and the right accent and I will move the world.
Joseph Conrad 1857–1924: *A Personal Record* (1919); see **Technology** 6

8 Even if I could be Shakespeare, I think I should still choose to be Faraday.
Aldous Huxley 1894–1963: in 1925, attributed; Walter M. Elsasser *Memoirs of a Physicist in the Atomic Age* (1978)

9 Art is meant to disturb, science reassures.
Georges Braque 1882–1963: *Le Jour et la nuit: Cahiers 1917–52*

10 Science must begin with myths, and with the criticism of myths.
Karl Popper 1902–94: 'The Philosophy of Science'; C. A. Mace (ed.) *British Philosophy in the Mid-Century* (1957)

11 Once or twice I have been provoked and have asked the company how many of them could describe the Second Law of Thermodynamics. The response was cold: it was also negative. Yet I was asking something which is about the scientific equivalent of: *Have you read a work of Shakespeare's?*
C. P. Snow 1905–80: *The Two Cultures* (1959); see **Physical Sciences** 4

12 When I find myself in the company of scientists, I feel like a shabby curate who has strayed by mistake into a drawing room full of dukes.
W. H. Auden 1907–73: *The Dyer's Hand* (1963) 'The Poet and the City'

13 If a scientist were to cut his ear off, no one would take it as evidence of a heightened sensibility.
Peter Medawar 1915–87: 'J. B. S.' (1968)

14 Shakespeare would have grasped wave functions, Donne would have understood complementarity and relative time. They would have been excited. What richness! They would have plundered this new science for their imagery. And they would have educated their audiences too. But you 'arts' people, you're not only ignorant of these magnificent things, you're rather proud of knowing nothing.
Ian McEwan 1948– : *The Child in Time* (1987)

15 Scientists are explorers, philosophers are tourists.
Richard Feynman 1918–88: Christopher Sykes (ed.) *No Ordinary Genius* (1994)

16 If Watson and Crick had not discovered the nature of DNA, one can be virtually certain that other scientists would eventually have determined it. With art—whether painting, music or literature — it is quite different. If Shakespeare had not written *Hamlet*, no other playwright would have done so.
Lewis Wolpert 1929– : *The Unnatural Nature of Science* (1993)

⇥ Australia ⇤

see also **Towns and Cities**

PROVERBS AND SAYINGS

1 **Advance Australia.**
catchphrase used as a patriotic slogan or motto, mid 19th century onwards; see 17 below

2 **Australians wouldn't give a XXXX for anything else.**
advertising slogan for Castlemaine lager, 1986 onwards

PHRASES

3 **Apple Island**
Tasmania, popularly identified as an apple-growing region

4 **beyond the black stump**
in the remote outback; *black stump* an imaginary marker at the limits of settled and, by implication, civilized country

5 **Cabbage Garden**
the state of Victoria

6 **First Fleet**
the eleven British ships under the command of Arthur Phillip, first governor of New South Wales, which arrived in Australia in January 1788

7 **the Lucky Country**
Australia; see 24 below

8 the Never Never Land
the unpopulated northern part of the Northern
Territory and Queensland; the desert country of the
interior of Australia

9 stolen generation
the Aboriginal people forcibly removed from their
families as children between the 1900s and the

1960s, to be brought up by white foster families or in
institutions; see 32 below

10 Top End
(the northern part of) the Northern Territory of
Australia

QUOTATIONS

11 From what I have said of the natives of New
Holland, they may appear to some to be the
most wretched people upon earth; but in
reality they are far happier than we
Europeans; being wholly unacquainted not
only with the superfluous but the necessary
conveniences so much sought after in
Europe, they are happy in not knowing the
use of them.
James Cook 1728–79: diary, August 1770

12 The loss of America what can repay?
New colonies seek for at Botany Bay.
John Freeth 1731–1808: 'Botany Bay' (1786)

13 True patriots we; for be it understood,
We left our country for our country's good.
prologue, written for, but not recited at, the opening
of the Playhouse, Sydney, New South Wales, 16
January 1796, when the actors were principally
convicts
Henry Carter d. 1806: A. W. Jose and H. J. Carter
(eds.) *The Australian Encyclopaedia* (1927); previously
attributed to George Barrington (b. 1755)

14 Who knows but that England may revive in
New South Wales when it has sunk in
Europe.
Joseph Banks 1743–1820: letter to Governor
Hunter, 30 March 1797

15 I have been disappointed in all my
expectations of Australia, except as to its
wickedness; for it is far more wicked than I
have conceived it possible for any place to
be, or than it is possible for me to describe to
you in England.
Henry Parkes 1815–95: letter, 1 May 1840 *An
Emigrant's Home Letters* (1896)

16 Earth is here so kind, that just tickle her
with a hoe and she laughs with a harvest.
Douglas Jerrold 1803–57: *The Wit and Opinions of
Douglas Jerrold* (1859)

17 In joyful strains then let us sing
Advance Australia fair.
the national anthem of Australia, which officially
replaced 'God Save the Queen' in 1984; see 1 above
P. D. McCormick 1834–1916: 'Advance Australia
Fair' (*c.*1878 song)

18 The crimson thread of kinship runs through
us all.
on Australian federation
Henry Parkes 1815–95: speech at banquet in
Melbourne 6 February 1890; *The Federal Government
of Australasia* (1890)

19 Once a jolly swagman camped by a
billabong,
Under the shade of a coolibah tree;
And he sang as he watched and waited till
his 'Billy' boiled:
'You'll come a-waltzing, Matilda, with me.'
'Banjo' Paterson 1864–1941: 'Waltzing Matilda'
(1903 song)

20 Australia has a marvellous sky and air and
blue clarity, and a hoary sort of land
beneath it, like a Sleeping Princess on whom
the dust of ages has settled.
D. H. Lawrence 1885–1930: letter to Jan Juta, 20
May 1922

21 What Great Britain calls the Far East is to us
the near north.
Robert Gordon Menzies 1894–1978: in *Sydney
Morning Herald* 27 April 1939

22 Down under we send soldiers and wool
abroad but keep poets and wine at home.
John Streeter Manifold 1915–85: attributed,
Selected Verse (1948)

23 Above our writers—and other artists—looms
the intimidating mass of Anglo-Saxon
culture. Such a situation almost inevitably
produces the characteristic Australian
Cultural Cringe.
Arthur Angell Phillips 1900–85: *Meanjin* (1950)
'The Cultural Cringe'; see 30 below

24 Australia is a lucky country run mainly by
second-rate people who share its luck.
Donald Richmond Horne 1921– : *The Lucky
Country: Australia in the Sixties* (1964); see 7 above

25 In all directions stretched the great
Australian Emptiness, in which the mind is
the least of possessions.
Patrick White 1912–90: *The Vital Decade* (1968)
'The Prodigal Son'

26 Waiting for the Australian republic is like
waiting for the other shoe to drop.
Les Murray 1938– : 'The Coming Republic' in
Quadrant April 1976

27 I wanted to know the true nature of the 'otherness' I had been born into. It was not a European thing. I wanted to paint the great purity and implacability of the landscape. I wanted a visual form of the 'otherness' of the thing not seen.
Sidney Nolan 1917–93: Elwyn Lynn *Sidney Nolan—Australia* (1979)

28 Australia is the flattest, driest, ugliest place on earth. Only those who can be possessed by her can know what secret beauty she holds.
Eric Paul Willmot 1936– : *Australia The Last Experiment* (1987)

29 We wish no harm to England's native people. We are here to bring you good manners, refinement and an opportunity to make a *Koompartoo*, a fresh start.
planting an Aboriginal flag on the white cliffs of Dover and 'claiming' England for the Aboriginal people
Burnum Burnum 1936–97: on 26 January 1988, the year of Australia's bicentenary

30 Even as it [Great Britain] walked out on you and joined the Common Market, you were still looking for your MBEs and your knighthoods, and all the rest of the regalia that comes with it. You would take Australia right back down the time tunnel to the cultural cringe where you have always come from.
addressing Australian Conservative supporters of Great Britain
Paul Keating 1944– : on 27 February 1992; see 23 above

31 When New Zealanders emigrate to Australia, it raises the average IQ of both countries.
Robert Muldoon 1921–92: attributed

32 I was so angry because they were denying they had done anything wrong, denying that a whole generation was stolen.
of official response to concerns about the 'stolen generation'
Cathy Freeman 1973– : interview in *Daily Telegraph* 16 July 2000; see 9 above

➤➤ Beauty ◄◄

see also **The Body**

PROVERBS AND SAYINGS

1 **Beauty draws with a single hair.**
asserting the powerful attraction of a woman's beauty (often shown as outdoing great physical strength); see **Strength** 20, **Women** 24; English proverb, late 16th century

2 **Beauty is a good letter of introduction.**
American proverb, mid 20th century; see 10 below

3 **Beauty is in the eye of the beholder.**
beauty is not judged objectively, but according to the beholder's estimation; English proverb, mid 18th century

4 **Beauty is only skin deep.**
physical beauty is no guarantee of a good character or temperament; English proverb, early 17th century; see 32 below

PHRASES

9 **Beauty and the Beast**
characters in a fairy story by the French writer for children Madame de Beaumont (1711–80), translated into English in 1757. In the story Beauty, the youngest daughter of a merchant, goes to live in the Beast's palace and agrees to marry him; she

5 **Beauty is power.**
advertising slogan for Helena Rubinstein's Valaze Skin Food, 1904

6 **Mirror, mirror on the wall, Who is the fairest of them all?**
in the early 19th-century translation of the Grimm Brothers' *Fairytales*, the customary invocation of Snow White's wicked stepmother, which in due time received the reply that Snow White rather than herself was now the most beautiful

7 **Monday's child is fair of face.**
traditional rhyme, mid 19th century; see also **Gifts** 2, **Sorrow** 2, **Travel** 6, **Work** 6

8 **Please your eye and plague your heart.**
contrasting the pleasure given by the appearance of a beautiful person with the heartache they may cause; English proverb, early 17th century

discovers that he is a prince who has been put under a spell, which is destroyed by her love for him, and her ability to see his true worth beneath the hideous exterior; see 31 below

QUOTATIONS

10 A beautiful face is a mute recommendation.
Publilius Syrus: *Sententiae*; see 2 above

11 Consider the lilies of the field, how they grow; they toil not, neither do they spin: And yet I say unto you, That even Solomon in all his glory was not arrayed like one of these.
Bible: St Matthew

12 And she was fayr as is the rose in May.
Geoffrey Chaucer 1343–1400: *The Legend of Good Women* 'Cleopatra'

13 Was this the face that launched a thousand ships,
And burnt the topless towers of Ilium?
Sweet Helen, make me immortal with a kiss!
Christopher Marlowe 1564–93: *Doctor Faustus* (1604)

14 Love built on beauty, soon as beauty, dies.
John Donne 1572–1631: *Elegies* 'The Anagram' (c.1595)

15 O! she doth teach the torches to burn bright.
It seems she hangs upon the cheek of night
Like a rich jewel in an Ethiop's ear;
Beauty too rich for use, for earth too dear.
William Shakespeare 1564–1616: *Romeo and Juliet* (1595)

16 There is no excellent beauty that hath not some strangeness in the proportion.
Francis Bacon 1561–1626: *Essays* (1625) 'Of Beauty'

17 Beauty is the lover's gift.
William Congreve 1670–1729: *The Way of the World* (1700)

18 The flowers anew, returning seasons bring; But beauty faded has no second spring.
Ambrose Philips 1675–1749: *The First Pastoral* (1708)

19 Beauty is no quality in things themselves. It exists merely in the mind which contemplates them.
David Hume 1711–76: *Essays, Moral, Political, and Literary* (ed. T. H. Green and T. H. Grose, 1875) 'Of the Standard of Taste' (1757)

20 She walks in beauty, like the night
Of cloudless climes and starry skies.
Lord Byron 1788–1824: 'She Walks in Beauty' (1815)

21 A thing of beauty is a joy for ever.
John Keats 1795–1821: *Endymion* (1818); see Men 15

22 'Beauty is truth, truth beauty,'—that is all
Ye know on earth, and all ye need to know.
John Keats 1795–1821: 'Ode on a Grecian Urn' (1820); see **Truth 28**

23 There is nothing ugly; *I never saw an ugly thing in my life*: for let the form of an object be what it may,—light, shade, and perspective will always make it beautiful.
John Constable 1776–1837: C. R. Leslie *Memoirs of the Life of John Constable* (1843)

24 Remember that the most beautiful things in the world are the most useless; peacocks and lilies for instance.
John Ruskin 1819–1900: *Stones of Venice* vol. 1 (1851)

25 If you get simple beauty and naught else, You get about the best thing God invents.
Robert Browning 1812–89: 'Fra Lippo Lippi' (1855)

26 The awful thing is that beauty is mysterious as well as terrible. God and devil are fighting there, and the battlefield is the heart of man.
Fedor Dostoevsky 1821–81: *The Brothers Karamazov* (1879–80)

27 I have a left shoulder-blade that is a miracle of loveliness. People come miles to see it. My right elbow has a fascination that few can resist.
W. S. Gilbert 1836–1911: *The Mikado* (1885)

28 When a woman isn't beautiful, people always say, 'You have lovely eyes, you have lovely hair.'
Anton Chekhov 1860–1904: *Uncle Vanya* (1897)

29 Beauty is all very well at first sight; but who ever looks at it when it has been in the house three days?
George Bernard Shaw 1856–1950: *Man and Superman* (1903)

30 A pretty girl is like a melody
That haunts you night and day.
Irving Berlin 1888–1989: 'A Pretty Girl is like a Melody' (1919 song)

31 Oh no, it wasn't the aeroplanes. It was Beauty killed the Beast.
James Creelman 1901–41 and **Ruth Rose**: *King Kong* (1933 film) final words; see 9 above

32 I'm tired of all this nonsense about beauty being only skin-deep. That's deep enough. What do you want—an adorable pancreas?
Jean Kerr 1923– : *The Snake has all the Lines* (1958); see 4 above

33 There are no ugly women, only lazy ones.
Helena Rubinstein 1882–1965: *My Life for Beauty* (1966)

34 At some point in life the world's beauty becomes enough. You don't need to photograph, paint or even remember it. It is enough.
Toni Morrison 1931– : *Tar Baby* (1981)

35 The beauty myth moves for men as a mirage; its power lies in its ever-receding nature. When the gap is closed, the lover embraces only his own disillusion.
Naomi Wolf 1962– : *The Beauty Myth* (1990)

36 'Form follows profit' is the aesthetic principle of our times.
Richard Rogers 1933– : in *The Times* 13 February 1991; see **Architecture** 11

37 Beauty is handed out as undemocratically as inherited peerages, and beautiful people have done nothing to deserve their astonishing reward.
John Mortimer 1923– : in *Observer* 21 March 1999

38 Being thought of as a beautiful woman has spared me nothing in life. No heartache, no trouble. Beauty is essentially meaningless.
Halle Berry 1968– : in *Observer* 8 August 2004

➤➤ Beginning ◄◄

see also **Change, Ending**

PROVERBS AND SAYINGS

1 **Are you sitting comfortably? Then we'll begin.**
Julia Lang (1921–), introduction to stories on *Listen with Mother*, BBC Radio programme for small children, 1950–82

2 **First impressions are the most lasting.**
English proverb, early 18th century

3 **The golden rule of life is, make a beginning.**
American proverb, mid 20th century

4 **A good beginning makes a good ending.**
getting things right at the outset is likely to ensure success; English proverb, early 14th century

5 **It is easier to raise the Devil than to lay him.**
sometimes used to mean that it is easier to start a process than to stop it; English proverb, mid 17th century

6 **It is the first step that is difficult.**
English proverb, late 16th century; see **Achievement** 18

PHRASES

13 **back to square one**
back to the starting-point, with no progress made (*square one* may be a reference to a board-game such as Snakes and Ladders, or derive from the notional division of a football pitch into eight numbered sections for the purpose of early radio commentaries)

14 **back to the drawing board**
used to indicate that an idea, scheme, or proposal has been unsuccessful and that a new one must be devised; *drawing board* = a large flat board on which paper may be spread for artists or designers to work on; see **Inventions** 22

7 **It was a dark and stormy night.**
one variant of an opening line intended to convey a threatening and doom-laden atmosphere; in this form used by the novelist Edward Bulwer-Lytton (1803–73) in his novel *Paul Clifford* (1830)

8 **I've started so I'll finish.**
said by Magnus Magnusson when a contestant's time runs out while a question is being put, on *Mastermind*, BBC television (1972–97)

9 **The longest journey begins with a single step.**
often used to emphasize how important a single decision may be; late 20th century saying, ultimately derived from Lao Tzu: see 20 below

10 **The sooner begun, the sooner done.**
used as a warning against putting off a necessary but unwanted task; English proverb, late 16th century

11 **There is always a first time.**
English proverb, late 16th century

12 **Well begun is half done.**
emphasizing the importance of a successful beginning to the completion of a project; English proverb, early 15th century

15 **First Cause**
in philosophy, a supposed ultimate cause of all events, which does not itself have a cause, identified with God; see **God** 13

16 **fons et origo**
the source and origin; Latin, earliest in *fons et origo mali* (*mali* = of evil)

17 **primum mobile**
an originator of an action or event, an initiator, an initial source of activity; medieval Latin, literally 'first moving thing', in the medieval version of the Ptolemaic system, an outermost sphere supposed to revolve round the earth in twenty-four hours, carrying with it the inner spheres

18 vita nuova

a fresh start or new direction in life, especially after some powerful emotional experience; Italian = new life, a work by Dante describing his love for Beatrice

QUOTATIONS

19 In the beginning God created the heaven and the earth. And the earth was without form, and void; and darkness was upon the face of the deep. And the Spirit of God moved upon the face of the waters. And God said, Let there be light: and there was light.
Bible: Genesis

20 A tower of nine storeys begins with a heap of earth.
The journey of a thousand *li* starts from where one stands.
Lao Tzu *c.*604–*c.*531 BC: *Tao-te Ching*; see 9 above

21 Ere time and place were, time and place were not;
Where primitive nothing something straight begot;

Then all proceeded from the great united what.
John Wilmot, Lord Rochester 1647–80: 'Upon Nothing' (1680)

22 'Where shall I begin, please your Majesty?' he asked. 'Begin at the beginning,' the King said, gravely, 'and go on till you come to the end: then stop.'
Lewis Carroll 1832–98: *Alice's Adventures in Wonderland* (1865)

23 In my beginning is my end.
T. S. Eliot 1888–1965: *Four Quartets* 'East Coker' (1940); see **Ending 6**

24 All this will not be finished in the first 100 days. Nor will it be finished in the first 1,000 days, nor in the life of this Administration, nor even perhaps in our lifetime on this planet. But let us begin.
John F. Kennedy 1917–63: inaugural address, 20 January 1961

→→ Behaviour ←←

see also **Manners, Words and Deeds**

PROVERBS AND SAYINGS

1 Be what you would seem to be.
English proverb, late 14th century; earlier in classical sources

2 By a sweet tongue and kindness, you can drag an elephant by a hair.
Middle Eastern proverb; commonly found in this form in Arabic, the equivalent proverb in Persian has 'drag a snake'

3 Cleanliness is next to godliness.
next here means 'immediately following', as in serial order, and is now often used humorously to mean, 'the second most desirable quality possible'; English proverb, late 18th century; see **Dress 8**

4 Evil communications corrupt good manners.
proper conduct is harmfully influenced by false information or knowledge; the saying is also used to assert the deleterious effect of bad example; English proverb, early 15th century, from the Bible: see **Manners 10**

5 Good behaviour is the last refuge of mediocrity.
American proverb, mid 20th century

6 Handsome is as handsome does.
handsome here originally referred to chivalrous or genteel behaviour, although it is often popularly taken to refer to good looks; English proverb, late 16th century; see 8 below

7 He is a good dog who goes to church.
good character is shown by moral custom and practice; English proverb, early 19th century

8 Pretty is as pretty does.
American proverb, mid 19th century, equivalent of 6 above

9 When in Rome, do as the Romans do.
English proverb, late 15th century, from St Ambrose; see 19 below

PHRASES

10 add insult to injury
act in a way that makes a bad or displeasing situation worse, from Edward Moore's *The Foundling* (1748), 'This is adding insult to injuries'

11 beyond the pale
outside the bounds of acceptable behaviour; *pale* = former term for an area within determined bounds, or subject to a particular jurisdiction, as in *the Pale*, used to designate the English Pale in medieval Ireland, the territory of Calais in northern France when under English jurisdiction, and those areas of Tsarist Russia to which Jewish residence was restricted (known more fully as the Pale of Settlement)

12 conduct unbecoming
unsuitable or inappropriate behaviour, from *Articles of War* (1872) 'Any officer who shall behave in a scandalous manner, unbecoming the character of an officer and a gentleman shall . . . be CASHIERED'; the Naval Discipline Act, 10 August 1860 uses the words 'conduct unbecoming the character of an Officer'

13 dirty work at the crossroads
dishonourable, illicit, or underhand behaviour. The term may reflect a view of *crossroads* as a sinister place, where suicides were traditionally buried

14 prunes and prisms
(marked by) prim, mincing affectation of speech; offered by Mrs General in Dickens's *Little Dorrit* (1857) as a phrase giving 'a pretty form to the lips'

15 the Queensberry Rules
standard rules of polite or acceptable behaviour; a code of rules drawn up in 1867 under the supervision of Sir John Sholto Douglas (1844–1900), eighth Marquis of *Queensberry*, to govern the sport of boxing in Great Britain; the standard rules of modern boxing

16 sweetness and light
extreme (and uncharacteristic) mildness and reason in manner and behaviour, from Swift (1704): see **Virtue** 25

17 to the manner born
naturally fitted for some position or employment, from Shakespeare *Hamlet*: see **Custom** 11

QUOTATIONS

18 *O tempora, O mores!*
Oh, the times! Oh, the manners!
Cicero 106–43 BC: *In Catilinam*

19 When I go to Rome, I fast on Saturday, but here [Milan] I do not. Do you also follow the custom of whatever church you attend, if you do not want to give or receive scandal.
St Ambrose c.339–397: 'Letter 54 to Januarius' (AD c.400); see 9 above

20 This noble ensample to his sheep he yaf,
That first he wroghte, and afterward he taughte.
Geoffrey Chaucer 1343–1400: *The Canterbury Tales* 'The General Prologue'

21 Careless she is with artful care,
Affecting to seem unaffected.
William Congreve 1670–1729: 'Amoret'

22 Take the tone of the company that you are in.
Lord Chesterfield 1694–1773: *Letters to his Son* (1774) 16 October 1747

23 They teach the morals of a whore, and the manners of a dancing master.
of the *Letters* of Lord Chesterfield
Samuel Johnson 1709–84: James Boswell *Life of Samuel Johnson* (1791) 1754

24 Always ding, dinging Dame Grundy into my ears—what will Mrs Grundy zay? What will Mrs Grundy think?
Thomas Morton 1764–1838: *Speed the Plough* (1798); see **Morality** 9

25 May I ask whether these pleasing attentions proceed from the impulse of the moment, or are the result of previous study?
Jane Austen 1775–1817: *Pride and Prejudice* (1813)

26 There was a little girl
Who had a little curl
Right in the middle of her forehead,
When she was good
She was very, very good,
But when she was bad she was horrid.
composed for, and sung to, his second daughter while a babe in arms, c.1850
Henry Wadsworth Longfellow 1807–82: B. R. Tucker-Macchetta *The Home Life of Henry W. Longfellow* (1882)

27 He only does it to annoy,
Because he knows it teases.
Lewis Carroll 1832–98: *Alice's Adventures in Wonderland* (1865)

28 Go directly—see what she's doing, and tell her she mustn't.
Punch: 1872

29 Conduct is three-fourths of our life and its largest concern.
Matthew Arnold 1822–88: *Literature and Dogma* (1873)

30 Be a good animal, true to your instincts.
D. H. Lawrence 1885–1930: *The White Peacock* (1911)

31 Vulgarity has its uses. Vulgarity often cuts ice which refinement scrapes at vainly.
Max Beerbohm 1872–1956: letter 21 May 1921

32 Being tactful in audacity is knowing how far one can go too far.
Jean Cocteau 1889–1963: *Le Rappel à l'ordre* (1926)

33 Private faces in public places
Are wiser and nicer
Than public faces in private places.
W. H. Auden 1907–73: *Orators* (1932)

34 I get too hungry for dinner at eight.
I like the theatre, but never come late.
I never bother with people I hate.
That's why the lady is a tramp.
Lorenz Hart 1895–1943: 'The Lady is a Tramp' (1937 song)

35 The basis of all good human behaviour is kindness.
Eleanor Roosevelt 1884–1962: *Book of Common Sense Etiquette* (1962)

36 When people are on their best behaviour they aren't always at their best.
Alan Bennett 1934– : *Dinner at Noon* (BBC television, 1988)

37 I would have love to have had such a positive role model.
describing herself in her book offering advice to teenagers
Serena Williams 1981– : in *Sunday Times* 27 March 2005

⤜ Belief ⤝

see also **Certainty and Doubt, Faith**

PROVERBS AND SAYINGS

1 **Believe nothing of what you hear, and only half of what you see.**
English proverb, mid 19th century; a related Middle English saying warns that you should not believe everything that is said or that you hear

2 **A believer is a songless bird in a cage.**
American proverb, late 19th century; see 24 below

3 **Believing has a core of unbelieving.**
American proverb, mid 19th century

4 **Pigs may fly, but they are very unlikely birds.**
English proverb, mid 19th century; see 8 below

5 **Seeing is believing.**
acceptance of the existence of something depends on actual demonstration; English proverb, early 17th century

6 **Tell that to the marines.**
a scornful expression of disbelief, from the saying *that will do for the marines but the sailors won't believe it* (the marines were originally soldiers enlisted and trained to serve on board ship); see 21 below. The expression is recorded from the early 19th century, although a late 19th-century hoax attributing the origin to a remark made by Charles II to Samuel Pepys has been widely reprinted

PHRASES

7 **a doubting Thomas**
a person who refuses to believe something without incontrovertible proof; a sceptic, from the story of the apostle *Thomas*, who said that he would not believe that Christ had risen again until he had seen and touched his wounds; from the Bible (John)

8 **pigs might fly**
an expression of ironical disbelief, from the proverb: see 4 above

9 **swallow a camel**
make no difficulty about something incredible or unreasonable, from the Bible (Matthew) 'Ye blind guides, which strain at a gnat, and swallow a camel'

10 **take something with a pinch (or grain) of salt**
regard something as exaggerated; believe only part of something (from the modern Latin phrase *cum grano salis* 'with a grain of salt', recorded from the mid 17th century)

QUOTATIONS

11 It is convenient that there be gods, and, as it is convenient, let us believe that there are.
Ovid 43–c.17: *Ars Amatoria*

12 Lord, I believe; help thou mine unbelief.
Bible: St Mark

13 Except ye see signs and wonders, ye will not believe.
Bible: St John

14 *Certum est quia impossibile est.*
It is certain because it is impossible.
often quoted as '*Credo quia impossibile* [I believe because it is impossible]'
Tertullian c.AD 160–c.225: *De Carne Christi*

15 Say to the unbelievers: 'You shall be overthrown, and mustered into Gehenna— an evil cradling!'
The Koran: sura 3

16 For what a man would like to be true, that he more readily believes.
Francis Bacon 1561–1626: *Novum Organum* (1620)

17 By night an atheist half believes a God.
Edward Young 1683–1765: *Night Thoughts* (1742–5) 'Night 5'

18 Truth, Sir, is a cow, that will yield such people [sceptics] no more milk, and so they are gone to milk the bull.
Samuel Johnson 1709–84: James Boswell *Life of Samuel Johnson* (1791) 21 July 1763

19 Confidence is a plant of slow growth in an aged bosom: youth is the season of credulity.
William Pitt, Earl of Chatham 1708–78: speech, House of Commons, 14 January 1766

20 Credulity is the man's weakness, but the child's strength.
Charles Lamb 1775–1834: *Essays of Elia* (1823) 'Witches, and Other Night-Fears'

21 Tell that to the marines—the sailors won't believe it.
Sir Walter Scott 1771–1832: *Redgauntlet* (1824); see 6 above

22 *We can believe what we choose.* We are answerable for what we choose to believe.
John Henry Newman 1801–90: letter to Mrs William Froude, 27 June 1848

23 Why, sometimes I've believed as many as six impossible things before breakfast.
Lewis Carroll 1832–98: *Through the Looking-Glass* (1872)

24 A believer is a songless bird in a cage, a freethinker is an eagle parting the clouds with tireless wings.
Robert G. Ingersoll 1833–99: *An Arraignment of the Church, and a Plea for Individuality* (1877); see 2 above

25 I do not pretend to know where many ignorant men are sure — that is all that agnosticism means.
Clarence Darrow 1857–1938: speech at the trial of John Thomas Scopes, 15 July 1925

26 Of course not, but I am told it works even if you don't believe in it.
when asked whether he really believed a horseshoe hanging over his door would bring him luck, c.1930
Niels Bohr 1885–1962: A. Pais *Inward Bound* (1986)

27 The dust of exploded beliefs may make a fine sunset.
Geoffrey Madan 1895–1947: *Livre sans nom: Twelve Reflections* (privately printed 1934)

28 When men stop believing in God they don't believe in nothing; they believe in anything.
G. K. Chesterton 1874–1936: widely attributed, although not traced in his works

29 Man is a credulous animal, and must believe *something*; in the absence of good grounds for belief, he will be satisfied with bad ones.
Bertrand Russell 1872–1970: *Unpopular Essays* (1950) 'Outline of Intellectual Rubbish'

30 If it were an innocent, passive gullibility it would be excusable; but all too clearly, alas, it is an active willingness to be deceived.
Peter Medawar 1915–87: review of Teilhard de Chardin *The Phenomenon of Man* (1961)

31 I do not believe . . . I know.
Carl Gustav Jung 1875–1961: L. van der Post *Jung and the Story of our Time* (1976)

32 I confused things with their names: that is belief.
Jean-Paul Sartre 1905–80: *Les Mots* (1964)

33 No matter how I probe and prod
I cannot quite believe in God.
But oh! I hope to God that he
Unswervingly believes in me.
E. Y. Harburg 1898–1981: 'The Agnostic' (1965)

34 Of course, Behaviourism 'works'. So does torture. Give me a no-nonsense, down-to-earth behaviourist, a few drugs, and simple electrical appliances, and in six months I will have him reciting the Athanasian Creed in public.
W. H. Auden 1907–73: *A Certain World* (1970)

35 It is harder for some people to believe that God loves them than to believe that he exists.
Basil Hume 1923–99: in *Guardian* 18 June 1999

⇥ The Bible ⇤

PHRASES

1 the Authorized Version
the King James Bible of 1611; this translation became widely popular following its publication, and although in fact never officially 'authorized' it remained for centuries the Bible of every English-speaking country; see 3 below

2 the Breeches Bible
the Geneva bible of 1560, so named because the word *breeches* is used in Genesis 3:7 for the garments made by Adam and Eve, rendered *aprons* in the King James bible

3 the King James Bible
the 1611 English translation of the Bible, ordered to be made by James I, and produced by about fifty scholars; see 1 above

4 Sin On Bible
an edition of 1716, the first English-language Bible to be printed in Ireland, so named because John 5:14 reads 'sin on more' instead of 'sin no more'

5 the Treacle Bible
a translation which has 'treacle' where other translations have 'balm', as in Jeremiah 8:22 'Is there no treacle in Gilead?'

6 the Wicked Bible
an edition of 1631, in which the seventh commandment was misprinted 'Thou shalt commit adultery'

QUOTATIONS

7 Holy writ is the scripture of peoples, for it is made, that all peoples should know it.
St Jerome c.AD 342–420: attributed

8 The devil can cite Scripture for his purpose.
William Shakespeare 1564–1616: *The Merchant of Venice* (1596–8); see **Quotations** 1

9 The pencil of the Holy Ghost hath laboured more in describing the afflictions of Job than the felicities of Solomon.
Francis Bacon 1561–1626: *Essays* (1625) 'Of Adversity'

10 *Scrutamini scripturas* [Let us look at the scriptures]. These two words have undone the world.
John Selden 1584–1654: *Table Talk* (1689) 'Bible Scripture'

11 We present you with this Book, the most valuable thing that this world affords. Here is wisdom; this is the royal Law; these are the lively Oracles of God.
Coronation Service 1689: The Presenting of the Holy Bible

12 The English Bible, a book which, if everything else in our language should perish, would alone suffice to show the whole extent of its beauty and power.
Lord Macaulay 1800–59: 'John Dryden' (1828)

13 There's a great text in Galatians,
Once you trip on it, entails
Twenty-nine distinct damnations,
One sure, if another fails.
Robert Browning 1812–89: 'Soliloquy of the Spanish Cloister' (1842)

14 We have used the Bible as if it was a constable's handbook—an opium-dose for keeping beasts of burden patient while they are being overloaded.
Charles Kingsley 1819–75: *Letters to the Chartists*

15 LORD ILLINGWORTH: The Book of Life begins with a man and a woman in a garden.
MRS ALLONBY: It ends with Revelations.
Oscar Wilde 1854–1900: *A Woman of No Importance* (1893)

16 An apology for the Devil: It must be remembered that we have only heard one side of the case. God has written all the books.
Samuel Butler 1835–1902: *Notebooks* (1912)

17 It ain't necessarily so,
It ain't necessarily so,
De t'ings dat yo' li'ble
To read in de Bible
It ain't necessarily so.
Du Bose Heyward 1885–1940 and **Ira Gershwin** 1896–1989: 'It ain't necessarily so' (1935)

18 I know of no book which has been a source of brutality and sadistic conduct, both public and private, that can compare with the Bible.
Reginald Paget 1908–90: in *Observer* 28 June 1964

19 There's a Bible on that shelf there. But I keep it next to Voltaire—poison and antidote.
Bertrand Russell 1872–1970: in *Kenneth Harris Talking To* (1971) 'Bertrand Russell'

20 Anyone who thinks that politics and
religion don't mix is not reading the same
Bible I am.
Desmond Tutu 1931– : attributed; David Rogers
Politics, Prayer and Parliament (2000)

⇥ Biography ⇤

PHRASES

1 lues Boswelliana
a biographer's tendency to magnify his or her
subject, regarded as a disease, from Latin *lues* (=
plague) and the name of James *Boswell* (1740–95) as
the friend and biographer of Samuel Johnson

2 who's who
a list or directory of facts about notable people; the
annual biographical dictionary *Who's Who* was first

issued in 1849 but took its present form in 1897. The
entries are compiled with the assistance of the
subjects themselves, and contain some agreeable
eccentricities particularly in the section labelled
'Recreations'; see **Leisure 16**

QUOTATIONS

3 Many brave men lived before Agamemnon's
time; but they are all, unmourned and
unknown, covered by the long night,
because they lack their sacred poet.
Horace 65–8 BC: *Odes*; see **Reputation 1**

4 I am writing biography, not history, and the
truth is that the most brilliant exploits often
tell us nothing of the virtues or vices of the
men who performed them, while on the
other hand a chance remark or a joke may
reveal far more of a man's character than the
mere feat of winning battles in which
thousands fall, or of marshalling great
armies, or laying siege to cities.
Plutarch c.AD 46–c.120: *Parallel Lives* 'Alexander'

5 Nobody can write the life of a man, but
those who have eat and drunk and lived in
social intercourse with him.
Samuel Johnson 1709–84: James Boswell *Life of
Samuel Johnson* (1791) 31 March 1772

6 Lives of great men all remind us
We can make our lives sublime,
And, departing, leave behind us
Footprints on the sands of time.
Henry Wadsworth Longfellow 1807–82: 'A
Psalm of Life' (1838)

7 A well-written Life is almost as rare as a well-
spent one.
Thomas Carlyle 1795–1881: *Critical and
Miscellaneous Essays* (1838) 'Jean Paul Friedrich
Richter'

8 There is properly no history; only
biography.
Ralph Waldo Emerson 1803–82: *Essays* (1841)
'History'

9 Then there is my noble and biographical
friend who has added a new terror to death.
on Lord Campbell's *Lives of the Lord Chancellors*
being written without the consent of heirs or
executors
Charles Wetherell 1770–1846: Lord St Leonards
*Misrepresentations in Campbell's Lives of Lyndhurst
and Brougham* (1869); also attributed to Lord
Lyndhurst (1772–1863)

10 *refusing an offer to write his memoirs:*
I should be trading on the blood of my men.
Robert E. Lee 1807–70: attributed, perhaps
apocryphal

11 Every great man nowadays has his disciples,
and it is always Judas who writes the
biography.
Oscar Wilde 1854–1900: *Intentions* (1891) 'The
Critic as Artist'

12 It is not a Life at all. It is a Reticence, in three
volumes.
on J. W. Cross's *Life of George Eliot*
W. E. Gladstone 1809–98: E. F. Benson *As We Were*
(1930)

13 The Art of Biography
Is different from Geography.
Geography is about Maps,
But Biography is about Chaps.
Edmund Clerihew Bentley 1875–1956: *Biography
for Beginners* (1905)

14 And kept his heart a secret to the end
From all the picklocks of biographers.
of Robert E. Lee
Stephen Vincent Benét 1898–1943: *John Brown's
Body* (1928)

15 Discretion is not the better part of biography.
Lytton Strachey 1880–1932: Michael Holroyd *Lytton Strachey* vol. 1 (1967)

16 Reformers are always finally neglected, while the memoirs of the frivolous will always eagerly be read.
Chips Channon 1897–1958: diary 7 July 1936

17 To write one's memoirs is to speak ill of everybody except oneself.
Henri Philippe Pétain 1856–1951: in *Observer* 26 May 1946

18 If you really want to hear about it, the first thing you'll probably want to know is where I was born, and what my lousy childhood was like, and how my parents were occupied and all before they had me, and all that David Copperfield kind of crap, but I don't feel like going into it.
J. D. Salinger 1919– : *Catcher in the Rye* (1951)

19 An autobiography is an obituary in serial form with the last instalment missing.
Quentin Crisp 1908–99: *The Naked Civil Servant* (1968)

20 It's an excellent life of somebody else. But I've really lived inside myself, and she can't get in there.
on a biography of himself
Robertson Davies 1913–95: interview in *The Times* 4 April 1995

21 Nobody likes being written about in their lifetime, it's as though the FBI and the CIA were suddenly to splash your files in the paper.
Saul Bellow 1915–2005: in *Guardian* 10 September 1997

22 Biography is the mesh through which real life escapes.
Tom Stoppard 1937– : *The Invention of Love* (1997)

➤➤ Birds ◄◄

see also **Animals**

PROVERBS AND SAYINGS

1 **A mockingbird has no voice of his own.**
the mockingbird is noted for its mimicry of the calls and songs of other birds; American proverb, mid 19th century

2 **One for sorrow; two for mirth; three for a wedding, four for a birth.**
a traditional rhyme found in a variety of forms, referring to the number of magpies seen on a particular occasion; English proverb, mid 19th century

3 **The robin and the wren are God's cock and hen; the martin and the swallow are God's mate and marrow.**
there was a traditional belief that the robin and the wren were sacred birds, and that to harm them in any way would be unlucky (*marrow* = 'companion'); English proverb, late 18th century

4 **The white heron is a bird of a single flight.**
the white heron is very rare; Maori proverb; see **Originality** 3

PHRASES

5 **the bird of Jove**
the eagle

6 **the bird of Juno**
the peacock

7 **Mother Carey's chicken**
the storm petrel

QUOTATIONS

8 The silver swan, who, living had no note, When death approached unlocked her silent throat.
Orlando Gibbons 1583–1625: 'The Silver Swan' (1612 song)

9 A robin red breast in a cage Puts all Heaven in a rage.
William Blake 1757–1827: 'Auguries of Innocence' (*c*.1803)

10 O Cuckoo! Shall I call thee bird, Or but a wandering voice?
William Wordsworth 1770–1850: 'To the Cuckoo' (1807)

11 Hail to thee, blithe Spirit! Bird thou never wert, That from Heaven, or near it, Pourest thy full heart

In profuse strains of unpremeditated art.
Percy Bysshe Shelley 1792–1822: 'To a Skylark' (1819)

12 Alone and warming his five wits,
The white owl in the belfry sits.
Alfred, Lord Tennyson 1809–92: 'Song—The Owl' (1830)

13 That's the wise thrush; he sings each song
     twice over,
  Lest you should think he never could
     recapture
  The first fine careless rapture!
Robert Browning 1812–89: 'Home-Thoughts, from Abroad' (1845)

14 I once had a sparrow alight upon my shoulder for a moment while I was hoeing in a village garden, and I felt that I was more distinguished by that circumstance than I should have been by any epaulette I could have worn.
Henry David Thoreau 1817–62: *Walden* (1854) 'Winter Animals'

15 I caught this morning morning's minion,
     kingdom of daylight's dauphin, dapple-
     dawn-drawn Falcon.
Gerard Manley Hopkins 1844–89: 'The Windhover' (written 1877)

16 It was the Rainbow gave thee birth,
  And left thee all her lovely hues.
W. H. Davies 1871–1940: 'Kingfisher' (1910)

17 Oh, a wondrous bird is the pelican!
  His beak holds more than his belican.
  He takes in his beak
  Food enough for a week.
  But I'll be darned if I know how the helican.
usually quoted as, ' . . . But I'm damned if I see how the helican'
Dixon Lanier Merritt 1879–1972: in *Nashville Banner* 22 April 1913

18 It took the whole of Creation
  To produce my foot, my each feather:
  Now I hold Creation in my foot.
Ted Hughes 1930–98: 'Hawk Roosting' (1960)

19 Blackbirds are the cellos of the deep farms.
Anne Stevenson 1933– : 'Green Mountain, Black Mountain' (1982)

20 I live in a city. I know sparrows from starlings. After that everything's a duck as far as I'm concerned.
Terry Pratchett 1948– : *Monstrous Regiment* (2003)

Birth see **Pregnancy and Birth**

➤➤ The Body ◀◀

see also **Appearance, The Senses**

PROVERBS AND SAYINGS

1 **Cold hands, warm heart.**
the outward sign may contradict the inward reality; English proverb, early 20th century

2 **The eyes are the window of the soul.**
it is in the eyes that a person's true nature can be discerned; English proverb, mid 16th century

3 **The larger the body, the bigger the heart.**
American proverb, mid 20th century

PHRASES

4 **a boneless wonder**
a contortionist; see **Politicians** 27

5 **crowning glory**
a woman's hair; the most beautiful feature or possession, the greatest achievement; see 10 below

6 **Cupid's bow**
a particular shape of (the upper edge of) the upper lip, referring to the double-curved bow traditionally carried by Cupid

7 **lump of clay**
the human body regarded as purely material, without a soul; linked to the biblical use of *clay* = a

material of which the human body was formed, as in Genesis: 'I also am formed out of the clay'

8 **unruly member**
the tongue, after the Bible (James) 'the tongue is a little member . . . the tongue can no man tame; it is an unruly evil'

QUOTATIONS

9 I will give thanks unto thee, for I am
fearfully and wonderfully made.
Bible: Psalm 139

10 Doth not even nature itself teach you, that if
a man have long hair, it is a shame
unto him?
But if a woman have long hair, it is a glory
to her.
Bible: I Corinthians; see 5 above

11 Raised by that curious engine, your white
hand.
John Webster 1580– : *The Duchess of Malfi* (1623)

12 Her feet beneath her petticoat,
Like little mice, stole in and out.
John Suckling 1609–42: 'A Ballad upon a
Wedding' (1646)

13 The hands are a sort of feet, which serve us
in our passage towards Heaven, curiously
distinguished into joints and fingers, and fit
to be applied to any thing which reason can
imagine or desire.
Thomas Traherne 1637–74: *Meditations on the Six
Days of Creation* (1717)

14 Why has not man a microscopic eye?
For this plain reason, man is not a fly.
Alexander Pope 1688–1744: *An Essay on Man*
Epistle 1 (1733)

15 And our carcases, which are to rise again, are
they worth raising? I hope, if mine is, that I
shall have a better pair of legs than I have
moved on these two-and-twenty years, or I
shall be sadly behind in the squeeze into
Paradise.
Lord Byron 1788–1824: letter 13 September 1811

16 I sing the body electric.
Walt Whitman 1819–92: title of poem (1855)

17 Our body is a machine for living. It is
organized for that, it is its nature. Let life go
on in it unhindered and let it defend itself,
it will do more than if you paralyse it by
encumbering it with remedies.
Leo Tolstoy 1828–1910: *War and Peace* (1865–9)

18 A large nose is in fact the sign of an affable
man, good, courteous, witty, liberal,
courageous, such as I am.
Edmond Rostand 1868–1918: *Cyrano de Bergerac*
(1897)

19 An impersonal and scientific knowledge of
the structure of our bodies is the surest
safeguard against prurient curiosity and
lascivious gloating.
Marie Stopes 1880–1958: *Married Love* (1918)

20 Anatomy is destiny.
Sigmund Freud 1856–1939: *Collected Writings*
(1924)

21 There is more felicity on the far side of
baldness than young men can possibly
imagine.
Logan Pearsall Smith 1865–1946: *Afterthoughts*
(1931)

22 Only God, my dear,
Could love you for yourself alone
And not your yellow hair.
W. B. Yeats 1865–1939: 'Anne Gregory' (1932)

23 Imprisoned in every fat man a thin one is
wildly signalling to be let out.
Cyril Connolly 1903–74: *The Unquiet Grave* (1944)

24 I came in here in all good faith to help my
country. I don't mind giving a reasonable
amount [of blood], but a pint . . . why that's
very nearly an armful.
Ray Galton 1930– and **Alan Simpson** 1929– :
The Blood Donor (1961 BBC television programme)
words spoken by Tony Hancock

25 A woman watches her body uneasily, as
though it were an unreliable ally in the
battle for love.
Leonard Cohen 1934– : *The Favourite Game* (1963)

26 My brain? It's my second favourite organ.
Woody Allen 1935– : *Sleeper* (1973 film, with
Marshall Brickman)

27 Fat is a feminist issue.
Susie Orbach 1946– : title of book (1978)

28 The leg, a source of much delight,
which carries weight and governs height.
Ian Dury 1942–2000: 'The Body Song' (1981)

29 Entrails don't care for travel,
Entrails don't care for stress:
Entrails are better kept folded inside you
For outside, they make a mess.
Connie Bensley 1929– : 'Entrails' (1987)

30 My disability is that I cannot use my legs.
My handicap is your negative perception of
that disability, and thus of me.
Rick Hansen 1957– : *Rick Hansen: Man in Motion*
(1987, with Jim Taylor)

31 I think with my hands. I just like
manipulation. I began to like it as a child
and it's continued to be a pleasure.
Dorothy Hodgkin 1910–94: Lewis Wolpert and
Alison Richards *A Passion for Science* (1988)

32 Modern body building is ritual, religion,
sport, art, and science, awash in Western
chemistry and mathematics. Defying
nature, it surpasses it.
Camille Paglia 1947– : *Sex, Art, and American
Culture* (1992)

⇥ Books ⇤

see also **Fiction and Story-telling, Libraries, Reading, Writing**

PROVERBS AND SAYINGS

1 **A book is like a garden carried in the pocket.**
American proverb, mid 20th century

2 **A great book is a great evil.**
a long book is likely to be verbose and badly written; English proverb, early 17th century: a contraction of Callimachus (c.305–c.240 BC) 'the great book is equal to a great evil'

3 **It is a tie between men to have read the same book.**
American proverb, mid 19th century

QUOTATIONS

4 Of making many books there is no end; and much study is a weariness of the flesh.
Bible: Ecclesiastes

5 There is no book so bad that some good cannot be got out of it.
Pliny the Elder AD 23–79: Pliny the Younger *Letters*

6 Some books are to be tasted, others to be swallowed, and some few to be chewed and digested; that is, some books are to be read only in parts; others to be read but not curiously; and some few to be read wholly, and with diligence and attention. Some books also may be read by deputy, and extracts made of them by others.
Francis Bacon 1561–1626: *Essays* (1625) 'Of Studies'

7 A good book is the precious lifeblood of a master spirit, embalmed and treasured up on purpose to a life beyond life.
John Milton 1608–74: *Areopagitica* (1644)

8 An empty book is like an infant's soul, in which anything may be written. It is capable of all things, but containeth nothing.
Thomas Traherne 1637–74: *Centuries of Meditations*

9 I hate books; they only teach us to talk about things we know nothing about.
Jean-Jacques Rousseau 1712–78: *Émile* (1762)

10 The reading or non-reading a book—will never keep down a single petticoat.
Lord Byron 1788–1824: letter to Richard Hoppner, 29 October 1819

11 Your *borrowers of books*—those mutilators of collections, spoilers of the symmetry of shelves, and creators of odd volumes.
Charles Lamb 1775–1834: *Essays of Elia* (1823) 'The Two Races of Men'

12 A good book is the best of friends, the same to-day and for ever.
Martin Tupper 1810–89: *Proverbial Philosophy* Series I (1838) 'Of Reading'

13 No furniture so charming as books.
Sydney Smith 1771–1845: Lady Holland *Memoir* (1855)

14 'What is the use of a book', thought Alice, 'without pictures or conversations?'
Lewis Carroll 1832–98: *Alice's Adventures in Wonderland* (1865)

15 There is no such thing as a moral or an immoral book. Books are well written, or badly written.
Oscar Wilde 1854–1900: *The Picture of Dorian Gray* (1891)

16 '*Classic*'. A book which people praise and don't read.
Mark Twain 1835–1910: *Following the Equator* (1897)

17 A bad book is as much of a labour to write as a good one; it comes as sincerely from the author's soul.
Aldous Huxley 1894–1963: *Point Counter Point* (1928)

18 A best-seller is the gilded tomb of a mediocre talent.
Logan Pearsall Smith 1865–1946: *Afterthoughts* (1931)

19 Books can not be killed by fire. People die, but books never die. No man and no force can abolish memory . . . In this war, we know, books are weapons. And it is a part of your dedication always to make them weapons for man's freedom.
Franklin D. Roosevelt 1882–1945: 'Message to the Booksellers of America' 6 May 1942

20 The principle of procrastinated rape is said to be the ruling one in all the great best-sellers.
V. S. Pritchett 1900–97: *The Living Novel* (1946) 'Clarissa'

21 I suggest that the only books that influence us are those for which we are ready, and which have gone a little farther down our

particular path than we have yet got ourselves.
E. M. Forster 1879–1970: *Two Cheers for Democracy* (1951)

22 Some books are undeservedly forgotten; none are undeservedly remembered.
W. H. Auden 1907–73: *The Dyer's Hand* (1963) 'Reading'

23 The possession of a book becomes a substitute for reading it.
Anthony Burgess 1917–93: in *New York Times Book Review* 4 December 1966

24 Long books, when read, are usually overpraised, because the reader wishes to convince others and himself that he has not wasted his time.
E. M. Forster 1879–1970: note from commonplace book; O. Stallybrass (ed.) *Aspects of the Novel and Related Writings* (1974)

25 The good of a book lies in its being read.
Umberto Eco 1932– : *The Name of the Rose* (1981)

26 Books say: she did this because. Life says: she did this. Books are where things are explained to you; life is where things aren't.
Julian Barnes 1946– : *Flaubert's Parrot* (1984)

27 Russian literature saved my soul. When I was a young girl in school and I asked what is good and what is evil, no one in that corrupt system could show me.
Irina Ratushinskaya 1954– : in *Observer* 15 October 1989

28 What literature can and should do is change the people who teach the people who don't read the books.
A. S. Byatt 1936– : interview in *Newsweek* 5 June 1995

⤝ Boredom ⤜

PHRASES

1 **been there, done that**
used to express past experience of or familiarity with something, especially something now regarded as boring or unwelcome; see **Travel** 1

2 **harp on the same string**
dwell tediously on the same subject; see 3 below

QUOTATIONS

3 Harp not on that string.
William Shakespeare 1564–1616: *Richard III* (1591); see 2 above

4 The secret of being a bore . . . is to tell everything.
Voltaire 1694–1778: *Discours en vers sur l'homme* (1737)

5 He is not only dull in himself, but the cause of dullness in others.
on a law lord
Samuel Foote 1720–77: James Boswell *Life of Samuel Johnson* (1791) 1783

6 Society is now one polished horde, Formed of two mighty tribes, the *Bores* and *Bored*.
Lord Byron 1788–1824: *Don Juan* (1819–24)

7 A desire for desires—boredom.
Leo Tolstoy 1828–1910: *Anna Karenina* (1873–6)

8 Boredom is . . . a vital problem for the moralist, since half the sins of mankind are caused by the fear of it.
Bertrand Russell 1872–1970: *The Conquest of Happiness* (1930)

9 Someone has somewhere commented on the fact that millions long for immortality who don't know what to do with themselves on a rainy Sunday afternoon.
Susan Ertz 1894–1985: *Anger in the Sky* (1943)

10 Nothing happens, nobody comes, nobody goes, it's awful!
Samuel Beckett 1906–89: *Waiting for Godot* (1955)

11 Nothing, like something, happens anywhere.
Philip Larkin 1922–85: 'I Remember, I Remember' (1955)

12 Life, friends, is boring. We must not say so
. . .
And moreover my mother told me as a boy (repeatedly) 'Ever to confess you're bored means you have no
Inner Resources.' I conclude now I have no inner resources, because I am heavy bored.
John Berryman 1914–72: *77 Dream Songs* (1964) no. 14

13 What's wrong with being a boring kind of guy?
during the campaign for the Republican nomination
George Bush 1924– : in *Daily Telegraph* 28 April 1988

Borrowing see Debt and Borrowing

⇥⇥Britain ⇤⇤

see also **England, Scotland, Wales**

PHRASES

1 Cool Britannia
Britain, perceived as a stylish and fashionable place, especially (in the late 1990s) as represented by the international success of and interest in contemporary British art, popular music, film, and fashion

2 from Land's End to John o'Groats
from one end of Britain to the other; *Land's End* a rocky promontory in SW Cornwall, which forms the westernmost point of England; *John o'Groats* a village at the extreme NE point of the Scottish mainland

3 the Mother of Parliaments
the British parliament, from Bright: see **Parliament** 21

4 the red, white, and blue
the Union flag of the United Kingdom, from the colours of the three crosses making up the Union flag, the red on white cross of St George (for England), the white on blue cross saltire of St Andrew (for Scotland), and the red on white cross saltire of St Patrick (for Ireland)

5 twist the lion's tail
provoke the resentment of the British; a *lion* as the symbol of the British Empire

QUOTATIONS

6 Rule, Britannia, rule the waves;
Britons never will be slaves.
James Thomson 1700–48: *Alfred: a Masque* (1740)

7 It must be owned, that the Graces do not seem to be natives of Great Britain; and I doubt, the best of us here have more of rough than polished diamond.
Lord Chesterfield 1694–1773: *Letters to his Son* (1774) 18 November 1748

8 Born and educated in this country, I glory in the name of Briton.
George III 1738–1820: *The King's Speech on Opening the Session* 18 November 1760

9 He [the Briton] is a barbarian, and thinks that the customs of his tribe and island are the laws of nature.
George Bernard Shaw 1856–1950: *Caesar and Cleopatra* (1901)

10 Other nations use 'force'; we Britons alone use 'Might'.
Evelyn Waugh 1903–66: *Scoop* (1938)

11 The British nation is unique in this respect. They are the only people who like to be told how bad things are, who like to be told the worst.
Winston Churchill 1874–1965: speech in the House of Commons, 10 June 1941

12 Britain will be honoured by historians more for the way she disposed of an empire than for the way in which she acquired it.
Lord Harlech 1918–85: in *New York Times* 28 October 1962

13 Great Britain has lost an empire and has not yet found a role.
Dean Acheson 1893–1971: speech at the Military Academy, West Point, 5 December 1962

14 A soggy little island huffing and puffing to keep up with Western Europe.
John Updike 1932– : 'London Life' (written 1969)

15 [The Commonwealth] is a largely meaningless relic of Empire—like the smile on the face of the Cheshire Cat which remains when the cat has disappeared.
Nigel Lawson 1932– : attributed, 1993; see **Cats** 3

16 Fifty years on from now, Britain will still be the country of long shadows on county [cricket] grounds, warm beer, invincible green suburbs, dog lovers, and—as George Orwell said—old maids bicycling to Holy Communion through the morning mist.
John Major 1943– : speech to the Conservative Group for Europe, 22 April 1993; see **England** 24

17 What you have within the UK is three small nations who've been under the cosh of the English.
Jack Straw 1946– : in *Sunday Times* 6 January 2000

18 Most of all I would like to thank all those people in Britain who work hard to make sure the rivers in this country never run with blood, only with water.
Andrea Levy 1956– : speech on winning the Whitbread Book of the Year, 25 January 2005; see **Race** 27

➤➤ British Towns and Regions ➤➤

PROVERBS AND SAYINGS

1 Essex stiles, Kentish miles, Norfolk wiles, many a man beguiles.
traditional saying, early 17th century

2 From Hell, Hull, and Halifax, good Lord deliver us.
traditional saying, late 16th century

3 Glasgow's miles better.
slogan introduced by Provost Michael Kelly, 1980s

4 Kirton was a borough town When Exon was a vuzzy down.
on the relative age of Crediton (*Kirton*) and Exeter (*Exon*); traditional saying

5 Lincoln was, London is, and York shall be.
referring to which is the greatest city; traditional saying, late 16th century

6 London Bridge is broken down My fair lady.
traditional nursery rhyme, early 18th century

7 May God in His mercy look down on Belfast.
traditional refrain; see 44 below

8 Northamptonshire for squires and spires.
traditional saying, late 19th century

9 Peebles for pleasure.
the town of *Peebles* in the Scottish Borders has traditionally been a favoured holiday resort; traditional saying, late 19th century

10 Some places of Kent have health and no wealth, some wealth and no health, some health and wealth.
referring to the north and east of the county, Romney Marsh, and the Weald respectively; traditional saying, late 16th century

11 Sussex won't be druv.
asserting that Sussex people have minds of their own, and cannot be forced against their will (*druv* is a dialect version of *drove*, meaning *driven*); English proverb, early 20th century

12 What Manchester says today, the rest of England says tomorrow.
English proverb, late 19th century, occurring in a variety of forms

13 Yorkshire born and Yorkshire bred, strong in the arm and weak in the head.
the names of other (chiefly northern) English counties and towns are also used instead of Yorkshire; English proverb, mid 19th century

PHRASES

14 the Athens of the North
Edinburgh, alluding to its academic and intellectual traditions, and to the predominantly neoclassical style of architecture in its city centre

15 Auld Reekie
Edinburgh, literally 'Old Smoky'

16 the big Smoke
London

17 City of Bon-accord
Aberdeen; *bon-accord* in Scottish usage (from French) means 'good will, fellowship'

18 City of Dreaming Spires
Oxford, deriving originally from Matthew Arnold's 'Thyrsis' (1866): 'And that sweet City with her dreaming Spires'; see **Universities 25**

19 the garden of England
Kent; the Vale of Evesham

20 the Granite City
the city of Aberdeen, Scotland

21 the great wen
London, as the type of a large and overcrowded city, from William Cobbett *Rural Rides* (1822) 'But what is to be the fate of the great wen of all?'

22 the land of the broad acres
Yorkshire, NE England

QUOTATIONS

23 London, thou art the flower of cities all!
Anonymous: 'London' (poem of unknown authorship, previously attributed to William Dunbar, c.1465–c.1530)

24 That shire which we the Heart of England well may call.
of Warwickshire
Michael Drayton 1563–1631: *Poly-Olbion* (1612–22)

25 When a man is tired of London, he is tired of life; for there is in London all that life can afford.
Samuel Johnson 1709–84: James Boswell *Life of Samuel Johnson* (1791) 20 September 1777; see 45 below

26 Earth has not anything to show more fair:
Dull would he be of soul who could pass by
A sight so touching in its majesty:
This City now doth like a garment wear
The beauty of the morning.
William Wordsworth 1770–1850: 'Composed upon Westminster Bridge' (1807)

27 *Was für Plunder!*
What rubbish!
of London as seen from the Monument in June 1814; often misquoted as '*Was für plündern* [What a place to plunder]!'
Gebhard Lebrecht Blücher 1742–1819: Evelyn Princess Blücher *Memoirs of Prince Blücher* (1932)

28 One has no great hopes from Birmingham. I always say there is something direful in the sound.
Jane Austen 1775–1817: *Emma* (1816)

29 Oh! who can ever be tired of Bath?
Jane Austen 1775–1817: *Northanger Abbey* (1818)

30 It is from the midst of this putrid sewer that the greatest river of human industry springs up and carries fertility to the whole world. From this foul drain pure gold flows forth.
of Manchester
Alexis de Tocqueville 1805–59: *Voyage en Angleterre et en Irlande de 1835* 2 July 1835

31 Kent, sir—everybody knows Kent—apples, cherries, hops, and women.
Charles Dickens 1812–70: *Pickwick Papers* (1837)

32 Towery city and branchy between towers;
Cuckoo-echoing, bell-swarmèd, lark-charmèd, rook-racked, river-rounded.
Gerard Manley Hopkins 1844–89: 'Duns Scotus's Oxford' (written 1879)

33 St Andrews by the Northern sea,
A haunted town it is to me!
Andrew Lang 1844–1912: 'Almae Matres' (1884)

34 When Adam and Eve were dispossessed
Of the garden hard by Heaven,
They planted another one down in the west,
'Twas Devon, glorious Devon!
Harold Edwin Boulton 1859–1935: 'Glorious Devon' (1902)

35 God gives all men all earth to love,
But since man's heart is small,
Ordains for each one spot shall prove
Belovèd over all.
Each to his choice, and I rejoice
The lot has fallen to me
In a fair ground—in a fair ground—

Yea, Sussex by the sea!
Rudyard Kipling 1865–1936: 'Sussex' (1903)

36 The folk that live in Liverpool, their heart is in their boots;
They go to hell like lambs, they do, because the hooter hoots.
G. K. Chesterton 1874–1936: 'Me Heart' (1914)

37 For Cambridge people rarely smile,
Being urban, squat, and packed with guile.
Rupert Brooke 1887–1915: 'The Old Vicarage, Grantchester' (1915)

38 I belong to Glasgow
Dear Old Glasgow town!
Will Fyffe 1885–1947: 'I Belong to Glasgow' (1920 song)

39 Bugger Bognor.
comment made either in 1929, when it was proposed that the town be renamed Bognor Regis following the king's convalescence there; or on his deathbed when someone said 'Cheer up, your Majesty, you will soon be at Bognor again.'
George V 1865–1936: Kenneth Rose *King George V* (1983)

40 Very flat, Norfolk.
Noël Coward 1899–1973: *Private Lives* (1930)

41 London Pride has been handed down to us.
London Pride is a flower that's free.
London Pride means our own dear town to us,
And our pride it for ever will be.
Noël Coward 1899–1973: 'London Pride' (1941 song)

42 Maybe it's because I'm a Londoner
That I love London so.
Hubert Gregg 1914–2004: 'Maybe It's Because I'm a Londoner' (1947 song)

43 With the possible exceptions of Jerusalem and Mecca, Belfast must be the most religion-conscious city in the world.
Tyrone Guthrie 1900–71: *A Life in the Theatre* (1959)

44 O the bricks they will bleed and the rain it will weep
And the damp Lagan fog lull the city to sleep;
It's to hell with the future and live on the past:
May the Lord in His mercy be kind to Belfast.
Maurice James Craig 1919– : 'Ballad to a Traditional Refrain' (1974); see 7 above

45 'A man who is tired of London is tired of life'—no, I was tired of hunting for parking places.
Paul Theroux 1941– : *The Kingdom by the Sea* (1983); see 25 above

46 Try Manchester after midnight and you'll
think you've walked into the Book of
Revelations.
Howard Jacobson: *The Mighty Waltzer* (1999)

➤➤ Broadcasting ➤➤

PROVERBS AND SAYINGS

**1 Always turn the radio on before you
listen to it.**
American saying, mid 20th century

2 Assistant heads must roll!
traditional solution to management problems in
broadcasting

3 Nation shall speak peace unto nation.
motto of the BBC, adapted from the Bible (Isaiah) by
Montague John Rendall (1862–1950); see **Peace** 7

4 So much chewing gum for the eyes.
small boy's definition of certain television
programmes, 1950s

PHRASES

5 couch potato
a person who takes little or no exercise and watches
a lot of television, coined in the US from a pun on
boob tube as a slang expression for television;
someone given to continuous viewing was a *boob
tuber*, and the cartoonist Robert Armstrong drew the
most familiar tuber, a potato, reclining on a couch
watching TV

6 jump the shark
(of a television series) reach a point when the
inclusion of far-fetched events for the sake of novelty
marks a decline. The origin is said to be an episode in
the long-running US television series *Happy Days*, in
which the central character (the Fonz) jumped over a
shark when waterskiing

QUOTATIONS

7 He who prides himself on giving what he
thinks the public wants is often creating a
fictitious demand for lower standards which
he will then satisfy.
Lord Reith 1889–1971: memo to Crawford
Committee 1926; Andrew Boyle *Only the Wind Will
Listen* (1972)

8 *Television*? The word is half Greek, half
Latin. No good can come of it.
C. P. Scott 1846–1932: Asa Briggs *The BBC: the First
Fifty Years* (1985)

9 I hate television. I hate it as much as
peanuts. But I can't stop eating peanuts.
Orson Welles 1915–85: in *New York Herald Tribune*
12 October 1956

10 It's just like having a licence to print your
own money.
on the profitability of commercial television in Britain
Roy Thomson 1894–1976: R. Braddon *Roy Thomson*
(1965)

11 It used to be that we in films were the lowest
form of art. Now we have something to look
down on.
of television
Billy Wilder 1906–2002: A. Madsen *Billy Wilder*
(1968)

12 Adams' first law of television: the weight of
the backside is greater than the force of the
intellect.
Phillip Adams 1939– : in 1970; attributed,
Stephen Murray-Smith (ed.) *The Dictionary of
Australian Quotations* (1984)

13 Television brought the brutality of war into
the comfort of the living room. Vietnam
was lost in the living rooms of America—not
the battlefields of Vietnam.
Marshall McLuhan 1911–80: in *Montreal Gazette*
16 May 1975

14 Let's face it, there are no plain women on
television.
Anna Ford 1943– : in *Observer* 23 September 1979

15 Television is simultaneously blamed, often
by the same people, for worsening the world
and for being powerless to change it.
Clive James 1939– : *Glued to the Box* (1981)

16 Television contracts the imagination and
radio expands it.
Terry Wogan 1938– : attributed, 1984

17 Get a life!
to Star Trek fans on *Saturday Night Live*, 1986
William Shatner 1931– : William Shatner *Get a
Life!* (1999)

18 Television . . . thrives on unreason, and unreason thrives on television . . . [It] strikes at the emotions rather than the intellect.
Robin Day 1923–2000: *Grand Inquisitor* (1989)

19 Television has made dictatorship impossible, but democracy unbearable.
Shimon Peres 1923– : at a Davos meeting, in *Financial Times* 31 January 1995

20 A terminal blight has hit the TV industry nipping fun in the bud and stunting our growth. This blight is management—the dreaded Four M's: male, middle class, middle-aged and mediocre.
Janet Street-Porter 1946– : MacTaggart Lecture, Edinburgh Television Festival, 25 August 1995

21 Television today has replaced the theatre of the 20th century, the novels of the 19th, the Bible of the 17th, the folktales of the village, the bedtime stories parents told their children.
Jonathan Sacks 1948– : *Culture and Communications* (2001)

⇢ Business ⇠

see also **Buying and Selling**

PROVERBS AND SAYINGS

1 Business before pleasure.
often used to encourage a course of action; English proverb, mid 19th century

2 Business goes where it is invited and stays where it is well-treated.
American proverb, mid 20th century

3 Business is like a car: it will not run by itself except downhill.
American proverb, mid 20th century

4 Business is war.
modern saying, said to derive from a Japanese proverb

5 Business neglected is business lost.
North American proverb, mid 20th century

6 The customer is always right.
English proverb, early 20th century; see 35 below

7 If you don't speculate, you can't accumulate.
outlay (and some degree of risk) is necessary if real gain is to be achieved; English proverb, mid 20th century

8 I liked it so much, I bought the company!
advertising slogan for Remington Shavers, coined by owner Victor Kiam (1926–2001)

9 Keep your own shop and your shop will keep you.
recommending attention to what is essential to one's livelihood; English proverb, early 17th century

10 Never knowingly undersold.
motto, from *c*.1920, of the John Lewis partnership

11 No cure, no pay.
known principally from its use on Lloyd's of London's Standard Form of Salvage Agreement; English proverb, late 19th century

12 No penny, no paternoster.
if you want a thing you must pay for it (the reference is to priests insisting on being paid for performing services); English proverb, early 16th century

13 Pay beforehand was never well served.
payment in advance removes the incentive to finish the work; English proverb, late 16th century

14 Pile it high, sell it cheap.
slogan coined by Jack Cohen (1898–1979), founder of the Tesco supermarket chain

15 Sell in May and go away (come back on St Leger's day).
saying relating to the cycle of activity on the London Stock Exchange. May, shortly after the start of the financial year, was traditionally a busy time, but during the summer months trading was slack as Londoners (including stockbrokers) took their holiday breaks away from the capital. The full form of the saying refers to the classic *St Leger* horse race, taken as marking the end of the English summer social calendar

16 There are tricks in every trade.
the practice of every skill is likely to involve some trickery or dishonesty; English proverb, mid 17th century

17 Trade follows the flag.
commercial development is likely to follow military intervention; English proverb, late 19th century

PHRASES

18 bear market

a market in which share prices are falling encouraging selling. In Stock Exchange usage, a *bear* is a person who sells shares hoping to buy them back again later at a lower price. The dealer in this kind of stock was known as the bearskin jobber, and it seems likely that the original phrase was 'sell the bearskin'; see **Optimism** 8. The associated *bull* is of later date, and may perhaps have been suggested by the existence of *bear* in this sense: see 20 below

19 blue-chip

denoting companies or their shares considered to be a reliable investment, though less secure than gilt-edged stock; US, early 20th century, from the *blue chip* used in gambling games, which usually has a high value

20 bull market

a market in which share prices are rising, encouraging buying; see 18 above

21 Chinese wall

on the Stock Exchange, a prohibition against the passing of confidential information from one department of a financial institution to another, alluding to the Great Wall of China, as an insurmountable barrier to understanding

22 the triple-witching hour

in the US, informal name for the unpredictable final hour of trading on the US Stock Exchange before the simultaneous expiry of three different kinds of options; a development of *witching* hour: see **Day and Night** 4

23 a white knight

a welcome company bidding for a company facing an unwelcome takeover bid, likened to a traditional figure of chivalry rescuing someone from danger

QUOTATIONS

24 A merchant shall hardly keep himself from doing wrong.
Bible: Ecclesiasticus

25 They [corporations] cannot commit treason, nor be outlawed, nor excommunicate, for they have no souls.
Edward Coke 1552–1634: *The Reports of Sir Edward Coke* (1658) 'The case of Sutton's Hospital'; see 31 below

26 A Company for carrying on an undertaking of Great Advantage, but no one to know what it is.
Anonymous: Company Prospectus at the time of the South Sea Bubble (1711)

27 There is nothing more requisite in business than dispatch.
Joseph Addison 1672–1719: *The Drummer* (1716)

28 It is the nature of all greatness not to be exact; and great trade will always be attended with considerable abuses.
Edmund Burke 1729–97: *On American Taxation* (1775)

29 People of the same trade seldom meet together, even for merriment and diversion, but the conversation ends in a conspiracy against the public, or in some contrivance to raise prices.
Adam Smith 1723–90: *Wealth of Nations* (1776)

30 To found a great empire for the sole purpose of raising up a people of customers, may at first sight appear a project fit only for a nation of shopkeepers. It is, however, a project altogether unfit for a nation of shopkeepers; but extremely fit for a nation whose government is influenced by shopkeepers.
Adam Smith 1723–90: *Wealth of Nations* (1776); see **England** 14

31 Corporations have neither bodies to be punished, nor souls to be condemned, they therefore do as they like.
often quoted as 'Did you ever expect a corporation to have a conscience, when it has no soul to be damned, and no body to be kicked?'
Lord Thurlow 1731–1806: John Poynder *Literary Extracts* (1844); see 25 above

32 Here's the rule for bargains: 'Do other men, for they would do you.' That's the true business precept.
Charles Dickens 1812–70: *Martin Chuzzlewit* (1844)

33 The public be damned! I'm working for my stockholders.
William H. Vanderbilt 1821–85: comment to a news reporter, 2 October 1882

34 The growth of a large business is merely a survival of the fittest . . . The American beauty rose can be produced in the splendour and fragrance which bring cheer to its beholder only by sacrificing the early buds which grow up around it.
John D. Rockefeller 1839–1937: W. J. Ghent *Our Benevolent Feudalism* (1902); see **Life Sciences** 8

35 *Le client n'a jamais tort.*
The customer is never wrong.
César Ritz 1850–1918: R. Nevill and C. E. Jerningham *Piccadilly to Pall Mall* (1908); see 6 above

36 The best of all monopoly profits is a quiet life.
J. R. Hicks 1904–89: *Econometrica* (1935)

37 For a salesman, there is no rock bottom to the life . . . A salesman is got to dream, boy. It comes with the territory.
Arthur Miller 1915–2005: *Death of a Salesman* (1949)

38 How to succeed in business without really trying.
Shepherd Mead 1914– : title of book (1952)

39 For years I thought what was good for our country was good for General Motors and vice versa.
Charles E. Wilson 1890–1961: testimony to the Senate Armed Services Committee on his proposed nomination for Secretary of Defence, 15 January 1953

40 You cannot be a success in any business without believing that it is the greatest business in the world . . . You have to put your heart in the business and the business in your heart.
Thomas Watson Snr. 1874–1956: Robert Sobel *IBM: Colossus in Transition* (1981)

41 Consumer wants can have bizarre, frivolous, or even immoral origins, and an admirable case can still be made for a society that seeks to satisfy them. But the case cannot stand if it is the process of satisfying wants that creates the wants.
J. K. Galbraith 1908– : *The Affluent Society* (1958)

42 Accountants are the witch-doctors of the modern world and willing to turn their hands to any kind of magic.
Lord Justice Harman 1894–1970: speech, February 1964; A. Sampson *The New Anatomy of Britain* (1971)

43 If business always made the right decisions, business wouldn't be business.
J. Paul Getty 1892–1976: *How to be Rich* (1965)

44 Could Henry Ford produce the Book of Kells? Certainly not. He would quarrel initially with the advisability of such a project and then prove it was impossible.
Flann O'Brien 1911–66: *Myles Away from Dublin* (1990)

45 In the factory we make cosmetics; in the store we sell hope.
Charles Revson 1906–75: A. Tobias *Fire and Ice* (1976)

46 The most striking thing about modern industry is that it requires so much and accomplishes so little. Modern industry seems to be inefficient to a degree that surpasses one's ordinary powers of imagination. Its inefficiency therefore remains unnoticed.
E. F. Schumacher 1911–77: *Small is Beautiful* (1973)

47 The salary of the chief executive of the large corporation is not a market reward for achievement. It is frequently in the nature of a warm personal gesture by the individual to himself.
J. K. Galbraith 1908– : *Annals of an Abiding Liberal* (1979)

48 Deals are my art form. Other people paint beautifully on canvas or write wonderful poetry. I like making deals, preferably big deals. That's how I get my kicks.
Donald Trump 1946– : Donald Trump and Tony Schwartz *The Art of the Deal* (1987)

49 Nothing is illegal if one hundred well-placed business men decide to do it.
Andrew Young 1932– : Morris K. Udall *Too Funny to be President* (1988)

50 There is only one boss. The customer. And he can fire everybody in the company from the chairman on down, simply by spending his money somewhere else.
Sam Walton 1919–92: *Sam Walton: Made in America, My Story*, with J. Huey (1990)

51 We even sell a pair of earrings for under £1, which is cheaper than a prawn sandwich from Marks & Spencers. But I have to say the earrings probably won't last as long.
Gerald Ratner 1949– : speech to the Institute of Directors, Albert Hall, 23 April 1991

52 We used to build civilizations. Now we build shopping malls.
Bill Bryson 1951– : *Neither Here Nor There* (1991)

53 I think that business practices would improve immeasurably if they were guided by 'feminine' principles—qualities like love and care and intuition.
Anita Roddick 1942– : *Body and Soul* (1991)

54 Only the paranoid survive.
dictum on which he has long run his company, the Intel Corporation
Andrew Grove 1936– : in *New York Times* 18 December 1994

55 Business is becoming more and more akin to intellectual sumo wrestling.
John Harvey-Jones 1924– : *All Together Now* (1994)

Buying and Selling

see also **Business**

PROVERBS AND SAYINGS

1 The buyer has need of a hundred eyes, the seller of but one.
stressing the responsibility of a purchaser to examine goods on offer; English proverb, mid 17th century

2 Let the buyer beware.
warning that it is up to the buyer to establish the nature and value of a purchase before completing the transaction; English proverb, early 16th century. The Latin tag *caveat emptor* is also found

3 You buy land, you buy stones; you buy meat, you buy bones.
every purchase has its drawbacks; English proverb, late 17th century

QUOTATIONS

4 It is naught, it is naught, saith the buyer: but when he is gone his way, then he boasteth.
Bible: Proverbs

5 I have heard of a man who had a mind to sell his house, and therefore carried a piece of brick in his pocket, which he showed as a pattern to encourage purchasers.
Jonathan Swift 1667–1745: *The Drapier's Letters* (1724)

6 I often wonder what the Vintners buy
One half so precious as the Goods they sell.
Edward Fitzgerald 1809–83: *The Rubáiyát of Omar Khayyám* (1859)

7 Every one lives by selling something.
Robert Louis Stevenson 1850–94: *Across the Plains* (1892) 'Beggars'

8 The car, the furniture, the wife, the children—everything has to be disposable. Because you see the main thing today is—shopping.
Arthur Miller 1915–2005: *The Price* (1968)

9 The consumer, so it is said, is the king . . . each is a voter who uses his money as votes to get the things done that he wants done.
Paul A. Samuelson 1915– : *Economics* (8th ed., 1970)

10 In a consumer society there are inevitably two kinds of slaves: the prisoners of addiction and the prisoners of envy.
Ivan Illich 1926– : *Tools for Conviviality* (1973)

11 The source of status is no longer the ability to make things but simply the ability to purchase them.
Harry Braverman: *Labour and Monopoly Capital* (1974)

12 Buying is much more American than thinking and I'm as American as they come.
Andy Warhol 1927–87: *Philosophy of Andy Warhol (From A to B and Back Again)* (1975)

13 Let me teach you how to sell.
remark to employees more than 40 years after founding eponymous company
Estée Lauder 1910– : in *Time* April 1998

14 Women are people who shop. Shopping is the festival of the female oppressed.
Germaine Greer 1939– : in *Sunday Times* 23 July 2000

Canada

PROVERBS AND SAYINGS

1 A mari usque ad mare.
Latin, *From sea unto sea*, motto of Canada, taken from the Bible (Psalm 72) 'He shall have dominion also from sea to sea, and from the river unto the ends of the earth'

2 The Mounties always get their man.
unofficial motto of the Royal Canadian Mounted Police

PHRASES

3 the land God gave to Cain
a name for Labrador, from Cartier (see 5 below), referring to Cain's banishment by God to a desolate land 'east of Eden'; see also **Murder** 7, **Order** 8, **Travel** 11

4 the Land of the Little Sticks
the subarctic tundra region of northern Canada, characterized by its stunted vegetation; Chinook *stik* = wood, tree, forest

QUOTATIONS

5 I am rather inclined to believe that this is the land God gave to Cain.
on discovering the northern shore of the Gulf of St Lawrence in 1534; see 3 above
Jacques Cartier 1491–1557: *La Première Relation*

6 These two nations have been at war over a few acres of snow near Canada, and . . . they are spending on this fine struggle more than Canada itself is worth.
of the struggle between the French and the British for the control of colonial north Canada
Voltaire 1694–1778: *Candide* (1759)

7 Fair these broad meads, these hoary woods are grand;
But we are exiles from our fathers' land.
John Galt 1779–1839: 'Canadian Boat Song' (1829); translated from the Gaelic; attributed

8 I expected to find a contest between a government and a people: I found two nations warring in the bosom of a single state.
John George Lambton, Lord Durham 1792–1840: *Report of the Affairs of British North America* (1839)

9 Dusty, cobweb-covered, maimed, and set at naught,
Beauty crieth in an attic, and no man regardeth.
O God! O Montreal!
Samuel Butler 1835–1902: 'Psalm of Montreal' (1878)

10 The twentieth century belongs to Canada.
encapsulation of a view expressed in a speech to the Canadian Club of Ottawa, 18 January 1904, 'The nineteenth century was the century of the United States. I think we can claim that it is Canada that shall fill the twentieth century'
Wilfrid Laurier 1841–1919: popularly attributed in this form

11 We have in our country the patriotism of Ontarians, the patriotism of Quebecers and the patriotism of westerners . . . but there is no Canadian patriotism, and there will not be a Canadian nation as long as we do not have a Canadian patriotism.
Henri Bourassa 1868–1952: speech, the Canadian Club of Toronto, 22 January 1907

12 *O Canada! Terre de nos aïeux,*
Ton front est ceint de fleurons glorieux!
Car ton bras sait porter l'épée,
Il sait porter la croix!

O Canada! Our home and native land!
True patriot love in all thy sons command.
With glowing hearts we see thee rise,
The True North strong and free!
Robert Stanley Weir 1856–1926: 'Oh Canada' (1908 song); French words written in 1880 by Adolphe-Basile Routhier (1839–1920)

13 Building that railroad would have made a Canadian out of the German Emperor.
on the construction of the Canadian Pacific Railway
William Cornelius Van Horne 1843–1915: in *Canadian Encyclopedia* (1988) vol. 1

14 If some countries have too much history, we have too much geography.
William Lyon Mackenzie King 1874–1950: speech on Canada as an international power, 18 June 1936

15 We French, we English, never lost our civil war,
endure it still, a bloodless civil bore;
no wounded lying about, no Whitman wanted.
It's only by our lack of ghosts we're haunted.
Earle Birney 1904– : 'Can.Lit.' (1962)

16 *Mon pays ce n'est pas un pays, c'est l'hiver.*
My country is not a country, it is winter.
Gilles Vigneault 1928– : 'Mon Pays' (1964)

17 Canada could have enjoyed:
English government,
French culture,
and American know-how.
Instead it ended up with:
English know-how,
French government,
and American culture.
a similar (prose) summary has been attributed to Lester Pearson (1897–1972), 'Canada was supposed to get British government, French culture, and American know-how. Instead it got French government, American culture, and British know-how'
John Robert Colombo 1936– : 'O Canada' (1965)

18 *Vive Le Québec Libre.*
Long Live Free Quebec.
Charles de Gaulle 1890–1970: speech in Montreal, 24 July 1967

19 When the white man came we had the land and they had the bibles; now they have the land and we have the bibles.
Dan George 1899–1981: Gerald Walsh *Indians in Transition: An Inquiry Approach* (1971)

20 People put down Canadian literature and ask us why there isn't a *Moby Dick*. The reason there isn't a *Moby Dick* is that if a Canadian did a *Moby Dick*, it would be done from the point of view of the whale.
Margaret Atwood 1939– : in *Saturday Night* November 1972

21 A Canadian is somebody who knows how to make love in a canoe.
Pierre Berton 1920–2004: in *The Canadian* 22 December 1973

22 In the Maritimes, politics is a disease, in Quebec a religion, in Ontario a business, on the Prairies a protest and in British Columbia entertainment.
Allan Fotheringham 1932– : in 1975; *Last Page First* (1999)

23 Canadians are Americans with no Disneyland.
Margaret Mahy 1936– : *The Changeover* (1984)

24 I see Canada as a country torn between a very northern, rather extraordinary, mystical spirit which it fears and its desire to present itself to the world as a Scotch banker.
Robertson Davies 1913–95: *The Enthusiasms of Robertson Davies* (1990)

25 Canada is . . . a country always dressed in its Sunday go-to-meeting clothes. A country you wouldn't ask to dance a second waltz. Clean. Christian. Dull. Quiescent. But growing.
Carol Shields 1935–2003: *The Stone Diaries* (1993)

26 North of the 49th parallel we value equality; south of it, they treasure freedom.
Michael Adams: *Sex in the Snow* (1997)

27 I don't have a moral plan. I'm a Canadian.
David Cronenberg 1943– : attributed

➤➤Capitalism and Communism ◄◄

see also **Class, Political Parties**

PROVERBS AND SAYINGS

1 **All power to the Soviets.**
slogan of workers in Petrograd, 1917

2 **Are you now or have you ever been a member of the Communist Party?**
formal question put to those appearing before the Committee on UnAmerican Activities during the McCarthy campaign of 1950–4 against alleged Communists in the US government and other institutions; the allusive form *are you now or have you ever been?* derives from this

3 **Better red than dead.**
slogan of nuclear disarmament campaigners, late 1950s

4 **We pretend to work, and they pretend to pay us.**
Russian saying of the Soviet era

PHRASES

5 **the bamboo curtain**
a political and economic barrier between China and non-Communist countries, after *iron curtain*: see 7 below

6 **dictatorship of the proletariat**
the Communist ideal of proletarian supremacy following the overthrow of capitalism and preceding the classless state

7 **the iron curtain**
a notional barrier to the passage of people and information between the Soviet bloc and the West; in this specific sense from Churchill (see 20 below), but the figurative use of *iron curtain* (literally a fire-curtain in a theatre) is recorded earlier; see also 5 above

8 **reds under the bed**
denoting an exaggerated fear of the presence and harmful influence of Communist sympathizers within a society or institution

QUOTATIONS

9 The Riches and Goods of Christians are not common, as touching the right, title, and possession of the same, as certain Anabaptists do falsely boast.
The Book of Common Prayer 1662: *Articles of Religion* (1562)

10 In the first stone which he [the savage] flings at the wild animals he pursues, in the first stick that he seizes to strike down the fruit which hangs above his reach, we see the appropriation of one article for the

purpose of aiding in the acquisition of another, and thus discover the origin of capital.
Robert Torrens 1780–1864: *An Essay on the Production of Wealth* (1821)

11 A spectre is haunting Europe—the spectre of Communism.
Karl Marx 1818–83 and **Friedrich Engels** 1820–95: *The Communist Manifesto* (1848)

12 What is a communist? One who hath yearnings
For equal division of unequal earnings.
Ebenezer Elliott 1781–1849: 'Epigram' (1850)

13 Communism is a Russian autocracy turned upside down.
Alexander Ivanovich Herzen 1812–70: *The Development of Revolutionary Ideas in Russia* (1851)

14 All I know is that I am not a Marxist.
Karl Marx 1818–83: attributed in a letter from Friedrich Engels to Conrad Schmidt, 5 August 1890

15 Imperialism is the monopoly stage of capitalism.
Lenin 1870–1924: *Imperialism as the Last Stage of Capitalism* (1916) 'Briefest possible definition of imperialism'

16 I have seen the future; and it works.
following a visit to the Soviet Union in 1919
Lincoln Steffens 1866–1936: *Letters* (1938)

17 Communism is Soviet power plus the electrification of the whole country.
Lenin 1870–1924: Report to 8th Congress, 1920

18 The State is an instrument in the hands of the ruling class, used to break the resistance of the adversaries of that class.
Joseph Stalin 1879–1953: *Foundations of Leninism* (1924)

19 Communism is like prohibition, it's a good idea but it won't work.
Will Rogers 1879–1935: in 1927; *Weekly Articles* (1981)

20 From Stettin in the Baltic to Trieste in the Adriatic an iron curtain has descended across the Continent.
the expression 'iron curtain' previously had been applied by others to the Soviet Union or her sphere of influence
Winston Churchill 1874–1965: speech at Westminster College, Fulton, Missouri, 5 March 1946; see 7 above

21 Whether you like it or not, history is on our side. We will bury you.
Nikita Khrushchev 1894–1971: speech to Western diplomats in Moscow, 18 November 1956

22 Capitalism, it is said, is a system wherein man exploits man. And communism—is vice versa.
quoting 'a Polish intellectual'
Daniel Bell 1919– : *The End of Ideology* (1960)

23 Normally speaking, it may be said that the forces of a capitalist society, if left unchecked, tend to make the rich richer and the poor poorer and thus increase the gap between them.
Jawaharlal Nehru 1889–1964: 'Basic Approach' in Vincent Shean *Nehru . . .* (1960)

24 History suggests that capitalism is a necessary condition for political freedom. Clearly it is not a sufficient condition for it.
Milton Friedman 1912– : *Capitalism and Freedom* (1962)

25 Capitalism is using its money; we socialists throw it away.
Fidel Castro 1927– : in *Observer* 8 November 1964

26 Left wing, chicken wing, it's all the same to me.
Woody Guthrie 1912–67: Joe Klein *Woody Guthrie: a life* (1980)

27 In the service of the people we followed such a policy that socialism would not lose its human face.
Alexander Dubček 1921–92: in *Rudé Právo* 19 July 1968

28 The unpleasant and unacceptable face of capitalism.
on the Lonrho affair
Edward Heath 1916–2005: speech, House of Commons, 15 May 1973

29 It is as wholly wrong to blame Marx for what was done in his name, as it is to blame Jesus for what was done in his.
Tony Benn 1925– : Alan Freeman *The Benn Heresy* (1982)

30 Transformations in Eastern Europe seem to have been fuelled by people's desire to buy rather than their desire to vote, by dreams of purchasing rather than dreams of participating.
Rosabeth Moss Kanter 1943– : *World Class* (1995)

31 It would be simplistic to say that Divine Providence caused the fall of communism. It fell by itself as a consequence of its own mistakes and abuses. It fell by itself because of its own inherent weaknesses.
Pope John Paul II 1920–2005: Carl Bernstein and Marco Politi *His Holiness: John Paul II and the Hidden History of our Time* (1996)

32 Yes to the market economy, No to the market society.
Lionel Jospin 1937– : in *Independent* 16 September 1998

⤙ Cats ⤘

see also **Animals**

PROVERBS AND SAYINGS

1 **A cat has nine lives.**
traditional saying

2 **Touch not the cat but a glove.**
but = without, the cat here is a wild cat; Scottish
proverb, early 19th century

PHRASES

3 **Cheshire cat**
a cat depicted with a broad fixed grin, as
popularized through Lewis Carroll's *Alice's
Adventures in Wonderland* (1865). The origin is
unknown, but it is said that *Cheshire* cheeses used to
be marked with the face of a smiling cat; see **Britain**
15, **God** 31

4 **fight like Kilkenny cats**
two cats from Kilkenny in Ireland which, according
to legend, fought until only their tails remained

QUOTATIONS

5 When I play with my cat, who knows
whether she isn't amusing herself with me
more than I am with her?
Montaigne 1533–92: *Essais* (1580)

6 For I will consider my Cat Jeoffrey. . . .
For he counteracts the powers of darkness by
   his electrical skin and glaring eyes.
For he counteracts the Devil, who is death,
   by brisking about the life.
Christopher Smart 1722–71: *Jubilate Agno*
(*c*.1758–63)

7 When I observed he was a fine cat, saying,
'Why yes, Sir, but I have had cats whom I
liked better than this'; and then as if
perceiving Hodge to be out of countenance,
adding, 'but he is a very fine cat, a very fine
cat indeed.'
Samuel Johnson 1709–84: James Boswell *Life of
Samuel Johnson* (1791) 1783

8 Cruel, but composed and bland,
Dumb, inscrutable and grand,
So Tiberius might have sat,
Had Tiberius been a cat.
Matthew Arnold 1822–88: 'Poor Matthias' (1885)

9 He walked by himself, and all places were
alike to him.
Rudyard Kipling 1865–1936: *Just So Stories* (1902)
'The Cat that Walked by Himself'

10 Cats, no less liquid than their shadows,
Offer no angles to the wind.
They slip, diminished, neat, through
   loopholes
Less than themselves.
A. S. J. Tessimond 1902–62: *Cats* (1934)

11 The Naming of Cats is a difficult matter,
It isn't just one of your holiday games;
You may think at first I'm as mad as a hatter
When I tell you, a cat must have THREE
   DIFFERENT NAMES.
T. S. Eliot 1888–1965: 'The Naming of Cats' (1939);
see **Madness** 2

12 The trouble with a kitten is
THAT
Eventually it becomes a
CAT.
Ogden Nash 1902–71: 'The Kitten' (1940)

13 Cats seem to go on the principle that it
never does any harm to ask for what you
want.
Joseph Wood Krutch 1893–1970: *Twelve Seasons*
(1949)

14 If a fish is the movement of water embodied,
given shape, then cat is a diagram and
pattern of subtle air.
Doris Lessing 1919– : *Particularly Cats* (1967)

⤜Causes and Consequences ⤛

PROVERBS AND SAYINGS

1 After the feast comes the reckoning.
a period of pleasure or indulgence has to be paid for;
English proverb, early 17th century, but now chiefly
in modern North American use

2 As you bake so shall you brew.
as you begin, so shall you proceed; English proverb,
late 16th century

3 As you brew, so shall you bake.
your circumstances will be shaped by your own
initial actions; English proverb, late 16th century

**4 As you make your bed, so you must lie
upon it.**
as you begin, so shall you proceed; English proverb,
late 16th century

5 As you sow, so you reap.
you will have to endure the consequences of your
actions; English proverb, late 15th century; see 11,
18, 20 below

6 Good seed makes a good crop.
something which has a sound basis will do well;
English proverb, mid 16th century

7 Great oaks from little acorns grow.
great results may ensue from apparently small
beginnings; English proverb, late 14th century

**8 He who plants thorns must not expect
to gather roses.**
Arabic proverb; see **Change** 17

**9 If you want to see heaven, you have to
die yourself.**
Indian proverb

**10 The mother of mischief is no bigger
than a midge's wing.**
the origin of difficulties can be very small; English
proverb, early 17th century

**11 They that sow the wind, shall reap the
whirlwind.**
those who have initiated a dangerous course must
suffer the consequences; English proverb, late 16th
century; see 5 above, 18, 20 below

**12 Who won't be ruled by the rudder
must be ruled by the rock.**
a ship which is not being steered on its course will
run on to a rock; English proverb, mid 17th century

PHRASES

13 the butterfly effect
the effect of a very small change in the initial
conditions of a system which makes a significant
difference to the outcome, from Lorenz: see
Chance 35

14 a grain of mustard seed
a small thing capable of vast development, from the
great height attained by black mustard in Palestine,
as in the Bible (Matthew) 'a mustard seed . . . indeed
is the least of all seeds: but when it is grown, it is the
greatest among herbs'

15 hoist with one's own petard
ruined by one's own devices against others; literally
blown up by one's own bomb, after Shakespeare

Hamlet 'For 'tis the sport to have the engineer Hoist
with his own petar'; *petar* = a petard, a small bomb
made of a metal or wooden box filled with powder,
used to blow in a door or to make a hole in a wall

16 poetic justice
the ideal justice in distribution of rewards and
punishments supposed to befit a poem or other
work of imagination; well-deserved unforeseen
retribution or reward; from Pope *The Dunciad* 'Poetic
Justice, with her lifted scale'

QUOTATIONS

17 He that diggeth a pit shall fall into it.
Bible: Ecclesiastes

18 They have sown the wind, and they shall
reap the whirlwind.
Bible: Hosea; see 5, 11 above, 20 below

19 Whenever anything which has several parts
is such that the whole is something over
and above its parts, and not just the sum of
them all, like a heap, then it always has
some cause.
Aristotle 384–322 BC: *Metaphysica*; see **Quantities
and Qualities** 12

20 Whatsoever a man soweth, that shall he also
reap.
Bible: Galatians; see 5, 11, 18 above

21 One leak will sink a ship, and one sin will
destroy a sinner.
John Bunyan 1628–88: *The Pilgrim's Progress*
(1684)

22 Whoever wills the end, wills also (so far as reason decides his conduct) the means in his power which are indispensably necessary thereto.
Immanuel Kant 1724–1804: *Fundamental Principles of the Metaphysics of Ethics* (1785)

23 Sow an act, and you reap a habit. Sow a habit and you reap a character. Sow a character, and you reap a destiny.
Charles Reade 1814–84: attributed; in *Notes and Queries* 17 October 1903

24 The present contains nothing more than the past, and what is found in the effect was already in the cause.
Henri Bergson 1859–1941: *L'Évolution créatrice* (1907)

25 The captain is in his bunk, drinking bottled ditch-water; and the crew is gambling in the forecastle. She will strike and sink and split. Do you think the laws of God will be suspended in favour of England because you were born in it?
George Bernard Shaw 1856–1950: *Heartbreak House* (1919)

26 As it will be in the future, it was at the birth of Man—
There are only four things certain since Social Progress began:
That the Dog returns to his Vomit and the Sow returns to her Mire,
And the burnt Fool's bandaged finger goes wabbling back to the Fire;
And that after this is accomplished, and the brave new world begins
When all men are paid for existing and no man must pay for his sins,
As surely as Water will wet us, as surely as Fire will burn,

The Gods of the Copybook Headings with terror and slaughter return!
Rudyard Kipling 1865–1936: 'The Gods of the Copybook Headings' (1919); see **Reputation** 14

27 You have broader considerations that might follow what you might call the 'falling domino' principle. You have a row of dominoes set up. You knock over the first one, and what will happen to the last one is that it will go over very quickly. So you have the beginning of a disintegration that would have the most profound influences.
Dwight D. Eisenhower 1890–1969: speech at press conference, 7 April 1954

28 The structure of a play is always the story of how the birds came home to roost.
Arthur Miller 1915–2005: in *Harper's Magazine* August 1958

29 Every positive value has its price in negative terms . . . The genius of Einstein leads to Hiroshima.
Pablo Picasso 1881–1973: F. Gilot and C. Lake *Life With Picasso* (1964)

30 I fear we have only awakened a sleeping giant, and his reaction will be terrible.
of the attack on Pearl Harbor
Larry Forrester et al.: *Tora! Tora! Tora!* (1970 film); said by the Japanese admiral Isoruko Yamamoto (1884–1943), although there is no evidence that Yamamoto used these words

31 If you wish to make an apple pie from scratch, you must first invent the universe.
Carl Sagan 1934–96: *Cosmos* (1980)

32 Instead of having one [Osama] bin Laden, we will have 100 bin Ladens.
on the probable result of a western invasion of Iraq
Hosni Mubarak 1928– : in *Newsweek* 14 April 2003

⤞ Caution ⤝

see also **Danger**

PROVERBS AND SAYINGS

1 **Better be safe than sorry.**
urging the wisdom of taking precautions; English proverb, mid 19th century

2 **A bird in the hand is worth two in the bush.**
it is better to accept what one has than to try to get more and risk losing everything; English proverb, mid 15th century; see **Certainty** 4

3 **A cat in gloves catches no mice.**
deliberate restraint and caution (or 'pussyfooting')

often result in nothing being achieved; English proverb, late 16th century

4 **Caution is the parent of safety.**
American proverb, early 18th century

5 **Delhi is far away.**
warning that unexpected events may intervene; Indian proverb, deriving from the response of the 14th-century Sufi mystic Nizamuddin Aulia to a threat from the Sultan of Delhi: the Sultan died before arriving home. Compare **Government** 3, 4

6 Discretion is the better part of valour.
often used to explain caution, and sometimes with allusion to Shakespeare's *1 Henry IV* (1597), 'The better part of valour is discretion'; English proverb, late 16th century

7 Don't put all your eggs in one basket.
you should not chance everything on a single venture, but spread the risk; English proverb, mid 17th century; see 32 below

8 Full cup, steady hand.
used especially to caution against spoiling a comfortable or otherwise enviable situation by careless action; English proverb, early 11th century

9 He who fights and runs away, may live to fight another day.
English proverb, mid 16th century

10 He who has been scalded by hot milk, blows even on cold lassi before drinking it.
lassi = an Indian drink, traditionally based on diluted buttermilk or yoghurt, and usually served chilled; Indian proverb; see 19 below, **Experience** 8

11 He who sups with the Devil should have a long spoon.
one should be cautious when dealing with dangerous persons; English proverb, late 14th century

12 If you can't be good, be careful.
often used as a humorous warning; English proverb, early 20th century. The same idea is found in 11th-century Latin, *si non caste tamen caute*

13 Let's be careful out there.
catchphrase from *Hill Street Blues* (police procedural television series, 1981 onwards), written by Steven Bochco and Michael Kozoll

14 Let sleeping dogs lie.
something which may be dangerous or difficult to handle is better left undisturbed; English proverb, late 14th century; see 20 below

15 Let well alone.
often used as a warning against raising problems which will then be difficult to resolve; English proverb, late 16th century

16 Look before you leap.
used to advise caution before committing oneself to a course of action; English proverb, mid 14th century

17 The more you stir it [a turd] the worse it stinks.
disturbance of something naturally unpleasant will only make it more disagreeable; English proverb, mid 16th century

18 Never trouble trouble till trouble troubles you.
another version of the advice that one should let well alone; English proverb, late 19th century

19 Once bitten by a snake, a man will be afraid of a piece of rope for three years.
Chinese proverb; see 10 above, **Experience** 8, **Trust** 40

20 Poke a bush, a snake comes out.
warning against unnecessary disturbance; Japanese proverb: see 14 above

21 Safe bind, safe find.
something kept securely will be readily found again; English proverb, mid 16th century

22 Second thoughts are best.
it is dangerous to act on one's first impulse without due thought; English proverb, late 16th century; see 30 below

23 A stitch in time saves nine.
a small but timely intervention will ensure against the need for much more substantial repair later; English proverb, early 18th century

24 Stop-look-and-listen.
road safety slogan, current in the US from 1912

25 Those who play at bowls must look out for rubbers.
one must beware of difficulties associated with a particular activity; a *rubber* here is an alteration of *rub*, an obstacle or impediment to the course of a bowl; English proverb, mid 18th century

26 Trust in Allah, but tie up your camel.
Arab proverb; see **Practicality** 3

QUOTATIONS

27 Happy is that city which in time of peace thinks of war.
inscription found in the armoury of Venice
Anonymous: Robert Burton *The Anatomy of Melancholy* (1621–51)

28 Beware of desperate steps. The darkest day (Live till tomorrow) will have passed away.
William Cowper 1731–1800: 'The Needless Alarm' (written c.1790)

29 Prudence is a rich, ugly, old maid courted by Incapacity.
William Blake 1757–1827: *The Marriage of Heaven and Hell* (1790–3) 'Proverbs of Hell'

30 Have no truck with first impulses for they are always generous ones.
Casimir, Comte de Montrond 1768–1843: attributed; Comte J. d'Estourmel *Derniers Souvenirs* (1860), where the alternative attribution to Talleyrand is denied; see 22 above

31 Tar-baby ain't sayin' nuthin', en Brer Fox, he
lay low.
Joel Chandler Harris 1848–1908: *Uncle Remus
and His Legends of the Old Plantation* (1881)

32 Put all your eggs in the one basket,
and—WATCH THAT BASKET.
Mark Twain 1835–1910: *Pudd'nhead Wilson*
(1894); see 7 above

33 Them that asks no questions isn't told a lie.
Watch the wall, my darling, while the
Gentlemen go by!
Rudyard Kipling 1865–1936: 'A Smuggler's Song'
(1906)

34 Of all forms of caution, caution in love is
perhaps the most fatal to true happiness.
Bertrand Russell 1872–1970: *The Conquest of
Happiness* (1930)

35 All the same, sir, I would put some of the
colonies in your wife's name.
Joseph Herman Hertz 1872–1946: the Chief Rabbi
to George VI, summer 1940; Chips Channon diary 3
June 1943

36 All the security around the American
president is just to make sure the man who
shoots him gets caught.
Norman Mailer 1923– : in *Sunday Telegraph* 4
March 1990

37 You can put up a sign on the door, 'beware
of the dog', without having a dog.
Hans Blix 1928– : in *Guardian* (online edition) 18
September 2003; see **Dogs** 1

Celebrations see Festivals and Celebrations

➤➤ Censorship ◄◄

PHRASES

1 **blue-pencil**
censor or make cuts in a manuscript; a blue 'lead'
pencil was traditionally used for marking corrections
and deletions; see **Culture** 25

2 **thought control**
the attempt to restrict ideas and impose opinions
through censorship and the control of curricula in
schools

QUOTATIONS

3 If these writings of the Greeks agree with
the book of God, they are useless and need
not be preserved; if they disagree, they are
pernicious and ought to be destroyed.
on burning the library of Alexandria, AD *c.*641
Caliph Omar d. 644: Edward Gibbon *The Decline
and Fall of the Roman Empire* (1776–88)

4 As good almost kill a man as kill a good
book: who kills a man kills a reasonable
creature, God's image; but he who destroys a
good book, kills reason itself, kills the image
of God, as it were in the eye.
John Milton 1608–74: *Areopagitica* (1644)

5 It is a bad cause which cannot bear the
words of a dying man.
as drums and trumpets were ordered to sound at his
execution to drown anything he might say
Henry Vane 1613–62: Charles Dickens *A Child's
History of England* (1853)

6 I disapprove of what you say, but I will
defend to the death your right to say it.
his attitude towards Helvétius following the burning
of the latter's *De l'esprit* in 1759
Voltaire 1694–1778: attributed to Voltaire, the
words are in fact S. G. Tallentyre's summary; *The
Friends of Voltaire* (1907)

7 Wherever books will be burned, men also, in
the end, are burned.
Heinrich Heine 1797–1856: *Almansor* (1823)

8 Those whom books will hurt will not be
proof against events. Events, not books,
should be forbid.
Herman Melville 1819–91: *The Piazza Tales* (1856)

9 You have not converted a man, because you
have silenced him.
Lord Morley 1838–1923: *On Compromise* (1874)

10 Assassination is the extreme form of
censorship.
George Bernard Shaw 1856–1950: *The Showing-
Up of Blanco Posnet* (1911)

11 Everybody favours free speech in the slack
moments when no axes are being ground.
Heywood Broun 1888–1939: in *New York World* 23
October 1926

12 It is obvious that 'obscenity' is not a term
capable of exact legal definition; in the
practice of the Courts, it means 'anything
that shocks the magistrate'.
Bertrand Russell 1872–1970: *Sceptical Essays*
(1928) 'The Recrudescence of Puritanism'

13 Don't you see that the whole aim of Newspeak is to narrow the range of thought? In the end we shall make thoughtcrime literally impossible, because there will be no words in which to express it.
George Orwell 1903–50: *Nineteen Eighty-Four* (1949)

14 Those who want the Government to regulate matters of the mind and spirit are like men who are so afraid of being murdered that they commit suicide to avoid assassination.
Harry S. Truman 1884–1972: address at the National Archives, Washington, D.C., 15 December 1952

15 We are paid to have dirty minds.
on British Film Censors
John Trevelyan: in *Observer* 15 November 1959

16 Is it a book you would even wish your wife or your servants to read?
of D. H. Lawrence's *Lady Chatterley's Lover*
Mervyn Griffith-Jones 1909–79: speech for the prosecution at the Central Criminal Court, Old Bailey, 20 October 1960

17 It's red hot, mate. I hate to think of this sort of book getting into the wrong hands. As soon as I've finished this, I shall recommend they ban it.
Ray Galton 1930– and **Alan Simpson** 1929– : *The Missing Page* (1960 BBC television programme) words spoken by Tony Hancock

18 The state has no place in the nation's bedrooms.
Pierre Trudeau 1919–2000: interview, Ottawa, 22 December 1967

19 If decade after decade the truth cannot be told, each person's mind begins to roam irretrievably. One's fellow countrymen become harder to understand than Martians.
Alexander Solzhenitsyn 1918– : *Cancer Ward* (1968)

20 One does not put Voltaire in the Bastille.
when asked to arrest Sartre, in the 1960s
Charles de Gaulle 1890–1970: in *Encounter* June 1975

21 Vietnam was the first war ever fought without censorship. Without censorship, things can get terribly confused in the public mind.
William C. Westmoreland 1914– : attributed, 1982

22 To portray only what you would like to be true is the beginning of censorship.
David Hare 1947– : *The History Plays* (1984)

23 What is freedom of expression? Without the freedom to offend, it ceases to exist.
Salman Rushdie 1947– : in *Weekend Guardian* 10 February 1990

⤍ Certainty and Doubt ⤎

see also **Belief, Faith, Indecision**

PROVERBS AND SAYINGS

1 Does she . . . or doesn't she?
advertising slogan for Clairol hair colouring, 1950s

2 Don't be vague, ask for Haig.
advertising slogan for Haig whisky, *c.*1936

3 Nothing is certain but death and taxes.
summarizing what in life is inevitable and inescapable; English proverb, early 18th century; see **Pregnancy 10, Taxes 15**

PHRASES

4 a bird in the hand
something certain (as implicitly contrasted with the prospect of a greater but less certain advantage), from the proverb: see **Caution 2**

5 Lombard Street to a China orange
great wealth against one ordinary object, virtual certainty; *Lombard Street* a street in London, originally occupied by Lombard bankers and still containing many of the principal London banks; *China orange* taken as the type of something worthless

6 twist in the wind
be left in a state of suspense or uncertainty; see **Haste 22**

QUOTATIONS

7 How long halt ye between two opinions?
Bible: I Kings

8 I lived uncertain, I die doubtful: O thou
Being of beings, have mercy upon me!
Aristotle 384–322 BC: attributed last words,
probably apocryphal; a Latin version was current in
the early 17th century

9 O thou of little faith, wherefore didst thou
doubt?
Bible: St Matthew

10 If a man will begin with certainties, he shall
end in doubts; but if he will be content to
begin with doubts, he shall end in
certainties.
Francis Bacon 1561–1626: *The Advancement of
Learning* (1605)

11 I beseech you, in the bowels of Christ, think
it possible you may be mistaken.
Oliver Cromwell 1599–1658: letter to the General
Assembly of the Kirk of Scotland, 3 August 1650

12 Negative Capability, that is when man is
capable of being in uncertainties, mysteries,
doubts, without any irritable reaching after
fact and reason.
John Keats 1795–1821: letter to George and
Thomas Keats, 21 December 1817

13 My deplorable mania for analysis exhausts
me. I doubt everything, even my doubt.
Gustave Flaubert 1821–80: letter, 8–9
August 1846

14 I wish I was as cocksure of anything as Tom
Macaulay is of everything.
Lord Melbourne 1779–1848: Lord Cowper's
preface to *Lord Melbourne's Papers* (1889)

15 There lives more faith in honest doubt,
Believe me, than in half the creeds.
Alfred, Lord Tennyson 1809–92: *In Memoriam A.
H. H.* (1850)

16 Ah, what a dusty answer gets the soul
When hot for certainties in this our life!
George Meredith 1828–1909: *Modern Love*
(1862); see **Satisfaction** 12

17 Ten thousand difficulties do not make one
doubt.
John Henry Newman 1801–90: *Apologia pro Vita
Sua* (1864)

18 What, never?
No, never!

What, *never?*
Hardly ever!
W. S. Gilbert 1836–1911: *HMS Pinafore* (1878)

19 I am too much of a sceptic to deny the
possibility of anything.
T. H. Huxley 1825–95: letter to Herbert Spencer, 22
March 1886

20 Oh! let us never, never doubt
What nobody is sure about!
Hilaire Belloc 1870–1953: 'The Microbe' (1897)

21 Life is doubt,
And faith without doubt is nothing but
death.
Miguel de Unamuno 1864–1937: 'Salmo II' (1907)

22 I respect faith but doubt is what gets you an
education.
Wilson Mizner 1876–1933: H. L. Mencken *A New
Dictionary of Quotations* (1942)

23 My mind is not a bed to be made and
re-made.
James Agate 1877–1947: *Ego 6* (1944) 9 June 1943

24 We often call a certainty a hope, to bring it
luck.
Elizabeth Bibesco 1897–1945: *Haven* (1951)

25 Human beings are perhaps never more
frightening than when they are convinced
beyond doubt that they are right.
Laurens van der Post 1906–96: *The Lost World of
the Kalahari* (1958)

26 The trouble with the world is that the stupid
are cocksure and the intelligent are full of
doubt.
Bertrand Russell 1872–1970: attributed

27 I'm a man of no convictions. At least, I
think I am.
Christopher Hampton 1946– : *The Philanthropist*
(1970)

28 When a Southern Irishman says 'Not an
inch', he means no more than four or five
inches, and certainly not, at any rate for the
next five or six years. But when an
Ulsterman says 'Not an inch', that's it: he
means not the tiniest fraction of an inch,
from now until the last syllable of recorded
time. And when he says 'No Surrender' he
means just that, no surrender, ever.
Tony Gray 1928– : *St Patrick's People* (1996); see
Defiance 2

-»- Chance and Luck -«-

PROVERBS AND SAYINGS

1 Accidents will happen (in the best-regulated families).
the most orderly arrangements cannot prevent accidents from occurring; English proverb, mid 18th century

2 Blind chance sweeps the world along.
American proverb, mid 20th century

3 The devil looks after his own.
often used to comment on the good fortune of someone undeserving; English proverb, early 18th century; see 4 below

4 The devil's children have the devil's luck.
commenting on the good fortune of someone undeserving; English proverb, late 17th century; see 3 above

5 Diligence is the mother of good luck.
success results more from application and practice than from good fortune; English proverb, late 16th century

6 Fools for luck.
a foolish person is traditionally fortunate; English proverb, mid 19th century

7 It could be you.
advertising slogan for the British national lottery, 1994

8 It is better to be born lucky than rich.
often with the implication that riches can be lost or spent, but that good luck gives one the capacity to improve one's fortunes; English proverb, mid 17th century

9 Lightning never strikes the same place twice.
often used as an encouragement that a particular misfortune will not be repeated; English proverb, mid 19th century

10 Lucky at cards, unlucky in love.
suggesting that good fortune in gambling is balanced by lack of success in love; English proverb, mid 19th century

11 Moses took a chance.
used to urge someone to take a risk; American proverb, mid 20th century

12 See a pin and pick it up, all the day you'll have good luck; see a pin and let it lie, bad luck you'll have all day.
extolling the virtues of thrift in small matters; English proverb, mid 19th century

13 There is luck in odd numbers.
English proverb, late 16th century

14 Third time lucky.
reflecting the idea that three is a lucky number; often used to suggest making another effort after initial failure; English proverb, mid 19th century

15 You have two chances, Buckley's and none.
Australian proverb; see 18 below

PHRASES

16 Aladdin's lamp
a talisman enabling the holder to gratify any wish; in the *Arabian Nights*, an old lamp found by Aladdin in a cave, which when rubbed brought a genie to obey his will; see **Wealth 7**

17 a bow at a venture
a chance attempt at something; from the Bible: see 21 below

18 Buckley's chance
in Australia, a slim chance, no chance at all, sometimes said to be from the name of William Buckley (died 1856), who, despite dire predictions as to his chances of survival, lived with the Aboriginals for many years; see 15 above

19 in the lap of the gods
subject to fate; see **Fate 11**

20 wheel of Fortune
the wheel which the deity Fortune is represented as turning as a symbol of random luck or change; see **Circumstance 10**

QUOTATIONS

21 And a certain man drew a bow at a venture, and smote the king of Israel between the joints of the harness.
Bible: I Kings; see 17 above

22 Cast thy bread upon the waters: for thou shalt find it after many days.
Bible: Ecclesiastes; see **Future 8**

23 Care and diligence bring luck.
Thomas Fuller 1654–1734: *Gnomologia* (1732)

24 The chapter of knowledge is a very short, but the chapter of accidents is a very long one.
Lord Chesterfield 1694–1773: letter to Solomon Dayrolles, 16 February 1753; see **Misfortunes 9**

25 O! many a shaft, at random sent,
Finds mark the archer little meant!
And many a word, at random spoken,
May soothe or wound a heart that's broken.
Sir Walter Scott 1771–1832: *The Lord of the Isles*
(1813)

26 All you know about it [luck] for certain is
that it's bound to change.
Bret Harte 1836–1902: *The Outcasts of Poker Flat*
(1871)

27 Some folk want their luck buttered.
Thomas Hardy 1840–1928: *The Mayor of
Casterbridge* (1886)

28 A throw of the dice will never eliminate
chance.
Stéphane Mallarmé 1842–98: title of poem
(1897)

29 There is much good luck in the world, but it
is luck. We are none of us safe. We are
children, playing or quarrelling on the line.
E. M. Forster 1879–1970: *The Longest Journey*
(1907)

30 At any rate, I am convinced that *He* [God]
does not play dice.
often quoted as 'God does not play dice'
Albert Einstein 1879–1955: letter to Max Born, 4
December 1926

31 If an army of monkeys were strumming on
typewriters they *might* write all the books in
the British Museum.
Arthur Eddington 1882–1944: *The Nature of the
Physical World* (1928); see **Computers** 17

32 The best mascot is a good mechanic.
Amelia Earhart 1898–1937: Mary S. Lovell *The
Sound of Wings* (1989)

33 Miracles do happen, but one has to work
very hard for them.
Chaim Weizmann 1874–1952: Isaiah Berlin
Personal Impressions (1998)

34 Mr Bond, they have a saying in Chicago:
'Once is happenstance. Twice is
coincidence. The third time it's enemy
action.'
Ian Fleming 1908–64: *Goldfinger* (1959)

35 Predictability: Does the flap of a butterfly's
wings in Brazil set off a tornado in Texas?
Edward N. Lorenz: title of paper given to the
American Association for the Advancement of
Science, Washington, 29 December 1979; see
Causes 13

36 What we call luck is the inner man
externalized. We make things happen to us.
Robertson Davies 1913–95: *What's Bred in the
Bone* (1985)

⤜ Change ⤛

see also **Beginning, Ending, Progress**

PROVERBS AND SAYINGS

1 **And now for something completely
different.**
catchphrase popularized in *Monty Python's Flying
Circus* (BBC TV programme, 1969–74)

2 **A change is as good as a rest.**
suggesting that a change of activity can be
refreshing; English proverb, late 19th century

3 **It is never too late to mend.**
one can always try to improve; English proverb, late
16th century

4 **The leopard does not change his spots.**
a person cannot change their essential nature, from
the Bible: see 20, 28 below, **Character** 4; English
proverb, mid 16th century

5 **Never say never.**
used as a warning against over-confidence that
circumstances cannot change; late 20th century
saying; see **Time** 4

6 **New brooms sweep clean.**
often used in the context of someone newly
appointed to a post who is making changes in

personnel and procedures; English proverb, mid
16th century

7 **New lords, new laws.**
new authorities are likely to change existing rules;
English proverb, mid 16th century

8 **No matter how long a log floats in the
river, it will never become a crocodile.**
essential characteristics will not change; African
proverb; see **Character** 8

9 **No more Mr Nice Guy.**
said to assert that one will no longer be amiable or
cooperative; mid 20th century saying

10 **Nothing is for ever.**
late 20th century saying

11 **Other times, other manners.**
used in resignation or consolation; English proverb,
late 16th century

12 **Semper eadem.**
Latin, *ever the same*, motto of Elizabeth I
(1533–1603)

13 **There are no birds in last year's nest.**
circumstances have changed, and former
opportunities are no longer there; English proverb,
early 17th century

14 **Three removals are as bad as a fire.**
moving house is so disruptive and unsettling, that
the effects of doing it three times are as destructive
as a house fire; English proverb, mid 18th century

15 **Times change and we with time.**
we adapt in response to changes in the world
around us; English proverb, late 16th century

PHRASES

18 **be subdued to what one works in**
become reduced in capacity or ability to the
standard of one's material; in allusion to Shakespeare
Sonnets: see **Circumstance** 24

19 **change horses in midstream**
change one's ideas or plans in the middle of a
project or process; also in proverbial form, 'Don't
change horses in midstream'

20 **change one's skin**
undergo a change of character regarded as
fundamentally impossible, probably originally with
reference to the Bible (Jeremiah): see 4 above, 28
below

21 **fresh fields and pastures new**
new areas of activity, from a misquotation of Milton:
see 32 below

22 **the law of the Medes and Persians**
a rule which cannot be altered in any circumstances,
from the Bible (Daniel) 'The thing is true, according
to the law of the Medes and Persians, which
altereth not'

QUOTATIONS

28 Can the Ethiopian change his skin, or the
leopard his spots?
Bible: Jeremiah; see 4, 20 above

29 Everything flows and nothing stays . . . You
can't step twice into the same river.
Heraclitus *c.*540–*c.*480 BC: Plato *Cratylus*

30 Times go by turns, and chances change by
course,
From foul to fair, from better hap to worse.
Robert Southwell 1561–95: 'Times go by Turns'
(1595)

31 He that will not apply new remedies must
expect new evils; for time is the greatest
innovator.
Francis Bacon 1561–1626: *Essays* (1625) 'Of
Innovations'

32 At last he rose, and twitched his mantle
blue:
Tomorrow to fresh woods, and pastures new.
John Milton 1608–74: 'Lycidas' (1638); see 21
above

16 **Variety is the spice of life.**
English proverb, late 18th century, originally with
allusion to Cowper: see 36 below

17 **You can't put new wine in old bottles.**
often used in relation to the introduction of new
ideas or practices; English proverb, early 20th
century, from the Bible (Matthew) 'Neither do men
put new wine into old bottles: else the bottles break,
and the wine runneth out, and the bottles perish';
see 25 below

23 **mover and shaker**
a person who influences events, a person who gets
things done; see **Musicians** 6

24 **move the goalposts**
unfairly alter the conditions or rules of a procedure
during its course. The term has been current since
the late 1980s, and provides a useful image for the
idea of making an important (and usually
unheralded) alteration to terms and conditions
previously agreed

25 **new wine in old bottles**
something new or innovatory added to an existing
or established system or organization; from the
proverb: see 17 above

26 **road to Damascus**
a sudden and complete personal conversion to a
cause or principle which one has formerly rejected,
in allusion to the conversion of St Paul on the road to
Damascus, told in the Bible (Acts); see 52 below

27 **sea change**
a profound or notable transformation, from
Shakespeare's *Tempest*: see **The Sea** 10

33 When it is not necessary to change, it is
necessary not to change.
Lucius Cary, Lord Falkland 1610–43: 'A Speech
concerning Episcopacy' delivered in 1641

34 Change is not made without inconvenience,
even from worse to better.
Samuel Johnson 1709–84: *A Dictionary of the
English Language* (1755)

35 If we do not find anything pleasant, at least
we shall find something new.
Voltaire 1694–1778: *Candide* (1759)

36 Variety's the very spice of life,
That gives it all its flavour.
William Cowper 1731–1800: *The Task* (1785) bk. 2
'The Timepiece'; see 16 above

37 There is a certain relief in change, even
though it be from bad to worse . . . it is often
a comfort to shift one's position and be
bruised in a new place.
Washington Irving 1783–1859: *Tales of a Traveller*
(1824)

38 There are three things which the public will always clamour for, sooner or later: namely, novelty, novelty, novelty.
Thomas Hood 1799–1845: *Announcement of Comic Annual for 1836*

39 A foolish consistency is the hobgoblin of little minds, adored by little statesmen and philosophers and divines. With consistency a great soul has simply nothing to do.
Ralph Waldo Emerson 1803–82: *Essays* (1841) 'Self-Reliance'

40 Forward, forward let us range,
Let the great world spin for ever down the ringing grooves of change.
Alfred, Lord Tennyson 1809–92: 'Locksley Hall' (1842)

41 Change and decay in all around I see;
O Thou, who changest not, abide with me.
Henry Francis Lyte 1793–1847: 'Abide with Me' (probably written in 1847)

42 *Plus ça change, plus c'est la même chose.*
The more things change, the more they are the same.
Alphonse Karr 1808–90: *Les Guêpes* January 1849

43 There is in all change something at once sordid and agreeable, which smacks of infidelity and household removals. This is sufficient to explain the French Revolution.
Charles Baudelaire 1821–67: *Journaux intimes* (1887) 'Mon coeur mis à nu'

44 The old order changeth, yielding place to new,
And God fulfils himself in many ways,
Lest one good custom should corrupt the world.
Alfred, Lord Tennyson 1809–92: *Idylls of the King* 'The Passing of Arthur' (1869)

45 All conservatism is based upon the idea that if you leave things alone you leave them as they are. But you do not. If you leave a thing alone you leave it to a torrent of change.
G. K. Chesterton 1874–1936: *Orthodoxy* (1908)

46 Most of the change we think we see in life
Is due to truths being in and out of favour.
Robert Frost 1874–1963: 'The Black Cottage' (1914)

47 All changed, changed utterly:
A terrible beauty is born.
W. B. Yeats 1865–1939: 'Easter, 1916' (1921)

48 Consistency is contrary to nature, contrary to life. The only completely consistent people are the dead.
Aldous Huxley 1894–1963: *Do What You Will* (1929)

49 Toto, I've a feeling we're not in Kansas any more.
Noel Langley 1911– et al.: *The Wizard of Oz* (1939 film)

50 God, give us the serenity to accept what cannot be changed;
Give us the courage to change what should be changed;
Give us the wisdom to distinguish one from the other.
Reinhold Niebuhr 1892–1971: prayer said to have been first published in 1951; Richard Wightman Fox *Reinhold Niebuhr* (1985)

51 If we want things to stay as they are, things will have to change.
Giuseppe di Lampedusa 1896–1957: *The Leopard* (1957)

52 You don't reach Downing Street by pretending you've travelled the road to Damascus when you haven't even left home.
of Neil Kinnock
Margaret Thatcher 1925– : in *Independent* 14 October 1989; see 26 above

53 I sometimes sense the world is changing almost too fast for its inhabitants, at least for us older ones.
Elizabeth II 1926– : on a tour of Pakistan, 8 October 1997

Chaos see Order and Chaos

->- Character -<-

see also **Human Nature**

1 **An ape's an ape, a varlet's a varlet, though they be clad in silk or scarlet.**
inward nature cannot be overcome by outward show; English proverb, mid 16th century

2 **A bad penny always turns up.**
referring to the inevitable return of an unwanted or disreputable person; English proverb, mid 18th century

3 Better a good cow than a cow of a good kind.

good character is more important than distinguished lineage; English proverb, early 20th century

4 By seeing one spot, you know the entire leopard.

Japanese proverb; see **Change** 4

5 Character is what we are; reputation is what others think we are.

American proverb, mid 20th century

6 The child is the father of the man.

asserting the unity of character from childhood to adult life; English proverb, early 19th century, from Wordsworth, see **Children** 14

7 Eagles don't catch flies.

great or important persons do not concern themselves with trifling matters; English proverb, mid 16th century

8 Feeding a snake with milk will not change its poisonous nature.

kindness will not alter a bad character; Indian proverb; see **Change** 8

9 It takes all sorts to make a world.

often used in recognition that a particular group may encompass a wide range of character and background; English proverb, early 17th century

10 Like a fence, character cannot be strengthened by whitewash.

American proverb, mid 20th century

11 The man who is born in a stable is not a horse.

sometimes attributed to the Duke of Wellington, who asserted that being born in Ireland did not make him Irish; English proverb, mid 19th century

12 Once a —, always a —.

a particular way of life produces traits that cannot be eradicated; English proverb, early 17th century, see **Clergy** 4

PHRASES

22 a curate's egg

something of very mixed character, partly good and partly bad; from the *Punch* cartoon: see **Satisfaction** 32

23 feet of clay

fundamental weakness in a person who has appeared to be of great merit; from the Bible (Daniel) 'This image's head was of fine gold . . . his feet part of iron and part of clay'

24 heart of oak

a person with a strong, courageous nature; literally, the solid central part of the tree; see **Armed Forces** 23

25 Jekyll-and-Hyde

someone with violent and unpredictable changes of mood and personality; from the central character of

13 The same fire that hardens the egg melts the butter.

different people will react in different ways to the same experiences; modern saying, see **Similarity** 17

14 Still waters run deep.

now commonly used to assert that a placid exterior hides a passionate nature; English proverb, early 15th century

15 A stream cannot rise above its source.

used to suggest that a person's natural level is set by their ultimate origin; English proverb, mid 17th century

16 The tree is known by its fruit.

a person is judged by what they do and produce; English proverb, early 16th century

17 There's many a good cock come out of a tattered bag.

something good may emerge from unpromising surroundings (the reference is to cockfighting); English proverb, late 19th century

18 What can you expect from a pig but a grunt.

used rhetorically of coarse or boorish behaviour; English proverb, mid 18th century

19 What's bred in the bone will come out in the flesh.

inherent characteristics will in the end become apparent; English proverb, late 15th century

20 When the going gets tough, the tough get going.

pressure acts as a stimulus to the strong; English proverb, mid 20th century, often used by Joseph Kennedy (1888–1969) as an injunction to his children

21 You cannot dream yourself into a character, you must forge one out for yourself.

American proverb, mid 20th century

Robert Louis Stevenson's story *The Strange Case of Dr Jekyll and Mr Hyde* (1886). He discovers a drug which creates a separate personality (appearing in the character of Mr Hyde) into which Jekyll's evil impulses are channelled

26 a man for all seasons

a person who is ready for any situation or contingency, or adaptable to any circumstance; from Whittington on Thomas More: see **31** below

27 neither fish, nor flesh, nor good red herring

of indefinite character; from distinctions made by early religious dietary laws; see **Food** 9

28 of shreds and patches

made up of rags or scraps, patched together; from Shakespeare *Hamlet* 'A King of shreds and patches'; see **Singing** 10

29 A man's character is his fate.
Heraclitus c.540–c.480 BC: *On the Universe*

30 He was a verray, parfit gentil knyght.
Geoffrey Chaucer 1343–1400: *The Canterbury Tales* 'The General Prologue'

31 As time requireth, a man of marvellous mirth and pastimes, and sometime of as sad gravity, as who say: a man for all seasons.
of Sir Thomas More
Robert Whittington c.1480–1553?: *Vulgaria* (1521); see 26 above

32 Nature is often hidden, sometimes overcome, seldom extinguished.
Francis Bacon 1561–1626: *Essays* (1625) 'Of Nature in Men'

33 Youth, what man's age is like to be doth show;
We may our ends by our beginnings know.
John Denham 1615–69: 'Of Prudence' (1668)

34 It is not in the still calm of life, or the repose of a pacific station, that great characters are formed . . . Great necessities call out great virtues.
Abigail Adams 1744–1818: letter to John Quincy Adams, 19 January 1780

35 Talent develops in quiet places, character in the full current of human life.
Johann Wolfgang von Goethe 1749–1832: *Torquato Tasso* (1790)

36 Qualities too elevated often unfit a man for society. We don't take ingots with us to market; we take silver or small change.
Nicolas-Sébastien Chamfort 1741–94: *Maximes et Pensées* (1796)

37 I am not at all the sort of person you and I took me for.
Jane Carlyle 1801–66: letter to Thomas Carlyle, 7 May 1822

38 Affection beaming in one eye, and calculation shining out of the other.
Charles Dickens 1812–70: *Martin Chuzzlewit* (1844)

39 The great qualities, the imperious will, the rapid energy, the eager nature fit for a great crisis are not required—are impediments—in common times.
Walter Bagehot 1826–77: *The English Constitution* (1867)

40 Though I've belted you and flayed you,
By the livin' Gawd that made you,
You're a better man than I am, Gunga Din!
Rudyard Kipling 1865–1936: 'Gunga Din' (1892)

41 A man of great common sense and good taste, meaning thereby a man without originality or moral courage.
George Bernard Shaw 1856–1950: *Notes to Caesar and Cleopatra* (1901) 'Julius Caesar'

42 McKinley has no more backbone than a chocolate éclair!
Theodore Roosevelt 1858–1919: H. T. Peck *Twenty Years of the Republic* (1906)

43 If you can trust yourself when all men doubt you,
But make allowance for their doubting too;
If you can wait and not be tired by waiting,
Or being lied about, don't deal in lies,
Or being hated, don't give way to hating,
And yet don't look too good, nor talk too wise.
Rudyard Kipling 1865–1936: 'If—' (1910)

44 Slice him where you like, a hellhound is always a hellhound.
P. G. Wodehouse 1881–1975: *The Code of the Woosters* (1938)

45 It is the nature, and the advantage, of strong people that they can bring out the crucial questions and form a clear opinion about them. The weak always have to decide between alternatives that are not their own.
Dietrich Bonhoeffer 1906–45: *Widerstand und Ergebung* (Resistance and Submission, 1951)

46 There exists a great chasm between those, on one side, who relate everything to a single central vision . . . and, on the other side, those who pursue many ends, often unrelated and even contradictory . . . The first kind of intellectual and artistic personality belongs to the hedgehogs, the second to the foxes.
Isaiah Berlin 1909–97: *The Hedgehog and the Fox* (1953); see **Knowledge** 17

47 A thick skin is a gift from God.
Konrad Adenauer 1876–1967: in *New York Times* 30 December 1959

48 We are all worms. But I do believe that I am a glow-worm.
Winston Churchill 1874–1965: Violet Bonham-Carter *Winston Churchill as I Knew Him* (1965)

49 Fame vaporizes, money goes with the wind, and all that's left is character.
O. J. Simpson 1947– : *Juice: O. J. Simpson's Life* (1977)

50 Those who stand for nothing fall for anything.
Alex Hamilton 1936– : 'Born Old' (radio broadcast), in *Listener* 9 November 1978

⤜⋗⋗⋖⋗⋗⋖⋗⋗⋖⋗⋗⋖⋗⋗⋖⋗⋗⋖⋗⋗⋖⋗⋗⋖⋗⋗⋖⋗⋗⋖⋗⋗⋖⋗⋗⋖⋗⋗⋖⋗⋗⋖⋗⋗⋖⋗⋗⋖⋗⋗⋖⋗⋗

51 You can tell a lot about a fellow's character by his way of eating jellybeans.
Ronald Reagan 1911–2004: in *New York Times* 15 January 1981

52 Claudia's the sort of person who goes through life holding on to the sides.
Alice Thomas Ellis 1932–2005: *The Other Side of the Fire* (1983)

53 Nice guys, when we turn nasty, can make a terrible mess of it, usually because we've had so little practice, and have bottled it up for too long.
Matthew Parris 1949– : in *The Spectator* 27 February 1993

54 If you have bright plumage, people will take pot shots at you.
Alan Clark 1928–99: in *Independent* 25 June 1994

55 Do not underestimate the determination of a quiet man.
Iain Duncan Smith 1954– : speech to the Conservative Party Conference, 10 October 2002

⤜⋗ Charity ⋖⋗

see also **Gifts**

PROVERBS AND SAYINGS

1 **Charity begins at home.**
you should look first to needs in your immediate vicinity; English proverb, late 14th century

2 **Charity is not a bone you throw to a dog but a bone you share with a dog.**
the recipient of one's charity should not be treated as an inferior; American proverb, mid 20th century

3 **Give a man a fish, and you feed him for a day; show him how to catch fish, and you feed him for a lifetime.**
mid 20th century saying, perhaps deriving from a Chinese proverb: see **Teaching** 5

4 **Keep your own fish-guts for your own sea-maws.**
any surplus product should be offered first to those in need who are closest to you; Scottish proverb, early 18th century

5 **The roots of charity are always green.**
true generosity constantly renews itself; American proverb, mid 20th century

6 **Service is the rent we pay for our room on earth.**
modern saying, deriving from the admission ceremony of Toc H, a society, originally of ex-servicemen and women, founded by Tubby Clayton (1885–1972) after the First World War to promote Christian fellowship and social service

PHRASES

7 **blood out of a stone**
pity from the hard-hearted or money from the impecunious or avaricious; see **Futility** 5

8 **a good Samaritan**
a charitable or helpful person; from the Bible (Luke) 'A certain Samaritan . . . had compassion on him', in the parable of the man who fell among thieves, in which the succouring Samaritan had been preceded by a priest and a Levite, both of whom 'passed by on the other side'; see 13, 25 below

9 **ladies who lunch**
women who organize and take part in fashionable lunches to raise funds for charitable projects; from 'The Ladies who Lunch', 1970 song by Stephen Sondheim (1930–) 'A toast to that invincible bunch . . . Let's hear it for the ladies who lunch'

10 **a ministering angel**
a kind-hearted person, especially a woman, who nurses or comforts others; originally from Shakespeare *Hamlet* 'A ministering angel shall my sister be, When thou liest howling'; later reinforced by Scott: see **Women** 30

11 **a widow's mite**
a person's modest contribution to a cause or charity, representing the most the giver can manage; from the Bible (Mark) in the parable of the poor widow who contributed two *mites* (coins of low value) to the treasury, and of whom Jesus said that 'this poor widow hath cast more in, than all they which have cast into the treasury', because she 'of her want did cast in all that she had'

QUOTATIONS

12 When thou doest alms, let not thy left hand know what thy right hand doeth.
Bible: St Matthew

13 He passed by on the other side.
Bible: St Luke; see 8 above

14 Friends, I have lost a day.
on reflecting that he had done nothing to help anybody all day
Titus AD 39–81: Suetonius *Lives of the Caesars* 'Titus'

15 Thy necessity is yet greater than mine.
on giving his water-bottle to a dying soldier on the battle-field of Zutphen, 1586; commonly quoted 'thy need is greater than mine'
Philip Sidney 1554–86: Fulke Greville *Life of Sir Philip Sidney* (1652)

16 'Tis not enough to help the feeble up,
But to support him after.
William Shakespeare 1564–1616: *Timon of Athens* (c.1607)

17 Defer not charities till death; for certainly, if a man weigh it rightly, he that doth so is rather liberal of another man's than of his own.
Francis Bacon 1561–1626: *Essays* (1625) 'Of Riches'

18 For Charity is cold in the multitude of possessions, and the rich are covetous of their crumbs.
Christopher Smart 1722–71: *Jubilate Agno* (c.1758–63)

19 The living need charity more than the dead.
George Arnold 1834–65: 'The Jolly Old Pedagogue' (1866)

20 People often feed the hungry so that nothing may disturb their own enjoyment of a good meal.
W. Somerset Maugham 1874–1965: *A Writer's Notebook* (1949) written in 1896

21 Without trampling down twelve others You cannot help one poor man.
Bertolt Brecht 1898–1956: *The Good Woman of Setzuan* (1938)

22 I have always depended on the kindness of strangers.
Tennessee Williams 1911–83: *A Streetcar Named Desire* (1947)

23 Keeping books on charity is capitalist nonsense! I just use the money for the poor. I can't stop to count it.
Eva Perón 1919–52: Fleur Cowles *Bloody Precedent: the Peron Story* (1952)

24 We ourselves feel that what we are doing is just a drop in the ocean. But if that drop was not in the ocean, I think the ocean would be less because of that missing drop.
Mother Teresa 1910–97: *A Gift for God* (1975)

25 No one would remember the Good Samaritan if he'd only had good intentions. He had money as well.
Margaret Thatcher 1925– : television interview, 6 January 1980; see 8 above

26 Feed the world
Let them know it's Christmas time again.
Bob Geldof 1954– and **Midge Ure** 1953– : 'Do They Know it's Christmas?' (1984 song)

27 Charity begins today. Today somebody is suffering, today somebody is in the street, today somebody is hungry. Our work is for today, yesterday has gone, tomorrow has not yet come. We have only today.
Mother Teresa 1910–97: in *Osservatore Romano* 8 April 1991; see **The Present** 3

28 Foreign aid is a system of taking money from poor people in rich countries and giving it to rich people in poor countries.
Lord Bauer 1915–2002: attributed

29 The soup of human kindness needs to be getting people off the streets, not giving them a reason to stay on the streets. No one's come up with a soup that gets people off the street.
John Bird 1946– : in *Observer* 25 September 2005; see **Sympathy** 8

⤳ Child Care ⤲

see also **Children, The Family, Parents**

PROVERBS AND SAYINGS

1 The art of being a parent consists of sleeping when the baby isn't looking.
American proverb, mid 20th century

2 It takes a (whole) village to raise a child.
many in the community have a role in a child's development; African proverb (Yoruba)

3 Spare the rod and spoil the child.
the result of not disciplining a child is to spoil it;
English proverb, early 11th century, see **Crime** 19

QUOTATIONS

4 Train up a child in the way he should go:
and when he is old, he will not depart
from it.
Bible: Proverbs

5 Diogenes struck the father when the son
swore.
Robert Burton 1577–1640: *The Anatomy of
Melancholy* (1621–51)

6 Who ran to help me when I fell,
And would some pretty story tell,
Or kiss the place to make it well?
My Mother.
Ann Taylor 1782–1866 and **Jane Taylor**
1783–1824: 'My Mother' (1804)

7 There never was a child so lovely but his
mother was glad to get asleep.
Ralph Waldo Emerson 1803–82: *Journal* 1836

8 Her bringing me up by hand, gave her no
right to bring me up by jerks.
Charles Dickens 1812–70: *Great Expectations*
(1861)

9 You will find as the children grow up that as
a rule children are a bitter
disappointment—their greatest object being
to do precisely what their parents do not
wish and have anxiously tried to prevent.
Queen Victoria 1819–1901: letter to the Crown
Princess of Prussia, 5 January 1876

10 If there is anything that we wish to change
in the child, we should first examine it and
see whether it is not something that could
better be changed in ourselves.
Carl Gustav Jung 1875–1961: 'Vom Werden der
Persönlichkeit' (1932)

11 Oh, what a tangled web do parents weave
When they think that their children are
naïve.
Ogden Nash 1902–71: 'Baby, What Makes the Sky
Blue' (1940); after Scott: see **Deception** 21

12 There is no finer investment for any
community than putting milk into babies.
Winston Churchill 1874–1965: radio broadcast, 21
March 1943

13 Parentage is a very important profession,
but no test of fitness for it is ever imposed in
the interest of the children.
George Bernard Shaw 1856–1950: *Everybody's
Political What's What?* (1944)

14 You know more than you think you do.
Benjamin Spock 1903–98: *Baby and Child Care*
(1946) opening words

15 If you bungle raising your children I don't
think whatever else you do well matters very
much.
Jacqueline Kennedy Onassis 1929–94: Theodore
C. Sorenson *Kennedy* (1965)

16 The art of dealing with children might be
defined as *knowing what not to say.*
A. S. Neill 1883–1973: Jonathan Croall *Neill of
Summerhill: The Permanent Rebel* (1983)

17 They fuck you up, your mum and dad.
They may not mean to, but they do.
They fill you with the faults they had
And add some extra, just for you.
Philip Larkin 1922–85: 'This Be The Verse' (1974)

18 The first child is made of glass, the second
porcelain, the rest of rubber, steel, and
granite.
Richard J. Needham 1939– : in *Toronto Globe and
Mail* 25 January 1977

19 It is only in our advanced and synthetic
civilization that mothers no longer sing to
the babies they are carrying.
Yehudi Menuhin 1916–99: in *Observer* 4
January 1987

20 I don't work that way . . . The very idea that
all children want to be cuddled by a
complete stranger, I find completely
amazing.
on her work for Save the Children
Anne, Princess Royal 1950– : in *Daily Telegraph*
17 January 1998

21 Quality time? There's always another load of
washing.
Julian Barnes 1946– : *Love, Etc.* (2000)

⟶ Children ⟵

see also **The Family, Parents, Schools, Youth**

PROVERBS AND SAYINGS

1 Children should be seen and not heard.
originally applied specifically to (young) women; English proverb, early 15th century

2 Children: one is one, two is fun, three is a houseful.
American proverb, mid 20th century

PHRASES

3 the young idea
the child's mind, from Thomson: see **Teaching** 11

QUOTATIONS

4 Like as the arrows in the hand of the giant: even so are the young children.
Happy is the man that hath his quiver full of them.
Bible: Psalm 127

5 Suffer the little children to come unto me, and forbid them not: for of such is the kingdom of God.
Bible: St Mark

6 A child is owed the greatest respect; if you ever have something disgraceful in mind, don't ignore your son's tender years.
Juvenal c.AD 60–c.130: *Satires*

7 A child is not a vase to be filled, but a fire to be lit.
François Rabelais c.1494–c.1553: attributed; see **The Mind** 7

8 It should be noted that children at play are not playing about; their games should be seen as their most serious-minded activity.
Montaigne 1533–92: *Essais* (1580)

9 At first the infant,
Mewling and puking in the nurse's arms.
And then the whining schoolboy, with his satchel,
And shining morning face, creeping like snail
Unwillingly to school.
William Shakespeare 1564–1616: *As You Like It* (1599)

10 Children sweeten labours, but they make misfortunes more bitter.
Francis Bacon 1561–1626: *Essays* (1625) 'Of Parents and Children'

11 Men are generally more careful of the breed of their horses and dogs than of their children.
William Penn 1644–1718: *Some Fruits of Solitude* (1693)

12 Behold the child, by Nature's kindly law
Pleased with a rattle, tickled with a straw.
Alexander Pope 1688–1744: *An Essay on Man* Epistle 2 (1733)

13 Alas, regardless of their doom,
The little victims play!
Thomas Gray 1716–71: *Ode on a Distant Prospect of Eton College* (1747)

14 The Child is father of the Man;
And I could wish my days to be
Bound each to each by natural piety.
William Wordsworth 1770–1850: 'My heart leaps up when I behold' (1807); see **Character** 6

15 Oh, for an hour of Herod!
at the first night of J. M. Barrie's *Peter Pan* in 1904; see **Festivals** 28
Anthony Hope 1863–1933: Denis Mackail *The Story of JMB* (1941)

16 Childhood is the kingdom where nobody dies.
Nobody that matters, that is.
Edna St Vincent Millay 1892–1950: 'Childhood is the Kingdom where Nobody dies' (1934)

17 There is no end to the violations committed by children on children, quietly talking alone.
Elizabeth Bowen 1899–1973: *The House in Paris* (1935)

18 There is always one moment in childhood when the door opens and lets the future in.
Graham Greene 1904–91: *The Power and the Glory* (1940)

19 A baby is God's opinion that life should go on.
Carl Sandburg 1878–1967: *Remembrance Rock* (1948)

20 The summer that I was ten—
Can it be there was only one
summer that I was ten? It must

have been a long one then.
May Swenson 1919–89: 'The Centaur' (1958)

21 Literature is mostly about having sex and not much about having children. Life is the other way round.
David Lodge 1935– : *The British Museum is Falling Down* (1965)

22 A child becomes an adult when he realizes that he has a right not only to be right but also to be wrong.
Thomas Szasz 1920– : *The Second Sin* (1973)

23 Childhood is Last Chance Gulch for happiness. After that, you know too much.
Tom Stoppard 1937– : *Where Are They Now?* (1973); see **Opportunity** 21

24 There is no such thing as other people's children.
Hillary Rodham Clinton 1947– : in *Newsweek* 15 January 1996

25 Since you arrived, days have melted into night and back again and we are learning a new grammar, a long sentence whose punctuation marks are feeding and winding and nappy changing and these occasional moments of quiet.
Fergal Keane 1961– : *Letter to Daniel* BBC Radio 4 (1996)

->- Choice -<-

see also **Indecision**

PROVERBS AND SAYINGS

1 **Different strokes for different folks.**
different ways of doing something are appropriate for different people (the saying is of US origin, and *strokes* here means, 'comforting gestures of approval'); late 20th century saying

2 **A door must be either shut or open.**
said of two mutually exclusive alternatives; English proverb, mid 18th century

3 **He that has a choice has trouble.**
choosing between two things or persons may cause difficulties; American proverb, mid 20th century

4 **No man can serve two masters.**
English proverb, early 14th century; see **Money** 26

5 **The obvious choice is usually a quick regret.**
selection on outward appearance alone soon disappoints; American proverb, mid 20th century

6 **Of two evils choose the less.**
English proverb, late 14th century; see 12, 25 below

7 **Small choice in rotten apples.**
if all options are unpalatable there is little choice to be had; English proverb, late 16th century

8 **They offered death so you would be happy with a fever.**
a worse possibility makes something inherently unwelcome acceptable; Persian proverb

9 **Whose finger do you want on the trigger?**
headline in *Daily Mirror* 21 September 1951, alluding to the atom bomb, apropos the failure of both the Labour and Conservative parties to purge their leaders of proven failures

10 **You pays your money and you takes your choice.**
said when there is little or nothing to choose between two options; English proverb, mid 19th century

PHRASES

11 **Hobson's choice**
the option of taking what is offered or nothing; no choice; from *Hobson* (1554–1631), a Cambridge carrier who gave his customers a choice between the next horse or none at all.

12 **the lesser of two evils**
the less harmful of two evil things; the alternative that has fewer drawbacks; see 6 above, 25 below

13 **Morton's fork**
a situation in which there are two choices or alternatives whose consequences are equally unpleasant, from John *Morton* (*c.*1420–1500) Archbishop of Canterbury and minister of Henry VII; *Morton's fork* = the argument (used by Morton to extract loans) that the obviously rich must have money and the frugal must have savings

QUOTATIONS

14 For many are called, but few are chosen.
Bible: St Matthew

15 To be, or not to be: that is the question.
William Shakespeare 1564–1616: *Hamlet* (1601)

16 How happy could I be with either,
Were t'other dear charmer away!
John Gay 1685–1732: *The Beggar's Opera* (1728)

17 From this day you must be a stranger to one
of your parents.—Your mother will never see
you again if you do *not* marry Mr Collins,
and I will never see you again if you *do*.
Jane Austen 1775–1817: *Pride and Prejudice* (1813)

18 What man wants is simply *independent*
choice, whatever that independence may
cost and wherever it may lead.
Fedor Dostoevsky 1821–81: *Notes from
Underground* (1864)

19 A woman can hardly ever choose . . . she is
dependent on what happens to her. She
must take meaner things, because only
meaner things are within her reach.
George Eliot 1819–80: *Felix Holt* (1866)

20 White shall not neutralize the black,
nor good
Compensate bad in man, absolve him so:
Life's business being just the terrible choice.
Robert Browning 1812–89: *The Ring and the Book*
(1868–9)

21 Any customer can have a car painted any
colour that he wants so long as it is black.
on the Model T Ford, 1909
Henry Ford 1863–1947: *My Life and Work* (with
Samuel Crowther, 1922)

22 Two roads diverged in a wood, and I—
I took the one less travelled by,
And that has made all the difference.
Robert Frost 1874–1963: 'The Road Not Taken'
(1916)

23 If it has to choose who is to be crucified, the
crowd will always save Barabbas.
Jean Cocteau 1889–1963: *Le Rappel à l'ordre*
(1926)

24 Many men would take the death-sentence
without a whimper to escape the life-
sentence which fate carries in her other
hand.
T. E. Lawrence 1888–1935: *The Mint* (1955)

25 Between two evils, I always pick the one I
never tried before.
Mae West 1892–1980: *Klondike Annie* (1936 film);
see 6, 12 above

26 If one cannot catch the bird of paradise,
better take a wet hen.
Nikita Khrushchev 1894–1971: in *Time* 6
January 1958

27 Chips with everything.
Arnold Wesker 1932– : title of play (1962)

28 Was there ever in anyone's life span a point
free in time, devoid of memory, a night
when choice was any more than the sum of
all the choices gone before?
Joan Didion 1934– : *Run River* (1963)

29 I'll make him an offer he can't refuse.
Mario Puzo 1920–99: *The Godfather* (1969)

30 There is no real alternative.
popularly encapsulated in the acronym TINA
Margaret Thatcher 1925– : speech at
Conservative Women's Conference, 21 May 1980

31 A compromise in the sense that being bitten
in half by a shark is a compromise with
being swallowed whole.
P. J. O'Rourke 1947– : *Parliament of Whores* (1991)

32 DUMBLEDORE: It is our choices, Harry, that
show what we truly are, far more than our
abilities.
J. K. Rowling 1965– : *Harry Potter and the Chamber
of Secrets* (1998)

⊷ The Christian Church ⊰⊷

see also **Clergy, God, Religion**

PROVERBS AND SAYINGS

1 **The blood of the martyrs is the seed of
the Church.**
persecution causes the Church to grow; English
proverb, mid 16th century, see 16 below

2 **Christ has no body now on earth but
yours, no hands but yours, no feet but
yours, yours are the eyes through
which he looks compassion on this
world, yours are the feet with which
he is to go about doing good.**
modern saying, often attributed to St Teresa of Ávila
(1512–82), but not found in her writings

3 **The Christians to the lions!**
saying reported by the Roman theologian Tertullian
(c.160–c.225): 'If the Tiber rises, if the Nile does not
rise, if the heavens give no rain, if there is an

earthquake, famine, or pestilence, straightway the cry is . . . ' *Apologeticus* ch. 40; see **Danger** 25, **Haste** 18

4 **A church is God between four walls.**
American proverb, mid 20th century

5 **The church is an anvil which has worn out many hammers.**
the passive strength of Christianity will outlast aggression; English proverb, mid 19th century

6 **The nearer the church, the farther from God.**
sometimes used to indicate a lack of true spirituality where it is most likely to be found; English proverb, early 14th century, see 19 below

7 **Meat and mass never hindered man.**
indicating human need for physical and spiritual sustenance; English proverb, early 17th century

8 **You can't build a church with stumbling-blocks.**
members of a church need to work together in fellowship; American proverb, mid 20th century

PHRASES

9 **God's Acre**
a churchyard; German *Gottesacker* = 'God's seed-field' in which the bodies of the dead are 'sown'; from the Bible (I Corinthians)

10 **muscular Christianity**
Christian life characterized by cheerful physical activity or robust good works; Christianity without asceticism; as described in the writings of Charles Kingsley; see 28 below

11 **the Old Hundredth**
the traditional tune to which the hymn 'All people that on earth do dwell' is sung, and the hymn itself.

The hymn (which appears first in the Geneva Psalter of 1561) is an early metrical version of Psalm 100

12 **the second Adam**
Jesus Christ; from the Bible (I Corinthians) 'The first man Adam was made a living soul; the last Adam was made a quickening spirit . . . The second man is the Lord from heaven'; see **Human Nature** 5

13 **the Sermon on the Mount**
the discourse in the Bible (Matthew) in which teachings of Jesus, including the Lord's Prayer and the Beatitudes, are presented. It is introduced by the words, 'he went up into a mountain . . . and taught them, saying'; see **Science and Religion** 15

QUOTATIONS

14 Thou art Peter, and upon this rock I will build my church; and the gates of hell shall not prevail against it.
Bible: St Matthew

15 I am the way, the truth, and the life: no man cometh unto the Father, but by me.
Bible: St John; see also **Custom** 8

16 As often as we are mown down by you, the more we grow in numbers; the blood of Christians is the seed.
Tertullian c.AD 160–c.225: *Apologeticus*; see 1 above

17 He cannot have God for his father who has not the church for his mother.
St Cyprian c.AD 200–258: *De Ecclesiae Catholicae Unitate*

18 *In hoc signo vinces.*
In this sign shalt thou conquer.
traditional form of Constantine's vision of the cross (AD 312)
Constantine the Great c.AD 288–337: reported in Greek 'By this, conquer'; Eusebius *Life of Constantine*

19 Take heed of thinking, *The farther you go from the church of Rome, the nearer you are to God.*
Henry Wotton 1568–1639: Izaak Walton *Reliquiae Wottonianae* (1651); see 6 above

20 The papacy is not other than the ghost of the deceased Roman Empire, sitting crowned upon the grave thereof.
Thomas Hobbes 1588–1679: *Leviathan* (1651)

21   As some to church repair,
Not for the doctrine, but the music there.
Alexander Pope 1688–1744: *An Essay on Criticism* (1711)

22 The Gospel of Christ knows of no religion but social; no holiness but social holiness.
John Wesley 1703–91: *Hymns and Sacred Poems* (1739) preface

23 The Christian religion not only was at first attended with miracles, but even at this day cannot be believed by any reasonable person without one.
David Hume 1711–76: *An Enquiry Concerning Human Understanding* (1748)

24 Christians have burnt each other, quite persuaded
That all the Apostles would have done as they did.
Lord Byron 1788–1824: *Don Juan* (1819–24)

25 He who begins by loving Christianity better than Truth will proceed by loving his own sect or church better than Christianity, and end by loving himself better than all.
Samuel Taylor Coleridge 1772–1834: *Aids to Reflection* (1825)

26 He may be one of its [the Church's] buttresses, but certainly not one of its pillars, for he is never found within it.
of John Scott, Lord Eldon (1751–1838)
Anonymous: H. Twiss *Public and Private Life of Eldon* (1844); later attributed to Lord Melbourne

27 If the Church of England were to fail, it would be found in my parish.
John Keble 1792–1866: D. Newsome *The Parting of Friends* (1966)

28 His Christianity was muscular.
Benjamin Disraeli 1804–81: *Endymion* (1880); see 10 above

29 Scratch the Christian and you find the pagan—spoiled.
Israel Zangwill 1864–1926: *Children of the Ghetto* (1892)

30 The Christian ideal has not been tried and found wanting. It has been found difficult; and left untried.
G. K. Chesterton 1874–1936: *What's Wrong with the World* (1910)

31 The Church should go forward along the path of progress and be no longer satisfied only to represent the Conservative Party at prayer.
Maude Royden 1876–1956: address at Queen's Hall, London, 16 July 1917

32 Christianity is the most materialistic of all great religions.
William Temple 1881–1944: *Readings in St John's Gospel* vol. 1 (1939)

33 The chief contribution of Protestantism to human thought is its massive proof that God is a bore.
H. L. Mencken 1880–1956: *Minority Report* (1956)

34 I want to throw open the windows of the Church so that we can see out and the people can see in.
Pope John XXIII 1881–1963: attributed

35 You have no idea how much nastier I would be if I was not a Catholic. Without supernatural aid I would hardly be a human being.
Evelyn Waugh 1903–66: Noel Annan *Our Age* (1990)

36 We're more popular than Jesus now; I don't know which will go first—rock 'n' roll or Christianity.
of The Beatles
John Lennon 1940–80: interview in *Evening Standard* 4 March 1966

37 The Church can no longer contain the fizzy, explosive stuff that the true wine of the bottle ought to be.
Donald Soper 1903–98: in *Methodist Recorder* 18 January 1968

38 Our cathedrals are like abandoned computers now, but they used to be prayer factories once.
Lawrence Durrell 1912–90: in *Listener* 20 April 1978

39 We are an Easter people and Alleluia is our song.
Pope John Paul II 1920–2005: speech in Harlem, New York, 2 October 1979

40 The Catholic Church has never really come to terms with women. What I object to is being treated either as Madonnas or Mary Magdalenes.
Shirley Williams 1930– : in *Observer* 22 March 1981

41 If you're going to do a thing, you should do it thoroughly. If you're going to be a Christian, you may as well be a Catholic.
Muriel Spark 1918– : in *Independent* 2 August 1989

42 We must recall that the Church is always 'one generation away from extinction.'
George Carey 1935– : Working Party Report *Youth A Part: Young People and the Church* (1996) foreword

➤➤ Christmas ◄◄

PROVERBS AND SAYINGS

1 **A green Yule makes a fat churchyard.**
a mild winter is traditionally unhealthy (*Yule* = archaic term for Christmas); English proverb, mid 17th century; see **Weather** 42

2 **Only — shopping days to Christmas.**
the imminence of Christmas expressed in commercial terms

PHRASES

3 **the twelve days of Christmas**
the traditional period of Christmas festivities, from Christmas Day to the Feast of the Epiphany; see **Gifts** 6

4 **a white Christmas**
Christmas with snow on the ground, from Irving Berlin: see 13 below

QUOTATIONS

5 For unto us a child is born, unto us a son is given: and the government shall be upon his shoulder: and his name shall be called Wonderful, Counsellor, The mighty God, The everlasting Father, The Prince of Peace.
Bible: Isaiah

6 She brought forth her firstborn son, and wrapped him in swaddling clothes, and laid him in a manger; because there was no room for them in the inn.
Bible: St Luke

7 Welcome, all wonders in one sight! Eternity shut in a span.
Richard Crashaw 1612–49: 'Hymn of the Nativity' (1652)

8 'Twas the night before Christmas, when all through the house
Not a creature was stirring, not even a mouse.
Clement C. Moore 1779–1863: 'A Visit from St Nicholas' (December 1823)

9 'Bah,' said Scrooge. 'Humbug!'
Charles Dickens 1812–70: *A Christmas Carol* (1843)

10 Christmas won't be Christmas without any presents.
Louisa May Alcott 1832–88: *Little Women* (1868–9)

11 It is Christmas Day in the Workhouse.
George R. Sims 1847–1922: 'In the Workhouse—Christmas Day' (1879)

12 Yes, Virginia, there is a Santa Claus.
replying to a letter from eight-year-old Virginia O'Hanlon
Francis Pharcellus Church 1839–1906: editorial in New York *Sun*, 21 September 1897

13 I'm dreaming of a white Christmas, Just like the ones I used to know.
Irving Berlin 1888–1989: 'White Christmas' (1942 song); see 4 above

14 And girls in slacks remember Dad, And oafish louts remember Mum, And sleepless children's hearts are glad, And Christmas-morning bells say 'Come!'
John Betjeman 1906–84: 'Christmas' (1954)

15 Still xmas is a good time with all those presents and good food and i hope it will never die out or at any rate not until i am grown up and hav to pay for it all.
Geoffrey Willans 1911–58 and **Ronald Searle** 1920– : *How To Be Topp* (1954)

16 Christmas is the Disneyfication of Christianity.
Don Cupitt 1934– : in *Independent* 19 December 1996

⤜ The Cinema ⤛

see also **Acting, The Theatre**

PROVERBS AND SAYINGS

1 **Come with me to the Casbah.**
often attributed to Charles Boyer in the film *Algiers* (1938), but not found there

2 **Have gun, will travel.**
supposedly characteristic statement of a hired gunman in a western; popularized as the title of an American television series (1957–64)

3 **Play it again, Sam.**
popular misquotation of Humphrey Bogart in *Casablanca* (1942), subsequently used as the title of a play (1969) and film (1972) by Woody Allen

4 **You dirty rat.**
frequently attributed to James Cagney in a gangster part, but not found in this precise form in any of his films

QUOTATIONS

5 It is like writing history with lightning. And my only regret is that it is all so terribly true.
on seeing D. W. Griffith's film *The Birth of a Nation*
Woodrow Wilson 1856–1924: at the White House, 18 February 1915

6 The lunatics have taken charge of the asylum.
on the take-over of United Artists by Charles Chaplin, Mary Pickford, Douglas Fairbanks and D. W. Griffith
Richard Rowland 1881–1947: Terry Ramsaye *A Million and One Nights* (1926)

7 There is only one thing that can kill the movies, and that is education.
Will Rogers 1879–1935: *Autobiography of Will Rogers* (1949)

8 *on being asked which film he would like to see while convalescing:*
Anything except that damned Mouse.
George V 1865–1936: George Lyttelton letter to Rupert Hart-Davis, 12 November 1959

9 Bring on the empty horses!
said while directing the 1936 film *The Charge of the Light Brigade*
Michael Curtiz 1888–1962: David Niven *Bring on the Empty Horses* (1975)

10 If we'd had as many soldiers as that, we'd have won the war!
on seeing the number of Confederate troops in *Gone with the Wind* at the 1939 premiere
Margaret Mitchell 1900–49: W. G. Harris *Gable and Lombard* (1976)

11 If my books had been any worse, I should not have been invited to Hollywood, and if they had been any better, I should not have come.
Raymond Chandler 1888–1959: letter to Charles W. Morton, 12 December 1945

12 This is the biggest electric train a boy ever had!
of the RKO studios
Orson Welles 1915–85: Roy Fowler *Orson Welles* (1946)

13 JOE GILLIS: You used to be in pictures. You used to be big.
NORMA DESMOND: I am big. It's the pictures that got small.
Charles Brackett 1892–1969, **Billy Wilder** 1906–2002, and **D.M. Marshman Jr.**: *Sunset Boulevard* (1950 film)

14 If I made Cinderella, the audience would immediately be looking for a body in the coach.
Alfred Hitchcock 1899–1980: in *Newsweek* 11 June 1956

15 Why should people go out and pay to see bad movies when they can stay at home and see bad television for nothing?
Sam Goldwyn 1882–1974: in *Observer* 9 September 1956

16 Photography is truth. The cinema is truth 24 times per second.
Jean-Luc Godard 1930– : *Le Petit Soldat* (1960 film)

17 All I need to make a comedy is a park, a policeman and a pretty girl.
Charlie Chaplin 1889–1977: *My Autobiography* (1964)

18 The words 'Kiss Kiss Bang Bang' which I saw on an Italian movie poster, are perhaps the briefest statement imaginable of the basic appeal of movies.
Pauline Kael 1919– : *Kiss Kiss Bang Bang* (1968)

19 Pictures are for entertainment, messages should be delivered by Western Union.
Sam Goldwyn 1882–1974: Arthur Marx *Goldwyn* (1976)

20 [The camera] is so refined that it makes it possible for us to shed light on the human soul, to reveal it the more brutally and thereby add to our knowledge new dimensions of the 'real'.
Ingmar Bergman 1918– : in *New York Times* 22 January 1978

21 GEORGES FRANJU: Movies should have a beginning, a middle and an end.
JEAN-LUC GODARD: Certainly. But not necessarily in that order.
Jean-Luc Godard 1930– : in *Time* 14 September 1981; see **Fiction 21**, **Quantities 22**

22 There are no rules in filmmaking. Only sins. And the cardinal sin is dullness.
Frank Capra 1897–1991: in *People* 16 September 1991

23 If you gave him a good script, actors and technicians, Mickey Mouse could direct a movie.
Nicholas Hytner 1956– : in *Daily Telegraph* 24 February 1994

⇥ Circumstance and Situation ⇤

PROVERBS AND SAYINGS

1 **Circumstances alter cases.**
a general principle may be modified in the light of particular circumstances; English proverb, late 17th century

2 **If you live in the river, you should make friends with the crocodile.**
Indian proverb

3 **May you live in interesting times.**
used ironically, as eventful times are generally dangerous or unpleasant; modern saying, said to derive from a Chinese curse, but likely to be apocryphal; see 34 below

4 **New circumstances, new controls.**
American proverb, mid 20th century

5 **No rose without a thorn.**
even the pleasantest circumstances have their drawbacks; English proverb, mid 15th century; see **Practicality 2**, **Satisfaction 4**

6 **One day honey, one day onions.**
Arab proverb

7 **One man's loss is another man's gain.**
often said by the gainer in self-congratulation; English proverb, early 16th century

8 There's a time and place for everything.
often used as a warning against doing or saying something at a particular time or in a particular situation; English proverb, early 16th century

9 There's no great loss without some gain.
said in consolation or resignation; English proverb, mid 17th century

PHRASES

11 catch-22
a dilemma or difficult circumstance from which there is no escape because of mutually conflicting or dependent conditions, from Joseph Heller's novel: see **Madness** 14

12 cuckoo in the nest
an unwelcome intruder in a place or situation

13 dig oneself into a hole
get oneself into an awkward or restrictive situation; see **Apology** 8

14 elephant in the room
an unwelcome fact which is not directly referred to but of which everyone is aware; other variants include *moose on the table*

15 a fish out of water
a person in a completely unsuitable environment or situation

16 in the wrong box
unsuitably or awkwardly placed; in a difficulty, at a disadvantage

QUOTATIONS

21 Every honourable action has its proper time and season, or rather it is this propriety or observance which distinguishes an honourable action from its opposite.
Agesilaus 444–360 BC: Plutarch *Lives* 'Agesilaus'

22 But for the grace of God there goes John Bradford.
on seeing a group of criminals being led to their execution; usually quoted as, 'There but for the grace of God go I'
John Bradford 1510–55: in *Dictionary of National Biography* (1917–)

23 The time is out of joint; O cursèd spite, That ever I was born to set it right!
William Shakespeare 1564–1616: *Hamlet* (1601)

24   My nature is subdued
To what it works in, like the dyer's hand.
William Shakespeare 1564–1616: sonnet 111; see **Change** 18

25 And, spite of Pride, in erring Reason's spite, One truth is clear, 'Whatever IS, is RIGHT.'
Alexander Pope 1688–1744: *An Essay on Man* Epistle 1 (1733)

10 The wheel has come full circle.
the situation has returned to what it was in the past, as if completing a cycle, with reference to Shakespeare's *King Lear* 'The wheel is come full circle'; see **Chance** 20

17 on the horns of a dilemma
faced with a decision involving equally unfavourable alternatives; *dilemma* in Rhetoric, a form of argument involving an adversary in the choice of two alternatives (the 'horns'), either of which is or appears to be equally unfavourable

18 the plot thickens
the situation becomes more difficult and complex, from George Villiers *The Rehearsal* (1671): see **Theatre** 9

19 a square peg in a round hole
a person in a situation unsuited to his or her capacities or disposition, a misfit; see 27 below

20 swings and roundabouts
a state of affairs in which different actions result in no eventual gain or loss, from the saying: see **Winning** 3

26 *No se puede mirar.*
One cannot look at this.
Goya 1746–1828: *The Disasters of War* (1863) title of etching

27 We shall generally find that the triangular person has got into the square hole, the oblong into the triangular, and a square person has squeezed himself into the round hole. The officer and the office, the doer and the thing done, seldom fit so exactly that we can say they were almost made for each other.
Sydney Smith 1771–1845: *Sketches of Moral Philosophy* (1849); see 19 above

28 For of all sad words of tongue or pen, The saddest are these: 'It might have been!'
John Greenleaf Whittier 1807–92: 'Maud Muller' (1854); see 30 below

29 It was the best of times, it was the worst of times, it was the age of wisdom, it was the age of foolishness, it was the epoch of belief, it was the epoch of incredulity, it was the season of Light, it was the season of Darkness, it was the spring of hope, it was the winter of despair, we had everything

before us, we had nothing before us, we were all going direct to Heaven, we were all going direct the other way.
Charles Dickens 1812–70: *A Tale of Two Cities* (1859)

30 If, of all words of tongue and pen,
The saddest are, 'It might have been,'
More sad are these we daily see:
'It is, but hadn't ought to be!'
Bret Harte 1836–1902: 'Mrs Judge Jenkins' (1867); see 28 above

31 Watch out w'en you'er gittin all you want. Fattenin' hogs ain't in luck.
Joel Chandler Harris 1848–1908: *Uncle Remus: His Songs and His Sayings* (1880)

32 We are so made, that we can only derive intense enjoyment from a contrast, and only very little from a state of things.
Sigmund Freud 1856–1939: *Civilization and its Discontents* (1930)

33 I love to feel events overlapping each other, crawling over one another like wet crabs in a basket.
Lawrence Durrell 1912–90: *Balthazar* (1958)

34 There is a Chinese curse which says 'May he live in interesting times.' Like it or not we live in interesting times. They are times of danger and uncertainty; but they are also more open to the creative energy of men than any other time in history.
Robert Kennedy 1925–68: speech, Cape Town, 6 June 1966; see 3 above

35 Anyone who isn't confused doesn't really understand the situation.
on the Vietnam War
Ed Murrow 1908–65: Walter Bryan *The Improbable Irish* (1969)

36 The whole world seemed so unequal, so unfair. Some people were created with all the good things ready-made for them, others were just created like mistakes. God's mistakes.
Buchi Emecheta 1944– : *Second-Class Citizen* (1974)

Cities see Towns and Cities

Civilization see Culture and Civilization

⟿ Class ⟸

see also **Capitalism and Communism, Rank and Title**

PROVERBS AND SAYINGS

1 **It takes three generations to make a gentleman.**
English proverb, early 19th century; the idea that it took three generations before the possession of wealth conferred the status of gentleman occurs from the late 16th century

2 **When Adam delved and Eve span, who was then the gentleman?**
traditional rhyme from Richard Rolle (see 9 below), taken in this form by John Ball as the text of his revolutionary sermon on the outbreak of the Peasants' Revolt, 1381

PHRASES

3 **airs and graces**
an affectation of superiority

4 **Essex man**
derogatory term for a type of British Conservative voter in the late 1980s, associated particularly with the county of Essex, and characterized as a brash, amoral, self-made young businessman, of right-wing views and few or no cultural or intellectual interests, devoted to the acquisition of goods and material wealth; see **Women** 11

5 **the gentlemen and the players**
distinguishing between the amateur (gentlemen) and professional (players) players of cricket, and

hence other sports; figuratively, a player means a lower-class person

6 **Islington person**
a middle-class, socially aware person with left-wing views, characteristics supposedly typical of Islington residents, seen as a typical supporter of New Labour who, while rejecting the brash self-interest of Essex man, is nevertheless similarly insulated by material wealth from the harshest pressures of modern society

7 **the many-headed monster**
an archaic term for the people, the populace, after Horace *Epistles* 'The people are a many-headed beast'; see **Theatre** 11

8 Sloane Ranger
a fashionable and conventional upper-class young woman, especially one living in London; a play on

Sloane Square, London, and *Lone Ranger*, a fictitious cowboy hero; coined in 1975 in the magazine *Harpers & Queen*

QUOTATIONS

9 When Adam dalfe and Eve spane
Go spire if thou may spede,
Where was than the pride of man
That now merres his mede?
Richard Rolle de Hampole 1290–1349: G. G. Perry *Religious Pieces* (1914); see 2 above

10 I must have the gentleman to haul and draw with the mariner, and the mariner with the gentleman . . . I would know him, that would refuse to set his hand to a rope, but I know there is not any such here.
Francis Drake 1540–96: J. S. Corbett *Drake and the Tudor Navy* (1898)

11 That in the captain's but a choleric word, Which in the soldier is flat blasphemy.
William Shakespeare 1564–1616: *Measure for Measure* (1604)

12 He told me . . . that mine was the middle state, or what might be called the upper station of low life, which he had found by long experience was the best state in the world, the most suited to human happiness.
Daniel Defoe 1660–1731: *Robinson Crusoe* (1719)

13 O let us love our occupations,
Bless the squire and his relations,
Live upon our daily rations,
And always know our proper stations.
Charles Dickens 1812–70: *The Chimes* (1844) 'The Second Quarter'

14 The proletarians have nothing to lose but their chains. They have a world to win.
WORKING MEN OF ALL COUNTRIES, UNITE!
commonly rendered as 'Workers of the world, unite!'
Karl Marx 1818–83 and **Friedrich Engels** 1820–95: *The Communist Manifesto* (1848); see 25 below

15 The rich man in his castle,
The poor man at his gate,
God made them, high or lowly,
And ordered their estate.
Cecil Frances Alexander 1818–95: 'All Things Bright and Beautiful' (1848)

16 *Il faut épater le bourgeois.*
One must astonish the bourgeois.
Charles Baudelaire 1821–67: attributed; also attributed to Privat d'Anglemont (c.1820–59) in the form *'Je les ai épatés, les bourgeois* [I flabbergasted them, the bourgeois]'

17 The so called immorality of the lower classes is not to be named on the same day with that of the higher and highest. This is a

thing which makes my blood boil, and they will pay for it.
Queen Victoria 1819–1901: letter to the Crown Princess of Prussia, 26 June 1872

18 All the world over, I will back the masses against the classes.
W. E. Gladstone 1809–98: speech in Liverpool, 28 June 1886

19 The bourgeois are other people.
Jules Renard 1864–1910: diary, 28 January 1890

20 Bourgeois . . . is an epithet which the riff-raff apply to what is respectable, and the aristocracy to what is decent.
Anthony Hope 1863–1933: *The Dolly Dialogues* (1894)

21 You may tempt the upper classes
With your villainous demi-tasses,
But; Heaven will protect a working-girl!
Edgar Smith 1857–1938: 'Heaven Will Protect the Working-Girl' (1909 song)

22 Dear me, I never knew that the lower classes had such white skins.
supposedly said when watching troops bathing during the First World War
Lord Curzon 1859–1925: K. Rose *Superior Person* (1969)

23 The bourgeois prefers comfort to pleasure, convenience to liberty, and a pleasant temperature to the deathly inner consuming fire.
Hermann Hesse 1877–1962: *Der Steppenwolf* (1927)

24 Civilization has made the peasantry its pack animal. The bourgeoisie in the long run only changed the form of the pack.
Leon Trotsky 1879–1940: *History of the Russian Revolution* (1933)

25 We of the sinking middle class . . . may sink without further struggles into the working class where we belong, and probably when we get there it will not be so dreadful as we feared, for, after all, we have nothing to lose but our aitches.
George Orwell 1903–50: *The Road to Wigan Pier* (1937); see 14 above

26 Ladies were ladies in those days; they did not do things themselves.
Gwen Raverat 1885–1957: *Period Piece* (1952)

27 I can't help feeling wary when I hear anything said about the masses. First you take their faces from 'em by calling 'em the

masses and then you accuse 'em of not having any faces.
J. B. Priestley 1894–1984: *Saturn Over the Water* (1961)

28 Will the people in the cheaper seats clap your hands? All the rest of you, if you'll just rattle your jewellery.
John Lennon 1940–80: at the Royal Variety Performance, 4 November 1963

29 The real solvent of class distinction is a proper measure of self-esteem—a kind of unselfconsciousness . . . What keeps us in our place is embarrassment.
Alan Bennett 1934– : *Dinner at Noon* (BBC television, 1988)

30 The worst fault of the working classes is telling their children they're not going to succeed, saying: 'There is life, but it's not for you.'
John Mortimer 1923– : in *Daily Mail* 31 May 1988

31 I was born in the real world, not with a silver spoon in my mouth. If you plant a rose in the best soil it'll grow whatever you do. It's a lot harder growing in concrete, understand what I'm saying?
Vinnie Jones 1965– : in *Radio Times* 8 July 2000; see **Wealth** 8

⤞ Clergy ⤝

see also **The Christian Church**

PROVERBS AND SAYINGS

1 **Clergymen's sons always turn out badly.**
the implication is that the weight of expectation on clergyman's children is often in itself damaging; English proverb, late 19th century

2 **Like people, like priest.**
English proverb, late 16th century; from the Bible (Hosea) 'And there shall be like people, like priest'

PHRASES

5 **the Angelic Doctor**
St Thomas Aquinas (1225–74), Italian philosopher, theologian, and Dominican friar

6 **benefit of clergy**
historically, exemption from ordinary courts of law because of membership of the clergy or (later)

3 **Nobody is born learned; bishops are made of men.**
American proverb, mid 20th century

4 **Once a priest, always a priest.**
English proverb, mid 19th century; see **Character** 12

literacy or scholarship; exemption from the sentence for certain first offences because of literacy; see **Appearance** 17

QUOTATIONS

7 A bishop then must be blameless, the husband of one wife, vigilant, sober, of good behaviour, given to hospitality, apt to teach; Not given to wine, no striker, not greedy of filthy lucre; but patient, not a brawler, not covetous.
Bible: I Timothy; see **Money** 19

8 In old time we had treen chalices and golden priests, but now we have treen priests and golden chalices.
John Jewel 1522–71: *Certain Sermons Preached Before the Queen's Majesty* (1609)

9 A single life doth well with churchmen, for charity will hardly water the ground where it must first fill a pool.
Francis Bacon 1561–1626: *Essays* (1625) 'Of Marriage and the Single Life'

10 New *Presbyter* is but old *Priest* writ large.
John Milton 1608–74: 'On the New Forcers of Conscience under the Long Parliament' (1646)

11 And of all plagues with which mankind are curst,
Ecclesiastic tyranny's the worst.
Daniel Defoe 1660–1731: *The True-Born Englishman* (1701)

12 I look upon all the world as my parish.
John Wesley 1703–91: *Journal* 11 June 1739

13 In all ages of the world, priests have been enemies of liberty.

David Hume 1711–76: *Essays, Moral, Political, and Literary* (1875) 'Of the Parties of Great Britain' (1741–2)

14 I never saw, heard, nor read, that the clergy were beloved in any nation where Christianity was the religion of the country. Nothing can render them popular, but some degree of persecution.

Jonathan Swift 1667–1745: *Thoughts on Religion* (1765)

15 *Merit*, indeed! . . . We are come to a pretty pass if they talk of *merit* for a bishopric.

John Fane, Lord Westmorland 1759–1841: Lady Salisbury's diary, 9 December 1835

16 How can a bishop marry? How can he flirt? The most he can say is, 'I will see you in the vestry after service.'

Sydney Smith 1771–1845: Lady Holland *Memoir* (1855)

17 Pray remember, Mr Dean, no dogma, no Dean.

Benjamin Disraeli 1804–81: W. Monypenny and G. Buckle *Life of Benjamin Disraeli* vol. 4 (1916)

18 I wouldn't take the Pope too seriously. He's a Pole first, a pope second, and maybe a Christian third.

Muriel Spark 1918– : in *International Herald Tribune* 29 May 1989

19 Pastors need to start where people are and not where we think they should be.

Basil Hume 1923–99: in *Independent* 18 June 1999

Communism see **Capitalism and Communism**

⤳ Computers and the Internet ⤙

PROVERBS AND SAYINGS

1 **Do not fold, spindle or mutilate.**
instruction on punched cards (1950s, and in differing forms from the 1930s)

2 **Garbage in, garbage out.**
in computing, incorrect or faulty input will always cause poor output; mid 20th century saying; see 10 below

3 **It's not a bug, it's a feature.**
bug = an error in a computer program or system; late 20th century saying

4 **No manager ever got fired for buying IBM.**
IBM advertising slogan

5 **To err is human but to really foul things up requires a computer.**
late 20th century saying; see **Mistakes 6**

PHRASES

6 **bells and whistles**
in computing, speciously attractive but superfluous facilities, with allusion to the various bells and whistles of old fairground organs

7 **Moore's law**
the principle that a new type of microprocessor chip is released every 12 to 24 months, with each new version having approximately twice as many logical elements as its predecessor, and that this trend is likely to continue, resulting in an exponential rise in computing power per chip over a period of time; an

observation and prediction originally made in 1965 by Gordon Earle *Moore* (1929–)

8 **Trojan horse**
a computing program that breaches the security of a computer system, especially by ostensibly functioning as part of a legitimate program, in order to erase, corrupt, or remove data; from a hollow wooden statue of a horse in which the Greeks are said to have concealed themselves to enter Troy; see **Trust and Treachery 16**

QUOTATIONS

9 The Analytical Engine weaves algebraic patterns just as the Jacquard loom weaves flowers and leaves.

of Babbage's mechanical computer

Ada Lovelace 1815–52: Luigi Menabrea *Sketch of the Analytical Engine invented by Charles Babbage* (1843), translated and annotated by Ada Lovelace, Note A

10 His patience in explaining his machine in those days was really exemplary . . . A lady, to whom he had sacrificed some very precious time, on the supposition that she understood as much as she assumed to do, finished by saying, 'Now, Mr Babbage, there is only one thing that I want to know. If you

put the question in wrong, will the answer come out right?'
of Charles Babbage (1791–1871), inventor of the mechanical computer; see 2 above
Harriet Martineau 1802–76: *Autobiography* (1877)

11 We used to have lots of questions to which there were no answers. Now with the computer there are lots of answers to which we haven't thought up the questions.
Peter Ustinov 1921–2004: in *Illustrated London News* 1 June 1968

12 Computers are composed of nothing more than logic gates stretched out to the horizon in a vast numerical irrigation system.
Stan Augarten: *State of the Art: A Photographic History of the Integrated Circuit* (1983)

13 A modern computer hovers between the obsolescent and the nonexistent.
Sydney Brenner 1927– : attributed in *Science* 5 January 1990

14 The PC is the LSD of the '90s.
Timothy Leary 1920–96: remark made in the early 1990s; in *Guardian* 1 June 1996

15 On the Internet, nobody knows you're a dog.
Peter Steiner 1940– : cartoon caption in *New Yorker* 5 July 1993

16 The Internet is an elite organisation; most of the population of the world has never even made a phone call.
Noam Chomsky 1928– : in *Observer* 18 February 1996

17 We've all heard that a million monkeys banging on a million typewriters will eventually reproduce the entire works of Shakespeare. Now, thanks to the Internet, we know this is not true.
Robert Wilensky 1951– : in *Mail on Sunday* 16 February 1997; see **Chance** 31

18 The symbol of the atomic age, which tended to centralise power, was a nucleus with electrons held in tight orbit; the symbol of the digital age is the Web, with countless centres of power all equally networked.
Walter Isaacson 1952– : in *Time* 29 December 1997

19 The Web is a tremendous grassroots revolution. All these people coming from very different directions achieved a change. There's a tremendous message of hope for humanity in that.
Tim Berners-Lee 1955– : in *Independent* 17 May 1999

20 [The Internet is] a whining Californian mall rat, forever demanding that the real world be redefined to suit its whims.
Terry Pratchett 1948– : in *Bookseller* 15 September 2000

21 It turns out people want keyboards. When Apple first started out, people couldn't type. We realized: Death would eventually take care of this.
Steve Jobs 1955– : interview, 28 May 2003

22 The encyclopedia was the first book to go. It's way cheaper, way more up-to-date. It doesn't smell as good, but otherwise we're a winner.
comparing books to the tablet computer
Bill Gates 1955– : in *Times Online* 29 October 2005

⤻ Conformity ⤺

PROVERBS AND SAYINGS

1 **The nail that sticks up is certain to be hammered down.**
Japanese proverb

2 **Obey orders, if you break owners.**
the saying is nautical, and means that orders should be followed even if it is clear that they are wrong; English proverb, late 18th century

PHRASES

3 **be all things to all men**
please everyone, typically by fitting in with their needs or expectations; originally probably in allusion to the Bible (I Corinthians) 'I am made all things to all men'

4 **marching to a different drum**
conforming to different principles and practices from those around one; ultimately from Thoreau: see 9 below

QUOTATIONS

5 While we were talking came by several poor
creatures carried by, by constables, for being
at a conventicle . . . I would to God they
would either conform, or be more wise, and
not be catched!
Samuel Pepys 1633–1703: diary 7 August 1664

6 'It's always best on these occasions to do
what the mob do.' 'But suppose there are
two mobs?' suggested Mr Snodgrass. 'Shout
with the largest,' replied Mr Pickwick.
Charles Dickens 1812–70: *Pickwick Papers* (1837)

7 Whoso would be a man must be a
nonconformist.
Ralph Waldo Emerson 1803–82: *Essays* (1841)
'Self-Reliance'

8 Teach him to think for himself? Oh, my
God, teach him rather to think like other
people!
on her son's education
Mary Shelley 1797–1851: Matthew Arnold *Essays in
Criticism* Second Series (1888) 'Shelley'

9 If a man does not keep pace with his
companions, perhaps it is because he hears a
different drummer. Let him step to the
music which he hears, however measured or
far away.
Henry David Thoreau 1817–62: *Walden* (1854);
see 4 above

10 My duty is to obey orders.
Thomas Jonathan 'Stonewall' Jackson
1824–63: attributed

11 You cannot make a man by standing a sheep
on its hind-legs. But by standing a flock of
sheep in that position you can make a crowd
of men.
Max Beerbohm 1872–1956: *Zuleika Dobson* (1911)

12 Imitation lies at the root of most human
actions. A respectable person is one who
conforms to custom. People are called good
when they do as others do.
Anatole France 1844–1924: *Crainquebille* (1923)

13 The Party line is that there is no Party line.
Milovan Djilas 1911– : comment on reforms of the
Yugoslavian Communist Party, November 1952;
Fitzroy Maclean *Disputed Barricade* (1957)

14 These are the days when men of all social
disciplines and all political faiths seek the
comfortable and the accepted; when the
man of controversy is looked upon as a
disturbing influence; when originality is
taken to be a mark of instability; and when,
in minor modification of the scriptural
parable, the bland lead the bland.
J. K. Galbraith 1908– : *The Affluent Society* (1958);
see **Leadership 9**

15 Never forget that only dead fish swim with
the stream.
Malcolm Muggeridge 1903–90: quoting a
supporter; in *Radio Times* 9 July 1964

16 The Normal is the good smile in a child's
eyes—all right. It is also the dead stare in a
million adults. It both sustains and
kills—like a God. It is the Ordinary made
beautiful; it is also the Average made lethal.
Peter Shaffer 1926– : *Equus* (1983 ed.)

17 To be like everyone else. Isn't that what we
all want in the end?
Carol Shields 1935–2003: *Larry's Party* (1997)

18 My parents were convinced that I would one
day become Mr Average, but almost 30 years
on I am still an A1 freak.
Boy George 1961– : in *Independent on Sunday* 28
March 1999

⇢ Conscience ⇠

see also **Forgiveness and Repentance, Sin**

PROVERBS AND SAYINGS

1 **A clean conscience is a good pillow.**
a clear conscience enables its possessor to sleep
soundly; English proverb, early 18th century

2 **Conscience gets a lot of credit that
belongs to cold feet.**
American proverb, mid 20th century

3 **Do right and fear no man.**
English proverb, mid 15th century

4 **Evil doers are evil dreaders.**
someone engaged in wrongdoing is likely to be
nervous and suspicious of others; English proverb,
mid 16th century

5 **A guilty conscience needs no accuser.**
awareness of one's own guilt has the same effect as
an accusation; English proverb, late 14th century

6 **Let your conscience be your guide.**
American proverb, mid 20th century

7 A quiet conscience sleeps in thunder.
someone with an untroubled conscience will sleep undisturbed whatever the noise; English proverb, late 16th century

PHRASES

8 agenbite of inwit
remorse, used as a conscious archaism derived from James Joyce's *Ulysses*; see 17 below

9 prick of conscience
compunction, remorse, guilt; used as the title of a devotional treatise by the English mystic Richard Rolle of Hampole (*c.*1290–1349)

QUOTATIONS

10 Then I, however, showed again, by action, not in word only, that I did not care a whit for death . . . but that I did care with all my might not to do anything unjust or unholy.
on being ordered by the Thirty Commissioners to take part in the liquidation of Leon of Salamis
Socrates 469–399 BC: Plato *Apology*

11 *O dignitosa coscienza e netta,*
Come t'è picciol fallo amaro morso!
O pure and noble conscience, how bitter a sting to thee is a little fault!
Dante 1265–1321: *Divina Commedia* 'Purgatorio'

12 Every subject's duty is the king's; but every subject's soul is his own.
William Shakespeare 1564–1616: *Henry V* (1599)

13 Thus conscience doth make cowards of us all.
William Shakespeare 1564–1616: *Hamlet* (1601)

14 If I am obliged to bring religion into after-dinner toasts (which indeed does not seem quite the thing) I shall drink—to the Pope, if you please—still, to Conscience first, and to the Pope afterwards.
John Henry Newman 1801–90: *A Letter Addressed to the Duke of Norfolk . . .* (1875)

15 Conscience is thoroughly well-bred and soon leaves off talking to those who do not wish to hear it.
Samuel Butler 1835–1902: *Further Extracts from Notebooks* (1934)

16 Conscience: the inner voice which warns us that someone may be looking.
H. L. Mencken 1880–1956: *A Little Book in C major* (1916)

17 They wash and tub and scrub. Agenbite of inwit. Conscience.
James Joyce 1882–1941: *Ulysses* (1922); see 8 above

18 Most people sell their souls, and live with a good conscience on the proceeds.
Logan Pearsall Smith 1865–1946: *Afterthoughts* (1931)

19 Sufficient conscience to bother him, but not sufficient to keep him straight.
of Ramsay MacDonald
David Lloyd George 1863–1945: A. J. Sylvester *Life with Lloyd George* (1975)

20 I cannot and will not cut my conscience to fit this year's fashions.
Lillian Hellman 1905–84: letter to John S. Wood, 19 May 1952

Consequences see Causes and Consequences

Consolation see Sympathy and Consolation

↠ Constancy and Inconstancy ↞

PROVERBS AND SAYINGS

1 Love me little, love me long.
love of great intensity is unlikely to last; English proverb, early 16th century

2 Quickly come, quickly go.
English proverb, late 16th century

3 A rolling stone gathers no moss.
used to imply that someone who does not settle down will not prosper, or form lasting ties; English proverb, mid 14th century

PHRASES

4 true as Troilus
completely devoted, alluding to Shakespeare *Troilus and Cressida* ' "As true as Troilus" shall crown up the verse'

QUOTATIONS

5 My true love hath my heart and I have his,
By just exchange one for the other giv'n.
Philip Sidney 1554–86: *Arcadia* (1581)

6 But I am constant as the northern star,
Of whose true-fixed and resting quality
There is no fellow in the firmament.
William Shakespeare 1564–1616: *Julius Caesar* (1599)

7 I loved thee once. I'll love no more,
Thine be the grief, as is the blame;
Thou art not what thou wast before,
What reason I should be the same?
Robert Aytoun 1570–1638: 'To an Inconstant Mistress'

8 Tell me no more of constancy,
that frivolous pretence,
Of cold age, narrow jealousy,
disease and want of sense.
John Wilmot, Lord Rochester 1647–80: 'Against Constancy' (1676)

9 An inconstant woman, tho' she has no chance to be very happy, can never be very unhappy.
John Gay 1685–1732: 'Polly' (1729)

10 No, the heart that has truly loved never forgets,
But as truly loves on to the close,
As the sunflower turns on her god, when he sets,
The same look which she turned when he rose.
Thomas Moore 1779–1852: 'Believe me, if all those endearing young charms' (1807)

11 Bright star, would I were steadfast as thou art—.
John Keats 1795–1821: 'Bright star, would I were steadfast as thou art' (written 1819)

12 There is no infidelity when there has been no love.
Honoré de Balzac 1799–1850: letter to Mme Hanska, August 1833; in *The Penguin Book of Infidelities* (1994)

13 His honour rooted in dishonour stood,
And faith unfaithful kept him falsely true.
Alfred, Lord Tennyson 1809–92: *Idylls of the King* 'Lancelot and Elaine' (1859)

14 I have been faithful to thee, Cynara! in my fashion.
Ernest Dowson 1867–1900: 'Non Sum Qualis Eram' (1896); also known as 'Cynara'; see 15 below; Memory 15

15 But I'm always true to you, darlin', in my fashion.
Yes I'm always true to you, darlin', in my way.
Cole Porter 1891–1964: 'Always True to You in my Fashion' (1949 song); see 14 above

16 Your idea of fidelity is not having more than one man in bed at the same time.
Frederic Raphael 1931– : *Darling* (1965)

17 You're . . . turning into a kind of serial monogamist.
Richard Curtis 1956– : *Four Weddings and a Funeral* (1994 film)

⤖ Conversation ⥽

see also **Gossip, Speech, Speeches**

PROVERBS AND SAYINGS

1 It's good to talk.
advertising slogan for British Telecom, from 1994

PHRASES

2 feast of reason
intellectual discussion, from Pope 'The feast of reason and the flow of soul'; see 3 below

3 flow of soul
genial conversation, as complementary to intellectual discussion, from Pope: see 2 above

4 glittering generalities
platitudes, clichés, superficially convincing but
empty phrases; see **Human Rights** 11

QUOTATIONS

5 All use metaphors in conversation, as well as
proper and appropriate words.
Aristotle 384–322 BC: *The Art of Rhetoric*

6 Must I always be a mere listener?
Juvenal c.AD 60–c.130: *Satires*

7 I am not bound to please thee with my
answer.
William Shakespeare 1564–1616: *The Merchant of
Venice* (1596–8)

8 With thee conversing I forget all time.
John Milton 1608–74: *Paradise Lost* (1667)

9 JOHNSON: Well, we had a good talk.
BOSWELL: Yes, Sir; you tossed and gored
several persons.
James Boswell 1740–95: *Life of Samuel Johnson*
(1791) Summer 1768

10 Religion is by no means a proper subject of
conversation in a mixed company.
Lord Chesterfield 1694–1773: *Letters . . . to his
Godson and Successor* (1890) Letter 142

11 Questioning is not the mode of
conversation among gentlemen. It is
assuming a superiority.
Samuel Johnson 1709–84: James Boswell *Life of
Samuel Johnson* (1791) 25 March 1776

12 He talked on for ever; and you wished him
to talk on for ever.
of Coleridge
William Hazlitt 1778–1830: *Lectures on the English
Poets* (1818)

13 Two may talk and one may hear, but three
cannot take part in a conversation of the
most sincere and searching sort.
Ralph Waldo Emerson 1803–82: *Essays* (1841)
'Friendship'

14 The fun of talk is to find what a man really
thinks, and then contrast it with the
enormous lies he has been telling all dinner,
and, perhaps, all his life.
Benjamin Disraeli 1804–81: *Lothair* (1870)

15 'The time has come,' the Walrus said,
'To talk of many things:
Of shoes—and ships—and sealing wax—
Of cabbages—and kings.
Lewis Carroll 1832–98: *Through the Looking-Glass*
(1872)

16 It is the province of knowledge to speak and
it is the privilege of wisdom to listen.
Oliver Wendell Holmes 1809–94: *The Poet at the
Breakfast-Table* (1872)

17 He speaks to Me as if I was a public meeting.
of Gladstone
Queen Victoria 1819–1901: G. W. E. Russell
Collections and Recollections (1898)

18 Although there exist many thousand
subjects for elegant conversation, there are
persons who cannot meet a cripple without
talking about feet.
Ernest Bramah 1868–1942: *The Wallet of Kai Lung*
(1900)

19 There is no such thing as conversation. It is
an illusion. There are intersecting
monologues, that is all.
Rebecca West 1892–1983: *There is No Conversation*
(1935)

20 Too much agreement kills a chat.
Eldridge Cleaver 1935–98: *Soul on Ice* (1968)
'Letters from Prison'

21 How time flies when you's doin' all the
talking.
Harvey Fierstein 1954– : *Torch Song Trilogy* (1979)

⇥ Cooking and Eating ⇤

see also **Food and Drink, Greed**

PROVERBS AND SAYINGS

**1 After dinner rest a while, after supper
walk a mile.**
the implication is that dinner is a heavy meal, while
supper is a light one; English proverb, late 16th
century

2 After meat, mustard.
traditional comment on some essential ingredient
which is brought too late of be of use; English
proverb, late 16th century

**3 All are not cooks who sport white
caps and carry long knives.**
American proverb, mid 20th century

4 **A cook is no better than her stove.**
American proverb, mid 20th century

5 **Eat to live, not live to eat.**
distinguishing between necessity and indulgence;
English proverb, late 14th century

6 **Fingers were made before forks.**
commonly used as a polite excuse for eating with
one's hands at table; English proverb, mid 18th
century. The earlier variant 'God made hands before
knives' is found in the mid 16th century

7 **God sends meat, but the Devil sends
cooks.**
anything which is in itself good or useful may be
spoiled or perverted by the use to which it is put;
English proverb, mid 16th century

8 **Go to work on an egg.**
advertising slogan for the British Egg Marketing
Board, from 1957; perhaps written by Fay Weldon or
Mary Gowing

9 **Hunger is the best sauce.**
food which is needed will be received most readily;
English proverb, early 16th century

10 **We must eat a peck of dirt before
we die.**
often used as a consolatory remark in literal
contexts; English proverb, mid 18th century

11 **You are what you eat.**
English proverb, mid 20th century; see 19 below

PHRASES

12 **Barmecide feast**
an illusory or imaginary feast, from the name of a
prince in the *Arabian Nights*, who gave a beggar a
feast consisting of ornate but empty dishes

13 **dine with Duke Humphrey**
in archaic usage, go without dinner, go hungry;
possibly originally associated with a part of Old St
Paul's, wrongly believed to be the site of the tomb of
Duke Humphrey of Gloucester, where people walked
instead of dining

QUOTATIONS

14 You won't be surprised that diseases are
innumerable—count the cooks.
Seneca c.4 BC–AD 65: *Epistles*

15 Now good digestion wait on appetite,
And health on both!
William Shakespeare 1564–1616: *Macbeth* (1606)

16 Strange to see how a good dinner and
feasting reconciles everybody.
Samuel Pepys 1633–1703: diary 9 November 1665

17 I look upon it, that he who does not mind
his belly will hardly mind anything else.
Samuel Johnson 1709–84: James Boswell *Life of
Samuel Johnson* (1791) 5 August 1763

18 Some have meat and cannot eat,
Some cannot eat that want it:
But we have meat and we can eat,
Sae let the Lord be thankit.
Robert Burns 1759–96: 'The Kirkudbright Grace'
(1790), also known as 'The Selkirk Grace'

19 Tell me what you eat and I will tell you what
you are.
Anthelme Brillat-Savarin 1755–1826: *Physiologie
du Goût* (1825); see 11 above

20 Cooking is the most ancient of the arts, for
Adam was born hungry.
Anthelme Brillat-Savarin 1755–1826: *Physiologie
du Goût* (1825)

21 Anyone who tells a lie has not a pure heart,
and cannot make a good soup.
Ludwig van Beethoven 1770–1827: Ludwig Nohl
Beethoven Depicted by his Contemporaries (1880)

22 I'll fill hup the chinks wi' cheese.
R. S. Surtees 1805–64: *Handley Cross* (1843)

23 Let onion atoms lurk within the bowl,
And, scarce-suspected, animate the whole.
Sydney Smith 1771–1845: Lady Holland *Memoir*
(1855) 'Receipt for a Salad'

24 Kissing don't last: cookery do!
George Meredith 1828–1909: *The Ordeal of
Richard Feverel* (1859)

25 We each day dig our graves with our teeth.
Samuel Smiles 1812–1904: *Duty* (1880)

26 He sows hurry and reaps indigestion.
Robert Louis Stevenson 1850–94: *Virginibus
Puerisque* (1881) 'An Apology for Idlers'

27 The healthy stomach is nothing if not
conservative. Few radicals have good
digestions.
Samuel Butler 1835–1902: *Notebooks* (1912)

28 The cook was a good cook, as cooks go; and
as cooks go, she went.
Saki 1870–1916: *Reginald* (1904)

29 Time for a little something.
A. A. Milne 1882–1956: *Winnie-the-Pooh* (1926)

30 Be content to remember that those who can
make omelettes properly can do nothing
else.
Hilaire Belloc 1870–1953: *A Conversation with a
Cat* (1931)

31 Good food is always a trouble and its preparation should be regarded as a labour of love.
Elizabeth David 1913–92: *French Country Cooking* (1951) introduction

32 Hot on Sunday,
Cold on Monday,
Hashed on Tuesday,
Minced on Wednesday,
Curried Thursday,
Broth on Friday,
Cottage pie Saturday.
Dorothy Hartley 1893–1985: *Food in England* (1954) 'Vicarage Mutton'

33 Gluttony is an emotional escape, a sign something is eating us.
Peter De Vries 1910–93: *Comfort Me With Apples* (1956)

34 Lunch? You gotta be kidding. Lunch is for wimps.
Stanley Weiser and **Oliver Stone** 1946– : *Wall Street* (1987 film)

35 You cannot trust people who have such bad cuisine. It is the country with the worst food after Finland.
on the British
Jacques Chirac 1932– : in *Times* 5 July 2005

Cooperation

PROVERBS AND SAYINGS

1 A chain is no stronger than its weakest link.
often used when identifying a particular point of vulnerability; English proverb, mid 19th century; see **Strength and Weakness 9**

2 Dog does not eat dog.
people of the same profession should not attack each other; English proverb, mid 16th century

3 Each of us at a handle of the basket.
Maori proverb

4 Every little helps.
English proverb, early 17th century

5 Four eyes see more than two.
two people are more observant than one alone; English proverb, late 16th century

6 Hawks will not pick out hawks' eyes.
powerful people from the same group will not attack one another; English proverb, late 16th century

7 If you don't believe in cooperation, watch what happens to a wagon when one wheel comes off.
American proverb, mid 20th century

8 If you think cooperation is unnecessary, just try running your car a while on three wheels.
American proverb, mid 20th century

9 It takes two to make a bargain.
often used to imply that both parties must be prepared to give some ground; English proverb, late 16th century

10 It takes two to tango.
meaning that a cooperative venture requires a contribution from both participants; mid 20th century saying, from the 1952 song by Al Hoffman and Dick Manning

11 Little birds that can sing and won't sing must be made to sing.
those who refuse to obey or cooperate will be forced to do so; English proverb, late 17th century

12 Many hands make light work.
often used as an encouragement to join in with assistance; English proverb, mid 14th century

13 One good turn deserves another.
English proverb, early 15th century

14 One hand washes the other.
referring to cooperation between two closely linked persons or organizations; English proverb, late 16th century

15 Phone a friend.
advice to contestants uncertain of the correct answer, said by Chris Tarrant, host of the ITV quiz show *Who Wants to be a Millionaire* (1998–)

16 There is honour among thieves.
sometimes used ironically; English proverb, early 19th century

17 A trouble shared is a trouble halved.
discussing a problem will lessen its impact; English proverb, mid 20th century

18 Union is strength.
English proverb, mid 17th century; *unity* is a popular alternative for *union*, especially when used as a trade-union slogan

19 United we stand, divided we fall.
a watchword of the American Revolution, English proverb, late 18th century; see **America 12**

20 When spider webs unite, they can tie up a lion.
African proverb

21 **With your food basket, and with my food basket, the guest will have enough.**
Maori proverb

QUOTATIONS

22 The wolf also shall dwell with the lamb, and the leopard shall lie down with the kid; and the calf and the young lion and the fatling together; and a little child shall lead them.
Bible: Isaiah; see 32 below

23 If a house be divided against itself, that house cannot stand.
Bible: St Mark

24 If someone claps his hand a sound arises. Listen to the sound of the single hand!
Hakuin 1686–1769: attributed

25 When bad men combine, the good must associate; else they will fall, one by one, an unpitied sacrifice in a contemptible struggle.
Edmund Burke 1729–97: *Thoughts on the Cause of the Present Discontents* (1770)

26 We must indeed all hang together, or, most assuredly, we shall all hang separately.
Benjamin Franklin 1706–90: at the signing of the Declaration of Independence, 4 July 1776; possibly not original

27 Now who will stand on either hand,
And keep the bridge with me?
Lord Macaulay 1800–59: 'Horatius' (1842)

28 All for one, one for all.
motto of the Three Musketeers
Alexandre Dumas 1802–70: *Les Trois Mousquetaires* (1844); see **Friendship** 7

29 Government and cooperation are in all things the laws of life; anarchy and competition the laws of death.
John Ruskin 1819–1900: *Unto this Last* (1862)

30 Why don't you do something to *help* me?
Stan Laurel 1890–1965: *Drivers' Licence Sketch* (1947 film); words spoken by Oliver Hardy

31 We must learn to live together as brothers or perish together as fools.
Martin Luther King 1929–68: speech at St Louis, 22 March 1964

32 The lion and the calf shall lie down together but the calf won't get much sleep.
Woody Allen 1935– : in *New Republic* 31 August 1974; see 22 above

33 'Solidarity' means taking care of the person standing next to you.
Lech Wałęsa 1943– : speech, Gdansk, Poland, May 1988

34 In a place where 'please' is pronounced 'I s'pose you couldn't'
it is rare to meet with any belief in help.
Les A. Murray 1938– : *The Boys Who Stole the Funeral* (1989)

➤➤ Corruption ⤙⤙

PROVERBS AND SAYINGS

1 **Corruption will find a dozen alibis for its evil deeds.**
American proverb, mid 20th century

2 **Every man has his price.**
everyone is susceptible to the right bribe; English proverb, mid 18th century, see 13 below

3 **A golden key can open any door.**
any access is guaranteed if enough money is offered; English proverb, late 16th century

PHRASES

6 **itching palm**
avarice, originally with reference to Shakespeare; see 10 below

4 **It's not what you know, it's who you know.**
stressing the importance of personal influence; late 20th century saying

5 **The rotten apple injures its neighbour.**
often used to mean that one corrupt person in an organization is likely to affect others; English proverb, mid 14th century

QUOTATIONS

7 A venal city ripe to perish, if a buyer can be found.
of Rome
Sallust 86–35 BC: *Jugurtha*

8 . . . *Omnia Romae*
Cum pretio.
Everything in Rome—at a price.
Juvenal c.AD 60–c.130: *Satires*

9 If gold ruste, what shall iren do?
Geoffrey Chaucer 1343–1400: *The Canterbury Tales* 'The General Prologue'

10 Let me tell you, Cassius, you yourself
Are much condemned to have an itching palm.
William Shakespeare 1564–1616: *Julius Caesar* (1599); see 6 above

11 Nothing to be done without a bribe I find, in love as well as law.
Susannah Centlivre 1669–1723: *The Perjured Husband* (1700)

12 All those men have their price.
of fellow parliamentarians
Robert Walpole 1676–1745: W. Coxe *Memoirs of Sir Robert Walpole* (1798); see 2 above

13 I am not worth purchasing, but such as I am, the King of Great Britain is not rich enough to do it.
replying to an offer from Governor George Johnstone of £10,000, and any office in the Colonies in the King's gift, if he were able successfully to promote a Union between Britain and America
Joseph Reed 1741–85: W. B. Read *Life and Correspondence of Joseph Reed* (1847)

14 But the jingling of the guinea helps the hurt that Honour feels.
Alfred, Lord Tennyson 1809–92: 'Locksley Hall' (1842)

15 And that is called paying the Dane-geld;
But we've proved it again and again,
That if once you have paid him the
Dane-geld
You never get rid of the Dane.
Rudyard Kipling 1865–1936: 'What Dane-geld means' (1911)

16 When their lordships asked Bacon
How many bribes he had taken
He had at least the grace
To get very red in the face.
Edmund Clerihew Bentley 1875–1956: 'Bacon' (1939)

17 Men are more often bribed by their loyalties and ambitions than money.
Robert H. Jackson 1892–1954: dissenting opinion in *United States v. Wunderlich* 1951

18 I stuffed their mouths with gold.
on his handling of the consultants during the establishment of the National Health Service
Aneurin Bevan 1897–1960: Brian Abel-Smith *The Hospitals 1800–1948* (1964)

19 The flood of money that gushes into politics today is a pollution of democracy.
Theodore H. White 1915–86: in *Time* 19 November 1984

⇥ Countries and Peoples ⇤

see also **Africa, America, Australia, Canada, England, France, International Relations, Ireland, Russia, Scotland, Towns and Cities, Wales**

PROVERBS AND SAYINGS

1 **Every land has its own law.**
Scottish proverb, early 17th century, used to emphasize the individuality of a nation or group

PHRASES

2 **the Celestial Empire**
Imperial China; translation of a Chinese honorific title

3 **the children of Israel**
the Jewish people; people whose descent is traditionally traced from the patriarch Jacob (also called *Israel*), each of whose twelve sons became the founder of a tribe

4 **the chosen people**
the Jewish people; the people specially favoured by God; compare the Bible (1 Peter) 'but ye are a chosen generation, a royal priesthood, an holy nation, a peculiar people'

5 **the Holy Land**
a region on the eastern shores of the Mediterranean, in what is now Israel and Palestine, with religious significance for Judaism, Christianity, and Islam;

medieval Latin *terra sancta*, French *la terre sainte*, applied to the region with reference to its having been the scene of the Incarnation and also to the existing sacred sites there, especially the Holy Sepulchre at Jerusalem

6 the Land of the Long White Cloud
New Zealand

7 land of the midnight sun
any of the most northerly European countries, in which it never gets fully dark during the summer months

8 land of the rising sun
Japan; the Japanese name of the country is *Nippon*, literally 'rising sun'

9 the Lost Tribes
Asher, Dan, Gad, Issachar, Levi, Manasseh, Naphtali, Reuben, Simeon, and Zebulun, ten of the twelve divisions of ancient Israel, each traditionally descended from one of the sons of Jacob; the ten tribes of Israel taken away *c.*720 BC by Sargon II to captivity in Assyria, from which they are believed never to have returned, while the tribes of Benjamin and Judah remained

10 on which the sun never sets
(of an empire, originally the Spanish and later the British) worldwide

11 the sick man of Europe
Turkey in the late 19th century, originally with reference to the view expressed by Nicholas I, Russian Emperor from 1825, 'Turkey is a dying man. We may endeavour to keep him alive, but we shall not succeed. He will, he must die'

QUOTATIONS

12 If there is a paradise on earth, it is this, it is this, it is this.
Amir Khusrau 1253–1325: inscribed on the wall of the Diwan-i-Khas [the hall of special audience] in the Red Fort at Delhi

13 The Netherlands have been for many years, as one may say, the very cockpit of Christendom.
James Howell 1594–1666: *Instructions for Foreign Travel* (1642); see **Europe** 1

14 This agglomeration which was called and which still calls itself the Holy Roman Empire was neither holy, nor Roman, nor an empire.
Voltaire 1694–1778: *Essai sur l'histoire générale et sur les moeurs et l'esprit des nations* (1756)

15 She has made me in love with a cold climate, and frost and snow, with a northern moonlight.
on Mary Wollstonecraft's letters from Sweden and Norway
Robert Southey 1774–1843: letter to his brother Thomas, 28 April 1797

16 I look upon Switzerland as an inferior sort of Scotland.
Sydney Smith 1771–1845: letter to Lord Holland, 1815

17 The isles of Greece, the isles of Greece! Where burning Sappho loved and sung.
Lord Byron 1788–1824: *Don Juan* (1819–24)

18 A nation is the universality of citizens speaking the same tongue.
Giuseppe Mazzini 1805–72: in *La Giovine Italia*, 1832

19 Holland . . . lies so low they're only saved by being dammed.
Thomas Hood 1799–1845: *Up the Rhine* (1840)

20 A quiet, pilfering, unprotected race.
John Clare 1793–1864: 'The Gipsy Camp' (1841)

21 Some people . . . may be Rooshans, and others may be Prooshans; they are born so, and will please themselves. Them which is of other naturs thinks different.
Charles Dickens 1812–70: *Martin Chuzzlewit* (1844)

22 Except the blind forces of Nature, nothing moves in this world which is not Greek in its origin.
Henry Maine 1822–88: *Village Communities* (3rd ed., 1876)

23 I'm Charley's aunt from Brazil—where the nuts come from.
Brandon Thomas 1856–1914: *Charley's Aunt* (1892)

24 The traveller who has gone to Italy to study the tactile values of Giotto, or the corruption of the Papacy, may return remembering nothing but the blue sky and the men and women under it.
E. M. Forster 1879–1970: *Room with a View* (1908)

25 He is crazed with the spell of far Arabia, They have stolen his wits away.
Walter de la Mare 1873–1956: 'Arabia' (1912)

26 Poor Mexico, so far from God and so close to the United States.
Porfirio Diaz 1830–1915: attributed

27 What cleanliness everywhere! You dare not throw your cigarette into the lake. No graffiti in the urinals. Switzerland is proud of this; but I believe this is just what she lacks: manure.
André Gide 1869–1951: diary, Lucerne, 10 August 1917

28 Nothing in India is identifiable, the mere asking of a question causes it to disappear or to merge in something else.
E. M. Forster 1879–1970: *A Passage to India* (1924)

29 Were I to . . . take a [Yugoslav] peasant by the shoulders and whisper to him, 'In your lifetime, have you known peace?' wait for his answer, shake his shoulders and transform him into his father, and ask him the same question, and transform him in turn into his father, I would never hear the word 'yes' if I carried my questioning of the dead back for a thousand years.
Rebecca West 1892–1983: *Black Lamb and Grey Falcon* (1940)

30 Latins are tenderly enthusiastic. In Brazil they throw flowers at you. In Argentina they throw themselves.
Marlene Dietrich 1901–92: in *Newsweek* 24 August 1959

31 A country is a piece of land surrounded on all sides by boundaries, usually unnatural.
Joseph Heller 1923–99: *Catch-22* (1961)

32 There are very few Eskimos, but millions of Whites, just like mosquitoes. It is something very special and wonderful to be an Eskimo—they are like the snow geese. If an Eskimo forgets his language and Eskimo ways, he will be nothing but just another mosquito.
Abraham Okpik d. 1997: attributed, 1966

33 Nothing and no one can destroy the Chinese people. They are relentless survivors. They are the oldest civilized people on earth. Their civilization passes through phases but its basic characteristics remain the same. They yield, they bend to the wind, but they do not break.
Pearl S. Buck 1892–1973: *China, Past and Present* (1972)

34 Whereas in England all is permitted that is not expressly prohibited, it has been said that in Germany all is prohibited unless expressly permitted and in France all is permitted that is expressly prohibited. In the European Common Market (as it then was) no-one knows what is permitted and it all costs more.
Robert Megarry 1910– : 'Law and Lawyers in a Permissive Society' (5th Riddell Lecture delivered in Lincoln's Inn Hall 22 March 1972); see **Europe** 2

35 India . . . is not a place that one can pick up and put down again as if nothing had happened. In a way it's not so much a country as an experience, and whether it turns out to be a good or a bad one depends, I suppose, on oneself.
Ruth Prawer Jhabvala 1927– : *Travellers* (1973)

36 In Turkey it was always 1952, in Malaysia 1937; Afghanistan was 1910 and Bolivia 1949. It is twenty years ago in the Soviet Union, ten in Norway, five in France. It is always last year in Australia and next week in Japan.
Paul Theroux 1941– : *The Kingdom by the Sea* (1983)

37 The Third World is an artificial construction of the West—an ideological empire on which the sun is always setting.
Shiva Naipaul 1945–85: *An Unfinished Journey* (1986); see **International Relations** 9

38 If you take Greece apart, in the end you will see remaining to you an olive tree, a vineyard and a ship. Which means: with just so much you can put her back together.
Odysseus Elytis 1911– : 'The Little Seafarer' (1988)

39 The Japanese are full of surprises, because the women are so refined and elegant and the men fundamentally so crude and tough.
Harold Acton 1904–94: Naim Attallah *Singular Encounters* (1990)

The Country and the Town

see also **Farming**

PROVERBS AND SAYINGS

1 **An everyday story of country folk.**
traditional summary of the BBC's long-running radio soap opera *The Archers*

2 **God made the country and man made the town.**
contrasting rural and urban life; English proverb, mid 17th century, in this form from Cowper: see **10** below

3 **You can take the boy out of the country but you can't take the country out of the boy.**
even when a person moves away from the place they were brought up in, they retain its essential manners and customs; English proverb, mid 20th century

PHRASES

4 **concrete jungle**
a city with a high density of large, unattractive, modern buildings and which is perceived as an unpleasant living environment, after Morris: see 25 below

5 **a country mouse**
a person from a rural area unfamiliar with urban life, from one of Aesop's fables in which the *country mouse* and the *town mouse* visit each other, and each in the end is convinced of the superiority of its own home; see 7 below

6 **rus in urbe**
an illusion of countryside created by a building or garden within a city; an urban building which has this effect; Latin, literally 'country in city', from Martial (AD *c*.40–*c*.104)

7 **a town mouse**
a person with an urban lifestyle unfamiliar with rural life; see 5 above

QUOTATIONS

8 As one who long in populous city pent,
Where houses thick and sewers annoy
   the air,
Forth issuing on a summer's morn to
   breathe
Among the pleasant villages and farms
Adjoined, from each thing met conceives
   delight.
John Milton 1608–74: *Paradise Lost* (1667)

9 God the first garden made, and the first city
Cain.
Abraham Cowley 1618–67: 'The Garden' (1668); see 10 below

10 God made the country, and man made the town.
William Cowper 1731–1800: *The Task* (1785) bk. 1 'The Sofa'; see 2, 9 above

11 'Tis distance lends enchantment to the view,
And robes the mountain in its azure hue.
Thomas Campbell 1777–1844: *Pleasures of Hope* (1799); see **Appearance** 5

12 We do not look in great cities for our best morality.
Jane Austen 1775–1817: *Mansfield Park* (1814)

13 There is nothing good to be had in the country, or if there is, they will not let you have it.
William Hazlitt 1778–1830: *The Round Table* (1817) 'Observations on Mr Wordsworth's Poem *The Excursion*'

14 If you would be known, and not know, vegetate in a village; if you would know, and not be known, live in a city.
Charles Caleb Colton 1780–1832: *Lacon* (1820)

15 I have no relish for the country; it is a kind of healthy grave.
Sydney Smith 1771–1845: letter to Miss G. Harcourt, 1838

16 Anybody can be good in the country.
Oscar Wilde 1854–1900: *The Picture of Dorian Gray* (1891)

17 It is my belief, Watson, founded upon my experience, that the lowest and vilest alleys in London do not present a more dreadful record of sin than does the smiling and beautiful countryside.
Arthur Conan Doyle 1859–1930: *The Adventures of Sherlock Holmes* (1892) 'The Copper Beeches'

18 Wiv a ladder and some glasses,
You could see to 'Ackney Marshes,
If it wasn't for the 'ouses in between.
Edgar Bateman and **George Le Brunn**: 'If it wasn't for the 'Ouses in between' (1894 song)

19 So *that's* what hay looks like.
said at Badminton House, where she was evacuated during the Second World War
Queen Mary 1867–1953: James Pope-Hennessy *Life of Queen Mary* (1959)

20 Oh, give me land, lots of land under starry skies above,
Don't fence me in.
Let me ride through the wide open country that I love,
Don't fence me in.
Cole Porter 1891–1964: 'Don't Fence Me In' (1944 song); see **Solitude** 20

21 The modern city is a place for banking and prostitution and very little else.
Frank Lloyd Wright 1867–1959: Robert C. Twombly *Frank Lloyd Wright* (1973)

22 Green belts should be the start of the countryside, not a ditch between Subtopias.
Hugh Gaitskell 1906–63: in *Observer* 1 January 1961

23 The materials of city planning are sky, space, trees, steel and cement in that order and in that hierarchy.
Le Corbusier 1887–1965: in *The Times* 1965

24 An industrial worker would sooner have a £5 note but a countryman must have praise.
Ronald Blythe 1922– : *Akenfield* (1969)

25 The city is not a concrete jungle, it is a human zoo.
Desmond Morris 1928– : *The Human Zoo* (1969); see 4 above

26 I come from suburbia . . . and I don't ever want to go back. It's the one place in the world that's further away than anywhere else.
Frederic Raphael 1931– : *The Glittering Prizes* (1976)

27 Villages, unlike towns, have always been ruled by conformism, isolation, petty surveillance, boredom and repetitive malicious gossip about the same families.

Which is a precise enough description of the global spectacle's present vulgarity.
on the concept of the 'global village'
Guy Debord 1931–94: *Comments on the Society of the Spectacle* (1988); see **The Earth 6, Technology 17**

28 Judaism, Christianity and Islam all took root among nomads who had recently settled, and all three characterize nomadic traits—the shepherd, the pilgrim, the wanderer in the wilderness—as godly, and the life of the city as degenerate.
George Monbiot: *No Man's Land* (1994)

➤➤ Courage ◄◄

see also **Fear**

PROVERBS AND SAYINGS

1 **Attack is the best form of defence.**
English proverb, late 18th century; see 2 below

2 **The best defence is a good offence.**
late 20th-century American version of 1 above

3 **A bully is always a coward.**
English proverb, early 19th century

4 **Courage is fear that has said its prayers.**
American proverb, mid 20th century

5 **Courage without conduct is like a ship without ballast.**
American proverb, mid 20th century

6 **Don't cry before you're hurt.**
sometimes used as a warning against appealing for sympathy on the assumption of an unpleasant outcome; English proverb, mid 16th century

7 **Faint heart never won fair lady.**
often used as an encouragement to action; English proverb, mid 16th century

8 **Fortune favours the brave.**
a person who acts bravely is likely to be successful; English proverb, late 14th century, originally often with allusion to Terence *Phormio* 'Fortune assists the brave' and Virgil *Aeneid* 'Fortune assists the bold'

9 **None but the brave deserve the fair.**
English proverb, late 17th century, from Dryden: see 18 below

10 **You never know what you can do till you try.**
often used as encouragement to the reluctant; English proverb, early 19th century

PHRASES

11 **grasp the nettle**
tackle a difficulty or danger with courage or boldness; see 19 below, **Danger 28**

QUOTATIONS

12 The wicked flee when no man pursueth: but the righteous are bold as a lion.
Bible: Proverbs

13 Happiness depends on being free, and freedom depends on being courageous.
Thucydides *c*.455–*c*.400 BC: *History of the Peloponnesian War*

14 Cowards die many times before their deaths;
The valiant never taste of death but once.
William Shakespeare 1564–1616: *Julius Caesar* (1599); see **Fear 2**

15 Boldness be my friend!
Arm me, audacity.
William Shakespeare 1564–1616: *Cymbeline* (1609–10)

16 He either fears his fate too much,
Or his deserts are small,
That puts it not unto the touch
To win or lose it all.
James Graham, Marquess of Montrose 1612–50: 'My Dear and Only Love' (written *c*.1642)

17 For all men would be cowards if they durst.
John Wilmot, Lord Rochester 1647–80: 'A Satire against Mankind' (1679)

18 None but the brave deserves the fair.
John Dryden 1631–1700: *Alexander's Feast* (1697); see 9 above

19 Tender-handed stroke a nettle,
And it stings you for your pains;
Grasp it like a man of mettle,
And it soft as silk remains.
Aaron Hill 1685–1750: 'Verses Written on a Window in Scotland'; see 11 above, **Danger** 28

20 Perhaps those, who, trembling most,
maintain a dignity in their fate, are the
bravest: resolution on reflection is real
courage.
Horace Walpole 1717–97: *Memoirs of the Reign of King George II* (1757)

21 My valour is certainly going!—it is sneaking
off!—I feel it oozing out as it were at the
palms of my hands!
Richard Brinsley Sheridan 1751–1816: *The Rivals* (1775)

22 It is thus that mutual cowardice keeps us in
peace. Were one half of mankind brave and
one half cowards, the brave would be always
beating the cowards. Were all brave, they
would lead a very uneasy life; all would be
continually fighting: but being all cowards,
we go on very well.
Samuel Johnson 1709–84: James Boswell *Life of Samuel Johnson* (1791) 28 April 1778

23 Boldness, and again boldness, and always
boldness!
Georges Jacques Danton 1759–94: speech to the Legislative Committee of General Defence, 2 September 1792

24 As to moral courage, I have very rarely met
with two o'clock in the morning courage: I
mean instantaneous courage.
Napoleon I 1769–1821: E. A. de Las Cases *Mémorial de Ste-Hélène* (1823) 4–5 December 1815

25 Was none who would be foremost
To lead such dire attack;
But those behind cried 'Forward!'
And those before cried 'Back!'
Lord Macaulay 1800–59: 'Horatius' (1842)

26 No coward soul is mine,
No trembler in the world's storm-troubled
  sphere:

I see Heaven's glories shine,
And faith shines equal, arming me from
  fear.
Emily Brontë 1818–48: 'No coward soul is mine' (1846)

27 In the fell clutch of circumstance,
I have not winced nor cried aloud:
Under the bludgeonings of chance
My head is bloody, but unbowed.
W. E. Henley 1849–1903: 'Invictus. In Memoriam R.T.H.B.' (1888)

28 Had we lived, I should have had a tale to tell
of the hardihood, endurance, and courage
of my companions which would have stirred
the heart of every Englishman. These rough
notes and our dead bodies must tell the tale.
Robert Falcon Scott 1868–1912: 'Message to the Public' in late editions of *The Times* 11 February 1913

29 Courage is the thing. All goes if courage
goes!
J. M. Barrie 1860–1937: Rectorial Address at St Andrews, 3 May 1922

30 Courage is the price that Life exacts for
  granting peace,
The soul that knows it not, knows no release
From little things.
Amelia Earhart 1898–1937: 'Courage' (1927)

31 Grace under pressure.
when asked what he meant by 'guts', in an interview with Dorothy Parker
Ernest Hemingway 1899–1961: in *New Yorker* 30 November 1929

32 Courage is rightly esteemed the first of
human qualities because as has been said, it
is the quality which guarantees all others.
Winston Churchill 1874–1965: *Great Contemporaries* (1932)

33 For every ten men who are willing to face
the guns of an enemy there is only one
willing to brave the disapproval of his
fellow, the censure of his colleagues, the
wrath of his society. Moral courage is a rarer
commodity than bravery in battle or great
intelligence.
Robert Kennedy 1925–68: speech in Cape Town, 7 June 1966

34 What's courage? Failure of planning,
that's all.
David Hare 1947– : Bertolt Brecht *Mother Courage and her Children* (1995 version for the National Theatre)

➤➤ Courtship ◄◄

see also **Love**

PROVERBS AND SAYINGS

1 **Can you make me a cambric shirt,
Parsley, sage, rosemary, and thyme,
Without any seam or needlework?
And you shall be a true lover of mine.**
traditional song

2 **Happy's the wooing that is not long
a-doing.**
English proverb, late 16th century, reflecting a
traditional belief

QUOTATIONS

3 She is a woman, therefore may be wooed;
She is a woman, therefore may be won.
William Shakespeare 1564–1616: *Titus Andronicus*
(1590)

4 Why so pale and wan, fond lover?
Prithee, why so pale?
Will, when looking well can't move her,
Looking ill prevail?
John Suckling 1609–42: *Aglaura* (1637)

5 Had we but world enough, and time,
This coyness, lady, were no crime.
Andrew Marvell 1621–78: 'To His coy Mistress'
(1681)

6 Courtship to marriage, as a very witty
prologue to a very dull play.
William Congreve 1670–1729: *The Old Bachelor*
(1693)

7 There are very few of us who have heart
enough to be really in love without
encouragement. In nine cases out of ten, a
woman had better show *more* affection than
she feels.
Jane Austen 1775–1817: *Pride and Prejudice* (1813)

8 If you want to win her hand,
Let the maiden understand
That she's not the only pebble on the beach.
Harry Braisted: 'You're Not the Only Pebble on the
Beach' (1896 song)

9 Holding hands at midnight
'Neath a starry sky,
Nice work if you can get it,
And you can get it if you try.
Ira Gershwin 1896–1989: 'Nice Work If You Can
Get It' (1937 song); see **Envy 6**

10 Wooing, so tiring.
Nancy Mitford 1904–73: *The Pursuit of Love* (1945)

11 A man chases a girl (until she catches him).
Irving Berlin 1888–1989: title of song (1949)

12 Ten years of courtship is carrying celibacy to
extremes.
Alan Bennett 1934– : *Habeas Corpus* (1973)

13 Everyone knows that dating in your thirties
is not the happy-go-lucky free-for-all it was
when you were twenty-two.
Helen Fielding 1958– : *Bridget Jones's Diary*
(1996)

14 If you want to get to know someone better,
you shouldn't take them out for a candlelit
dinner, you should watch them at work.
When they're full of concentration, only
not concentrating on you.
Julian Barnes 1946– : *Love, etc.* (2000)

➤➤ Creativity ◄◄

PROVERBS AND SAYINGS

1 **If you don't make mistakes you don't
make anything.**
English proverb, late 19th century; see **Mistakes** 21

PHRASES

2 the tenth Muse
a spirit of inspiration; a muse of inspiration imagined
as added to the nine of classical mythology; see **Arts
and Sciences** 1

QUOTATIONS

3 Nothing can be created out of nothing.
Lucretius *c.*94–55 BC: *De Rerum Natura*

4 All things were made by him; and without
him was not any thing made that was made.
Bible: St John

5 The whole, though it be long, stands almost
complete and finished in my mind, so that I
can survey it, like a fine picture or a
beautiful statue, at a glance. Nor do I hear in
my imagination the parts *successively*, but I
hear them, as it were, all at once. What a
delight this is I cannot tell!
on his method of composition
Wolfgang Amadeus Mozart 1756–91: letter,
Edward Holmes *The Life of Mozart* (1845)

6 The urge for destruction is also a creative
urge!
Michael Bakunin 1814–76: *Jahrbuch für
Wissenschaft und Kunst* (1842) 'Die Reaktion in
Deutschland' (under the pseudonym 'Jules Elysard')

7 Urge and urge and urge,
Always the procreant urge of the world.
Walt Whitman 1819–92: 'Song of Myself' (written
1855)

8 Alas! the Muses . . . are hard to tempt into a
gilded cage, however amusingly made.
Charles Kingsley 1819–75: *Alexandria* (1857); see
Wealth 9

9 Birds build—but not I build; no, but strain,
Time's eunuch, and not breed one work that
wakes.

Mine, O thou lord of life, send my roots
rain.
Gerard Manley Hopkins 1844–89: 'Thou art
indeed just, Lord' (written 1889)

10 Poems are made by fools like me,
But only God can make a tree.
Joyce Kilmer 1886–1918: 'Trees' (1914)

11 Like a piece of ice on a hot stove the poem
must ride on its own melting. A poem may
be worked over once it is in being, but may
not be worried into being.
Robert Frost 1874–1963: *Collected Poems* (1939)
'The Figure a Poem Makes'

12 Think before you speak is criticism's motto;
speak before you think creation's.
E. M. Forster 1879–1970: *Two Cheers for Democracy*
(1951)

13 All men are creative but few are artists.
Paul Goodman 1911–72: *Growing up Absurd* (1961)

14 Creating is a harrowing business. I work in a
state of anguish all year. I shut myself up,
don't go out. It's a hard life, which is why I
understand Proust so well; I have such an
admiration for what he has written about
the agony of creation.
Yves Saint Laurent 1936– : Nicholas Coleridge
The Fashion Conspiracy (1988)

15 The worst crime is to leave a man's hands
empty.
Men are born makers, with that primal
simplicity
In every maker since Adam.
Derek Walcott 1930– : *Omeros* (1990)

⤜ Cricket ⤛

PHRASES

1 barmy army
a self-designation of (a group of) the supporters of a
particular team, particularly a group of young,
vociferous followers of the England cricket team

2 break one's duck
in cricket, score one's first run, in allusion to the
origin of duck for a score of 0, as resembling a duck's
egg in shape

3 sticky wicket
a cricket pitch that has been drying after rain and is
difficult to bat on; figuratively, a tricky or awkward
situation

QUOTATIONS

4 It's more than a game. It's an institution.
of cricket
Thomas Hughes 1822–96: *Tom Brown's Schooldays* (1857)

5 In Affectionate Remembrance
of
ENGLISH CRICKET,
Which Died at The Oval
on
29th August, 1882.
Deeply lamented by a large circle of
sorrowing friends and acquaintances.
R. I. P.
N. B.—The body will be cremated and
the ashes taken to Australia.
following England's defeat by the Australians
Anonymous: in *Sporting Times* 2 September 1882

6 There's a breathless hush in the Close
       to-night—
Ten to make and the match to win—
A bumping pitch and a blinding light,
An hour to play and the last man in.
Henry Newbolt 1862–1938: 'Vitaï Lampada'
(1897); see **Sports** 11

7 Then ye returned to your trinkets; then ye
       contented your souls
With the flannelled fools at the wicket or
       the muddied oafs at the goals.
Rudyard Kipling 1865–1936: 'The Islanders'
(1903)

8 If everything else in this nation of ours were
lost but cricket—her Constitution and the
laws of England of Lord Halsbury—it would
be possible to reconstruct from the theory
and practice of cricket all the eternal
Englishness which has gone to the

establishment of that Constitution and the
laws aforesaid.
Neville Cardus 1889–1975: *Cricket* (1930)

9 Personally, I have always looked on cricket
as organized loafing.
William Temple 1881–1944: attributed

10 It is hard to tell where the MCC ends and
the Church of England begins.
J. B. Priestley 1894–1984: in *New Statesman* 20
July 1962

11 Cricket—a game which the English, not
being a spiritual people, have invented in
order to give themselves some conception of
eternity.
Lord Mancroft 1914–87: *Bees in Some Bonnets*
(1979)

12 Bowl fast, bowl faster. When you play Test
cricket you don't give Englishmen an inch.
Play it tough, all the way. Grind them into
the dust.
Don Bradman 1908–2001: Jack Fingleton *Batting
from Memory* (1981)

13 Cricket civilizes people and creates good
gentlemen. I want everyone to play cricket
in Zimbabwe; I want ours to be a nation of
gentlemen.
Robert Mugabe 1924– : in *Sunday Times* 26
February 1984

14 I have learnt to think of three words all the
time—what, when and why. That means
always knowing what I am going to bowl,
when I am going to bowl it and to be clear
why I have chosen that option.
Shane Warne 1969– : *My Autobiography* (2001)

⇥ Crime and Punishment ⇤

see also **Guilt and Innocence, Justice, The Law, Murder**

PROVERBS AND SAYINGS

1 **A conservative is a liberal who's been
mugged.**
American saying, 1980s; see 48 below

2 **Crime doesn't pay.**
American proverb, early 20th century; a slogan of
the FBI and the cartoon detective Dick Tracy

3 **Crime must be concealed by crime.**
American proverb, mid 20th century

4 **Hang a thief when he's young, and
he'll no' steal when he's old.**
Scottish proverbial saying, early 19th century

5 **If there were no receivers, there would
be no thieves.**
English proverb, late 14th century

6 **Ill gotten goods never thrive.**
something which is acquired dishonestly is unlikely
to be the basis of lasting prosperity; English proverb,
early 16th century

7 **Little thieves are hanged, but great
ones escape.**
sufficient power and influence can ensure that a
wrongdoer is not punished; English proverb, mid
17th century

8 **Opportunity makes a thief.**
often used to imply that the carelessness of the person who is robbed has contributed to the crime; English proverb, early 13th century

9 **Three strikes and you're out.**
referring to legislation which provides that an offender's third felony is punishable by life imprisonment or other severe sentence; deriving from the terminology of baseball, in which a batter who has had three strikes, or three fair opportunities of hitting the ball, is out; late 20th century saying

PHRASES

12 **cruel and unusual punishment**
punishment which is seen to exceed the bounds of what is regarded as an appropriate penal remedy for a civilized society; from the Eighth Amendment (1791): see 27 below

13 **dead-end kid**
a young slum-dwelling tough, a juvenile delinquent; the *Dead End Kids* were the juvenile delinquents in the films *Dead End* (1937) and *Angels with Dirty Faces* (1938)

14 **lash of scorpions**
an instrument of vengeance or repression; a whip of torture made of knotted cords or armed with metal spikes, especially in allusion to the Bible (1 Kings): see 20 below

15 **read the Riot Act**
reprimand or caution sternly; the *Riot Act*, passed in 1715 and repealed in 1967, made it a felony for an

10 **When thieves fall out, honest men come by their own.**
meaning that it is through thieves quarrelling over their stolen goods that they are likely to be caught, and the goods recovered; English proverb, mid 16th century

11 **You'll die facing the monument.**
warning of the end of a life of crime; in Glasgow, prisoners were hanged facing Nelson's Monument on Glasgow Green; Scottish proverb

assembly of more than twelve people to refuse to disperse after the reading of a specified portion of it by lawful authority

16 **short sharp shock**
a form of corrective treatment for young offenders in which the deterrent value was seen in the harshness of the regime rather than the length of the sentence; advocated by the Home Secretary, William Whitelaw, to the Conservative Party Conference in 1979; see 37 below

17 **smite hip and thigh**
punish unsparingly, originally referring to the Bible (Judges) 'He smote them hip and thigh with a mighty plague'

QUOTATIONS

18 I the Lord thy God am a jealous God, visiting the iniquity of the fathers upon the children unto the third and fourth generation of them that hate me.
'the sins of the fathers' in the Book of Common Prayer (1662)
Bible: Exodus; see **The Family** 29

19 He that spareth his rod hateth his son.
Bible: Proverbs; see **Child Care** 3

20 My father hath chastised you with whips, but I will chastise you with scorpions.
Bible: I Kings; see **14** above

21 This is the first of punishments, that no guilty man is acquitted if judged by himself.
Juvenal c.AD 60–c.130: *Satires*

22 Severity breedeth fear, but roughness breedeth hate. Even reproofs from authority ought to be grave, and not taunting.
Francis Bacon 1561–1626: *Essays* (1625) 'Of Great Place'

23 I went out to Charing Cross, to see Major-general Harrison hanged, drawn, and quartered; which was done there, he

looking as cheerful as any man could do in that condition.
Samuel Pepys 1633–1703: diary 13 October 1660

24 Hanging is too good for him, said Mr Cruelty.
John Bunyan 1628–88: *The Pilgrim's Progress* (1678)

25 Men are not hanged for stealing horses, but that horses may not be stolen.
Lord Halifax 1633–95: *Political, Moral, and Miscellaneous Thoughts and Reflections* (1750) 'Of Punishment'

26 All punishment is mischief: all punishment in itself is evil.
Jeremy Bentham 1748–1832: *Principles of Morals and Legislation* (1789)

27 Excessive bail shall not be required, nor excessive fines imposed, nor cruel and unusual punishment inflicted.
Constitution of the United States 1787– : *Eighth Amendment* (1791); see **12** above

28 Lay then the axe to the root, and teach governments humanity. It is their sanguinary punishments which corrupt mankind.
Thomas Paine 1737–1809: *The Rights of Man* (1791)

29 Whenever the offence inspires less horror than the punishment, the rigour of penal law is obliged to give way to the common feelings of mankind.
Edward Gibbon 1737–94: attributed

30 Punishment is not for revenge, but to lessen crime and reform the criminal.
Elizabeth Fry 1780–1845: Rachel E. Cresswell and Katharine Fry *Memoir of the Life of Elizabeth Fry* (1848)

31 A clever theft was praiseworthy amongst the Spartans; and it is equally so amongst Christians, provided it be on a sufficiently large scale.
Herbert Spencer 1820–1903: *Social Statics* (1850)

32 The best of us being unfit to die, what an inexpressible absurdity to put the worst to death!
Nathaniel Hawthorne 1804–64: diary 13 October 1851

33 Better build schoolrooms for 'the boy', Than cells and gibbets for 'the man'.
Eliza Cook 1818–89: 'A Song for the Ragged Schools' (1853)

34 Thou shalt not steal; an empty feat, When it's so lucrative to cheat.
Arthur Hugh Clough 1819–61: 'The Latest Decalogue' (1862)

35 To crush, to annihilate a man utterly, to inflict on him the most terrible punishment so that the most ferocious murderer would shudder at it beforehand, one need only give him work of an absolutely, completely useless and irrational character.
Fedor Dostoevsky 1821–81: *House of the Dead* (1862)

36 The boy learns not to fear sin, but the *punishment* for it, and thus he learns to lie.
Charles Kingsley 1819–75: F. G. Kingsley *Charles Kingsley* (1877)

37 Awaiting the sensation of a short, sharp shock,
From a cheap and chippy chopper on a big black block.
W. S. Gilbert 1836–1911: *The Mikado* (1885); see 16 above

38 My object all sublime
I shall achieve in time—
To let the punishment fit the crime—
The punishment fit the crime.
W. S. Gilbert 1836–1911: *The Mikado* (1885)

39 Singularity is almost invariably a clue. The more featureless and commonplace a crime is, the more difficult is it to bring it home.
Arthur Conan Doyle 1859–1930: *The Adventures of Sherlock Holmes* (1892) 'The Boscombe Valley Mystery'

40 Thieves respect property. They merely wish the property to become their property that they may more perfectly respect it.
G. K. Chesterton 1874–1936: *The Man who was Thursday* (1908)

41 For de little stealin' dey gits you in jail soon or late. For de big stealin' dey makes you Emperor and puts you in de Hall o' Fame when you croaks.
Eugene O'Neill 1888–1953: *The Emperor Jones* (1921)

42 Once in the racket you're always in it.
Al Capone 1899–1947: in *Philadelphia Public Ledger* 18 May 1929

43 Major Strasser has been shot. Round up the usual suspects.
Julius J. Epstein 1909–2001 et al.: *Casablanca* (1942 film)

44 Crime isn't a disease, it's a symptom. Cops are like a doctor that gives you aspirin for a brain tumour.
Raymond Chandler 1888–1959: *The Long Good-Bye* (1953)

45 The fear of burglars is not only the fear of being robbed, but also the fear of a sudden and unexpected clutch out of the darkness.
Elias Canetti 1905–94: *Crowds and Power* (1960)

46 I hate victims who respect their executioners.
Jean-Paul Sartre 1905–80: *Les Séquestrés d'Altona* (1960)

47 The thoughts of a prisoner—they're not free either. They keep returning to the same things.
Alexander Solzhenitsyn 1918– : *One Day in the Life of Ivan Denisovich* (1962)

48 A liberal is a conservative who has been arrested.
Tom Wolfe 1931– : *The Bonfire of the Vanities* (1987); see 1 above

49 Society needs to condemn a little more and understand a little less.
John Major 1943– : interview with *Mail on Sunday* 21 February 1993

50 Labour is the party of law and order in Britain today. Tough on crime and tough on the causes of crime.
Tony Blair 1953– : speech at the Labour Party Conference, 30 September 1993

⇥ Crises ⇤

PROVERBS AND SAYINGS

1 Duck and cover.
US advice in the event of a missile attack, c.1950; associated particularly with children's cartoon character 'Bert the Turtle'

2 Go in, stay in, tune in.
British government advice on preparing for emergencies, 2004

3 Ohhh, I don't *believe* it!
catchphrase used by Victor Meldrew in *One Foot in the Grave* (BBC television series, 1989–2000), written by David Renwick

4 We won't make a drama out of a crisis.
advertising slogan for Commercial Union insurance

PHRASES

5 cross the Rubicon
take a decisive or irrevocable step; the *Rubicon* was a stream in North-East Italy which marked the ancient boundary with Cisalpine Gaul; by taking his army across it into Italy from his own province in 49 BC, Julius Caesar broke the law forbidding a general to lead an army out of his province, and so committed himself to war against the Senate and Pompey; see 11 below

6 the Dunkirk spirit
the refusal to surrender or despair in a time of crisis; from the evacuation of the British Expeditionary Force from Dunkirk in 1940; see 21 below, **World War II** 11

7 the final straw
a slight addition to a burden or difficulty that makes it finally unbearable, from the proverb: see **Excess** 5

8 moment of truth
a crisis, a turning-point; a testing situation; Spanish *el momento de la verdad* = the time of the final sword-thrust in a bullfight

9 the parting of the ways
the moment at which a choice must be made; after the Bible (Ezekiel) 'The king of Babylon stood at the parting of the ways'

10 the sky is falling
a warning of imminent disaster, especially one which is regarded as unduly alarmist; from the nursery story in which Chicken Little and other animals repeatedly warn the king that the sky is falling down; see **Fear** 4

QUOTATIONS

11 The die is cast.
at the crossing of the Rubicon (see 5 above); often quoted in Latin *'Iacta alea est'* but originally spoken in Greek
Julius Caesar 100–44 BC: Suetonius *Lives of the Caesars* 'Divus Julius'; Plutarch *Parallel Lives* 'Pompey'

12 For it is your business, when the wall next door catches fire.
Horace 65–8 BC: *Epistles*

13 Whatever might be the extent of the individual calamity, I do not consider it of a nature worthy to interrupt the proceedings on so great a national question.
on hearing that his theatre was on fire, during a debate on the campaign in Spain
Richard Brinsley Sheridan 1751–1816: speech, House of Commons 24 February 1809

14 We have the wolf by the ears; and we can neither hold him, nor safely let him go. Justice is in one scale, and self-preservation in the other.
on slavery
Thomas Jefferson 1743–1826: letter to John Holmes, 22 April 1820; see **Danger** 17

15 Moments of crisis produce in man a redoubling of life.
François-René Chateaubriand 1768–1848: *Mémoires d'outre-tombe* (1849–50)

16 Swimming for his life, a man does not see much of the country through which the river winds.
W. E. Gladstone 1809–98: diary, 31 December 1868

**17 If you can keep your head when all about you
Are losing theirs and blaming it on you . . .**
Rudyard Kipling 1865–1936: 'If—' (1910); see 20 below

18 The British people have taken for themselves this motto—'Business carried on as usual during alterations on the map of Europe'.
Winston Churchill 1874–1965: speech at Guildhall, 9 November 1914

19 Comin' in on a wing and a pray'r.
the contemporary comment of a war pilot, speaking from a disabled plane to ground control
Harold Adamson 1906–80: title of song (1943); see **Necessity** 15

20 As someone pointed out recently, if you can keep your head when all about you are losing theirs, it's just possible you haven't grasped the situation.
Jean Kerr 1923–2003: *Please Don't Eat the Daisies* (1957); see 17 above

21 I myself have always deprecated . . . in crisis after crisis, appeals to the Dunkirk spirit as an answer to our problems.
Harold Wilson 1916–95: in the House of Commons, 26 July 1961; see 6 above

22 We're eyeball to eyeball, and I think the other fellow just blinked.
on the Cuban missile crisis
Dean Rusk 1909– : comment, 24 October 1962; see **Defiance** 6

23 In bygone days, commanders were taught that when in doubt, they should march their troops towards the sound of gunfire. I intend to march my troops towards the sound of gunfire.
Jo Grimond 1913–93: speech at Liberal Party Annual Assembly, 14 September 1963

24 There cannot be a crisis next week. My schedule is already full.
Henry Kissinger 1923– : in *New York Times Magazine* 1 June 1969

25 Does any one know where the love of God goes
When the waves turn the minutes to hours?
Gordon Lightfoot 1938– : 'The Wreck of the Edmund Fitzgerald' (1976 song)

26 Crisis? What Crisis?
headline summarizing James Callaghan's remark of 10 January 1979: 'I don't think other people in the world would share the view there is mounting chaos'
Anonymous: in *Sun* 11 January 1979

27 Don't panic.
Douglas Adams 1952–2001: *Hitch Hiker's Guide to the Galaxy* (1979)

28 We do not experience and thus we have no measure of the disasters we prevent.
J. K. Galbraith 1908– : *A Life in our Times* (1981)

⤞ Criticism ⤝

see also **Likes and Dislikes, Taste**

PROVERBS AND SAYINGS

1 **The best place for criticism is in front of your mirror.**
judge yourself before others; American proverb, mid 20th century

2 **Criticism is something you can avoid by saying nothing, doing nothing, and being nothing.**
abstaining from criticism will result in complete inaction; American proverb, mid 20th century

3 **Don't judge a man till you've walked two moons in his moccasins.**
warning against judging without understanding circumstances; modern saying, said to be of native American origin

PHRASES

4 **cast the first stone**
be the first to make an accusation, especially when not oneself guiltless, with allusion to the Bible (John): see **Guilt** 7

5 **the pot calling the kettle black**
used to convey that the criticisms a person is aiming at someone else could equally well apply to themselves

QUOTATIONS

6 There is more business in interpreting interpretations than in interpreting things, and more books on books than on any other subject: all we do is gloss each other. All is a-swarm with commentaries: of authors there is a dearth.
Montaigne 1533–92: *Essais* (1580, ed. M. Rat, 1958)

7 Critics are like brushers of noblemen's clothes.
Henry Wotton 1568–1639: Francis Bacon *Apophthegms New and Old* (1625)

8 One should look long and carefully at oneself before one considers judging others.
Molière 1622–73: *Le Misanthrope* (1666)

9 How science dwindles, and how volumes swell,
How commentators each dark passage shun,
And hold their farthing candle to the sun.
Edward Young 1683–1765: *The Love of Fame* (1725–8)

10 You *may* abuse a tragedy, though you cannot write one. You may scold a carpenter who has made you a bad table, though you cannot make a table. It is not your trade to make tables.
on literary criticism
Samuel Johnson 1709–84: James Boswell *Life of Samuel Johnson* (1791) 25 June 1763

11 I have always suspected that the reading is right, which requires many words to prove it wrong; and the emendation wrong, that cannot without so much labour appear to be right.
Samuel Johnson 1709–84: *Plays of William Shakespeare . . .* (1765)

12 A man must serve his time to every trade Save censure—critics all are ready made.
Lord Byron 1788–1824: *English Bards and Scotch Reviewers* (1809)

13 This will never do.
on Wordsworth's *The Excursion* (1814)
Francis, Lord Jeffrey 1773–1850: in *Edinburgh Review* November 1814

14 I never read a book before reviewing it; it prejudices a man so.
Sydney Smith 1771–1845: H. Pearson *The Smith of Smiths* (1934)

15 You know who the critics are? The men who have failed in literature and art.
Benjamin Disraeli 1804–81: *Lothair* (1870)

16 The good critic is he who relates the adventures of his soul in the midst of masterpieces.
Anatole France 1844–1924: *La Vie littéraire* (1888)

17 I am sitting in the smallest room of my house. I have your review before me. In a moment it will be behind me.
responding to a savage review by Rudolph Louis in *Münchener Neueste Nachrichten*, 7 February 1906
Max Reger 1873–1916: Nicolas Slonimsky *Lexicon of Musical Invective* (1953)

18 She was one of the people who say 'I don't know anything about music really, but I know what I like.'
Max Beerbohm 1872–1956: *Zuleika Dobson* (1911)

19 People ask you for criticism, but they only want praise.
W. Somerset Maugham 1874–1965: *Of Human Bondage* (1915)

20 Parodies and caricatures are the most penetrating of criticisms.
Aldous Huxley 1894–1963: *Point Counter Point* (1928)

21 Remember, a statue has never been set up in honour of a critic!
Jean Sibelius 1865–1957: Bengt de Törne *Sibelius: A Close-Up* (1937)

22 Whom the gods wish to destroy they first call promising.
Cyril Connolly 1903–74: *Enemies of Promise* (1938); see **Madness** 1

23 When the reviews are bad I tell my staff that they can join me as I cry all the way to the bank.
Liberace 1919–87: *Autobiography* (1973); joke coined in the mid-1950s

24 Interpretation is the revenge of the intellect upon art.
Susan Sontag 1933–2004: in *Evergreen Review* December 1964

25 A critic is a man who knows the way but can't drive the car.
Kenneth Tynan 1927–80: in *New York Times Magazine* 9 January 1966

26 *Il n'y a pas de hors-texte.*
There is nothing outside of the text.
Jacques Derrida 1930–2004: *Of Grammatology* (1967)

27 I doubt that art needed Ruskin any more than a moving train needs one of its passengers to shove it.
Tom Stoppard 1937– : in *Times Literary Supplement* 3 June 1977

28 If you are not criticized, you may not be doing much.
Donald Rumsfeld 1932– : *Rumsfeld's Rules* (2001)

⊷Cruelty ⊰⊱

PROVERBS AND SAYINGS

1 **It takes 40 dumb animals to make a fur coat, but only one to wear it.**
slogan of an anti-fur campaign poster, 1980s, sometimes attributed to David Bailey (1938–)

PHRASES

2 **out-Herod Herod**
behave with extreme cruelty or tyranny; *Herod* = a blustering tyrant in miracle plays, representing Herod the ruler of Judaea at the time of Jesus' birth (see **Festivals 28**); after Shakespeare *Hamlet* 'I would have such a fellow whipp'd for o'erdoing Termagant; it out-herods Herod'

3 **Roman holiday**
an event occasioning enjoyment or profit derived from the suffering or discomfort of others, from Byron: see 8 below

QUOTATIONS

4 Boys throw stones at frogs for fun, but the frogs don't die for 'fun', but in sober earnest.
Bion c.325–c.255 BC: Plutarch *Moralia*

5 Strike him so that he can feel that he is dying.
Caligula AD 12–41: Suetonius *Lives of the Caesars* 'Gaius Caligula'

6 I must be cruel only to be kind.
William Shakespeare 1564–1616: *Hamlet* (1601); see 11 below

7 Man's inhumanity to man
Makes countless thousands mourn!
Robert Burns 1759–96: 'Man was made to Mourn' (1786)

8 *There* were his young barbarians all at play,
There was their Dacian mother—he, their sire,
Butchered to make a Roman holiday.
Lord Byron 1788–1824: *Childe Harold's Pilgrimage* (1812–18); see 3 above

9 Cruelty, like every other vice, requires no motive outside itself—it only requires opportunity.
George Eliot 1819–80: *Scenes of Clerical Life* (1858)

10 The infliction of cruelty with a good conscience is a delight to moralists. That is why they invented Hell.
Bertrand Russell 1872–1970: *Sceptical Essays* (1928) 'On the Value of Scepticism'

11 Being cruel to be kind is just ordinary cruelty with an excuse made for it . . . And it is right that it should be more resented, as it is.
Ivy Compton-Burnett 1884–1969: *Daughters and Sons* (1937); see 6 above

12 The healthy man does not torture others—generally it is the tortured who turn into torturers.
Carl Gustav Jung 1875–1961: in *Du* May 1941

13 The wish to hurt, the momentary intoxication with pain, is the loophole through which the pervert climbs into the minds of ordinary men.
Jacob Bronowski 1908–74: *The Face of Violence* (1954)

14 Our language lacks words to express this offence, the demolition of a man.
of a year spent in Auschwitz
Primo Levi 1919–87: *If This is a Man* (1958)

15 Nothing there is in nature as thoughtlessly cruel as a small boy, unless it be a small girl.
John Steinbeck 1902–68: *America and Americans* (1966)

16 It is cruel to break people's legs, even if the statement is made by someone in the habit of breaking their arms.
Brigid Brophy 1929– : S. and R. Godlovitch and J. Harris (eds.) *Animals, Men and Morals* (1972)

Culture and Civilization

PROVERBS AND SAYINGS

1 **An ace caff with quite a nice museum attached.**
advertising slogan for the Victoria and Albert Museum, February 1989

2 **A man without culture is like a zebra without stripes.**
African proverb (Masai)

PHRASES

3 **the age of reason**
the late 17th and 18th centuries in western Europe, during which cultural life was characterized by faith in human reason; the enlightenment

4 **the end of civilization as we know it**
the complete collapse of ordered society; supposedly a cinematic cliché, and actually used in the film *Citizen Kane* (1941) 'a project which would mean the end of civilization as we know it'

5 **the golden age**
an idyllic past time of prosperity, happiness, and innocence; the period of a nation's greatest prosperity or literary and artistic merit

6 **the noble savage**
primitive man, conceived of in the manner of Rousseau as morally superior to civilized man; see also 9 below

QUOTATIONS

7 Our love of what is beautiful does not lead to extravagance; our love of the things of the mind does not make us soft.
Pericles c.495–429 BC: funeral oration, Athens, 430 BC; Thucydides *History of the Peloponnesian War*

8 In the youth of a state arms do flourish; in the middle age of a state, learning; and then both of them together for a time; in the declining age of a state, mechanical arts and merchandise.
Francis Bacon 1561–1626: *Essays* (1625) 'Of Vicissitude of Things'

9 I am as free as nature first made man,
Ere the base laws of servitude began,
When wild in woods the noble savage ran.
John Dryden 1631–1700: *The Conquest of Granada* (1670); see 6 above

10 I must study politics and war that my sons may have liberty to study mathematics and philosophy. My sons ought to study mathematics and philosophy, geography, natural history, naval architecture, navigation, commerce, and agriculture, in order to give their children a right to study painting, poetry, music, architecture, statuary, tapestry, and porcelain.
John Adams 1735–1826: letter to Abigail Adams, 12 May 1780

11 If a nation expects to be ignorant and free, in a state of civilization, it expects what never was and never will be.
Thomas Jefferson 1743–1826: letter to Colonel Charles Yancey, 6 January 1816

12 The three great elements of modern civilization, Gunpowder, Printing, and the Protestant Religion.
Thomas Carlyle 1795–1881: *Critical and Miscellaneous Essays* (1838) 'The State of German Literature'; see **Inventions 6**

13 Civilized ages inherit the human nature which was victorious in barbarous ages, and that nature is, in many respects, not at all suited to civilized circumstances.
Walter Bagehot 1826–77: *Physics and Politics* (1872) 'The Age of Discussion'

14 What are we waiting for, gathered in the market-place?
The barbarians are to arrive today.
Constantine Cavafy 1863–1933: 'Waiting for the Barbarians' (1904)

15 You think that a wall as solid as the earth separates civilization from barbarism. I tell you the division is a thread, a sheet of glass.
John Buchan 1875–1940: *The Power House* (1916)

16 Civilization advances by extending the number of important operations which we can perform without thinking about them.
Alfred North Whitehead 1861–1947: *Introduction to Mathematics* (1911)

17 Mrs Ballinger is one of the ladies who pursue Culture in bands, as though it were dangerous to meet it alone.
Edith Wharton 1862–1937: *Xingu and Other Stories* (1916)

18 All civilization has from time to time become a thin crust over a volcano of revolution.
Havelock Ellis 1859–1939: *Little Essays of Love and Virtue* (1922)

19 Cultured people are merely the glittering scum which floats upon the deep river of production.
on hearing his son Randolph criticize the lack of culture of the Calgary oil magnates, probably *c.*1929
Winston Churchill 1874–1965: Martin Gilbert *In Search of Churchill* (1994)

20 JOURNALIST: Mr Gandhi, what do you think of modern civilization?
GANDHI: That would be a good idea.
Mahatma Gandhi 1869–1948: on arriving in England in 1930; E. F. Schumacher *Good Work* (1979)

21 Whenever I hear the word culture . . . I release the safety-catch of my Browning!
often quoted: 'Whenever I hear the word culture, I reach for my pistol!'
Hanns Johst 1890–1978: *Schlageter* (1933); often attributed to Hermann Goering; see 25 below

22 Culture may even be described simply as that which makes life worth living.
T. S. Eliot 1888–1965: *Notes Towards a Definition of Culture* (1948)

23 In Italy for thirty years under the Borgias they had warfare, terror, murder, bloodshed —they produced Michelangelo, Leonardo da Vinci and the Renaissance. In Switzerland they had brotherly love, five hundred years of democracy and peace and what did that produce . . . ? The cuckoo clock.
Orson Welles 1915–85: *The Third Man* (1949 film); words added by Welles to Graham Greene's script

24 The soul of any civilization on earth has ever been and still is Art and Religion, but neither has ever been found in commerce, in government or the police.
Frank Lloyd Wright 1867–1959: *A Testament* (1957)

25 When politicians and civil servants hear the word 'culture' they feel for their blue pencils.
Lord Esher 1913– : speech, House of Lords, 2 March 1960; see 21 above, **Censorship** 1

26 Sooner or later we must absorb Islam if our own culture is not to die of anaemia.
Basil Bunting 1900–85: Omar Pound *Arabic and Persian Poems* (1970) foreword

27 If civilization had been left in female hands, we would still be living in grass huts.
Camille Paglia 1947– : *Sexual Personae* (1990)

28 A cultural Chernobyl.
of Euro Disney
Ariane Mnouchkine 1934– : in *Harper's Magazine* July 1992; see 29 below

29 Some refer to it as a cultural Chernobyl. I think of it as a cultural Stalingrad.
of Euro Disney
J. G. Ballard 1930– : in *Daily Telegraph* 2 July 1994; see 28 above

30 Popular culture is a contradiction in terms. If it's popular, it's not culture. If everyone loves it, it's not original.
Vivienne Westwood 1941– : in *Independent on Sunday* 8 November 1998

31 The culture of the 1990s can be summed up by Neighbours and football.
Spike Milligan 1918–2002: in *Sunday Times* 2 January 2000

⊷Custom and Habit ⊷

PROVERBS AND SAYINGS

1 **Custom is mummified by habit and glorified by law.**
American proverb, mid 20th century

2 **Old habits die hard.**
it is difficult to break long-established habits; English proverb, mid 18th century

3 **What is new cannot be true.**
used to imply that innovation is less soundly based than custom which has been proved by experience; English proverb, mid 17th century

4 **You cannot shift an old tree without it dying.**
often used to suggest the risk involved in moving an elderly person who has lived in the same place for many years; English proverb, early 16th century

5 **You can't teach an old dog new tricks.**
someone who is already set in their ways is not able to learn new ways of doing things; English proverb, mid 16th century

PHRASES

6 pass on the torch

pass on a tradition, from Lucretius 'Some races increase, others are reduced, and in a short while the generations of living creatures are changed and like runners relay the torch of life'

QUOTATIONS

7 If one were to order all mankind to choose the best set of rules in the world, each group would, after due consideration, choose its own customs; each group regards its own as being by far the best.
Herodotus c.485–c.425 BC: *Histories*

8 The Lord says in the gospel; 'I am the Truth'. He does not say 'I am custom'. Therefore, when the truth is made manifest, custom must give way to truth.
Bishop Libosus of Vaga fl. 256 AD: St Augustine of Hippo *On Baptism*; see **The Christian Church** 15

9 *Consuetudo est altera natura.*
Habit is second nature.
Auctoritates Aristotelis: a compilation of medieval propositions

10 Everyone calls barbarism what is not customary to him.
Montaigne 1533–92: *Essais* (1580, ed. M. Rat, 1958)

11 But to my mind,—though I am native here,
And to the manner born,—it is a custom
More honoured in the breach than the observance.
William Shakespeare 1564–1616: *Hamlet* (1601); see **Behaviour** 17

12 Custom that is before all law, Nature that is above all art.
Samuel Daniel 1563–1619: *A Defence of Rhyme* (1603)

13 Custom, that unwritten law,
By which the people keep even kings in awe.
Charles D'Avenant 1656–1714: *Circe* (1677)

14 Custom reconciles us to everything.
Edmund Burke 1729–97: *On the Sublime and Beautiful* (1757)

15 Habit with him was all the test of truth,
'It must be right: I've done it from my youth.'
George Crabbe 1754–1832: *The Borough* (1810)

16 People wish to be settled: only as far as they are unsettled is there any hope for them.
Ralph Waldo Emerson 1803–82: *Essays* (1841) 'Circles'

17 The tradition of all the dead generations weighs like a nightmare on the brain of the living.
Karl Marx 1818–83: *The Eighteenth Brumaire of Louis Bonaparte* (1852)

18 Laws are sand, customs are rock. Laws can be evaded and punishment escaped, but an openly transgressed custom brings sure punishment.
Mark Twain 1835–1910: *The Gorky Incident* (1906)

19 Tradition means giving votes to the most obscure of all classes, our ancestors. It is the democracy of the dead.
G. K. Chesterton 1874–1936: *Orthodoxy* (1908)

20 Every public action, which is not customary, either is wrong, or, if it is right, is a dangerous precedent. It follows that nothing should ever be done for the first time.
Francis M. Cornford 1874–1943: *Microcosmographia Academica* (1908)

21 One can't carry one's father's corpse about everywhere.
Guillaume Apollinaire 1880–1918: *Les peintres cubistes* (1965) 'Méditations esthétiques: Sur la peinture'

22 Tradition is entirely different from habit, even from an excellent habit, since habit is by definition an unconscious acquisition and tends to become mechanical, whereas tradition results from a conscious and deliberate acceptance . . . Tradition presupposes the reality of what endures.
Igor Stravinsky 1882–1971: *Poetics of Music* (1947)

23 The air is full of our cries. (*He listens*) But habit is a great deadener.
Samuel Beckett 1906–89: *Waiting for Godot* (1955)

24 Routine, in an intelligent man, is a sign of ambition.
W. H. Auden 1907–73: 'The Life of That-There Poet' (1958)

25 I don't think you can make a conscious decision about tradition. I mean, you're either of it, or you're not. I don't think you belong to a tradition by aping it.
Harrison Birtwistle 1934– : Andrew Ford *Composer to Composer* (1993)

Cynicism see Disillusion and Cynicism

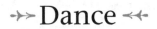

Dance

PROVERBS AND SAYINGS

1 **When you go to dance, take heed whom you take by the hand.**
English proverb, early 17th century

2 **You need more than dancing shoes to be a dancer.**
American proverb, mid 20th century

PHRASES

3 **antic hay**
an absurd dance, from Marlowe; see 5 below

4 **trip the light fantastic**
dance, originally with allusion to Milton: see 8 below

QUOTATIONS

5 My men, like satyrs grazing on the lawns,
Shall with their goat feet dance an antic hay.
Christopher Marlowe 1564–93: *Edward II* (1593);
see 3 above

6 This wondrous miracle did Love devise,
For dancing is love's proper exercise.
John Davies 1569–1626: 'Orchestra, or a Poem of
Dancing' (1596)

7 A dance is a measured pace, as a verse is a
measured speech.
Francis Bacon 1561–1626: *The Advancement of
Learning* (1605)

8 Come, and trip it as ye go
On the light fantastic toe.
John Milton 1608–74: 'L'Allegro' (1645); see 4
above

9 On with the dance! let joy be unconfined.
Lord Byron 1788–1824: *Childe Harold's Pilgrimage*
(1812–18)

10 Will you, won't you, will you, won't you,
will you join the dance?
Lewis Carroll 1832–98: *Alice's Adventures in
Wonderland* (1865)

11 I wish I could shimmy like my sister Kate,
She shivers like the jelly on a plate.
Armand J. Piron: *Shimmy like Kate* (1919 song)

12 O body swayed to music, O brightening
glance

How can we know the dancer from the
dance?
W. B. Yeats 1865–1939: 'Among School Children'
(1928)

13 Heaven—I'm in Heaven—And my heart
beats so that I can hardly speak;
And I seem to find the happiness I seek
When we're out together dancing cheek-
to-cheek.
Irving Berlin 1888–1989: 'Cheek-to-Cheek' (1935
song)

14 There may be trouble ahead,
But while there's moonlight and music and
love and romance,
Let's face the music and dance.
Irving Berlin 1888–1989: 'Let's Face the Music and
Dance' (1936 song)

15 [Dancing is] a perpendicular expression of a
horizontal desire.
George Bernard Shaw 1856–1950: in *New
Statesman* 23 March 1962

16 The truest expression of a people is in its
dances and its music. Bodies never lie.
Agnes de Mille 1908– : in *New York Times
Magazine* 11 May 1975

17 Dance is the hidden language of the soul.
Martha Graham 1894–1991: *Blood Memory* (1991)

⤳ Danger ⤝

see also **Caution, Courage**

PROVERBS AND SAYINGS

1 **Adventures are to the adventurous.**
the person who wants exciting things to happen must take the initiative; English proverb, mid 19th century

2 **A common danger causes common action.**
American proverb, mid 20th century

3 **Heaven protects children, sailors, and drunken men.**
often used (in a number of variant forms) to imply that someone unable to look after themselves has been undeservedly lucky; English proverb, mid 19th century

4 **He who rides a tiger is afraid to dismount.**
once a dangerous or troublesome venture is begun, the safest course is to carry it through to the end; see 16, 22 below; English proverb, late 19th century

5 **If you play with fire you get burnt.**
if you involve yourself with something potentially dangerous you are likely to be hurt; English proverb, late 19th century

6 **Just when you thought it was safe to go back in the water.**
advertising copy for the film *Jaws 2* (1978), featuring the return of the great white shark

7 **Light the blue touch paper and retire immediately.**
traditional instruction for lighting fireworks

8 **More than one yew bow in Chester.**
you may escape danger once, but not a second time (*Chester* representing the English, the traditional enemy); Welsh proverb

9 **The post of honour is the post of danger.**
English proverb, mid 16th century

10 **When the lion shows its teeth, don't assume that it is smiling.**
a warning sign should not be taken lightly; Arab proverb

11 **Who dares wins.**
motto of the British Special Air Service regiment, from 1942

12 **Women and children first.**
order given on a ship in difficulty, indicating that women and children should be allowed on to the lifeboats before men; in allusive (and often humorous) use, warning of a risky or unpleasant situation; from the mid 19th century

PHRASES

13 **bell the cat**
take the danger of a shared enterprise upon oneself, from the fable in which mice proposed hanging a bell around a cat's neck so as to be warned of its approach

14 **cry wolf**
raise repeated false alarms, so that a genuine cry for help goes unheeded, from the fable of the shepherd boy who tricked people with false cries of 'Wolf!'; when he was actually attacked and killed, his genuine appeals for help were ignored

15 **firebell in the night**
a warning of danger; from Thomas Jefferson's expression of alarm at the implications of the Missouri Compromise (which established that slavery should be excluded from the northern states); see **America** 16

16 **have a tiger by the tail**
have embarked on a course of action which proves unexpectedly difficult but which cannot easily or safely be abandoned; see 4 above

17 **have a wolf by the ears**
be in a precarious situation; be in a predicament where any course of action presents problems; see **Crises** 14

18 **a lion in the way**
a danger or obstacle, especially an imaginary one; from the Bible (Proverbs) 'The slothful man saith, There is a lion in the way'

19 **the lion's mouth**
a place or situation of great peril, with reference to the Bible (Psalms) 'Save me from the lion's mouth' and (2 Timothy) 'I was delivered out of the mouth of the lion'

20 **a pad in the straw**
a lurking or hidden danger; *pad* = a toad, regarded as a venomous creature

21 **pull the chestnuts out of the fire**
succeed in a hazardous undertaking on behalf of or through the agency of another, in allusion to the fable of a monkey using a cat's paw to get roasting chestnuts from a fire; see **Duty** 6

22 ride a tiger
take on a responsibility or embark on a course of
action which subsequently cannot easily or safely be
abandoned, from the proverb: see 4 above

23 a snake in the grass
a secret enemy, a lurking danger; after Virgil *Eclogues*
'There's a snake hidden in the grass'

24 a sword of Damocles
an imminent danger; a constant threat, especially in
the midst of prosperity; *Damocles* = a legendary
courtier who extravagantly praised the happiness of

QUOTATIONS

27 I am escaped with the skin of my teeth.
Bible: Job

28 Out of this nettle, danger, we pluck this
flower, safety.
William Shakespeare 1564–1616: *Henry IV, Part 1*
(1597); see **Courage** 11

29 It is the bright day that brings forth the
adder;
And that craves wary walking.
William Shakespeare 1564–1616: *Julius Caesar*
(1599)

30 Our God and soldiers we alike adore
Ev'n at the brink of danger; not before:
After deliverance, both alike requited,
Our God's forgotten, and our soldiers
slighted.
Francis Quarles 1592–1644: 'Of Common
Devotion' (1632); see **Human Nature** 10

31 When there is no peril in the fight, there is
no glory in the triumph.
Pierre Corneille 1606–84: *Le Cid* (1637)

32 Dangers by being despised grow great.
Edmund Burke 1729–97: speech on the Petition of
the Unitarians, 11 May 1792

33 In skating over thin ice, our safety is in our
speed.
Ralph Waldo Emerson 1803–82: *Essays* (1841)
'Prudence'

Dionysius I, ruler of Syracuse, and whom Dionysius
feasted while a sword hung by a hair above him

25 throw someone to the lions
to put in an unpleasant or dangerous situation,
originally with reference to the practice in imperial
Rome of throwing religious and political dissidents,
especially Christians, to wild beasts as a method of
execution; see **Christian Church** 3

26 the valley of the shadow of death
a place or period of intense gloom or peril, from the
Bible (Psalms) 'Though I walk through the valley of
the shadow of death, I will fear no evil'

34 We took risks, we knew we took them;
things have come out against us, and
therefore we have no cause for complaint.
Robert Falcon Scott 1868–1912: 'The Last
Message' in *Scott's Last Expedition* (1913)

35 Anyone who expects to meet a lunatic
brandishing a hatchet and instead finds a
man hiding a revolver in his trouser pocket
is bound to feel relieved. But that doesn't
prevent a revolver from being more
dangerous than a hatchet.
Leon Trotsky 1879–1940: in *Bulletin of the
Opposition* 1933

36 Security is mostly a superstition. It does not
exist in nature, nor do the children of men
as a whole experience it. Avoiding danger is
no safer in the long run than outright
exposure. Life is either a daring adventure,
or nothing.
Helen Keller 1880–1968: *The Open Door* (1957)

37 Security is when everything is settled, when
nothing can happen to you; security is the
denial of life.
Germaine Greer 1939– : *The Female Eunuch*
(1970)

38 They found more dangerous chemicals in
Coca-Cola's Dasani mineral water than they
did in the whole of Iraq.
Robin Cook 1946–2005: in *Observer* 29
August 2004

⤛ Day and Night ⤜

PROVERBS AND SAYINGS

**1 Be the day weary or be the day long,
at last it ringeth to evensong.**
even the most difficult time will come to an end;
English proverb, early 16th century

**2 The morning daylight appears plainer
when you put out your candle.**
American proverb

PHRASES

3 the watches of the night
the night-time; *watch* = originally each of the three
or four periods of time, during which a watch or
guard was kept, into which the night was divided by
the Jews and Romans

4 the witching hour
midnight; the time when witches are proverbially
active; after Shakespeare: see 6 below; see also
Business 22

QUOTATIONS

5 Night's candles are burnt out, and
    jocund day
Stands tiptoe on the misty mountain tops.
William Shakespeare 1564–1616: *Romeo and
Juliet* (1595)

6 'Tis now the very witching time of night,
When churchyards yawn and hell itself
    breathes out
Contagion to this world.
William Shakespeare 1564–1616: *Hamlet* (1601);
see 4 above

7 Lighten our darkness, we beseech thee, O
Lord; and by thy great mercy defend us from
all perils and dangers of this night.
The Book of Common Prayer 1662: *Evening
Prayer*

8 Now came still evening on, and
    twilight grey
Had in her sober livery all things clad.
John Milton 1608–74: *Paradise Lost* (1667)

9 The curfew tolls the knell of parting day,
The lowing herd wind slowly o'er the lea,
The ploughman homeward plods his
    weary way,
And leaves the world to darkness and to me.
Thomas Gray 1716–71: *Elegy Written in a Country
Churchyard* (1751)

10 The Sun's rim dips; the stars rush out;
At one stride comes the dark.
Samuel Taylor Coleridge 1772–1834: 'The Rime
of the Ancient Mariner' (1798)

11 The cares that infest the day
Shall fold their tents, like the Arabs,
And as silently steal away.
Henry Wadsworth Longfellow 1807–82: 'The
Day is Done' (1844)

12 Awake! for Morning in the bowl of night
Has flung the stone that puts the stars to
    flight:

And Lo! the Hunter of the East has caught
The Sultan's turret in a noose of light.
Edward Fitzgerald 1809–83: *The Rubáiyát of Omar
Khayyám* (1859)

13 There midnight's all a glimmer, and noon a
    purple glow,
And evening full of the linnet's wings.
W. B. Yeats 1865–1939: 'The Lake Isle of Innisfree'
(1892)

14 Let us go then, you and I,
When the evening is spread out against
    the sky
Like a patient etherized upon a table.
T. S. Eliot 1888–1965: 'The Love Song of J. Alfred
Prufrock' (1917); see **Poetry** 32

15 I have a horror of sunsets, they're so
romantic, so operatic.
Marcel Proust 1871–1922: *Cities of the Plain* (1922)

16 I have been one acquainted with the night.
Robert Frost 1874–1963: 'Acquainted with the
Night' (1928)

17 Morning has broken
Like the first morning,
Blackbird has spoken
Like the first bird.
Eleanor Farjeon 1881–1965: 'A Morning Song (for
the First Day of Spring)' (1957)

18 I cannot walk through the suburbs in the
solitude of the night without thinking that
the night pleases us because it suppresses
idle details, just as our memory does.
Jorge Luis Borges 1899–1986: *Labyrinths* (1962)

19 What are days for?
Days are where we live.
Philip Larkin 1922–85: 'Days' (1964)

20 It's been a hard day's night.
John Lennon 1940–80 and **Paul McCartney**
1942– : 'A Hard Day's Night' (1964 song)

⇥ Death ⇤

see also **Mourning, Murder, Suicide**

PROVERBS AND SAYINGS

1 As a tree falls, so shall it lie.

one should not change from one's long established practices and customs because of approaching death; English proverb, mid 16th century, from the Bible (Ecclesiastes) 'in the place where the tree falleth, there let it lie.'

2 Blessed are the dead that the rain rains on.

English proverb, early 17th century

3 [Death is] nature's way of telling you to slow down.

American life insurance saying, in *Newsweek* 25 April 1960

4 Death is the great leveller.

all people will be equal in death, whatever their material prosperity; English proverb, early 18th century

5 Death pays all debts.

the death of a person cancels out their obligations; English proverb, early 17th century, see 36 below

6 Et in Arcadia ego.

Latin tomb inscription 'And I too in Arcadia', of disputed meaning, often depicted in classical paintings, notably by Poussin in 1655

7 One funeral makes many.

sometimes with the implication that attendance at a deathbed or funeral may have fatal consequences; English proverb, late 19th century

8 Stone-dead hath no fellow.

traditionally used by advocates of the death penalty, or to suggest that only when a dangerous person is dead can one be sure that they will cause no further trouble; English proverb, mid 17th century

9 There is a remedy for everything except death.

English proverb, mid 15th century

10 This ae nighte, this ae nighte,
—Every nighte and alle,
Fire and fleet and candle-lighte,
And Christe receive thy saule.

'Lyke-Wake Dirge', traditional ballad; *fleet* = corruption of *flet*: see **The Home** 11

11 You can only die once.

used to encourage someone in a dangerous or difficult enterprise; English proverb, mid 15th century

12 Young men may die, but old men must die.

death is inevitable for all, and can at best be postponed until old age; English proverb, mid 16th century

PHRASES

13 beyond the veil

in the unknown state of being after death; originally with reference to Tyndale 'Christ hath brought us all in into the inner temple within the veil', taken as referring to the next world

14 go the way of all flesh

die; alteration of the Bible (I Kings) 'I go the way of all the earth' (Douay Bible 1609 'I enter into the way of all flesh')

15 hic jacet

an epitaph; Latin, literally 'here lies', the traditional first two words of a Latin epitaph; see 37 below

16 join the great majority

die; Edward Young *The Revenge* (1721) 'Death joins us to the great majority'; see 28 below

17 memento mori

an object serving as a warning or reminder of death, such as a skull; Latin, literally 'remember (that you have) to die'

18 the potter's field

a burial place for paupers or strangers, in reference to the Bible (Matthew), of how the chief priests and elders made use of the thirty pieces of silver returned to them by Judas after the Crucifixion, 'And they took counsel, and bought with them the potter's field, to bury strangers in'; see **Trust and Treachery** 15

19 Seven Last Words

the last seven utterances of Christ on the Cross

20 smite under the fifth rib

stab to the heart, kill; originally with reference to the Bible (II Samuel) 'Abner . . . smote him under the fifth rib'

21 turn one's face to the wall

(of a dying person) turn away one's face in awareness of impending death

QUOTATIONS

22 I would rather be tied to the soil as another man's serf, even a poor man's, who hadn't much to live on himself, than be King of all these the dead and destroyed.
Homer: *The Odyssey*

23 For dust thou art, and unto dust shalt thou return.
Bible: Genesis; see 44 below

24 If any man thinks he slays, and if another thinks he is slain, neither knows the ways of truth. The Eternal in man cannot kill: the Eternal in man cannot die.
The Upanishads c.800–200 BC: *Katha Upanishad*

25 Death, therefore, the most awful of evils, is nothing to us, seeing that, when we are death is not come, and when death is come, we are not.
Epicurus 341–271 BC: Diogenes Laertius *Lives of Eminent Philosophers*

26 *Non omnis moriar.*
I shall not altogether die.
Horace 65–8 BC: *Odes*

27 O death, where is thy sting? O grave, where is thy victory?
Bible: I Corinthians; see **World War I** 20

28 *Abiit ad plures.*
He's gone to join the majority [the dead].
Petronius d. AD 65: *Satyricon*; see 16 above

29 Anyone can stop a man's life, but no one his death; a thousand doors open on to it.
Seneca ('the Younger') c.4 BC–AD 65: *Phoenissae*; see 39 below

30 Finally he paid the debt of nature.
Robert Fabyan d. 1513: *The New Chronicles of England and France* (1516)

31 I am going to seek a great perhaps.
François Rabelais c.1494–c.1553: attributed last words, though none of his contemporaries authenticated the remark, which has become part of the 'Rabelaisian legend'; Jean Fleury *Rabelais et ses oeuvres* (1877)

32 I care not; a man can die but once; we owe God a death.
William Shakespeare 1564–1616: *Henry IV, Part 2* (1597); see 11 above

33   To die, to sleep;
To sleep: perchance to dream: ay, there's the rub;
For in that sleep of death what dreams may come
When we have shuffled off this mortal coil, Must give us pause.
William Shakespeare 1564–1616: *Hamlet* (1601); see **Life** 15, **Problems** 15

34 Nothing in his life
Became him like the leaving it.
William Shakespeare 1564–1616: *Macbeth* (1606)

35 Death be not proud, though some have called thee
Mighty and dreadful, for thou art not so.
John Donne 1572–1631: *Holy Sonnets* (1609)

36 He that dies pays all debts.
William Shakespeare 1564–1616: *The Tempest* (1611); see 5 above

37 O eloquent, just, and mighty Death! . . . thou hast drawn together all the farstretched greatness, all the pride, cruelty, and ambition of man, and covered it all over with these two narrow words, *Hic jacet*.
Walter Ralegh 1552–1618: *The History of the World* (1614); see 15 above

38 Only we die in earnest, that's no jest.
Walter Ralegh 1552–1618: 'On the Life of Man'

39 I know death hath ten thousand several doors
For men to take their exits.
John Webster 1580– : *The Duchess of Malfi* (1623); see 29 above

40 Any man's death diminishes me, because I am involved in Mankind; And therefore never send to know for whom the bell tolls; it tolls for thee.
John Donne 1572–1631: *Devotions upon Emergent Occasions* (1624)

41 The long habit of living indisposeth us for dying.
Thomas Browne 1605–82: *Hydriotaphia* (Urn Burial, 1658)

42 We shall die alone.
Blaise Pascal 1623–62: *Pensées* (1670)

43 In the midst of life we are in death.
The Book of Common Prayer 1662: *The Burial of the Dead*; see **Debt** 19

44 Forasmuch as it hath pleased Almighty God of his great mercy to take unto himself the soul of our dear brother here departed, we therefore commit his body to the ground; earth to earth, ashes to ashes, dust to dust; in sure and certain hope of the Resurrection to eternal life.
The Book of Common Prayer 1662: *The Burial of the Dead* Interment; see 23 above, **Adversity** 12

45 I am about to take my last voyage, a great leap in the dark.
Thomas Hobbes 1588–1679: last words; John Watkins *Anecdotes of Men of Learning* (1808)

46 Death never takes the wise man by surprise;
he is always ready to go.
Jean de la Fontaine 1621–95: *Fables* (1678–9) 'La
Mort et le Mourant'

47 They that die by famine die by inches.
Matthew Henry 1662–1714: *An Exposition on the
Old and New Testament* (1710)

48 Can storied urn or animated bust
Back to its mansion call the fleeting breath?
Thomas Gray 1716–71: *Elegy Written in a Country
Churchyard* (1751)

49 It matters not how a man dies, but how he
lives. The act of dying is not of importance,
it lasts so short a time.
Samuel Johnson 1709–84: James Boswell *Life of
Samuel Johnson* (1791) 26 October 1769

50 Depend upon it, Sir, when a man knows he
is to be hanged in a fortnight, it
concentrates his mind wonderfully.
on the execution of Dr Dodd
Samuel Johnson 1709–84: James Boswell *Life of
Samuel Johnson* (1791) 19 September 1777

51 My name is Death: the last best friend am I.
Robert Southey 1774–1843: 'The Lay of the
Laureate' (1816)

52 Now more than ever seems it rich to die,
To cease upon the midnight with no pain.
John Keats 1795–1821: 'Ode to a Nightingale'
(1820)

53 The cemetery is an open space among the
ruins, covered in winter with violets and
daisies. It might make one in love with
death, to think that one should be buried in
so sweet a place.
Percy Bysshe Shelley 1792–1822: *Adonais* (1821)

54 He'd make a lovely corpse.
Charles Dickens 1812–70: *Martin Chuzzlewit*
(1844)

55 Death must be distinguished from dying,
with which it is often confused.
Sydney Smith 1771–1845: H. Pearson *The Smith of
Smiths* (1934)

56 Just try and set death aside. It sets you aside,
and that's the end of it!
Ivan Turgenev 1818–83: *Fathers and Sons* (1862)

57 This quiet Dust was Gentlemen and Ladies
And Lads and Girls—
Was laughter and ability and Sighing
And Frocks and Curls.
Emily Dickinson 1830–86: 'This quiet Dust was
Gentlemen and Ladies' (c.1864)

58 Die, my dear Doctor, that's the last thing I
shall do!
Lord Palmerston 1784–1865: last words, E.
Latham *Famous Sayings and their Authors* (1904)

59 And all our calm is in that balm—
Not lost but gone before.
Caroline Norton 1808–77: 'Not Lost but Gone
Before'

60 For though from out our bourne of time and
place
The flood may bear me far,
I hope to see my pilot face to face
When I have crossed the bar.
Alfred, Lord Tennyson 1809–92: 'Crossing the
Bar' (1889)

61 In the arts of life man invents nothing; but
in the arts of death he outdoes Nature
herself, and produces by chemistry and
machinery all the slaughter of plague,
pestilence and famine.
George Bernard Shaw 1856–1950: *Man and
Superman* (1903)

62 Death is nothing at all; it does not count. I
have only slipped away into the next room.
Henry Scott Holland 1847–1918: sermon
preached on Whitsunday 1910

63 Why fear death? It is the most beautiful
adventure in life.
Charles Frohman 1860–1915: before drowning in
the *Lusitania*, 7 May 1915; see 66 below

64 Webster was much possessed by death
And saw the skull beneath the skin.
T. S. Eliot 1888–1965: 'Whispers of Immortality'
(1919)

65 A man's dying is more the survivors' affair
than his own.
Thomas Mann 1875–1955: *The Magic Mountain*
(1924)

66 To die will be an awfully big adventure.
J. M. Barrie 1860–1937: *Peter Pan* (1928); see 63
above

67 Ain't it grand to be blooming well dead?
Leslie Sarony 1897–1985: title of song (1932)

68 If this is dying, then I don't think much
of it.
Lytton Strachey 1880–1932: last words, Michael
Holroyd *Lytton Strachey* vol. 2 (1968)

69 Nor dread nor hope attend
A dying animal;
A man awaits his end
Dreading and hoping all.
W. B. Yeats 1865–1939: 'Death' (1933)

70 Though lovers be lost love shall not;
And death shall have no dominion.
Dylan Thomas 1914–53: 'And death shall have no
dominion' (1936)

71 He shouts play death more sweetly this
Death is a master from Deutschland.
Paul Celan 1920–70: 'Deathfugue' (written 1944)

72   This is death.
   To die and know it. This is the Black Widow,
   death.
   Robert Lowell 1917–77: 'Mr Edwards and the
   Spider' (1950)

73 One death is a tragedy, a million deaths a
   statistic.
   Joseph Stalin 1879–1953: attributed

74 If there wasn't death, I think you couldn't
   go on.
   Stevie Smith 1902–71: in *Observer* 9
   November 1969

75 This parrot is no more! It has ceased to be!
   It's expired and gone to meet its maker! This
   is a late parrot! It's a stiff! Bereft of life it rests
   in peace — if you hadn't nailed it to the
   perch it would be pushing up the daisies! It's
   rung down the curtain and joined the choir
   invisible! THIS IS AN EX-PARROT!
   Graham Chapman 1941–89, **John Cleese**
   1939– , et al.: *Monty Python's Flying Circus* (BBC TV
   programme, 1969)

76 Death is nothing if one can approach it as
   such. I was just a tiny night-light, suffocated
   in its own wax, and on the point of
   expiring.
   E. M. Forster 1879–1970: Philip Gardner (ed.) *E. M.
   Forster: Commonplace Book* (1985)

77 It's not that I'm afraid to die. I just don't
   want to be there when it happens.
   Woody Allen 1935– : *Death* (1975)

78 Deception is not as creative as truth. We do
   best in life if we look at it with clear eyes,
   and I think that applies to coming up to
   death as well.
   of the Hospice movement
   Cicely Saunders 1916– : in *Time* 5 September 1988

79 Even death is unreliable: instead of zero it
   may be some ghastly hallucination, such as
   the square root of minus one.
   Samuel Beckett 1906–89: attributed

80 We die containing a richness of lovers and
   tribes, tastes we have swallowed, bodies we
   have plunged into and swum up as if rivers
   of wisdom, characters we have climbed into
   as if trees, fears we have hidden as if in
   caves.
   Michael Ondaatje 1943– : *The English Patient*
   (1992)

Debt and Borrowing

see also **Thrift and Extravagance**

PROVERBS AND SAYINGS

1 **Access—your flexible friend.**
   advertising slogan for Access credit card, 1981
   onwards

2 **American Express? . . . That'll do
   nicely, sir.**
   advertising slogan for American Express credit card,
   1970s

3 **He that goes a-borrowing, goes a
   sorrowing.**
   involving oneself in debt is likely to lead to
   unhappiness; English proverb, late 15th century

4 **Lend your money and lose your
   friend.**
   debt puts a strain on friendship; English proverb, late
   15th century

5 **A man in debt is caught in a net.**
   American proverb, mid 20th century

6 **A national debt, if it is not excessive,
   will be to us a national blessing.**
   American proverb; often attributed to Alexander
   Hamilton (*c.*1757–1804)

7 **Neither a borrower, nor a lender be.**
   advising caution in financial dealings with others;
   English proverb, early 17th century, from
   Shakespeare: see 13 below

8 **Out of debt, out of danger.**
   someone in debt is vulnerable and at risk from
   others; English proverb, mid 17th century

9 **Short reckonings make long friends.**
   the prompt settlement of any debt between friends
   ensures that their friendship will not be damaged;
   English proverb, mid 16th century

◆▸◅◆▸▸◅◆▸▸◅◆▸▸◅◆▸▸◅◆▸▸◅◆▸▸◅◆▸▸◅◆▸▸◅◆▸▸◅◆▸▸◅◆▸▸◅◆▸▸◅◆▸▸

PHRASES

10 a pound of flesh
a payment or penalty which is strictly due but which
it is ruthless or inhuman to demand, with allusion to
Shakespeare *The Merchant of Venice*, and Shylock's
insistence that he had the right to take the pound of
Antonio's flesh promised in the bargain
between them

11 rob Peter to pay Paul
take away from one person to pay another;
discharge one debt by incurring another; probably
referring to the Apostles St *Peter* and St *Paul* as
founders of the Church; see **Government** 35

QUOTATIONS

12 Be not made a beggar by banqueting upon
borrowing.
Bible: Ecclesiasticus

13 Neither a borrower, nor a lender be;
For loan oft loses both itself and friend,
And borrowing dulls the edge of husbandry.
William Shakespeare 1564–1616: *Hamlet* (1601);
see 7 above

14 The human species, according to the best
theory I can form of it, is composed of two
distinct races, *the men who borrow*, and *the
men who lend*.
Charles Lamb 1775–1834: *Essays of Elia* (1823)
'The Two Races of Men'

15 Dreading that climax of all human ills,
The inflammation of his weekly bills.
Lord Byron 1788–1824: *Don Juan* (1819–24)

16 Three things I never lends—my 'oss, my
wife, and my name.
R. S. Surtees 1805–64: *Hillingdon Hall* (1845)

17 Annual income twenty pounds, annual
expenditure nineteen nineteen six, result
happiness. Annual income twenty pounds,
annual expenditure twenty pounds ought
and six, result misery.
Charles Dickens 1812–70: *David Copperfield*
(1850)

18 One must have some sort of occupation
nowadays. If I hadn't my debts I shouldn't
have anything to think about.
Oscar Wilde 1854–1900: *A Woman of No
Importance* (1893)

19 In the midst of life we are in debt.
Ethel Watts Mumford 1878–1940 et al.: *Altogether
New Cynic's Calendar* (1907); see **Death** 43

20 To take usury is contrary to Scripture; it is
contrary to Aristotle; it is contrary to nature,
for it is to live without labour; it is to sell

time, which belongs to God, for the
advantage of wicked men; it is to rob those
who use the money lent, and to whom,
since they make it profitable, the profits
should belong.
R. H. Tawney 1880–1962: *Religion and the Rise of
Capitalism* (1926)

21 The National Debt is a very Good Thing and
it would be dangerous to pay it off, for fear
of Political Economy.
W. C. Sellar 1898–1951 and **R. J. Yeatman**
1898–1968: *1066 and All That* (1930)

22 They hired the money, didn't they?
on the subject of war debts incurred by England and
others
Calvin Coolidge 1872–1933: John H. McKee
Coolidge: Wit and Wisdom (1933)

23 Sixteen tons, what do you get?
Another day older and deeper in debt.
Say brother, don't you call me 'cause I
can't go
I owe my soul to the company store.
Merle Travis 1917–83: 'Sixteen Tons' (1947 song)

24 Should we really let our people starve so we
can pay our debts?
Julius Nyerere 1922–99: in *Guardian* 21
March 1985

25 You can't put your VISA bill on your
American Express card.
P. J. O'Rourke 1947– : *The Bachelor Home
Companion* (1987)

26 I don't borrow on credit cards because it is
too expensive.
view of the chief executive of Barclays Bank
Matt Barrett 1944– : in *Independent* 17
October 2003

⇥ Deception ⇤

see also **Hypocrisy, Lies**

PROVERBS AND SAYINGS

1 Cheats never prosper.
English proverb, early 19th century

2 Deceit is a lie that wears a smile.
American proverb, mid 20th century

3 Fool me once, shame on you; fool me twice, shame on me.
if someone is deceived twice their own stupidity is to blame; late 20th century saying

PHRASES

4 all done with mirrors
an apparent achievement with an element of trickery, alluding to explanations of the art of a conjuror

5 be caught with chaff
be easily deceived or trapped; *chaff* = the husks of corn separated from the grain by threshing; from the proverb: see **Experience** 12

6 borrowed plumes
a pretentious display not of one's own making, with reference to the fable of the jay which decked itself in the peacock's feathers

7 hand a person a lemon
pass off a substandard article as good; swindle a person, do a person down; *lemon* = the type of a bad, unsatisfactory, or disappointing thing; see **Satisfaction** 2

8 mare's nest
an illusory discovery, originally in the phrase *to have found* (or *spied*) *a mare's nest* (i.e. something that

does not exist), used in the sense 'to have discovered something amazing'

9 a Potemkin village
a sham or unreal thing; any of a number of sham villages reputedly built on the orders of *Potemkin*, favourite of Empress Catherine II of Russia, for her tour of the Crimea in 1787

10 smell a rat
begin to suspect trickery or deception; see 20 below

11 a wolf in sheep's clothing
a person whose hostile or malicious intentions are concealed by a pretence of gentleness or friendliness, with reference to the Bible (Matthew): see **Hypocrisy** 9

12 wooden nutmeg
in US usage, a false or fraudulent thing, from a piece of wood shaped to resemble a nutmeg and fraudulently sold; see **American Cities** 31

QUOTATIONS

13 Deceive boys with toys, but men with oaths.
Lysander d. 395 BC: Plutarch *Parallel Lives* 'Lysander'

14 And if, to be sure, sometimes you need to conceal a fact with words, do it in such a way that it does not become known, or, if it does become known, that you have a ready and quick defence.
Niccolò Machiavelli 1469–1527: 'Advice to Raffaello Girolami when he went as Ambassador to the Emperor' (October 1522)

15 A false report, if believed during three days, may be of great service to a government.
Catherine de' Medici 1518–89: Isaac D'Israeli *Curiosities of Literature* Second Series vol. 2 (1849)

16 Doubtless the pleasure is as great
Of being cheated, as to cheat.
As lookers-on feel most delight,
That least perceive a juggler's sleight.
Samuel Butler 1612–80: *Hudibras* pt. 2 (1664)

17 One is easily fooled by that which one loves.
Molière 1622–73: *Le Tartuffe* (1669)

18 An open foe may prove a curse,
But a pretended friend is worse.
John Gay 1685–1732: *Fables* (1727) 'The Shepherd's Dog and the Wolf'

19   Wise fear, you know,
Forbids the robbing of a foe;
But what, to serve our private ends,
Forbids the cheating of our friends?
Charles Churchill 1731–64: *The Ghost* (1763)

20 Mr Speaker, I smell a rat; I see him forming in the air and darkening the sky; but I'll nip him in the bud.
Boyle Roche 1743–1807: attributed; see 10 above

21 O what a tangled web we weave,
When first we practise to deceive!
Sir Walter Scott 1771–1832: *Marmion* (1808); see **Child Care** 11

22 You may fool all the people some of the time; you can even fool some of the people all the time; but you can't fool all of the people all the time.
Abraham Lincoln 1809–65: Alexander K. McClure *Lincoln's Yarns and Stories* (1904); also attributed to Phineas Barnum; see **Politics** 21

23 It was beautiful and simple as all truly great swindles are.
O. Henry 1862–1910: *Gentle Grafter* (1908)

24 A deception that elevates us is dearer than a host of low truths.
Marina Tsvetaeva 1892–1941: *Pushkin and Pugachev* (1937)

25 In wartime . . . truth is so precious that she should always be attended by a bodyguard of lies.
Winston Churchill 1874–1965: *The Second World War* vol. 5 (1951)

26 Propaganda is a soft weapon: hold it in your hands too long, and it will move about like a snake, and strike the other way.
Jean Anouilh 1910–87: *The Lark* (adapted by Lillian Hellman, 1955)

27 It is now a very good day to get out anything we want to bury.
email sent in the aftermath of the terrorist action in America, 11 September 2001; often quoted as 'a good day to bury bad news'
Jo Moore: in *Daily Telegraph* 10 October 2001

Deeds see **Words and Deeds**

⤚ **Defiance** ⤙

see also **Determination and Perseverance**

PROVERBS AND SAYINGS

1 Nemo me impune lacessit.
Latin, *No one provokes me with impunity*, motto of the Crown of Scotland and of all Scottish regiments

2 No surrender!
Protestant Northern Irish slogan originating with the defenders of Derry against the Catholic forces of James II in 1689; see **Certainty** 28

3 They haif said: Quhat say they? Lat thame say.
motto of the Earls Marischal of Scotland, inscribed at Marischal College, Aberdeen, 1593; a similarly

defiant motto in Greek has been found engraved in remains from classical antiquity

4 You can take a horse to the water, but you can't make him drink.
even if you create the right circumstances, you cannot persuade someone to do something against their will; English proverb, late 12th century

PHRASES

5 die in the last ditch
die desperately defending something, die fighting to the last extremity; see 14 below

6 eyeball to eyeball
confronting closely; with neither party yielding; see **Crises** 22

7 kick against the pricks
rebel, be recalcitrant, especially to one's own hurt; with reference to the Bible (Acts) 'It is hard for thee to kick against the pricks'

8 nail one's colours to the mast
persist, refuse to give in; be undeterred in one's support for a party or plan of action; *colours* = the flag or ensign of a ship; see **Indecision** 15

QUOTATIONS

9 They are as venomous as the poison of a serpent: even like the deaf adder that stoppeth her ears;
Which refuseth to hear the voice of the charmer: charm he never so wisely.
Bible: Psalm 58; see **Senses** 2

10 He will give him seven feet of English ground, or as much more as he may be taller than other men.
his offer to the invader Harald Hardrada, before the battle of Stamford Bridge
Harold II 1019–66: Snorri Sturluson *Heimskringla* (*c.*1260) 'King Harald's Saga'

11 If I had heard that as many devils would set on me in Worms as there are tiles on the roofs, I should none the less have ridden there.
Martin Luther 1483–1546: to the Princes of Saxony, 21 August 1524; *Sämmtliche Schriften* vol. 16 (1745)

12 I grow, I prosper;
Now, gods, stand up for bastards!
William Shakespeare 1564–1616: *King Lear* (1605–6)

13 . . . What though the field be lost?
All is not lost; the unconquerable will,
And study of revenge, immortal hate,
And courage never to submit or yield:
And what is else not to be overcome?
John Milton 1608–74: *Paradise Lost* (1667)

14 'Do you not see your country is lost?' asked the Duke of Buckingham. 'There is one way never to see it lost' replied William, 'and that is to die in the last ditch.'
William III 1650–1702: Bishop Gilbert Burnet *History of My Own Time* (1838 ed.); see 5 above

15 Should the whole frame of nature round him break,

In ruin and confusion hurled,
He, unconcerned, would hear the mighty crack,
And stand secure amidst a falling world.
Joseph Addison 1672–1719: translation of Horace *Odes*

16 I was ever a fighter, so—one fight more,
The best and the last!
Robert Browning 1812–89: 'Prospice' (1864)

17 *No pasarán.*
They shall not pass.
Dolores Ibarruri 1895–1989: radio broadcast, Madrid, 19 July 1936; see **World War I** 1

18 Get up, stand up
Stand up for your rights
Get up, stand up
Never give up the fight.
Bob Marley 1945–81: 'Get up, Stand up' (1973 song)

19 She won't go quietly, that's the problem. I'll fight to the end.
Diana, Princess of Wales 1961–97: interview on *Panorama*, BBC1 TV, 20 November 1995

Delay see **Haste and Delay**

➤➤ Democracy ◀◀

see also **Elections, Politics**

PROVERBS AND SAYINGS

1 **Democracy is better than tyranny.**
an imperfect system is better than a bad one; American proverb

2 **The voice of the people is the voice of God.**
English version of the Latin *vox populi, vox dei*; English proverb, early 15th century, see 3 below

QUOTATIONS

3 And those people should not be listened to who keep saying the voice of the people is the voice of God, since the riotousness of the crowd is always very close to madness.
Alcuin 735–804: letter 164; *Works* (1863); see 2 above

4 Let no one oppose this belief of mine with that well-worn proverb: 'He who builds on the people builds on mud.'
Niccolò Machiavelli 1469–1527: *The Prince* (written 1513)

5 Nor is the people's judgement always true:
The most may err as grossly as the few.
John Dryden 1631–1700: *Absalom and Achitophel* (1681)

6 I never could believe that Providence had sent a few men into the world, ready booted and spurred to ride, and millions ready saddled and bridled to be ridden.
Richard Rumbold 1622–85: on the scaffold; T. B. Macaulay *History of England* vol. 1 (1849)

7 If one must serve, I hold it better to serve a well-bred lion, who is naturally stronger than I am, than two hundred rats of my own breed.
Voltaire 1694–1778: letter to a friend; Alexis de Tocqueville *The Ancien Régime* (1856)

8 One man shall have one vote.
John Cartwright 1740–1824: *The People's Barrier Against Undue Influence* (1780)

9 All, too, will bear in mind this sacred principle, that though the will of the majority is in all cases to prevail, that will to be rightful must be reasonable; that the minority possess their equal rights, which equal law must protect, and to violate would be oppression.
Thomas Jefferson 1743–1826: inaugural address, 4 March, 1801

10 It is impossible that the whisper of a faction should prevail against the voice of a nation.
Lord John Russell 1792–1878: reply to an Address from a meeting of 150,000 persons at Birmingham on the defeat of the second Reform Bill, October 1831

11 Minorities . . . are almost always in the right.
Sydney Smith 1771–1845: H. Pearson *The Smith of Smiths* (1934)

12 A majority is always the best repartee.
Benjamin Disraeli 1804–81: *Tancred* (1847)

13 Fourscore and seven years ago our fathers brought forth upon this continent a new nation, conceived in liberty, and dedicated to the proposition that all men are created equal . . . we here highly resolve that the dead shall not have died in vain, that this nation, under God, shall have a new birth of freedom; and that government of the people, by the people, and for the people, shall not perish from the earth.
the Lincoln Memorial inscription reads 'by the people, for the people'
Abraham Lincoln 1809–65: address at the Dedication of the National Cemetery at Gettysburg, 19 November 1863, as reported the following day

14 The cure for the ills of Democracy is more Democracy.
Jane Addams 1860–1935: *Democracy and Social Ethics* (1902)

15 Democracy substitutes election by the incompetent many for appointment by the corrupt few.
George Bernard Shaw 1856–1950: *Man and Superman* (1903) 'Maxims: Democracy'

16 The world must be made safe for democracy.
Woodrow Wilson 1856–1924: speech to Congress, 2 April 1917

17 No, Democracy is *not* identical with majority rule. Democracy is a *State* which recognizes the subjection of the minority to the majority, that is, an organization for the systematic use of *force* by one class against the other, by one part of the population against another.
Lenin 1870–1924: *State and Revolution* (1919)

18 Man's capacity for justice makes democracy possible, but man's inclination to injustice makes democracy necessary.
Reinhold Niebuhr 1892–1971: *Children of Light and Children of Darkness* (1944)

19 No one pretends that democracy is perfect or all-wise. Indeed, it has been said that democracy is the worst form of Government except all those other forms that have been tried from time to time.
Winston Churchill 1874–1965: speech, House of Commons, 11 November 1947

20 After each war there is a little less democracy to save.
Brooks Atkinson 1894–1984: *Once Around the Sun* (1951)

21 So Two cheers for Democracy: one because it admits variety and two because it permits criticism. Two cheers are quite enough: there is no occasion to give three. Only Love the Beloved Republic deserves that.
E. M. Forster 1879–1970: *Two Cheers for Democracy* (1951)

22 Democracy means government by discussion, but it is only effective if you can stop people talking.
Clement Attlee 1883–1967: speech at Oxford, 14 June 1957

23 It's not the voting that's democracy, it's the counting.
Tom Stoppard 1937– : *Jumpers* (1972); see Elections 16

24 Every government is a parliament of whores. The trouble is, in a democracy the whores are us.
P. J. O'Rourke 1947– : *Parliament of Whores* (1991)

25 Democracy is not worth a brass farthing if it is being installed by bayonets.
Alexander Solzhenitsyn 1918– :in *Mail on Sunday* 12 June 2005

⇢ Despair ⇠

see also **Hope, Optimism and Pessimism, Sorrow**

PHRASES

1 black dog
a metaphorical representation of melancholy or depression, used particularly by Samuel Johnson (see 6 below) and later by Winston Churchill when alluding to his own periodic bouts of depression

2 dark night of the soul
a period of anguish or despair; a period of spiritual aridity suffered by a mystic, 'Dark night of the soul' being a translation of the Spanish title of a work by St John of the Cross, known in English as *The Ascent of Mount Carmel* (1578–80); see 14 below

3 legion of the lost ones
people who are destitute or abandoned, regarded as beyond hope or help, after Kipling 'Gentleman-Rankers' (1892) 'To the legion of the lost ones, to the cohort of the damned, to my brethren in their sorrow overseas'

QUOTATIONS

4 My God, my God, look upon me; why hast thou forsaken me?
Bible: Psalm 22

5 Magnanimous Despair alone
Could show me so divine a thing,
Where feeble Hope could ne'er have flown
But vainly flapped its tinsel wing.
Andrew Marvell 1621–78: 'The Definition of Love' (1681)

6 The black dog I hope always to resist, and in time to drive, though I am deprived of almost all those that used to help me.
on his attacks of melancholia
Samuel Johnson 1709–84: letter to Mrs Thrale, 28 June 1783; see 1 above

7 Everywhere I see bliss, from which I alone am irrevocably excluded.
Mary Shelley 1797–1851: *Frankenstein* (1818)

8 I am in that temper that if I were under water I would scarcely kick to come to the top.
John Keats 1795–1821: letter to Benjamin Bailey, 25 May 1818

9 I give the fight up: let there be an end,
A privacy, an obscure nook for me.
I want to be forgotten even by God.
Robert Browning 1812–89: *Paracelsus* (1835)

10 Take thy beak from out my heart, and take thy form from off my door!
Quoth the Raven, 'Nevermore'.
Edgar Allan Poe 1809–49: 'The Raven' (1845)

11 There is no despair so absolute as that which comes with the first moments of our first great sorrow, when we have not yet known what it is to have suffered and be healed, to have despaired and have recovered hope.
George Eliot 1819–80: *Adam Bede* (1859)

12 In despair there are the most intense enjoyments, especially when one is very acutely conscious of the hopelessness of one's position.
Fedor Dostoevsky 1821–81: *Notes from Underground* (1864)

13 Not, I'll not, carrion comfort, Despair, not feast on thee;
Not untwist—slack they may be—these last strands of man
In me or, most weary, cry *I can no more*.
I can;
Can something, hope, wish day come, not choose not to be.
Gerard Manley Hopkins 1844–89: 'Carrion Comfort' (written 1885)

14 In a real dark night of the soul it is always three o'clock in the morning.
F. Scott Fitzgerald 1896–1940: 'Handle with Care' in *Esquire* March 1936; see 2 above

15 Human life begins on the far side of despair.
Jean-Paul Sartre 1905–80: *Les Mouches* (1943)

16 Despair is the price one pays for setting oneself an impossible aim.
Graham Greene 1904–91: *Heart of the Matter* (1948)

17 Despair, in short, seeks its own environment as surely as water finds its own level.
Alfred Alvarez 1929– : *The Savage God* (1971)

⇢─Determination and Perseverance ⇠─

see also **Defiance**

PROVERBS AND SAYINGS

1 Constant dropping wears away a stone.
primarily used to mean that persistence will achieve a difficult or unlikely objective; English proverb, mid 13th century; see 30 below

2 A determined fellow can do more with a rusty monkey wrench than a lot of people can with a machine shop.
American proverb, mid 20th century

3 Fall seven times, stand up eight.
Japanese proverb; see 6 below

4 He that will to Cupar maun to Cupar.
if someone is determined on an end they will not be dissuaded; *Cupar* is a town in Fife, Scotland; Scottish traditional saying, early 18th century

5 He who wills the end, wills the means.
someone sufficiently determined upon an outcome will also be ready to accept whatever is necessary to achieve it; English proverb, late 17th century

6 If at first you don't succeed, try, try, try again.
English proverb, mid 19th century; see 47 below

7 It is idle to swallow the cow and choke on the tail.
when a serious matter has been accepted, there is no point in quibbling over a trifle, or that it is senseless to give up when a great task is almost completed; English proverb, mid 17th century

8 It's dogged as does it.
steady perseverance will bring success; English proverb, mid 19th century

9 Little strokes fell great oaks.
a person or thing of size and stature can be brought down by a series of small blows; English proverb, early 15th century

10 Nil carborundum illegitimi.
cod Latin for 'Don't let the bastards grind you down', in circulation during the Second World War, though possibly of earlier origin; often quoted as, '*nil carborundum*' or '*illegitimi non carborundum*'.

11 Put a stout heart to a stey brae.
determination is needed to climb a steep ('stey') hillside; Scottish proverb, late 16th century

12 Revenons à ces moutons.
an exhortation to stop digressing and get back to the subject in hand; French, literally 'Let us return to these sheep', with allusion to the confused court scene in the Old French *Farce de Maistre Pierre Pathelin* (*c*.1470)

13 The show must go on.
American proverb, mid 19th century

14 Slow and steady wins the race.
from the story of the race between the hare and the tortoise, in Aesop's *Fables*, in which the winner was the slow but persistent tortoise and not the swift but easily distracted hare; mid 18th century saying; see 22 below

15 A stern chase is a long chase.
a *stern chase* is a chase in which the pursuing ship follows directly in the wake of the pursued; English proverb, early 19th century

16 The third time pays for all.
success after initial failure makes up for earlier disappointment; English proverb, late 16th century

17 We shall not be moved.
title of labour and civil rights song (1931), adapted from an earlier gospel hymn

18 We shall overcome.
title of song, originating from before the American Civil War, adapted as a Baptist hymn ('I'll Overcome Some Day', 1901) by C. Albert Tindley; revived in 1946 as a protest song by black tobacco workers, and in 1963 during the black Civil Rights Campaign

19 Where there's a will there's a way.
anything can be done if one has sufficient determination; English proverb, mid 17th century

20 A wilful man must have his way.
a person set on their own ends will disregard advice in pursuing their chosen course; English proverb, early 19th century

PHRASES

21 gird up one's loins
prepare oneself for mental and physical effort, summon one's courage and determination; of biblical origin, as in II Kings 'Then said he to Gehazi, Gird up thy loins, and take my staff in thine hand, and go thy way'

22 hare and tortoise
the defeat of ability by persistence, in allusion to Aesop's fable: see 14 above

23 make a spoon or spoil a horn
make a determined effort to achieve something, whatever the cost. With reference to the practice of making spoons out of the horns of cattle or sheep

24 put one's hand to the plough
undertake a task; enter on a course of life or
conduct, from the Bible (Luke): see 26 below

QUOTATIONS

25 Faint, yet pursuing.
Bible: Judges

26 No man, having put his hand to the plough,
and looking back, is fit for the kingdom
of God.
Bible: St Luke; see 24 above

27 *Hoc volo, sic iubeo, sit pro ratione voluntas.*
I will have this done, so I order it done; let
my will replace reasoned judgement.
Juvenal c.AD 60–c.130: *Satires*

28 Thought shall be the harder, heart the
keener, courage the greater, as our might
lessens.
Anonymous: *The Battle of Maldon* (c.1000)

29 Here stand I. I can do no other. God help
me. Amen.
Martin Luther 1483–1546: speech at the Diet of
Worms, 18 April 1521; attributed

30 The drop of rain maketh a hole in the stone,
not by violence, but by oft falling.
Hugh Latimer 1485–1555: *The Second Sermon
preached before the King's Majesty*, 19 April 1549; see
1 above

31　　　　Perseverance, dear my lord,
Keeps honour bright.
William Shakespeare 1564–1616: *Troilus and
Cressida* (1602)

32 Obstinacy in a bad cause, is but constancy in
a good.
Thomas Browne 1605–82: *Religio Medici* (1643)

33 Who would true valour see,
Let him come hither;
One here will constant be,
Come wind, come weather.
There's no discouragement
Shall make him once relent
His first avowed intent
To be a pilgrim.
John Bunyan 1628–88: *The Pilgrim's Progress*
(1684)

34 Obstinacy, Sir, is certainly a great vice . . . It
happens, however, very unfortunately, that
almost the whole line of the great and
masculine virtues, constancy, gravity,
magnanimity, fortitude, fidelity, and
firmness are closely allied to this
disagreeable quality.
Edmund Burke 1729–97: *On American Taxation*
(1775)

35 I have not yet begun to fight.
as his ship was sinking, 23 September 1779, having
been asked whether he had lowered his flag
John Paul Jones 1747–92: Mrs Reginald De Koven
Life and Letters of John Paul Jones (1914)

36 I have only one eye,—I have a right to be
blind sometimes . . . I really do not see the
signal!
at the battle of Copenhagen
Horatio, Lord Nelson 1758–1805: Robert Southey
Life of Nelson (1813); see **Ignorance** 13

37 I am in earnest—I will not equivocate—I will
not excuse—I will not retreat a single
inch—and I will be heard!
William Lloyd Garrison 1805–79: in *The Liberator*
1 January 1831

38 Let us, then, be up and doing,
With a heart for any fate;
Still achieving, still pursuing,
Learn to labour and to wait.
Henry Wadsworth Longfellow 1807–82: 'A
Psalm of Life' (1838); see **Achievement** 8

39　　　　That which we are, we are;
One equal temper of heroic hearts,
Made weak by time and fate, but strong
　　in will
To strive, to seek, to find, and not to yield.
Alfred, Lord Tennyson 1809–92: 'Ulysses' (1842)

40 I purpose to fight it out on this line, if it
takes all summer.
Ulysses S. Grant 1822–85: dispatch to Washington,
from head-quarters in the field, 11 May 1864

41 The best way out is always through.
Robert Frost 1874–1963: 'A Servant to Servants'
(1914)

42 Keep right on to the end of the road,
Keep right on to the end.
Harry Lauder 1870–1950: 'The End of the Road'
(1924 song)

43 One man that has a mind and knows it can
always beat ten men who haven't and don't.
George Bernard Shaw 1856–1950: *The Apple Cart*
(1930)

44 Nothing in the world can take the place of
persistence. Talent will not; nothing is more
common than unsuccessful men with
talent. Genius will not; unrewarded genius
is almost a proverb. Education will not; the
world is full of educated derelicts.
Persistence and determination are
omnipotent. The slogan 'press on' has

solved and always will solve the problems of the human race.

Calvin Coolidge 1872–1933: attributed in the programme of a memorial service for Coolidge in 1933

45 Pick yourself up,
Dust yourself off,
Start all over again.

Dorothy Fields 1905–74: 'Pick Yourself Up' (1936 song)

46 The capacity women have for just hanging on is depressing to contemplate.

Stevie Smith 1902–71: in *Tribune* c.1945

47 If at first you don't succeed, try, try again. Then quit. No use being a damn fool about it.

W. C. Fields 1880–1946: attributed; see 6 above

48 But above all
we have
the ability
to sort peas,
to cup water in our hands,
to seek
the right screw
under the sofa
for hours.

Miroslav Holub 1923– : 'Wings' (1967)

49 On, on, on.

last words after collapsing on Mont Ventoux in the Tour de France; commonly quoted as, 'Put me back on my bike'

Tom Simpson 1937–67: William Fotheringham *Put Me Back on My Bike* (2002)

50 We shall not be diverted from our course. To those waiting with bated breath for that favourite media catchphrase, the U-turn, I have only this to say. 'You turn if you want; the lady's not for turning.'

final line from alteration of the title of Christopher Fry's 1949 play *The Lady's Not For Burning*

Margaret Thatcher 1925– : speech at Conservative Party Conference in Brighton, 10 October 1980

51 Got to kick at the darkness 'til it bleeds daylight.

Bruce Cockburn 1945– : 'Lovers in a Dangerous Time' (1984 song)

52 The comeback kid!

Bill Clinton 1946– : description of himself after coming second in the New Hampshire primary, 1992

53 I will fight for what I believe in until I drop dead. And that's what keeps you alive.

Barbara Castle 1910–2002: in *Guardian* 14 January 1998

54 I can only go one way. I've not got a reverse gear.

Tony Blair 1953– : speech, Labour Party Conference, Bournemouth, 30 September 2003

Difference see Similarity and Difference

⊷ Diplomacy ⊷

see also **International Relations**

PROVERBS AND SAYINGS

1 **A soft answer turneth away wrath.**

refraining from defending oneself against verbal attack may defuse a situation; English proverb, late 14th century, from the Bible: see **Anger 7**

2 **We have no friends but the mountains.**

inhospitable terrain is more reliable than an ally as a source of safety; Kurdish proverb

PHRASES

3 **coalition of the willing**

a group of nations agreeing to act together, especially with military involvement; particularly associated with those countries giving active support to American intervention in Iraq in 2003

4 **honest broker**

an impartial mediator in international, industrial, or other disputes, from Bismarck: see **9 below**

QUOTATIONS

5 An ambassador is an honest man sent to lie abroad for the good of his country.

Henry Wotton 1568–1639: written in the album of Christopher Fleckmore in 1604; Izaak Walton *Reliquiae Wottonianae* (1651)

6 We are prepared to go to the gates of Hell—but no further.

attempting to reach an agreement with Napoleon, c.1800–1

Pope Pius VII 1742–1823: J. M. Robinson *Cardinal Consalvi* (1987)

7 The Congress makes no progress; it dances.
on the Congress of Vienna
Charles-Joseph, Prince de Ligne 1735–1814:
Auguste de la Garde-Chambonas *Souvenirs du Congrès de Vienne* (1820)

8 The compact which exists between the North and the South is 'a covenant with death and an agreement with hell'.
William Lloyd Garrison 1805–79: resolution adopted by the Massachusetts Anti-Slavery Society, 27 January 1843; in allusion to the Bible (Isaiah) 'We have made a covenant with death, and with hell are we at agreement'

9 I do not regard the procuring of peace as a matter in which we should play the role of arbiter between different opinions . . . more that of an honest broker who really wants to press the business forward.
Otto von Bismarck 1815–98: speech to the Reichstag, 19 February 1878; see 4 above

10 The agonies of a man who has to finish a difficult negotiation, and at the same time to entertain four royalties at a country house can be better imagined than described.
Lord Salisbury 1830–1903: letter to Lord Lyons, 5 June 1878

11 There is a homely old adage which runs: 'Speak softly and carry a big stick; you will go far.' If the American nation will speak softly, and yet build and keep at a pitch of the highest training a thoroughly efficient navy, the Monroe Doctrine will go far.
Theodore Roosevelt 1858–1919: speech in Chicago, 3 April 1903; **International Relations 6, Woman's Role 34**

12 You can no more make an agreement with those leaders of Colombia than you can nail currant jelly to the wall. And the failure to

nail currant jelly to the wall is not due to the nail. It's due to the currant jelly.
at the time of the Panama revolution, 1903
Theodore Roosevelt 1858–1919: attributed; see **Futility 10**

13 An appeaser is one who feeds a crocodile hoping it will eat him last.
Winston Churchill 1874–1965: in the House of Commons, January 1940

14 Personally I feel happier now that we have no allies to be polite to and to pamper.
George VI 1895–1952: to Queen Mary, 27 June 1940; John Wheeler-Bennett *King George VI* (1958)

15 Negotiating with de Valera . . . is like trying to pick up mercury with a fork.
to which de Valera replied, 'Why doesn't he use a spoon?'
David Lloyd George 1863–1945: M. J. MacManus *Eamon de Valera* (1944)

16 To jaw-jaw is always better than to war-war.
Winston Churchill 1874–1965: speech at White House, 26 June 1954

17 Mr Khrushchev holds out an olive branch and at the same time tries to hit us over the head with it.
Lyndon Baines Johnson 1908–73: in *Observer* 1 January 1961 'Sayings of the Year 1960'; see **Peace 5**

18 Let us never negotiate out of fear. But let us never fear to negotiate.
John F. Kennedy 1917–63: inaugural address, 20 January 1961

19 One of the things I learnt when I was negotiating was that until I changed myself I could not change others.
Nelson Mandela 1918– : in *Sunday Times* 16 April 2000

Discontent see Satisfaction and Discontent

Discoveries see Inventions and Discoveries

Disillusion and Cynicism

PROVERBS AND SAYINGS

1 **Blessed is he who expects nothing, for he shall never be disappointed.**
English proverb, early 18th century; see 12 below

PHRASES

2 Dead Sea fruit
any outwardly desirable object which on attainment turns out to be worthless; any hollow disappointing thing; from a legendary fruit, of attractive appearance, which dissolved into smoke and ashes when held; see 3, 5 below; **Power** 35

3 dust and ashes
used to convey a feeling of great disappointment or disillusion about something; originally with allusion to the legend of the Dead Sea fruit; see 2 above, **Adversity** 12

4 take the gilt off the gingerbread
strip something of its attractions; gingerbread was traditionally made in decorative forms which were then gilded

5 turn to ashes in a person's mouth
turn out to be utterly disappointing or worthless; probably originally with allusion to the legend of Dead Sea fruit: see 2 above

6 vanitas vanitatum
vanity of vanities, futility (frequently as an exclamation of disillusionment or pessimism); late Latin, from the Vulgate translation of the Bible; see **Futility** 16, **Satisfaction and Discontent** 28

QUOTATIONS

7 To get practice in being refused.
on being asked why he was begging for alms from a statue
Diogenes 404–323 BC: Diogenes Laertius *Lives of the Philosophers*

8 Kill them all; God will recognize his own.
when asked how the true Catholics could be distinguished from the heretics at the massacre of Béziers, 1209
Arnald-Amaury, abbot of Cîteaux d. 1225: Jonathan Sumption *The Albigensian Crusade* (1978)

9 Paris is well worth a mass.
Henri of Navarre, a Huguenot, on becoming King of France
Henri IV 1553–1610: attributed to Henri IV; alternatively to his minister Sully, in conversation with Henri

10 What makes all doctrines plain and clear?
About two hundred pounds a year.
And that which was proved true before,
Prove false again? Two hundred more.
Samuel Butler 1612–80: *Hudibras* pt. 3 (1680)

11 Everything has been said, and we are more than seven thousand years of human thought too late.
Jean de la Bruyère 1645–96: *Les Caractères ou les moeurs de ce siècle* (1688)

12 'Blessed is the man who expects nothing, for he shall never be disappointed' was the ninth beatitude.
Alexander Pope 1688–1744: letter to Fortescue, 23 September 1725; see 1 above

13 And finds, with keen discriminating sight,
Black's not so black;—nor white so very white.
George Canning 1770–1827: 'New Morality' (1821)

14 Never glad confident morning again!
Robert Browning 1812–89: 'The Lost Leader' (1845)

15 Take the life-lie away from the average man and straight away you take away his happiness.
Henrik Ibsen 1828–1906: *The Wild Duck* (1884)

16 A man who knows the price of everything and the value of nothing.
definition of a cynic
Oscar Wilde 1854–1900: *Lady Windermere's Fan* (1892)

17 And nothing to look backward to with pride,
And nothing to look forward to with hope.
Robert Frost 1874–1963: 'The Death of the Hired Man' (1914)

18 Cynicism is an unpleasant way of saying the truth.
Lillian Hellman 1905–84: *The Little Foxes* (1939)

19 Reason and Progress, the old firm, is selling out! Everyone get out while the going's good. Those forgotten shares you had in the old traditions, the old beliefs are going up—up and up and up.
John Osborne 1929–94: *Look Back in Anger* (1956)

20 If someone tells you he is going to make a 'realistic decision', you immediately understand that he has resolved to do something bad.
Mary McCarthy 1912–89: *On the Contrary* (1961) 'American Realist Playwrights'

21 Like all dreamers, I mistook disenchantment for truth.
Jean-Paul Sartre 1905–80: *Les Mots* (1964) 'Écrire'

22 Man hands on misery to man.
It deepens like a coastal shelf.
Get out as early as you can,
And don't have any kids yourself.
Philip Larkin 1922–85: 'This Be The Verse' (1974)

23 Cynicism is our shared common language, the Esperanto that actually caught on.
Nick Hornby 1957– : *How to be Good* (2001)

Dislikes see Likes and Dislikes

Dogs

see also **Animals**

PROVERBS AND SAYINGS

1 **Cave canem.**
Latin, *beware of the dog*; deriving originally from
Petronius (d. AD 65); see **Caution** 37

2 **A dog is for life, not just for**
Christmas.
slogan of the National Canine Defence League (now
Dogs Trust), from 1978

3 **There is no good flock without a good**
shepherd, and no good shepherd
without a good dog.
motto of the International Sheep Dog Society, said to
derive from a Scottish proverb

QUOTATIONS

4 There will be little dogs, with golden hair,
shining like precious stones.
Martin Luther 1483–1546: sermon on the
resurrection, Easter Sunday, 1544

5 I am his Highness' dog at Kew;
Pray, tell me sir, whose dog are you?
Alexander Pope 1688–1744: 'Epigram Engraved
on the Collar of a Dog which I gave to his Royal
Highness' (1738)

6 My dog! what remedy remains,
Since, teach you all I can,
I see you, after all my pains,
So much resemble man!
William Cowper 1731–1800: 'On a Spaniel called
Beau, killing a young bird' (written 1793)

7 Near this spot are deposited the remains of
one who possessed beauty without vanity,
strength without insolence, courage
without ferocity, and all the virtues of Man,
without his vices.
Lord Byron 1788–1824: 'Inscription on the
Monument of a Newfoundland Dog' (1808)

8 The more one gets to know of men, the
more one values dogs.
also attributed to Mme Roland in the form 'The more
I see of men, the more I like dogs'
A. Toussenel 1803–85: *L'Esprit des bêtes* (1847)

9 We were regaled by a dogfight . . . How odd
that people of sense should find any
pleasure in being accompanied by a beast
who is always spoiling conversation.
Lord Macaulay 1800–59: G. O. Trevelyan *Life and
Letters of Macaulay* (1876)

10 The great pleasure of a dog is that you may
make a fool of yourself with him and not
only will he not scold you, but he will make
a fool of himself too.
Samuel Butler 1835–1902: *Notebooks* (1912)

11 Brothers and Sisters, I bid you beware
Of giving your heart to a dog to tear.
Rudyard Kipling 1865–1936: 'The Power of the
Dog' (1909)

12 Any man who hates dogs and babies can't be
all bad.
of W. C. Fields, and often attributed to him
Leo Rosten 1908–97: speech at Masquers' Club
dinner, 16 February 1939

13 A door is what a dog is perpetually on the
wrong side of.
Ogden Nash 1902–71: 'A Dog's Best Friend is his
Illiteracy' (1953)

14 Happiness is a warm puppy.
Charles Monroe Schulz 1922– : title of book
(1962); see **Happiness** 29

15 That indefatigable and unsavoury engine of
pollution, the dog.
John Sparrow 1906–92: letter to *The Times* 30
September 1975

16 Outside of a dog, a book is a man's best
friend. Inside of a dog, it's too dark to read.
Groucho Marx 1890–1977: Groucho Marx and
Stefan Kanfer *The Essential Groucho* (2000)

Doubt see **Certainty and Doubt**

Drawing see **Painting and Drawing**

⇥ Dreams ⇤

see also **Sleep**

PROVERBS AND SAYINGS

1 **Dream of a funeral and you hear of a marriage.**
English proverb, mid 17th century

2 **Dreams go by contraries.**
English proverb, early 15th century

3 **Dreams retain the infirmities of our character.**
American proverb, late 19th century

4 **Morning dreams come true.**
English proverb, mid 16th century, recording a traditional superstition

PHRASES

5 **the gate of horn**
in Greek legend, the gates through which true dreams pass

6 **the ivory gate**
in Greek legend, the gate through which false dreams pass; see 8 below

QUOTATIONS

7 O God! I could be bounded in a nut-shell, and count myself a king of infinite space, were it not that I have bad dreams.
William Shakespeare 1564–1616: *Hamlet* (1601)

8 That children dream not in the first half year, that men dream not in some countries, are to me sick men's dreams, dreams out of the ivory gate, and visions before midnight.
Thomas Browne 1605–82: 'On Dreams'; see 6 above

9 The dream of reason produces monsters.
Goya 1746–1828: *Los Caprichos* (1799)

10 Was it a vision, or a waking dream?
Fled is that music:—do I wake or sleep?
John Keats 1795–1821: 'Ode to a Nightingale' (1820)

11   The quick Dreams,
The passion-wingèd Ministers of thought.
Percy Bysshe Shelley 1792–1822: *Adonais* (1821)

12 I have spread my dreams under your feet;
Tread softly because you tread on my dreams.
W. B. Yeats 1865–1939: 'He Wishes for the Cloths of Heaven' (1899)

13 The interpretation of dreams is the royal road to a knowledge of the unconscious activities of the mind.
often quoted as, 'Dreams are the royal road to the unconscious'
Sigmund Freud 1856–1939: *The Interpretation of Dreams* (2nd ed., 1909)

14 How many of our daydreams would darken into nightmares if there seemed any danger of their coming true!
Logan Pearsall Smith 1865–1946: *Afterthoughts* (1931)

15 Have you noticed . . . there is never any third act in a nightmare? They bring you to a climax of terror and then leave you there. They are the work of poor dramatists.
Max Beerbohm 1872–1956: S. N. Behrman *Conversations with Max* (1960)

16 All the things one has forgotten scream for help in dreams.
Elias Canetti 1905–94: *Die Provinz der Menschen* (1973)

17 When we dream that we are dreaming, the moment of awakening is at hand.
J. M. Coetzee 1940– : *In the Heart of the Country* (1977)

⇥ Dress ⇤

see also **Fashion**

PROVERBS AND SAYINGS

1 **Clothes make the man.**
what one wears is taken by others as an essential signal of status; English proverb, early 15th century; see 20 below

2 **Fine feathers make fine birds.**
beautiful clothes confer beauty or style on the wearer; English proverb, late 16th century

3 **If you want to get ahead, get a hat.**
advertising slogan for the British Hat Council, 1965

4 **Ne'er cast a clout till May be out.**
warning against leaving off old or warm clothes until the end of the month of May (the saying is

sometimes mistakenly understood to refer to may blossom); English proverb, early 18th century

5 **Nine tailors make a man.**
literally, a gentleman must select his attire from a number of sources (later also associated with bell-ringing, with the *nine tailors* or *tellers* indicating the nine knells traditionally rung for the death of a man); English proverb, early 17th century

QUOTATIONS

6 Costly thy habit as thy purse can buy,
But not expressed in fancy; rich, not gaudy;
For the apparel oft proclaims the man.
William Shakespeare 1564–1616: *Hamlet* (1601)

7 She wears her clothes, as if they were thrown on her with a pitchfork.
Jonathan Swift 1667–1745: *Polite Conversation* (1738)

8 Let it be observed, that slovenliness is no part of religion; that neither this, nor any text of Scripture, condemns neatness of apparel. Certainly this is a duty, not a sin. 'Cleanliness is, indeed, next to godliness.'
John Wesley 1703–91: *Sermons on Several Occasions* (1788); see **Behaviour** 3

9 Beware of all enterprises that require new clothes.
Henry David Thoreau 1817–62: *Walden* (1854) 'Economy'

10 The sense of being well-dressed gives a feeling of inward tranquillity which religion is powerless to bestow.
Miss C. F. Forbes 1817–1911: R. W. Emerson *Letters and Social Aims* (1876)

11 You should never have your best trousers on when you go out to fight for freedom and truth.
Henrik Ibsen 1828–1906: *An Enemy of the People* (1882)

12 His socks compelled one's attention without losing one's respect.
Saki 1870–1916: *Chronicles of Clovis* (1911)

13 When you're all dressed up and have no place to go.
George Whiting: title of song (1912)

14 Satan himself can't save a woman who wears thirty-shilling corsets under a thirty-guinea costume.
Rudyard Kipling 1865–1936: *Debits and Credits* (1926)

15 From the cradle to the grave, underwear first, last and all the time.
Bertolt Brecht 1898–1956: *The Threepenny Opera* (1928)

16 Where's the man could ease a heart like a satin gown?
Dorothy Parker 1893–1967: 'The Satin Dress' (1937)

17 The trick of wearing mink is to look as though you were wearing a cloth coat. The trick of wearing a cloth coat is to look as though you are wearing mink.
Pierre Balmain 1914–82: in *Observer* 25 December 1955

18 When I was young, I found out that the big toe always ends up making a hole in a sock. So I stopped wearing socks.
Albert Einstein 1879–1955: to Philippe Halsman; A. P. French *Einstein: A Centenary Volume* (1979)

19 *on being asked what she wore in bed:*
Chanel No. 5.
Marilyn Monroe 1926–62: Pete Martin *Marilyn Monroe* (1956)

20 Clothes don't make the man . . . but they go a long way toward making a businessman.
Thomas Watson Snr. 1874–1956: Robert Sobel *IBM: Colossus in Transition* (1981); see 1 above

21 Life is an adventure, so I make clothes to have adventures in.
Vivienne Westwood 1941– : in 1981; Jane Mulvagh *Vivienne Westwood: An Unfashionable Life* (1998)

22 Haute Couture should be fun, foolish and almost unwearable.
Christian Lacroix 1951– : attributed, 1987

23 It is totally impossible to be well dressed in cheap shoes.
Hardy Amies 1909–2003: *The Englishman's Suit* (1994)

24 Every time you open your wardrobe, you look at your clothes and you wonder what you are going to wear. What you are really saying is 'Who am I going to be today?'
Fay Weldon 1931– : in *New Yorker* 26 June 1995

25 The clothes in themselves do not make a statement. The woman makes the statement and the dress helps.
Jean Muir 1928–95: in *Vogue* August 1995

Drink see Food and Drink

⤳ Drugs ⤝

PROVERBS AND SAYINGS

1 **Just say no.**
motto of the Nancy Reagan Drug Abuse Fund, founded 1985

PHRASES

2 **chase the dragon**
take heroin by heating it on a piece of folded tin foil and inhaling the fumes. The term is said to be translated from Chinese, and to arise from the fact that the fumes and the molten heroin powder move up and down the piece of tin foil with an undulating movement resembling the tail of the dragon in Chinese myths

3 **cold turkey**
the abrupt and complete cessation of taking a drug to which one is addicted; the phrase derives from one of the symptoms, the development of 'goose-flesh' on the skin from a sudden chill, caused by this

QUOTATIONS

4 Almighty God hath not bestowed on mankind a remedy of so universal an extent and so efficacious in curing divers maladies as opiates.
Thomas Sydenham 1624–89: *Observationes Medicae* (1676); MS version given in 1991 ed.

5 Thou hast the keys of Paradise, oh just, subtle, and mighty opium!
Thomas De Quincey 1785–1859: *Confessions of an English Opium Eater* (1822)

6 Cocaine habit-forming? Of course not. I ought to know. I've been using it for years.
Tallulah Bankhead 1903–68: *Tallulah* (1952)

7 In this country, don't forget, a habit is no damn private hell. There's no solitary confinement outside of jail. A habit is hell for those you love.
Billie Holiday 1915–59: *Lady Sings the Blues* (1956, with William F. Duffy)

8 Junk is the ideal product . . . the ultimate merchandise. No sales talk necessary. The client will crawl through a sewer and beg to buy.
William S. Burroughs 1914–97: *The Naked Lunch* (1959)

9 Every form of addiction is bad, no matter whether the narcotic be alcohol or morphine or idealism.
Carl Gustav Jung 1875–1961: *Erinnerungen, Träume, Gedanken* (1962)

10 I'll die young, but it's like kissing God.
on his drug addiction
Lenny Bruce 1925–66: attributed

11 LSD? Nothing much happened, but I did get the distinct impression that some birds were trying to communicate with me.
W. H. Auden 1907–73: George Plimpton (ed.) *The Writer's Chapbook* (1989)

12 A drug is neither moral or immoral—it's a chemical compound. The compound itself is not a menace to society until a human being

treats it as if consumption bestowed a temporary licence to act like an asshole.
Frank Zappa 1940–93: *The Real Frank Zappa Book* (1989)

13 I experimented with marijuana a time or two. And I didn't like it, and I didn't inhale.
Bill Clinton 1946– : in *Washington Post* 30 March 1992

14 Sure thing, man. I used to be a laboratory myself once.
on being asked to autograph a fan's school chemistry book
Keith Richards 1943– : in *Independent on Sunday* 7 August 1994

15 Go. Get busy living, or get busy dying.
advice to his son, a drug addict
Pierce Brosnan 1953– : in *Sunday Times* 13 November 2005

⇥ Drunkenness ⇤

see also **Alcohol**

PROVERBS AND SAYINGS

1 **The drunkard's cure is drink again.**
American proverb, mid 20th century

2 **He that drinks beer, thinks beer.**
warning against the effects of intoxication; English proverb, early 19th century

3 **There is truth in wine.**
a person who is drunk is more likely to speak the truth; English proverb, mid 16th century, the saying is found earlier in Latin as *in vino veritas*

4 **When the wine is in, the wit is out.**
when one is drunk one is likely to be indiscreet or to speak or act foolishly; English proverb, late 14th century

QUOTATIONS

5 Drink, sir, is a great provoker of three things . . . nose-painting, sleep, and urine. Lechery, sir, it provokes, and unprovokes; it provokes the desire, but it takes away the performance.
William Shakespeare 1564–1616: *Macbeth* (1606)

6 Lo! the poor toper whose untutored sense,
Sees bliss in ale, and can with wine dispense;
Whose head proud fancy never taught to steer,
Beyond the muddy ecstasies of beer.
George Crabbe 1754–1832: 'Inebriety' (1775); see Ignorance 17

7 A man who exposes himself when he is intoxicated, has not the art of getting drunk.
Samuel Johnson 1709–84: James Boswell *Life of Samuel Johnson* (1791) 24 April 1779

8 Not drunk is he, who from the floor
Can rise alone and still drink more;
But drunk is he, who prostrate lies,
Without the power to drink or rise.
Thomas Love Peacock 1785–1866: *The Misfortunes of Elphin* (1829)

9 It would be better that England should be free than that England should be compulsorily sober.
William Connor Magee 1821–91: speech on the Intoxicating Liquor Bill, House of Lords, 2 May 1872

10 Licker talks mighty loud w'en it git loose fum de jug.
Joel Chandler Harris 1848–1908: *Uncle Remus: His Songs and His Sayings* (1880)

11 But I'm not so think as you drunk I am.
J. C. Squire 1884–1958: 'Ballade of Soporific Absorption' (1931)

12 Till a lady passing by was heard to say:
'You can tell a man who "boozes" by the company he chooses'
And the pig got up and slowly walked away.
of a pig and a drunk lying side by side in the gutter
Benjamin Hapgood Burt 1880–1950: 'The Pig Got Up and Slowly Walked Away' (1933 song)

13 After a man has had his coffee it's tomorrow: it has to be! . . . And tomorrow it's just a hangover; you ain't still drunk tomorrow.
William Faulkner 1897–1962: *Pylon* (1935)

14 Love makes the world go round? Not at all. Whisky makes it go round twice as fast.
Compton Mackenzie 1883–1972: *Whisky Galore* (1947); see Love 8

15 A man you don't like who drinks as much as you do.
definition of an alcoholic
Dylan Thomas 1914–53: Constantine Fitzgibbon *Life of Dylan Thomas* (1965)

16 One more drink and I'd have been under the host.

Dorothy Parker 1893–1967: Howard Teichmann *George S. Kaufman* (1972)

17 You're not drunk if you can lie on the floor without holding on.

Dean Martin 1917– : Paul Dickson *Official Rules* (1978)

⇢⇢Duty and Responsibility ⇠⇠

PROVERBS AND SAYINGS

1 Don't care was made to care.

traditional rebuke to someone who asserts their lack of concern; first words of a children's rhyme ('Don't care was *made* to care, don't care was hung'); English saying, mid 20th century

2 Everybody's business is nobody's business.

when something is of some interest to everyone, no single person takes full responsibility for it; English proverb, early 17th century

3 Every herring must hang by its own gill.

everyone is accountable for their own actions; English proverb, early 17th century

4 Take what you want, and pay for it, says God.

traditional saying

5 Those who eat salty fish will have to accept being thirsty.

everyone is responsible for the consequences of their own actions; Chinese proverb

PHRASES

6 cat's paw

a person who is used by another, typically to carry out an unpleasant or dangerous task; originally with allusion to the fable of a monkey which asked a cat to extract its roasted chestnuts from the fire; see **Danger 21**

7 pass the buck

shift the responsibility for something to another person; *buck* = an article placed as a reminder before

a player whose turn it is to deal at poker; see 26 below

8 wash one's hands of

renounce responsibility for; refuse to have any further dealings with; originally with allusion to the Bible; see **Guilt 6, Indifference 13**

QUOTATIONS

9 And do thy duty, even if it be humble, rather than another's, even if it be great. To die in one's duty is life: to live in another's is death.

Bhagavadgita 250 BC–AD 250: ch. 3

10 It is much safer to be in a subordinate position than in authority.

Thomas à Kempis 1380–1471: *The Imitation of Christ*

11 Had I but served God as diligently as I have served the King, he would not have given me over in my grey hairs.

Thomas Wolsey 1475–1530: George Cavendish *Negotiations of Thomas Wolsey* (1641)

12 Do your duty, and leave the outcome to the Gods.

Pierre Corneille 1606–84: *Horace* (1640)

13 I could not love thee, Dear, so much, Loved I not honour more.

Richard Lovelace 1618–58: 'To Lucasta, Going to the Wars' (1649)

14 England expects that every man will do his duty.

Horatio, Lord Nelson 1758–1805: at the battle of Trafalgar, 21 October 1805; Robert Southey *Life of Nelson* (1813)

15 Stern daughter of the voice of God! O Duty!

William Wordsworth 1770–1850: 'Ode to Duty' (1807)

16 The brave man inattentive to his duty, is worth little more to his country, than the coward who deserts her in the hour of danger.

to troops who had abandoned their lines during the battle of New Orleans, 8 January 1815

Andrew Jackson 1767–1845: attributed

17 Do the work that's nearest, Though it's dull at whiles, Helping, when we meet them, Lame dogs over stiles.

Charles Kingsley 1819–75: 'The Invitation. To Tom Hughes' (1856)

18 On an occasion of this kind it becomes more than a moral duty to speak one's mind. It becomes a pleasure.
Oscar Wilde 1854–1900: *The Importance of Being Earnest* (1895)

19 Take up the White Man's burden—
Send forth the best ye breed—
Go, bind your sons to exile
To serve your captives' need.
Rudyard Kipling 1865–1936: 'The White Man's Burden' (1899); see **Race** 5

20 When a stupid man is doing something he is ashamed of, he always declares that it is his duty.
George Bernard Shaw 1856–1950: *Caesar and Cleopatra* (1901)

21 If we believe a thing to be bad, and if we have a right to prevent it, it is our duty to try to prevent it and to damn the consequences.
Lord Milner 1854–1925: speech in Glasgow, 26 November 1909

22 People will do things from a sense of duty which they would never attempt as a pleasure.
Saki 1870–1916: *The Chronicles of Clovis* (1911)

23 A sense of duty is useful in work, but offensive in personal relations. People wish to be liked, not to be endured with patient resignation.
Bertrand Russell 1872–1970: *The Conquest of Happiness* (1930)

24 Power without responsibility: the prerogative of the harlot throughout the ages.
summing up Lord Beaverbrook's political standpoint as a newspaper editor; Stanley Baldwin, Kipling's cousin, subsequently obtained permission to use the phrase in a speech in London on 18 March 1931
Rudyard Kipling 1865–1936: in *Kipling Journal* December 1971

25 I know this—a man got to do what he got to do.
John Steinbeck 1902–68: *Grapes of Wrath* (1939)

26 The buck stops here.
Harry S. Truman 1884–1972: unattributed motto on Truman's desk; see 7 above

27 Duty is what no-one else will do at the moment.
Penelope Fitzgerald 1916–2000: *Offshore* (1979)

⤗ The Earth ⤛

see also **Nature, Pollution and the Environment, The Universe**

PROVERBS AND SAYINGS

1 Touch the earth lightly.
modern saying, said to derive from an Australian Aboriginal proverb

2 We do not inherit the earth from our parents, we borrow it from our children.
modern saying, said to be of native American origin

PHRASES

3 flood and field
sea and land, after Shakespeare *Othello* 'Of moving accidents by flood and field'

4 Gaia hypothesis
the theory, put forward by the English scientist James Lovelock (1919–) in 1969, that living matter on the earth collectively defines and regulates the material conditions necessary for the continuance of life; *Gaia* = in Greek mythology, the Earth personified as a goddess, daughter of Chaos; see 18 below

5 the glimpses of the moon
the earth by night; sublunary scenes; after Shakespeare *Hamlet* 'That thou, dead corse again in complete steel, Revisit'st thus the glimpses of the moon'

6 global village
the world considered as a single community linked by telecommunications, from McLuhan: see **Technology** 17; see also **The Country and the Town** 27

7 under the sun
on earth; in existence (used in expressions emphasizing the large number of something); see **Familiarity** 12, **Progress** 6

QUOTATIONS

8 The earth is the Lord's, and all that therein is: the compass of the world, and they that dwell therein.
Bible: Psalm 24

9 Need for a knowledge of geography is greater than the need of gardens for water after the stars have failed to fulfil their promise of rain.
Yāqūt d. 1229: attributed

10 Above the smoke and stir of this dim spot, Which men call earth.
John Milton 1608–74: *Comus* (1637)

11 As low as where this earth Spins like a fretful midge.
Dante Gabriel Rossetti 1828–82: 'The Blessed Damozel' (1870)

12 Topography displays no favourites; North's as near as West.
More delicate than the historians' are the map-makers' colours.
Elizabeth Bishop 1911–79: 'The Map' (1946)

13 Now there is one outstandingly important fact regarding Spaceship Earth, and that is that no instruction book came with it.
R. Buckminster Fuller 1895–1983: *Operating Manual for Spaceship Earth* (1969)

14 God owns heaven but He craves the earth.
Anne Sexton 1928–74: 'The Earth' (1975)

15 The Alps, the Rockies and all other mountains are related to the earth, the Himalayas to the heavens.
J. K. Galbraith 1908– : *A Life in our Times* (1981)

16 How inappropriate to call this planet Earth when it is clearly Ocean.
Arthur C. Clarke 1917– : in *Nature* 1990; attributed

17 To me, it underscores our responsibility to deal more kindly with one another, and to preserve and cherish the pale blue dot, the only home we've ever known.
of Earth as photographed by Voyager 1
Carl Sagan 1934–96: *Pale Blue Dot* (1995)

18 Gaia is a tough bitch. People think the earth is going to die and they have to save it, that's ridiculous . . . There's no doubt that Gaia can compensate for our output of greenhouse gases, but the environment that's left will not be happy for any people.
Lynn Margulis 1938– : in *New York Times Biographical Service* January 1996; see 4 above

Eating see Cooking and Eating

➤➤ Economics ◄◄

see also **Business, Debt and Borrowing, Money, Thrift and Extravagance**

PROVERBS AND SAYINGS

1 **Buy in the cheapest market and sell in the dearest.**
sometimes with an implication of sharp practice; English proverb, late 16th century

2 **The only free cheese is in a mousetrap.**
Russian proverb; see also **Preparation** 10

3 **There's no such thing as a free lunch.**
colloquial axiom in American economics from the 1960s, much associated with Milton Friedman; first found in printed form in Robert Heinlein *The Moon is a Harsh Mistress* (1966); see **Universe** 19

PHRASES

4 **the dismal science**
economics, from Thomas Carlyle *The Nigger Question* (1849), in a play on *gay science*: see **Poetry** 1

5 **green shoots of recovery**
signs of growth or renewal, especially of economic recovery; popular form of phrasing used by Norman Lamont: see 22 below

6 **selling off the family silver**
parting with a valuable resource for immediate advantage; the reference is to Harold Macmillan's comparison of privatization to the sale of family assets by impoverished landowners: see 19 below

QUOTATIONS

7 Finance is, as it were, the stomach of the country, from which all the other organs take their tone.
W. E. Gladstone 1809–98: article on finance, 1858; H. C. G. Matthew *Gladstone 1809–1874* (1986)

8 There can be no economy where there is no efficiency.
Benjamin Disraeli 1804–81: address to his constituents, 1 October 1868

9 Lenin was right. There is no subtler, no surer means of overturning the existing basis of society than to debauch the currency.
John Maynard Keynes 1883–1946: *The Economic Consequences of the Peace* (1919)

10 We have always known that heedless self-interest was bad morals; we know now that it is bad economics.
Franklin D. Roosevelt 1882–1945: second inaugural address, 20 January 1937

11 What a country calls its vital economic interests are not the things which enable its citizens to live, but the things which enable it to make war.
Simone Weil 1909–43: W. H. Auden *A Certain World* (1971)

12 Everyone is always in favour of general economy and particular expenditure.
Anthony Eden 1897–1977: in *Observer* 17 June 1956

13 It's a recession when your neighbour loses his job; it's a depression when you lose yours.
Harry S. Truman 1884–1972: in *Observer* 13 April 1958

14 In a community where public services have failed to keep abreast of private consumption things are very different. Here, in an atmosphere of private opulence and public squalor, the private goods have full sway.
J. K. Galbraith 1908– : *The Affluent Society* (1958)

15 Expenditure rises to meet income.
C. Northcote Parkinson 1909–93: *The Law and the Profits* (1960)

16 When I have to read economic documents I have to have a box of matches and start moving them into position to simplify and illustrate the points to myself.
Alec Douglas-Home, Lord Home 1903–95: in *Observer* 16 September 1962

17 Small is beautiful. A study of economics as if people mattered.
E. F. Schumacher 1911–77: title of book (1973); see **Quantities** 8

18 Inflation is the one form of taxation that can be imposed without legislation.
Milton Friedman 1912– : in *Observer* 22 September 1974

19 First of all the Georgian silver goes, and then all that nice furniture that used to be in the saloon. Then the Canalettos go.
on privatization; see 6 above
Harold Macmillan 1894–1986: speech to the Tory Reform Group, 8 November 1985

20 If the policy isn't hurting, it isn't working.
on controlling inflation
John Major 1943– : speech in Northampton, 27 October 1989

21 Balancing the budget is like going to heaven. Everybody wants to do it, but nobody wants to do what you have to do to get there.
Phil Gramm 1942– : in a television interview, 16 September 1990

22 The green shoots of economic spring are appearing once again.
Norman Lamont 1942– : speech at Conservative Party Conference, 9 October 1991; see 5 above

23 Trickle-down theory—the less than elegant metaphor that if one feeds the horse enough oats, some will pass through to the road for the sparrows.
J. K. Galbraith 1908– : *The Culture of Contentment* (1992)

24 There are two kinds of Chancellor. Those who fail and those who get out in time.
Gordon Brown 1951– : habitual saying recalled by Anthony Howard; in *The Times* 8 February 2005

⇥ Education ⇤

see also **Schools, Teaching, Universities**

PROVERBS AND SAYINGS

1 **As the twig is bent, so is the tree inclined.**
early influences have a permanent effect; English proverb, early 18th century

2 **Education doesn't come by bumping your head against the school house.**
American proverb, mid 20th century

3 **Give me a child for the first seven years, and you may do what you like with him afterwards.**
traditionally regarded as a Jesuit maxim; recorded in *Lean's Collectanea* vol. 3 (1903)

4 **The ink of a scholar is holier than the blood of a martyr.**
modern saying, said to derive from an Arab proverb, but of uncertain origin

5 **It is never too late to learn.**
English proverb, late 17th century

6 **Never let your education interfere with your intelligence.**
American proverb, mid 20th century

7 **Never too old to learn.**
English proverb, late 16th century

8 **There is no royal road to learning.**
English proverb, early 19th century, deriving from Euclid; see **Mathematics 8**

9 **When the pupil is ready, the master arrives.**
Indian proverb, deriving from Sanskrit

PHRASES

10 **the groves of Academe**
the academic community, from the Roman poet Horace (65–8 BC) *Epistles* 'And seek for truth in the groves of Academe'

QUOTATIONS

11 Get learning with a great sum of money, and get much gold by her.
Bible: Ecclesiasticus

12 In education there should be no class distinction.
Confucius 551–479 BC: *Analects*

13 Whereas then a rattle is a suitable occupation for infant children, education serves as a rattle for young people when older.
Aristotle 384–322 BC: *Politics*

14 Say not, When I have leisure I will study; perchance thou wilt never have leisure.
Hillel 'The Elder' *c.*60 BC–C.AD 9: in *Talmud* Mishnah 'Pirqei Avot'

15 Study as if you were to live for ever; live as if you were to die tomorrow.
St Edmund of Abingdon *c.*1175–1240: John Crozier *St Edmund of Abingdon* (1982)

16 And gladly wolde he lerne and gladly teche.
Geoffrey Chaucer 1343–1400: *The Canterbury Tales* 'The General Prologue'

17 That lyf so short, the craft so long to lerne.
Geoffrey Chaucer 1343–1400: *The Parliament of Fowls*; see **Arts 2**, **Medicine 9**

18 Studies serve for delight, for ornament, and for ability.
Francis Bacon 1561–1626: *Essays* (1625) 'Of Studies'

19 Wear your learning, like your watch in a private pocket: and do not merely pull it out and strike it, merely to show that you have one.
Lord Chesterfield 1694–1773: *Letters to his Son* (1774) 22 February 1748

20 Gie me ae spark o' Nature's fire, That's a' the learning I desire.
Robert Burns 1759–96: 'Epistle to J. L[aprai]k' (1786)

21 Example is the school of mankind, and they will learn at no other.
Edmund Burke 1729–97: *Two Letters on the Proposals for Peace with the Regicide Directory* (9th ed., 1796)

22 What does education often do? It makes a straight-cut ditch of a free, meandering brook.
Henry David Thoreau 1817–62: *Journal* *c.*November 1850

23 Education makes a people easy to lead, but difficult to drive; easy to govern, but impossible to enslave.
Lord Brougham 1778–1868: attributed

24 Soap and education are not as sudden as a massacre, but they are more deadly in the long run.
Mark Twain 1835–1910: *A Curious Dream* (1872) 'Facts concerning the Recent Resignation'

25 Education is an admirable thing, but it is well to remember from time to time that nothing that is worth knowing can be taught.
Oscar Wilde 1854–1900: *Intentions* (1891)

26 The aim of education is the knowledge not of facts but of values.
William Ralph Inge 1860–1954: 'The Training of the Reason' in A. C. Benson (ed.) *Cambridge Essays on Education* (1917)

27 The best thing for being sad . . . is to learn something.
T. H. White 1906–64: *The Sword in the Stone* (1938)

28 To live for a time close to great minds is the best kind of education.
John Buchan 1875–1940: *Memory Hold-the-Door* (1940)

29 The empires of the future are the empires of the mind.
Winston Churchill 1874–1965: speech at Harvard, 6 September 1943

30 If you educate a man you educate one person, but if you educate a woman you educate a family.
Ruby Manikan: in *Observer* 30 March 1947

31 Education is the ability to listen to almost anything without losing your temper or your self-confidence.
Robert Frost 1874–1963: in *Reader's Digest* April 1960

32 Education is what survives when what has been learned has been forgotten.
B. F. Skinner 1904–90: in *New Scientist* 21 May 1964

33 The liberally educated person is one who is able to resist the easy and preferred answers, not because he is obstinate but because he knows others worthy of consideration.
Allan Bloom 1930–92: *The Closing of the American Mind* (1987)

34 Ask me my three main priorities for Government, and I tell you: education, education and education.
Tony Blair 1953– : speech at the Labour Party Conference, 1 October 1996; see **Politics** 15

⊶ Effort ⊷

see also **Achievement**

PROVERBS AND SAYINGS

1 **And all because the lady loves Milk Tray.**
advertising slogan for Cadbury's Milk Tray chocolates, 1968 onwards, showing the obstacles overcome to deliver the chocolates

2 **Easy come, easy go.**
something which is acquired without effort will be lost without regret; English proverb, mid 17th century

3 **He that would eat the fruit must climb the tree.**
someone who wishes to attain success must first make the necessary effort; English proverb, early 18th century

4 **I didn't get where I am today without—.**
managerial catchphrase in BBC television series *The Fall and Rise of Reginald Perrin* (1976–80), written by David Nobbs

5 **If a thing's worth doing, it's worth doing well.**
if something is worth any effort at all, it should be taken seriously; English proverb, mid 18th century; see 27 below, **Women** 40

6 **If the sky falls we shall catch larks.**
used dismissively to indicate that something will be attainable only in the most unlikely circumstances; English proverb, mid 15th century

7 **Much cry and little wool.**
referring to a disturbance without tangible result; in early usage, the image was that of shearing a pig, which cried loudly but produced no wool; English proverb, late 15th century

8 **No pain, no gain.**
nothing worth having can be achieved without effort; English proverb, late 16th century

9 **One cannot become a good sailor sailing in a tranquil sea.**
a person must be disciplined and educated to become a useful citizen; Chinese proverb

10 **We're number two. We try harder.**
advertising slogan for Avis car rentals

PHRASES

11 **burn the candle at both ends**
draw on one's resources from two directions; especially, overtax one's strength by going to bed late and getting up early; see **Transience** 15

12 **improve the shining hour**
make good use of time; make the most of one's time; after Isaac Watts (1674–1748): see **Work** 26

13 **leave no stone unturned**
try every possible expedient; the expression is used by Pliny in his Letters. The term was said by the

sophist Zenobius to derive from a story of hidden Persian treasure

14 smell of the lamp
show signs of laborious study and effort; the reference is to an oil-lamp, and according to Plutarch the criticism was once made of the work of Demosthenes, 'His impromptus smell of the lamp', meaning that his speeches were written rather than spoken orations

QUOTATIONS

15 *Parturient montes, nascetur ridiculus mus.*
Mountains will go into labour, and a silly little mouse will be born.
Horace 65–8 BC: *Ars Poetica*

16 Also say to them, that they suffer him this day to win his spurs.
speaking of the Black Prince at the battle of Crécy, 1346, and commonly quoted as 'Let the boy win his spurs'; see **Success** 21
Edward III 1312–77: *The Chronicle of Froissart* (translated by John Bourchier 1523–5)

17 Things won are done; joy's soul lies in the doing.
William Shakespeare 1564–1616: *Troilus and Cressida* (1602)

18 I had done all that I could; and no man is well pleased to have his all neglected, be it ever so little.
Samuel Johnson 1709–84: letter to Lord Chesterfield, 7 February 1755

19 But the fruit that can fall without shaking, Indeed is too mellow for me.
Lady Mary Wortley Montagu 1689–1762: 'Answered, for Lord William Hamilton' (1758)

20 Oh, how I am tired of the struggle!
Johann Wolfgang von Goethe 1749–1832: *Wandrers Nachtlied* (1821)

21 It is a folly to expect men to do all that they may reasonably be expected to do.
Richard Whately 1787–1863: *Apophthegms* (1854)

22 Say not the struggle naught availeth, The labour and the wounds are vain,

The enemy faints not, nor faileth, And as things have been, things remain.
Arthur Hugh Clough 1819–61: 'Say not the struggle naught availeth' (1855)

23 Now, *here*, you see, it takes all the running *you* can do, to keep in the same place. If you want to get somewhere else, you must run at least twice as fast as that!
Lewis Carroll 1832–98: *Through the Looking-Glass* (1872); said by the Red Queen: see **Life Sciences 6**

24 Superhuman effort isn't worth a damn unless it achieves results.
Ernest Shackleton 1874–1922: to his navigator Frank Worsley, 1916; F. P. Worsley *Endurance* (1931)

25 The world is divided into people who do things and people who get the credit. Try, if you can, to belong to the first class. There's far less competition.
Dwight Morrow 1873–1931: letter to his son; Harold Nicolson *Dwight Morrow* (1935)

26 The world is an oyster, but you don't crack it open on a mattress.
Arthur Miller 1915–2005: *Death of a Salesman* (1949)

27 If something is worth doing, then it's worth overdoing.
Justin Hawkins 1975– : in *Observer* 22 February 2004; see 5 above

⇥ Elections ⇤

see also **Democracy**

PROVERBS AND SAYINGS

1 **As Maine goes, so goes the nation.**
American political saying, c.1840; see 11 below

2 **A straw vote only shows which way the hot air blows.**
American proverb, early 20th century

3 **Vote early and vote often.**
American election slogan, already current when quoted by William Porcher Miles in the House of Representatives, 31 March 1858

QUOTATIONS

4 Anyone who campaigns for public office becomes disqualified for holding any office at all.
Thomas More 1478–1535: *Utopia* (1516)

5 The English people believes itself to be free; it is gravely mistaken; it is free only during the election of Members of Parliament; as soon as the Members are elected, the people is enslaved; it is nothing.
Jean-Jacques Rousseau 1712–78: *Du Contrat social* (1762)

6 The right of election is the very essence of the constitution.
'Junius': *Public Advertiser* 24 April 1769

7 To give victory to the right, not bloody bullets, but peaceful ballots only, are necessary.
usually quoted 'The ballot is stronger than the bullet'
Abraham Lincoln 1809–65: speech, 18 May 1858

8 An election is coming. Universal peace is declared, and the foxes have a sincere interest in prolonging the lives of the poultry.
George Eliot 1819–80: *Felix Holt* (1866)

9 One of the nuisances of the ballot is that when the oracle has spoken you never know what it means.
Lord Salisbury 1830–1903: after the Renfrew by-election of October 1877; Andrew Roberts *Salisbury: Victorian Titan* (1999)

10 As for our majority . . . one is enough.
now often associated with Churchill
Benjamin Disraeli 1804–81: *Endymion* (1880)

11 As Maine goes, so goes Vermont.
after predicting correctly that Franklin D. Roosevelt would carry all but two states in the election of 1936
James A. Farley 1888–1976: statement to the press, 4 November 1936; see 1 above

12 If there had been any formidable body of cannibals in the country he would have promised to provide them with free missionaries fattened at the taxpayer's expense.
of Harry Truman's success in the 1948 presidential campaign
H. L. Mencken 1880–1956: in *Baltimore Sun* 7 November 1948

13 Hell, I never vote *for* anybody. I always vote *against*.
W. C. Fields 1880–1946: Robert Lewis Taylor *W. C. Fields* (1950)

14 Don't buy a single vote more than necessary. I'll be damned if I'm going to pay for a landslide.
telegraphed message from his father, read at a Gridiron dinner in Washington, 15 March 1958, and almost certainly JFK's invention
John F. Kennedy 1917–63: J. F. Cutler *Honey Fitz* (1962)

15 Vote for the man who promises least; he'll be the least disappointing.
Bernard Baruch 1870–1965: Meyer Berger *New York* (1960)

16 You won the elections, but I won the count.
replying to an accusation of ballot-rigging
Anastasio Somoza 1925–80: in *Guardian* 17 June 1977; see **Democracy** 23

17 You campaign in poetry. You govern in prose.
Mario Cuomo 1932– : in *New Republic*, Washington, DC, 8 April 1985

18 If voting changed anything, they'd abolish it.
Ken Livingstone 1945– : title of book, 1987

19 Instead of rocking the cradle, they rocked the system.
in her victory speech as President, paying tribute to the women of Ireland
Mary Robinson 1944– : in *The Times* 10 November 1990; see **Women** 3

20 I earned capital in the campaign, political capital, and I intend to spend it.
on his re-election as President
George W. Bush 1946– : in *New York Times* 5 November 2004 (online edition)

⤙ Emotions ⤚

PROVERBS AND SAYINGS

1 Out of the fullness of the heart the mouth speaks.
overwhelming feeling will express itself in speech; English proverb, late 14th century, originally with allusion to the Bible (Matthew), 'Out of the abundance of the heart the mouth speaketh'

2 Sing before breakfast, cry before night.
warning against overconfidence in early happiness presaging a reversal of good fortune; English proverb, early 17th century

PHRASES

3 hard as the nether millstone
callous and unyielding, without sympathy or pity;
nether millstone = the lower of the two millstones by
which corn is ground; with allusion to Job in the
Geneva Bible (1560) 'His heart is as strong as a stone,
and as hard as the nether millstone'

4 in cold blood
without feeling or mercy, ruthlessly. According to
medieval physiology, blood was naturally hot, so this
phrase refers to an unnatural state in which someone
can do a (hot-blooded) deed of passion or violence
without the normal heating of the blood; see
Violence 8

5 the pathetic fallacy
the attribution of human emotion or responses to
inanimate things or animals, especially in art and
literature; from John Ruskin *Modern Painters* (1856)
'All violent feelings . . . produce . . . a falseness in . . .
impressions of external things, which I would
generally characterize as the "Pathetic fallacy"'

6 wear one's heart on one's sleeve
allow one's feelings to be obvious, from
Shakespeare: see 9 below

7 wring the withers
stir the emotions or sensibilities, after Shakespeare
Hamlet 'let the galled jade wince, our withers are
unwrung'

QUOTATIONS

8 Even as rain breaks not through a well-
thatched house, passions break not through
a well-guarded mind.
Pali Tripitaka c. 2nd century BC: *Dhammapada*

9 But I will wear my heart upon my sleeve
For daws to peck at: I am not what I am.
William Shakespeare 1564–1616: *Othello*
(1602–4); see 6 above

10   A man whose blood
Is very snow-broth; one who never feels
The wanton stings and motions of the sense.
William Shakespeare 1564–1616: *Measure for
Measure* (1604)

11 Our passions are most like to floods and
streams;
The shallow murmur, but the deep are
dumb.
Walter Ralegh 1552–1618: 'Sir Walter Ralegh to
the Queen' (1655)

12 The heart has its reasons which reason
knows nothing of.
Blaise Pascal 1623–62: *Pensées* (1670)

13 Calm of mind, all passion spent.
John Milton 1608–74: *Samson Agonistes* (1671)

14 The ruling passion, be it what it will,
The ruling passion conquers reason still.
Alexander Pope 1688–1744: *Epistles to Several
Persons* 'To Lord Bathurst' (1733)

15 We shall never learn to feel and respect our
real calling and destiny, unless we have
taught ourselves to consider every thing as
moonshine, compared with the education
of the heart.
Sir Walter Scott 1771–1832: to J. G. Lockhart,
August 1825

16 There are strings . . . in the human heart
that had better not be wibrated.
Charles Dickens 1812–70: *Barnaby Rudge* (1841)

17 Nothing great was ever achieved without
enthusiasm.
Ralph Waldo Emerson 1803–82: *Essays* (1841)
'Circles'

18 As you pass from the tender years of youth
into harsh and embittered manhood, make
sure you take with you on your journey all
the human emotions! Don't leave them on
the road, for you will not pick them up
afterwards!
Nikolai Gogol 1809–52: *Dead Souls* (1842)

19 *on being told there was no English word
equivalent to* sensibilité:
Yes we have. Humbug.
Lord Palmerston 1784–1865: attributed

20 We do not expect people to be deeply
moved by what is not unusual. That element
of tragedy which lies in the very fact of
frequency, has not yet wrought itself into
the coarse emotion of mankind.
George Eliot 1819–80: *Middlemarch* (1871–2)

21 The heart gets tired too; and it falls apart bit
by bit, like an old cloth wears out in the
wash.
Giovanni Verga 1840–1922: *I Malavoglia* (The
House by the Medlar Tree, 1881), tr. R. Rosenthal

22 There is a road from the eye to the heart
that does not go through the intellect.
G. K. Chesterton 1874–1936: *The Defendant* (1901)

23 Time cools, time clarifies; no mood can be
maintained quite unaltered through the
course of hours.
Thomas Mann 1875–1955:*The Magic Mountain*
(1924), tr. H. T. Lowe-Porter

24 In the realm of the emotions, the real is
indistinguishable from the imaginary.
André Gide 1869–1951: *Les Faux Monnayeurs*
(1925)

25 The desires of the heart are as crooked as
   corkscrews.
   W. H. Auden 1907–73: 'Death's Echo' (1937)

26 Now that my ladder's gone
   I must lie down where all ladders start
   In the foul rag and bone shop of the heart.
   W. B. Yeats 1865–1939: 'The Circus Animals'
   Desertion' (1939)

27 Oh heavens, how I long for a little ordinary
   human enthusiasm. Just enthusiasm—that's
   all. I want to hear a warm, thrilling voice cry
   out Hallelujah! Hallelujah! I'm alive!
   John Osborne 1929–94: Look Back in Anger (1956)

28 A man who has not passed through the
   inferno of his passions has never overcome
   them.
   Carl Gustav Jung 1875–1961: Erinnerungen,
   Träume, Gedanken (1962)

29 Sentimentality is the emotional promiscuity
   of those who have no sentiment.
   Norman Mailer 1923– : Cannibals and Christians
   (1966)

30 The heart is an organ of fire.
   Michael Ondaatje 1943– : The English Patient
   (1992)

31 The human heart likes a little disorder in its
   geometry.
   Louis de Bernières 1954– : Captain Corelli's
   Mandolin (1994)

⇥ Employment ⇤

see also **Work**

PROVERBS AND SAYINGS

1 **The labourer is worthy of his hire.**
someone should be properly recompensed for
effort; English proverb, late 14th century, deriving
from the Bible (Luke)

2 **Like master, like man.**
English proverb, mid 16th century; man here means
'servant'

PHRASES

3 **the butcher, the baker, the
candlestick-maker**
people of all trades, from the nursery rhyme 'Rub-
a-dub-dub, Three men in a tub'

4 **the oldest profession**
traditional euphemism for prostitution; see also
Politics 30

5 **winter of discontent**
a period of difficulty, especially political or industrial
unrest; particularly applied to the winter of 1978–79
in Britain, when widespread strikes forced the
government out of power; after Shakespeare Richard
III 'Now is the winter of our discontent'; see 26
below

QUOTATIONS

6 For promotion cometh neither from the
east, nor from the west: nor yet from the
south.
Bible: Psalm 75

7 He who does not teach his son a craft,
teaches him brigandage.
The Talmud: Babylonian Talmud Qiddushin

8 I hold every man a debtor to his profession.
Francis Bacon 1561–1626: The Elements of the
Common Law (1596)

9 Thou art not for the fashion of these times,
Where none will sweat but for promotion.
William Shakespeare 1564–1616: As You Like It
(1599)

10 It is wonderful, when a calculation is made,
how little the mind is actually employed in
the discharge of any profession.
Samuel Johnson 1709–84: James Boswell Life of
Samuel Johnson (1791) 6 April 1775

11 To do nothing and get something, formed a
boy's ideal of a manly career.
Benjamin Disraeli 1804–81: Sybil (1845)

12 Which of us . . . is to do the hard and dirty
work for the rest—and for what pay? Who is
to do the pleasant and clean work, and for
what pay?
John Ruskin 1819–1900: Sesame and Lilies (1865)

13 Naturally, the workers are perfectly free; the
manufacturer does not force them to take
his materials and his cards, but he says to
them . . . 'If you don't like to be frizzled in

-}>-<-}>-<-}>-<-}>-<-}>-<-}>-<-}>-<-}>-<-}>-<-}>-<-}>-<-}>-<-}>-<-}>-<-}>-<-}>-<-}>-<-}>-<-}>-<-}>-<-}>-<-}>

my frying pan, you can take a walk into the fire'.

Friedrich Engels 1820–95: *The Condition of the Working Class in England in 1844* (1892); see **Misfortunes** 12

14 The labour of women in the house, certainly, enables men to produce more wealth than they otherwise could; and in this way women are economic factors in society. But so are horses.

Charlotte Perkins Gilman 1860–1935: *Women and Economics* (1898)

15 When domestic servants are treated as human beings it is not worth while to keep them.

George Bernard Shaw 1856–1950: *Man and Superman* (1903)

16 Lord Finchley tried to mend the Electric Light
Himself. It struck him dead: And serve him right!
It is the business of the wealthy man
To give employment to the artisan.

Hilaire Belloc 1870–1953: 'Lord Finchley' (1911)

17 All professions are conspiracies against the laity.

George Bernard Shaw 1856–1950: *The Doctor's Dilemma* (1911)

18 The world's civilization started from the day on which everyone received reward for labour.

Andrew Carnegie 1835–1919: *Autobiography* (1920)

19 Not a penny off the pay, not a second on the day.

often quoted with 'minute' substituted for 'second'
A. J. Cook 1885–1931: speech at York, 3 April 1926

20 Had the employers of past generations all of them dealt fairly with their men there would have been no unions.

Stanley Baldwin 1867–1947: speech in Birmingham, 14 January 1931

21 Work is of two kinds: first, altering the position of matter at or near the earth's surface relatively to other such matter; second, telling other people to do so. The

first kind is unpleasant and ill paid; the second is pleasant and highly paid.

Bertrand Russell 1872–1970: *In Praise of Idleness and Other Essays* (1986) title essay (1932)

22 A professional is a man who can do his job when he doesn't feel like it. An amateur is a man who can't do his job when he does feel like it.

James Agate 1877–1947: diary 19 July 1945

23 By working faithfully eight hours a day, you may eventually get to be a boss and work twelve hours a day.

Robert Frost 1874–1963: attributed

24 It is difficult to get a man to understand something when his salary depends on his not understanding it.

Upton Sinclair 1878–1968: attributed

25 You don't get me I'm part of the union.

John Ford 1948– and **Richard Hudson** 1948– : 'Part of the Union' (1974 song)

26 I had known it was going to be a 'winter of discontent'.

James Callaghan 1912– : television interview, 8 February 1979; see 5 above

27 Always suspect any job men willingly vacate for women.

Jill Tweedie 1936–93: *It's Only Me* (1980)

28 McJob: A low-pay, low-prestige, low-dignity, low benefit, no-future job in the service sector.

Douglas Coupland 1961– : *Generation X* (1991)

29 We spend most of our lives working. So why do so few people have a good time doing it? Virgin is the possibility of good times.

Richard Branson 1950– : interview in *New York Times* 28 February 1993

30 I have that normal male thing of valuing myself according to the job I do. When I can't tell someone in one word what I am, then something is missing. I don't represent anything any more.

Michael Portillo 1953– : in *Independent on Sunday* 20 June 1999

⊰⊱ Ending ⊰⊱

see also **Beginning, Change**

PROVERBS AND SAYINGS

1 All good things must come to an end.
nothing lasts; although the addition of 'good' is a later development; English proverb, mid 15th century

2 All's well that ends well.
often used with the implication that difficulties have been successfully negotiated; English proverb, late 14th century

3 And they all lived happily ever after.
traditional ending for a fairy story; see **Optimism** 39

4 The end crowns the work.
the fulfilment of a process is its finest and most notable part; English proverb, early 16th century

5 Everything has an end.
no condition lasts for ever; English proverb, late 14th century

6 In my end is my beginning.
motto of Mary, Queen of Scots (1542–87); see **Beginning** 23

7 The opera isn't over till the fat lady sings.
using an informal description of the culmination of a traditional opera to indicate that a process is not yet complete; late 20th century saying

PHRASES

8 crack of doom
in archaic usage, the thunder-peal supposed to proclaim the Day of Judgement; originally often as a quotation from Shakespeare's *Macbeth*

9 the four last things
the four things (death, judgement, heaven, and hell) studied in eschatology

10 the last of the Mohicans
the sole survivors of a particular race or kind; in Fenimore Cooper's novel of that name (1826), the

American Indian Uncas, the last survivor of the Mohicans (= Mohegans), an Algonquian people formerly inhabiting Connecticut and Massachusetts

11 when the kissing has to stop
when the honeymoon period finishes; when one is forced to recognize harsh realities; from Browning: see **Kissing** 7

QUOTATIONS

12 Better is the end of a thing than the beginning thereof.
Bible: Ecclesiastes

13 The rest is silence.
William Shakespeare 1564–1616: *Hamlet* (1601)

14 Finish, good lady; the bright day is done, And we are for the dark.
William Shakespeare 1564–1616: *Antony and Cleopatra* (1606–7)

15 What if this present were the world's last night?
John Donne 1572–1631: *Holy Sonnets* (after 1609)

16 This is the beginning of the end.
on the announcement of Napoleon's Pyrrhic victory at Borodino, 1812
Charles-Maurice de Talleyrand 1754–1838: attributed; Sainte-Beuve *M. de Talleyrand* (1870); see 19 below

17 All tragedies are finished by a death, All comedies are ended by a marriage;

The future states of both are left to faith.
Lord Byron 1788–1824: *Don Juan* (1819–24)

18 This is the way the world ends Not with a bang but a whimper.
T. S. Eliot 1888–1965: 'The Hollow Men' (1925)

19 Now this is not the end. It is not even the beginning of the end. But it is, perhaps, the end of the beginning.
on the Battle of Egypt
Winston Churchill 1874–1965: speech at the Mansion House, London, 10 November 1942; see 16 above

20 The party's over, it's time to call it a day.
Betty Comden 1919– and **Adolph Green** 1915– : 'The Party's Over' (1956 song)

21 They think it's all over—it is now.
Kenneth Wolstenholme 1920–2002: television commentary in closing moments of the World Cup Final, 30 July 1966

22 Eternity's a terrible thought. I mean,
where's it all going to end?
Tom Stoppard 1937– : *Rosencrantz and
Guildenstern are Dead* (1967)

23 It ain't over till it's over.
Yogi Berra 1925– : comment on National League
pennant race, 1973, quoted in many versions

⇥ Enemies ⇤

see also **Hatred**

PROVERBS AND SAYINGS

1 Dead men don't bite.
killing an enemy puts an end to danger; English
proverb, mid 16th century; see **Practicality 6**

**2 Do not call a wolf to help you against
the dogs.**
advising against allying with an enemy which will
destroy you in your turn; Russian proverb

3 The enemy of my enemy is my friend.
shared enmity provides common ground; American
proverb, mid 20th century, said to be 'an old Arab
proverb'; compare **Family 10**

**4 Love your enemy—but don't put a gun
in his hand.**
indicating the practical limitations of charity;
American proverb, mid 20th century, see 9 below

5 There is no little enemy.
any enemy can be dangerous; English proverb, mid
17th century

QUOTATIONS

6 If thine enemy be hungry, give him bread to
eat; and if he be thirsty, give him water to
drink.
For thou shalt heap coals of fire upon his
head, and the Lord shall reward thee.
Bible: Proverbs; see **Forgiveness 7**

7 *Delenda est Carthago.*
Carthage must be destroyed.
warning included in every speech made by Cato,
whatever the subject; see **Peace 4**
Cato the Elder 234–149 BC: Pliny the Elder
Naturalis Historia

8 He that is not with me is against me.
Bible: St Matthew

9 Love your enemies, do good to them which
hate you.
Bible: St Luke; see **4 above, Forgiveness 14**

10 There is nothing in the whole world so
painful as feeling that one is not liked. It
always seems to me that people who hate
me must be suffering from some strange
form of lunacy.
Sei Shōnagon c.966–c.1013: *The Pillow Book*

11 Heat not a furnace for your foe so hot
That it do singe yourself.
William Shakespeare 1564–1616: *Henry VIII*
(1613)

12 People wish their enemies dead—but I do
not; I say give them the gout, give them the
stone!
Lady Mary Wortley Montagu 1689–1762: letter
from Horace Walpole to George Harcourt, 17
September 1778

13 He that wrestles with us strengthens our
nerves, and sharpens our skill. Our
antagonist is our helper.
Edmund Burke 1729–97: *Reflections on the
Revolution in France* (1790)

14 Respect was mingled with surprise,
And the stern joy which warriors feel
In foemen worthy of their steel.
Sir Walter Scott 1771–1832: *The Lady of the Lake*
(1810)

15 He makes no friend who never made a foe.
Alfred, Lord Tennyson 1809–92: *Idylls of the King*
'Lancelot and Elaine' (1859)

16 A man cannot be too careful in the choice of
his enemies.
Oscar Wilde 1854–1900: *The Picture of Dorian Gray*
(1891)

17 You shall judge of a man by his foes as well
as by his friends.
Joseph Conrad 1857–1924: *Lord Jim* (1900)

18 Scratch a lover, and find a foe.
Dorothy Parker 1893–1967: 'Ballade of a Great
Weariness' (1937)

19 Not while I'm alive 'e ain't!
reply to the observation that Nye Bevan was
sometimes his own worst enemy
Ernest Bevin 1881–1951: Roderick Barclay *Ernest Bevin and the Foreign Office* (1975)

20 I ain't got no quarrel with the Viet Cong.
refusing to be drafted to fight in Vietnam
Muhammad Ali 1942– : at a press conference in Miami, Florida, February 1966

21 Better to have him inside the tent pissing out, than outside pissing in.
of J. Edgar Hoover
Lyndon Baines Johnson 1908–73: David Halberstam *The Best and the Brightest* (1972)

22 Fidel Castro is right. You do not quieten your enemy by talking with him like a priest, but by burning him.
at a Communist Party meeting 17 December 1989
Nicolae Ceausescu 1918–89: in *Guardian* 11 January 1990

⇢ England ⇠

see also **Britain, British Towns and Regions**

PROVERBS AND SAYINGS

1 **England is the paradise of women, the hell of horses, and the purgatory of servants.**
English proverb, late 16th century

2 **An Englishman's word is his bond.**
a promise given is regarded as having the force of a legal agreement; English proverb, early 16th century

PHRASES

3 **Anglo-Saxon attitudes**
behaviour regarded as typically English. The phrase was coined by Lewis Carroll in *Through the Looking-Glass* (1872) as a description of the Messenger who approaches 'skipping and wriggling', and with his hands spread out fanlike from his sides: 'He's an Anglo-Saxon Messenger—and those are Anglo-Saxon attitudes.' (The image may reflect the depiction of figures in medieval manuscripts)

4 **perfidious Albion**
England; translation of French *la perfide Albion*, of late 18th century origin, with reference to England's

alleged habitual treachery to other nations; *Albion* is probably of Celtic origin and related to Latin *albus* 'white', in allusion to the white cliffs of Dover; see 5 below

5 **white cliffs of Dover**
the chalk cliffs on the Kent coast near Dover, taken as a national and patriotic symbol; see 4 above

QUOTATIONS

6 *Non Angli sed Angeli.*
Not Angles but Angels.
summarizing Bede *Historia Ecclesiastica* 'They answered that they were called Angles. "It is well," he said, "for they have the faces of angels, and such should be the co-heirs of the angels of heaven"'
Gregory the Great AD 540–604: oral tradition

7 This royal throne of kings, this sceptered isle,
This earth of majesty, this seat of Mars,
This other Eden, demi-paradise,
This fortress built by Nature for herself
Against infection and the hand of war,
This happy breed of men, this little world,
This precious stone set in the silver sea . . .
This blessèd plot, this earth, this realm, this England.
William Shakespeare 1564–1616: *Richard II* (1595)

8 Let not England forget her precedence of teaching nations how to live.
John Milton 1608–74: *The Doctrine and Discipline of Divorce* (1643)

9 The English are busy; they don't have time to be polite.
Montesquieu 1689–1755: *Pensées et fragments inédits . . .* vol. 2 (1901)

10 The English plays are like their English puddings: nobody has any taste for them but themselves.
Voltaire 1694–1778: Joseph Spence *Anecdotes* (ed. J. M. Osborn, 1966)

11 In England there are sixty different religions, and only one sauce.
Francesco Caracciolo 1752–99: attributed

12 We must be free or die, who speak the tongue

That Shakespeare spake; the faith and
 morals hold
Which Milton held.
William Wordsworth 1770–1850: 'It is not to be
thought of that the Flood' (1807)

13 I will not cease from mental fight,
Nor shall my sword sleep in my hand,
Till we have built Jerusalem,
In England's green and pleasant land.
William Blake 1757–1827: *Milton* (1804–10) 'And
did those feet in ancient time'

14 England is a nation of shopkeepers.
the phrase 'nation of shopkeepers' had been used
earlier by Samuel Adams and Adam Smith
Napoleon I 1769–1821: Barry E. O'Meara *Napoleon
in Exile* (1822); see **Business** 30

15 For he might have been a Roosian,
A French, or Turk, or Proosian,
Or perhaps Ital-ian!
But in spite of all temptations
To belong to other nations,
He remains an Englishman!
W. S. Gilbert 1836–1911: *HMS Pinafore* (1878)

16 Winds of the World, give answer! They are
 whimpering to and fro—
And what should they know of England
 who only England know?
Rudyard Kipling 1865–1936: 'The English Flag'
(1892)

17 Ask any man what nationality he would
prefer to be, and ninety-nine out of a
hundred will tell you that they would prefer
to be Englishmen.
Cecil Rhodes 1853–1902: Gordon Le Seur *Cecil
Rhodes* (1913)

18 Englishmen never will be slaves: they are
free to do whatever the Government and
public opinion allow them to do.
George Bernard Shaw 1856–1950: *Man and
Superman* (1903)

19 Mad dogs and Englishmen
Go out in the midday sun.
Noël Coward 1899–1973: 'Mad Dogs and
Englishmen' (1931 song)

20 Down here it was still the England I had
known in my childhood: the railway
cuttings smothered in wild flowers . . . the
red buses, the blue policemen—all sleeping
the deep, deep sleep of England, from which
I sometimes fear that we shall never wake till
we are jerked out of it by the roar of bombs.
George Orwell 1903–50: *Homage to Catalonia*
(1938)

21 There'll always be an England
While there's a country lane,
Wherever there's a cottage small
Beside a field of grain.
Ross Parker 1914–74 and **Hugh Charles** 1907– :
'There'll always be an England' (1939 song)

22 I am American bred,
I have seen much to hate here—much to
 forgive,
But in a world where England is finished
 and dead,
I do not wish to live.
Alice Duer Miller 1874–1942: *The White Cliffs*
(1940)

23 Think of what our Nation stands for,
Books from Boots' and country lanes,
Free speech, free passes, class distinction,
Democracy and proper drains.
John Betjeman 1906–84: 'In Westminster Abbey'
(1940)

24 Old maids biking to Holy Communion
through the mists of the autumn mornings
. . . these are not only fragments, but
characteristic fragments, of the English
scene.
George Orwell 1903–50: *The Lion and the Unicorn*
(1941) 'England Your England'; see **Britain** 16

25 An Englishman, even if he is alone, forms an
orderly queue of one.
George Mikes 1912– : *How to be an Alien* (1946)

26 England's not a bad country . . . It's just a
mean, cold, ugly, divided, tired, clapped-
out, post-imperial, post-industrial slag-heap
covered in polystyrene hamburger cartons.
Margaret Drabble 1939– : *A Natural Curiosity*
(1989)

The Environment see **Pollution and the Environment**

⇢ Envy and Jealousy ⇠

PROVERBS AND SAYINGS

1 **Better be envied than pitied.**
even if one is unhappy it is preferable to be rich and
powerful than poor and vulnerable; English proverb,
mid 16th century

2 **Envy feeds on the living; it ceases
when they are dead.**
American proverb, mid 20th century

3 The grass is always greener on the other side of the fence.
something just out of reach always appears more desirable than what one already has; English proverb, mid 20th century

PHRASES

4 the green-eyed monster
jealousy, from Shakespeare: see 10 below

5 keep up with the Joneses
strive not to be outdone socially by one's neighbours, from a comic-strip title, 'Keeping up with the Joneses—by Pop' in the New York *Globe* 1913

6 nice work if you can get it
expressing envy of what is perceived to be another's more favourable situation; title of Gershwin song (1937); see **Courtship 9**

QUOTATIONS

7 Thou shalt not covet thy neighbour's house, thou shalt not covet thy neighbour's wife, nor his manservant, nor his maidservant, nor his ox, nor his ass, nor any thing that is thy neighbour's.
Bible: Exodus; see 14 below, **Lifestyles** 10

8 Love is strong as death; jealousy is cruel as the grave.
Bible: Song of Solomon

9 Though jealousy be produced by love, as ashes are by fire, yet jealousy extinguishes love as ashes smother the flame.
Marguerite d'Angoulême 1492–1549: *The Heptameron* (1558)

10   O! beware, my lord, of jealousy;
It is the green-eyed monster which
     doth mock
The meat it feeds on.
William Shakespeare 1564–1616: *Othello* (1602–4); see 4 above

11 Malice is of a low stature, but it hath very long arms.
Lord Halifax 1633–95: *Political, Moral, and Miscellaneous Thoughts and Reflections* (1750) 'Of Malice and Envy'

12 Fools out of favour grudge at knaves in place.
Daniel Defoe 1660–1731: *The True-Born Englishman* (1701)

13 If something pleasant happens to you, don't forget to tell it to your friends, to make them feel bad.
Casimir, Comte de Montrond 1768–1843: attributed; Comte J. d'Estourmel *Derniers Souvenirs* (1860)

14 Thou shalt not covet; but tradition Approves all forms of competition.
Arthur Hugh Clough 1819–61: 'The Latest Decalogue' (1862); see 7 above

15 Do we want laurels for ourselves most, Or most that no one else shall have any?
Amy Lowell 1874–1925: 'La Ronde du Diable' (1925); see **Success 20**

16 Jealousy is no more than feeling alone against smiling enemies.
Elizabeth Bowen 1899–1973: *The House in Paris* (1935)

17 To jealousy, nothing is more frightful than laughter.
Françoise Sagan 1935–2004: *La Chamade* (1965)

18 Jealousy is all the fun you *think* they had.
Erica Jong 1942– : *How to Save Your Own Life* (1977)

19 May good confront the man on top and the man below. But let him who is jealous of another's position choke with his envy.
Chinua Achebe 1930– : *Arrow of God* (1988)

⤞ Equality ⤝

see also **Human Rights**

PROVERBS AND SAYINGS

1 A cat may look at a king.
even someone in a lowly position has a right to observe a person of power and influence; English proverb, mid 16th century

2 Diamond cuts diamond.
used of persons who are evenly matched in wit or cunning (only a diamond is hard enough to cut

another diamond); English proverb, early 17th century

3 Jack is as good as his master.
Jack is used variously as a familiar name for a sailor, a member of the common people, a serving man, and

QUOTATIONS

4 He maketh his sun to rise on the evil and on the good, and sendeth rain on the just and on the unjust.
Bible: St Matthew; see **Weather** 46

5 SHYLOCK: If you prick us, do we not bleed? if you tickle us, do we not laugh? if you poison us, do we not die? and if you wrong us, shall we not revenge?
William Shakespeare 1564–1616: *The Merchant of Venice* (1596–8)

6 Night makes no difference 'twixt the Priest and Clerk;
Joan as my Lady is as good i' th' dark.
Robert Herrick 1591–1674: 'No Difference i' th' Dark' (1648)

7 Sir, there is no settling the point of precedency between a louse and a flea.
on the relative merits of two minor poets
Samuel Johnson 1709–84: James Boswell *Life of Samuel Johnson* (1791) 1783

8 A man's a man for a' that.
Robert Burns 1759–96: 'For a' that and a' that' (1790)

9 There is no method by which men can be both free and equal.
Walter Bagehot 1826–77: in *The Economist* 5 September 1863 'France or England'

10 Make all men equal today, and God has so created them that they shall all be unequal tomorrow.
Anthony Trollope 1815–82: *Autobiography* (1883)

11 When every one is somebodee,
Then no one's anybody.
W. S. Gilbert 1836–1911: *The Gondoliers* (1889)

12 Oh, East is East, and West is West, and never the twain shall meet,
Till Earth and Sky stand presently at God's great Judgement Seat;
But there is neither East nor West, Border, nor Breed, nor Birth,
When two strong men stand face to face, tho' they come from the ends of earth!
Rudyard Kipling 1865–1936: 'The Ballad of East and West' (1892); see **Similarity** 4

13 While there is a lower class, I am in it; while there is a criminal element, I am of it; while there is a soul in prison, I am not free.
Eugene Victor Debs 1855–1926: speech at his trial for sedition in Cleveland, Ohio, 14 September 1918

14 The constitution does not provide for first and second class citizens.
Wendell Willkie 1892–1944: *An American Programme* (1944)

15 All animals are equal but some animals are more equal than others.
George Orwell 1903–50: *Animal Farm* (1945)

16 I have a dream that one day on the red hills of Georgia the sons of former slaves and the sons of former slave owners will be able to sit down together at the table of brotherhood.
Martin Luther King 1929–68: speech at Civil Rights March in Washington, 28 August 1963

17 You can have equality or equality of opportunity; you cannot have both. Equality will mean the holding back (or the new deprivation) of the brighter children.
Brian Cox 1928– and **Rhodes Boyson** 1925– : *Black Paper 1975* (1975)

⇢ Europe ⇠

see also **Countries and Peoples, International Relations**

PHRASES

1 the cockpit of Europe
Belgium; see **Countries and Peoples** 13

2 the Common Market
a name for the European Economic Community or European Union, used especially in the 1960s and 1970s; see **Countries and Peoples** 34

3 the Garden of Europe
a traditional name for Italy

QUOTATIONS

4   Pray enter
You are learned Europeans and we worse
Than ignorant Americans.
Philip Massinger 1583–1640: *The City Madam*
(1658)

5 The age of chivalry is gone.— That of
sophisters, economists, and calculators, has
succeeded; and the glory of Europe is
extinguished for ever.
Edmund Burke 1729–97: *Reflections on the
Revolution in France* (1790)

6 Roll up that map; it will not be wanted these
ten years.
of a map of Europe, on hearing of Napoleon's victory
at Austerlitz, December 1805
William Pitt 1759–1806: Earl Stanhope *Life of the
Rt. Hon. William Pitt* vol. 4 (1862)

7 Better fifty years of Europe than a cycle of
Cathay.
Alfred, Lord Tennyson 1809–92: 'Locksley Hall'
(1842)

8 Whoever speaks of Europe is wrong, [it is] a
geographical concept.
Otto von Bismarck 1815–98: marginal note on a
letter from the Russian Chancellor Gorchakov,
November 1876

9 We are part of the community of Europe
and we must do our duty as such.
Lord Salisbury 1830–1903: speech at Caernarvon,
10 April 1888

10 The European view of a poet is not of much
importance unless the poet writes in
Esperanto.
A. E. Housman 1859–1936: in *Cambridge
Review* 1915

11 Purity of race does not exist. Europe is a
continent of energetic mongrels.
H. A. L. Fisher 1856–1940: *A History of Europe*
(1935)

12 Fog in Channel—Continent isolated.
Russell Brockbank 1913– : newspaper placard in
cartoon, *Round the Bend with Brockbank* (1948)

13 If you open that Pandora's Box, you never
know what Trojan 'orses will jump out.
on the Council of Europe
Ernest Bevin 1881–1951: Roderick Barclay *Ernest
Bevin and the Foreign Office* (1975); see **Problems** 11

14 Yes, it is Europe, from the Atlantic to the
Urals, it is Europe, it is the whole of Europe,
that will decide the fate of the world.
Charles de Gaulle 1890–1970: speech to the
people of Strasbourg, 23 November 1959

15 Without Britain Europe would remain only
a torso.
Ludwig Erhard 1897–1977: remark on West
German television, 27 May 1962

16 It means the end of a thousand years of
history.
on a European federation
Hugh Gaitskell 1906–63: speech at Labour Party
Conference, 3 October 1962

17 'We went in,' he said, 'to screw the French
by splitting them off from the Germans. The
French went in to protect their inefficient
farmers from commercial competition. The
Germans went in to cleanse themselves of
genocide and apply for readmission to the
human race.'
on the European Community
Jonathan Lynn 1943– and **Antony Jay** 1930– :
Yes, Minister (1982) vol. 2

18 In the eighteenth and nineteenth centuries
you weren't considered cultured unless you
made the European tour, and so it
should be.
Edward Heath 1916– : in *Observer* 18
November 1990

19 The policy of European integration is in
reality a question of war and peace in the
21st century.
Helmut Kohl 1930– : speech at Louvain University,
2 February 1996

20 In my lifetime all our problems have come
from mainland Europe and all the solutions
have come from the English-speaking
nations of the world.
Margaret Thatcher 1925– : in *Times* 6
October 1999

21 You're thinking of Europe as Germany and
France. I don't. I think that's old Europe.
to journalists who asked him about European
hostility to a possible war, 22 January 2003
Donald Rumsfeld 1932– : in *Independent* 21
February 2003

22 We are not on the outskirts of Europe, we
are at the centre of Europe.
view of the President of Ukraine
Viktor Yushchenko 1954– : in *Independent* 24
January 2005

Evil see **Good and Evil**

➤➤ Excellence ◄◄

see also **Perfection**

PROVERBS AND SAYINGS

1 Corruptio optimi pessima.
Latin saying, *Corruption of the best becomes the worst*; found in English from the early 17th century

2 If something sounds too good to be true, it probably is.
late 20th century saying

3 Jack of all trades and master of none.
a person who tries to master too many skills will learn none of them properly; English proverb, early 17th century; see **Ability 8, 16**

PHRASES

4 an admirable Crichton
a person who excels in all kinds of studies and pursuits, or who is noted for supreme competence; originally from James *Crichton* of Clunie (1560–85?), a Scottish prodigy of intellectual and knightly accomplishments; later in allusion to J. M. Barrie's play *The Admirable Crichton* (1902) of which the eponymous hero is a butler who takes charge when his master's family is shipwrecked on a desert island

5 the blue ribbon
the greatest distinction, the first place or prize; a ribbon of blue silk, especially that of the Order of the Garter, worn as a badge of honour; see also **Sports** 3

6 eighth wonder of the world
a particularly impressive object; something worthy to rank with the Seven Wonders of the ancient world; see **Architecture 5**

7 ne plus ultra
the furthest limit reached or attainable; the point of highest attainment, the acme or highest point of a quality; Latin = not further beyond, the supposed inscription on the Pillars of Hercules (Strait of Gibraltar) prohibiting passage by ships

8 with flying colours
with distinction. In former military parlance, *flying colours* meant having the regimental flag flying as a sign of success or victory; a conquered army usually had to *lower* (or *strike*) *its colours*

QUOTATIONS

9 Between us and excellence, the gods have placed the sweat of our brows.
Hesiod fl. *c.*700 BC: *Works and Days*

10 Nature made him, and then broke the mould.
Ludovico Ariosto 1474–1533: *Orlando Furioso* (1532); see **Originality 2**

11 The danger chiefly lies in acting well;
No crime's so great as daring to excel.
Charles Churchill 1731–64: *An Epistle to William Hogarth* (1763)

12 The best is the enemy of the good.
Voltaire 1694–1778: *Contes* (1772) 'La Begueule'; derived from an Italian proverb

13 The pretension is nothing; the performance every thing. A good apple is better than an insipid peach.
Leigh Hunt 1784–1859: *The Story of Rimini* (1832 ed.)

14 The best is the best, though a hundred judges have declared it so.
Arthur Quiller-Couch 1863–1944: *Oxford Book of English Verse* (1900) preface

15 The dullard's envy of brilliant men is always assuaged by the suspicion that they will come to a bad end.
Max Beerbohm 1872–1956: *Zuleika Dobson* (1911)

16 The best lack all conviction, while the worst
Are full of passionate intensity.
W. B. Yeats 1865–1939: 'The Second Coming' (1921)

17 There's only one real sin, and that is to persuade oneself that the second-best is anything but the second-best.
Doris Lessing 1919– : *Golden Notebook* (1962)

18 I'm not the greatest. I'm the best available.
of his election as Canadian Conservative leader
Joe Clark 1939– : in *Maclean's* 21 February 1977

19 You don't look tall if you surround yourself by short grasses.
on Iain Duncan Smith
Michael Portillo 1953– : in *Independent* 22 February 2003

⟶ Excess and Moderation ⟵

PROVERBS AND SAYINGS

1 Do not add legs to the snake after you have finished drawing it.
advising against making superfluous and undesirable additions; Chinese proverb

2 Enough is as good as a feast.
used as a warning against overindulgence, or overdoing something; English proverb, late 14th century

3 Enough is enough.
originally used as an expression of content or satisfaction, but now more usually employed as a reprimand, warning someone against persisting in an inappropriate or excessive course of action; English proverb, mid 16th century

4 The half is better than the whole.
advising economy or restraint; English proverb, mid 16th century, from Hesiod *Works and Days* 'The half is greater than the whole'

5 It is the last straw that breaks the camel's back.
the addition of one quite minor problem may prove crushing to someone who is already overburdened; English proverb, mid 17th century; see **Crises** 7

6 Keep no more cats than will catch mice.
recommending efficiency and the ethic of steady work to justify one's place; English proverb, late 17th century

7 The last drop makes the cup run over.
in which the addition of something in itself quite minor causes an excess; English proverb, mid 17th century

8 Less is more.
something simple often has more effect; English proverb, mid 19th century; see **Architecture** 17

9 Moderation in all things.
English proverb, mid 19th century, from Hesiod *Works and Days* 'Observe due measure; moderation is best in all things'; see 11 below

10 The pitcher will go to the well once too often.
one should not repeat a risky action too often, or push one's luck too far; English proverb, mid 14th century

11 There is measure in all things.
English proverb, late 14th century; see 9 above

12 You can have too much of a good thing.
excess even of something which is good in itself can be damaging; English proverb, late 15th century

PHRASES

13 break a butterfly on a wheel
use unnecessary force in destroying something fragile; *break on the wheel* = fracture the bones of or dislocate on a wheel as a form of punishment or torture; from Pope: see **Futility** 21

14 corn in Egypt
a plentiful supply; from the Bible (Genesis) 'Behold, I have heard that there is corn in Egypt: get you down thither and buy for us from thence'

15 embarras de richesse(s)
a superfluity of something, more than one needs or wants; French = embarrassment of riches, from *L'embarras des richesses* (1726), title of comedy by Abbé d'Allainval

16 gild the lily
embellish excessively, add ornament where none is needed; from alteration of Shakespeare: see 25 below

17 the golden mean
the avoidance of extremes, moderation; from the Roman poet Horace (65–8 BC) *Odes* 'Someone who loves the golden mean'

18 the Matthew principle
the principle that more will be given to those who already have; after the Bible (Matthew) 'Unto every one that hath shall be given, and he shall have abundance'

19 pile Ossa upon Pelion
add further problems to an existing difficulty; from Virgil 'three times they endeavoured to pile Ossa on Pelion, no less, and to roll leafy Olympus on top of Ossa', referring to the Greek legend of how the giants used the Thessalian mountains of Ossa and Pelion in an attempt to scale the heavens and overthrow the gods

QUOTATIONS

20 Nothing in excess.
Anonymous: inscribed on the temple of Apollo at Delphi, and variously ascribed to the Seven Wise Men

21 May temperance befriend me, the gods' most lovely gift.
Euripides c.485–c.406 BC: *Medea*

22 You will go most safely by the middle way.
Ovid 43–c.17: *Metamorphoses*

23 Because thou art lukewarm, and neither cold nor hot, I will spew thee out of my mouth.
Bible: Revelation

24 To many, total abstinence is easier than perfect moderation.
St Augustine of Hippo AD 354–430: *On the Good of Marriage* (AD 401)

25 To gild refinèd gold, to paint the lily . . . Is wasteful and ridiculous excess.
William Shakespeare 1564–1616: *King John* (1591–8); see 16 above

26 By God, Mr Chairman, at this moment I stand astonished at my own moderation!
Lord Clive 1725–74: reply during Parliamentary cross-examination, 1773; G. R. Gleig *The Life of Robert, First Lord Clive* (1848)

27 I know many have been taught to think that moderation, in a case like this, is a sort of treason.
Edmund Burke 1729–97: *Letter to the Sheriffs of Bristol* (1777)

28 The road of excess leads to the palace of wisdom.
William Blake 1757–1827: *The Marriage of Heaven and Hell* (1790–3) 'Proverbs of Hell'

29 Above all, gentlemen, not the slightest zeal.
Charles-Maurice de Talleyrand 1754–1838: P. Chasles *Voyages d'un critique à travers la vie et les livres* (1868)

30 Our life is frittered away by detail . . . Simplify, simplify.
Henry David Thoreau 1817–62: *Walden* (1854)

31 Moderation is a fatal thing, Lady Hunstanton. Nothing succeeds like excess.
Oscar Wilde 1854–1900: *A Woman of No Importance* (1893)

32 Fanaticism consists in redoubling your effort when you have forgotten your aim.
George Santayana 1863–1952: *The Life of Reason* (1905)

33 Up to a point, Lord Copper.
meaning no
Evelyn Waugh 1903–66: *Scoop* (1938)

34 We know what happens to people who stay in the middle of the road. They get run down.
Aneurin Bevan 1897–1960: in *Observer* 6 December 1953

35 I would remind you that extremism in the defence of liberty is no vice! And let me remind you also that moderation in the pursuit of justice is no virtue!
Barry Goldwater 1909–98: accepting the presidential nomination, 16 July 1964

36 There's nothing in the middle of the road but yellow stripes and dead armadillos.
Jim Hightower 1943– : attributed, 1984

Excuses see **Apology and Excuses**

➤➤ Experience ◅◅

see also **Maturity**

PROVERBS AND SAYINGS

1 **Appetite comes with eating.**
desire or facility increases as an activity proceeds; English proverb, mid 17th century

2 **A burnt child dreads the fire.**
the memory of past hurt may act as a safeguard in the future; English proverb, mid 13th century

3 **Experience is a comb which fate gives a man when his hair is all gone.**
American proverb, mid 20th century; see **Wars** 28

4 **Experience is the best teacher.**
sometimes used with the implication that learning by experience may be painful; English proverb, mid 16th century; see 18 below

5 **Experience is the father of wisdom.**
real understanding of something comes only from direct experience of it; English proverb, mid 16th century

6 **Experience keeps a dear school.**
lessons learned from experience can be painful; English proverb, mid 18th century

7 Live and learn.
often as a resigned or rueful comment on a disagreeable experience; English proverb, early 17th century

8 Once bitten, twice shy.
someone who has suffered an injury will in the future be very cautious of the cause; English proverb, mid 19th century; see **Caution** 19

9 Some folks speak from experience; others, from experience, don't speak.
American proverb, mid 20th century

10 They that live longest, see most.
often used to comment on the experience of old age; English proverb, early 17th century

11 Walking ten thousand miles is better than reading ten thousand books.
theoretical knowledge must be consolidated by practical experience; Chinese proverb, compare **Knowledge** 11

12 You cannot catch old birds with chaff.
the wise and experienced are not easily fooled; English proverb, late 15th century: see **Deception** 5

13 You cannot put an old head on young shoulders.
you cannot expect someone who is young and inexperienced to show the wisdom and maturity of an older person; English proverb, late 16th century

14 You should make a point of trying every experience once, excepting incest and folk-dancing.
20th century saying, repeated by Arnold Bax in *Farewell My Youth* (1943), quoting 'a sympathetic Scot'

PHRASES

15 babes in the wood
inexperienced people in a situation calling for experience, with reference to an old ballad *The Children in the Wood*, in which a wicked uncle who wishes to steal the children's inheritance causes them to be abandoned in a forest where they die

16 walk before one can run
understand elementary points before proceeding to anything more difficult, from the proverb: see **Patience** 19

QUOTATIONS

17 *Experto credite.*
Trust one who has gone through it.
Virgil 70–19 BC: *Aeneid*

18 *Experientia docuit.*
Experience has taught.
commonly quoted as '*Experientia docet* [experience teaches]'
Tacitus c.AD 56–after 117: *The Histories*; see 4 above, 26 below

19 No man's knowledge here can go beyond his experience.
John Locke 1632–1704: *An Essay concerning Human Understanding* (1690)

20 Courts and camps are the only places to learn the world in.
Lord Chesterfield 1694–1773: *Letters to his Son* (1774) 2 October 1747

21 The courtiers who surround him have forgotten nothing and learnt nothing.
of Louis XVIII, at the time of the Declaration of Verona, September 1795
Charles François du Périer Dumouriez 1739–1823: *Examen impartial d'un Écrit intitulé Déclaration de Louis XVIII* (1795); quoted by Napoleon in his Declaration to the French on his return from Elba; a similar saying is attributed to Talleyrand

22 He went like one that hath been stunned, And is of sense forlorn:

A sadder and a wiser man,
He rose the morrow morn.
Samuel Taylor Coleridge 1772–1834: 'The Rime of the Ancient Mariner' (1798)

23 The light which experience gives is a lantern on the stern, which shines only on the waves behind us!
Samuel Taylor Coleridge 1772–1834: *Table Talk* (1835) 18 December 1831

24 The years teach much which the days never know.
Ralph Waldo Emerson 1803–82: *Essays. Second Series* (1844) 'Experience'

25 Grace is given of God, but knowledge is bought in the market.
Arthur Hugh Clough 1819–61: *The Bothie of Tober-na-Vuolich* (1848)

26 Experientia does it—as papa used to say.
said by Mrs Micawber
Charles Dickens 1812–70: *David Copperfield* (1850); see 18 above

27 *in his case against Ruskin, replying to the question, 'For two days' labour, you ask two hundred guineas?':*
No, I ask it for the knowledge of a lifetime.
James McNeill Whistler 1834–1903: D. C. Seitz *Whistler Stories* (1913)

28 Experience is the name every one gives to their mistakes.
Oscar Wilde 1854–1900: *Lady Windermere's Fan* (1892)

29 All experience is an arch to build upon.
Henry Brooks Adams 1838–1918: *The Education of Henry Adams* (1907)

30 Experience is not what happens to a man; it is what a man does with what happens to him.
Aldous Huxley 1894–1963: *Texts and Pretexts* (1932)

31 I've been things and seen places.
Mae West 1892–1980: *I'm No Angel* (1933 film)

32 It's a funny old world—a man's lucky if he gets out of it alive.
Walter de Leon and **Paul M. Jones**: *You're Telling Me* (1934 film); spoken by W. C. Fields

33 Experience isn't interesting till it begins to repeat itself—in fact, till it does that, it hardly *is* experience.
Elizabeth Bowen 1899–1973: *Death of the Heart* (1938)

34 We had the experience but missed the meaning.
T. S. Eliot 1888–1965: *Four Quartets* 'The Dry Salvages' (1941)

35 I've looked at life from both sides now,
From win and lose and still somehow
It's life's illusions I recall;
I really don't know life at all.
Joni Mitchell 1945– : 'Both Sides Now' (1967 song)

36 Education is when you read the fine print; experience is what you get when you don't.
Pete Seeger 1919– : L. Botts *Loose Talk* (1980)

37 Damaged people are dangerous. They know they can survive.
Josephine Hart: *Damage* (1991)

✈ Exploration ✦

see also **Travel**

PROVERBS AND SAYINGS

1 **Here be dragons.**
alluding to a traditional indication of early map-makers that a region was unexplored and potentially dangerous

PHRASES

2 **to boldly go**
explore freely, unhindered by fear of the unknown; from the brief given to the *Enterprise* in the television series *Star Trek*, written by Gene Roddenberry (from 1966), 'These are the voyages of the starship Enterprise. Its five-year mission . . . to boldly go where no man has gone before'

QUOTATIONS

3 Now the boundary of Britain is revealed, and everything unknown is held to be glorious.
reporting the speech of a British leader, Calgacus
Tacitus c.AD 56–after 117: *Agricola*

4 There is no land unhabitable nor sea innavigable.
Robert Thorne d. 1527: Richard Hakluyt *The Principal Navigations, Voyages, and Discoveries of the English Nation* (1589)

5 They are ill discoverers that think there is no land, when they can see nothing but sea.
Francis Bacon 1561–1626: *The Advancement of Learning* (1605)

6 So geographers, in Afric-maps,
With savage-pictures fill their gaps;
And o'er unhabitable downs
Place elephants for want of towns.
Jonathan Swift 1667–1745: 'On Poetry' (1733)

7 Go West, young man, go West!
John L. B. Soule 1815–91: in *Terre Haute* [Indiana] *Express* (1851); see **America** 20

8 It was a melancholy day for human nature when that stupid Lord Anson, after beating about for three years, found himself again at Greenwich. The circumnavigation of our globe was accomplished, but the illimitable

was annihilated and a fatal blow [dealt] to all imagination.
Benjamin Disraeli 1804–81: written 1860, in *Reminiscences* (ed. H. and M. Swartz, 1975)

9 [Faust] never reached a place where he wanted to 'remain'. I cannot even glimpse anywhere worth the attempt.
Fridtjof Nansen 1861–1930: diary, 1909; Alistair Horne (ed.) *Telling Lives* (2000)

10 Why do people so love to wander? I think the civilized parts of the world will suffice for me in the future.
Mary Cassatt 1844–1926: letter to Louisine Havemeyer, 11 February 1911

11 What on earth good accrues from going to the North and South Poles? I never could understand—no one is going there when they can go to Monte Carlo!
John Arbuthnot Fisher 1841–1920: Roland Huntford *The Last Place on Earth* (2000)

12 Polar exploration is at once the cleanest and most isolated way of having a bad time which has been devised.
Apsley Cherry-Garrard 1882–1959: *The Worst Journey in the World* (1922)

13 We shall not cease from exploration
And the end of all our exploring
Will be to arrive where we started
And know the place for the first time.
T. S. Eliot 1888–1965: *Four Quartets* 'Little Gidding' (1942)

14 For a joint scientific and geographical piece of organization, give me Scott; for a Winter Journey, Wilson; for a dash to the pole and nothing else, Amundsen: and if I am in the devil of a hole and want to get out of it, give me Shackleton every time.
Apsley Cherry-Garrard 1882–1959: F. A. Worsley *Shackleton's Boat Journey* (1999)

15 Slim [Lindbergh] flew through miserable weather and stretched science and the art of navigation to find Le Bourget. We could see our destination throughout our entire voyage.
Neil Armstrong 1930– : accepting Lindbergh Award, 10 May 1997

Extravagance see **Thrift and Extravagance**

Fact see **Hypothesis and Fact**

Failure see **Success and Failure**

➵➵ Faith ➵➵

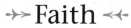

see also **Belief**

PROVERBS AND SAYINGS

1 **Faith will move mountains.**
with the help of faith something naturally impossible can be achieved; English proverb, late 19th century, in allusion to the Bible: see 3 below

PHRASES

2 **born-again**
relating to or denoting a person who has converted to a personal faith in Christ, alluding to the Bible (John) 'Except a man be born again, he cannot see the kingdom of God'; figuratively, newly converted to and very enthusiastic about an idea or cause; see 8 below

QUOTATIONS

3 If ye have faith as a grain of mustard seed, ye shall say unto this mountain, Remove hence to yonder place; and it shall remove.
Bible: St Matthew; see 1 above

4 Faith without works is dead.
Bible: James

5 The confidence and faith of the heart alone
make both God and an idol.
Martin Luther 1483–1546: *Large Catechism* (1529)
'The First Commandment'

6 Be of good comfort Master Ridley, and play
the man. We shall this day light such a
candle by God's grace in England, as (I trust)
shall never be put out.
prior to being burned for heresy, 16 October 1555
Hugh Latimer 1485–1555: John Foxe *Actes and
Monuments* (1570 ed.)

7 A man with God is always in the majority.
John Knox 1505–72: inscription on the Reformation
Monument, Geneva

8 At last, by singing and repeating
enthusiastic amorous hymns, and
ignorantly applying particular texts of
scripture, I got my imagination to the
proper pitch, and thus was I born again in
an instant.
James Lackington 1746–1815: *Memoirs* (1792 ed.);
see 2 above

9 It is necessary to the happiness of man that
he be mentally faithful to himself. Infidelity
does not consist in believing, or in
disbelieving, it consists in professing to
believe what one does not believe.
Thomas Paine 1737–1809: *The Age of Reason* pt. 1
(1794)

10 The faith that stands on authority is not
faith.
Ralph Waldo Emerson 1803–82: *Essays* (1841)
'The Over-Soul'

11 The Sea of Faith
Was once, too, at the full, and round earth's
shore
Lay like the folds of a bright girdle furled.
But now I only hear

Its melancholy, long, withdrawing roar.
Matthew Arnold 1822–88: 'Dover Beach' (1867)

12 You can do very little with faith, but you
can do nothing without it.
Samuel Butler 1835–1902: *Notebooks* (1912)
ch. 20

13 The great act of faith is when a man decides
he is not God.
Oliver Wendell Holmes Jr. 1841–1935: letter to
William James, 24 March 1907

14 And I said to the man who stood at the gate
of the year: 'Give me a light that I may tread
safely into the unknown.'
And he replied:
'Go out into the darkness and put your
hand into the Hand of God. That shall be to
you better than light and safer than a
known way.'
quoted by King George VI in his Christmas
broadcast, 25 December 1939
Minnie Louise Haskins 1875–1957: *Desert* (1908)
'God Knows'

15 Booth died blind and still by faith he trod,
Eyes still dazzled by the ways of God.
Vachel Lindsay 1879–1931: 'General William Booth
Enters into Heaven' (1913)

16 A miracle, my friend, is an event which
creates faith. That is the purpose and nature
of miracles....Frauds deceive. An event
which creates faith does not deceive:
therefore it is not a fraud, but a miracle.
George Bernard Shaw 1856–1950: *Saint Joan*
(1924)

17 A faith is something you die for; a doctrine
is something you kill for: there is all the
difference in the world.
Tony Benn 1925– : in *Observer* 16 April 1989

⇢⇢ Fame ⇠⇠

see also **Reputation**

PROVERBS AND SAYINGS

1 **More people know Tom Fool than Tom
Fool knows.**
English proverb, mid 17th century; *Tom Fool* was a
name given to the part of the fool in a play or morris
dance

2 **Who he?**
an editorial interjection after the name of a
(supposedly) little-known person, associated
particularly with Harold Ross (1892–1951), editor of
the *New Yorker*; repopularized in Britain by the
satirical magazine *Private Eye*

PHRASES

3 backing into the limelight
apparently shrinking from attention while actually
seeking it; *limelight* = an intense white light obtained
by heating lime, formerly used in theatres;
figuratively, the focus of public attention. The phrase
is particularly associated with T. E. Lawrence
(1888–1935), and has been ascribed by oral tradition
to Lord Berners. However, see 21 below

4 famous for fifteen minutes
enjoying a brief period of fame before fading back
into obscurity; coined by the American artist Andy
Warhol: see 26 below

5 a legend in their own lifetime
a very famous or notorious person; someone whose
fame is comparable to that of a hero of legend or
about whom similar stories are told; see 29 below

6 nine days' wonder
a person who or thing which is briefly famous

7 a tall poppy
a privileged or distinguished person; perhaps
originally in allusion to the legendary Roman king
Tarquin striking the heads off poppies in his garden
to demonstrate how to treat the leaders of a
conquered city

QUOTATIONS

8 Let us now praise famous men, and our
fathers that begat us.
Bible: Ecclesiasticus

9 Cattle die, kinsmen die,
the self must also die;
but glory never dies,
for the man who is able to achieve it.
Anonymous: *Hávamál* ('Sayings of the High One'),
c.10th century

10 So long as men can breathe, or eyes can see,
So long lives this, and this gives life to thee.
William Shakespeare 1564–1616: sonnet 18

11 Fame is like a river, that beareth up things
light and swollen, and drowns things
weighty and solid.
Francis Bacon 1561–1626: *Essays* (1625) 'Of Praise'

12 Fame is the spur that the clear spirit doth
raise
(That last infirmity of noble mind)
To scorn delights, and live laborious days;
John Milton 1608–74: 'Lycidas' (1638)

13 To be nameless in worthy deeds exceeds an
infamous history.
Thomas Browne 1605–82: *Hydriotaphia* (Urn
Burial, 1658)

14 Seven wealthy towns contend for
HOMER dead
Through which the living HOMER begged
his bread.
Anonymous: epilogue to *Aesop at Tunbridge; or, a
Few Selected Fables in Verse By No Person of Quality*
(1698)

15 Full many a flower is born to blush unseen,
And waste its sweetness on the desert air.
Thomas Gray 1716–71: *Elegy Written in a Country
Churchyard* (1751)

16 Every man has a lurking wish to appear
considerable in his native place.
Samuel Johnson 1709–84: letter to Joshua
Reynolds, 17 July 1771; see **Familiarity** 15

17 I awoke one morning and found myself
famous.
on the instantaneous success of *Childe Harold*
Lord Byron 1788–1824: Thomas Moore *Letters and
Journals of Lord Byron* (1830)

18 The deed is all, the glory nothing.
Johann Wolfgang von Goethe 1749–1832: *Faust*
pt. 2 (1832) 'Hochgebirg'

19 Martyrdom . . . the only way in which a
man can become famous without ability.
George Bernard Shaw 1856–1950: *The Devil's
Disciple* (1901)

20 I don't care what you say about me, as long
as you say *something* about me, and as long
as you spell my name right.
said to a newspaperman in 1912
George M. Cohan 1878–1942: John McCabe
George M. Cohan (1973)

21 You always hide just in the middle of the
limelight.
to T. E. Lawrence, who had complained of Press
attention
George Bernard Shaw 1856–1950: Charles
Kessler *The Diaries of a Cosmopolitan 1918-1937*
(1971) 14 November 1929; see 3 above

22 Now who is responsible for this work of
development on which so much depends?
To whom must the praise be given? To the
boys in the back rooms. They do not sit in
the limelight. But they are the men who do
the work.
Lord Beaverbrook 1879–1964: in *Listener* 27
March 1941; see **Science** 3

23 The celebrity is a person who is known for
his well-knownness.
Daniel J. Boorstin 1914– : *The Image* (1961)

24 I'm world famous, Dr Parks said, all over
Canada.
Mordecai Richler 1931–2001: *The Incomparable
Atuk* (1963)

25 There's no such thing as bad publicity except your own obituary.
Brendan Behan 1923–64: Dominic Behan *My Brother Brendan* (1965); see **Advertising 1**

26 In the future everybody will be world famous for fifteen minutes.
Andy Warhol 1927–87: *Andy Warhol* (1968); see 4 above

27 Celebrity is a mask that eats into the face.
John Updike 1932– : *Self-Consciousness: Memoirs* (1989)

28 The best fame is a writer's fame: it's enough to get a table at a good restaurant, but not enough that you get interrupted when you eat.
Fran Lebowitz 1946– : in *Observer* 30 May 1993 'Sayings of the Week'

29 She's not a legend. She's a beginner.
on Nicole Kidman
Lauren Bacall 1924– : in *Independent* 9 September 2004; see 5 above

30 After a while you learn that privacy is something you can sell, but you can't buy it back.
Bob Dylan 1941– : *Chronicles Volume One* (2004)

Familiarity

PROVERBS AND SAYINGS

1 **Better the devil you know than the devil you don't know.**
understanding of the nature of a danger may give one an advantage, and is preferable to something which is completely unknown, and which may well be worse; English proverb, mid 19th century

2 **Better wed over the mixen than over the moor.**
it is better to marry a neighbour than a stranger (a *mixen* is a midden); English proverb, early 17th century

3 **Blue are the hills that are far away.**
a distant view lends enchantment; English proverb, 19th century

4 **Come live with me and you'll know me.**
the implication is that only by living with a person will you learn their real nature; English proverb, early 20th century

5 **Familiarity breeds contempt.**
we value least the things which are most familiar; English proverb, late 14th century; see 22 below

6 **Good fences make good neighbours.**
this reduces the possibility of disputes over adjoining land; English proverb, mid 17th century

7 **If you lie down with dogs, you will get up with fleas.**
asserting that human failings, such as dishonesty and foolishness, are contagious; English proverb, late 16th century (earlier in Latin)

8 **Local ginger is not hot.**
modern saying, said to derive from a Chinese proverb; see 11 below

9 **A man is known by the company he keeps.**
originally used as a moral maxim or exhortation in the context of preparation for marriage; English proverb, mid 16th century

10 **No man is a hero to his valet.**
English proverb, mid 18th century; see **Heroes 5**

11 **A prophet is not without honour save in his own country.**
English proverb, late 15th century, from the Bible: see 8 above, 15 below

12 **There is nothing new under the sun.**
English proverb, late 16th century, from the Bible; see **Earth 7, Progress 6**

13 **What a neighbour gets is not lost.**
one is likely to benefit from the gain of a neighbour or friend; English proverb, mid 16th century

14 **You should know a man seven years before you stir his fire.**
used as a caution against over-familiarity on slight acquaintance; English proverb, early 19th century

QUOTATIONS

15 A prophet is not without honour, save in his own country, and in his own house.
Bible: St Matthew; see 11 above, **Fame 16**

16 There is nothing that God hath established in a constant course of nature, and which therefore is done every day, but would seem

a Miracle, and exercise our admiration, if it were done but once.
John Donne 1572–1631: *LXXX Sermons* (1640) Easter Day, 25 March 1627

17 Old friends are best. King James used to call for his old shoes; they were easiest for his feet.
John Selden 1584–1654: *Table Talk* (1689) 'Friends'

18 We can scarcely hate any one that we know.
William Hazlitt 1778–1830: *Table Talk* (1822) 'On Criticism'

19 Think you, if Laura had been Petrarch's wife, He would have written sonnets all his life?
Lord Byron 1788–1824: *Don Juan* (1819–24)

20 A maggot must be born i' the rotten cheese to like it.
George Eliot 1819–80: *Adam Bede* (1859)

21 There are no conditions of life to which a man cannot get accustomed, especially if he sees them accepted by everyone about him.
Leo Tolstoy 1828–1910: *Anna Karenina* (1875–7)

22 Familiarity breeds contempt—and children.
Mark Twain 1835–1910: *Notebooks* (1935); see 5 above

23 Only the unknown frightens men. But once a man has faced the unknown, that terror becomes known.
Antoine de Saint-Exupéry 1900–44: *Wind, Sand and Stars* (1939)

24 I've grown accustomed to the trace Of something in the air; Accustomed to her face.
Alan Jay Lerner 1918–86: 'I've Grown Accustomed to her Face' (1956 song)

25 The mind loves the unknown. It loves images whose meaning is unknown, since the meaning of the mind itself is unknown.
René Magritte 1898–1967: Suzy Gablik *Magritte* (1970)

⇥ The Family ⇤

see also **Child Care, Children, Parents**

PROVERBS AND SAYINGS

1 **The apple never falls far from the tree.**
family characteristics will assert themselves; English proverb, mid 19th century

2 **Blood is thicker than water.**
in the end family ties will always count; English proverb, early 19th century; see 21 below

3 **Blood will tell.**
family characteristics or heredity will in the end be dominant; English proverb, mid 19th century

4 **The child of a frog is a frog.**
Japanese proverb

5 **Children are certain cares, but uncertain comforts.**
emphasizing the continuing responsibility and anxiety of parenthood; English proverb, mid 17th century

6 **Dragons beget dragons, phoenixes beget phoenixes, and burglars' children learn how to break into houses.**
Chinese proverb; see 8 below

7 **I belong by blood relationship; therefore I am.**
on the importance of family ties in a sense of identity; African proverb

8 **Like father, like son.**
often used to call attention to similarities in behaviour; English proverb, mid 14th century

9 **Like mother, like daughter.**
English proverb, early 14th century; the ultimate allusion is to the Bible (Ezekiel), 'As is the mother, so is her daughter'

10 **My brother and I against my cousin and my cousin and I against the stranger.**
Arab proverb; compare **Enemies** 2

11 **The shoemaker's son always goes barefoot.**
the family of a skilled or knowledgeable person are often the last to benefit from their expertise; English proverb, mid 16th century

PHRASES

12 black sheep
a member of a family or group who is regarded as a disgrace to it

13 a chip off the old block
a child resembling a parent or ancestor, especially in character; *chip* = something forming a portion of, or derived from, a larger or more important thing, of which it retains the characteristic qualities; see **Speeches** 11

QUOTATIONS

14 Thy wife shall be as the fruitful vine: upon the walls of thine house.
Thy children like the olive-branches: round about thy table.
Bible: Psalm 128

15 A little more than kin, and less than kind.
William Shakespeare 1564–1616: *Hamlet* (1601)

16 He that hath wife and children hath given hostages to fortune; for they are impediments to great enterprises, either of virtue or mischief.
Francis Bacon 1561–1626: *Essays* (1625) 'Of Marriage and the Single Life'

17 We begin our public affections in our families. No cold relation is a zealous citizen.
Edmund Burke 1729–97: *Reflections on the Revolution in France* (1790)

18 If a man's character is to be abused, say what you will, there's nobody like a relation to do the business.
William Makepeace Thackeray 1811–63: *Vanity Fair* (1847–8)

19 All happy families resemble one another, but each unhappy family is unhappy in its own way.
Leo Tolstoy 1828–1910: *Anna Karenina* (1875–7)

20 Family! . . . the home of all social evil, a charitable institution for comfortable women, an anchorage for house-fathers, and a hell for children.
August Strindberg 1849–1912: *The Son of a Servant* (1886)

21 I detest collaterals. Blood may be thicker than water, but it is also a great deal nastier.
Edith Œ Somerville 1858–1949 and **Martin Ross** 1862–1915: *Some Experiences of an Irish R.M.* (1899)

22 The awe and dread with which the untutored savage contemplates his mother-in-law are amongst the most familiar facts of anthropology.
James George Frazer 1854–1941: *The Golden Bough* (2nd ed., 1900)

23 I am the family face;
Flesh perishes, I live on.
Thomas Hardy 1840–1928: 'Heredity' (1917)

24 One would be in less danger
From the wiles of the stranger
If one's own kin and kith
Were more fun to be with.
Ogden Nash 1902–71: 'Family Court' (1931)

25 Believe me, family solidarity is after all the only good thing. I have been deprived of it, so I know.
Marie Curie 1867–1934: to her sister Bronia in 1932; Eve Curie *Madame Curie* (1937)

26 The family—that dear octopus from whose tentacles we never quite escape.
Dodie Smith 1896–1990: *Dear Octopus* (1938)

27 It is no use telling me that there are bad aunts and good aunts. At the core, they are all alike. Sooner or later, out pops the cloven hoof.
P. G. Wodehouse 1881–1975: *The Code of the Woosters* (1938); see **Good and Evil** 9

28 Far from being the basis of the good society, the family, with its narrow privacy and tawdry secrets, is the source of all our discontents.
Edmund Leach 1910–89: BBC Reith Lectures, 1967

29 The truth is that it is not the sins of the fathers that descend unto the third generation, but the sorrows of the mothers.
Marilyn French 1929– : *Her Mother's Daughter* (1987); see **Crime** 18

30 Having one child makes you a parent; having two you are a referee.
David Frost 1939– : in *Independent* 16 September 1989

31 [It is] time to turn our attention to pressing challenges like . . . how to make American families more like the Waltons and a little bit less like the Simpsons.
George Bush 1924– : speech, Neenah, Wisconsin, 27 July 1992

Farming

PROVERBS AND SAYINGS

1 **Candlemas day, put beans in the clay; put candles and candlesticks away.**
recording the tradition that the feast of Candlemas, on 2 February, was the time for planting beans; English proverb, late 17th century

2 **One for the mouse, one for the crow, one to rot, one to grow.**
traditionally used when sowing seed, and enumerating the ways in which some of the crop will be lost leaving a proportion to germinate; English proverb, mid 19th century

3 **On Saint Thomas the Divine kill all turkeys, geese and swine.**
21 December, the traditional feast-day in the Western Church of St Thomas the Apostle, taken as marking the season at which domestic animals not kept through the winter were to be slaughtered; English proverb, mid 18th century

4 **Three acres and a cow.**
regarded as the requirement for self-sufficiency; late 19th century political slogan

PHRASES

5 **first fruits**
the first agricultural produce of a season, especially when given as an offering to God; originally alluding to the Bible (Numbers), 'the first fruits of them which they shall offer unto the Lord'

QUOTATIONS

6 A farm is like a man—however great the income, if there is extravagance but little is left.
Cato the Elder 234–149 BC: *On Agriculture*

7 For of all gainful professions, nothing is better, nothing more pleasing, nothing more delightful, nothing better becomes a well-bred man than agriculture.
Cicero 106–43 BC: *De Officiis*

8 O farmers excessively fortunate if only they recognized their blessings!
Virgil 70–19 BC: *Georgics*

9 Cultivators of the earth are the most valuable citizens. They are the most vigorous, the most independent, the most virtuous, and they are tied to their country and wedded to its liberty and interests by the most lasting bands.
Thomas Jefferson 1743–1826: letter to John Jay, 23 August 1785

10 Agriculture is the foundation of manufactures; since the productions of nature are the materials of art.
Edward Gibbon 1737–94: *The Decline and Fall of the Roman Empire* (1776–88)

11 We plough the fields, and scatter
The good seed on the land,
But it is fed and watered
By God's almighty hand.
Jane Montgomery Campbell 1817–78: 'We plough the fields, and scatter' (1861 hymn)

12 Our salvation can only come through the farmer. Neither the lawyers, nor the doctors, nor the rich landlords are going to secure it.
Mahatma Gandhi 1869–1948: speech, Benares, 4 February 1916

13 The Farmer will never be happy again;
He carries his heart in his boots;
For either the rain is destroying his grain
Or the drought is destroying his roots.
A. P. Herbert 1890–1971: 'The Farmer' (1922)

14 Farming looks mighty easy when your plough is a pencil, and you're a thousand miles from the corn field.
Dwight D. Eisenhower 1890–1969: speech, Peoria, 25 September 1956

15 Death may be inevitable but cruelty is not. If we must eat meat, then we must ensure that the animals we kill for our food live the best possible lives before they die.
Desmond Morris 1928– : *The Animal Contract* (1990)

➤➤Fashion ◄◄

see also **Dress**

PHRASES

1 all the world and his wife
everyone with pretensions to fashion, from Swift
Polite Conversation (1738) 'Pray, Madam, who were
the Company? . . . Why, there was all the world, and
his wife'

2 flavour of the month
the current fashion; a person who or thing which is
especially popular at a given time; a marketing
phrase used in US ice-cream parlours in the 1940s,
when a particular flavour of ice-cream would be
singled out for the month for special promotion

3 the new black
something which is suddenly extremely popular or
fashionable, from its use to describe a colour in such
vogue with clothing designers as to rival the
traditional role of black as a staple or background
colour for garments; compare 13 below

4 radical chic
the fashionable affectation of radical left-wing views
or an associated style of dress or life, coined by Tom
Wolfe: see 11 below

QUOTATIONS

5 The women come to see the show, they
come to make a show themselves.
Ovid 43–c.17: *Ars Amatoria*

6 It is charming to totter into vogue.
Horace Walpole 1717–97: letter to George Selwyn,
2 December 1765

7 A little of what you call frippery is very
necessary towards looking like the rest of
the world.
Abigail Adams 1744–1818: letter to John Adams, 1
May 1780

8 Fashion, though Folly's child, and guide of
fools,
Rules e'en the wisest, and in learning rules.
George Crabbe 1754–1832: 'The Library' (1808)

9 Fashion is something barbarous, for it
produces innovation without reason and
imitation without benefit.
George Santayana 1863–1952: *The Life of Reason*
(1905)

10 You cannot be both fashionable and first-
rate.
Logan Pearsall Smith 1865–1946: *Afterthoughts*
(1931) 'In the World'

11 Radical Chic . . . is only radical in Style; in its
heart it is part of Society and its
tradition—Politics, like Rock, Pop, and
Camp, has its uses.
Tom Wolfe 1931– : in *New York* 8 June 1970; see 4
above

12 Fashion isn't made to be canned. Fashion in
cans becomes quickly obsolete.
Coco Chanel 1883–1971: A. Madsen *Coco Chanel*
(1990)

13 Pink is the navy blue of India.
Diana Vreeland 1903–89: in *Rolling Stone* 11
August 1977; compare 3 above

14 Fashion is more usually a gentle progression
of revisited ideas.
Bruce Oldfield 1950– : in *Independent* 9
September 1989

15 I never cared for fashion much. Amusing
little seams and witty little pleats. It was the
girls I liked.
David Bailey 1938– : in *Independent* 5
November 1990

16 You dress elegant and sophisticated women,
I dress sluts.
Gianni Versace 1946–97: to Giorgio Armani,
attributed; in *Independent* 15 September 2000

17 Sometimes fashion moves from the moment
to the moment to the moment. But where is
the integrity in design?
Donna Karan 1948– : in *Detroit News*
February 2000

⊷ Fate ⊷

PROVERBS AND SAYINGS

1 **Fate can be taken by the horns, like a goat, and pushed in the right direction.**
with sufficient determination one need not be a helpless victim of fate; American proverb, mid 20th century

2 **Hanging and wiving go by destiny.**
an expression of fatalism about the course of one's life; English proverb, mid 16th century

3 **If you're born to be hanged then you'll never be drowned.**
used to qualify apparent good luck which may have an unhappy outcome; English proverb, late 16th century

4 **Man proposes, God disposes.**
often now said in consolation or resignation when plans have been disrupted; English proverb, mid 15th century

5 **The mills of God grind slowly, yet they grind exceeding small.**
English proverb, mid 17th century; the current form is from Longfellow: see **God** 18

6 **We're here
Because
We're here
Because
We're here
Because we're here.**
soldiers' song of the First World War, sung to the tune of 'Auld Lang Syne'

7 **What goes up must come down.**
commonly associated with wartime bombing and anti-aircraft shrapnel, and often used with the implication that an exhilarating rise must be followed by a fall; early 20th century saying

8 **What must be, must be.**
used to acknowledge the force of circumstances; English proverb, late 14th century

PHRASES

9 **appointment in Samarra**
an unavoidable meeting with death or fate, from a story by Somerset Maugham in the play *Sheppey* (1933), in which a man sees Death in Baghdad and flees to distant Samarra to escape, not realizing that Death had always intended to meet him that night in Samarra; see 22 below

10 **have a person's name and number on it**
(of a bullet) be destined to kill a particular person; see 18 below

11 **in the lap of the gods**
beyond human control, from Homer *The Iliad* 'It lies in the lap of the gods'; see **Chance** 19

12 **the three sisters**
the three goddesses of destiny, the Fates

QUOTATIONS

13 Canst thou bind the sweet influences of Pleiades, or loose the bands of Orion?
Bible: Job

14 Each man is the smith of his own fortune.
Appius Claudius Caecus fl. 312–279 BC: Sallust *Ad Caesarem Senem de Re Publica Oratio*; see **Self** 2

15 　　*Dis aliter visum.*
The gods thought otherwise.
Virgil 70–19 BC: *Aeneid*

16 There's a divinity that shapes our ends,
Rough-hew them how we will.
William Shakespeare 1564–1616: *Hamlet* (1601)

17 We are merely the stars' tennis-balls, struck and bandied
Which way please them.
John Webster 1580– : *The Duchess of Malfi* (1623)

18 Every bullet has its billet.
William III 1650–1702: John Wesley's diary, 6 June 1765; see 10 above

19 Must it be? It must be.
Ludwig van Beethoven 1770–1827: String Quartet in F Major, Opus 135, epigraph

20 What we call fate does not come into us from the outside, but emerges from us.
Rainer Maria Rilke 1875–1926: *Letters to a Young Poet* (1929) 12 August 1904, tr. S. Mitchell

21 There once was an old man who said,
　　'Damn!
It is borne in upon me I am
An engine that moves
In determinate grooves,
I'm not even a bus, I'm a tram.'
Maurice Evan Hare 1886–1967: 'Limerick' (1905)

22 I [Death] was astonished to see him in Baghdad, for I had an appointment with him tonight in Samarra.
W. Somerset Maugham 1874–1965: *Sheppey* (1933); see 9 above

23 Fate is not an eagle, it creeps like a rat.
Elizabeth Bowen 1899–1973: *The House in Paris* (1935)

24 I go the way that Providence dictates with the assurance of a sleepwalker.
Adolf Hitler 1889–1945: speech in Munich, 15 March 1936

25 We may become the makers of our fate when we have ceased to pose as its prophets.
Karl Popper 1902–94: *The Open Society and its Enemies* (1945)

Fear

PROVERBS AND SAYINGS

1 **Be afraid. Be very afraid.**
advertising copy for the film *The Fly* (1986)

2 **Cowards may die many times before their death.**
English proverb, late 16th century; see **Courage** 14

3 **In space no one can hear you scream.**
advertising copy for the film *Alien* (1979)

PHRASES

4 **Chicken Little**
an alarmist, a person who panics at the first sign of a problem; from the name of a character in a nursery story who repeatedly warns that the sky is falling down; see **Crises** 10

5 **freeze one's blood**
fill one with a sudden feeling of great fear or horror. The idea of the blood congealing at such a moment goes back to the late medieval period; the actual

phrase is used in *Hamlet*, when the Ghost tells his son that he 'could a tale unfold whose lightest word Would . . . freeze thy young blood.'; see **Style** 14

6 **make one's flesh creep**
frighten, horrify, or disgust, especially with dread of the supernatural; indicating that there is a physical sensation of something crawling over the skin, and causing goose-pimples; see 13 below

QUOTATIONS

7 Thou shalt not be afraid for any terror by night: nor for the arrow that flieth by day; For the pestilence that walketh in darkness: nor for the sickness that destroyeth in the noon-day.
Bible: Psalm 91

8 Letting 'I dare not' wait upon 'I would,' Like the poor cat i' the adage?
William Shakespeare 1564–1616: *Macbeth* (1606)

9 Present fears
Are less than horrible imaginings.
William Shakespeare 1564–1616: *Macbeth* (1606)

10 Every drop of ink in my pen ran cold.
Horace Walpole 1717–97: letter to George Montagu, 30 July 1752

11 No passion so effectually robs the mind of all its powers of acting and reasoning as fear.
Edmund Burke 1729–97: *On the Sublime and Beautiful* (1757)

12 Wee, sleekit, cow'rin', tim'rous beastie, O what a panic's in thy breastie!
Robert Burns 1759–96: 'To a Mouse' (1786)

13 I wants to make your flesh creep.
The Fat Boy
Charles Dickens 1812–70: *Pickwick Papers* (1837); see 6 above

14 Better be killed than frightened to death.
R. S. Surtees 1805–64: *Mr Facey Romford's Hounds* (1865)

15 It is my belief that six out of every dozen people who go out hunting are disagreeably conscious of a nervous system, and two out of six are in what is brutally called 'a blue funk'.
Edith Œ Somerville 1858–1949 and **Martin Ross** 1862–1915: *Some Experiences of an Irish R.M.* (1899)

16 The horror! The horror!
Joseph Conrad 1857–1924: *Heart of Darkness* (1902)

17 I will show you fear in a handful of dust.
T. S. Eliot 1888–1965: *The Waste Land* (1922)

18 To fear love is to fear life, and those who fear life are already three parts dead.
Bertrand Russell 1872–1970: *Marriage and Morals* (1929)

19 The only thing we have to fear is fear itself.
Franklin D. Roosevelt 1882–1945: inaugural
address, 4 March 1933

20 We must travel in the direction of our fear.
John Berryman 1914–72: 'A Point of Age' (1942)

21 Cowardice, as distinguished from panic, is
almost always simply a lack of ability to
suspend the functioning of the imagination.
Ernest Hemingway 1899–1961: *Men at War*
(1942)

22 There is no terror in a bang, only in the
anticipation of it.
Alfred Hitchcock 1899–1980: attributed

23 Terror . . . often arises from a pervasive sense
of disestablishment; that things are in the
unmaking.
Stephen King 1947– : *Danse Macabre* (1981)

⇥ Festivals and Celebrations ⇤

see also **Christmas**

PROVERBS AND SAYINGS

**1 Barnaby bright, Barnaby bright, the
longest day and the shortest night.**
in the Old Style calendar St Barnabas' Day, 11 June,
was reckoned the longest day of the year; English
proverb, mid 17th century

**2 The better the day, the better the
deed.**
frequently used to justify working on a Sunday or
Holy Day; English proverb, early 17th century

PHRASES

5 All Saints' Day
1 November, on which there is a general
commemoration of the blessed dead, sometimes
known as All Hallows Day; see 56 below

6 All Souls' Day
2 November, on which the Roman Catholic Church
makes supplications on behalf of the dead

7 April Fool's Day
the first of April; the custom of playing tricks on this
day has been observed in many countries for
hundreds of years, but its origin is unknown

8 Ash Wednesday
the first day of Lent, from the custom of marking the
foreheads of penitents with ashes on that day

9 Bastille Day
14 July, celebrated as a national holiday in France;
the date of the storming of the Bastille in 1789

10 Bonfire Night
5 November, Guy Fawkes Night; see 24 below

11 Burns Night
25 January; the annual celebration in honour of the
Scottish poet Robert *Burns* (1759–96), held
worldwide on his birthday

12 Canada Day
1 July, observed as a public holiday in Canada,
marking the day in 1867 when four of the former
colonial provinces were united under one
government as the Dominion of Canada

**3 If Saint Paul's day be fair and clear, it
will betide a happy year.**
the feast of the conversion of St Paul is 25 January;
English proverb, late 16th century

4 A penny for the guy.
traditional saying, used by children displaying a guy
to ask for money toward celebrations of Guy Fawkes
Night; *guy* = an effigy representing Guy Fawkes: see
24 below

13 counting of the omer
in the Jewish religion, the formal enumeration of the
49 days from the offering at Passover to Pentecost;
omer = a sheaf of corn presented as an offering on
the second day of Passover

14 Day of Atonement
Yom Kippur; see 60 below

15 Ember days
a group of three days in each season, observed as
days of fasting and prayer in some Christian
Churches, and now associated almost entirely with
the ordination of ministers; *Ember* = perhaps
alteration of Old English *ymbryne* = period,
revolution of time; at first, there were apparently
only three groups, perhaps taken over from pagan
religious observances connected with seed-time,
harvest, and autumn vintage

16 Father's Day
a day, usually the third Sunday in June, established
for a special tribute to fathers

17 festival of lights
Hanukkah (Hebrew 'consecration'), an eight-day
Jewish festival with lights beginning in December,
commemorating the rededication of the Temple in
165 BC after its desecration by the Syrians; Diwali,
(from Hindustani 'row of lights') a Hindu festival
with lights, held over three nights in the period
October to November to celebrate the new season at
the end of the monsoon, and particularly associated
with Lakshmi, the goddess of prosperity

18 first-foot
the first person to cross a threshold in the New Year, in accordance with a Scottish custom

19 Forefathers' Day
in US usage, 21 December, the anniversary of the landing of the first settlers at Plymouth, Massachusetts

20 Fourth of July
4 July, a national holiday in the United States, the anniversary of the adoption of the Declaration of Independence in 1776; see 21, 27 below

21 the Glorious Fourth
the Fourth of July; see 20 above

22 the glorious Twelfth
12 August, on which the grouse-shooting season opens

23 Good Friday
the Friday before Easter Day, observed as the anniversary of Jesus' Crucifixion

24 Guy Fawkes Night
5 November, Bonfire Night; *Guy Fawkes*, conspirator in the Gunpowder Plot to blow up James I and his Parliament on 5 November 1605, who was arrested in the cellars of the Houses of Parliament the day before the scheduled attack and betrayed his colleagues under torture; he was subsequently executed, and the plot is commemorated by bonfires and fireworks, with the burning of an effigy of Guy Fawkes, annually on 5 November; see 3, 10 above, **Trust and Treachery** 2

25 harvest home
the festival (now rarely held) celebrating bringing in the harvest

26 Holy Week
the week before Easter Sunday, after Italian *la settimana santa*, French *la semaine sainte*

27 Independence Day
the Fourth of July; see 20 above

28 Innocents' Day
28 December, commemorating the massacre of the *innocents*, the young children killed by Herod the Great after the birth of Jesus; see **Children** 15, **Cruelty** 2

29 kill the fatted calf
celebrate, especially at a prodigal's return; from the Bible (Luke): see **Hospitality** 8, **Forgiveness** 8

30 Labour Day
1 May in many places; the first Monday of September in North America; a day celebrated in honour of workers, often as a public holiday

31 Lady Day
25 March, the feast of the Annunciation to the Virgin Mary

32 Lammas Day
1 August; *Lammas* from Old English 'loaf mass', later interpreted as from *lamb*; formerly observed as an English harvest festival at which loaves made from the first ripe corn were consecrated

33 Low Sunday
the Sunday after Easter, perhaps so named in contrast to the high days of Holy Week and Easter

34 many happy returns of the day
a greeting to a person on his or her birthday

35 Mardi Gras
Shrove Tuesday in some Catholic countries; French, = fat Tuesday, in reference to celebrations before the beginning of Lent; see 53 below

36 mark with a white stone
regard as specially fortunate or happy, with allusion to the ancient practice of using a white stone as a memorial of a happy event

37 Maundy Thursday
the Thursday before Good Friday; *Maundy* comes ultimately from Latin *mandatum* commandment, mandate in *mandatum novum* a new commandment (with reference to the Bible (John) 'A new commandment give I unto you'), the opening of the first antiphon sung at the Maundy ceremony of washing the feet of a number of poor people, performed by royal or other eminent people or by ecclesiastics, on the Thursday before Easter, and commonly followed by the distribution of clothing, food, or money

38 May Day
1 May; a day of traditional springtime celebrations, probably associated with pre-Christian fertility rites; May Day was designated an international labour day by the International Socialist congress of 1889

39 Memorial Day
in the United States, 30 May, or the last Monday in May; a day on which those who died on active service are remembered

40 Midsummer Day
24 June, traditionally taken as marking the summer solstice

41 Mothers' Day
in North America, the second Sunday in May; in Britain, Mothering Sunday; a day on which mothers are particularly honoured; see 42 below

42 Mothering Sunday
the fourth Sunday in Lent; *mothering* = the custom of visiting, communicating with, or giving presents to one's mother (formerly, one's parents) on this day; see 41 above

43 New Year's Day
1 January; the first day of the year

44 Oak-Apple Day
29 May, the anniversary of Charles II's restoration in 1660, when oak-apples or oak-leaves were worn in memory of his hiding in an oak after the battle of Worcester, 1651

45 Palm Sunday
the Sunday before Easter, on which Jesus's entry into Jerusalem is commemorated by processions in which branches of palms are carried

46 Pancake Day
Shrove Tuesday, on which pancakes are traditionally eaten; see 53 below

47 Poppy Day
Remembrance Day, from the artificial red poppies made for wearing on Remembrance Day and sold in aid of needy ex-servicemen and ex-servicewomen (see **World War I** 3); see 49 below

48 red letter day
a pleasantly memorable, fortunate, or happy day; a saint's day or church festival traditionally indicated in the calendar by red letters

49 Remembrance Day
the Sunday nearest to 11 November, anniversary of the signing of the armistice that ended the First World War on 11 November 1918, when those killed in the wars of 1914–18 and 1939–45 are commemorated; see 47 above

50 Rogation Sunday
the Sunday before Ascension Day; *rogation(s)* = solemn prayers consisting of the litany of the saints chanted on the three days before Ascension Day

51 Rosh Hashana
the Jewish New Year, celebrated on the first (and sometimes second) day of the month Tishri (September–October); Hebrew, = beginning (literally 'head') of the year

52 St Valentine's day
14 February, traditionally associated with the choosing of sweethearts and the mating of birds

53 Shrove Tuesday
the Tuesday before Ash Wednesday; *shrove* = past tense of *shrive* = hear the confession of, assign penance to, and absolve; the day preceding the start of Lent, when it was formerly customary to be shriven and to take part in festivities; see 35, 46 above; see also **Food** 10

54 Stir-up Sunday
the Sunday before the Sunday on which Advent begins, so called from the opening words of the collect for the day: 'Stir up, we beseech thee, O Lord, the hearts of thy faithful people'

55 Trafalgar Day
21 October, the anniversary of the battle of Trafalgar, 1805

56 trick or treat
a children's custom of calling at houses at Hallowe'en (31 October, the eve of All Saints' Day) with the threat of pranks if they are not given a small gift; Hallowe'en is of pre-Christian origin, being associated with Samhain, the Celtic festival marking the end of the year and the beginning of winter, when ghosts and spirits were thought to be abroad; it was adopted as a Christian festival but gradually became a secular rather than a Christian observance, involving the dressing up and wearing of masks, and was particularly strong in Scotland; these secular customs were popularized in the US in the late 19th century and later developed into the custom of children playing *trick or treat*; see 5 above

57 Trinity Sunday
the next Sunday after Whit Sunday, celebrated in honour of the Holy Trinity

58 Twelfth Night
the evening of 5 January, the eve of the Epiphany, formerly the last day of the Christmas festivities.

59 Whit Sunday
the seventh Sunday after Easter, literally 'white Sunday', probably from the white robes of the newly baptized at Pentecost; commemorating the descent of the Holy Spirit on the disciples

60 Yom Kippur
the most solemn religious fast of the Jewish Year, the last of the ten days of penitence that begin with Rosh Hashana, the Jewish New Year; Hebrew; see 14 above

QUOTATIONS

61 *Natalis grate numeras?*
Do you count your birthdays thankfully?
Horace 65–8 BC: *Epistles*

62 Our birthdays are feathers in the broad wing of time.
Jean Paul Richter 1763–1825: *Titan* (1803)

63 Tomorrow 'ill be the happiest time of all the glad New-year;
Of all the glad New-year, mother, the maddest merriest day;
For I'm to be Queen o' the May, mother, I'm to be Queen o' the May.
Alfred, Lord Tennyson 1809–92: 'The May Queen' (1832)

64 Gay are the Martian Calends:
December's Nones are gay:
But the proud Ides, when the squadron rides,
Shall be Rome's whitest day!
Lord Macaulay 1800–59: *Lays of Ancient Rome* (1842) 'The Battle of the Lake Regillus'

65 Ring out the old, ring in the new,
Ring, happy bells, across the snow:
The year is going, let him go;
Ring out the false, ring in the true.
Alfred, Lord Tennyson 1809–92: *In Memoriam A. H. H.* (1850)

66 Seasons pursuing each other the indescribable
crowd is gathered, it is the fourth of Seventh-
month, (what salutes of cannon and small-arms!)
Walt Whitman 1819–92: 'Song of Myself' (written 1855)

67 The holiest of all holidays are those
Kept by ourselves in silence and apart;

The secret anniversaries of the heart.
Henry Wadsworth Longfellow 1807–82: 'Holidays' (1877)

68 *April 1.* This is the day upon which we are reminded of what we are on the other three hundred and sixty-four.
Mark Twain 1835–1910: *Pudd'nhead Wilson* (1894)

69 Hogmanay, like all festivals, being but a bank from which we can only draw what we put in.
J. M. Barrie 1860–1937: *Sentimental Tommy* (1896)

70 Time has no divisions to mark its passage, there is never a thunderstorm or blare of trumpets to announce the beginning of a new month or year. Even when a new century begins it is only we mortals who ring bells and fire off pistols.
Thomas Mann 1875–1955: *The Magic Mountain* (1924)

71 EEYORE: But after all, what *are* birthdays? Here today and gone tomorrow.
A. A. Milne 1882–1956: *The House at Pooh Corner* (1928)

72 One of the sadder things, I think,
Is how our birthdays slowly sink:
Presents and parties disappear,
The cards grow fewer year by year.
Philip Larkin 1922–85: 'Dear Charles, My Muse, alive or dead' (1982)

73 Never ask the children to tell the class what they did for Easter or Christmas or Confirmation or St Patrick's Day . . . Nothing points up the inequality of people's lives more starkly than asking innocent children to tell you how they spent what was meant to be a festival.
Maeve Binchy 1940– : in *Irish Times* 14 March 1998

⤞ Fiction and Story-telling ⤝

see also **Writers, Writing**

PROVERBS AND SAYINGS

1 **Fact is stranger than fiction.**
English proverb, mid 19th century; see **Truth 5, 29**

2 **A long time ago in a galaxy far, far away . . .**
advertising copy for the film *Star Wars* (1977)

PHRASES

3 **a Canterbury tale**
a long tedious story; one of those told on the pilgrimage to the shrine of St Thomas at *Canterbury* in Chaucer's *Canterbury Tales*

4 **a cock and bull story**
a rambling inconsequential tale, an incredible story; probably originally with reference to a particular fable

5 **shaggy-dog story**
a long, rambling story or joke, typically one that is amusing only because it is absurdly inconsequential

or pointless. The expression comes from an anecdote of this type, about a shaggy-haired dog (1945)

6 **a tale of a tub**
in archaic usage, an apocryphal or incredible tale; used as the title for a comedy by Jonson (1633) and a satire by Swift (1704), but of earlier origin

7 **a whole Megillah**
a long, tedious, or complicated story; *Megillah* = each of five books of the Hebrew Scriptures (the Song of Solomon, Ruth, Lamentations, Ecclesiastes, and Esther) appointed to be read on certain Jewish notable days

QUOTATIONS

8 Storys to rede ar delitabill,
Suppos that thai be nocht bot fabill.
John Barbour 1320–95: *The Bruce* (1375)

9 With a tale forsooth he [the poet] cometh unto you, with a tale which holdeth children from play, and old men from the chimney corner.
Philip Sidney 1554–86: *The Defence of Poetry* (1595)

10 If this were played upon a stage now, I could condemn it as an improbable fiction.
William Shakespeare 1564–1616: *Twelfth Night* (1601)

11 'Oh! it is only a novel! . . . only Cecilia, or Camilla, or Belinda:' or, in short, only some work in which the most thorough knowledge of human nature, the happiest delineation of its varieties, the liveliest

effusions of wit and humour are conveyed to the world in the best chosen language.
Jane Austen 1775–1817: *Northanger Abbey* (1818)

12 I hate things all *fiction* . . . there should always be some foundation of fact for the most airy fabric and pure invention is but the talent of a liar.
Lord Byron 1788–1824: letter to John Murray, 2 April 1817

13 A novel is a mirror which passes over a highway. Sometimes it reflects to your eyes the blue of the skies, at others the churned-up mud of the road.
Stendhal 1783–1842: *Le Rouge et le noir* (1830)

14 Merely corroborative detail, intended to give artistic verisimilitude to an otherwise bald and unconvincing narrative.
W. S. Gilbert 1836–1911: *The Mikado* (1885)

15 The good ended happily, and the bad unhappily. That is what fiction means.
Oscar Wilde 1854–1900: *The Importance of Being Earnest* (1895)

16 Literature is a luxury; fiction is a necessity.
G. K. Chesterton 1874–1936: *The Defendant* (1901) 'A Defence of Penny Dreadfuls'

17 The Story is just the spoiled child of art.
Henry James 1843–1916: *The Ambassadors* (1909 ed.) preface

18 Yes—oh dear yes—the novel tells a story.
E. M. Forster 1879–1970: *Aspects of the Novel* (1927)

19 When in doubt have a man come through the door with a gun in his hand.
Raymond Chandler 1888–1959: attributed

20 Men must have legends, else they will die of strangeness.
Les Murray 1938– : 'The Noonday Axeman' (1965)

21 A beginning, a muddle, and an end.
on the 'classic formula' for a novel
Philip Larkin 1922–85: in *New Fiction* January 1978; see **Cinema 21**, **Quantities 22**

22 The central function of imaginative literature is to make you realize that other people act on moral convictions different from your own.
William Empson 1906–84: *Milton's God* (1981)

23 No stories! No stories! Imagine a world without stories!
But that's exactly what you would have, if all the women were wise.
Margaret Atwood 1939– : *Good Bones* (1992) 'Let Us Now Praise Stupid Women'

24 Most modern fantasy just rearranges the furniture in Tolkien's attic.
Terry Pratchett 1948– : Stan Nicholls (ed.) *Wordsmiths of Wonder* (1993)

Fitness see **Health and Fitness**

Flattery see **Praise and Flattery**

 Flowers

PROVERBS AND SAYINGS

1 **Say it with flowers.**
slogan for the Society of American Florists, from 1917

QUOTATIONS

2 That wel by reson men it calle may
The 'dayesye,' or elles the 'ye of day,'
The emperice and flour of floures alle.
Geoffrey Chaucer 1343–1400: *The Legend of Good Women* 'The Prologue'

3 I know a bank whereon the wild thyme blows,
Where oxlips and the nodding violet grows
Quite over-canopied with luscious woodbine.
With sweet musk-roses, and with eglantine.
William Shakespeare 1564–1616: *A Midsummer Night's Dream* (1595–6)

4   Daffodils,
That come before the swallow dares,
and take
The winds of March with beauty.
William Shakespeare 1564–1616: *The Winter's Tale* (1610–11)

5 I wandered lonely as a cloud
That floats on high o'er vales and hills,
When all at once I saw a crowd,
A host, of golden daffodils;
Beside the lake, beneath the trees,
Fluttering and dancing in the breeze.
William Wordsworth 1770–1850: 'I wandered lonely as a cloud' (1815 ed.)

6 Here are sweet peas, on tiptoe for a flight.
John Keats 1795–1821: 'I stood tip-toe upon a little hill' (1817)

7 Flowers . . . are a proud assertion that a ray of beauty outvalues all the utilities of the world.
Ralph Waldo Emerson 1803–82: *Essays* (Second Series, 1844)

8 Summer set lip to earth's bosom bare,
And left the flushed print in a poppy there.
Francis Thompson 1859–1907: 'The Poppy' (1913)

9 Oh, no man knows
Through what wild centuries
Roves back the rose.
Walter de la Mare 1873–1956: 'All That's Past' (1912)

10 Unkempt about those hedges blows
An English unofficial rose.
Rupert Brooke 1887–1915: 'The Old Vicarage, Grantchester' (1915)

11 The rose of all the world is not for me.
I want for my part
Only the little white rose of Scotland
That smells sharp and sweet—and breaks
the heart.
Hugh MacDiarmid 1892–1978: 'The Little White Rose' (1934)

12 Hey, buds below, up is where to grow,
Up with which below can't compare with.
Hurry! It's lovely up here! *Hurry!*
Alan Jay Lerner 1918–86: 'It's Lovely Up Here' (1965)

13 People from a planet without flowers would think we must be mad with joy the whole time to have such things about us.
Iris Murdoch 1919–99: *A Fairly Honourable Defeat* (1970)

⤙ Food and Drink ⤚

see also **Alcohol, Cooking and Eating**

PROVERBS AND SAYINGS

1 An apple-pie without some cheese is like a kiss without a squeeze.
traditional saying, early 20th century

2 Don't eat oysters unless there is an R in the month.
from the tradition that oysters were likely to be unsafe to eat in the warmer months between May and August

3 God never sends mouths but He sends meat.
used in resignation or consolation; English proverb, late 14th century

4 A hungry man is an angry man.
someone deprived of a basic necessity will not be easily placated; English proverb, mid 17th century

5 It's ill speaking between a full man and a fasting.
someone in need is never on good terms with someone who has all they want; English proverb, mid 17th century

6 No dinner without bread.
Russian proverb

7 Oxo gives a meal man-appeal.
advertising slogan for Oxo beef extract, *c.* 1960

PHRASES

8 bread and water
a frugal diet that is eaten in poverty, chosen in abstinence, or given as a punishment

9 fish, flesh, and fowl
meat of all kinds, comprising fish, animals excluding birds, and poultry, originally relating to distinctions made by religious dietary laws; see **Character** 27

10 Lenten fare
food without meat; food appropriate to *Lent*, the period from Ash Wednesday to Holy Saturday, of which the 40 weekdays are devoted to fasting and penitence in commemoration of Jesus's fasting in the wilderness; see **Festivals** 53

11 staff of life
bread, or a similar staple food of an area or people; from the Biblical phrase *break the staff of bread* diminish or cut off the supply of food (Leviticus)

QUOTATIONS

12 Methinks sometimes I have no more wit than a Christian or an ordinary man has; but I am a great eater of beef, and I believe that does harm to my wit.
William Shakespeare 1564–1616: *Twelfth Night* (1601)

13 Doubtless God could have made a better berry, but doubtless God never did.
on the strawberry
William Butler 1535–1618: Izaak Walton *The Compleat Angler* (3rd ed., 1661)

14 Coffee, (which makes the politician wise, And see thro' all things with his half-shut eyes).
Alexander Pope 1688–1744: *The Rape of the Lock* (1714)

15 A cucumber should be well sliced, and dressed with pepper and vinegar, and then thrown out, as good for nothing.
Samuel Johnson 1709–84: James Boswell *Journal of a Tour to the Hebrides* (1785) 5 October 1773

16 Fair fa' your honest, sonsie face, Great chieftain o' the puddin'-race!
Robert Burns 1759–96: 'To a Haggis' (1787)

17 An egg boiled very soft is not unwholesome.
Jane Austen 1775–1817: *Emma* (1816)

18 Many's the long night I've dreamed of cheese—toasted, mostly.
Robert Louis Stevenson 1850–94: *Treasure Island* (1883)

19 Cauliflower is nothing but cabbage with a college education.
Mark Twain 1835–1910: *Pudd'nhead Wilson* (1894)

20 Look here, Steward, if this is coffee, I want tea; but if this is tea, then I wish for coffee.
Punch: 1902

21 Tea, although an Oriental, Is a gentleman at least; Cocoa is a cad and coward, Cocoa is a vulgar beast.
G. K. Chesterton 1874–1936: 'Song of Right and Wrong' (1914)

22 MOTHER: It's broccoli, dear.
CHILD: I say it's spinach, and I say the hell with it.
E. B. White 1899–1985: *New Yorker* 8 December 1928 (cartoon caption)

23 The ethical value of uncooked food is incomparable. Economically this food has possibilities which no cooked food can have.
Mahatma Gandhi 1869–1948: in *Young India* 13 June 1929

24 The ordinary human being would sooner starve than live on brown bread and raw carrots. And the peculiar evil is this, that the less money you have, the less inclined you feel to spend it on wholesome food . . . When you are underfed, harassed, bored and miserable, you don't *want* to eat dull wholesome food. You want something a little bit 'tasty.'
George Orwell 1903–50: *The Road to Wigan Pier* (1937)

25 Shake and shake
The catsup bottle.
None will come,
And then a lot'll.
Richard Armour 1906–89: 'Going to Extremes' (1949)

26 Milk's leap toward immortality.
of cheese
Clifton Fadiman 1904– : *Any Number Can Play* (1957)

27 Take away that pudding—it has no theme.
Winston Churchill 1874–1965: Lord Home *The Way the Wind Blows* (1976)

28 In Europe, spices were the jewels and furs and brocades of the kitchen and the still-room.
Elizabeth David 1913–92: *Spices, Salt and Aromatics in the English Kitchen* (1970)

29 I'm President of the United States, and I'm not going to eat any more broccoli!
George Bush 1924– : in *New York Times* 23 March 1990

30 A hen's egg is, quite simply, a work of art, a masterpiece of design and construction with, it has to be said, brilliant packaging.
Delia Smith: *How To Cook* (1998)

⤞ Fools ⤛

see also **Intelligence**

PROVERBS AND SAYINGS

1 Ask a silly question and you get a silly answer.

often used to indicate that the answer is so obvious that the question should not have been asked; English proverb, early 14th century

2 Empty vessels make the most sound.

foolish and empty-headed people make the most noise; English proverb, mid 15th century

3 A fool and his money are soon parted.

English proverb, late 16th century

4 Fools build houses and wise men live in them.

a shrewd person chooses to save themselves trouble, and benefit from the effort expended by another; English proverb, late 17th century

5 Fortune favours fools.

a foolish person is traditionally fortunate; English proverb, mid 16th century

PHRASES

6 suffer fools (gladly)

tolerate incompetence or foolishness (usually in negative contexts), from the Bible: see 13 below

7 wear motley

play the fool; *motley* = the multicoloured costume of a jester; see 14 below

8 a wise man of Gotham

a fool; *Gotham* = a village proverbial for the folly of its inhabitants

9 with egg on one's face

appearing foolish or ridiculous; see 29 below

QUOTATIONS

10 Answer not a fool according to his folly, lest thou also be like unto him.
Answer a fool according to his folly, lest he be wise in his own conceit.
Bible: Proverbs

11 As the crackling of thorns under a pot, so is the laughter of a fool.
Bible: Ecclesiastes

12 *Misce stultitiam consiliis brevem:*
Dulce est desipere in loco.
Mix a little foolishness with your prudence: it's good to be silly at the right moment.
Horace 65–8 BC: *Odes*

13 For ye suffer fools gladly, seeing ye yourselves are wise.
Bible: II Corinthians; see 6 above

14 A worthy fool! Motley's the only wear.
William Shakespeare 1564–1616: *As You Like It* (1599); see 7 above

15 The world is full of fools, and he who would not see it should live alone and smash his mirror.
Anonymous: adaptation from an original form attributed to Claude Le Petit (1640–65); *Discours satiriques* (1686)

16 A knowledgeable fool is a greater fool than an ignorant fool.
Molière 1622–73: *Les Femmes savantes* (1672)

17 The rest to some faint meaning make pretence,
But Shadwell never deviates into sense.
John Dryden 1631–1700: *MacFlecknoe* (1682)

18 For fools rush in where angels fear to tread.
Alexander Pope 1688–1744: *An Essay on Criticism* (1711)

19 Be wise with speed;
A fool at forty is a fool indeed.
Edward Young 1683–1765: *The Love of Fame* (1725–8)

20 'Tis hard if all is false that I advance
A fool must now and then be right, by chance.
William Cowper 1731–1800: 'Conversation' (1782)

21 A fool sees not the same tree that a wise man sees.
William Blake 1757–1827: *The Marriage of Heaven and Hell* (1790–3) 'Proverbs of Hell'

22 With stupidity the gods themselves struggle in vain.
Friedrich von Schiller 1759–1805: *Die Jungfrau von Orleans* (1801)

23 The ae half of the warld thinks the tither daft.
Sir Walter Scott 1771–1832: *Redgauntlet* (1824)

24 The ultimate result of shielding men from the effects of folly, is to fill the world with fools.
Herbert Spencer 1820–1903: *Essays* (1891) vol. 3 'State Tamperings with Money and Banks'

25 There's a sucker born every minute.
Phineas T. Barnum 1810–91: attributed

26 Better to keep your mouth shut and appear stupid than to open it and remove all doubt.
Mark Twain 1835–1910: James Munson (ed.) *The Sayings of Mark Twain* (1992); attributed, perhaps apocryphal

27 Never give a sucker an even break.
W. C. Fields 1880–1946: title of a W. C. Fields film (1941); the catchphrase (Fields's own) is said to have originated in the musical comedy *Poppy* (1923)

28 So dumb he can't fart and chew gum at the same time.
of Gerald Ford
Lyndon Baines Johnson 1908–73: Richard Reeves *A Ford, not a Lincoln* (1975)

29 We don't just have egg on our face. We have omelette all over our suits.
after the networks twice called the Florida election results prematurely and then had to retract
Tom Brokaw 1940– : in *Atlanta Constitution-Journal* 9 November 2000 (online edition); see 9 above

⇥⇥Football ⇤⇤

see also **Sports and Games**

PHRASES

1 **the beautiful game**
football; associated with Pelé: see 8 below

2 **golden goal**
the first goal scored during extra time which ends the match and gives victory to the scoring side

QUOTATIONS

3 Football, wherein is nothing but beastly fury, and extreme violence, whereof proceedeth hurt, and consequently rancour and malice do remain with them that be wounded.
Thomas Elyot 1499–1546: *Book of the Governor* (1531)

4 Then ye returned to your trinkets; then ye contented your souls
With the flannelled fools at the wicket or the muddied oafs at the goals.
Rudyard Kipling 1865–1936: 'The Islanders' (1903)

5 To say that these men paid their shillings to watch twenty-two hirelings kick a ball is merely to say that a violin is wood and catgut, that *Hamlet* is so much paper and ink. For a shilling the Bruddersford United AFC offered you Conflict and Art.
J. B. Priestley 1894–1984: *Good Companions* (1929)

6 Oh, he's football crazy, he's football mad
And the football it has robbed him o' the wee bit sense he had.
And it would take a dozen skivvies, his clothes to wash and scrub,

Since our Jock became a member of that terrible football club.
Jimmie McGregor 1932– : 'Football Crazy' (1960 song)

7 The great fallacy is that the game is first and last about winning. It is nothing of the kind. The game is about glory, it is about doing things in style and with a flourish, about going out and beating the lot, not waiting for them to die of boredom.
Danny Blanchflower 1926–93: attributed, 1972

8 My life and the beautiful game.
Pelé 1940– : title of autobiography (1977); see 1 above

9 Some people think football is a matter of life and death . . . I can assure them it is much more serious than that.
Bill Shankly 1914–81: in *Sunday Times* 4 October 1981

10 The goal was scored a little bit by the hand of God, another bit by head of Maradona.
on his controversial goal against England in the 1986 World Cup
Diego Maradona 1960– : in *Guardian* 1 July 1986

11 The nice aspect about football is that, if things go wrong, it's the manager who gets the blame.
before his first match as captain of England
Gary Lineker 1960– : in *Independent* 12 September 1990

12 The natural state of the football fan is bitter disappointment, no matter what the score.
Nick Hornby 1957– : *Fever Pitch* (1992)

13 Football is an art more central to our culture than anything the Arts Council deigns to recognize.
Germaine Greer 1939– : in *Independent* 28 June 1996

Foresight

see also **The Future**

PROVERBS AND SAYINGS

1 **If a man's foresight were as good as his hindsight, we would all get somewhere.**
American proverb, mid 20th century

2 **It is easy to be wise after the event.**
the difficult thing is to make a correct judgement without the benefit of hindsight; English proverb, early 17th century

3 **It's too late to shut the stable-door after the horse has bolted.**
preventive measures taken after things have gone wrong are of little effect; English proverb, mid 14th century; see **Mistakes** 11

4 **Nothing is certain but the unforeseen.**
warning against an overconfident belief in a future occurrence; English proverb, late 19th century

5 **Prevention is better than cure.**
English proverb, early 17th century

PHRASES

6 **cross a person's palm with silver**
give a person a coin as payment for fortune-telling; originally, make the sign of the cross with a coin in the fortune-teller's palm

7 **famous last words**
said as an ironic comment on or reply to an overconfident assertion that may well be proved wrong by events

8 **a pricking in one's thumbs**
a premonition, a foreboding, with allusion to Shakespeare *Macbeth*: see **Good** 26

QUOTATIONS

9 For which of you, intending to build a tower, sitteth not down first, and counteth the cost, whether he have sufficient to finish it?
Bible: St Luke

10 The best way to suppose what may come, is to remember what is past.
Lord Halifax 1633–95: *Political, Moral, and Miscellaneous Thoughts and Reflections* (1750) 'Miscellaneous: Experience'

11 Prognostics do not always prove prophecies,—at least the wisest prophets make sure of the event first.
Horace Walpole 1717–97: letter to Thomas Walpole, 19 February 1785

12 The best laid schemes o' mice an' men Gang aft a-gley.
Robert Burns 1759–96: 'To a Mouse' (1786); see **Life** 14

13 You can never plan the future by the past.
Edmund Burke 1729–97: *Letter to a Member of the National Assembly* (1791)

14 She felt that those who prepared for all the emergencies of life beforehand may equip themselves at the expense of joy.
E. M. Forster 1879–1970: *Howards End* (1910)

15 The man who has fed the chicken every day throughout its life at last wrings its neck instead, showing that a more refined view as to the uniformity of nature would have been useful to the chicken.
Bertrand Russell 1872–1970: *The Problems of Philosophy* (1912)

16 God damn you all: I told you so.
suggestion for his own epitaph, in conversation with
Sir Ernest Barker, 1939
H. G. Wells 1866–1946: Ernest Barker *Age and Youth*
(1953)

17 Some of the jam we thought was for
tomorrow, we've already eaten.
Tony Benn 1925– : attributed, 1969; see **The
Present** 11

18 The best way to predict the future is to
invent it.
Alan Kay 1940– : in 1971, at the Palo Alto Research
Center

19 Science fiction writers foresee the inevitable,
and although problems and catastrophes
may be inevitable, solutions are not.
Isaac Asimov 1920–92: in *Natural History*
April 1975

20 It was déjà vu all over again.
Yogi Berra 1925– : attributed

⇥ Forgiveness and Repentance ⇤

PROVERBS AND SAYINGS

1 **Charity covers a multitude of sins.**
charity as a virtue outweighs many faults; English
proverb, early 17th century; see 13 below

2 **A fault confessed is half redressed.**
by confessing what you have done wrong you have
begun to make amends; English proverb, mid 16th
century

3 **Good to forgive, best to forget.**
it is even better to forget that you have been injured
than to forgive the injury; North American proverb,
mid 20th century

4 **Never let the sun go down on your
anger.**
recommending a swift reconciliation after a quarrel;
from the Bible: English proverb, mid 17th century;
see **Anger** 9

5 **Offenders never pardon.**
the experience of having wronged someone often
fosters a continuing resentment of the victim;
English proverb, mid 17th century

6 **To know all is to forgive all.**
English proverb, mid 20th century; see **Insight** 11

PHRASES

7 **heap coals of fire on a person's head**
cause remorse by returning good for evil; with
allusion to the Bible (Proverbs): see **Enemies** 6

8 **a prodigal son**
a spendthrift who subsequently regrets such
behaviour; a returned and repentant wanderer; from
the parable in the Bible (Luke) telling the story of the
wastrel younger son who repented and was received
back and forgiven by his father, who killed the fatted
calf to celebrate his return; see **Festivals** 29,
Hospitality 8

9 **turn the other cheek**
refuse to retaliate, permit or invite another blow or
attack; alluding to the Bible (Matthew): see
Violence 4

10 **wipe the slate clean**
forgive or forget past faults or offences, make a fresh
start. Shopkeepers and landlords used formerly to
keep a record of what was owing to them by writing
on a tablet or slate; a *clean slate* was one on which
no debts were recorded

QUOTATIONS

11 Though your sins be as scarlet, they shall be
as white as snow.
Bible: Isaiah

12 Lord, how oft shall my brother sin against
me, and I forgive him? till seven times?
Jesus saith unto him I say not unto thee,
Until seven times: but Until seventy times
seven.
Bible: St Matthew

13 Charity shall cover the multitude of sins.
Bible: I Peter; see 1 above

14 We read that we ought to forgive our
enemies; but we do not read that we ought
to forgive our friends.
speaking of what Bacon refers to as 'perfidious
friends'
Cosimo de' Medici 1389–1464: Francis Bacon
Apophthegms (1625); see **Enemies** 9

15 And forgive us our trespasses, As we forgive
them that trespass against us.
The Book of Common Prayer 1662: *Morning
Prayer* The Lord's Prayer

16 Repentance is but want of power to sin.
John Dryden 1631–1700: *Palamon and Arcite* (1700)

17 To err is human; to forgive, divine.
Alexander Pope 1688–1744: *An Essay on Criticism* (1711); see **Computers** 5, **Mistakes** 6

18 This is no time for making new enemies.
on being asked to renounce the Devil on his deathbed
Voltaire 1694–1778: attributed

19 Remorse, the fatal egg by pleasure laid.
William Cowper 1731–1800: 'The Progress of Error' (1782)

20 But with the morning cool repentance came.
Sir Walter Scott 1771–1832: *Rob Roy* (1817)

21 And blessings on the falling out
That all the more endears,
When we fall out with those we love
And kiss again with tears!
Alfred, Lord Tennyson 1809–92: *The Princess* (1847), song (added 1850)

22 God will pardon me, it is His trade.
on his deathbed
Heinrich Heine 1797–1856: Alfred Meissner *Heinrich Heine. Erinnerungen* (1856); see **Power** 22

23 After such knowledge, what forgiveness?
T. S. Eliot 1888–1965: 'Gerontion' (1920)

24 I never forgive but I always forget.
Arthur James Balfour 1848–1930: R. Blake *Conservative Party* (1970)

25 Every one says forgiveness is a lovely idea, until they have something to forgive.
C. S. Lewis 1898–1963: *Mere Christianity* (1952)

26 I ain't sayin' you treated me unkind
You could have done better but I don't mind
You just kinda wasted my precious time
But don't think twice, it's all right.
Bob Dylan 1941– : 'Don't Think Twice, It's All Right' (1963 song)

27 The stupid neither forgive nor forget; the naïve forgive and forget; the wise forgive but do not forget.
Thomas Szasz 1920– : *The Second Sin* (1973)

28 God of forgiveness, do not forgive those murderers of Jewish children here.
at an unofficial ceremony at Auschwitz on 26 January 1995, commemorating the 50th anniversary of its liberation
Elie Wiesel 1928– : in *The Times* 27 January 1995

29 True reconciliation does not consist in merely forgetting the past.
Nelson Mandela 1918– : speech, 7 January 1996

France

see also **Countries and Peoples, International Relations, Towns and Cities**

PROVERBS AND SAYINGS

1 **One Englishman can beat three Frenchmen.**
a boastful statement now used of other nationalities and in different proportions; English proverb, late 16th century

PHRASES

2 **la Belle France**
the country of France, especially viewed in a nostalgic or patriotic manner

3 **the Corsican ogre**
Napoleon I (1769–1821), Emperor of France, in reference to his Corsican birthplace; see **Armed Forces** 13

4 **the Maid of Orleans**
Joan of Arc (c.1412–31); translation of French *la Pucelle*; *Orleans* in reference to her relieving of the besieged city in 1429

QUOTATIONS

5 France, mother of arts, of warfare, and of laws.
Joachim Du Bellay 1522–60: *Les Regrets* (1558)

6 That sweet enemy, France.
Philip Sidney 1554–86: *Astrophil and Stella* (1591)

7 Tilling and grazing are the two breasts by which France is fed.
Maximilien de Béthune, Duc de Sully 1559–1641: *Mémoires* (1638)

❯-❯-≺≺-❮-❯-≺≺-❯-❯-≺≺-❯-❯-≺≺-❯-❯-≺≺-❯-❯-≺≺-❯-❯-≺≺-❮-❯-≺≺-❯-❯-≺≺-❯-❯-≺≺-❮-❯-≺≺-❯-❯-

8 They order, said I, this matter better in France.
Laurence Sterne 1713–68: *A Sentimental Journey* (1768)

9 What is not clear is not French.
Antoine de Rivarol 1753–1801: *Discours sur l'Universalité de la Langue Française* (1784)

10 France has more need of me than I have need of France.
Napoleon I 1769–1821: speech, Paris, 31 December 1813

11 Yet, who can help loving the land that has taught us
Six hundred and eighty-five ways to dress eggs?
Thomas Moore 1779–1852: *The Fudge Family in Paris* (1818)

12 France was long a despotism tempered by epigrams.
Thomas Carlyle 1795–1881: *History of the French Revolution* (1837)

13 France, famed in all great arts, in none supreme.
Matthew Arnold 1822–88: 'To a Republican Friend—Continued' (1849)

14 The French soul is stronger than the French mind, and Voltaire shatters against Joan of Arc.
Victor Hugo 1802–85: *Tas de pierres* (1942)

15 If the French noblesse had been capable of playing cricket with their peasants, their chateaux would never have been burnt.
G. M. Trevelyan 1876–1962: *English Social History* (1942)

16 Everything ends this way in France. Weddings, christenings, duels, burials, swindlings, affairs of state—everything is a pretext for a good dinner.
Jean Anouilh 1910–87: *Cécile* (1951)

17 How can you govern a country which has 246 varieties of cheese?
Charles de Gaulle 1890–1970: Ernest Mignon *Les Mots du Général* (1962)

18 France is the only place where you can make love in the afternoon without people hammering on your door.
Barbara Cartland 1901–2000: in *Guardian* 24 December 1984

19 We have a country which loves ideology, and we need pragmatism.
Jean-Pierre Raffarin 1948– : in *Independent* 11 May 2002

20 *Vive la différence, mais vive l'entente cordiale.*
Long live the difference, but long live the Entente Cordiale.
Elizabeth II 1926– : speech, Paris, 5 April 2004

❯❯ Friendship ≺≺

see also **Relationships**

PROVERBS AND SAYINGS

1 **Be kind to your friends: if it weren't for them, you would be a total stranger.**
American proverb, mid 20th century

2 **A friend in need is a friend indeed.**
a *friend in need* is one who helps when one is in need or difficulty; English proverb, mid 11th century

3 **Love me, love my dog.**
English proverb, early 16th century

4 **Oh, the comfort—the inexpressible comfort of feeling safe with a person, having neither to weigh thoughts, nor measure words, but pouring them all out, just as they are, chaff and grain together; knowing that a faithful hand will take and sift them—keep what is worth keeping— and with the breath of kindness blow the rest away.**
19th century saying, often attributed to George Eliot or Dinah Mulock Craik (1826–87)

5 **Save us from our friends.**
the earnest help of friends can sometimes be unintentionally damaging; English proverb, late 15th century; see 18 below

6 **Two is company, but three is none.**
often used with the alternative ending 'three's a crowd'; English proverb, early 18th century

PHRASES

7 three musketeers
three close associates, three inseparable friends; translation of French *Les Trois Mousquetaires* by Alexandre Dumas père; see **Cooperation** 28

QUOTATIONS

8 Intreat me not to leave thee, or to return from following after thee: for whither thou goest, I will go; and where thou lodgest, I will lodge: thy people shall be my people, and thy God my God.
Bible: Ruth

9 There is a friend that sticketh closer than a brother.
Bible: Proverbs

10 One soul inhabiting two bodies.
reply when asked 'What is a friend?'
Aristotle 384–322 BC: Diogenes Laertius *Lives of Philosophers*

11 To like and dislike the same things, that is indeed true friendship.
Sallust 86–35 BC: *Catiline*

12 I count myself in nothing else so happy
As in a soul remembering my good friends.
William Shakespeare 1564–1616: *Richard II* (1595)

13 It redoubleth joys, and cutteth griefs in halves.
Francis Bacon 1561–1626: *Essays* (1625) 'Of Friendship'

14 It is more shameful to doubt one's friends than to be duped by them.
Duc de la Rochefoucauld 1613–80: *Maximes* (1678)

15 If a man does not make new acquaintance as he advances through life, he will soon find himself left alone. A man, Sir, should keep his friendship in constant repair.
Samuel Johnson 1709–84: James Boswell *Life of Samuel Johnson* (1791) 1755

16 The bird a nest, the spider a web, man friendship.
William Blake 1757–1827: *The Marriage of Heaven and Hell* (1790–3) 'Proverbs of Hell'

17 Should auld acquaintance be forgot
And never brought to mind?
Robert Burns 1759–96: 'Auld Lang Syne' (1796)

18 Give me the avowed, erect and manly foe;
Firm I can meet, perhaps return the blow;
But of all plagues, good Heaven, thy wrath can send,
Save me, oh, save me, from the candid friend.
George Canning 1770–1827: 'New Morality' (1821); see 5 above

19 The only reward of virtue is virtue; the only way to have a friend is to be one.
Ralph Waldo Emerson 1803–82: *Essays* (1841) 'Friendship'

20 [Grant] stood by me when I was crazy, and I stood by him when he was drunk; and now we stand by each other always.
William Sherman 1820–91: in 1864; Geoffrey C. Ward *The Civil War* (1991)

21 Friendships begin with liking or gratitude—roots that can be pulled up.
George Eliot 1819–80: *Daniel Deronda* (1876)

22 I have lost friends, some by death . . . others through sheer inability to cross the street.
Virginia Woolf 1882–1941: *The Waves* (1931)

23 Think where man's glory most begins
and ends
And say my glory was I had such friends.
W. B. Yeats 1865–1939: 'The Municipal Gallery Re-visited' (1939)

24 To find a friend one must close one eye. To keep him—two.
Norman Douglas 1868–1952: *Almanac* (1941)

25 HUMPHREY BOGART: Louis, I think this is the beginning of a beautiful friendship.
Julius J. Epstein 1909–2001 et al.: *Casablanca* (1942 film)

26 My life is spent in a perpetual alternation between two rhythms, the rhythm of attracting people for fear I may be lonely, and the rhythm of trying to get rid of them because I know that I am bored.
C. E. M. Joad 1891–1953: in *Observer* 12 December 1948

27 Friends . . . are God's apology for relations.
Hugh Kingsmill 1889–1949: Michael Holroyd *The Best of Hugh Kingsmill* (1970)

28 Champagne for my real friends, real pain for my sham friends.
Francis Bacon 1909–92: in the 1950s; Michael Peppiatt *Francis Bacon* (1996)

29 Oh I get by with a little help from my friends,
Mm, I get high with a little help from my friends.
John Lennon 1940–80 and **Paul McCartney** 1942– : 'With a Little Help From My Friends' (1967 song)

30 I do not believe that friends are necessarily
the people you like best, they are merely the
people who got there first.
Peter Ustinov 1921–2004: *Dear Me* (1977)

⭢Futility ⭠

PROVERBS AND SAYINGS

1 **Dogs bark, but the caravan goes on.**
trivial criticism will not deflect the progress of
something important; English proverb, late 19th
century

2 **In vain the net is spread in the sight of
the bird.**
a person who has seen the process by which
someone intends to harm them is unlikely to be in
danger; English proverb, late 14th century

3 **Sue a beggar and catch a louse.**
it is pointless to try to obtain restitution from
someone without resources; English proverb, mid
17th century

4 **You cannot get a quart into a pint pot.**
used of any situation in which the prospective
contents are too large for the container; English
proverb, late 19th century

5 **You cannot get blood from a stone.**
often used, as a resigned admission, to mean that it
is hopeless to try to extort money or sympathy from
those who have none; English proverb, mid 17th
century; see **Charity** 7

6 **You cannot make bricks without
straw.**
nothing can be made or achieved if one does not
have the correct materials; English proverb, mid 17th
century, from the Bible (Exodus): see **Problems** 9

7 **You can't make a silk purse out of a
sow's ear.**
inherent nature cannot be overcome by nurture;
English proverb, early 16th century

PHRASES

8 **cast pearls before swine**
offer a good or valuable thing to a person incapable
of appreciating it, with allusion to the Bible
(Matthew): see **Value** 22

9 **caviar to the general**
a good thing unappreciated by the ignorant, from
Shakespeare *Hamlet*: see **Taste** 3

10 **nail jelly to the wall**
the type of an impossible task; see **Diplomacy** 12

11 **plough the sand**
labour uselessly; a proverbial type of fruitless activity;
see **Revolution** 15

12 **rearrange the deckchairs on the
Titanic**
to make trivial improvements in a major crisis; see 30
below

13 **tilt at windmills**
attack an imaginary enemy or wrong, from a story in
Cervantes *Don Quixote* (1605–15) in which Don
Quixote attacked a group of windmills believing
them to be giants

14 **a voice in the wilderness**
an unheeded advocate of reform, with allusion to
the Bible (Matthew) 'The voice of one crying in the
wilderness'; see also **Preparation** 16

15 **a wild-goose chase**
a foolish, fruitless, or hopeless quest, a pursuit of
something unattainable; from a horse-race in which
the second or any succeeding horse had to follow
accurately the course of the leader, like a flight of
wild geese; later, an erratic course taken by one
person (or thing) and followed (or that may be
followed) by another

QUOTATIONS

16 Vanity of vanities, saith the Preacher, vanity
of vanities; all is vanity.
Bible: Ecclesiastes; see **Disillusion** 6

17 You will never make a crab walk straight.
Aristophanes c.450–c.385 BC: *Peace*

18 How weary, stale, flat, and unprofitable
Seem to me all the uses of this world.
William Shakespeare 1564–1616: *Hamlet* (1601)

19 To enlarge or illustrate this power and effect
of love is to set a candle in the sun.
Robert Burton 1577–1640: *The Anatomy of
Melancholy* (1621–51)

20 To endeavour to work upon the vulgar with
fine sense, is like attempting to hew blocks
with a razor.
Alexander Pope 1688–1744: *Miscellanies* (1727)
'Thoughts on Various Subjects'

21 Who breaks a butterfly upon a wheel?
Alexander Pope 1688–1744: 'An Epistle to Dr Arbuthnot' (1735); see **Excess** 13

22 'My name is Ozymandias, king of kings: Look on my works, ye Mighty, and despair!' Nothing beside remains. Round the decay Of that colossal wreck, boundless and bare The lone and level sands stretch far away.
Percy Bysshe Shelley 1792–1822: 'Ozymandias' (1819)

23 Useless! Useless!
John Wilkes Booth 1838–65: last words; Philip van Doren Stern *The Man Who Killed Lincoln* (1939)

24 Pathos, piety, courage—they exist, but are identical, and so is filth. Everything exists, nothing has value.
E. M. Forster 1879–1970: *A Passage to India* (1924)

25 We are the hollow men We are the stuffed men Leaning together Headpiece filled with straw. Alas!
T. S. Eliot 1888–1965: 'The Hollow Men' (1925)

26 Nothing to be done.
Samuel Beckett 1906–89: *Waiting for Godot* (1955)

27 Nothingness haunts being.
Jean-Paul Sartre 1905–80: *Being and Nothingness* (1956)

28 There aren't any good, brave causes left. If the big bang does come, and we all get killed off, it won't be in aid of the old-fashioned, grand design. It'll just be for the Brave New-nothing-very-much-thank-you. About as pointless and inglorious as stepping in front of a bus.
John Osborne 1929–94: *Look Back in Anger* (1956)

29 He's a real nowhere man Sitting in his nowhere land Making all his nowhere plans for nobody.
John Lennon 1940–80 and **Paul McCartney** 1942– : 'Nowhere Man' (1966 song)

30 I'm not going to rearrange the furniture on the deck of the Titanic.
having lost five of the last six primaries as President Ford's campaign manager
Rogers Morton 1914–79: *Washington Post* 16 May 1976; see 12 above

31 It seems that I have spent my entire time trying to make life more rational and that it was all wasted effort.
A. J. Ayer 1910–89: in *Observer* 17 August 1986

⤜The Future ⤚

see also **Foresight**

PROVERBS AND SAYINGS

1 **Coming events cast their shadow before.**
some initial effects indicating the nature of an event may be felt before it takes place; English proverb, early 19th century

2 **The future's bright, the future's Orange.**
advertising slogan for Orange telecom company, mid 1990s

3 **He that follows freits, freits will follow him.**
someone who looks for portents of the future will find himself dogged by them (*freits* are omens); Scottish proverb, early 18th century

PHRASES

8 **cast one's bread upon the waters**
give generously in the expectation of future repayment for one's present kindness, from the Bible (Ecclesiastes): see **Chance** 22

4 **There is no future like the present.**
American proverb, mid 20th century

5 **Today you; tomorrow me.**
often used in the context of the inevitability of death to each person; English proverb, mid 13th century

6 **Tomorrow is another day.**
English proverb, early 16th century; see **Hope** 20

7 **Tomorrow never comes.**
used in the context of something which is constantly predicted to be imminent, but which never occurs; English proverb, early 16th century

9 **the shape of things to come**
the way in which future events will develop; the form the future will take; from the title of a book by H. G. Wells, 1933

10 **a straw in the wind**
a small but significant indicator of the future course of events; proverbial: see **Meaning** 2

11 **the writing on the wall**
evidence or a sign of approaching disaster; an
ominously significant event or situation; with
allusion to the biblical story in Daniel of the writing

that appeared on the palace wall at a feast given by
Belshazzar, last king of Babylon, foretelling that he
would be killed and the city sacked; see also
Success 19

QUOTATIONS

12 Boast not thyself of to morrow; for thou
knowest not what a day may bring forth.
Bible: Proverbs

13 Lord! we know what we are, but know not
what we may be.
William Shakespeare 1564–1616: *Hamlet* (1601)

14 For present joys are more to flesh and blood
Than a dull prospect of a distant good.
John Dryden 1631–1700: *The Hind and the Panther*
(1687)

15 'We are always doing', says he, 'something
for Posterity, but I would fain see Posterity
do something for us.'
Joseph Addison 1672–1719: in *The Spectator* 20
August 1714

16 The next Augustan age will dawn on the
other side of the Atlantic. There will,
perhaps, be a Thucydides at Boston, a
Xenophon at New York, and, in time, a
Virgil at Mexico, and a Newton at Peru. At
last, some curious traveller from Lima will
visit England and give a description of the
ruins of St Paul's, like the editions of Balbec
and Palmyra.
Horace Walpole 1717–97: letter to Horace Mann,
24 November 1774

17 People will not look forward to posterity,
who never look backward to their ancestors.
Edmund Burke 1729–97: *Reflections on the
Revolution in France* (1790)

18 You cannot fight against the future. Time is
on our side.
W. E. Gladstone 1809–98: speech on the Reform
Bill, House of Commons, 27 April 1866

19 You will eat, bye and bye,
In that glorious land above the sky;
Work and pray, live on hay,
You'll get pie in the sky when you die.
Joe Hill 1879–1915: 'Preacher and the Slave' (1911
song)

20 Make me a beautiful word for doing things
tomorrow; for that surely is a great and
blessed invention.
George Bernard Shaw 1856–1950: *Back to
Methuselah* (1921)

21 *In the long run* we are all dead.
John Maynard Keynes 1883–1946: *A Tract on
Monetary Reform* (1923)

22 I never think of the future. It comes soon
enough.
Albert Einstein 1879–1955: in an interview given
on the *Belgenland*, December 1930

23 We have trained them [men] to think of the
Future as a promised land which favoured
heroes attain—not as something which
everyone reaches at the rate of sixty minutes
an hour, whatever he does, whoever he is.
C. S. Lewis 1898–1963: *The Screwtape Letters* (1942)

24 If you want a picture of the future, imagine a
boot stamping on a human face—for ever.
George Orwell 1903–50: *Nineteen Eighty-Four*
(1949)

25 They spend their time mostly looking
forward to the past.
John Osborne 1929–94: *Look Back in Anger* (1956)

26 Predictions can be very difficult—especially
about the future.
Niels Bohr 1885–1962: H. Rosovsky *The University:
An Owners Manual* (1991)

27 The future ain't what it used to be.
Yogi Berra 1925– : attributed

28 And now, we can see a new world coming
into view. A world in which there is the very
real prospect of a new world order.
George Bush 1924– : speech, in *New York Times* 7
March 1991; see **International Relations 7**

Games see **Sports and Games**

⊷ Gardens ⊶

see also **Flowers**

PROVERBS AND SAYINGS

1 **All the flowers of tomorrow are in the seeds of today.**
Indian proverb; see **Trees 3**

2 **The answer lies in the soil.**
traditional gardening advice

3 **Dig for victory.**
Second World War slogan, encouraging production of food in gardens and allotments

4 **If you would be happy for a week take a wife; if you would be happy for a month kill a pig; but if you would be happy all your life plant a garden.**
the saying exists in a variety of forms, but marriage is nearly always given as one of the ephemeral forms of happiness; English proverb, mid 17th century

5 **It is not enough for a gardener to love flowers; he must also hate weeds.**
American proverb, mid 20th century

6 **One year's seeding makes seven years weeding.**
the allusion is to the danger of allowing weeds to grow and seed themselves; English proverb, late 19th century

7 **Parsley seed goes nine times to the Devil.**
it is often slow to germinate; there was a superstition that parsley, which belonged to the Devil, had to be sown nine times before it would come up; English proverb, mid 17th century

8 **Select a proper site for your garden and half your work is done.**
Chinese proverb

9 **Sow dry and set wet.**
seeds should be sown in dry ground and then given water; English proverb, mid 17th century

10 **Walnuts and pears you plant for your heirs.**
both trees are traditionally slow growing, so that the benefit will be felt by future generations; English proverb, mid 17th century

QUOTATIONS

11 And the Lord God planted a garden eastward in Eden.
Bible: Genesis

12 Sowe Carrets in your Gardens, and humbly praise God for them, as for a singular and great blessing.
Richard Gardiner b. c.1533: *Profitable Instructions for the Manuring, Sowing and Planting of Kitchen Gardens* (1599)

13 Nothing is more pleasant to the eye than green grass kept finely shorn.
Francis Bacon 1561–1626: *Essays* (1625) 'Of Gardens'

14 Annihilating all that's made
To a green thought in a green shade.
Andrew Marvell 1621–78: 'The Garden' (1681)

15 All gardening is landscape-painting.
Alexander Pope 1688–1744: Joseph Spence *Anecdotes* (1966)

16 But though an old man, I am but a young gardener.
Thomas Jefferson 1743–1826: letter to Charles Willson Peale, 20 August 1811

17 What is a weed? A plant whose virtues have not been discovered.
Ralph Waldo Emerson 1803–82: *Fortune of the Republic* (1878)

18 The Glory of the Garden lies in more than meets the eye.
Rudyard Kipling 1865–1936: 'The Glory of the Garden' (1911)

19 The kiss of the sun for pardon,
The song of the birds for mirth,
One is nearer God's Heart in a garden
Than anywhere else on earth.
Dorothy Frances Gurney 1858–1932: 'God's Garden' (1913)

20 As long as one has a garden, one has a future; and as long as one has a future one is alive.
Frances Hodgson Burnett 1849–1924: *In the Garden* (1925)

21 Weeds are not supposed to grow,
But by degrees
Some achieve a flower, although
No one sees.
Philip Larkin 1922–85: 'Modesties' (1951)

22 Perennials are the ones that grow like weeds, biennials are the ones that die this year instead of next and hardy annuals are the ones that never come up at all.
Katharine Whitehorn 1928– : *Observations* (1970)

23 I just come and talk to the plants, really—very important to talk to them, they respond I find.
Prince Charles 1948– : television interview, 21 September 1986

24 There can be no other occupation like gardening in which, if you were to creep behind someone at their work, you would find them smiling.
Mirabel Osler: *A Gentle Plea for Chaos* (1989)

25 Gardening is the new rock'n'roll. When I was little, it was all fuddy-duddy Percy Thrower. Now it's very social and very, very fashionable.
Ali Ward: in *Independent* 13 June 1998

➤➤The Generation Gap ◀◀

see also **Old Age, Youth**

PROVERBS AND SAYINGS

1 **Young folks think old folks to be fools, but old folks know young folks to be fools.**
asserting the value of the experience of life which comes with age over youth and inexperience; English proverb, late 16th century

PHRASES

2 **an angry young man**
a young man who feels and expresses anger at the conventional values of the society around him; originally, a member of a group of socially conscious writers in the 1950s, including particularly the playwright John Osborne; the phrase, the title of a book (1951) by Leslie Paul, was used of Osborne in the publicity material for his play *Look Back in Anger* (1956), in which the characteristic views were articulated by the anti-hero Jimmy Porter; see **Anger 4 Writers 2**

3 **baby boomer**
a person born during the temporary marked increase in the birth rate following the Second World War

4 **Generation X**
the generation born after that of the baby boomers (roughly from the early 1960s to mid 1970s), typically perceived to be disaffected and directionless; popularized by Douglas Coupland's book *Generation X: tales for an accelerated culture* (1991)

QUOTATIONS

5 Tiresome, complaining, a praiser of past times, when he was a boy, a castigator and censor of the young generation.
Horace 65–8 BC: *Ars Poetica*

6 Age is deformed, youth unkind,
We scorn their bodies, they our mind.
Thomas Bastard 1566–1618: *Chrestoleros* (1598)

7 Crabbed age and youth cannot live together:
Youth is full of pleasance, age is full of care.
William Shakespeare 1564–1616: *The Passionate Pilgrim* (1599)

8 O Man! that from thy fair and shining youth

Age might but take the things Youth needed not!
William Wordsworth 1770–1850: 'The Small Celandine' (1807)

9 Youth, which is forgiven everything, forgives itself nothing: age, which forgives itself everything, is forgiven nothing.
George Bernard Shaw 1856–1950: *Man and Superman* (1903)

10 When I was a boy of 14, my father was so ignorant I could hardly stand to have the old man around. But when I got to be 21, I was astonished at how much the old man had learned in seven years.
Mark Twain 1835–1910: attributed in *Reader's Digest* September 1939, but not traced in his works

11 The young man who has not wept is a savage, and the old man who will not laugh is a fool.
George Santayana 1863–1952: *Dialogues in Limbo* (1925)

12 Every generation revolts against its fathers and makes friends with its grandfathers.
Lewis Mumford 1895–90: *The Brown Decades* (1931)

13 Grown-ups never understand anything for themselves, and it is tiresome for children to be always and forever explaining things to them.
Antoine de Saint-Exupéry 1900–44: *Le Petit Prince* (1943)

14 It is the one war in which everyone changes sides.
Cyril Connolly 1903–74: Tom Driberg speech in House of Commons, 30 October 1959

15 Come mothers and fathers,
Throughout the land
And don't criticize
What you can't understand.
Your sons and your daughters
Are beyond your command
Your old road is
Rapidly agin'
Please get out of the new one
If you can't lend your hand
For the times they are a-changin'!
Bob Dylan 1941– : 'The Times They Are A-Changing' (1964 song)

16 When I was young, the old regarded me as an outrageous young fellow, and now that I'm old the young regard me as an outrageous old fellow.
Fred Hoyle 1915–2001: in *Scientific American* March 1995

⤚⤙ Genius ⤙⤚

PROVERBS AND SAYINGS

1 **Genius is an infinite capacity for taking pains.**
English proverb, late 19th century

2 **Genius without education is like silver in the mine.**
American proverb, mid 18th century

QUOTATIONS

3 Great wits are sure to madness near allied,
And thin partitions do their bounds divide.
John Dryden 1631–1700: *Absalom and Achitophel* (1681)

4 When a true genius appears in the world, you may know him by this sign, that the dunces are all in confederacy against him.
Jonathan Swift 1667–1745: *Thoughts on Various Subjects* (1711)

5 There is more beauty in the works of a great genius who is ignorant of all the rules of art, than in the works of a little genius, who not only knows but scrupulously observes them.
Joseph Addison 1672–1719: in *The Spectator* 10 September 1714

6 The true genius is a mind of large general powers, accidentally determined to some particular direction.
Samuel Johnson 1709–84: *Lives of the English Poets* (1779–81) 'Cowley'

7 Many a genius has been slow of growth. Oaks that flourish for a thousand years do not spring up into beauty like a reed.
G. H. Lewes 1817–78: *The Spanish Drama* (1846)

8 Since when was genius found respectable?
Elizabeth Barrett Browning 1806–61: *Aurora Leigh* (1857)

9 Genius does what it must, and Talent does what it can.
Owen Meredith 1831–91: 'Last Words of a Sensitive Second-Rate Poet' (1868)

10 I have nothing to declare except my genius.
Oscar Wilde 1854–1900: at the New York Custom House; Frank Harris *Oscar Wilde* (1918)

11 Genius is one per cent inspiration, ninety-nine per cent perspiration.
Thomas Alva Edison 1847–1931: said c.1903, in *Harper's Monthly Magazine* September 1932

12 Little minds are interested in the extraordinary; great minds in the commonplace.
Elbert Hubbard 1859–1915: *Thousand and One Epigrams* (1911)

13 Everybody has talent at twenty-five. The difficult thing is to have it at fifty.
Edgar Degas 1834–1917: R. H. Ives Gammell *The Shop-Talk of Edgar Degas* (1961)

14 Geniuses are the luckiest of mortals because what they must do is the same as what they most want to do.
W. H. Auden 1907–73: Dag Hammarskjöld *Markings* (1964)

15 Airing one's dirty linen never makes for a masterpiece.
François Truffaut 1932–84: *Bed and Board* (1972)

16 Genius is always allowed some leeway, once the hammer has been pried from its hands and the blood has been cleaned up.
Terry Pratchett 1948– : *Thief of Time* (2001)

⤜ Gifts ⤛

see also **Charity**

PROVERBS AND SAYINGS

1 A bird never flew on one wing.
frequently used to justify a further gift, especially another drink; early 18th century proverb, mainly Scottish and Irish

2 Friday's child is loving and giving.
English proverb, mid 19th century; see also **Beauty** 7, **Sorrow** 2, **Travel** 6, **Work** 6

3 Give a thing, and take a thing, to wear the devil's gold ring.
a schoolchildren's rhyme, chanted when a person gives something and then asks for it back; English proverb, late 16th century

4 He gives twice who gives quickly.
associating readiness to give with generosity; English proverb, mid 16th century

PHRASES

8 Greek gift
a gift given with intent to harm, in allusion to Virgil: see **Trust and Treachery** 1, 19

9 manna from heaven
an unexpected or gratuitous benefit; *manna* in the Bible (Exodus), the substance miraculously supplied

5 It is better to give than to receive.
English proverb, late 14th century; see 13 below

6 On the first day of Christmas my true love sent to me
A partridge in a pear tree.
'The Twelve Days of Christmas', traditional song listing gifts sent on each day of the Christmas season; see **Christmas** 3

7 A small gift usually gets small thanks.
American proverb, mid 20th century

each day as food to the Israelites in the wilderness; see **Satisfaction** 22

QUOTATIONS

10 A gift though small is welcome.
Homer 8th century BC: *Odyssey*

11 Enemies' gifts are no gifts and do no good.
Sophocles c.496–406 BC: *Ajax*

12 Give, and it shall be given unto you; good measure, pressed down, and shaken together, and running over.
Bible: St Luke

13 It is more blessed to give than to receive.
Bible: Acts of the Apostles; see 5 above

14 God loveth a cheerful giver.
Bible: II Corinthians

15 Teach us, good Lord, to serve Thee as Thou deservest:

To give and not to count the cost;
To fight and not to heed the wounds;
To toil and not to seek for rest;
To labour and not to ask for any reward
Save that of knowing that we do Thy will.
St Ignatius Loyola 1491–1556: 'Prayer for Generosity' (1548)

16 I am not in the giving vein to-day.
William Shakespeare 1564–1616: *Richard III* (1591)

17 Presents, I often say, endear Absents.
Charles Lamb 1775–1834: *Essays of Elia* (1823) 'A Dissertation upon Roast Pig'

18 Behold, I do not give lectures or a little charity,

When I give I give myself.
Walt Whitman 1819–92: 'Song of Myself' (written 1855)

19 They gave it me,—for an un-birthday present.
Lewis Carroll 1832–98: *Through the Looking-Glass* (1872)

20 One must be poor to know the luxury of giving.
George Eliot 1819–80: *Middlemarch* (1871–2)

21 Why is it no one ever sent me yet
One perfect limousine, do you suppose?
Ah no, it's always just my luck to get
One perfect rose.
Dorothy Parker 1893–1967: 'One Perfect Rose' (1937)

22 'The more we ask, the more we have. And, it is fair enough: asking is not always easy.'
'And it is said to be hard to accept . . . So no wonder we have so little.'
Ivy Compton-Burnett 1884–1969: *The Mighty and their Fall* (1961)

23 I know it's not much, but it's the best I can do,
My gift is my song and this one's for you.
Elton John 1947– and **Bernie Taupin** 1950– : 'Your Song' (1970 song)

24 Giving presents is one of the most possessive of things we do . . . It's the way we keep a hold on other people. Plant ourselves in their lives.
Penelope Lively 1933– : *Moon Tiger* (1987)

⇥ God ⇤

see also **Belief, The Bible, The Christian Church, Religion**

PROVERBS AND SAYINGS

1 **All things are possible with God.**
English proverb, late 17th century; see 9 below

2 **God helps them that helps themselves.**
often used in urging someone to action; English proverb, mid 16th century

3 **The nature of God is a circle of which the centre is everywhere and the circumference is nowhere.**
medieval saying, said to have been traced to a lost treatise of Empedocles; quoted in the *Roman de la Rose*, and by St Bonaventura in *Itinerarius Mentis in Deum*

PHRASES

4 **the Ancient of Days**
God; a scriptural title in the Bible (Daniel) 'the Ancient of Days did sit, whose garments were white as snow'

5 **the Lord of Sabaoth**
the Lord of Hosts, God; Hebrew *Sabaoth* = the heavenly hosts

6 **Pascal's wager**
the argument that it is in one's own best interest to behave as if God exists, since the possibility of eternal punishment in hell outweighs any advantage in believing otherwise; see 19 below

QUOTATIONS

7 The Lord is my shepherd: therefore can I lack nothing.
He shall feed me in a green pasture: and lead me forth beside the waters of comfort.
Bible: Psalm 23

8 God is always doing geometry.
Plato 429–347 BC: Plutarch *Moralia*; see **The Universe 16**

9 With men this is impossible; but with God all things are possible.
Bible: St Matthew; see 1 above

10 He that loveth not knoweth not God; for God is love.
Bible: I John

11 A living man is the glory of God.
St Irenaeus c.AD 130–c.200: *Against the Heresies*

12 Praise belongs to God, the Lord of all Being, the All-merciful, the All-compassionate, the Master of the Day of Doom.
The Koran: sura 1

13 Therefore it is necessary to arrive at a prime mover, put in motion by no other; and this everyone understands to be God.
St Thomas Aquinas 1225–74: *Summa Theologicae* (c.1265); see **Beginning 15**

14 Whatever your heart clings to and confides in, that is really your God.
Martin Luther 1483–1546: *Large Catechism* (1529) 'The First Commandment'

15 'Twas only fear first in the world made gods.
Ben Jonson 1573–1637: *Sejanus* (1603)

16 Batter my heart, three-personed God;
for, you
As yet but knock, breathe, shine, and seek to
mend.
John Donne 1572–1631: *Holy Sonnets* (after 1609)

17 I had rather believe all the fables in the
legend, and the Talmud, and the Alcoran,
than that this universal frame is without a
mind.
Francis Bacon 1561–1626: *Essays* (1625) 'Of
Atheism'

18 Though the mills of God grind slowly, yet
they grind exceeding small;
Though with patience He stands waiting,
with exactness grinds He all.
Friedrich von Logau 1604–55: *Sinngedichte*
(1654) translated by Longfellow; Von Logau's first
line is itself a translation of an anonymous verse in
Sextus Empiricus *Adversus Mathematicos*; see **Fate 5**

19 'God is or he is not.' But to which side shall
we incline? . . . Let us weigh the gain and
the loss in wagering that God is. Let us
estimate the two chances. If you gain, you
gain all; if you lose, you lose nothing. Wager
then without hesitation that he is.
Blaise Pascal 1623–62: *Pensées* (1670); see **6** above

20 As you know, God is usually on the side of
the big squadrons against the small.
Comte de Bussy-Rabutin 1618–93: letter to the
Comte de Limoges, 18 October 1677; see **Armed
Forces 8, Warfare 23**

21 If the triangles were to make a God they
would give him three sides.
Montesquieu 1689–1755: *Lettres Persanes* (1721)

22 If God did not exist, it would be necessary to
invent him.
Voltaire 1694–1778: *Épîtres* no. 96 'A l'Auteur du
livre des trois imposteurs'

23 God moves in a mysterious way
His wonders to perform.
William Cowper 1731–1800: 'Light Shining out of
Darkness' (1779 hymn)

24 Suppose I had found a *watch* upon the
ground, and it should be enquired how the
watch happened to be in that place . . . the
inference, we think, is inevitable; that the
watch must have had a maker; that there
must have existed, at some time and at some
place or other, an artificer or artificers, who
formed it for the purpose which we find it
actually to answer; who comprehended its
construction, and designed its use.
William Paley 1743–1805: *Natural Theology*
(1802); see **Life Sciences 26**

25 Mine eyes have seen the glory of the coming
of the Lord:

He is trampling out the vintage where the
grapes of wrath are stored;
He hath loosed the fateful lightning of his
terrible swift sword:
His truth is marching on.
Julia Ward Howe 1819–1910: 'Battle Hymn of the
Republic' (1862)

26 I will call no being good, who is not what I
mean when I apply that epithet to my
fellow-creatures; and if such a being can
sentence me to hell for not so calling him,
to hell I will go.
John Stuart Mill 1806–73: *Examination of Sir
William Hamilton's Philosophy* (1865)

27 An honest God is the noblest work of man.
after Pope *Essay on Man* (1734) 'An honest man's the
noblest work of God'
Robert G. Ingersoll 1833–99: *The Gods* (1876)

28 God is dead: but considering the state the
species Man is in, there will perhaps be
caves, for ages yet, in which his shadow will
be shown.
Friedrich Nietzsche 1844–1900: *Die fröhliche
Wissenschaft* (1882)

29 God is subtle but he is not malicious.
Albert Einstein 1879–1955: remark made at
Princeton University, May 1921; R. W. Clark *Einstein*
(1973)

30 It is a mistake to suppose that God is only, or
even chiefly, concerned with religion.
William Temple 1881–1944: R. V. C. Bodley *In
Search of Serenity* (1955)

31 Operationally, God is beginning to resemble
not a ruler but the last fading smile of a
cosmic Cheshire cat.
Julian Huxley 1887–1975: *Religion without
Revelation* (1957 ed.); see **Cats 3**

32 God has been replaced, as he has all over the
West, with respectability and air-
conditioning.
Imamu Amiri Baraka 1934– : *Midstream* (1963)

33 God seems to have left the receiver off the
hook, and time is running out.
Arthur Koestler 1905–83: *The Ghost in the
Machine* (1967)

34 The Buddha, the Godhead, resides quite as
comfortably in the circuits of a digital
computer or the gears of a cycle
transmission as he does at the top of a
mountain or in the petals of a flower.
Robert M. Pirsig 1928– : *Zen and the Art of
Motorcycle Maintenance* (1974)

35 Any God I ever felt in church I brought in with me. And I think all the other folks did too. They come to church to *share* God not find God.

Alice Walker 1944– : *The Colour Purple* (1982)

36 I am not clear that God manoeuvres physical things . . . After all, a conjuring trick with bones only proves that it is as clever as a conjuring trick with bones.

of the Resurrection

David Jenkins 1925– : 'Poles Apart' (BBC radio, 4 October 1984)

37 I think you have to be very careful when you say, 'God is on my side.' I much prefer to say, 'I am on God's side'.

Ann Widdecombe 1947– : Anthony Clare *In the Psychiatrist's Chair III* (1998)

38 Even God has become female. God is no longer the bearded patriarch in the sky. He has had a sex change and turned into Mother Nature.

Fay Weldon 1931– : in *The Times* 29 August 1998

➤➤ Good and Evil ◄◄

see also **Sin, Virtue**

PROVERBS AND SAYINGS

1 The greater the sinner, the greater the saint.

a sinner who has reformed is likely to be more virtuous that someone who is morally neutral; English proverb, late 18th century

2 He that touches pitch shall be defiled.

a person who chooses to put themselves in contact with wrongdoing will be marked by it; English proverb, early 14th century; see 15 below

3 Honi soit qui mal y pense.

French, *Evil be to him who evil thinks*, the motto of the Order of the Garter, originated by Edward III, probably on 23 April of 1348 or 1349

4 Ill weeds grow apace.

used to comment on the apparent success enjoyed by an ill-doer; English proverb, late 15th century

5 The sun loses nothing by shining into a puddle.

something which is naturally clear and radiant cannot be tainted or diminished by association; English proverb, early 14th century, of classical origin

6 Two blacks don't make a white.

one injury or instance of wrongdoing does not justify another; English proverb, early 18th century

7 Two wrongs don't make a right.

a first injury does not justify a second in retaliation; English proverb, late 18th century; see 43 below

8 Where God builds a church, the Devil will build a chapel.

the establishment of something which in itself good may also create the opening for something evil; English proverb, mid 16th century; see 24 below

PHRASES

9 cloven hoof

the mark of an inherently evil nature; a divided hoof, as that of a goat, ascribed to a satyr, the god Pan, or to the Devil; see **The Family** 27

10 Lord of the Flies

Satan, the Devil; the meaning of the Hebrew word which is the origin of *Beelzebub*, in the Bible (II Kings) the god of the Philistine city Ekron, and in the Gospels, the prince of the devils, often identified with the Devil

11 the Prince of this world

Satan, the Devil; from the Bible (John) 'the prince of this world is judged'

12 separate the sheep from the goats

sort the good persons or things from the bad or inferior, from the Bible (Matthew) 'He shall separate the one from another, as a shepherd divideth his sheep from his goats. And he shall set the sheep on his right hand, but the goats on his left'

13 three wise monkeys

a conventional sculptured group of three monkeys; used allusively to refer to a person who chooses to ignore or keep silent about wrongdoing. One monkey is depicted with its paws over its mouth (taken as connoting 'speak no evil'), one with its paws over its eyes ('see no evil'), and one with its paws over its ears ('hear no evil'); see **Virtue** 5

>->-<-->--><-<--->->-<--->-><-<--->->-<--->-><-<--->->-<--->-><-<--->->-<--->-><-<--->->-<--->-><-<--->->-<--->-><-<--->->-<-->

QUOTATIONS

14 There is no peace, saith the Lord, unto the wicked.
Bible: Isaiah; see **Action** 15

15 He that toucheth pitch shall be defiled therewith.
Bible: Ecclesiasticus; see 2 above

16 It is never right to do wrong or to requite wrong with wrong, or when we suffer evil to defend ourselves by doing evil in return.
Socrates 469–399 BC: Plato *Crito*

17 Every art and every investigation, and likewise every practical pursuit or undertaking, seems to aim at some good: hence it has been well said that the Good is That at which all things aim.
Aristotle 384–322 BC: *Nicomachean Ethics*

18 How can Satan cast out Satan?
Bible: St Mark; see also **Warfare** 34

19 For the good that I would I do not: but the evil which I would not, that I do.
Bible: Romans

20 Unto the pure all things are pure.
Bible: Titus; see 38 below

21 With love for mankind and hatred of sins.
often quoted as 'Love the sinner but hate the sin'
St Augustine of Hippo AD 354–430: letter 211; J.-P. Migne (ed.) *Patrologiae Latinae* (1845)

22 Good and evil shall not be held equal. Turn away evil with that which is better; and behold the man between whom and thyself there was enmity, shall become, as it were, thy warmest friend.
The Koran: sura 41

23 If all evil were prevented, much good would be absent from the universe. A lion would cease to live, if there were no slaying of animals; and there would be no patience of martyrs if there were no tyrannical persecution.
St Thomas Aquinas 1225–74: *Summa Theologicae* (c.1265)

24 For, where God built a church, there the devil would also build a chapel . . . In such sort is the devil always God's ape.
Martin Luther 1483–1546: *Colloquia Mensalia* (1566); see 8 above

25 There is nothing either good or bad, but thinking makes it so.
William Shakespeare 1564–1616: *Hamlet* (1601)

26   By the pricking of my thumbs, Something wicked this way comes.
William Shakespeare 1564–1616: *Macbeth* (1606); see **Foresight** 8

27 Farewell remorse! All good to me is lost; Evil, be thou my good.
John Milton 1608–74: *Paradise Lost* (1667)

28 But if he does really think that there is no distinction between virtue and vice, why, Sir, when he leaves our houses, let us count our spoons.
Samuel Johnson 1709–84: James Boswell *Life of Samuel Johnson* (1791) 14 July 1763

29 Don't let us make imaginary evils, when you know we have so many real ones to encounter.
Oliver Goldsmith 1728–74: *The Good-Natured Man* (1768)

30 It is necessary only for the good man to do nothing for evil to triumph.
Edmund Burke 1729–97: attributed (in a number of forms) to Burke, but not found in his writings

31 One impulse from a vernal wood
May teach you more of man,
Of moral evil and of good,
Than all the sages can.
William Wordsworth 1770–1850: 'The Tables Turned' (1798)

32 He who would do good to another, must do it in minute particulars
General good is the plea of the scoundrel, hypocrite and flatterer.
William Blake 1757–1827: *Jerusalem* (1815)

33 It is better to fight for the good, than to rail at the ill.
Alfred, Lord Tennyson 1809–92: *Maud* (1855)

34 Imagine that you are creating a fabric of human destiny with the object of making men happy in the end, giving them peace and rest at last, but that it was essential and inevitable to torture to death only one tiny creature . . . and to found that edifice on its unavenged tears, would you consent to be the architect on those conditions?
Fedor Dostoevsky 1821–81: *The Brothers Karamazov* (1879–80)

35 A belief in a supernatural source of evil is not necessary; men alone are quite capable of every wickedness.
Joseph Conrad 1857–1924: *Under Western Eyes* (1911)

36 In my humble opinion, non-cooperation with evil is as much a duty as is cooperation with good.
Mahatma Gandhi 1869–1948: speech in Ahmadabad, 23 March 1922

37 What we call evil is simply ignorance bumping its head in the dark.
Henry Ford 1863–1947: in *Observer* 16 March 1930

38 To the Puritan all things are impure, as
somebody says.
D. H. Lawrence 1885–1930: *Etruscan Places* (1932)
'Cerveteri'; see 20 above

39 I and the public know
What all schoolchildren learn,
Those to whom evil is done
Do evil in return.
W. H. Auden 1907–73: 'September 1, 1939' (1940)

40 As soon as men decide that all means are
permitted to fight an evil, then their good
becomes indistinguishable from the evil
that they set out to destroy.
Christopher Dawson 1889–1970: *The Judgement
of the Nations* (1942)

41 The face of 'evil' is always the face of total
need.
William S. Burroughs 1914–97: *The Naked Lunch*
(1959)

42 It was as though in those last minutes he
[Eichmann] was summing up the lessons
that this long course in human wickedness
had taught us—the lesson of the fearsome,
word-and-thought-defying *banality of evil*.
Hannah Arendt 1906–75: *Eichmann in Jerusalem*
(1963)

43 Two wrongs don't make a right, but they
make a good excuse.
Thomas Szasz 1920– : *The Second Sin* (1973); see 7
above

44 To respond to evil by committing another
evil does not eliminate evil but allows it to
go on forever.
Václav Havel 1936– : letter, 5 November 1989

45 Mostly, we are good when it makes sense. A
good society is one that makes sense of
being good.
Ian McEwan 1948– : *Enduring Love* (1998)

⤞ Gossip ⤝

see also **Reputation, Secrecy**

PROVERBS AND SAYINGS

1 Careless talk costs lives.
Second World War security slogan

**2 A dog that will fetch a bone will carry
a bone.**
someone given to gossip carries talk both ways;
English proverb, early 19th century

3 Give a dog a bad name and hang him.
once a person's reputation has been blackened his
plight is hopeless; English proverb, early 18th
century

4 Gossip is the lifeblood of society.
American proverb, mid 20th century

5 Gossip is vice enjoyed vicariously.
American proverb, early 20th century

**6 The greater the truth, the greater the
libel.**
English proverb, late 18th century

7 Loose lips sink ships.
American Second World war security slogan

8 A tale never loses in the telling.
implying that a story is often exaggerated when it is
repeated; English proverb, mid 16th century

**9 Those who live in glass houses
shouldn't throw stones.**
it is unwise to criticize or slander another if you are
vulnerable to retaliation; English proverb, mid 17th
century

10 What the soldier said isn't evidence.
hearsay evidence alone cannot be relied on; English
proverb, mid 19th century, originally from Dickens
Pickwick Papers (1837) 'You must not tell us what the
soldier, or any other man, said . . . it's not evidence'

PHRASES

11 bush telegraph
a rapid informal spreading of information or a
rumour; the network through which this takes place;
see 13 below

12 Chinese whispers
a game in which a message is distorted by being
passed around in a whisper; Russian scandal; see 14
below

13 hear on the grapevine
acquire information by rumour or unofficial
communication; originally from an American Civil
War usage, when news was said to be passed 'by
grapevine telegraph'; see 11 above

14 Russian scandal
Chinese whispers; see 12 above

QUOTATIONS

15 Many have fallen by the edge of the sword: but not so many as have fallen by the tongue.
Bible: Ecclesiasticus

16 *Che ti fa ciò che quivi pispiglia?*
Vien dietro a me, e lascia dir le genti.
What is it to thee what they whisper there? Come after me and let the people talk.
Dante Alighieri 1265–1321: *Divina Commedia* 'Purgatorio'

17 Enter Rumour, painted full of tongues.
William Shakespeare 1564–1616: *Henry IV, Part 2* (1597); stage direction

18 How these curiosities would be quite forgot, did not such idle fellows as I am put them down.
John Aubrey 1626–97: *Brief Lives* 'Venetia Digby'

19 Love and scandal are the best sweeteners of tea.
Henry Fielding 1707–54: *Love in Several Masques* (1728)

20 It is a matter of great interest what sovereigns are doing; but as to what Grand Duchesses are doing—Who cares?
Napoleon I 1769–1821: letter, 17 December 1811

21 Every man is surrounded by a neighbourhood of voluntary spies.
Jane Austen 1775–1817: *Northanger Abbey* (1818)

22 Everyone in a crowd has the power to throw dirt: nine out of ten have the inclination.
William Hazlitt 1778–1830: 'On Reading New Books' (1827)

23 There is only one thing in the world worse than being talked about, and that is not being talked about.
Oscar Wilde 1854–1900: *The Picture of Dorian Gray* (1891)

24 It takes your enemy and your friend, working together, to hurt you to the heart: the one to slander you and the other to get the news to you.
Mark Twain 1835–1910: *Following the Equator* (1897)

25 Like all gossip—it's merely one of those half-alive things that try to crowd out real life.
E. M. Forster 1879–1970: *A Passage to India* (1924)

26 No one gossips about other people's secret virtues.
Bertrand Russell 1872–1970: *On Education Especially in Early Childhood* (1926)

27 Blood sport is brought to its ultimate refinement in the gossip columns.
Bernard Ingham 1932– : speech, 5 February 1986

⤗ Government ⤖

see also **International Relations, Parliament, Politics, The Presidency, Society**

PROVERBS AND SAYINGS

1 **The cat, the rat, and Lovell the dog, rule all England under the hog.**
contemporary rhyme referring to William *Catesby*, Richard *Ratcliffe*, and Francis *Lovell*, favourites of Richard III (1452–85), whose personal emblem was a white *boar*

2 **Divide and rule.**
government control is more easily exercised if possible opponents are separated into factions; English proverb, early 17th century

PHRASES

5 **appeal to Caesar**
appeal to the highest possible authority; particularly with allusion to the Bible (Acts), in which Paul the Apostle exercised his right as a Roman citizen to have his case heard in Rome, with the words 'I appeal unto Caesar'

3 **God is high above, and the tsar is far away.**
the source of central power is out of the reach of local interests; Russian proverb; see 4 below, compare **Caution 5**

4 **The mountains are high, and the emperor is far away.**
the source of central power is out of the reach of local interests; Chinese proverb; see 3 above, compare **Caution 5**

6 **bread and circuses**
the public provision of subsistence and entertainment, especially to assuage the populace; from Juvenal: see 12 below

7 **checks and balances**
counterbalancing influences by which an organization or system is regulated, typically those

ensuring that power in political institutions is not concentrated in the hands of particular individuals or groups

8 the corridors of power
the senior levels of government or administration, where covert influence is regarded as being exerted and significant decisions are made; from the title of C. P. Snow's novel *The Corridors of Power* (1964)

QUOTATIONS

10 A ruler who governs his state by virtue is like the north polar star, which remains in its place while all the other stars revolve around it.
Confucius 551–479 BC: *Analects*

11 Let them hate, so long as they fear.
Accius 170–c.86 BC: from *Atreus*; Seneca *Dialogues*

12 . . . *Duas tantum res anxius optat,
Panem et circenses.*
Only two things does he [the modern citizen] anxiously wish for—bread and circuses.
Juvenal c.AD 60–c.130: *Satires*; see 6 above

13 Because it is difficult to join them together, it is much safer for a prince to be feared than loved, if he is to fail in one of the two.
Niccolò Machiavelli 1469–1527: *The Prince* (written 1513)

14 Though God hath raised me high, yet this I count the glory of my crown: that I have reigned with your loves.
Elizabeth I 1533–1603: The Golden Speech, 1601

15 I will govern according to the common weal, but not according to the common will.
James I 1566–1625: in December, 1621; J. R. Green *History of the English People* vol. 3 (1879)

16 *L'État c'est moi.*
I am the State.
Louis XIV 1638–1715: before the Parlement de Paris, 13 April 1655; probably apocryphal

17 It is a 'beautiful maxim' that it is necessary to save five *sous* on unessential things, and to pour out millions when it is a question of your glory.
Jean-Baptiste Colbert 1619–83: letter to Louis XIV, 1666

18 Governments need both shepherds and butchers.
Voltaire 1694–1778: 'The Piccini Notebooks' (c.1735–50)

19 I would not give half a guinea to live under one form of government rather than another. It is of no moment to the happiness of an individual.
Samuel Johnson 1709–84: James Boswell *Life of Samuel Johnson* (1791) 31 March 1772

9 the ship of state
the state and its affairs, especially when regarded as being subject to adverse or changing circumstances; a *ship* as the type of something subject to adverse or changing weather

20 A government of laws, and not of men.
John Adams 1735–1826: *Boston Gazette* (1774) 'Novanglus' papers; later incorporated in the Massachusetts Constitution (1780)

21 The happiness of society is the end of government.
John Adams 1735–1826: *Thoughts on Government* (1776)

22 Government, even in its best state, is but a necessary evil . . . Government, like dress, is the badge of lost innocence; the palaces of kings are built upon the ruins of the bowers of paradise.
Thomas Paine 1737–1809: *Common Sense* (1776)

23 My people and I have come to an agreement which satisfies us both. They are to say what they please, and I am to do what I please.
his interpretation of benevolent despotism
Frederick the Great 1712–86: attributed

24 When, in countries that are called civilized, we see age going to the workhouse and youth to the gallows, something must be wrong in the system of government.
Thomas Paine 1737–1809: *The Rights of Man* pt. 2 (1792)

25 Away with the cant of 'Measures not men'!—the idle supposition that it is the harness and not the horses that draw the chariot along. If the comparison must be made, if the distinction must be taken, men are everything, measures comparatively nothing.
George Canning 1770–1827: speech on the Army estimates, 8 December 1802; the phrase 'measures not men' may be found as early as 1742 (in a letter from Chesterfield to Dr Chevenix, 6 March)

26 To govern is to choose.
Duc de Lévis 1764–1830: *Maximes et Réflexions* (1812 ed.)

27 The best government is that which governs least.
John L. O'Sullivan 1813–95: *United States Magazine and Democratic Review* (1837)

28 No Government can be long secure without a formidable Opposition.
Benjamin Disraeli 1804–81: *Coningsby* (1844)

29 The Crown is, according to the saying, the 'fountain of honour'; but the Treasury is the spring of business.
Walter Bagehot 1826–77: *The English Constitution* (1867) 'The Cabinet'; see **Royalty** 24

30 A fainéant government is not the worst government that England can have. It has been the great fault of our politicians that they have all wanted to do something.
Anthony Trollope 1815–82: *Phineas Finn* (1869)

31 My faith in the people governing is, on the whole, infinitesimal; my faith in The People governed is, on the whole, illimitable.
Charles Dickens 1812–70: speech at Birmingham and Midland Institute, 27 September 1869

32 The State is not 'abolished', *it withers away.*
Friedrich Engels 1820–95: *Anti-Dühring* (1878)

33 The state is like the human body. Not all of its functions are dignified.
Anatole France 1844–1924: *Les Opinions de M. Jerome Coignard* (1893)

34 While the State exists, there can be no freedom. When there is freedom there will be no State.
Lenin 1870–1924: *State and Revolution* (1919)

35 A government which robs Peter to pay Paul can always depend on the support of Paul.
George Bernard Shaw 1856–1950: *Everybody's Political What's What?* (1944); see **Debt** 11

36 BIG BROTHER IS WATCHING YOU.
George Orwell 1903–50: *Nineteen Eighty-Four* (1949)

37 If the Government is big enough to give you everything you want, it is big enough to take away everything you have.
Gerald Ford 1909– : John F. Parker *If Elected* (1960)

38 The Civil Service is profoundly deferential — 'Yes, Minister! No, Minister! If you wish it, Minister!'
Richard Crossman 1907–74: diary, 22 October 1964

39 Many journalists have fallen for the conspiracy theory of government. I do assure you that they would produce more accurate work if they adhered to the cock-up theory.
Bernard Ingham 1932– : in *Observer* 17 March 1985

40 I think it will be a clash between the political will and the administrative won't.
Jonathan Lynn 1943– and **Antony Jay** 1930– : *Yes Prime Minister* (1987) vol. 2

41 We give the impression of being in office but not in power.
Norman Lamont 1942– : speech, House of Commons, 9 June 1993

42 Thank heavens we do not get all of the government that we are made to pay for.
Milton Friedman 1912– : quoted in the House of Lords, 24 November 1994

Gratitude and Ingratitude

PROVERBS AND SAYINGS

1 **The Devil was sick, the Devil a saint would be; the Devil was well, the devil a saint was he.**
promises made in adversity may not be kept in prosperity; English proverb, early 17th century

2 **Don't overload gratitude, if you do, she'll kick.**
American proverb, mid 18th century

3 **Never look a gift horse in the mouth.**
warning against questioning the quality or use of a lucky chance or gift; referring to the fact that it is by

a horse's teeth that its age is judged; English proverb, early 16th century

4 **You never miss the water till the well runs dry.**
applied to situations in which it is only when a source of support or sustenance has been withdrawn that its importance is understood; English proverb, early 17th century

PHRASES

5 **bite the hand that feeds one**
injure a benefactor, act ungratefully; see 15 below

QUOTATIONS

6 A joyful and pleasant thing it is to be thankful.
Bible: Psalm 147

7 Blow, blow, thou winter wind,
Thou art not so unkind
As man's ingratitude.
William Shakespeare 1564–1616: *As You Like It* (1599)

8 They say late thanks are ever best.
Francis Bacon 1561–1626: letter to Robert, Lord Cecil, July 1603

9 How sharper than a serpent's tooth it is
To have a thankless child!
William Shakespeare 1564–1616: *King Lear* (1605–6)

10 I once knew a man out of courtesy help a lame dog over a stile, and he for requital bit his fingers.
William Chillingworth 1602–44: *The Religion of Protestants* (1637)

11 In most of mankind gratitude is merely a secret hope for greater favours.
Duc de la Rochefoucauld 1613–80: *Maximes* (1678)

12 When I'm not thanked at all, I'm thanked enough,
I've done my duty, and I've done no more.
Henry Fielding 1707–54: *Tom Thumb the Great* (1731)

13 There are minds so impatient of inferiority, that their gratitude is a species of revenge, and they return benefits, not because recompense is a pleasure, but because obligation is a pain.
Samuel Johnson 1709–84: in *The Rambler* 15 January 1751

14 There's plenty of boys that will come hankering and grovelling around you when you've got an apple, and beg the core off of you; but when they've got one, and you beg for the core and remind them how you give them a core one time, they say thank you 'most to death, but there ain't-a-going to be no core.
Mark Twain 1835–1910: *Tom Sawyer Abroad* (1894)

15 That's the way with these directors, they're always biting the hand that lays the golden egg.
Sam Goldwyn 1882–1974: Alva Johnston *The Great Goldwyn* (1937); see 5 above, **Greed** 5

16 Never in the field of human conflict was so much owed by so many to so few.
on the skill and courage of British airmen
Winston Churchill 1874–1965: speech, House of Commons, 20 August 1940

17 Maybe the only thing worse than having to give gratitude constantly all the time, is having to accept it.
William Faulkner 1897–1962: *Requiem for a Nun* (1951) act 2, sc. 1

18 [Gratitude] is a sickness suffered by dogs.
Joseph Stalin 1879–1953: Nikolai Tolstoy *Stalin's Secret War* (1981)

19 My children are ungrateful: they don't care. That is my great reward. They are free.
Fay Weldon 1931– : *Praxis* (1978)

20 What have the Romans ever done for us?
Graham Chapman 1941–89 et al.: *Monty Python's Life of Brian* (1979 film)

⤞ Greatness ⤝

PROVERBS AND SAYINGS

1 If any man seek for greatness, let him forget greatness and seek truth.
American proverb, mid 20th century

QUOTATIONS

2 The beauty of Israel is slain upon thy high places: how are the mighty fallen!
Bible: II Samuel

3 But be not afraid of greatness: some men are born great, some achieve greatness, and some have greatness thrust upon them.
William Shakespeare 1564–1616: *Twelfth Night* (1601)

4 What millions died—that Caesar might be great!
Thomas Campbell 1777–1844: *Pleasures of Hope* (1799)

5 Fleas know not whether they are upon the body of a giant or upon one of ordinary size.
Walter Savage Landor 1775–1864: *Imaginary Conversations* (1824)

6 Is it so bad, then, to be misunderstood? Pythagoras was misunderstood, and Socrates, and Jesus, and Luther, and Copernicus, and Galileo, and Newton, and every pure and wise spirit that ever took flesh. To be great is to be misunderstood.
Ralph Waldo Emerson 1803–82: *Essays* (1841) 'Self-Reliance'

7   In me there dwells
No greatness, save it be some far-off touch
Of greatness to know well I am not great.
Alfred, Lord Tennyson 1809–92: *Idylls of the King* 'Lancelot and Elaine' (1859)

8 In historical events great men—so-called—are but labels serving to give a name to the event, and like labels they have the least possible connection with the event itself.
Leo Tolstoy 1828–1910: *War and Peace* (1868–9)

9 A man is seldom ashamed of feeling that he cannot love a woman so well when he sees a certain greatness in her: nature having intended greatness for men.
George Eliot 1819–80: *Middlemarch* (1871–2)

10 If I am a great man, then all great men are frauds.
Andrew Bonar Law 1858–1923: Lord Beaverbrook *Politicians and the War* (1932)

11 A man does not attain the status of Galileo merely because he is persecuted; he must also be right.
Stephen Jay Gould 1941–2002: *Ever since Darwin* (1977)

⤞ Greed ⤝

see also **Money**

PROVERBS AND SAYINGS

1 **The more you get the more you want.**
English proverb, mid 14th century

2 **Much would have more.**
the ownership of substantial possessions creates in the owner the desire for still more; English proverb, mid 14th century

3 **The sea refuses no river.**
the sea's capacity is so great that anyone who chooses may find a place there; English proverb, early 17th century

4 **Where the carcase is, there shall the eagles be gathered together.**
English proverb, mid 16th century, from the Bible (Matthew) 'Wheresoever the carcase is, there will the eagles be gathered together'; *eagles* here as the type of carrion bird

PHRASES

5 **kill the goose that lays the golden eggs**
sacrifice long-term advantage to short-term gain; referring to a traditional story, in which the owner of the goose killed it in the hope of possessing himself of a store of golden eggs instead of being contented with a daily ration; see **Gratitude** 15

QUOTATIONS

6 Greedy for the property of others, extravagant with his own.
Sallust 86–35 BC: *Catiline*

7   *Quid non mortalia pectora cogis,*
Auri sacra fames!
To what do you not drive human hearts, cursed craving for gold!
Virgil 70–19 BC: *Aeneid*

8 Bell, book, and candle shall not drive me back,

When gold and silver becks me to come on.
William Shakespeare 1564–1616: *King John* (1591–8); see **The Supernatural** 2

9   What a rare punishment
Is avarice to itself!
Ben Jonson 1573–1637: *Volpone* (1606)

10 £40,000 a year a moderate income—such a one as a man *might jog on with.*
Lord Durham 1792–1840: letter from Mr Creevey to Miss Elizabeth Ord, 13 September 1821

11 Please, sir, I want some more.
Charles Dickens 1812–70: *Oliver Twist* (1838)

12 I'll be sick tonight.

in reply to his mother's warning 'You'll be sick tomorrow', when stuffing himself with cakes at tea
Jack Llewelyn-Davies 1894–1959: Andrew Birkin *J. M. Barrie and the Lost Boys* (1979); Barrie used the line in *Little Mary* (1903)

13 If all the rich people in the world divided up their money among themselves there wouldn't be enough to go round.
Christina Stead 1902–83: *House of All Nations* (1938)

14 There is enough in the world for everyone's need, but not enough for everyone's greed.
Frank Buchman 1878–1961: *Remaking the World* (1947)

15 But the music that excels is the sound of oil wells

As they slurp, slurp, slurp into the barrels
. . .
I want an old-fashioned house
With an old-fashioned fence
And an old-fashioned millionaire.
Marve Fisher: 'An Old-Fashioned Girl' (1954 song)

16 Greed is all right . . . Greed is healthy. You can be greedy and still feel good about yourself.
Ivan F. Boesky 1937– : commencement address, Berkeley, California, 18 May 1986

17 Greed—for lack of a better word—is good. Greed is right. Greed works.
Stanley Weiser and **Oliver Stone** 1946– : *Wall Street* (1987 film)

Guilt and Innocence

PROVERBS AND SAYINGS

1 Confess and be hanged.

guilt must be confessed and the due punishment accepted for true repentance; English proverb, late 16th century

2 The guilty one always runs.

American proverb, mid 20th century

3 We are all guilty.

supposedly typical of the liberal view that all members of society bear responsibility for its

wrongs; used particularly as a catchphrase by the psychiatrist 'Dr Heinz Kiosk' in the satirical column of 'Peter Simple' (pseudonym of Michael Wharton)

4 We name the guilty men.

supposedly now a cliché of investigative journalism; *Guilty Men* (1940) was the title of a tract by Michael Foot, Frank Owen, and Peter Howard, published under the pseudonym of 'Cato', which attacked the supporters of Munich and the appeasement policy of Neville Chamberlain

QUOTATIONS

5 Everyone's quick to blame the alien.
Aeschylus *c.*525–456 BC: *The Suppliant Maidens*

6 When Pilate saw that he could prevail nothing . . . he took water, and washed his hands before the multitude, saying, I am innocent of the blood of this just person: see ye to it.
Bible: St Matthew; see **Duty 8**

7 He that is without sin among you, let him first cast a stone at her.
Bible: St John; see **Criticism 4**

8 Suspicion always haunts the guilty mind; The thief doth fear each bush an officer.
William Shakespeare 1564–1616: *Henry VI, Part 3* (1592)

9 Here's the smell of the blood still: all the perfumes of Arabia will not sweeten this little hand.
William Shakespeare 1564–1616: *Macbeth* (1606)

10 He that first cries out stop thief, is often he that has stolen the treasure.
William Congreve 1670–1729: *Love for Love* (1695)

11 It is better that ten guilty persons escape than one innocent suffer.
William Blackstone 1723–80: *Commentaries on the Laws of England* (1765)

12 What hangs people . . . is the unfortunate circumstance of guilt.
Robert Louis Stevenson 1850–94: *The Wrong Box* (with Lloyd Osbourne, 1889)

13 The innocent and the beautiful Have no enemy but time.
W. B. Yeats 1865–1939: 'In Memory of Eva Gore Booth and Con Markiewicz' (1933)

14 It is not only our fate but our business to lose innocence, and once we have lost that, it is futile to attempt a picnic in Eden.
Elizabeth Bowen 1899–1973: 'Out of a Book' in *Orion III* (1946)

15 Innocence always calls mutely for protection, when we would be so much wiser to guard ourselves against it: innocence is like a dumb leper who has lost

his bell, wandering the world meaning no harm.
Graham Greene 1904–91: *The Quiet American* (1955)

16 True guilt is guilt at the obligation one owes to oneself to be oneself. False guilt is guilt felt at not being what other people feel one ought to be or assume that one is.
R. D. Laing 1927–89: *Self and Others* (1961)

17 To be absolutely honest, what I feel really bad about is that I don't feel worse. That's the ineffectual liberal's problem in a nutshell.
Michael Frayn 1933– : in *Observer* 8 August 1965

18 I brought myself down. I gave them a sword. And they stuck it in.
Richard Nixon 1913–94: television interview, 19 May 1977

19 Guilt feelings so often arise from accusations rather than from crimes.
Iris Murdoch 1919–99: *The Sea, The Sea* (1978)

20 Good women always think it is their fault when someone else is being offensive. Bad women never take the blame for anything.
Anita Brookner 1928– : *Hotel du Lac* (1984)

21 *to Albert Speer, who having always denied knowledge of the Holocaust had said that he was at fault in having 'looked away':*
You cannot look away from something you don't know. If you looked away, then you knew.
Gitta Sereny 1923– : recalled on BBC2 *Reputations*, 2 May 1996

22 Innocence is a slippery substance. It seems you can't possess it and at the same time *know* you possess it.
Carol Shields 1935–2003: *Larry's Party* (1997)

Habit see Custom and Habit

⤚ Happiness ⤙

PROVERBS AND SAYINGS

1 **Blessings brighten as they take their flight.**
it is only when something is lost that one realizes its value; English proverb, mid 18th century

2 **Call no man happy till he dies.**
traditionally attributed to the Athenian statesman and poet Solon (*c.*640–after 556 BC) in the form 'Call no man happy before he dies, he is at best but fortunate'; English proverb, mid 16th century

3 **Happiness is what you make of it.**
American proverb, mid 19th century

4 **It is a poor heart that never rejoices.**
often used to explain a celebratory action, and implying that circumstances are not in general unrelievedly bad; English proverb, mid 19th century

PHRASES

5 **the gaiety of nations**
general gaiety or amusement; from Samuel Johnson on the death of David Garrick (1779), 'that stroke of death, which has eclipsed the gaiety of nations'

QUOTATIONS

6 The person who is searching for his own happiness should pull out the dart that he has stuck in himself, the arrow-head of grieving, of desiring, of despair.
Pali Tripitaka *c.* 2nd century BC: *Sutta-Nipāta* [Woven Cadences]

7 *Nil admirari prope res est una, Numici,*
Solaque quae possit facere et servare beatum.
To marvel at nothing is just about the one and only thing, Numicius, that can make a man happy and keep him that way.
Horace 65–8 BC: *Epistles*; see 14 below

8 Happiness lies in conquering one's enemies, in driving them in front of oneself, in taking their property, in savouring their despair, in outraging their wives and daughters.
Genghis Khan 1162–1227: Witold Rodzinski *The Walled Kingdom: A History of China* (1979)

9 Certainly there is no happiness within this circle of flesh, nor is it in the optics of these eyes to behold felicity; the first day of our Jubilee is death.
Thomas Browne 1605–82: *Religio Medici* (1643)

10 But headlong joy is ever on the wing.
John Milton 1608–74: 'The Passion' (1645)

11 One is never as unhappy as one thinks, nor as happy as one hopes.
Duc de la Rochefoucauld 1613–80: *Sentences et Maximes de Morale* (1664)

12 For all the happiness mankind can gain
Is not in pleasure, but in rest from pain.
John Dryden 1631–1700: *The Indian Emperor* (1665)

13 Mirth is like a flash of lightning that breaks through a gloom of clouds, and glitters for a moment: cheerfulness keeps up a kind of daylight in the mind, and fills it with a steady and perpetual serenity.
Joseph Addison 1672–1719: in *The Spectator* 17 May 1712

14 Not to admire, is all the art I know,
To make men happy, and to keep them so.
Alexander Pope 1688–1744: *Imitations of Horace* (1738); see 7 above

15 It cannot reasonably be doubted, but a little miss, dressed in a new gown for a dancing-school ball, receives as complete enjoyment as the greatest orator, who triumphs in the splendour of his eloquence, while he governs the passions and resolutions of a numerous assembly.
David Hume 1711–76: *Essays: Moral and Political* (1741–2) 'The Sceptic'

16 That all who are happy, are equally happy, is not true. A peasant and a philosopher may be equally *satisfied*, but not equally *happy*. Happiness consists in the multiplicity of agreeable consciousness.
Samuel Johnson 1709–84: James Boswell *Life of Samuel Johnson* (1791) February 1766

17 *Freude, schöner Götterfunken,*
Tochter aus Elysium.
Joy, beautiful radiance of the gods, daughter of Elysium.
Friedrich von Schiller 1759–1805: 'An die Freude' (1785)

18 Happiness is not an ideal of reason but of imagination.
Immanuel Kant 1724–1804: *Fundamental Principles of the Metaphysics of Ethics* (1785)

19 A large income is the best recipe for happiness I ever heard of. It certainly may secure all the myrtle and turkey part of it.
Jane Austen 1775–1817: *Mansfield Park* (1814)

20 Happiness is no laughing matter.
Richard Whately 1787–1863: *Apophthegms* (1854)

21 Cheerfulness gives elasticity to the spirit. Spectres fly before it.
Samuel Smiles 1812–1904: *Self-Help* (1859)

22 Ask yourself whether you are happy, and you cease to be so.
John Stuart Mill 1806–73: *Autobiography* (1873)

23 But a lifetime of happiness! No man alive could bear it: it would be hell on earth.
George Bernard Shaw 1856–1950: *Man and Superman* (1903)

24 For if unhappiness develops the forces of the mind, happiness alone is salutary to the body.
Marcel Proust 1871–1922: *Time Regained* (1926)

25 There may be Peace without Joy, and Joy without Peace, but the two combined make Happiness.
John Buchan 1875–1940: *Memory-Hold-the-Door* (1940)

26 Happiness makes up in height for what it lacks in length.
Robert Frost 1874–1963: title of poem (1942)

27 Point me out the happy man and I will point you out either egotism, selfishness, evil—or else an absolute ignorance.
Graham Greene 1904–91: *The Heart of the Matter* (1948)

28 Happiness washes away many things, just as suffering washes away many things.
Heinrich Böll 1917–85: *The Train was on Time* (1949)

29 Happiness is a warm gun.
John Lennon 1940–80: title of song (1968); see **Dogs** 14

30 Happiness is an imaginary condition, formerly often attributed by the living to the dead, now usually attributed by adults to children, and by children to adults.
Thomas Szasz 1920– : *The Second Sin* (1973)

31 I always say I don't think everyone has the right to happiness or to be loved. Even the Americans have written into their constitution that you have the right to the 'pursuit of happiness'. You have the right to try but that is all.
Claire Rayner 1931– : G. Kinnock and F. Miller (eds.) *By Faith and Daring* (1993); see **Human Rights** 7

➤Haste and Delay ◄

PROVERBS AND SAYINGS

1 Always in a hurry, always behind.
North American proverb, mid 20th century

2 Delays are dangerous.
used as a warning against procrastination; English proverb, late 16th century

3 Don't hurry—start early.
American proverb, mid 20th century

4 Haste is from the Devil.
often used to mean that undue haste results in work being done badly or carelessly; English proverb, mid 17th century

5 Haste makes waste.
hurried work is likely to be wasteful; English proverb, late 14th century

6 Make haste slowly.
advising a course of careful preparation; English proverb, late 16th century; see 13 below

7 More haste, less speed.
speed here meant originally success rather than swiftness, and the meaning is that hurried work is likely to be less successful; English proverb, mid 14th century

8 Never put off till tomorrow what you can do today.
English proverb, late 14th century

9 Procrastination is the thief of time.
someone who continually puts things off ultimately achieves little; English proverb, mid 18th century, from Edward Young *Night Thoughts* (1742–5)

PHRASES

10 at the eleventh hour
at the latest possible moment; with reference to the story in the Bible (Matthew) of the labourers who were hired 'about the eleventh hour' to work in the vineyard, and who were given the same payment as those who had worked all day

QUOTATIONS

11 Why tarry the wheels of his chariots?
Bible: Judges

12 He always hurries to the main event and whisks his audience into the middle of things as though they knew already.
Horace 65–8 BC: *Ars Poetica*

13 *Festina lente.*
Make haste slowly.
Augustus 63 BC–AD 14: Suetonius *Lives of the Caesars* 'Divus Augustus'; see 6 above

14 I'll put a girdle round about the earth
In forty minutes.
William Shakespeare 1564–1616: *A Midsummer Night's Dream* (1595–6)

15 I knew a wise man that had it for a by-word, when he saw men hasten to a conclusion. 'Stay a little, that we may make an end the sooner.'
Francis Bacon 1561–1626: *Essays* (1625) 'Of Dispatch'

16 Though I am always in haste, I am never in a hurry.
John Wesley 1703–91: letter to Miss March, 10 December 1777

17 No admittance till the week after next!
Lewis Carroll 1832–98: *Through the Looking-Glass* (1872)

18 Never be a pioneer. It's the Early Christian that gets the fattest lion.
Saki 1870–1916: *Reginald* (1904) 'Reginald's Choir Treat'; see **Christian Church** 3

19 Hesitating doesn't matter if only you win out.
Bertolt Brecht 1898–1956: *The Good Woman of Setzuan* (1938)

20 ESTRAGON: Charming spot. Inspiring prospects. Let's go.
VLADIMIR: We can't.
ESTRAGON: Why not?
VLADIMIR: We're waiting for Godot.
Samuel Beckett 1906–89: *Waiting for Godot* (1955)

21 If anyone believes that our smiles involve abandonment of the teaching of Marx, Engels and Lenin he deceives himself. Those who wait for that must wait until a shrimp learns to whistle.
Nikita Khrushchev 1894–1971: speech in Moscow, 17 September 1955

22 I think we ought to let him hang there. Let him twist slowly, slowly in the wind.
of Patrick Gray, regarding his nomination as director of the FBI, in a telephone conversation with John Dean
John Ehrlichman 1925–99: in *Washington Post* 27 July 1973; see **Certainty** 6

23 I never run for the bus.
   Linford Christie 1960– : in *Independent* 19
   May 1999

⇥⇥ Hatred ⇤⇤

see also **Enemies**

PROVERBS AND SAYINGS

1 **Better a dinner of herbs than a stalled
  ox where hate is.**
   simple food accompanied by goodwill and affection
   is preferable to luxury in an atmosphere of ill-will;
   English proverb, mid 16th century, see 3 below

2 **Curses, like chickens, come home to
  roost.**
   ill will directed at another is likely to rebound on the
   originator; English proverb, late 14th century

QUOTATIONS

3 Better is a dinner of herbs where love is,
  than a stalled ox and hatred therewith.
   Bible: Proverbs; see 1 above

4 For hate is not conquered by hate: hate is
  conquered by love. This is a law eternal.
   Pali Tripitaka *c.* 2nd century BC: *Dhammapada*

5 I have loved him too much not to feel any
  hatred for him.
   Jean Racine 1639–99: *Andromaque* (1667)

6 Now hatred is by far the longest pleasure;
  Men love in haste, but they detest at leisure.
   Lord Byron 1788–1824: *Don Juan* (1819–24)

7 The dupe of friendship, and the fool of love;
  have I not reason to hate and to despise
  myself? Indeed I do; and chiefly for not
  having hated and despised the world
  enough.
   William Hazlitt 1778–1830: *The Plain Speaker*
   (1826) 'On the Pleasure of Hating'

8 Gr-r-r—there go, my heart's abhorrence!
  Water your damned flower-pots, do!
  If hate killed men, Brother Lawrence,
  God's blood, would not mine kill you!
   Robert Browning 1812–89: 'Soliloquy of the
   Spanish Cloister' (1842)

9 I tell you there is such a thing as creative
  hate!
   Willa Cather 1873–1947: *The Song of the Lark*
   (1915)

10 If you hate a person, you hate something in
   him that is part of yourself. What isn't part
   of ourselves doesn't disturb us.
   Hermann Hesse 1877–1962: *Demian* (1919)

11 Any kiddie in school can love like a fool,
   But hating, my boy, is an art.
   Ogden Nash 1902–71: 'Plea for Less Malice Toward
   None' (1933)

12 I never hated a man enough to give him
   diamonds back.
   Zsa Zsa Gabor 1919– : in *Observer* 25 August 1957

13 Always remember, others may hate you.
   Those who hate you don't win unless you
   hate them. And then you destroy yourself.
   Richard Nixon 1913–94: address to members of his
   staff after his resignation, 9 August 1974

14 Hating gets going, it goes round, it gets older
   and tighter and older and tighter, until it
   holds a person inside it like a fist holds a
   stick.
   Ursula K. Le Guin 1929– : *Always Coming Home*
   (1985)

15 No one is born hating another person
   because of the colour of his skin, or his
   background, or his religion. People must
   learn to hate, and if they can learn to hate,
   they can be taught to love, for love comes
   more naturally to the human heart than its
   opposite.
   Nelson Mandela 1918– : *Long Walk to Freedom*
   (1994)

⤚ Health and Fitness ⤙

PROVERBS AND SAYINGS

1 **An apple a day keeps the doctor away.**
eating an apple each day keeps one healthy; English proverb, mid 19th century; compare 5 below

2 **Don't die of ignorance.**
Aids publicity campaign, 1987

3 **Drinka Pinta Milka Day.**
advertising slogan for National Dairy Council, 1958; coined by Bertrand Whitehead

4 **Early to bed and early to rise, makes a man healthy, wealthy, and wise.**
linking a healthy and sober lifestyle with material success; English proverb, late 15th century, see Sleep 18

5 **Eat leeks in March and ramsons in May, and all the year after physicians may play.**
ramsons = wild garlic; Welsh proverb; compare 1 above

6 **Even your closest friends won't tell you.**
advertising slogan for Listerine mouthwash, US, 1923

7 **Every good quality is contained in ginger.**
Indian proverb

8 **I was a seven-stone weakling.**
advertising slogan for Charles Atlas body-building, originally in US

9 **More die of food than famine.**
American proverb, mid 20th century

10 **Slip, slop, slap.**
sun protection slogan, meaning *slip* on a T-shirt, *slop* on some suncream, *slap* on a hat; Australian health education programme, 1980s

11 **There is nothing so good for the inside of a man as the outside of a horse.**
recommending the healthful effects of horse-riding; English proverb, early 20th century

12 **Those who do not find time for exercise will have to find time for illness.**
traditional saying

13 **Your food is your medicine.**
Indian proverb

QUOTATIONS

14 Life's not just being alive, but being well.
Martial c.AD 40–c.104: *Epigrammata*

15 *Orandum est ut sit mens sana in corpore sano.*
You should pray to have a sound mind in a sound body.
Juvenal c.AD 60–c.130: *Satires*

16 Look to your health; and if you have it, praise God, and value it next to a good conscience; for health is the second blessing that we mortals are capable of; a blessing that money cannot buy.
Izaak Walton 1593–1683: *The Compleat Angler* (1653)

17 The wise, for cure, on exercise depend;
God never made his work for man to mend.
John Dryden 1631–1700: Epistle 'To my honoured kinsman John Driden' (1700)

18 The sovereign invigorator of the body is exercise, and of all the exercises, walking is best.
Thomas Jefferson 1743–1826: letter to Thomas Mann Randolph Jr., 27 August 1786

19 Exercise is bunk. If you are healthy, you don't need it: if you are sick you shouldn't take it.
Henry Ford 1863–1947: attributed

20 Avoid running at all times.
Leroy ('Satchel') Paige 1906–82: *How To Stay Young* (1953)

21 I sometimes think that running has given me a glimpse of the greatest freedom a man can ever know, because it results in the simultaneous liberation of both body and mind.
Roger Bannister 1929– : *First Four Minutes* (1955)

22 Therapy has become what I think of as the tenth American muse.
Jacob Bronowski 1908–74: attributed

23 Exercise is the yuppie version of bulimia.
Barbara Ehrenreich 1941– : *The Worst Years of Our Lives* (1991) 'Food Worship'

24 The first law of dietetics seems to be: if it tastes good, it's bad for you.
Isaac Asimov 1920–92: attributed

25 The only exercise I take is walking behind the coffins of friends who took exercise.
Peter O'Toole 1932– : in *Mail on Sunday* 27 December 1998

26 It is not for doctors to advise people to live
their lives as patients, in order to die
healthy.
Richard Doll 1912–2005: in *The Times* 3
August 2005

⇥ Heaven and Hell ↤

PROVERBS AND SAYINGS

1 Hell is wherever heaven is not.
English proverb, late 16th century

PHRASES

2 Abraham's bosom
heaven, the place of rest for the souls of the blessed;
Abraham the Hebrew patriarch from whom all Jews
trace their descent; from the Bible (Luke) 'And it
came to pass, that the beggar died, and was carried
by the angels into Abraham's bosom'

3 fire and brimstone
torment in hell; deriving from biblical allusion, as in
Revelation 'These both were cast alive into a lake of
fire burning with brimstone'

4 the happy hunting-grounds
among Native Americans, a fabled country full of
game to which warriors go after death

5 Land of Beulah
heaven; from John Bunyan's *Pilgrim's Progress*, where
the Land of Beulah is a pleasant and fertile country
beyond the Valley of the Shadow of Death, and
within sight of the Heavenly City

6 New Jerusalem
the abode of the blessed in heaven; from the Bible
(Revelation) 'And I, John, saw the holy city, new
Jerusalem, coming down from God out of heaven'

QUOTATIONS

7 But the children of the kingdom shall be
cast out into outer darkness: there shall be
weeping and gnashing of teeth.
Bible: St Matthew

8 And I saw a new heaven and a new earth: for
the first heaven and the first earth were
passed away; and there was no more sea.
Bible: Revelation

9 PER ME SI VA NELLA CITTÀ DOLENTE,
PER ME SI VA NELL' ETERNO DOLORE,
PER ME SI VA TRA LA PERDUTA GENTE . . .
LASCIATE OGNI SPERANZA VOI CH'ENTRATE!
Through me is the way to the sorrowful city.
Through me is the way to eternal suffering.
Through me is the way to join the lost
people . . . Abandon all hope, you who
enter!
inscription at the entrance to Hell; the final sentence
now often quoted as 'Abandon hope, all ye who
enter here'
Dante Alighieri 1265–1321: *Divina Commedia*
'Inferno'

10 Why, this is hell, nor am I out of it:
Thinkst thou that I who saw the face
of God,
And tasted the eternal joys of heaven,
Am not tormented with ten thousand hells

In being deprived of everlasting bliss!
Christopher Marlowe 1564–93: *Doctor Faustus*
(1604)

11 Were the happiness of the next world as
closely apprehended as the felicities of this,
it were a martyrdom to live.
Thomas Browne 1605–82: *Hydriotaphia* (Urn
Burial, 1658)

12 He ascended into heaven, And sitteth on the
right hand of God the Father Almighty;
From thence he shall come to judge the
quick and the dead.
quick = an archaic term for the living
The Book of Common Prayer 1662: *Morning
Prayer* The Apostles' Creed; see **Transport** 15

13 Me miserable! which way shall I fly
Infinite wrath, and infinite despair?
Which way I fly is hell; myself am hell.
John Milton 1608–74: *Paradise Lost* (1667)

14 My idea of heaven is, eating *pâté de foie gras*
to the sound of trumpets.
the view of Smith's friend Henry Luttrell
Sydney Smith 1771–1845: H. Pearson *The Smith of
Smiths* (1934)

15 I will spend my heaven doing good on
earth.
St Teresa of Lisieux 1873–97: T. N. Taylor (ed.) *Soeur
Thérèse of Lisieux* (1912)

16 He has the look of a man who has been in
hell and seen there, not a hopeless suffering,
but meanness and frippery.
on Dostoevsky
W. Somerset Maugham 1874–1965: *A Writer's
Notebook* (1949) written in 1917

17 The true paradises are the paradises that we
have lost.
Marcel Proust 1871–1922: *Time Regained* (1926)

18 Hell, madam, is to love no more.
Georges Bernanos 1888–1948: *Journal d'un curé
de campagne* (1936)

19 Whose love is given over-well
Shall look on Helen's face in hell
Whilst they whose love is thin and wise

Shall see John Knox in Paradise.
Dorothy Parker 1893–1967: 'Partial Comfort'
(1937)

20 Hell is other people.
Jean-Paul Sartre 1905–80: *Huis Clos* (1944)

21 What is hell?
Hell is oneself,
Hell is alone, the other figures in it
Merely projections.
T. S. Eliot 1888–1965: *The Cocktail Party* (1950)

22 We are not bound for ever to the circles of
the world, and beyond them is more than
memory.
J. R. R. Tolkien 1892–1973: *The Lord of the Rings* pt.
3 *The Return of the King* (1955)

23 We may be surprised at the people we find
in heaven. God has a soft spot for sinners.
His standards are quite low.
Desmond Tutu 1931– : in *Sunday Times* 15
April 2001

⤳ Heroes ⤶

PROVERBS AND SAYINGS

**1 Better to have lived one day as a tiger
than a thousand years as a sheep.**
modern saying; see 7 below

2 For every Pharaoh there is a Moses.
a liberator will arise against every oppressor; Middle
Eastern proverb

PHRASES

3 the Age of Chivalry
the time when men behave with courage, honour,
and courtesy; the period during which the knightly
social and ethical system prevailed

4 knight in shining armour
a chivalrous rescuer or helper, especially of a woman

QUOTATIONS

5 No man is a hero to his valet.
Mme Cornuel 1605–94: *Lettres de Mlle Aïssé à
Madame C* (1787) Letter 13 'De Paris, 1728'; see 9
below; **Familiarity** 10

6 See, the conquering hero comes!
Sound the trumpets, beat the drums!
Thomas Morell 1703–84: *Judas Maccabeus* (1747)

7 In this world I would rather live two days
like a tiger, than two hundred years like a
sheep.
Tipu Sultan 1750–99: Alexander Beatson *A View of
the Origin and Conduct of the War with Tippoo
Sultaun* (1800); see 1 above

8 So faithful in love, and so dauntless in war,
There never was knight like the young
Lochinvar.
Sir Walter Scott 1771–1832: *Marmion* (1808)
'Lochinvar'

9 In short, he was a perfect cavaliero,
And to his very valet seemed a hero.
Lord Byron 1788–1824: *Beppo* (1818); see 5 above

10 Every hero becomes a bore at last.
Ralph Waldo Emerson 1803–82: *Representative
Men* (1850)

11 Hero-worship is strongest where there is
least regard for human freedom.
Herbert Spencer 1820–1903: *Social Statics* (1850)

12 Men reject their prophets and slay them,
but they love their martyrs and honour
those whom they have slain.
Fedor Dostoevsky 1821–81: *The Brothers
Karamazov* (1879–80)

13 Heroing is one of the shortest-lived
professions there is.
Will Rogers 1879–1935: newspaper article, 15
February 1925

14 ANDREA: Unhappy the land that has no
heroes! . . .
GALILEO: No. Unhappy the land that needs
heroes.
Bertolt Brecht 1898–1956: *The Life of Galileo*
(1939)

15 Show me a hero and I will write you a
tragedy.
F. Scott Fitzgerald 1896–1940: Edmund Wilson
(ed.) *The Crack-Up* (1945) 'Note-Books E'

16 Faster than a speeding bullet! . . . Look! Up
in the sky! It's a bird! It's a plane! It's
Superman!
Anonymous: *Superman* (US radio show, 1940
onwards)

17 If the myth gets bigger than the man, print
the myth.
Dorothy Johnson 1905–84: *Indian Country* (1953)
'The Man Who Shot Liberty Valance'; see also
Journalism 22

18 It was involuntary. They sank my boat.
on being asked how he became a war hero
John F. Kennedy 1917–63: Arthur M. Schlesinger
Jr. *A Thousand Days* (1965)

19 In such a regime, I say, you died a good
death if your life had inspired someone to
come forward and shoot your murderer in
the chest—without asking to be paid.
Chinua Achebe 1930– : *A Man of the People* (1966)

20 Ultimately a hero is a man who would argue
with the Gods, and so awakens devils to
contest his vision.
Norman Mailer 1923– : *The Presidential Papers*
(1976)

21 We can be heroes
Just for one day.
David Bowie 1947– : 'Heroes' (1977 song)

⇥ History ⇤

PROVERBS AND SAYINGS

**1 Happy is the country which has no
history.**
memorable events are likely to be unhappy and
disruptive; English proverb, early 19th century, see
13 below

2 History is a fable agreed upon.
American proverb, mid 20th century

**3 History is fiction with the truth
left out.**
American proverb, mid 20th century

PHRASES

7 the Father of History
Herodotus (5th century BC), Greek historian; the first
historian to collect materials systematically, test their
accuracy to a certain extent, and arrange them in a
well-constructed and vivid narrative

QUOTATIONS

9 I have written my work, not as an essay
which is to win the applause of the
moment, but as a possession for all time.
Thucydides c.455–c.400 BC: *History of the
Peloponnesian War*

10 History is philosophy from examples.
Dionysius of Halicarnassus fl. 30–7 BC: *Ars
Rhetorica*

4 History is written by the victors.
modern saying

5 History repeats itself.
English proverb, mid 19th century; see 17, 21 below

**6 Until the lions produce their own
historian, the story of the hunt will
glorify the hunter.**
African proverb

8 Whig historian
a historian who interprets history as the continuing
and inevitable victory of progress over reaction; first
recorded in George Bernard Shaw's preface to *St Joan*
(1924)

11 If history records good things of good men,
the thoughtful hearer is encouraged to
imitate what is good.
The Venerable Bede AD 673–735: *Ecclesiastical
History of the English People*

12 Whosoever, in writing a modern history,
shall follow truth too near the heels, it may
happily strike out his teeth.
Walter Ralegh 1552–1618: *The History of the World*
(1614)

13 Happy the people whose annals are blank in history-books!
Montesquieu 1689–1755: attributed to Montesquieu by Thomas Carlyle *History of Frederick the Great*; see 1 above

14 History . . . is, indeed, little more than the register of the crimes, follies, and misfortunes of mankind.
Edward Gibbon 1737–94: *The Decline and Fall of the Roman Empire* (1776–88)

15 What experience and history teach is this—that nations and governments have never learned anything from history, or acted upon any lessons they might have drawn from it.
G. W. F. Hegel 1770–1831: *Lectures on the Philosophy of World History: Introduction* (1830); see 17 below

16 History is the essence of innumerable biographies.
Thomas Carlyle 1795–1881: *Critical and Miscellaneous Essays* (1838) 'On History'

17 Hegel says somewhere that all great events and personalities in world history reappear in one fashion or another. He forgot to add: the first time as tragedy, the second as farce.
Karl Marx 1818–83: *The Eighteenth Brumaire of Louis Bonaparte* (1852); see 5, 15 above

18 History is a gallery of pictures in which there are few originals and many copies.
Alexis de Tocqueville 1805–59: *L'Ancien régime* (1856)

19 History is past politics, and politics is present history.
E. A. Freeman 1823–92: *Methods of Historical Study* (1886)

20 It has been said that though God cannot alter the past, historians can; it is perhaps because they can be useful to Him in this respect that He tolerates their existence.
Samuel Butler 1835–1902: *Erewhon Revisited* (1901); see **The Past** 18

21 History repeats itself; historians repeat one another.
Rupert Brooke 1887–1915: letter to Geoffrey Keynes, 4 June 1906; see 5 above

22 History is more or less bunk.
Henry Ford 1863–1947: interview with Charles N. Wheeler in *Chicago Tribune* 25 May 1916

23 Human history becomes more and more a race between education and catastrophe.
H. G. Wells 1866–1946: *The Outline of History* (1920)

24 History is not what you thought. *It is what you can remember.*
W. C. Sellar 1898–1951 and **R. J. Yeatman** 1898–1968: *1066 and All That* (1930)

25 History gets thicker as it approaches recent times.
A. J. P. Taylor 1906–90: *English History 1914–45* (1965) bibliography

26 What we may be witnessing is not just the end of the Cold War but the end of history as such: that is, the end point of man's ideological evolution and the universalism of Western liberal democracy.
Francis Fukuyama 1952– : in *Independent* 20 September 1989

27 A country's identity, its value and civilization resides in its history. If a country's civilization is looted, as ours has been here, its history ends.
an Iraqi archaeologist on the looting of the National Museum
Raid Abdul Ridhar Muhammad: in *The Times* 14 April 2003

⤛ The Home ⤜

see also **Housework**

PROVERBS AND SAYINGS

1 The dog is a lion in his own house.
Persian proverb

2 East, west, home's best.
English proverb, mid 19th century

3 An Englishman's home is his castle.
a person has the right to refuse entry to his home; reflecting a legal principle, as formulated by the English jurist Edward Coke (1552–1634) 'For a man's house is his castle, *et domus sua cuique est tutissimum refugium* [and each man's home is his safest refuge]'; English proverb, late 16th century

4 Every cock will crow upon his own dunghill.
everyone is confident and at ease on their home ground; English proverb, mid 13th century

-›>-<‹-›>-<‹-›>-<‹-›>-<‹-›>-<‹-›>-<‹-›>-<‹-›>-<‹-›>-<‹-›>-<‹-›>-<‹-›>-<‹-›>-<‹-›>-<‹-›>-<‹-›>-

5 Falling leaves have to return to their roots.

everything must ultimately return to its origins; Chinese proverb

6 Home is home though it's never so homely.

no place can compare with one's own home; English proverb, mid 16th century

7 Home is where the heart is.

one's true home is wherever the person one loves most is; English proverb, late 19th century

PHRASES

11 fire and flet

fire and houseroom; *flet* = a dwelling, a house; see Death 10

12 lares and penates

the home; Latin *lares* = the protective gods of the household worshipped in ancient Rome; *penates* =

QUOTATIONS

14 The foxes have holes, and the birds of the air have nests; but the Son of man hath not where to lay his head.
Bible: St Matthew

15 The accent of one's birthplace lingers in the mind and in the heart as it does in one's speech.
Duc de la Rochefoucauld 1613–80: *Maximes* (1678)

16 I am returned to my own Lares and Penates—to my dogs and cats.
Horace Walpole 1717–97: letter to Rev. William Mason, 25 October 1775; see 12 above

17 Mid pleasures and palaces though we may roam,
Be it ever so humble, there's no place like home.
J. H. Payne 1791–1852: *Clari, or, The Maid of Milan* (1823 opera) 'Home, Sweet Home'; see 10 above

18 The worst thing . . . is to leave your own town, where even the stones know you, and it must break your heart to leave them behind on the road.
Giovanni Verga 1840–1922: *I Malavoglia* (The House by the Medlar Tree, 1881), tr. R. Rosenthal

19 What's the good of a home if you are never in it?
George and Weedon Grossmith 1847–1912, 1854–1919: *The Diary of a Nobody* (1894)

8 Home is where the mortgage is.

American proverb, mid 20th century

9 Lang may yer lum reek!

long may your chimney smoke, often used as a toast; Scottish proverb

10 There's no place like home.

English proverb, late 16th century; the saying is found earlier in Greek, in the work of the Greek poet Hesiod (*c*.700 BC); see 17 below

the protective gods of the household, especially the storeroom; see 16 below

13 motherhood and apple pie

in North American usage, a cherished ideal of homeliness, representing the type of values regarded as deserving unquestioning support

20 Any old place I can hang my hat is home sweet home to me.
William Jerome 1865–1932: title of song (1901)

21 Home is the girl's prison and the woman's workhouse.
George Bernard Shaw 1856–1950: *Man and Superman* (1903) 'Maxims: Women in the Home'

22 We make our friends, we make our enemies; but God makes our next-door neighbour.
G. K. Chesterton 1874–1936: *Heretics* (1905)

23 Home is the place where, when you have to go there,
They have to take you in.
Robert Frost 1874–1963: 'The Death of the Hired Man' (1914)

24   The best
Thing we can do is to make wherever we're lost in
Look as much like home as we can.
Christopher Fry 1907– : *The Lady's not for Burning* (1949)

25 Home is where you come to when you have nothing better to do.
Margaret Thatcher 1925– : in *Vanity Fair* May 1991

⇢⇢Honesty ⇠⇠

see also **Deception, Lies, Truth**

PROVERBS AND SAYINGS

1 **Children and fools tell the truth.**
implying that they lack the cunning to see possible danger; tradition sometimes adds drunkards; English proverb, mid 16th century

2 **Confession is good for the soul.**
confession is essential to repentance and forgiveness; English proverb, mid 17th century

3 **Honesty is more praised than practised.**
it is easier to advise another person to be honest than to be honest oneself; American proverb, mid 20th century

4 **Honesty is the best policy.**
as well as being right, to be honest may also achieve a more successful outcome; English proverb, early 17th century; see 11 below

5 **It's a sin to steal a pin.**
even if what is stolen is of little value, the action is still wrong; English proverb, late 19th century

6 **Sell honestly, but not honesty.**
a play on words meaning that honesty is the essential virtue in commerce; American proverb, mid 20th century

QUOTATIONS

7 Honesty is praised and left to shiver.
Juvenal c.AD 60–c.130: *Satires*

8 Here lies he who neither feared nor flattered any flesh.
said of John Knox, as he was buried, 26 November 1572
James Douglas, Earl of Morton 1516–81: George R. Preedy *The Life of John Knox* (1940)

9 And those who paint 'em truest praise 'em most.
Joseph Addison 1672–1719: *The Campaign* (1705)

10 'But the Emperor has nothing on at all!' cried a little child.
Hans Christian Andersen 1805–75: *Danish Fairy Legends and Tales* (1846) 'The Emperor's New Clothes'

11 Honesty is the best policy; but he who is governed by that maxim is not an honest man.
Richard Whately 1787–1863: *Apophthegms* (1854); see 4 above

12 The louder he talked of his honour, the faster we counted our spoons.
Ralph Waldo Emerson 1803–82: *The Conduct of Life* (1860)

13 A little sincerity is a dangerous thing, and a great deal of it is absolutely fatal.
Oscar Wilde 1854–1900: *Intentions* (1891)

14 honesty is a good
thing but
it is not profitable to
its possessor
unless it is
kept under control.
Don Marquis 1878–1937: *archys life of mehitabel* (1933)

15 Integrity has no need of rules.
Albert Camus 1913–60: *The Myth of Sisyphus* (1942)

16 This is hard to answer, so I'll tell the truth.
David Ben-Gurion 1886–1973: at the Zionist Actions Committee session, London, 14 August 1945

17 Always be sincere, even if you don't mean it.
Harry S. Truman 1884–1972: attributed

18 I write the truth and it kills me.
Sarah Kane 1971–99: *Crave* (1998)

✈ Hope ✈

see also **Despair, Optimism and Pessimism**

PROVERBS AND SAYINGS

1 A drowning man will clutch at a straw.

when hope is slipping away one grasps at the slightest chance; English proverb, mid 16th century

2 He that lives in hope dances to an ill tune.

hoping for something better may constrain one's freedom of action; English proverb, late 16th century

3 Hope deferred makes the heart sick.

implying that it is worse to have had one's hopes raised and then dashed, than to have been resigned to not having something; English proverb, late 14th century, from the Bible: see 10 below

4 Hope is a good breakfast but a bad supper.

while it is pleasant to begin something in a hopeful mood, the hopes need to have been fulfilled by the time it ends; English proverb, mid 17th century

5 Hope springs eternal.

English proverb, mid 18th century, from Pope: see 13 below

6 If it were not for hope, the heart would break.

referring to the role of hope in warding off complete despair; English proverb, mid 13th century

7 In the kingdom of hope, there is no winter.

Russian proverb

8 It is better to travel hopefully than to arrive.

often with the implication that something long sought may be disappointing when achieved; English proverb, late 19th century, from Stevenson: see **Travel** 33

9 While there's life there's hope.

often used as encouragement not to despair in an unpromising situation; English proverb, mid 16th century

QUOTATIONS

10 Hope deferred maketh the heart sick: but when the desire cometh, it is a tree of life.
Bible: Proverbs; see 3 above

11 *Nil desperandum.*
Never despair.
Horace 65–8 BC: *Odes*

12 Who would have thought my shrivelled heart
Could have recovered greenness?
George Herbert 1593–1633: 'The Flower' (1633)

13 Hope springs eternal in the human breast:
Man never Is, but always To be blest.
Alexander Pope 1688–1744: *An Essay on Man* Epistle 1 (1733); see 5 above

14 He that lives upon hope will die fasting.
Benjamin Franklin 1706–90: *Poor Richard's Almanac* (1758)

15 What is hope? nothing but the paint on the face of Existence; the least touch of truth rubs it off, and then we see what a hollow-cheeked harlot we have got hold of.
Lord Byron 1788–1824: letter to Thomas Moore, 28 October 1815

16   O, Wind,
If Winter comes, can Spring be far behind?
Percy Bysshe Shelley 1792–1822: 'Ode to the West Wind' (1819)

17 Work without hope draws nectar in a sieve,
And hope without an object cannot live.
Samuel Taylor Coleridge 1772–1834: 'Work without Hope' (1828)

18 If hopes were dupes, fears may be liars.
Arthur Hugh Clough 1819–61: 'Say not the struggle naught availeth' (1855)

19 He who has never hoped can never despair.
George Bernard Shaw 1856–1950: *Caesar and Cleopatra* (1901)

20 After all, tomorrow is another day.
Margaret Mitchell 1900–49: *Gone with the Wind* (1936); see **The Future** 6

21 Walk on, walk on, with hope in your heart,
And you'll never walk alone.
Oscar Hammerstein II 1895–1960: 'You'll Never Walk Alone' (1945 song)

22 Hope is definitely not the same thing as optimism. It is not the conviction that something will turn out well, but the certainty that something makes sense, regardless of how it turns out.
Václav Havel 1936– : *Disturbing the Peace* (1986)

Hospitality

PROVERBS AND SAYINGS

1 **Always leave the party when you are still having a good time.**
implying that pleasure of this kind is transient; American proverb, mid 20th century

2 **The company makes the feast.**
the success of a social occasion depends on those present rather than on the food and drink provided; English proverb, mid 17th century

3 **The first day a guest, the second day a guest, the third day a calamity.**
Indian proverb; see 4 below

4 **Fish and guests stink after three days.**
one should not outstay one's welcome; English proverb, late 16th century; see 3 above

5 **Food without hospitality is medicine.**
American proverb, mid 20th century

6 **It is merry in hall when beards wag all.**
when conversation is in full flow; English proverb, early 14th century

7 **There isn't much to talk about at some parties until after one or two couples leave.**
American proverb, mid 20th century

QUOTATIONS

8 Bring hither the fatted calf, and kill it.
Bible: St Luke; see **Festivals** 29, **Forgiveness** 8

9 Be not forgetful to entertain strangers: for thereby some have entertained angels unawares.
Bible: Hebrews

10   Unbidden guests
Are often welcomest when they are gone.
William Shakespeare 1564–1616: *Henry VI, Part 1* (1592)

11 This day my wife made it appear to me that my late entertainment this week cost me above £12, an expense which I am almost ashamed of, though it is but once in a great while, and is the end for which, in the most part, we live, to have such a merry day once or twice in a man's life.
Samuel Pepys 1633–1703: diary 6 March 1669

12 He showed me his bill of fare to tempt me to dine with him; poh, said I, I value not your bill of fare, give me your bill of company.
Jonathan Swift 1667–1745: *Journal to Stella* 2 September 1711

13 For I, who hold sage Homer's rule the best,
Welcome the coming, speed the going guest.
Alexander Pope 1688–1744: *Imitations of Horace* (1734); 'speed the parting guest' in Pope's translation of *The Odyssey* (1725–6)

14 Like other parties of the kind, it was first silent, then talky, then argumentative, then disputatious, then unintelligible, then altogethery, then inarticulate, and then drunk.
Lord Byron 1788–1824: letter to Thomas Moore, 31 October 1815

15 The sooner every party breaks up the better.
Jane Austen 1775–1817: *Emma* (1816)

16 Come in the evening, or come in the morning,
Come when you're looked for, or come without warning.
Thomas Davis 1814–45: 'The Welcome' (1846)

17 Everyone knows that the real business of a ball is either to look out for a wife, to look after a wife, or to look after somebody else's wife.
R. S. Surtees 1805–64: *Mr Facey Romford's Hounds* (1865)

18 At a dinner party one should eat wisely but not too well, and talk well but not too wisely.
W. Somerset Maugham 1874–1965: *Writer's Notebook* (1949); written in 1896

19 Some people can stay longer in an hour than others can in a week.
William Dean Howells 1837–1920: attributed

20 Candy
Is dandy
But liquor
Is quicker.
Ogden Nash 1902–71: 'Reflections on Ice-breaking' (1931)

21 Guests can be, and often are, delightful, but they should never be allowed to get the upper hand.
Elizabeth, Countess von Arnim 1866–1941: *All the Dogs in My Life* (1936)

22 The tumult and the shouting dies,
The captains and the kings depart,
And we are left with large supplies
Of cold blancmange and rhubarb tart.
Ronald Knox 1888–1957: 'After the Party' (1959); see **Pride** 10

23 The best number for a dinner party is two—myself and a dam' good head waiter.
Nubar Gulbenkian 1896–1972: in *Daily Telegraph* 14 January 1965

24 Bachelors know all about parties. In fact, a good bachelor is a living, breathing party all by himself.
P. J. O'Rourke 1947– : *The Bachelor Home Companion* (1987)

25 Unless your life is going well you don't dream of giving a party. Unless you can look in the mirror and see a benign and generous and healthy human being, you shrink from acts of hospitality.
Carol Shields 1935–2003: *Larry's Party* (1997)

26 It's life's losers who really want to please—and wanting to please is a prerequisite of hospitality.
A. A. Gill 1954– : in *Sunday Times* 19 September 1999

⤞ Housework ⤛

see also **The Home**

PROVERBS AND SAYINGS

1 **He that will thrive must first ask his wife.**
the husband's material welfare depends on the way in which his wife manages the household; English proverb, late 15th century

2 **It beats as it sweeps as it cleans.**
advertising slogan for Hoover vacuum cleaners, 1919

3 **Persil washes whiter—and it shows.**
advertising slogan for Persil washing powder, 1970s

4 **They that wash on Monday**
Have all the week to dry;
They that wash on Tuesday
Are not so much awry;
They that wash on Wednesday
Are not so much to blame;
They that wash on Thursday
Wash for very shame;
They that wash on Friday
Wash in sorry need;
And they that wash on Saturday,
Are lazy folk indeed.
traditional rhyme

5 **A woman's work is never done.**
reflecting the traditional responsibilities of the housewife; English proverb, late 16th century

PHRASES

6 **lay up in lavender**
preserve carefully for future use; the flowers and stalks of *lavender* were customarily placed among linen or other clothes as a preservative against moths during storage

QUOTATIONS

7 There is scarcely any less bother in the running of a family than in that of an entire state. And domestic business is no less importunate for being less important.
Montaigne 1533–92: *Essais* (1580)

8 God walks among the pots and pans.
St Teresa of Ávila 1512–82: *Book of the Foundations* (1610)

9 Hatred of domestic work is a natural and admirable result of civilization.
Rebecca West 1892–1983: in *The Freewoman* 6 June 1912

10 The dust comes secretly day after day,
Lies on my ledge and dulls my shining things.
But O this dust that I shall drive away
Is flowers and Kings,
Is Solomon's temple, poets, Nineveh.
Viola Meynell 1886–1956: 'Dusting' (1919)

11 At the worst, a house unkempt cannot be so distressing as a life unlived.
Rose Macaulay 1881–1958 : *Problems of a Woman's Life* (1926)

12 Few tasks are more like the torture of Sisyphus than housework, with its endless repetition . . . The housewife wears herself out marking time: she makes nothing, simply perpetuates the present.
Simone de Beauvoir 1908–86: *The Second Sex* (1949)

13 There was no need to do any housework at all. After the first four years the dirt doesn't get any worse.
Quentin Crisp 1908–99: *The Naked Civil Servant* (1968)

14 Conran's Law of Housework—it expands to fill the time available plus half an hour.
Shirley Conran 1932– : *Superwoman 2* (1977)

15 'I hate discussions of feminism that end up with who does the dishes,' she said. So do I. But at the end, there are always the damned dishes.
Marilyn French 1929– : *The Women's Room* (1977)

16 All the rudiments of success in life can be found in ironing a pair of trousers.
Chris Eubank 1966– : in *Independent* 6 September 2003

➤➤ Human Nature ◄◄

see also **Behaviour, Character**

PROVERBS AND SAYINGS

1 The best of men are but men at best.
even someone of great moral worth is still human and fallible; English proverb, late 17th century

2 Man is a wolf to man.
English proverb, mid 16th century, from Plautus: see 7 below

3 There's nowt so queer as folk.
English proverb, early 20th century

4 Young saint, old devil.
unnaturally good and moral behaviour at an early age is likely to change in later life; English proverb, early 15th century

PHRASES

5 the old Adam
unregenerate human nature; fallen man as contrasted with the *second Adam*, Jesus Christ; see 11 below; **The Christian Church** 12

QUOTATIONS

6 By nature men are alike. Through practice they have become far apart.
Confucius 551–479 BC: *Analects*

7 A man is a wolf rather than a man to another man, when he hasn't yet found out what he's like.
Plautus c.250–184 BC: *Asinaria*; see 2 above

8 It is part of human nature to hate the man you have hurt.
Tacitus c.AD 56–after 117: *Agricola*

9 One touch of nature makes the whole world kin.
William Shakespeare 1564–1616: *Troilus and Cressida* (1602)

10 God and the doctor we alike adore
But only when in danger, not before;
The danger o'er, both are alike requited,
God is forgotten, and the Doctor slighted.
John Owen 1563–1622: *Epigrams*; see **Danger** 30

11 O merciful God, grant that the old Adam in this Child may be so buried, that the new man may be raised up in him.
The Book of Common Prayer 1662: *Public Baptism of Infants*; see 5 above

12 On ev'ry hand it will allow'd be,
He's just—nae better than he shou'd be.
Robert Burns 1759–96: 'A Dedication to G[avin] H[amilton]' (1786)

13 Subdue your appetites my dears, and you've conquered human natur.
Charles Dickens 1812–70: *Nicholas Nickleby* (1839)

14 But good God, people don't do such things!
Henrik Ibsen 1828–1906: *Hedda Gabler* (1890)

15 Adam was but human—this explains it all. He did not want the apple for the apple's sake; he wanted it only because it was forbidden.
Mark Twain 1835–1910: *Pudd'nhead Wilson* (1894)

16 The natural man has only two primal passions, to get and beget.
William Osler 1849–1919: *Science and Immortality* (1904)

17 The terrorist and the policeman both come from the same basket.
Joseph Conrad 1857–1924: *The Secret Agent* (1907)

18 That is ever the way. 'Tis all jealousy to the bride and good wishes to the corpse.
J. M. Barrie 1860–1937: *Quality Street* (1913)

19 Human nature is not black and white but black and grey.
Graham Greene 1904–91: 'The Lost Childhood' (1951)

20 There's a man all over for you, blaming on his boots the faults of his feet.
Samuel Beckett 1906–89: *Waiting for Godot* (1955)

⤏⤏ The Human Race ⤙⤙

PROVERBS AND SAYINGS

1 **God sleeps in the stone, dreams in the plant, stirs in the animal, and awakens in man.**
traditional saying, frequently said to be of Indian origin; the wording varies in different languages

2 **Man is the measure of all things.**
everything could be understood in terms of humankind; English proverb, mid 16th century; see 9 below

3 **What is the most important thing in life? It is people, people, people.**
Maori proverb

PHRASES

4 **a man and a brother**
a fellow human being; from the anti-slavery motto *Am I not a man and a brother?*: see **Race** 1

5 **the man on the Clapham omnibus**
the average man; attributed, in the *Law Reports* of 1903, to the English judge Lord Bowen (1853–94)

6 **the naked ape**
present-day humans regarded as a species, from the title of a book (1967) by Desmond Morris

7 **ship of fools**
the world, humankind; after *The shyp of folys of the worlde* (1509) translation of German work *Das Narrenschiff* (1494), literally a ship whose passengers represent various types of vice, folly, or human failings

QUOTATIONS

8 And God said, Let us make man in our image, after our likeness: and let them have dominion over the fish of the sea, and over the fowl of the air, and over the cattle, and over all the earth and over every creeping thing that creepeth upon the earth.
Bible: Genesis

9 Man is the measure of all things.
Protagoras b. *c*.485 BC: Plato *Theaetetus*; see 2 above

10 There are many wonderful things, and nothing is more wonderful than man.
Sophocles *c*.496–406 BC: *Antigone*

11 I am a man, I count nothing human foreign to me.
Terence *c*.190–159 BC: *Heauton Timorumenos*

12 *Considerate la vostra semenza:*
Fatti non foste a viver come bruti,
Ma per seguir virtute e conoscenza.
Consider your origins: you were not made to live as brutes, but to follow virtue and knowledge.
Dante Alighieri 1265–1321: *Divina Commedia* 'Inferno'

13 What a piece of work is a man! How noble in reason! how infinite in faculty! in form, in moving, how express and admirable! in action how like an angel! in apprehension how like a god! the beauty of the world! the paragon of animals! And yet, to me, what is this quintessence of dust?
William Shakespeare 1564–1616: *Hamlet* (1601)

14 How beauteous mankind is! O brave new world,
That has such people in't.
William Shakespeare 1564–1616: *The Tempest* (1611); see **Progress** 2

15 We carry within us the wonders we seek without us: there is all Africa and her prodigies in us.
Thomas Browne 1605–82: *Religio Medici* (1643)

16 Man is only a reed, the weakest thing in nature; but he is a thinking reed.
Blaise Pascal 1623–62: *Pensées* (1670)

17 What is man in nature? A nothing in respect of that which is infinite, an all in respect of nothing, a middle betwixt nothing and all.
Blaise Pascal 1623–62: *Pensées* (1670)

18 Principally I hate and detest that animal called man; although I heartily love John, Peter, Thomas, and so forth.
Jonathan Swift 1667–1745: letter to Pope, 29 September 1725

19 Know then thyself, presume not God to scan;
The proper study of mankind is man.
Alexander Pope 1688–1744: *An Essay on Man* Epistle 2 (1733)

20 Man is a tool-making animal.
Benjamin Franklin 1706–90: James Boswell *Life of Samuel Johnson* (1791) 7 April 1778

21 Out of the crooked timber of humanity no straight thing can ever be made.
Immanuel Kant 1724–1804: *Idee zu einer allgemeinen Geschichte in weltbürgerlicher Absicht* (1784)

22 Drinking when we are not thirsty and making love all year round, madam; that is all there is to distinguish us from other animals.
Pierre-Augustin Caron de Beaumarchais 1732–99: *Le Mariage de Figaro* (1785)

23 Is man an ape or an angel? Now I am on the side of the angels.
Benjamin Disraeli 1804–81: speech at Oxford, 25 November 1864; see **Life Sciences** 14

24 I teach you the superman. Man is something to be surpassed.
Friedrich Nietzsche 1844–1900: *Also Sprach Zarathustra* (1883)

25 Man is the Only Animal that Blushes. Or needs to.
Mark Twain 1835–1910: *Following the Equator* (1897)

26 Man, biologically considered, and whatever else he may be into the bargain, is simply the most formidable of all the beasts of prey, and, indeed, the only one that preys systematically on its own species.
William James 1842–1910: in *Atlantic Monthly* December 1904

27 Taking a very gloomy view of the future of the human race, let us suppose that it can only expect to survive for two thousand million years longer, a period about equal to the past age of the earth. Then, regarded as a being destined to live for three-score years and ten, humanity, although it has been born in a house seventy years old, is itself only three days old.
James Jeans 1877–1946: *Eos* (1928)

28   Human kind
Cannot bear very much reality.
T. S. Eliot 1888–1965: *Four Quartets* 'Burnt Norton' (1936)

29 What is man, when you come to think upon him, but a minutely set, ingenious machine for turning, with infinite artfulness, the red wine of Shiraz into urine?
Isak Dinesen 1885–1962: *Seven Gothic Tales* (1934) 'The Dreamers'

30 To say, for example, that a man is made up of certain chemical elements is a satisfactory description only for those who intend to use him as a fertilizer.
H. J. Muller 1890–1967: *Science and Criticism* (1943)

31 Man must be invented each day.
Jean-Paul Sartre 1905–80: *Qu'est-ce que la littérature?* (1948)

32 We're all of us guinea pigs in the laboratory of God. Humanity is just a work in progress.
Tennessee Williams 1911–83: *Camino Real* (1953)

33 In all my work what I try to say is that as human beings we are more alike than we are unalike.
Maya Angelou 1928– : interview in *New York Times* 20 January 1993

34 We have Africa in our blood and Africa has our bones. We are all Africans.
Richard Dawkins 1941– : *A Devil's Chaplain* (2003)

⊷Human Rights ⊷

see also **Equality, Justice**

PROVERBS AND SAYINGS

1 **Liberté! Égalité! Fraternité!**
French, *Freedom! Equality! Brotherhood!*: motto of
the French Revolution, 1789, but of earlier origin

PHRASES

2 **bread and roses**
slogan summarizing the right to food for both mind
and body; associated with a strike by textile workers
in Lawrence, Massachussetts in 1912; see 14 below,
Lifestyles 4

3 **the four freedoms**
four essential human freedoms as proclaimed in a
speech to Congress by Franklin D. Roosevelt in 1941;
see 16 below

4 **rights of man**
rights held to be justifiably belonging to any person;
human rights; associated with the Declaration of the
Rights of Man and of the Citizen, adopted by the
French National Assembly in 1789 and used as a
preface to the French Constitution of 1791

QUOTATIONS

5 No free man shall be taken or imprisoned or
dispossessed, or outlawed or exiled, or in
any way destroyed, nor will we go upon
him, nor will we send against him except by
the lawful judgement of his peers or by the
law of the land.
Magna Carta 1215: clause 39

6 Magna Charta is such a fellow, that he will
have no sovereign.
on the Lords' Amendment to the Petition of Right, 17
May 1628
Edward Coke 1552–1634: J. Rushworth *Historical
Collections* (1659)

7 We hold these truths to be self-evident, that
all men are created equal, that they are
endowed by their Creator with certain
unalienable rights, that among these are
life, liberty and the pursuit of happiness.
American Declaration of Independence: 4 July
1776; from a draft by Thomas Jefferson (1743–1826);
see **Happiness** 31

8 Whatever each man can separately do,
without trespassing upon others, he has a
right to do for himself; and he has a right to
a fair portion of all which society, with all
its combinations of skill and force, can do in
his favour.
Edmund Burke 1729–97: *Reflections on the
Revolution in France* (1790)

9 Any law which violates the inalienable
rights of man is essentially unjust and
tyrannical; it is not a law at all.
Maximilien Robespierre 1758–94: *Déclaration des
droits de l'homme* 24 April 1793

10 Natural rights is simple nonsense: natural
and imprescriptible rights, rhetorical
nonsense—nonsense upon stilts.
Jeremy Bentham 1748–1832: *Anarchical Fallacies*
(1843)

11 Its constitution the glittering and sounding
generalities of natural right which make up
the Declaration of Independence.
Rufus Choate 1799–1859: letter to the Maine Whig
State Central Committee, 9 August 1856; see
Conversation 4

12 The first duty of a State is to see that every
child born therein shall be well housed,
clothed, fed and educated, till it attain years
of discretion.
John Ruskin 1819–1900: *Time and Tide* (1867)

13 No man can put a chain about the ankle of
his fellow man without at last finding the
other end fastened about his own neck.
Frederick Douglass 1818–95: speech at Civil
Rights Mass Meeting, Washington, DC, 22
October 1883

14 Hearts starve as well as bodies: Give us
Bread, but give us Roses.
James Oppenheim 1882–1932: 'Bread and Roses'
(1911); see 2 above

15 The most stringent protection of free speech
would not protect a man falsely shouting
fire in a theatre and causing a panic.
sometimes quoted as, 'shouting fire in a crowded
theatre'
Oliver Wendell Holmes Jr. 1841–1935: in *Schenck
v. United States* (1919)

16 We look forward to a world founded upon four essential human freedoms. The first is freedom of speech and expression—everywhere in the world. The second is freedom of every person to worship God in his own way—everywhere in the world. The third is freedom from want . . . everywhere in the world. The fourth is freedom from fear . . . anywhere in the world.
Franklin D. Roosevelt 1882–1945: message to Congress, 6 January 1941; see 3 above

17 All human beings are born free and equal in dignity and rights.
Anonymous: *Universal Declaration of Human Rights* (1948) article 1

18 A right is not effectual by itself, but only in relation to the obligation to which it corresponds . . . An obligation which goes unrecognized by anybody loses none of the full force of its existence. A right which goes unrecognized by anybody is not worth very much.
Simone Weil 1909–43: *L'Enracinement* (1949)

19 Better to light a candle than curse the darkness.
Peter Benenson 1921– :the founder of Amnesty International, at a Human Rights Day ceremony, 10 December 1961; see **Action** 5

20 We have talked long enough in this country about equal rights. We have talked for a hundred years or more. It is time now to write the next chapter, and to write it in the books of law.
Lyndon Baines Johnson 1908–73: speech to Congress, 27 November 1963

21 We could live in a world which is airy-fairy, libertarian, where everybody does precisely what they like and we believe the best of everybody and then they destroy us.
David Blunkett 1947– : interview on London Weekend Television, 11 November 2001; see **Idealism** 2

Humility see **Pride and Humility**

Humour

see also **Wit**

PHRASES

1 **collapse of Stout Party**
standard dénouement in Victorian humour; *stout party* = a fat person; the phrase is supposed to come from *Punch*, as the characteristic finishing line of a joke, but no actual example has been traced

2 **Homeric laughter**
irrepressible laughter, proverbially like that of Homer's gods in the *Iliad* as they watched lame Hephaestus hobbling

3 **a merry Andrew**
a comic entertainer; a buffoon, a clown. The suggestion of the antiquary Thomas Hearne (1678–1735) that the original 'merry Andrew' was the traveller and physician Dr Andrew Boorde (1490?–1549) is thought improbable

QUOTATIONS

4 A merry heart doeth good like a medicine.
Bible: Proverbs; see **Medicine** 4

5 Delight hath a joy in it either permanent or present. Laughter hath only a scornful tickling.
Philip Sidney 1554–86: *The Defence of Poetry* (1595)

6 I love such mirth as does not make friends ashamed to look upon one another next morning.
Izaak Walton 1593–1683: *The Compleat Angler* (1653)

7 We must laugh before we are happy, for fear of dying without having laughed at all.
Jean de la Bruyère 1645–96: *Les Caractères ou les moeurs de ce siècle* (1688)

8 Among all kinds of writing, there is none in which authors are more apt to miscarry than in works of humour, as there is none in which they are more ambitious to excel.
Joseph Addison 1672–1719: in *The Spectator* 10 April 1711

9 Life is a jest; and all things show it.
I thought so once; but now I know it.
John Gay 1685–1732: 'My Own Epitaph' (1720)

10 I make myself laugh at everything, for fear of having to weep at it.
Pierre-Augustin Caron de Beaumarchais 1732–99: *Le Barbier de Séville* (1775)

11 Of all days, the one most surely wasted is the one on which one has not laughed.
Nicolas-Sébastien Chamfort 1741–94: *Maximes et Pensées* (1796) ch. 1

12 For what do we live, but to make sport for our neighbours, and laugh at them in our turn?
Jane Austen 1775–1817: *Pride and Prejudice* (1813)

13 Laughter is pleasant, but the exertion is too much for me.
Thomas Love Peacock 1785–1866: *Nightmare Abbey* (1818)

14 We are not amused.
Queen Victoria 1819–1901: attributed; Caroline Holland *Notebooks of a Spinster Lady* (1919) 2 January 1900

15 Everything is funny as long as it is happening to Somebody Else.
Will Rogers 1879–1935: *The Illiterate Digest* (1924)

16 Fun is fun but no girl wants to laugh all of the time.
Anita Loos 1893–1981: *Gentlemen Prefer Blondes* (1925)

17 What do you mean, funny? Funny-peculiar or funny ha-ha?
Ian Hay 1876–1952: *The Housemaster* (1938)

18 Whatever is funny is subversive, every joke is ultimately a custard pie . . . A dirty joke is a sort of mental rebellion.
George Orwell 1903–50: in *Horizon* September 1941 'The Art of Donald McGill'

19 The funniest thing about comedy is that you never know why people laugh. I know *what* makes them laugh but trying to get your hands on the *why* of it is like trying to pick an eel out of a tub of water.
W. C. Fields 1880–1946: R. J. Anobile *A Flask of Fields* (1972)

20 Good taste and humour . . . are a contradiction in terms, like a chaste whore.
Malcolm Muggeridge 1903–90: in *Time* 14 September 1953

21 Laughter would be bereaved if snobbery died.
Peter Ustinov 1921–2004: in *Observer* 13 March 1955

22 Freud's theory was that when a joke opens a window and all those bats and bogeymen fly out, you get a marvellous feeling of relief and elation. The trouble with Freud is that he never had to play the old Glasgow Empire on a Saturday night after Rangers and Celtic had both lost.
Ken Dodd 1931– : in *Guardian* 30 April 1991; quoted in many, usually much contracted, forms since the mid-1960s

23 The marvellous thing about a joke with a double meaning is that it can only mean one thing.
Ronnie Barker 1929–2005: *Sauce* (1977)

24 Comedy is tragedy that happens to *other* people.
Angela Carter 1940–92: *Wise Children* (1991)

⇥ Hunting, Shooting, and Fishing ⇤

PROVERBS AND SAYINGS

1 **The bleating of the lamb excites the tiger.**
Indian proverb; quoted by Kipling in the form 'The bleating of the kid . . . '

PHRASES

2 **big five**
a name given by hunters to the five largest and most dangerous of the African mammals: rhinoceros, elephant, buffalo, lion, and leopard.

3 **the one that got away**
traditional angler's description of a large fish that just eluded capture; from the comment 'you should have seen the one that got away'

QUOTATIONS

4 As no man is born an artist, so no man is born an angler.
Izaak Walton 1593–1683: *The Compleat Angler* (1653)

5 Most of their discourse was about hunting, in a dialect I understand very little.
Samuel Pepys 1633–1703: diary 22 November 1663

6 The dusky night rides down the sky,
And ushers in the morn;
The hounds all join in glorious cry,
The huntsman winds his horn:
And a-hunting we will go.
Henry Fielding 1707–54: *Don Quixote in England* (1733)

7 The sport of kings;
Image of war, without its guilt.
William Somerville 1675–1742: *The Chase* (1735); see 12 below, **Sports 5**

8 Fly fishing may be a very pleasant amusement; but angling or float fishing I can only compare to a stick and a string, with a worm at one end and a fool at the other.
Samuel Johnson 1709–84: attributed; Hawker *Instructions to Young Sportsmen* (1859); also attributed to Jonathan Swift, in *The Indicator* 27 October 1819

9 It is very strange, and very melancholy, that the paucity of human pleasures should persuade us ever to call hunting one of them.
Samuel Johnson 1709–84: Hester Lynch Piozzi *Anecdotes of . . . Johnson* (1786)

10 D'ye ken John Peel with his coat so grey?
D'ye ken John Peel at the break of the day?
D'ye ken John Peel when he's far far away
With his hounds and his horn in the morning?
John Woodcock Graves 1795–1886: 'John Peel' (1820)

11 It ar'n't that I loves the fox less, but that I loves the 'ound more.
R. S. Surtees 1805–64: *Handley Cross* (1843)

12 'Unting is all that's worth living for—all time is lost wot is not spent in 'unting—it is like the hair we breathe—if we have it not we die—it's the sport of kings, the image of war without its guilt, and only five-and-twenty per cent of its danger.
R. S. Surtees 1805–64: *Handley Cross* (1843); see 7 above

13 The English country gentleman galloping after a fox—the unspeakable in full pursuit of the uneatable.
Oscar Wilde 1854–1900: *A Woman of No Importance* (1893)

14 When a man wants to murder a tiger he calls it sport; when a tiger wants to murder him, he calls it ferocity.
George Bernard Shaw 1856–1950: *Man and Superman* (1903)

15 The fascination of shooting as a sport depends almost wholly on whether you are at the right or wrong end of a gun.
P. G. Wodehouse 1881–1975: in *Punch*, 1925; attributed

16 A sportsman is a man who, every now and then, simply has to get out and kill something. Not that he's cruel. He wouldn't hurt a fly. It's not big enough.
Stephen Leacock 1869–1944: *My Remarkable Uncle* (1942)

17 Fishing is unquestionably a form of madness but, happily, for the once-bitten there is no cure.
Lord Home 1903–95: *The Way the Wind Blows* (1976)

18 I love fishing. It's like transcendental meditation with a punch-line.
Billy Connolly 1942– : *Gullible's Travels* (1982)

19 They do you a decent death on the hunting-field.
John Mortimer 1923– : *Paradise Postponed* (1985)

20 If killing foxes is necessary for the safety and survival of other species, I—and several million others—will vote for it to continue. But the slaughter ought not to be fun.
Roy Hattersley 1932– : in *Guardian* 21 April 1990

↦ Hypocrisy ↤

see also **Deception**

PROVERBS AND SAYINGS

1 **Do as I say, not as I do.**
often used to imply hypocrisy; English proverb, mid 16th century

PHRASES

2 curry favour with

ingratiate oneself with someone through obsequious behaviour; from an alteration of Middle English *curry favel*, from the name (*Favel* or *Fauvel*) of a chestnut horse in a 14th-century French romance who became a symbol of cunning and duplicity; hence 'to rub down Favel' meant to use the cunning which he personified

3 holier than thou

characterized by an attitude of self-conscious virtue and piety, from the Bible (Isaiah) 'Stand by thyself, come not near to me; for I am holier than thou'

4 holy Willie

a pious hypocrite, from Robert Burns's poem 'Holy Willie's Prayer' (1785)

5 shed crocodile tears

put on a display of insincere grief; from the belief that crocodiles wept while devouring or alluring their prey

6 a whited sepulchre

a hypocrite, an ostensibly virtuous or pleasant person who is inwardly corrupt; from the Bible (Matthew): see 10 below

QUOTATIONS

7 Woe unto them that call evil good, and good evil.
Bible: Isaiah

8 My tongue swore, but my mind's unsworn.
on his breaking of an oath
Euripides *c*.485–*c*.406 BC: *Hippolytus*

9 Beware of false prophets, which come to you in sheep's clothing, but inwardly they are ravening wolves.
Bible: St Matthew; see **Deception** 11

10 Ye are like unto whited sepulchres, which indeed appear beautiful outward, but are within full of dead men's bones, and of all uncleanness.
Bible: St Matthew; see 6 above

11 I want that glib and oily art
To speak and purpose not.
William Shakespeare 1564–1616: *King Lear* (1605–6)

12 For neither man nor angel can discern
Hypocrisy, the only evil that walks
Invisible, except to God alone.
John Milton 1608–74: *Paradise Lost* (1667)

13 Hypocrisy is a tribute which vice pays to virtue.
Duc de la Rochefoucauld 1613–80: *Maximes* (1678)

14 Keep up appearances; there lies the test;
The world will give thee credit for the rest.
Outward be fair, however foul within;
Sin if thou wilt, but then in secret sin.
Charles Churchill 1731–64: *Night* (1761)

15 In the mouths of many men soft words are like roses that soldiers put into the muzzles of their muskets on holidays.
Henry Wadsworth Longfellow 1807–82: *Table-Talk* (1857) 'Driftwood'

16 I sit on a man's back, choking him and making him carry me, and yet assure myself and others that I am very sorry for him and wish to ease his lot by all possible means—except by getting off his back.
Leo Tolstoy 1828–1910: *What Then Must We Do?* (1886)

17 Hypocrisy is the most difficult and nerve-racking vice that any man can pursue; it needs an unceasing vigilance and a rare detachment of spirit. It cannot, like adultery or gluttony, be practised at spare moments; it is a whole-time job.
W. Somerset Maugham 1874–1965: *Cakes and Ale* (1930)

18 All Reformers, however strict their social conscience, live in houses just as big as they can pay for.
Logan Pearsall Smith 1865–1946: *Afterthoughts* (1931) 'Other People'

19 What makes it so plausible to assume that hypocrisy is the vice of vices is that integrity can indeed exist under the cover of all other vices except this one. Only crime and the criminal, it is true, confront us with the perplexity of radical evil; but only the hypocrite is really rotten to the core.
Hannah Arendt 1906–75: *On Revolution* (1963)

⇥ Hypothesis and Fact ⇤

see also **Science**

PROVERBS AND SAYINGS

1 The exception proves the rule.
originally this meant that the recognition of
something as an exception proved the existence of a
rule, but it is now more often used or understood as
justifying divergence from a rule; see 6 below;
English proverb, mid 17th century

2 Facts are stubborn things.
used to indicate a core of reality that cannot be
adjusted to people's wishes; English proverb, early
18th century

3 Nullius in verba.
Latin, *In the word of none*, motto of the Royal Society,
emphasizing reliance on experiment rather than

authority; adapted from Horace *Epistles*; see
Liberty 6

4 One story is good till another is told.
doubt may be cast on an apparently convincing
account by a second told from a different angle;
English proverb, late 16th century

**5 The proof of the pudding is in the
eating.**
the truth of an assertion will be demonstrated by
how things actually turn out; *proof* here means
'test'; English proverb, early 14th century

6 There is an exception to every rule.
English proverb, late 16th century; see 1 above

PHRASES

7 chapter and verse
exact reference or authority; the precise reference for
a passage of Scripture

8 dot the i's and cross the t's
particularize minutely, complete in every detail

QUOTATIONS

9 Whoever has fixed on his Cause, before he
has experimented, can hardly avoid fitting
his Experiment to his own Cause . . . rather
than the Cause to the truth of the
Experiment itself.
Thomas Sprat 1635–1713: *History of the Royal
Society* (1667)

10 *Hypotheses non fingo.*
I do not feign hypotheses.
Isaac Newton 1642–1727: *Principia Mathematica*
(1713 ed.)

11 It may be so, there is no arguing against
facts and experiments.
when told of an experiment which appeared to
destroy his theory
Isaac Newton 1642–1727: reported by John
Conduit, 1726; D. Brewster *Memoirs of Sir Isaac
Newton* (1855)

12 It is the nature of an hypothesis, when once
a man has conceived it, that it assimilates
every thing to itself, as proper nourishment;
and, from the first moment of your
begetting it, it generally grows the stronger
by every thing you see, hear, read, or
understand.
Laurence Sterne 1713–68: *Tristram Shandy*
(1759–67)

13 Nothing is too wonderful to be true, if it be
consistent with the laws of nature, and in
such things as these, experiment is the best
test of such consistency.
Michael Faraday 1791–1867: diary, 19 March 1849

14 Now, what I want is, Facts . . . Facts alone are
wanted in life.
Charles Dickens 1812–70: *Hard Times* (1854)

15 False views, if supported by some evidence,
do little harm, for everyone takes a salutary
pleasure in proving their falseness.
Charles Darwin 1809–82: *The Descent of Man*
(1871)

16 How seldom is it that theories stand the
wear and tear of practice!
Anthony Trollope 1815–82: *Thackeray* (1879)

17 It is a capital mistake to theorize before you
have all the evidence. It biases the
judgement.
Arthur Conan Doyle 1859–1930: *A Study in Scarlet*
(1888)

18 The great tragedy of Science—the slaying of
a beautiful hypothesis by an ugly fact.
T. H. Huxley 1825–95: *Collected Essays* (1893–4)
'Biogenesis and Abiogenesis'

19 Get your facts first, and then you can distort
'em as much as you please.
Mark Twain 1835–1910: Rudyard Kipling *From Sea
to Sea* (1899)

20 Roundabout the accredited and orderly fact of every science there ever floats a sort of dust cloud of exceptional observations, of occurrences minute and irregular and seldom met with, which it always proves more easy to ignore than to attend to.
William James 1842–1910: attributed

21 The best scale for an experiment is 12 inches to a foot.
John Arbuthnot Fisher 1841–1920: *Memories* (1919)

22 Facts do not cease to exist because they are ignored.
Aldous Huxley 1894–1963: *Proper Studies* (1927)

23 The grand aim of all science [is] to cover the greatest number of empirical facts by logical deduction from the smallest possible number of hypotheses or axioms.
Albert Einstein 1879–1955: Lincoln Barnett *The Universe and Dr Einstein* (1950 ed.)

24 Aristotle maintained that women have fewer teeth than men; although he was twice married, it never occurred to him to verify this statement by examining his wives' mouths.
Bertrand Russell 1872–1970: *The Impact of Science on Society* (1952)

25 If it looks like a duck, walks like a duck and quacks like a duck, then it just may be a duck.
as a test, during the McCarthy era, of Communist affiliations
Walter Reuther 1907–70: attributed

26 It is a good morning exercise for a research scientist to discard a pet hypothesis every day before breakfast. It keeps him young.
Konrad Lorenz 1903–89: *Das Sogenannte Böse* (1963; translated by Marjorie Latzke as *On Aggression*, 1966)

27 An experiment is a device to make Nature speak intelligibly. After that one has only to listen.
George Wald 1904–97: in *Science* vol. 162 (1968)

28 With five free parameters, a theorist could fit the profile of an elephant.
George Gamow 1904–68: attributed; in *Nature* 21 June 1990

29 If an elderly but distinguished scientist says that something is possible he is almost certainly right, but if he says that it is impossible he is very probably wrong.
Arthur C. Clarke 1917– : in *New Yorker* 9 August 1969; see 30 below

30 When, however, the lay public rallies around an idea that is denounced by distinguished but elderly scientists and supports that idea with great fervour and emotion—the distinguished but elderly scientists are then, after all, probably right.
corollary to Arthur C. Clarke's law; see 29 above
Isaac Asimov 1920–92: Arthur C. Clarke 'Asimov's Corollary' in K. Frazier (ed.) *Paranormal Borderlands of Science* (1981)

31 No *good* model ever accounted for *all* the facts since some data was bound to be misleading if not plain wrong.
James Watson 1928– : Francis Crick *Some Mad Pursuit* (1988)

32 Extraordinary claims require extraordinary evidence.
Carl Sagan 1934–96: *Billions and Billions: Thoughts on Life and Death at the Brink of the Millennium* (1997)

33 We have not found any smoking guns.
of weapons inspections in Iraq
Hans Blix 1928– : in *Newsweek* 20 January 2003; see **Secrecy** 22

⤞ Idealism ⤝

see also **Hope**

PROVERBS AND SAYINGS

1 Vision without action is a daydream. Action without vision is a nightmare.
recommending a balance between idealism and reality; modern saying, said to derive from a Japanese proverb

PHRASES

2 airy-fairy
impractical and foolishly idealistic. The phrase, originally used to mean 'delicate or light as a fairy', derives from Tennyson's 'airy, fairy Lilian' *(Lilian*, 1830); see **Human Rights** 21

3 flower power
the ideas of the flower people, hippies who wore flowers as symbols of peace and love; especially the promotion of these as a means of changing the world

4 starry-eyed
idealistic, uplifted, romantic

5 the vision thing
a political view encompassing the longer term, from the comment by George Bush: see 18 below

QUOTATIONS

6 Where there is no vision, the people perish.
Bible: Proverbs

7 Love and a cottage! Eh, Fanny! Ah, give me indifference and a coach and six!
George Colman, the Elder 1732–94 and **David Garrick** 1717–79: *The Clandestine Marriage* (1766); see **Love** 46, **Marriage** 15

8 Hitch your wagon to a star.
Ralph Waldo Emerson 1803–82: *Society and Solitude* (1870)

9 We are all in the gutter, but some of us are looking at the stars.
Oscar Wilde 1854–1900: *Lady Windermere's Fan* (1892)

10 I am an idealist. I don't know where I'm going but I'm on the way.
Carl Sandburg 1878–1967: *Incidentals* (1907)

11 A cause may be inconvenient, but it's magnificent. It's like champagne or high heels, and one must be prepared to suffer for it.
Arnold Bennett 1867–1931: *The Title* (1918)

12 When they come downstairs from their Ivory Towers, Idealists are very apt to walk straight into the gutter.
Logan Pearsall Smith 1865–1946: *Afterthoughts* (1931) 'Other People'; see **Reality** 5

13 If only Bapu knew the cost of setting him up in poverty!
of Mahatma Gandhi
Sarojini Naidu 1879–1949: A. Campbell-Johnson *Mission with Mountbatten* (1951)

14 I submit to you that if a man hasn't discovered something he will die for, he isn't fit to live.
Martin Luther King 1929–68: speech in Detroit, 23 June 1963

15 To dream the impossible dream,
To reach the unreachable star!
Joe Darion 1917–2001: 'The Quest' (1965 song)

16 Each time a man stands up for an ideal, or acts to improve the lot of others, or strikes out against injustice, he sends forth a tiny ripple of hope, and crossing each other from a million different centres of energy and daring those ripples build a current which can sweep down the mightiest walls of oppression and resistance.
Robert Kennedy 1925–68: speech, Cape Town, 6 June 1966

17 I'm not a dreamer . . . but I believe in miracles. I have to.
planning a fund-raising run across Canada; he completed two thirds of his 'Marathon of Hope'
Terry Fox 1958–81: letter to the Canadian Cancer Society, 15 October 1979

18 Oh, the vision thing.
responding to the suggestion that he turn his attention from short-term campaign objectives and look to the longer term
George Bush 1924– : in *Time* 26 January 1987; see 5 above

19 We Americans used to say that the American Dream is worth dying for. The new European Dream is worth living for.
Jeremy Rifkin 1945– : *The European Dream: How Europe's vision of the Future is Quietly Eclipsing the American Dream* (2004); see **America** 4

⇥ Ideas ⇤

see also **Hypothesis and Fact, The Mind, Problems and Solutions, Thinking**

PROVERBS AND SAYINGS

1 I have a cunning plan.
Baldrick's habitual overoptimistic promise, originally in *Blackadder II* (1987 television series, written by Richard Curtis and Ben Elton)

2 There is one thing stronger than all the armies in the world; and that is an idea whose time has come.
mid 20th century saying; see 7 below

PHRASES

3 invita Minerva
lacking inspiration; Latin = *Minerva* (the goddess of wisdom) unwilling

4 King Charles's head
an obsession, an *idée fixe*; with reference to 'Mr Dick', in Dickens's *David Copperfield* (1850), who could not write or speak on any subject without King Charles's head intruding

QUOTATIONS

5 New opinions are always suspected, and usually opposed, without any other reason but because they are not already common.
John Locke 1632–1704: *An Essay concerning Human Understanding* (1690)

6 General notions are generally wrong.
Lady Mary Wortley Montagu 1689–1762: letter to Edward Wortley Montagu, 28 March 1710

7 A stand can be made against invasion by an army; no stand can be made against invasion by an idea.
Victor Hugo 1802–85: *Histoire d'un Crime* (written 1851–2, published 1877); see 2 above

8 I share no one's ideas. I have my own.
Ivan Turgenev 1818–83: *Fathers and Sons* (1862)

9 You see things; and you say 'Why?' But I dream things that never were; and I say 'Why not?'
George Bernard Shaw 1856–1950: *Back to Methuselah* (1921)

10 Marvellous, what ideas the young people have these days. But I don't believe a word of it.
of the uncertainty principle
Albert Einstein 1879–1955: in 1927; see **Physical Sciences 9**

11 Nothing is more dangerous than an idea, when you have only one idea.
Alain 1868–1951: *Propos sur la religion* (1938)

12 No grand idea was ever born in a conference, but a lot of foolish ideas have died there.
F. Scott Fitzgerald 1896–1940: Edmund Wilson (ed.) *The Crack-Up* (1945) 'Note-Books E'

13 Madmen in authority, who hear voices in the air, are distilling their frenzy from some academic scribbler of a few years back.
John Maynard Keynes 1883–1946: *General Theory* (1947 ed.)

14 *Ideas won't keep.* Something must be done about them.
Alfred North Whitehead 1861–1947: *Dialogues* (1954) 28 April 1938

15 It is better to entertain an idea than to take it home to live with you for the rest of your life.
Randall Jarrell 1914–65: *Pictures from an Institution* (1954)

16 The English approach to ideas is not to kill them, but to let them die of neglect.
Jeremy Paxman 1950– : *The English: a portrait of a people* (1998)

⇥Idleness ⇤

see also **Action and Inaction, Words and Deeds**

PROVERBS AND SAYINGS

1 As good be an addled egg as an idle bird.

an idle person will produce nothing; English proverb, late 16th century

2 Better to wear out than to rust out.

it is better to remain active than to succumb to idleness; in this form frequently attributed to Richard Cumberland, Bishop of Peterborough (1631–1718); English proverb, mid 16th century

3 The devil finds work for idle hands to do.

someone who has no work to do will get into mischief; English proverb, early 18th century

4 An idle brain is the devil's workshop.

those who do not apply themselves to their work are most likely to get into trouble; English proverb, early 17th century

5 Idle people have the least leisure.

lazy people are the least able to manage their time efficiently; English proverb, late 17th century

6 Idleness is never enjoyable unless there is plenty to do.

American proverb, mid 20th century: see 21 below

7 Idleness is the root of all evil.

English proverb, early 15th century; the idea has been attributed to the French theologian, monastic reformer, and abbot St Bernard of Clairvaux (1090–1153); see **Money** 27

8 If you won't work you shan't eat.

essential sustenance is seen as a reward for industry; English proverb, mid 16th century, from the Bible: see **Work** 22

PHRASES

9 the bread of idleness

food or sustenance for which one has not worked, after the Bible (Proverbs) 'She . . . eateth not the bread of idleness'

10 lotus-eater

a person who spends their time indulging in pleasure and luxury rather than dealing with

practical concerns. The *lotus-eaters* in Greek mythology were a people who lived on the fruit of the lotus, said to cause a dreamy forgetfulness and an unwillingness to depart; see 17 below

QUOTATIONS

11 Go to the ant thou sluggard; consider her ways, and be wise.
Bible: Proverbs

12 Out ye whores, to work, to work, ye whores, go spin.
commonly quoted as 'Go spin, you jades, go spin'
William Herbert, Lord Pembroke 1501–70: John Aubrey *Brief Lives* (1898 ed.)

13 He that would thrive
Must rise at five;
He that hath thriven
May lie till seven.
John Clarke d. 1658: 'Diligentia' (1639)

14 Idleness is only the refuge of weak minds.
Lord Chesterfield 1694–1773: *Letters to his Son* (1774) 20 July 1749

15 If you are idle, be not solitary; if you are solitary, be not idle.
Samuel Johnson 1709–84: letter to Boswell, 27 October 1779

16 A man who has nothing to do with his own time has no conscience in his intrusion on that of others.
Jane Austen 1775–1817: *Sense and Sensibility* (1811)

17 Surely, surely, slumber is more sweet than toil, the shore
Than labour in the deep mid-ocean, wind and wave and oar;
Oh rest ye, brother mariners, we will not wander more.
Alfred, Lord Tennyson 1809–92: 'The Lotos-Eaters' (1832); see 10 above

18 The foul sluggard's comfort: 'It will last my time.'
Thomas Carlyle 1795–1881: *Critical and Miscellaneous Essays* (1838) 'Count Cagliostro. Flight Last'

19 How dull it is to pause, to make an end,
To rust unburnished, not to shine in use!
As though to breathe were life.
Alfred, Lord Tennyson 1809–92: 'Ulysses' (1842)

20 Never do to-day what you can put off till
to-morrow.
Punch: in 1849

21 It is impossible to enjoy idling thoroughly
unless one has plenty of work to do.
Jerome K. Jerome 1859–1927: *Idle Thoughts of an
Idle Fellow* (1886); see 6 above

22 Oh! how I hate to get up in the morning,
Oh! how I'd love to remain in bed.
Irving Berlin 1888–1989: *Oh! How I Hate to Get Up
in the Morning* (1918 song)

23 I was raised to feel that doing nothing was a
sin. I had to learn to do nothing.
Jenny Joseph 1932– : in *Observer* 19 April 1998

⤜ Ignorance ⤛

PROVERBS AND SAYINGS

1 **The husband is always the last to
know.**
relating to marital infidelity; English proverb, early
17th century

2 **Ignorance is bliss.**
English proverb, mid 18th century, from Gray: see 18
below

3 **Ignorance is a voluntary misfortune.**
one has chosen not to remedy the condition;
American proverb, mid 20th century

4 **The less you know, the better you
sleep.**
Russian saying of the Soviet era

5 **Man is the enemy of that of which he
is ignorant.**
fear is a common response to the unknown; Arab
proverb

6 **Nothing so bold as a blind mare.**
those who know least about a situation are least
likely to be deterred by it; English proverb, early 17th
century

7 **A slice off a cut loaf isn't missed.**
if something has already been diminished or
damaged, further damage may go unnoticed;
English proverb, late 16th century (first recorded in
Shakespeare's *Titus Andronicus*, 1592)

8 **What the eye doesn't see, the heart
doesn't grieve over.**
now sometimes used with the implication that
information is being withheld to prevent difficulties;
English proverb, mid 16th century

9 **What you don't know can't hurt you.**
English proverb, late 16th century

10 **When the blind lead the blind, both
shall fall into the ditch.**
when a person is guided by someone equally
inexperienced, both are likely to come to grief;
English proverb, late 9th century, from the Bible: see
Leadership 9

PHRASES

11 **all Greek to me**
completely unintelligible; *Greek* for unintelligible
language or gibberish is recorded from the late 16th
century; see 16 below

12 **invincible ignorance**
in theological terms, ignorance which the person
concerned does not have the means to overcome;
translation of scholastic Latin *ignorantia invincibilis*,
in the *Summa Theologiae* of Thomas Aquinas

13 **turn a Nelson eye to**
turn a blind eye to, overlook, pretend ignorance of.
Horatio *Nelson* (1758–1805), British admiral, was
killed in the battle of Trafalgar, having suffered the
loss of an eye and an arm in earlier conflicts: see
Determination 36

QUOTATIONS

14 I see no other single hindrance such as this
hindrance of ignorance, obstructed by
which mankind for a long long time runs on
and circles on.
Pali Tripitaka *c.* 2nd century BC: *Itivuttaka* [Thus
Was Said]

15 If one does not know to which port one is
sailing, no wind is favourable.
Seneca ('the Younger') *c.*4 BC–AD 65: *Epistulae
Morales*

16 But those that understood him smiled at
one another and shook their heads; but, for
mine own part, it was Greek to me.
William Shakespeare 1564–1616: *Julius Caesar*
(1599); see 11 above

17 Lo! the poor Indian, whose untutored mind
Sees God in clouds, or hears him in the
wind.
Alexander Pope 1688–1744: *An Essay on Man*
Epistle 1 (1733); see **Drunkenness 6**

18   Where ignorance is bliss,
'Tis folly to be wise.
Thomas Gray 1716–71: *Ode on a Distant Prospect of
Eton College* (1747); see 2 above

19 Ignorance, madam, pure ignorance.
on being asked why he had defined *pastern* as the
'knee' of a horse
Samuel Johnson 1709–84: James Boswell *Life of
Samuel Johnson* (1791) 1755

20 For most men, an ignorant enjoyment is
better than an informed one; it is better to
conceive the sky as a blue dome than a dark
cavity; and the cloud as a golden throne
than a sleety mist.
John Ruskin 1819–1900: *Modern Painters* (1856)

21 Ignorance is not innocence but sin.
Robert Browning 1812–89: *The Inn Album* (1875)

22 Ignorance is like a delicate exotic fruit;
touch it and the bloom is gone.
Oscar Wilde 1854–1900: *The Importance of Being
Earnest* (1895)

23 I know nothing—nobody tells me anything.
John Galsworthy 1867–1933: *Man of Property*
(1906)

24 You know everybody is ignorant, only on
different subjects.
Will Rogers 1879–1935: in *New York Times* 31
August 1924

25 Happy the hare at morning, for she
cannot read
The Hunter's waking thoughts.
W. H. Auden 1907–73: *Dog beneath the Skin* (with
Christopher Isherwood, 1935)

26 Ignorance is an evil weed, which dictators
may cultivate among their dupes, but which
no democracy can afford among its citizens.
William Henry Beveridge 1879–1963: *Full
Employment in a Free Society* (1944)

27 As any fule kno.
Geoffrey Willans 1911–58 and **Ronald Searle**
1920– : *Down with Skool!* (1953)

28 Nothing in all the world is more dangerous
than sincere ignorance and conscientious
stupidity.
Martin Luther King 1929–68: *Strength to Love*
(1963)

29 A bishop wrote gravely to the *Times* inviting
all nations to destroy 'the formula' of the
atomic bomb. There is no simple remedy for
ignorance so abysmal.
Peter Medawar 1915–87: *The Hope of Progress*
(1972)

30 It was absolutely marvellous working for
Pauli. You could ask him anything. There
was no worry that he would think a
particular question was stupid, since he
thought *all* questions were stupid.
Victor Weisskopf 1908–2002: in *American Journal
of Physics* 1977

31 Learn to say, 'I don't know'. If used when
appropriate, it will be often.
Donald Rumsfeld 1932– : 'Rumsfeld's Rules'
(2001)

⤛⤛Imagination ⤜⤜

PHRASES

1 **build castles in the air**
form unsubstantial or visionary projects

2 **a castle in Spain**
a visionary project, a daydream unlikely to be
realized; the expression is recorded from late Middle
English, and it is possible that *Spain*, as the nearest
Moorish country to Christendom, was taken as the

type of a region in which the prospective castle-
builder had no standing

3 **the vision splendid**
the dream of some glorious imagined time; from
Wordsworth 'And by the vision splendid is on his
way attended'

QUOTATIONS

4 For the imagination of man's heart is evil
from his youth.
Bible: Genesis

5 The lunatic, the lover, and the poet,
Are of imagination all compact.
William Shakespeare 1564–1616: *A Midsummer
Night's Dream* (1595–6)

6 Though our brother is on the rack, as long as we ourselves are at our ease, our senses will never inform us of what he suffers . . . It is by imagination that we can form any conception of what are his sensations.
Adam Smith 1723–90: *Theory of Moral Sentiments* (2nd ed., 1762)

7 Were it not for imagination, Sir, a man would be as happy in the arms of a chambermaid as of a Duchess.
Samuel Johnson 1709–84: James Boswell *Life of Samuel Johnson* (1791) 9 May 1778

8 Whither is fled the visionary gleam? Where is it now, the glory and the dream?
William Wordsworth 1770–1850: 'Ode. Intimations of Immortality' (1807)

9 The same that oft-times hath Charmed magic casements, opening on the foam Of perilous seas, in faery lands forlorn.
John Keats 1795–1821: 'Ode to a Nightingale' (1820)

10 His imagination resembled the wings of an ostrich. It enabled him to run, though not to soar.
Lord Macaulay 1800–59: T. F. Ellis (ed.) *Miscellaneous Writings of Lord Macaulay* (1860) 'John Dryden' (1828)

11 I dreamed that I dwelt in marble halls With vassals and serfs at my side.
Alfred Bunn c.1796–1860: *The Bohemian Girl* (1843) 'The Gipsy Girl's Dream'; see **Likes** 11

12 He said he should prefer not to know the sources of the Nile, and that there should be some unknown regions preserved as hunting-grounds for the poetic imagination.
George Eliot 1819–80: *Middlemarch* (1871–2)

13 Where there is no imagination there is no horror.
Arthur Conan Doyle 1859–1930: *A Study in Scarlet* (1888)

14 Must then a Christ perish in torment in every age to save those that have no imagination?
George Bernard Shaw 1856–1950: *Saint Joan* (1924)

15 All fantasy should have a solid base in reality.
Max Beerbohm 1872–1956: *Zuleika Dobson* (1946 ed.) note

16 The imagination is man's power over nature.
Wallace Stevens 1879–1955: 'Adagia' (1959)

17 When the imagination sleeps, words are emptied of their meaning.
Albert Camus 1913–60: *Resistance, Rebellion and Death* (1961)

18 Imagination isn't merely a surplus mental department meant for entertainment, but the most essential piece of machinery we have if we are going to live the lives of human beings.
Ted Hughes 1930–98: in *Children's Literature in Education* March 1970

19 Fantasy is like jam; you have to spread it on a solid slice of bread.
Italo Calvino 1923–85: attributed; in *New York Review of Books* 21 November 1985

Inaction see **Action and Inaction**

Inconstancy see **Constancy and Inconstancy**

⤙ Indecision ⤚

see also **Certainty and Doubt**

PROVERBS AND SAYINGS

1 Between two stools one falls to the ground.
inability to choose between, or accommodate oneself to, alternative viewpoints or courses of action may end in disaster; English proverb, late 14th century

2 The cat would eat fish, but would not wet her feet.
commenting on a situation in which desire for something is checked by unwillingness to risk discomfort in acquiring it; English proverb, early 13th century

3 Councils of war never fight.
people discussing matters in a group never reach the decision to fight, which an individual would make; English proverb, mid 19th century

4 First thoughts are best.
advice to trust an instinctive reaction, often used as a warning against indecision; English proverb, early 20th century

5 He who hesitates is lost.

often used to urge decisive action on someone; English proverb, early 18th century, early usages refer specifically to women, as in Addison *Cato* (1713) 'The woman that deliberates is lost'

6 If you run after two hares you will catch neither.

one must decide on one's goal; English proverb, early 16th century

7 Indecision is fatal, so make up your mind.

American proverb, mid 20th century

PHRASES

8 fudge and mudge

evade comment or avoid making a decision on an issue by waffling; apply facile solutions to decisions while trying to appear resolved; coined as a political catchphrase by the Labour politician David Owen in

an attack on the leadership of James Callaghan, 'We are fed up with fudging and mudging, with mush and slush. We need courage, conviction, and hard work'

QUOTATIONS

9 Now, the melancholy god protect thee, and the tailor make thy doublet of changeable taffeta, for thy mind is a very opal.
William Shakespeare 1564–1616: *Twelfth Night* (1601)

10 I must have a prodigious quantity of mind; it takes me as much as a week, sometimes, to make it up.
Mark Twain 1835–1910: *The Innocents Abroad* (1869)

11 There is no more miserable human being than one in whom nothing is habitual but indecision.
William James 1842–1910: *The Principles of Psychology* (1890)

12 The tragedy of a man who could not make up his mind.
Laurence Olivier 1907–89: introduction to his 1948 screen adaptation of *Hamlet*

13 I'll give you a definite maybe.
Sam Goldwyn 1882–1974: attributed

14 A wrong decision isn't forever; it can always be reversed. The losses from a delayed decision *are* forever; they can never be retrieved.
J. K. Galbraith 1908– : *A Life in our Times* (1981)

15 The archbishop is usually to be found nailing his colours to the fence.
of Archbishop Runcie
Frank Field 1942– : attributed in *Crockfords 1987/88* (1987); Geoffrey Madan records in his *Notebooks* a similar comment was made about A. J. Balfour, *c.*1904; see **Defiance 8**

16 A lack of decision is also a decision.
the President of Poland, on delaying his country's referendum on the European constitution
Alexander Kwasniewski 1954– : in *Sunday Times* 12 June 2005

Indifference

PHRASES

1 compassion fatigue

indifference to charitable appeals on behalf of those who are suffering, experienced as a result of the frequency or number of such appeals

2 leather or prunella

something to which one is completely indifferent; a misinterpretation of lines from Alexander Pope's

Essay on Man (1734): 'Worth makes the Man, and want of it the Fellow;/The rest, is all but Leather or Prunella.' In Pope's poem, a distinction is being drawn between the trade of a cobbler (*leather*) and the profession of a clergyman (*prunella* as the material from which a clerical gown is made). The phrase was however taken to denote something of no value

QUOTATIONS

3 They have mouths, and speak not: eyes have they, and see not.
They have ears, and hear not: noses have they, and smell not.

They have hands, and handle not: feet have they, and walk not: neither speak they through their throat.
Bible: Psalm 115

4 All colours will agree in the dark.
Francis Bacon 1561–1626: *Essays* (1625) 'Of Unity in Religion'

5 And this the burthen of his song,
For ever used to be,
I care for nobody, not I,
If no one cares for me.
Isaac Bickerstaffe 1733–c.1808: *Love in a Village* (1762) 'The Miller of Dee'

6 There is nothing upon the face of the earth so insipid as a medium. Give me love or hate! a friend that will go to jail for me, or an enemy that will run me through the body!
Fanny Burney 1752–1840: *Camilla* (1796)

7 Vacant heart and hand, and eye,—
Easy live and quiet die.
Sir Walter Scott 1771–1832: *The Bride of Lammermoor* (1819)

8 If Jesus Christ were to come to-day, people would not even crucify him. They would ask him to dinner, and hear what he had to say, and make fun of it.
Thomas Carlyle 1795–1881: D. A. Wilson *Carlyle at his Zenith* (1927)

9 The worst sin towards our fellow creatures is not to hate them, but to be indifferent to them: that's the essence of inhumanity.
George Bernard Shaw 1856–1950: *The Devil's Disciple* (1901)

10 Science may have found a cure for most evils; but it has found no remedy for the worst of them all—the apathy of human beings.
Helen Keller 1880–1968: *My Religion* (1927)

11 I wish I could care what you do or where you go but I can't . . . My dear, I don't give a damn.
'Frankly, my dear, I don't give a damn!' in the 1939 screen version by Sidney Howard
Margaret Mitchell 1900–49: *Gone with the Wind* (1936)

12 Cast a cold eye
On life, on death.
Horseman pass by!
W. B. Yeats 1865–1939: 'Under Ben Bulben' (1939)

13 Catholics and Communists have committed great crimes, but at least they have not stood aside, like an established society, and been indifferent. I would rather have blood on my hands than water like Pilate.
Graham Greene 1904–91: *The Comedians* (1966); see **Duty 8**

14 In Germany they came first for the Communists, and I didn't speak up because I wasn't a Communist; and then they came for the trade unionists, and I didn't speak up because I wasn't a trade unionist; and then they came for the Jews, and I didn't speak up because I wasn't a Jew; and then . . . they came for me . . . and by that time there was no-one left to speak up.
Martin Niemöller 1892–1984: quoted in many versions since the Second World War; this version, in *'Quote Unquote' Newsletter* April 2001, was approved by Niemöller as the original in 1971

15 I come from a people who gave the ten commandments to the world. Time has come to strengthen them by three additional ones, which we ought to adopt and commit ourselves to: thou shalt not be a perpetrator; thou shalt not be a victim; and thou shalt never, but never, be a bystander.
Yehuda Bauer 1926– : speech to the German Bundestag, 1998, quoted in his own speech to the Stockholm International Forum on the Holocaust, 26 July 2000; see **Lifestyles 10**

Ingratitude see **Gratitude and Ingratitude**

Innocence see **Guilt and Innocence**

⇢ Insight ↢

see also **Self-Knowledge**

PROVERBS AND SAYINGS

1 **I pointed out to you the stars and all you saw was the tip of my finger.**
African proverb

PHRASES

2 **the penny drops**
understanding dawns; referring to the mechanism of
a penny-in-the-slot machine

3 **scales fall from a person's eyes**
a person receives sudden enlightenment or
revelation; from the Bible (Acts) 'And immediately

there fell from his eyes as it had been scales: and he
received sight forthwith'

4 **third eye**
in Hinduism and Buddhism, the 'eye of insight' in
the forehead of an image of a deity, especially the
god Shiva

QUOTATIONS

5 For the Lord seeth not as man seeth: for
man looketh on the outward appearance,
but the Lord looketh on the heart.
Bible: I Samuel

6 He—in whose nature, is the ugly disposition
Sees not the peacock,—only his ugly foot.
Sadi c.1213–91: *The Bustan* (1257); see **Self-
Knowledge** 2

7 Each of us touches one place
and understands the whole in that way.
The palm and the fingers feeling in the
   dark are
how the senses explore the reality of the
   elephant.
If each of us held a candle there,
and if we went in together,
we could see it.
on the inferences drawn by men touching different
parts of an elephant in the dark
Jalal ad-Din ar-Rumi 1207–73: *Mathnawi*; see
Knowledge 25

8 Everything I have written seems like straw
by comparison with what I have seen and
what has been revealed to me.
following a mystical experience, after which he did
no more teaching or writing
St Thomas Aquinas 1225–74: on 6
December 1273

9 I have striven not to laugh at human
actions, not to weep at them, nor to hate
them, but to understand them.
Baruch Spinoza 1632–77: *Tractatus Politicus* (1677)

10 If the doors of perception were cleansed
everything would appear to man as it is,
infinite.
William Blake 1757–1827: *The Marriage of Heaven
and Hell* (1790–3)

11 *Tout comprendre rend très indulgent.*
To be totally understanding makes one very
indulgent.
Mme de Staël 1766–1817: *Corinne* (1807); see
Forgiveness 6

12 The veil of eternity was lifted. The one great
truth which underlies all human
experience, and is the key to all the
mysteries that philosophy has sought in

vain to solve, flashed upon me in a sudden
revelation . . . staggering to my desk, I wrote
. . . '*A strong smell of turpentine prevails
throughout.*'
of his experiences under the influence of ether
Oliver Wendell Holmes 1809–94: *Mechanism in
Thought and Morals* (1871)

13 If we had a keen vision and feeling of all
ordinary human life, it would be like
hearing the grass grow and the squirrel's
heart beat, and we should die of that roar
which lies on the other side of silence.
George Eliot 1819–80: *Middlemarch* (1871–2)

14 One sees great things from the valley; only
small things from the peak.
G. K. Chesterton 1874–1936: *The Innocence of
Father Brown* (1911)

15 It is only with the heart that one can see
rightly; what is essential is invisible to
the eye.
Antoine de Saint-Exupéry 1900–44: *Le Petit
Prince* (1943)

16 Come to the edge.
We might fall.
Come to the edge.
It's too high!
COME TO THE EDGE!
And they came
and he pushed
and they flew . . .
Christopher Logue 1926– : 'Come to the edge'
(1969)

17 The world is like a Mask dancing. If you
want to see it well you do not stand in one
place.
Chinua Achebe 1930– : *Arrow of God* (1988)

18 If we find the answer to that [why it is that
we and the universe exist], it would be the
ultimate triumph of human reason—for
then we would know the mind of God.
Stephen Hawking 1942– : *A Brief History of Time*
(1988)

19 Know what I mean, Harry?
Frank Bruno 1961– : supposed to have been said
in interview with sports commentator Harry
Carpenter, possibly apocryphal

⤛ Insults ⤜

PROVERBS AND SAYINGS

1 Don't add insult to injury.
recommending not to treat someone one has hurt
with contempt as well; American proverb, mid 18th
century

PHRASES

2 bite one's thumb at
insult by making the gesture of biting one's thumb;
in Shakespeare's *Romeo and Juliet* (1595), in a scene
between two quarrelling servants, one when
challenged says to the other, 'I do not bite my thumb
at you, sir; but I bite my thumb, sir'

QUOTATIONS

3 The devil damn thee black, thou cream-
faced loon!
Where gott'st thou that goose look?
William Shakespeare 1564–1616: *Macbeth* (1606)

4 How easy it is to call rogue and villain, and
that wittily! But how hard to make a man
appear a fool, a blockhead, or a knave,
without using any of those opprobrious
terms! To spare the grossness of the names,
and to do the thing yet more severely, is to
draw a full face, and to make the nose and
cheeks stand out, and yet not to employ any
depth of shadowing.
John Dryden 1631–1700: *Of Satire* (1693)

5 An injury is much sooner forgotten than an
insult.
Lord Chesterfield 1694–1773: *Letters to his Son*
(1774) 9 October 1746

6 To-day I pronounced a word which should
never come out of a lady's lips it was that I
called John a Impudent Bitch.
Marjory Fleming 1803–11: *Journals, Letters and
Verses* (1934)

7 The words she spoke of Mrs Harris, lambs
could not forgive . . . nor worms forget.
Charles Dickens 1812–70: *Martin Chuzzlewit*
(1844)

8 Silence is the most perfect expression of
scorn.
George Bernard Shaw 1856–1950: *Back to
Methuselah* (1921)

9 JUDGE: You are extremely offensive,
young man.
SMITH: As a matter of fact, we both are, and
the only difference between us is that I
am trying to be, and you can't help it.
F. E. Smith 1872–1930: 2nd Earl of Birkenhead *Earl
of Birkenhead* (1933)

10 Okie use' ta mean you was from Oklahoma.
Now it means you're a dirty son-of-a-bitch.
Okie means you're scum. Don't mean
nothing itself, it's the way they say it.
John Steinbeck 1902–68: *The Grapes of Wrath*
(1939)

11 BESSIE BRADDOCK: Winston, you're drunk.
CHURCHILL: Bessie, you're ugly. But
tomorrow I shall be sober.
Winston Churchill 1874–1965: J. L. Lane (ed.)
Sayings of Churchill (1992)

12 Like being savaged by a dead sheep.
on being criticized by Geoffrey Howe
Denis Healey 1917– : speech in the House of
Commons, 14 June 1978

13 I decided the worst thing you can call Paul
Keating, quite frankly, is Paul Keating.
John Hewson 1946– : Michael Gordon *A Question
of Leadership* (1993)

➤➤Intelligence and Intellectuals ◆◆

PROVERBS AND SAYINGS

1 Elementary, my dear Watson.
remark attributed to Sherlock Holmes, but not found
in this form in any book by Arthur Conan Doyle; first
found in P.G. Wodehouse *Psmith Journalist* (1915)

**2 To question and ask is a moment's
shame, but to question and not ask is
a lifetime's shame.**
Japanese proverb

PHRASES

3 the chattering classes
the articulate professional people given to free
expression of (especially liberal) opinions on society
and culture

4 know a hawk from a handsaw
have ordinary discernment; now chiefly in allusion to
Shakespeare *Hamlet*: see **Madness 5**

5 little grey cells
intelligence; the expression used by Agatha Christie's
detective Hercule Poirot; see 14 below

6 too clever by half
far more clever than is satisfactory or desirable; see
21 below

7 trahison des clercs
a betrayal of intellectual, artistic, or moral standards
by writers, academics, or artists; French, 'treason of
the scholars', title of a book by Julien Benda (1927)

QUOTATIONS

8 Mere cleverness is not wisdom.
Euripides *c.*485–*c.*406 BC: *Bacchae*

9 Whoever in discussion adduces authority
uses not intellect but rather memory.
Leonardo da Vinci 1452–1519: Edward McCurdy
(ed.) *Leonardo da Vinci's Notebooks* (1906)

10 The height of cleverness is to be able to
conceal it.
Duc de la Rochefoucauld 1613–80: *Maximes*
(1678)

11 You beat your pate, and fancy wit will come:
Knock as you please, there's nobody at
home.
Alexander Pope 1688–1744: 'Epigram: You beat
your pate' (1732)

12 Sir, I have found you an argument; but I am
not obliged to find you an understanding.
Samuel Johnson 1709–84: James Boswell *Life of
Samuel Johnson* (1791) June 1784

13 A man is not necessarily intelligent because
he has plenty of ideas, any more than he is a
good general because he has plenty of
soldiers.
Nicolas-Sébastien Chamfort 1741–94: *Maximes
et Pensées* (1796)

14 He [Hercule Poirot] tapped his forehead.
'These little grey cells. It is "up to them".'
Agatha Christie 1890–1976: *The Mysterious Affair
at Styles* (1920); see 5 above

15 No one in this world, so far as I know—and I
have searched the records for years, and
employed agents to help me—has ever lost

money by underestimating the intelligence
of the great masses of the plain people.
H. L. Mencken 1880–1956: in *Chicago Tribune* 19
September 1926

16 'Hullo! friend,' I call out, 'Won't you lend us
a hand?' 'I am an intellectual and don't drag
wood about,' came the answer. 'You're
lucky,' I reply. 'I too wanted to become an
intellectual, but I didn't succeed.'
Albert Schweitzer 1875–1965: *Mitteilungen aus
Lambarene* (1928)

17 What is a highbrow? He is a man who has
found something more interesting than
women.
Edgar Wallace 1875–1932: in *New York Times* 24
January 1932

18 As a human being, one has been endowed
with just enough intelligence to be able to
see clearly how utterly inadequate that
intelligence is when confronted with what
exists.
Albert Einstein 1879–1955: letter to Queen
Elisabeth of Belgium, 19 September 1932

19 To the man-in-the-street, who, I'm sorry
to say,
Is a keen observer of life,
The word 'Intellectual' suggests
straight away
A man who's untrue to his wife.
W. H. Auden 1907–73: *New Year Letter* (1941)

20 An intellectual is someone whose mind
watches itself.
Albert Camus 1913–60: *Carnets, 1935–42* (1962)

21 Too clever by half.

of Iain Macleod; the term had been applied by an earlier Lord Salisbury (1830–1903) to Disraeli's amendment on Disestablishment, 30 March 1868. See 6 above
Lord Salisbury 1893–1972: speech, House of Lords, 7 March 1961

22 It takes little talent to see clearly what lies under one's nose, a good deal of it to know in which direction to point that organ.
W. H. Auden 1907–73: *Dyer's Hand* (1963) 'Writing'

23 I am sure some people think I have not got the brains to be that clever, but I do have the brains.

on how he intentionally picked up a yellow card in England's World Cup match against Wales
David Beckham 1975– : in *Mail on Sunday* 17 October 2004

⊁⊱ International Relations ⊰⊁

see also **Countries and Peoples, Diplomacy, Government, Politics**

PHRASES

1 the Auld Alliance
the political relationship of France and Scotland between the 14th and the 16th centuries; *auld* is a Scottish form of old

2 the balance of power
a state of international equilibrium with no nation predominant; originally *the balance of power in Europe*, as in *London Gazette* 1701 'Your glorious design of re-establishing a just balance of power in Europe', and associated with the political aspirations of Robert Walpole (1676–1745)

3 the cold war
the hostility between the Soviet bloc countries and the Western powers which began after the Second World War with the Soviet takeover of the countries of eastern Europe, and which was formally ended in November 1990; from a speech to the South Carolina Legislature 16 April 1947, 'Let us not be deceived—we are today in the midst of a cold war' by Bernard Baruch (1870–1965); the expression *cold war* was suggested to him by H. B. Swope, former editor of the *New York World*

4 ethical foreign policy
the conduct of foreign policy according to ethical as well as national considerations; after the British general election of 1997, the aspiration was particularly associated with the incumbency of Robin Cook as Foreign Secretary, but its precise application in individual cases has been controversial

5 hands across the sea
promoting closer international links, recorded from the late 19th century; see 19, 25 below

6 the Monroe doctrine
a principle of US policy, that any intervention by external powers in the politics of the Americas is a potentially hostile act against the US, originated by President James Monroe in his annual message to Congress, 2 December 1823; see **Diplomacy** 11

7 a New World Order
a vision of a world ordered differently from the way it is at present; in particular, an optimistic view of the world order or balance of power following the end of the Cold War; see **The Future** 28

8 the special relationship
the relationship between Britain and the US, regarded as particularly close in terms of common origin and language; associated with Winston Churchill, as in the House of Commons 7 November 1945, 'We should not abandon our special relationship with the United States and Canada'

9 the Third World
the developing countries of Asia, Africa, and Latin America; the phrase was first applied in the 1950s by French commentators who used *tiers monde* to distinguish the developing countries from the capitalist and Communist blocs; see **Countries** 37, **Journalism** 24

10 watchful waiting
American policy towards Mexico during Mexico's revolutionary period, 1913–20; from Woodrow Wilson's State of the Union address, 2 December 1913, 'Our policy of watchful waiting'

QUOTATIONS

11 Excessive dealings with tyrants are not good for the security of free states.
Demosthenes c.384–c.322 BC: *Second Philippic*

12 *Il n'y a plus de Pyrénées.*
The Pyrenees are no more.
on the accession of his grandson to the throne of Spain, 1700
Louis XIV 1638–1715: attributed to Louis by Voltaire in *Siècle de Louis XIV* (1753); but to the Spanish

Ambassador to France in the *Mercure Galant* (Paris)
November 1700

13 Peace, commerce, and honest friendship
with all nations—entangling alliances with
none.
Thomas Jefferson 1743–1826: inaugural address,
4th of March 1801

14 If you wish to avoid foreign collision, you
had better abandon the ocean.
Henry Clay 1777–1852: speech in the House of
Representatives, 22 January 1812

15 In matters of commerce the fault of the
Dutch
Is offering too little and asking too much.
The French are with equal advantage
content,
So we clap on Dutch bottoms just twenty
per cent.
George Canning 1770–1827: dispatch, in cipher,
to the English ambassador at the Hague, 31
January 1826

16 The Continent will [not] suffer England to
be the workshop of the world.
Benjamin Disraeli 1804–81: speech, House of
Commons, 15 March 1838

17 Italy is a geographical expression.
discussing the Italian question with Palmerston
in 1847
Prince Metternich 1773–1859: *Mémoires,
Documents, etc. de Metternich publiés par son fils*
(1883)

18 We have no eternal allies and we have no
perpetual enemies. Our interests are eternal
and perpetual, and those interests it is our
duty to follow.
Lord Palmerston 1784–1865: speech, House of
Commons, 1 March 1848

19 Hands across the sea,
Feet on English ground,
The old blood is bold blood, the wide world
round.
Byron Webber b. 1838: 'Hands across the Sea'
(*c*.1860), in Burton Stevenson *The Home Book of
Quotations* (1967 ed.); see 5 above, 25 below

20 Lord Palmerston, with characteristic levity
had once said that only three men in Europe
had ever understood [the Schleswig-Holstein
question], and of these the Prince Consort
was dead, a Danish statesman (unnamed)
was in an asylum, and he himself had
forgotten it.
Lord Palmerston 1784–1865: R. W. Seton-Watson
Britain in Europe 1789-1914 (1937)

21 Nations touch at their summits.
Walter Bagehot 1826–77: *The English Constitution*
(1867)

22 This policy cannot succeed through
speeches, and shooting-matches, and songs;
it can only be carried out through blood and
iron.
Otto von Bismarck 1815–98: speech in the
Prussian House of Deputies, 28 January 1886; see
Warfare 5

23 In a word, we desire to throw no one into
the shade [in East Asia], but we also demand
our own place in the sun.
Bernhard von Bülow 1849–1929: speech,
Reichstag, 6 December 1897; see **Success 18**

24 Just for a word 'neutrality'—a word which in
wartime has so often been disregarded—just
for a scrap of paper, Great Britain is going to
make war on a kindred nation who desires
nothing better than to be friends with her.
Theobald von Bethmann Hollweg 1856–1921:
summary of a report by Sir E. Goschen to Sir Edward
Grey; *The Diary of Edward Goschen 1900-1914* (1980)
discusses the contentious origins of this statement;
see **Trust 13**

25 I have never used in peace or in war any
such expression as 'hands across the sea',
and I emphatically disapprove of what it
signifies save in so far as it means cordial
friendship between us and every other
nation that acts in accordance with the
standards that we deem just and right.
Theodore Roosevelt 1858–1919: in *Metropolitan*
October 1915; see 5, 19 above

26 Armed neutrality is ineffectual enough at
best.
Woodrow Wilson 1856–1924: speech to Congress,
2 April 1917

27 In the field of world policy I would dedicate
this Nation to the policy of the good
neighbour.
Franklin D. Roosevelt 1882–1945: inaugural
address, 4 March 1933

28 Since the day of the air, the old frontiers are
gone. When you think of the defence of
England you no longer think of the chalk
cliffs of Dover; you think of the Rhine. That
is where our frontier lies.
Stanley Baldwin 1867–1947: speech, House of
Commons, 30 July 1934

29 If Hitler invaded hell I would make at least a
favourable reference to the devil in the
House of Commons.
Winston Churchill 1874–1965: *The Second World
War* (1950) vol. 3

30 If you carry this resolution you will send
Britain's Foreign Secretary naked into the
conference chamber.
on a motion proposing unilateral nuclear
disarmament by the UK
Aneurin Bevan 1897–1960: speech at Labour Party
Conference in Brighton, 3 October 1957

31 We face neither East nor West: we face forward.
Kwame Nkrumah 1900–72: conference speech, Accra, 7 April 1960

32 *Ich bin ein Berliner.*
I am a Berliner.
expressing US commitment to the support and defence of West Berlin
John F. Kennedy 1917–63: speech in West Berlin, 26 June 1963

33 We hope that the world will not narrow into a neighbourhood before it has broadened into a brotherhood.
Lyndon Baines Johnson 1908–73: speech at the lighting of the Nation's Christmas Tree, 22 December 1963

34 The great nations have always acted like gangsters, and the small nations like prostitutes.
Stanley Kubrick 1928–99: in *Guardian* 5 June 1963

35 Living next to you is in some ways like sleeping with an elephant. No matter how friendly and even-tempered the beast, one is affected by every twitch and grunt.
on relations between Canada and the US
Pierre Trudeau 1919–2000: speech at National Press Club, Washington D. C., 25 March 1969

36 They're Germans. Don't mention the war.
John Cleese 1939– and **Connie Booth**: *Fawlty Towers* 'The Germans' (BBC TV programme, 1975)

37 We do not tilt on either side . . . we walk upright.
when asked by a reporter why India 'always tilted towards the Soviet Union'
Indira Gandhi 1917–84: in Washington, 1982; Inder Malhotra *Indira Gandhi* (1989)

38 If Kuwait grew carrots we wouldn't give a damn.
Lawrence Korb 1939– : in *International Herald Tribune* 21 August 1990

39 More than ever before in human history, we share a common destiny. We can master it only if we face it together. And that, my friends, is why we have the United Nations.
Kofi Annan 1938– : in *Sunday Times* 2 January 2000

40 This is not a battle betweeen the United States and terrorism, but between the free and democratic world and terrorism. We therefore here in Britain stand shoulder to shoulder with our American friends in this hour of tragedy and we, like them, will not rest until this evil is driven from our world.
Tony Blair 1953– : in Downing Street, London, 11 September 2001

41 States like these . . . constitute an axis of evil, arming to threaten the peace of this world.
of Iraq, Iran, and North Korea
George W. Bush 1946– : State of the Union address, in *Newsweek* 11 February 2002

42 Blair, keep your England and let me keep my Zimbabwe.
Robert Mugabe 1924– : at the Earth Summit in Johannesburg, 2 September 2002

The Internet see **Computers and the Internet**

Inventions and Discoveries

see also **Science, Technology**

PROVERBS AND SAYINGS

1 **Turkey, heresy, hops, and beer came into England all in one year.**
perhaps referring to 1521. The *turkey*, found domesticated in Mexico in 1518, was soon afterwards introduced into Europe, in 1521, the Pope conferred on Henry VIII the title Defender of the Faith, in recognition of his opposition to the Lutheran *heresy*, the *hop*-plant is believed to have been introduced into the south of England from Flanders between 1520 and 1524, and *beer* as the name of hopped malt liquor became common only in the 16th century; English proverb, late 16th century

PHRASES

2 **the best thing since sliced bread**
a particularly notable invention or discovery

3 **reinvent the wheel**
be forced by necessity to construct a basic requirement again from the beginning; the *wheel* as an essential requirement of modern civilization

QUOTATIONS

4 God hath made man upright; but they have sought out many inventions.
Bible: Ecclesiastes

5 *Eureka!*
I've got it!
Archimedes *c.*287–212 BC: Vitruvius Pollio *De Architectura*

6 It is well to observe the force and virtue and consequence of discoveries, and these are to be seen nowhere more conspicuously than in those three which were unknown to the ancients, and of which the origins, though recent, are obscure and inglorious; namely, printing, gunpowder, and the mariner's needle [the compass]. For these three have changed the whole face and state of things throughout the world.
Francis Bacon 1561–1626: *Novum Organum* (1620); see **Culture** 12

7 I don't know what I may seem to the world, but as to myself, I seem to have been only like a boy playing on the sea-shore and diverting myself in now and then finding a smoother pebble or a prettier shell than ordinary, whilst the great ocean of truth lay all undiscovered before me.
Isaac Newton 1642–1727: Joseph Spence *Anecdotes* (ed. J. Osborn, 1966)

8 What is the use of a new-born child?
when asked what was the use of a new invention
Benjamin Franklin 1706–90: J. Parton *Life and Times of Benjamin Franklin* (1864)

9 Then felt I like some watcher of the skies
When a new planet swims into his ken;
Or like stout Cortez when with eagle eyes
He stared at the Pacific—and all his men
Looked at each other with a wild surmise—
Silent, upon a peak in Darien.
John Keats 1795–1821: 'On First Looking into Chapman's Homer' (1817)

10 The discovery of a new dish does more for human happiness than the discovery of a star.
Anthelme Brillat-Savarin 1755–1826: *Physiologie du Goût* (1826)

11 Why sir, there is every possibility that you will soon be able to tax it!
to Gladstone, when asked about the usefulness of electricity
Michael Faraday 1791–1867: W. E. H. Lecky *Democracy and Liberty* (1899 ed.)

12 Name the greatest of all the inventors. Accident.
Mark Twain 1835–1910: *Notebook* (1935)

13 When man wanted to make a machine that would walk he created the wheel, which does not resemble a leg.
Guillaume Apollinaire 1880–1918: *Les Mamelles de Tirésias* (1918)

14 Yes, wonderful things.
when asked what he could see on first looking into the tomb of Tutankhamun, 26 November 1922; his notebook records the words as 'Yes, it is wonderful'
Howard Carter 1874–1939: H. V. F. Winstone *Howard Carter and the discovery of the tomb of Tutankhamun* (1993)

15 Whatever Nature has in store for mankind, unpleasant as it may be, men must accept, for ignorance is never better than knowledge.
Enrico Fermi 1901–54: Laura Fermi *Atoms in the Family* (1955)

16 Discovery consists of seeing what everybody has seen and thinking what nobody has thought.
Albert von Szent-Györgyi 1893–1986: Irving Good (ed.) *The Scientist Speculates* (1962)

17 Fleming was like a man who stumbles on a nugget of gold, shows it to a few friends, and then goes off to look for something else. Florey was like a man who goes back to the same spot and creates a gold mine.
Gwyn Macfarlane 1907–87: *Howard Florey* (1979)

18 It's true that by blundering about, we stumbled on gold, but the fact remains that we were looking for gold.
Francis Crick 1916–2004: *What Mad Pursuit* (1988)

19 praise without end the go-ahead zeal
of whoever it was invented the wheel;
but never a word for the poor soul's sake
that thought ahead, and invented the brake.
Howard Nemerov 1920–91: 'To the Congress of the United States, Entering Its Third Century' 26 February 1989

20 After the idea, there is plenty of time to learn the technology.
James Dyson 1947– : *Against the Odds* (1997)

21 The Patent Office is the gatekeeper to the new age.
Tom Stoppard 1937– : *The Invention of Love* (1997)

22 When the inventor of the drawing board messed things up, what did he go back to?
Bob Monkhouse 1928–2003: attributed; in *Guardian* 29 December 2003 (online edition); see **Beginning** 14

⤜ Ireland ⤛

PROVERBS AND SAYINGS

1 **England's difficulty is Ireland's opportunity.**
associated with the aspirations of Irish nationalism;
English proverb, mid 19th century

PHRASES

2 **Celtic twilight**
the romantic fairy tale atmosphere of Irish folklore;
literature conveying this; from the title of an
anthology collected by W. B. Yeats

3 **the Emerald Isle**
Ireland; from William Drennan *Erin* (1795) 'Nor one
feeling of vengeance presume to defile The cause, or
the men, of the Emerald Isle'

4 **the Flight of the Earls**
the flight into exile from Ireland of the two Catholic
leaders, Hugh O'Neill, Earl of Tyrone, and Rory
O'Donnell, Earl of Tyrconnell, 1607; see **22** below

5 **Land of Saints and Scholars**
Ireland; *saint* meaning 'monk' or 'anchorite',
alluding to the traditional view of medieval Ireland as
a monastic and scholarly land

6 **the Wild Geese**
the Irish Jacobites who fled from Ireland to the
Continent after the defeat of James II at the Battle of
the Boyne (1690), many of whom later took service
with the French forces; recorded in a poem by M. J.
Barry in *Spirit of the Nation* (1845) 'The wild
geese—the wild geese,—'Tis long since they flew,
O'er the billowy ocean's bright bosom of blue'

QUOTATIONS

7 Icham of Irlaunde
Ant of the holy londe of irlonde
Gode sir pray ich ye
for of saynte charite,
come ant daunce wyt me,
in irlaunde.
Anonymous: fourteenth century

8 I met wid Napper Tandy, and he took me by
   the hand,
And he said, 'How's poor ould Ireland, and
   how does she stand?'
She's the most disthressful country that iver
   yet was seen,
For they're hangin' men an' women for the
   wearin' o' the Green.
Anonymous: 'The Wearin' o' the Green' (*c.*1795
ballad)

9 The moment the very name of Ireland is
mentioned, the English seem to bid adieu to
common feeling, common prudence, and
common sense, and to act with the
barbarity of tyrants, and the fatuity of
idiots.
Sydney Smith 1771–1845: *Letters of Peter Plymley*
(1807)

10 The harp that once through Tara's halls
The soul of music shed,
Now hangs as mute on Tara's walls
As if that soul were fled.
Thomas Moore 1779–1852: 'The harp that once
through Tara's halls'(1807)

11 Thus you have a starving population, an
absentee aristocracy, and an alien Church,
and in addition the weakest executive in the
world. That is the Irish Question.
Benjamin Disraeli 1804–81: speech in the House
of Commons, 16 February 1844

12 I decided some time ago that if the G.O.M.
[Gladstone] went for Home Rule, the Orange
card would be the one to play. Please God it
may turn out the ace of trumps and not
the two.
Lord Randolph Churchill 1849–94: letter to Lord
Justice FitzGibbon, 16 February 1886; see **Ways and
Means 25**

13 Ulster will fight; Ulster will be right.
Lord Randolph Churchill 1849–94: public letter,
7 May 1886

14 For the great Gaels of Ireland
Are the men that God made mad,
For all their wars are merry,
And all their songs are sad.
G. K. Chesterton 1874–1936: *The Ballad of the
White Horse* (1911)

15 Ireland is the old sow that eats her farrow.
James Joyce 1882–1941: *A Portrait of the Artist as a
Young Man* (1916)

16 In Ireland the inevitable never happens and
the unexpected constantly occurs.
John Pentland Mahaffy 1839–1919: W. B.
Stanford and R. B. McDowell *Mahaffy* (1971)

17 Out of Ireland have we come.
Great hatred, little room,

Maimed us at the start.
W. B. Yeats 1865–1939: 'Remorse for Intemperate Speech' (1933)

18 Spenser's Ireland
has not altered;—
a place as kind as it is green,
the greenest place I've never seen.
Marianne Moore 1887–1972: 'Spenser's Ireland' (1941)

19 Clay is the word and clay is the flesh
Where the potato-gatherers like mechanized scarecrows move
Along the side-fall of the hill—Maguire and his men.
Patrick Kavanagh 1904–67: 'The Great Hunger' (1947)

20   The famous
Northern reticence, the tight gag of place

And times: yes, yes. Of the 'wee six' I sing.
Seamus Heaney 1939– : 'Whatever You Say Say Nothing' (1975)

21 Do you not feel that this island is moored only lightly to the sea-bed, and might be off for the Americas at any moment?
Sebastian Barry 1955– : Prayers of Sherkin (1991)

22 I've said and written a lot about emigration. But maybe soon I'll be writing The Flight of Earls in reverse—about everyone coming back home again.
Liam Reilly: in Irish Post 23 August 1997; see 4 above

23 I'm Irish. We think sideways.
Spike Milligan 1918–2002: in Independent on Sunday 20 June 1999

⤳ Jazz ⤲

see also **Music**

1 **beat generation**
a movement of young people in the 1950s and early 1960s who rejected conventional society, valuing free self-expression and favouring modern jazz; the phrase was supposedly coined by Jack Kerouac (1922–69) in the course of a conversation

QUOTATIONS

2 Jazz will endure, just as long as people hear it through their feet instead of their brains.
John Philip Sousa 1854–1932: Nat Shapiro (ed.) An Encyclopedia of Quotations about Music (1978)

3 It don't mean a thing
If it ain't got that swing.
Irving Mills 1894–1985: 'It Don't Mean a Thing' (1932 song; music by Duke Ellington)

4 Jazz music is to be played sweet, soft, plenty rhythm.
Jelly Roll Morton 1885–1941: Mister Jelly Roll (1950)

5 What a terrible revenge by the culture of the Negroes on that of the whites!
Ignacy Jan Paderewski 1860–1941: Nat Shapiro (ed.) An Encyclopedia of Quotations about Music (1978)

6 Playing 'Bop' is like scrabble with all the vowels missing.
Duke Ellington 1899–1974: in Look 10 August 1954

7 A jazz musician is a juggler who uses harmonies instead of oranges.
Benny Green 1927– : The Reluctant Art (1962)

8 Jazz is the only music in which the same note can be played night after night but differently each time.
Ornette Coleman 1930– : W. H. Mellers Music in a New Found Land (1964)

9 If you still have to ask . . . shame on you.
when asked what jazz is; sometimes quoted as, 'Man, if you gotta ask you'll never know'
Louis Armstrong 1901–71: Max Jones et al. Salute to Satchmo (1970)

10 [Charlie] Parker was a modern jazz player just as Picasso was a modern painter and Pound a modern poet. I hadn't realized that jazz had gone from Lascaux to Jackson Pollock in fifty years.
Philip Larkin 1922–85: Required Writing (1983)

Jealousy see Envy and Jealousy

➤➤Journalism ⤛⤛

see also **News**

PROVERBS AND SAYINGS

1 **All the news that's fit to print.**
motto of the *New York Times*, from 1896; coined by
Adolph S. Ochs (1858–1935)

2 **Top people take *The Times*.**
advertising slogan for *The Times* newspaper, from
January 1959

3 **Watch this space!**
further developments are expected and more
information will be given later; *space* = an area of a
newspaper available for a specific purpose,
especially for advertising

PHRASES

4 **the fourth estate**
the press; a group regarded as having power in the
land equivalent to that of one of the three Estates of
the Realm, the Crown, the House of Lords, and the
House of Commons; from Lord Macaulay in 1843,
'The gallery in which the reporters sit has become a
fourth estate of the realm'

5 **Page Three**
a British trademark term for a feature which formerly
appeared daily on page three of the *Sun* newspaper

and included a picture of a topless young woman;
see 28 below, **Women** 14

6 **the silly season**
the months of August and September, when
newspapers make up for the lack of serious news
with articles on trivial topics; the time when
Parliament and the law courts are in recess; recorded
in 1861, when the *Saturday Review* of 13 July spoke
of 'the Silly Season of 1861 setting in a month or two
before its time'

QUOTATIONS

7 Our liberty depends on freedom of the
press, and that cannot be limited without
being lost.
Thomas Jefferson 1743–1826: letter to James
Currie, 28 January 1786, in *Papers of Thomas
Jefferson* (1954) vol. 9

8 Nothing can now be believed which is seen
in a newspaper. Truth itself becomes
suspicious by being put into that polluted
vehicle.
Thomas Jefferson 1743–1826: letter to John
Norvell, 14 June 1807, in *The Portable Thomas
Jefferson* (1977)

9 *The Times* has made many ministries.
Walter Bagehot 1826–77: *The English Constitution*
(1867) 'The Cabinet'

10 There are laws to protect the freedom of the
press's speech, but none that are worth
anything to protect the people from the
press.
Mark Twain 1835–1910: 'License of the Press'
(1873)

11 You furnish the pictures and I'll furnish
the war.
message to the artist Frederic Remington in Havana,
Cuba, during the Spanish-American War of 1898
William Randolph Hearst 1863–1951: attributed

12 By office boys for office boys.
of the *Daily Mail*
Lord Salisbury 1830–1903: H. Hamilton Fyfe
Northcliffe, an Intimate Biography (1930)

13 The men with the muck-rakes are often
indispensable to the well-being of society;
but only if they know when to stop raking
the muck.
Theodore Roosevelt 1858–1919: speech in
Washington, 14 April 1906

14 A cynical, mercenary, demagogic, corrupt
press will produce in time a people as base as
itself.
Joseph Pulitzer 1847–1911: inscribed on the
gateway to the Columbia School of Journalism in
New York

15 The power of the press is very great, but not
so great as the power of suppress.
Lord Northcliffe 1865–1922: office message, *Daily
Mail* 1918; Reginald Rose and Geoffrey Harmsworth
Northcliffe (1959)

16 Comment is free, but facts are sacred.
C. P. Scott 1846–1932: in *Manchester Guardian* 5
May 1921; see 25 below

17 You cannot hope
to bribe or twist,
thank God! the
British journalist.
But, seeing what

the man will do
unbribed, there's
no occasion to.

Humbert Wolfe 1886–1940: 'Over the Fire' (1930)

18 Journalism—an ability to meet the
challenge of filling the space.

Rebecca West 1892–1983: in *New York Herald Tribune* 22 April 1956

19 Anyone here been raped and speaks English?

shouted by a British TV reporter in a crowd of
Belgian civilians waiting to be airlifted out of the
Belgian Congo, *c*.1960

Anonymous: Edward Behr *Anyone Here been Raped and Speaks English?* (1981)

20 A good newspaper, I suppose, is a nation
talking to itself.

Arthur Miller 1915–2005: in *Observer* 26 November 1961

21 Freedom of the press in Britain means
freedom to print such of the proprietor's
prejudices as the advertisers don't object to.

Hannen Swaffer 1879–1962: Tom Driberg *Swaff* (1974)

22 When the legend becomes fact, print the
legend.

Willis Goldbeck and **James Warner Bellah**: *The Man who Shot Liberty Valance* (1962 film); see also **Heroes** 17

23 Success in journalism can be a form of
failure. Freedom comes from lack of
possessions. The truth-divulging paper must
imitate the tramp and sleep under a hedge.

Graham Greene 1904–91: in *New Statesman* 31 May 1968

24 The Third World never sold a newspaper.

Rupert Murdoch 1931– : in *Observer* 1 January
1978; see **International Relations** 9

25 Comment is free but facts are on expenses.

Tom Stoppard 1937– : *Night and Day* (1978); see
16 above

26 Rock journalism is people who can't write
interviewing people who can't talk for
people who can't read.

Frank Zappa 1940–93: Linda Botts *Loose Talk* (1980)

27 Go to where the silence is and say
something.

accepting an award from Columbia University for her
coverage of the 1991 massacre in East Timor by
Indonesian troops

Amy Goodman 1957– : in *Columbia Journalism
Review* March/April 1994

28 I don't know. The editor did it when I was
away.

when asked why he had allowed Page 3 to develop

Rupert Murdoch 1931– : in *Guardian* 25 February
1994; see 5 above

29 When seagulls follow a trawler, it is because
they think sardines will be thrown into
the sea.

to the media at the end of a press conference, 31
March 1995

Eric Cantona 1966– : in *The Times* 1 April 1995

30 No government in history has been as
obsessed with public relations as this one
. . . Speaking for myself, if there is a message
I want to be off it.

Jeremy Paxman 1950– : in *Daily Telegraph* 3
July 1998

⟶Justice ⟵

see also **The Law**

PROVERBS AND SAYINGS

1 **All's fair in love and war.**

in certain conditions rules do not apply, and any
measures are acceptable; English proverb, early 17th
century

2 **Be just before you're generous.**

often used in the context of advising that one should
settle any obligations before indulging in generosity;
English proverb, mid 18th century

3 **A fair exchange is no robbery.**

sometimes used of an action regarded as cancelling
out an obligation which has been incurred; English
proverb, mid 16th century

4 **Fair play's a jewel.**

applauding the value of honest dealing; English
proverb, early 19th century

5 **Give and take is fair play.**

English proverb, late 18th century

6 **Give the Devil his due.**

one should acknowledge the strengths and
capabilities of even the most unpleasant person;
English proverb, late 16th century

7 **Justice delayed is justice denied.**

English proverb, late 20th century; see 23 below

8 **One law for the rich and another for
the poor.**

English proverb, mid 19th century

9 **There are two sides to every question.**
a problem can be seen from more than one angle;
English proverb, early 19th century

10 **Turn about is fair play.**
recommending equality of opportunity; English
proverb, mid 18th century

11 **We all love justice—at our neighbour's
expense.**
American proverb, mid 20th century

PHRASES

14 **a fair field and no favour**
equal conditions in a contest, not unduly favouring
or hindering either side

15 **Jedem das Seine**
German = 'To each his own'; inscription on the gate
of Buchenwald concentration camp, c. 1937; often
quoted as 'Everyone gets what he deserves'; see
World War II 25

QUOTATIONS

18 Life for life,
Eye for eye, tooth for tooth.
Bible: Exodus; see **Revenge** 3, 8

19 What I say is that 'just' or 'right' means
nothing but what is in the interest of the
stronger party.
spoken by Thrasymachus
Plato 429–347 BC: *The Republic*

20 Judge not, that ye be not judged.
Bible: St Matthew; see **Prejudice** 1

21 *Nulla iniuria est, quae in volentem fiat.*
No injustice is done to someone who wants
that thing done.
usually quoted as '*Volenti non fit iniuria*'
Ulpian d. 228: *Corpus Iuris Civilis* Digests

22 Justice is the constant and perpetual wish to
render to every one his due.
Justinian AD 483–565: *Institutes*

23 To no man will we sell, or deny, or delay,
right or justice.
Magna Carta 1215: clause 40; see 7 above

24 If the parties will at my hands call for
justice, then, all were it my father stood on
the one side, and the Devil on the other, his
cause being good, the Devil should have
right.
Thomas More 1478–1535: William Roper *Life of Sir
Thomas More*

25 *Fiat justitia et pereat mundus.*
Let justice be done, though the world
perish.
Ferdinand I 1503–64: motto; Johannes Manlius
Locorum Communium Collectanea (1563)

12 **What goes around comes around.**
often used as a comment on someone becoming
subject to what they have visited on others; late 20th
century, of US origin

13 **What's sauce for the goose is sauce for
the gander.**
originally meaning that what is suitable for a woman
is also suitable for a man, but now sometimes used
in wider contexts; English proverb, late 17th century

16 **Jedburgh justice**
summary justice; such as that meted out to Border
reivers at *Jedburgh* in southern Scotland in the 16th
century

17 **a Roland for an Oliver**
an appropriate retaliation for a verbal or physical
attack, a quid pro quo; *Roland* was the legendary
nephew of Charlemagne, celebrated with his
comrade *Oliver* in the medieval romance *Chanson de
Roland*

26 The quality of mercy is not strained,
It droppeth as the gentle rain from heaven
Upon the place beneath.
William Shakespeare 1564–1616: *The Merchant of
Venice* (1596–8)

27 You manifestly wrong even the poorest
ploughman, if you demand not his free
consent.
Charles I 1600–49: The King's Reasons for declining
the jurisdiction of the High Court of Justice, 21
January 1649

28 I'm armed with more than complete
steel—The justice of my quarrel.
Anonymous: *Lust's Dominion* (1657); attributed to
Marlowe, though of doubtful authorship

29 Consider what you think justice requires,
and decide accordingly. But never give your
reasons; for your judgement will probably be
right, but your reasons will certainly be
wrong.
advice to a newly appointed colonial governor
ignorant in the law
William Murray, Lord Mansfield 1705–93: Lord
Campbell *The Lives of the Chief Justices of England*
(1849)

30 Justice is truth in action.
Benjamin Disraeli 1804–81: speech, House of
Commons, 11 February 1851

31 When I hear of an 'equity' in a case like this,
I am reminded of a blind man in a dark
room—looking for a black hat—which isn't
there.
Lord Bowen 1835–94: John Alderson Foote *Pie-
Powder* (1911)

32 *J'accuse.*

I accuse.

on the Dreyfus affair

Émile Zola 1840–1902: title of an open letter to the President of the French Republic in *L'Aurore* 13 January 1898

33 A man who is good enough to shed his blood for the country is good enough to be given a square deal afterwards. More than that no man is entitled to, and less than that no man shall have.

Theodore Roosevelt 1858–1919: speech at the Lincoln Monument, Springfield, Illinois, 4 June 1903

34 In England, justice is open to all—like the Ritz Hotel.

James Mathew 1830–1908: R. E. Megarry *Miscellany-at-Law* (1955)

35 Injustice is relatively easy to bear; what stings is justice.

H. L. Mencken 1880–1956: *Prejudices, Third Series* (1922)

36 A long line of cases shows that it is not merely of some importance, but is of fundamental importance that justice should not only be done, but should manifestly and undoubtedly be seen to be done.

Gordon Hewart 1870–1943: Rex v Sussex Justices, 9 November 1923

37 Injustice anywhere is a threat to justice everywhere.

Martin Luther King 1929–68: letter from Birmingham Jail, Alabama, 16 April 1963

38 What good is an ounce of justice in an ocean of shit?

Sony Labou Tansi 1947–95: *The Antipeople* (1983)

39   Once in a lifetime

The longed-for tidal wave

Of justice can rise up

And hope and history rhyme.

Seamus Heaney 1939– : *The Cure at Troy* (version of Sophocles' *Philoctetes*, 1990)

40 If it falls to me to start a fight to cut out the cancer of bent and twisted journalism in our country with the simple sword of truth and the trusty shield of British fair play, so be it.

Jonathan Aitken 1942– : statement, London, 10 April 1995

➤➤ Kissing ◄◄

PROVERBS AND SAYINGS

1 Kissing goes by favour.

a kiss is often given as a reward for something done; English proverb, early 17th century

2 When the gorse is out of bloom, kissing's out of fashion.

the idea behind the saying is that gorse is always in flower somewhere: see **Love** 15; English proverb, mid 19th century

QUOTATIONS

3 *Da mi basia mille, deinde centum,*

Dein mille altera, dein secunda centum,

Deinde usque altera mille, deinde centum.

Give me a thousand kisses, then a hundred, then another thousand, then a second hundred, then yet another thousand, then a hundred.

Catullus c.84–c.54 BC: *Carmina*

4 I kissed thee ere I killed thee, no way but this,

Killing myself to die upon a kiss.

William Shakespeare 1564–1616: *Othello* (1602–4)

5 But indeed, dear, these kisses on paper are scarce worth keeping. You gave me one on my neck that night you were in such good-humour, and one on my lips on some forgotten occasion, that I would not part with for a hundred thousand paper ones.

Jane Carlyle 1801–66: letter to Thomas Carlyle, 3 October 1826

6 O Love, O fire! once he drew

With one long kiss my whole soul through

My lips, as sunlight drinketh dew.

Alfred, Lord Tennyson 1809–92: 'Fatima' (1832)

7 What of soul was left, I wonder, when the kissing had to stop?

Robert Browning 1812–89: 'A Toccata of Galuppi's' (1855); see **Ending 11**

8 I wonder who's kissing her now.

Frank Adams and **Will M. Hough**: title of song (1909)

9 You must remember this, a kiss is still a kiss,

A sigh is just a sigh;

The fundamental things apply,

As time goes by.
Herman Hupfeld 1894–1951: 'As Time Goes By' (1931 song)

10 A fine romance with no kisses.
A fine romance, my friend, this is.
Dorothy Fields 1905–74: 'A Fine Romance' (1936 song)

11 Where do the noses go? I always wondered where the noses would go.
Ernest Hemingway 1899–1961: *For Whom the Bell Tolls* (1940)

12 A kiss can be a comma, a question mark or an exclamation point. That's basic spelling that every woman ought to know.
Mistinguett 1875–1956: in *Theatre Arts* December 1955

13 I wasn't kissing her, I was just whispering in her mouth.
on being discovered by his wife with a chorus girl
Chico Marx 1891–1961: Groucho Marx and Richard J. Anobile *Marx Brothers Scrapbook* (1973)

14 Oh, innocent victims of Cupid,
Remember this terse little verse;
To let a fool kiss you is stupid,
To let a kiss fool you is worse.
E. Y. Harburg 1898–1981: 'Inscriptions on a Lipstick' (1965)

15 Kissing girls is not like science, nor is it like sport. It is the third thing when you thought there were only two.
Tom Stoppard 1937– : *The Invention of Love* (1997)

⤞ Knowledge ⤝

PROVERBS AND SAYINGS

1 **The cobbler to his last and the gunner to his linstock.**
a fanciful extension of 'Let the cobbler stick to his last' (see 7 below). The gunner's *linstock* was a long pole used to hold a match for firing a cannon; English proverb, mid 18th century

2 **Fools ask questions that wise men cannot answer.**
a foolish person may put a question to which there is no simple or easily given answer; English proverb, mid 17th century

3 **Knowledge and timber shouldn't be much used until they are seasoned.**
American proverb, mid 19th century

4 **Knowledge is power.**
English proverb, late 16th century; see 29 below, Arts 3

5 **The larger the shoreline of knowledge, the longer the shoreline of wonder.**
North American proverb, mid 20th century

6 **Learning is better than house and land.**
reflecting on the difference between knowledge and material, and therefore ephemeral, possessions; English proverb, late 18th century

7 **Let the cobbler stick to his last.**
people should only concern themselves with things they know something about (the cobbler's *last* is a

shoemaker's model for shaping or repairing a shoe or boot); English proverb, mid 16th century; see also 1 above

8 **A little knowledge is a dangerous thing.**
English proverb, early 18th century; alteration of Pope: see 32, 43 below

9 **Out of the mouths of babes—.**
young children may sometimes speak with disconcerting wisdom; English proverb, late 19th century, with allusion to the Bible (Psalms), 'Out of the mouth of very babes and sucklings hast thou ordained strength, because of thine enemies'

10 **The sea of learning has no end.**
Chinese proverb

11 **Walking ten thousand miles; reading ten thousand books.**
theoretical knowledge and practical experience are of equal value; Chinese proverb, compare **Experience** 11

12 **When house and land are gone and spent, then learning is most excellent.**
contrasting the value of learning with the ephemeral nature of material possessions; English proverb, mid 18th century

PHRASES

13 **have the right sow by the ear**
have the correct understanding of a situation; see **Practicality** 5

14 **milk for babes**
something easy and pleasant to learn; especially in allusion to the Bible (I Corinthians) 'I . . . speak unto

you . . . even as unto babes in Christ. I have fed you with milk, and not with meat'

15 'satiable curiosity
a thirst for knowledge that cannot be satisfied, as exemplified by the Elephant's Child in Kipling's *Just So Stories*, who was 'full of 'satiable curtiosity': see also 45 below

QUOTATIONS

17 The fox knows many things—the hedgehog one *big* one.
Archilochus 7th century BC: E. Diehl (ed.) *Anthologia Lyrica Graeca* (3rd ed., 1949–52); see **Character 46**

18 He who knows does not speak.
He who speaks does not know.
Lao Tzu c.604–c.531 BC: *Tao-te Ching*

19 He that increaseth knowledge increaseth sorrow.
Bible: Ecclesiastes

20 The price of wisdom is above rubies.
Bible: Job

21 I know nothing except the fact of my ignorance.
Socrates 469–399 BC: Diogenes Laertius *Lives of the Philosophers*

22 All men by nature desire knowledge.
Aristotle 384–322 BC: *Metaphysics*

23 Paul, thou art beside thyself; much learning doth make thee mad.
Bible: Acts of the Apostles

24 For now we see through a glass, darkly; but then face to face: now I know in part; but then shall I know even as also I am known.
Bible: I Corinthians

25 Each had but known one part, and no man all;
Hence into deadly error each did fall.
No way to know the All man's heart can find:
Can knowledge e'er accompany the blind?
on blind men's conclusions on touching different parts of an elephant
Sana'i d. c.1131: 'The Blind Men and the Elephant'; see **Insight 7**

26 Everyman, I will go with thee, and be thy guide,
In thy most need to go by thy side.
spoken by 'Knowledge'
Anonymous: *Everyman* (c.1509–19)

27 Knowledge without conscience is but the ruin of the soul.
François Rabelais c.1494–c.1553: *Gargantua and Pantagruel* (1532–64)

16 the tree of knowledge
knowledge in general, comprising all its branches; the tree in the Garden of Eden bearing the apple eaten by Eve

28 *Que sais-je?*
What do I know?
on the position of the sceptic
Montaigne 1533–92: *Essais* (1580)

29 Knowledge itself is power.
Francis Bacon 1561–1626: *Meditationes Sacrae* (1597) 'Of Heresies'; see **4 above**

30 What song the Syrens sang, or what name Achilles assumed when he hid himself among women, though puzzling questions, are not beyond all conjecture.
Thomas Browne 1605–82: *Hydriotaphia* (Urn Burial, 1658)

31 We have first raised a dust and then complain we cannot see.
George Berkeley 1685–1753: *A Treatise Concerning the Principles of Human Knowledge* (1710)

32 A little learning is a dangerous thing;
Drink deep, or taste not the Pierian spring.
Alexander Pope 1688–1744: *An Essay on Criticism* (1711); see **8 above, Poetry 3**

33 Knowledge may give weight, but accomplishments give lustre, and many more people see than weigh.
Lord Chesterfield 1694–1773: *Maxims* (1774)

34 Knowledge is of two kinds. We know a subject ourselves, or we know where we can find information upon it.
Samuel Johnson 1709–84: James Boswell *Life of Samuel Johnson* (1791) 18 April 1775

35 Wisdom is not the purchase of a day.
Thomas Paine 1737–1809: *The Crisis* (December 1776)

36 Only through beauty's gate, can you penetrate the land of knowledge.
Friedrich von Schiller 1759–1805: 'Die Künstler' (1789)

37 Knowledge advances by steps, and not by leaps.
Lord Macaulay 1800–59: T. F. Ellis (ed.) *Miscellaneous Writings of Lord Macaulay* (1860) 'History' (1828)

38 Knowledge comes, but wisdom lingers.
Alfred, Lord Tennyson 1809–92: 'Locksley Hall' (1842)

39 You will find it a very good practice always
to verify your references, sir!
Martin Joseph Routh 1755–1854: John William
Burgon *Lives of Twelve Good Men* (1888 ed.)

40 It is better to know nothing than to know
what ain't so.
Josh Billings 1818–85: *Proverb* (1874)

41 No lesson seems to be so deeply inculcated
by the experience of life as that you never
should trust experts. If you believe the
doctors, nothing is wholesome: if you
believe the theologians, nothing is
innocent: if you believe the soldiers,
nothing is safe. They all require to have their
strong wine diluted by a very large
admixture of insipid common sense.
Lord Salisbury 1830–1903: letter to Lord Lytton, 15
June 1877

42 Now that I do know it, I shall do my best to
forget it.
Arthur Conan Doyle 1859–1930: *A Study in Scarlet*
(1887)

43 If a little knowledge is dangerous, where is
the man who has so much as to be out of
danger?
T. H. Huxley 1825–95: *Collected Essays* vol. 3 (1895)
'On Elementary Instruction in Physiology' (written
1877); see 8 above

44 The motto of all the mongoose family is,
'Run and find out.'
Rudyard Kipling 1865–1936: *The Jungle Book*
(1894)

45 I keep six honest serving-men
(They taught me all I knew);
Their names are What and Why and When
And How and Where and Who.
Rudyard Kipling 1865–1936: *Just So Stories* (1902)
'The Elephant's Child'; see 15 above

46 There is no such thing on earth as an
uninteresting subject; the only thing that
can exist is an uninterested person.
G. K. Chesterton 1874–1936: *Heretics* (1905)

47 The clever men at Oxford
Know all that there is to be knowed.
But they none of them know one half
  as much

As intelligent Mr Toad!
Kenneth Grahame 1859–1932: *Wind in the
Willows* (1908)

48 For lust of knowing what should not be
  known,
We take the Golden Road to Samarkand.
James Elroy Flecker 1884–1915: *The Golden
Journey to Samarkand* (1913)

49 Owl hasn't exactly got Brain, but he Knows
Things.
A. A. Milne 1882–1956: *Winnie-the-Pooh* (1926)

50 Pedantry is the dotage of knowledge.
Holbrook Jackson 1874–1948: *Anatomy of
Bibliomania* (1930)

51 Where is the wisdom we have lost in
  knowledge?
Where is the knowledge we have lost in
  information?
T. S. Eliot 1888–1965: *The Rock* (1934)

52 We must know,
We will know.
David Hilbert 1862–1943: epitaph on his
tombstone

53 An expert is one who knows more and more
about less and less.
Nicholas Murray Butler 1862–1947:
commencement address at Columbia University;
attributed

54 An expert is someone who knows some of
the worst mistakes that can be made in his
subject and who manages to avoid them.
Werner Heisenberg 1901–76: *Der Teil und das
Ganze* (1969)

55 Not many people know that.
Michael Caine 1933– : title of book (1984)

56 That was a little bit more information than I
needed to know.
Quentin Tarantino 1963– : *Pulp Fiction* (1994
film); spoken by Uma Thurman

57 Knowledge is good. It does not have to look
good or sound good or even do good. And it is
good just by being knowledge. And the only
thing that makes it knowledge is that it is
true. You can't have too much of it and
there is no little too little to be worth
having.
Tom Stoppard 1937– : *The Invention of Love* (1997)

➤➤Language ◂◂

see also **Meaning, Speech, Swearing, Words**

PROVERBS AND SAYINGS

1 **The quick brown fox jumps over the lazy dog.**
traditional sentence used by keyboarders to ensure that all letters of the alphabet are functioning

PHRASES

2 **weasel words**
words or statements that are intentionally ambiguous or misleading; the expression was popularized by Theodore Roosevelt: see 18 below

3 **winged words**
highly significant or apposite words; travelling as directly as arrows to the mark; from Homer *The Iliad*

QUOTATIONS

4 A word fitly spoken is like apples of gold in pictures of silver.
Bible: Proverbs

5 The chief merit of language is clearness, and we know that nothing detracts so much from this as do unfamiliar terms.
Galen AD 129–199: *On the Natural Faculties*

6 Grammer, the ground of al.
William Langland c.1330–c.1400: *The Vision of Piers Plowman*

7 Syllables govern the world.
John Selden 1584–1654: *Table Talk* (1689)

8 Good heavens! For more than forty years I have been speaking prose without knowing it.
Molière 1622–73: *Le Bourgeois Gentilhomme* (1671)

9 The true use of speech is not so much to express our wants as to conceal them.
Oliver Goldsmith 1728–74: in *The Bee* 20 October 1759 'On the Use of Language'

10 Language is the dress of thought.
Samuel Johnson 1709–84: *Lives of the English Poets* (1779–81)

11 In language, the ignorant have prescribed laws to the learned.
Richard Duppa 1770–1831: *Maxims* (1830)

12 He who understands baboon would do more towards metaphysics than Locke.
Charles Darwin 1809–82: Notebook M (16 August 1838)

13 Language is fossil poetry.
Ralph Waldo Emerson 1803–82: *Essays. Second Series* (1844) 'The Poet'

14 It is hard for a woman to define her feelings in language which is chiefly made by men to express theirs.
Thomas Hardy 1840–1928: *Far from the Madding Crowd* (1874)

15 I will not go down to posterity talking bad grammar.
while correcting proofs of his last Parliamentary speech, 31 March 1881
Benjamin Disraeli 1804–81: Robert Blake *Disraeli* (1966)

16 The mystery of language was revealed to me. I knew then that 'w-a-t-e-r' meant the wonderful cool something that was flowing over my hand. That living word awakened my soul, gave it light, joy, set it free!
Helen Keller 1880–1968: *The Story of My Life* (1902)

17 A definition is the enclosing a wilderness of idea within a wall of words.
Samuel Butler 1835–1902: *Notebooks* (1912)

18 One of our defects as a nation is a tendency to use what have been called 'weasel words'. When a weasel sucks eggs the meat is sucked out of the egg. If you use a 'weasel word' after another, there is nothing left of the other.
Theodore Roosevelt 1858–1919: speech in St Louis, 31 May 1916; see 2 above

19 The limits of my language mean the limits of my world.
Ludwig Wittgenstein 1889–1951: *Tractatus Logico-Philosophicus* (1922)

20 One picture is worth ten thousand words.
Frederick R. Barnard: in *Printers' Ink* 10 March 1927; see **Words and Deeds** 5

21 The subjunctive mood is in its death throes, and the best thing to do is to put it out of its misery as soon as possible.
W. Somerset Maugham 1874–1965: *A Writer's Notebook* (1949) written in 1941

22 Would you convey my compliments to the purist who reads your proofs and tell him or her that I write in a sort of broken-down patois which is something like the way a Swiss waiter talks, and that when I split an infinitive, God damn it, I split it so it will stay split.
Raymond Chandler 1888–1959: letter to Edward Weeks, 18 January 1947

23 This is the sort of English up with which I will not put.
Winston Churchill 1874–1965: Ernest Gowers *Plain Words* (1948)

24 Colourless green ideas sleep furiously.
illustrating that grammatical structure is independent of meaning
Noam Chomsky 1928– : *Syntactic Structures* (1957)

25 Slang is a language that rolls up its sleeves, spits on its hands and goes to work.
Carl Sandburg 1878–1967: in *New York Times* 13 February 1959

26 Different persons growing up in the same language are like different bushes trimmed and trained to take the shape of identical elephants. The anatomical details of twigs and branches will fulfill the elephantine shape differently from bush to bush, but the overall outward results are alike.
W. V. O. Quine 1908–2000: *Word and Object* (1960)

27 Save the gerund and screw the whale.
Tom Stoppard 1937– : *The Real Thing* (1988 rev. ed.); see Pollution 2

28 I believe that political correctness can be a form of linguistic fascism, and it sends shivers down the spine of my generation who went to war against fascism.
P. D. James 1920– : in *Paris Review* 1995; see Prejudice 6

29 I hope to use the subjunctive until the end.
Tom Lehrer 1928– : attributed; in *The Times* 3 August 2000

⤖ Languages ⤚

see also **Translation**

PROVERBS AND SAYINGS

1 **A nation without a language is a nation without a heart.**
Welsh proverb; see 13 below

PHRASES

2 **the gift of tongues**
the power of speaking in unknown languages, regarded as one of the gifts of the Holy Spirit; from the account in the Bible (Acts) of the coming of the Holy Spirit to the disciples at Pentecost, after which those to whom the disciples preached 'heard them speak with tongues, and magnify God'

3 **the Tower of Babel**
a tower built in an attempt to reach heaven, which God frustrated by confusing the languages of its builders so that they could not understand one another; from the biblical story (Genesis), which was probably inspired by the Babylonian ziggurat, and may be an attempt to explain the existence of different languages; see 10 below

QUOTATIONS

4 And Frenssh she spak ful faire and fetisly,
After the scole of Stratford atte Bowe,
For Frenssh of Parys was to hire unknowe.
Geoffrey Chaucer 1343–1400: *The Canterbury Tales* 'The General Prologue'

5 To God I speak Spanish, to women Italian, to men French, and to my horse—German.
Charles V 1500–58: attributed; Lord Chesterfield *Letters to his Son* (1774)

6 It is a thing plainly repugnant to the Word of God, and the custom of the Primitive Church, to have publick Prayer in the Church, or to minister the Sacraments in a tongue not understood of the people.
The Book of Common Prayer 1662: *Articles of Religion* (1562)

7 So now they have made our English tongue a gallimaufry or hodgepodge of all other speeches.
Edmund Spenser 1552–99: *The Shepherd's Calendar* (1579)

8 Thou hadst small Latin, and less Greek.
Ben Jonson 1573–1637: 'To the Memory of My Beloved, the Author, Mr William Shakespeare' (1623)

9 Poets that lasting marble seek
Must carve in Latin or in Greek.
Edmund Waller 1606–87: 'Of English Verse' (1645)

10 I am not like a lady at the court of Versailles, who said: 'What a dreadful pity that the bother at the tower of Babel should have got language all mixed up; but for that, everyone would always have spoken French.'
Voltaire 1694–1778: letter to Catherine the Great, 26 May 1767; see 3 above

11 I am always sorry when any language is lost, because languages are the pedigree of nations.
Samuel Johnson 1709–84: James Boswell *Journal of a Tour to the Hebrides* (1785) 18 September 1773

12 My English text is chaste, and all licentious passages are left in the obscurity of a learned language.
parodied as 'decent obscurity' in the *Anti-Jacobin*, 1797–8
Edward Gibbon 1737–94: *Memoirs of My Life* (1796)

13 A people without a language of its own is only half a nation.
Thomas Davis 1814–45: 'The National Language'; see 1 above

14 The great breeding people had gone out and multiplied; colonies in every clime attest our success; French is the *patois* of Europe; English is the language of the world.
Walter Bagehot 1826–77: in *National Review* January 1856 'Edward Gibbon'

15 A language is a dialect with an army and a navy.
Max Weinreich 1894–1969: in *Yivo Bleter* January–February 1945

16 England and America are two countries divided by a common language.
George Bernard Shaw 1856–1950: attributed in this and other forms, but not found in Shaw's published writings

17 There even are places where English completely disappears.
In America, they haven't used it for years!
Why can't the English teach their children how to speak?
Alan Jay Lerner 1918–86: 'Why Can't the English?' (1956 song)

18 It is very much better to go out in a bowler and speaking Spanish than in a sombrero and speaking English.
Prince Philip, Duke of Edinburgh 1921– : in *Observer* 15 April 1962

19 Waiting for the German verb is surely the ultimate thrill.
Flann O'Brien 1911–66: *The Hair of the Dogma* (1977)

20 We are walking lexicons. In a single sentence of idle chatter we preserve Latin, Anglo-Saxon, Norse; we carry a museum inside our heads, each day we commemorate peoples of whom we have never heard.
Penelope Lively 1933– : *Moon Tiger* (1987)

⤞ The Law ⤝

see also **Crime and Punishment, Justice**

PROVERBS AND SAYINGS

1 **The devil makes his Christmas pies of lawyers' tongues and clerks' fingers.**
the lawyers' tongues and clerks' fingers stand for the words and actions of the legal profession as welcomed by the Devil; English proverb, late 16th century

2 **Gray's Inn for walks,
Lincoln's Inn for a wall,**
**The Inner Temple for a garden,
And the Middle Temple for a hall.**
on the four Inns of Court; traditional rhyme, mid 17th century

3 **Hard cases make bad law.**
difficult cases cause the clarity of the law to be obscured by exceptions and strained interpretations; the saying may now also be used to imply that a law

framed in response to a particularly distressing case may not be well-thought-out or well-based; English proverb, mid 19th century

4 Home is home, as the Devil said when he found himself in the Court of Session.

the *Court of Session* is the supreme civil tribunal of Scotland, established in 1532; Scottish proverbial saying, mid 19th century

5 Ignorance of the law is no excuse for breaking it.

English proverb, early 15th century; see 20 below

6 A man who is his own lawyer has a fool for his client.

English proverb, early 19th century

7 The more laws, the more thieves and bandits.

a rigid and over-detailed code of law is likely to foster rather than prevent lawbreaking; English proverb, late 16th century; see 15, 18 below

PHRASES

11 habeas corpus

a writ requiring a person under arrest to be brought before a judge or into court, especially to secure the person's release unless lawful grounds are shown for their detention; Latin, literally 'thou shalt have the body (in court)'; see 26 below

12 myrmidon of the law

a police officer, a minor administrative officer of the law; *Myrmidon* = a member of a warlike people of

QUOTATIONS

15 The more laws and orders are made
    prominent,
The more thieves and bandits there will be.
Lao Tzu c.604–c.531 BC: *Tao-te Ching*; see 7 above,
18 below

16 Written laws are like spider's webs; they will catch, it is true, the weak and poor, but would be torn in pieces by the rich and powerful.
Anacharsis 6th century BC: Plutarch *Parallel Lives* 'Solon'

17 *Salus populi suprema est lex.*
The good of the people is the chief law.
Cicero 106–43 BC: *De Legibus*

18 The more corrupt the state, the more numerous the laws.
Tacitus c.AD 56–after 117: *Annals*; see 7, 15 above

19 How long soever it hath continued, if it be against reason, it is of no force in law.
Edward Coke 1552–1634: *The First Part of the Institutes of the Laws of England* (1628)

8 No one should be judge in his own cause.

it is impossible to be impartial where your own interest is involved; English proverb, mid 15th century

9 Possession is nine points of the law.

although it does not reflect any specific legal ruling, in early use the satisfaction of ten (sometimes twelve) points was commonly asserted to attest to full entitlement or ownership; possession, represented by nine (or eleven) points is therefore the closest substitute for this; English proverb, early 17th century

10 Rules are made to be broken.

English proverb, mid 20th century; see 25 below

ancient Thessaly, whom, according to a Homeric story, Achilles led to the siege of Troy

13 the thin blue line

the police as a defensive barrier of the law; alteration of *thin red line*: see **The Armed Forces** 16

14 twelve good men and true

a jury; traditionally composed of twelve men

20 Ignorance of the law excuses no man; not that all men know the law, but because 'tis an excuse every man will plead, and no man can tell how to confute him.
John Selden 1584–1654: *Table Talk* (1689) 'Law';
see 5 above

21 Law is a bottomless pit.
John Arbuthnot 1667–1735: *The History of John Bull* (1712)

22 The hungry judges soon the sentence sign,
And wretches hang that jury-men may dine.
Alexander Pope 1688–1744: *The Rape of the Lock* (1714)

23 Laws, like houses, lean on one another.
Edmund Burke 1729–97: *A Tract on the Popery Laws* (planned c.1765)

24 Bad laws are the worst sort of tyranny.
Edmund Burke 1729–97: *Speech at Bristol, previous to the Late Election* (1780)

25 Laws were made to be broken.
Christopher North 1785–1854: in *Blackwood's Magazine* (May 1830); see 10 above

26 The have-his-carcase, next to the perpetual motion, is vun of the blessedest things as wos ever made.
Charles Dickens 1812–70: *Pickwick Papers* (1837); see 11 above

27 'If the law supposes that,' said Mr Bumble . . . 'the law is a ass—a idiot.'
Charles Dickens 1812–70: *Oliver Twist* (1838)

28 English law does not permit good persons, as such, to strangle bad persons, as such.
T. H. Huxley 1825–95: letter in *Pall Mall Gazette*, 31 October 1866

29 I know no method to secure the repeal of bad or obnoxious laws so effective as their stringent execution.
Ulysses S. Grant 1822–85: inaugural address, 4 March 1869

30 When constabulary duty's to be done, A policeman's lot is not a happy one.
W. S. Gilbert 1836–1911: *The Pirates of Penzance* (1879)

31 The Law is the true embodiment Of everything that's excellent. It has no kind of fault or flaw, And I, my Lords, embody the Law.
the Lord Chancellor
W. S. Gilbert 1836–1911: *Iolanthe* (1882)

32 However harmless a thing is, if the law forbids it most people will think it wrong.
W. Somerset Maugham 1874–1965: *A Writer's Notebook* (1949) written in 1896

33 I don't know as I want a lawyer to tell me what I cannot do. I hire him to tell me how to do what I want to do.
J. P. Morgan 1837–1913: Ida M. Tarbell *The Life of Elbert H. Gary* (1925)

34 Regulations—they're written for the obedience of fools and the guidance of wise men.
Harry Day: to Douglas Bader, 1931; Paul Brickhill *Reach for the Sky* (1954)

35 No poet ever interpreted nature as freely as a lawyer interprets the truth.
Jean Giraudoux 1882–1944: *La Guerre de Troie n'aura pas lieu* (1935)

36 A verbal contract isn't worth the paper it is written on.
Sam Goldwyn 1882–1974: Alva Johnston *The Great Goldwyn* (1937)

37 Everything not forbidden is compulsory.
T. H. White 1906–64: *The Sword in the Stone* (1938)

38 The art of cross-examination is not the art of examining crossly. It's the art of leading the witness through a line of propositions he agrees to until he's forced to agree to the *one fatal question*.
Clifford Mortimer d. 1960: John Mortimer *Clinging to the Wreckage* (1982)

39 Every society gets the kind of criminal it deserves. What is equally true is that every community gets the kind of law enforcement it insists on.
Robert Kennedy 1925–68: *The Pursuit of Justice* (1964)

40 Loopholes are not always of a fixed dimension. They tend to enlarge as the numbers that pass through wear them away.
Harold Lever 1914–95: speech to Finance Bill Committee, 22 May 1968

41 A lawyer with his briefcase can steal more than a hundred men with guns.
Mario Puzo 1920–99: *The Godfather* (1969)

42 Asking the ignorant to use the incomprehensible to decide the unknowable.
on the jury system
Hiller B. Zobel 1932– : 'The Jury on Trial' in *American Heritage* July–August 1995

43 Not only did we play the race card, we played it from the bottom of the deck.
on the defence's conduct of the O. J. Simpson trial
Robert Shapiro 1942– : interview, 3 October 1995, in *The Times* 5 October 1995; see **Ways and Means** 25

Leadership

PROVERBS AND SAYINGS

1 **As one fern frond dies, another is born to take its place.**
Maori proverb, applied particularly to chiefs

2 **The fish always stinks from the head downwards.**
as the freshness of a dead fish can be judged from the condition of its head, any corruption in a country or organization will be manifested first in its leaders; English proverb, late 16th century

3 **A good leader is also a good follower.**
American proverb, mid 20th century

4 **He that cannot obey cannot command.**
the experience of being under orders teaches one how they should be given; English proverb, late 15th century

PHRASES

7 **the Nelson touch**
a masterly or sympathetic approach to a problem by the person in charge, supposedly characteristic of Nelson's style of leadership: see 11 below

QUOTATIONS

8 A leader is best when people barely know he exists . . . He acts without unnecessary speech, and when the work is done the people say 'We did it ourselves'.
Lao Tzu c.604–c.531 BC: *Tao-te Ching*

9 They be blind leaders of the blind. And if the blind lead the blind, both shall fall into the ditch.
Bible: St Matthew; see **Conformity 14, Ignorance 10**

10 Since, then, a prince is necessitated to play the animal well, he chooses among the beasts the fox and the lion, because the lion does not protect himself from traps; the fox does not protect himself from wolves. The prince must be a fox, therefore, to recognize the traps and a lion to frighten the wolves.
Niccolò Machiavelli 1469–1527: *The Prince* (written 1513)

11 I believe my arrival was most welcome, not only to the Commander of the Fleet but almost to every individual in it; and when I came to explain to them the *'Nelson touch'*, it was like an electric shock. Some shed tears, all approved—'It was new—it was singular—it was simple!'
Horatio, Lord Nelson 1758–1805: letter to Lady Hamilton, 1 October 1805; see 7 above

12 I used to say of him [Napoleon] that his presence on the field made the difference of forty thousand men.
Duke of Wellington 1769–1852: Philip Henry Stanhope *Notes of Conversations with the Duke of Wellington* (1888) 2 November 1831

13 By the structure of the world we often want, at the sudden occurrence of a grave tempest, to change the helmsman—to replace the pilot of the calm by the pilot of the storm.
Walter Bagehot 1826–77: *The English Constitution* (1867) 'The Cabinet'

5 **If you are not the lead dog, the view never changes.**
Canadian saying

6 **Take me to your leader.**
catchphrase from science-fiction stories

14 The art of leadership . . . consists in consolidating the attention of the people against a single adversary and taking care that nothing will split up that attention.
Adolf Hitler 1889–1945: *Mein Kampf* (1925)

15 So long as men worship the Caesars and Napoleons, Caesars and Napoleons will duly arise and make them miserable.
Aldous Huxley 1894–1963: *Ends and Means* (1937)

16 The final test of a leader is that he leaves behind him in other men the conviction and the will to carry on.
Walter Lippmann 1889–1974: in *New York Herald Tribune* 14 April 1945

17 The loyalties which centre upon number one are enormous. If he trips he must be sustained. If he makes mistakes they must be covered. If he sleeps he must not be wantonly disturbed. If he is no good he must be pole-axed. But this last extreme process cannot be carried out every day; and certainly not in the days just after he has been chosen.
Winston Churchill 1874–1965: *The Second World War* vol. 2 (1949)

18 I know that the right kind of leader for the Labour Party is a desiccated calculating machine who must not in any way permit himself to be swayed by indignation.
generally taken as referring to Hugh Gaitskell, although Bevan specifically denied it
Aneurin Bevan 1897–1960: Michael Foot *Aneurin Bevan* (1973)

19 I don't mind how much my Ministers talk, so long as they do what I say.
Margaret Thatcher 1925– : in *Observer* 27 January 1980

20 Leadership means making people feel good.
Jean Chrétien 1934– : in *Toronto Star* 7 June 1984

21 To grasp and hold a vision, that is the very essence of successful leadership—not only on the movie set where I learned it, but everywhere.
Ronald Reagan 1911–2004: in *The Wilson Quarterly* Winter 1994; attributed

22 The art of leadership is saying no, not yes. It is very easy to say yes.
Tony Blair 1953– : in *Mail on Sunday* 2 October 1994

23 Leadership is not about being nice. It's about being right and being strong.
Paul Keating 1944– : in *Time* 9 January 1995

⤛Leisure⤜

see also **Work**

PROVERBS AND SAYINGS

1 **All work and no play makes Jack a dull boy.**
warning against a lifestyle without any form of relaxation; English proverb, mid 17th century

2 **The busiest men have the most leisure.**
someone who is habitually busy is likely to make best use of their time; English proverb, late 19th century

3 **Have a break, have a Kit-Kat.**
advertising slogan for Rowntree's Kit-Kat, from c.1955

QUOTATIONS

4 The wisdom of a learned man cometh by opportunity of leisure: and he that hath little business shall become wise.
Bible: Ecclesiasticus

5 The thing which is the most outstanding and chiefly to be desired by all healthy and good and well-off persons, is leisure with honour.
Cicero 106–43 BC: *Pro Sestio*

6 If all the year were playing holidays,
To sport would be as tedious as to work;
But when they seldom come, they wished for come.
William Shakespeare 1564–1616: *Henry IV, Part 1* (1597)

7 Diligent occupation, if not criminally perverted from its purposes, is at once the instrument of virtue and the secret of happiness. Man cannot be safely trusted with a life of leisure.
Hannah More 1745–1833: *Christian Morals* (1813)

8 What is this life if, full of care,
We have no time to stand and stare.
W. H. Davies 1871–1940: 'Leisure' (1911)

9 A perpetual holiday is a good working definition of hell.
George Bernard Shaw 1856–1950: *Parents and Children* (1914)

10 There's sand in the porridge and sand in the bed,
And if this is pleasure we'd rather be dead.
Noël Coward 1899–1973: 'The English Lido' (1928)

11 To be able to fill leisure intelligently is the last product of civilization.
Bertrand Russell 1872–1970: *The Conquest of Happiness* (1930)

12 Cannot avoid contrasting deliriously rapid flight of time when on a holiday with very much slower passage of days, and even hours, in other and more familiar surroundings.
E. M. Delafield 1890–1943: *The Diary of a Provincial Lady* (1930)

13 We are closer to the ants than to the butterflies. Very few people can endure much leisure.
Gerald Brenan 1894–1987: *Thoughts in a Dry Season* (1978)

14 To many people holidays are no voyage of discovery, but a ritual of reassurance.
Phillip Adams 1939– : in *Age* 10 September 1983

15 If I am doing nothing, I like to be doing nothing to some purpose. That is what leisure means.
Alan Bennett 1934– : *A Question of Attribution* (1989)

16 *Recreations*: growling, prowling, scowling and owling.
Nicholas Fairbairn 1933–95: entry in *Who's Who* 1990; see **Biography** 2

⇥ Letters ⇤

PROVERBS AND SAYINGS

1 **Do not close a letter without reading it.**
American proverb, mid 20th century

2 **A love letter sometimes costs more than a three-cent stamp.**
American proverb, mid 20th century

3 **Someone, somewhere, wants a letter from you.**
advertising slogan for the British Post Office in the 1960s

QUOTATIONS

4 Ye see how large a letter I have written unto you with mine own hand.
Bible: Galatians

5 There is nothing to write about, you say. Well then, write and let me know just this—that there is nothing to write about; or tell me in the good old style if you are well.
Pliny the Younger c.AD 61–c.112: *Letters*

6 Sir, more than kisses, letters mingle souls.
John Donne 1572–1631: 'To Sir Henry Wotton' (1597–8)

7 I knew one that when he wrote a letter he would put that which was most material in the postscript, as if it had been a bymatter.
Francis Bacon 1561–1626: *Essays* (1625) 'Of Cunning'

8 All letters, methinks, should be free and easy as one's discourse, not studied as an oration, nor made up of hard words like a charm.
Dorothy Osborne 1627–95: letter to William Temple, September 1653

9 I have made this [letter] longer than usual, only because I have not had the time to make it shorter.
Blaise Pascal 1623–62: *Lettres Provinciales* (1657)

10 A woman seldom writes her mind but in her postscript.
Richard Steele 1672–1729: in *The Spectator* 31 May 1711

11 It is not in my power to tell thee how I have been affected by this dearest of all letters—it was so unexpected—so new a thing to see the breathing of thy inmost heart upon paper.
Mary Wordsworth 1782–1859: letter to William Wordsworth, 1 August 1810

12 She'll vish there wos more, and that's the great art o' letter writin'.
Charles Dickens 1812–70: *Pickwick Papers* (1837–8)

13 Correspondences are like small-clothes before the invention of suspenders; it is impossible to keep them up.
Sydney Smith 1771–1845: letter to Catherine Crowe, 31 January 1841

14 I would any day as soon kill a pig as write a letter.
on his dislike of personal correspondence
Alfred, Lord Tennyson 1809–92: remark made in the 1850s; Ann Thwaite *Emily Tennyson* (1996)

15 It is wonderful how much news there is when people write every other day; if they wait for a month, there is nothing that seems worth telling.
O. Douglas 1877–1948: *Penny Plain* (1920)

16 Why it should be such an effort to write to the people one loves I can't imagine. It's none at all to write to those who don't really count.
Katherine Mansfield 1888–1923: *Journal of Katherine Mansfield* (1930)

17 Letters of thanks, letters from banks,
Letters of joy from girl and boy,
Receipted bills and invitations
To inspect new stock or to visit relations,
And applications for situations,
And timid lovers' declarations,
And gossip, gossip from all the nations.
W. H. Auden 1907–73: 'Night Mail' (1936)

18 A man seldom puts his authentic self into a letter. He writes it to amuse a friend or to get rid of a social or business obligation, which is to say, a nuisance.
H. L. Mencken 1880–1956: *Minority Report* (1956)

19 Don't think that this is a letter. It is only a small eruption of a disease called friendship.
Jean Renoir 1894–1979: letter to Janine Bazin, 12 June 1974

→→ Liberty ←←

PROVERBS AND SAYINGS

1 Lean liberty is better than fat slavery.
asserting that freedom matters more than any
material comfort; English proverb, early 17th century

PHRASES

2 the bird has flown
the prisoner or fugitive has escaped; see
Parliament 15

3 Liberty Hall
a place where one may do as one likes; from
Goldsmith's *She Stoops to Conquer* (1773): 'This is
Liberty-hall, gentlemen. You may do just as you
please'

4 Underground Railroad
in the US, a secret network for helping slaves escape
from the South to the North and Canada in the years
before the American Civil War

QUOTATIONS

5 Let my people go.
Bible: Exodus

6 Not bound to swear allegiance to any
master, wherever the wind takes me I travel
as a visitor.
Horace 65–8 BC: *Epistles*

7 One Cartwright brought a Slave from Russia,
and would scourge him, for which he was
questioned: and it was resolved, That
England was too pure an Air for Slaves to
breathe in.
Anonymous: 'In the 11th of Elizabeth'
(1568–1569); John Rushworth *Historical Collections*
(1680–1722)

8 Why should a man be in love with his
fetters, though of gold?
Francis Bacon 1561–1626: *Essay of Death* (1648)

9 Stone walls do not a prison make,
Nor iron bars a cage.
Richard Lovelace 1618–58: 'To Althea, From
Prison' (1649)

10 None can love freedom heartily, but good
men; the rest love not freedom, but licence.
John Milton 1608–74: *The Tenure of Kings and
Magistrates* (1649)

11 Liberty is, to the lowest rank of every nation,
little more than the choice of working or
starving.
Samuel Johnson 1709–84: 'The Bravery of the
English Common Soldier'; in *The British Magazine*
January 1760

12 Man was born free, and everywhere he is in
chains.
Jean-Jacques Rousseau 1712–78: *Du Contrat
social* (1762)

13 I know not what course others may take; but
as for me, give me liberty, or give me death!
Patrick Henry 1736–99: speech in Virginia
Convention, 23 March 1775

14 The tree of liberty must be refreshed from
time to time with the blood of patriots and
tyrants. It is its natural manure.
Thomas Jefferson 1743–1826: letter to W. S.
Smith, 13 November 1787

15 I believe there are more instances of the
abridgement of the freedom of the people
by gradual and silent encroachments of
those in power than by violent and sudden
usurpations.
James Madison 1751–1836: speech in Virginia
Convention, 16 June 1788

16 The condition upon which God hath given
liberty to man is eternal vigilance; which
condition if he break, servitude is at once
the consequence of his crime, and the
punishment of his guilt.
John Philpot Curran 1750–1817: speech on the
right of election of the Lord Mayor of Dublin, 10
July 1790

17 O liberty! O liberty! what crimes are
committed in thy name!
Mme Roland 1754–93: A. de Lamartine *Histoire des
Girondins* (1847)

18 If men are to wait for liberty till they
become wise and good in slavery, they may
indeed wait for ever.
Lord Macaulay 1800–59: *Essays Contributed to the
Edinburgh Review* (1843) 'Milton'

19 The liberty of the individual must be thus
far limited; he must not make himself a
nuisance to other people.
John Stuart Mill 1806–73: *On Liberty* (1859)

20 The word 'freedom' means for me not a point of departure but a genuine point of arrival. The point of departure is defined by the word 'order'. Freedom cannot exist without the concept of order.
Prince Metternich 1773–1859: *Mein Politisches Testament* (1880)

21 In giving freedom to the slave, we assure freedom to the free—honourable alike in what we give and what we preserve. We shall nobly save, or meanly lose, the last, best hope of earth.
Abraham Lincoln 1809–65: annual message to Congress, 1 December 1862

22 Liberty means responsibility. That is why most men dread it.
George Bernard Shaw 1856–1950: *Man and Superman* (1903) 'Maxims: Liberty and Equality'

23 Tyranny is always better organized than freedom.
Charles Péguy 1873–1914: *Basic Verities* (1943) 'War and Peace'

24 Freedom is always and exclusively freedom for the one who thinks differently.
Rosa Luxemburg 1871–1919: *Die Russische Revolution* (1918)

25 Liberty is precious—so precious that it must be rationed.
Lenin 1870–1924: Sidney and Beatrice Webb *Soviet Communism* (1936)

26 It's often better to be in chains than to be free.
Franz Kafka 1883–1924: *The Trial* (1925)

27 It is better to die on your feet than to live on your knees.
Dolores Ibarruri 1895–1989: speech in Paris, 3 September 1936; also attributed to Emiliano Zapata

28 I am condemned to be free.
Jean-Paul Sartre 1905–80: *L'Être et le néant* (1943)

29 The enemies of Freedom do not argue; they shout and they shoot.
William Ralph Inge 1860–1954: *End of an Age* (1948)

30 Freedom is the freedom to say that two plus two make four. If that is granted, all else follows.
George Orwell 1903–50: *Nineteen Eighty-Four* (1949)

31 The moment the slave resolves that he will no longer be a slave, his fetters fall. He frees himself and shows the way to others. Freedom and slavery are mental states.
Mahatma Gandhi 1869–1948: *Non-Violence in Peace and War* (1949)

32 Freedom is not something that one people can bestow on another as a gift. They claim it as their own and none can keep it from them.
Kwame Nkrumah 1900–72: speech in Accra, 10 July 1953

33 Liberty is always unfinished business.
American Civil Liberties Union: title of 36th Annual Report, 1 July 1955–30 June 1956

34 Ask the first man you meet what he means by defending freedom, and he'll tell you privately he means defending the standard of living.
Martin Niemöller 1892–1984: address at Augsburg, January 1958; James Bentley *Martin Niemöller* (1984)

35 Liberty is liberty, not equality or fairness or justice or human happiness or a quiet conscience.
Isaiah Berlin 1909–97: *Two Concepts of Liberty* (1958)

36 Let every nation know, whether it wishes us well or ill, that we shall pay any price, bear any burden, meet any hardship, support any friend, oppose any foe to assure the survival and the success of liberty.
John F. Kennedy 1917–63: inaugural address, 20 January 1961

37 Freedom's just another word for nothin' left to lose,
Nothin' ain't worth nothin', but it's free.
Kris Kristofferson 1936– : 'Me and Bobby McGee' (1969 song, with Fred Foster)

38 Freedom is about the willingness of every single human being to cede to lawful authority a great deal of discretion about what you do, and how you do it.
Rudy Giuliani 1944– : attributed, in *Independent* 10 July 1999

⇥ Libraries ⇤

see also **Books, Reading**

PROVERBS AND SAYINGS

1 **A library is a repository of medicine for the mind.**
American proverb, mid 20th century

QUOTATIONS

2 Medicine for the soul.
inscription on the library of Ramses II at Thebes (c.1292–1225 BC)
Anonymous: Diodorus Siculus *Bibliotheca Historica* 60–30 BC

3 Let your bookcases and your shelves be your gardens and your pleasure-grounds. Pluck the fruit that grows therein, gather the roses, the spices and the myrrh.
Judah Ibn Tibbon 1120–90: Israel Abrahams *Jewish Life in the Middle Ages* (1932)

4 Come, and take choice of all my library,
And so beguile thy sorrow.
William Shakespeare 1564–1616: *Titus Andronicus* (1590)

5 If it were so that I must be a prisoner, if I might have my wish, I would have no other prison than this library, and be chained together with these good authors.
referring to the Bodleian Library, Oxford
James I 1566–1625: attributed

6 No place affords a more striking conviction of the vanity of human hopes, than a public library.
Samuel Johnson 1709–84: in *The Rambler* 23 March 1751

7 With awe, around these silent walks I tread;
These are the lasting mansions of the dead.
George Crabbe 1754–1832: 'The Library' (1808)

8 What a sad want I am in of libraries, of books to gather facts from! Why is there not a Majesty's library in every county town? There is a Majesty's jail and gallows in every one.
Thomas Carlyle 1795–1881: diary 18 May 1832

9 We call ourselves a rich nation, and we are filthy and foolish enough to thumb each other's books out of circulating libraries!
John Ruskin 1819–1900: *Sesame and Lilies* (1865)

10 A man should keep his little brain attic stocked with all the furniture that he is likely to use, and the rest he can put away in the lumber room of his library, where he can get it if he wants it.
Arthur Conan Doyle 1859–1930: *The Adventures of Sherlock Holmes* (1892)

11 I've been drunk for about a week now, and I thought it might sober me up to sit in a library.
F. Scott Fitzgerald 1896–1940: *The Great Gatsby* (1925)

12 Cultures of East and West, the entire atlas,
Encyclopedias, centuries, dynasties,
Symbols, the cosmos, and cosmogonies
Are offered from the walls.
Jorge Luis Borges 1899–1986: 'Poem of the Gifts' (1972)

13 What is more important in a library than anything else—than everything else—is the fact that it exists.
Archibald MacLeish 1892–1982: 'The Premise of Meaning' in *American Scholar* 5 June 1972

14 If you file your waste-paper basket for 50 years, you have a public library.
Tony Benn 1925– : in *Daily Telegraph* 5 March 1994

⤛ Lies ⤜

see also **Deception, Truth**

PROVERBS AND SAYINGS

1 **An abomination unto the Lord, but a very present help in time of trouble.**
definition of a lie, an amalgamation of lines from the Bible (Proverbs and Psalms), often attributed to the American politician Adlai Stevenson (1900–65)

2 **Half the truth is often a whole lie.**
something which is partially true can still convey a completely false impression; English proverb, mid 18th century

3 **A liar ought to have a good memory.**
implying that one lie is likely to lead to the need for another; English proverb, mid 16th century, 1st century AD in Latin

4 **The liar's candle lasts till evening.**
a lie will be exposed sooner or later; Turkish proverb

5 **A lie can go around the world and back again while the truth is lacing up its boots.**
American proverb, late 19th century; see 17 below

6 **One seldom meets a lonely lie.**
implying that one lie is likely to lead to the need for another; American proverb, mid 20th century

7 **To tell a falsehood is like the cut of a sabre, for though the wound may heal the scar will remain.**
Persian proverb

PHRASES

8 **economical with the truth**
a person or statement that lies or deliberately withholds information; used euphemistically, and deriving from a statement given in evidence by Sir Robert Armstrong: see **Truth 42**

9 **the liar paradox**
the paradox involved in a speaker's statement that he or she is lying or is a (habitual) liar; said to have been created by the semi-legendary Cretan poet Epimenides, asserting that all Cretans are liars; by this definition, if he is a Cretan, then what he says cannot be true, and Cretans are honest

QUOTATIONS

10 It is the penalty of a liar, that should he even tell the truth, he is not listened to.
The Talmud: *Babylonian Talmud* Sanhedrin

11 The retort courteous . . . the quip modest . . . the reply churlish . . . the reproof valiant . . . the countercheck quarrelsome . . . the lie circumstantial . . . the lie direct.
of the degrees of a lie
William Shakespeare 1564–1616: *As You Like It* (1599)

12 A mixture of a lie doth ever add pleasure.
Francis Bacon 1561–1626: *Essays* (1625) 'Of Truth'

13 He replied that I must needs be mistaken, or that I *said the thing which was not.* (For they have no word in their language to express lying or falsehood.)
Jonathan Swift 1667–1745: *Gulliver's Travels* (1726)

14 Whoever would lie usefully should lie seldom.
Lord Hervey 1696–1743: *Memoirs of the Reign of George II* (ed. J. W. Croker, 1848)

15 Falsehood has a perennial spring.
Edmund Burke 1729–97: *On American Taxation* (1775)

16 *as a child, when asked whether he had cut down a cherry tree:*
I can't tell a lie, Pa; you know I can't tell a lie. I did cut it with my hatchet.
George Washington 1732–99: M. L. Weems *Life of George Washington* (10th ed., 1810); see 18 below

17 If you want truth to go round the world you must hire an express train to pull it; but if you want a lie to go round the world, it will fly: it is as light as a feather, and a breath will carry it. It is well said in the old proverb, 'a lie will go round the world while truth is pulling its boots on'.
C. H. Spurgeon 1834–92: *Gems from Spurgeon* (1859); see 5 above

18 I am different from Washington. I have a higher and grander stand of principle. Washington could not lie. I *can* lie but I won't.
Mark Twain 1835–1910: in *Chicago Tribune* 20 December 1871; see 16 above

19 The cruellest lies are often told in silence.
Robert Louis Stevenson 1850–94: *Virginibus Puerisque* (1881)

20 Matilda told such Dreadful Lies,
It made one Gasp and Stretch one's Eyes.
Hilaire Belloc 1870–1953: *Cautionary Tales* (1907) 'Matilda'

21 A little inaccuracy sometimes saves tons of explanation.
Saki 1870–1916: *The Square Egg* (1924)

22 Without lies humanity would perish of despair and boredom.
Anatole France 1844–1924: *La Vie en fleur* (1922)

23 The broad mass of a nation . . . will more easily fall victim to a big lie than to a small one.
Adolf Hitler 1889–1945: *Mein Kampf* (1925)

24 One sometimes sees more clearly in the man who lies than in the man who tells the truth. Truth, like the light, blinds. Lying, on the other hand, is a beautiful twilight, which gives to each object its value.
Albert Camus 1913–60: attributed; Lord Trevelyan *Diplomatic Channels* (1973)

25 In our country the lie has become not just a moral category but a pillar of the State.
Alexander Solzhenitsyn 1918– : 1974 interview, in *The Oak and the Calf* (1975)

⇥Life⇤

see also **Life Sciences, Lifestyles**

PROVERBS AND SAYINGS

1 **Be happy while y'er leevin,**
For y'er a lang time deid.
Scottish motto for a house

2 **Life is a sexually transmitted disease.**
graffito found on the London Underground

3 **Life is harder than crossing a field.**
Russian proverb

4 **Life isn't all beer and skittles.**
life is not unalloyed pleasure or relaxation; English proverb, mid 19th century

5 **Life is the best gift; the rest is extra.**
African proverb (Swahili)

6 **Life's a bitch, and then you die.**
modern saying, late 20th century

7 **A live dog is better than a dead lion.**
often used in the context of a lesser person taking the place of a greater one who has died; English proverb, late 14th century, from the Bible: see **Value 21**

8 **Man cannot live by bread alone.**
one needs spiritual as well as physical sustenance; English proverb, late 19th century, after the Bible (Matthew) 'Man shall not live by bread alone, but by every word that proceedeth out of the mouth of God'

9 **Tout passe, tout casse, tout lasse.**
French = everything passes, everything perishes, everything palls

PHRASES

10 **all flesh**
whatever has bodily life; from the Bible: see **Transience 7**

11 **all human life is there**
every variety of human experience; used as an advertising slogan for the *News of the World* in the late 1950s: see **36 below**

12 **the elixir of life**
a supposed drug or essence capable of prolonging life indefinitely; translation of medieval Latin *elixir vitae*

13 **life's rich pageant**
all the variety of human experience; the first recorded use is by Arthur Marshall (1910–89) in the monologue *The Games Mistress* (1937)

14 **mouse and man**
every living thing; alliterative association of the types of animal and human kind; probably popularized by Robert Burns: see **Foresight 12**

15 **this mortal coil**
the turmoil of life, from Shakespeare *Hamlet*: see **Death 33**

⇢⇢⊷⊶⇠⊶⇢⇢⊷⇠⊶⇢⇢⊷⇠⊶⇢⇢⊷⇠⊶⇢⇢⊷⇠⊶⇢⇢⊷⇠⊶⇢⇢⊷⇠⊶⇢⇢⊷⇠⊶⇢⇢⊷⇠⊶⇢⇢

QUOTATIONS

16 All that a man hath will he give for his life.
Bible: Job

17 Not to be born is, past all prizing, best.
Sophocles c.496–406 BC: *Oedipus Coloneus*; see 41 below

18 And life is given to none freehold, but it is leasehold for all.
Lucretius c.94–55 BC: *De Rerum Natura*

19 'Such,' he said, 'O King, seems to me the present life of men on earth, in comparison with that time which to us is uncertain, as if when on a winter's night you sit feasting with your ealdormen and thegns,—a single sparrow should fly swiftly into the hall, and coming in at one door, instantly fly out through another.'
The Venerable Bede AD 673–735: *Ecclesiastical History of the English People*

20 Life well spent is long.
Leonardo da Vinci 1452–1519: Edward McCurdy (ed.) *Leonardo da Vinci's Notebooks* (1906)

21 All the world's a stage,
And all the men and women merely players:
They have their exits and their entrances;
And one man in his time plays many parts,
His acts being seven ages.
William Shakespeare 1564–1616: *As You Like It* (1599)

22 Life's but a walking shadow, a poor player,
That struts and frets his hour upon the stage,
And then is heard no more; it is a tale
Told by an idiot, full of sound and fury,
Signifying nothing.
William Shakespeare 1564–1616: *Macbeth* (1606)

23 No arts; no letters; no society; and which is worst of all, continual fear and danger of violent death; and the life of man, solitary, poor, nasty, brutish, and short.
Thomas Hobbes 1588–1679: *Leviathan* (1651)

24 Life is an incurable disease.
Abraham Cowley 1618–67: 'To Dr Scarborough' (1656)

25 Man that is born of a woman hath but a short time to live, and is full of misery.
The Book of Common Prayer 1662: *The Burial of the Dead*

26 Man wants but little here below,
Nor wants that little long.
Oliver Goldsmith 1728–74: 'Edwin and Angelina, or the Hermit' (1766); see **Alcohol** 15

27 This world is a comedy to those that think, a tragedy to those that feel.
Horace Walpole 1717–97: letter to Anne, Countess of Upper Ossory, 16 August 1776

28 Life, like a dome of many-coloured glass,
Stains the white radiance of Eternity,
Until Death tramples it to fragments.
Percy Bysshe Shelley 1792–1822: *Adonais* (1821)

29 Life is real! Life is earnest!
And the grave is not its goal;
Dust thou art, to dust returnest,
Was not spoken of the soul.
Henry Wadsworth Longfellow 1807–82: 'A Psalm of Life' (1838); see **Death** 23

30 I slept, and dreamed that life was beauty;
I woke, and found that life was duty.
Ellen Sturgis Hooper 1816–41: 'Beauty and Duty' (1840)

31 Life must be understood backwards; but . . . it must be lived forwards.
Sören Kierkegaard 1813–55: *Journals and Papers* (1843)

32 Youth is a blunder; Manhood a struggle; Old Age a regret.
Benjamin Disraeli 1804–81: *Coningsby* (1844)

33 The mass of men lead lives of quiet desperation.
Henry David Thoreau 1817–62: *Walden* (1854)

34 Life would be tolerable but for its amusements.
George Cornewall Lewis 1806–63: in *The Times* 18 September 1872

35 Life is mostly froth and bubble,
Two things stand like stone,
Kindness in another's trouble,
Courage in your own.
Adam Lindsay Gordon 1833–70: *Ye Wearie Wayfarer* (1866)

36 Cats and monkeys—monkeys and cats—all human life is there!
Henry James 1843–1916: *The Madonna of the Future* (1879); see 11 above

37 Life is like playing a violin solo in public and learning the instrument as one goes on.
Samuel Butler 1835–1902: speech at the Somerville Club, 27 February 1895

38 Life is just one damned thing after another.
Elbert Hubbard 1859–1915: in *Philistine* December 1909; often attributed to Frank Ward O'Malley

39 I have measured out my life with coffee spoons.
T. S. Eliot 1888–1965: 'The Love Song of J. Alfred Prufrock' (1917)

40 Life is not a series of gig lamps symmetrically arranged; life is a luminous halo, a semi-transparent envelope surrounding us from the beginning of consciousness to the end.
Virginia Woolf 1882–1941: *The Common Reader* (1925)

41 Never to have lived is best, ancient
writers say;
Never to have drawn the breath of life, never
to have looked into the eye of day;
The second best's a gay goodnight and
quickly turn away.
W. B. Yeats 1865–1939: 'From *Oedipus at Colonus*'
(1928); see 17 above

42 Life is a horizontal fall.
Jean Cocteau 1889–1963: *Opium* (1930)

43 Life is just a bowl of cherries.
Lew Brown 1893–1958: title of song (1931)

44 Birth, and copulation, and death.
That's all the facts when you come to brass
tacks:
Birth, and copulation, and death.
I've been born, and once is enough.
T. S. Eliot 1888–1965: *Sweeney Agonistes* (1932)

45 All that matters is love and work.
Sigmund Freud 1856–1939: attributed

46 To live at all is miracle enough.
Mervyn Peake 1911–68: *The Glassblower* (1950)

47 Life is like a sewer. What you get out of it
depends on what you put into it.
Tom Lehrer 1928– : 'We Will All Go Together
When We Go' (1953 song)

48 Oh, isn't life a terrible thing, thank God?
Dylan Thomas 1914–53: *Under Milk Wood* (1954)

49 As far as we can discern, the sole purpose of
human existence is to kindle a light in the
darkness of mere being.
Carl Gustav Jung 1875–1961: *Erinnerungen,
Träume, Gedanken* (1962)

50 Life is first boredom, then fear.
Philip Larkin 1922–85: 'Dockery & Son' (1964)

51 There's a rule, I think. You get what you
want in life, but not your second choice too.
Alison Lurie 1926– : *Real People* (1969)

52 The Answer to the Great Question Of . . .
Life, the Universe and Everything . . . [is]
Forty-two.
Douglas Adams 1952–2001: *The Hitch Hiker's
Guide to the Galaxy* (1979)

53 Life is a rainbow which also includes black.
Yevgeny Yevtushenko 1933– : in *Guardian* 11
August 1987

54 My momma always said life was like a box of
chocolates . . . you never know what you're
gonna get.
Eric Ross: *Forrest Gump* (1994 film), based on the
novel (1986) by Winston Groom; spoken by Tom
Hanks

55 There seems to be a general overall pattern
in most lives, that nothing happens, and
nothing happens, and then all of a sudden
everything happens.
Fay Weldon 1931– : *Auto da Fay* (2002)

⤜⤜ Life Sciences ⤛⤛

see also **Life, Nature, Science, Science and Religion**

PROVERBS AND SAYINGS

1 **What's hit is history, what's missed is
mystery.**
on the importance of securing a dead specimen of a
new species; late 19th-century saying

PHRASES

2 **animal, vegetable, and mineral**
the three traditional divisions into which natural
objects have been classified, first recorded in English
in the early 18th century (earlier in Latin)

3 **hopeful monster**
in some theories of macroevolution, an organism
displaying a radical mutation which nevertheless
permits it to survive, produce offspring, and so
potentially give rise to a new and distinct group of
organisms

4 **the missing link**
a hypothetical intermediate type between humans
and apes; a Victorian concept, arising from a
simplistic picture of human evolution, representing
either a common evolutionary ancestor for both
humans and apes, or, in popular thought, some kind
of ape-man through which humans had evolved
from the other higher primates; it is now clear that
human evolution has been much more complex

5 **natural selection**
the process whereby organisms better adapted to
their environment tend to survive and produce more
offspring; the theory of its action was first fully
expounded by Charles Darwin and it is now believed
to be the main process that brings about evolution;
see 13, 15 below

6 Red Queen hypothesis

the hypothesis that organisms are constantly struggling to keep up with one another in an evolutionary race between predator and prey species, named from Lewis Carroll's Red Queen; see **Effort** 23, see also **Strength** 1

7 the selfish gene

hypothesized as the unit of heredity whose preservation is the ultimate explanation of and rationale for human existence; from the title of a book (1976) by Richard Dawkins, which did much to popularize the theory of sociobiology

8 survival of the fittest

the process or result of natural selection, from Spencer: see 15 below; see also 5 above, **Business** 34

QUOTATIONS

9 That which *is* grows, while that which *is not* becomes.
Galen AD 129–199: *On the Natural Faculties*

10 But what if one should tell such people in future that there are more animals living in the scum on the teeth in a man's mouth than there are men in a whole kingdom?
on his observations of micro-organisms
Antoni van Leeuwenhoek 1632–1723: letter to Francis Aston, 17 September 1683

11 Like following life thro' creatures you dissect,
You lose it in the moment you detect.
Alexander Pope 1688–1744: *Epistles to Several Persons* 'To Lord Cobham' (1734)

12 Population, when unchecked, increases in a geometrical ratio. Subsistence only increases in an arithmetical ratio.
Thomas Robert Malthus 1766–1834: *Essay on the Principle of Population* (1798)

13 I have called this principle, by which each slight variation, if useful, is preserved, by the term of Natural Selection.
Charles Darwin 1809–82: *On the Origin of Species* (1859); see 5 above

14 Was it through his grandfather or his grandmother that he claimed his descent from a monkey?
addressed to T. H. Huxley in the debate on Darwin's theory of evolution
Samuel Wilberforce 1805–73: at a meeting of British Association in Oxford, 30 June 1860; see **Human Race** 23, **Science and Religion** 10

15 This survival of the fittest which I have here sought to express in mechanical terms, is that which Mr Darwin has called 'natural selection, or the preservation of favoured races in the struggle for life'.
Herbert Spencer 1820–1903: *Principles of Biology* (1865); see 5, 13 above

16 It has, I believe, been often remarked that a hen is only an egg's way of making another egg.
Samuel Butler 1835–1902: *Life and Habit* (1877)

17 Men will not be content to manufacture life: they will want to improve on it.
J. D. Bernal 1901–71: *The World, the Flesh and the Devil* (1929)

18 Life exists in the universe only because the carbon atom possesses certain exceptional properties.
James Jeans 1877–1946: *The Mysterious Universe* (1930)

19 It has not escaped our notice that the specific pairing we have postulated immediately suggests a possible copying mechanism for the genetic material.
proposing the double helix as the structure of DNA, and hence the chemical mechanism of heredity
Francis Crick 1916–2004 and **James D. Watson** 1928– : in *Nature* 25 April 1953

20 We have discovered the secret of life!
on the discovery of the structure of DNA, 1953
Francis Crick 1916–2004: James D. Watson *The Double Helix* (1968)

21 Evolution advances, not by a priori design, but by the selection of what works best out of whatever choices offer. We are the products of editing, rather than of authorship.
George Wald 1904–97: in *Annals of the New York Academy of Sciences* vol. 69 1957

22 The history of the living world can be summarised as the elaboration of ever more perfect eyes within a cosmos in which there is always something more to be seen.
Pierre Teilhard de Chardin 1881–1955: *The Phenomenon of Man* (1959)

23 I'd lay down my life for two brothers or eight cousins.
J. B. S. Haldane 1892–1964: attributed; in *New Scientist* 8 August 1974

24 The biologist passes, the frog remains.
sometimes quoted as 'Theories pass. The frog remains'
Jean Rostand 1894–1977: *Inquiétudes d'un Biologiste* (1967)

25 Water is life's *mater* and *matrix*, mother and medium. There is no life without water.
Albert von Szent-Györgyi 1893–1986: in *Perspectives in Biology and Medicine* Winter 1971

26 [Natural selection] has no vision, no foresight, no sight at all. If it can be said to play the role of watchmaker in nature, it is the *blind* watchmaker.
Richard Dawkins 1941– : *The Blind Watchmaker* (1986); see **God** 24

27 The essence of life is statistical improbability on a colossal scale.
Richard Dawkins: *The Blind Watchmaker* (1986)

28 Almost all aspects of life are engineered at the molecular level, and without understanding molecules we can only have a very sketchy understanding of life itself.
Francis Crick 1916–2004: *What Mad Pursuit* (1988)

29 Life is a copiously branching bush, continually pruned by the grim reaper of extinction, not a ladder of predictable progress.
Stephen Jay Gould 1941–2002: *Wonderful Life* (1989)

30 Biology is the search for the chemistry that works.
R. J. P. Williams 1926– : lecture in Oxford, June 1996

31 Genes are not like engineering blueprints; they are more like recipes in a cookbook. They tell us what ingredients to use, in what quantities, and in what order—but they do not provide a complete, accurate plan of the final result.
Ian Stewart 1945– : *Life's Other Secret* (1998) preface

32 Students accept astonishing things happening in human genetics without turning a hair but worry about GM soya beans.
Steve Jones 1944– : in *Times Higher Education Supplement* 27 August 1999

⤜⤜ Lifestyles ⤛⤛

see also **Life**

PROVERBS AND SAYINGS

1 **Do as you would be done by.**
English proverb, late 16th century; in Charles Kingsley's *The Water-Babies* (1863), Mrs *Doasyouwouldbedoneby* is the motherly and benevolent figure who is contrasted with her stern sister, Mrs *Bedonebyasyoudid*

2 **Do unto others as you would they should do unto you.**
English proverb; early 10th century, from the Bible (Matthew): see 15 below; see also **Likes and Dislikes** 14

3 **Eat, drink and be merry, for tomorrow we die.**
a conflation of two biblical sayings, Ecclesiastes, 'A man hath no better thing under the sun, than to eat, and to drink, and to be merry', and Isaiah, 'Let us eat and drink; for to morrow we shall die'; English proverb, late 19th century

4 **If you have two coins, use one to buy bread, the other to buy hyacinths.**
both the mind and the body should be fed; Middle Eastern proverb (sometimes roses or lilies are suggested instead); see 28 below, **Human Rights** 2

5 **Make love not war.**
student slogan, 1960s

PHRASES

6 **the eleventh commandment**
a rule of conduct regarded as coming next in importance to the Ten Commandments; often defined as 'Thou shalt not be found out'; see 10 below

7 **plain living and high thinking**
a frugal and philosophic lifestyle, from Wordsworth: see **Satisfaction** 25

8 **rake's progress**
a progressive degeneration or decline, especially through self-indulgence; from the title of a series of engravings (1735) by William Hogarth, tracing the rake's life from indulged childhood to the gallows

9 **sow one's wild oats**
commit youthful follies or excesses before settling down; *wild oat* = a wild grass related to the cultivated oat which was traditionally a weed of cornfields

10 **the Ten Commandments**
the divine rules of conduct given by God to Moses on Mount Sinai, as recounted in the Bible (Exodus); the commandments are generally enumerated as: have no other gods; do not make or worship idols; do not take the name of the Lord in vain; keep the sabbath holy; honour one's father and mother; do not kill; do not commit adultery; do not steal; do not

give false evidence; do not covet another's property

QUOTATIONS

11 Thou shalt love thy neighbour as thyself.
Bible: Leviticus; see also St Matthew

12 A man hath no better thing under the sun, than to eat, and to drink, and to be merry.
Bible: Ecclesiastes

13 We live, not as we wish to, but as we can.
Menander 342–c.292 BC: *The Lady of Andros*

14 1) Refraining from taking life. 2) Refraining from taking what is not given. 3) Refraining from incontinence. 4) Refraining from falsehood. 5) Refraining from strong drink, intoxicants, and liquor, which are occasions of carelessness.
The Five Precepts
Pali Tripitaka c. 2nd century BC: *Vinaya, Mahāv.* [Book of Discipline]

15 Therefore all things whatsoever ye would that men should do to you, do ye even so to them: for this is the law and the prophets.
Bible: Matthew; see 2 above, **Success** 16

16 Love and do what you will.
St Augustine of Hippo AD 354–430: *In Epistolam Joannis ad Parthos* (AD 413)

17 *Fay ce que vouldras.*
Do what you like.
François Rabelais c.1494–c.1553: *Gargantua* (1534); see 29 below

18 Living is my job and my art.
Montaigne 1533–92: *Essais* (1580)

19 Six hours in sleep, in law's grave study six, Four spend in prayer, the rest on Nature fix.
Edward Coke 1552–1634: translation of a quotation from Justinian *The Pandects*

20 For my part I keep the Commandments, I love my neighbour as my self, and to avoid coveting my neighbour's wife I desire to be coveted by her; which you know is quite another thing.
William Congreve 1670–1729: letter to Mrs Edward Porter, 27 September 1700; see 10 above, Envy 7

21 Life is all a VARIORUM,
We regard not how it goes;
Let them cant about DECORUM,
Who have characters to lose.
Robert Burns 1759–96: 'The Jolly Beggars' (1799)

22 Just trust yourself and you'll learn the art of living.
Johann Wolfgang von Goethe 1749–1832: *Faust* pt. 1 (1808) 'Studierzimmer'

or wife; see **Envy** 7, **Murder** 8, **Parents** 6; see also 6 above, 20 below, **Indifference** 15

23 A man should have the fine point of his soul taken off to become fit for this world.
John Keats 1795–1821: letter to J. H. Reynolds, 22 November 1817

24 Take short views, hope for the best, and trust in God.
Sydney Smith 1771–1845: Lady Holland *Memoir* (1855)

25 Believe me! The secret of reaping the greatest fruitfulness and the greatest enjoyment from life is *to live dangerously!*
Friedrich Nietzsche 1844–1900: *Die fröhliche Wissenschaft* (1882)

26 *Bramo assai, poco spero, nulla chieggio.*
I essay much, I hope little, I ask nothing.
Edward Elgar 1857–1934: inscribed at the end of *Enigma Variations* (1899); from Torquato Tasso (1544–95)

27 Live all you can; it's a mistake not to. It doesn't so much matter what you do in particular, so long as you have your life. If you haven't had that, what *have* you had?
Henry James 1843–1916: *The Ambassadors* (1903)

28 If I had but two loaves of bread I would sell one of them, and buy White Hyacinths to feed my soul.
Elbert Hubbard 1859–1915: *White Hyacinths* (1907); see 4 above

29 Do what thou wilt shall be the whole of the Law.
Aleister Crowley 1875–1947: *Book of the Law* (1909); see 17 above

30 We had better live as we think, otherwise sooner or later we shall end up by thinking as we have lived.
Paul Bourget 1852–1935: *Le Démon de Midi* (1914)

31 Where is the Life we have lost in living?
T. S. Eliot 1888–1965: *The Rock* (1934)

32 Never play cards with a man called Doc. Never eat at a place called Mom's. Never sleep with a woman whose troubles are worse than your own.
Nelson Algren 1909– : in *Newsweek* 2 July 1956

33 Man is born to live, not to prepare for life.
Boris Pasternak 1890–1960: *Doctor Zhivago* (1958)

34 Turn on, tune in and drop out.
Timothy Leary 1920– : lecture, June 1966; *The Politics of Ecstasy* (1968)

35 I've lived a life that's full, I've travelled each and ev'ry highway

And more, much more than this. I did it my way.
Paul Anka 1941– : 'My Way' (1969 song)

36 Expect nothing. Live frugally on surprise.
Alice Walker 1944– : 'Expect nothing' (1973)

37 Everybody's a mad scientist, and life is their lab. We're all trying to experiment to find a way to live, to solve problems, to fend off madness and chaos.
David Cronenberg 1943– : Chris Rodley (ed.) *Cronenberg on Cronenberg* (1992)

38 Another person's life, observed from outside, always has a shape and definition that one's own life lacks.
Pat Barker 1943– : *The Ghost Road* (1995)

39 You only live once, and the way I live, once is enough.
Frank Sinatra 1915–98: attributed, in *The Times* 16 May 1998

40 Do what you love and love what you do and everything else is detail.
Martina Navratilova 1956– : in *The Times* 3 July 2004

41 What is the secret of my long life? I really don't know—cigarettes, whisky and wild, wild women!
the oldest British survivor of the First World War
Henry Allingham 1896– : in *Daily Telegraph* 10 November 2005 (online edition)

⤛ Likes and Dislikes ⤜

see also **Criticism, Taste**

PROVERBS AND SAYINGS

1 **Every man to his taste.**
often used to comment on someone else's choice: English proverb, late 16th century

2 **One man's meat is another man's poison.**
pointing out that what may be necessary to one person is injurious to another; English proverb, late 16th century

3 **Tastes differ.**
different people will like or approve of different things; English proverb, early 19th century

PHRASES

7 **mother's milk**
in figurative usage, something providing sustenance or regarded by a person as entirely appropriate to them; see **Alcohol 22**

QUOTATIONS

8 To business that we love we rise betime, And go to 't with delight.
William Shakespeare 1564–1616: *Antony and Cleopatra* (1606–7)

9 I do not love thee, Dr Fell.
The reason why I cannot tell;
But this I know, and know full well,
I do not love thee, Dr Fell.
written while an undergraduate at Christ Church, Oxford, of which Dr Fell was Dean
Thomas Brown 1663–1704: translation of an epigram by Martial AD *c.*40–*c.*104

4 **There is no accounting for tastes.**
often used in recognition of a difference in choice between two people; English proverb, late 18th century

5 **You can't please everyone.**
English proverb, late 15th century

6 **You're going to like this . . . not a lot . . . but you'll like it!**
catchphrase used by Paul Daniels in his conjuring act, especially on television from 1981 onwards

10 People who like this sort of thing will find this the sort of thing they like.
judgement of a book
Abraham Lincoln 1809–65: G. W. E. Russell *Collections and Recollections* (1898)

11 For I've read in many a novel that, unless they've souls that grovel,
Folks *prefer* in fact a hovel to your dreary marble halls.
C. S. Calverley 1831–84: 'In the Gloaming' (1872); see **Imagination 11**

12 I don't care anything about reasons, but I know what I like.
Henry James 1843–1916: *Portrait of a Lady* (1881)

13 Take care to get what you like or you will be forced to like what you get.
George Bernard Shaw 1856–1950: *Man and Superman* (1903) 'Maxims: Stray Sayings'

14 Do not do unto others as you would that they should do unto you. Their tastes may not be the same.
George Bernard Shaw 1856–1950: *Man and Superman* (1903) 'Maxims for Revolutionists: The Golden Rule'; see **Lifestyles 2, Success 16**

15 A little of what you fancy does you good.
Fred W. Leigh d. 1924 and **George Arthurs**: title of song (1915)

16 Tiggers don't like honey.
A. A. Milne 1882–1956: *House at Pooh Corner* (1928)

17 One-fifth of the people are against everything all the time.
Robert Kennedy 1925–68: speech, University of Pennsylvania, 6 May 1964

18 The hippies wanted peace and love. We wanted Ferraris, blondes and switchblades.
Alice Cooper 1948– : in *Independent* 5 May 2001

19 I am old Labour. I like kippers, not oysters.
John Prescott 1938– : in *Observer* 23 May 2004

⤳ Logic and Reason ⤲

PROVERBS AND SAYINGS

1 **There is reason in the roasting of eggs.**
however odd an action may seem, there is a reason for it; English proverb, mid 17th century

PHRASES

2 **chop logic**
engage in pedantically logical arguments; *chop* = exchange or bandy words, later wrongly understood as 'cut into small pieces, mince'

3 **ex pede Herculem**
inferring the whole of something from an insignificant part; Latin, *from the foot of Hercules*, alluding to the story that Pythagoras calculated Hercules's height from the size of Hercules's foot

4 **lucus a non lucendo**
a paradoxical or otherwise absurd derivation; something of which the qualities are the opposite of what its name suggests; Latin, literally 'a grove from its not shining', i.e. *lucus* (a grove) is derived from *lucere* (shine) because there is no light there

5 **method in one's madness**
sense or reason in what appears to be foolish or abnormal behaviour, from Shakespeare: see **Madness 6**

6 **a red herring**
a distraction introduced to a discussion or argument to divert attention from a more serious question or matter; from the practice of using the scent of a smoked herring to train hounds to follow a trail

QUOTATIONS

7 I have no other but a woman's reason:
I think him so, because I think him so.
William Shakespeare 1564–1616: *The Two Gentlemen of Verona* (1592–3)

8 Reasons are not like garments, the worse for wearing.
Robert Devereux, Earl of Essex 1566–1601: letter to Lord Willoughby, 4 January 1599

9 What ever sceptic could inquire for;
For every why he had a wherefore.
Samuel Butler 1612–80: *Hudibras* pt. 1 (1663)

10 I have never yet been able to perceive how anything can be known for truth by consecutive reasoning—and yet it must be.
John Keats 1795–1821: letter to Benjamin Bailey, 22 November 1817

11 I'll not listen to reason . . . Reason always means what someone else has got to say.
Elizabeth Gaskell 1810–65: *Cranford* (1853)

12 'Contrariwise,' continued Tweedledee, 'if it was so, it might be; and if it were so, it would be: but as it isn't, it ain't. That's logic.'
Lewis Carroll 1832–98: *Through the Looking-Glass* (1872)

13 Logical consequences are the scarecrows of fools and the beacons of wise men.
T. H. Huxley 1825–95: *Science and Culture and Other Essays* (1881) 'On the Hypothesis that Animals are Automata'

14 [Logic] is neither a science nor an art, but a dodge.
Benjamin Jowett 1817–93: Lionel A. Tollemache *Benjamin Jowett* (1895)

15 'Is there any other point to which you would wish to draw my attention?'
'To the curious incident of the dog in the night-time.'
'The dog did nothing in the night-time.'
'That was the curious incident,' remarked Sherlock Holmes.
Arthur Conan Doyle 1859–1930: *The Memoirs of Sherlock Holmes* (1894)

16 After all, what was a paradox but a statement of the obvious so as to make it sound untrue?
Ronald Knox 1888–1957: *A Spiritual Aeneid* (1918)

17 Logic must take care of itself.
Ludwig Wittgenstein 1889–1951: *Tractatus Logico-Philosophicus* (1922)

18 If we would guide by the light of reason, we must let our minds be bold.
Louis D. Brandeis 1856–1941: *Jay Burns Baking Co. v. Bryan* (1924) (dissenting)

19 You can't think rationally on an empty stomach, and a whole lot of people can't do it on a full stomach either.
Lord Reith 1889–1971: D. Parker *Radio: The Great Years* (1977)

20 Even logical positivists are capable of love.
A. J. Ayer 1910–89: Kenneth Tynan *Profiles* (1989)

Losing see **Winning and Losing**

➤➤ Love ◄◄

see also **Courtship, Kissing, Marriage, Relationships, Sex**

PROVERBS AND SAYINGS

1 The course of true love never did run smooth.
English proverb, late 16th century, originally from Shakespeare: see 31 below

2 It is best to be off with the old love before you are on with the new.
English proverb, early 19th century

3 Jove but laughs at lover's perjury.
English proverb, mid 16th century; from the Roman poet Tibullus (*c.*50–19 BC) and ultimately from the Greek poet Hesiod (*c.*700 BC)

4 Love and a cough cannot be hid.
love can no more be concealed than a cough can be suppressed; English proverb, early 14th century

5 Love begets love.
English proverb, early 16th century

6 Love is blind.
Cupid, the god of love, was traditionally portrayed as blind, shooting his arrows at random, but the saying is generally used to mean that a person is often unable to see faults in the one they love; English proverb, late 14th century; see **Relationships** 3

7 Love laughs at locksmiths.
love is too strong a force to be denied by ordinary barriers; English proverb, early 19th century, from the title of a play (1808) by George Colman, the Younger (1762–1836)

8 Love makes the world go round.
English proverb, mid 19th century, from a traditional French song; see **Drunkenness** 15; **Money** 43

9 Love means never having to say you're sorry.
advertising copy for the film *Love Story* (1970); from the novel (1970) by Erich Segal (1937–)

10 Love will find a way.
love is a force which cannot be stemmed or denied; English proverb, early 17th century

11 One cannot love and be wise.
English proverb, early 16th century; the statement 'to love and be wise is scarcely allowed to God' is found in Latin in the writings of the 1st-century Roman writer Publilius Syrus; see **Taxes** 10

12 The quarrel of lovers is the renewal of love.
love can be renewed through reconciliation; English proverb, early 16th century

13 There are as good fish in the sea as ever came out of it.
now often used as a consolation to rejected lovers in the form, 'there are plenty more fish in the sea'; English proverb, late 16th century

14 'Tis better to have loved and lost, than never to have loved at all.
English proverb, early 18th century; see 53 below

15 When the furze is in bloom, my love's in tune.

with the implication that some furze can always be found in bloom; English proverb, mid 18th century; see also **Kissing 2**

PHRASES

16 Cupid's dart

the conquering power of love; *Cupid* the Roman god of love, son of Mercury and Venus, represented as a beautiful naked winged boy with a bow and arrows

17 love's young dream

the relationship of young lovers; the object of someone's love; a man regarded as a perfect lover; see 45 below

18 moonlight and roses

romance; title of song by Black and Moret, 1925

19 star-crossed lovers

ill-fated lovers, from Shakespeare *Romeo and Juliet* 'A pair of star-crossed lovers'

20 tender passion

romantic love; the term is first recorded in Sheridan's *Duenna* (1775)

QUOTATIONS

21 Many waters cannot quench love, neither can the floods drown it.
Bible: Song of Solomon

22 *Omnia vincit Amor: et nos cedamus Amori.*
Love conquers all things: let us too give in to Love.
Virgil 70–19 BC: *Eclogues*

23 And now abideth faith, hope, charity, these three; but the greatest of these is charity.
Bible: I Corinthians

24 There is no fear in love; but perfect love casteth out fear.
Bible: I John

25 You who seek an end of love, love will yield to business: be busy, and you will be safe.
Ovid 43–c.17: *Remedia Amoris*

26 Lord, make me an instrument of Your peace! Where there is hatred let me sow love.
St Francis of Assisi 1181–1226: 'Prayer of St Francis'; attributed

27 The love that moves the sun and the other stars.
Dante Alighieri 1265–1321: *Divina Commedia* 'Paradiso'

28 I find no peace, and I am not at war, I fear and hope, and burn and I am ice.
Petrarch 1304–74: *Canzoniere* no. 134 (*c.*1352) tr. Mark Musa

29 God defend me, said Dinadan, for the joy of love is too short, and the sorrow thereof, and what cometh thereof, dureth over long.
Thomas Malory d. 1471: *Le Morte D'Arthur* (1485)

30 Where both deliberate, the love is slight; Who ever loved that loved not at first sight?
Christopher Marlowe 1564–93: *Hero and Leander* (1598)

31 The course of true love never did run smooth.
William Shakespeare 1564–1616: *A Midsummer Night's Dream* (1595–6); see 1 above

32 Whoever loves, if he do not propose The right true end of love, he's one that goes To sea for nothing but to make him sick.
John Donne 1572–1631: 'Love's Progress' (*c.*1600)

33 Then, must you speak Of one that loved not wisely but too well.
William Shakespeare 1564–1616: *Othello* (1602–4)

34 Love is like linen often changed, the sweeter.
Phineas Fletcher 1582–1650: *Sicelides* (performed 1614)

35 Let me not to the marriage of true minds Admit impediments. Love is not love Which alters when it alteration finds.
William Shakespeare 1564–1616: sonnet 116

36 But true love is a durable fire, In the mind ever burning, Never sick, never old, never dead, From itself never turning.
Walter Ralegh 1552–1618: 'Walsinghame'

37 No cord nor cable can so forcibly draw, or hold so fast, as love can do with a twined thread.
Robert Burton 1577–1640: *The Anatomy of Melancholy* (1621–51)

38 Love is the fart Of every heart: It pains a man when 'tis kept close, And others doth offend, when 'tis let loose.
John Suckling 1609–42: 'Love's Offence' (1646)

39 It's no longer a burning within my veins: it's Venus entire latched onto her prey.
Jean Racine 1639–99: *Phèdre* (1677)

40 There is no disguise which can hide love for long where it exists, or feign it where it does not.
Duc de la Rochefoucauld 1613–80: *Maximes* (1678) no. 70

41 Say what you will, 'tis better to be left than never to have been loved.
William Congreve 1670–1729: *The Way of the World* (1700); see 53 below

42 If I were young and handsome as I was, instead of old and faded as I am, and you could lay the empire of the world at my feet, you should never share the heart and hand that once belonged to John, Duke of Marlborough.
refusing an offer of marriage from the Duke of Somerset
Sarah, Duchess of Marlborough 1660–1744: W. S. Churchill *Marlborough: His Life and Times* vol. 4 (1938)

43 O, my Luve's like a red, red rose That's newly sprung in June.
Robert Burns 1759–96: 'A Red Red Rose' (1796); derived from various folk-songs

44 If I love you, what does that matter to you!
Johann Wolfgang von Goethe 1749–1832: *Wilhelm Meister's Apprenticeship* (1795-6)

45 No, there's nothing half so sweet in life As love's young dream.
Thomas Moore 1779–1852: 'Love's Young Dream' (1807); see 17 above

46 Love in a hut, with water and a crust, Is—Love, forgive us!—cinders, ashes, dust; Love in a palace is perhaps at last More grievous torment than a hermit's fast.
John Keats 1795–1821: 'Lamia' (1820); see Idealism 7

47 The magic of first love is our ignorance that it can ever end.
Benjamin Disraeli 1804–81: *Henrietta Temple* (1837)

48 In the spring a young man's fancy lightly turns to thoughts of love.
Alfred, Lord Tennyson 1809–92: 'Locksley Hall' (1842)

49 What love is, if thou wouldst be taught, Thy heart must teach alone— Two souls with but a single thought, Two hearts that beat as one.
Friedrich Halm 1806–71: *Der Sohn der Wildnis* (1842)

50 If you could see my legs when I take my boots off, you'd form some idea of what unrequited affection is.
Charles Dickens 1812–70: *Dombey and Son* (1848)

51 If thou must love me, let it be for nought Except for love's sake only.
Elizabeth Barrett Browning 1806–61: *Sonnets from the Portuguese* (1850) no. 14

52 How do I love thee? Let me count the ways. I love thee to the depth and breadth and height My soul can reach.
Elizabeth Barrett Browning 1806–61: *Sonnets from the Portuguese* (1850) no. 43

53 'Tis better to have loved and lost Than never to have loved at all.
Alfred, Lord Tennyson 1809–92: *In Memoriam A. H. H.* (1850); see 14, 41 above

54 Love's like the measles—all the worse when it comes late in life.
Douglas Jerrold 1803–57: *The Wit and Opinions of Douglas Jerrold* (1859)

55 The love that lasts longest is the love that is never returned.
W. Somerset Maugham 1874–1965: *A Writer's Notebook* (1949) written in 1894

56 Christianity has done a great deal for love by making a sin of it.
Anatole France 1844–1924: *Le Jardin d'Épicure* (1895)

57 I am the Love that dare not speak its name.
Lord Alfred Douglas 1870–1945: 'Two Loves' (1896)

58 Yet each man kills the thing he loves, By each let this be heard, Some do it with a bitter look, Some with a flattering word. The coward does it with a kiss, The brave man with a sword!
Oscar Wilde 1854–1900: *The Ballad of Reading Gaol* (1898)

59 Love consists in this, that two solitudes protect and touch and greet each other.
Rainer Maria Rilke 1875–1926: *Letters to a Young Poet* (1929) 14 May 1904 (tr. Hugh MacLennan)

60 The fate of love is that it always seems too little or too much.
Amelia E. Barr 1831–1919: *The Belle of Bolling Green* (1904)

61 Love is so short, forgetting is so long.
Pablo Neruda 1904–73: 'Tonight I Can Write' (1924)

62 Even memory is not necessary for love. There is a land of the living and a land of the dead and the bridge is love, the only survival, the only meaning.
Thornton Wilder 1897–1975: *The Bridge of San Luis Rey* (1927), closing words

63 Experience shows us that love does not consist in gazing at each other but in looking together in the same direction.
Antoine de Saint-Exupéry 1900–44: *Wind, Sand and Stars* (1939)

64 If I can't love Hitler, I can't love at all.
Rev. A. J. Muste 1885–1967: at a Quaker meeting 1940; in *New York Times* 12 February 1967

65 The life that I have
Is all that I have
And the life that I have
Is yours.
The love that I have
Of the life that I have
Is yours and yours and yours.
given to the British secret agent Violette Szabo (1921–45), for use with the Special Operations Executive
Leo Marks 1920–2001: 'The Life that I Have' (written 1943)

66 How alike are the groans of love to those of the dying.
Malcolm Lowry 1909–57: *Under the Volcano* (1947)

67 Birds do it, bees do it,
Even educated fleas do it.
Let's do it, let's fall in love.
Cole Porter 1891–1964: 'Let's Do It' (1954 song; words added to the 1928 original)

68 Love. Of course, love. Flames for a year, ashes for thirty.
Guiseppe di Lampedusa 1896–1957: *The Leopard* (1957)

69 What will survive of us is love.
Philip Larkin 1922–85: 'An Arundel Tomb' (1964)

70 All you need is love.
John Lennon 1940–80 and **Paul McCartney** 1942– : title of song (1967)

71 Love doesn't just sit there, like a stone, it has to be made, like bread; remade all the time, made new.
Ursula K. Le Guin 1929– : *The Lathe of Heaven* (1971)

72 Love is mutually feeding each other, not one living on another like a ghoul.
Bessie Head 1937–86: *A Question of Power* (1973)

73 If grass can grow through cement, love can find you at every time in your life.
Cher 1946– : in *The Times* 30 May 1998

Luck see Chance and Luck

Luxury see Wealth and Luxury

⤜ Madness ⤛

see also **Fools, The Mind**

PROVERBS AND SAYINGS

1 **Whom the gods would destroy, they first make mad.**
often used to comment on a foolish action seen as self-destructive in its effect; English proverb, early 17th century; see 4 below, **Criticism** 22

PHRASES

2 **mad as a hatter**
completely insane. Hat-makers sometimes suffered from mercury poisoning as a result of the use of mercurous nitrate in the manufacture of felt hats, and the idea was personified in one of the two eccentric hosts (the *Mad Hatter*) at the 'mad tea party' in Lewis Carroll's *Alice's Adventures in Wonderland* (1865); see 3 below, see also **Cats** 11

3 **mad as a March hare**
completely insane; the allusion here is to the running and leaping of hares in the breeding season, and was reinforced by the character created by Lewis Carroll in *Alice's Adventures in Wonderland* (1865); see 2 above

QUOTATIONS

4 Whenever God prepares evil for a man, He first damages his mind, with which he deliberates.
Anonymous: scholiastic annotation to Sophocles's *Antigone*; see 1 above

5 I am but mad north-north-west; when the wind is southerly, I know a hawk from a handsaw.
William Shakespeare 1564–1616: *Hamlet* (1601); see **Intelligence** 4

6 Though this be madness, yet there is method in't.
William Shakespeare 1564–1616: *Hamlet* (1601); see **Logic** 5

7   There is a pleasure sure,
In being mad, which none but madmen know!
John Dryden 1631–1700: *The Spanish Friar* (1681)

8 They called me mad, and I called them mad, and damn them, they outvoted me.
Nathaniel Lee 1653–92: R. Porter *A Social History of Madness* (1987)

9 Mad, is he? Then I hope he will *bite* some of my other generals.
replying to the Duke of Newcastle, who had complained that General Wolfe was a madman
George II 1683–1760: Henry Beckles Willson *Life and Letters of James Wolfe* (1909)

10 Babylon in all its desolation is a sight not so awful as that of the human mind in ruins.
Scrope Davies 1783–1852: letter to Thomas Raikes, May 1835

11 Dear Sir,—I am in a madhouse and quite forget your name or who you are.
John Clare 1793–1864: letter, 1860

12 Every one is more or less mad on one point.
Rudyard Kipling 1865–1936: *Plain Tales from the Hills* (1888)

13 As an experience, madness is terrific . . . and in its lava I still find most of the things I write about.
Virginia Woolf 1882–1941: letter to Ethel Smyth, 22 June 1930

14 There was only one catch and that was Catch-22, which specified that a concern for one's own safety in the face of dangers that were real and immediate was the process of a rational mind . . . Orr would be crazy to fly more missions and sane if he didn't, but if he was sane he had to fly them. If he flew them he was crazy and didn't have to; but if he didn't want to he was sane and had to.
Joseph Heller 1923–99: *Catch-22* (1961); see **Circumstance** 11

15 Madness need not be all breakdown. It may also be break-through.
R. D. Laing 1927–89: *The Politics of Experience* (1967)

16 If you talk to God, you are praying; if God talks to you, you have schizophrenia. If the dead talk to you, you are a spiritualist; if God talks to you, you are a schizophrenic.
Thomas Szasz 1920– : *The Second Sin* (1973)

17 The psychopath is the furnace that gives no heat.
Derek Raymond 1931–94: *The Hidden Files* (1992)

Management

see also **Administration**

PROVERBS AND SAYINGS

1 **The eye of a master does more work than both his hands.**
employees work harder when the person who is in charge is present; English proverb, mid 18th century

2 **We trained hard . . . but it seemed that every time we were beginning to form up into teams we would be reorganized. I was to learn later in life that we tend to meet any new situation by reorganizing; and a wonderful method it can be for creating the illusion of progress while producing confusion, inefficiency, and demoralization.**
late 20th century saying, frequently (and wrongly) attributed to Roman satirist Petronius Arbiter (d. AD 65)

3 **Why keep a dog and bark yourself?**
often used to advise against carrying out work which can be done for you by somebody else; English proverb, late 16th century

PHRASES

4 the Peter Principle
the principle that members of a hierarchy are
promoted until they reach a level at which they are
no longer competent; from title of book by US
educationalist and author Laurence J. Peter (see
Administration 19); compare **Achievement** 32

5 pour encourager les autres
as an example to others, to encourage others;
French, from Voltaire: see **Ways and Means** 28

QUOTATIONS

6 There is nothing in the world which does
not have its decisive moment, and the
masterpiece of good management is to
recognize and grasp this moment.
Cardinal de Retz 1613–79: *Mémoires* (1717); see
Photography 4

7 Every time I make an appointment, I create
a hundred malcontents and one ingrate.
Louis XIV 1638–1715: Voltaire *Siècle de Louis XIV*
(1768 ed.)

8 Some great men owe most of their greatness
to the ability of detecting in those they
destine for their tools the exact quality of
strength that matters for their work.
Joseph Conrad 1857–1924: *Lord Jim* (1900)

9 Safe and sane business management . . .
reduces itself in the main to a sagacious use
of sabotage.
Thorstein Veblen 1857–1929: *The Nature of Peace*
(1917)

10 I tell you, sir, the only safeguard of order
and discipline in the modern world is a
standardized worker with interchangeable
parts. That would solve the entire problem
of management.
Jean Giraudoux 1882–1944: *The Madwoman of
Chaillot* (1945)

11 A good plan violently executed *Now* is better
than a perfect plan next week.
George S. Patton 1885–1945: *War As I Knew It*
(1947)

12 Perfection of planned layout is achieved
only by institutions on the point of collapse.
C. Northcote Parkinson 1909–93: *Parkinson's
Law* (1958)

13 Who's in charge of the clattering train?
habitual question about an organization
Lord Beaverbrook 1879–1964: A. Chisholm and
M. Davie *Beaverbrook* (1992)

14 Surround yourself with the best people you
can find, delegate authority, and don't
interfere.
Ronald Reagan 1911–2004: in *Fortune*
September 1986

15 If you want people motivated to do a good
job, give them a good job to do.
Frederick Herzberg 1923– : in *Industry Week* 21
September 1987

16 Every organization of today has to build into
its very structure the *management of change*.
Peter F. Drucker 1909– : *Post-Capitalist Society*
(1993)

17 Management that wants to change an
institution must first show it loves that
institution.
John Tusa 1936– : in *Observer* 27 February 1994

18 When you're up to your ears in alligators, it
is difficult to remember that the reason
you're there is to drain the swamp.
Donald Rumsfeld 1932– : *Rumsfeld's Rules* (2001)

⇥ Manners ⟨

see also **Behaviour**

PROVERBS AND SAYINGS

1 Civility costs nothing.
one should behave with at least minimal courtesy;
English proverb, early 18th century

**2 A civil question deserves a civil
answer.**
English proverb, mid 19th century

**3 Everyone speaks well of the bridge
which carries him over.**
someone is naturally well-disposed towards a source
of help, whether or not it has been beneficial to
others; English proverb, late 17th century

4 Manners maketh man.
motto of William of Wykeham (1324–1404), bishop
of Winchester and founder of Winchester College;
English proverb, mid 14th century

5 **Striking manners are bad manners.**
American proverb, mid 20th century

6 **The test of good manners is being able to put up pleasantly with bad ones.**
American proverb, mid 20th century

QUOTATIONS

8 Leave off first for manners' sake.
Bible: Ecclesiasticus

9 An insolent reply from a polite person is a bad sign.
Hippocrates c.460–c.370 BC: Prorrhetic

10 Evil communications corrupt good manners.
Bible: I Corinthians; see **Behaviour** 4

11 Immodest words admit of no defence,
For want of decency is want of sense.
Wentworth Dillon, Lord Roscommon 1633–85: Essay on Translated Verse (1684)

12 In my mind, there is nothing so illiberal and so ill-bred, as audible laughter.
Lord Chesterfield 1694–1773: Letters to his Son (1774) 9 March 1748

13 He is the very pineapple of politeness!
Richard Brinsley Sheridan 1751–1816: The Rivals (1775)

14 A man, indeed, is not genteel when he gets drunk; but most vices may be committed very genteelly: a man may debauch his friend's wife genteelly: he may cheat at cards genteelly.
James Boswell 1740–95: Life of Samuel Johnson (1791) 6 April 1775

15 The art of pleasing consists in being pleased.
William Hazlitt 1778–1830: The Round Table (1817) 'On Manner'

16 Ceremony is an invention to take off the uneasy feeling which we derive from knowing ourselves to be less the object of love and esteem with a fellow-creature than some other person is.
Charles Lamb 1775–1834: Essays of Elia (1823) 'A Bachelor's Complaint of the Behaviour of Married People'

17 Curtsey while you're thinking what to say. It saves time.
Lewis Carroll 1832–98: Through the Looking-Glass (1872)

18 It is worse than a crime, Violet; it is an impropriety.
Mary Elizabeth Braddon 1837–1915: Vixen (1879)

7 **There is nothing lost by civility.**
English proverb, late 19th century

19 Very notable was his distinction between coarseness and vulgarity (coarseness, revealing something; vulgarity, concealing something).
E. M. Forster 1879–1970: The Longest Journey (1907)

20 Of Courtesy, it is much less
Than Courage of Heart or Holiness,
Yet in my Walks it seems to me
That the Grace of God is in Courtesy.
Hilaire Belloc 1870–1953: 'Courtesy' (1910)

21 Good breeding consists in concealing how much we think of ourselves and how little we think of the other person.
Mark Twain 1835–1910: Notebooks (1935)

22 When suave politeness, tempering bigot zeal,
Corrected I believe to One does feel.
Ronald Knox 1888–1957: 'Absolute and Abitofhell' (1913)

23 THUMPER: If you can't say something nice
. . . don't say nothing at all.
Larry Morey 1905–71: Bambi (1942 film); from the novel by Felix Salten (1869–1945)

24 Phone for the fish-knives, Norman
As Cook is a little unnerved;
You kiddies have crumpled the serviettes
And I must have things daintily served.
John Betjeman 1906–84: 'How to get on in Society' (1954)

25 To Americans, English manners are far more frightening than none at all.
Randall Jarrell 1914–65: Pictures from an Institution (1954)

26 Manners are especially the need of the plain. The pretty can get away with anything.
Evelyn Waugh 1903–66: in Observer 15 April 1962

27 The Japanese have perfected good manners and made them indistinguishable from rudeness.
Paul Theroux 1941– : The Great Railway Bazaar (1975)

28 Good manners are a combination of intelligence, education, taste, and style mixed together so that you don't need any of those things.
P. J. O'Rourke 1947– : Modern Manners (1984)

⇥ Marriage ⇤

see also **Courtship, Love, Sex, The Single Life, Weddings**

PROVERBS AND SAYINGS

1 **Better be an old man's darling than a young man's slave.**
English proverb, mid 16th century

2 **Better one house spoiled than two.**
said of two wicked or foolish people joined in marriage; English proverb, late 16th century

3 **Change the name and not the letter, change for the worse and not the better.**
it is unlucky for a woman to marry a man whose surname begins with the same letter as her own; English proverb, mid 19th century

4 **A deaf husband and a blind wife are always a happy couple.**
each will remain unaware of drawbacks in the other. The saying is sometimes reversed to a blind husband and a deaf wife; English proverb, late 16th century

5 **The grey mare is the better horse.**
the wife rules, or is more competent than, the husband; English proverb, mid 16th century

6 **Marriage is a lottery.**
referring either to one's choice of partner, or more generally to the element of chance involved in how a marriage will turn out; English proverb, mid 17th century

7 **Marriages are made in heaven.**
often used ironically; English proverb, mid 16th century

8 **Marry in haste and repent at leisure.**
the formula is also applied to rash steps taken in other circumstances; English proverb, mid 16th century; see 28 below

9 **Needles and pins, needles and pins, when a man marries, his trouble begins.**
traditional saying (originally a nursery rhyme), perhaps reflecting on the pressures of domestic life; English proverb, mid 19th century

10 **Never marry for money, but marry where money is.**
distinguishing between monetary gain as a primary objective and a side benefit; English proverb, late 19th century

11 **There goes more to marriage than four bare legs in a bed.**
physical compatibility is not enough for a successful marriage; English proverb, mid 16th century

12 **Wedlock is a padlock.**
English proverb, late 17th century

13 **You do not marry the person you love, you love the person you marry.**
Indian proverb

14 **A young man married is a young man marred.**
often used as an argument against marrying too young; English proverb, late 16th century; see 23 below

PHRASES

15 **love in a cottage**
marriage with insufficient means; after Colman: see **Idealism** 7

16 **May and January**
a young woman and an old man as husband and wife, as in Chaucer's *Merchant's Tale* (c.1395)

17 **the weaker vessel**
a wife, a female partner; originally in allusion to the Bible (I Peter) 'Giving honour unto the wife, as unto the weaker vessel'

QUOTATIONS

18 Therefore shall a man leave his father and his mother, and shall cleave unto his wife: and they shall be one flesh.
Bible: Genesis

19 Man's best possession is a sympathetic wife.
Euripides c.485–c.406 BC: fragment no. 164; Augustus Nauck *Tragicorum Graecorum Fragmenta*

20 What therefore God hath joined together, let not man put asunder.
Bible: St Matthew

21 It is better to marry than to burn.
Bible: I Corinthians

22 I am your clay.
You are my clay.
In life we share a single quilt.
In death we will share one coffin.
Kuan Tao-sheng 1262–1319: 'Married Love'

23 A young man married is a man that's
marred.
William Shakespeare 1564–1616: *All's Well that
Ends Well* (1603–4); see 14 above

24 Wives are young men's mistresses,
companions for middle age, and old men's
nurses.
Francis Bacon 1561–1626: *Essays* (1625) 'Of
Marriage and the Single Life'

25 Then be not coy, but use your time;
And while ye may, go marry:
For having lost but once your prime,
You may for ever tarry.
Robert Herrick 1591–1674: 'To the Virgins, to
Make Much of Time' (1648)

26 Marriage is nothing but a civil contract.
John Selden 1584–1654: *Table Talk* (1689)
'Marriage'

27 To have and to hold from this day forward,
for better for worse, for richer for poorer, in
sickness and in health, to love, cherish, and
to obey, till death us do part.
The Book of Common Prayer 1662:
Solemnization of Matrimony Betrothal; see 57 below

28 SHARPER: Thus grief still treads upon the
heels of pleasure:
Married in haste, we may repent at leisure.
SETTER: Some by experience find those
words mis-placed:
At leisure married, they repent in haste.
William Congreve 1670–1729: *The Old Bachelor*
(1693); see 8 above

29 I . . . chose my wife, as she did her wedding
gown, not for a fine glossy surface, but such
qualities as would wear well.
Oliver Goldsmith 1728–74: *The Vicar of Wakefield*
(1766)

30 The triumph of hope over experience.
of a man who remarried immediately after the death
of a wife with whom he had been unhappy
Samuel Johnson 1709–84: James Boswell *Life of
Samuel Johnson* (1791) 1770

31 My definition of marriage . . . it resembles a
pair of shears, so joined that they cannot be
separated; often moving in opposite
directions, yet always punishing anyone
who comes between them.
Sydney Smith 1771–1845: Lady Holland *Memoir*
(1855)

32 What man thinks of changing himself so as
to suit his wife? And yet men expect that
women shall put on altogether new
characters when they are married, and girls
think that they can do so.
Anthony Trollope 1815–82: *Phineas Redux* (1874)

33 Marriage is like life in this—that it is a field
of battle, and not a bed of roses.
Robert Louis Stevenson 1850–94: *Virginibus
Puerisque* (1881)

34 It was very good of God to let Carlyle and
Mrs Carlyle marry one another and so make
only two people miserable instead of four.
Samuel Butler 1835–1902: letter to Miss E. M. A.
Savage, 21 November 1884

35 The chains of marriage are so heavy that it
takes two to bear them, and sometimes
three.
Alexandre Dumas 1824–95: Léon Treich *L'Esprit
d'Alexandre Dumas*

36 In married life three is company and two
none.
Oscar Wilde 1854–1900: *The Importance of Being
Earnest* (1895)

37 Love the quest; marriage the conquest;
divorce the inquest.
Helen Rowland 1875–1950: *Reflections of a
Bachelor Girl* (1903)

38 Marriage is popular because it combines the
maximum of temptation with the
maximum of opportunity.
George Bernard Shaw 1856–1950: *Man and
Superman* (1903) 'Maxims: Marriage'

39 Being a husband is a whole-time job. That is
why so many husbands fail. They cannot
give their entire attention to it.
Arnold Bennett 1867–1931: *The Title* (1918)

40 You shall be together when the white wings
of death scatter your days.
Ay, you shall be together even in the silent
memory of God.
But let there be spaces in your togetherness,
And let the winds of the heavens dance
between you.
Kahlil Gibran 1883–1931: *The Prophet* (1923) 'On
Marriage'

41 Marriage isn't a word . . . it's a *sentence*!
King Vidor 1895–1982: *The Crowd* (1928 film)

42 The deep, deep peace of the double-bed
after the hurly-burly of the chaise-longue.
on her recent marriage
Mrs Patrick Campbell 1865–1940: Alexander
Woollcott *While Rome Burns* (1934)

43 If you cannot have your dear husband for a
comfort and a delight, for a breadwinner
and a crosspatch, for a sofa, chair or a hot-
water bottle, one can use him as a Cross to
be Borne.
Stevie Smith 1902–71: *Novel on Yellow Paper*
(1936); see **Suffering** 5

44 Marriage is a bribe to make a housekeeper think she's a householder.
Thornton Wilder 1897–1975: *The Merchant of Yonkers* (1939)

45 So they were married—to be the more together—
And found they were never again so much together,
Divided by the morning tea,
By the evening paper,
By children and tradesmen's bills.
Louis MacNeice 1907–63: 'Les Sylphides' (1941)

46 The value of marriage is not that adults produce children but that children produce adults.
Peter De Vries 1910–93: *The Tunnel of Love* (1954)

47 Love and marriage, love and marriage, Go together like a horse and carriage.
Sammy Cahn 1913–93: *Love and Marriage* (1955 song)

48 One doesn't have to get anywhere in a marriage. It's not a public conveyance.
Iris Murdoch 1919–99: *A Severed Head* (1961)

49 I think everybody really will concede that on this, of all days, I should begin my speech with the words 'My husband and I'.
Elizabeth II 1926– : speech at Guildhall, London, on her 25th wedding anniversary, 20 November 1972

50 A divorce is like an amputation; you survive, but there's less of you.
Margaret Atwood 1939– : in *Time*, 1973

51 Marriage is a wonderful invention; but, then again, so is a bicycle repair kit.
Billy Connolly 1942– : Duncan Campbell *Billy Connolly* (1976)

52 Chains do not hold a marriage together. It is threads, hundreds of tiny threads which sew people together through the years. That is what makes a marriage last—more than passion or even sex!
Simone Signoret 1921–85: in *Daily Mail* 4 July 1978

53 The heart of marriage is memories.
Bill Cosby 1937– : *Love and Marriage* (1989)

54 There were three of us in this marriage, so it was a bit crowded.
Diana, Princess of Wales 1961–97: interview on *Panorama*, BBC1 TV, 20 November 1995

55 Maybe the Smug Marrieds only mix with other Smug Marrieds and don't know how to relate to individuals any more.
Helen Fielding 1958– : *Bridget Jones's Diary* (1996)

56 I learnt a long time ago that the only people who count in any marriage are the two that are in it.
Hillary Rodham Clinton 1947– : television interview with NBC, 27 January 1998

57 I think we explored the further reaches of 'for better or for worse'.
on her marriage during the 1980s
Mary Archer 1944– : at Jeffrey Archer's trial for perjury, London, 29 June 2001; see 27 above

Mathematics

see also **Quantities and Qualities, Statistics**

PROVERBS AND SAYINGS

1 **The good Christian should beware of mathematicians, and all those who make empty prophecies. The danger already exists that mathematicians have made a covenant with the Devil to darken the spirit and to confine man in the bonds of Hell.**
mistranslation of St Augustine's *De Genesi ad Litteram*; the Latin word *mathematicus* means both 'mathematician' and 'astrologer': see **The Supernatural 10**

PHRASES

2 **Delian problem**
the problem of finding geometrically the side of a cube having twice the volume of a given cube; from the Delian oracle's pronouncement that a plague in Athens would cease if the cubical altar to Apollo were doubled in size

3 **Fermat's last theorem**
the conjecture that if *n* is greater than 2 then there is no integer whose *n*th power can be expressed as the sum of two smaller *n*th powers. The French lawyer and mathematician Pierre de *Fermat* (1601–65) noted that he had 'a truly wonderful proof' of the conjecture, but never wrote it down. In 1995 a general proof was published by the Princeton-based British mathematician Andrew Wiles

4 **the golden section**
the division of a line so that the whole is to the greater part as that part is to the smaller part, a

proportion which is considered to be particularly pleasing to the eye; although the proportion has been known since the 4th century BC, and occurs in Euclid, the name *golden section* (now the usual term) is not recorded before the 19th century

5 pons asinorum

the fifth proposition of the first book of Euclid; Latin, = bridge of asses; so called from the difficulty which beginners find in 'getting over' it

6 square the circle

construct a square equal in area to a given circle (a problem incapable of a purely geometrical solution); thus, do something that is considered to be impossible

QUOTATIONS

7 Let no one enter who does not know geometry [mathematics].
inscription on Plato's door, probably at the Academy at Athens
Anonymous: Elias Philosophus *In Aristotelis Categorias Commentaria*

8 There is no 'royal road' to geometry.
Euclid fl. *c*.300 BC: addressed to Ptolemy I; Proclus *Commentary on the First Book of Euclid's Elementa*; see **Education 8**

9 If in other sciences we should arrive at certainty without doubt and truth without error, it behoves us to place the foundations of knowledge in mathematics.
Roger Bacon *c*.1220–*c*.92: *Opus Majus*

10 Philosophy is written in that great book which ever lies before our eyes—I mean the universe . . . This book is written in mathematical language and its characters are triangles, circles and other geometrical figures, without whose help . . . one wanders in vain through a dark labyrinth.
often quoted as 'The book of nature is written . . . '
Galileo 1564–1642: *The Assayer* (1623)

11 They are neither finite quantities, or quantities infinitely small, nor yet nothing. May we not call them the ghosts of departed quantities?
on Newton's infinitesimals
George Berkeley 1685–1753: *The Analyst* (1734)

12 The most devilish thing is 8 times 8 and 7 times 7 it is what nature itselfe cant endure.
Marjory Fleming 1803–11: *Journals, Letters and Verses* (ed. A. Esdaile, 1934)

13 Mathematics are a species of Frenchman; if you say something to them, they translate it into their own language and presto! it is something entirely different.
Johann Wolfgang von Goethe 1749–1832: attributed; R. L. Weber *A Random Walk in Science* (1973)

14 What would life be like without arithmetic, but a scene of horrors?
Sydney Smith 1771–1845: letter to Miss [Lucie Austen], 22 July 1835

15 I used to love mathematics for its own sake, and I still do, because it allows for no hypocrisy and no vagueness, my two *bêtes noires*.
Stendhal 1783–1842: *La Vie d'Henri Brulard* (1890)

16 'What's the good of *Mercator's* North Poles and Equators,
Tropics, Zones and Meridian lines?'
So the Bellman would cry: and the crew would reply,
'They are merely conventional signs!'
Lewis Carroll 1832–98: *The Hunting of the Snark* (1876)

17 God made the integers, all the rest is the work of man.
Leopold Kronecker 1823–91: *Jahrsberichte der Deutschen Mathematiker Vereinigung*

18 I never could make out what those damned dots meant.
on decimal points
Lord Randolph Churchill 1849–94: W. S. Churchill *Lord Randolph Churchill* (1906)

19 Mathematics, rightly viewed, possesses not only truth, but supreme beauty—a beauty cold and austere, like that of sculpture.
Bertrand Russell 1872–1970: *Philosophical Essays* (1910)

20 Beauty is the first test: there is no permanent place in the world for ugly mathematics.
Godfrey Harold Hardy 1877–1947: *A Mathematician's Apology* (1940)

21 One must divide one's time between politics and equations. But our equations are much more important to me.
Albert Einstein 1879–1955: C. P. Snow 'Einstein' in M. Goldsmith et al. (eds.) *Einstein* (1980)

22 In mathematics you don't understand things. You just get used to them.
John von Neumann 1903–57: Gary Zukav *The Dancing Wu Li Masters* (1979)

23 It is more important to have beauty in one's equations than to have them fit experiment.
he went on to say 'The discrepancy may well be due to minor features . . . that will get cleared up with further developments'
Paul Dirac 1902–84: in *Scientific American* May 1963

24 No-one could study mathematics intensively for more than five hours a day and remain sane.

J. B. S. Haldane 1892–1964: in *Perspectives in Biology and Medicine* (1966) 'An Autobiography in Brief'

25 Points
Have no parts or joints
How then can they combine
To form a line?

J. A. Lindon: M. Gardner *Wheels, Life and Other Mathematical Amusements* (1983)

26 Someone told me that each equation I included in the book would halve the sales.

Stephen Hawking 1942– : *A Brief History of Time* (1988)

27 Prime numbers are what is left when you have taken all the patterns away. I think prime numbers are like life.

Mark Haddon 1962– : *The Curious Incident of the Dog in the Night-time* (2003)

28 There are 10 types of people in the country: those who understand binary and those who don't.

Jeremy Paxman 1950– : in *Sunday Telegraph* 28 December 2003

➤➤ Maturity ◄◄

see also **Experience**

PROVERBS AND SAYINGS

1 Never send a boy to do a man's job.

someone who is young and inexperienced should not be given too much responsibility; English proverb, mid 20th century

2 Soon ripe, soon rotten.

a warning against precocity, meaning that notably early achievement is unlikely to be long-lasting; English proverb, late 14th century (earlier in Latin)

QUOTATIONS

3 More childish valorous than manly wise.

Christopher Marlowe 1564–93: *Tamburlaine the Great* (1590)

4 And so, from hour to hour, we ripe and ripe,
And then from hour to hour, we rot and rot:
And thereby hangs a tale.

William Shakespeare 1564–1616: *As You Like It* (1599)

5 Is not old wine wholesomest, old pippins toothsomest, old wood burn brightest, old linen wash whitest? Old soldiers, sweethearts, are surest, and old lovers are soundest.

John Webster 1580– : *Westward Hoe* (1607)

6 Men are but children of a larger growth;
Our appetites as apt to change as theirs,
And full as craving too, and full as vain.

John Dryden 1631–1700: *All for Love* (1678)

7 At twenty years of age, the will reigns; at thirty, the wit; and at forty, the judgement.

Benjamin Franklin 1706–90: *Poor Richard's Almanac* (1741)

8 The imagination of a boy is healthy, and the mature imagination of a man is healthy; but there is a space of life between, in which the soul is in a ferment, the character undecided, the way of life uncertain, the ambition thick-sighted: thence proceeds mawkishness.

John Keats 1795–1821: *Endymion* (1818) preface

9 If you can talk with crowds and keep your virtue,
Or walk with Kings—nor lose the common touch,
If neither foes nor loving friends can hurt you,
If all men count with you, but none too much;
If you can fill the unforgiving minute
With sixty seconds' worth of distance run,
Yours is the Earth and everything that's in it,
And—which is more—you'll be a Man, my son!

Rudyard Kipling 1865–1936: 'If—' (1910)

10 To be adult is to be alone.

Jean Rostand 1894–1977: *Pensées d'un biologiste* (1954)

11 Immature love says: 'I love you because I need you.' Mature love says: 'I need you because I love you.'

Erich Fromm 1900–80: *The Art of Loving* (1956)

12 One's prime is elusive. You little girls, when
you grow up, must be on the alert to
recognise your prime at whatever time of
your life it may occur.
Muriel Spark 1918– : *The Prime of Miss Jean Brodie*
(1961)

13 How many roads must a man walk down
Before you can call him a man? . . .
The answer, my friend, is blowin' in the
wind,
The answer is blowin' in the wind.
Bob Dylan 1941– : 'Blowin' in the Wind' (1962
song)

14 One of the most obvious facts about grown-
ups, to a child, is that they have forgotten
what it is like to be a child.
Randall Jarrell 1914–65: Christina Stead *The Man
Who Loved Children* (1965)

15 Whereas nature turns girls into women,
society has to make boys into men.
Anthony Stevens: *Archetype* (1982)

16 I gave my beauty and my youth to men. I
am going to give my wisdom and experience
to animals.
Brigitte Bardot 1934– : attributed, June 1987

17 I had always thought that once you grew up
you could do anything you wanted—stay up
all night or eat ice-cream straight out of the
container.
Bill Bryson 1951– : *The Lost Continent* (1989)

18 When adults stop being infants, children
can be children.
Rowan Williams 1950– : in *Mail on Sunday* 17
April 2005

⇢⇢ Meaning ⇠⇠

see also **Words**

PROVERBS AND SAYINGS

1 **Every picture tells a story.**
advertisement for Doan's Backache Kidney Pills (early
1900s)

2 **Straws tell which way the wind blows.**
English proverb, mid 17th century; see **The
Future** 10

PHRASES

3 **gammon and spinach**
nonsense, humbug; with a pun on *gammon* bacon,
ham. The words *gammon and spinach* are part of the
refrain to the song 'A frog he would a-wooing go',
and the term is used by Dickens in *David Copperfield*
and *Bleak House*

QUOTATIONS

4 I pray thee, understand a plain man in his
plain meaning.
William Shakespeare 1564–1616: *The Merchant of
Venice* (1596–8)

5 Where more is meant than meets the ear.
John Milton 1608–74: 'Il Penseroso' (1645)

6 Egad I think the interpreter is the hardest to
be understood of the two!
Richard Brinsley Sheridan 1751–1816: *The Critic*
(1779)

7 God and I both knew what it meant once;
now God alone knows.
also attributed to Browning, apropos *Sordello*, in the
form 'When it was written, God and Robert
Browning knew what it meant; now only God
knows'
Friedrich Klopstock 1724–1803: C. Lombroso *The
Man of Genius* (1891)

8 'Then you should say what you mean,' the
March Hare went on. 'I do,' Alice hastily
replied; 'at least—at least I mean what I
say—that's the same thing, you know.' 'Not
the same thing a bit!' said the Hatter. 'Why,
you might just as well say that "I see what I
eat" is the same thing as "I eat what I see!" '
Lewis Carroll 1832–98: *Alice's Adventures in
Wonderland* (1865)

9 You see it's like a portmanteau—there are
two meanings packed up into one word.
Lewis Carroll 1832–98: *Through the Looking-Glass*
(1872)

10 The meaning doesn't matter if it's only idle
chatter of a transcendental kind.
W. S. Gilbert 1836–1911: *Patience* (1881)

11 No one means all he says, and yet very few
say all they mean, for words are slippery and
thought is viscous.
Henry Brooks Adams 1838–1918: *The Education
of Henry Adams* (1907)

12 The little girl had the making of a poet in her who, being told to be sure of her meaning before she spoke, said, 'How can I know what I think till I see what I say?'
Graham Wallas 1858–1932: *The Art of Thought* (1926)

13 Any general statement is like a cheque drawn on a bank. Its value depends on what is there to meet it.
Ezra Pound 1885–1972: *The ABC of Reading* (1934)

14 It all depends what you mean by . . .
C. E. M. Joad 1891–1953: answering questions on 'The Brains Trust' (formerly 'Any Questions'), BBC radio (1941–8)

15 It depends on what the meaning of 'is' is.
Bill Clinton 1946– : videotaped evidence to the grand jury; tapes broadcast 21 September 1998

Means see **Ways and Means**

Medicine

see also **Sickness**

PROVERBS AND SAYINGS

1 **The best doctors are Dr Diet, Dr Quiet, and Dr Merryman.**
outline to an appropriate regime for someone who is ill; English proverb, mid 16th century

2 **Dr Williams' pink pills for pale people.**
patent medicine advertisement, from 1890 on

3 **Keep taking the tablets.**
supposedly traditional advice from a doctor, especially when little change in the patient's condition is envisaged; see **Pregnancy** 19

4 **Laughter is the best medicine.**
late 20th century saying; the idea is an ancient one: see **Humour** 4

5 **Medicine can prolong life, but death will seize the doctor, too.**
American proverb, mid 20th century

6 **Similia similibus curantur.**
Latin, 'Like cures like'; motto of homeopathic medicine attributed to S. Hahnemann (1755–1843), although not found in this form in Hahnemann's writings

PHRASES

7 **the Lady of the Lamp**
Florence Nightingale (1820–1910), English nurse and medical reformer; from her nightly rounds in army hospital at Scutari in the Crimean War

QUOTATIONS

8 Honour a physician with the honour due unto him for the uses which ye may have of him: for the Lord hath created him.
Bible: Ecclesiasticus

9 Life is short, the art long.
Hippocrates c.460–357 BC: *Aphorisms*; see **The Arts** 2

10 Healing is a matter of time, but it is sometimes also a matter of opportunity.
Hippocrates c.460–357 BC: *Precepts*

11 Physician, heal thyself.
Bible: St Luke

12 Confront disease at its onset.
Persius AD 34–62: *Satires*

13 There can be no surgeon who is not also a physician . . . Where the physician is not also a surgeon he is an idol that is nothing but a painted monkey.
Paracelsus 1493–1541: Walter Pagel *Paracelsus: An introduction to Philosophical Medicine in the Era of the Renaissance* (1958)

14 　　　　Diseases desperate grown,
By desperate appliances are relieved,
Or not at all.
William Shakespeare 1564–1616: *Hamlet* (1601); see **Necessity** 3

15 Throw physic to the dogs; I'll none of it.
William Shakespeare 1564–1616: *Macbeth* (1606)

16 The remedy is worse than the disease.
Francis Bacon 1561–1626: *Essays* (1625) 'Of Seditions and Troubles'

17 Physicians of all men are most happy; what good success soever they have, the world proclaimeth, and what faults they commit, the earth covereth.
Francis Quarles 1592–1644: *Hieroglyphics of the Life of Man* (1638); see **Architecture** 18

18 Cured yesterday of my disease,
I died last night of my physician.
Matthew Prior 1664–1721: 'The Remedy Worse than the Disease' (1727)

19 In disease Medical Men guess: if they cannot ascertain a disease, they call it nervous.
John Keats 1795–1821: J. A. Gere and John Sparrow (eds.) *Geoffrey Madan's Notebooks* (1981); attributed

20 It may seem a strange principle to enunciate as the very first requirement in a Hospital that it should do the sick no harm.
Florence Nightingale 1820–1910: *Notes on Hospitals* (1863 ed.) preface

21 Ah, well, then, I suppose that I shall have to die beyond my means.
at the mention of a huge fee for a surgical operation
Oscar Wilde 1854–1900: R. H. Sherard *Life of Oscar Wilde* (1906)

22 If a lot of cures are suggested for a disease, it means that the disease is incurable.
Anton Chekhov 1860–1904: *The Cherry Orchard* (1904)

23 There is at bottom only one genuinely scientific treatment for all diseases, and that is to stimulate the phagocytes.
George Bernard Shaw 1856–1950: *The Doctor's Dilemma* (1911)

24 Every day, in every way, I am getting better and better.
to be said 15 to 20 times, morning and evening
Émile Coué 1857–1926: *De la suggestion et de ses applications* (1915); see **Ability** 12

25 The young physician starts life with twenty drugs for each disease, and the old physician ends life with one drug for twenty diseases.
William Osler 1849–1919: *Aphorisms from His Bedside Teachings and Writings* (1950)

26 One finger in the throat and one in the rectum makes a good diagnostician.
William Osler 1849–1919: *Aphorisms from his Bedside Teachings* (1961)

27 We shall have to learn to refrain from doing things merely because we know how to do them.
Theodore Fox 1899–1989: speech to Royal College of Physicians, 18 October 1965

28 When our organs have been transplanted
And the new ones made happy to lodge
  in us,
Let us pray one wish be granted—
We retain our zones erogenous.
E. Y. Harburg 1898–1981: 'Seated One Day at the Organ' (1965)

29 Formerly, when religion was strong and science weak, men mistook magic for medicine; now, when science is strong and religion weak, men mistake medicine for magic.
Thomas Szasz 1920– : *The Second Sin* (1973)

30 A cousin of mine who was a casualty surgeon in Manhattan tells me that he and his colleagues had a one-word nickname for bikers: Donors.
Stephen Fry 1957– : *Paperweight* (1992)

31 The irony is that the healthier Western society becomes, the more medicine it craves.
Roy Porter 1946–2002: *The Greatest Benefit to Mankind* (1998)

⤜ Meeting and Parting ⤛

PROVERBS AND SAYINGS

1 The best of friends must part.
no friendship is so close that separation is impossible; English proverb, early 17th century

2 Nice to see you—to see you, nice.
catchphrase used by Bruce Forsyth in 'The Generation Game' on BBC Television, 1973 onwards

3 Talk of the Devil, and he is bound to appear.
to speak of the Devil may be to invite his presence; often abbreviated to *talk of the Devil*, and used when a person just spoken of is seen; English proverb, mid 17th century

PHRASES

4 nunc dimittis
permission to depart, dismissal; Latin = now you let (your servant) depart, a canticle forming part of the Christian liturgy at evensong and compline, comprising the song of Simeon in the Bible (Luke) (in the Vulgate beginning *Nunc dimittis, Domine*)

5 ships that pass in the night

people whose contact or acquaintance is necessarily
fleeting or transitory; from Longfellow: see
Relationships 12

QUOTATIONS

6 *Atque in perpetuum, frater, ave atque vale.*
And so, my brother, hail, and farewell
    evermore!
Catullus *c.*84–*c.*54 BC: *Carmina*

7 Fare well my dear child and pray for me, and
I shall for you and all your friends that we
may merrily meet in heaven.
Thomas More 1478–1535: last letter to his
daughter Margaret Roper, 5 July 1535

8 Good-night, good-night! parting is such
    sweet sorrow.
William Shakespeare 1564–1616: *Romeo and
Juliet* (1595)

9 Ill met by moonlight, proud Titania.
William Shakespeare 1564–1616: *A Midsummer
Night's Dream* (1595–6)

10 When shall we three meet again
In thunder, lightning, or in rain?
William Shakespeare 1564–1616: *Macbeth* (1606)

11 Since there's no help, come let us kiss and
    part,
Nay, I have done: you get no more of me.
Michael Drayton 1563–1631: *Idea* (1619)
sonnet 61

12 Gin a body meet a body
Comin thro' the rye,
Gin a body kiss a body
Need a body cry?
Robert Burns 1759–96: 'Comin thro' the rye'
(1796)

13 Not many sounds in life, and I include all
urban and all rural sounds, exceed in
interest a knock at the door.
Charles Lamb 1775–1834: *Essays of Elia* (1823)
'Valentine's Day'

14 In every parting there is an image of death.
George Eliot 1819–80: *Scenes of Clerical Life* (1858)

15 Neither could find anything to say. There
comes a moment during leave-taking when
the loved one is no longer with us.
Gustave Flaubert 1821–80: *A Sentimental
Education* (1869) tr. D. Parmée

16 Dr Livingstone, I presume?
Henry Morton Stanley 1841–1904: *How I found
Livingstone* (1872)

17 Parting is all we know of heaven,
And all we need of hell.
Emily Dickinson 1830–86: 'My life closed twice
before its close'

18 'Is there anybody there?' said the Traveller,
Knocking on the moonlit door.
Walter de la Mare 1873–1956: 'The Listeners'
(1912)

19 We live our lives, for ever taking leave.
Rainer Maria Rilke 1875–1926: *Duineser Elegien*
(1948)

20 Goodnight, children . . . everywhere.
Derek McCulloch 1897–1967: *Children's Hour* (BBC
Radio programme; closing words normally spoken
by 'Uncle Mac' in the 1930s and 1940s)

21 Why don't you come up sometime, and
see me?
usually quoted as 'Why don't you come up and see
me sometime?'
Mae West 1892–1980: *She Done Him Wrong* (1933
film)

22 We'll meet again, don't know where,
Don't know when,
But I know we'll meet again some
    sunny day.
Ross Parker 1914–74 and **Hugh Charles** 1907– :
'We'll Meet Again' (1939 song)

23 HUMPHREY BOGART: Of all the gin joints in
all the towns in all the world, she walks into
mine.
Julius J. Epstein 1909–2001 et al.: *Casablanca*
(1942 film)

24 Some enchanted evening,
You may see a stranger,
You may see a stranger,
Across a crowded room.
Oscar Hammerstein II 1895–1960: 'Some
Enchanted Evening' (1949 song)

25 I'll be back.
James Cameron 1954– : *The Terminator* (1984 film,
with Gale Anne Hurd); spoken by Arnold
Schwarzenegger

Memory

PROVERBS AND SAYINGS

1 Our memory is always at fault, never our judgement.
American proverb, mid 20th century

PHRASES

2 down memory lane
recalling a pleasant past; *Down Memory Lane* (1949) title of a compilation of Mack Sennett comedy shorts

3 Kim's game
a memory-testing game in which players try to remember as many as possible of a set of objects briefly shown to them; *Kim* (the eponymous hero of) a book by Rudyard Kipling (1865–1936), in which a similar game is played.

4 recherche du temps perdu
an evocation of one's early life; French, literally 'in search of the lost time', title of Proust's novel sequence of 1913–27 (in English translation of 1922–31, 'Remembrance of things past'): see 8, 16 below, **The Past** 17

QUOTATIONS

5 Maybe one day it will be cheering to remember even these things.
Virgil 70–19 BC: *Aeneid*

6 The memories of long love gather like drifting snow, poignant as the mandarin ducks who float side by side in sleep.
Murasaki Shikibu c.978–c.1031: *The Tale of Genji*

7 Old men forget: yet all shall be forgot,
But he'll remember with advantages
What feats he did that day.
William Shakespeare 1564–1616: *Henry V* (1599)

8 When to the sessions of sweet silent thought
I summon up remembrance of things past.
William Shakespeare 1564–1616: sonnet 30; see 4 above

9 We'll tak a cup o' kindness yet,
For auld lang syne.
Robert Burns 1759–96: 'Auld Lang Syne' (1796); see **The Past** 10

10 You may break, you may shatter the vase, if you will,
But the scent of the roses will hang round it still.
Thomas Moore 1779–1852: 'Farewell!—but whenever' (1807)

11 In looking on the happy autumn-fields,
And thinking of the days that are no more.
Alfred, Lord Tennyson 1809–92: *The Princess* (1847) song (added 1850)

12 And we forget because we must
And not because we will.
Matthew Arnold 1822–88: 'Absence' (1852)

13 Better by far you should forget and smile
Than that you should remember and be sad.
Christina Rossetti 1830–94: 'Remember' (1862)

14 I've a grand memory for forgetting, David.
Robert Louis Stevenson 1850–94: *Kidnapped* (1886)

15 I have forgot much, Cynara! gone with the wind,
Flung roses, roses, riotously, with the throng,
Dancing, to put thy pale, lost lilies out of mind.
Ernest Dowson 1867–1900: 'Non Sum Qualis Eram' (1896); also known as 'Cynara'; see **Absence** 7, **Constancy** 14

16 And suddenly the memory revealed itself. The taste was that of the little piece of madeleine which on Sunday mornings at Combray . . . my aunt Léonie used to give me, dipping it first in her own cup of tea or tisane.
Marcel Proust 1871–1922: *Swann's Way* (1913, vol. 1 of *Remembrance of Things Past*); see 4 above

17 Midnight shakes the memory
As a madman shakes a dead geranium.
T. S. Eliot 1888–1965: 'Rhapsody on a Windy Night' (1917)

18 Someone said that God gave us memory so that we might have roses in December.
J. M. Barrie 1860–1937: Rectorial Address at St Andrew's, 3 May 1922

19 In plucking the fruit of memory one runs the risk of spoiling its bloom.
Joseph Conrad 1857–1924: *The Arrow of Gold* (1924 ed.)

20 What beastly incidents our memories insist
on cherishing! . . . the ugly and disgusting
. . . the beautiful things we have to keep
diaries to remember!
Eugene O'Neill 1888–1953: *Strange Interlude*
(1928)

21 A cigarette that bears a lipstick's traces,
An airline ticket to romantic places;
And still my heart has wings
These foolish things
Remind me of you.
Holt Marvell: 'These Foolish Things Remind Me of
You' (1935 song)

22 There should be an invention that bottles
up a memory like a perfume, and it never
faded, never got stale, and whenever I
wanted to I could uncork the bottle, and live
the memory all over again.
Daphne Du Maurier 1907–89: *Rebecca* (1938)

23 Our memories are card-indexes consulted,
and then put back in disorder by authorities
whom we do not control.
Cyril Connolly 1903–74: *The Unquiet Grave* (1944)

24 We met at nine.
We met at eight.
I was on time.
No, you were late.
Ah yes! I remember it well.
Alan Jay Lerner 1918–86: 'I Remember it Well'
(1958 song)

25 Poor people's memory is less nourished
than that of the rich; it has fewer landmarks
in space because they seldom leave the place
where they live, and fewer reference points
in time.
Albert Camus 1913–60: *The First Man* (1994)

26 Memories are not shackles, Franklin, they
are garlands.
Alan Bennett 1934– : *Forty Years On* (1969)

27 Everyone seems to remember with great
clarity what they were doing on November
22nd, 1963, at the precise moment they
heard President Kennedy was dead.
Frederick Forsyth 1938– : *The Odessa File* (1972)

28 Your memory is a monster; *you* forget—*it*
doesn't. It simply files things away. It keeps
things for you, or hides things from
you—and summons them to your recall
with a will of its own. You think you have a
memory; but it has you!
John Irving 1942– : *A Prayer for Owen Meany*
(1989)

⊱ Men ⊰

1 **Boys will be boys.**
English proverb, early 17th century, often used
ironically

2 **I married my husband for life, not for
lunch.**
20th century saying, origin unknown

3 **The way to a man's heart is through
his stomach.**
English proverb, early 19th century

4 **dead white European male**
regarded as the stereotypical figure on which
literary, cultural, and philosophical studies have
traditionally centred; the acronym DWEM derives
from this

5 **good ol' boy**
in US usage, a (usually white) male from the
Southern States of America, regarded as one of a
group conforming to a social and cultural masculine
stereotype

6 Sigh no more, ladies, sigh no more,
Men were deceivers ever.
William Shakespeare 1564–1616: *Much Ado
About Nothing* (1598–9)

7 In matters of love men's eyes are always
bigger than their bellies. They have violent
appetites, 'tis true; but they have soon
dined.
John Vanbrugh 1664–1726: *The Relapse* (1696)

8 Man is to be held only by the *slightest*
chains, with the idea that he can break
them at pleasure, he submits to them in
sport.
Maria Edgeworth 1767–1849: *Letters for Literary
Ladies* (1795)

9 Men have had every advantage of us in telling their own story. Education has been theirs in so much higher a degree; the pen has been in their hands.
Jane Austen 1775–1817: *Persuasion* (1818)

10 A man . . . is *so* in the way in the house!
Elizabeth Gaskell 1810–65: *Cranford* (1853)

11 The three most important things a man has are, briefly, his private parts, his money, and his religious opinions.
Samuel Butler 1835–1902: *Further Extracts from Notebooks* (1934)

12 Every man over forty is a scoundrel.
George Bernard Shaw 1856–1950: *Man and Superman* (1903) 'Maxims: Stray Sayings'

13 If you wish—
. . . I'll be irreproachably tender;
not a man, but—a cloud in trousers!
Vladimir Mayakovsky 1893–1930: 'The Cloud in Trousers' (1915)

14 Men build bridges and throw railroads across deserts, and yet they contend successfully that the job of sewing on a button is beyond them. Accordingly, they don't have to sew buttons.
Heywood Broun 1888–1939: *Seeing Things at Night* (1921)

15 Somehow a bachelor never quite gets over the idea that he is a thing of beauty and a boy forever.
Helen Rowland 1875–1950: *A Guide to Men* (1922); see **Beauty** 21

16 It's not the men in my life that counts—it's the life in my men.
Mae West 1892–1980: *I'm No Angel* (1933 film)

17 There is, of course, no reason for the existence of the male sex except that sometimes one needs help with moving the piano.
Rebecca West 1892–1983: in *Sunday Telegraph* 28 June 1970

18 Whatever they may be in public life, whatever their relations with men, in their relations with women, all men are rapists, and that's all they are. They rape us with their eyes, their laws, and their codes.
Marilyn French 1929– : *The Women's Room* (1977)

19 Men—athletes especially—have to be like King Kong. When we lose, we can't cry and we can't pout.
Carl Lewis 1961– : in *Observer* 29 July 1984

20 Years ago, manhood was an opportunity for achievement, and now it is a problem to be overcome.
Garrison Keillor 1942– : *The Book of Guys* (1994)

21 Men would rather take their trousers off in public when they're drunk than open the shield of their hearts when they are sober.
Stephen Fry 1957– : comment on the work of the Samaritans, 17 May 1996

22 Give me macho, or give me death.
Madonna 1958– : in *Sunday Times* 29 July 2001

⊱ Men and Women ⊰

see also **Men, Woman's Role, Women**

PROVERBS AND SAYINGS

1 **Every Jack has his Jill.**
all lovers have found a mate; English proverb, early 17th century

2 **A good Jack makes a good Jill.**
used of the effect of a husband on his wife; English proverb, early 17th century

3 **A man is as old as he feels, and a woman as old as she looks.**
both parts of the proverb are sometimes used on their own; English proverb, late 19th century

QUOTATIONS

4   Just such disparity
As is 'twixt air and angels' purity,
'Twixt women's love, and men's will ever be.
John Donne 1572–1631: 'Air and Angels'

5 He for God only, she for God in him.
John Milton 1608–74: *Paradise Lost* (1667)

6 In every age and country, the wiser, or at least the stronger, of the two sexes, has usurped the powers of the state, and confined the other to the cares and pleasures of domestic life.
Edward Gibbon 1737–94: *The Decline and Fall of the Roman Empire* (1776–88)

7 Man's love is of man's life a thing apart,
'Tis woman's whole existence.
Lord Byron 1788–1824: *Don Juan* (1819–24)

8 The man's desire is for the woman; but the woman's desire is rarely other than for the desire of the man.
Samuel Taylor Coleridge 1772–1834: *Table Talk* (1835) 23 July 1827

9 Man is the hunter; woman is his game.
Alfred, Lord Tennyson 1809–92: *The Princess* (1847)

10 'Tis strange what a man may do, and a woman yet think him an angel.
William Makepeace Thackeray 1811–63: *The History of Henry Esmond* (1852)

11 Man dreams of fame while woman wakes to love.
Alfred, Lord Tennyson 1809–92: *Idylls of the King* 'Merlin and Vivien' (1859)

12 I expect that Woman will be the last thing civilized by Man.
George Meredith 1828–1909: *The Ordeal of Richard Feverel* (1859)

13 Any woman who is sure of her own wits is a match at any time for a man who is not sure of his own temper.
Wilkie Collins 1824–89: *The Woman in White* (1860)

14 Take my word for it, the silliest woman can manage a clever man; but it takes a very clever woman to manage a fool.
Rudyard Kipling 1865–1936: *Plain Tales from the Hills* (1888)

15 All women become like their mothers. That is their tragedy. No man does. That's his.
Oscar Wilde 1854–1900: *The Importance of Being Earnest* (1895)

16 Where young boys plan for what they will achieve and attain, young girls plan for whom they will achieve and attain.
Charlotte Perkins Gilman 1860–1935: *Women and Economics* (1898)

17 Of all human struggles there is none so treacherous and remorseless as the struggle between the artist man and the mother woman.
George Bernard Shaw 1856–1950: *Man and Superman* (1903)

18 Women deprived of the company of men pine, men deprived of the company of women become stupid.
Anton Chekhov 1860–1904: *Notebooks* (1921)

19 A woman can forgive a man for the harm he does her, but she can never forgive him for the sacrifices he makes on her account.
W. Somerset Maugham 1874–1965: *The Moon and Sixpence* (1919)

20 Women have served all these centuries as looking-glasses possessing the magic and delicious power of reflecting the figure of a man at twice its natural size.
Virginia Woolf 1882–1941: *A Room of One's Own* (1929)

21 Me Tarzan, you Jane.
summing up his role in *Tarzan, the Ape Man* (1932 film)
Johnny Weissmuller 1904–84: in *Photoplay Magazine* June 1932; the words occur neither in the film nor the original novel, by Edgar Rice Burroughs

22 It is not in giving life but in risking life that man is raised above the animal; that is why superiority has been accorded in humanity not to the sex that brings forth but to that which kills.
Simone de Beauvoir 1908–86: *The Second Sex* (1949)

23 There is more difference within the sexes than between them.
Ivy Compton-Burnett 1884–1969: *Mother and Son* (1955)

24 Why can't a woman be more like a man? Men are so honest, so thoroughly square; Eternally noble, historically fair.
Alan Jay Lerner 1918–86: 'A Hymn to Him' (1956 song)

25 Every woman adores a Fascist,
The boot in the face, the brute
Brute heart of a brute like you.
Sylvia Plath 1932–63: 'Daddy' (1963)

26 Whatever women do they must do twice as well as men to be thought half as good.
Charlotte Whitton 1896–1975: in *Canada Month* June 1963

27 Stand by your man.
Tammy Wynette 1942–98 and **Billy Sherrill**: title of song (1968)

28 Women have very little idea of how much men hate them.
Germaine Greer 1939– : *The Female Eunuch* (1971)

29 My mother said it was simple to keep a man, you must be a maid in the living room, a cook in the kitchen and a whore in the bedroom. I said I'd hire the other two and take care of the bedroom bit.
Jerry Hall: in *Observer* 6 October 1985

30 A man has every season, while a woman has only the right to spring.
Jane Fonda 1937– : in *Daily Mail* 13 September 1989

31 A woman without a man is like a fish without a bicycle.
Gloria Steinem 1934– : attributed

32 Men are from Mars, women are from Venus.
John Gray 1951– : title of book (1992)

33 In societies where men are truly confident of their own worth, women are not merely tolerated but valued.
Aung San Suu Kyi 1945– : videotape speech at NGO Forum on Women, China, early September 1995

Middle Age

PROVERBS AND SAYINGS

1 A fool at forty is a fool indeed.
someone who has not learned wisdom by the age of forty will never learn it; in this form from Edward Young *Universal Passion* (1725) 'Be wise with speed; A fool at forty is a fool indeed'; English proverb, early 16th century

2 Life begins at forty.
English proverb, mid 20th century, from title of book (1932) by Walter B. Pitkin

QUOTATIONS

3 *Nel mezzo del cammin di nostra vita.*
Midway along the path of our life.
Dante Alighieri 1265–1321: *Divina Commedia* 'Inferno'

4 I am resolved to grow fat and look young till forty, and then slip out of the world with the first wrinkle and the reputation of five-and-twenty.
John Dryden 1631–1700: *The Maiden Queen* (1668)

5 He who thinks to realize when he is older the hopes and desires of youth is always deceiving himself, for every decade of a man's life possesses its own kind of happiness, its own hopes and prospects.
Johann Wolfgang von Goethe 1749–1832: *Elective Affinities* (1809)

6 My days are in the yellow leaf;
The flowers and fruits of love are gone;
The worm, the canker, and the grief
Are mine alone!
Lord Byron 1788–1824: 'On This Day I Complete my Thirty-Sixth Year' (1824); see **Old Age** 14

7 I am past thirty, and three parts iced over.
Matthew Arnold 1822–88: letter to Arthur Hugh Clough, 12 February 1853

8 Few women, I fear, have had such reason as I have to think the long sad years of youth were worth living for the sake of middle age.
George Eliot 1819–80: letter, 1857

9 Thirty-five is a very attractive age. London society is full of women of the very highest birth who have, of their own free choice, remained thirty-five for years.
Oscar Wilde 1854–1900: *The Importance of Being Earnest* (1895)

10 At eighteen our convictions are hills from which we look; at forty-five they are caves in which we hide.
F. Scott Fitzgerald 1896–1940: 'Bernice Bobs her Hair' (1920)

11 The afternoon of human life must also have a significance of its own and cannot be merely a pitiful appendage to life's morning.
Carl Gustav Jung 1875–1961: *The Stages of Life* (1930)

12 One of the pleasures of middle age is to *find out* that one WAS right, and that one was much righter than one knew at say 17 or 23.
Ezra Pound 1885–1972: *ABC of Reading* (1934)

13 I have a bone to pick with Fate.
Come here and tell me, girlie,
Do you think my mind is maturing late,
Or simply rotted early?
Ogden Nash 1902–71: 'Lines on Facing Forty' (1942)

14 Years ago we discovered the exact point, the dead centre of middle age. It occurs when you are too young to take up golf and too old to rush up to the net.
Franklin P. Adams 1881–1960: *Nods and Becks* (1944)

15 At forty-five,
What next, what next?
At every corner,
I meet my Father,
my age, still alive.
Robert Lowell 1917–77: 'Middle Age' (1964)

16 After forty a woman has to choose between losing her figure or her face. My advice is to keep your face, and stay sitting down.
Barbara Cartland 1901–2000: Libby Purves 'Luncheon à la Cartland'; in *The Times* 6 October 1993

17 By the time you hit 50, I reckon you've earned your wrinkles, so why not be proud of them?
Twiggy 1949– : in *Observer* 8 September 2002

➤➤ The Mind ◄◄

see also **Ideas, Logic and Reason, Madness, Thinking**

PROVERBS AND SAYINGS

1 Mind has no sex.
modern saying, from Mary Wollstonecraft: see 14 below

2 A mind is a terrible thing to waste.
motto of the United Negro College Fund; see 27 below

PHRASES

3 the five wits
the five (bodily) senses of hearing, sight, smell, taste, and touch

4 the ghost in the machine
the mind viewed as distinct from the body; a term coined by the philosopher Gilbert Ryle in *The Concept of Mind* (1949), for a viewpoint which he regarded as completely misleading

5 nature and nurture
heredity and environment as influences on, or the determinants of, personality or behaviour; there has been a long debate on which, if either, is dominant; see 29 below

QUOTATIONS

6 The mind of the perfect man is like a mirror. It does not lean forward or backward in its response to things. It responds to things but conceals nothing of its own.
Zhuangzi c.369–286 BC: *Chuang Tzu*

7 The mind does not require filling like a bottle, but rather, like wood, it only requires kindling to create in it an impulse to think independently and an ardent desire for the truth.
Plutarch c.AD 46–c.120: *Moralia*; see **Children** 7

8 My mind to me a kingdom is.
Such perfect joy therein I find.
Edward Dyer d. 1607: 'In praise of a contented mind' (1588); attributed

9 It is not enough to have a good mind; the main thing is to use it well.
René Descartes 1596–1650: *Le Discours de la méthode* (1637) pt. 1

10 The mind is its own place, and in itself Can make a heaven of hell, a hell of heaven.
John Milton 1608–74: *Paradise Lost* (1667)

11 Everyone complains of his memory, and no one complains of his judgement.
Duc de la Rochefoucauld 1613–80: *Maximes* (1678)

12 The mind is but a barren soil; a soil which is soon exhausted, and will produce no crop, or only one, unless it be continually fertilized and enriched with foreign matter.
Joshua Reynolds 1723–92: *Discourses on Art* 10 December 1774

13 When people will not weed their own minds, they are apt to be overrun with nettles.
Horace Walpole 1717–97: letter to Caroline, Countess of Ailesbury, 10 July 1779

14 To give a sex to mind was not very consistent with the principles of a man [Rousseau] who argued so warmly, and so well, for the immortality of the soul.
Mary Wollstonecraft 1759–97: *A Vindication of the Rights of Woman* (1792); see 1 above

15 The only means of strengthening one's intellect is to make up one's mind about nothing—to let the mind be a thoroughfare for all thoughts. Not a select party.
John Keats 1795–1821: letter to George and Georgiana Keats, 24 September 1819

16 What is Matter?—Never mind.
What is Mind?—No matter.
Punch: 1855

17 On earth there is nothing great but man; in man there is nothing great but mind.
William Hamilton 1788–1856: *Lectures on Metaphysics and Logic* (1859); attributed in a Latin form to Favorinus in Pico di Mirandola (1463–94) *Disputationes Adversus Astrologiam Divinatricem*

18 The great regions of the mind correspond to the great regions of the brain.
Paul Broca 1824–80: at the Société Anatomique, August 1861

19 To be conscious is an illness—a real thorough-going illness.
Fedor Dostoevsky 1821–81: *Notes from Underground* (1864)

20 With me the horrid doubt always arises whether the convictions of man's mind which has been developed from the mind of the lower animals, are of any value or at all trustworthy.
Charles Darwin 1809–82: Francis Darwin (ed.) *The Life and Letters of Charles Darwin* (1887)

21 O the mind, mind has mountains; cliffs of fall
Frightful, sheer, no-man-fathomed. Hold them cheap
May who ne'er hung there.
Gerard Manley Hopkins 1844–89: 'No worst, there is none' (written 1885)

22 Minds are like parachutes. They only function when they are open.
James Dewar 1842–1923: attributed

23 If my mental processes are determined wholly by the motions of atoms in my brain, I have no reason for supposing that my beliefs are true. They may be sound chemically, but that does not make them sound logically. And hence I have no reason for supposing my brain to be composed of atoms.
J. B. S. Haldane 1892–1964: *Possible Worlds* (1927)

24 Purple haze is in my brain
Lately things don't seem the same.
Jimi Hendrix 1942–70: 'Purple Haze' (1967 song)

25 That's the classical mind at work, runs fine inside but looks dingy on the surface.
Robert M. Pirsig 1928– : *Zen and the Art of Motorcycle Maintenance* (1974)

26 Those who are caught in mental cages can often picture freedom, it just has no attractive power.
Iris Murdoch 1919–99: *The Sea, The Sea* (1978)

27 What a waste it is to lose one's mind, or not to have a mind. How true that is.
Dan Quayle 1947– : speech to the United Negro College Fund, in *The Times* 26 May 1989; see 2 above

28 Consciousness *isn't* intolerable. It is beautiful: the eternal creation and dissolution of mental forms.
Martin Amis 1949– : *Time's Arrow* (1991)

29 Every human brain is born not as a blank tablet (a *tabula rasa*) waiting to be filled in by experience but as 'an exposed negative waiting to be slipped into developer fluid'.
on the nature v. nurture debate; see 5 above
Edward O. Wilson 1929– : attributed

⤞ Misfortunes ⤝

see also **Adversity**

PROVERBS AND SAYINGS

1 **Bad things come in threes.**
the belief that an accident or misfortune is likely to be accompanied by two more is traditional, although in this form it is only recorded from the late 20th century

2 **The bread never falls but on its buttered side.**
if something goes wrong, the outcome is likely to be as bad as possible; English proverb, mid 19th century

3 **Help you to salt, help you to sorrow.**
in which salt is regarded as a sign of bad luck (especially if spilt at table); English proverb, mid 17th century

4 **I cried because I had no shoes, until I met a man who had no feet.**
modern saying, deriving from a Persian original; see 18 below

5 **If anything can go wrong, it will.**
modern saying reflecting a supposed law of nature, said to have been coined in 1949 by George Nichols. Nichols is said to have developed the maxim from a remark made by a colleague, Captain E. Murphy, and the rule is otherwise known as Murphy's Law. See 11 below

6 **It is no use crying over spilt milk.**
it is pointless to repine when it is too late to prevent the misfortune; English proverb, mid 17th century

7 It never rains but it pours.

if one thing has gone wrong, worse will follow;
English proverb, early 18th century

PHRASES

9 a chapter of accidents

a series of misfortunes; see **Chance** 24

10 damnosa hereditas

an inheritance or tradition bringing more burden
than profit; Latin = inheritance that causes loss, from
The Institutes of the Roman jurist Gaius (AD
c.110–c.180)

11 Murphy's law

any of various aphoristic expressions of the apparent
perverseness and unreasonableness of things; see 5
above

12 out of the frying-pan into the fire

from one unfortunate situation into an even worse
one; see **Employment** 13

13 a poisoned chalice

an assignment, award, or honour which is likely to
prove a disadvantage or source of problems to the
recipient; originally from Shakespeare's *Macbeth*
(1606): 'This even-handed justice Commends

8 Misfortunes never come singly.

English proverb, early 14th century

th'ingredience of our poison'd chalice To our own
lips'

14 shirt of Nessus

a destructive or expurgatory force or influence; from
the classical story of the centaur Nessus slain by
Hercules, whose blood later poisoned Hercules after
he was given a garment smeared with it to wear

15 skeleton at the feast

something that spoils one's pleasure; an intrusive
worry or cause of grief; originally in allusion to an
ancient Egyptian custom recorded in Herodotus's
Histories, which tells of a wooden corpse in a coffin
being carried round at parties, and shown to guests
with the words, 'Look on this, for this will be your lot
when you are dead'

16 sow dragon's teeth

take action that (perhaps unintentionally) brings
about trouble; from the teeth of the dragon killed by
Cadmus in Greek legend, which when sown in the
ground sprouted up as armed men

QUOTATIONS

17 Man is born unto trouble, as the sparks fly
upward.
Bible: Job

18 I never complained at the vicissitudes of
fortune, nor murmured at the ordinances of
Heaven, excepting once, when my feet were
bare, and I had not the means of procuring
myself shoes. I entered the great mosque at
Cufah with a heavy heart when I beheld a
man who had no feet. I offered up praise
and thanksgiving to God for his bounty, and
bore with patience the want of shoes.
Sadi 1213–91: *The Rose Garden* (1258); see 4 above

19 Misery acquaints a man with strange
bedfellows.
William Shakespeare 1564–1616: *The Tempest*
(1611); see **Adversity** 1

20 All the misfortunes of men derive from one
single thing, which is their inability to be at
ease in a room.
Blaise Pascal 1623–62: *Pensées* (1670)

21 In the misfortune of our best friends, we
always find something which is not
displeasing to us.
Duc de la Rochefoucauld 1613–80: *Réflexions ou
Maximes Morales* (1665)

22 If Gladstone fell into the Thames, that
would be misfortune; and if anybody pulled
him out, that, I suppose, would be a
calamity.
Benjamin Disraeli 1804–81: Leon Harris *The Fine
Art of Political Wit* (1965)

23 I had never had a piece of toast
Particularly long and wide,
But fell upon the sanded floor,
And always on the buttered side.
James Payn 1830–98: in *Chambers's Journal* 2
February 1884; see 2 above

24 I left the room with silent dignity, but
caught my foot in the mat.
George and Weedon Grossmith 1847–1912,
1854–1919: *The Diary of a Nobody* (1894)

25 And always keep a-hold of Nurse
For fear of finding something worse.
Hilaire Belloc 1870–1953: *Cautionary Tales* (1907)
'Jim'

26 One likes people much better when they're
battered down by a prodigious siege of
misfortune than when they triumph.
Virginia Woolf 1882–1941: diary 13 August 1921

27 My only solution for the problem of
habitual accidents . . . is to stay in bed all
day. Even then, there is always the chance
that you will fall out.
Robert Benchley 1889–1945: *Chips off the old
Benchley* (1949)

28   People will take balls,
Balls will be lost always, little boy,
And no one buys a ball back.
John Berryman 1914–72: 'The Ball Poem' (1948)

29 Well, don't you think it's at least possible,
just possible that things can happen to us so
bad that we don't ever get over them?
Doris Lessing 1919– : *The Golden Notebook* (1962)

30 The fatal law of gravity: when you are down
everything falls on you.
Sylvia Townsend Warner 1893–1978: attributed

31 In the words of one of my more sympathetic
correspondents, it has turned out to be an
'annus horribilis'.
Elizabeth II 1926– : speech at Guildhall, London,
24 November 1992; see **Time** 10

32 I've no sympathy with people to whom
things happen. It may be that their luck was
bad, but is that to count in their favour?
Cormac McCarthy 1933– : *All the Pretty Horses*
(1993)

➤➤ Mistakes ◄◄

PROVERBS AND SAYINGS

1 **Even monkeys sometimes fall off a
tree.**
even the most adept can be careless and make
errors; Japanese proverb

2 **Homer sometimes nods.**
even the greatest expert may make a mistake (*nods*
here means 'becomes drowsy', implying a
momentary lack of attention); English proverb, late
fourteenth century; see 13 below

3 **A miss is as good as a mile.**
if you miss the target, it hardly matters by how
much; the syntax has been distorted by
abridgement: the original form was ' an inch in a
miss is as good as an ell' (an *ell* being a former
measure of length equal to about 1.1 metres);
English proverb, early 17th century

PHRASES

8 **a beam in one's eye**
a fault great compared to another's; from the Bible
(Matthew): see **Self-Knowledge** 4; see also 10 below

9 **an error in the first concoction**
a fault in the initial stage; the first of three stages of
digestion formerly recognized

10 **a mote in a person's eye**
a fault observed in another person by a person who
ignores a greater fault of his or her own; *mote* = an

QUOTATIONS

12 I would rather be wrong, by God, with Plato
. . . than be correct with those men.
on Pythagoreans
Cicero 106–43 BC: *Tusculanae Disputationes*

13 I'm aggrieved when sometimes even
excellent Homer nods.
Horace 65–8 BC: *Ars Poetica*; see 2 above, **Poets** 18

14 Leave no rubs nor botches in the work.
William Shakespeare 1564–1616: *Macbeth* (1606)

4 **Shome mishtake, shurely?**
catchphrase in *Private Eye* magazine, from the 1980s

5 **There's many a slip 'twixt cup and lip.**
much can go wrong between the initiation of a
process and its completion, often used as a warning;
English proverb, mid 16th century

6 **To err is human (to forgive divine).**
English proverb, late 16th century (in its quoted
form, from Pope, see **Forgiveness** 17); see also 30
below, **Computers** 5

7 **Wink at sma' fauts, ye hae great anes
yoursel.**
avoid criticizing the mistakes of others, your own
may be greater; Scottish proverb; see **Self-
Knowledge** 4

irritating particle in the eye; from the Bible
(Matthew): see 8 above

11 **shut the stable door when the horse
has bolted**
take preventive measures too late; from the proverb:
see **Foresight** 3

15 Errors, like straws, upon the surface flow;
He who would search for pearls must dive
    below.
John Dryden 1631–1700: *All for Love* (1678)

16 Crooked things may be as stiff and unflexible as straight: and men may be as positive in error as in truth.
John Locke 1632–1704: *An Essay concerning Human Understanding* (1690)

17 Truth lies within a little and certain compass, but error is immense.
Henry St John, Lord Bolingbroke 1678–1751: *Reflections upon Exile* (1716)

18 It is worse than a crime, it is a blunder.
on hearing of the execution of the Duc d'Enghien, 1804
Antoine Boulay de la Meurthe 1761–1840: C.-A. Sainte-Beuve *Nouveaux Lundis* (1870)

19 As she frequently remarked when she made any such mistake, it would be all the same a hundred years hence.
Charles Dickens 1812–70: *Nicholas Nickleby* (1839)

20 'Forward, the Light Brigade!'
Was there a man dismayed?
Not though the soldier knew
Some one had blundered.
Alfred, Lord Tennyson 1809–92: 'The Charge of the Light Brigade' (1854)

21 The man who makes no mistakes does not usually make anything.
Edward John Phelps 1822–1900: speech at the Mansion House, London, 24 January 1889; see **Creativity** 1

22 To lose one parent, Mr Worthing, may be regarded as a misfortune; to lose both looks like carelessness.
Oscar Wilde 1854–1900: *The Importance of Being Earnest* (1895)

23 The report of my death was an exaggeration.
usually quoted as 'Reports of my death have been greatly exaggerated'
Mark Twain 1835–1910: in *New York Journal* 2 June 1897

24 Well, if I called the wrong number, why did you answer the phone?
James Thurber 1894–1961: cartoon caption in *New Yorker* 5 June 1937

25 One Galileo in two thousand years is enough.
on being asked to proscribe the works of Teilhard de Chardin
Pope Pius XII 1876–1958: attributed; Stafford Beer *Platform for Change* (1975)

26 The weak have one weapon: the errors of those who think they are strong.
Georges Bidault 1899–1983: in *Observer* 15 July 1962

27 Mistakes are a fact of life
It is the response to error that counts.
Nikki Giovanni 1943– : 'Of Liberation' (1970)

28 When people thought the Earth was flat, they were wrong. When people thought the Earth was spherical, they were wrong. But if *you* think that thinking the Earth is spherical is *just as wrong* as thinking the Earth is flat, then your view is wronger than both of them put together.
Isaac Asimov 1920–92: *The Relativity of Wrong* (1989)

29 If all else fails, immortality can always be assured by a spectacular error.
J. K. Galbraith 1908– : attributed

30 To err is human, but it feels divine.
Dolly Parton 1946– : in *Observer* 7 August 2005; also attributed to Mae West (1892–1980); see 6 above

Moderation see **Excess and Moderation**

➤➤ Money ◀◀

see also **Greed, Poverty, Thrift and Extravagance, Wealth**

PROVERBS AND SAYINGS

1 Bad money drives out good.
money of lower intrinsic value tends to circulate more freely than money of higher intrinsic and equal nominal value, through what is recognized as money of higher value being hoarded, known as Gresham's law; English proverb, early 20th century; see 21 below

2 The best things in life are free.
English proverb, early 20th century; see **Possessions** 24

3 Get the money honestly if you can.
American proverb, early 19th century; see 25 below

4 He that cannot pay, let him pray.
if you have no material resources, prayer is your only resort; English proverb, early 17th century

-▷-◁-(••)-▷-◁-(••)-▷-◁-(••)-▷-◁-(••)-▷-◁-(••)-▷-◁-(••)-▷-◁-(••)-▷-◁-(••)-▷-◁-(••)-▷-◁-(••)-▷-◁-(••)-▷-◁-(••)-▷-◁-(••)-▷-◁-(••)-▷

5 Money can't buy happiness.
English proverb, mid 19th century

6 Money has no smell.
English proverb, early 20th century in this form, but originally deriving from a comment made by the Emperor Vespasian (AD 9–79); see **Taxes** 5

7 Money isn't everything.
often said in consolation or resignation; English proverb, early 20th century

8 Money is power.
English proverb, mid 18th century

9 Money is the root of all evil.
English proverb, mid 15th century, of biblical origin; see 27 below

10 Money, like manure, does no good till it is spread.
English proverb, early 19th century; see 28 below

11 Money makes the mare to go.
referring to money as a source of power; English proverb, late 15th century

12 Money talks.
money has influence; English proverb, mid 17th century; see 42 below

13 Shrouds have no pockets.
worldly wealth cannot be kept and used after death; English proverb, mid 19th century

14 Time is money.
often used to mean that time spent fruitlessly on something represents a real loss of money which could have been earned in that time; English proverb, late 16th century; see **Time** 35

15 Where there's muck there's brass.
dirty or unpleasant activities are also lucrative (*brass* here means 'money'); English proverb, late 17th century; see 28 below

16 You cannot serve God and Mammon.
now generally used of wealth regarded as an evil influence; English proverb, mid 16th century; see 26 below

PHRASES

17 the almighty dollar
the power of money; originally with allusion to the American writer Washington Irving (1783–1859): 'The almighty dollar, that great object of universal veneration throughout our land'

18 feather one's own nest
make money, usually illicitly and at someone else's expense. With reference to the habit of some birds of using feathers (their own or another bird's) to line the interior of their nests

19 filthy lucre
money, especially when regarded as sordid or distasteful or gained in a dishonourable way; of biblical origin: see **Clergy** 7

20 the gnomes of Zurich
Swiss financiers or bankers, regarded as having sinister influence; the phrase was popularized by the British Labour statesman Harold Wilson (1916–95)

21 Gresham's Law
the tendency for debased money to circulate more freely than money of higher intrinsic and equal nominal value; after Thomas *Gresham* (d. 1579), English financier and founder of the Royal Exchange; see 1 above

22 the Old Lady of Threadneedle Street
the Bank of England; *Threadneedle Street* in the City of London containing the premises of the Bank of England; the name is derived from *three-needle*, possibly from a tavern with the arms of the City of London Guild of Needlemakers

23 a penny more and up goes the donkey
inviting contributions to complete a sum of money; from the cry of a travelling showman

QUOTATIONS

24 Wine maketh merry: but money answereth all things.
Bible: Ecclesiastes

25 If possible honestly, if not, somehow, make money.
Horace 65–8 BC: *Epistles*; see 3 above, **Wealth** 22

26 No man can serve two masters . . . Ye cannot serve God and mammon.
Bible: St Matthew; see 16 above, **Choice** 4, **Wealth** 10

27 The love of money is the root of all evil.
Bible: I Timothy; see 9 above, **Idleness** 7

28 Money is like muck, not good except it be spread.
Francis Bacon 1561–1626: *Essays* (1625) 'Of Seditions and Troubles'; see 10, 15 above

29 Money speaks sense in a language all nations understand.
Aphra Behn 1640–89: *The Rover* pt. 2 (1681)

30 Money is the sinews of love, as of war.
George Farquhar 1678–1707: *Love and a Bottle* (1698); see **Warfare** 14

31 Take care of the pence, and the pounds will take care of themselves.
William Lowndes 1652–1724: Lord Chesterfield *Letters to his Son* (1774) 5 February 1750; see **Thrift** 9

32 Money . . . is none of the wheels of trade: it is the oil which renders the motion of the wheels more smooth and easy.
David Hume 1711–76: *Essays: Moral and Political* (1741–2) 'Of Money'

33 I want the whole of Europe to have one currency; it will make trading much easier.
Napoleon I 1769–1821: letter to his brother Louis, 6 May 1807

34 The force of the guinea you have in your pocket depends wholly on the default of a guinea in your neighbour's pocket. If he did not want it, it would be of no use to you.
John Ruskin 1819–1900: *Unto this Last* (1862)

35 Money is like a sixth sense without which you cannot make a complete use of the other five.
W. Somerset Maugham 1874–1965: *Of Human Bondage* (1915)

36 I'm tired of Love: I'm still more tired of Rhyme.
But Money gives me pleasure all the time.
Hilaire Belloc 1870–1953: 'Fatigued' (1923)

37 What is robbing a bank compared with founding a bank?
Bertolt Brecht 1898–1956: *Die Dreigroschenoper* (1928)

38 'My boy,' he says, 'always try to rub up against money, for if you rub up against money long enough, some of it may rub off on you.'
Damon Runyon 1884–1946: in *Cosmopolitan* August 1929, 'A Very Honourable Guy'

39 A bank is a place that will lend you money if you can prove that you don't need it.
Bob Hope 1903–2003: Alan Harrington *Life in the Crystal Palace* (1959)

40 Money, it turned out, was exactly like sex, you thought of nothing else if you didn't have it and thought of other things if you did.
James Baldwin 1924–87: in *Esquire* May 1961 'Black Boy looks at the White Boy'

41 For I don't care too much for money, For money can't buy me love.
John Lennon 1940–80 and **Paul McCartney** 1942– : 'Can't Buy Me Love' (1964 song)

42 Money doesn't talk, it swears.
Bob Dylan 1941– : 'It's Alright, Ma (I'm Only Bleeding)' (1965 song); see 12 above

43 Money makes the world go around.
Fred Ebb 1932–2004: 'Money Money' (1965 song), from the musical *Cabaret*; see **Love** 8

44 From now the pound abroad is worth 14 per cent or so less in terms of other currencies. It does not mean, of course, that the pound here in Britain, in your pocket or purse or in your bank, has been devalued.
Harold Wilson 1916–95: ministerial broadcast, 19 November 1967

45 Those who have some means think that the most important thing in the world is love. The poor know that it is money.
Gerald Brenan 1894–1987: *Thoughts in a Dry Season* (1978)

46 Pennies don't fall from heaven. They have to be earned on earth.
Margaret Thatcher 1925– : in *Observer* 18 November 1979; see **Optimism** 32

⤙ Morality ⤚

PROVERBS AND SAYINGS

1 **It is one thing to keep your morals on high plane; it's another to keep up with them.**
American proverb, mid 20th century

2 **Never do evil that good may come of it.**
the prospect of a good outcome cannot justify wrongdoing; English proverb, late 16th century

QUOTATIONS

3 Moral principles please our minds as beef and mutton and pork please our mouths.
Meng-tzu 371–289 BC: *The Book of Mencius*

4 Waste no more time arguing what a good man should be. Be one.
Marcus Aurelius AD 121–180: *Meditations*

5 *Cum finis est licitus, etiam media sunt licita.*
The end justifies the means.
Hermann Busenbaum 1600–68: *Medulla Theologiae Moralis* (1650); literally 'When the end is allowed, the means also are allowed'; see 20 below; **Ways and Means** 3

6 That action is best, which procures the greatest happiness for the greatest numbers.
Francis Hutcheson 1694–1746: *An Inquiry into the Original of our Ideas of Beauty and Virtue* (1725); see **Society** 10

7 State a moral case to a ploughman and a professor. The former will decide it as well, and often better than the latter, because he has not been led astray by artificial rules.
Thomas Jefferson 1743–1826: letter to Peter Carr, 10 August 1787

8 We know no spectacle so ridiculous as the British public in one of its periodical fits of morality.
Lord Macaulay 1800–59: *Essays Contributed to the Edinburgh Review* (1843) 'Moore's *Life of Lord Byron*'

9 And many are afraid of God—
And more of Mrs Grundy.
Frederick Locker-Lampson 1821–95: 'The Jester's Plea' (1868); see **Behaviour** 24

10 The highest possible stage in moral culture is when we recognize that we ought to control our thoughts.
Charles Darwin 1809–82: *The Descent of Man* (1871)

11 Morality is the herd-instinct in the individual.
Friedrich Nietzsche 1844–1900: *Die fröhliche Wissenschaft* (1882)

12 If your morals make you dreary, depend upon it they are wrong.
Robert Louis Stevenson 1850–94: 'A Christmas Sermon' (1888)

13 Morality is a private and costly luxury.
Henry Brooks Adams 1838–1918: *The Education of Henry Adams* (1907)

14 The nation's morals are like its teeth: the more decayed they are the more it hurts to touch them.
George Bernard Shaw 1856–1950: *The Shewing-up of Blanco Posnet* (1911)

15 Moral indignation is jealousy with a halo.
H. G. Wells 1866–1946: *The Wife of Sir Isaac Harman* (1914)

16 You can't learn too soon that the most useful thing about a principle is that it can always be sacrificed to expediency.
W. Somerset Maugham 1874–1965: *The Circle* (1921)

17 Food comes first, then morals.
Bertolt Brecht 1898–1956: *Die Dreigroschenoper* (1928)

18 In olden days a glimpse of stocking
Was looked on as something shocking
Now, heaven knows,
Anything goes.
Cole Porter 1891–1964: 'Anything Goes' (1934 song)

19 The last temptation is the greatest treason:
To do the right deed for the wrong reason.
T. S. Eliot 1888–1965: *Murder in the Cathedral* (1935)

20 The end cannot justify the means, for the simple and obvious reason that the means employed determine the nature of the ends produced.
Aldous Huxley 1894–1963: *Ends and Means* (1937); see 5 above

21 It is always easier to fight for one's principles than to live up to them.
Alfred Adler 1870–1937: Phyllis Bottome *Alfred Adler* (1939)

22 Morality's *not* practical. Morality's a gesture. A complicated gesture learned from books.
Robert Bolt 1924–95: *A Man for All Seasons* (1960)

23 Even a purely moral act that has no hope of any immediate and visible political effect can gradually and indirectly, over time, gain in political significance.
Václav Havel 1936– : letter to Alexander Dubček, August 1969

24 Values are tapes we play on the Walkman of the mind: any tune we choose so long as it does not disturb others.
Jonathan Sacks 1948– : *The Persistence of Faith* (1991)

25 There is no good or evil, there is only power, and those too weak to seek it.
J. K. Rowling 1965– : *Harry Potter and the Philosopher's Stone* (1997)

Mourning

see also **Sorrow**

PROVERBS AND SAYINGS

1 **A bellowing cow soon forgets her calf.**
the person who laments most loudly is the one who is soonest comforted; English proverb, late 19th century

2 **Grief is the price we pay for love.**
late 20th century saying; see 25 below

3 **Let the dead bury the dead.**
often used to mean that the past should be left undisturbed; English proverb, early 19th century,

PHRASES

6 **sackcloth and ashes**
a sign of penitence or mourning; used with biblical allusion to the wearing of sackcloth and having ashes sprinkled on the head, as in Matthew, 'if the mighty works, which were done in you, had been done in Tyre and Sidon, they would have repented long ago in sackcloth and ashes'

QUOTATIONS

8 Blessed are they that mourn: for they shall be comforted.
Bible: St Matthew

9 Grief fills the room up of my absent child,
Lies in his bed, walks up and down with me.
William Shakespeare 1564–1616: *King John* (1591–8)

10   All my pretty ones?
Did you say all? O hell-kite! All?
What! all my pretty chickens and their dam,
At one fell swoop?
William Shakespeare 1564–1616: *Macbeth* (1606); see **Thoroughness 6**

11 He first deceased; she for a little tried
To live without him: liked it not, and died.
Henry Wotton 1568–1639: 'Upon the Death of Sir Albertus Moreton's Wife' (1651)

12 How often are we to die before we go quite off this stage? In every friend we lose a part of ourselves, and the best part.
Alexander Pope 1688–1744: letter to Jonathan Swift, 5 December 1732

13 She lived unknown, and few could know
When Lucy ceased to be;
But she is in her grave, and, oh,
The difference to me!
William Wordsworth 1770–1850: 'She dwelt among the untrodden ways' (1800)

14 I have had playmates, I have had companions,

from the Bible (Matthew) 'Let the dead bury their dead'

4 **No flowers by request.**
an intimation that no flowers are desired at a funeral; see **Style 19**

5 **You can shed tears that she is gone or you can smile because she has lived.**
preface to the Order of Service at the funeral of Queen Elizabeth the Queen Mother, 2002

7 **wear the green willow**
grieve for the loss of a loved one, be in mourning; a branch or the leaves of the *willow* as a symbol of grief for unrequited love or the loss of a loved one

In my days of childhood, in my joyful school-days,—
All, all are gone, the old familiar faces.
Charles Lamb 1775–1834: 'The Old Familiar Faces'

15 Bombazine would have shown a deeper sense of her loss.
Elizabeth Gaskell 1810–65: *Cranford* (1853)

16 They told me, Heraclitus, they told me you were dead,
They brought me bitter news to hear and bitter tears to shed.
I wept as I remembered how often you and I
Had tired the sun with talking and sent him down the sky.
William Cory 1823–92: 'Heraclitus' (1858); translation of Callimachus 'Epigram'

17 Dead! and . . . never called me mother.
Mrs Henry Wood 1814–87: *East Lynne* (dramatized by T. A. Palmer, 1874, the words do not occur in the novel of 1861)

18 Do not stand at my grave and weep:
I am not there. I do not sleep.
I am a thousand winds that blow.
I am the diamond glints on snow . . .
Do not stand at my grave and cry;
I am not there, I did not die.
quoted in letter left by British soldier Stephen Cummins when killed by the IRA, March 1989
Mary E. Frye 1905–2004: originally circulated privately from 1932 on

19 He was my North, my South, my East and
  West,
  My working week and my Sunday rest,
  My noon, my midnight, my talk, my song;
  I thought that love would last for ever: I was
    wrong.
  W. H. Auden 1907–73: 'Funeral Blues' (1936)

20 Bereavement is a universal and integral part
  of our experience of love. It follows marriage
  as normally as marriage follows courtship or
  as autumn follows summer.
  C. S. Lewis 1898–1963: *A Grief Observed* (1961)

21 All I have I would have given gladly not to
  be standing here today.
  following the assassination of J. F. Kennedy
  Lyndon Baines Johnson 1908–73: first speech to
  Congress as President, 27 November 1963

22 Widow. The word consumes itself.
  Sylvia Plath 1932–63: 'Widow' (1971)

23 I can't think of a more wonderful
  thanksgiving for the life I have had than
  that everyone should be jolly at my funeral.
  Lord Mountbatten 1900–79: Richard Hough
  Mountbatten (1980)

24 The number of casualties will be more than
  any of us can bear.
  following the destruction of the World Trade Center
  in New York, 11 September 2001
  Rudy Giuliani 1944– : in *The Times* 12
  September 2001

25 Nothing that can be said can begin to take
  away the anguish and pain of these
  moments. Grief is the price we pay for love.
  Elizabeth II 1926– : message to prayer service for
  the families of British victims of the terrorist attacks in
  New York, 21 September 2001; see 2 above

⤙ Murder ⤚

see also **Death**

PROVERBS AND SAYINGS

1 **Blood will have blood.**
  killing will provoke further killing; English proverb,
  mid 15th century: in this form from Shakespeare
  Macbeth 'It will have blood, they say blood will have
  blood'

2 **Guns don't kill people; people kill
  people.**
  National Rifle Association slogan; see 22 below

3 **Killing no murder.**
  English proverb, mid 17th century; see 13 below

4 **Lizzie Borden took an axe
  And gave her mother forty whacks;**

**When she saw what she had done
She gave her father forty-one!**
popular rhyme in circulation after the acquittal of
Lizzie Borden, in June 1893, from the charge of
murdering her father and stepmother at Fall River,
Massachusetts on 4 August 1892

5 **Murder will out.**
  the crime of murder can never be successfully
  concealed; English proverb, early 14th century; see
  11 below

PHRASES

6 **licensed to kill**
  supposedly indicating that an agent is authorized by
  the Security Service to kill when engaged in counter-
  espionage; associated particularly with Ian Fleming's
  thriller-hero James Bond

7 **mark of Cain**
  the stigma of a murderer, a sign of infamy; the sign
  placed on Cain after the murder of Abel, originally as
  a sign of divine protection in exile; see also **Canada**
  3, **Order** 8, **Travel** 11

QUOTATIONS

8 Thou shalt not kill.
  Bible: Exodus; see 17 below; **Lifestyles** 10

9 Whoso slays a soul not to retaliate for a soul
  slain, nor for corruption done in the land,
  shall be as if he had slain mankind
  altogether.
  The Koran: sura 5

10 Will no one rid me of this turbulent priest?
  of Thomas Becket, Archbishop of Canterbury,
  murdered in Canterbury Cathedral, December 1170
  Henry II 1133–89: oral tradition

11 Mordre wol out; that se we day by day.
  Geoffrey Chaucer 1343–1400: *The Canterbury
  Tales* 'The Nun's Priest's Tale'; see 5 above

12 Murder most foul, as in the best it is;
But this most foul, strange, and unnatural.
William Shakespeare 1564–1616: *Hamlet* (1601)

13 Killing no murder briefly discourt in three questions.
an apology for tyrannicide
Edward Sexby d. 1658: title of pamphlet (1657); see 3 above

14 Assassination is the quickest way.
Molière 1622–73: *Le Sicilien* (1668)

15 Murder considered as one of the fine arts.
Thomas De Quincey 1785–1859: in *Blackwood's Magazine* February 1827; essay title

16 In that case, if we are to abolish the death penalty, let the murderers take the first step.
Alphonse Karr 1808–90: in *Les Guêpes* January 1849

17 Thou shalt not kill; but need'st not strive Officiously to keep alive.
Arthur Hugh Clough 1819–61: 'The Latest Decalogue' (1862); see 8 above

18 Kill a man, and you are an assassin. Kill millions of men, and you are a conqueror. Kill everyone, and you are a god.
Jean Rostand 1894–1977: *Pensées d'un biologiste* (1939)

19 Roast beef and Yorkshire, or roast pork and apple sauce, followed up by suet pudding and driven home, as it were, by a cup of mahogany-brown tea, have put you in just the right mood. Your pipe is drawing sweetly, the sofa cushions are soft underneath you, the fire is well alight, the air is warm and stagnant. In these blissful circumstances, what is it that you want to read about?
Naturally, about a murder.
George Orwell 1903–50: *Decline of the English Murder and other essays* (1965) title essay, written 1946

20 Television has brought back murder into the home—where it belongs.
Alfred Hitchcock 1899–1980: in *Observer* 19 December 1965

21 It might or might not be right to kill, but sometimes it is necessary.
Gerry Adams 1948– : view of the protagonist in a short story; *Before the Dawn* (1996)

22 The National Rifle Association says guns don't kill people, people do. But I think the gun helps. Just standing there, going 'Bang!'—that's not going to kill too many people.
Eddie Izzard 1962– : *Dress to Kill* (stageshow, San Francisco, 1998); see 2 above

23 I love you . . . That is what they were all saying down their phones, from the hijacked planes and the burning towers. There is only love, and then oblivion. Love was all they had to set against the hatred of their murderers.
of the last messages received from those trapped by terrorist attacks, 11 September 2001
Ian McEwan 1948– : in *Guardian* 15 September 2001

⇥ Music ⇤

see also **Jazz, Musicians, Singing**

PROVERBS AND SAYINGS

1 **Every good boy deserves favour.**
traditional mnemonic for the notes (E, G. B, D, F) on the lines of the treble clef stave

2 **It takes seven years to make a piper.**
Scottish proverb

3 **Music helps not the toothache.**
English proverb, mid 17th century

PHRASES

4 **music of the spheres**
the harmonious sound supposed to be produced by the motion of the celestial globes imagined by the older astronomers as revolving round the earth and respectively carrying with them the moon, sun, planets, and fixed stars; see **The Universe** 3

5 **Tin Pan Alley**
the world of composers and publishers of popular music; from the name given to a district in New York (28th Street, between 5th Avenue and Broadway) where many songwriters, arrangers, and music publishers were formerly based

6 **the tune the old cow died of**
a tedious badly played piece of music

QUOTATIONS

7 If music be the food of love, play on;
Give me excess of it, that, surfeiting,
The appetite may sicken, and so die.
William Shakespeare 1564–1616: *Twelfth Night*
(1601)

8 Music has charms to soothe a savage breast.
William Congreve 1670–1729: *The Mourning Bride*
(1697)

9 Too beautiful for our ears, and much too
many notes, dear Mozart.
of *The Abduction from the Seraglio* (1782)
Joseph II 1741–90: F. X. Niemetschek *Life of Mozart*
(1798)

10 Melody is the essence of music. I compare a
good melodist to a fine racer, and
counterpoints to hack post-horses.
Wolfgang Amadeus Mozart 1756–91: remark to
Michael Kelly, 1786; Michael Kelly *Reminiscences*
(1826)

11 A carpenter's hammer, in a warm summer
noon, will fret me into more than
midsummer madness. But those
unconnected, unset sounds are nothing to
the measured malice of music.
Charles Lamb 1775–1834: *Elia* (1823)

12 Hark, the dominant's persistence till it must
be answered to!
Robert Browning 1812–89: 'A Toccata of
Galuppi's' (1855)

13 But I struck one chord of music,
Like the sound of a great Amen.
Adelaide Ann Procter 1825–64: 'A Lost Chord'
(1858)

14 Hell is full of musical amateurs: music is the
brandy of the damned.
George Bernard Shaw 1856–1950: *Man and
Superman* (1903)

15 There is music in the air.
Edward Elgar 1857–1934: R. J. Buckley *Sir Edward
Elgar* (1905)

16 The symphony must be like the world. It
must embrace everything.
Gustav Mahler 1860–1911: remark to Sibelius,
Helsinki, 1907

17 It is only that which cannot be expressed
otherwise that is worth expressing in music.
Frederick Delius 1862–1934: in *Sackbut*
September 1920 'At the Crossroads'

18 Art is not national. It is international. Music
is not written in red, white and blue; it is
written with the heart's blood of the
composer.
Nellie Melba 1861–1931: *Melodies and Memories*
(1925)

19 Extraordinary how potent cheap music is.
Noël Coward 1899–1973: *Private Lives* (1930)

20 Music begins to atrophy when it departs too
far from the dance . . . poetry begins to
atrophy when it gets too far from music.
Ezra Pound 1885–1972: *The ABC of Reading* (1934)

21 The whole trouble with a folk song is that
once you have played it through there is
nothing much you can do except play it
over again and play it rather louder.
Constant Lambert 1905–51: *Music Ho!* (1934)

22 Down the road someone is practising scales,
The notes like little fishes vanish with a
wink of tails.
Louis MacNeice 1907–63: 'Sunday Morning'
(1935)

23 The whole problem can be stated quite
simply by asking, 'Is there a meaning to
music?' My answer to that would be, 'Yes.'
And 'Can you state in so many words what
the meaning is?' My answer to that would
be, 'No.'
Aaron Copland 1900–90: *What to Listen for in
Music* (1939)

24 If I don't practise for one day, I know it; if I
don't practise for two days, the critics know
it; if I don't practise for three days, the
audience knows it.
Ignacy Jan Paderewski 1860–1941: attributed;
Nat Shapiro *An Encyclopedia of Quotations about
Music* (1978)

25 Good music is that which penetrates the ear
with facility and quits the memory with
difficulty.
Thomas Beecham 1879–1961: speech, *c.*1950; in
New York Times 9 March 1961

26 The notes I handle no better than many
pianists. But the pauses between the
notes—ah, that is where the art resides!
Artur Schnabel 1882–1951: in *Chicago Daily News*
11 June 1958

27 Music is your own experience, your
thoughts, your wisdom. If you don't live it,
it won't come out of your horn.
Charlie Parker 1920–55: Nat Shapiro and Nat
Hentoff *Hear Me Talkin' to Ya* (1955)

28 I don't know whether I like it, but it's what I
meant.
on his 4th symphony
Ralph Vaughan Williams 1872–1958:
Christopher Headington *Bodley Head History of
Western Music* (1974)

29 The hills are alive with the sound of music,
With songs they have sung for a thousand
years.
Oscar Hammerstein II 1895–1960: 'The Sound of
Music' (1959 song)

30 You just pick a chord, go twang, and you've got music.
Sid Vicious 1957–79: attributed

31 Music is spiritual. The music business is not.
Van Morrison: in *The Times* 6 July 1990

32 Why waste money on psychotherapy when you can listen to the B Minor Mass?
Michael Torke 1961– : in *Observer* 23 September 1990 'Sayings of the Week'

33 Improvisation is too good to leave to chance.
Paul Simon 1942– : in *Observer* 30 December 1990

34 Rock is like a battery that must always go back to blues to get recharged.
Eric Clapton 1945– : attributed; M. Palmer *Small Talk, Big Names* (1993)

35 All of this music is only made with 12 miserable tones. It's extraordinary. This is the miracle of music.
Daniel Barenboim 1942– : in *Guardian* 13 August 2004

⇥Musicians ⇤

see also **Jazz**, **Music**

PHRASES

1 **The Fab Four**
George Harrison, John Lennon, Paul McCartney, and Ringo Starr; the four members of the pop and rock group the Beatles

2 **the waltz king**
Johann Strauss (1825–99), who composed many famous waltzes, such as *The Blue Danube* (1867)

QUOTATIONS

3 Tallis is dead and Music dies.
William Byrd 1543–1623: 'Ye Sacred Muses'

4 Difficult do you call it, Sir? I wish it were impossible.
on the performance of a celebrated violinist
Samuel Johnson 1709–84: William Seward *Supplement to the Anecdotes of Distinguished Persons* (1797)

5 Hats off, gentlemen—a genius!
on Chopin
Robert Schumann 1810–56: 'An Opus 2' (1831); H. Pleasants (ed.) *Schumann on Music* (1965)

6 We are the music makers,
We are the dreamers of dreams . . .
We are the movers and shakers
Of the world for ever, it seems.
Arthur O'Shaughnessy 1844–81: 'Ode' (1874); see **Change** 23

7 Please do not shoot the pianist. He is doing his best.
printed notice in a dancing saloon
Anonymous: Oscar Wilde *Impressions of America* 'Leadville' (c.1882–3)

8 I have been told that Wagner's music is better than it sounds.
Bill Nye 1850–96: Mark Twain *Autobiography* (1924)

9 It will be generally admitted that Beethoven's Fifth Symphony is the most sublime noise that has ever penetrated into the ear of man.
E. M. Forster 1879–1970: *Howards End* (1910)

10 Ravel refuses the Legion of Honour, but all his music accepts it.
Erik Satie 1866–1925: Jean Cocteau *Le Discours d'Oxford* (1956)

11 Bach almost persuades me to be a Christian.
Roger Fry 1866–1934: Virginia Woolf *Roger Fry* (1940)

12 Children are given Mozart because of the small *quantity* of the notes; grown-ups avoid Mozart because of the great *quality* of the notes.
Artur Schnabel 1882–1951: *My Life and Music* (1961)

13 There are two golden rules for an orchestra: start together and finish together. The public doesn't give a damn what goes on in between.
Thomas Beecham 1879–1961: Harold Atkins and Archie Newman *Beecham Stories* (1978)

14 If I play Tchaikovsky I play his melodies and skip his spiritual struggles . . . If there's any time left over I fill in with a lot of runs up and down the keyboard.
Liberace 1919–87: Stuart Hall and Paddy Whannel (eds.) *The Popular Arts* (1964)

15 Whether the angels play only Bach in praising God I am not quite sure; I am sure, however, that en famille they play Mozart.
Karl Barth 1886–1968: in *New York Times* 11 December 1968

16 A musician, if he's a messenger, is like a child who hasn't been handled too many times by man, hasn't had too many fingerprints across his brain.
Jimi Hendrix 1942–70: in *Life Magazine* (1969)

17 Most people get into bands for three very simple rock and roll reasons: to get laid, to get fame, and to get rich.
Bob Geldof 1954– : in *Melody Maker* 27 August 1977

18 If anyone has conducted a Beethoven performance, and then doesn't have to go to an osteopath, then there's something wrong.
Simon Rattle 1955– : in *Guardian* 31 May 1990

19 Beethoven tells you what it's like to be Beethoven and Mozart tells you what it's like to be human. Bach tells you what it's like be the universe.
Douglas Adams 1952–2001: attributed, in *Independent* 17 May 2001

⇢ Names ⇠

PROVERBS AND SAYINGS

1 By Tre, Pol, and Pen, you shall know the Cornish men.
traditional saying, referring to the frequency of these elements in Cornish names; English proverb, mid 16th century

2 If the cap fits, wear it.
used with reference to the assumed suitability of a name or description to a person's behaviour; English proverb, mid 18th century

3 If the shoe fits, wear it.
one has to accept it when a particular comment is shown to apply to oneself; found mainly in the US; English proverb, late 18th century

4 Only the camel knows the hundredth name of God.
saying from Arab folklore; see 5 below

PHRASES

5 ninety-nine names of God
in Islam, the names for Allah (in the main taken or derived from the Koran); see 5 above

6 a rose by any other name
an allusive reference to Shakespeare, referring to the arbitrary nature of names: see 8 below

QUOTATIONS

7 God hath also highly exalted him, and given him a name which is above every name:
That at the name of Jesus every knee should bow.
Bible: Philippians

8 What's in a name? that which we call a rose By any other name would smell as sweet.
William Shakespeare 1564–1616: *Romeo and Juliet* (1595); see 6 above

9 JAQUES: I do not like her name.
ORLANDO: There was no thought of pleasing you when she was christened.
William Shakespeare 1564–1616: *As You Like It* (1599)

10 If you should have a boy do not christen him John . . . 'Tis a bad name and goes against a man. If my name had been Edmund I should have been more fortunate.
John Keats 1795–1821: letter to his sister-in-law, 13 January 1820

11 A nickname is the heaviest stone that the devil can throw at a man.
William Hazlitt 1778–1830: *Sketches and Essays* (1839) 'Nicknames'

12 With a name like yours, you might be any shape, almost.
Lewis Carroll 1832–98: *Through the Looking-Glass* (1872)

13 I have fallen in love with American names, The sharp, gaunt names that never get fat, The snakeskin-titles of mining-claims, The plumed war-bonnet of Medicine Hat,

Tucson and Deadwood and Lost Mule Flat.
Stephen Vincent Benét 1898–1943: 'American Names' (1927)

14 Dear 338171 (May I call you 338?).
Noël Coward 1899–1973: letter to T. E. Lawrence, 25 August 1930

15 A self-made man may prefer a self-made name.
on Samuel Goldfish changing his name to Samuel Goldwyn
Learned Hand 1872–1961: Bosley Crowther *Lion's Share* (1957)

16 The name of a man is a numbing blow from which he never recovers.
Marshall McLuhan 1911–80: *Understanding Media* (1964)

17 Proper names are poetry in the raw. Like all poetry they are untranslatable.
W. H. Auden 1907–73: *A Certain World* (1970)

18 Every Tom, Dick and Harry is called Arthur.
to Arthur Hornblow, who was planning to name his son Arthur
Sam Goldwyn 1882–1974: Michael Freedland *The Goldwyn Touch* (1986)

19 No, I'm breaking it in for a friend.
when asked if Groucho were his real name
Groucho Marx 1890–1977: attributed

20 Just as crystallization of surnames was one of the steps in human civilization, their relinquishment gradually increases as we revert to savagery.
Anthony Powell 1905–2000: *Fisher King* (1986)

21 We do have these extraordinary names . . . When you see the sign 'African Primates Meeting' you expect someone to produce bananas.
at his retirement service as Archbishop of Cape Town, 23 June 1996
Desmond Tutu 1931– : in *Daily Telegraph* 24 June 1996

⤜ Nature ⤛

see also **The Earth, Life Sciences**

PROVERBS AND SAYINGS

1 **Nature abhors a vacuum.**
English proverb, mid 16th century; see 20 below

2 **You can drive out nature with a pitchfork but she keeps on coming back.**
English proverb, mid 16th century, from the Roman poet Horace (65–8 BC) *Epistles* 'You may drive out nature with a pitchfork, but she will always return'

PHRASES

3 **balance of nature**
a state of equilibrium produced by the interaction of living organisms, ecological balance

4 **Nature red in tooth and claw**
a ruthless personification of the creative and regulative physical power conceived of as operating in the material world; from Tennyson: see 13 below

QUOTATIONS

5 Nature does nothing without purpose or uselessly.
Aristotle 384–322 BC: *Politics*

6 It is far from easy to judge whether she has proved a kind parent to man or a harsh step-mother.
on nature
Pliny the Elder AD 23–79: *Historia Naturalis*

7 Be not blind, but open-eyed, to the great wonders of Nature, familiar, everyday objects though they be to thee. But men are more wont to be astonished at the sun's eclipse than at his unfailing rise.
Orchoth Zadikkim c.15th century: *Orchoth Zaddikim*

8 In her inventions nothing is lacking, and nothing is superfluous.
Leonardo da Vinci 1452–1519: Edward McCurdy (ed.) *Leonardo da Vinci's Notebooks* (1906)

9 And this our life, exempt from public haunt, Finds tongues in trees, books in the running brooks,

Sermons in stones, and good in everything.
William Shakespeare 1564–1616: *As You Like It* (1599)

10 The subtlety of nature is greater many times over than the subtlety of the senses and understanding.
Francis Bacon 1561–1626: *Novum Organum* (1620) tr. J. Spedding

11 All things are artificial, for nature is the art of God.
Thomas Browne 1605–82: *Religio Medici* (1643)

12 There is a pleasure in the pathless woods,
There is a rapture on the lonely shore,
There is society, where none intrudes,
By the deep sea, and music in its roar:
I love not man the less, but nature more.
Lord Byron 1788–1824: *Childe Harold's Pilgrimage* (1812–18)

13 Who trusted God was love indeed
And love Creation's final law—
Though Nature, red in tooth and claw
With ravine, shrieked against his creed.
Alfred, Lord Tennyson 1809–92: *In Memoriam A. H. H.* (1850); see 4 above

14 I believe a leaf of grass is no less than the journey-work of the stars,
And the pismire is equally perfect, and a grain of sand, and the egg of the wren,
And the tree toad is a chef-d'oeuvre for the highest,
And the running blackberry would adorn the parlours of heaven.
Walt Whitman 1819–92: 'Song of Myself' (written 1855)

15 What a book a devil's chaplain might write on the clumsy, wasteful, blundering, low, and horridly cruel works of nature!
Charles Darwin 1809–82: letter to J. D. Hooker, 13 July 1856

16 Nature is not a temple, but a workshop, and man's the workman in it.
Ivan Turgenev 1818–83: *Fathers and Sons* (1862)

17 In nature there are neither rewards nor punishments—there are consequences.
Robert G. Ingersoll 1833–99: *Some Reasons Why* (1881)

18 For nature, heartless, witless nature,
Will neither care nor know
What stranger's feet may find the meadow
And trespass there and go.
A. E. Housman 1859–1936: *Last Poems* (1922) no. 40

19 Nature, Mr Allnutt, is what we are put into this world to rise above.
James Agee 1909–55: *The African Queen* (1951 film); not in the novel by C. S. Forester

20 BRICK: Well, they say nature hates a vacuum, Big Daddy.
BIG DADDY: That's what they say, but sometimes I think that a vacuum is a hell of a lot better than some of the stuff that nature replaces it with.
Tennessee Williams 1911–83: *Cat on a Hot Tin Roof* (1955); see 1 above

21 Christianity deposes Mother Nature and begets, on her prostrate body, Science, which proceeds to destroy Nature.
Ted Hughes 1930–98: in *Your Environment* Summer 1970

22 People thought they could explain and conquer nature—yet the outcome is that they destroyed it and disinherited themselves from it.
Václav Havel 1936– : Lewis Wolpert *The Unnatural Nature of Science* (1993)

⤳ Necessity ⤲

1 **Any port in a storm.**
when one is in trouble or difficulty, support or shelter from any source is welcome; English proverb, mid 18th century

2 **Beggars can't be choosers.**
someone who is destitute is in no position to criticize what may be offered; English proverb, mid 16th century

3 **Desperate diseases must have desperate remedies.**
in a difficult or dangerous situation it may be necessary to take extreme and risky measures;

English proverb, mid 16th century; see **Medicine** 14, **Revolution** 5

4 **Even a worm will turn.**
even a meek person will resist or retaliate if pushed too far; English proverb, mid 16th century

5 **Hunger drives the wolf out of the wood.**
even the fiercest animal will be driven from shelter by acute need; English proverb, late 15th century

6 If the mountain will not come to Mahomet, Mahomet must go to the mountain.

used in the context of an apparently insoluble situation. The saying refers to a story of Muhammad recounted by Bacon in his *Essays*, in which the Prophet called a hill to him, and when it did not move, made this remark; English proverb, early 17th century

7 Make a virtue of necessity.

one should do with a good grace what is unavoidable; English proverb, late 14th century; see 17 below

8 Necessity is the mother of invention.

need is often a spur to the creative process; English proverb, mid 16th century

9 Necessity knows no law.

someone in extreme need will disregard rules or prohibitions; English proverb, late 14th century; see 20 below

10 Necessity sharpens industry.

American proverb, mid 20th century; see 8 above

11 Needs must when the devil drives.

used in recognition of overwhelming force of circumstance; English proverb, mid 15th century

12 When all fruit fails, welcome haws.

often used of someone taking of necessity an older or otherwise unsuitable lover (*haws*, the red fruit of the hawthorn, are contrasted with fruits generally eaten as food); English proverb, early 18th century

13 Who says A must say B.

only recorded in English from North American sources, and meaning that if a first step is taken, the second will inevitably follow; English proverb, mid 19th century

PHRASES

14 the breath of life

a necessity for continuing existence; from the Bible (Genesis) 'all in whose nostrils was the breath of life'

15 a wing and a prayer

reliance on hope or the slightest chance in a desperate situation; from a song (1943) by H.

Adamson, recounting an emergency landing by an aircraft: see **Crises** 19

QUOTATIONS

16 Nothing have I found stronger than Necessity.
Euripides c.485–c.406 BC: *Alcestis*

17 All places that the eye of heaven visits
Are to a wise man ports and happy havens.
Teach thy necessity to reason thus;
There is no virtue like necessity.
William Shakespeare 1564–1616: *Richard II* (1595); see 7 above

18 Must! Is *must* a word to be addressed to princes? Little man, little man! thy father, if he had been alive, durst not have used that word.
to Robert Cecil, on his saying she must go to bed
Elizabeth I 1533–1603: J. R. Green *A Short History of the English People* (1874)

19 Cruel necessity.
on the execution of Charles I, 1649
Oliver Cromwell 1599–1658: Joseph Spence *Anecdotes* (1820)

20 Necessity hath no law. Feigned necessities, imaginary necessities . . . are the greatest cozenage that men can put upon the Providence of God, and make pretences to break known rules by.
Oliver Cromwell 1599–1658: speech to Parliament, 12 September 1654; see 9 above

21 Necessity never made a good bargain.
Benjamin Franklin 1706–90: *Poor Richard's Almanac* (1735)

22 The superfluous, a very necessary thing.
Voltaire 1694–1778: *Le Mondain* (1736)

23 Necessity is the plea for every infringement of human freedom: it is the argument of tyrants; it is the creed of slaves.
William Pitt 1759–1806: speech, House of Commons, 18 November 1783

24 What throws a monkey wrench in
A fella's good intention?
That nasty old invention—
Necessity!
E. Y. Harburg 1898–1981: 'Necessity' (1947)

25 Necessity has the face of a dog.
Gabriel García Márquez 1928– : *In Evil Hour* (1968)

→→ News ←←

see also **Journalism**

PROVERBS AND SAYINGS

1 Bad news travels fast.
bad news is more likely to be talked about; English proverb, late 16th century

2 No news is good news.
often used in consolation or resignation; English proverb, early 17th century

3 One who sees something good must tell of it.
African proverb

PHRASES

4 dodgy dossier
informal name for a government briefing document on Iraqi weaponry which was later withdrawn; from a reference in the leading article in the *Observer* newspaper, 9 February 2003, to 'Downing Street's dodgy dossier of "intelligence" about Iraq'

5 shoot the messenger
treat the bearer of bad news as if they were to blame for it; often in the form, *don't shoot (or kill) the messenger!*; see 10 below

QUOTATIONS

6 Tell it not in Gath, publish it not in the streets of Askelon.
Bible: II Samuel

7 How beautiful upon the mountains are the feet of him that bringeth good tidings.
Bible: Isaiah

8 What news on the Rialto?
William Shakespeare 1564–1616: *The Merchant of Venice* (1596–8)

9 Ill news hath wings, and with the wind doth go,
Comfort's a cripple and comes ever slow.
Michael Drayton 1563–1631: *The Barons' Wars* (1603)

10 The nature of bad news infects the teller.
William Shakespeare 1564–1616: *Antony and Cleopatra* (1606–7); see 5 above

11 A master passion is the love of news.
George Crabbe 1754–1832: 'The Newspaper' (1785)

12 When a dog bites a man, that is not news, because it happens so often. But if a man bites a dog, that is news.
John B. Bogart 1848–1921: F. M. O'Brien *The Story of the* [New York] *Sun* (1918); often attributed to Charles A. Dana

13 News is what a chap who doesn't care much about anything wants to read. And it's only news until he's read it. After that it's dead.
Evelyn Waugh 1903–66: *Scoop* (1938)

14 You might get bigger audiences for 'Noble Rover, the labrador, who saved beautiful baby in fire', but that ain't news—just an insidious form of patronising propaganda.
on the desirability of promoting 'good news' stories
John Simpson 1944– : interview in *Radio Times* 9 August 1997

Night see **Day and Night**

→→ Old Age ←←

see also **Middle Age**

PROVERBS AND SAYINGS

1 The gods send nuts to those who have no teeth.
opportunities or pleasures often come too late to be enjoyed; English proverb, early 20th century

2 The older the ginger the more pungent its flavour.
older people have more knowledge and experience than the young; Chinese proverb

3 An old horse does not spoil the furrow.

Russian proverb; see 4 below

4 There's many a good tune played on an old fiddle.

someone's abilities to not depend on their being young; English proverb, early 20th century

5 There's no fool like an old fool.

often used to suggest that folly in an older person, who should be wiser, is particularly acute; English proverb, mid 16th century

6 When an elder dies, it is as if a whole library has burned down.

African proverb

7 When drinking water, remember the source.

advocating filial piety; Chinese proverb

PHRASES

8 Indian summer

a tranquil late period of life; a period of fine weather in late autumn: see **Weather** 25

9 threescore and ten

the age of seventy; in reference to the biblical span of a person's life: see 11 below

QUOTATIONS

10 Then shall ye bring down my grey hairs with sorrow to the grave.
Bible: Genesis

11 The days of our age are threescore years and ten; and though men be so strong that they come to fourscore years: yet is their strength then but labour and sorrow; so soon passeth it away, and we are gone.
Bible: Psalm 90; see 9 above

12   Last scene of all,
That ends this strange eventful history,
Is second childishness, and mere oblivion,
Sans teeth, sans eyes, sans taste, sans everything.
William Shakespeare 1564–1616: *As You Like It* (1599)

13 No spring, nor summer beauty hath such grace,
As I have seen in one autumnal face.
John Donne 1572–1631: 'The Autumnal' (*c.*1600)

14 I have lived long enough: my way of life
Is fall'n into the sear, the yellow leaf.
William Shakespeare 1564–1616: *Macbeth* (1606); see **Middle Age** 6

15 Age will not be defied.
Francis Bacon 1561–1626: *Essays* (1625) 'Of Regimen of Health'

16 Every man desires to live long; but no man would be old.
Jonathan Swift 1667–1745: *Thoughts on Various Subjects* (1727 ed.)

17 Those that desire to write or say anything to me have no time to lose; for time has shaken me by the hand and death is not far behind.
John Wesley 1703–91: letter to Ezekiel Cooper, 1 February 1791

18 Age does not make us childish, as men tell,
It merely finds us children still at heart.
Johann Wolfgang von Goethe 1749–1832: *Faust* pt. 1 (1808)

19 Grow old along with me!
The best is yet to be.
Robert Browning 1812–89: 'Rabbi Ben Ezra' (1864)

20 It is better to be seventy years young than forty years old!
Oliver Wendell Holmes 1809–94: reply to invitation from Julia Ward Howe to her seventieth birthday party, 27 May 1889

21 The tragedy of old age is not that one is old, but that one is young.
Oscar Wilde 1854–1900: *The Picture of Dorian Grey* (1891)

22 When you are old and grey and full of sleep,
And nodding by the fire, take down
    this book
And slowly read and dream of the soft look
Your eyes had once, and of their shadows deep.
W. B. Yeats 1865–1939: 'When You Are Old' (1893)

23 Oh, to be seventy again!
on seeing a pretty girl on his eightieth birthday
Georges Clemenceau 1841–1929: James Agate diary, 19 April 1938; also attributed to Oliver Wendell Holmes Jnr.

24 From the earliest times the old have rubbed it into the young that they are wiser than they, and before the young had discovered what nonsense this was they were old too, and it profited them to carry on the imposture.
W. Somerset Maugham 1874–1965: *Cakes and Ale* (1930)

25 Old age is the most unexpected of all things that happen to a man.
Leon Trotsky 1879–1940: diary 8 May 1935

26 You will recognize, my boy, the first sign of old age: it is when you go out into the streets of London and realize for the first time how young the policemen look.
Seymour Hicks 1871–1949: C. R. D. Pulling *They Were Singing* (1952)

27 Do not go gentle into that good night,
Old age should burn and rave at close
   of day;
Rage, rage against the dying of the light.
Dylan Thomas 1914–53: 'Do Not Go Gentle into that Good Night' (1952)

28 To me old age is always fifteen years older than I am.
Bernard Baruch 1870–1965: in *Newsweek* 29 August 1955

29 Considering the alternative, it's not too bad at all.
when asked what he felt about the advancing years on his seventy-second birthday
Maurice Chevalier 1888–1972: Michael Freedland *Maurice Chevalier* (1981)

30 Hope I die before I get old.
Pete Townshend 1945– : 'My Generation' (1965 song)

31 Will you still need me, will you still feed me, When I'm sixty four?
John Lennon 1940–80 and **Paul McCartney** 1942– : 'When I'm Sixty Four' (1967 song)

32 What is called the serenity of age is only perhaps a euphemism for the fading power to feel the sudden shock of joy or sorrow.
Arthur Bliss 1891–1975: *As I Remember* (1970)

33 The man who works and is not bored is never old.
Pablo Casals 1876–1973: J. Lloyd Webber (ed.) *Song of the Birds* (1985)

34 When I am an old woman I shall wear
   purple
With a red hat which doesn't go, and
   doesn't suit me.
Jenny Joseph 1932– : 'Warning' (1974)

35 While there's snow on the roof, it doesn't mean the fire has gone out in the furnace.
John G. Diefenbaker 1895–1979: approaching his 80th birthday, Ottawa, 17 September 1975

36 With full-span lives having become the norm, people may need to learn how to be aged as they once had to learn how to be adult.
Ronald Blythe 1922– : *The View in Winter* (1979)

37 The unending problem of growing old was not how he changed, but how things did.
Toni Morrison 1931– : *Tar Baby* (1981)

38 I saw how hard it is for our own society ever to become wise while old people are ostracized.
George Monbiot: *No Man's Land* (1994)

39 Old people have one advantage compared with young ones. They have been young themselves, and young people haven't been old.
Lord Longford 1905–2001: in *Independent* 6 March 1999

Opinion

PROVERBS AND SAYINGS

1 **He that complies against his will is of his own opinion still.**
English proverb, late 17th century, from Samuel Butler: see 15 below

2 **So many men, so many opinions.**
the greater the number of people involved, the greater the number of different opinions there will be; English proverb, late 14th century, from Terence (*c*.190–159 BC) *Phormio* 'There are as many opinions as there are people: each has his own correct way'

3 **Those who never retract their opinions, love themselves more than they love truth.**
American proverb, mid 20th century

4 **Thought is free.**
while speech and action can be limited, one's powers of imagination and speculation cannot be regulated; English proverb, late 14th century

5 **The wish is father to the thought.**
one's opinions are often influenced by one's wishes; English proverb, late 16th century, from Shakespeare *2 Henry IV* 'Thy wish was father, Harry, to that thought'

PHRASES

6 appeal from Philip drunk to Philip sober
suggest that an opinion or decision represents a passing mood only; alluding to Philip of Macedon, father of Alexander the Great, who is said to have been the subject of such an appeal

7 hearts and minds
people as represented by their emotions and intellect; originally with biblical allusion: see **Peace** 8; see 10 below, **Speeches** 14

8 no comment
I do not intend to express an opinion; traditional expression of refusal to answer journalists' questions

9 vox populi
expressed general opinion; Latin = voice of the people; see **Democracy 2**

10 win hearts and minds
gain emotional or intellectual support; especially used in the context of the Vietnam War: see 7 above

QUOTATIONS

11 People who only see one side of things
Engage in quarrels and disputes.
Pali Tripitaka c. 2nd century BC: *The Udāna* [Solemn Utterances]

12 A plague of opinion! a man may wear it on both sides, like a leather jerkin.
William Shakespeare 1564–1616: *Troilus and Cressida* (1602)

13 Opinion in good men is but knowledge in the making.
John Milton 1608–74: *Areopagitica* (1644)

14 They that approve a private opinion, call it opinion; but they that mislike it, heresy: and yet heresy signifies no more than private opinion.
Thomas Hobbes 1588–1679: *Leviathan* (1651)

15 He that complies against his will,
Is of his own opinion still.
Samuel Butler 1612–80: *Hudibras* pt. 3 (1680); see 1 above

16 Some praise at morning what they blame at night;
But always think the last opinion right.
Alexander Pope 1688–1744: *An Essay on Criticism* (1711)

17 Have not the wisest of men in all ages, not excepting Solomon himself,—have they not had their Hobby-Horses . . . and so long as a man rides his Hobby-Horse peaceably and quietly along the King's highway, and neither compels you or me to get up behind him,—pray, Sir, what have either you or I to do with it?
Laurence Sterne 1713–68: *Tristram Shandy* (1759–67)

18 Every man has a right to utter what he thinks truth, and every other man has a right to knock him down for it. Martyrdom is the test.
Samuel Johnson 1709–84: James Boswell *Life of Samuel Johnson* (1791) 1780

19 A man can brave opinion, a woman must submit to it.
Mme de Staël 1766–1817: *Delphine* (1802)

20 If all mankind minus one were of one opinion, and only one person were of the contrary opinion, mankind would be no more justified in silencing that one person, than he, if he had the power, would be justified in silencing mankind.
John Stuart Mill 1806–73: *On Liberty* (1859)

21 There are nine and sixty ways of constructing tribal lays,
And—every—single—one—of—them—is—right!
Rudyard Kipling 1865–1936: 'In the Neolithic Age' (1893)

22 It were not best that we should all think alike; it is difference of opinion that makes horse-races.
Mark Twain 1835–1910: *Pudd'nhead Wilson* (1894)

23 Thank God, in these days of enlightenment and establishment, everyone has a right to his own opinions, and chiefly to the opinion that nobody else has a right to theirs.
Ronald Knox 1888–1957: *Reunion All Round* (1914)

24 An intellectual hatred is the worst,
So let her think opinions are accursed.
W. B. Yeats 1865–1939: 'A Prayer for My Daughter' (1920)

25 The opinions that are held with passion are always those for which no good ground exists; indeed the passion is the measure of the holder's lack of rational conviction.
Bertrand Russell 1872–1970: *Sceptical Essays* (1928)

26 Why should you mind being wrong if someone can show you that you are?
A. J. Ayer 1910–89: attributed

27 You might very well think that. I couldn't possibly comment.
the Chief Whip's habitual response to questioning
Michael Dobbs 1948– : *House of Cards* (televised 1990)

28 I've never had a humble opinion. If you've got an opinion, why be humble about it?
Joan Baez 1941– : in *Observer* 29 February 2004

Opportunity

PROVERBS AND SAYINGS

1 All is fish that comes to the net.
everything can be used to advantage; English proverb, early 16th century

2 All is grist that comes to the mill.
all experience or knowledge is useful (*grist* is corn that is ground to make flour); English proverb, mid 17th century

3 A bleating sheep loses a bite.
opportunities may be lost through idle chatter; English proverb, late 16th century

4 Every dog has his day.
everyone, however insignificant, has a moment of strength and power; English proverb, mid 16th century

5 He that will not when he may, when he will he shall have nay.
if an opportunity is not taken when offered, it may well not occur again; English proverb, late 10th century

6 It's not what you know, but whom you know.
American proverb, mid 20th century

7 Make hay while the sun shines.
one should take advantage of favourable circumstances which may not last; English proverb, mid 16th century

8 The mill cannot grind with the water that is past.
an opportunity that has been missed cannot then be used; English proverb, early 17th century

9 No time like the present.
often used to urge swift and immediate action; English proverb, mid 16th century

10 Opportunities look for you when you are worth finding.
North American proverb, mid 20th century; see also 12 below

11 Opportunity never knocks twice at any man's door.
a chance once missed will not occur again; English proverb, mid 16th century

12 Opportunity never knocks for persons not worth a rap.
American proverb, mid 20th century; see also 10 above

13 A person who misses his chance, and the monkey who misses his branch, can't be saved.
Indian proverb; see 11 above

14 A postern door makes a thief.
referring to the opportunity offered by a back or side entrance; English proverb, mid 15th century

15 Strike while the iron is hot.
one should take advantage of opportunity; the allusion was originally to the work of a blacksmith; English proverb, late 14th century; see 32 below

16 Take the goods the gods provide.
one should accept and be grateful for unearned benefits; English proverb, late 17th century

17 Time and tide wait for no man.
often used as an exhortation to act, in the knowledge that a favourable moment will not last for ever; English proverb, late 14th century

18 When one door shuts, another opens.
as one possible course of action is closed off, another opportunity offers; English proverb, late 16th century

19 When the cat's away, the mice will play.
many will take advantage of a situation in which rules are not enforced or authority is lacking; English proverb, early 17th century

20 The world is one's oyster.
opportunities are unlimited; an *oyster* as a delicacy and a source of pearls. Perhaps originally with allusion to Shakespeare's *Merry Wives of Windsor* (1597), 'the world's mine oyster, which I, with sword will open'; English proverb, early 17th century

PHRASES

21 in the last chance saloon
having been allowed one final opportunity to improve or get things right, from the fanciful idea of a saloon bar with this name; see **Children** 23

22 room at the top
opportunity to join an élite or the top ranks of a profession; see **Ambition** 5

23 second bite at the cherry
another attempt or opportunity to do something; a *cherry* as the type of something to be consumed in a single bite (in original proverbial use, to *take two bites at the cherry* indicated a person's behaving with affected nicety)

24 streets paved with gold
proverbial view of a city in which opportunities for advancement are easy; as in George Colman the

Younger's *The Heir at Law* (1797) 'Oh, London is a fine town, A very famous city, Where all the streets are paved with gold'

25 take time by the forelock

not let a chance slip away; from the personification of Time as bald except for a forelock; see 31 below

QUOTATIONS

27 Time is that wherein there is opportunity, and opportunity is that wherein there is no great time.
Hippocrates *c.*460–357 BC: *Precepts*

28 How oft the sight of means to do ill deeds Makes ill deeds done!
William Shakespeare 1564–1616: *King John* (1591–8)

29 There is a tide in the affairs of men, Which, taken at the flood, leads on to fortune.
William Shakespeare 1564–1616: *Julius Caesar* (1599)

30 If any man can shew any just cause, why they may not lawfully be joined together, let him now speak, or else hereafter for ever hold his peace.
The Book of Common Prayer 1662: *Solemnization of Matrimony*

31 But on occasion's forelock watchful wait.
John Milton 1608–74: *Paradise Regained* (1671); see 25 above

32 We must beat the iron while it is hot, but we may polish it at leisure.
John Dryden 1631–1700: *Aeneis* (1697); see 15 above

26 window of opportunity

a free or suitable interval or period of time for a particular event or action; deriving from *launch window*, a period outside which the planned launch of a spacecraft cannot take place if the journey is to be completed, owing to the changing positions of the planets; especially used in connection with the US–Soviet arms race

33 *La carrière ouverte aux talents.*
The career open to the talents.
Napoleon I 1769–1821: Barry E. O'Meara *Napoleon in Exile* (1822); see 34 below

34 To the very last he [Napoleon] had a kind of idea; that, namely, of *La carrière ouverte aux talents*, The tools to him that can handle them.
Thomas Carlyle 1795–1881: *Critical and Miscellaneous Essays* (1838) 'Sir Walter Scott'; see 33 above

35 Never the time and the place And the loved one all together!
Robert Browning 1812–89: 'Never the Time and the Place' (1883)

36 If only I could get down to Sidcup! I've been waiting for the weather to break. He's got my papers, this man I left them with, it's got it all down there, I could prove everything.
Harold Pinter 1930– : *The Caretaker* (1960)

37 She's got a ticket to ride, but she don't care.
John Lennon 1940–80 and **Paul MacCartney** 1942– : 'Ticket to Ride' (1965 song)

38 I opened the door for a lot of people, and they just ran through and left me holding the knob.
Bo Diddley 1928– : in 1971; M. Wrenn *Bitch, Bitch, Bitch* (1988)

⤜ Optimism and Pessimism ⤛

see also **Despair, Hope**

PROVERBS AND SAYINGS

1 All's for the best in the best of all possible worlds.

English proverb, early 20th century, from Voltaire; see 20 below

2 Another day, another dollar.

a world-weary comment on routine toil to earn a living, originally referring to the custom of paying sailors by the day, so that the longer the voyage, the greater the financial reward; American proverb, mid 20th century

3 Chickens are counted in autumn.

Russian proverb; compare 6 below

4 The darkest hour is just before dawn.

suggesting that the experience of complete despair may mean that matters have reached the lowest point and may shortly improve; English proverb, mid 17th century

5 Don't bargain for fish that are still in the water.

Indian proverb; see 8 below

6 **Don't count your chickens before they are hatched.**

one should not make, or act upon, an assumption (usually favourable) which may turn out to be ill-founded; English proverb, late 16th century; see 17 below; compare 3 above

7 **Don't halloo till you are out of the wood.**

you should not exult until danger and difficulty are past (*halloo* means shout in order to attract attention); English proverb, late 18th century

8 **Don't sell the skin till you have caught the bear.**

do not act upon an assumption of success which may turn out to be ill-founded; English proverb, late 16th century. Early versions have *lion* or *beast*; see also **Business 18**

9 **Every cloud has a silver lining.**

even the gloomiest circumstance has some hopeful element in it; English proverb, mid 19th century; see 34 below

10 **God's in his heaven; all's right with the world.**

English proverb, from early 16th century in the form 'God is where he was'; now largely replaced by this quotation from Browning; see 22 below

11 **If ifs and ands were pots and pans, there'd be no work for tinkers' hands.**

traditional response to an over-optimistic conditional expression, in which *ands* is the plural form of *and* = 'if'; English proverb, mid 19th century

12 **If wishes were horses, beggars would ride.**

what one wishes is often far from reality; English proverb, early 17th century

13 **It's an ill wind that blows nobody any good.**

good luck may arise from the source of another's misfortune; English proverb, mid 16th century

14 **The sharper the storm, the sooner it's over.**

the more intense something is, the shorter time it is likely to last; English proverb, late 19th century

15 **Turn your face to the sun, and the shadows fall behind you.**

recommending a positive attitude; modern saying, said to derive from a Maori proverb

16 **When things are at the worst they begin to mend.**

when a bad situation has reached its worst possible point, the next change must reflect at least a small improvement; English proverb, mid 18th century

PHRASES

17 **count one's chickens**

be overoptimistic, assume too much; from the proverb: see 6 above

QUOTATIONS

18 Sin is behovely, but all shall be well and all shall be well and all manner of thing shall be well.

behovely = expedient, necessary
Julian of Norwich 1343–after 1416: *Revelations of Divine Love*

19 Yet where an equal poise of hope and fear
Does arbitrate the event, my nature is
That I incline to hope, rather than fear,
And gladly banish squint suspicion.
John Milton 1608–74: *Comus* (1637)

20 In this best of possible worlds . . . all is for the best.

usually quoted as 'All is for the best in the best of all possible worlds'
Voltaire 1694–1778: *Candide* (1759); see 1 above, 30 below

21 There's a gude time coming.
Sir Walter Scott 1771–1832: *Rob Roy* (1817)

22 The lark's on the wing;
The snail's on the thorn:
God's in his heaven—
All's right with the world!
Robert Browning 1812–89: *Pippa Passes* (1841); see 10 above

23 I have known him come home to supper with a flood of tears, and a declaration that nothing was now left but a jail; and go to bed making a calculation of the expense of putting bow-windows to the house, 'in case anything turned up,' which was his favourite expression.

of Mr Micawber
Charles Dickens 1812–70: *David Copperfield* (1850)

24 In front the sun climbs slow, how slowly,
But westward, look, the land is bright.
Arthur Hugh Clough 1819–61: 'Say not the struggle naught availeth' (1855)

25 Nothing to do but work,
Nothing to eat but food,
Nothing to wear but clothes
To keep one from going nude.
Benjamin Franklin King 1857–94: 'The Pessimist'

26 If way to the Better there be, it exacts a full look at the worst.
Thomas Hardy 1840–1928: 'De Profundis' (1902)

27 Are we downhearted?
No! Let 'em all come!
Charles Knight and **Kenneth Lyle**: 'Here we are!
Here we are again!!' (1914 song)

28 'Twixt the optimist and pessimist
The difference is droll:
The optimist sees the doughnut
But the pessimist sees the hole.
McLandburgh Wilson b. 1892: *Optimist and
Pessimist* (c.1915)

29 Cheer up! the worst is yet to come!
Philander Chase Johnson 1866–1939: in
Everybody's Magazine May 1920

30 The optimist proclaims that we live in the
best of all possible worlds; and the pessimist
fears this is true.
James Branch Cabell 1879–1958: *The Silver
Stallion* (1926); see 20 above

31 Leave your worry on the doorstep,
Just direct your feet
To the sunny side of the street.
Dorothy Fields 1905–74: 'On the Sunny Side of the
Street' (1930 song)

32 Every time it rains, it rains
Pennies from heaven.
Don't you know each cloud contains
Pennies from heaven?
Johnny Burke 1908–64: 'Pennies from Heaven'
(1936 song); see **Money 46, Surprise 6**

33 You've got to ac-cent-tchu-ate the positive
Elim-my-nate the negative
Latch on to the affirmative
Don't mess with Mister In-between.
Johnny Mercer 1909–76: 'Ac-cent-tchu-ate the
Positive' (1944 song)

34 There are bad times just around the corner,
There are dark clouds travelling through
the sky
And it's no good whining
About a silver lining
For we know from experience that they
won't roll by.
Noël Coward 1899–1973: 'There are Bad Times Just
Around the Corner' (1953 song); see 9 above

35 Everything's coming up roses.
Stephen Sondheim 1930– : title of song (1959)

36 When you're depressed, there *are* no
molehills.
Randall Jarrell 1914–65: William H. Pritchard
Randall Jarrell: A Literary Life (1990); see **Value 16**

37 If we see light at the end of the tunnel,
It's the light of the oncoming train.
Robert Lowell 1917–77: 'Since 1939' (1977); see
Adversity 7

38 I don't consider myself a pessimist. I think
of a pessimist as someone who is waiting for
it to rain. And I feel soaked to the skin.
Leonard Cohen 1934– : in *Observer* 2 May 1993

39 I don't mind grappling with the fact that
there is no Santa Claus, but I still want to be
allowed to believe in living happily ever
after.
Vanessa Feltz 1962– : in *Sunday Times* 2
September 2001; see **Ending 3**

⤞ Order and Chaos ⤝

PROVERBS AND SAYINGS

1 **The Devil is in the details.**
the most difficult part of planning and achieving
something is the detailed specification rather than
the overall concept; English proverb, late 20th
century; see **Architecture 20**

2 **One day of chaos is worse than a
thousand years of tyranny.**
stability under an oppressive regime may be
preferable to anarchy (the number of years may

fluctuate); modern saying, said to derive from an
Arab proverb

3 **A place for everything, and
everything in its place.**
English proverb, mid 17th century, often associated
with the 19th-century writer on self-help Samuel
Smiles; see **Administration 9**

PHRASES

4 **alarms and excursions**
confused noise and bustle; *alarums and excursions*
an old stage-direction occurring in Shakespeare *3
Henry VI* and *Richard III*

5 **all hell let loose**
a state of utter confusion and uproar, utter
pandemonium; from Milton: see 13 below

6 flutter the dovecots

startle or perturb a sedate or conventionally-minded community; from Shakespeare's *Coriolanus* 'like an eagle in a dove-cote, I Fluttered your Volscians in Corioli'

7 a pretty kettle of fish

an awkward state of affairs, a mess; *kettle* = a long pan for cooking fish in liquid

8 raise Cain

make a disturbance, cause trouble; *Cain* the eldest son of Adam, who in the Bible (Genesis) is said to have murdered his younger brother Abel; see also **Canada** 3, **Murder** 7, **Travel** 11

9 shipshape and Bristol fashion

with all in good order; *Bristol* a city and port in the west of England; originally a nautical expression

10 Sturm und Drang

(a period of) emotion, stress, or turbulence; German, literally 'storm and stress', title of a 1776 play by Friedrich Maximilian Klinger (1752–1831)

11 to the (four) winds

in all directions; so as to be abandoned or neglected, from Milton's *Paradise Lost*: 'And fear of death deliver to the winds'; *the four winds* blowing from each of the points of the compass, and often personified as such

QUOTATIONS

12 All things began in order, so shall they end, and so shall they begin again; according to the ordainer of order and mystical mathematics of the city of heaven.
Thomas Browne 1605–82: *The Garden of Cyrus* (1658)

13 But wherefore thou alone? Wherefore with thee
Came not all hell broke loose?
said by Gabriel to Satan
John Milton 1608–74: *Paradise Lost* (1667); see 5 above

14 With ruin upon ruin, rout on rout,
Confusion worse confounded.
John Milton 1608–74: *Paradise Lost* (1667)

15 Good order is the foundation of all good things.
Edmund Burke 1729–97: *Reflections on the Revolution in France* (1790)

16 Chaos often breeds life, when order breeds habit.
Henry Brooks Adams 1838–1918: *The Education of Henry Adams* (1907)

17 Things fall apart; the centre cannot hold;
Mere anarchy is loosed upon the world,
The blood-dimmed tide is loosed, and everywhere
The ceremony of innocence is drowned.
W. B. Yeats 1865–1939: 'The Second Coming' (1921)

18 I'm interested in anything about revolt, disorder, chaos, especially activity that appears to have no meaning. It seems to me to be the road toward freedom.
Jim Morrison 1943–71: in *Time* 24 January 1968

19 I'm at my best in a messy, middle-of-the-road muddle.
Harold Wilson 1916–95: remark in Cabinet, 21 January 1975; Philip Ziegler *Wilson* (1993)

⤜ Originality ⤛

PHRASES

1 an Arabian bird

a unique specimen; a phoenix, in allusion to Shakespeare *Cymbeline* 'She is alone the Arabian bird, and I Have lost the wager'

2 break the mould

make impossible the repetition of a certain type of creation; put an end to a pattern of events or behaviour by setting markedly different standards; originally with reference to Ariosto: see **Excellence** 10

3 rara avis

a person or thing of a kind rarely encountered; a unique or exceptional person; Latin, from the Roman satirist Juvenal (c.60–c.140) *Rara avis in terris nigroque simillima cycno.* 'A rare bird on this earth, like nothing so much as a black swan'; see **Birds** 4

4 a white crow

a rare thing or event; recorded from the 16th century

QUOTATIONS

5 The saying of the noble and glorious Aeschylus, who declared that his tragedies were large cuts taken from Homer's mighty dinners.
Aeschylus c.525–456 BC: Athenaeus *Deipnosophistae*

6 Nothing has yet been said that's not been said before.
Terence c.190–159 BC: *Eunuchus*

7 It could be said of me that in this book I have only made up a bunch of other men's flowers, providing of my own only the string that ties them together.
Montaigne 1533–92: *Essais* (1580)

8 They lard their lean books with the fat of others' works.
Robert Burton 1577–1640: *The Anatomy of Melancholy* (1621–51)

9 Not wrung from speculations and subtleties, but from common sense, and observation; not picked from the leaves of any author, but bred among the weeds and tares of mine own brain.
Thomas Browne 1605–82: *Religio Medici* (1643)

10 The original writer is not he who refrains from imitating others, but he who can be imitated by none.
François-René Chateaubriand 1768–1848: *Le Génie du Christianisme* (1802)

11 Never forget what I believe was observed to you by Coleridge, that every great and original writer, in proportion as he is great and original, must himself create the taste by which he is to be relished.
William Wordsworth 1770–1850: letter to Lady Beaumont, 21 May 1807

12 Make copies, young man, many copies. You can only become a good artist by copying the masters.
Jean Ingres 1780–1867: to Degas; A. Vollard *Souvenirs d'un marchand de tableaux* (1937)

13 The truth is that the propensity of man to imitate what is before him is one of the strongest parts of his nature.
Walter Bagehot 1826–77: *Physics and Politics* (1872) 'Nation-Making'

14 Immature poets imitate; mature poets steal.
T. S. Eliot 1888–1965: *The Sacred Wood* (1920) 'Philip Massinger'

15 If you steal from one author, it's plagiarism; if you steal from many, it's research.
Wilson Mizner 1876–1933: Alva Johnston *The Legendary Mizners* (1953)

16 No plagiarist can excuse the wrong by showing how much of his work he did not pirate.
Learned Hand 1872–1961: *Sheldon v. Metro-Goldwyn Pictures Corp.* 1936

17 It is sometimes necessary to repeat what we all know. All map-makers should place the Mississippi in the same location, and avoid originality.
Saul Bellow 1915–2005: *Mr Sammler's Planet* (1969)

18 Let's have some new clichés.
Sam Goldwyn 1882–1974: attributed, perhaps apocryphal

Painting and Drawing

see also **The Arts, Photography, Sculpture**

PROVERBS AND SAYINGS

1 **A good painter can draw a devil as well as an angel.**
English proverb, late 16th century

2 **Not a day without a line.**
traditional saying, attributed to the Greek artist Apelles (fl. 325 BC) by Pliny the Elder

PHRASES

3 **Giotto's O**
the perfect circle supposedly drawn freehand by the Italian painter Giotto (*c.*1267–1337)

4 **warts and all**
including features or qualities that are not appealing or attractive; from Cromwell: see 6 below

QUOTATIONS

5 Good painters imitate nature, bad ones spew it up.
Cervantes 1547–1616: *El Licenciado Vidriera* (1613)

6 Remark all these roughnesses, pimples, warts, and everything as you see me; otherwise I will never pay a farthing for it.
to the painter Lely; see 4 above
Oliver Cromwell 1599–1658: Horace Walpole *Anecdotes of Painting in England* vol. 3 (1763)

7 An imitation in lines and colours on any surface of all that is to be found under the sun.
of painting
Nicolas Poussin 1594–1665: letter to M. de Chambray, 1665

8 A mere copier of nature can never produce anything great.
Joshua Reynolds 1723–92: *Discourses on Art* 14 December 1770

9 The sound of water escaping from mill-dams, etc., willows, old rotten planks, slimy posts, and brickwork . . . those scenes made me a painter and I am grateful.
John Constable 1776–1837: letter to John Fisher, 23 October 1821

10 *Le dessin est la probité de l'art.*
Drawing is the true test of art.
J. A. D. Ingres 1780–1867: *Pensées d'Ingres* (1922)

11 I have seen, and heard, much of Cockney impudence before now; but never expected to hear a coxcomb ask two hundred guineas for flinging a pot of paint in the public's face.
on Whistler's *Nocturne in Black and Gold*
John Ruskin 1819–1900: *Fors Clavigera* (1871–84) letter 79, 18 June 1877

12 I own I like definite form in what my eyes are to rest upon; and if landscapes were sold, like the sheets of characters of my boyhood, one penny plain and twopence coloured, I should go the length of twopence every day of my life.
Robert Louis Stevenson 1850–94: *Travels with a Donkey* (1879); see **Style** 3

13 You should not paint the chair, but only what someone has felt about it.
Edvard Munch 1863–1944: written c.1891; R. Heller *Munch* (1984)

14 Treat nature in terms of the cylinder, the sphere, the cone, all in perspective.
Paul Cézanne 1839–1906: letter to Emile Bernard, 1904; Emile Bernard *Paul Cézanne* (1925)

15 Monet is only an eye, but what an eye!
Paul Cézanne 1839–1906: attributed

16 What I dream of is an art of balance, of purity and serenity devoid of troubling or depressing subject matter . . . a soothing, calming influence on the mind, rather like a good armchair which provides relaxation from physical fatigue.
Henri Matisse 1869–1954: *Notes d'un peintre* (1908)

17 It's with my brush that I make love.
often quoted as 'I paint with my prick'
Pierre Auguste Renoir 1841–1919: A. André *Renoir* (1919)

18 An active line on a walk, moving freely without a goal. A walk for walk's sake.
Paul Klee 1879–1940: *Pedagogical Sketchbook* (1925)

19 Every time I paint a portrait I lose a friend.
John Singer Sargent 1856–1925: N. Bentley and E. Esar *Treasury of Humorous Quotations* (1951)

20 No, painting is not made to decorate apartments. It's an offensive and defensive weapon against the enemy.
Pablo Picasso 1881–1973: interview with Simone Téry, 24 March 1945, in Alfred H. Barr *Picasso* (1946)

21 A picture equals a movement in space.
Emily Carr 1871–1945: *Hundreds and Thousands: The Journals of Emily Carr* (1966) August 1935

22 I am a painter and I nail my pictures together.
Kurt Schwitters 1887–1948: R. Hausmann *Am Anfang war Dada* (1972)

23 I paint my own reality.
Frida Kahlo 1907–54: Hayden Herrera *Frida* (1983)

24 When I was the age of these children I could draw like Raphael: it took me many years to learn how to draw like these children.
to Herbert Read, when visiting an exhibition of childen's drawings
Pablo Picasso 1881–1973: quoted in letter from Read to *The Times* 27 October 1956

25 There was a reviewer a while back who wrote that my pictures didn't have any beginning or any end. He didn't mean it as a compliment, but it was. It was a fine compliment.
Jackson Pollock 1912–56: Francis V. O'Connor *Jackson Pollock* (1967)

26 Painting is saying 'Ta' to God.
Stanley Spencer 1891–1959: letter from Spencer's daughter Shirin to *Observer* 7 February 1988

27 If Botticelli were alive today he'd be working for *Vogue*.
Peter Ustinov 1921–2004: in *Observer* 21 October 1962

28 A product of the untalented, sold by the unprincipled to the utterly bewildered.
on abstract art
Al Capp 1907–79: in *National Observer* 1 July 1963

29 I rarely draw what I see—I draw what I feel in my body.
Barbara Hepworth 1903–75: Alan Bowness *Barbara Hepworth—Drawings from a Sculptor's Landscape* (1966)

30 When you are interested in life more than you are in painting, then your paintings can come to life.
Jack Chambers 1931–78: William Withrow *Contemporary Painting in Canada* (1972)

31 All painting, no matter what you're painting, is abstract in that it's got to be organized.
David Hockney 1937– : *David Hockney* (1976)

32 I find a particular delight in taking the caricature as far as I can. It satisfies me to stretch the human frame about and recreate it and yet keep a likeness.
Gerald Scarfe 1936– : *Scarfe by Scarfe* (1986)

33 Mostly painting is like putting a message in a bottle and flinging it into the sea.
Howard Hodgkin 1932– : in *Observer* 10 June 2001

The Paranormal

see also **The Supernatural**

PROVERBS AND SAYINGS

1 **It's life, Jim, but not as we know it.**
late 20th century saying associated with the television series *Star Trek* (1966–); the saying does not occur in the series but derives from the 1987 song 'Star Trekkin' ' sung by The Firm

2 **The truth is out there.**
catchphrase from *The X Files* (American television series, 1993–), created by Chris Carter (1957–), in which two special agents repeatedly investigate cases which appear to involve the paranormal; final proof of extra-terrestrial activity, however, is always lacking

3 **We are not alone.**
advertising copy for the film *Close Encounters of the Third Kind* (1977); see 5 below

PHRASES

4 **Bermuda triangle**
a place where people or objects vanish without explanation; from an area of the West Atlantic Ocean where a disproportionately large number of ships and aeroplanes are said to have been mysteriously lost

5 **Close Encounter**
term used for a supposed encounter with a UFO; divided into categories, from a *Close Encounter of the First Kind* (sighting but no physical evidence), through Second (physical evidence left) and Third (extra-terrestrials beings observed) to a *Close Encounter of the Fourth Kind*, which involves abduction by aliens; see 8 below

6 **Fermi paradox**
a paradox suggested by a question asked by the Italian-born American physicist Enrico Fermi (see 14 below): if extraterrestrial civilizations exist throughout the galaxy, then they would have developed the technology to contact others, and evidence of such contact should be apparent on earth. But no such evidence has been observed

7 **near-death experience**
an unusual experience taking place on the brink of death and recounted by a person on recovery; see 17, 19 below

8 **Unidentified Flying Object**
a mysterious object seen in the sky for which it is claimed no orthodox scientific explanation can be found; often abbreviated to UFO. It is often supposed that UFOs, if real, must be vehicles carrying extraterrestrials, although other theories are put forward; see 5 above

QUOTATIONS

9 When the consciousness-principle getteth outside [the body it sayeth to itself] 'Am I dead or am I not dead?' It cannot determine. It seeth its relatives and connections as it had been used to seeing them before. It even heareth the wailings.
The Tibetan Book of the Dead 8th century: bk. 1, pt. 1

10 GLENDOWER: I can call spirits from the vasty deep.
HOTSPUR: Why, so can I, or so can any man;
But will they come when you do call for them?
William Shakespeare 1564–1616: *Henry IV, Part 1* (1597)

11 No testimony is sufficient to establish a miracle, unless the testimony be of such a kind, that its falsehood would be more miraculous than the fact which it endeavours to establish.
David Hume 1711–76: 'Of Miracles' (1748)

12 From the astrologer came the astronomer, from the alchemist the chemist, from the mesmerist the experimental psychologist. The quack of yesterday is the professor of tomorrow.
Arthur Conan Doyle 1859–1930: *Tales of Terror and Mystery* (1922)

13 Indubitably, Magic is one of the subtlest and most difficult of the sciences and arts. There is more opportunity for errors of comprehension, judgement and practice than in any other branch of physics.
Aleister Crowley 1875–1947: *The Confessions of Aleister Crowley* (1929)

14 But where is everybody?
on the existence of extraterrestrials
Enrico Fermi 1901–54: attributed, c.1950; see 6 above

15 About astrology and palmistry: they are good because they make people vivid and full of possibilities. They are communism at its best. Everybody has a birthday and almost everybody has a palm.
Kurt Vonnegut 1922– : *Wampeters, Foma and Granfalloons* (1974)

16 The fancy that extraterrestrial life is by definition of a higher order than our own is one that soothes all children, and many writers.
Joan Didion 1934– : *The White Album* (1979)

17 This was reality and all else an illusion.
on his near-death experience; see 7 above
Michael Bentine 1922–96: *The Door Marked Summer* (1981)

18 Black magic operates most effectively in preconscious, marginal areas. Casual curses are the most effective.
William S. Burroughs 1914–97: *The Western Lands* (1987)

19 Did you know that I was dead? The first time that I tried to cross the river I was frustrated, but my second attempt succeeded. It was most extraordinary. My thoughts became persons.
on his near-death experience; see 7 above
A. J. Ayer 1910–89: in *Sunday Telegraph* 28 August 1988

20 Mr Geller may have psychic powers by means of which he can bend spoons; if so, he appears to be doing it the hard way.
James Randi 1928– : *The Supernatural A-Z: the truth and the lies* (1995)

21 I don't believe in astrology; I'm a Sagittarius and we're sceptical.
Arthur C. Clarke 1917– : attributed; Nigel Rees *Cassell Dictionary of Humorous Quotations* (1999)

22 There is no such thing as magic, only acting.
Paul Daniels 1938– : *Under No Illusion* (2000, with Chris Gidney)

⇢ Parents ⇠

see also **Child Care, The Family**

PROVERBS AND SAYINGS

1 **It is a wise child that knows its own father.**
a child's legal paternity might not reflect an actual blood link; English proverb, late 16th century; see 8 below

2 **My son is my son till he gets him a wife, but my daughter's my daughter all the days of her life.**
while a man who establishes his own family relegates former blood ties to second place, a woman's filial role is not affected by her marriage; English proverb, late 17th century

QUOTATIONS

6 Honour thy father and thy mother.
Bible: Exodus; see **Lifestyles** 10

7 A wise son maketh a glad father: but a foolish son is the heaviness of his mother.
Bible: Proverbs

3 **Parents want their children to become dragons.**
parents want their children to be successful; Chinese proverb

4 **Praise the child, and you make love to the mother.**
English proverb, early 19th century

5 **To understand your parents' love, you must raise children yourself.**
Chinese proverb

8 It is a wise father that knows his own child.
William Shakespeare 1564–1616: *The Merchant of Venice* (1596–8); see 1 above

9 The joys of parents are secret, and so are their griefs and fears.
Francis Bacon 1561–1626: *Essays* (1625) 'Of Parents and Children'

10 After God comes my Papa—that was ever the motto, the axiom of my childhood and I cling to it still!
Wolfgang Amadeus Mozart 1756–91: letter to his father and sister, 7 March 1778

11 A slavish bondage to parents cramps every faculty of the mind.
Mary Wollstonecraft 1759–97: *A Vindication of the Rights of Woman* (1792)

12 The mother's yearning, that completest type of the life in another life which is the essence of real human love, feels the presence of the cherished child even in the debased, degraded man.
George Eliot 1819–80: *Adam Bede* (1859)

13 What *do* girls do who haven't any mothers to help them through their troubles?
Louisa May Alcott 1832–88: *Little Women* (1869)

14 For the hand that rocks the cradle
Is the hand that rules the world.
William Ross Wallace d. 1881: 'What rules the world' (1865); see **Women 3**

15 If I were damned of body and soul,
I know whose prayers would make me whole,
Mother o' mine, O mother o' mine.
Rudyard Kipling 1865–1936: *The Light That Failed* (1891)

16 Children begin by loving their parents; after a time they judge them; rarely, if ever, do they forgive them.
Oscar Wilde 1854–1900: *A Woman of No Importance* (1893)

17 Few misfortunes can befall a boy which bring worse consequences than to have a really affectionate mother.
W. Somerset Maugham 1874–1965: *A Writer's Notebook* (1949); written in 1896

18 The natural term of the affection of the human animal for its offspring is six years.
George Bernard Shaw 1856–1950: *Heartbreak House* (1919)

19 Your children are not your children.
They are the sons and daughters of Life's longing for itself.
They came through you but not from you
And though they are with you yet they belong not to you.
Kahlil Gibran 1883–1931: *The Prophet* (1923) 'On Children'

20 The affection you get back from children is sixpence given as change for a sovereign.
Edith Nesbit 1858–1924: J. Briggs *A Woman of Passion* (1987)

21 The fundamental defect of fathers, in our competitive society, is that they want their children to be a credit to them.
Bertrand Russell 1872–1970: *Sceptical Essays* (1928) 'Freedom versus Authority in Education'

22 Children aren't happy with nothing to ignore,
And that's what parents were created for.
Ogden Nash 1902–71: 'The Parent' (1933)

23 Nothing has a stronger influence on their children than the unlived lives of their parents.
Carl Gustav Jung 1875–1961: attributed; in *Boston Magazine* June 1978

24 There is no good father, that's the rule. Don't lay the blame on men but on the bond of paternity, which is rotten. To beget children, nothing better; to *have* them, what iniquity!
Jean-Paul Sartre 1905–80: *Les Mots* (1964) 'Lire'

25 No matter how old a mother is she watches her middle-aged children for signs of improvement.
Florida Scott-Maxwell: *Measure of my Days* (1968)

26 In our society mothers take the place elsewhere occupied by the Fates, the System, Negroes, Communism or Reactionary Imperialist Plots; mothers go on getting blamed until they're eighty, but shouldn't take it personally.
Katharine Whitehorn 1928– : *Observations* (1970)

27 Children always assume the sexual lives of their parents come to a grinding halt at their conception.
Alan Bennett 1934– : *Getting On* (1972)

28 It doesn't matter who my father was; it matters who I remember he was.
Anne Sexton 1928–74: diary, 1 January 1972

29 There must be many fathers around the country who have experienced the cruellest, most crushing rejection of all: their children have ended up supporting the wrong team.
Nick Hornby 1957– : *Fever Pitch* (1992)

30 I have reached the age when a woman begins to perceive that she is growing into the person she least plans to resemble: her mother.
Anita Brookner 1928– : *Incidents in the Rue Laugier* (1995)

31 Parents are the bones on which children sharpen their teeth.

Peter Ustinov 1921–2004: attributed, in *The Times* 30 March 2004

32 You can't understand it until you experience the simple joy of the first time your son points at a seagull and says 'duck'.

on fatherhood

Russell Crowe 1932– : in *Observer* 29 May 2005

➤➤ Parliament ⤜⤛

PROVERBS AND SAYINGS

1 I spy strangers!
the conventional formula demanding the exclusion from the House of Commons of non-members to whose presence attention is thus drawn

2 Who goes home?
formal question asked by the doorkeeper when the House of Commons adjourns

PHRASES

3 Administration of All the Talents
a coalition government, ironically regarded; the Ministry of Lord Grenville, 1806–7, a short-lived coalition ironically regarded as possessing all possible talents in its members

4 another place
the other House of Parliament (traditionally used in the Commons to refer to the Lords, and vice versa)

5 apply for the Chiltern Hundreds
resign from the House of Commons; *Chiltern Hundreds* a crown manor, the administration of which is a nominal office under the Crown and so requires an MP to vacate his or her seat

6 the best club in London
the House of Commons

7 Father of the House of Commons
the member with the longest continuous service

8 the Five Members
the members of the Long Parliament, Pym, Hampden, Haselrig, Holles, and Strode, whose arrest was unsuccessfully attempted by Charles I on 4 January 1642 in the House of Commons

9 His or Her Majesty's Opposition
the principal party opposed to the governing party in the British Parliament; John Cam Hobhouse, in

Recollections of a Long Life (1865), said of a debate in 1826, 'When I invented the phrase 'His Majesty's Opposition' [Canning] paid me a compliment on the fortunate hit'

10 Leader of the House
(in the House of Commons) an MP chosen from the party in office to plan the Government's legislative programme and arrange the business of the House; (in the House of Lords) the peer who acts as spokesman for the Government

11 Mr Balfour's poodle
the House of Lords; title of a book by Roy Jenkins (1954), in allusion to Lloyd George's comment: see 25 below

12 the West Lothian question
the constitutional anomaly that MPs for Scottish and Welsh constituencies are unable to vote on Scottish or Welsh matters that have been devolved to those assemblies, but are able to vote on equivalent matters concerning England, whilst MPs for English constituencies have no reciprocal influence on Scottish or Welsh policy. *West Lothian* is the name of a former parliamentary constituency in Central Scotland, whose MP, Tam Dalyell, persistently raised this question in Parliament in debates on Scottish and Welsh devolution during 1977–8

QUOTATIONS

13 A parliament can do any thing but make a man a woman, and a woman a man.

Henry Herbert, Lord Pembroke 1534–1601: quoted in 4th Earl of Pembroke's speech, 11 April 1648, proving himself Chancellor of Oxford

14 I have neither eye to see, nor tongue to speak here, but as the House is pleased to direct me.

the Speaker, on being asked if he had seen any of the five MPs whom the King had ordered to be arrested

William Lenthall 1591–1662: to Charles I, 4 January 1642; John Rushworth *Historical Collections. The Third Part* (1692)

15 I see all the birds are flown.

after attempting to arrest the Five Members; see 8 above

Charles I 1600–49: in the House of Commons, 4 January 1642; see **Liberty** 2

16 Take away that fool's bauble, the mace.

often quoted as, 'Take away these baubles'

Oliver Cromwell 1599–1658: at the dismissal of the Rump Parliament, 20 April 1653

17 Your representative owes you, not his industry only, but his judgement; and he betrays, instead of serving you, if he sacrifices it to your opinion.
Edmund Burke 1729–97: speech, Bristol, 3 November 1774

18 Though we cannot out-vote them we will out-argue them.
on the practical value of speeches in the House of Commons
Samuel Johnson 1709–84: James Boswell *Life of Samuel Johnson* (1791) 3 April 1778

19 The duty of an Opposition [is] very simple . . . to oppose everything, and propose nothing.
Edward Stanley, 14th Earl of Derby 1799–1869: quoting 'Mr Tierney, a great Whig authority', in the House of Commons, 4 June 1841

20 Your business is not to govern the country but it is, if you think fit, to call to account those who do govern it.
W. E. Gladstone 1809–98: speech to the House of Commons, 29 January 1855

21 England is the mother of Parliaments.
John Bright 1811–89: speech at Birmingham, 18 January 1865; see **Britain** 3

22 A cabinet is a combining committee—a *hyphen* which joins, a *buckle* which fastens, the legislative part of the state to the executive part of the state.
Walter Bagehot 1826–77: *The English Constitution* (1867) 'The Cabinet'

23 I am dead; dead, but in the Elysian fields.
to a peer, on his elevation to the House of Lords
Benjamin Disraeli 1804–81: W. Monypenny and G. Buckle *Life of Benjamin Disraeli* vol. 5 (1920)

24 When in that House MPs divide,
If they've a brain and cerebellum too,
They have to leave that brain outside,
And vote just as their leaders tell 'em to.
W. S. Gilbert 1836–1911: *Iolanthe* (1882)

25 The leal and trusty mastiff which is to watch over our interests, but which runs away at the first snarl of the trade unions . . . A

mastiff? It is the right hon. Gentleman's poodle.
on the House of Lords and A. J. Balfour
David Lloyd George 1863–1945: speech, House of Commons, 26 June 1907; see **11** above

26 They [parliament] are a lot of hard-faced men who look as if they had done very well out of the war.
Stanley Baldwin 1867–1947: J. M. Keynes *Economic Consequences of the Peace* (1919)

27 Think of it! A second Chamber selected by the Whips. A seraglio of eunuchs.
Michael Foot 1913– : speech, *Hansard* 3 February 1969

28 Parliament itself would not exist in its present form had people not defied the law.
Arthur Scargill 1938– : evidence to House of Commons Select Committee on Employment, 2 April 1980

29 The only safe pleasure for a parliamentarian is a bag of boiled sweets.
Julian Critchley 1930–2000: in *Listener* 10 June 1982

30 Being an MP is a good job, the sort of job all working-class parents want for their children—clean, indoors and no heavy lifting.
Diane Abbott 1953– : in *Independent* 18 January 1994

31 Being an MP feeds your vanity and starves your self-respect.
Matthew Parris 1949– : in *The Times* 9 February 1994

32 There can be no place in a 21st-century parliament for people with 15th-century titles upholding 19th-century prejudices.
Paddy Ashdown 1941– : comment, 24 November 1998

33 In the last Parliament, the House of Commons had more MPs called John than all the women MPs put together.
Tessa Jowell 1947– : in *Independent on Sunday* 14 March 1999 'Quotes'

34 To say that change at Westminster happens at a snail's pace is to insult the pace of snails.
Oona King 1967– : in *The Times* 25 November 2000

Parting see Meeting and Parting

->- The Past -<-

see also **History, Memory, The Present**

PROVERBS AND SAYINGS

1 Nostalgia isn't what it used to be.
graffito; taken as title of book by Simone
Signoret, 1978

2 Old sins cast long shadows.
current usage is likely to refer to the wrong done by
one generation affecting its descendants; English
proverb, early 20th century

**3 The past always looks better than it
was; it's only pleasant because it isn't
here.**
American proverb, late 19th century

4 The past at least is secure.
American proverb, early 19th century

5 The past is always ahead of us.
the past is a reminder of what has been and what
may be; Maori proverb

6 Things past cannot be recalled.
what has already happened cannot be changed;
English proverb, late 15th century

7 What's done cannot be undone.
English proverb, mid 15th century

**8 You have drunk from wells you did
not dig, and been warmed by fires you
did not build.**
the present generation depends on those who have
gone before; modern saying, said to be of native
American origin

PHRASES

9 ancien régime
the old system or style of things; French = former
regime, the system of government in France before
the Revolution of 1789

10 auld lang syne
times long past; literally 'old long since'; especially
as the title and refrain of a traditional song (see
Memory 9)

11 a fly in amber
a curious relic of the past, preserved into the
present; alluding to the fossilized bodies of insects
often found trapped in amber

12 the good old days
the past; regarded as better than the present; see 34
below, **The Present 16**

13 the naughty nineties
the 1890s; regarded as a time of liberalism and
permissiveness, especially in Britain and France

14 once upon a time
at some vague time in the past; usually as a
conventional opening of a story

15 the roaring twenties
the 1920s; regarded as a period of postwar
buoyancy following the end of the First World War

16 the swinging sixties
the 1960s; regarded as a period of release from
accepted social and cultural conventions

17 temps perdu
the past, contemplated with nostalgia and a sense of
irretrievability; French, literally 'time lost', originally
with allusion to Proust: see **Memory 4**

QUOTATIONS

18 Even a god cannot change the past.
literally 'The one thing which even God cannot do is
to make undone what has been done'
Agathon b. c.445 BC–: Aristotle *Nicomachaean
Ethics*; see **History 20**

19 *Mais où sont les neiges d'antan?*
But where are the snows of yesteryear?
François Villon b. c.1431: *Le Grand Testament*
(1461) 'Ballade des dames du temps jadis'

20 O! call back yesterday, bid time return.
William Shakespeare 1564–1616: *Richard II*
(1595)

21 Antiquities are history defaced, or some
remnants of history which have casually
escaped the shipwreck of time.
Francis Bacon 1561–1626: *The Advancement of
Learning* (1605)

22 There never was a merry world since the
fairies left off dancing, and the Parson left
conjuring.
John Selden 1584–1654: *Table Talk* (1689)

23 Old mortality, the ruins of forgotten times.
Thomas Browne 1605–82: *Hydriotaphia* (Urn
Burial, 1658)

24 Think of it, soldiers; from the summit of these pyramids, forty centuries look down upon you.
Napoleon I 1769–1821: speech, 21 July 1798, before the Battle of the Pyramids

25 Thy Naiad airs have brought me home, To the glory that was Greece And the grandeur that was Rome.
Edgar Allan Poe 1809–49: 'To Helen' (1831)

26 The splendour falls on castle walls And snowy summits old in story.
Alfred, Lord Tennyson 1809–92: *The Princess* (1847), song (added 1850)

27 The moving finger writes; and, having writ, Moves on: nor all thy piety nor wit Shall lure it back to cancel half a line, Nor all thy tears wash out a word of it.
Edward Fitzgerald 1809–83: *The Rubáiyát of Omar Khayyám* (1859)

28 I have gazed upon the face of Agamemnon.
on discovering a gold mask at Mycenae, 1876; traditional version of his telegram to the minister at Athens: 'This one is very like the picture which my imagination formed of Agamemnon long ago'
Heinrich Schliemann 1822–90: W. M. Calder and D. A. Traill *Myth, Scandal, and History* (1986)

29 What are those blue remembered hills, What spires, what farms are those? That is the land of lost content, I see it shining plain, The happy highways where I went And cannot come again.
A. E. Housman 1859–1936: *A Shropshire Lad* (1896)

30 Those who cannot remember the past are condemned to repeat it.
George Santayana 1863–1952: *The Life of Reason* (1905)

31 Stands the Church clock at ten to three? And is there honey still for tea?
Rupert Brooke 1887–1915: 'The Old Vicarage, Grantchester' (1915)

32 I tell you the past is a bucket of ashes.
Carl Sandburg 1878–1967: 'Prairie' (1918)

33 Things ain't what they used to be.
Ted Persons: title of song (1941)

34 In every age 'the good old days' were a myth. No one ever thought they were good at the time. For every age has consisted of crises that seemed intolerable to the people who lived through them.
Brooks Atkinson 1894–1984: *Once Around the Sun* (1951); see 12 above

35 The past is never dead. It's not even past.
William Faulkner 1897–1962: *Requiem for a Nun* (1951)

36 The past is a foreign country: they do things differently there.
L. P. Hartley 1895–1972: *The Go-Between* (1953)

37 An old teapot, used daily, can tell me more of my past than anything I recorded of it. Continuity . . . continuity . . . it is that which we cannot write down, it is that we cannot compass, record or control.
Sylvia Townsend Warner 1893–1978: letter to Alyse Gregory, 26 May 1953

38 People who are always praising the past And especially the times of faith as best Ought to go and live in the Middle Ages And be burnt at the stake as witches and sages.
Stevie Smith 1902–71: 'The Past' (1957)

39 Yesterday, all my troubles seemed so far away, Now it looks as though they're here to stay. Oh I believe in yesterday.
John Lennon 1940–80 and **Paul McCartney** 1942– : 'Yesterday' (1965 song)

40 Every age has the Stonehenge it deserves—or desires.
Jacquetta Hawkes 1910–96: in *Antiquity* no. 41, 1967

41 Hindsight is always twenty-twenty.
Billy Wilder 1906–2002: J. R. Columbo *Wit and Wisdom of the Moviemakers* (1979)

42 The past is like a collection of photographs: some are familiar and on constant display, others need searching for in dusty drawers.
John Mortimer 1923– : *Clinging to the Wreckage* (1982)

43 Reading about sex in yesterday's novels is like watching people smoke in old films.
Fay Weldon 1931– : in *Guardian* 1 December 1989

44 Thanks to modern technology . . . history now comes equipped with a fast-forward button.
Gore Vidal 1925– : *Screening History* (1992)

45 I think that today's youth have a tendency to live in the present and work for the future—and to be totally ignorant of the past.
Steven Spielberg 1947– : in *Independent on Sunday* 22 August 1999

⤞ Patience ⤝

see also **Determination, Haste and Delay**

PROVERBS AND SAYINGS

1 All commend patience, but none can endure to suffer.
American proverb, mid 20th century

2 All things come to those who wait.
often used as an adjuration to patience; English proverb, early 16th century

3 Bear and forbear.
recommending patience and tolerance; English proverb, late 16th century

4 Don't put the cart before the horse.
don't reverse the proper order of things; English proverb, early 16th century

5 First things first.
English proverb, late 19th century

6 Hurry no man's cattle.
sometimes used as an injunction to be patient with someone; English proverb, early 19th century

7 If you sit by the river long enough, you will see the body of your enemy float by.
advocating patience in the face of wrongs; modern saying, said to derive from a Japanese proverb

8 I sit on the shore, and wait for the wind.
what is expected will arrive sooner or later; Russian proverb

9 It is a long lane that has no turning.
commonly used as an assertion that an unfavourable situation will eventually change for the better; English proverb, mid 19th century

10 The longest way round is the shortest way home.
not trying to take a short cut is often the most effective way; English proverb, mid 17th century

11 Nothing should be done in haste but gripping a flea.
used as a warning against rash action; English proverb, mid 17th century

12 One step at a time.
recommending cautious progression along a desired route; English proverb, mid 19th century

13 Patience is a virtue.
often used as an exhortation; English proverb, late 14th century

14 Rome was not built in a day.
used to warn against trying to achieve too much at once; English proverb, mid 16th century

15 Slow but sure.
sure here means 'sure-footed, deliberate'; English proverb, late 17th century

16 Softly, softly, catchee monkey.
advocating caution or guile as the best way to achieve an end; English proverb, early 20th century

17 There is luck in leisure.
it is often advisable to wait before acting; English proverb, late 17th century

18 A watched pot never boils.
to pay too close an attention to the development of a desired event appears to inhibit the result; English proverb, mid 19th century

19 We must learn to walk before we can run.
a solid foundation is necessary for faster progress; English proverb, mid 14th century; see **Experience 16**

20 What can't be cured must be endured.
there is no point in complaining about what is unavoidable; English proverb, late 16th century

21 Where water flows, a channel is formed.
success will come when conditions are ripe; Chinese proverb

PHRASES

22 the patience of Job
unending patience; from the patriarch *Job*, whose patience and exemplary piety were tried by dire and undeserved misfortunes, and who, in spite of his bitter lamentations, remained finally confident in the goodness and justice of God (see 23 below); see **Sympathy 7**

-⇥-◅⟨-▻-⟩◦◅⟨-▻-⟩◦◅⟨-▻-⟩◦◅⟨-▻-⟩◦◅⟨-▻-⟩◦◅⟨-▻-⟩◦◅⟨-▻-⟩◦◅⟨-▻-⟩◦◅⟨-▻-⟩◦◅⟨-▻-⟩◦◅⟨-▻-⟩◦◅⟨-▻-⟩◦◅⟨-▻-⟩

QUOTATIONS

23 The Lord gave, and the Lord hath taken away; blessed be the name of the Lord.
Bible: Job; see 22 above

24 Let patience have her perfect work.
Bible: James

25 Let nothing trouble you, nothing frighten you. All things are passing; God never changes. Patient endurance attains all things.
St Teresa of Ávila 1512–82: 'St Teresa's Bookmark'; found in her breviary after her death

26 Still have I borne it with a patient shrug, For sufferance is the badge of all our tribe.
spoken by Shylock
William Shakespeare 1564–1616: *The Merchant of Venice* (1596–8)

27 Beware the fury of a patient man.
John Dryden 1631–1700: *Absalom and Achitophel* (1681)

28 Our patience will achieve more than our force.
Edmund Burke 1729–97: *Reflections on the Revolution in France* (1790)

29 Patience, that blending of moral courage with physical timidity.
Thomas Hardy 1840–1928: *Tess of the d'Urbervilles* (1891)

30 We had better wait and see.
referring to the rumour that the House of Lords was to be flooded with new Liberal peers to ensure the passage of the Finance Bill
Herbert Asquith 1852–1928: phrase used repeatedly in speeches in 1910; Roy Jenkins *Asquith* (1964)

31 Perhaps there is only one cardinal sin: impatience. Because of impatience we were driven out of Paradise; because of impatience we cannot return.
Franz Kafka 1883–1924: *Collected Aphorisms* no. 3

32 I am extraordinarily patient, provided I get my own way in the end.
Margaret Thatcher 1925– : in *Observer* 4 April 1989

⇢⟩⟩Patriotism ◅◅⟨

PROVERBS AND SAYINGS

1 **I'm backing Britain.**
slogan coined by workers at the Colt factory, Surbiton, Surrey in 1968, and subsequently used in a national campaign

2 **It's an ill bird that fouls its own nest.**
a condemnation of a person who brings his own family, home, or country into disrepute by his words or actions; English proverb, mid 13th century

3 **Lousy but loyal.**
London East End slogan at George V's Jubilee (1935)

PHRASES

4 **King and country**
the objects of allegiance for a patriot whose head of State is a king; see 26 below

5 **Queen and country**
the objects of allegiance for a patriot whose head of State is a queen

QUOTATIONS

6 I am not Athenian or Greek but a citizen of the world.
Socrates 469–399 BC: Plutarch *Moralia*

7 *Dulce et decorum est pro patria mori.*
Lovely and honourable it is to die for one's country.
Horace 65–8 BC: *Odes*; see **Warfare** 38

8 Not that I loved Caesar less, but that I loved Rome more.
Brutus' reason for killing Caesar
William Shakespeare 1564–1616: *Julius Caesar* (1599)

9 Never was patriot yet, but was a fool.
John Dryden 1631–1700: *Absalom and Achitophel* (1681)

10   What pity is it
That we can die but once to serve our country!
Joseph Addison 1672–1719: *Cato* (1713)

11   Be England what she will,
With all her faults, she is my country still.
Charles Churchill 1731–64: *The Farewell* (1764)

12 Patriotism is the last refuge of a scoundrel.
Samuel Johnson 1709–84: James Boswell *Life of Samuel Johnson* (1791) 7 April 1775

13 I only regret that I have but one life to lose for my country.
prior to his execution by the British for spying
Nathan Hale 1755–76: Henry Phelps Johnston *Nathan Hale, 1776* (1914)

14 These are the times that try men's souls. The summer soldier and the sunshine patriot will, in this crisis, shrink from the service of their country; but he that stands it *now*, deserves the love and thanks of men and women.
Thomas Paine 1737–1809: *The Crisis* (December 1776)

15 Breathes there the man, with soul so dead, Who never to himself hath said, This is my own, my native land!
Sir Walter Scott 1771–1832: *The Lay of the Last Minstrel* (1805)

16 Our country! In her intercourse with foreign nations, may she always be in the right; but our country, right or wrong.
Stephen Decatur 1779–1820: toast at Norfolk, Virginia, April 1816; A. S. Mackenzie *Life of Stephen Decatur* (1846); see 17 below

17 My toast would be, may our country be always successful, but whether successful or otherwise, always right.
John Quincy Adams 1767–1848: letter to John Adams, 1 August 1816; see 16 above

18 A steady patriot of the world alone, The friend of every country but his own.
on the Jacobins, extreme political radicals
George Canning 1770–1827: 'New Morality' (1821)

19 We don't want to fight, yet by jingo! if we do,
We've got the ships, we've got the men, and got the money too.
the origin of the term *jingoism*
G. W. Hunt ?1829–1904: 'We Don't Want to Fight' (1878 song)

20 If I should die, think only this of me: That there's some corner of a foreign field That is for ever England.
Rupert Brooke 1887–1915: 'The Soldier' (1914)

21 Standing, as I do, in view of God and eternity, I realize that patriotism is not enough. I must have no hatred or bitterness towards anyone.
on the eve of her execution for helping Allied soldiers to escape from occupied Belgium
Edith Cavell 1865–1915: in *The Times* 23 October 1915

22 I vow to thee, my country—all earthly things above—
Entire and whole and perfect, the service of my love.
Cecil Spring-Rice 1859–1918: 'I Vow to Thee, My Country' (1918)

23 You'll never have a quiet world till you knock the patriotism out of the human race.
George Bernard Shaw 1856–1950: *O'Flaherty V.C.* (1919)

24 You think you are dying for your country; you die for the industrialists.
Anatole France 1844–1924: in *L'Humanité* 18 July 1922

25 Patriotism is a lively sense of collective responsibility. Nationalism is a silly cock crowing on its own dunghill.
Richard Aldington 1892–1962: *The Colonel's Daughter* (1931)

26 That this House will in no circumstances fight for its King and Country.
D. M. Graham 1911–99: motion worded by Graham for a debate at the Oxford Union, of which he was Librarian, 9 February 1933 (passed by 275 votes to 153); see 4 above

27 *on H. G. Wells's comment on 'an alien and uninspiring court':*
I may be uninspiring, but I'll be damned if I'm an alien!
George V 1865–1936: Sarah Bradford *George VI* (1989); attributed, perhaps apocryphal

28 If I had to choose between betraying my country and betraying my friend, I hope I should have the guts to betray my country.
E. M. Forster 1879–1970: *Two Cheers for Democracy* (1951)

29 And so, my fellow Americans: ask not what your country can do for you—ask what you can do for your country.
John F. Kennedy 1917–63: inaugural address, 20 January 1961

30 I would die for my country but I could never let my country die for me.
Neil Kinnock 1942– : speech at Labour Party Conference, 30 September 1986

31 The cricket test—which side do they cheer for? . . . Are you still looking back to where you came from or where you are?
on the loyalties of Britain's immigrant population
Norman Tebbit 1931– : interview in *Los Angeles Times*; in *Daily Telegraph* 20 April 1990

32 I worry that patriotism run amok will trample the very values that the country seeks to defend.
Dan Rather 1931– : in *Independent* 18 May 2002

⤑ Peace ⤐

see also **Warfare**

PROVERBS AND SAYINGS

1 After a storm comes a calm.
often used with the implication that a calm situation is only achieved after stress and turmoil; English proverb, late 14th century

2 Ban the bomb.
US anti-nuclear slogan, 1953 onwards, adopted by the Campaign for Nuclear Disarmament

3 Nothing can bring you peace but yourself.
American proverb, mid 19th century

PHRASES

4 a Carthaginian peace
a peace settlement which imposes very severe terms on the defeated side; referring to the ultimate destruction of Carthage by Rome in the Punic Wars; see **Enemies** 7

5 an olive branch
a branch of an olive tree as an emblem of peace; any token of peace or goodwill; alluding to the Bible

(Genesis) 'And the dove came in to him in the evening; and lo, in her mouth was an olive leave pluckt off: so Noah knew that the waters were abated from off the earth'; see **Diplomacy** 17

6 peace with honour
a phrase recorded from the 17th century, used most famously by Disraeli: see **13** below

QUOTATIONS

7 They shall beat their swords into plowshares, and their spears into pruninghooks: nation shall not lift up sword against nation, neither shall they learn war any more.
Bible: Isaiah; see **Broadcasting** 3

8 The peace of God, which passeth all understanding, shall keep your hearts and minds through Christ Jesus.
Bible: Philippians; see **Opinion** 7

9 They make a wilderness and call it peace.
Tacitus c.AD 56–after 117: *Agricola*

10 . . . Peace hath her victories
No less renowned than war.
John Milton 1608–74: 'To the Lord General Cromwell' (written 1652)

11 It's a maxim not to be despised, 'Though peace be made, yet it's interest that keeps peace.'
Oliver Cromwell 1599–1658: speech to Parliament, 4 September 1654

12 Give peace in our time, O Lord.
The Book of Common Prayer 1662: *Morning Prayer*; see **20** below

13 Lord Salisbury and myself have brought you back peace—but a peace I hope with honour.
Benjamin Disraeli 1804–81: speech on returning from the Congress of Berlin, 16 July 1878; see **6** above, **20** below

14 In the arts of peace Man is a bungler.
George Bernard Shaw 1856–1950: *Man and Superman* (1903)

15 War makes rattling good history; but Peace is poor reading.
Thomas Hardy 1840–1928: *The Dynasts* (1904)

16 It is easier to make war than to make peace.
Georges Clemenceau 1841–1929: speech at Verdun, 20 July 1919

17 Peace is indivisible.
Maxim Litvinov 1876–1951: note to the Allies, 25 February 1920

18 I have many times asked myself whether there can be more potent advocates of peace upon earth through the years to come than this massed multitude of silent witnesses to the desolation of war.
George V 1865–1936: message read at Terlincthun Cemetery, Boulogne, 13 May 1922

19 I am not only a pacifist but a militant pacifist. I am willing to fight for peace. Nothing will end war unless the people themselves refuse to go to war.
Albert Einstein 1879–1955: interview with G. S. Viereck, January 1931

❖❖❖

20 This is the second time in our history that there has come back from Germany to Downing Street peace with honour. I believe it is peace for our time.
Neville Chamberlain 1869–1940: speech from 10 Downing Street, 30 September 1938; see 12, 13 above

21 One observes, they have gone too long without a war here. Where is morality to come from in such a case, I ask? Peace is nothing but slovenliness, only war creates order.
Bertolt Brecht 1898–1956: *Mother Courage* (1939)

22 Go placidly amid the noise and the haste, and remember what peace there may be in silence.
Max Ehrmann 1872–1945: 'Desiderata' (1948); often wrongly dated to 1692, the date of foundation of a church in Baltimore whose vicar circulated the poem in 1956

23 The work, my friend, is peace. More than an end of this war—an end to the beginnings of all wars.
Franklin D. Roosevelt 1882–1945: undelivered address for Jefferson Day, 13 April 1945 (the day after Roosevelt died)

24 The grim fact is that we prepare for war like precocious giants and for peace like retarded pygmies.
Lester Pearson 1897–1972: speech in Toronto, 14 March 1955

25 I think that people want peace so much that one of these days governments had better get out of the way and let them have it.
Dwight D. Eisenhower 1890–1969: broadcast discussion, 31 August 1959

26 You can't separate peace from freedom because no one can be at peace unless he has his freedom.
Malcolm X 1925–65: speech in New York, 7 January 1965

27 Give peace a chance.
John Lennon 1940–80 and **Paul McCartney** 1942– : title of song (1969)

28 Kissinger brought peace to Vietnam the same way Napoleon brought peace to Europe: by losing.
Joseph Heller 1923–99: *Good as Gold* (1979)

29 Enough of blood and tears. Enough.
Yitzhak Rabin 1922–95: at the signing of the Israel-Palestine Declaration, Washington, 13 September 1993

30 A war can perhaps be won single-handedly. But peace—lasting peace—cannot be secured without the support of all.
Luiz Inácio Lula da Silva 1945– : speech, United Nations, 23 September 2003

Peoples see Countries and Peoples

❖❖ Perfection ❖❖

see also Excellence

PROVERBS AND SAYINGS

1 **Trifles make perfection, but perfection is no trifle.**
American proverb, mid 20th century; from Michelangelo: see 4 below

PHRASES

2 **not the rose but near it**
not ideal but approaching or near this; the earliest version in English is found in an early 19th century translation of the *Gulistan* by the Persian poet Sadi (*c.*1213–*c.*1291)

QUOTATIONS

3 Nothing is an unmixed blessing.
Horace 65–8 BC: *Odes*

4 Trifles make perfection, and perfection is no trifle.
Michelangelo 1475–1564: attributed; Samuel Smiles *Self-Help* (1859); see 1 above

5 How many things by season seasoned are To their right praise and true perfection!
William Shakespeare 1564–1616: *The Merchant of Venice* (1596–8)

6 Perfection is the child of Time.
Joseph Hall 1574–1656: *Works* (1625)

7 Whoever thinks a faultless piece to see,
   Thinks what ne'er was, nor is, nor e'er
      shall be.
   Alexander Pope 1688–1744: *An Essay on Criticism*
   (1711)

8 Pictures of perfection as you know make me
   sick and wicked.
   Jane Austen 1775–1817: letter to Fanny Knight, 23
   March 1817

9 Faultily faultless, icily regular, splendidly
      null,
   Dead perfection, no more.
   Alfred, Lord Tennyson 1809–92: *Maud* (1855)

10 Faultless to a fault.
   Robert Browning 1812–89: *The Ring and the Book*
   (1868–9)

11 The pursuit of perfection, then, is the
   pursuit of sweetness and light . . . He who
   works for sweetness and light united, works
   to make reason and the will of God prevail.
   Matthew Arnold 1822–88: *Culture and Anarchy*
   (1869); see **Virtue 25**

12 Finality is death. Perfection is finality.
   Nothing is perfect. There are lumps in it.
   James Stephens 1882–1950: *The Crock of Gold*
   (1912)

13 The intellect of man is forced to choose
   Perfection of the life, or of the work.
   W. B. Yeats 1865–1939: 'The Choice' (1933)

14 Perfection is finally attained not when there
   is no longer anything to add but when there
   is no longer anything to take away, when a
   body has been stripped down to its
   nakedness.
   Antoine de Saint-Exupéry 1900–44: *Wind, Sand
   and Stars* (1939)

15 Perfection is terrible, it cannot have
      children.
   Sylvia Plath 1932–63: 'The Munich Mannequins'
   (1965)

Perseverance see **Determination and Perseverance**

Pessimism see **Optimism and Pessimism**

➤➤ Philosophy ◄◄

see also **Logic and Reason**

PROVERBS AND SAYINGS

1 **How many angels can dance on the
   head of a pin?**
   regarded satirically as a characteristic speculation of
   scholastic philosophy, particularly as exemplified by

'Doctor Scholasticus' (Anselm of Laon, d. 1117) and
as used in medieval comedies; see **8** below

PHRASES

2 **Occam's razor**
   the principle that in explaining a thing no more
   assumptions should be made than are necessary; an
   ancient philosophical principle often attributed to
   the English scholastic philosopher William of *Occam*
   (c.1285–1349), but earlier in origin; see **6** below

3 **the Socratic method**
   engaging in dialogue with others in an attempt to
   reach understanding and ethical concepts by
   exposing and dispelling error, after the Athenian
   philosopher *Socrates* (469–399 BC); see **17** below

QUOTATIONS

4 The unexamined life is not worth living.
   Socrates 469–399 BC: Plato *Apology*

5 There is nothing so absurd but some
   philosopher has said it.
   Cicero 106–43 BC: *De Divinatione*

6 No more things should be presumed to exist
   than are absolutely necessary.
   William of Occam 1285–1349: not found in this
   form in his writings, although he frequently used

similar expressions, e.g. 'Plurality should not be
assumed unnecessarily'; *Quodlibeta* (c.1324); see **2**
above

7 How charming is divine philosophy!
   Not harsh and crabbèd, as dull fools
      suppose,
   But musical as is Apollo's lute.
   John Milton 1608–74: *Comus* (1637)

8 Some who are far from atheists, may make themselves merry with that conceit of thousands of spirits dancing at once upon a needle's point.
Ralph Cudworth 1617–88: *The True Intellectual System of the Universe* (1678); see 1 above

9 The same principles which at first lead to scepticism, pursued to a certain point bring men back to common sense.
George Berkeley 1685–1753: *Three Dialogues between Hylas and Philonous* (1734)

10 Superstition sets the whole world in flames; philosophy quenches them.
Voltaire 1694–1778: *Dictionnaire philosophique* (1764) 'Superstition'

11 I have tried too in my time to be a philosopher; but, I don't know how, cheerfulness was always breaking in.
Oliver Edwards 1711–91: James Boswell *Life of Samuel Johnson* (1791) 17 April 1778

12 I am tempted to say of metaphysicians what Scaliger used to say of the Basques: they are said to understand one another, but I don't believe a word of it.
Nicolas-Sébastien Chamfort 1741–94: *Maximes et Pensées* (1796)

13 When philosophy paints its grey on grey, then has a shape of life grown old. By philosophy's grey on grey it cannot be rejuvenated but only understood. The owl of Minerva spreads its wings only with the falling of the dusk.
G. W. F. Hegel 1770–1831: *Philosophy of Right* (1821)

14 The philosophers have only interpreted the world in various ways; the point is to change it.
Karl Marx 1818–83: *Theses on Feuerbach* (written 1845, published 1888)

15 Metaphysics is the finding of bad reasons for what we believe upon instinct; but to find these reasons is no less an instinct.
F. H. Bradley 1846–1924: *Appearance and Reality* (1893)

16 What I understand by 'philosopher': a terrible explosive in the presence of which everything is in danger.
Friedrich Nietzsche 1844–1900: *Ecce Homo* (1908) 'Die Unzeitgemässen'

17 The Socratic manner is not a game at which two can play.
Max Beerbohm 1872–1956: *Zuleika Dobson* (1911); see 3 above

18 He [Wittgenstein] thinks nothing empirical is Knowable—I asked him to admit that there was not a rhinoceros in the room, but he wouldn't.
Bertrand Russell 1872–1970: letter to Lady Ottoline Morrell, November 1911

19 The safest general characterization of the European philosophical tradition is that it consists of a series of footnotes to Plato.
Alfred North Whitehead 1861–1947: *Process and Reality* (1929)

20 To ask the hard question is simple.
W. H. Auden 1907–73: title of poem (1933)

21 What is your aim in philosophy?—To show the fly the way out of the fly-bottle.
Ludwig Wittgenstein 1889–1951: *Philosophische Untersuchungen* (1953)

22 Students of the heavens are separable into astronomers and astrologers as readily as are the minor domestic ruminants into sheep and goats, but the separation of philosophers into sages and cranks seems to be more sensitive to frames of reference.
W. V. O. Quine 1908–2000: *Theories and Things* (1981)

23 What we do today, we don't have to do tomorrow. We don't even *think* about tomorrow. I was tellin' somebody that the other day; they say that's *existentialism*. I say, well, they probably copied that off of me.
Miles Davis 1926–91: Charles Shaar Murray *Shots From the Hip* (1991)

⇢⇢ Photography ⇠⇠

PROVERBS AND SAYINGS

1 **The camera never lies.**
20th century saying; see 8 below

2 **You press the button, we do the rest.**
advertising slogan to launch Kodak camera 1888, coined by George Eastman (1854–1932)

PHRASES

3 candid camera
the technique of photographing or filming people without their knowledge, chiefly in situations set up for the amusement of television viewers

4 decisive moment
the moment in which a photographer recognizes the precise significance and organization of the picture

QUOTATIONS

5 I longed to arrest all beauty that came before me, and at length the longing has been satisfied.
Julia Margaret Cameron 1815–79: *Annals of My Glass House* (1874)

6 The photographer is like the cod which produces a million eggs in order that one may reach maturity.
George Bernard Shaw 1856–1950: introduction to the catalogue for Alvin Langdon Coburn's exhibition at the Royal Photographic Society, 1906; Bill Jay and Margaret Moore *Bernard Shaw and Photography* (1989)

7 If your pictures aren't good enough, you aren't close enough.
of photojournalism
Robert Capa 1913–54: Russell Miller *Magnum: Fifty years at the Front Line of History* (1997)

8 The camera's eye
Does not lie,
But it cannot show
The life within.
W. H. Auden 1907–73: 'Runner' (1962); see 1 above

9 Nothing attracts me like a closed door. I cannot let my camera rest until I have pried it open.
Margaret Bourke-White 1906–71: *Portrait of Myself* (1964)

10 A photograph is a secret about a secret. The more it tells you the less you know.
Diane Arbus 1923–71: Patricia Bosworth *Diane Arbus: a Biography* (1985)

to be taken; used as the title of an exhibition and book by the French photographer Henri Cartier-Bresson in 1952, and deriving ultimately from de Retz: see **Management 6**

11 In photography you've got to be quick, quick, quick, like an animal and a prey.
Henri Cartier-Bresson 1908–2004: interview, 1979

12 It takes a lot of imagination to be a good photographer. You need less imagination to be a painter, because you can invent things. But in photography everything is so ordinary; it takes a lot of looking before you learn to see the ordinary.
David Bailey 1938– : interview in *The Face* December 1984

13 All you can do with most ordinary photographs is stare at them—they stare back, blankly—and presently your concentration begins to fade. They stare you down. I mean, photography is all right if you don't mind looking at the world from the point of view of a paralysed cyclops—*for a split second*.
David Hockney 1937– : as told to Lawrence Weschler, *Cameraworks* (1984)

14 Most things in life are moments of pleasure and a lifetime of embarrassment; photography is a moment of embarrassment and a lifetime of pleasure.
Tony Benn 1925– : in *Independent* 21 October 1989

15 It's more important to click with people than to click the shutter.
Alfred Eisenstaedt 1898–1995: in *Life* 24 August 1995

⤞ Physical Sciences ⤝

see also **Science**

PROVERBS AND SAYINGS

1 Laws of Thermodynamics:
1) **You cannot win, you can only break even.**
2) **You can only break even at absolute zero.**

3) **You cannot reach absolute zero.**
folklore amongst physicists; see 4 below

PHRASES

2 cold fusion
nuclear fusion occurring at or close to room temperature; claims for its discovery in 1989 are generally held to have been mistaken

3 fourth dimension
a postulated spatial dimension additional to those determining length, area, and volume; the phrase is recorded from the late 19th century, and is now also used in physics to denote time as analogous to linear dimensions

4 laws of thermodynamics
three laws describing the general direction of physical change in the universe; see 1 above, 11, 16 below; see also **Arts and Sciences** 11

5 Maxwell's demon
a hypothetical being imagined as controlling a hole in a partition dividing a gas-filled container into two parts, and allowing only fast-moving molecules to pass in one direction, and slow-moving molecules in the other. This would result in one side of the container becoming warmer and the other colder, in violation of the second law of thermodynamics. The name derives from the Scottish physicist James Clerk *Maxwell* (1831–79); see 16 below

6 perpetual motion
the motion of a hypothetical machine which, once activated, would run forever unless subject to an external force or to wear. Although impossible according to the first and second laws of thermodynamics, the development of such a mechanism has been attempted by many inventors; see 4 above

7 quark confinement
the hypothesis that free quarks can never be seen in isolation; *quark* = any of a number of subatomic particles carrying a fractional electric charge, postulated as building blocks of the hadrons. The name (originally *quork*) was invented in the 1960s by Murray Gell-Mann; it was changed by association with the line 'Three quarks for Muster Mark' in James Joyce's *Finnegans Wake* (1939)

8 Schrödinger's cat
a paradox concerning a cat in a sealed box containing a lethal device triggered by radioactive decay; an outside observer cannot know whether the device has been set off and the cat killed. According to quantum mechanics the cat is in an indeterminate state, some combination of alive and dead, until the box is opened, at which point it will be found to be one or the other. The paradox was suggested in 1935 by the Austrian theoretical physicist Erwin Schrödinger (1887–1961), to illustrate the conceptual difficulties of quantum mechanics

9 uncertainty principle
the principle that the momentum and position of a particle cannot both be precisely determined at the same time; see **Ideas** 10, **Science** 27

QUOTATIONS

10 There was a young lady named Bright,
Whose speed was far faster than light;
She set out one day
In a relative way
And returned on the previous night.
Arthur Buller 1874–1944: 'Relativity' in *Punch* 19 December 1923

11 If someone points out to you that your pet theory of the universe is in disagreement with Maxwell's equations—then so much the worse for Maxwell's equations. If it is found to be contradicted by observation—well, these experimentalists do bungle things sometimes. But if your theory is found to be against the second law of thermodynamics I can give you no hope; there is nothing for it but to collapse in deepest humiliation.
Arthur Eddington 1882–1944: *The Nature of the Physical World* (1928); see 4 above

12 If we assume that the last breath of, say, Julius Caesar has by now become thoroughly scattered through the atmosphere, then the chances are that each of us inhales one molecule of it with every breath we take.
now usually quoted as the 'dying breath of Socrates'
James Jeans 1877–1946: *An Introduction to the Kinetic Theory of Gases* (1940)

13 I remembered the line from the Hindu scripture, the *Bhagavad Gita* . . . 'I am become death, the destroyer of worlds.'
on the explosion of the first atomic bomb near Alamogordo, New Mexico, 16 July 1945
J. Robert Oppenheimer 1904–67: Len Giovannitti and Fred Freed *The Decision to Drop the Bomb* (1965)

14 In some sort of crude sense which no vulgarity, no humour, no overstatement can quite extinguish, the physicists have known sin; and this is a knowledge which they cannot lose.
J. Robert Oppenheimer 1904–67: lecture at Massachusetts Institute of Technology, 25 November 1947

15 If I could remember the names of all these particles I'd be a botanist.
Enrico Fermi 1901–54: R. L. Weber *More Random Walks in Science* (1973)

16 Heat won't pass from a cooler to a hotter,
You can try it if you like but you'd far better
notter.
Michael Flanders 1922–75 and **Donald Swann**
1923–94: 'The First and Second Law' (1956 song);
see 4, 5 above

17 It would be a poor thing to be an atom in a
world without physicists. And physicists are
made of atoms. A physicist is an atom's way
of knowing about atoms.
George Wald 1904–97: foreword to L. J. Henderson
The Fitness of the Environment (1958)

18 We do not know why they have the masses
they do; we do not know why they
transform into another the way they do; we
do not know anything! The one concept
that stands like the Rock of Gibraltar in our
sea of confusion is the Pauli [exclusion]
principle.
of elementary particles
George Gamow 1904–68: in *Scientific American*
July 1959

19 Anybody who is not shocked by this subject
has failed to understand it.
of quantum mechanics
Niels Bohr 1885–1962: attributed; in *Nature* 23
August 1990

20 Neutrinos, they are very small
They have no charge and have no mass
And do not interact at all.
John Updike 1932– : 'Cosmic Gall ' (1964)

21 There is no democracy in physics. We can't
say that some second-rate guy has as much
right to opinion as Fermi.
Luis Walter Alvarez 1911–88: D. S. Greenberg *The
Politics of Pure Science* (1969)

22 I am acutely aware of the fact that the
marriage between mathematics and physics,
which was so enormously fruitful in past
centuries, has recently ended in divorce.
Freeman Dyson 1923– : in *Bulletin of the American
Mathematical Society* September 1972

⇥ Pleasure ⇤

PROVERBS AND SAYINGS

1 A good time was had by all.
title of a collection of poems published in 1937 by
Stevie Smith (1902–71), taken from the characteristic
conclusion of accounts of social events in parish
magazines

2 Stop me and buy one.
Wall's ice cream, from spring 1922

PHRASES

3 cakes and ale
merrymaking, good things; from Shakespeare
Twelfth Night: see **Virtue** 22

4 forbidden fruit
illicit pleasure; the fruit forbidden to Adam in the
Bible (Genesis) 'But of the tree of the knowledge of
good and evil, thou shalt not eat of it'

5 pleased as Punch
showing or feeling great pleasure; *Punch* the
grotesque hook-nosed humpbacked principal
character of *Punch and Judy*, a traditional puppet-
show in which Punch is shown nagging, beating,
and finally killing a succession of characters,
including his wife Judy

6 the primrose path
the pursuit of pleasure, especially with disastrous
consequences; in allusion to Shakespeare *Hamlet*:
see **Words and Deeds** 12

7 a song in one's heart
a feeling of joy or pleasure; originally with allusion to
Lorenz Hart 'With a Song in my Heart', 1930 song

8 teddy bears' picnic
an occasion of innocent enjoyment; from a song
(c.1932) by Jimmy Kennedy and J. W. Bratton

9 wine, women, and song
proverbially required by men for carefree
entertainment and pleasure; see 12 below

QUOTATIONS

10 Everyone is dragged on by their favourite
pleasure.
Virgil 70–19 BC: *Eclogues*

11 The less we indulge our pleasures the more
we enjoy them.
Juvenal c.AD 60–c.130: *Satires*

12 Who loves not woman, wine, and song
Remains a fool his whole life long.
Martin Luther 1483–1546: attributed; later
inscribed in the Luther room in the Wartburg, but
with no proof of authorship; see 9 above, 19 below

13 Pleasure is nothing else but the intermission of pain.
John Selden 1584–1654: *Table Talk* (1689) 'Pleasure'

14 I shouldn't be surprised if the greatest rule of all weren't to give pleasure.
Molière 1622–73: *La Critique de l'école des femmes* (1663)

15 Music and women I cannot but give way to, whatever my business is.
Samuel Pepys 1633–1703: diary 9 March 1666

16 Great lords have their pleasures, but the people have fun.
Montesquieu 1689–1755: *Pensées et fragments inédits . . .* vol. 2 (1901)

17 A man enjoys the happiness he feels, a woman the happiness she gives.
Pierre Choderlos de Laclos 1741–1803: *Les Liaisons dangereuses* (1782)

18 One half of the world cannot understand the pleasures of the other.
Jane Austen 1775–1817: *Emma* (1816)

19 Let us have wine and women, mirth and laughter,
Sermons and soda-water the day after.
Lord Byron 1788–1824: *Don Juan* (1819–24); see 12 above

20 The greatest pleasure I know, is to do a good action by stealth, and to have it found out by accident.
Charles Lamb 1775–1834: 'Table Talk by the late Elia' in *The Athenaeum* 4 January 1834

21 The Puritan hated bear-baiting, not because it gave pain to the bear, but because it gave pleasure to the spectators.
Lord Macaulay 1800–59: *History of England* vol. 1 (1849)

22 The great pleasure in life is doing what people say you cannot do.
Walter Bagehot 1826–77: in *Prospective Review* 1853 'Shakespeare'

23 A fool bolts pleasure, then complains of moral indigestion.
Minna Antrim 1861–1950: *Naked Truth and Veiled Allusions* (1902)

24 Lying in bed would be an altogether perfect and supreme experience if only one had a coloured pencil long enough to draw on the ceiling.
G. K. Chesterton 1874–1936: *Tremendous Trifles* (1909) 'On Lying in Bed'

25 It is a curious thing that people only ask if you are enjoying yourself when you aren't.
Edith Nesbit 1858–1924: *Five of Us, and Madeline* (1925)

26 People must not do things for fun. We are not here for fun. There is no reference to fun in any Act of Parliament.
A. P. Herbert 1890–1971: *Uncommon Law* (1935)

27 All the things I really like to do are either illegal, immoral, or fattening.
Alexander Woollcott 1887–1943: R. E. Drennan *Wit's End* (1973)

28 There's no greater bliss in life than when the plumber eventually comes to unblock your drains. No writer can give that sort of pleasure.
Victoria Glendinning 1937– : in *Observer* 3 January 1993

29 No pleasure is worth giving up for the sake of two more years in a geriatric home in Weston-super-Mare.
Kingsley Amis 1922–95: in *The Times* 21 June 1994; attributed

⤜ Poetry ⤛

see also **Writing**

PHRASES

1 **the gay science**
the art of poetry; Provencal *gai saber*; see Economics 4

2 **Mount Parnassus**
poetry; after a mountain in central Greece, just north of Delphi. Held to be sacred by the ancient Greeks, it was associated with Apollo and the Muses

3 **the Pierian spring**
the source of poetic inspiration; from Pieria, a district in northern Thessaly, that in classical mythology was reputed home of the Muses and the location of a spring sacred to them; see **Knowledge** 32

4 **stuffed owl**
of poetry which treats trivial or inconsequential subjects in a grandiose manner; *the stuffed owl* title of 'an anthology of bad verse' (1930); ultimately from Wordsworth *Miscellaneous Sonnets* (1827) 'The presence even of a stuffed owl for her Can cheat the time'

QUOTATIONS

5 Skilled or unskilled, we all scribble poems.
Horace 65–8 BC: *Epistles*

6 Poetry is devil's wine.
St. Augustine of Hippo AD 354–430: *Contra Academicos*

7 'By God,' quod he, 'for pleynly, at a word,
Thy drasty rymyng is nat worth a toord!'
Geoffrey Chaucer 1343–1400: *The Canterbury Tales* 'Sir Thopas'

8 I am two fools, I know,
For loving, and for saying so
In whining poetry.
John Donne 1572–1631: 'The Triple Fool'

9 All poets are mad.
Robert Burton 1577–1640: *The Anatomy of Melancholy* (1621–51) 'Democritus to the Reader'

10 For rhyme the rudder is of verses,
With which like ships they steer their courses.
Samuel Butler 1612–80: *Hudibras* pt. 1 (1663)

11 Rhyme being no necessary adjunct or true ornament of poem or good verse, in longer works especially, but the invention of a barbarous age, to set off wretched matter and lame metre.
John Milton 1608–74: *Paradise Lost* (1667) 'The Verse' (preface, added 1668)

12 All that is not prose is verse; and all that is not verse is prose.
Molière 1622–73: *Le Bourgeois Gentilhomme* (1671)

13 BOSWELL: Sir, what is poetry?
JOHNSON: Why Sir, it is much easier to say what it is not. We all *know* what light is; but it is not easy to *tell* what it is.
Samuel Johnson 1709–84: James Boswell *Life of Samuel Johnson* (1791) 12 April 1776

14 Some rhyme a neebor's name to lash;
Some rhyme (vain thought!) for needfu' cash;
Some rhyme to court the countra clash,
An' raise a din;
For me, an aim I never fash;
I rhyme for fun.
Robert Burns 1759–96: 'To J. S[mith]' (1786)

15 Poetry is the spontaneous overflow of powerful feelings: it takes its origin from emotion recollected in tranquillity.
William Wordsworth 1770–1850: *Lyrical Ballads* (2nd ed., 1802)

16 That willing suspension of disbelief for the moment, which constitutes poetic faith.
Samuel Taylor Coleridge 1772–1834: *Biographia Literaria* (1817)

17 If poetry comes not as naturally as the leaves to a tree it had better not come at all.
John Keats 1795–1821: letter to John Taylor, 27 February 1818

18 Poetry is the record of the best and happiest moments of the happiest and best minds.
Percy Bysshe Shelley 1792–1822: *A Defence of Poetry* (written 1821)

19 Poets are the unacknowledged legislators of the world.
Percy Bysshe Shelley 1792–1822: *A Defence of Poetry* (written 1821)

20 Prose = words in their best order;—poetry = the *best* words in the best order.
Samuel Taylor Coleridge 1772–1834: *Table Talk* (1835) 12 July 1827

21 Scorn not the Sonnet; Critic, you have frowned,
Mindless of its just honours; with this key
Shakespeare unlocked his heart.
William Wordsworth 1770–1850: 'Scorn not the Sonnet' (1827)

22 Prose is when all the lines except the last go on to the end. Poetry is when some of them fall short of it.
Jeremy Bentham 1748–1832: M. St. J. Packe *The Life of John Stuart Mill* (1954)

23 The difference between genuine poetry and the poetry of Dryden, Pope, and all their school, is briefly this: their poetry is conceived and composed in their wits, genuine poetry is conceived and composed in the soul.
Matthew Arnold 1822–88: *Essays in Criticism Second Series* (1888) 'Thomas Gray'

24 I said 'a line will take us hours maybe,
Yet if it does not seem a moment's thought
Our stitching and unstitching has been naught.'
W. B. Yeats 1865–1939: 'Adam's Curse' (1904)

25 All a poet can do today is warn.
Wilfred Owen 1893–1918: preface (written 1918) in *Poems* (1963)

26 Poetry is not a turning loose of emotion, but an escape from emotion; it is not the expression of personality but an escape from personality.
T. S. Eliot 1888–1965: *The Sacred Wood* (1920) 'Tradition and Individual Talent'

27 A poem should not mean
But be.
Archibald MacLeish 1892–1982: 'Ars Poetica' (1926)

28 In our language rhyme is a barrel. A barrel of dynamite. The line is a fuse. The line smoulders to the end and explodes; and the town is blown sky-high in a stanza.
Vladimir Mayakovsky 1893–1930: 'Conversation with an Inspector of Taxes about Poetry' (1926)

29 Experience has taught me, when I am shaving of a morning, to keep watch over my thoughts, because, if a line of poetry strays into my memory, my skin bristles so that the razor ceases to act . . . The seat of this sensation is the pit of the stomach.
A. E. Housman 1859–1936: lecture at Cambridge, 9 May 1933

30 Poetry is not the most important thing in life . . . I'd much rather lie in a hot bath reading Agatha Christie and sucking sweets.
Dylan Thomas 1914–53: Joan Wyndham *Love is Blue* (1986) 6 July 1943

31 There's nothing in the world for which a poet will give up writing, not even when he is a Jew and the language of his poems is German.
Paul Celan 1920–70: letter to relatives, 2 August 1948

32 For twenty years I've stared my level best
To see if evening—any evening —would suggest
A patient etherized upon a table;
In vain. I simply wasn't able.
on contemporary poetry
C. S. Lewis 1898–1963: 'A Confession' (1964); see Day 14

33 I'd as soon write free verse as play tennis with the net down.
Robert Frost 1874–1963: Edward Lathem *Interviews with Robert Frost* (1966)

34 Most people ignore most poetry
because
most poetry ignores most people.
Adrian Mitchell 1932– : *Poems* (1964)

35 It is barbarous to write a poem after Auschwitz.
Theodor Adorno 1903–69: I. Buruma *Wages of Guilt* (1994)

36 A poet's hope: to be,
like some valley cheese,
local, but prized elsewhere.
W. H. Auden 1907–73: 'Shorts II' (1976)

37 The notion of expressing sentiments in short lines having similar sounds at their ends seems as remote as mangoes on the moon.
Philip Larkin 1922–85: letter to Barbara Pym, 22 January 1975

38 My favourite poem is the one that starts 'Thirty days hath September' because it actually tells you something.
Groucho Marx 1890–1977: Ned Sherrin *Cutting Edge* (1984); attributed

39 I think poetry should be alive. You should be able to dance it.
Benjamin Zephaniah 1958– : in *Sunday Times* 23 August 1987

40 As well as between tongue and teeth, poetry happens between the ears and behind the left nipple.
Douglas Dunn 1942– : in *Observer* 23 March 1997

⤞ Poets ⤝

PHRASES

1 **the Father of English poetry**
Geoffrey Chaucer (c.1342–1400), regarded as traditional starting-point for English literature and as the first great English poet

2 **the fleshly school of poetry**
a group of late 19th-century poets associated with Dante Gabriel Rossetti; the term was coined in the *Contemporary Review* of October 1871 by the Scottish writer Robert Buchanan

3 **the Good Gray Poet**
the American poet Walt Whitman (1819–92); the sobriquet was first applied to him in a book of this title (1866) by his friend, the journalist William O'Connor

4 **the Lake Poets**
the poets Samuel Taylor Coleridge, Robert Southey, and William Wordsworth; they lived in and were inspired by the Lake District

5 **the Peasant Poet**
John Clare (1793–1864); his popularity became part of a vogue for rural poetry and 'ploughman' poets

6 **Poet Laureate**
an eminent poet appointed as a member of the British royal household; the Poet Laureate was formerly expected to write poems for state occasions, but since Victorian times the post has carried no specific duties

7 the Theban eagle
the Greek lyric poet Pindar (c.518–c.438 BC); the name derives from three passages in poems by Pindar in which an eagle is mentioned without its connection to the context being clear; traditionally, the bird has been taken as an image of the poet

QUOTATIONS

8 The worshipful father and first founder and embellisher of ornate eloquence in our English, I mean Master Geoffrey Chaucer.
William Caxton 1421–91: Caxton's edition (c.1478) of Chaucer's translation of Boethius *De Consolacione Philosophie*

9 Dr Donne's verses are like the peace of God; they pass all understanding.
James I 1566–1625: remark recorded by Archdeacon Plume (1630–1704)

10 'Tis sufficient to say, according to the proverb, that here is God's plenty.
of Chaucer
John Dryden 1631–1700: *Fables Ancient and Modern* (1700)

11 Ev'n copious Dryden, wanted, or forgot, The last and greatest art, the art to blot.
Alexander Pope 1688–1744: *Imitations of Horace* (1737)

12 The living throne, the sapphire-blaze, Where angels tremble, while they gaze, He saw; but blasted with excess of light, Closed his eyes in endless night.
of Milton
Thomas Gray 1716–71: *The Progress of Poesy* (1757)

13 Milton, Madam, was a genius that could cut a Colossus from a rock; but could not carve heads upon cherry-stones.
to Hannah More, who had expressed a wonder that the poet who had written *Paradise Lost* should write such poor sonnets
Samuel Johnson 1709–84: James Boswell *Life of Samuel Johnson* (1791) 13 June 1784

14 The reason Milton wrote in fetters when he wrote of Angels and God, and at liberty when of Devils and Hell, is because he was a true Poet, and of the Devil's party without knowing it.
William Blake 1757–1827: *The Marriage of Heaven and Hell* (1790–3)

15 Mad, bad, and dangerous to know.
of Byron, after their first meeting
Lady Caroline Lamb 1785–1828: diary, March 1812; Elizabeth Jenkins *Lady Caroline Lamb* (1932)

16 With Donne, whose muse on dromedary trots, Wreathe iron pokers into true-love knots.
Samuel Taylor Coleridge 1772–1834: 'On Donne's Poetry' (1818)

17 A cloud-encircled meteor of the air, A hooded eagle among blinking owls.
of Coleridge
Percy Bysshe Shelley 1792–1822: 'Letter to Maria Gisborne' (1820)

18 We learn from Horace, Homer sometimes sleeps; We feel without him: Wordsworth sometimes wakes.
Lord Byron 1788–1824: *Don Juan* (1819–24); see **Mistakes 13**

19 In poetry, no less than in life, he is 'a beautiful and ineffectual angel, beating in the void his luminous wings in vain'.
Matthew Arnold 1822–88: *Essays in Criticism* Second Series (1888) 'Shelley' (quoting from his own essay on Byron in the same work)

20 Chaos, illumined by flashes of lightning.
on Robert Browning's 'style'
Oscar Wilde 1854–1900: Ada Leverson *Letters to the Sphinx* (1930)

21 You who desired so much—in vain to ask— Yet fed your hunger like an endless task, Dared dignify the labor, bless the quest— Achieved that stillness ultimately best, Being, of all, least sought for: Emily, hear!
Hart Crane 1899–1932: 'To Emily Dickinson' (1927)

22 How unpleasant to meet Mr Eliot! With his features of clerical cut, And his brow so grim And his mouth so prim And his conversation, so nicely Restricted to What Precisely And If and Perhaps and But.
T. S. Eliot 1888–1965: 'Five-Finger Exercises' (1936)

23 The high-water mark, so to speak, of Socialist literature is W. H. Auden, a sort of gutless Kipling.
George Orwell 1903–50: *The Road to Wigan Pier* (1937)

24 You were silly like us; your gift survived it all: The parish of rich women, physical decay, Yourself. Mad Ireland hurt you into poetry.
W. H. Auden 1907–73: 'In Memory of W. B. Yeats' (1940)

25 *Hugo—hélas!*
Hugo—alas!
when asked who was the greatest 19th-century poet
André Gide 1869–1951: Claude Martin *La Maturité d'André Gide* (1977)

26 To see him fumbling with our rich and delicate language is to experience all the horror of seeing a Sèvres vase in the hands of a chimpanzee.
of Stephen Spender
Evelyn Waugh 1903–66: in *The Tablet* 5 May 1951

27 Self-contempt, well-grounded.
on the foundation of T. S. Eliot's work
F. R. Leavis 1895–1978: in *Times Literary Supplement* 21 October 1988; see **Self-Esteem** 14

28 He is the poet of rational light, a light that has its own luminous beauty but which has also the effect of exposing clearly the truths which it touches.
of Philip Larkin
Seamus Heaney 1939– : *Finder's Keepers: Selected prose 1971–2001* (2002)

⟶ Political Parties ⟵

see also **Capitalism and Communism, Politicians, Politics**

PROVERBS AND SAYINGS

1 **I am a Marxist—of the Groucho tendency.**
slogan found at Nanterre in Paris, 1968

2 **Labour isn't working.**
on a poster showing a long queue outside an unemployment office; British Conservative Party slogan, 1978

3 **Meet the challenge—make the change.**
Labour Party slogan, 1989

4 **Not to be a republican at twenty is proof of want of heart; to be one at thirty is proof of want of head.**
often used in the form 'Not to be a socialist . . . '; saying attributed by Georges Clemenceau (1841–1929) to François Guizot (1787–1874)

PHRASES

5 **Big Blue Machine**
in Canada, informal name for the Ontario Progressive Conservative party, especially during the premiership of William Davis (1971–85), or for the group of people responsible for the party's campaigns and political organization

6 **big tent**
the doctrine or belief that a political party (or coalition of parties) should permit and encourage a broad spectrum of views and opinions among its members rather than insist on strict adherence to party policy; a party run on these lines

7 **clear blue water**
as seen by some Conservatives, the gap between their political aims and aspirations and those of the Labour Party; from blend of *clear water*, the distance between two boats, and *blue water*, the open sea, with a play on *blue* as the traditional colour of Conservatism

8 **the Grand Old Party**
the American Republican Party, recorded from the late 19th century

9 **the magic circle**
an inner group of politicians viewed as choosing the leader of the Conservative Party before this became an electoral matter; coined by Iain Macleod in a critical article in the *Spectator* on the 'emergence' of Alec Douglas-Home in succession to Harold Macmillan in 1963

10 **Selsdon man**
an advocate or adherent of the policies outlined at a conference of Conservative Party leaders held at the Selsdon Park Hotel, January 1970, from the view of a political opponent; from the *Selsdon* Park Hotel, Croydon, Surrey, after *Piltdown man* a fraudulent fossil composed of a human cranium and an ape jaw that was presented in 1912 as a genuine hominid of great antiquity

11 **somewhere to the right of Genghis Khan**
holding right-wing views of the most extreme kind; *Genghis Khan* (1162–1227), the founder of the Mongol empire, as the type of a repressive and tyrannical ruler

12 **yellow-dog Democrat**
in the US, a diehard Democrat, who will vote for a Democratic candidate, regardless of their personal qualities; the term implies someone who would vote for even a *yellow dog* if it were on the party ticket

---

QUOTATIONS

13 Party is little less than an inquisition, where
men are under such a discipline in carrying
on the common cause, as leaves no liberty
of private opinion.
Lord Halifax 1633–95: *Political, Moral, and
Miscellaneous Thoughts and Reflections* (1750) 'Of
Parties'

14 Party-spirit, which at best is but the
madness of many for the gain of a few.
Alexander Pope 1688–1744: letter to Edward
Blount, 27 August 1714

15 I have always said, the first Whig was the
Devil.
Samuel Johnson 1709–84: James Boswell *Life of
Johnson* (1791) 28 April 1778; see 19 below

16 PRINCE OF WALES: True blue and Mrs Crewe.
MRS CREWE: Buff and blue and all of you.
toast proposed by George IV when Prince of Wales to
Mrs Crewe, in honour of her support for the Whigs
and Charles James Fox in the Westminster election of
1784 (buff and blue were the Whig colours)
George IV 1762–1830: at a dinner at Carlton House,
May 1784; Amanda Foreman *Georgiana Duchess of
Devonshire* (1998); see **Trust and Treachery** 17

17 If I could not go to Heaven but with a party,
I would not go there at all.
Thomas Jefferson 1743–1826: letter to Francis
Hopkinson, 13 March 1789

18 Let me . . . warn you in the most solemn
manner against the baneful effects of the
spirit of party.
George Washington 1732–99: President's address
retiring from public life, 17 September 1796

19 God will not always be a Tory.
Lord Byron 1788–1824: letter 2 February 1821; see
15 above

20 I always voted at my party's call,
And I never thought of thinking for myself
at all.
W. S. Gilbert 1836–1911: *HMS Pinafore* (1878)

21 Damn your principles! Stick to your party.
Benjamin Disraeli 1804–81: attributed to Disraeli
and believed to have been said to Edward Bulwer-
Lytton; E. Latham *Famous Sayings and their Authors*
(1904)

22 We are Republicans and don't propose to
leave our party and identify ourselves with
the party whose antecedents are rum,
Romanism, and rebellion.
Samuel Dickinson Burchard 1812–91: speech at
the Fifth Avenue Hotel, New York, 29 October 1884

23 We are all socialists now.
during the passage of the 1888 budget, noted for
the reduction of the National Debt
William Harcourt 1827–1904: attributed; Hubert
Bland 'The Outlook' in G. B. Shaw (ed.) *Fabian
Essays in Socialism* (1889)

24 Then raise the scarlet standard high!
Within its shade we'll live or die.
Tho' cowards flinch and traitors sneer,
We'll keep the red flag flying here.
James M. Connell 1852–1929: 'The Red Flag'
(1889 song)

25 When in office, the Liberals forget their
principles and the Tories remember their
friends.
Thomas Kettle 1880–1916: Nicholas Mansergh *The
Irish Question* (ed. 3, 1975)

26 I never dared be radical when young
For fear it would make me conservative
when old.
Robert Frost 1874–1963: 'Precaution' (1936)

27 To the ordinary working man, the sort you
would meet in any pub on Saturday night,
Socialism does not mean much more than
better wages and shorter hours and nobody
bossing you about.
George Orwell 1903–50: *The Road to Wigan Pier*
(1937)

28 I am reminded of four definitions: A Radical
is a man with both feet firmly planted—in
the air. A Conservative is a man with two
perfectly good legs who, however, has never
learned to walk forward. A Reactionary is a
somnambulist walking backwards. A Liberal
is a man who uses his legs and his hands at
the behest—at the command—of his head.
Franklin D. Roosevelt 1882–1945: radio address
to *New York Herald Tribune* Forum, 26 October 1939

29 Conservatives do not believe that the
political struggle is the most important
thing in life . . . The simplest of them prefer
fox-hunting—the wisest religion.
Lord Hailsham 1907–2001: *The Case for
Conservatism* (1947)

30 The language of priorities is the religion of
Socialism.
Aneurin Bevan 1897–1960: speech at Labour Party
Conference in Blackpool, 8 June 1949

31 If they [the Republicans] will stop telling lies
about the Democrats, we will stop telling
the truth about them.
Adlai Stevenson 1900–65: speech during 1952
Presidential campaign; J. B. Martin *Adlai Stevenson
and Illinois* (1976)

32 Under democracy one party always devotes
its energies to trying to prove that the other
party is unfit to rule—and both commonly
succeed and are right.
H. L. Mencken 1880–1956: *Minority Report* (1956)

33 I am a free man, an American, a United States Senator, and a Democrat, in that order.
Lyndon Baines Johnson 1908–73: in *Texas Quarterly* Winter 1958

34 Fascism is not in itself a new order of society. It is the future refusing to be born.
Aneurin Bevan 1897–1960: Leon Harris *The Fine Art of Political Wit* (1965)

35 There are some of us . . . who will fight and fight and fight again to save the Party we love.
Hugh Gaitskell 1906–63: speech at Labour Party Conference, 5 October 1960

36 As usual the Liberals offer a mixture of sound and original ideas. Unfortunately none of the sound ideas is original and none of the original ideas is sound.
Harold Macmillan 1894–1986: speech to London Conservatives, 7 March 1961

37 Loyalty is the Tory's secret weapon.
Lord Kilmuir 1900–67: Anthony Sampson *Anatomy of Britain* (1962)

38 This party is a moral crusade or it is nothing.
Harold Wilson 1916–95: speech at the Labour Party Conference, 1 October 1962

39 The Labour Party owes more to Methodism than to Marxism.
Morgan Phillips 1902–63: James Callaghan *Time and Chance* (1987)

40 An independent is a guy who wants to take the politics out of politics.
Adlai Stevenson 1900–65: Bill Adler *The Stevenson Wit* (1966)

41 This party is a bit like an old stage-coach. If you drive along at a rapid rate, everyone aboard is either so exhilarated or so seasick that you don't have a lot of difficulty.
of the Labour Party
Harold Wilson 1916–95: Anthony Sampson *The Changing Anatomy of Britain* (1982)

42 Socialism can only arrive by bicycle.
José Antonio Viera Gallo 1943– : Ivan Illich *Energy and Equity* (1974) epigraph

43 The longest suicide note in history.
on the Labour Party's election manifesto *New Hope for Britain* (1983)
Gerald Kaufman 1930– : Denis Healey *The Time of My Life* (1989)

44 I have only one firm belief about the American political system, and that is this: God is a Republican and Santa Claus is a Democrat.
P. J. O'Rourke 1947– : *Parliament of Whores* (1991)

45 International life is right-wing, like nature. The social contract is left-wing, like humanity.
Régis Debray 1940– : *Charles de Gaulle* (1994)

46 No man or woman is indispensable and no individual is more important than the party and thereby the democratic health of our country.
William Hague 1961– : resignation speech as Conservative leader, 8 June 2001

47 You know what some people call us: the nasty party.
Theresa May 1956– : speech to the Conservative Conference, 7 October 2002

⇢ Politicians ⇠

see also **Political Parties, Politics, Speeches**

PROVERBS AND SAYINGS

1 **Mummy, what's that man for?**
remark by a small child to its mother; commonly cited as originally said of a late 19th/early 20th century politician; the earliest known instance is a cartoon in *Punch* in 1906 where it is applied to a man carrying a bag of golf clubs; see also 14 below

2 **A politician is an animal who can sit on a fence and yet keep both ears to the ground.**
American proverb, mid 20th century

PHRASES

3 **the Grand Old Man**
William Ewart Gladstone (1809–98); recorded from 1882, and popularly abbreviated as *GOM*; Gladstone won his last election in 1892 at the age of eighty-three

4 **the Iron Lady**
Margaret Thatcher (1925–); name given to Margaret Thatcher in 1976 by the Soviet newspaper *Red Star*, which accused her of trying to revive the cold war

➤━◄━▶━◄━▶━◄━▶━◄━▶━◄━▶━◄━▶━◄━▶━◄━▶━◄━▶━◄━▶━◄━▶━◄━▶━◄━▶━◄━▶━

5 the People's William
William Ewart Gladstone (1809–98), British Liberal statesman; coined by the newspaper proprietor Edward Levy-Lawson (1833–1916)

6 spend more time with one's family
now used (often ironically) in the context of a politician's ostensible reason for resigning office, paraphrasing Norman Fowler's resignation in 1990: see 39 below

QUOTATIONS

7 You have all the characteristics of a popular politician: a horrible voice, bad breeding and a vulgar manner.
Aristophanes c.450–c.385 BC: *The Knights* (424 BC)

8 Politicians also have no leisure, because they are always aiming at something beyond political life itself, power and glory, or happiness.
Aristotle 384–322 BC: *Nicomachean Ethics*

9 This judgement I have of you that you will not be corrupted by any manner of gift and that you will be faithful to the state; and that without respect of my private will you will give me that counsel which you think best.
to William Cecil, appointing him her Secretary of State in 1558
Elizabeth I 1533–1603: Conyers Read *Mr Secretary Cecil and Queen Elizabeth* (1955)

10 He that goeth about to persuade a multitude, that they are not so well governed as they ought to be, shall never want attentive and favourable hearers.
Richard Hooker 1554–1600: *Of the Laws of Ecclesiastical Polity* (1593)

11   Get thee glass eyes;
And, like a scurvy politician, seem
To see the things thou dost not.
William Shakespeare 1564–1616: *King Lear* (1605–6)

12 The greatest art of a politician is to render vice serviceable to the cause of virtue.
Henry St John, Lord Bolingbroke 1678–1751: comment (c.1728); Joseph Spence *Observations, Anecdotes, and Characters* (1820)

13 A minister who moves about in society is in a position to read the signs of the times even in a festive gathering, but one who remains shut up in his office learns nothing.
Duc de Choiseul 1719–85: Jack F. Bernard *Talleyrand* (1973)

14 What is that fat gentleman in such a passion about?
as a child, on hearing Charles James Fox speak in Parliament
Charles Shaw-Lefevre, Lord Eversley 1794–1888: G. W. E. Russell *Collections and Recollections* (1898); see also 1 above

15 If a due participation of office is a matter of right, how are vacancies to be obtained? Those by death are few; by resignation none.
usually quoted as, 'Few die and none resign'
Thomas Jefferson 1743–1826: letter to E. Shipman and others, 12 July 1801

16 The seagreen Incorruptible.
of Robespierre
Thomas Carlyle 1795–1881: *History of the French Revolution* (1837)

17 What I want is men who will support me when I am in the wrong.
replying to a politician who said 'I will support you as long as you are in the right'
Lord Melbourne 1779–1848: Lord David Cecil *Lord M* (1954)

18 The greatest gift of any statesman rests not in knowing what concessions to make, but recognising when to make them.
Prince Metternich 1773–1859: *Concessionen und Nichtconcessionen* (1852)

19 With malice toward none; with charity for all; with firmness in the right, as God gives us to see the right, let us strive on to finish the work we are in.
Abraham Lincoln 1809–65: Second Inaugural Address, 4 March 1865

20 A constitutional statesman is in general a man of common opinion and uncommon abilities.
Walter Bagehot 1826–77: *Biographical Studies* (1881) 'The Character of Sir Robert Peel'

21 An honest politician is one who when he's bought stays bought.
Simon Cameron 1799–1889: attributed

22 He knows nothing; and he thinks he knows everything. That points clearly to a political career.
George Bernard Shaw 1856–1950: *Major Barbara* (1907)

23 'Do you pray for the senators, Dr Hale?' 'No, I look at the senators and I pray for the country.'
Edward Everett Hale 1822–1909: Van Wyck Brooks *New England Indian Summer* (1940)

24 He [Labouchere] did not object to the old man always having a card up his sleeve, but he did object to his insinuating that the Almighty had placed it there.
on Gladstone's 'frequent appeals to a higher power'
Henry Labouchere 1831–1912: Earl Curzon *Modern Parliamentary Eloquence* (1913); see **Secrecy** 18

25 We all know that Prime Ministers are wedded to the truth, but like other married couples they sometimes live apart.
Saki 1870–1916: *The Unbearable Bassington* (1912)

26 If you want to succeed in politics, you must keep your conscience well under control.
David Lloyd George 1863–1945: Lord Riddell, diary, 23 April 1919

27 I remember, when I was a child, being taken to the celebrated Barnum's circus, which contained an exhibition of freaks and monstrosities, but the exhibit on the programme which I most desired to see was the one described as 'The Boneless Wonder'. My parents judged that that spectacle would be too revolting and demoralizing for my youthful eyes, and I have waited 50 years to see the boneless wonder sitting on the Treasury Bench.
of Ramsay MacDonald
Winston Churchill 1874–1965: speech in the House of Commons, 28 January 1931; see **The Body** 4

28 Forever poised between a cliché and an indiscretion.
on the life of a Foreign Secretary
Harold Macmillan 1894–1986: in *Newsweek* 30 April 1956

29 I am not going to spend any time whatsoever in attacking the Foreign Secretary . . . If we complain about the tune, there is no reason to attack the monkey when the organ grinder is present.
during a debate on the Suez crisis
Aneurin Bevan 1897–1960: speech, House of Commons, 16 May 1957; see **Power** 13

30 A statesman is a politician who's been dead 10 or 15 years.
Harry S. Truman 1884–1972: in *New York World Telegram and Sun* 12 April 1958

31 The ability to foretell what is going to happen tomorrow, next week, next month, and next year. And to have the ability afterwards to explain why it didn't happen.
describing the qualifications desirable in a prospective politician
Winston Churchill 1874–1965: B. Adler *Churchill Wit* (1965)

32 I think a Prime Minister has to be a butcher and know the joints. That is perhaps where I have not been quite competent, in knowing all the ways that you can cut up a carcass.
R. A. Butler 1902–82: in *Listener* 28 June 1966

33 In politics, if you want anything said, ask a man. If you want anything done, ask a woman.
Margaret Thatcher 1925– : in 1970; in *People* (New York) 15 September 1975

34 A statesman is a politician who places himself at the service of the nation. A politician is a statesman who places the nation at his service.
Georges Pompidou 1911–74: in *Observer* 30 December 1973

35 The average footslogger in the New South Wales Right . . . generally speaking carries a dagger in one hand and a Bible in the other and doesn't put either to really elegant use.
Neville Wran 1926– : in 1973; Michael Gordon *A Question of Leadership* (1993)

36 All political lives, unless they are cut off in midstream at a happy juncture, end in failure, because that is the nature of politics and of human affairs.
Enoch Powell 1912–98: *Joseph Chamberlain* (1977)

37 It is not necessary that every time he rises he should give his famous imitation of a semi-house-trained polecat.
of Norman Tebbit
Michael Foot 1913– : speech, House of Commons, 2 March 1978

38 In politics you must always keep running with the pack. The moment that you falter and they sense that you are injured, the rest will turn on you like wolves.
R. A. Butler 1902–82: Dennis Walters *Not Always with the Pack* (1989)

39 I have a young family and for the next few years I should like to devote more time to them.
Margaret Thatcher replied that she understood 'your wish to be able to spend more time with your family': see 6 above
Norman Fowler 1938– : resignation letter to the Prime Minister, in *Guardian* 4 January 1990

40 There are no true friends in politics. We are all sharks circling, and waiting, for traces of blood to appear in the water.
Alan Clark 1928–99: diary 30 November 1990

41 Politicians are entitled to change their minds. But when they adjust their principles some explanation is necessary.
Roy Hattersley 1932– : in *Observer* 21 March 1999

⇥Politics ⇤

see also **Democracy, Elections, Government, International Relations, Parliament, Political Parties, Politicians, The Presidency**

PROVERBS AND SAYINGS

1 In politics a man must learn to rise above principle.
American proverb, mid 20th century

2 It'll play in Peoria.
catchphrase of the Nixon administration (early 1970s) meaning 'it will be acceptable to middle America', but originating in a standard music hall joke of the 1930s

3 The personal is political.
1970s feminist slogan, coined by Carol Hanisch (1945–)

4 Politics makes strange bedfellows.
political alliances in a common cause may bring together those of widely differing views; English proverb, mid 19th century

PHRASES

5 midnight appointment
in US politics, an appointment made during the last hours of an administration; originally with particular reference to those made by the 2nd President John Adams (1735–1826)

6 October surprise
in the US, an unexpected but popular political act or speech made just prior to a November election in an attempt to win votes; used especially with reference to an alleged conspiracy in which members of the 1980 Republican campaign team are said to have made an arms deal with Iran to delay the release of US hostages in Iran until after the election

7 a smoke-filled room
regarded as the characteristic venue of those in control of a party meeting to arrange a political decision; from Kirke Simpson news report, filed 12 June 1920, '[Warren] Harding of Ohio was chosen by a group of men in a smoke-filled room early today as

Republican candidate for President'; usually attributed to Harry Daugherty, one of Harding's supporters, who appears merely to have concurred with this version of events, when pressed for comment by Simpson.

8 the third way
in politics, a middle way between conventional right- and left-wing ideologies or policies; an ideology founded on political centrism or neutrality. In the 1990s the *third way* became identified with the political programmes of centre-left parties in Western Europe and North America, characterized by both market-driven economic policy and a concern for social justice

9 the two nations
the rich and poor members of a society seen as effectively divided into separate nations by the presence or absence of wealth; from Disraeli: see **Wealth 25**

QUOTATIONS

10 Man is by nature a political animal.
Aristotle 384–322 BC: *Politics*

11 State business is a cruel trade; good nature is a bungler in it.
Lord Halifax 1633–95: *Political, Moral, and Miscellaneous Thoughts and Reflections* (1750) 'Wicked Ministers'

12 Most schemes of political improvement are very laughable things.
Samuel Johnson 1709–84: James Boswell *Life of Samuel Johnson* (1791) 26 October 1769

13 Magnanimity in politics is not seldom the truest wisdom; and a great empire and little minds go ill together.
Edmund Burke 1729–97: *On Conciliation with America* (1775)

14 I agree with you that in politics the middle way is none at all.
John Adams 1735–1826: letter to Horatio Gates, 23 March 1776

15 What is the first part of politics? Education. The second? Education. And the third? Education.
Jules Michelet 1798–1874: *Le Peuple* (1846); see **Education 34**

16 Finality is not the language of politics.
Benjamin Disraeli 1804–81: speech, House of Commons, 28 February 1859

17 Politics is the art of the possible.
Otto von Bismarck 1815–98: in conversation with Meyer von Waldeck, 11 August 1867; see 27, 32 below, **Science 25**

18 In politics, there is no use looking beyond the next fortnight.
Joseph Chamberlain 1836–1914: letter from A. J. Balfour to 3rd Marquess of Salisbury, 24 March 1886; see **28** below

19 A statesman . . . must wait until he hears the steps of God sounding through events; then leap up and grasp the hem of his garment.
Otto von Bismarck 1815–98: A. J. P. Taylor *Bismarck* (1955)

20 Politics is war without bloodshed while war is politics with bloodshed.
Mao Zedong 1893–1976: lecture, 1938; *Selected Works* (1965)

21 The trouble with this country is that there are too many politicians who believe, with a conviction based on experience, that you can fool all of the people all of the time.
Franklin P. Adams 1881–1960: *Nods and Becks* (1944); see **Deception 22**

22 All reactionaries are paper tigers. In appearance, the reactionaries are terrifying, but in reality they are not so powerful. From a long-term point of view, it is not the reactionaries but the people who are really powerful.
Mao Zedong 1893–1976: interview with Anne Louise Strong, August 1946; *Selected Works* (1961)

23 We have a great objective—the light on the hill—which we aim to reach by working for the betterment of mankind not only here but anywhere we may give a helping hand.
Joseph Benedict 'Ben' Chifley 1885–1951: speech to the Annual Conference of the New South Wales branch of the Australian Labor Party, 12 June 1949

24 Political language . . . is designed to make lies sound truthful and murder respectable, and to give an appearance of solidity to pure wind.
George Orwell 1903–50: *Shooting an Elephant* (1950) 'Politics and the English Language'

25 Men enter local politics solely as a result of being unhappily married.
C. Northcote Parkinson 1909–93: *Parkinson's Law* (1958)

26 Politics are too serious a matter to be left to the politicians.
responding to Attlee's remark that 'De Gaulle is a very good soldier and a very bad politician'
Charles de Gaulle 1890–1970: Clement Attlee *A Prime Minister Remembers* (1961); see **Warfare 40**

27 Politics is not the art of the possible. It consists in choosing between the disastrous and the unpalatable.
J. K. Galbraith 1908– : letter to President Kennedy, 2 March 1962; see **17** above

28 A week is a long time in politics.
probably first said at the time of the 1964 sterling crisis
Harold Wilson 1916–95: Nigel Rees *Sayings of the Century* (1984); see **18** above

29 The liberals can understand everything but people who don't understand them.
Lenny Bruce 1925–66: John Cohen (ed.) *The Essential Lenny Bruce* (1967)

30 Politics is supposed to be the second oldest profession. I have come to realize that it bears a very close resemblance to the first.
Ronald Reagan 1911–2004: at a conference in Los Angeles, 2 March 1977; see **Employment 4**

31 The opposition of events.
on his biggest problem; popularly quoted as, 'Events, dear boy. Events'
Harold Macmillan 1894–1986: David Dilks *The Office of Prime Minister in Twentieth Century Britain* (1993)

32 Let us teach ourselves and others that politics can be not only the art of the possible, especially if this means the art of speculation, calculation, intrigue, secret deals, and pragmatic manoeuvring, but that it can even be the art of the impossible, namely, the art of improving ourselves and the world.
Václav Havel 1936– : speech, Prague, 1 January 1990; see **17** above

33 Politics is a marathon, not a sprint.
Ken Livingstone 1945– : in *New Statesman* 10 October 1997

34 When you want to get to the suites, start in the streets.
her rule for political activism
Florynce Kennedy 1916–2000: attributed; in *Los Angeles Times* 28 December 2000

⤞ Pollution and the Environment ⤛

see also **The Earth, Nature**

PROVERBS AND SAYINGS

1 **Kills all known germs.**
advertising slogan for Domestos bleach, 1959

2 **Save the whale.**
environmental slogan associated with the alarm over
the rapidly declining whale population which led in
1985 to a moratorium on commercial whaling; see
also **Language 27**

3 **Think globally, act locally.**
Friends of the Earth slogan, *c*.1985

4 **When the last tree is cut, the last river
poisoned, and the last fish dead, we
will discover that we can't eat money.**
Canadian saying, sometimes said to be of native
American origin

QUOTATIONS

5 Woe to her that is filthy and polluted, to the
oppressing city!
Bible: Zephaniah

6 Woe unto them that join house to house,
that lay field to field, till there be no place.
Bible: Isaiah

7 This most excellent canopy, the air, look
you, this brave o'erhanging firmament, this
majestical roof fretted with golden fire, why,
it appears no other thing to me but a foul
and pestilent congregation of vapours.
William Shakespeare 1564–1616: *Hamlet* (1601)

8 O all ye Green Things upon the Earth, bless
ye the Lord: praise him, and magnify him
for ever.
The Book of Common Prayer 1662: Benedicite

9 The parks are the lungs of London.
William Pitt, Earl of Chatham 1708–78: speech
by William Windham, House of Commons, 30
June 1808

10 And did the Countenance Divine
Shine forth upon our clouded hills?
And was Jerusalem builded here
Among these dark Satanic mills?
William Blake 1757–1827: *Milton* (1804–10) 'And
did those feet in ancient time'

11 The river Rhine, it is well known,
Doth wash your city of Cologne;
But tell me, Nymphs, what power divine
Shall henceforth wash the river Rhine?
Samuel Taylor Coleridge 1772–1834: 'Cologne'
(1834)

12 What would the world be, once bereft
Of wet and wildness? Let them be left,
O let them be left, wildness and wet;
Long live the weeds and the wilderness yet.
Gerard Manley Hopkins 1844–89: 'Inversnaid'
(written 1881)

13 Dirt is only matter out of place.
John Chipman Gray 1839–1915: *Restraints on the
Alienation of Property* (2nd ed., 1895)

14 Man has been endowed with reason, with
the power to create, so that he can add to
what he's been given. But up to now he
hasn't been a creator, only a destroyer.
Forests keep disappearing, rivers dry up,
wild life's become extinct, the climate's
ruined and the land grows poorer and uglier
every day.
Anton Chekhov 1860–1904: *Uncle Vanya* (1897)

15 The sanitary and mechanical age we are now
entering makes up for the mercy it grants to
our sense of smell by the ferocity with
which it assails our sense of hearing. As
usual, what we call 'progress' is the
exchange of one nuisance for another
nuisance.
Havelock Ellis 1859–1939: *Impressions and
Comments* (1914)

16 I think that I shall never see
A billboard lovely as a tree.
Perhaps, unless the billboards fall,
I'll never see a tree at all.
Ogden Nash 1902–71: 'Song of the Open Road'
(1933); see **Trees 17**

17 Clear the air! clean the sky! wash the wind!
T. S. Eliot 1888–1965: *Murder in the Cathedral*
(1935)

18 Come, friendly bombs, and fall on Slough!
It isn't fit for humans now,
There isn't grass to graze a cow.
Swarm over, Death!
John Betjeman 1906–84: 'Slough' (1937)

19 Over increasingly large areas of the United
States, spring now comes unheralded by the
return of the birds, and the early mornings

are strangely silent where once they were
filled with the beauty of bird song.
Rachel Carson 1907–64: *The Silent Spring* (1962)

20 Make it a *green* peace.
Bill Darnell: at a meeting of the Don't Make a Wave
Committee, which preceded the formation of
Greenpeace, in Vancouver, 1970; Robert Hunter *The
Greenpeace Chronicle* (1979)

21 We have met the enemy and he is us.
the cartoon-strip character, Pogo the opossum,
looking at litter under a tree; used as an Earth Day
poster in 1971
Walt Kelly 1913–73: *Pogo* cartoon, 1970

22 The sea is the universal sewer.
Jacques Cousteau 1910–97: testimony before the
House Committee on Science and Astronautics, 28
January 1971

23 There should be supermarkets that sell
things and supermarkets that buy things
back, and until that equalizes, there'll be
more waste than there should be.
Andy Warhol 1927–87: *Philosophy of Andy Warhol
(From A to B and Back Again)* (1975)

24 It is not what they built. It is what they
knocked down.
It is not the houses. It is the spaces between
the houses.
It is not the streets that exist. It is the streets
that no longer exist.
James Fenton 1949– : *German Requiem* (1981)

25 If I were a Brazilian without land or money
or the means to feed my children, I would
be burning the rain forest too.
Sting 1951– : in *International Herald Tribune* 14
April 1989

26 The poor tread lightest upon the earth. The
higher our income, the more resources we
control and the more havoc we wreak.
Paul Harrison 1936– : in *Guardian* 1 May 1992

27 The greenest political party there has ever
been was the Nazi party. The Nazis were
great believers in purity, that nature should
not be interfered with.
Steve Jones 1944– : in *Times Higher Education
Supplement* 27 August 1999

Possessions

PROVERBS AND SAYINGS

1 **Finders keepers (losers weepers).**
English proverb, early 19th century

2 **Findings keepings.**
English proverb, mid 19th century

3 **Keep a thing seven years and you'll
always find a use for it.**
recommending caution and thrift; English proverb,
early 17th century

4 **Light come, light go.**
something gained without effort can be lost without
much regret; English proverb, late 14th century

5 **What you have, hold.**
with reference to an uncompromising position based
on a refusal to make any concessions; English
proverb, mid 15th century

6 **What you spend, you have.**
the only real possessions one has are those of which
one can dispose; English proverb, early 14th century

7 **You cannot lose what you never had.**
used in consolation or resignation; English proverb,
late 16th century

PHRASES

8 **dead men's shoes**
a property or position coveted by a prospective
successor but available only on a person's death;
from the proverb: see **Ambition 3**

9 **ewe lamb**
a person's most cherished possession; from the Bible:
see **12 below**

10 **goods and chattels**
all kinds of personal property; a *chattel* is a movable
possession

QUOTATIONS

11 The sage does not accumulate for himself.
The more he uses for others, the more he
has himself.

The more he gives to others, the more he
possesses of his own.
Lao Tzu *c.*604–*c.*531 BC: *Tao-te Ching*

12 The poor man had nothing, save one little
ewe lamb.
Bible: II Samuel; see 9 above

13 How many things I can do without!
on looking at a multitude of wares exposed for sale
Socrates 469–399 BC: Diogenes Laertius *Lives of the
Philosophers*

14 For we brought nothing into this world, and
it is certain we can carry nothing out.
Bible: I Timothy

15 All my possessions for a moment of time.
Elizabeth I 1533–1603: attributed last words, but
almost certainly apocryphal

16 There are only two families in the world, as a
grandmother of mine used to say: the haves
and the have-nots.
Cervantes 1547–1616: *Don Quixote* (1605)

17 Well! some people talk of morality, and
some of religion, but give me a little snug
property.
Maria Edgeworth 1767–1849: *The Absentee* (1812)

18 Property has its duties as well as its rights.
Thomas Drummond 1797–1840: letter to the Earl
of Donoughmore, 22 May 1838

19 Property is theft.
Pierre-Joseph Proudhon 1809–65: *Qu'est-ce que
la propriété?* (1840)

20 Things are in the saddle,
And ride mankind.
Ralph Waldo Emerson 1803–82: 'Ode' Inscribed
to W. H. Channing (1847)

21 Have nothing in your houses that you do
not know to be useful, or believe to be
beautiful.
William Morris 1834–96: *Hopes and Fears for Art*
(1882) 'Making the Best of It'

22 Conspicuous consumption of valuable
goods is a means of reputability to the
gentleman of leisure.
Thorstein Veblen 1857–1929: *Theory of the Leisure
Class* (1899)

23 Never be afraid of throwing away what you
have, if you *can* throw it away, it is not really
yours.
R. H. Tawney 1880–1962: diary 1912, in *Dictionary
of National Biography 1961–1970* (1981)

24 The moon belongs to everyone,
The best things in life are free.
Buddy De Sylva 1895–1950 and **Lew Brown**
1893–1958: 'The Best Things in Life are Free' (1927
song); see **Money 2**

25 People don't resent having nothing nearly
as much as too little.
Ivy Compton-Burnett 1884–1969: *A Family and a
Fortune* (1939)

26 Man must choose whether to be rich in
things or in the freedom to use them.
Ivan Illich 1926– : *Deschooling Society* (1971)

27 The thrill was in the trying on, in the
buying. The moment after she had acquired
something new it became meaningless
to her.
Judith Krantz 1932– : *Scruples* (1978)

28 If men are to respect each other for what
they are, they must cease to respect each
other for what they own.
A. J. P. Taylor 1906–90: *Politicians, Socialism and
Historians* (1980)

29 People who get through life dependent on
other people's possessions are always the
first to lecture you on how little possessions
count.
Ben Elton 1959– : *Stark* (1989)

30 The metamorphosis of consumption from
vice to virtue is one of the most important
yet least examined phenomena of the
twentieth century.
Jeremy Rifkin 1945– : *The End of Work* (1995)

⤜ Poverty ⤛

see also **Money, Wealth**

PROVERBS AND SAYINGS

1 **Both poverty and prosperity come
from spending money—prosperity
from spending it wisely.**
American proverb, mid 20th century

2 **Empty sacks will never stand upright.**
those in an extremity of need cannot survive; English
proverb, mid 17th century

3 **Make poverty history.**
slogan of a campaign launched in 2005 by a
coalition of charities and other groups to pressure
governments to take action to reduce poverty

4 **A moneyless man goes fast through the market.**
someone without resources is unable to pause to buy anything (or, in a modern variant, rushes to wherever what they lack may be found); English proverb, early 18th century

5 **Poverty comes from God, but not dirt.**
American proverb, mid 20th century

6 **Poverty is no disgrace, but it's a great inconvenience.**
English proverb, late 16th century

7 **Poverty is not a crime.**
English proverb, late 16th century

8 **When poverty comes in at the door, love flies out of the window.**
the strains of living in poverty often destroy a loving relationship; English proverb, mid 17th century

PHRASES

9 **on one's beam-ends**
at the end of one's financial resources; *beam-ends* are the ends of a ship's beams, and a ship *on her beam-ends* is one on its side, almost capsizing

10 **on the breadline**
in the poorest conditions in which it is possible to live; the *breadline* in North American usage was a queue of people waiting to receive free food

11 **poor as Job**
very poor; in the Bible (Job), the formerly wealthy figure of Job, deprived of his possessions, becomes a type of abject poverty

12 **the submerged tenth**
the supposed fraction of the population permanently living in poverty; from William Booth (1829–1912) *In Darkest England* (1890) 'This Submerged Tenth—is it, then, beyond the reach of the nine-tenths in the midst of whom they live?'

QUOTATIONS

13 What mean ye that ye beat my people to pieces, and grind the faces of the poor?
Bible: Isaiah

14 The poor always ye have with you.
Bible: St John

15 The misfortunes of poverty carry with them nothing harder to bear than that it makes men ridiculous.
Juvenal c.AD 60–c.130: *Satires*

16 I can get no remedy against this consumption of the purse: borrowing only lingers and lingers it out, but the disease is incurable.
William Shakespeare 1564–1616: *Henry IV, Part 2* (1597)

17 I want there to be no peasant in my kingdom so poor that he is unable to have a chicken in his pot every Sunday.
Henri IV (of France) 1553–1610: Hardouin de Péréfixe *Histoire de Henry le Grand* (1681); see **Progress** 17

18 Come away; poverty's catching.
Aphra Behn 1640–89: *The Rover* pt. 2 (1681)

19 Give me not poverty lest I steal.
Daniel Defoe 1660–1731: in *Review* 15 September 1711; later incorporated into *Moll Flanders* (1721)

20 Laws grind the poor, and rich men rule the law.
Oliver Goldsmith 1728–74: *The Traveller* (1764)

21 Resolve not to be poor: whatever you have, spend less. Poverty is a great enemy to human happiness; it certainly destroys liberty, and it makes some virtues impracticable, and others extremely difficult.
Samuel Johnson 1709–84: letter to Boswell, 7 December 1782

22 The murmuring poor, who will not fast in peace.
George Crabbe 1754–1832: 'The Newspaper' (1785)

23 The poor are Europe's blacks.
Nicolas-Sébastien Chamfort 1741–94: *Maximes et Pensées* (1796)

24 Oh! God! that bread should be so dear, And flesh and blood so cheap!
Thomas Hood 1799–1845: 'The Song of the Shirt' (1843)

25 Economy was always 'elegant', and money-spending always 'vulgar' and ostentatious— a sort of sour-grapeism, which made us very peaceful and satisfied.
Elizabeth Gaskell 1810–65: *Cranford* (1853)

26 Like dear St Francis of Assisi I am wedded to Poverty: but in my case the marriage is not a success.
Oscar Wilde 1854–1900: letter June 1899

27 The greatest of evils and the worst of crimes is poverty.
George Bernard Shaw 1856–1950: *Major Barbara* (1907)

28 The poor cannot always reach those whom they want to love, and they can hardly ever escape from those whom they no longer love.
E. M. Forster 1879–1970: *Howards End* (1910)

29 There's nothing surer,
The rich get rich and the poor get children.
Gus Kahn 1886–1941 and **Raymond B. Egan** 1890–1952: 'Ain't We Got Fun' (1921 song)

30 Brother can you spare a dime?
E. Y. Harburg 1898–1981: title of song (1932)

31 How can you frighten a man whose hunger is not only in his own cramped stomach but in the wretched bellies of his children? You can't scare him—he has known a fear beyond every other.
John Steinbeck 1902–68: *The Grapes of Wrath* (1939)

32 Anyone who has ever struggled with poverty knows how extremely expensive it is to be poor.
James Baldwin 1924–87: *Nobody Knows My Name* (1961) 'Fifth Avenue, Uptown: a letter from Harlem'

33 Born down in a dead man's town
The first kick I took was when I hit the ground.
Bruce Springsteen 1949– : 'Born in the USA' (1984 song)

34 Where mass hunger reigns, we cannot speak of peace.
Willy Brandt 1913–92: *World Armament and World Hunger* (1986)

35 When I give food to the poor they call me a saint. When I ask why the poor have no food they call me a communist.
Helder Camara 1909–99: attributed

36 I never saw a beggar yet who would recognise guilt if it bit him on his unwashed ass.
Tony Parsons 1953– : *Dispatches from the Front Line of Popular Culture* (1994)

37 Poverty is a lot like childbirth—you know it is going to hurt before it happens, but you'll never know how much until you experience it.
J. K. Rowling 1965– : in *Mail on Sunday* 16 June 2002

38 Overcoming poverty is not a gesture of charity. It is an act of justice.
Nelson Mandela 1918– : speech in Trafalgar Square, London, 3 February 2005

➵ Power ⤖

PROVERBS AND SAYINGS

1 **Big fish eat little fish.**
the rich and powerful are likely to prey on those who are less strong, and often used with the implication that each predator is in turn victim to a stronger one; English proverb, early 13th century

2 **He who pays the piper calls the tune.**
the person financially responsible for something can control what is done; English proverb, late 19th century; see 14 below

3 **Kings have long arms.**
a king's power reaches a long way; English proverb, mid 16th century

4 **Might is right.**
English proverb, early 14th century

5 **A mouse may help a lion.**
alluding to Aesop's fable of the lion and the rat, in which a rat saved a lion which had become trapped in a net by gnawing through the cords which bound it; English proverb, mid 16th century

6 **Power corrupts.**
English proverb, late 19th century; see 28 below

7 **Set a beggar on horseback, and he'll ride to the Devil.**
a person unused to power will make unwise use of it; English proverb, late 16th century

8 **They that dance must pay the fiddler.**
you must be prepared to make recompense for the provision of an essential service; English proverb, mid 17th century

9 **We have ways of making you talk.**
supposedly the characteristic threat of an inquisitor in a 1930s film, but not traced in this form; 'We have ways of making men talk' occurs in *Lives of a Bengal Lancer* (1935)

10 **When elephants fight, it is the grass that gets hurt.**
the weak are likely to suffer as a result of the conflicts of the strong and powerful; African proverb (Swahili)

PHRASES

11 éminence grise
a person who exercises power or influence in a certain sphere without holding an official position; the term was originally applied to Cardinal Richelieu's grey-cloaked private secretary, Père Joseph (1577–1638)

12 on the hip
at a disadvantage (sometimes with allusion to Shakespeare's *Merchant of Venice*, 'Now, infidel, I have you on the hip')

13 organ-grinder
a person who is more important or powerful than another (usually contrasted with *monkey*). The allusion is to an itinerant street musician who played a barrel organ which was turned by hand, and who often had a pet monkey; see **Politicians** 29

14 pay the piper (and call the tune)
pay the cost of (and so have the right to control) an activity or undertaking; from the proverb: see 2 above

15 the powers that be
the authorities concerned, the people exercising political or social control; from the Bible (Romans), 'For there is no power but of God: the powers that be are ordained of God'

16 speak truth to power
challenge those who have a responsibility to act with the realities of a situation; the phrase was used in 1955 as the title of a document issued by the American Friends Service Committee, which claimed to derive the phrase from a charge given to Eighteenth Century Friends

QUOTATIONS

17   Man, proud man,
Drest in a little brief authority.
William Shakespeare 1564–1616: *Measure for Measure* (1604)

18 All rising to great place is by a winding stair.
Francis Bacon 1561–1626: *Essays* (1625) 'Of Great Place'

19 Power is so apt to be insolent and Liberty to be saucy, that they are very seldom upon good terms.
Lord Halifax 1633–95: *Political, Moral, and Miscellaneous Thoughts and Reflections* (1750) 'Of Prerogative, Power and Liberty'

20 Nature has left this tincture in the blood, That all men would be tyrants if they could.
Daniel Defoe 1660–1731: *The History of the Kentish Petition* (1712–13)

21 Those who have been once intoxicated with power, and have derived any kind of emolument from it, even though for but one year, can never willingly abandon it.
Edmund Burke 1729–97: *Letter to a Member of the National Assembly* (1791)

22 I shall be an autocrat: that's my trade. And the good Lord will forgive me: that's his.
Catherine the Great 1729–96: attributed; see **Forgiveness** 22

23   The good old rule
Sufficeth them, the simple plan,
That they should take who have the power,
And they should keep who can.
William Wordsworth 1770–1850: 'Rob Roy's Grave' (1807)

24 The fundamental article of my political creed is that despotism, or unlimited sovereignty, or absolute power, is the same in a majority of a popular assembly, an aristocratic council, an oligarchical junto, and a single emperor.
John Adams 1735–1826: letter to Thomas Jefferson, 13 November 1815

25 Power concedes nothing without a demand. It never did, and it never will.
Frederick Douglass 1818–95: letter to Gerrit Smith, 30 March 1849

26 I claim not to have controlled events, but confess plainly that events have controlled me.
Abraham Lincoln 1809–65: letter to A. G. Hodges, 4 April 1864

27 'The question is,' said Humpty Dumpty, 'which is to be master—that's all.'
Lewis Carroll 1832–98: *Through the Looking-Glass* (1872)

28 Power tends to corrupt and absolute power corrupts absolutely.
Lord Acton 1834–1902: letter to Bishop Mandell Creighton, 3 April 1887; see 6 above

29 Whatever happens we have got
The Maxim Gun, and they have not.
Hilaire Belloc 1870–1953: *The Modern Traveller* (1898)

30 Every Communist must grasp the truth, 'Political power grows out of the barrel of a gun'.
Mao Zedong 1893–1976: speech, 6 November 1938

31 The finest plans are always ruined by the littleness of those who ought to carry them out, for the Emperors can actually do nothing.
Bertolt Brecht 1898–1956: *Mother Courage* (1939)

32 Who controls the past controls the future: who controls the present controls the past.
George Orwell 1903–50: *Nineteen Eighty-Four* (1949)

33 You only have power over people as long as you don't take *everything* away from them. But when you've robbed a man of *everything* he's no longer in your power — he's free again.
Alexander Solzhenitsyn 1918– : *The First Circle* (1968)

34 Power is the great aphrodisiac.
Henry Kissinger 1923– : in *New York Times* 19 January 1971

35 Power? It's like a Dead Sea fruit. When you achieve it, there is nothing there.
Harold Macmillan 1894–1986: Anthony Sampson *The New Anatomy of Britain* (1971); see **Disillusion** 2

36 When you make your peace with authority, you become an authority.
Jim Morrison 1943–71: Andrew Doe and John Tobler *In Their Own Words: The Doors* (1988)

37 The struggle of man against power is the struggle of memory against forgetting.
Milan Kundera 1929– : *The Book of Laughter and Forgetting* (1979)

38 Every dictator uses religion as a prop to keep himself in power.
Benazir Bhutto 1953– : interview on *60 Minutes*, CBS-TV, 8 August 1986

⊱ Practicality ⊰

PROVERBS AND SAYINGS

1 Cut your coat according to your cloth.
actions taken should suit one's circumstances or resources; English proverb, mid 16th century

2 He who wants a rose must respect the thorn.
someone wanting a desirable object needs to be aware of the dangers it brings with it; Persian proverb; see **Circumstance** 5, **Satisfaction** 4

3 Put your trust in God, and keep your powder dry.
often attributed to Oliver Cromwell (1599–1658); English proverb, mid 19th century; see **Caution** 26

4 You cannot make an omelette without breaking eggs.
often used in the context of a regrettable political necessity which is said to be justified because it will benefit the majority; English proverb, mid 19th century

QUOTATIONS

5 This man hath the right sow by the ear.
of Thomas Cranmer, June 1529
Henry VIII 1491–1547: *Acts and Monuments of John Foxe* ['Fox's Book of Martyrs'], 1570; see **Knowledge** 13

6 A dead woman bites not.
pressing for the execution of Mary Queen of Scots in 1587
Patrick, Lord Gray d. 1612: oral tradition; William Camden *Annals of the Reign of Queen Elizabeth* (1615); see **Enemies** 1

7 My lord, we make use of you, not for your bad legs, but for your good head.
to William Cecil, who suffered from gout
Elizabeth I 1533–1603: F. Chamberlin *Sayings of Queen Elizabeth* (1923)

8 Common sense is the best distributed commodity in the world, for every man is convinced that he is well supplied with it.
René Descartes 1596–1650: *Le Discours de la méthode* (1637)

9 And he gave it for his opinion, that whoever could make two ears of corn or two blades of grass to grow upon a spot of ground where only one grew before, would deserve better of mankind, and do more essential service to his country than the whole race of politicians put together.
Jonathan Swift 1667–1745: *Gulliver's Travels* (1726) 'A Voyage to Brobdingnag'

10 'Tis use alone that sanctifies expense, And splendour borrows all her rays from sense.
Alexander Pope 1688–1744: *Epistles to Several Persons* 'To Lord Burlington' (1731)

11 Common sense is not so common.
Voltaire 1694–1778: *Dictionnaire philosophique* (1765) 'Sens Commun'

12 Whenever our neighbour's house is on fire, it cannot be amiss for the engines to play a little on our own.
Edmund Burke 1729–97: *Reflections on the Revolution in France* (1790)

13 It's grand, and you canna expect to be baith grand and comfortable.
J. M. Barrie 1860–1937: *The Little Minister* (1891)

14 Praise the Lord and pass the ammunition.
moving along a line of sailors passing ammunition by hand to the deck
Howell Forgy 1908–83: at Pearl Harbor, 7 December 1941; later the title of a song by Frank Loesser, 1942

15 Common sense is nothing more than a deposit of prejudices laid down in the mind before you reach eighteen.
Albert Einstein 1879–1955: Lincoln Barnett *The Universe and Dr Einstein* (1950 ed.)

16 Life is too short to stuff a mushroom.
Shirley Conran 1932– : *Superwoman* (1975)

17 I'm up to my neck in the real world, every day. Just you try doing your VAT return with a head full of goblins.
Terry Pratchett 1948– : in *Sunday Times* 27 February 2000

➤➤ Praise and Flattery ◄◄

PROVERBS AND SAYINGS

1 **Flattery is soft soap, and soft soap is ninety percent lye.**
lye = a strongly alkaline solution, especially of potassium hydroxide, used for washing or cleansing; American proverb, mid 19th century

2 **Flattery, like perfume, should be smelled, not swallowed.**
American proverb, mid 19th century; see 18 below

3 **Give credit where credit is due.**
English proverb, late 18th century

4 **Imitation is the sincerest form of flattery.**
English proverb, early 19th century, from Charles Caleb Colton (1780–1832) *Lacon* (1820)

5 **Praise from Sir Hubert is praise indeed.**
popular saying, from Thomas Morton: see 15 below

PHRASES

6 **damn with faint praise**
commend so feebly as to imply disapproval; from Pope: see 13 below

7 **turn geese into swans**
exaggerate the merits of people; see **Self-Esteem** 16

QUOTATIONS

8 But when I tell him he hates flatterers,
He says he does, being then most flattered.
William Shakespeare 1564–1616: *Julius Caesar* (1599)

9 It has been well said that 'the arch-flatterer with whom all the petty flatterers have intelligence is a man's self.'
Francis Bacon 1561–1626: *Essays* (1625) 'Of Love'

10 Nothing so soon the drooping spirits can raise
As praises from the men, whom all men praise.
Abraham Cowley 1618–67: 'Ode upon a Copy of Verses of My Lord Broghill's' (1663)

11 Of whom to be dispraised were no small praise.
John Milton 1608–74: *Paradise Regained* (1671)

12 He who discommendeth others obliquely commendeth himself.
Thomas Browne 1605–82: *Christian Morals* (1716)

13 Damn with faint praise, assent with civil leer,
And without sneering, teach the rest to sneer.
Alexander Pope 1688–1744: 'An Epistle to Dr Arbuthnot' (1735); see 6 above

14 Madam, before you flatter a man so grossly to his face, you should consider whether or not your flattery is worth his having.
Samuel Johnson 1709–84: Fanny Burney's diary, August 1778

15 Approbation from Sir Hubert Stanley is praise indeed.
Thomas Morton c.1764–1838: *A Cure for the Heartache* (1797); see 5 above

16 And even the ranks of Tuscany
Could scarce forbear to cheer.
Lord Macaulay 1800–59: *Lays of Ancient Rome* (1842) 'Horatius'

17 The advantage of doing one's praising for oneself is that one can lay it on so thick and exactly in the right places.
Samuel Butler 1835–1902: *The Way of All Flesh* (1903)

18 I suppose flattery hurts no one, that is, if he doesn't inhale.
Adlai Stevenson 1900–65: television broadcast, 30 March 1952; see 2 above

19 If you are flattering a woman, it pays to be a little more subtle. You don't have to bother with men, they believe any compliment automatically.
Alan Ayckbourn 1939– : *Round and Round the Garden* (1975)

20 I can't think of many toadies that have prospered, or many toadies who have become household names.
Betty Boothroyd 1929– : in *Mail on Sunday* 12 April 1998

⊸⊱ Prayer ⊰⊷

PROVERBS AND SAYINGS

1 The family that prays together stays together.
motto devised by Al Scalpone for the Roman Catholic Family Rosary Crusade, 1947

2 Laborare est orare.
Latin, *To work is to pray*, a traditional motto of the Benedictine order, also found in the form '*Ora, lege, et labora* [Pray, read, and work]'

PHRASES

3 the Lord's Prayer
the prayer taught by Christ to his disciples, beginning 'Our Father'; the term is a translation of Latin *oratio Dominica*, and is first recorded in the Book of Common Prayer of 1549

4 sacrifice of praise (and thanksgiving)
an offering of praise to God; with reference to the Bible (Leviticus) 'He shall offer with the sacrifice of thanksgiving unleavened cakes mingled with oil'

5 tell one's beads
say one's prayers; the *beads* of a rosary or paternoster, used for keeping count of the prayers said

QUOTATIONS

6 O gods, grant me this in return for my piety.
Catullus *c*.84–*c*.54 BC: *Carmina*

7 Ask, and it shall be given you; seek, and ye shall find; knock, and it shall be opened unto you.
Bible: St Matthew; see **Action** 11

8 A man's prayer is only answered if he takes his heart into his hand.
The Talmud: *Babylonian Talmud* Taanit

9 Christ beside me,
Christ before me,
Christ behind me,
Christ within me,
Christ beneath me,
Christ above me.
St Patrick fl. 5th cent.: 'St Patrick's Breastplate'

10 Perform the prayer
at the sinking of the sun to the darkening of the night
and the recital of dawn.
The Koran: sura 17

11 God be in my head,
And in my understanding.
Anonymous: *Sarum Missal* (11th century)

12 Prayer in my opinion is nothing else than an intimate sharing between friends.
St Teresa of Ávila 1512–82: *Life of the Mother Teresa of Jesus* (1611)

13 My words fly up, my thoughts remain below:
Words without thoughts never to heaven go.
William Shakespeare 1564–1616: *Hamlet* (1601)

14 I throw myself down in my Chamber, and I call in, and invite God, and his Angels thither, and when they are there, I neglect God and his Angels, for the noise of a fly, for the rattling of a coach, for the whining of a door.
John Donne 1572–1631: *LXXX Sermons* (1640) 12 December 1626 'At the Funeral of Sir William Cokayne'

15 O Lord! thou knowest how busy I must be this day: if I forget thee, do not thou forget me.
prayer before the Battle of Edgehill, 1642
Jacob Astley 1579–1652: Sir Philip Warwick *Memoires* (1701)

16 At my devotion I love to use the civility of my knee, my hat, and hand.
Thomas Browne 1605–82: *Religio Medici* (1643)

17 Be still and cool in thy own mind and spirit from thy own thoughts, and then thou wilt feel the principle of God to turn thy mind to the Lord God.
George Fox 1624–91: diary 1658

18 No praying, it spoils business.
Thomas Otway 1652–85: *Venice Preserved* (1682)

19 O God, if there be a God, save my soul, if I have a soul!
prayer of a common soldier before the battle of Blenheim, 1704
Anonymous: in *Notes and Queries* 9 October 1937

20 One single grateful thought raised to heaven is the most perfect prayer.
G. E. Lessing 1729–81: *Minna von Barnhelm* (1767)

21   Did not God
Sometimes withhold in mercy what we ask,
We should be ruined at our own request.
Hannah More 1745–1833: *Moses in the Bulrushes* (1782)

22 He prayeth well, who loveth well
Both man and bird and beast.
Samuel Taylor Coleridge 1772–1834: 'The Rime of the Ancient Mariner' (1798)

23 Enjoy yourself—that's the best way to pray.
Georg Büchner 1813–37: *Danton's Death* (1835)

24 And lips say, 'God be pitiful,'
Who ne'er said, 'God be praised.'
Elizabeth Barrett Browning 1806–61: 'The Cry of the Human' (1844)

25   More things are wrought by prayer
Than this world dreams of.
Alfred, Lord Tennyson 1809–92: *Idylls of the King* 'The Passing of Arthur' (1869)

26 Whatever a man prays for, he prays for a miracle. Every prayer reduces itself to this: Great God, grant that twice two be not four.
Ivan Turgenev 1818–83: *Poems in Prose* (1881) 'Prayer'

27 To lift up the hands in prayer gives God glory, but a man with a dungfork in his hand, a woman with a slop-pail, give him glory too. He is so great that all things give him glory if you mean they should.
Gerard Manley Hopkins 1844–89: 'The Principle or Foundation' (1882)

28 You can't pray a lie.
Mark Twain 1835–1910: *Adventures of Huckleberry Finn* (1885)

29 Frederick Douglass used to tell me that when he was a Maryland slave, and a good Methodist, he would go into the farthest corner of the tobacco fields and pray to God to bring him liberty; but God never answered his prayers until he prayed with his heels.
Susan B. Anthony 1820–1906: R. C. Dorr *Susan B. Anthony* (1928)

30 Often when I pray I wonder if I am not posting letters to a non-existent address.
C. S. Lewis 1898–1963: letter to Arthur Greeves, 24 December 1930; W. Hooper (ed.) *They Stand Together* (1979)

31 The wish for prayer is a prayer in itself.
Georges Bernanos 1888–1948: *Journal d'un curé de campagne* (1936)

32 School prayer . . . bears about as much resemblance to real spiritual experience as that freeze-dried astronaut food bears to a nice standing rib roast.
Anna Quindlen 1953– : in *New York Times* 7 December 1994

33 The prayers of the dying are especially precious to God, because they will soon be in His presence.
Basil Hume 1923–99: in *Independent* 18 June 1999

⊷ Pregnancy and Birth ⊶

PROVERBS AND SAYINGS

1 **And the child that is born of the Sabbath day,
Is bonny, and blithe, and good and gay.**
traditional rhyme, mid 19th century; see also **Beauty 7, Gifts 2, Sorrow 2, Travel 6, Work 6**

2 **Jeannie Jeannie, full of hopes
Read a book by Marie Stopes
But to judge from her condition
She must have read the wrong edition.**
1920s skipping rhyme; Marie Stopes (1880–1958) was a Scottish birth-control campaigner

3 No moon, no man.
recording the traditional belief that a child born at the time of the new moon or just before its appearance will not live to grow up; English proverb, late 19th century

QUOTATIONS

4 In sorrow thou shalt bring forth children.
Bible: Genesis

5 The queen of Scots is this day leichter of a fair son, and I am but a barren stock.
Elizabeth I 1533–1603: in 1566; Sir James Melville *Memoirs of His Own Life* (1827 ed.)

6 Our birth is but a sleep and a forgetting . . .
Not in entire forgetfulness,
And not in utter nakedness,
But trailing clouds of glory do we come.
William Wordsworth 1770–1850: 'Ode. Intimations of Immortality' (1807)

7 What you say of the pride of giving life to an immortal soul is very fine, dear, but I own I can not enter into that; I think much more of our being like a cow or a dog at such moments; when our poor nature becomes so very animal and unecstatic.
Queen Victoria 1819–1901: letter to the Princess Royal, 15 June 1858

8 In the dark womb where I began
My mother's life made me a man.
Through all the months of human birth
Her beauty fed my common earth.
I cannot see, nor breathe, nor stir,
But through the death of some of her.
John Masefield 1878–1967: 'C. L. M.' (1910)

9 We want better reasons for having children than not knowing how to prevent them.
Dora Russell 1894–1986: *Hypatia* (1925)

10 Death and taxes and childbirth! There's never any convenient time for any of them.
Margaret Mitchell 1900–49: *Gone with the Wind* (1936); see **Certainty** 3

11 I am not yet born; O fill me
With strength against those who would freeze my
humanity, would dragoon me into a lethal automaton,
would make me a cog in a machine, a thing with
one face, a thing.
Louis MacNeice 1907–63: 'Prayer Before Birth' (1944)

12 Abortions will not let you forget.
You remember the children you got that you did not get . . .
Gwendolyn Brooks 1917–2000: 'The Mother' (1945)

13 Love set you going like a fat gold watch.
The midwife slapped your footsoles, and your bald cry
Took its place among the elements.
Sylvia Plath 1932–63: 'Morning Song' (1965)

14 A fast word about oral contraception. I asked a girl to go to bed with me and she said 'no'.
Woody Allen 1935– : at a nightclub in Washington, April 1965

15 If men could get pregnant, abortion would be a sacrament.
Florynce Kennedy 1916–2000: in *Ms.* March 1973

16 No phallic hero, no matter what he does to himself or to another to prove his courage, ever matches the solitary, existential courage of the woman who gives birth.
Andrea Dworkin 1946–2005: *Our Blood* (1976)

17 No test tube can breed love and affection. No frozen packet of semen ever read a story to a sleepy child.
Shirley Williams 1930– : in *Daily Mirror* 2 March 1978

18 If men had to have babies, they would only ever have one each.
Diana, Princess of Wales 1961–97: in *Observer* 29 July 1984

19 Protestant women may take the pill. Roman Catholic women must keep taking The Tablet.
Irene Thomas 1919–2001: in *Guardian* 28 December 1990; see **Medicine** 3

Prejudice and Tolerance

see also **Race and Racism**

PROVERBS AND SAYINGS

1 **Judge not, that ye be not judged.**
used as a warning against overhasty criticism of someone; English proverb, late 15th century, from the Bible (Matthew): see **Justice** 20

2 **Live and let live.**
often used in the context of coexistence between deeply divided groups; English proverb, early 17th century

3 **No tree takes so deep a root as a prejudice.**
emphasizing how difficult it is to eradicate prejudice; American proverb, mid 20th century

4 **There's none so blind as those who will not see.**
used in reference to someone who is unwilling to recognize unwelcome facts; English proverb, mid 16th century

5 **There's none so deaf as those who will not hear.**
used to refer to someone who chooses not to listen to unwelcome information; English proverb, mid 16th century

PHRASES

6 **political correctness**
the avoidance of forms of expression or action that are perceived to exclude, marginalize, or insult groups of people who are socially disadvantaged or discriminated against; see **Language** 28

QUOTATIONS

7 *Sine ira et studio.*
With neither anger nor partiality.
Tacitus c.AD 56–after 117: *Annals*

8 Hear the other side.
St Augustine of Hippo AD 354–430: *De Duabus Animabus contra Manicheos*

9 Sir Roger told them, with the air of a man who would not give his judgement rashly, that much might be said on both sides.
Joseph Addison 1672–1719: in *The Spectator* 20 July 1711

10 There is, however, a limit at which forbearance ceases to be a virtue.
Edmund Burke 1729–97: *Observations on a late Publication on the Present State of the Nation* (2nd ed., 1769)

11 Drive out prejudices through the door, and they will return through the window.
Frederick the Great 1712–86: letter to Voltaire, 19 March 1771

12 When prejudice commands, reason is silent.
Helvétius 1715–71: *De l'homme* (1773)

13 Prejudice is the child of ignorance.
William Hazlitt 1778–1830: 'On Prejudice' (1830)

14 Who's 'im, Bill?
A stranger!
'Eave 'arf a brick at 'im.
Punch: 1854

15 Tolerance is only another name for indifference.
W. Somerset Maugham 1874–1965: *A Writer's Notebook* (1949) written in 1896

16 Make hatred hated!
to public school teachers
Anatole France 1844–1924: speech in Tours, August 1919; Carter Jefferson *Anatole France: The Politics of Scepticism* (1965)

17 I decline utterly to be impartial as between the fire brigade and the fire.
replying to complaints of his bias in editing the *British Gazette* during the General Strike
Winston Churchill 1874–1965: speech, House of Commons, 7 July 1926

18 Bigotry tries to keep truth safe in its hand
With a grip that kills it.
Rabindranath Tagore 1861–1941: *Fireflies* (1928)

19 Oh who is that young sinner with the handcuffs on his wrists?
And what has he been after that they groan and shake their fists?
And wherefore is he wearing such a conscience-stricken air?
Oh they're taking him to prison for the colour of his hair.
A. E. Housman 1859–1936: *Collected Poems* (1939) 'Additional Poems' no. 18

20 Intolerance of groups is often, strangely enough, exhibited more strongly against small differences than against fundamental ones.
Sigmund Freud 1856–1939: *Moses and Monotheism* (1938)

21 You might as well fall flat on your face as lean over too far backward.
James Thurber 1894–1961: 'The Bear Who Let It Alone' in *New Yorker* 29 April 1939

22 Four legs good, two legs bad.
George Orwell 1903–50: *Animal Farm* (1945)

23 We should therefore claim, in the name of tolerance, the right not to tolerate the intolerant.
Karl Popper 1902–94: *The Open Society and Its Enemies* (1945)

24 When people feel deeply, impartiality is bias.
Lord Reith 1889–1971: *Into the Wind* (1945)

25 PLEASE ACCEPT MY RESIGNATION. I DON'T WANT TO BELONG TO ANY CLUB THAT WILL ACCEPT ME AS A MEMBER.
Groucho Marx 1890–1977: *Groucho and Me* (1959)

26 What is objectionable, what is dangerous about extremists is not that they are extreme but that they are intolerant.
Robert Kennedy 1925–68: *The Pursuit of Justice* (1964)

27 Human diversity makes tolerance more than a virtue, it makes it a requirement for survival.
René Dubos 1901–82: *Celebrations of Life* (1981)

⤞ Preparation and Readiness ⤝

PROVERBS AND SAYINGS

1 Be prepared.
motto of the Scout and Guide organizations, deriving from the initials of Robert Baden-Powell (1857–1941), the founder

2 Don't cross the bridge till you come to it.
warning that you should not concern yourself with possible difficulties unless and until they arise; English proverb, mid 19th century

3 The early bird catches the worm.
someone who is energetic and efficient is most likely to be successful; English proverb, mid 17th century; see 10 below

4 The early man never borrows from the late man.
someone who has made their preparations has no need to turn to someone less efficient; English proverb, mid 17th century

5 Forewarned is forearmed.
if one has been warned in advance about a problem one can make preparations for dealing with it; English proverb, early 16th century

6 For want of a nail the shoe was lost; for want of a shoe the horse was lost; and for want of a horse the man was lost.
often quoted allusively to imply that one apparently small circumstance can result in a large-scale disaster; English proverb, early 17th century, late 15th century in French

7 Here's one I made earlier.
catchphrase popularized by children's television programme *Blue Peter*, from 1963, as a culmination to directions for making a model out of empty yoghurt pots, coat-hangers, and similar domestic items

8 Hope for the best and prepare for the worst.
recommending a balance between optimism and realism; English proverb, mid 16th century

9 If you want peace, you must prepare for war.
a country in a state of military preparedness is unlikely to be attacked; English proverb, mid 16th century; see **Warfare** 12

10 It's the second mouse that gets the cheese.
modern addition to 3 above, suggesting the dangers of being the first to make a venture, and the possible benefits of following directly behind a pioneer; see also **Economics** 2

11 Measure seven times, cut once.
care taken in preparation will prevent errors (originally referring to carpentry and needlework); Russian proverb

12 No one was ever lost on a straight road.
if you know where you are going you will not make mistakes; Indian proverb

13 No plan survives first contact with the enemy.
modern saying, from von Moltke: see 22 below

14 To fail to prepare is to prepare to fail.
modern saying

PHRASES

15 armed at all points
prepared in every particular; recorded from late
Middle English, but often referring directly to a First
Folio variant reading of Shakespeare *Hamlet*

QUOTATIONS

16 The voice of him that crieth in the
wilderness, Prepare ye the way of the Lord.
Bible: Isaiah; see **Futility** 14

17 Watch therefore: for ye know not what hour
your Lord doth come.
Bible: St Matthew

18   Not a mouse
Shall disturb this hallowed house:
I am sent with broom before,
To sweep the dust behind the door.
William Shakespeare 1564–1616: *A Midsummer
Night's Dream* (1595–6)

19 No time like the present.
Mrs Manley 1663–1724: *The Lost Lover* (1696)

20 Barkis is willin'.
Charles Dickens 1812–70: *David Copperfield*
(1850)

21 I think the necessity of being *ready*
increases. Look to it.
Abraham Lincoln 1809–65: the whole of a letter
to Governor Andrew Curtin of Pennsylvania, 8
April 1861

22 No plan of operations reaches with any
certainty beyond the first encounter with
the enemy's main force.
Helmuth von Moltke 1800–91: *Kriegsgechichtiche
Einzelschriften* (1880); see 13 above

23 If we had had more time for discussion we
should probably have made a great many
more mistakes.
Leon Trotsky 1879–1940: *My Life* (1930)

24 In preparing for battle I have always found
that plans are useless, but planning is
indispensable.
Dwight D. Eisenhower 1890–1969: Richard Nixon
Six Crises (1962); attributed

25 First things first, second things never.
Shirley Conran 1932– : *Superwoman* (1975)

26 Go ahead, make my day.
Joseph C. Stinson 1947– : *Sudden Impact* (1983
film); spoken by Clint Eastwood

27 We are ready for any unforeseen event
which may or may not happen.
George W. Bush 1946– : in *Guardian* 30
December 2000

⊱ The Present ⊰

see also **The Past**

PROVERBS AND SAYINGS

**1 Enjoy the present moment and don't
grieve for the future.**
American proverb, mid 20th century

**2 Jam tomorrow and jam yesterday, but
never jam today.**
English proverb, late 19th century, from Carroll: see
11 below

**3 Yesterday has gone, tomorrow is yet to
be. Today is the miracle.**
modern saying; see 4 below, **Charity** 27

**4 Yesterday is ashes; tomorrow is wood.
Only today does the fire burn brightly.**
emphasizing the importance of enjoying and valuing
the present rather than dwelling in the past, which
cannot be changed, or the future, which has not yet
happened; Canadian saying, said to be of Inuit
origin; see 3 above

QUOTATIONS

5 *Carpe diem, quam minimum credula postero.*
Seize the day, put no trust in the future.
Horace 65–8 BC: *Odes*

6 Take therefore no thought for the morrow:
for the morrow shall take thought for the
things of itself. Sufficient unto the day is the
evil thereof.
Bible: St Matthew; see **Worry** 4

7 Can ye not discern the signs of the times?
Bible: St Matthew

8 Praise they that will times past, I joy to see
My self now live: this age best pleaseth me.
Robert Herrick 1591–1674: 'The Present Time Best
Pleaseth' (1648)

9 The present is the funeral of the past,
And man the living sepulchre of life.
John Clare 1793–1864: 'The present is the funeral
of the past' (written 1845)

10 Unborn TO-MORROW, and dead YESTERDAY,
Why fret about them if TO-DAY be sweet!
Edward Fitzgerald 1809–83: *The Rubáiyát of Omar
Khayyám* (1859)

11 The rule is, jam to-morrow and jam
yesterday—but never jam today.
Lewis Carroll 1832–98: *Through the Looking-Glass*
(1872); see 2 above, **Foresight** 17

12 To-morrow for the young the poets
    exploding like bombs,
The walks by the lake, the weeks of perfect
    communion;
To-morrow the bicycle races
Through the suburbs on summer evenings:
    but to-day the struggle.
W. H. Auden 1907–73: 'Spain 1937' (1937)

13 Exhaust the little moment. Soon it dies.
And be it gash or gold it will not come
Again in this identical disguise.
Gwendolyn Brooks 1917–2000: 'Exhaust the little
moment' (1949)

14 Life is one tenth Here and Now, nine-tenths
a history lesson. For most of the time the
Here and Now is neither now nor here.
Graham Swift 1949– : *Waterland* (1984)

15 Things are both more trivial than they ever
were, and more important than they ever
were, and the difference between the trivial
and the important doesn't seem to matter.
But the nowness of everything is absolutely
wondrous.
on his heightened awareness of things, in the face of
his imminent death
Dennis Potter 1935–94: interview with Melvyn
Bragg on Channel 4, March 1994, in *Seeing the
Blossom* (1994)

16 It's not perfect, but to me on balance Right
Now is a lot better than the Good Old Days.
Maeve Binchy 1940– : in *Irish Times* 15 November
1997; see **The Past** 12

⇥ The Presidency ⇤

see also **America, Politicians**

PHRASES

1 **bully pulpit**
a public office or position of authority that provides
its occupant with an outstanding opportunity to
speak out on any issue; from Roosevelt's personal
view of the presidency: see 7 below

2 **just a heart-beat away from the
Presidency**
the vice-president's position; from Adlai Stevenson
(1900–65), speech at Cleveland, Ohio, 23 October
1952, 'The Republican party did not have to . . .
encourage the excesses of its Vice-Presidential
nominee [Richard Nixon]—the young man who asks
you to set him one heart-beat from the Presidency of
the United States'

QUOTATIONS

3 My country has in its wisdom contrived for
me the most insignificant office that ever
the invention of man contrived or his
imagination conceived.
of the vice-presidency
John Adams 1735–1826: letter to Abigail Adams, 19
December 1793

4 A citizen, first in war, first in peace, and first
in the hearts of his countrymen.
Henry Lee 1756–1818: *Funeral Oration on the death
of General Washington* (1800)

5 I have learned to expect that it will rarely
fall to the lot of imperfect man to retire from
this station with the reputation and the
favour which bring him into it.
Thomas Jefferson 1743–1826: first inaugural
address, 4 March 1801

6 As President, I have no eyes but
constitutional eyes; I cannot see you.
Abraham Lincoln 1809–65: reply to the South
Carolina Commissioners; attributed

7 I have got such a bully pulpit!
Theodore Roosevelt 1858–1919: in *Outlook* (New York) 27 February 1909; see 1 above, 19 below

8 Log-cabin to White House.
William Roscoe Thayer 1859–1923: title of biography (1910) of James Garfield (1831–81)

9 To announce that there must be no criticism of the president, or that we are to stand by the president, right or wrong, is not only unpatriotic and servile, but is morally treasonable to the American public.
Theodore Roosevelt 1858–1919: in *Kansas City Star* 7 May 1918

10 When I was a boy I was told that anybody could become President. I'm beginning to believe it.
Clarence Darrow 1857–1938: Irving Stone *Clarence Darrow for the Defence* (1941)

11 No easy problems ever come to the President of the United States. If they are easy to solve, somebody else has solved them.
Dwight D. Eisenhower 1890–1969: in *Parade Magazine* 8 April 1962

12 The lines he loved to hear were: 'Don't let it be forgot, that once there was a spot, for one brief shining moment that was known as Camelot.' . . . There'll be great Presidents again . . . but there'll never be another Camelot again.
on the Kennedy White House, quoting Alan Jay Lerner
Jacqueline Kennedy Onassis 1929–94: in *Life* 6 December 1963

13 The vice-presidency isn't worth a pitcher of warm piss.
John Nance Garner 1868–1967: O. C. Fisher *Cactus Jack* (1978)

14 The answer to the runaway Presidency is not the messenger-boy Presidency. The American democracy must discover a middle way between making the President a tsar and making him a puppet.
Arthur M. Schlesinger Jr. 1917– : *The Imperial Presidency* (1973) preface

15 There can be no whitewash at the White House.
on Watergate
Richard Nixon 1913–94: television speech, 30 April 1973

16 The US presidency is a Tudor monarchy plus telephones.
Anthony Burgess 1917–93: George Plimpton (ed.) *Writers at Work* 4th Series (1977)

17 When the President does it, that means that it is not illegal.
Richard Nixon 1913–94: David Frost *I Gave Them a Sword* (1978)

18 Ronald Reagan . . . is attempting a great breakthrough in political technology—he has been perfecting the Teflon-coated Presidency. He sees to it that nothing sticks to him.
Patricia Schroeder 1940– : speech in the US House of Representatives, 2 August 1983

19 If the President has a bully pulpit, then the First Lady has a white glove pulpit . . . more refined, restricted, ceremonial, but it's a pulpit all the same.
Nancy Reagan 1923– : in *New York Times* 10 March 1988; see 7 above

20 Poor George [Bush], he can't help it—he was born with a silver foot in his mouth.
Ann Richards 1933– : keynote speech at the Democratic convention, in *Independent* 20 July 1988; see **Wealth** 8

21 Somewhere out in this audience may even be someone who will one day follow in my footsteps, and preside over the White House as the President's spouse. I wish him well!
Barbara Bush 1925– : remarks at Wellesley College Commencement, 1 June 1990

22 To those of you who received honours, awards and distinctions, I say well done. And to the C students, I say you, too, can be president of the United States.
George W. Bush 1946– : in *Sunday Times* 27 May 2001

➤➤ Pride and Humility ◄◄

see also **Self-Esteem and Self-Assertion**

PROVERBS AND SAYINGS

1 **Pride feels no pain.**
implying that inordinate self-esteem will not allow the admission that one might be suffering; English proverb, early 17th century

2 **Pride goes before a fall.**
often with the implication that proud and haughty behaviour will contribute to its own downfall; English proverb, late 14th century; see 4 below

PHRASES

3 as proud as Lucifer
very proud, arrogant; *Lucifer* = the rebel angel whose fall from heaven Jerome and other early Christian

writers considered was alluded to in the Bible (Isaiah, where the word is an epithet of the king of Babylon), and equivalent to Satan, the Devil

QUOTATIONS

4 Pride goeth before destruction, and an haughty spirit before a fall.
Bible: Proverbs; see 2 above

5 Blessed are the meek: for they shall inherit the earth.
Bible: St Matthew; see 11 below

6 He that is down needs fear no fall,
He that is low no pride.
He that is humble ever shall
Have God to be his guide.
John Bunyan 1628–88: *The Pilgrim's Progress* (1684) 'Shepherd Boy's Song'

7 We are so very 'umble.
Charles Dickens 1812–70: *David Copperfield* (1850)

8 Pride helps us; and pride is not a bad thing when it only urges us to hide our own hurts, not to hurt others.
George Eliot 1819–80: *Middlemarch* (1871–2)

9 I can trace my ancestry back to a protoplasmal primordial atomic globule. Consequently, my family pride is something in-conceivable. I can't help it. I was born sneering.
W. S. Gilbert 1836–1911: *The Mikado* (1885)

10 The tumult and the shouting dies—
The captains and the kings depart—

Still stands Thine ancient Sacrifice,
An humble and a contrite heart.
Lord God of Hosts, be with us yet,
Lest we forget—lest we forget!
Rudyard Kipling 1865–1936: 'Recessional' (1897); see **Hospitality** 22

11 We have the highest authority for believing that the meek shall inherit the earth; though I have never found any particular corroboration of this aphorism in the records of Somerset House.
F. E. Smith 1872–1930: *Contemporary Personalities* (1924); see 5 above

12 I have often wished I had time to cultivate modesty . . . But I am too busy thinking about myself.
Edith Sitwell 1887–1964: in *Observer* 30 April 1950

13 No one can make you feel inferior without your consent.
Eleanor Roosevelt 1884–1962: in *Catholic Digest* August 1960

14 In 1969 I published a small book on Humility. It was a pioneering work which has not, to my knowledge, been superseded.
Lord Longford 1905–2001: in *Tablet* 22 January 1994

⇢⇢ Problems and Solutions ⇠⇠

see also **Ways and Means**

PROVERBS AND SAYINGS

1 If you lead your mule to the top of the minaret, then you must lead him down again.
if you get yourself into a difficult position, you will have to extricate yourself; Arab proverb

2 Jim'll fix it.
catchphrase of a BBC television series (1975–94) starring Jimmy Savile in which participants had their wishes fulfilled

3 Never bid the Devil good morrow until you meet him.
a warning against trying to deal with problems or difficulties before they have actually occurred;

English proverb, late 19th century, said to be an old Irish saying

4 When all you have is a hammer, everything looks like a nail.
often used to comment on the wholesale application of one solution or method to the solution of any problem; English proverb, late 20th century (chiefly North American)

5 Why did the chicken cross the road?
traditional puzzle question, to which the answer is, to get to the other side; mid 19th century

PHRASES

6 a chicken-and-egg problem

an unresolved question as to which of two things caused the other; from the riddle, *Which came first, the chicken or the egg?*

7 cut the Gordian knot

solve a problem by force or by evading the conditions; in allusion to an intricate knot tied by Gordius, king of Gordium, Phrygia, and cut through by Alexander the Great in response to the prophecy that only the future ruler of Asia could loosen it

8 Frankenstein's monster

something which has developed beyond the management or control of its originator; *Frankenstein* the title of a novel (1818) by Mary Shelley whose eponymous main character constructed and gave life to a human monster

9 make bricks without straw

perform a task without provision of the necessary materials or means; from the Bible (Exodus), in allusion to Pharaoh's decree to the taskmasters set over the Israelites in Egypt 'Ye shall no more give the people straw to make brick, as heretofore: let them go and gather straw for themselves'; see **Futility** 6

10 Open Sesame

a (marvellous or irresistible) means of securing access to what would usually be inaccessible; the magic words by which, in the tale of Ali Baba and the Forty Thieves in the *Arabian Nights*, the door of the robbers' cave was made to open

11 Pandora's box

a thing which once activated will give rise to many unmanageable problems; in Greek mythology, the gift of Jupiter to *Pandōra*, 'all-gifted', the first mortal woman, on whom, when made by Vulcan, all the gods and goddesses bestowed gifts; the box enclosed all human ills, which flew out when it was foolishly opened (or in a later version, it contained all the blessings of the gods, which with the exception of hope escaped and were lost when the box was opened); see **Europe** 13

12 philosophers' stone

a universal cure or solution; the supreme object of alchemy, a substance supposed to change any metal into gold or silver and (according to some) to cure all diseases and prolong life indefinitely

13 the sixty-four thousand dollar question

the crucial issue, a difficult question, a dilemma; the top prize in a broadcast quiz show

14 sorcerer's apprentice

a person who having instigated a process is unable to control it; translating French *l'apprenti sorcier*, a symphonic poem by Paul Dukas (1897) after *der Zauberlehrling*, a ballad by Goethe (1797)

15 there's the rub

there is the difficulty; a *rub* here is literally an impediment in bowls by which a bowl is hindered in or diverted from its proper course; from Shakespeare: see **Death** 33

QUOTATIONS

16 Probable impossibilities are to be preferred to improbable possibilities.
Aristotle 384–322 BC: *Poetics*

17 One hears only those questions for which one is able to find answers.
Friedrich Nietzsche 1844–1900: *The Gay Science* (1882)

18 How often have I said to you that when you have eliminated the impossible, whatever remains, *however improbable*, must be the truth?
Arthur Conan Doyle 1859–1930: *The Sign of Four* (1890)

19 The fascination of what's difficult
Has dried the sap out of my veins, and rent
Spontaneous joy and natural content
Out of my heart.
W. B. Yeats 1865–1939: 'The Fascination of What's Difficult' (1910)

20 For most of my life I refused to work at any problem unless its solution seemed to be capable of being put to commercial use.
Thomas Alva Edison 1847–1931: interview, in *New York Sun* February 1917

21 There is always a well-known solution to every human problem—neat, plausible, and wrong.
Henry Louis Mencken 1880–1956: *Prejudices* 2nd series (1920)

22 Another nice mess you've gotten me into.
Stan Laurel 1890–1965: *Another Fine Mess* (1930 film) and many other Laurel and Hardy films; spoken by Oliver Hardy

23 It isn't that they can't see the solution. It is that they can't see the problem.
G. K. Chesterton 1874–1936: *Scandal of Father Brown* (1935)

24 We haven't got the money, so we've got to think!
Ernest Rutherford 1871–1937: in *Bulletin of the Institute of Physics* (1962); see 29 below

25 Let me have the best solution worked out. Don't argue the matter. The difficulties will argue for themselves.
on the Mulberry floating harbours
Winston Churchill 1874–1965: minute to Lord Mountbatten, 30 May 1942

26 What we're saying today is that you're either part of the solution or you're part of the problem.
Eldridge Cleaver 1935–98: speech in San Francisco, 1968; R. Scheer *Eldridge Cleaver, Post Prison Writings and Speeches* (1969)

27 Problems worthy
of attack
prove their worth
by hitting back.
Piet Hein 1905– : 'Problems' (1969)

28 Houston, we've had a problem.
on Apollo 13 space mission, 14 April 1970
James Lovell 1928– : in *The Times* 15 April 1970

29 Rutherford was a disaster. He started the 'something for nothing' tradition . . . the notion that research can always be done on the cheap . . . The war taught us differently.

If you want quick and effective results you must put the money in.
Edward Bullard 1907–80: P. Grosvenor and J. McMillan *The British Genius* (1973); see 24 above

30 If a problem is too difficult to solve, one cannot claim that it is solved by pointing at all the efforts made to solve it.
Hannes Alfven 1908–95: quoted by Lord Flowers in 1976; A. Sampson *The Changing Anatomy of Britain* (1982)

31 What I cannot create, I do not understand. Know how to solve every problem that has been solved.
written on his blackboard at Caltech, as he left it for the last time in January 1988
Richard Feynman 1918–88: Christopher Sykes (ed.) *No Ordinary Genius* (1994)

32   Most of life's problems can be solved
By running fast and kicking something.
U. A. Fanthorpe 1929– : 'Autumn Offer' (2000)

⊱⊱ Progress ⊰⊰

see also **Change**

PROVERBS AND SAYINGS

1 Be sure you can better your condition before you make a change.
American proverb, mid 20th century

PHRASES

2 brave new world
utopia produced by technological and social advance; title of a satirical novel by Aldous Huxley (1932), after Shakespeare *Tempest*: see **Human Race** 14

3 future shock
a state of distress or disorientation due to rapid social or technological change; from Alvin Toffler in *Horizon* 1965, 'The dizzying disorientation brought on by the premature arrival of the future'; definition of *future shock*

4 Great Leap Forward
an unsuccessful attempt made under Mao Zedong in China 1958–60 to hasten the process of industrialization and improve agricultural production

5 quantum leap
a sudden, significant or very evident (usually large) increase or advance; from the term *quantum jump* in Physics, referring to an abrupt transition from one quantum state to another

QUOTATIONS

6 The thing that hath been, it is that which shall be; and that which is done is that which shall be done: and there is no new thing under the sun.
Bible: Ecclesiastes; see **Earth** 7, **Familiarity** 12

7 Forgetting those things which are behind, and reaching forth unto those things which are before,
I press toward the mark.
Bible: Philippians

8 We are like dwarfs on the shoulders of giants, so that we can see more than they, and things at a greater distance, not by virtue of any sharpness of sight on our part, or any physical distinction, but because we are carried high and raised up by their giant size.
Bernard of Chartres d. *c.*1130: John of Salisbury *The Metalogicon* (1159); see 9 below

9 If I have seen further it is by standing on the shoulders of giants.
Isaac Newton 1642–1727: letter to Robert Hooke, 5 February 1676; see 8 above

10 Not to go back, is somewhat to advance, And men must walk at least before they dance.
Alexander Pope 1688–1744: *Imitations of Horace*

11 Nothing in progression can rest on its original plan. We may as well think of rocking a grown man in the cradle of an infant.
Edmund Burke 1729–97: *Letter to the Sheriffs of Bristol* (1777)

12 The European talks of progress because by an ingenious application of some scientific acquirements he has established a society which has mistaken comfort for civilization.
Benjamin Disraeli 1804–81: *Tancred* (1847)

13 Belief in progress is a doctrine of idlers and Belgians. It is the individual relying upon his neighbours to do his work.
Charles Baudelaire 1821–67: *Journaux intimes* (1887) 'Mon coeur mis à nu'

14 The reasonable man adapts himself to the world: the unreasonable one persists in trying to adapt the world to himself. Therefore all progress depends on the unreasonable man.
George Bernard Shaw 1856–1950: *Man and Superman* (1903)

15 One step forward two steps back.
Lenin 1870–1924: title of book (1904)

16 The new growth in the plant swelling against the sheath, which at the same time imprisons and protects it, must still be the truest type of progress.
Jane Addams 1860–1935: *Democracy and Social Ethics* (1907)

17 The slogan of progress is changing from the full dinner pail to the full garage.
sometimes paraphrased as, 'a car in every garage and a chicken in every pot'
Herbert Hoover 1874–1964: speech in New York, 22 October 1928; see **Poverty** 17

18 In time to come, I tell them, we'll be equal to any living now. If cripples, then no matter; we shall just have been run over by 'New Man' in the wagon of his 'Plan'.
Boris Pasternak 1890–1960: 'When I Grow Weary' (1932)

19 Want is one only of five giants on the road of reconstruction . . . the others are Disease, Ignorance, Squalor and Idleness.
William Henry Beveridge 1879–1963: *Social Insurance and Allied Services* (1942)

20 'Change' is scientific, 'progress' is ethical; change is indubitable, whereas progress is a matter of controversy.
Bertrand Russell: *Unpopular Essays* (1950) 'Philosophy and Politics'

21 Man aspires to the stars. But if he can get his sewage and refuse distributed and utilised in orderly fashion he will be doing very well.
Roy Bridger: in *The Times* 13 July 1959

22 Is it progress if a cannibal uses knife and fork?
Stanislaw Lec 1909–66: *Unkempt Thoughts* (1962)

23 The march of social progress is like a long and straggling parade, with the seers and prophets at its head and a smug minority bringing up the rear.
Pierre Berton 1920– : *The Smug Minority* (1968)

24 Things can only get better.
Jamie Petrie and **Peter Cunnah**: title of song (1992), used as a slogan by the Labour party in the 1997 general election campaign

25 For 80 per cent of humanity the Middle Ages ended suddenly in the 1950s; or perhaps better still, they were *felt* to end in the 1960s.
Eric Hobsbawm 1917– : *Age of Extremes* (1994)

26 Progress is not made by the cynics and the doubters, it is made by those who believe everything is possible.
Carly Fiorina 1954– : speech, Las Vegas, 18 November 2002

⤳ Publishing ⤶

see also **Books**

PHRASES

1 **printer's devil**
an errand-boy or junior assistant in a printing office; *devil* = a person employed in a subordinate position

to work under the direction of or for a particular person; see 8 below

2 river of white
a white line or streak down a printed page where spaces between words on consecutive lines are close together

QUOTATIONS

3 I, according to my copy, have done set it in imprint, to the intent that noble men may see and learn the noble acts of chivalry, the gentle and virtuous deeds that some knights used in those days.
William Caxton 1421–91: Thomas Malory *Le Morte D'Arthur* (1485) prologue

4 You shall see them on a beautiful quarto page where a neat rivulet of text shall meander through a meadow of margin.
Richard Brinsley Sheridan 1751–1816: *The School for Scandal* (1777)

5 Never literary attempt was more unfortunate than my Treatise of Human Nature. It fell *dead-born from the press.*
David Hume 1711–76: *My Own Life* (1777)

6 The poem will please if it is lively—if it is stupid it will fail—but I will have none of your damned cutting and slashing.
Lord Byron 1788–1824: letter to his publisher John Murray, 6 April 1819

7 Publish and be damned.
replying to Harriette Wilson's blackmail threat, c. 1825
Duke of Wellington 1769–1852: attributed

8 For you know, dear—I may, without vanity, hint—
Though an angel should write, still 'tis *devils* must print.
Thomas Moore 1779–1852: *The Fudges in England* (1835); see 1 above

9 Now Barabbas was a publisher.
alteration in a Bible of the verse 'Now Barabbas was a robber'
Thomas Campbell 1777–1844: attributed, in Samuel Smiles *A Publisher and his Friends* (1891); also attributed, wrongly, to Byron

10 University printing presses exist, and are subsidised by the Government for the purpose of producing books which no one can read; and they are true to their high calling.
Francis M. Cornford 1874–1943: *Microcosmographia Academica* (1908)

11 For several days after my first book was published I carried it about in my pocket, and took surreptitious peeps at it to make sure that the ink had not faded.
J. M. Barrie 1860–1937: speech at the Critics' Circle in London, 26 May 1922

12 Of all the literary scenes
Saddest this sight to me:
The graves of little magazines
Who died to make verse free.
Keith Preston 1884–1927: 'The Liberators'

13 Gutenberg made everybody a reader. Xerox makes everybody a publisher.
Marshall McLuhan 1911–80: in *Guardian Weekly* 12 June 1977

14 The whole world of publishing has changed. The accountants have moved in. It's now the bottom line, not is it a good book?
Hammond Innes 1913– : interview in *Daily Telegraph* 3 August 1996

⤜Punctuality⤛

PROVERBS AND SAYINGS

1 **Better late than never.**
even if one has missed the first chance of doing something, it is better to attempt it than not to do it at all; English proverb, early 14th century

2 **Cathedral time is five minutes later than standard time.**
order of service leaflet, Christ Church Cathedral, Oxford, 1990s

3 **First come, first served.**
English proverb, late 14th century

4 **Punctuality is the art of guessing correctly how late the other party is going to be.**
American proverb, mid 20th century

5 **Punctuality is the politeness of princes.**
English proverb, mid 19th century; see 10 below

6 **Punctuality is the soul of business.**
English proverb, mid 19th century

QUOTATIONS

7 You come most carefully upon your hour.
William Shakespeare 1564–1616: *Hamlet* (1601)

8 I was nearly kept waiting.
Louis XIV 1638–1715: attribution queried, among others, by E. Fournier in *L'Esprit dans l'Histoire* (1857)

9 Recollect that painting and punctuality mix like oil and vinegar, and that genius and regularity are utter enemies, and must be to the end of time.
Thomas Gainsborough 1727–88: letter to the Hon. Edward Stratford, 1 May 1772

10 Punctuality is the politeness of kings.
Louis XVIII 1755–1824: *Souvenirs de J. Lafitte* (1844); attributed; see 5 above

11 The only way of catching a train I have ever discovered is to miss the train before.
G. K. Chesterton 1874–1936: *Tremendous Trifles* (1909)

12 An artist must organize his life. Here is the exact timetable of my daily activities. Get up: 7.18 am; be inspired: 10.23 to 11.47 am. I take lunch at 12.11 pm and leave the table at 12.14 pm.
Erik Satie 1866–1925: *Memoirs of an Amnesiac* (1914)

13 But think how early I go.
when criticized for continually arriving late for work in the City in 1919
Lord Castlerosse 1891–1943: Leonard Mosley *Castlerosse* (1956); remark also claimed by Howard Dietz at MGM

14 We've been waiting 700 years, you can have the seven minutes.
on arriving at Dublin Castle for the handover by British forces on 16 January 1922, and being told that he was seven minutes late
Michael Collins 1880–1922: Tim Pat Coogan *Michael Collins* (1990); attributed, perhaps apocryphal

15 I have noticed that the people who are late are often so much jollier than the people who have to wait for them.
E. V. Lucas 1868–1938: *365 Days and One More* (1926)

16 We must leave exactly on time . . . From now on everything must function to perfection.
to a station-master
Benito Mussolini 1883–1945: Giorgio Pini *Mussolini* (1939)

17 My Aunt Minnie would always be punctual and never hold up production, but who would pay to see my Aunt Minnie?
on Marilyn Monroe's unpunctuality
Billy Wilder 1906–2002: P. F. Boller and R. L. Davis *Hollywood Anecdotes* (1988)

18 Punctuality is the virtue of the bored.
Evelyn Waugh 1903–66: diary 26 March 1962

19 I will surprise God because I'm late. I was always very punctual with the Devil.
on his imminent death
Jeffrey Bernard 1932–97: in *Guardian* 6 September 1997

20 I love deadlines. I love the whooshing noise they make as they go by.
Douglas Adams 1952–2001: in *Guardian* 14 May 2001

Punishment see **Crime and Punishment**

Quantities and Qualities

PROVERBS AND SAYINGS

1 **Drops that gather one by one finally become a sea.**
Persian proverb

2 **How long is a piece of string?**
traditional saying, used to indicate that something cannot be given a finite measurement

3 **Little fish are sweet.**
small gifts are always acceptable; English proverb, early 19th century

4 **Many a little makes a mickle.**
the proper form of the next proverb (*mickle* in Scottish usage means 'a great quantity or amount'); English proverb, mid 13th century

5 **Many a mickle makes a muckle.**
an alteration of the previous proverb which is actually nonsensical, since *muckle* is a variant of *mickle* and both mean 'a large quantity or amount'; English proverb, late 18th century

6 **The more the merrier.**
English proverb, late 14th century

7 **The nearer the bone, the sweeter the meat.**
the juiciest meat lies next to the bone, or that the meat closest to the bone is particularly precious because it may represent one's last scrap of food; English proverb, late 14th century

8 **Never mind the quality, feel the width.**

used as the title of a television comedy series (1967–9) about a tailoring business in the East End of London, ultimately probably an inversion of a cloth trade saying

9 **One spoonful of tar spoils a barrel of honey.**

Russian proverb

10 **Small is beautiful.**

title of a book by E. F. Schumacher, 1973; see **Economics** 17

PHRASES

13 **Benjamin's portion**

the largest share; the youngest son of the patriarch Jacob, who according to the Bible (Genesis) was given a larger share than his other brothers by his brother Joseph, 'He took and sent messes [portions of food] unto them before him: but Benjamin's mess was five times so much as any of theirs'

14 **the eye of a needle**

a minute opening or space through which it is difficult to pass; chiefly in echoes of the Bible (Matthew): see **Wealth** 16

15 **horn of plenty**

a cornucopia, an overflowing stock; an abundant source; translation of Latin *cornu copiae* a mythical horn able to provide whatever is desired

16 **the lion's share**

the largest share of something

17 **the number of the beast**

six hundred and sixty-six; after the Bible (Revelation) 'Let him that hath understanding count the number of the beast: for it is the number of a man: and his

QUOTATIONS

22 A whole is that which has a beginning, a middle, and an end.
Aristotle 384–322 BC: *Poetics*; see **Cinema** 21, **Fiction** 21

23 The works of Creation are described as being completed in six days, the same formula for a day being repeated six times. The reason for this is that six is the number of perfection.
St. Augustine of Hippo AD 354–430: *The City of God*

24 Nobody can remember more than seven of anything.
reason for omitting the eight beatitudes from his catechism
Cardinal Robert Bellarmine 1542–1621: John Bossy *Christianity in the West 1400–1700* (1985)

25 Thick as autumnal leaves that strew the brooks
In Vallombrosa.
John Milton 1608–74: *Paradise Lost* (1667)

11 **There is safety in numbers.**

now with the implication that a number of people will be unscathed where an individual might be in danger; English proverb, late 17th century

12 **The whole is more than the sum of the parts.**

traditional saying, probably deriving from Aristotle; see **Causes and Consequences** 19

number is six hundred threescore and six' (the beast was traditionally identified with Antichrist)

18 **their name is legion**

they are innumerable; from the story in the Bible (Mark) of the reply of the 'man with an unclean spirit' who was to be healed by Jesus, 'My name is Legion, for we are many'

19 **tip of the iceberg**

a known or recognizable part of something (especially a difficulty) evidently much larger; the part of an iceberg visible above the water

20 **Uncle Tom Cobley and all**

a whole lot of people; the last of a long list of people in the song 'Widecombe Fair'

21 **a widow's cruse**

a seemingly slight resource which is in fact not readily exhausted; in allusion to the story in the Bible (I Kings) of the cruse of oil and handful of meal belonging to the widow to whom Elijah was sent for sustenance: by God's decree neither meal nor oil were exhausted

26 So, naturalists observe, a flea
Hath smaller fleas that on him prey;
And these have smaller fleas to bite 'em,
And so proceed *ad infinitum*.
Jonathan Swift 1667–1745: 'On Poetry' (1733)

27 Nothing is more contrary to the organization of the mind, of the memory, and of the imagination . . . It's just tormenting the people with trivia!!!
on the introduction of the metric system
Napoleon I 1769–1821: *Mémoires . . . écrits à Ste-Hélène* (1823–5)

28 Oh, the little more, and how much it is!
And the little less, and what worlds away!
Robert Browning 1812–89: 'By the Fireside' (1855)

29 I think no virtue goes with size.
Ralph Waldo Emerson 1803–82: 'The Titmouse' (1867)

30 It is our national joy to mistake for the first-rate, the fecund rate.
Dorothy Parker 1893–1967: review of Sinclair Lewis *Dodsworth*; in *New Yorker* 16 March 1929

31 Less is a bore.
Robert Venturi 1925– : *Complexity and Contradiction in Architecture* (1966); see **Architecture** 17, **Excess** 8

32 I'm only a four-dimensional creature. Haven't got a clue how to visualise infinity. Even Einstein hadn't. I know because I asked him.
Patrick Moore 1923– : in *Sunday Times* 15 April 2001

⇥ Quotations ⇤

PROVERBS AND SAYINGS

1 **The devil can quote Scripture for his own ends.**
it is possible for someone engaged in wrongdoing to quote selectively from the Bible in apparent support of their position, and alluding to the temptation of Christ by the Devil in the Bible (Matthew); English proverb, late 16th century: see **The Bible** 8

2 **Proverbs are the coins of the people.**
Russian proverb

3 **There is no proverb without a grain of truth.**
Russian proverb

4 **To understand the people acquaint yourself with their proverbs.**
Arab proverb

PHRASES

5 **cap verses**
reply to one previously quoted with another, that begins with the final or initial letter of the first, or that rimes or otherwise corresponds with it

QUOTATIONS

6 Confound those who have said our remarks before us.
Aelius Donatus 4th century AD: St Jerome *Commentary on Ecclesiastes*

7 Classical quotation is the *parole* of literary men all over the world.
Samuel Johnson 1709–84: James Boswell *Life of Samuel Johnson* (1791) 8 May 1781

8 A proverb is one man's wit and all men's wisdom.
Lord John Russell 1792–1878: R. J. Mackintosh *Sir James Mackintosh* (1835)

9 I hate quotation. Tell me what you know.
Ralph Waldo Emerson 1803–82: diary May 1849

10 He wrapped himself in quotations—as a beggar would enfold himself in the purple of emperors.
Rudyard Kipling 1865–1936: *Many Inventions* (1893)

11 OSCAR WILDE: How I wish I had said that. WHISTLER: You will, Oscar, you will.
James McNeill Whistler 1834–1903: R. Ellman *Oscar Wilde* (1987)

12 But I have long thought that if you knew a column of advertisements by heart, you could achieve unexpected felicities with them. You can get a happy quotation anywhere if you have the eye.
Oliver Wendell Holmes Jr. 1841–1935: letter to Harold Laski, 31 May 1923

13 It is a good thing for an uneducated man to read books of quotations.
Winston Churchill 1874–1965: *My Early Life* (1930)

14 I always have a quotation for everything—it saves original thinking.
Dorothy L. Sayers 1893–1957: *Have His Carcase* (1932)

15 Misquotation is, in fact, the pride and privilege of the learned. A widely-read man never quotes accurately, for the rather obvious reason that he has read too widely.
Hesketh Pearson 1887–1964: *Common Misquotations* (1934)

16 Brush up your Shakespeare,
Start quoting him now.
Brush up your Shakespeare

And the women you will wow.
Cole Porter 1891–1964: 'Brush Up your Shakespeare' (1948 song)

17 People who like quotations love meaningless generalizations.
Graham Greene 1904–91: *Travels With My Aunt* (1969)

18 Windbags can be right. Aphorists can be wrong. It is a tough world.
James Fenton 1949– : in *Times* 21 February 1985

19 A quotation is what a speaker wants to say—unlike a soundbite which is all that an interviewer allows you to say.
Tony Benn 1925– : letter to Antony Jay, August 1996

→→ Race and Racism ←←

see also **Equality, Prejudice and Tolerance**

PROVERBS AND SAYINGS

1 **Am I not a man and a brother.**
motto on the seal of the British and Foreign Anti-Slavery Society, 1787, depicting a kneeling slave in chains uttering these words (subsequently a popular Wedgwood cameo); see **Human Race** 4

2 **Black is beautiful.**
slogan of American civil rights campaigners, mid-1960s

3 **Power to the people.**
slogan of the Black Panther movement, from *c.*1968 onwards

PHRASES

4 **rainbow coalition**
a political alliance of minority peoples and other disadvantaged groups; from Jesse Jackson: see 30 below

5 **the white man's burden**
the supposed task of whites to civilize blacks; from Kipling, originally in specific allusion to the United States' role in the Philippines: see **Duty** 19

QUOTATIONS

6 You call me misbeliever, cut-throat dog,
And spit upon my Jewish gabardine,
And all for use of that which is mine own.
William Shakespeare 1564–1616: *The Merchant of Venice* (1596–8), spoken by Shylock

7 When I recovered a little I found some black people about me . . . I asked them if we were not to be eaten by those white men with horrible looks, red faces, and loose hair.
Olaudah Equiano c.1745–c.97: *Narrative of the Life of Olaudah Equiano* (1789)

8 You have seen how a man was made a slave; you shall see how a slave was made a man.
Frederick Douglass 1818–95: *Narrative of the Life of Frederick Douglass* (1845)

9 The only good Indian is a dead Indian.
at Fort Cobb, January 1869
Philip Henry Sheridan 1831–88: attributed

10 Because a man has a black face and a different religion from our own, there is no reason why he should be treated as a brute.
Edward VII 1841–1910: letter to Lord Granville, 30 November 1875

11 The gentleman will please remember that when his half-civilized ancestors were hunting the wild boar in Silesia, mine were princes of the earth.
in reply to a taunt by a Senator of German descent
Judah Benjamin 1811–84: B. Perley Poore *Perley's Reminiscences* (1886)

12 The so-called white races are really pinko-grey.
E. M. Forster 1879–1970: *A Passage to India* (1924)

13 How odd
Of God
To choose
The Jews.
to which Cecil Browne replied: 'But not so odd/As those who choose/A Jewish God/But spurn the Jews.'
William Norman Ewer 1885–1976: *Week-End Book* (1924)

14 I, too, sing America.
I am the darker brother.
They send me to eat in the kitchen
When company comes.
Langston Hughes 1902–67: 'I, Too' (1925)

15 If my theory of relativity is proven correct, Germany will claim me as a German and France will declare that I am a citizen of the world. Should my theory prove untrue, France will say that I am a German and Germany will declare that I am a Jew.
Albert Einstein 1879–1955: address at the Sorbonne, Paris, possibly early December 1929; in *New York Times* 16 February 1930

16 After all, who remembers today the extermination of the Armenians?
Adolf Hitler 1889–1945: comment, 22 August 1939

17 I herewith commission you to carry out all preparations with regard to . . . a *total solution* of the Jewish question in those territories of Europe which are under German influence.
Hermann Goering 1893–1946: instructions to Heydrich, 31 July 1941; W. L. Shirer *The Rise and Fall of the Third Reich* (1962)

18 Some of my best friends are white boys.
when I meet 'em
I treat 'em
just the same as if they was people.
Ray Durem 1915–63: 'Broadminded' (written 1951)

19 The white man was *created* a devil, to bring chaos upon this earth.
Malcolm X 1925–65: speech, c.1953; Malcolm X with Alex Haley *The Autobiography of Malcolm X* (1965)

20 You gotta say this for the white race—its self-confidence knows no bounds. Who else could go to a small island in the South Pacific where there's no poverty, no crime, no unemployment, no war and no worry—and call it a 'primitive society'?
Dick Gregory 1932– : *From the Back of the Bus* (1962)

21 I want to be the white man's brother, not his brother-in-law.
Martin Luther King 1929–68: in *New York Journal-American* 10 September 1962

22 Segregation now, segregation tomorrow and segregation forever!
George Wallace 1919– : inaugural speech as Governor of Alabama, 14 January 1963

23 There are no 'white' or 'coloured' signs on the foxholes or graveyards of battle.
John F. Kennedy 1917–63: message to Congress on proposed Civil Rights Bill, 19 June 1963

24 Being a star has made it possible for me to get insulted in places where the average Negro could never *hope* to go and get insulted.
Sammy Davis Jnr. 1925–90: *Yes I Can* (1965)

25 It comes as a great shock around the age of 5, 6 or 7 to discover that the flag to which you have pledged allegiance, along with everybody else, has not pledged allegiance to you. It comes as a great shock to see Gary Cooper killing off the Indians and, although you are rooting for Gary Cooper, that the Indians are you.
speaking for the proposition that 'The American Dream is at the expense of the American Negro'; see **America** 4
James Baldwin 1924–87: Cambridge Union, England, 17 February 1965

26 Though it be a thrilling and marvellous thing to be merely young and gifted in such times, it is doubly so, doubly dynamic—to be young, gifted and *black*.
Lorraine Hansberry 1930–65: *To be young, gifted and black: Lorraine Hansberry in her own words* (1969) adapted by Robert Nemiroff

27 As I look ahead, I am filled with foreboding. Like the Roman, I seem to see 'the River Tiber foaming with much blood'.
on the probable consequences of immigration
Enoch Powell 1912–98: speech at the Annual Meeting of the West Midlands Area Conservative Political Centre, Birmingham, 20 April 1968; see **Warfare** 15; see also **Britain** 18

28 And if the white man thought that Asians were a low, filthy nation, Asians could still smile with relief—at least, they were not Africans. And if the white man thought that Africans were a low, filthy nation, Africans in southern Africa could still smile—at least, they were not bushmen. They all have their monsters.
Bessie Head 1937–86: *Maru* (1971)

29 There are no 'mixed' marriages. It just looks that way. People don't mix races; they abandon them or pick them.
Toni Morrison 1931– : *Tar Baby* (1981)

30 When I look out at this convention, I see the face of America, red, yellow, brown, black, and white. We are all precious in God's sight—the real rainbow coalition.
Jesse Jackson 1941– : speech at Democratic National Convention, Atlanta, 19 July 1988; see 4 above

31 Growing up, I came up with this name: I'm a Cablinasian.
explaining his rejection of 'African-American' as the term to describe his Caucasian, Afro-American, Native American, Thai, and Chinese ancestry
Tiger Woods 1975– : interview, 21 April 1997

32 When the Founding Fathers said 'we the people', they did not mean me. My ancestors were three-fifths of a man.
Condoleezza Rice 1954– : in *Independent* 3 April 2004; see **America** 13, **Taxes** 13

⇥ Rank and Title ⇤

see also **Class**

see also **Class**

PROVERBS AND SAYINGS

1 **Everybody loves a lord.**
English proverb, mid 19th century

2 **If two ride on a horse, one must ride behind.**
of two people engaged on the same task, one must take a subordinate role; English proverb, late 16th century

3 **Where Macgregor sits is the head of the table.**
sometimes attributed to 'Rob Roy' MacGregor. Other names are used as well as Macgregor; English proverb, mid 19th century

4 **You may know a gentleman by his horse, his hawk, and his greyhound.**
traditional accoutrements of leisure for those of rank; Welsh proverb

QUOTATIONS

5 Virtue is the one and only nobility.
Juvenal c.AD 60–c.130: *Satires*

6 This love of place and precedency rocks us in our cradles, it lies down with us in our graves.
John Donne 1572–1631: *LXXX Sermons* (1640) 19 December 1619

7 I made the carles lords, but who made the carlines ladies?
of the wives of Scots Lords of Session
James I 1566–1625: E. Grenville Murray *Embassies and Foreign Courts* (1855)

8 'Tis from high life high characters are drawn;
A saint in crape is twice a saint in lawn.
Alexander Pope 1688–1744: 'To Lord Cobham' (1734)

9 I bow to no man for I am considered a prince among my own people. But I will gladly shake your hand.
Canadian Mohawk leader, on being presented to George III
Joseph Brant (Thayendanegea) 1742–1807: attributed

10 Nobility is a graceful ornament to the civil order. It is the Corinthian capital of polished society.
Edmund Burke 1729–97: *Reflections on the Revolution in France* (1790)

11 The rank is but the guinea's stamp,
The man's the gowd for a' that!
Robert Burns 1759–96: 'For a' that and a' that' (1790)

12 I am an ancestor.
taunted on his lack of ancestry when made Duke of Abrantes by Napoleon, 1807
Marshal Junot 1771–1813: attributed

13 Kind hearts are more than coronets,
And simple faith than Norman blood.
Alfred, Lord Tennyson 1809–92: 'Lady Clara Vere de Vere' (1842)

14 What I like about the Order of the Garter is that there is no damned merit about it.
Lord Melbourne 1779–1848: Lord David Cecil *The Young Melbourne* (1939)

15 The stately homes of England,
How beautiful they stand!
Amidst their tall ancestral trees,
O'er all the pleasant land.
Felicia Hemans 1793–1835: 'The Homes of England' (1849); see 20 below

16 The order of nobility is of great use, too, not only in what it creates, but in what it prevents. It prevents the rule of wealth—the religion of gold. This is the obvious and natural idol of the Anglo-Saxon.
Walter Bagehot 1826–77: *The English Constitution* (1867)

17 Titles distinguish the mediocre, embarrass the superior, and are disgraced by the inferior.
George Bernard Shaw 1856–1950: *Man and Superman* (1903)

18 A fully-equipped duke costs as much to keep up as two Dreadnoughts; and dukes are just as great a terror and they last longer.
David Lloyd George 1863–1945: speech at Newcastle, 9 October 1909

19 When I want a peerage, I shall buy it like an honest man.
Lord Northcliffe 1865–1922: Tom Driberg *Swaff* (1974)

20 The Stately Homes of England,
How beautiful they stand,
To prove the upper classes

Have still the upper hand.
Noël Coward 1899–1973: 'The Stately Homes of England' (1938 song); see 15 above

21 A medal glitters, but it also casts a shadow.
a reference to the envy caused by the award of honours
Winston Churchill 1874–1965: in 1941; Kenneth Rose *King George V* (1983)

22 Not a reluctant peer but a persistent commoner.
of his ultimately successful fight to disclaim his inherited title of Viscount Stansgate
Tony Benn 1925– : at a press conference, 23 November 1960

23 There is no stronger craving in the world than that of the rich for titles, except perhaps that of the titled for riches.
Hesketh Pearson 1887–1964: *The Pilgrim Daughters* (1961)

24 What harm have I ever done to the Labour Party?
declining the offer of a peerage
R. H. Tawney 1880–1962: in *Evening Standard* 18 January 1962

25 People fail you, children disappoint you, thieves break in, moths corrupt, but an OBE goes on for ever.
Fay Weldon 1931– : *Praxis* (1978)

26 She needed no royal title to continue to generate her particular brand of magic.
of his sister, Diana, Princess of Wales
Lord Spencer 1964– : tribute at her funeral, 7 September 1997

Readiness see **Preparation and Readiness**

⇢ Reading ⇠

see also **Books**

PROVERBS AND SAYINGS

1 **Have you read any good books lately?**
catchphrase used by Richard Murdoch in radio comedy series *Much-Binding-in-the-Marsh*, written by Richard Murdoch and Kenneth Horne, started 2 January 1947

2 **He that runs may read.**
meaning very clear and readable; English proverb, late 16th century, originally with allusion to the Bible (Habakkuk), reinforced by John Keble's 'Septuagesima' (1827), 'There is a book, who runs may read'

3 **The man who reads is the man who leads.**
American proverb, mid 20th century

QUOTATIONS

4 When he was reading, he drew his eyes along over the leaves, and his heart searched into the sense, but his voice and tongue were silent.
of St Ambrose
St Augustine of Hippo AD 354–430: *Confessions* (AD 397–8)

5 POLONIUS: What do you read, my lord?
HAMLET: Words, words, words.
William Shakespeare 1564–1616: *Hamlet* (1601)

6 Choose an author as you choose a friend.
Wentworth Dillon, Lord Roscommon 1633–85: *Essay on Translated Verse* (1684)

7 He had read much, if one considers his long life; but his contemplation was much more than his reading. He was wont to say that if he had read as much as other men, he should have known no more than other men.
John Aubrey 1626–97: *Brief Lives* 'Thomas Hobbes'

8 Reading is to the mind what exercise is to the body.
Richard Steele 1672–1729: in *The Tatler* 18 March 1710

9 The bookful blockhead, ignorantly read, With loads of learned lumber in his head.
Alexander Pope 1688–1744: *An Essay on Criticism* (1711)

10 A man ought to read just as inclination leads him; for what he reads as a task will do him little good.
Samuel Johnson 1709–84: James Boswell *Life of Samuel Johnson* (1791) 14 July 1763

11 Digressions, incontestably, are the sunshine;—they are the life, the soul of reading;—take them out of this book for instance,—you might as well take the book along with them.
Laurence Sterne 1713–68: *Tristram Shandy* (1759–67)

12 Much have I travelled in the realms of gold, And many goodly states and kingdoms seen.
John Keats 1795–1821: 'On First Looking into Chapman's Homer' (1817)

13 People say that life is the thing, but I prefer reading.
Logan Pearsall Smith 1865–1946: *Afterthoughts* (1931) 'Myself'

14 What do we ever get nowadays from reading to equal the excitement and the revelation in those first fourteen years?
Graham Greene 1904–91: *The Lost Childhood and Other Essays* (1951) title essay

15 What really knocks me out is a book that, when you're all done reading it, you wish the author that wrote it was a terrific friend of yours and you could call him up on the phone whenever you felt like it.
J. D. Salinger 1919– : *Catcher in the Rye* (1951)

16 Curiously enough, one cannot *read* a book: one can only reread it. A good reader, a major reader, an active and creative reader is a rereader.
Vladimir Nabokov 1899–1977: *Lectures on Literature* (1980) 'Good Readers and Good Writers'

17 Any writer worth his salt knows that only a small proportion of literature does more than partly compensate people for the damage they have suffered in learning to read.
Rebecca West 1892–1983: Peter Vansittart *Path from a White Horse* (1985)

18 The world may be full of fourth-rate writers but it's also full of fourth-rate readers.
Stan Barstow 1928– : in *Daily Mail* 15 August 1989

⤛⤜ Reality ⤛⤜

see also **Appearance, Hypothesis and Fact**

PROVERBS AND SAYINGS

1 **All that glitters is not gold.**
an attractive appearance is not necessarily evidence of intrinsic value; English proverb, early 13th century

2 **Where's the beef?**
advertising slogan for Wendy's Hamburgers in campaign launched 9 January 1984, and subsequently taken up by Walter Mondale in a televised debate with Gary Hart from Atlanta, 11 March 1984: 'When I hear your new ideas I'm reminded of that ad, "Where's the beef?" '

PHRASES

3 **cloud cuckoo land**
a state of unrealistic or absurdly over-optimistic fantasy; a translation of Greek *Nephelokokkugia*, the name of the city built by the birds in the Greek poet Aristophanes' comedy *Birds* (414 BC)

4 **in the cold light of day**
when one has had time to consider a situation objectively

5 **ivory tower**
a state of privileged seclusion or separation from the facts and practicalities of the real world, translating French *tour d'ivoire*, used by the writer Sainte-Beuve (1804–69); see **Idealism 12**

6 **opium of the people**
something regarded as inducing a false and unrealistic sense of contentment among people; from Marx: see **Religion 19**; see also **Sports 25**

7 **the real McCoy**
the real thing, the genuine article; it is suggested that this originated from the phrase *the real Mackay*, an advertising slogan used by G. Mackay and Co, whisky distillers in Edinburgh in 1870. The form *McCoy* appears to be of US origin

8 **the real Simon Pure**
the real or genuine person or thing; a character in Centlivre's *A Bold Stroke for a Wife* (1717), who is impersonated by another character during part of the play

QUOTATIONS

9 Every thing, saith Epictetus, hath two handles, the one to be held by, the other not.
Robert Burton 1577–1640: *The Anatomy of Melancholy* (1621–51)

10 I refute it *thus*.
kicking a large stone by way of refuting Bishop Berkeley's theory of the non-existence of matter
Samuel Johnson 1709–84: James Boswell *Life of Samuel Johnson* (1791) 6 August 1763

11 All theory, dear friend, is grey, but the golden tree of actual life springs ever green.
Johann Wolfgang von Goethe 1749–1832: *Faust* pt. 1 (1808) 'Studierzimmer'

12 What is rational is actual and what is actual is rational.
G. W. F. Hegel 1770–1831: *Grundlinien der Philosophie des Rechts* (1821)

13 All that we see or seem
Is but a dream within a dream.
Edgar Allan Poe 1809–49: 'A Dream within a Dream' (1849)

14 Do you think that the things people make fools of themselves about are any less real and true than the things they behave sensibly about? They are more true: they are the only things that are true.
George Bernard Shaw 1856–1950: *Candida* (1898)

15 Between the idea
And the reality
Between the motion
And the act
Falls the Shadow.
T. S. Eliot 1888–1965: 'The Hollow Men' (1925)

16 They said, 'You have a blue guitar,
You do not play things as they are.'
The man replied, 'Things as they are
Are changed upon the blue guitar.'
Wallace Stevens 1879–1955: 'The Man with the Blue Guitar' (1937)

17 BLANCHE: I don't want realism.
MITCH: Naw, I guess not.
BLANCHE: I'll tell you what I want. Magic!
Tennessee Williams: *A Streetcar Named Desire* (1947)

18 Reality goes bounding past the satirist like a cheetah laughing as it lopes ahead of the greyhound.
Claud Cockburn 1904–81: *Crossing the Line* (1958)

19 Perhaps the rare and simple pleasure of being seen for what one is compensates for the misery of being it.
Margaret Drabble 1939– : *A Summer Bird-Cage* (1963)

20 The camera makes everyone a tourist in other people's reality, and eventually in one's own.
Susan Sontag 1933–2004: in *New York Review of Books* 18 April 1974

21 Each person experiences his own reality, and no one else can be the judge of what that reality really is.
Shirley Maclaine 1934– : *Out on a Limb* (1983)

22 I keep trying to understand reality, but it always defeats me. I reinvent the world so that I can handle it.
Terry Gilliam 1940– : in *Observer* 12 September 2004

Reason see **Logic and Reason**

Rebellion see **Revolution and Rebellion**

⇢ Relationships ⇠

see also **Friendship, Hatred, Love**

PROVERBS AND SAYINGS

1 **I am because we are; we are because I am.**
whatever affects the individual affects the whole community and whatever affects the whole community affects the individual; African proverb

2 **It is easy to kindle a fire on a familiar hearth.**
a relationship which has once existed can be revived; Welsh proverb

3 **L'amour est aveugle; l'amitié ferme les yeux.**
Love is blind; friendship closes its eyes; French proverb; see **Love 6**

4 **There is always one who kisses, and one who turns (offers) the cheek.**
traditional saying, said to be French in origin

5 **Treat a man as he is, and that is what he remains. Treat a man as he can be, and that is what he becomes.**
modern saying, from Goethe: see 11 below

QUOTATIONS

6 Am I my brother's keeper?
Bible: Genesis

7 Difficult or easy, pleasant or bitter, you are the same you: I cannot live with you—or without you.
Martial c.AD 40–c.104: *Epigrammata*

8 He who has a thousand friends has not a friend to spare,
And he who has one enemy will meet him everywhere.
Ali ibn-Abi-Talib 602–661: *A Hundred Sayings*

9 In necessary things, unity; in doubtful things, liberty; in all things, charity.
Richard Baxter 1615–91: motto

10 Friendship is a disinterested commerce between equals; love, an abject intercourse between tyrants and slaves.
Oliver Goldsmith 1728–74: *The Good-Natured Man* (1768)

11 When we take people, thou wouldst say, merely as they are, we make them worse; when we treat them as if they were what they should be, we improve them as far as they can be improved.
Johann Wolfgang von Goethe 1749–1832: *Wilhelm Meisters Lehrjare* (1795–6), tr. Carlyle; see 5 above

12 Ships that pass in the night, and speak each other in passing;
Only a signal shown and a distant voice in the darkness;
So on the ocean of life we pass and speak one another,
Only a look and a voice; then darkness again and a silence.
Henry Wadsworth Longfellow 1807–82: *Tales of a Wayside Inn* pt. 3 (1874); see **Meeting 5**

13 Love, friendship, respect do not unite people as much as common hatred for something.
Anton Chekhov 1860–1904: *Notebooks* (1921)

14 Personal relations are the important thing for ever and ever, and not this outer life of telegrams and anger.
E. M. Forster 1879–1970: *Howards End* (1910)

15 I may be wrong, but I have never found deserting friends conciliates enemies.
Margot Asquith 1864–1945: *Lay Sermons* (1927)

16 No human relation gives one possession in another—every two souls are absolutely different. In friendship or in love, the two side by side raise hands together to find what one cannot reach alone.
Kahlil Gibran 1883–1931: *Beloved Prophet: the love letters of Kahlil Gibran and Mary Haskell and her private journal* (1972)

17 The meeting of two personalities is like the contact of two chemical substances: if there is any reaction, both are transformed.
Carl Gustav Jung 1875–1961: *Modern Man in Search of a Soul* (1933)

18 In human relations kindness and lies are worth a thousand truths.
Graham Greene 1904–91: *The Heart of the Matter* (1948)

19 She experienced all the cosiness and irritation which can come from living with thoroughly nice people with whom one has nothing in common.
Barbara Pym 1913–80: *Less than Angels* (1955)

20 Human relationships don't belong to engineering, mathematics, chess, which offer problems that can be perfectly solved. Human relationships grow, like trees.
J. B. Priestley 1894–1984: J. B. Priestley and Jacquetta Hawkes *Journey Down a Rainbow* (1957 rev. ed.)

21 It is easier to live through someone else than to become complete yourself.
Betty Friedan 1921– : *The Feminine Mystique* (1963)

22 And it seems to me you lived your life
Like a candle in the wind.
Never knowing who to cling to
When the rain set in . . .
Elton John 1947– and **Bernie Taupin** 1950– : 'Candle in the Wind' (song, 1973)

23 Never marry a man who hates his mother, because he'll end up hating you.
Jill Bennett 1931–90: in *Observer* 12 September 1982

24 The ones we choose to love become our anchor
when the hawser of the blood-tie's hacked, or frays.
Tony Harrison 1937– : *v* (1985)

25 Men love women, women love children; children love hamsters—it's quite hopeless.
Alice Thomas Ellis 1932–2005: attributed, 1987

26 There are those who never stretch out the hand for fear it will be bitten. But those who never stretch out the hand will never feel it clasped in friendship.
Michael Heseltine 1933– : *Where There's a Will* (1987)

27 Here's how men think. Sex, work—and those are reversible, depending on age—sex, work, food, sports and lastly, begrudgingly, relationships. And here's how women think. Relationships, relationships, relationships, work, sex, shopping, weight, food.
Carrie Fisher 1956– : *Surrender the Pink* (1990)

28 Their relationship consisted
In discussing if it existed.
Thom Gunn 1929–2004: 'Jamesian' (1992)

29 We have to learn to be human alongside all sorts of others, the ones whose company we don't greatly like.
Rowan Williams 1950– : in *Independent* 1 March 2003

⤛ Religion ⤜

see also **The Bible, The Christian Church, Clergy, God, Prayer, Science and Religion**

PROVERBS AND SAYINGS

1 **Man's extremity is God's opportunity.**
great distress or danger may prompt a person to turn to God for help; English proverb, early 17th century

PHRASES

2 **graven image**
an idol; in allusion to the second commandment in the Bible (Exodus) 'Thou shalt not make unto thee any graven image'; see **Lifestyles** 10

3 **people of the Book**
the Jews and Christians as regarded by Muslims; those whose religion entails adherence to a book of divine revelation

QUOTATIONS

4 Is that which is holy loved by the gods because it is holy, or is it holy because it is loved by the gods?
Plato 429–347 BC: *Euthyphro*

5 *Tantum religio potuit suadere malorum.*
So much wrong could religion induce.
Lucretius *c*.94–55 BC: *De Rerum Natura*

6 Render therefore unto Caesar the things which are Caesar's; and unto God the things that are God's.
Bible: St Matthew

7 I go into the Muslim mosque and the Jewish synagogue and the Christian church and I see one altar.
Jalal ad-Din ar-Rumi 1207–73: Coleman Barks and John Moyne (eds.) *The Essential Rumi* (1999)

8 I count religion but a childish toy,
And hold there is no sin but ignorance.
Christopher Marlowe 1564–93: *The Jew of Malta* (*c*.1592)

9 One religion is as true as another.
Robert Burton 1577–1640: *The Anatomy of Melancholy* (1621–51)

10 They are for religion when in rags and contempt; but I am for him when he walks in his golden slippers, in the sunshine and with applause.
John Bunyan 1628–88: *The Pilgrim's Progress* (1678)

11 'People differ in their discourse and profession about these matters, but men of sense are really but of one religion.' . . . 'Pray, my lord, what religion is that which men of sense agree in?' 'Madam,' says the earl immediately, 'men of sense never tell it.'
1st Earl of Shaftesbury 1621–83: Bishop Gilbert Burnet *History of My Own Time* vol. 1 (1724)

12 We have just enough religion to make us hate, but not enough to make us love one another.
Jonathan Swift 1667–1745: *Thoughts on Various Subjects* (1711)

13 I went to America to convert the Indians; but oh, who shall convert me?
John Wesley 1703–91: diary 24 January 1738

14 Putting moral virtues at the highest, and religion at the lowest, religion must still be allowed to be a collateral security, at least, to virtue; and every prudent man will sooner trust to two securities than to one.
Lord Chesterfield 1694–1773: *Letters to his Son* (1774) 8 January 1750

15 Orthodoxy is my doxy; heterodoxy is another man's doxy.
William Warburton 1698–1779: to Lord Sandwich; Joseph Priestley *Memoirs* (1807)

16 My country is the world, and my religion is to do good.
Thomas Paine 1737–1809: *The Rights of Man* pt. 2 (1792)

17 Any system of religion that has any thing in it that shocks the mind of a child cannot be a true system.
Thomas Paine 1737–1809: *The Age of Reason* pt. 1 (1794)

18 In vain with lavish kindness
The gifts of God are strown;
The heathen in his blindness
Bows down to wood and stone.
Reginald Heber 1783–1826: 'From Greenland's icy mountains' (1821 hymn); see **Armed Forces** 34

19 Religion . . . is the opium of the people.
Karl Marx 1818–83: *A Contribution to the Critique of Hegel's Philosophy of Right* (1843–4); see **Reality** 6

20 Things have come to a pretty pass when religion is allowed to invade the sphere of private life.
on hearing an evangelical sermon
Lord Melbourne 1779–1848: G. W. E. Russell *Collections and Recollections* (1898)

21 So long as man remains free he strives for nothing so incessantly and so painfully as to find someone to worship.
Fedor Dostoevsky 1821–81: *The Brothers Karamazov* (1879–80)

22 So many gods, so many creeds,
So many paths that wind and wind,
While just the art of being kind

Is all the sad world needs.
Ella Wheeler Wilcox 1855–1919: 'The World's Need'

23 To become a popular religion, it is only necessary for a superstition to enslave a philosophy.
William Ralph Inge 1860–1954: *Idea of Progress* (1920)

24 There's no reason to bring religion into it. I think we ought to have as great a regard for religion as we can, so as to keep it out of as many things as possible.
Sean O'Casey 1880–1964: *The Plough and the Stars* (1926)

25 Religion is the frozen thought of men out of which they build temples.
Jiddu Krishnamurti 1895–1986: in *Observer* 22 April 1928

26 Zen . . . does not confuse spirituality with thinking about God while one is peeling potatoes. Zen spirituality is just to peel the potatoes.
Alan Watts 1915–73: *The Way of Zen* (1957)

27 If even a dog's tooth is truly worshipped it glows with light. The venerated object is endowed with power, that is the simple sense of the ontological proof.
Iris Murdoch 1919–99: *The Sea, The Sea* (1978)

28 Religion to me has always been the wound, not the bandage.
Dennis Potter 1935–94: interview with Melvyn Bragg on Channel 4, March 1994, in *Seeing the Blossom* (1994)

29 A sense of the sacred without a sense of humour becomes leaden.
Robert Runcie 1921–2000: on *Loose Ends*, BBC Radio 4, 15 April 2000

30 It is time the West confronted its ignorance of Islam. Jews, Muslims and Christians are all children of Abraham.
Tony Blair 1953– : Labour Party conference, Brighton, 2 October 2001

Repentance see Forgiveness and Repentance

Reputation

see also **Fame**

PROVERBS AND SAYINGS

1 **Brave men lived before Agamemnon.**
to be remembered the exploits of a hero must be recorded; English proverb, early 19th century, from Horace: see **Biography** 3

2 **Common fame is seldom to blame.**
reputation is generally founded on fact rather than rumour; English proverb, mid 17th century

3 De mortuis nil nisi bonum.
Latin, literally 'Of the dead, speak kindly or not at all'; see 8 below

4 The devil is not so black as he is painted.
someone may not be as bad as their reputation; English proverb, mid 16th century

5 A good reputation stands still; a bad one runs.
American proverb, mid 20th century

6 He that has an ill name is half hanged.
someone with a bad reputation is already half way to being condemned on any charge brought against him; English proverb, late 14th century

7 A man's best reputation for his future is his record of the past.
American proverb, mid 20th century

8 Never speak ill of the dead.
English proverb, mid 16th century; see 3 above

PHRASES

14 blot one's copybook
tarnish one's good reputation; a *copybook* was a book in which copies were written or printed for pupils to imitate, and *copybook* is applied allusively to maxims of a conventional or commonplace character; see **Causes** 26

15 a blot on one's escutcheon
a mark on one's reputation; *escutcheon* = an heraldic shield or emblem bearing one's coat of arms

QUOTATIONS

18 A good name is rather to be chosen than great riches.
Bible: Proverbs

19 And some there be, which have no memorial . . . and are become as though they had never been born . . .
But these were merciful men, whose righteousness hath not been forgotten . . .
Their bodies are buried in peace; but their name liveth for evermore.
Bible: Ecclesiasticus

20 Caesar's wife must be above suspicion.
Julius Caesar 100–44 BC: oral tradition, based on Plutarch *Parallel Lives* 'Julius Caesar'; see 16 above

21 Woe unto you, when all men shall speak well of you!
Bible: St Luke

22 *Non è il mondan romore altro che un fiato di vento, ch'or vien quinci ed or qien quindi, e muta nome perchè muta lato.*
The reputation which the world bestows is like the wind, that shifts now here now there,

9 No smoke without fire.
rumour is generally founded on fact; English proverb, late 14th century, earlier in French and Latin

10 One man may steal a horse, while another may not look over a hedge.
while one person is endlessly indulged, another is treated with suspicion on the slightest evidence; English proverb, mid 16th century

11 Speak as you find.
English proverb, late 16th century

12 Throw dirt enough, and some will stick.
persistent slander will in the end be believed; English proverb, mid 17th century

13 When a tiger dies it leaves its skin. When a man dies he leaves his name.
a person leaves behind more than a body; Japanese proverb

16 Caesar's wife
a person required to be above suspicion; Julius Caesar, according to oral tradition, had divorced his wife after unfounded allegations were made against her: see 20 below

17 rest on one's laurels
cease to strive for further glory; *laurels* = leaves of the bay-tree as an emblem of victory or distinction; see **Success** 20

its name changed with the quarter whence it blows.
Dante Alighieri 1265–1321: *Divina Commedia* 'Purgatorio'

23 Who steals my purse steals trash; 'tis something, nothing;
'Twas mine, 'tis his, and has been slave to thousands;
But he that filches from me my good name
Robs me of that which not enriches him,
And makes me poor indeed.
William Shakespeare 1564–1616: *Othello* (1602–4)

24 They come together like the Coroner's Inquest, to sit upon the murdered reputations of the week.
William Congreve 1670–1729: *The Way of the World* (1700)

25 At ev'ry word a reputation dies.
Alexander Pope 1688–1744: *The Rape of the Lock* (1714)

26 We owe respect to the living; to the dead we owe only truth.
Voltaire 1694–1778: 'Première Lettre sur Oedipe' in *Oeuvres* (1785)

27 What is merit? The opinion one man
   entertains of another.
   Lord Palmerston 1784–1865: Thomas Carlyle
   Shooting Niagara: and After? (1867)

28 Always providing you have enough
   courage—or money—you can do without a
   reputation.
   Margaret Mitchell 1900–49: *Gone with the Wind*
   (1936)

29 Honour is like a match, you can only use it
   once.
   Marcel Pagnol 1895–1974: *Marius* (1946)

30 I'm the girl who lost her reputation and
   never missed it.
   Mae West 1892–1980: P. F. Boller and R. L. Davis
   Hollywood Anecdotes (1988)

31 You can't shame or humiliate modern
   celebrities. What used to be called shame
   and humiliation is now called publicity.
   P. J. O'Rourke 1947– : *Give War a Chance* (1992)

32 I think that's just another word for a
   washed-up has-been.
   on being an 'icon'
   Bob Dylan 1941– : in *Mail on Sunday* 18
   January 1998

⤙ Revenge ⤚

PROVERBS AND SAYINGS

1 **Don't cut off your nose to spite your
  face.**
  warning against spiteful revenge which is likely to
  result in your own hurt or loss; English proverb, mid
  16th century

2 **Don't get mad, get even.**
  late 20th century saying; see 25 below

3 **An eye for an eye makes the whole
  world blind.**
  modern saying, often attributed to Mahatma Gandhi
  (1869–1948); see 8 below, **Justice** 18

PHRASES

8 **an eye for an eye**
  revenge, retaliation in kind; from the Bible (Exodus):
  see 3 above, **Justice** 18

QUOTATIONS

10 Vengeance is mine; I will repay, saith the
   Lord.
   Bible: Romans

11 Indeed, revenge is always the pleasure of a
   paltry, feeble, tiny mind.
   Juvenal c.AD 60–c.130: *Satires*

12 Men should be either treated generously or
   destroyed, because they take revenge for
   slight injuries—for heavy ones they cannot.
   Niccolò Machiavelli 1469–1527: *The Prince*
   (written 1513)

13   Caesar's spirit, ranging for revenge,
   With Ate by his side, come hot from hell,
   Shall in these confines, with a monarch's
        voice
   Cry, 'Havoc!' and let slip the dogs of war.
   William Shakespeare 1564–1616: *Julius Caesar*
   (1599); see **Warfare** 6

4 **He laughs best who laughs last.**
  the most successful person is the one who is finally
  triumphant; English proverb, early 17th century

5 **He who laughs last, laughs longest.**
  early 20th century development of 4 above

6 **Revenge is a dish that can be eaten
  cold.**
  vengeance need not be exacted immediately; English
  proverb, late 19th century

7 **Revenge is sweet.**
  English proverb, mid 16th century; see 19 below

9 **squeeze until the pips squeak**
  exact the maximum payment from; originally with
  reference to Eric Geddes: see 21 below

14 Revenge is a kind of wild justice, which the
   more man's nature runs to, the more ought
   law to weed it out.
   Francis Bacon 1561–1626: *Essays* (1625) 'Of
   Revenge'

15 A man that studieth revenge keeps his own
   wounds green.
   Francis Bacon 1561–1626: *Essays* (1625) 'Of
   Revenge'

16 Heaven has no rage, like love to hatred
        turned,
   Nor Hell a fury, like a woman scorned.
   William Congreve 1670–1729: *The Mourning Bride*
   (1697); see **Women** 4

17 We hand folks over to God's mercy, and
   show none ourselves.
   George Eliot 1819–80: *Adam Bede* (1859)

18 *Sic semper tyrannis!* The South is avenged.
having shot President Lincoln, 14 April 1865
John Wilkes Booth 1838–65: '*Sic semper tyrannis*
[Thus always to tyrants]'—motto of the State of
Virginia; in *New York Times* 15 April 1865 (the second
part of the statement possibly apocryphal)

19 It may be that vengeance is sweet, and that
the gods forbade vengeance to men because
they reserved for themselves so delicious
and intoxicating a drink. But no one should
drain the cup to the bottom. The dregs are
often filthy-tasting.
Winston Churchill 1874–1965: *The River War*
(1899); see 7 above

20 Beware of the man who does not return
your blow: he neither forgives you nor
allows you to forgive yourself.
George Bernard Shaw 1856–1950: *Man and
Superman* (1903)

21 The Germans, if this Government is
returned, are going to pay every penny; they
are going to be squeezed as a lemon is
squeezed—until the pips squeak.
Eric Geddes 1875–1937: speech at Cambridge, 10
December 1918; see 9 above

22 If you start throwing hedgehogs under me, I
shall throw a couple of porcupines
under you.
Nikita Khrushchev 1894–1971: in *New York Times*
7 November 1963

23 Get your retaliation in first.
Carwyn James 1929–83: attributed, 1971

24 You can't be fuelled by bitterness. It can eat
you up, but it cannot drive you.
Benazir Bhutto 1953– : *Daughter of Destiny*
(1989)

25 Don't get mad, get everything.
advice to wronged wives
Ivana Trump 1949– : spoken in *The First Wives Club*
(1996 film); see 2 above

⤜ Revolution and Rebellion ⤛

PROVERBS AND SAYINGS

1 **Every revolution was first a thought
in one man's mind.**
American proverb, mid 19th century

2 **Revolutions are not made by men in
spectacles.**
American proverb, late 19th century; see 3 below

3 **Revolutions are not made with
rosewater.**
revolutions involve violence and ruthless behaviour;
English proverb, early 19th century

4 **Whosoever draws his sword against
the prince must throw the scabbard
away.**
anyone who tries to assassinate or depose a monarch
must remain constantly on the defence; English
proverb, early 17th century; see **Warfare** 7, 11

QUOTATIONS

5 A desperate disease requires a dangerous
remedy.
Guy Fawkes 1570–1606: remark, 6 November
1605; see **Necessity** 3

6 The surest way to prevent seditions (if the
times do bear it) is to take away the matter
of them.
Francis Bacon 1561–1626: *Essays* (1625) 'Of
Seditions and Troubles'

7 Rebellion to tyrants is obedience to God.
John Bradshaw 1602–59: supposititious epitaph;
Henry S. Randall *Life of Thomas Jefferson* (1865)

8 When the people contend for their liberty,
they seldom get anything by their victory
but new masters.
Lord Halifax 1633–95: *Political, Moral, and
Miscellaneous Thoughts and Reflections* (1750) 'Of
Prerogative, Power and Liberty'

9 He wished . . . that all the great men in the
world and all the nobility could be hanged,
and strangled with the guts of priests.
quoting 'an ignorant, uneducated man'; often
quoted as 'I should like . . . the last of the kings to be
strangled with the guts of the last priest'
Jean Meslier 1664–1733: *Testament* (1864)

10 *Après nous le déluge.*
After us the deluge.
Madame de Pompadour 1721–64: Madame du Hausset *Mémoires* (1824)

11 A little rebellion now and then is a good thing.
Thomas Jefferson 1743–1826: letter to James Madison, 30 January 1787

12 There was reason to fear that the Revolution, like Saturn, might devour in turn each one of her children.
Pierre Vergniaud 1753–93: Alphonse de Lamartine *Histoire des Girondins* (1847) bk. 38, ch. 20

13 Bliss was it in that dawn to be alive,
But to be young was very heaven!
William Wordsworth 1770–1850: 'The French Revolution, as it Appeared to Enthusiasts' (1809)

14 A share in two revolutions is living to some purpose.
Thomas Paine 1737–1809: Eric Foner *Tom Paine and Revolutionary America* (1976)

15 Those who have served the cause of the revolution have ploughed the sea.
Simón Bolívar 1783–1830: attributed; see Futility 11

16 Maximilien Robespierre was nothing but the hand of Jean Jacques Rousseau, the bloody hand that drew from the womb of time the body whose soul Rousseau had created.
Heinrich Heine 1797–1856: *Zur Geschichte der Religion und Philosophie in Deutschland* (1834)

17 Revolutions are not made; they come. A revolution is as natural a growth as an oak. It comes out of the past. Its foundations are laid far back.
Wendell Phillips 1811–84: speech, 8 January 1852

18 The social order destroyed by a revolution is almost always better than that which immediately preceded it, and experience shows that the most dangerous moment for a bad government is generally that in which it sets about reform.
Alexis de Tocqueville 1805–59: *L'Ancien régime* (1856)

19 Better to abolish serfdom from above than to wait till it begins to abolish itself from below.
Tsar Alexander II 1818–81: speech in Moscow, 30 March 1856

20 I will die like a true-blue rebel. Don't waste any time in mourning—organize.
prior to his death by firing squad
Joe Hill 1879–1915: farewell telegram to Bill Haywood, 18 November 1915

21 The Germans turned upon Russia the most grisly of all weapons. They transported Lenin in a sealed truck, like a plague bacillus, from Switzerland into Russia.
Winston Churchill 1874–1965: *The World Crisis* (1929)

22 Not believing in force is the same thing as not believing in gravitation.
Leon Trotsky 1879–1940: G. Maximov *The Guillotine at Work* (1940)

23 What is a rebel? A man who says no.
Albert Camus 1913–60: *L'Homme révolté* (1951)

24 History will absolve me.
Fidel Castro 1927– : title of pamphlet (1953)

25 Would it not be easier
In that case for the government
To dissolve the people
And elect another?
on the 1953 uprising in East Germany
Bertolt Brecht 1898–1956: 'The Solution' (1953)

26 Those who make peaceful revolution impossible will make violent revolution inevitable.
John F. Kennedy 1917–63: speech at the White House, 13 March 1962

27 The Revolution is made by man, but man must forge his revolutionary spirit from day to day.
Ernesto ('Che') Guevara 1928–67: *Socialism and Man in Cuba* (1968)

28 Ev'rywhere I hear the sound of marching, charging feet, boy,
'Cause summer's here and the time is right for fighting in the street, boy.
Mick Jagger 1943– and **Keith Richards** 1943– : 'Street Fighting Man' (1968 song)

29 The most radical revolutionary will become a conservative on the day after the revolution.
Hannah Arendt 1906–75: in *New Yorker* 12 September 1970

30 We must try to find ways to starve the terrorist and the hijacker of the oxygen of publicity on which they depend.
Margaret Thatcher 1925– : speech, 15 July 1985

31 We will make no distinction between the terrorists who committed these acts and those who harbour them.
after the terrorist attacks of 11 September
George W. Bush 1946– : televised address, 11 September 2001

⇥ Rivers ⇤

PROVERBS AND SAYINGS

1 **All rivers run into the sea.**
English proverb, early 16th century; originally with biblical allusion to the Bible (Ecclesiastes), 'All the rivers run into the sea; yet the sea is not full; unto the place from whence the rivers come, thither they return again'

2 **Says Tweed to Till—**
'What gars ye rin sae still?'

Says Till to Tweed—
'Though ye rin with speed
And I rin slaw,
For ae man that ye droon
I droon twa.'
traditional Scottish rhyme

PHRASES

3 **the Father of Waters**
the Mississippi; see 4 below

4 **Old Man River**
the Mississippi; see 3 above, 15 below

QUOTATIONS

5 Because of you your land never pleads for showers, nor does its parched grass pray to Jupiter the Rain-giver.
of the River Nile
Tibullus c.50–19 BC: *Elegies*

6 Sweet Thames, run softly, till I end my song.
Edmund Spenser 1552–99: *Prothalamion* (1596)

7 I love any discourse of rivers, and fish and fishing.
Izaak Walton 1593–1683: *The Compleat Angler* (1653)

8 Oh, Tiber! father Tiber
To whom the Romans pray,
A Roman's life, a Roman's arms,
Take thou in charge this day!
Lord Macaulay 1800–59: *Lays of Ancient Rome* (1842) 'Horatius'

9 I come from haunts of coot and hern,
I make a sudden sally
And sparkle out among the fern,
To bicker down a valley.
Alfred, Lord Tennyson 1809–92: 'The Brook' (1855)

10 Even the weariest river
Winds somewhere safe to sea.
Algernon Charles Swinburne 1837–1909: 'The Garden of Proserpine' (1866)

11 The great grey-green, greasy, Limpopo River, all set about with fever trees.
Rudyard Kipling 1865–1936: *Just So Stories* (1902) 'The Elephant's Child'

12 For soft is the song my paddle sings.
Pauline Johnson (Tekahionwake) 1861–1913: 'The Song My Paddle Sings'

13 Then I saw the Congo, creeping through the black,
Cutting through the forest with a golden track.
Vachel Lindsay 1879–1931: 'The Congo' (1914)

14 I've known rivers:
I've known rivers ancient as the world and older than the flow of human blood in human veins.
Langston Hughes 1902–67: 'The Negro Speaks of Rivers' (1921)

15 Ol' man river, dat ol' man river,
He must know sumpin', but don't say nothin',
He jus' keeps rollin',
He jus' keeps rollin' along.
Oscar Hammerstein II 1895–1960: 'Ol' Man River' (1927 song); see 4 above

16 I do not know much about gods; but I think that the river
Is a strong brown god—sullen, untamed and intractable.
T. S. Eliot 1888–1965: *Four Quartets* 'The Dry Salvages' (1941)

17 The Thames is liquid history.
to an American who had compared the Thames disparagingly with the Mississippi
John Burns 1858–1943: in *Daily Mail* 25 January 1943

18 I may be smelly, and I may be old,
Rough in my pebbles, reedy in my pools,
But where my fish float by I bless their swimming

And I like people to bathe in me, especially
women.
Stevie Smith 1902–71: 'The River God' (1950)

►►Royalty ◄◄

PROVERBS AND SAYINGS

1 Camels, fleas and princes exist everywhere.

referring to the large numbers of offspring of some rulers; Persian proverb

2 The king can do no wrong.

something cannot be wrong if it is done by someone of sovereign power, who alone is not subject to the laws of the land; translation of the Latin legal maxim

rex non potest peccare; English proverb, mid 17th century

3 A king's chaff is worth more than other men's corn.

even minor benefits available to those attending on a sovereign are more substantial than the best that can be offered by those of lesser status; English proverb, early 17th century

PHRASES

4 the Black Prince

Edward, Prince of Wales (1330–76), eldest son of Edward III of England; the name Black Prince apparently derives from the black armour he wore when fighting

5 Bonnie Prince Charlie

Charles Edward Stuart, the Young Pretender; Scottish appellation for Charles Edward Stuart, who led the Jacobite uprising of 1745–6; see 18 below

6 born in the purple

born into an imperial or royal reigning family; *purple* the dye traditionally used for fabric worn by persons of imperial or royal rank; see 15 below

7 the Chrysanthemum Throne

the throne of Japan; the chrysanthemum is the crest of the imperial family

8 the divine right of kings

the doctrine that monarchs have authority from God alone, independently of their subjects' will; see 29 below

9 the King over the Water

an exiled sovereign as seen by those loyal to his cause; 18th-century Jacobite toast to James Francis Edward Stuart (1688–1766) and his son Charles Edward Stuart (1720–88), who from exile in France and Italy asserted their right to the British throne against the House of Hanover; see 12, 18, 31 below

10 the Merry Monarch

Charles II (1630–85); from Rochester: see 27 below

11 the Nine Days' Queen

Lady Jane Grey (1537–54); named as his successor by her cousin, the dying Edward VI, she was deposed after nine days on the throne, and was executed in the following year

12 the Old Pretender

James Stuart (1688–1766), the son of the exiled James II of England, and focus of Jacobite loyalties; from his assertion of his claim to the British throne against the house of Hanover; see 18, 31 below, Writers 22

13 the Peacock Throne

the former throne of the Kings of Delhi, later that of the Shahs of Iran; adorned with precious stones forming an expanded peacock's tail, the throne was taken to Persia by Nadir Shah (1688–1747), king of Persia, who in 1739 captured Delhi

14 Stupor Mundi

Frederick II (1194–1250), Holy Roman Emperor; Latin = wonder of the world

15 wear the purple

hold the office of a sovereign or emperor; *purple* the dye traditionally used for fabric worn by persons of imperial or royal rank; see 6 above

16 the Widow at Windsor

Queen Victoria (1819–1901); the Queen's husband, Prince Albert, predeceased her by forty years

17 the Young Chevalier

Charles Edward Stuart, the Young Pretender; his father, James Stuart, the Old Pretender, was known by the sobriquet of *The Chevalier* (*de St George*); see 5 above, 18 below

18 the Young Pretender

Charles Edward Stuart (1720–88); son of James Stuart, the Old Pretender, who asserted the Stuart claim to the British throne against the house of Hanover: see 5, 12, 17 above, 31 below

QUOTATIONS

19 Whoso pulleth out this sword of this stone and anvil is rightwise King born of all England.
Thomas Malory d. 1471: *Le Morte D'Arthur* (1470)

20 The anger of the sovereign is death.
Duke of Norfolk 1473–?1554: William Roper *Life of Sir Thomas More*

21 I know I have the body of a weak and feeble woman, but I have the heart and stomach of a king, and of a king of England too.
Elizabeth I 1533–1603: speech to the troops at Tilbury on the approach of the Armada, 1588

22 Not all the water in the rough rude sea Can wash the balm from an anointed king.
William Shakespeare 1564–1616: *Richard II* (1595)

23 Uneasy lies the head that wears a crown.
William Shakespeare 1564–1616: *Henry IV, Part 2* (1597)

24 He is the fountain of honour.
Francis Bacon 1561–1626: *An Essay of a King* (1642); attribution doubtful; see **Government** 29

25 A subject and a sovereign are clean different things.
Charles I 1600–49: speech on the scaffold, 30 January 1649

26 But methought it lessened my esteem of a king, that he should not be able to command the rain.
Samuel Pepys 1633–1703: diary 19 July 1662

27 A merry monarch, scandalous and poor.
John Wilmot, Lord Rochester 1647–80: 'A Satire on King Charles II' (1697); see 10 above

28 Titles are shadows, crowns are empty things, The good of subjects is the end of kings.
Daniel Defoe 1660–1731: *The True-Born Englishman* (1701)

29 The Right Divine of Kings to govern wrong.
Alexander Pope 1688–1744: *The Dunciad* (1742); see 8 above

30 God save our gracious king!
Long live our noble king!
God save the king!
Anonymous: 'God save the King', attributed to various authors of the mid eighteenth century, including Henry Carey c.1687–1743

31 God bless the King, I mean the Faith's Defender;
God bless—no harm in blessing—the Pretender;
But who Pretender is, or who is King,
God bless us all—that's quite another thing.
John Byrom 1692–1763: 'To an Officer in the Army, Extempore, Intended to allay the Violence of Party-Spirit' (1773); see 9 above, **People** 12, 18

32 The influence of the Crown has increased, is increasing, and ought to be diminished.
John Dunning 1731–83: resolution passed in the House of Commons, 6 April 1780

33 Monarchy is only the string that ties the robber's bundle.
Percy Bysshe Shelley 1792–1822: *A Philosophical View of Reform* (written 1819–20)

34 The king neither administers nor governs, he reigns.
Louis Adolphe Thiers 1797–1877: in *Le National*, 4 February 1830

35 I will be good.
on being shown a chart of the line of succession, 11 March 1830
Queen Victoria 1819–1901: Theodore Martin *The Prince Consort* (1875)

36 The Emperor is everything, Vienna is nothing.
Prince Metternich 1773–1859: letter to Count Bombelles, 5 June 1848

37 Above all things our royalty is to be reverenced, and if you begin to poke about it you cannot reverence it . . . Its mystery is its life. We must not let in daylight upon magic.
Walter Bagehot 1826–77: *The English Constitution* (1867)

38 The Sovereign has, under a constitutional monarchy such as ours, three rights—the right to be consulted, the right to encourage, the right to warn.
Walter Bagehot 1826–77: *The English Constitution* (1867)

39 Everyone likes flattery; and when you come to Royalty you should lay it on with a trowel.
Benjamin Disraeli 1804–81: to Matthew Arnold; G. W. E. Russell *Collections and Recollections* (1898)

40 We could not go anywhere without sending word ahead so that life might be put on parade for us.
Infanta Eulalia of Spain 1864–1958: *Court Life from Within* (1915)

41 At long last I am able to say a few words of my own . . . you must believe me when I tell you that I have found it impossible to carry the heavy burden of responsibility and to discharge my duties as King as I would wish to do without the help and support of the woman I love.
Edward VIII 1894–1972: radio broadcast following his abdication, 11 December 1936

42 The whole world is in revolt. Soon there will be only five Kings left—the King of England, the King of Spades, the King of Clubs, the King of Hearts and the King of Diamonds.
King Farouk 1920–65: addressed to the author at a conference in Cairo, 1948; Lord Boyd-Orr *As I Recall* (1966)

43 The family firm.
description of the British monarchy
George VI 1895–1952: attributed

44 Royalty is the gold filling in a mouthful of decay.
John Osborne 1929–94: 'They call it cricket' in T. Maschler (ed.) *Declaration* (1957)

45 To be Prince of Wales is not a position. It is a predicament.
Alan Bennett 1934– : *The Madness of King George* (1995 film)

46 I'd like to be a queen in people's hearts but I don't see myself being Queen of this country.
Diana, Princess of Wales 1961–97: interview on *Panorama*, BBC1 TV, 20 November 1995

47 She was the People's Princess, and that is how she will stay . . . in our hearts and in our memories forever.
Tony Blair 1953– : on hearing of the death of Diana, Princess of Wales, 31 August 1997

⤛ Russia ⤜

PROVERBS AND SAYINGS

1 Scratch a Russian and you find a Tartar.
if a person is harmed their real national character will be revealed; English proverb, early 19th century

QUOTATIONS

2 God of frostbite, God of famine,
beggars, cripples by the yard,
farms with no crops to examine—
that's him, that's your Russian God.
Prince Peter Vyazemsky 1792–1878: 'The Russian God' (1828)

3 A land that does not like doing things by halves.
Nikolai Gogol 1809–52: *Dead Souls* (1842), tr. D. Magarshak

4 Russia has two generals in whom she can confide—Generals Janvier [January] and Février [February].
Nicholas I 1796–1855: attributed; *Punch* 10 March 1855

5 Every country has its own constitution; ours is absolutism moderated by assassination.
Anonymous: Ernst Friedrich Herbert, Count Münster, quoting 'an intelligent Russian', in *Political Sketches of the State of Europe, 1814–1867* (1868)

6 The Lord God has given us vast forests, immense fields, wide horizons; surely we ought to be giants, living in such a country as this.
Anton Chekhov 1860–1904: *The Cherry Orchard* (1904)

7 I cannot forecast to you the action of Russia. It is a riddle wrapped in a mystery inside an enigma.
Winston Churchill 1874–1965: radio broadcast, 1 October 1939

8 [Russian Communism is] the illegitimate child of Karl Marx and Catherine the Great.
Clement Attlee 1883–1967: speech at Aarhus University, 11 April 1956

9 The Soviet Union has indeed been our greatest menace, not so much because of what it has done, but because of the excuses it has provided us for our failures.
J. William Fulbright 1905–95: in *Observer* 21 December 1958

10 The idea of restructuring [perestroika] . . . combines continuity and innovation, the historical experience of Bolshevism and the contemporaneity of socialism.
Mikhail Sergeevich Gorbachev 1931– : speech on the seventieth anniversary of the Russian Revolution, 2 November 1987

11 Russia can be an empire or a democracy, but it cannot be both.
Zbigniew Brzezinski 1928– : in *Foreign Affairs* March/April 1994

12 Today is the last day of an era past.
at a Berlin ceremony to end the Soviet military presence in Germany
Boris Yeltsin 1931– : in *Guardian* 1 September 1994

⤛Satisfaction and Discontent ⤜

PROVERBS AND SAYINGS

1 Acorns were good till bread was found.

until something better is found, what one has will be judged satisfactory; English proverb, late 16th century

2 The answer is a lemon.

a *lemon* as the type of something unsatisfactory, perhaps referring to the least valuable symbol in a fruit machine; English proverb, early 20th century; see **Deception 7**

3 Better are small fish than an empty dish.

a little is preferable to nothing at all; English proverb, late 17th century

4 Do not grieve that rose trees have thorns, rather rejoice that thorny bushes bear roses.

advocating an emphasis on positive aspects; Arab proverb; see **Circumstance 5, Practicality 2**

5 Go further and fare worse.

it is often wise to take what is on offer; English proverb, mid 16th century

6 Half a loaf is better than no bread.

to have part of something is better than having nothing at all; English proverb, mid 16th century

7 Something is better than nothing.

even a possession of intrinsically little value is preferable to being empty-handed; English proverb, mid 16th century

8 What you've never had you never miss.

English proverb, early 20th century

PHRASES

9 all gas and gaiters

a satisfactory state of affairs; originally recorded in Dickens *Nicholas Nickleby* (1839) 'all is gas and gaiters'

10 all Sir Garnet

highly satisfactory, all right; Sir *Garnet* Wolseley (1833–1913), leader of several successful military expeditions; see **Armed Forces 33**

11 a chip on one's shoulder

a deeply ingrained grievance, typically about a particular thing. The phrase (originally US) is recorded from the 19th century, and may originate in a practice described in the *Long Island Telegraph* (Hempstead, New York), 20 May 1830, 'When two churlish boys were *determined* to fight, a *chip* would be placed on the shoulder of one, and the other demanded to knock it off at his peril'

12 a dusty answer

an unsatisfactory answer, a disappointing response; from Meredith: see **Certainty 16**

13 a fly in the ointment

a trifling circumstance that spoils the enjoyment or agreeableness of a thing; after the Bible (Ecclesiastes) 'Dead flies cause the ointment of the apothecary to send forth a stinking savour'

14 sour grapes

an expression or attitude of deliberate disparagement of a desired but unattainable object; alluding to Aesop's fable of 'The Fox and the Grapes', in which a fox unable to reach the grapes contented himself with the reflection that they must be sour

QUOTATIONS

15 My soul, do not seek immortal life, but exhaust the realm of the possible.
Pindar 518–438 BC: *Pythian Odes*

16 Those who are contented and at ease when the occasion comes and live in accord with the course of Nature cannot be affected by sorrow or joy. This is what the ancients called release from bondage. Those who cannot release themselves are so because they are bound by material things.
Zhuangzi c.369–286 BC: *Chuang Tzu*

17 It is called Nirvana because of the getting rid of craving.
Pali Tripitaka c. 2nd century BC: *Samyutta-nikāya* [Kindred Sayings]

18 So long as the great majority of men are not deprived of either property or honour, they are satisfied.
Niccolò Machiavelli 1469–1527: *The Prince* (written 1513)

19 Some have too much, yet still do crave;
I little have, and seek no more.
They are but poor, though much they have,

And I am rich with little store.
Edward Dyer d. 1607: 'In praise of a contented mind' (1588)

20 'Tis just like a summer birdcage in a garden; the birds that are without despair to get in, and the birds that are within despair, and are in a consumption, for fear they shall never get out.
John Webster 1580– : *The White Devil* (1612)

21 About six or seven o'clock, I walk out into a common that lies hard by the house, where a great many young wenches keep sheep and cows and sit in the shade singing of ballads . . . I talk to them, and find they want nothing to make them the happiest people in the world, but the knowledge that they are so.
Dorothy Osborne 1627–95: letter to William Temple, 2 June 1653

22 We loathe our manna, and we long for quails.
John Dryden 1631–1700: *The Medal* (1682); see Gifts 9

23 The stoical scheme of supplying our wants, by lopping off our desires, is like cutting off our feet when we want shoes.
Jonathan Swift 1667–1745: *Thoughts on Various Subjects* (1711)

24 Contented wi' little and cantie wi' mair,
Whene'er I forgather wi' Sorrow and Care,
I gie them a skelp, as they're creeping alang,
Wi' a cog o' gude swats and an auld Scotish sang.
Robert Burns 1759–96: 'Contented wi' little' (1796)

25 Plain living and high thinking are no more:
The homely beauty of the good old cause
Is gone.
William Wordsworth 1770–1850: 'O friend! I know not which way I must look' (1807); see Lifestyles 7

26 That all was wrong because not all was right.
George Crabbe 1754–1832: 'The Convert' (1812)

27 In pale contented sort of discontent.
John Keats 1795–1821: 'Lamia' (1820)

28 Ah! *Vanitas Vanitatum!* Which of us is happy in this world? Which of us has his desire? or, having it, is satisfied?—Come, children, let us shut up the box and the puppets, for our play is played out.
William Makepeace Thackeray 1811–63: *Vanity Fair* (1847–8); see Disillusion 6, Futility 16

29 It is better to be a human being dissatisfied than a pig satisfied; better to be Socrates dissatisfied than a fool satisfied.
John Stuart Mill 1806–73: *Utilitarianism* (1863)

30 It is an uneasy lot at best, to be what we call highly taught and yet not to enjoy: to be present at this great spectacle of life and never to be liberated from a small hungry shivering self.
George Eliot 1819–80: *Middlemarch* (1871–2)

31 A book of verses underneath the bough,
A jug of wine, a loaf of bread—and Thou
Beside me singing in the wilderness—
Oh, wilderness were paradise enow!
Edward Fitzgerald 1809–83: *The Rubáiyát of Omar Khayyám* (1879 ed.)

32 I'm afraid you've got a bad egg, Mr Jones. Oh no, my Lord, I assure you! Parts of it are excellent!
Punch: cartoon caption, 1895, showing a curate breakfasting with his bishop; see **Character** 22

33 As long as I have a want, I have a reason for living. Satisfaction is death.
George Bernard Shaw 1856–1950: *Overruled* (1916)

34 He spoke with a certain what-is-it in his voice, and I could see that, if not actually disgruntled, he was far from being gruntled.
P. G. Wodehouse 1881–1975: *The Code of the Woosters* (1938)

35 When you don't have any money, the problem is food. When you have money, it's sex. When you have both it's health.
J. P. Donleavy 1926– : *The Ginger Man* (1955)

36 Let us be frank about it: most of our people have never had it so good.
Harold Macmillan 1894–1986: speech at Bedford, 20 July 1957; 'You Never Had It So Good' was the Democratic Party slogan during the 1952 US election campaign

37 I've had this business that anything is better than nothing. There are times when nothing has to be better than anything.
Penelope Gilliatt 1933–93: *Sunday, Bloody Sunday* (1971)

38 You ask if they were happy. This is not a characteristic of a European. To be contented—that's for the cows.
Coco Chanel 1883–1971: A. Madsen *Coco Chanel* (1990)

⊹⊱ Schools ⊰⊹

see also **Children, Education, Teaching**

PROVERBS AND SAYINGS

1 **No more Latin, no more French,
No more sitting on a hard board
bench.**
traditional children's rhyme for the end of
school term

PHRASES

2 **the happiest days of your life**
school days; from the title of a film (1950) based on a
play by John Dighton

QUOTATIONS

3 Public schools are the nurseries of all vice
and immorality.
Henry Fielding 1707–54: *Joseph Andrews* (1742)

4 There is now less flogging in our great
schools than formerly, but then less is
learned there; so that what the boys get at
one end they lose at the other.
Samuel Johnson 1709–84: James Boswell *Life of
Samuel Johnson* (1791) 1775

5 My object will be, if possible, to form
Christian men, for Christian boys I can
scarcely hope to make.
on appointment to the Headmastership of Rugby
School
Thomas Arnold 1795–1842: letter to Revd John
Tucker, 2 March 1828

6 EDUCATION.—At Mr Wackford Squeers's
Academy, Dotheboys Hall, at the delightful
village of Dotheboys, near Greta Bridge in
Yorkshire, Youth are boarded, clothed,
booked, furnished with pocket-money,
provided with all necessaries, instructed in
all languages living and dead, mathematics,
orthography, geometry, astronomy,
trigonometry, the use of the globes, algebra,
single stick (if required), writing, arithmetic,
fortification, and every other branch of
classical literature. Terms, twenty guineas
per annum. No extras, no vacations, and
diet unparalleled.
Charles Dickens 1812–70: *Nicholas Nickleby* (1839)

7 'I don't care a straw for Greek particles, or
the digamma, no more does his mother.
What is he sent to school for? . . . If he'll
only turn out a brave, helpful, truth-telling
Englishman, and a gentleman, and a
Christian, that's all I want,' thought the
Squire.
Thomas Hughes 1822–96: *Tom Brown's Schooldays*
(1857)

8 You send your child to the schoolmaster,
but 'tis the schoolboys who educate him.
Ralph Waldo Emerson 1803–82: *Conduct of Life*
(1860) 'Culture'

9 Forty years on, when afar and asunder
Parted are those who are singing to-day.
E. E. Bowen 1836–1901: 'Forty Years On' (Harrow
School Song, published 1886)

10 Headmasters have powers at their disposal
with which Prime Ministers have never yet
been invested.
Winston Churchill 1874–1965: *My Early Life*
(1930)

11 The only good things about skool are the
BOYS wizz who are noble brave fearless etc.
although you hav various swots, bulies,
cissies, milksops, greedy guts and oiks with
whom i am forced to mingle hem-hem.
Geoffrey Willans 1911–58 and **Ronald Searle**
1920– : *Down With Skool!* (1953)

12 The dread of beatings! Dread of being late!
And, greatest dread of all, the dread of
games!
John Betjeman 1906–84: *Summoned by Bells*
(1960)

13 I am putting old heads on your young
shoulders . . . all my pupils are the crème de
la crème.
Muriel Spark 1918– : *The Prime of Miss Jean Brodie*
(1961)

14 Schools are for schooling, not social
engineering.
Brian Cox 1928– and **Rhodes Boyson** 1925– :
Black Paper 1975 (1975)

15 Dear Parents

If you don't believe everything your child tells you about school, I will not believe everything your child tells me about home.
John Rae 1931– : *Letters from School* (1987)

16 The day of the bog-standard comprehensive is over.
Alastair Campbell 1957– : press briefing, 12 February 2001

17 Life isn't like coursework, baby. It's one damn essay crisis after another.
Boris Johnson 1964– : in *Observer* 15 May 2005

⤞ Science ⤝

see also **Arts and Sciences, Hypothesis and Fact, Inventions and Discoveries, Life Sciences, Physical Sciences, Science and Religion, Technology**

PROVERBS AND SAYINGS

1 Much science, much sorrow.
suggesting that learning may increase one's awareness of difficult questions; English proverb, early 17th century

2 Science has no enemy but the ignorant.
English proverb, mid 16th century, from Latin *Scientia non habet inimicum nisi ignorantem*

PHRASES

3 backroom boys
people who provide vital scientific and technical support for those in the field who become public figures; the expression derives from Lord Beaverbrook: see **Fame 22**

QUOTATIONS

4 Lucky is he who has been able to understand the causes of things.
of Lucretius
Virgil 70–19 BC: *Georgics*

5 If anyone wishes to observe the works of nature, he should put his trust not in books of anatomy but in his own eyes.
Galen AD 129–199: *On the Usefulness of the Parts of the Body*

6 Books must follow sciences, and not sciences books.
Francis Bacon 1561–1626: *Resuscitatio* (1657)

7 The changing of bodies into light, and light into bodies, is very conformable to the course of Nature, which seems delighted with transmutations.
Isaac Newton 1642–1727: *Opticks* (1730 ed.)

8 Nature, and Nature's laws lay hid in night. God said, *Let Newton be!* and all was light.
Alexander Pope 1688–1744: 'Epitaph: Intended for Sir Isaac Newton' (1730); see **17 below**

9 Where observation is concerned, chance favours only the prepared mind.
Louis Pasteur 1822–95: address given on the inauguration of the Faculty of Science, University of Lille, 7 December 1854

10 Scientific truth should be presented in different forms, and should be regarded as equally scientific, whether it appears in the robust form and the vivid colouring of a physical illustration, or in the tenuity and paleness of a symbolic expression.
James Clerk Maxwell 1831–79: address to the British Association, 15 September 1870

11 When you can measure what you are speaking about, and express it in numbers, you know something about it; but when you cannot measure it, when you cannot express it in numbers, your knowledge is of a meagre and unsatisfactory kind: it may be the beginning of knowledge, but you have scarcely, in your thoughts, advanced to the stage of *science*, whatever the matter may be.
often quoted as 'If you cannot measure it, then it is not science'
Lord Kelvin 1824–1907: *Popular Lectures and Addresses* vol. 1 (1889) 'Electrical Units of Measurement', delivered 3 May 1883

12 Science is nothing but trained and organized common sense, differing from the latter only as a veteran may differ from a raw recruit: and its methods differ from those of common sense only as far as the guardsman's cut and thrust differ from the manner in which a savage wields his club.
T. H. Huxley 1825–95: *Collected Essays* (1893–4) 'The Method of Zadig'

13 In science, we must be interested in things, not in persons.
Marie Curie 1867–1934: in c.1904; Eve Curie *Madame Curie* (1937)

14 Science is built up of facts, as a house is built of stones; but an accumulation of facts is no more a science than a heap of stones is a house.
Henri Poincaré 1854–1912: *Science and Hypothesis* (1905)

15 The outcome of any serious research can only be to make two questions grow where one question grew before.
Thorstein Veblen 1857–1929: *University of California Chronicle* (1908) 'Evolution of the Scientific Point of View'

16 In science the credit goes to the man who convinces the world, not to the man to whom the idea first occurs.
Francis Darwin 1848–1925: in *Eugenics Review* April 1914 'Francis Galton'

17 It did not last: the Devil howling 'Ho! Let Einstein be!' restored the status quo.
J. C. Squire 1884–1958: 'In continuation of Pope on Newton' (1926); see 8 above

18 I ask you to look both ways. For the road to a knowledge of the stars leads through the atom; and important knowledge of the atom has been reached through the stars.
Arthur Eddington 1882–1944: *Stars and Atoms* (1928)

19 It is much easier to make measurements than to know exactly what you are measuring.
J. W. N. Sullivan 1886–1937: comment, 1928; R. L. Weber *More Random Walks in Science* (1982)

20 All science is either physics or stamp collecting.
Ernest Rutherford 1871–1937: J. B. Birks *Rutherford at Manchester* (1962)

21 The aim of science is not to open the door to infinite wisdom, but to set a limit to infinite error.
Bertolt Brecht 1898–1956: *Life of Galileo* (1939)

22 The importance of a scientific work can be measured by the number of previous publications it makes it superfluous to read.
David Hilbert 1862–1943: attributed; Lewis Wolpert *The Unnatural Nature of Science* (1993)

23 A new scientific truth does not triumph by convincing its opponents and making them see the light, but rather because its opponents eventually die, and a new generation grows up that is familiar with it.
Max Planck 1858–1947: *A Scientific Autobiography* (1949)

24 The scientific method, as far as it is a method, is nothing more than doing one's damnedest with one's mind, no holds barred.
Percy Williams Bridgeman 1882–1961: *Reflections of a Physicist* (1955)

25 If politics is the art of the possible, research is surely the art of the soluble. Both are immensely practical-minded affairs.
Peter Medawar 1915–87: in *New Statesman* 19 June 1964; see **Politics** 17

26 Basic research is what I am doing when I don't know what I am doing.
Wernher von Braun 1912–77: R. L. Weber *A Random Walk in Science* (1973)

27 In effect, we have redefined the task of science to be the discovery of laws that will enable us to predict events up to the limits set by the uncertainty principle.
Stephen Hawking 1942– : *A Brief History of Time* (1988); see **Physical Sciences** 9

28 Science is an integral part of culture. It's not this foreign thing, done by an arcane priesthood. It's one of the glories of human intellectual tradition.
Stephen Jay Gould 1941–2002: in *Independent* 24 January 1990

⤞ Science and Religion ⤛

PHRASES

1 **creation science**
the reinterpretation of scientific knowledge in accord with belief in the literal truth of the Bible; especially regarding the origin of matter, life, and humankind described in Genesis

2 **God of the gaps**
God as an explanation for phenomena not yet explained by science; God thought of as acting only in those spheres not otherwise accounted for; see 12 below

3 intelligent design

the theory that life, or the universe, cannot have arisen by chance and was designed and created by some intelligent entity

QUOTATIONS

4 Science is for the cultivation of religion, not for worldly enjoyment.
Sadi 1213–91: *The Rose Garden* (1258)

5 In disputes about natural phenomena one must begin not with the authority of Scriptural passage but with sensory experience and necessary demonstrations. For the Holy Scripture and nature derive equally from the Godhead, the former as the dictation of the Holy Spirit and the latter as the most obedient executrix of God's orders.
Galileo 1564–1642: letter to Christina Lotharinga, Archduchess of Tuscany

6 It is God who is the ultimate reason of things, and the knowledge of God is no less the beginning of science than his essence and will are the beginning of beings.
Gottfried Wilhelm Leibniz 1646–1716: *Letter on a General Principle Useful in Explaining the Laws of Nature* (1687)

7 An Aristotle was but the rubbish of an Adam, and Athens but the rudiments of Paradise.
Robert South 1634–1716: *Twelve Sermons . . .* (1692)

8 If ignorance of nature gave birth to the Gods, knowledge of nature is destined to destroy them.
Paul Henri, Baron d'Holbach 1723–89: *Système de la Nature* (1770)

9 The atoms of Democritus
And Newton's particles of light
Are sands upon the Red Sea shore
Where Israel's tents do shine so bright.
William Blake 1757–1827: *MS Note-Book*

10 I asserted—and I repeat—that a man has no reason to be ashamed of having an ape for his grandfather. If there were an ancestor whom I should feel shame in recalling it would rather be a *man*—a man of restless and versatile intellect—who, not content with an equivocal success in his own sphere of activity, plunges into scientific questions with which he has no real acquaintance, only to obscure them by an aimless rhetoric, and distract the attention of his hearers from the real point at issue by eloquent

digressions and skilled appeals to religious prejudice.
replying to Bishop Samuel Wilberforce in the debate on Darwin's theory of evolution
T. H. Huxley 1825–95: at a meeting of the British Association in Oxford, 30 June 1860; see **Life Sciences** 14

11 Terms like grace, new birth, justification . . . terms, in short, which with St Paul are literary terms, theologians have employed as if they were scientific terms.
Matthew Arnold 1822–88: *Literature and Dogma* (1873)

12 There are reverent minds who ceaselessly scan the fields of Nature and the books of Science in search of gaps—gaps which they will fill up with God. As if God lived in gaps?
Henry Drummond 1851–97: *The Ascent of Man* (1894); see 2 above

13 The theory, coarsely enough, and to my Father's great indignation, was defined by a hasty press as being this—that God hid the fossils in the rocks in order to tempt geologists into infidelity.
on Philip Gosse's fundamentalist interpretation of geology (in *Omphalos*, 1857), subsequently applied to evolution
Edmund Gosse 1849–1928: *Father and Son* (1907)

14 Science without religion is lame, religion without science is blind.
Albert Einstein 1879–1955: *Science, Philosophy and Religion: a Symposium* (1941)

15 We have grasped the mystery of the atom and rejected the Sermon on the Mount.
Omar Bradley 1893–1981: speech on Armistice Day, 1948; see **The Christian Church** 13

16 There is no evil in the atom; only in men's souls.
Adlai Stevenson 1900–65: speech at Hartford, Connecticut, 18 September 1952

17 The means by which we live have outdistanced the ends for which we live. Our scientific power has outrun our spiritual power. We have guided missiles and misguided men.
Martin Luther King 1929–68: *Strength to Love* (1963)

18 The priest persuades humble people to endure their hard lot; the politician urges them to rebel against it; and the scientist

thinks of a method that does away with the hard lot altogether.

Max Perutz 1914– : *Is Science Necessary* (1989)

19 How is it that hardly any major religion has looked at science and concluded, 'This is better than we thought! The Universe is much bigger than our prophets said, grander, more subtle, more elegant'?

Carl Sagan 1934–96: *Pale Blue Dot* (1995)

⇢⇢ Scotland ⇠⇠

see also **British Towns and Regions**

PHRASES

1 **the curse of Scotland**
the nine of diamonds in a pack of cards; perhaps from its resemblance to the armorial bearings, nine lozenges on a saltire, of Lord Stair, from his part in sanctioning the Massacre of Glencoe in 1692; see 6 below

2 **the land of cakes**
Scotland; *cake* = a piece of thin oaten bread

QUOTATIONS

3 So long as there shall but one hundred of us remain alive, we will never subject ourselves to the dominion of the English. For it is not glory, it is not riches, neither is it honour, but it is freedom alone that we fight and contend for, which no honest man will lose but with his life.
to the Pope, asserting the independence of Scotland
Declaration of Arbroath: letter sent by the Scottish Parliament, 6 April 1320

4 It came with a lass, and it will pass with a lass.
of the crown of Scotland, which had come to the Stuarts through the female line, on learning of the birth of Mary Queen of Scots, December 1542
James V 1512–42: Robert Lindsay of Pitscottie (c.1500–65) *History of Scotland* (1728)

5 Stands Scotland where it did?
William Shakespeare 1564–1616: *Macbeth* (1606)

6 It's a great work of charity to be exact in rooting out that damnable sept, the worst in all the Highlands.
on hearing that Alasdair Maclan, chief of the Glencoe MacDonalds, had been too late in taking the required oath of loyalty to William III; see 1 above
Lord Stair 1648–1707: letter to Thomas Livingston, 11 January 1692

7 Now there's ane end of ane old song.
as he signed the engrossed exemplification of the Act of Union, 1706; see 20 below
James Ogilvy, Lord Seafield 1664–1730: *The Lockhart Papers* (1817)

8 The noblest prospect which a Scotchman ever sees, is the high road that leads him to England!
Samuel Johnson 1709–84: James Boswell *Life of Samuel Johnson* (1791) 6 July 1763

9 My heart's in the Highlands, my heart is not here;
My heart's in the Highlands a-chasing the deer.
Robert Burns 1759–96: 'My Heart's in the Highlands' (1790)

10 Scots, wha hae wi' Wallace bled,
Scots, wham Bruce has aften led,
Welcome to your gory bed,—
Or to victorie.
Robert Burns 1759–96: 'Robert Bruce's March to Bannockburn' (1799) (also known as 'Scots, Wha Hae')

11 O Caledonia! stern and wild,
Meet nurse for a poetic child!
Sir Walter Scott 1771–1832: *The Lay of the Last Minstrel* (1805)

12 From the lone shieling of the misty island
Mountains divide us, and the waste of seas—
Yet still the blood is strong, the heart is Highland,
And we in dreams behold the Hebrides!
John Galt 1779–1839: 'Canadian Boat Song' (1829); translated from the Gaelic; attributed

13 They have barred us by barbed wire fences from the bens and glens: the peasant has been ruthlessly swept aside to make room for the pheasant, and the mountain hare

now brings forth her young on the
hearthstone of the Gael!
Tom Johnston 1881–1965: *Our Scots Noble Families*
(1909)

14 There are few more impressive sights in the
world than a Scotsman on the make.
J. M. Barrie 1860–1937: *What Every Woman Knows*
(1918)

15 It is never difficult to distinguish between a
Scotsman with a grievance and a ray of
sunshine.
P. G. Wodehouse 1881–1975: *Blandings Castle and
Elsewhere* (1935)

16 O flower of Scotland, when will we see your
like again,
that fought and died for your wee bit hill
and glen
and stood against him, proud Edward's
army,
and sent him homeward tae think again.
Roy Williamson 1936–90: 'O Flower of Scotland'
(1968)

17 Scotland, land of the omnipotent No.
Alan Bold 1943– : 'A Memory of Death' (1969)

18 Scotland small? Our multiform, our infinite
Scotland *small*?
Only as a patch of hillside may be a cliché
corner
To a fool who cries 'Nothing but heather!'
Hugh MacDiarmid 1892–1978: *Direadh 1* (1974)

19 I don't want a Stormont. I don't want a wee
pretendy government in Edinburgh.
on the prospective Scottish Parliament; often quoted
as 'a wee pretendy Parliament'
Billy Connolly 1942– : interview on *Breakfast with
Frost* (BBC TV), 9 February 1997

20 The Scottish Parliament which adjourned
on 25 March in the year 1707 is hereby
reconvened.
Winifred Ewing 1929– : in the Scottish
Parliament, 12 May 1999; see 7 above

⟶ Sculpture ⟵

PHRASES

1 **Elgin Marbles**
a collection of classical Greek marble sculptures and
architectural fragments, chiefly from the frieze and
pediment of the Parthenon in Athens; they were
brought to England in 1802–12 by the diplomat and
art connoisseur Thomas Bruce (1766–1841), the 7th
Earl of Elgin

2 **fig leaf**
representation of the leaf of a fig tree, often used for
concealing the genitals in paintings and sculpture;
with particular reference to the story of Adam and
Eve in the Bible (Genesis), when having eaten of the
tree of the knowledge of good and evil and become
ashamed of their nakedness, 'they sewed fig leaves
together, and made themselves aprons'

QUOTATIONS

3 The marble not yet carved can hold
the form
Of every thought the greatest artist has.
Michelangelo 1475–1564: Sonnet 15

4 All his statues are so constrained by agony
that they seem to wish to break themselves.
They all seem ready to succumb to the
pressure of despair that fills them.
of Michelangelo
Auguste Rodin 1840–1917: *On Art and Artists*
(1911)

5 Carving is interrelated masses conveying an
emotion: a perfect relationship between the
mind and the colour, light and weight
which is the stone, made by the hand which
feels.
Barbara Hepworth 1903–75: Herbert Read (ed.)
Unit One (1934)

6 The first hole made through a piece of stone
is a revelation.
Henry Moore 1898–1986: in *Listener* 18
August 1937

7 The old ideas of nobility and sacrifice have
become a howitzer squatting at Hyde Park
like a petrified toad, and the hero has
become a cabinet minister on a pedestal in
bronze boots.
on modern sculpture
Geoffrey Grigson 1905–85: *Henry Moore* (1944)

8 Why don't they stick to murder and leave
art to us?
on hearing that his statue of Lazarus in New College
chapel, Oxford, kept Khrushchev awake at night
Jacob Epstein 1880–1959: attributed

9 Most statues seem sad and introspective,
they hold their breath between coming and
going,

They lament their devoured, once
   shuddering stone.
Dannie Abse 1923– : 'At the Tate'

10 It's amazing what you can do with an E in
A-level art, twisted imagination and a
chainsaw.
after winning the 1995 Turner Prize
Damien Hirst 1965– : in *Observer* 3
December 1995

➤➤ The Sea ◄◄

PROVERBS AND SAYINGS

1 **The good seaman is known in bad
weather.**
American proverb, mid 18th century

2 **He that would go to sea for pleasure
would go to hell for a pastime.**
with reference to the dangers involved in going to
sea; English proverb, late 19th century

3 **One hand for oneself and one for the
ship.**
literally, hold on with one hand, and work the ship
with the other; English proverb, late 18th century

PHRASES

4 **Davy Jones's locker**
the deep, especially as the grave of those who are
drowned at sea; *Davy Jones* = the evil spirit of the sea

5 **the long forties**
the sea area between the NE coast of Scotland and
the SW coast of Norway; from its depth of over 40
fathoms

6 **price of admiralty**
the cost of maintaining command of the seas, often
with reference to Kipling's line, 'If blood be the price

of admiralty Good God, we ha' paid in full' ('Song of
the English', 1893)

7 **the roaring forties**
stormy ocean tracts between latitude 40 and 50
degrees south

8 **the seven seas**
the Arctic, Antarctic, North and South Pacific, North
and South Atlantic, and Indian Oceans

QUOTATIONS

9 They that go down to the sea in ships: and
occupy their business in great waters;
These men see the works of the Lord: and
his wonders in the deep.
Bible: Psalm 107

10 Full fathom five thy father lies;
Of his bones are coral made:
Those are pearls that were his eyes:
Nothing of him that doth fade,
But doth suffer a sea-change
Into something rich and strange.
William Shakespeare 1564–1616: *The Tempest*
(1611); see **Change** 27

11 Whosoever commands the sea commands
the trade; whosoever commands the trade of
the world commands the riches of the
world, and consequently the world itself.
Walter Ralegh 1552–1618: 'A Discourse of the
Invention of Ships, Anchors, Compass, &c.'

12 The dominion of the sea, as it is an ancient
and undoubted right of the crown of
England, so it is the best security of the land

. . . The wooden walls are the best walls of
this kingdom.
Thomas Coventry 1578–1640: speech to the
Judges, 17 June 1635; see **Armed Forces** 17

13 What is a ship but a prison?
Robert Burton 1577–1640: *The Anatomy of
Melancholy* (1621–51)

14 Water, water, everywhere,
And all the boards did shrink;
Water, water, everywhere,
Nor any drop to drink.
Samuel Taylor Coleridge 1772–1834: 'The Rime
of the Ancient Mariner' (1798)

15 It [the Channel] is a mere ditch, and will be
crossed as soon as someone has the courage
to attempt it.
Napoleon I 1769–1821: letter to Consul
Cambacérès, 16 November 1803

16 A wet sheet and a flowing sea,
A wind that follows fast
And fills the white and rustling sail

And bends the gallant mast.
Allan Cunningham 1784–1842: 'A Wet Sheet and a Flowing Sea' (1825)

17 Rocked in the cradle of the deep.
Emma Hart Willard 1787–1870: title of song (1840), inspired by a prospect of the Bristol Channel

18 Break, break, break,
On thy cold grey stones, O Sea!
And I would that my tongue could utter
The thoughts that arise in me.
Alfred, Lord Tennyson 1809–92: 'Break, Break, Break' (1842)

19 I must go down to the sea again, to the
    lonely sea and the sky,
And all I ask is a tall ship and a star to steer
    her by,
And the wheel's kick and the wind's song
    and the white sail's shaking,
And a grey mist on the sea's face and a grey
    dawn breaking.
John Masefield 1878–1967: 'Sea Fever'; 'I must down to the seas' in the original of 1902, possibly a misprint

20 'A man who is not afraid of the sea will soon be drownded,' he said 'for he will be going out on a day he shouldn't. But we do be afraid of the sea, and we do only be drownded now and again.'
John Millington Synge 1871–1909: *The Aran Islands* (1907)

21 The dragon-green, the luminous, the dark,
    the serpent-haunted sea.
James Elroy Flecker 1884–1915: 'The Gates of Damascus' (1913)

22 The snotgreen sea. The scrotumtightening sea.
James Joyce 1882–1941: *Ulysses* (1922)

23 The sea hates a coward!
Eugene O'Neill 1888–1953: *Mourning becomes Electra* (1931)

24 It is an interesting biological fact that all of us have in our veins the exact same percentage of salt in our blood that exists in the ocean, and therefore, we have salt in our blood, in our sweat, in our tears. We are tied to the ocean. And when we go back to the sea—whether it is to sail or to watch it—we are going back from whence we came.
John F. Kennedy 1917–63: speech, Newport, Rhode Island, 14 September 1962

25 The sea is as near as we come to another world.
Anne Stevenson 1933– : 'North Sea off Carnoustie' (1977)

26 The sea has such extraordinary moods that sometimes you feel this is the only sort of life—and 10 minutes later you're praying for death.
Prince Philip, Duke of Edinburgh 1921– : in *Independent* 31 December 1998

27 When you are up there, it's like trying to hang on to a telegraph pole in an earthquake.
90 feet up the mast of her boat *Kingfisher*
Ellen MacArthur 1977– : in *Daily Telegraph* 16 February 2001

⇥ The Seasons ⇤

see also **Weather**

PROVERBS AND SAYINGS

1 **A cherry year, a merry year; a plum year, a dumb year.**
recording the tradition that a good crop of cherries is a promising sign for the year; English proverb, late 17th century

2 **It is not spring until you can plant your foot upon twelve daisies.**
mild spring weather is only assured when daisies are flowering thickly on the grass; English proverb, mid 19th century

3 **May chickens come cheeping.**
the weakness of chickens born in May is apparent from their continuous feeble cries. The proverb has also been linked to the idea that marriage in May is unlucky, and that children of such marriages are less likely to survive; English proverb, late 19th century; see **Weddings** 3

4 **One swallow does not make a summer.**
a single sign such as the arrival of one migratory swallow does not mean that the summer's settled weather has fully arrived; English proverb, mid 16th century

5 **On the first of March, the crows begin to search.**
crows traditionally pair off on this day; English proverb, mid 19th century

6 **A swarm in May is worth a load of hay; a swarm in June is worth a silver spoon; but a swarm in July is not worth a fly.**
traditional beekeepers' saying, meaning that the later in the year it is, the less time there will be for bees to collect pollen from flowers in blossom; English proverb, mid 17th century

7 **Winter never rots in the sky.**
the arrival of winter is not delayed; English proverb, early 17th century

PHRASES

8 **a blackthorn winter**
a period of cold weather in early spring, at the time when the blackthorn is in flower

9 **fall of the leaf**
autumn

10 **February fill-dyke**
the month of February; referring to the month's rain and snows; see **Weather 4**

QUOTATIONS

11 Sumer is icumen in,
Lhude sing cuccu!
Anonymous: 'Cuckoo Song' (c.1250), sung annually at Reading Abbey gateway and first recorded by John Fornset, a monk of Reading Abbey; see 23 below

12 In a somer seson, whan softe was the sonne.
William Langland c.1330–c.1400: *The Vision of Piers Plowman*

13 Whan that Aprill with his shoures soote
The droghte of March hath perced to the roote.
Geoffrey Chaucer 1343–1400: *The Canterbury Tales* 'The General Prologue'

14 I sing of brooks, of blossoms, birds, and bowers:
Of April, May, of June, and July-flowers.
I sing of May-poles, Hock-carts, wassails, wakes,
Of bride-grooms, brides, and of their bridal-cakes.
Robert Herrick 1591–1674: 'The Argument of his Book' from *Hesperides* (1648)

15 Early autumn—
rice field, ocean,
one green.
Matsuo Basho 1644–94: translated by Lucien Stryk

16 The way to ensure summer in England is to have it framed and glazed in a comfortable room.
Horace Walpole 1717–97: letter to Revd William Cole, 28 May 1774

17 Snowy, Flowy, Blowy,
Showery, Flowery, Bowery,
Hoppy, Croppy, Droppy,
Breezy, Sneezy, Freezy.
George Ellis 1753–1815: 'The Twelve Months'

18 Season of mists and mellow fruitfulness,
Close bosom-friend of the maturing sun;
Conspiring with him how to load and bless
With fruit the vines that round the thatch-eaves run.
John Keats 1795–1821: 'To Autumn' (1820)

19 A tedious season they await
Who hear November at the gate.
Alexander Pushkin 1799–1837: *Eugene Onegin* (1833)

20 No warmth, no cheerfulness, no healthful ease,
No comfortable feel in any member—
No shade, no shine, no butterflies, no bees,
No fruits, no flowers, no leaves, no birds,—
November!
Thomas Hood 1799–1845: 'No!' (1844)

21 Oh, to be in England
Now that April's there.
Robert Browning 1812–89: 'Home-Thoughts, from Abroad' (1845)

22 In winter I get up at night
And dress by yellow candle-light.
In summer, quite the other way,—
I have to go to bed by day.
Robert Louis Stevenson 1850–94: 'Bed in Summer' (1885)

23 Winter is icummen in,
Lhude sing Goddamm.
Ezra Pound 1885–1972: 'Ancient Music' (1917); see 11 above

24 April is the cruellest month, breeding
Lilacs out of the dead land, mixing
Memory and desire, stirring
Dull roots with spring rain.
T. S. Eliot 1888–1965: *The Waste Land* (1922)

25 I want to go south, where there is no autumn, where the cold doesn't crouch over one like a snow-leopard waiting to pounce. The heart of the North is dead, and the fingers of cold are corpse fingers.
D. H. Lawrence 1885–1930: letter to J. Middleton Murry, 3 October 1924

26 Summer time an' the livin' is easy,
Fish are jumpin' an' the cotton is high.
Du Bose Heyward 1885–1940 and **Ira Gershwin**
1896–1983: 'Summertime' (1935 song)

27 It is about five o'clock in an evening that the
first hour of spring strikes—autumn arrives
in the early morning, but spring at the close
of a winter day.
Elizabeth Bowen 1899–1973: *The Death of the
Heart* (1938)

28 June is bustin' out all over.
Oscar Hammerstein II 1895–1960: title of song
(1945)

29 August creates as she slumbers, replete and
satisfied.
Joseph Wood Krutch 1893–1970: *Twelve Seasons*
(1949)

30 What of October, that ambiguous month,
the month of tension, the unendurable
month?
Doris Lessing 1919– : *Martha Quest* (1952)

31 For man, autumn is a time of harvest, of
gathering together. For nature, it is a time of
sowing, of scattering abroad.
Edwin Way Teale 1899–1980: *Autumn Across
America* (1956)

32 Work seethes in the hands of spring,
That strapping dairymaid.
Boris Pasternak 1890–1960: *Doctor Zhivago*
(1958) 'Zhivago's Poems: March'

⊶Secrecy ⊷

PROVERBS AND SAYINGS

1 **Dead men tell no tales.**
often used to imply that a person's knowledge of a
secret will die with them; English proverb, mid 17th
century

2 **Don't ask, don't tell.**
summary of the Clinton administration's
compromise policy on homosexuals serving in the
armed forces, as described by Sam Nunn (1938–) in
May 1993

3 **Fields have eyes and woods have ears.**
one may always be spied on by unseen watchers or
listeners; English proverb, early 13th century

4 **Listeners never hear any good of
themselves.**
English proverb, mid 17th century

5 **Little pitchers have large ears.**
children overhear what is not meant for them (a
pitcher's *ears* are its handles); English proverb, mid
16th century

6 **My lips are sealed.**
used to convey that one will not discuss or reveal
something; popular version of Stanley Baldwin's
speech on the Abyssinian crisis, 10 December 1935,
when he told the House of Commons, 'My lips are
not yet unsealed. Were these troubles over I would
make a case, and I guarantee that not a man would
go into the lobby against us.'

7 **Never tell tales out of school.**
a warning against indiscretion; English proverb, mid
16th century

8 **No names, no pack-drill.**
if nobody is named as being responsible, nobody
can be blamed or punished (*pack-drill* = a military
punishment of walking up and down carrying full
equipment); English proverb, early 20th century, the
expression is now used generally to express an
unwillingness to provide detailed information

9 **One does not wash one's dirty linen in
public.**
discreditable matters should be dealt with privately;
English proverb, early 19th century

10 **Sch . . . you know who.**
advertising slogan for Schweppes mineral drinks,
1960s

11 **A secret is either too good to keep or
too bad not to tell.**
American proverb, mid 20th century

12 **See all your best work go unnoticed.**
advertisement for staff for MI5, 2005

13 **Those who hide can find.**
those who have concealed something know where it
is to be found; English proverb, early 15th century

14 **Three may keep a secret, if two of
them are dead.**
the only way to keep a secret is to tell no-one else;
English proverb, mid 16th century

15 **Walls have ears.**
care should be taken for possible eavesdroppers;
English proverb, late 16th century

16 **Will the real — please stand up?**
catchphrase from an American TV game show
(1955–66) in which a panel was asked to identify the
'real' one of three candidates all claiming to be a
particular person; after the guesses were made, the
compère would request the 'real' candidate to
stand up

17 You can't hide an awl in a sack.
some things are too conspicuous to hide; Russian proverb

PHRASES

18 an ace up one's sleeve
something effective held in reserve, a hidden advantage; an *ace* as the card of highest value in a card-game; see **Politicians** 24

19 hidden agenda
a secret or ulterior motive for something

20 quiet American
a person suspected of being an undercover agent or spy; with allusion to Graham Greene's *The Quiet American* (1955)

21 a skeleton in the cupboard
a secret source of discredit, pain, or shame; brought into literary use by Thackeray in 1845, 'there is a skeleton in every house'; see 38 below

22 a smoking pistol
a piece of incontrovertible incriminating evidence; on the assumption that a person found with a

smoking pistol or gun must be the guilty party; particularly associated with Barber B. Conable's comment on a Watergate tape revealing President Nixon's wish to limit FBI involvement in the investigation: 'I guess we have found the smoking pistol, haven't we?'; see **Hypothesis** 33

23 something nasty in the woodshed
a traumatic experience or a concealed unpleasantness in a person's background; from Stella Gibbons *Cold Comfort Farm* (1932), the repeated assertion 'I saw something nasty in the woodshed' being Aunt Ada Doom's method of ensuring her family's continued attendance on her

24 under the rose
in secret, sometimes found in Latin = *sub rosa*; there is reason to believe that the phrase originated in Germany

QUOTATIONS

25 And whatsoever I shall see or hear in the course of my profession, as well as outside my profession in my intercourse with men, if it be what should not be published abroad, I will never divulge holding such things to be holy secrets.
Hippocrates *c.*460–357 BC: *The Hippocratic Oath* (tr. W. H. S. Jones)

26 DUKE: And what's her history?
VIOLA: A blank, my lord. She never told her love,
But let concealment, like a worm i' the bud, Feed on her damask cheek.
William Shakespeare 1564–1616: *Twelfth Night* (1601)

27 I would not open windows into men's souls.
Elizabeth I 1533–1603: oral tradition, the words very possibly originating in a letter drafted by Bacon; J. B. Black *Reign of Elizabeth 1558-1603* (1936)

28 For secrets are edged tools,
And must be kept from children and from fools.
John Dryden 1631–1700: *Sir Martin Mar-All* (1667)

29 The necessity of procuring good intelligence is apparent and need not be further urged.
George Washington 1732–99: letter, 26 July 1777

30 Secrets with girls, like loaded guns with boys,
Are never valued till they make a noise.
George Crabbe 1754–1832: *Tales of the Hall* (1819) 'The Maid's Story'

31 We never knows wot's hidden in each other's hearts; and if we had glass winders there, we'd need keep the shutters up, some on us, I do assure you!
Charles Dickens 1812–70: *Martin Chuzzlewit* (1844)

32 After the first silence the small man said to the other: 'Where does a wise man hide a pebble?' And the tall man answered in a low voice: 'On the beach.' The small man nodded, and after a short silence said: 'Where does a wise man hide a leaf?' And the other answered: 'In the forest.'
G. K. Chesterton 1874–1936: *The Innocence of Father Brown* (1911)

33 We dance round in a ring and suppose,
But the Secret sits in the middle and knows.
Robert Frost 1874–1963: 'The Secret Sits' (1942)

34 Once the toothpaste is out of the tube, it is awfully hard to get it back in.
on the Watergate affair
H. R. Haldeman 1929– : to John Dean, 8 April 1973

35 That's another of those irregular verbs, isn't it? I give confidential briefings; you leak; he has been charged under Section 2a of the Official Secrets Act.
Jonathan Lynn 1943– and **Antony Jay** 1930– : *Yes Prime Minister* (1987) vol. 2 'Man Overboard'

36 Truth is suppressed, not to protect the country from enemy agents but to protect the Government of the day against the people.
Roy Hattersley 1932– : in *Independent* 18 February 1995

37 I am deeply troubled about asserting these rights, because it may be perceived by some that I have something to hide.
invoking his Fifth Amendment protection and declining to answer Congress's questions on the Enron collapse; see **Self-Interest** 19
Kenneth L. Lay 1942– : in *Newsweek* 25 February 2002

38 If there was some terrible secret about me waiting to come out, I wouldn't be standing in front of you now.
responding to a question about skeletons in cupboards; see 21 above
David Cameron 1966– : debate with David Davis, *Question Time* BBC TV, 3 November 2005

⤳ The Self ⤫

PROVERBS AND SAYINGS

1 Deny self for self's sake.
the result of self-denial is likely to be self-improvement; American proverb, mid 18th century

2 Every man is the architect of his own fortune.
each person is ultimately responsible for what happens to them; English proverb, mid 16th century; see **Fate** 14

QUOTATIONS

3 The commander of three armies may be taken away but the will of even a common man may not be taken away from him.
Confucius 551–479 BC: *Analects*

4 If a man should conquer in battle a thousand and a thousand more, and another man should conquer himself, his would be the greater victory, because the greatest of victories is the victory over oneself.
Pali Tripitaka c. 2nd century BC: *Dhammapada*

5 If I am not for myself who is for me; and being for my own self what am I? If not now when?
Hillel 'The Elder' c.60 BC–c.AD 9: *Pirqe Aboth*

6 I am made all things to all men.
Bible: I Corinthians

7 Every man's ordure well to his own sense doth smell.
Montaigne 1533–92: *Essais* (1580, Florio's translation of 1603), quoting the Latin of Erasmus (c.1469–1536)

8 This above all: to thine own self be true, And it must follow, as the night the day, Thou canst not then be false to any man.
William Shakespeare 1564–1616: *Hamlet* (1601)

9 Who is it that can tell me who I am?
William Shakespeare 1564–1616: *King Lear* (1605–6)

10 But I do nothing upon my self, and yet I am mine own *Executioner.*
John Donne 1572–1631: *Devotions upon Emergent Occasions* (1624)

11 It is the nature of extreme self-lovers, as they will set a house on fire, and it were but to roast their eggs.
Francis Bacon 1561–1626: *Essays* (1625) 'Of Wisdom for a Man's Self'

12 The self is hateful.
Blaise Pascal 1623–62: *Pensées* (1670)

13 It is not contrary to reason to prefer the destruction of the whole world to the scratching of my finger.
David Hume 1711–76: *A Treatise upon Human Nature* (1739)

14 I am—yet what I am, none cares or knows; My friends forsake me like a memory lost: I am the self-consumer of my woes.
John Clare 1793–1864: 'I Am' (1848)

15 Do I contradict myself? Very well then I contradict myself, (I am large, I contain multitudes.)
Walt Whitman 1819–92: 'Song of Myself' (written 1855)

16 It matters not how strait the gate, How charged with punishments the scroll, I am the master of my fate: I am the captain of my soul.
W. E. Henley 1849–1903: 'Invictus. In Memoriam R.T.H.B.' (1888)

17 Rose is a rose is a rose is a rose, is a rose.
Gertrude Stein 1874–1946: *Sacred Emily* (1913)

18 I am I plus my surroundings, and if I do not preserve the latter I do not preserve myself.
José Ortega y Gasset 1883–1955: *Meditaciones del Quijote* (1914)

19 Through the Thou a person becomes I.
Martin Buber 1878–1965: *Ich und Du* (1923)

20 We are all serving a life-sentence in the dungeon of self.
Cyril Connolly 1903–74: *The Unquiet Grave* (1944)

21 The whole human way of life has been destroyed and ruined. All that's left is the bare, shivering human soul, stripped to the last shred, the naked force of the human psyche for which nothing has changed because it was always cold and shivering and reaching out to its nearest neighbour, as cold and lonely as itself.
Boris Pasternak 1890–1960: *Doctor Zhivago* (1958)

22 The image of myself which I try to create in my own mind in order that I may love myself is very different from the image which I try to create in the minds of others in order that they may love me.
W. H. Auden 1907–73: *Dyer's Hand* (1963) 'Hic et Ille'

23 I am not a number, I am a free man!
Patrick McGoohan 1928– et al.: Number Six, in *The Prisoner* (TV series 1967–68)

24 My one regret in life is that I am not someone else.
Woody Allen 1935– : Eric Lax *Woody Allen and his Comedy* (1975)

25 Personal isn't the same as important.
Terry Pratchett 1948– : *Men at Arms* (1993)

26 'You' your joys and your sorrows, your memories and ambitions, your sense of personal identity and free will, are in fact no more than the behaviour of a vast assembly of nerve cells and their associated molecules.
Francis Crick 1916–2004: *The Astonishing Hypothesis: The Scientific Search for the Soul* (1994)

27 Each child hunts for a solution to the boredom of being no one but itself.
Candia McWilliam 1955– : *Debatable Land* (1994)

⤳ Self-Esteem and Self-Assertion ⤶

see also **Pride and Humility**

PROVERBS AND SAYINGS

1 **Because I'm worth it.**
advertising slogan for L'Oreal beauty products, from mid 1980s

2 **Clever hawks conceal their claws.**
it is not necessary to boast of one's abilities; Japanese proverb

3 **A frog in a well knows nothing of the ocean.**
one should be aware of the limitations of one's own experience; Japanese proverb

4 **Here's tae us; wha's like us?**
Gey few, and they're a' deid.
Scottish toast, probably of 19th-century origin

5 **The kumara does not speak of its own sweetness.**
one should not praise oneself (*kumara* = a sweet potato); Maori proverb

6 **Self-praise is no recommendation.**
a person's own favourable account of themselves is of dubious worth; English proverb, early 19th century

PHRASES

7 **a fly on the wheel**
a person who overestimates his or her own influence; see 13 below

8 **hide one's light under a bushel**
conceal one's merits; with allusion to the Bible (Matthew) 'Neither do men light a candle, and put it under a bushel, but on a candlestick; and it giveth light unto all that are in the house'

9 **little tin god**
a self-important person; *tin* implicitly contrasted with precious metals; an object of unjustified veneration

10 **pooh-bah**
a person having much influence or holding many offices at the same time, especially one perceived as pompously self-important; from the name of a character in W. S. Gilbert's *The Mikado* (1885)

QUOTATIONS

11 Seest thou a man wise in his own conceit?
There is more hope of a fool than of him.
Bible: Proverbs

12 Lord I am not worthy that thou shouldest
come under my roof.
Bible: St Matthew

13 It was prettily devised of Aesop, 'The fly sat
upon the axletree of the chariot-wheel and
said, what a dust do I raise.'
Francis Bacon 1561–1626: *Essays* (1625) 'Of Vain-Glory'; see 7 above

14   Oft-times nothing profits more
Than self esteem, grounded on just and
     right
Well managed.
John Milton 1608–74: *Paradise Lost* (1667); see
Poets 27

15 Where he falls short, 'tis Nature's fault
alone;
Where he succeeds, the merit's all his own.
of the actor, Thomas Sheridan
Charles Churchill 1731–64: *The Rosciad* (1761)

16 All his own geese are swans, as the swans of
others are geese.
of Joshua Reynolds
Horace Walpole 1717–97: letter to Anne, Countess
of Upper Ossory, 1 December 1786; see **Praise** 7

17 The axis of the earth sticks out visibly
through the centre of each and every town
or city.
Oliver Wendell Holmes 1809–94: *The Autocrat of
the Breakfast-Table* (1858)

18 He was like a cock who thought the sun had
risen to hear him crow.
George Eliot 1819–80: *Adam Bede* (1859)

19 To be commonly above others, still more to
think yourself above others, is to be below
them every now and then, and sometimes
much below.
Walter Bagehot 1826–77: in *National Review* July
1859 'John Milton'

20 As for conceit, what man will do any good
who is not conceited? Nobody holds a good
opinion of a man who has a low opinion of
himself.
Anthony Trollope 1815–82: *Orley Farm* (1862)

21 *on the suggestion that his attacks on John Bright
were too harsh as Bright was a self-made man:*
I know he is and he adores his maker.
Benjamin Disraeli 1804–81: Leon Harris *The Fine
Art of Political Wit* (1965)

22 You must stir it and stump it,
And blow your own trumpet,
Or trust me, you haven't a chance.
W. S. Gilbert 1836–1911: *Ruddigore* (1887)

23 It is easy—terribly easy— to shake a man's
faith in himself. To take advantage of that to
break a man's spirit is devil's work.
George Bernard Shaw 1856–1950: *Candida*
(1898)

24 Anything you can do, I can do better,
I can do anything better than you.
Irving Berlin 1888–1989: 'Anything You Can Do'
(1946 song)

25 When I was young I hoped that one day I
should be able to go into a post office to buy
a stamp without feeling nervous and shy:
now I realize that I never shall.
Edmund Blunden 1896–1974: Rupert Hart-Davis
letter to George Lyttelton, 5 August 1956

26 Early in life I had to choose between honest
arrogance and hypocritical humility. I chose
honest arrogance and have seen no occasion
to change.
Frank Lloyd Wright 1867–1959: Herbert Jacobs
Frank Lloyd Wright (1965)

27 I'm the greatest.
Muhammad Ali (Cassius Clay) 1942– :
catchphrase used from 1962, in *Louisville Times* 16
November 1962

28 It's easy to be independent when you've got
money. But to be independent when you
haven't got a thing—that's the Lord's test.
Mahalia Jackson 1911–72: *Movin' On Up* (with
Evan McLoud Wylie 1966)

29 That's it baby, when you got it, flaunt it.
Mel Brooks 1926– : *The Producers* (1968 film)

30 Pretentious? *Moi?*
John Cleese 1939– and **Connie Booth**: *Fawlty
Towers* 'The Psychiatrist' (BBC TV programme, 1979)

31 Well, I don't want to be any more egotistical
than possible. I have total confidence in my
ability.
Robert Hawke 1929– : on entering Parliament,
1980; T. Thompson and E. Butel (eds.) *The World
According to Hawke* (1983)

32 Shyness is egotism out of its depth.
Penelope Keith 1940– : in *Daily Mail* 27 June 1988

33 In the company of those she found
unimportant, her spirits sank: she felt
insignificant, plain and ordinary as though
ordinariness was contagious.
Alice Thomas Ellis 1932– : *The Inn at the Edge of
the World* (1990)

34 Our deepest fear is not that we are
inadequate. Our deepest fear is that we are
powerful beyond measure. It is our light, not
our darkness, that most frightens us.
Marianne Williamson 1953– : *A Return to Love*
(1992)

35 Our mistreatment was just not right, and I was tired of it.

of her refusal, on 1 December 1955, to surrender her seat on a segregated bus in Alabama to a white man
Rosa Parks 1913–2005: *Quiet Strength* (1994)

36 Arrogance is a highly under-appreciated character trait.
Sting 1951– : in *Independent* 23 June 2001

⤝ Self-Interest ⤛

see also **Self-Sacrifice**

PROVERBS AND SAYINGS

1 **Every man for himself and God for us all.**

ultimately God is concerned for humankind while individuals are concerned only for themselves; English proverb, mid 16th century

2 **Every man for himself, and the Devil take the hindmost.**

each person must look out for their own interests, and that the weakest is likely to come to disaster; English proverb, early 16th century

3 **Hear all, see all, say nowt, tak'all, keep all, gie nowt, and if tha ever does owt for nowt do it for thysen.**

now associated with Yorkshire, and caricaturing supposedly traditional Yorkshire attributes, in the picture of someone who is shrewd, taciturn, grasping, and selfish; English proverb, early 15th century

4 **If you want a thing done well, do it yourself.**

no-one else has so much interest in your own welfare; English proverb, mid 17th century

5 **If you would be well served, serve yourself.**

no-one else has so much interest in your own welfare; English proverb, mid 17th century

6 **Near is my kirtle, but nearer is my smock.**

used as a justification for putting one's own interests first (a *kirtle* is a woman's skirt or gown, and a *smock* is an undergarment); English proverb, mid 15th century

7 **Near is my shirt, but nearer is my skin.**

a justification of self-interest; English proverb, late 16th century

8 **A satisfied person does not know the hungry person.**

African proverb

9 **Self-interest is the rule, self-sacrifice the exception.**

American proverb, mid 20th century

10 **Self-preservation is the first law of nature.**

the instinct for self-preservation is inbuilt and instinctive; English proverb, mid 17th century

PHRASES

11 **bow down in the house of Rimmon**

pay lip-service to a principle; sacrifice one's principles for the sake of conformity; *Rimmon* a deity worshipped in ancient Damascus; after the Bible (2 Kings) 'I bow myself in the house of Rimmon'

12 **cultivate one's garden**

attend to one's own affairs; after Voltaire: see 26 below

13 **dog in the manger**

a person who selfishly refuses to let others enjoy benefits for which he or she personally has no use; from Aesop's fable of a dog which jumped into a manger and would not let the ox or horse eat the hay

14 **an eye to the main chance**

consideration for one's own interests; the *main chance* literally, in the game of hazard, a number (5, 6, 7, or 8) called by a player before throwing the dice

15 **I'm all right, Jack**

expressing selfish complacency and unconcern for others; originally in nautical use

16 **law of the jungle**

a system in which brute force and self-interest are paramount; the supposed code of survival in jungle life

17 **like turkeys voting for Christmas**

used to suggest that a particular action or decision is hopelessly self-defeating; see 34 below

18 **not in my back yard**

expressing an objection to the siting of something regarded as unpleasant in one's own locality, while by implication finding it acceptable elsewhere; originating in the United States in derogatory references to the anti-nuclear movement, and in Britain particularly associated with reports of the then Environment Secretary Nicholas Ridley's opposition in 1988 to housing developments near his home; the acronym NIMBY derives from this

19 **take the Fifth (Amendment)**
in America, decline to incriminate oneself; appeal to Article V of the ten original amendments (1791) to the Constitution of the United States, which states that 'no person . . . shall be compelled in any criminal case to be a witness against himself'; see **Secrecy** 37

20 **throw someone to the wolves**
sacrifice another person in order to avert danger or difficulties for oneself; probably in allusion to stories of wolves in a pack pursuing travellers in a horse-drawn sleigh

QUOTATIONS

21 *Cui bono?*
To whose profit?
Cicero 106–43 BC: *Pro Roscio Amerino*; quoting L. Cassius Longinus Ravilla

22 Men are nearly always willing to believe what they wish.
Julius Caesar 100–44 BC: *De Bello Gallico*

23 To rise by other's fall
I deem a losing gain;
All states with others' ruins built
To ruin run amain.
Robert Southwell 1561–95: 'Content and Rich' (1595)

24 Thus God and nature linked the gen'ral frame,
And bade self-love and social be the same.
Alexander Pope 1688–1744: *An Essay on Man* Epistle 3 (1733)

25 And this is law, I will maintain,
Unto my dying day, Sir,
That whatsoever King shall reign,
I will be the Vicar of Bray, sir!
Anonymous: 'The Vicar of Bray' (1734 song)

26 *Il faut cultiver notre jardin.*
We must cultivate our garden.
Voltaire 1694–1778: *Candide* (1759); see 12 above

27 It is not from the benevolence of the butcher, the brewer, or the baker, that we expect our dinner, but from their regard to their own interest. We address ourselves not to their humanity but to their self love.
Adam Smith 1723–90: *Wealth of Nations* (1776)

28 All sensible people are selfish, and nature is tugging at every contract to make the terms of it fair.
Ralph Waldo Emerson 1803–82: *The Conduct of Life* (1860)

29 We are all special cases. We all want to appeal against something! Everyone insists on his innocence, at all costs, even if it means accusing the rest of the human race and heaven.
Albert Camus 1913–60: *La Chute* (1956)

30 He would, wouldn't he?
on being told that Lord Astor claimed that her allegations, concerning himself and his house parties at Cliveden, were untrue
Mandy Rice-Davies 1944– : at the trial of Stephen Ward, 29 June 1963

31 Selflessness . . . is always the greatest insult to the ghetto, for selflessness is a luxury to the poor, it beckons to the spineless, the undifferentiated, the inept, the derelict, the drowning—a poor man is nothing without the fierce thorns of his ego.
Norman Mailer 1923– : *Miami and the Siege of Chicago* (1968)

32 Fourteen heart attacks and he had to die in my week. In MY week.
when ex-President Eisenhower's death prevented her photograph appearing on the cover of *Newsweek*
Janis Joplin 1943–70: in *New Musical Express* 12 April 1969

33 We are now in the Me Decade—seeing the upward roll of . . . the third great religious wave in American history . . . and this one has the mightiest, holiest roll of all, the beat that goes . . . *Me . . . Me . . . Me . . . Me.*
Tom Wolfe 1931– : *Mauve Gloves and Madmen* (1976)

34 It's the first time in recorded history that turkeys have been known to vote for an early Christmas.
on the collapse of the pact between Labour and the Liberals; see 17 above
James Callaghan 1912–2005: in the House of Commons, 28 March 1979

⤵ Self-Knowledge ⤴

PROVERBS AND SAYINGS

1 Know thyself.
English proverb, late fourteenth century, inscribed in Greek on the temple of Apollo at Delphi; Plato, in *Protagoras*, ascribes the saying to the Seven Wise Men of the 6th century BC

2 The peacock is always happy because it never looks at its ugly feet.
a person does not see their own faults; Persian proverb: see **Insight 6**

QUOTATIONS

3 I do not know whether I was then a man dreaming I was a butterfly, or whether I am now a butterfly dreaming I am a man.
Zhuangzi c.369–286 BC: *Chuang Tzu*

4 Why beholdest thou the mote that is in thy brother's eye, but considerest not the beam that is in thine own eye?
Bible: St Matthew; see **Mistakes 7, 8, 10**

5 The path of self knowledge must never be abandoned, nor is there on this journey a soul so much a giant that it has no need to return often to the stage of an infant and suckling.
St Teresa of Ávila 1512–82: *Life of the Mother Teresa of Jesus* (1611)

6 He knows the universe and does not know himself.
Jean de la Fontaine 1621–95: *Fables* (1678–9) 'Démocrite et les Abdéritains'

7 Satire is a sort of glass, wherein beholders do generally discover everybody's face but their own.
Jonathan Swift 1667–1745: *The Battle of the Books* (1704)

8 All our knowledge is, ourselves to know.
Alexander Pope 1688–1744: *An Essay on Man* Epistle 4 (1734)

9 O wad some Pow'r the giftie gie us
To see oursels as others see us!
Robert Burns 1759–96: 'To a Louse' (1786)

10 How little do we know that which we are!
How less what we may be!
Lord Byron 1788–1824: *Don Juan* (1819–24)

11 I do not know myself, and God forbid that I should.
Johann Wolfgang von Goethe 1749–1832: J. P. Eckermann *Gespräche mit Goethe* (1836–48) 10 April 1829

12 Resolve to be thyself: and know, that he
Who finds himself, loses his misery.
Matthew Arnold 1822–88: 'Self-Dependence' (1852)

13 No, when the fight begins within himself,
A man's worth something.
Robert Browning 1812–89: 'Bishop Blougram's Apology' (1855)

14 The tragedy of a man who has found himself out.
J. M. Barrie 1860–1937: *What Every Woman Knows* (performed 1908, published 1918)

15 To enter into your own mind you need to be armed to the teeth.
Paul Valéry 1871–1945: *Oeuvres* (1960) vol. 2 'Quelques pensées de Monsieur Teste'

16 The chief requirement of the good life, is to live without any image of oneself.
Iris Murdoch 1919–99: *The Bell* (1958)

17 Between the ages of twenty and forty we are engaged in the process of discovering who we are, which involves learning the difference between accidental limitations which it is our duty to outgrow and the necessary limitations of our nature beyond which we cannot trespass with impunity.
W. H. Auden 1907–73: *Dyer's Hand* (1963) 'Reading'

18 There are few things more painful than to recognize one's own faults in others.
John Wells 1936– : in *Observer* 23 May 1982

19 [Alfred Hitchcock] thought of himself as looking like Cary Grant. That's tough, to think of yourself one way and look another.
Tippi Hedren 1935– : interview in California, 1982; P. F. Boller and R. L. Davis *Hollywood Anecdotes* (1988)

⇥ Self-Sacrifice ⇤

see also **Self-Interest**

PHRASES

1 labour of love
a task undertaken for the love of a person or for the work itself; from the Bible (I Thessalonians) 'Your work of faith and labour of love'

2 the supreme sacrifice
the laying down of one's life for another or for one's country; see 13 below

QUOTATIONS

3 Go, tell the Spartans, thou who passest by,
That here obedient to their laws we lie.
epitaph for the Spartans who died at Thermopylae
Simonides c.556–468 BC: attributed; Herodotus *Histories*

4 Greater love hath no man than this, that a man lay down his life for his friends.
Bible: St John; see **Trust and Treachery** 37

5 True martyrdom is not determined by the penalty suffered, but by the cause.
St. Augustine of Hippo AD 354–430: Epistle 89 in Alois Goldbacher *S. Aureli Augustini Hipponensis Episcopi Epistulae* (1895) vol. 2

6 I am no longer my own, but yours. Put me to what you will, rank me with whom you will; put me to doing, put me to suffering; let me be employed for you or laid aside for you, exalted for you or brought low for you; let me be full, let me be empty; let me have all things, let me have nothing.
Methodist Service Book: The Covenant Prayer (based on the words of Richard Alleine in the First Covenant Service, 1782)

7 Deny yourself! You must deny yourself! That is the song that never ends.
Johann Wolfgang von Goethe 1749–1832: *Faust* pt. 1 (1808) 'Studierzimmer'

8 It is a far, far better thing that I do, than I have ever done; it is a far, far better rest that I go to, than I have ever known.
Sydney Carton's thoughts on the steps of the guillotine, taking the place of Charles Darnay whom he has smuggled out of prison
Charles Dickens 1812–70: *A Tale of Two Cities* (1859)

9 From the standpoint of pure reason, there are no good grounds to support the claim that one should sacrifice one's own happiness to that of others.
W. Somerset Maugham 1874–1965: *A Writer's Notebook* (1949) written in 1896

10 Self-sacrifice enables us to sacrifice other people without blushing.
George Bernard Shaw 1856–1950: *Man and Superman* (1903) 'Maxims: Self-Sacrifice'

11 I am just going outside and may be some time.
walking to his death in a blizzard
Captain Lawrence Oates 1880–1912: Scott's diary entry, 16–17 March 1912

12 I gave my life for freedom — This I know:
For those who bade me fight had told me so.
William Norman Ewer 1885–1976: 'Five Souls' (1917)

13 The love that never falters, the love that pays the price,
The love that makes undaunted the final sacrifice.
Cecil Spring-Rice 1859–1918: 'I Vow to Thee, My Country' (1918); see 2 above

14 A woman will always sacrifice herself if you give her the opportunity. It is her favourite form of self-indulgence.
W. Somerset Maugham 1874–1965: *The Circle* (1921)

15 I do not think you have ever realised the shock, which the attitude you took up caused your family and the whole nation. It seemed inconceivable to those who had made such sacrifices during the war that you, as their King, refused a lesser sacrifice.
Queen Mary 1867–1953: letter to the Duke of Windsor, July 1938

16 I have nothing to offer but blood, toil, tears and sweat.
Winston Churchill 1874–1965: speech, House of Commons, 13 May 1940

17 She's the sort of woman who lives for others—you can always tell the others by their hunted expression.
C. S. Lewis 1898–1963: *The Screwtape Letters* (1942)

18 To gain that which is worth having, it may be necessary to lose everything else.
Bernadette Devlin McAliskey 1947– : preface to *The Price of My Soul* (1969)

19 Perhaps only those who sacrifice themselves completely are truly memorable.
Paul Scott 1920–78: letter to F. Weinbaum, 26 October 1975

20 I'd give up all my Shirley Temple dolls to get
Liza back.
the estranged husband of Liza Minnelli
David Gest: attributed; in *Sunday Times* 14
December 2003

Selling see **Buying and Selling**

➤➤ The Senses ➤➤

see also **The Body**

PROVERBS AND SAYINGS

1 **When a pine needle falls in the forest,
the eagle sees it, the deer hears it, and
the bear smells it.**
modern saying, said to be of native American origin

PHRASES

2 **deaf as an adder**
completely deaf; after the Bible: see **Defiance 9**

3 **the five senses**
the special bodily faculties of sight, hearing, smell,
taste, and touch

QUOTATIONS

4 I have heard of thee by the hearing of the
ear: but now mine eye seeth thee.
The Bible: Job

5 By convention there is colour, by
convention sweetness, by convention
bitterness, but in reality there are atoms and
space.
Democritus *c.*460–*c.*370 BC: fragment 125

6 When in recollection he withdraws all his
senses from the attractions of the pleasures
of sense, even as a tortoise withdraws all its
limbs, then his is a serene wisdom.
Bhagavadgita: ch. 2, v. 58

7 Nor will the sweetest delight of gardens
afford much comfort in sleep; wherein the
dullness of that sense shakes hands with
delectable odours; and though in the bed of
Cleopatra, can hardly with any delight raise
up the ghost of a rose.
Thomas Browne 1605–82: *The Garden of Cyrus*
(1658)

8 When I consider how my light is spent,
E're half my days, in this dark world and
wide,
And that one talent which is death to hide
Lodged with me useless.
on his blindness
John Milton 1608–74: 'When I consider how my
light is spent' (1673)

9 Whatever withdraws us from the power of
our senses; whatever makes the past, the
distant, or the future predominate over the
present, advances us in the dignity of
thinking beings.
Samuel Johnson 1709–84: *A Journey to the Western
Islands of Scotland* (1775)

10 O for a life of sensations rather than of
thoughts!
John Keats 1795–1821: letter to Benjamin Bailey, 22
November 1817

11   Any nose
May ravage with impunity a rose.
Robert Browning 1812–89: *Sordello* (1840)

12 Friday I tasted life. It was a vast morsel. A
Circus passed the house—still I feel the red
in my mind though the drums are out. The
Lawn is full of south and the odours tangle,
and I hear to-day for the first time the river
in the tree.
Emily Dickinson 1830–86: letter to Mrs J. G.
Holland, May 1866

13 You see, but you do not observe.
Arthur Conan Doyle 1859–1930: *The Adventures
of Sherlock Holmes* (1892)

14 Fortissimo at last!
on seeing Niagara Falls
Gustav Mahler 1860–1911: K. Blaukopf *Gustav
Mahler* (1973)

15 Does it matter?—losing your sight? . . .
There's such splendid work for the blind;
And people will always be kind,
As you sit on the terrace remembering
And turning your face to the light.
Siegfried Sassoon 1886–1967: 'Does it Matter?'
(1918)

16 I test my bath before I sit,
And I'm always moved to wonderment
That what chills the finger not a bit
Is so frigid upon the fundament.
Ogden Nash 1902–71: 'Samson Agonistes' (1942)

17 Each day I live in a glass room
Unless I break it with the thrusting
Of my senses and pass through

The splintered walls to the great landscape.
Mervyn Peake 1911–68: 'Each day I live in a glass
room' (1967)

18 My left hand is my thinking hand. The right
is only a motor hand.
Barbara Hepworth 1903–75: *A Pictorial
Autobiography* (1970)

19 I can hear people smile.
David Blunkett 1947– : in *Independent* 14
July 2001

20 To be able to feel the lightest touch is really
a gift.
regaining some movement after being paralysed in a
riding accident seven years before
Christopher Reeve 1952–2004: in *Sunday Times*
15 September 2002

⇸ Sex ⇷

see also **Love, Marriage, The Single Life**

PROVERBS AND SAYINGS

1 Did the earth move for you?
supposedly said to one's partner after sexual
intercourse, after Hemingway: see 26 below

2 Dirty water will quench fire.
mainly used to mean that a man's sexual needs can
be satisfied by any woman, however ugly or
immoral; English proverb, mid 16th century

3 Post coitum omne animal triste.
Latin = After coition every animal is sad

PHRASES

4 the beast with two backs
a man and woman having sexual intercourse; from
Shakespeare *Othello*: see 13 below

5 a gay Lothario
a libertine, a rake; from Nicholas Rowe (1674–1718)
The Fair Penitent (1703) 'Is this that haughty, gallant,
gay Lothario?'

6 nudge nudge (wink wink)
used to draw attention to a sexual innuendo in the
previous statement; a catchphrase from *Monty
Python's Flying Circus*: see 31 below; **Words** 31

QUOTATIONS

7 Someone asked Sophocles, 'How is your sex-
life now? Are you still able to have a
woman?' He replied, 'Hush, man; most
gladly indeed am I rid of it all, as though I
had escaped from a mad and savage master.'
Sophocles c.496–406 BC: Plato *Republic*

8 I have never yet seen anyone whose desire to
build up his moral power was as strong as
sexual desire.
Confucius 551–479 BC: *Analects*

9 Give me chastity and continency—but
not yet!
St Augustine of Hippo AD 354–430: *Confessions*
(AD 397–8)

10 And after wyn on Venus moste I thynke,
For al so siker as cold engendreth hayl,
A likerous mouth moste han a likerous tayl.
Geoffrey Chaucer 1343–1400: *The Canterbury
Tales* 'The Wife of Bath's Prologue'

11 Licence my roving hands, and let them go,
Behind, before, above, between, below.
O my America, my new found land,
My kingdom, safeliest when with one man
manned.
John Donne 1572–1631: 'To His Mistress Going to
Bed' (c.1595)

12 Is it not strange that desire should so many
years outlive performance?
William Shakespeare 1564–1616: *Henry IV, Part 2*
(1597)

13 Your daughter and the Moor are now
making the beast with two backs.
William Shakespeare 1564–1616: *Othello*
(1602–4); see 4 above

14 This trivial and vulgar way of coition; it is
the foolishest act a wise man commits in all
his life, nor is there any thing that will more
deject his cooled imagination, when he
shall consider what an odd and unworthy
piece of folly he hath committed.
Thomas Browne 1605–82: *Religio Medici* (1643)

15 The Duke returned from the wars today and
did pleasure me in his top-boots.
Sarah, Duchess of Marlborough 1660–1744: oral
tradition, attributed in various forms; see I. Butler
Rule of Three (1967)

16 I'll come no more behind your scenes,
David; for the silk stockings and white
bosoms of your actresses excite my amorous
propensities.
Samuel Johnson 1709–84: James Boswell *Life of
Samuel Johnson* (1791) 1750

17 The pleasure is momentary, the position
ridiculous, and the expense damnable.
Lord Chesterfield 1694–1773: attributed

18 Not tonight, Josephine.
Napoleon I 1769–1821: attributed, but probably
apocryphal; R. H. Horne *The History of Napoleon*
(1841) describes the circumstances in which the
affront may have occurred

19 'Tisn't beauty, so to speak, nor good talk
necessarily. It's just It. Some women'll stay
in a man's memory if they once walked
down a street.
Rudyard Kipling 1865–1936: *Traffics and
Discoveries* (1904); see **Women** 13

20 When I hear his steps outside my door I lie
down on my bed, close my eyes, open my
legs, and think of England.
Lady Hillingdon 1857–1940: diary 1912 (original
untraced, perhaps apocryphal); J. Gathorne-Hardy
The Rise and Fall of the British Nanny (1972)

21 i like my body when it is with your
body. It is so quite new a thing.
Muscles better and nerves more.
e. e. cummings 1894–1962: 'Sonnets–Actualities'
no. 8 (1925)

22 You're neither unnatural, nor abominable,
nor mad; you're as much a part of what
people call nature as anyone else; only

you're unexplained as yet—you've not got
your niche in creation.
on lesbianism
Radclyffe Hall 1883–1943: *The Well of Loneliness*
(1928)

23 Chastity—the most unnatural of all the
sexual perversions.
Aldous Huxley 1894–1963: *Eyeless in Gaza* (1936)

24 Pornography is the attempt to insult sex, to
do dirt on it.
D. H. Lawrence 1885–1930: *Phoenix* (1936)
'Pornography and Obscenity'

25 Give a man a free hand and he'll try to put it
all over you.
Mae West 1892–1980: *Klondike Annie* (1936 film)

26 But did thee feel the earth move?
Ernest Hemingway 1899–1961: *For Whom the Bell
Tolls* (1940); see 1 above

27 It doesn't matter what you do in the
bedroom as long as you don't do it in the
street and frighten the horses.
Mrs Patrick Campbell 1865–1940: Daphne
Fielding *The Duchess of Jermyn Street* (1964)

28 The only unnatural sex act is that which you
cannot perform.
Alfred Kinsey 1894–1956: attributed; in *Time* 21
January 1966

29 I can't get no satisfaction
I can't get no girl reaction
Mick Jagger 1943– and **Keith Richards** 1943– :
'(I Can't Get No) Satisfaction' (1965 song)

30 The orgasm has replaced the Cross as the
focus of longing and the image of
fulfilment.
Malcolm Muggeridge 1903–90: *Tread Softly*
(1966)

31 Your wife interested in . . . *photographs*? Eh?
Know what I mean—*photographs*? He asked
him knowingly . . . nudge nudge, snap snap,
grin grin, wink wink, say no more.
Graham Chapman 1941–89, **John Cleese**
1939– , et al.: *Monty Python's Flying Circus* (BBC TV
programme, 1969); see 6 above

32 Is sex dirty? Only if it's done right.
Woody Allen 1935– : *Everything You Always
Wanted to Know about Sex* (1972 film)

33 Traditionally, sex has been a very private,
secretive activity. Herein perhaps lies its
powerful force for uniting people in a strong
bond. As we make sex less secretive, we may
rob it of its power to hold men and women
together.
Thomas Szasz 1920– : *The Second Sin* (1973)

34 Sexual intercourse began
In nineteen sixty-three
(Which was rather late for me) —
Between the end of the *Chatterley* ban

And the Beatles' first LP.
Philip Larkin 1922–85: 'Annus Mirabilis' (1974)

35 Is that a gun in your pocket, or are you just glad to see me?
usually quoted as 'Is that a pistol in your pocket . . . '
Mae West 1892–1980: Joseph Weintraub *Peel Me a Grape* (1975)

36 On bisexuality: It immediately doubles your chances for a date on Saturday night.
Woody Allen 1935– : in *New York Times* 1 December 1975

37 Seduction is often difficult to distinguish from rape. In seduction, the rapist bothers to buy a bottle of wine.
Andrea Dworkin 1946–2005: speech to women at Harper & Row, 1976; in *Letters from a War Zone* (1988)

38 Don't knock masturbation. It's sex with someone I love.
Woody Allen 1935– : *Annie Hall* (1977 film, with Marshall Brickman)

39 That [sex] was the most fun I ever had without laughing.
Woody Allen 1935– : *Annie Hall* (1977 film, with Marshall Brickman)

40 Sex has never been an obsession with me. It's just like eating a bag of crisps. Quite nice, but nothing marvellous. Sex is not simply black and white. There's a lot of grey.
Boy George 1961– : in *Sun* 21 October 1982

41 Love is two minutes fifty-two seconds of squishing noises.
Johnny Rotten 1957– : in *Daily Mirror*, 1983

42 I'll have what she's having.
woman to waiter, seeing Sally acting an orgasm
Nora Ephron 1941– : *When Harry Met Sally* (1989 film)

43 Gay men may seek sex without emotion; lesbians often end up in emotion without sex.
Camille Paglia 1947– : in *Esquire* October 1991

44 Sex and taxes are in many ways the same. Tax does to cash what males do to genes. It dispenses assets among the population as a whole. Sex, not death, is the great leveller.
Steve Jones 1944– : speech to the Royal Society; in *Independent* 25 January 1997

⇥ Sickness ⇤

see also **Health and Fitness, Medicine**

PROVERBS AND SAYINGS

1 **Coughs and sneezes spread diseases. Trap the germs in your handkerchief.**
Second World War health slogan (1942)

2 **A creaking door hangs longest.**
someone who is apparently in poor health may well outlive the ostensibly stronger; English proverb, late 17th century

3 **Feed a cold and starve a fever.**
probably intended as two separate admonitions, but sometimes interpreted to mean that if you feed a cold you will have to starve a fever later; English proverb, mid 19th century

PHRASES

4 **the Black Death**
the great epidemic of plague in Europe in the 14th century; the name 'black death' is modern, and was apparently introduced by Mrs. Penrose (Mrs. Markham) in 1823; earlier writers call it the (great) pestilence, the plague, or the great death

5 **the falling sickness**
an archaic term for epilepsy

6 **the king's evil**
scrofula, from the belief that a cure could be obtained by the sovereign's touching the sores

7 **white death**
tuberculosis, after Black Death

QUOTATIONS

8 Here am I, dying of a hundred good symptoms.
Alexander Pope 1688–1744: to George, Lord Lyttelton, 15 May 1744; Joseph Spence *Anecdotes* (ed. J. Osborn, 1966)

9 To know ourselves diseased, is half our cure.
Edward Young 1683–1765: *Night Thoughts* (1742–5) 'Night 9'

10 How few of his friends' houses would a man choose to be at when he is sick.
Samuel Johnson 1709–84: James Boswell *Life of Samuel Johnson* (1791) 1783

11 It is a most extraordinary thing, but I never read a patent medicine advertisement without being impelled to the conclusion that I am suffering from the particular disease therein dealt with in its most virulent form.
Jerome K. Jerome 1859–1927: *Three Men in a Boat* (1889)

12 'Ye can call it influenza if ye like,' said Mrs Machin. 'There was no influenza in my young days. We called a cold a cold.'
Arnold Bennett 1867–1931: *The Card* (1911)

13 The desire to take medicine is perhaps the greatest feature which distinguishes man from animals.
William Osler 1849–1919: H. Cushing *Life of Sir William Osler* (1925)

14 I enjoy convalescence. It is the part that makes illness worth while.
George Bernard Shaw 1856–1950: *Back to Methuselah* (1921)

15 Illness is the doctor to whom we pay most heed; to kindness, to knowledge, we make promise only; pain we obey.
Marcel Proust 1871–1922: *Cities of the Plain* (1922)

16 Human nature seldom walks up to the word 'cancer'.
Rudyard Kipling 1865–1936: *Debits and Credits* (1926)

17 My final word, before I'm done,
Is 'Cancer can be rather fun'.
Thanks to the nurses and Nye Bevan
The NHS is quite like heaven
Provided one confronts the tumour
With a sufficient sense of humour.
J. B. S. Haldane 1892–1964: 'Cancer's a Funny Thing' (1968)

18 Did God who gave us flowers and trees,
Also provide the allergies?
E. Y. Harburg 1898–1981: 'A Nose is a Nose is a Nose' (1965)

19 Everyone I've met so far has a cold. The entire population of the British Isles seems to do absolutely nothing from one year's end to another except shuffle round in small circles sneezing voluptuously into each other's faces . . . a sort of merry-go-round of reinfection. What chance of survival has one got?
Lawrence Durrell 1912–90: Gerald Durrell *Birds, Beasts and Relatives* (1969)

20 A man's illness is his private territory and, no matter how much he loves you and how close you are, you stay an outsider. You are healthy.
Lauren Bacall 1924– : *By Myself* (1978)

21 Illness is not something a person *has*; it's another way of *being*.
Jonathan Miller 1934– : *The Body in Question* (1978)

22 Societies need to have one illness which becomes identified with evil, and attaches blame to its 'victims'.
Susan Sontag 1933–2004: *AIDS and its Metaphors* (1989)

23 Meningitis. It was a word you had to bite on to say it. It had a fright and a hiss in it.
Seamus Deane 1940– : *Reading in the Dark* (1996)

24 People mean well and do not see how distancing insistent cheeriness is, how it denies another's reality, denies a sick person the space or right to be sick and in pain.
Marilyn French 1929– : *A Season in Hell* (1998)

25 It's all about losing your brain without losing your mind.
on his fight against Parkinson's disease
Michael J. Fox 1961– : in *The Times* 16 September 2000

⥤ Silence ⥢

see also **Speech**

PROVERBS AND SAYINGS

1 **A shut mouth catches no flies.**
a warning against the dangers of idle talk; English proverb, late 16th century

2 **Silence is a still noise.**
American proverb, late 19th century

3 **Silence means consent.**
English proverb, late 14th century; translation of a Latin tag, '*qui tacet consentire videtur* [he who is silent seems to consent]', said to have been spoken by Thomas More (1478–1535) when asked at his trial why he was silent on being asked to acknowledge the king's supremacy over the Church. The principle is not accepted in modern English law

4 Speech is silver, but silence is golden.
discretion can be more valuable than the most eloquent words; English proverb, mid 19th century; see **Speech** 5

QUOTATIONS

6 Silence is a woman's finest ornament.
Auctoritates Aristotelis: a compilation of medieval propositions

7 Shallow brooks murmur most, deep silent slide away.
Philip Sidney 1554–86: *Arcadia* (1581)

8 Silence is the virtue of fools.
Francis Bacon 1561–1626: *De Dignitate et Augmentis Scientiarum* (1623)

9 No voice; but oh! the silence sank
Like music on my heart.
Samuel Taylor Coleridge 1772–1834: 'The Rime of the Ancient Mariner' (1798)

10 Thou still unravished bride of quietness,
Thou foster-child of silence and slow time.
John Keats 1795–1821: 'Ode on a Grecian Urn' (1820)

11 Under all speech that is good for anything there lies a silence that is better. Silence is deep as Eternity; speech is shallow as Time.
Thomas Carlyle 1795–1881: *Critical and Miscellaneous Essays* (1838) 'Sir Walter Scott'

5 A still tongue makes a wise head.
a person who is not given to idle talk, and who listens to others, is likely to be wise; English proverb, mid 16th century

12 Speech is often barren; but silence also does not necessarily brood over a full nest. Your still fowl, blinking at you without remark, may all the while be sitting on one addled egg; and when it takes to cackling will have nothing to announce but that addled delusion.
George Eliot 1819–80: *Felix Holt* (1866)

13 Elected Silence, sing to me
And beat upon my whorlèd ear.
Gerard Manley Hopkins 1844–89: 'The Habit of Perfection' (written 1866)

14 People talking without speaking
People hearing without listening
People writing songs that voices never share
And no one dare disturb the sound of silence.
Paul Simon 1942– : 'Sound of Silence' (1964 song)

15 Silence is often a good policy on some subjects in politics, but silence is regarded as a sort of sin now, and it has to be filled with a lot of gossip and sound bites.
Douglas Hurd 1930– : in *Independent* 23 April 2001

⤞Similarity and Difference ⤝

PROVERBS AND SAYINGS

1 All cats are grey in the dark.
darkness obscures inessential differences; English proverb, mid 16th century

2 Birds of a feather flock together.
people of the same (usually, unscrupulous) character associated together; English proverb, mid 16th century; see 13 below

3 Comparisons are odious.
often used to suggest that to compare two different things or persons is unhelpful or misleading; English proverb, mid 15th century; see 16 below

4 East is east, and west is west.
an assertion of ineradicable racial and cultural differences; English proverb, late 19th century, from Kipling: see **Equality** 12

5 Extremes meet.
opposite extremes have much in common; English proverb, mid 18th century

6 From the sweetest wine, the tartest vinegar.
the strongest hate comes from former love; English proverb, late 16th century

7 Like breeds like.
a particular kind of event may well be the genesis of a similar occurrence; English proverb, mid 16th century

8 Like will to like.
those of similar nature and inclination are drawn together; English proverb, late 14th century

9 One nail drives out another.
like will counter like; English proverb, mid 13th century

10 Two of a trade never agree.
close association with someone makes disagreement over policy and principles more likely; English proverb, early 17th century

11 Two swords do not fit in one scabbard.
Indian proverb; see 10 above

12 **When Greek meets Greek, then comes the tug of war.**
when two people of a similar kind are opposed, there is a struggle for supremacy; English proverb, late 17th century; see 19 below

PHRASES

13 **birds of a feather**
those of like character; from the proverb: see 2 above

14 **of the same leaven**
of the same sort or character; *leaven* = an agency which exercises a transforming influence from

within, of biblical origin as in Matthew, 'Take heed and beware of the leaven of the Pharisees'; see **Sin** 3

QUOTATIONS

15 The road up and the road down are one and the same.
Heraclitus c.540–c.480 BC: H. Diels and W. Kranz *Die Fragmente der Vorsokratiker* (7th ed., 1954) fragment 60

16 Comparisons are odorous.
William Shakespeare 1564–1616: *Much Ado About Nothing* (1598–9); see 3 above

17 In one and the same fire, clay grows hard and wax melts.
Francis Bacon 1561–1626: *History of Life and Death* (1623); see **Character** 13

18   Feel by turns the bitter change
Of fierce extremes, extremes by change more fierce.
John Milton 1608–74: *Paradise Lost* (1667)

19 When Greeks joined Greeks, then was the tug of war!
Nathaniel Lee 1653–92: *The Rival Queens* (1677); see 12 above

20 No caparisons, Miss, if you please!—Caparisons don't become a young woman.
Richard Brinsley Sheridan 1751–1816: *The Rivals* (1775)

21   Near all the birds
Will sing at dawn,—and yet we do not take
The chaffering swallow for the holy lark.
Elizabeth Barrett Browning 1806–61: *Aurora Leigh* (1857)

22 One of the most common defects of half-instructed minds is to think much of that in which they differ from others, and little of that in which they agree with others.
on the evils of sectarianism
Walter Bagehot 1826–77: in *Economist* 11 June 1870

23 If every one were cast in the same mould, there would be no such thing as beauty.
Charles Darwin 1809–82: *The Descent of Man* (1871)

24 Whatever you may be sure of, be sure at least of this, that you are dreadfully like other people.
James Russell Lowell 1819–91: *My Study Windows* (1871)

25 Out of intense complexities intense simplicities emerge.
Winston Churchill 1874–1965: *The World Crisis* (1923–9)

26 World is crazier and more of it than we think,
Incorrigibly plural. I peel and portion
A tangerine and spit the pips and feel
The drunkenness of things being various.
Louis MacNeice 1907–63: 'Snow' (1935)

27 If we cannot end now our differences, at least we can help make the world safe for diversity.
John F. Kennedy 1917–63: address at American University, Washington, DC, 10 June 1963

28 Without deviation from the norm, progress is not possible.
Frank Zappa 1940–93: attributed, in *New York* 20 June 1994

⇢➤ Sin ⥝⥼

see also **Good and Evil**

PROVERBS AND SAYINGS

1 Satan rebuking sin.

originally meaning that the worst possible stage has been reached; in later use, an ironic comment on the nature of the person delivering the rebuke; English proverb, early 17th century

2 What is got over the Devil's back is spent under his belly.

what is gained improperly will be spent on folly and debauchery; English proverb, late 16th century

PHRASES

3 the old leaven

traces of an unregenerate condition; *leaven* = an agency which exercises a transforming influence from within, as in the Bible (1 Corinthians) 'Purge out therefore the old leaven'; see **Similarity** 14

4 original sin

the tendency to evil supposedly innate in all humans, held to be inherited from Adam in consequence of the Fall of Man

5 the seven deadly sins

those entailing damnation; traditionally pride, covetousness, lust, envy, gluttony, anger, and sloth

6 the sin against the Holy Ghost

the only sin regarded as putting its perpetrator beyond redemption; an ultimate and irredeemable wrong; in Christian theology, based on the interpretation of several Gospel passages: see 8 below

QUOTATIONS

7 Be sure your sin will find you out.
Bible: Numbers

8 The blasphemy against the Holy Ghost shall not be forgiven unto men.
Bible: St Matthew; see 6 above

9 The wages of sin is death.
Bible: Romans

10 No one ever suddenly became depraved.
Juvenal c.AD 60–c.130: *Satires*

11 We make ourselves a ladder out of our vices if we trample the vices themselves underfoot.
St Augustine of Hippo AD 354–430: Sermon no. 176 ('On the Ascension of the Lord')

12 I have sinned exceedingly in thought, word, and deed, through my fault, through my fault, through my most grievous fault.
The Missal: *The Ordinary of the Mass*

13 Commit
The oldest sins the newest kind of ways.
William Shakespeare 1564–1616: *Henry IV, Part 2* (1597)

14 Nothing emboldens sin so much as mercy.
William Shakespeare 1564–1616: *Timon of Athens* (c.1607)

15 I should renounce the devil and all his works, the pomps and vanity of this wicked world, and all the sinful lusts of the flesh.
The Book of Common Prayer 1662: *Catechism*; see **Temptation** 4

16 We have erred, and strayed from thy ways like lost sheep. We have followed too much the devices and desires of our own hearts.
The Book of Common Prayer 1662: *Morning Prayer* General Confession

17 It is public scandal that constitutes offence, and to sin in secret is not to sin at all.
Molière 1622–73: *Le Tartuffe* (1669)

18 Vice came in always at the door of necessity, not at the door of inclination.
Daniel Defoe 1660–1731: *Moll Flanders* (1721)

19 I waive the quantum o' the sin;
The hazard of concealing;
But och! it hardens a' within,
And petrifies the feeling!
Robert Burns 1759–96: 'Epistle to a Young Friend' (1786)

20 Vice is detestable; I banish all its appearances from my coteries; and I would banish its reality, too, were I sure I should then have any thing but empty chairs in my drawing-room.
Fanny Burney 1752–1840: *Camilla* (1796)

21 That Calvinistic sense of innate depravity and original sin from whose visitations, in some shape or other, no deeply thinking mind is always and wholly free.
Herman Melville 1819–91: *Hawthorne and His Mosses* (1850)

22 She [the Catholic Church] holds that it were better for sun and moon to drop from heaven, for the earth to fail, and for all the

many millions who are upon it to die of starvation in extremest agony, as far as temporal affliction goes, than that one soul, I will not say, should be lost, but should commit one single venial sin, should tell one wilful untruth . . . or steal one poor farthing without excuse.
John Henry Newman 1801–90: *Lectures on Anglican Difficulties* (1852)

23 For the sin ye do by two and two ye must pay for one by one!
Rudyard Kipling 1865–1936: 'Tomlinson' (1892)

24 The only difference between the saint and the sinner is that every saint has a past, and every sinner has a future.
Oscar Wilde 1854–1900: *A Woman of No Importance* (1893)

25 When I'm good, I'm very, very good, but when I'm bad, I'm better.
Mae West 1892–1980: *I'm No Angel* (1933 film)

26 *when asked by Mrs Coolidge what a sermon had been about:*
'Sins,' he said. 'Well, what did he say about sin?' 'He was against it.'
Calvin Coolidge 1872–1933: John H. McKee *Coolidge: Wit and Wisdom* (1933); perhaps apocryphal

27 All sins are attempts to fill voids.
Simone Weil 1909–43: *La Pesanteur et la grâce* (1948)

28 There are different kinds of wrong. The people sinned against are not always the best.
Ivy Compton-Burnett 1884–1969: *The Mighty and their Fall* (1961)

29 All sin tends to be addictive, and the terminal point of addiction is what is called damnation.
W. H. Auden 1907–73: *A Certain World* (1970) 'Hell'

30 Sins become more subtle as you grow older. You commit sins of despair rather than lust.
Piers Paul Read 1941– : in *Daily Telegraph* 3 October 1990

⤞ Singing ⤝

see also **Music**

PROVERBS AND SAYINGS

1 **Why should the devil have all the best tunes?**
commonly attributed to the English evangelist Rowland Hill (1744–1833); many hymns are sung to popular secular melodies, and this practice was especially favoured by the Methodists

QUOTATIONS

2 The exercise of singing is delightful to Nature, and good to preserve the health of man. It doth strengthen all parts of the breast, and doth open the pipes.
William Byrd 1543–1623: *Psalms, Sonnets and Songs* (1588)

3 I can suck melancholy out of a song as a weasel sucks eggs.
William Shakespeare 1564–1616: *As You Like It* (1599)

4 If a man were permitted to make all the ballads, he need not care who should make the laws of a nation.
Andrew Fletcher of Saltoun 1655–1716: 'An Account of a Conversation concerning a Right Regulation of Government for the Good of Mankind. In a Letter to the Marquis of Montrose' (1704)

5 Nothing is capable of being well set to music that is not nonsense.
Joseph Addison 1672–1719: in *The Spectator* 21 March 1711

6 An exotic and irrational entertainment, which has been always combated, and always has prevailed.
of Italian opera
Samuel Johnson 1709–84: *Lives of the English Poets* (1779–81) 'Hughes'

7 Sentimentally I am disposed to harmony. But organically I am incapable of a tune.
Charles Lamb 1775–1834: *Essays of Elia* (1823) 'A Chapter on Ears'

8 Nothing can be more disgusting than an oratorio. How absurd to see 500 people fiddling like madmen about Israelites in the Red Sea!
Sydney Smith 1771–1845: Hesketh Pearson *The Smith of Smiths* (1934)

9 Every tone [of the songs of the slaves] was a testimony against slavery, and a prayer to God for deliverance from chains.
Frederick Douglass 1818–95: *Narrative of the Life of Frederick Douglass* (1845)

10 A wandering minstrel I—
A thing of shreds and patches.
Of ballads, songs and snatches,
And dreamy lullaby!
W. S. Gilbert 1836–1911: *The Mikado* (1885); see Character 28

11 You think that's noise—you ain't heard nuttin' yet!
first said in a café, competing with the din from a neighbouring building site, in 1906; subsequently an aside in the 1927 film *The Jazz Singer*
Al Jolson 1886–1950: Martin Abramson *The Real Story of Al Jolson* (1950); also the title of a Jolson song, 1919, in the form 'You Ain't Heard Nothing Yet'

12 Everyone suddenly burst out singing;
And I was filled with such delight
As prisoned birds must find in freedom.
Siegfried Sassoon 1886–1967: 'Everyone Sang' (1919)

13 Tenors get women by the score.
James Joyce 1882–1941: *Ulysses* (1922)

14 A good lyric should be rhymed conversation.
Ira Gershwin 1896–1983: Philip Furia *Ira Gershwin* (1966)

15 Words make you think a thought. Music makes you feel a feeling. A song makes you feel a thought.
E. Y. Harburg 1898–1981: lecture given at the New York YMCA in 1970

16 In writing songs I've learned as much from Cézanne as I have from Woody Guthrie.
Bob Dylan 1941– : Clinton Heylin *Dylan: Behind the Shades* (1991)

17 It's the only song I've ever written where I get goose bumps every time I play it.
of 'Candle in the Wind'
Elton John 1947– : in *Daily Telegraph* 9 September 1997

⤛ The Single Life ⤜

see also **Marriage**

PROVERBS AND SAYINGS

1 **Why buy a cow when milk is so cheap?**
putting forward an argument for choosing the least troublesome alternative; frequently used as an argument against marriage; English proverb, mid 17th century

PHRASES

2 **old maid**
a single woman regarded as too old for marriage; figuratively, a prim and fussy person; see 10 below

QUOTATIONS

3 I would be married, but I'd have no wife, I would be married to a single life.
Richard Crashaw 1612–49: 'On Marriage' (1646)

4 Marriage has many pains, but celibacy has no pleasures.
Samuel Johnson 1709–84: *Rasselas* (1759)

5 It is amusing that a virtue is made of the vice of chastity; and it's a pretty odd sort of chastity at that, which leads men straight into the sin of Onan, and girls to the waning of their colour.
Voltaire 1694–1778: letter to M. Mariott, 28 March 1766

6 It is a truth universally acknowledged, that a single man in possession of a good fortune, must be in want of a wife.
Jane Austen 1775–1817: *Pride and Prejudice* (1813)

7 Marriage may often be a stormy lake, but celibacy is almost always a muddy horsepond.
Thomas Love Peacock 1785–1866: *Melincourt* (1817)

8 Single women have a dreadful propensity for being poor—which is one very strong argument in favour of matrimony.
Jane Austen 1775–1817: letter to Fanny Knight, 13 March 1817

9 Even quarrels with one's husband are preferable to the ennui of a solitary existence.
Elizabeth Patterson Bonaparte 1785–1879: Eugene L. Didier *The Life and Letters of Madame Bonaparte* (1879)

10 Being an old maid is like death by drowning, a really delightful sensation after you cease to struggle.
Edna Ferber 1887–1968: R. E. Drennan *Wit's End* (1973); see 2 above

11 Nobody dies from lack of sex. It's lack of love we die from.
Margaret Atwood 1939– : *The Handmaid's Tale* (1986)

12 We are a select group, without personal obligation, social encumbrance, or any socks that match.
P. J. O'Rourke 1947– : *The Bachelor Home Companion* (1987)

13 Deep down, we remain human, very human and have all the desires to love and be loved by one person . . . Every time I did a marriage, every time I see people married, I say: 'That could have been me.'
Basil Hume 1923–99: attributed; in 1992

Situation see **Circumstance and Situation**

⤜ The Skies ⤛

see also **The Universe**

PHRASES

1 the evening star
the planet Venus, seen shining in the western sky after sunset; see 15 below

2 the Great Bear
in astronomy, the constellation Ursa Major; named from the story in Greek mythology that the nymph Callisto was turned into a bear and placed as a constellation in the heavens by Zeus. The seven brightest stars form a familiar formation variously called the Plough, Big Dipper, or Charles's Wain, and include the Pointers; see 7 below

3 the merry dancers
in Scotland, the aurora borealis; see 5 below

4 the mother of the months
the moon

5 the northern lights
the aurora borealis; alluding to the streamers of light appearing in the sky; see 3 above

6 the queen of tides
the moon

7 the seven stars
a former name for the Pleiades and the Great Bear; there are six stars in the Pleiades visible to the naked eye: the eldest Pleiad, Merope, was 'the lost Pleiad'; see also 2 above

QUOTATIONS

8 And God made two great lights; the greater light to rule the day, and the lesser light to rule the night: he made the stars also.
Bible: Genesis

9 And ther he saugh, with ful avysement
The erratik sterres, herkenyng armonye
With sownes ful of hevenyssh melodie.
Geoffrey Chaucer 1343–1400: *Troilus and Criseyde*

10 The fool will turn the whole art of astronomy inside out! But, as the Holy Scripture reports, Joshua ordered the sun to stand still and not the earth.
on Copernicus' suggestion that the earth moved round the sun
Martin Luther 1483–1546: *Table Talk*, 4 June 1539

11 Queen and huntress, chaste and fair,
Now the sun is laid to sleep,

Seated in thy silver chair,
State in wonted manner keep:
Hesperus entreats thy light,
Goddess, excellently bright.
Ben Jonson 1573–1637: *Cynthia's Revels* (1600)

12   The moon's an arrant thief,
And her pale fire she snatches from the sun.
William Shakespeare 1564–1616: *Timon of Athens* (c.1607)

13 Busy old fool, unruly sun,
Why dost thou thus,
Through windows, and through curtains call on us?
John Donne 1572–1631: 'The Sun Rising'

14 But it does move.
   after his recantation, that the earth moves around
   the sun, in 1632
   Galileo Galilei 1564–1642: attributed; Baretti
   Italian Library (1757) possibly has the earliest
   appearance of the phrase

15   The evening star,
   Love's harbinger.
   John Milton 1608–74: *Paradise Lost* (1667); see 1
   above

16 The hornèd Moon, with one bright star
   Within the nether tip.
   Samuel Taylor Coleridge 1772–1834: 'The Rime
   of the Ancient Mariner' (1798)

17 Twinkle, twinkle, little star,
   How I wonder what you are!
   Up above the world so high,
   Like a diamond in the sky!
   Ann Taylor 1782–1866 and **Jane Taylor**
   1783–1824: 'The Star' (1806)

18 I am the daughter of Earth and Water,
   And the nursling of the Sky;
   I pass through the pores of the ocean and
       shores;
   I change, but I cannot die.
   Percy Bysshe Shelley 1792–1822: 'The Cloud'
   (1819)

19 Look at the stars! look, look up at the skies!
   O look at all the fire-folk sitting in the air!
   Gerard Manley Hopkins 1844–89: 'The Starlight
   Night' (written 1877)

20 The night has a thousand eyes,
   And the day but one;
   Yet the light of the bright world dies,
   With the dying sun.
   F. W. Bourdillon 1852–1921: 'Light' (1878)

21 Slowly, silently, now the moon
   Walks the night in her silver shoon.
   Walter de la Mare 1873–1956: 'Silver' (1913)

22 I have loved the stars too fondly to be fearful
   of the night.
   Sarah Williams: 'The Old Astronomer to His Pupil'
   (1920)

23 The heaventree of stars hung with humid
   nightblue fruit.
   James Joyce 1882–1941: *Ulysses* (1922)

24 We have seen
   The moon in lonely alleys make
   A grail of laughter of an empty ash can.
   Hart Crane 1899–1932: 'Chaplinesque' (1926)

25 Had I been a man I might have explored the
   Poles, or climbed Mount Everest, but as it
   was, my spirit found outlet in the air.
   Amy Johnson 1903–41: Margot Asquith (ed.)
   Myself When Young (1938)

26 Don't tell me that man doesn't belong out
   there. Man belongs wherever he wants to
   go—and he'll do plenty well when he gets
   there.
   Wernher von Braun 1912–77: in *Time* 17
   February 1958

27 Houston, Tranquillity Base here. The Eagle
   has landed.
   Neil Armstrong 1930– : on landing on the moon,
   on 20 July 1969

28 Space isn't remote at all. It's only an hour's
   drive away if your car could go straight
   upwards.
   Fred Hoyle 1915–2001: in *Observer* 9
   September 1979

29 Nothing is more symptomatic of the
   enervation, of the decompression of the
   Western imagination, than our incapacity to
   respond to the landings on the Moon. Not a
   single great poem, picture, metaphor has
   come of this breathtaking act, of
   Prometheus' rescue of Icarus or of Phaeton
   in flight towards the stars.
   George Steiner 1926– : 'Modernity, Mythology
   and Magic', lecture at the 1994 Salzburg Festival

⤞ Sleep ⤝

see also **Dreams**

PROVERBS AND SAYINGS

1 **The morning knows more than the
   evening.**
   the mind is clearer after sleep; Russian proverb

2 **One hour's sleep before midnight is
   worth two after.**
   English proverb, mid 17th century

3 **Six hours sleep for a man, seven for a woman, and eight for a fool.**
implying that the more sleep a person needs, the less vigorous and effective they are likely to be; English proverb, early 17th century

4 **Some sleep five hours; nature requires seven, laziness nine, and wickedness eleven.**
American proverb, mid 20th century

5 **We never sleep.**
motto of the American detective agency founded by Allan Pinkerton (c.1855)

PHRASES

6 **the land of Nod**
sleep; a pun on the biblical place-name in the Bible (Genesis) of the land to which Cain was exiled after the killing of Abel, after Swift *Polite Conversation* (1731–8) 'I'm going to the Land of Nod'; see also **Canada** 3

QUOTATIONS

7 The sleep of a labouring man is sweet.
Bible: Ecclesiastes

8 Care-charmer Sleep, son of the sable Night, Brother to Death, in silent darkness born.
Samuel Daniel 1563–1619: *Delia* (1592) sonnet 54

9 Not to be a-bed after midnight is to be up betimes.
William Shakespeare 1564–1616: *Twelfth Night* (1601)

10 Golden slumbers kiss your eyes, Smiles awake you when you rise.
Thomas Dekker 1570–1641: *Patient Grissil* (1603)

11 Methought I heard a voice cry, 'Sleep no more!
Macbeth does murder sleep,' the innocent sleep,
Sleep that knits up the ravelled sleave of care,
The death of each day's life, sore labour's bath,
Balm of hurt minds, great nature's second course.
William Shakespeare 1564–1616: *Macbeth* (1606)

12 What hath night to do with sleep?
John Milton 1608–74: *Comus* (1637)

13 And so to bed.
Samuel Pepys 1633–1703: diary 20 April 1660

14 Tired Nature's sweet restorer, balmy sleep!
Edward Young 1683–1765: *Night Thoughts* (1742–5)

15 Turn the key deftly in the oilèd wards, And seal the hushèd casket of my soul.
John Keats 1795–1821: 'Sonnet to Sleep' (written 1819)

16 Must we to bed indeed? Well then, Let us arise and go like men, And face with an undaunted tread The long black passage up to bed.
Robert Louis Stevenson 1850–94: 'North-West Passage. Good-Night' (1885)

17   The cool kindliness of sheets,
            that soon
Smooth away trouble; and the rough male kiss
Of blankets.
Rupert Brooke 1887–1915: 'The Great Lover' (1914)

18 Early to rise and early to bed makes a male healthy and wealthy and dead.
James Thurber 1894–1961: 'The Shrike and the Chipmunks' in *New Yorker* 18 February 1939; see **Health** 4

19 Sleep is when all the unsorted stuff comes flying out as from a dustbin upset in a high wind.
William Golding 1911–93: *Pincher Martin* (1956)

20 I love sleep because it is both pleasant and safe to use.
Fran Lebowitz 1946– : *Metropolitan Life* (1978)

⇥ Smoking ⇤

PROVERBS AND SAYINGS

1 **Coffee without tobacco is like a Jew without a rabbi.**
Moroccan proverb

2 **Happiness is a cigar called Hamlet.**
advertising slogan for Hamlet cigars, UK

3 **Smoking can seriously damage your health.**
government health warning now required by British law to be printed on cigarette packets; in form 'Smoking can damage your health' from early 1970s

4 **You're never alone with a Strand.**
advertising slogan for Strand cigarettes, 1960; the
image of loneliness was so strongly conveyed by the

solitary smoker that sales were in fact adversely
affected

QUOTATIONS

5 I do hold it, and will affirm it (before any
prince in Europe) to be the most sovereign
and precious weed that ever the earth
tendered to the use of man.
of tobacco
Ben Jonson 1573–1637: *Every Man in His Humour*
(1598)

6 A custom loathsome to the eye, hateful to
the nose, harmful to the brain, dangerous to
the lungs, and in the black, stinking fume
thereof, nearest resembling the horrible
Stygian smoke of the pit that is bottomless.
James I 1566–1625: *A Counterblast to Tobacco*
(1604)

7 He who lives without tobacco is not worthy
to live.
Molière 1622–73: *Don Juan* (performed 1665)

8 This very night I am going to leave off
tobacco! Surely there must be some other
world in which this unconquerable purpose
shall be realized.
Charles Lamb 1775–1834: letter to Thomas
Manning, 26 December 1815

9 The roots of tobacco plants must go clear
through to hell.
Thomas Alva Edison 1847–1931: in *American
Heritage* 12 July 1885

10 A cigarette is the perfect type of a perfect
pleasure. It is exquisite, and it leaves one
unsatisfied. What more can one want?
Oscar Wilde 1854–1900: *The Picture of Dorian Gray*
(1891)

11 The wretcheder one is, the more one
smokes; and the more one smokes, the
wretcheder one gets—a vicious circle!
George du Maurier 1834–96: *Peter Ibbetson*
(1892)

12 What this country needs is a really good
5-cent cigar.
Thomas R. Marshall 1854–1925: in *New York
Tribune* 4 January 1920

13 I smoked my first cigarette and kissed my
first woman on the same day. I have never
had time for tobacco since.
Arturo Toscanini 1867–1957: in *Observer* 30
June 1946

14 It has been said that cigarettes are the only
product that, if used according to the
manufacturer's instructions, have a very
high chance of killing you.
Michael Buerk 1946– : in *Sunday Times* 11
July 1999

⤛ Society ⤜

see also **Government, Human Race**

PROVERBS AND SAYINGS

1 **If every man would sweep his own
doorstep the city would soon be clean.**
if everyone fulfils their own responsibilities, what is
necessary will be done; English proverb, early 17th
century

2 **One half of the world does not know
how the other half lives.**
often used to comment on a lack of communication
between neighbouring groups; English proverb,
early 17th century

PHRASES

3 **body politic**
the state viewed as an aggregate of its invidual
members; organized society

4 **pillar of society**
a person regarded as a particularly responsible
citizen, a mainstay of the social fabric; *pillar* in the

sense of a person regarded as a mainstay or support
for something is recorded from Middle English;
Pillars of Society was the English title (1888) of a play
by Ibsen

QUOTATIONS

5 No man is an Island, entire of it self; every man is a piece of the Continent, a part of the main; if a clod be washed away by the sea, Europe is the less, as well as if a promontory were.
John Donne 1572–1631: *Devotions upon Emergent Occasions* (1624)

6 The only way by which any one divests himself of his natural liberty and puts on the bonds of civil society is by agreeing with other men to join and unite into a community.
John Locke 1632–1704: *Second Treatise of Civil Government* (1690)

7 Society is indeed a contract . . . it becomes a partnership not only between those who are living, but between those who are living, those who are dead, and those who are to be born.
Edmund Burke 1729–97: *Reflections on the Revolution in France* (1790)

8 The general will rules in society as the private will governs each separate individual.
Maximilien Robespierre 1758–94: *Lettres à ses commettans* (2nd series) 5 January 1793

9 Only in the state does man have a rational existence . . . Man owes his entire existence to the state, and has his being within it alone. Whatever worth and spiritual reality he possesses are his solely by virtue of the state.
G. W. F. Hegel 1770–1831: *Lectures on the Philosophy of World History: Introduction* (1830)

10 The greatest happiness of the greatest number is the foundation of morals and legislation.
Jeremy Bentham 1748–1832: *The Commonplace Book*; Bentham claimed that either Joseph Priestley (1733–1804) or Cesare Beccaria (1738–94) passed on the 'sacred truth'; see **Morality** 6

11 Wherever a man goes, men will pursue him and paw him with their dirty institutions, and, if they can, constrain him to belong to their desperate oddfellow society.
Henry David Thoreau 1817–62: *Walden* (1854) 'The Village'

12 When society requires to be rebuilt, there is no use in attempting to rebuild it on the old plan.
John Stuart Mill 1806–73: *Dissertations and Discussions* vol. 1 (1859) 'Essay on Coleridge'

13 From each according to his abilities, to each according to his needs.
Karl Marx 1818–83: *Critique of the Gotha Programme* (written 1875, but of earlier origin)

14 The Social Contract is nothing more or less than a vast conspiracy of human beings to lie to and humbug themselves and one another for the general Good. Lies are the mortar that bind the savage individual man into the social masonry.
H. G. Wells 1866–1946: *Love and Mr Lewisham* (1900)

15 There is no such thing as the State
And no one exists alone;
Hunger allows no choice
To the citizen or the police;
We must love one another or die.
W. H. Auden 1907–73: 'September 1, 1939' (1940)

16 Society is based on the assumption that everyone is alike and no one is alive.
Hugh Kingsmill 1889–1949: Michael Holroyd *Hugh Kingsmill* (1964)

17 If a free society cannot help the many who are poor, it cannot save the few who are rich.
John F. Kennedy 1917–63: inaugural address, 20 January 1961

18 In your time we have the opportunity to move not only toward the rich society and the powerful society, but upward to the Great Society.
Lyndon Baines Johnson 1908–73: speech at University of Michigan, 22 May 1964

19 The citizen's first duty is unrest.
Günter Grass 1927– : *The Citizen's First Duty* address delivered 1967; in *Speak Out!* (1968)

20 We started off trying to set up a small anarchist community, but people wouldn't obey the rules.
Alan Bennett 1934– : *Getting On* (1972)

21 There is no such thing as Society. There are individual men and women, and there are families.
Margaret Thatcher 1925– : in *Woman's Own* 31 October 1987

Solitude

1 **Better alone than in bad company.**
American proverb, late 17th century

2 **He travels fastest who travels alone.**
implying that single-minded pursuit of an objective is more easily achieved by someone without family commitments; English proverb, late 19th century; see 13 below

3 **The lone sheep is in danger of the wolf.**
stressing the importance of mutual support; English proverb, late 16th century

PHRASES

4 **send to Coventry**
refuse to speak to; ostracize; perhaps after circumstances recorded in Clarendon *The History of the Rebellion* (1703) 'At Bromicham, a town so generally wicked, that it had risen upon small parties of the King's, and killed, or taken them prisoners, and sent them to Coventry' (Coventry being then strongly held for Parliament)

QUOTATIONS

5 It is not good that the man should be alone; I will make him an help meet for him.
Bible: Genesis; see 18, 19 below

6 He who is unable to live in society, or who has no need because he is sufficient for himself, must be either a beast or a god.
Aristotle 384–322 BC: *Politics*

7 Never less idle than when wholly idle, nor less alone than when wholly alone.
Scipio Africanus 236–c.184 BC: Cicero *De Officiis*

8 In solitude
What happiness? who can enjoy alone,
Or all enjoying, what contentment find?
John Milton 1608–74: *Paradise Lost* (1667)

9 I am monarch of all I survey,
My right there is none to dispute;
From the centre all round to the sea
I am lord of the foul and the brute.
William Cowper 1731–1800: 'Verses Supposed to be Written by Alexander Selkirk' (1782); Selkirk (1621–1721) was the prototype of 'Robinson Crusoe'

10 Anythin' for a quiet life, as the man said wen he took the sitivation at the lighthouse.
Charles Dickens 1812–70: *Pickwick Papers* (1837)

11 I long for scenes where man hath never trod
A place where woman never smiled or wept
There to abide with my Creator God.
John Clare 1793–1864: 'I Am' (1848)

12 It is a fine thing to be out on the hills alone.
A man can hardly be a beast or a fool alone
on a great mountain.
Francis Kilvert 1840–79: diary 29 May 1871

13 Down to Gehenna or up to the Throne,
He travels the fastest who travels alone.
Rudyard Kipling 1865–1936: 'The Winners' (*The Story of the Gadsbys*, 1890); see 2 above

14 My heart is a lonely hunter that hunts on a lonely hill.
Fiona McLeod 1855–1905: 'The Lonely Hunter' (1896); reworked by Carson McCullers as 'The heart is a lonely hunter' for the title of a novel, 1940

15 Man goes into the noisy crowd to drown his own clamour of silence.
Rabindranath Tagore 1861–1941: 'Stray Birds' (1916)

16 I want to be alone.
Greta Garbo 1905–90: *Grand Hotel* (1932 film), the phrase already being associated with Garbo

17 You come into the world alone and you go out of the world alone yet it seems to me you are more alone while living than even going and coming.
Emily Carr 1871–1945: *Hundreds and Thousands: The Journals of Emily Carr* (1966) 16 July 1933

18 God created man and, finding him not sufficiently alone, gave him a companion to make him feel his solitude more keenly.
Paul Valéry 1871–1945: *Tel Quel 1* (1941); see 5 above

19 [Barrymore] would quote from Genesis the text which says, 'It is not good for man to be alone,' and then add, 'But O my God, what a relief.'
John Barrymore 1882–1942: Alma Power-Waters *John Barrymore* (1941); see 5 above

20 Please fence me in baby the world's too big out here and I don't like it without you.
Humphrey Bogart 1899–1957: telegram to Lauren Bacall; Lauren Bacall *By Myself* (1978); see **The Country and the Town** 20

21 Oh, no no no, it was too cold always
(Still the dead one lay moaning)
I was much too far out all my life

And not waving but drowning.
Stevie Smith 1902–71: 'Not Waving but Drowning'
(1957)

22 We're all of us sentenced to solitary
confinement inside our own skins, for life!
Tennessee Williams 1911–83: *Orpheus Descending*
(1958)

23 How does it feel
To be on your own
With no direction home
Like a complete unknown
Like a rolling stone?
Bob Dylan 1941– : *Like a Rolling Stone* (1965 song)

24 All the lonely people, where do they all
come from?
John Lennon 1940–80 and **Paul McCartney**
1942– : 'Eleanor Rigby' (1966 song)

25 What Chekhov saw in our failure to
communicate was something positive and
precious: the private silence in which we
live, and which enables us to endure our
own solitude.
V. S. Pritchett 1900–97: *Myth Makers* (1979)

26 Thirty years is a very long time to live alone
and life doesn't get any nicer.
on widowhood, at the age of 92
Frances Partridge 1900–2004: G. Kinnock and F.
Miller *By Faith and Daring* (1993)

Solutions see Problems and Solutions

⇥ Sorrow ⇤

see also **Mourning, Suffering**

PROVERBS AND SAYINGS

1 **Misery loves company.**
English proverb, late 16th century, now
predominantly current in the United States

2 **Wednesday's child is full of woe.**
traditional rhyme, mid 19th century; see **Beauty 7,
Gifts 2, Travel 6, Work 6**

PHRASES

4 **de profundis**
a cry of appeal from the depths (of sorrow); Latin =
from the depths, the initial words of Psalm 130: see
Suffering 8

3 **You cannot prevent the birds of
sorrow from flying overhead, but you
can prevent them from building nests
in your hair.**
sorrow may be unavoidable, but one can respond to
it in different ways; Chinese proverb

5 **Man of Sorrows**
a name for Jesus Christ, deriving from a prophecy in
the Bible (Isaiah), 'He is despised and rejected of
men; a man of sorrows, and acquainted with grief'

QUOTATIONS

6 By the waters of Babylon we sat down and
wept: when we remembered thee, O Sion.
Bible: Psalm 137

7 *Sunt lacrimae rerum et mentem mortalia
tangunt.*
There are tears shed for things even here and
mortality touches the heart.
Virgil 70–19 BC: *Aeneid*

8 Small sorrows speak; great ones are silent.
Seneca ('the Younger') c.4 BC–AD 65: *Hippolytus*

9 . . . *Nessun maggior dolore,
Che ricordarsi del tempo felice
Nella miseria.*
There is no greater pain than to remember a
happy time when one is in misery.
Dante Alighieri 1265–1321: *Divina Commedia*
'Inferno'

10 If you have tears, prepare to shed them now.
William Shakespeare 1564–1616: *Julius Caesar*
(1599)

11 When sorrows come, they come not single
spies,
But in battalions.
William Shakespeare 1564–1616: *Hamlet* (1601)

12 We think caged birds sing, when indeed
they cry.
John Webster 1580– : *The White Devil* (1612)

13 All my joys to this are folly,
Naught so sweet as Melancholy.
Robert Burton 1577–1640: *The Anatomy of
Melancholy* (1621–51)

14 Nothing is here for tears.
John Milton 1608–74: *Samson Agonistes* (1671)

15 Grief is a species of idleness.
Samuel Johnson 1709–84: letter to Mrs Thrale, 17 March 1773

16 For a tear is an intellectual thing;
And a sigh is the sword of an Angel King.
William Blake 1757–1827: *Jerusalem* (1815)

17 I tell you, hopeless grief is passionless.
Elizabeth Barrett Browning 1806–61: 'Grief' (1844)

18 Tears, idle tears, I know not what they mean,
Tears from the depth of some divine despair.
Alfred, Lord Tennyson 1809–92: *The Princess* (1847), song (added 1850)

19 Áh! ás the heart grows older
It will come to such sights colder
By and by, nor spare a sigh
Though worlds of wanwood leafmeal lie;
And yet you *will* weep and know why.
Gerard Manley Hopkins 1844–89: 'Spring and Fall: to a young child' (written 1880)

20 MEDVEDENKO: Why do you wear black all the time?
MASHA: I'm in mourning for my life, I'm unhappy.
Anton Chekhov 1860–1904: *The Seagull* (1896)

21 Laugh and the world laughs with you;
Weep, and you weep alone.
Ella Wheeler Wilcox 1855–1919: 'Solitude'; see Sympathy 3

22 All the old statues of Victory have wings: but Grief has no wings. She is the unwelcome lodger that squats on the hearth-stone between us and the fire and will not move or be dislodged.
Arthur Quiller-Couch 1863–1944: Armistice Day anniversary sermon, Cambridge, November 1923

23 Now laughing friends deride tears I cannot hide,
So I smile and say 'When a lovely flame dies, Smoke gets in your eyes.'
Otto Harbach 1873–1963: 'Smoke Gets in your Eyes' (1933 song)

24 He felt the loyalty we all feel to unhappiness—the sense that that is where we really belong.
Graham Greene 1904–91: *The Heart of the Matter* (1948)

25 How small and selfish is sorrow. But it bangs one about until one is senseless.
shortly after the death of George VI
Queen Elizabeth, the Queen Mother 1900–2002: letter to Edith Sitwell, 1952; Victoria Glendinning *Edith Sitwell* (1983)

26 No one ever told me that grief felt so like fear.
C. S. Lewis 1898–1963: *A Grief Observed* (1961)

27 Total grief is like a minefield. No knowing when one will touch the tripwire.
Sylvia Townsend Warner 1893–1978: diary 11 December 1969

➤➤ Speech ◄◄

see also **Conversation**

PROVERBS AND SAYINGS

1 **How now, brown cow?**
a traditional elocution exercise

2 **Length begets loathing.**
in reference to verbosity; English proverb, mid 18th century

PHRASES

4 **have kissed the Blarney stone**
be eloquent and persuasive; a stone, at *Blarney* castle near Cork in Ireland, said to give the gift of persuasive speech to anyone who kisses it; the verb *to blarney* 'talk flatteringly' derives from this

5 **a silver tongue**
a gift of eloquence or persuasiveness; see Silence 4

3 **Who knows most, speaks least.**
English proverb, mid 17th century

6 **without hesitation, deviation, or repetition**
instruction for contestants' monologues on the panel show *Just a Minute* (BBC Radio, 1967–)

QUOTATIONS

7 The words of his mouth were softer than
butter, having war in his heart: his words
were smoother than oil, and yet they be
very swords.
Bible: Psalm 55

8 Then said they unto him, Say now
Shibboleth: and he said Sibboleth: for he
could not frame to pronounce it right. Then
they took him, and slew him.
Bible: Judges

9 The reason why we have two ears and only
one mouth is that we may listen the more
and talk the less.
to a youth who was talking nonsense
Zeno 333–261 BC: Diogenes Laertius *Lives of the
Philosophers*

10 The tongue can no man tame; it is an unruly
evil.
Bible: James; see **The Body** 8

11 Somwhat he lipsed, for his wantownesse,
To make his Englissh sweete upon his tonge.
Geoffrey Chaucer 1343–1400: *The Canterbury
Tales* 'The General Prologue'

12 It has been well said, that heart speaks to
heart, whereas language only speaks to the
ears.
St Francis de Sales 1567–1622: letter to the
Archbishop of Bourges, 5 October 1604, which John
Henry Newman paraphrased for his motto as '*cor ad
cor loquitur* [heart speaks to heart]'

13   Her voice was ever soft,
Gentle and low, an excellent thing in
woman.
William Shakespeare 1564–1616: *King Lear*
(1605–6)

14 I do not much dislike the matter, but
The manner of his speech.
William Shakespeare 1564–1616: *Antony and
Cleopatra* (1606–7)

15 Continual eloquence is tedious.
Blaise Pascal 1623–62: *Pensées* (1670)

16 Most men make little other use of their
speech than to give evidence against their
own understanding.
Lord Halifax 1633–95: *Political, Moral, and
Miscellaneous Thoughts and Reflections* (1750) 'Of
Folly and Fools'

17 Faith, that's well said, as if I had said it
myself.
Jonathan Swift 1667–1745: *Polite Conversation*
(1738)

18 *when asked if he found his stammering very
inconvenient:*
No, Sir, because I have time to think before I
speak, and don't ask impertinent questions.
Erasmus Darwin 1731–1802: 'Reminiscences of
My Father's Everyday Life', an appendix by Francis
Darwin to his edition of Charles Darwin
Autobiography (1877)

19 When you have nothing to say, say nothing.
Charles Caleb Colton 1780–1832: *Lacon* (1820)

20 And, when you stick on conversation's
burrs,
Don't strew your pathway with those
dreadful *urs*.
Oliver Wendell Holmes 1809–94: 'A Rhymed
Lesson' (1848)

21 Human speech is like a cracked kettle on
which we tap crude rhythms for bears to
dance to, while we long to make music that
will melt the stars.
Gustave Flaubert 1821–80: *Madame Bovary*
(1857)

22 Take care of the sense, and the sounds will
take care of themselves.
Lewis Carroll 1832–98: *Alice's Adventures in
Wonderland* (1865); see **Thrift** 9

23 Half the sorrows of women would be averted
if they could repress the speech they know
to be useless; nay, the speech they have
resolved not to make.
George Eliot 1819–80: *Felix Holt* (1866)

24 I don't want to talk grammar, I want to talk
like a lady.
George Bernard Shaw 1856–1950: *Pygmalion*
(1916)

25 What can be said at all can be said clearly;
and whereof one cannot speak thereof one
must be silent.
Ludwig Wittgenstein 1889–1951: *Tractatus
Logico-Philosophicus* (1922)

26 Speech is civilization itself. The word, even
the most contradictory word, preserves
contact — it is silence which isolates.
Thomas Mann 1875–1955: *The Magic Mountain*
(1924)

27 You like potato and I like po-tah-to,
You like tomato and I like to-mah-to;
Potato, po-tah-to, tomato, to-mah-to—
Let's call the whole thing off!
Ira Gershwin 1896–1983: 'Let's Call the Whole
Thing Off' (1937 song)

28   Speech impelled us
To purify the dialect of the tribe
And urge the mind to aftersight and
foresight.
T. S. Eliot 1888–1965: *Four Quartets* 'Little Gidding'
(1942)

29 Nagging is the repetition of unpalatable truths.
Edith Summerskill 1901–80: speech to the Married Women's Association, House of Commons, 14 July 1960

30 Never express yourself more clearly than you think.
Niels Bohr 1885–1962: Abraham Pais *Einstein Lived Here* (1994)

31 Sentence structure is innate but whining is acquired.
Woody Allen 1935– : 'Remembering Needleman' (1976)

⇥ Speeches ⇤

1 Unaccustomed as I am . . .
clichéistic opening words by a public speaker

PHRASES

2 the rubber chicken circuit
the circuit followed by professional speakers; referring to what is regarded as the customary menu for the lunch or dinner preceding the speech

3 the Rupert of Debate
Edward Stanley (1799–1869), later 14th Earl of Derby; a description by the British novelist and politician Edward Bulwer-Lytton (1803–73), likening his parliamentary style to the dashing cavalry charges of Prince Rupert

4 talking to Buncombe
ostentatious and irrelevant speechmaking; from Felix Walker, excusing a long, dull, irrelevant speech in the House of Representatives, c.1820, 'I'm talking to Buncombe', *Buncombe* being his constituency; the word *bunkum* derives from this

QUOTATIONS

5 What worse change can any one bring against an orator than that his words and his sentiments do not tally?
Demosthenes c.384–c.322 BC: *On the Crown*

6 When asked what was first in oratory, [he] replied to his questioner, 'action,' what second, 'action,' and again third, 'action'.
Demosthenes c.384–c.322 BC: Cicero *Brutus*

7 Grasp the subject, the words will follow.
Cato the Elder 234–149 BC: Caius Julius Victor *Ars Rhetorica*

8 Friends, Romans, countrymen, lend me your ears.
William Shakespeare 1564–1616: *Julius Caesar* (1599)

9 But all was false and hollow; though his tongue
Dropped manna, and could make the worse appear
The better reason.
John Milton 1608–74: *Paradise Lost* (1667)

10 And adepts in the speaking trade
Keep a cough by them ready made.
Charles Churchill 1731–64: *The Ghost* (1763)

11 Not merely a chip of the old 'block', but the old block itself.
on the younger Pitt's maiden speech, February 1781
Edmund Burke 1729–97: N. W. Wraxall *Historical Memoirs of My Own Time* (1904 ed.); see **The Family** 13

12 The Right Honourable gentleman is indebted to his memory for his jests, and to his imagination for his facts.
Richard Brinsley Sheridan 1751–1816: speech in reply to Mr Dundas; T. Moore *Life of Sheridan* (1825)

13 A sophistical rhetorician, inebriated with the exuberance of his own verbosity.
of Gladstone
Benjamin Disraeli 1804–81: in *The Times* 29 July 1878

14 [My ability] to put into words what is in their hearts and minds but not in their mouths.
when asked by Douglas MacArthur in 1906 to what he attributed his popularity
Theodore Roosevelt 1858–1919: William Safire *New Political Dictionary* (1978); see **Opinion** 7

15 He [Lord Charles Beresford] is one of those orators of whom it was well said, 'Before they get up, they do not know what they are going to say; when they are speaking, they do not know what they are saying; and

when they have sat down, they do not know what they have said.'
Winston Churchill 1874–1965: speech, House of Commons, 20 December 1912

16 M. Clemenceau . . . is one of the greatest living orators, but he knows that the finest eloquence is that which gets things done and the worst is that which delays them.
David Lloyd George 1863–1945: speech at Paris Peace Conference, 18 January 1919

17 If I am to speak for ten minutes, I need a week for preparation; if fifteen minutes, three days; if half an hour, two days; if an hour, I am ready now.
Woodrow Wilson 1856–1924: Josephus Daniels *The Wilson Era* (1946)

18 If you don't say anything, you won't be called on to repeat it.
Calvin Coolidge 1872–1933: attributed

19 He [Winston Churchill] mobilized the English language and sent it into battle to steady his fellow countrymen and hearten those Europeans upon whom the long dark night of tyranny had descended.
Ed Murrow 1908–65: broadcast, 30 November 1954

20 I do not object to people looking at their watches when I am speaking. But I strongly object when they start shaking them to make certain they are still going.
Lord Birkett 1883–1962: in *Observer* 30 October 1960

21 Do you remember that in classical times when Cicero had finished speaking, the people said, 'How well he spoke', but when Demosthenes had finished speaking, they said, 'Let us march.'
introducing John F. Kennedy in 1960
Adlai Stevenson 1900–65: Bert Cochran *Adlai Stevenson*

22 This is not a time for soundbites.
of the final stage of the Northern Irish negotiations
Tony Blair 1953– : speech, Belfast, 8 April 1998

⤞ Sports and Games ⤝

see also **Cricket, Football, Hunting, Shooting, and Fishing, Winning and Losing**

PROVERBS AND SAYINGS

1 Chess is a sea where a gnat may drink and an elephant may bathe.
the game may be played at many levels; modern saying, said to derive from an Indian proverb

2 Nice guys finish last.
modern saying, after Leo Durocher: see 18 below

PHRASES

3 the blue ribbon of the turf
the Derby, from Disraeli *Lord George Bentinck* (1852); a horse bred and sold by Lord George subsequently won the Derby, and Lord George coined this phrase in explaining to Disraeli his bitter disappointment at not still owning the horse, with the words 'you do not know what the Derby is'; see **Excellence 5**

4 rumble in the jungle
the boxing match between Muhammad Ali and George Foreman in Zaire in 1974

5 the sport of kings
horse-racing; the term was originally applied to war and later hunting; see **Hunting 7**

QUOTATIONS

6 There is plenty of time to win this game, and to thrash the Spaniards too.
receiving news of the Armada while playing bowls on Plymouth Hoe
Francis Drake 1540–96: attributed, in *Dictionary of National Biography* (1917–)

7   Chaos umpire sits,
And by decision more embroils the fray.
John Milton 1608–74: *Paradise Lost* (1667)

8 I am sorry I have not learned to play at cards. It is very useful in life: it generates kindness and consolidates society.
Samuel Johnson 1709–84: James Boswell *Journal of a Tour to the Hebrides* (1785) 21 November 1773

9 What a sad old age you are preparing for yourself.
to a young diplomat who boasted of his ignorance of whist
Charles-Maurice de Talleyrand 1754–1838: J. Amédée Pichot *Souvenirs Intimes sur M. de Talleyrand* (1870)

10 The harmless art of knucklebones has seen
the fall of the Roman empire and the rise of
the United States.
Robert Louis Stevenson 1850–94: *Across the
Plains* (1892) 'The Lantern-Bearers'

11 And it's not for the sake of a ribboned coat,
Or the selfish hope of a season's fame,
But his Captain's hand on his shoulder
smote—
'Play up! play up! and play the game!'
Henry Newbolt 1862–1938: 'Vitaï Lampada'
(1897)

12 To play billiards well is a sign of an ill-spent
youth.
Charles Roupell: attributed; D. Duncan *Life of
Herbert Spencer* (1908)

13 Take me out to the ball game,
Take me out with the crowd.
Buy me some peanuts and cracker-jack—
I don't care if I never get back.
Jack Norworth 1879–1959: 'Take Me Out to the
Ball Game' (1908 song)

14 Golf is a good walk spoiled.
Mark Twain 1835–1910: Alex Ayres *Greatly
Exaggerated: the Wit and Wisdom of Mark Twain*
(1988); attributed

15 We was robbed!
after Jack Sharkey beat Max Schmeling (of whom
Jacobs was manager) in the heavyweight title fight,
21 June 1932
Joe Jacobs 1896–1940: Peter Heller *In This Corner*
(1975)

16 For when the One Great Scorer comes to
mark against your name,
He writes—not that you won or lost—but
how you played the Game.
Grantland Rice 1880–1954: 'Alumnus Football'
(1941)

17 Love-thirty, love-forty, oh! weakness of joy,
The speed of a swallow, the grace of a boy,
With carefullest carelessness, gaily you won,
I am weak from your loveliness, Joan Hunter
Dunn.
John Betjeman 1906–84: 'A Subaltern's Love-Song'
(1945)

18 I called off his players' names as they came
marching up the steps behind him . . . All
nice guys. They'll finish last. Nice guys.
Finish last.
casual remark at a practice ground in the presence of
a number of journalists, July 1946
Leo Durocher 1906–91: *Nice Guys Finish Last*
(1975); see 2 above

19 *when asked by the coroner if he had intended to
'get Doyle in trouble':*
Mister, it's my *business* to get him in trouble.
following the death of Jimmy Doyle from his injuries
after fighting Robinson, 24 June 1947
Sugar Ray Robinson 1920–89: Sugar Ray
Robinson with Dave Anderson *Sugar Ray* (1970)

20 Serious sport has nothing to do with fair
play . . . It is war minus the shooting.
George Orwell 1903–50: *Shooting an Elephant*
(1950) 'I Write as I Please'

21 Don't look back. Something may be gaining
on you.
a baseball pitcher's advice
Satchel Paige 1906–82: in *Collier's* 13 June 1953

22 If you watch a game, it's fun. If you play it,
it's recreation. If you work at it, it's golf.
Bob Hope 1903–2003: in *Reader's Digest*
October 1958

23 What I know most surely about morality
and the duty of man I owe to sport.
often quoted as, ' . . . I owe to football'
Albert Camus 1913–60: Herbert R. Lottman *Albert
Camus* (1979)

24 Float like a butterfly, sting like a bee.
summary of his boxing strategy
Muhammad Ali 1942– : G. Sullivan *Cassius Clay
Story* (1964); probably originated by Drew 'Bundini'
Brown

25 In America, it is sport that is the opiate of
the masses.
Russell Baker 1925– : in *New York Times* 3 October
1967; see **Reality 6**

26 It's gonna be a thrilla, a chilla, and a killa,
When I get the gorilla in Manila.
of his fight with Joe Frazier
Muhammad Ali 1942– : in 1975

27 All you have to do is keep the five players
who hate your guts away from the five who
are undecided.
on baseball
Casey Stengel 1891–1975: John Samuel (ed.) *The
Guardian Book of Sports Quotes* (1985)

28 Sports do not build character. They reveal it.
Haywood Hale Broun 1918– : attributed; James
Michener *Sports in America* (1976)

29 You cannot be serious!
John McEnroe 1959– : said to tennis umpire at
Wimbledon, early 1980s

30 If people don't want to come out to the ball
park, nobody's going to stop 'em.
Yogi Berra 1925– : attributed

31 The thing about sport, any sport, is that
swearing is very much part of it.
Jimmy Greaves 1940– : in *Observer* 1 January 1989

32 I hated the easy assumption that girls had to be slower than boys.
Dawn Fraser 1937– : attributed; Colin Jarman *Guinness Dictionary of Sports Quotations* (1990)

33 Baseball, it is said, is only a game. True. And the Grand Canyon is only a hole in Arizona. Not all holes, or games, are created equal.
George F. Will 1941– : *Men At Work: The Craft of Baseball* (1990)

34 Everything about sport is derived from the hunt: there is no sport in existence that does not base itself either on the chase or on aiming, the two key elements of primeval hunting.
Desmond Morris 1928– : *The Animal Contract* (1990)

35 Boxing's just show business with blood.
Frank Bruno 1961– : in *Guardian* 20 November 1991; also attributed to David Belasco in 1915

36 Running's like breathing. It's something that comes really naturally.
Cathy Freeman 1973– : interview in *Daily Telegraph* 16 July 2000

37 If you can keep playing tennis when somebody is shooting a gun down the street, that's concentration. I didn't grow up playing at the country club.
Serena Williams 1981– : in *Sunday Times* 2 June 2002

38 We all get cut and we all get stitched up. We get stud marks down our bodies, we break bones and we lose teeth. We play rugby.
Martin Johnson 1970– : *Martin Johnson Autobiography* (2003)

⤜ Statistics ⤛

see also **Mathematics, Quantities and Qualities**

PHRASES

1 the law of averages
the supposed principle that future events are likely to turn out so that they balance any past deviation from a presumed average. The term derives initially from Henry Thomas Buckle's *The History of Civilization in England* (1857): 'The great advance made by the statisticians consists in applying to these inquiries [into crime] the doctrine of averages, which no one thought of doing before the eighteenth century'. The first (sceptical) reference to 'Mr Buckle's "Law of Averages" ' is found in 1875

2 vital statistics
quantitative data concerning the population, such as the number of births, marriages, and deaths; informally, the measurements of a woman's bust, waist, and hips

QUOTATIONS

3 We are just statistics, born to consume resources.
Horace 65–8 BC: *Epistles*

4 A witty statesman said, you might prove anything by figures.
Thomas Carlyle 1795–1881: *Chartism* (1839)

5 Every moment dies a man,
Every moment one is born.
Alfred, Lord Tennyson 1809–92: 'The Vision of Sin' (1842); see 6 below

6 Every moment dies a man,
Every moment 1$\frac{1}{16}$ is born.
Charles Babbage 1792–1871: parody of Tennyson's 'Vision of Sin' in an unpublished letter to the poet; in *New Scientist* 4 December 1958; see 5 above

7 There are three kinds of lies: lies, damned lies and statistics.
Benjamin Disraeli 1804–81: attributed; Mark Twain *Autobiography* (1924)

8 Long and painful experience has taught me one great principle in managing business for other people, viz., if you want to inspire confidence, *give plenty of statistics.*
Lewis Carroll 1832–98: C. L. Dodgson *Three Years in a Curatorship by One Whom It Has Tried* (1886)

9 He uses statistics as a drunken man uses lampposts—for support rather than for illumination.
Andrew Lang 1844–1912: attributed

10 [The War Office kept three sets of figures:] one to mislead the public, another to mislead the Cabinet, and the third to mislead itself.
Herbert Asquith 1852–1928: Alistair Horne *Price of Glory* (1962)

11 If your experiment needs statistics, you ought to have done a better experiment.
Ernest Rutherford 1871–1937: Norman T. J. Bailey *The Mathematical Approach to Biology and Medicine* (1967)

12 Statistics are the triumph of the quantitative method, and the quantitative method is the victory of sterility and death.
Hilaire Belloc 1870–1953: *The Silence of the Sea* (1941)

13 The so-called science of poll-taking is not a science at all but a mere necromancy. People are unpredictable by nature, and although you can take a nation's pulse, you can't be sure that the nation hasn't just run up a flight of stairs.
E. B. White 1899–1985: in *New Yorker* 13 November 1948

14 From the fact that there are 400,000 species of beetles on this planet, but only 8,000 species of mammals, he [Haldane] concluded that the Creator, if He exists, has a special preference for beetles.
J. B. S. Haldane 1892–1964: report of lecture, 7 April 1951

15 One of the thieves was saved. (*Pause*) It's a reasonable percentage.
Samuel Beckett 1906–89: *Waiting for Godot* (1955)

16 Counting counts only when we have learnt how to count what counts.
Alan Ryan 1940– : in *Independent* 26 April 2001

Story-telling see **Fiction and Story-telling**

⤞ Strength and Weakness ⤙

PROVERBS AND SAYINGS

1 **The caribou feeds the wolf, but it is the wolf that keeps the caribou strong.**
stressing the interrelationship between predator and prey; Inuit proverb; see **Life Sciences 6**

2 **Every tub must stand on its own bottom.**
it is necessary to support oneself by one's own efforts; English proverb, mid 16th century

3 **If you don't like the heat, get out of the kitchen.**
if you choose to work in a particular sphere you must also deal with its pressures; English proverb, mid 20th century; see 28 below

4 **It is the pace that kills.**
used as a warning against working under extreme pressure; English proverb, mid 19th century

5 **Only an elephant can bear an elephant's load.**
heavy responsibilities require significant strength; Indian proverb (Marathi)

6 **A reed before the wind lives on, while mighty oaks do fall.**
something which bends to the force of the wind is less likely to be broken than something which tries to withstand it; English proverb, late 14th century

7 **Strength through joy.**
German Labour Front slogan from 1933, coined by Robert Ley (1890–1945)

8 **The weakest go to the wall.**
usually said to derive from the installation of seating (around the walls) in the churches of the late Middle Ages; English proverb, early 16th century

9 **You are the weakest link . . . goodbye.**
catchphrase used by Anne Robinson on the television game-show *The Weakest Link* (2000–); see **Cooperation 1**

PHRASES

10 **Achilles heel**
a person's only vulnerable spot, a weak point; from the legend of the only point at which Achilles could be wounded after he was dipped into the River Styx, his mother having held him so that his heel was protected from the river water by her grasp

11 **broken reed**
a person who fails to give support, a weak or ineffectual person; from the Bible (Isaiah) 'thou trustest in the staff of this broken reed, on Egypt'

12 **built on sand**
lacking a firm foundation; unstable; ephemeral; from the parable in the Bible (Matthew) of the two houses founded respectively on rock and on sand

➤➤◄◄➤➤◄◄➤➤◄◄➤➤◄◄➤➤◄◄➤➤◄◄➤➤◄◄➤➤◄◄➤➤◄◄➤➤◄◄➤➤◄◄➤➤

13 steal someone's thunder
use another person's idea, and spoil the effect the
originator hoped to achieve by acting on it first;
originally *thunder* as a stage effect, after John Dennis:
see **The Theatre** 10

14 a tiger in one's tank
energy, spirit, animation; from an Esso petrol
advertising slogan: see **Transport** 3

QUOTATIONS

16 A threefold cord is not quickly broken.
Bible: Ecclesiastes

17 All the world knows that the weak
overcomes the strong and the soft
overcomes the hard.
But none can practice it.
Lao Tzu c.604–c.531 BC: *Tao-te Ching*

18 If God be for us, who can be against us?
Bible: Romans

19 The gods are on the side of the stronger.
Tacitus c.AD 56–after 117: *Histories*; see **Armed Forces** 8

20 One hair of a woman can draw more than a
hundred pair of oxen.
James Howell 1593–1666: *Familiar Letters*
(1645–55); see **Beauty** 1

21 The concessions of the weak are the
concessions of fear.
Edmund Burke 1729–97: *On Conciliation with America* (1775)

22 The thing is, you see, that the strongest man
in the world is the man who stands most
alone.
Henrik Ibsen 1828–1906: *An Enemy of the People* (1882)

23 A lath of wood painted to look like iron.
of Lord Salisbury
Otto von Bismarck 1815–98: attributed, but
vigorously denied by Sidney Whitman in *Personal Reminiscences of Prince Bismarck* (1902)

15 a tower of strength
a source of strong and reliable support; perhaps
originally alluding to the *Book of Common Prayer* 'O
Lord . . . be unto them a tower of strength'

24 The weak are strong because they are
reckless. The strong are weak because they
have scruples.
Otto von Bismarck 1815–98: quoted by Henry
Kissinger to James Callaghan, 1975; James Callaghan
Time and Chance (1987)

25 I am as strong as a bull moose and you can
use me to the limit.
'Bull Moose' subsequently became the popular
name of the Progressive Party
Theodore Roosevelt 1858–1919: letter to Mark
Hanna, 27 June 1900

26 This is the law of the Yukon, that only the
Strong shall thrive;
That surely the Weak shall perish, and only
the Fit survive.
Robert W. Service 1874–1958: 'The Law of the
Yukon' (1907)

27 Nothing is wasted, nothing is in vain:
The seas roll over but the rocks remain.
A. P. Herbert 1890–1971: *Tough at the Top*
(operetta c.1949)

28 If you can't stand the heat, get out of the
kitchen.
Harry Vaughan: in *Time* 28 April 1952; associated
with Harry S. Truman, but attributed by him to
Vaughan, his 'military jester'; see 3 above

29 The most potent weapon in the hands of the
oppressor is the mind of the oppressed.
Steve Biko 1946–77: statement as witness, 3
May 1976

30 Toughness doesn't have to come in a
pinstripe suit.
Dianne Feinstein 1933– : in *Time* 4 June 1984

➤➤ Style ◄◄

see also **Language**

PROVERBS AND SAYINGS

1 The style is the man.
one's chosen style reflects one's essential
characteristics; English proverb, early 20th century;
see 13 below

PHRASES

2 neat but not gaudy
characterized by an elegant simplicity; see 11 below

3 penny plain
plain and simple; with reference to prints of
characters sold for toy theatres, costing one penny

for black-and-white ones, and two pennies for
coloured ones; see **Painting** 12

4 purple patch
an ornate or elaborate passage in a literary
composition; from Horace: see 6 below

QUOTATIONS

5 I strive to be brief, and I become obscure.
Horace 65–8 BC: *Ars Poetica*

6 Works of serious purpose and grand
promises often have a purple patch or two
stitched on, to shine far and wide.
Horace 65–8 BC: *Ars Poetica*; see 4 above

7 I have revered always not crude verbosity,
but holy simplicity.
St Jerome c.AD 342–420: letter 'Ad Pammachium'

8 More matter with less art.
William Shakespeare 1564–1616: *Hamlet* (1601)

9 He does it with a better grace, but I do it
more natural.
William Shakespeare 1564–1616: *Twelfth Night*
(1601)

10 When we see a natural style, we are quite
surprised and delighted, for we expected to
see an author and we find a man.
Blaise Pascal 1623–62: *Pensées* (1670)

11 Style is the dress of thought; a modest dress,
Neat, but not gaudy, will true critics please.
Samuel Wesley 1662–1735: 'An Epistle to a Friend
concerning Poetry' (1700); see 2 above

12 True wit is Nature to advantage dressed,
What oft was thought, but ne'er so well
expressed.
Alexander Pope 1688–1744: *An Essay on Criticism*
(1711)

13 These things [subject matter] are external to
the man; style is the man.
Comte de Buffon 1707–88: *Discours sur le style*;
address given to the Académie Française, 25 August
1753; see 1 above

14 The moving accident is not my trade;
To freeze the blood I have no ready arts:
'Tis my delight, alone in summer shade,
To pipe a simple song for thinking hearts.
William Wordsworth 1770–1850: 'Hart-Leap
Well' (1800); see **Fear** 5

15 Style is life! It is the very life-blood of
thought!
Gustave Flaubert 1821–80: letter to Louise Colet,
7 September 1853

16 People think that I can teach them style.
What stuff it all is! Have something to say,
and say it as clearly as you can. That is the
only secret of style.
Matthew Arnold 1822–88: G. W. E. Russell
Collections and Recollections (1898)

17 I don't wish to sign my name, though I am
afraid everybody will know who the writer
is: one's style is one's signature always.
sending a letter for publication
Oscar Wilde 1854–1900: letter to the *Daily
Telegraph*, 2 February 1891

18 As to the Adjective: when in doubt, strike
it out.
Mark Twain 1835–1910: *Pudd'nhead Wilson* (1894)

19 No flowers, by request.
summarizing the principle of conciseness for
contributors to the *Dictionary of National Biography*
Alfred Ainger 1837–1904: speech to contributors,
8 July 1897; see **Mourning** 4

20 No iron can stab the heart with such force as
a full stop put just at the right place.
Isaac Babel 1894–1940: *Guy de Maupassant* (1932)

21 'Feather-footed through the plashy fen
passes the questing vole' . . . 'Yes,' said the
Managing Editor. 'That must be good style.'
Evelyn Waugh 1903–66: *Scoop* (1938)

22 The Mandarin style . . . is beloved by literary
pundits, by those who would make the
written word as unlike as possible to the
spoken one.
Cyril Connolly 1903–74: *Enemies of Promise* (1938)

23 I am well aware that an addiction to silk
underwear does not necessarily imply that
one's feet are dirty. Nonetheless, style, like
sheer silk, too often hides eczema.
Albert Camus 1913–60: *The Fall* (1956)

24 It's not what I do, but the way I do it. It's not
what I say, but the way I say it.
Mae West 1892–1980: G. Eells and S. Musgrove
Mae West (1989)

⇥ Success and Failure ⇤

see also **Winning and Losing**

PROVERBS AND SAYINGS

1 The bigger they are, the harder they fall.
English proverb, early 20th century, commonly attributed in its current form to the fighter Robert Fitzsimmons, prior to a fight *c.*1900

2 From clogs to clogs is only three generations.
the *clog*, a shoe with a thick wooden sole, was worn by manual workers in the north of England. The implication is that the energy and ability required to raise a person's material status from poverty is often not continued to the third generation, and that the success is therefore not sustained; English proverb, late 19th century, said to be a Lancashire proverb

3 From shirtsleeves to shirtsleeves in three generations.
wealth gained in one generation will be lost by the third; English proverb, early 20th century. The saying is often attributed to the Scottish-born American industrialist and philanthropist Andrew Carnegie (1835–1919) but is not found in his writings

4 From the sublime to the ridiculous is only one step.
English proverb, late 19th century; see 32, 33 below

5 Let them laugh that win.
triumphant laughter should be witheld until success is assured; English proverb, mid 16th century

6 Nothing succeeds like success.
someone already regarded as successful is likely to attract more support; English proverb, mid 19th century

7 The only place where success comes before work is in a dictionary.
modern saying

8 The race is not to the swift, nor the battle to the strong.
the person with the most apparent advantages will not necessarily be successful; English proverb, mid 17th century; see 22 below

9 A rising tide lifts all boats.
usually taken to mean that a prosperous society benefits everybody; in America the expression was particularly associated with John Fitzgerald Kennedy (1917–63); English proverb, mid 20th century

10 Rooster today, feather duster tomorrow.
one who is currently successful may subsequently find that circumstances change dramatically; Australian saying

11 Success has many fathers, while failure is an orphan.
once something is seen to succeed many people will claim to have initiated it, while responsibility for failure is likely to be disclaimed; English proverb, mid 20th century: see 45 below

12 Up like a rocket, down like a stick.
sudden marked success is likely to be followed by equally sudden failure; English proverb, late 19th century; see 31 below

13 When an elephant is in trouble, even a frog can kick him.
the weak can attack the strong when they are in difficulty; Indian proverb

14 You win a few, you lose a few.
one has to accept failure as well as success, and used as an expression of consolation or resignation; English proverb, mid 20th century

PHRASES

15 the bitch goddess
material or worldly success as an object of attainment; from William James: see 38 below

16 the golden rule
a basic principle which should always be followed to ensure success in general or in a particular activity. The term is sometimes specifically used of the injunction given by Jesus in the Bible: see **Lifestyles 15, Likes 14**

17 one's finest hour
the time of one's greatest success; now particularly associated with Churchill: see **World War II 13**

18 place in the sun
one's share of good fortune or prosperity; a favourable situation or position, prominence; associated with German nationalism (see **International Relations 23**) but earlier recorded in the writings of Pascal (translation 1688)

19 weighed in the balance and found wanting
having failed to meet the test of a particular situation; in the Bible (Daniel), part of the judgement made on King Belshazzar by the *writing on the wall*: see **The Future 11**

20 win one's laurels
succeed publicly, achieve one's due reward of acknowledgement and praise; *laurels* the foliage of

the bay-tree (real or imaginary) as an emblem of victory or of distinction; see **Envy** 15, **Reputation** 17, **Youth** 15

21 win one's spurs
attain distinction, achieve one's first honours; *spurs* as an emblem of knighthood, especially gained by an act of valour; see **Effort** 16

QUOTATIONS

22 The race is not to the swift, nor the battle to the strong.
Bible: Ecclesiastes; see 8 above

23 *Veni, vidi, vici.*
I came, I saw, I conquered.
Julius Caesar 100–44 BC: inscription displayed in Caesar's Pontic triumph, according to Suetonius *Lives of the Caesars* 'Divus Julius'; or, according to Plutarch *Parallel Lives* 'Julius Caesar', written in a letter by Caesar, announcing the victory of Zela which concluded the Pontic campaign

24 For what shall it profit a man, if he shall gain the whole world, and lose his own soul?
Bible: St Mark; see **Wales** 9

25 You do well to weep as a woman over what you could not defend as a man.
reproach to her son Boabdil (Muhammad XI, the last Sultan of Granada), who had surrendered Granada to Ferdinand and Isabella
Ayesha fl. 1492: traditional attribution; Washington Irving *The Alhambra* (1832; rev. ed. 1851) ch. 18

26 Of all I had, only honour and life have been spared.
usually quoted 'All is lost save honour'
Francis I of France 1494–1547: letter to his mother following his defeat at Pavia, 1525

27 MACBETH: If we should fail,—
LADY MACBETH: We fail!
But screw your courage to the sticking-place,
And we'll not fail.
William Shakespeare 1564–1616: *Macbeth* (1606)

28 'Tis not in mortals to command success,
But we'll do more, Sempronius; we'll
   deserve it.
Joseph Addison 1672–1719: *Cato* (1713)

29 In most things success depends on knowing how long it takes to succeed.
Montesquieu 1689–1755: *Pensées et fragments inédits . . .* vol. 1 (1901)

30 The conduct of a losing party never appears right: at least it never can possess the only infallible criterion of wisdom to vulgar judgements—success.
Edmund Burke 1729–97: *Letter to a Member of the National Assembly* (1791)

31 As he rose like a rocket, he fell like the stick.
on Edmund Burke losing the parliamentary debate on the French Revolution to Charles James Fox
Thomas Paine 1737–1809: *Letter to the Addressers on the late Proclamation* (1792); see 12 above

32 The sublime and the ridiculous are often so nearly related, that it is difficult to class them separately. One step above the sublime, makes the ridiculous; and one step above the ridiculous, makes the sublime again.
Thomas Paine 1737–1809: *The Age of Reason* pt. 2 (1795); see 4 above, 33 below

33 There is only one step from the sublime to the ridiculous.
to De Pradt, Polish ambassador, after the retreat from Moscow in 1812
Napoléon I 1769–1821: D. G. De Pradt *Histoire de l'Ambassade dans le grand-duché de Varsovie en 1812* (1815); see 4, 32 above

34 It was roses, roses, all the way.
Robert Browning 1812–89: 'The Patriot' (1855)

35 I have climbed to the top of the greasy pole.
on becoming Prime Minister
Benjamin Disraeli 1804–81: W. Monypenny and G. Buckle *Life of Benjamin Disraeli* vol. 4 (1916)

36 Success is a science; if you have the conditions, you get the result.
Oscar Wilde 1854–1900: letter ?March–April 1883

37 All you need in this life is ignorance and confidence; then success is sure.
Mark Twain 1835–1910: letter to Mrs Foote, 2 December 1887

38 The moral flabbiness born of the exclusive worship of the bitch-goddess *success*.
William James 1842–1910: letter to H. G. Wells, 11 September 1906; see 15 above

39 The world continues to offer glittering prizes to those who have stout hearts and sharp swords.
F. E. Smith 1872–1930: Rectorial Address, Glasgow University, 7 November 1923

40 Anybody seen in a bus over the age of 30 has been a failure in life.
Loelia, Duchess of Westminster 1902–93: in *The Times* 4 November 1993 (obituary); habitual remark

41 You [the Mensheviks] are pitiful isolated individuals; you are bankrupts; your role is played out. Go where you belong from now on — into the dustbin of history!
Leon Trotsky 1879–1940: *History of the Russian Revolution* (1933)

42 How to win friends and influence people.
Dale Carnegie 1888–1955: title of book (1936)

43 History to the defeated
May say Alas but cannot help or pardon.
W. H. Auden 1907–73: 'Spain 1937' (1937)

44 Success is relative:
It is what we can make of the mess we have
made of things.
T. S. Eliot 1888–1965: *The Family Reunion* (1939)

45 Victory has a hundred fathers, but no-one
wants to recognise defeat as his own.
Count Galeazzo Ciano 1903–44: diary, 9
September 1942; see 11 above

46 If *A* is a success in life, then *A* equals *x* plus *y*
plus *z*. Work is *x*; *y* is play; and *z* is keeping
your mouth shut.
Albert Einstein 1879–1955: in *Observer* 15
January 1950

47 For a writer, success is always temporary,
success is only a delayed failure. And it is
incomplete.
Graham Greene 1904–91: *A Sort of Life* (1971)

48 Whenever a friend succeeds, a little
something in me dies.
Gore Vidal 1925– : in *Sunday Times Magazine* 16
September 1973

49 Is it possible to succeed without any act of
betrayal?
Jean Renoir 1894–1979: *My Life and My Films*
(1974)

50 Ever tried. Ever failed. No matter. Try again.
Fail again. Fail better.
Samuel Beckett 1906–89: *Worstward Ho* (1983)

51 In the United States there's a Puritan ethic
and a mythology of success. He who is
successful is good. In Latin countries, in
Catholic countries, a successful person is a
sinner.
Umberto Eco 1932– : in *International Herald
Tribune* 14 December 1988

⟶ Suffering ⟵

see also **Mourning, Sorrow, Sympathy and Consolation**

PROVERBS AND SAYINGS

1 **Beauty without cruelty.**
slogan for Animal Rights

2 **Crosses are ladders that lead to
heaven.**
the way to heaven is through suffering; *crosses* refers
either to the crucifix, or more generally to troubles or
misfortunes; English proverb, early 17th century

3 **Ee, it was agony, Ivy.**
catchphrase from *Ray's a Laugh* (BBC radio
programme, 1949–61), written by Ted Ray

4 **No cross, no crown.**
cross is here used punningly, as in 2 above; English
proverb, early 17th century; see 17 below

PHRASES

5 **have one's cross to bear**
suffer the troubles that life brings. The allusion is to
Jesus (or Simon of Cyrene) carrying the Cross to

Calvary for the Crucifixion; see 12 below,
Marriage 43

QUOTATIONS

6 Have patience, heart. Once you endured
worse than this.
Homer: *The Odyssey*

7 They that sow in tears: shall reap in joy.
Bible: Psalm 126

8 Out of the deep have I called unto thee, O
Lord: Lord, hear my voice.
Bible: Psalm 130; see **Sorrow** 4

9 Justice inclines her scales so that wisdom
comes at the price of suffering.
Aeschylus c.525–456 BC: *Agamemnon* l. 250

10 Nothing happens to anybody which he is
not fitted by nature to bear.
Marcus Aurelius AD 121–80: *Meditations*

11 All those who suffer in the world do so
because of their desire for their own
happiness.
Shantideva 685–763: *Bodhicaryāvatāra* ch. 8,
v. 129

12 If you bear the cross gladly, it will bear you.
Thomas à Kempis 1380–1471: *The Imitation of
Christ*; see 5 above

13 Be grateful for, not blind to the many, many
sufferings which thou art spared; thou art
no better than those who have been
searched out and racked by them.
Orchoth Zadikkim c.15th century: *Orchoth
Zaddikim*

14 He jests at scars, that never felt a wound.
William Shakespeare 1564–1616: *Romeo and
Juliet* (1595)

15   The worst is not,
So long as we can say, 'This is the worst.'
William Shakespeare 1564–1616: *King Lear*
(1605–6)

16 Our torments also may in length of time
Become our elements.
John Milton 1608–74: *Paradise Lost* (1667)

17 No pain, no palm; no thorns, no throne; no
gall, no glory; no cross, no crown.
William Penn 1644–1718: *No Cross, No Crown*
(1669 pamphlet); see 4 above

18 To each his suff'rings, all are men,
Condemned alike to groan;
The tender for another's pain,
Th' unfeeling for his own.
Thomas Gray 1716–71: *Ode on a Distant Prospect of
Eton College* (1747)

19 Thank you, madam, the agony is abated.
aged four, having had hot coffee spilt over his legs
Lord Macaulay 1800–59: G. O. Trevelyan *Life and
Letters of Lord Macaulay* (1876)

20 Misery such as mine has no pride. I care not
who knows that I am wretched.
Jane Austen 1775–1817: *Sense and Sensibility* (1811)

21 Sorrow and silence are strong, and patient
endurance is godlike.
Henry Wadsworth Longfellow 1807–82:
Evangeline (1847)

22   For frequent tears have run
The colours from my life.
Elizabeth Barrett Browning 1806–61: *Sonnets
from the Portuguese* (1850)

23 After great pain, a formal feeling comes—
The Nerves sit ceremonious, like Tombs—
The stiff Heart questions was it He, that
          bore,
And Yesterday, or Centuries before?
Emily Dickinson 1830–86: 'After great pain, a
formal feeling comes' (1862)

24 The toad beneath the harrow knows
Exactly where each tooth-point goes;
The butterfly upon the road
Preaches contentment to that toad.
Rudyard Kipling 1865–1936: 'Pagett, MP' (1886);
see **Adversity** 11

25 What does not kill me makes me stronger.
Friedrich Nietzsche 1844–1900: *Twilight of the
Idols* (1889)

26 Nothing begins, and nothing ends,
That is not paid with moan;
For we are born in other's pain,
And perish in our own.
Francis Thompson 1859–1907: 'Daisy' (1913)

27 Tragedy ought really to be a great kick at
misery.
D. H. Lawrence 1885–1930: letter to A. W.
McLeod, 6 October 1912

28 It is not true that suffering ennobles the
character; happiness does that sometimes,
but suffering, for the most part, makes men
petty and vindictive.
W. Somerset Maugham 1874–1965: *The Moon
and Sixpence* (1919)

29 Too long a sacrifice
Can make a stone of the heart.
O when may it suffice?
W. B. Yeats 1865–1939: 'Easter, 1916' (1921)

30 The point is that nobody likes having salt
rubbed into their wounds, even if it is the
salt of the earth.
Rebecca West 1892–1983: *The Salt of the Earth*
(1935); see **Virtue** 11

31 About suffering they were never wrong,
The Old Masters: how well they understood
Its human position; how it takes place
While someone else is eating or opening a
          window or just walking dully along.
W. H. Auden 1907–73: 'Musée des Beaux Arts'
(1940)

32 Willy Loman never made a lot of money. His
name was never in the paper. He's not the
finest character that ever lived. But he's a
human being, and a terrible thing is
happening to him. So attention must be
paid.
Arthur Miller 1915–2005: *Death of a Salesman*
(1949)

33 How can you expect a man who's warm to
understand one who's cold?
Alexander Solzhenitsyn 1918– : *One Day in the
Life of Ivan Denisovich* (1962)

34 Children's talent to endure stems from their
ignorance of alternatives.
Maya Angelou 1928– : *I Know Why The Caged Bird
Sings* (1969)

35 The most extreme agony is to feel that one
has been utterly forsaken.
Bruno Bettelheim 1903–90: *Surviving and other
essays* (1979)

36 Scars have the strange power to remind us
that our past is real.
Cormac McCarthy 1933– : *All the Pretty Horses*
(1993)

⇥Suicide ⇤

PHRASES

1 assisted suicide
the suicide of a patient suffering from an incurable disease, effected by the taking of lethal drugs provided by a doctor for this purpose

2 kamikaze pilot
in the Second World War, the pilot of a Japanese aircraft loaded with explosives and making a deliberate suicidal crash on an enemy target; *kamikaze* = Japanese, from *kami* 'divinity' + *kaze* 'wind', originally referring to the gale that, in Japanese tradition, destroyed the fleet of invading Mongols in 1281

QUOTATIONS

3 For who would bear the whips and scorns of time,
The oppressor's wrong, the proud man's contumely,
The pangs of disprized love, the law's delay
. . .
When he himself might his quietus make
With a bare bodkin?
William Shakespeare 1564–1616: *Hamlet* (1601)

4 In chains and darkness, wherefore should I stay,
And mourn in prison, while I keep the key?
Lady Mary Wortley Montagu 1689–1762: 'Verses on Self-Murder' (1749)

5 All this buttoning and unbuttoning.
Anonymous: 18th-century suicide note

6   Nor at all can tell
Whether I mean this day to end myself,
Or lend an ear to Plato where he says,
That men like soldiers may not quit the post
Allotted by the Gods.
Alfred, Lord Tennyson 1809–92: 'Lucretius' (1868)

7 The thought of suicide is a great source of comfort: with it a calm passage is to be made across many a bad night.
Friedrich Nietzsche 1844–1900: *Jenseits von Gut und Böse* (1886)

8 In this life there's nothing new in dying,
But nor, of course, is living any newer.
his final poem, written in his own blood the day before he hanged himself in his Leningrad hotel room
Sergei Yesenin 1895–1925: 'Goodbye, my Friend, Goodbye' (1925)

9 Guns aren't lawful;
Nooses give;
Gas smells awful;
You might as well live.
Dorothy Parker 1893–1967: 'Résumé' (1937)

10 A suicide kills two people, Maggie, that's what it's for!
Arthur Miller 1915–2005: *After the Fall* (1964)

11 It's better to burn out
Than to fade away.
Neil Young 1945– : 'My My, Hey Hey (Out of the Blue)' (1978 song, with Jeff Blackburn); quoted by Kurt Cobain in his suicide note, 8 April 1994

12 Suicide is no more than a trick played on the calendar.
Tom Stoppard 1937– : *The Dog It Was That Died* (1983)

13 Without the possibility of suicide, I would have killed myself long ago.
E. M. Cioran 1911–95: in *Independent* 2 December 1989

⇥The Supernatural ⇤

see also **The Paranormal**

PROVERBS AND SAYINGS

**1 From ghoulies and ghosties and long-leggety beasties
And things that go bump in the night,**

Good Lord, deliver us!
'The Cornish or West Country Litany'; see 4 below

PHRASES

2 bell, book, and candle
the formulaic requirements for laying a curse on
someone; with allusion to the rite of
excommunication, 'Do to the book, quench the
candle, ring the bell'; see **Greed 8**

3 the good neighbours
fairies; witches

4 things that go bump in the night
supernatural manifestations as a source of night-time
terror; from 'The Cornish or West Country Litany':
see 1 above

5 the wee folk
fairies

6 a witch of Endor
a medium; from the story in the Bible (I Samuel) of 'a
woman that hath a familiar spirit at Endor', who with
its help conjured up the spirit of the dead prophet
Samuel for Saul; see 20 below

QUOTATIONS

7 Then a spirit passed before my face; the hair
of my flesh stood up.
Bible: Job

8 May the gods avert this omen.
Cicero 106–43 BC: *Third Philippic*

9 For we wrestle not against flesh and blood,
but against principalities, against powers,
against the rulers of the darkness of this
world, against spiritual wickedness in high
places.
Bible: Ephesians

10 Hence, a devout Christian must avoid
astrologers and all impious soothsayers,
especially when they tell the truth, for fear
of leading his soul into error by consorting
with demons and entangling himself with
the bonds of such association.
St Augustine of Hippo AD 354–430: *De Genesi ad
Litteram*; see **Mathematics 1**

11 There are more things in heaven and earth,
    Horatio,
Than are dreamt of in your philosophy.
William Shakespeare 1564–1616: *Hamlet* (1601);
see **Universe 10**

12 Double, double toil and trouble;
Fire burn and cauldron bubble.
William Shakespeare 1564–1616: *Macbeth* (1606)

13 There is a superstition in avoiding
superstition.
Francis Bacon 1561–1626: *Essays* (1625) 'Of
Superstition'

14 All argument is against it; but all belief is
for it.
of the existence of ghosts
Samuel Johnson 1709–84: James Boswell *Life of
Samuel Johnson* (1791) 31 March 1778

15 He dug up a fairy-mount against my advice,
and had no luck afterwards.
Maria Edgeworth 1767–1849: *Castle Rackrent*
(1800)

16 Superstition is the poetry of life.
Johann Wolfgang von Goethe 1749–1832:
Maximen und Reflexionen (1819) 'Literatur und
Sprache'

17 Up the airy mountain,
Down the rushy glen,
We daren't go a-hunting,
For fear of little men.
William Allingham 1824–89: 'The Fairies' (1850)

18 The Universe of Magic is in the mind of a
man: the setting is but Illusion even to the
thinker.
Aleister Crowley 1875–1947: in *Equinox* 1909

19 There are fairies at the bottom of our
garden!
Rose Fyleman 1877–1957: 'The Fairies' (1918)

20 Oh, the road to En-dor is the oldest road
And the craziest road of all!
Straight it runs to the Witch's abode
As it did in the days of Saul,
And nothing has changed of the sorrow in
    store
For such as go down on the road to En-dor!
Rudyard Kipling 1865–1936: 'En-dor' (1914–19);
see 6 above

21 Every time a child says 'I don't believe in
fairies' there is a little fairy somewhere that
falls down dead.
J. M. Barrie 1860–1937: *Peter Pan* (1928)

22 Do not meddle in the affairs of Wizards, for
they are subtle and quick to anger.
J. R. R. Tolkien 1892–1973: *The Lord of the Rings* pt.
1 *The Fellowship of the Ring* (1954)

23 The twilight is the crack between the worlds.
It is the door to the unknown.
Carlos Castaneda 1925–98: *Tales of Power* (1974)

24 In every generation there is a Chosen One.
She alone will stand against the vampires,
the demons, and the forces of darkness. She
is the Slayer.
Joss Whedon 1964– : *Buffy the Vampire Slayer* (TV
series, 1997–2003), episode 1, opening words

Surprise

PROVERBS AND SAYINGS

1 The age of miracles is past.
often used ironically, or as a comment on failure;
English proverb, late 16th century

2 Nobody expects the Spanish Inquisition.
from a *Monty Python* script: see 14 below

3 The unexpected always happens.
warning against an overconfident belief that
something cannot occur; English proverb, late 19th
century

4 Wonders will never cease.
often used ironically to comment on an unusual
circumstance; English proverb, late 18th century

5 You could have knocked me down with a feather.
expressing great surprise; English proverb, mid 19th
century saying

PHRASES

6 pennies from heaven
unexpected benefits, especially financial ones; song-
title, 1936: see **Optimism 32**

7 a Scarborough warning
very short notice, no notice at all; proverbial;
explained by Thomas Fuller as relating to the

surprise capture of Scarborough Castle by Thomas
Stafford in 1557, but the first recorded use predates
this by eleven years

QUOTATIONS

8 O wonderful, wonderful, and most
wonderful wonderful! and yet again
wonderful, and after that, out of all
whooping!
William Shakespeare 1564–1616: *As You Like It*
(1599)

9 Surprises are foolish things. The pleasure is
not enhanced, and the inconvenience is
often considerable.
Jane Austen 1775–1817: *Emma* (1816)

10 I'm Gormed—and I can't say no fairer than
that!
Charles Dickens 1812–70: *David Copperfield*
(1850)

11 'Curiouser and curiouser!' cried Alice.
Lewis Carroll 1832–98: *Alice's Adventures in
Wonderland* (1865)

12 I turned to Aunt Agatha, whose demeanour
was now rather like that of one who, picking
daisies on the railway, has just caught the
down express in the small of the back.
P. G. Wodehouse 1881–1975: *The Inimitable Jeeves*
(1923)

13 It was quite the most incredible event that
has ever happened to me in my life. It was
almost as incredible as if you fired a 15-inch
shell at a piece of tissue paper and it came
back and hit you.
on the back-scattering effect of metal foil on alpha-
particles
Ernest Rutherford 1871–1937: E. N. da C.
Andrade *Rutherford and the Nature of the Atom*
(1964)

14 Nobody expects the Spanish Inquisition!
Our chief weapon is surprise—surprise and
fear . . . fear and surprise . . . our two
weapons are fear and surprise—and ruthless
efficiency . . .
Graham Chapman 1941–89 et al.: *Monty Python's
Flying Circus* (BBC TV programme, 1970); see 2
above

⤜ Swearing ⤛

PROVERBS AND SAYINGS

1 Excuse (or pardon) my French.
an informal apology for swearing

PHRASES

2 four-letter word
any of several short words referring to sexual or
excretory functions, regarded as coarse or offensive

3 not Pygmalion likely
not bloody likely; a humorous euphemism deriving
from Shaw's *Pygmalion* (1916), which caused a
public sensation at the time of the first London
production; see **Transport** 13

QUOTATIONS

4 Swear not at all; neither by heaven; for it is
God's throne:
Nor by the earth; for it is his footstool.
Bible: St Matthew

5 You taught me language; and my profit on't
Is, I know how to curse: the red plague
rid you,
For learning me your language!
William Shakespeare 1564–1616: *The Tempest*
(1611)

6 'Our armies swore terribly in Flanders,' cried
my uncle Toby,—'but nothing to this.'
Laurence Sterne 1713–68: *Tristram Shandy*
(1759–67)

7 Though 'Bother it' I may
Occasionally say,
I never use a big, big D—
W. S. Gilbert 1836–1911: *HMS Pinafore* (1878)

8 If ever I utter an oath again may my soul be
blasted to eternal damnation!
George Bernard Shaw 1856–1950: *Saint Joan*
(1924)

9 Orchestras only need to be sworn at, and a
German is consequently at an advantage
with them, as English profanity, except in
America, has not gone beyond the limited
terminology of perdition.
George Bernard Shaw 1856–1950: Harold
Schonberg *The Great Conductors* (1967)

10 I doubt if there are very many rational
people in this world to whom the word
'fuck' is particularly diabolical or revolting
or totally forbidden.
Kenneth Tynan 1927–80: *BBC-3* (television
programme) 13 November 1965

11 The man who first abused his fellows with
swear words instead of bashing their brains
out with a club should be counted among
those who laid the foundations of
civilization.
John Cohen 1911– : in *Observer* 21 November 1965

12 Don't swear, boy. It shows a lack of
vocabulary.
Alan Bennett 1934– : *Forty Years On* (1969)

13 Expletive deleted.
Anonymous: *Submission of Recorded Presidential
Conversations to the Committee on the Judiciary of the
House of Representatives by President Richard M.
Nixon* 30 April 1974

14 All pro athletes are bilingual. They speak
English and profanity.
Gordie Howe 1928– : in *Toronto Star* 27 May 1975

15 Swear words are neutral; they only become
objectionable when someone is offended by
them. The art of good manners (as well as
bad manners) is knowing who will be
offended by what.
John Rae 1931– : *Letters from School* (1987)

⤳ Sympathy and Consolation ⤶

PROVERBS AND SAYINGS

1 **God makes the back to the burden.**
an assertion that nothing is truly insupportable used in resignation or consolation; English proverb, early 19th century

2 **God tempers the wind to the shorn lamb.**
God so arranges it that bad luck does not unduly plague the weak or unfortunate; English proverb, mid 17th century

3 **Laugh and the world laughs with you, weep and you weep alone.**
English proverb, late 19th century; see **Sorrow** 21

4 **Nothing so bad but it might have been worse.**
used in resignation or consolation; English proverb, late 19th century

5 **One kind word warms three winter months.**
Japanese proverb

6 **Pity is akin to love.**
English proverb, early 17th century

PHRASES

7 **a Job's comforter**
a person who aggravates distress while seeking to give comfort; *Job* the biblical patriarch, who responded to the exhortations of his friends, 'miserable comforters are ye all'; see **Patience** 22

8 **milk of human kindness**
compassion, sympathy; originally from Shakespeare's Lady Macbeth: see 16 below; see also **Charity** 29

9 **tea and sympathy**
hospitality and consolation offered to a distressed person; the phrase was used as a film title in 1956

10 **tender mercies**
a biblical phrase usually used ironically to refer to attention or treatment not in the best interests of its recipients; see **Animals** 13

QUOTATIONS

11 Heaven and Earth are not ruthful;
To them the Ten Thousand Things are but as
    straw dogs.
Ten Thousand Things all life forms; *straw dogs* sacrificial tokens
Lao Tzu c.604–c.531 BC: *Tao-Te Ching*

12 If you want me to weep, you must first feel grief yourself.
Horace 65–8 BC: *Ars Poetica*

13 O divine Master, grant that I may not so
    much seek
To be consoled as to console;
To be understood as to understand.
St Francis of Assisi 1181–1226: 'Prayer of St Francis'; attributed

14 For pitee renneth soone in gentil herte.
Geoffrey Chaucer 1343–1400: *The Canterbury Tales* 'The Knight's Tale'

15 But yet the pity of it, Iago! O! Iago, the pity of it, Iago!
William Shakespeare 1564–1616: *Othello* (1602–4)

16 Yet I do fear thy nature;
It is too full o' the milk of human kindness
To catch the nearest way.
William Shakespeare 1564–1616: *Macbeth* (1606); see 8 above

17 We are all strong enough to bear the misfortunes of others.
Duc de la Rochefoucauld 1613–80: *Maximes* (1678)

18 If a madman were to come into this room with a stick in his hand, no doubt we should pity the state of his mind; but our primary consideration would be to take care of ourselves. We should knock him down first, and pity him afterwards.
Samuel Johnson 1709–84: House of Commons, 3 April 1776

19 Our sympathy is cold to the relation of distant misery.
Edward Gibbon 1737–94: *The Decline and Fall of the Roman Empire* (1776–88)

20 Then cherish pity, lest you drive an angel from your door.
William Blake 1757–1827: 'Holy Thursday' (1789)

21 [Edmund Burke] is not affected by the reality of distress touching his heart, but by the showy resemblance of it striking his imagination. He pities the plumage, but forgets the dying bird.
on Burke's *Reflections on the Revolution in France*
Thomas Paine 1737–1809: *The Rights of Man* (1791)

22 Nobody can tell what I suffer! But it is always so. Those who do not complain are never pitied.
Jane Austen 1775–1817: *Pride and Prejudice* (1813)

23 They charge me with fanaticism. If to be feelingly alive to the sufferings of my fellow-creatures is to be a fanatic, I am one of the most incurable fanatics ever permitted to be at large.
William Wilberforce 1759–1833: in House of Commons, 19 June 1816

24 Hatred is a tonic, it makes one live, it inspires vengeance; but pity kills, it makes our weakness weaker.
Honoré de Balzac 1799–1850: *La Peau de Chagrin* (1831)

25 Only the hopeless are starkly sincere and . . . only the unhappy can either give or take sympathy.
Jean Rhys 1890–1979: *The Left Bank* (1927)

26 If you see anybody fallen by the wayside and lying in the ditch, it isn't much good climbing into the ditch and lying by his side.
Dick Sheppard 1880–1937: Carolyn Scott *Dick Sheppard* (1977)

27 Any victim demands allegiance.
Graham Greene 1904–91: *The Heart of the Matter* (1948)

28 The fact that I have no remedy for the sorrows of the world is no reason for my accepting yours. It simply supports the strong probability that yours is a fake.
H. L. Mencken 1880–1956: *Minority Report* (1956)

29 When times get rough,
And friends just can't be found
Like a bridge over troubled water
I will lay me down.
Paul Simon 1942– : 'Bridge over Troubled Water' (1970 song)

30 You can't cry on a shoulder that's wearing a shoulder pad.
Steven Spielberg 1947– : in *Rolling Stone* 22 July 1982

→→ Taste ←←

PHRASES

1 **arbiter elegantiarum**
an authority on matters of taste or etiquette; Latin: see 2 below

QUOTATIONS

2 *Elegantiae arbiter.*
The arbiter of taste.
of Petronius
Tacitus c.AD 56–after 117: *Annals*; see 1 above

3 The play, I remember, pleased not the million; 'twas caviar to the general.
William Shakespeare 1564–1616: *Hamlet* (1601); see **Futility 9**

4 Between good sense and good taste there is the same difference as between cause and effect.
Jean de la Bruyère 1645–96: *Les Caractères ou les moeurs de ce siècle* (1688) 'Des Jugements'

5 Our tastes greatly alter. The lad does not care for the child's rattle, and the old man does not care for the young man's whore.
Samuel Johnson 1709–84: James Boswell *Life of Samuel Johnson* (1791) Spring 1766

6 Could we teach taste or genius by rules, they would be no longer taste and genius.
Joshua Reynolds 1723–92: *Discourses on Art* 14 December 1770

7 Rules and models destroy genius and art.
William Hazlitt 1778–1830: *Sketches and Essays* (1839) 'On Taste'

8   She had
A heart—how shall I say?—too soon made glad,
Too easily impressed; she liked whate'er She looked on, and her looks went everywhere.
Robert Browning 1812–89: 'My Last Duchess' (1842)

9 A difference of taste in jokes is a great strain on the affections.
George Eliot 1819–80: *Daniel Deronda* (1876)

10 It's worse than wicked, my dear, it's vulgar.
Punch: Almanac (1876)

11 Taste is the feminine of genius.
Edward Fitzgerald 1809–83: letter to J. R. Lowell, October 1877

12 Nowhere probably is there more true feeling, and nowhere worse taste, than in a churchyard.
Benjamin Jowett 1817–93: Evelyn Abbott and Lewis Campbell (eds.) *Letters of Benjamin Jowett* (1899)

13 *of the wallpaper in the room where he was dying:*
One of us must go.
Oscar Wilde 1854–1900: attributed, probably apocryphal

14 Good taste is better than bad taste, but bad taste is better than no taste, and men without individuality have no taste — at any rate no taste that they can impose on their publics.
Arnold Bennett 1867–1931: in *Evening Standard* 21 August 1930

15 The kind of people who always go on about whether a thing is in good taste invariably have very bad taste.
Joe Orton 1933–67: in *Transatlantic Review* Spring 1967

⇢ Taxes ⇠

PROVERBS AND SAYINGS

1 **Can't pay, won't pay.**
anti-Poll Tax slogan, *c.*1990; see 3 below

PHRASES

2 **Peter's pence**
an annual tax of one penny from every householder having land of a certain value, paid to the papal see at Rome from Anglo-Saxon times until discontinued in 1534 after Henry VIII's break with Rome; St *Peter* regarded by Roman Catholics as the first bishop of the Church at Rome

3 **poll tax**
a tax levied on every adult, without reference to their income or resources. Such taxes were levied in

England in 1377, 1379, and 1380; the last of these is generally regarded as having contributed to the 1381 Peasants' Revolt. From the mid 1980s, the term was used informally for the community charge, a usage which reflected the tax's deep unpopularity; see 1 above

QUOTATIONS

4 It is the part of the good shepherd to shear his flock, not skin it.
to governors who recommended burdensome taxes
Tiberius 42 BC–AD 37: Suetonius *Lives of the Caesars* 'Tiberius'

5 Money has no smell.
quashing an objection to a tax on public lavatories
Vespasian AD 9–79: traditional summary; Suetonius *Lives of the Caesars* 'Vespasian'; see **Money** 6

6 Neither will it be, that a people overlaid with taxes should ever become valiant and martial.
Francis Bacon 1561–1626: *Essays* (1625) 'Of the True Greatness of Kingdoms'

7 The art of taxation consists in so plucking the goose as to obtain the largest possible amount of feathers with the smallest possible amount of hissing.
Jean-Baptiste Colbert 1619–83: attributed

8 *Excise.* A hateful tax levied upon commodities.
Samuel Johnson 1709–84: *A Dictionary of the English Language* (1755)

9 Taxation without representation is tyranny.
James Otis 1725–83: watchword (*c.*1761) of the American Revolution; in *Dictionary of American Biography*

10 To tax and to please, no more than to love and to be wise, is not given to men.
Edmund Burke 1729–97: *On American Taxation* (1775); see **Love** 11

11 There is no art which one government sooner learns of another than that of draining money from the pockets of the people.
Adam Smith 1723–90: *Wealth of Nations* (1776)

12 The art of government is to make two-thirds of a nation pay all it possibly can pay for the benefit of the other third.
Voltaire 1694–1778: attributed; Walter Bagehot *The English Constitution* (1867)

13 Representatives and direct taxes shall be apportioned among the several States which may be included within this Union, according to their respective numbers, which shall be determined by adding to the whole number of free persons, including those bound to service for a term of years, and excluding Indians not taxed, three fifths of all other persons.
Constitution of the United States 1787:article 1, sect. 2; see also **Race** 32

14 All taxes must, at last, fall upon agriculture.
Edward Gibbon 1737–94: quoting Artaxerxes, in *The Decline and Fall of the Roman Empire* (1776–88)

15 In this world nothing can be said to be certain, except death and taxes.
Benjamin Franklin 1706–90: letter to Jean Baptiste Le Roy, 13 November 1789; see **Certainty** 3

16 The Chancellor of the Exchequer is a man whose duties make him more or less of a taxing machine. He is intrusted with a certain amount of misery which it is his duty to distribute as fairly as he can.
Robert Lowe 1811–92: speech, House of Commons, 11 April 1870

17 Death is the most convenient time to tax rich people.
David Lloyd George 1863–1945: in *Lord Riddell's Intimate Diary of the Peace Conference and After, 1918–23* (1933)

18 Income Tax has made more Liars out of the American people than Golf.
Will Rogers 1879–1935: *The Illiterate Digest* (1924) 'Helping the Girls with their Income Taxes'

19 Only the little people pay taxes.
Leona Helmsley 1920– : addressed to her housekeeper in 1983, and reported at her trial for tax evasion; in *New York Times* 12 July 1989

20 Read my lips: no new taxes.
campaign pledge on taxation
George Bush 1924– : in *New York Times* 19 August 1988

➤➤Teaching ◀◀

see also **Education, Schools, Universities**

PROVERBS AND SAYINGS

1 **He teaches ill who teaches all.**
English proverb, early 17th century

2 **He that teaches himself has a fool for his master.**
English proverb, early 17th century

3 **Nobody forgets a good teacher.**
Teacher Training Agency slogan, late 20th century

4 **Tell me and I'll forget. Show me and I'll remember. Involve me and I'll be changed forever.**
Japanese proverb

5 **Who teaches me for a day is my father for a lifetime.**
Chinese proverb; see **Charity** 3

QUOTATIONS

6 A man who reviews the old so as to find out the new is qualified to teach others.
Confucius 551–479 BC: *Analects*

7 Even while they teach, men learn.
Seneca ('the Younger') c.4 BC–AD 65: *Epistulae Morales*

8 Re-hashed cabbage wore out the wretched teachers.
Juvenal c.AD 60–c.130: *Satires*

9 There is no such whetstone, to sharpen a good wit and encourage a will to learning, as is praise.
Roger Ascham 1515–68: *The Schoolmaster* (1570)

10 Men must be taught as if you taught them not,
And things unknown proposed as things forgot.
Alexander Pope 1688–1744: *An Essay on Criticism* (1711)

11 Delightful task! to rear the tender thought, To teach the young idea how to shoot.
James Thomson 1700–48: *The Seasons* (1746) 'Spring'; see **Children** 3

12 It is no matter what you teach them [children] first, any more than what leg you shall put into your breeches first.
Samuel Johnson 1709–84: James Boswell *Life of Samuel Johnson* (1791) 26 July 1763

13 Few have been taught to any purpose who have not been their own teachers.
Joshua Reynolds 1723–92: *Discourses on Art* 11 December 1769

14 C-l-e-a-n, clean, verb active, to make bright, to scour. W-i-n, win, d-e-r, der, winder, a casement. When the boy knows this out of the book, he goes and does it.
Charles Dickens 1812–70: *Nicholas Nickleby* (1839)

15 Be a governess! Better be a slave at once!
Charlotte Brontë 1816–55: *Shirley* (1849)

16 He who can, does. He who cannot, teaches.
George Bernard Shaw 1856–1950: *Man and Superman* (1903)

17 A teacher affects eternity; he can never tell where his influence stops.
Henry Brooks Adams 1838–1918: *The Education of Henry Adams* (1907)

18 For every person who wants to teach there are approximately thirty who don't want to learn—much.
W. C. Sellar 1898–1951 and **R. J. Yeatman** 1898–1968: *And Now All This* (1932)

19 We teachers can only help the work going on, as servants wait upon a master.
Maria Montessori 1870–1952: *The Absorbent Mind* (1949)

20 That is the difference between good teachers and great teachers: good teachers make the best of a pupil's means: great teachers foresee a pupil's ends.
Maria Callas 1923–77: *Kenneth Harris Talking To* (1971) 'Maria Callas'

21 A teacher should have maximal authority and minimal power.
Thomas Szasz 1920– : *The Second Sin* (1973) 'Education'

22 Knowledge has to be sucked into the brain, not pushed into it.
Victor Weisskopf 1908–2002: *The Privilege of Being a Physicist* (1989)

23 I wouldn't wish teaching on my worst enemy's dog.
Louis de Bernières 1954– : in *Sunday Times* 18 March 2001

⤞ Technology ⤝

see also **Inventions and Discoveries, Science**

PROVERBS AND SAYINGS

1 **Let your fingers do the walking.**
1960s advertisement for Bell system Telephone Directory Yellow Pages

2 **Science finds, industry applies, man conforms.**
subtitle of guidebook to 1933 Chicago World's Fair

3 **Vorsprung durch Technik.**
German = Progress through technology; advertising slogan for Audi motors, from 1986

PHRASES

4 **grey goo**
a mass of self-replicating nanoscale machines proliferating uncontrollably and destroying or damaging the biosphere, postulated as a danger of the use of nanotechnology

5 **the white heat of technology**
the most advanced form of technology; from a misquotation of Harold Wilson: see 18 below

QUOTATIONS

6 Give me but one firm spot on which to stand, and I will move the earth.
on the action of a lever
Archimedes *c.*287–212 BC: Pappus *Synagoge*; see Arts and Sciences 7

7 I sell here, Sir, what all the world desires to have—POWER.
of his engineering works
Matthew Boulton 1728–1809: James Boswell *Life of Samuel Johnson* (1791) 22 March 1776

8 Man is a tool-using animal . . . Without tools he is nothing, with tools he is all.
Thomas Carlyle 1795–1881: *Sartor Resartus* (1834)

9 This extraordinary metal [iron], the soul of every manufacture, and the mainspring perhaps of civilized society.
Samuel Smiles 1812–1904: *Men of Invention and Industry* (1884)

10 One machine can do the work of fifty ordinary men. No machine can do the work of one extraordinary man.
Elbert Hubbard 1859–1915: *Thousand and One Epigrams* (1911)

11 Machines are worshipped because they are beautiful, and valued because they confer power; they are hated because they are hideous, and loathed because they impose slavery.
Bertrand Russell 1872–1970: *Sceptical Essays* (1928) 'Machines and Emotions'

12 This is not the age of pamphleteers. It is the age of the engineers. The spark-gap is mightier than the pen.
Lancelot Hogben 1895–1975: *Science for the Citizen* (1938); see **Ways and Means 16**

13 One servant is worth a thousand gadgets.
Joseph Alois Schumpeter 1883–1950: J. K. Galbraith *A Life in our Times* (1981)

14 When you see something that is technically sweet, you go ahead and do it and you argue about what to do about it only after you have had your technical success. That is the way it was with the atomic bomb.
J. Robert Oppenheimer 1904–67: in *In the Matter of J. Robert Oppenheimer, USAEC Transcript of Hearing Before Personnel Security Board* (1954)

15 It has been said that an engineer is a man who can do for ten shillings what any fool can do for a pound.
Nevil Shute 1899–1960: *Slide Rule* (1954)

16 Technology . . . the knack of so arranging the world that we need not experience it.
Max Frisch 1911–91: *Homo Faber* (1957)

17 The new electronic interdependence recreates the world in the image of a global village.
Marshall McLuhan 1911–80: *The Gutenberg Galaxy* (1962); see **The Country and the Town 27, The Earth 6**

18 The Britain that is going to be forged in the white heat of this revolution will be no place for restrictive practices or for outdated methods on either side of industry.
referring to the 'technological revolution'
Harold Wilson 1916–95: speech at the Labour Party Conference, 1 October 1963; see 5 above

19 The medium is the message.
Marshall McLuhan 1911–80: *Understanding Media* (1964)

20 When this circuit learns your job, what are you going to do?
Marshall McLuhan 1911–80: *The Medium is the Massage* (1967)

21 Inanimate objects are classified scientifically into three major categories—those that don't work, those that break down, and those that get lost.
Russell Baker 1925– : in *New York Times* 18 June 1968

22 The first rule of intelligent tinkering is to save all the parts.
Paul Ralph Ehrlich 1932– : in *Saturday Review* 5 June 1971

23 Any sufficiently advanced technology is indistinguishable from magic.
Arthur C. Clarke 1917– : *The Lost Worlds of 2001* (1972)

24 For a successful technology, reality must take precedence over public relations, for nature cannot be fooled.
Richard Phillips Feynman 1918–88: Appendix to the *Rogers Commission Report on the Space Shuttle Challenger Accident* 6 June 1986

25 Machines are the new proletariat. The working class is being given its walking papers.
Jacques Attali 1943– : *Millenium: Winners and Losers in the Coming World Order* (1991)

26 The thing with high-tech is that you always end up using scissors.
David Hockney 1937– : in *Observer* 10 July 1994

27 Technology happens. It's not good, it's not bad. Is steel good or bad?
Andrew Grove 1936– : in *Time* 29 December 1997

➵ Temptation ◅┼

PROVERBS AND SAYINGS

1 **Naughty but nice.**
advertising slogan for cream-cakes in the first half of the 1980s; earlier, the title of a 1939 film

2 **Stolen fruit is sweet.**
the knowledge that something is forbidden makes it more attractive; English proverb, early 17th century

3 **Stolen waters are sweet.**
something which has been obtained secretly or
illicitly seems particularly attractive; English proverb,
late 14th century

PHRASES

4 **the pomps and vanities of this wicked
world**
ostentatious display as a type of worldly temptation;
after the answer in the *Catechism*: see **Sin** 15

5 **the world, the flesh, and the devil**
the temptations of earthly life; from *Book of Common
Prayer*: see 10 below

QUOTATIONS

6 Get thee behind me, Satan.
Bible: St Matthew

7 And lead us not into temptation, but deliver
us from evil.
Bible: St Matthew

8 Watch and pray, that ye enter not into
temptation: the spirit indeed is willing but
the flesh is weak.
Bible: St Matthew

9 Is this her fault or mine?
The tempter or the tempted, who sins most?
William Shakespeare 1564–1616: *Measure for
Measure* (1604)

10 From all the deceits of the world, the flesh,
and the devil,
Good Lord, deliver us.
The Book of Common Prayer 1662: *The Litany*;
see 5 above

11 What's done we partly may compute,
But know not what's resisted.
Robert Burns 1759–96: 'Address to the Unco Guid'
(1787); see **Virtue** 13

12 It may almost be a question whether such
wisdom as many of us have in our mature
years has not come from the dying out of
the power of temptation, rather than as the
results of thought and resolution.
Anthony Trollope 1815–82: *The Small House at
Allington* (1864)

13 I can resist everything except temptation.
Oscar Wilde 1854–1900: *Lady Windermere's Fan*
(1892)

14 There are several good protections against
temptations, but the surest is cowardice.
Mark Twain 1835–1910: *Following the Equator*
(1897)

15 If we are to be punished for the sins we have
committed, at least we should be praised for
our yearning for the sins we have not
committed.
paraphrasing the poet Mirza Ghalib (1797–1849)
Jawaharlal Nehru 1889–1964: letter to Indira
Gandhi, 7 May 1943

16 The Lord above made liquor for temptation
To see if man could turn away from sin.
The Lord above made liquor for
temptation—but
With a little bit of luck,
With a little bit of luck,
When temptation comes you'll give right in!
Alan Jay Lerner 1918–86: 'With a Little Bit of Luck'
(1956 song)

17 This extraordinary pride in being exempt
from temptation that you have not yet risen
to the level of! Eunuchs boasting of their
chastity!
C. S. Lewis 1898–1963: 'Unreal Estates' in Kingsley
Amis and Robert Conquest (eds.) *Spectrum IV* (1965)

18 I've looked on a lot of women with lust. I've
committed adultery in my heart many
times. This is something that God
recognizes I will do — and I have done it —
and God forgives me for it.
Jimmy Carter 1924– : in *Playboy* November 1976

19 Who was it said a temptation resisted is a
true measure of character? Certainly no one
in Beverly Hills.
Joan Collins 1933– : in *Independent* 18 July 1998

⇥ The Theatre ⇤

see also **Acting**

PHRASES

1 the ghost walks
money is available and salaries will paid; has been
explained by the story that an actor playing the
ghost of Hamlet's father refused to 'walk again' until
the cast's overdue salaries had been paid

2 a mess of plottage
a theatrical production with a poorly constructed
plot; by analogy with *mess of pottage*: see **Value** 17

3 the Scottish play
Shakespeare's *Macbeth*; in theatrical tradition it is
regarded as unlucky to speak of this play by its title

QUOTATIONS

4 Tragedy is thus a representation of an action
that is worth serious attention, complete in
itself and of some amplitude . . . by means of
pity and fear bringing about the purgation
of such emotions.
Aristotle 384–322 BC: *Poetics*

5 For what's a play without a woman in it?
Thomas Kyd 1558–94: *The Spanish Tragedy* (1592)

6   Can this cockpit hold
The vasty fields of France? or may we cram
Within this wooden O the very casques
That did affright the air at Agincourt?
William Shakespeare 1564–1616: *Henry V* (1599)

7   The play's the thing
Wherein I'll catch the conscience of the
   king.
William Shakespeare 1564–1616: *Hamlet* (1601)

8 Then to the well-trod stage anon,
If Jonson's learnèd sock be on,
Or sweetest Shakespeare fancy's child,
Warble his native wood-notes wild.
John Milton 1608–74: 'L'Allegro' (1645); see
Acting 3

9 Ay, now the plot thickens very much
upon us.
George Villiers, Duke of Buckingham 1628–87:
The Rehearsal (1672); see **Circumstance** 18

10 Damn them! They will not let my play run,
but they steal my thunder!
on hearing his new thunder effects used at a
performance of *Macbeth*, following the withdrawal
of one of his own plays after only a short run
John Dennis 1657–1734: William S. Walsh *A Handy-
Book of Literary Curiosities* (1893); see **Strength** 13

11 There still remains, to mortify a wit,
The many-headed monster of the pit.
Alexander Pope 1688–1744: *Imitations of Horace*;
see **Class** 7

12 The composition of a tragedy requires
testicles.
on being asked why no woman had ever written 'a
tolerable tragedy'
Voltaire 1694–1778: letter from Byron to John
Murray, 2 April 1817

13 We should show life neither as it is nor as it
ought to be, but as we see it in our dreams.
Anton Chekhov 1860–1904: *The Seagull* (1896)

14 Things on stage should be as complicated
and as simple as in life. People dine, just
dine, while their happiness is made and
their lives are smashed. If in Act 1 you have
a pistol hanging on the wall, then it must
fire in the last act.
Anton Chekhov 1860–1904: attributed; Donald
Rayfield *Anton Chekhov* (1997)

15 *Étonne-moi.*
Astonish me.
Sergei Diaghilev 1872–1929: to Jean Cocteau;
Wallace Fowlie (ed.) *Journals of Jean Cocteau* (1956)

16 There's no business like show business.
Irving Berlin 1888–1989: title of song (1946)

17 We never closed.
of the Windmill Theatre, London, during the Second
World War
Vivian van Damm 1889–1960: *Tonight and Every
Night* (1952)

18 It's a sound you can't get in the movies or
television . . . the sound of a wonderful,
deep silence that means you've hit them
where they live.
Shelley Winters 1922– : in *Theatre Arts* June 1956

19 Don't clap too hard—it's a very old building.
John Osborne 1929–94: *The Entertainer* (1957)

20 The theatre is the only institution in the
world which has been dying for four
thousand years and has never succumbed.
John Steinbeck 1902–68: *Once There Was a War*
(1958)

21 Satire is what closes Saturday night.
George S. Kaufman 1889–1961: Scott Meredith *George S. Kaufman and his Friends* (1974)

22 The weasel under the cocktail cabinet.
on being asked what his plays were about
Harold Pinter 1930– : J. Russell Taylor *Anger and After* (1962)

23 I go to the theatre to be entertained, I want to be taken out of myself, I don't want to see lust and rape and incest and sodomy and so on, I can get all that at home.
Alan Bennett 1934– : Alan Bennett et al. *Beyond the Fringe* (1963) 'Man of Principles'

24 I can do you blood and love without the rhetoric, and I can do you blood and rhetoric without the love, and I can do you all three concurrent or consecutive, but I can't do you love and rhetoric without the blood. Blood is compulsory—they're all blood, you see.
Tom Stoppard 1937– : *Rosencrantz and Guildenstern are Dead* (1967)

25 I've never much enjoyed going to plays . . . The unreality of painted people standing on a platform saying things they've said to each other for months is more than I can overlook.
John Updike 1932– : George Plimpton (ed.) *Writers at Work* 4th Series (1977)

26 The theatre exists in movement.
Peter Brook 1925– : *Threads of Time* (1998)

⤞ Thinking ⤝

see also **Ideas, The Mind**

PROVERBS AND SAYINGS

1 **Great minds think alike.**
English proverb, early 17th century, now often used ironically

2 **Perish the thought!**
saying used, often ironically, to show that one finds a suggestion or idea completely ridiculous; the phrase probably derives from 'perish that thought!' in Colley Cibber's *Richard III* (1700)

3 **Two heads are better than one.**
it is advisable to discuss a problem with another person; English proverb, late 14th century

PHRASES

4 **an agonizing reappraisal**
a reassessment of a policy or position painfully forced on one by a radical change of circumstance, or by a realization of what the existing circumstances really are; from John Foster Dulles (1888–1959) in 1953, 'If . . . the European Defence Community should not be effective; if France and Germany remain apart . . . That would compel an agonizing reappraisal of basic United States policy'

5 **lateral thinking**
a way of thinking which seeks the solution to intractable problems through unorthodox methods, or elements which would normally be ignored by logical thinking; from Edward de Bono (1933–) The *Use of Lateral Thinking* (1967) 'Some people are aware of another sort of thinking which . . . leads to those simple ideas that are obvious only after they have been thought of . . . the term "lateral thinking" has been coined to describe this other sort of thinking; "vertical thinking" is used to denote the conventional logical process'

6 **positive thinking**
the practice or result of concentrating one's mind on the good and constructive aspects of a matter so as to eliminate destructive attitudes and emotions; *The Power of Positive Thinking* title of a book (1952) by Norman Vincent Peale (1898–1993)

QUOTATIONS

7 His thinking does not produce smoke after the flame, but light after smoke.
Horace 65–8 BC: *Ars Poetica*

8 Whatsoever things are true, whatsoever things are honest, whatsoever things are just, whatsoever things are pure, whatsoever things are lovely, whatsoever things are of good report; if there be any virtue and if there be any praise, think on these things.
Bible: Philippians

9 To change your mind and to follow him who sets you right is to be nonetheless the free agent that you were before.
Marcus Aurelius AD 121–80: *Meditations*

10 The important thing is not to think much but to love much.
St Teresa of Ávila 1512–82: *The Interior Castle* (1588)

11 Yond' Cassius has a lean and hungry look; He thinks too much: such men are dangerous.
William Shakespeare 1564–1616: *Julius Caesar* (1599)

12 *Je pense, donc je suis.*
I think, therefore I am.
usually quoted as, 'Cogito, ergo sum', from the 1641 Latin edition
René Descartes 1596–1650: *Le Discours de la méthode* (1637); see 28 below

13 A man, doubtful of his dinner, or trembling at a creditor, is not much disposed to abstracted meditation, or remote enquiries.
Samuel Johnson 1709–84: *Lives of the English Poets* (1779–81) 'Collins'

14 Two things fill the mind with ever new and increasing wonder and awe, the more often and the more seriously reflection concentrates upon them: the starry heaven above me and the moral law within me.
Immanuel Kant 1724–1804: *Critique of Practical Reason* (1788)

15 Stung by the splendour of a sudden thought.
Robert Browning 1812–89: 'A Death in the Desert' (1864)

16 How often misused words generate misleading thoughts.
Herbert Spencer 1820–1903: *Principles of Ethics* (1879)

17 It is quite a three-pipe problem, and I beg that you won't speak to me for fifty minutes.
Arthur Conan Doyle 1859–1930: *The Adventures of Sherlock Holmes* (1892)

18 Three minutes' thought would suffice to find this out; but thought is irksome and three minutes is a long time.
A. E. Housman 1859–1936: *D. Iunii Iuvenalis Saturae* (1905)

19 Sometimes I sits and thinks, and then again I just sits.
Punch: 1906

20 How can I tell what I think till I see what I say?
E. M. Forster 1879–1970: *Aspects of the Novel* (1927)

21 Pooh began to feel a little more comfortable, because when you are a Bear of Very Little Brain, and you Think of Things, you find sometimes that a Thing which seemed very Thingish inside you is quite different when it gets out into the open and has other people looking at it.
A. A. Milne 1882–1956: *The House at Pooh Corner* (1928)

22 A man of action forced into a state of thought is unhappy until he can get out of it.
John Galsworthy 1867–1933: *Maid in Waiting* (1931)

23 *Doublethink* means the power of holding two contradictory beliefs in one's mind simultaneously, and accepting both of them.
George Orwell 1903–50: *Nineteen Eighty-Four* (1949)

24 He can't think without his hat.
Samuel Beckett 1906–89: *Waiting for Godot* (1955)

25 It is a far, far better thing to have a firm anchor in nonsense than to put out on the troubled seas of thought.
J. K. Galbraith 1908– : *The Affluent Society* (1958)

26 What was once thought can never be unthought.
Friedrich Dürrenmatt 1921– : *The Physicists* (1962)

27 The real question is not whether machines think but whether men do.
B. F. Skinner 1904–90: *Contingencies of Reinforcement* (1969)

28 *I think, therefore I am* is the statement of an intellectual who underrates toothaches.
Milan Kundera 1929– : *Immortality* (1991); see 12 above

⇥ Thoroughness ⇤

see also **Determination and Perseverance**

PROVERBS AND SAYINGS

1 **Do not spoil the ship for a ha'porth of tar.**
used generally to warn against risking loss or failure through unwillingness to allow relatively trivial expenditure; *ship* is a dialectal pronunciation of *sheep*, and the original literal sense was 'do not allow sheep to die for the lack of a trifling amount of tar', tar being used to protect sores and wounds on sheep from flies; English proverb, early 17th century

✦➤◄✦➤◄✦➤◄✦➤◄✦➤◄✦➤◄✦➤◄✦➤◄✦➤◄✦➤◄✦➤◄✦➤◄✦➤◄✦➤◄✦➤

2 In for a penny, in for a pound.
if one is to be involved at all, it may as well be fully;
English proverb, late 17th century

3 Nothing venture, nothing gain.
a later variant of *nothing venture, nothing have*;
English proverb, early 17th century

4 Nothing venture, nothing have.
one must be prepared to take some risks to achieve a
desired end; English proverb, late 14th century

PHRASES

6 at one fell swoop
at a single blow, in one go; *swoop* = the sudden
pouncing of a bird of prey from a height on its
quarry, especially with allusion to Shakespeare
Macbeth: see **Mourning** 10

7 flesh and fell
entirely; the whole substance of the body (*fell* = the
skin)

8 go the extra mile
make an extra effort, do more than is strictly asked or
required; in a revue song (1957) by Joyce Grenfell,

**5 One might as well be hanged for a
sheep as a lamb.**
if one is going to incur a severe penalty it may as well
be for something substantial; English proverb, late
17th century

'Ready . . . To go the extra mile', but perhaps
ultimately in allusion to the Bible (Matthew) 'And
whosoever shall compel thee to go a mile, go with
him twain'

9 to destroy root and branch
to destroy thoroughly, radically; perhaps originally
with reference to the Bible (Malachi), 'The day that
cometh shall burn them up . . . that it shall leave
them neither root nor branch'

QUOTATIONS

10 Whatsoever thy hand findeth to do, do it
with thy might.
Bible: Ecclesiastes

11 There must be a beginning of any great
matter, but the continuing unto the end
until it be thoroughly finished yields the
true glory.
Francis Drake 1540–96: dispatch to Sir Francis
Walsingham, 17 May 1587

12 The shortest way to do many things is to do
only one thing at once.
Samuel Smiles 1812–1904: *Self-Help* (1859)

13 Climb ev'ry mountain, ford ev'ry stream
Follow ev'ry rainbow, till you find your
    dream!
Oscar Hammerstein II 1895–1960: *Climb Ev'ry
Mountain* (1959 song)

➤➤Thrift and Extravagance ◄◄

see also **Debt and Borrowing, Poverty, Wealth**

PROVERBS AND SAYINGS

1 Bang goes sixpence.
ironic commentary on regretted expenditure,
deriving from a cartoon in *Punch* of 5 December
1868, featuring a miserly Scotsman. The caption
read: 'a had na' been the-erre abune Twa Hoours
when—Bang—went Saxpence!'

2 Make do and mend.
wartime slogan, 1940s

**3 Most people consider thrift a fine
virtue in ancestors.**
American proverb, mid 20th century

4 A penny saved is a penny earned.
used as an exhortation to thrift; English proverb, mid
17th century

5 Penny wise and pound foolish.
too much concern with saving small sums may result
in larger loss if necessary expenditure on
maintenance and safety has been withheld; English
proverb, early 17th century

**6 Spare at the spigot, and let out the
bung-hole.**
referring to the practice of being overcareful on the
one hand, and carelessly generous on the other. A
spigot is a peg or pin used to regulate the flow of
liquid through a tap on a cask, and a *bung-hole* is a
hole through which a cask is filled or emptied, and
which is closed by a bung; English proverb, mid 17th
century

7 Spare well and have to spend.

the person who is thrifty and careful with their resources can use them lavishly when the occasion offers; English proverb, mid 16th century

8 Stretch your arm no further than your sleeve will reach.

you should not spend more than you can afford; English proverb, mid 16th century

9 Take care of the pence and the pounds will take care of themselves.

thrift and small savings will grow to substantial wealth; English proverb, mid 18th century; see **Money** 31, **Speech** 22

10 Thrift is a great revenue.

care with expenditure is one of the best ways of providing an income for oneself; English proverb, mid 17th century

11 Wilful waste makes woeful want.

deliberate misuse of resources is likely to lead to severe shortage; English proverb, early 18th century

PHRASES

12 play ducks and drakes with

trifle with; treat frivolously or wastefully; *ducks and drakes* a game of throwing flat stones so that they skim along the surface of water

QUOTATIONS

13 Plenty has made me poor.

Ovid 43–*c*.17: *Metamorphoses*

14 Thrift, thrift, Horatio! the funeral baked meats
Did coldly furnish forth the marriage tables.

William Shakespeare 1564–1616: *Hamlet* (1601)

15 In squandering wealth was his peculiar art:
Nothing went unrewarded, but desert.
Beggared by fools, whom still he found too late:
He had his jest, and they had his estate.

John Dryden 1631–1700: *Absalom and Achitophel* (1681)

16 Economy is going without something you do want in case you should, some day, want something you probably won't want.

Anthony Hope 1863–1933: *The Dolly Dialogues* (1894)

17 From the foregoing survey of conspicuous leisure and consumption, it appears that the utility of both alike for the purposes of reputability lies in the element of waste that is common to both. In the one case it is a waste of time and effort, in the other it is a waste of goods.

Thorstein Veblen 1857–1929: *Theory of the Leisure Class* (1899)

18 All decent people live beyond their incomes nowadays, and those who aren't respectable live beyond other peoples'.

Saki 1870–1916: *Chronicles of Clovis* (1911)

19 We could have saved sixpence. We have saved fivepence. (*Pause*) But at what cost?

Samuel Beckett 1906–89: *All That Fall* (1957)

20 If a champion spends his money foolishly, they ridicule him for that, and if he doesn't spend it, they call him cheap. Well, I'd rather have them criticize me for not spending it and wind up keeping my money.

Rocky Marciano 1923–69: Everett M. Skehan *Rocky Marciano* (1983)

21 Prudence is the other woman in Gordon's life.

of Gordon Brown, Chancellor of the Exchequer
Anonymous: an unidentified aide, in March 1998

⤞ Time ⤝

see also **Transience**

PROVERBS AND SAYINGS

1 Give us back our eleven days.

slogan protesting against the adoption of the Gregorian Calendar in 1752, which meant that 14 September followed immediately after 2 September; see 14 below

2 An inch of gold cannot buy an inch of time.

time cannot be bought by money; Chinese proverb

3 **Man fears Time, but Time fears the Pyramids.**

Egyptian proverb; see **Architecture** 24

4 **Never is a long time.**

often used to indicate that circumstances may ultimately change; English proverb, late 14th century; see **Change** 5

5 **Spring forward, fall back.**

a reminder that clocks are moved *forward* in *spring* and *back* in the *fall* (autumn)

6 **There is a time for everything.**

there is always a suitable time to do something; English proverb, late 14th century, from the Bible: see 20 below

PHRASES

10 **annus mirabilis**

a remarkable or auspicious year; modern Latin = wonderful year in *Annus Mirabilis: the year of wonders*, title of poem (1667) by Dryden; see **Misfortunes** 31

11 **at the Greek Calends**

never; *calends* = the first day of the month in the ancient Roman calendar; the Greek Calends will never come as the Greeks did not use calends in reckoning time

12 **for the duration**

until the end of something, especially a war; hence, informally, for a very long time; used first of the 1914–18 war from the term of enlistment 'for four years or the duration of the war'

13 **a movable feast**

an event which takes place at no regular time; a religious feast day (especially Easter Day and the other Christian holy days whose dates are related to it) which does not occur on the same calendar date each year; see **Towns and Cities** 26

14 **Old Style**

the method of calculating dates using the Julian calendar; in England and Wales it was superseded by the use of the Gregorian calendar in 1752; see 1 above

15 **once in a blue moon**

very rarely, practically never; *to say that the moon is blue* is recorded in the sixteenth century as a

QUOTATIONS

20 To every thing there is a season, and a time to every purpose under the heaven:
A time to be born, and a time to die . . .
A time to weep, and a time to laugh; a time to mourn, and a time to dance.
Bible: Ecclesiastes; see 6 above

21 *Sed fugit interea, fugit inreparabile tempus.*
But meanwhile it is flying, irretrievable time is flying.
usually quoted as '*tempus fugit* [time flies]'
Virgil 70–19 BC: *Georgics*; see **Transience** 3

7 **Time is a great healer.**

initial pain is felt less keenly with the passage of time; English proverb, late 14th century; see 47 below

8 **Time will tell.**

the true nature of something is likely to emerge over a period of time, and that conversely it is only after time has passed that something can be regarded as settled; English proverb, mid 16th century

9 **Time works wonders.**

often used to suggest that with the passage of time something initially unknown and unwelcome will become familiar and acceptable; English proverb, late 16th century

proverbial assertion of something that could not be true

16 **till kingdom come**

for an indefinitely long period; *kingdom come* = the next world, eternity; from *thy kingdom come* in the Lord's Prayer

17 **time immemorial**

legally, a time up to the beginning of the reign of Richard I in 1189; generally, a longer time than anyone can remember or trace

18 **time's arrow**

the direction of travel from past to future in time considered as a physical dimension; from Arthur Eddington (1882–1944) *The Nature of the Physical World* (1928) 'Let us draw an arrow arbitrarily. If as we follow the arrow we find more and more of the random element in the world, then the arrow is pointing towards the future; if the random element decreases the arrow points towards the past . . . I shall use the phrase "time's arrow" to express this one-way property of time which has no analogue in space.'

19 **world without end**

for ever, eternally; translation of Late Latin *in saecula saeculorum* = to the ages of ages, as used in *Morning Prayer* and other services, 'As it was in the beginning, is now, and ever shall be: world without end.'

22 *Tempus edax rerum.*
Time the devourer of everything.
Ovid 43–c.17: *Metamorphoses*

23 Every instant of time is a pinprick of eternity.
Marcus Aurelius AD 121–80: *Meditations*

24 I am Time grown old to destroy the world,
Embarked on the course of world annihilation.
Bhagavadgita 250 BC–AD 250: ch. 11

25 Time is . . . Time was . . . Time is past.
Robert Greene 1560–92: *Friar Bacon and Friar Bungay* (1594)

26 I wasted time, and now doth time waste me.
William Shakespeare 1564–1616: *Richard II* (1595)

27 Time hath, my lord, a wallet at his back,
Wherein he puts alms for oblivion.
William Shakespeare 1564–1616: *Troilus and Cressida* (1602)

28 To-morrow, and to-morrow, and to-morrow,
Creeps in this petty pace from day to day,
To the last syllable of recorded time;
And all our yesterdays have lighted fools
The way to dusty death.
William Shakespeare 1564–1616: *Macbeth* (1606)

29 Even such is Time, which takes in trust
Our youth, our joys, and all we have,
And pays us but with age and dust.
Walter Ralegh 1552–1618: written the night before his death, and found in his Bible in the Gatehouse at Westminster

30 There was never any thing by the wit of man so well devised, or so sure established, which in continuance of time hath not been corrupted.
The Book of Common Prayer 1662: *The Preface Concerning the Service of the Church*

31 But at my back I always hear
Time's wingèd chariot hurrying near:
And yonder all before us lie
Deserts of vast eternity.
Andrew Marvell 1621–78: 'To His Coy Mistress' (1681)

32 Days and months are travellers of eternity. So are the years that pass by.
Matsuo Basho 1644–94: *The Narrow Road to the Deep North*, tr. Nobuyuki Yuasa

33 Time, like an ever-rolling stream,
Bears all its sons away.
Isaac Watts 1674–1748: 'O God, our help in ages past' (1719 hymn)

34 I recommend to you to take care of minutes: for hours will take care of themselves.
Lord Chesterfield 1694–1773: *Letters to his Son* (1774) 6 November 1747

35 Remember that time is money.
Benjamin Franklin 1706–90: *Advice to a Young Tradesman* (1748); see **Money** 14

36 O aching time! O moments big as years!
John Keats 1795–1821: 'Hyperion: A Fragment' (1820)

37 Men talk of killing time, while time quietly kills them.
Dion Boucicault 1820–90: *London Assurance* (1841)

38 He said, 'What's time? Leave Now for dogs and apes!
Man has Forever.'
Robert Browning 1812–89: 'A Grammarian's Funeral' (1855)

39 Lost, yesterday, somewhere between Sunrise and Sunset, two golden hours, each set with sixty diamond minutes. No reward is offered, for they are gone forever.
Horace Mann 1796–1859: 'Lost, Two Golden Hours'

40 Time is a great teacher but unfortunately it kills all its pupils.
Hector Berlioz 1803–69: attributed; in *Almanach des lettres françaises et étrangères* (1924) 11 May

41 Time is
Too slow for those who wait,
Too swift for those who fear,
Too long for those who grieve,
Too short for those who rejoice;
But for those who love,
Time is eternity.
Henry Van Dyke 1852–1933: 'Time is too slow for those who wait' (1905), read at the funeral of Diana, Princess of Wales; the original form of the last line is 'Time is not'

42 Time, you old gypsy man,
Will you not stay,
Put up your caravan
Just for one day?
Ralph Hodgson 1871–1962: 'Time, You Old Gipsy Man' (1917)

43 Ah! the clock is always slow;
It is later than you think.
Robert W. Service 1874–1958: 'It Is Later Than You Think' (1921)

44 Half our life is spent trying to find something to do with the time we have rushed through life trying to save.
Will Rogers 1879–1935: letter in *New York Times* 29 April 1930

45 Time present and time past
Are both perhaps present in time future,
And time future contained in time past.
T. S. Eliot 1888–1965: *Four Quartets* 'Burnt Norton' (1936)

46 Three o'clock is always too late or too early for anything you want to do.
Jean-Paul Sartre 1905–80: *La Nausée* (1938)

47 Time has too much credit . . . It is not a great healer. It is an indifferent and perfunctory one. Sometimes it does not heal at all. And sometimes when it seems to, no healing has been necessary.
Ivy Compton-Burnett 1884–1969: *Darkness and Day* (1951); see 7 above

48 VLADIMIR: That passed the time.
ESTRAGON: It would have passed in any case.

VLADIMIR: Yes, but not so rapidly.
Samuel Beckett 1906–89: *Waiting for Godot* (1955)

49 The distinction between past, present and future is only an illusion, however persistent.
Albert Einstein 1879–1955: letter to Michelangelo Besso, 21 March 1955

50 And meanwhile time goes about its immemorial work of making everyone look and feel like shit.
Martin Amis 1949– : *London Fields* (1989)

Title see **Rank and Title**

Tolerance see **Prejudice and Tolerance**

The Town see **The Country and the Town**

Towns and Cities

see also **American Cities and States, British Towns and Regions**

PROVERBS AND SAYINGS

1 **All roads lead to Rome.**
English proverb, late 14th century, earlier in Latin

2 **Isfahan is half the world.**
Isfahan was the capital of Persia from 1598 until 1722; Persian proverb

3 **Next year in Jerusalem!**
traditionally the concluding words of the Jewish Passover service, expressing the hope of the Diaspora that Jews dispersed throughout the world would once more be reunited

4 **See Naples and die.**
implying that after seeing Naples, one could have nothing left on earth to wish for; Goethe noted it as an Italian proverb in his diary in 1787

PHRASES

5 **the cities of the plain**
Sodom and Gomorrah, on the plain of Jordan in ancient Palestine; from the Bible (Genesis), the ancient cities destroyed by fire from heaven, because of the wickedness of their inhabitants

6 **the City of the Seven Hills**
Rome

7 **City of the Tribes**
Galway; the term *tribes of Galway* was used for Irish families or communities having the same surname

8 **City of the Violated Treaty**
Limerick; referring to the Treaty of Limerick of 1691

9 **City of the Violet Crown**
Athens; translating an epithet used by Pindar (*c*.518–*c*.438 BC) and Aristophanes (*c*.450–*c*.385 BC)

10 **the Eternal City**
Rome; translating the Latin *urbs aeterna*, occurring in Ovid and Tibullus, and frequently found in the official documents of the Empire

11 **the Forbidden City**
Lhasa; the centre of Tibetan Buddhism, closed to foreign visitors until the 20th century. The name *Forbidden City* is also given to an area of Beijing (Peking) containing the former imperial palaces

12 **the Holy City**
Jerusalem

13 **the Venice of the North**
St Petersburg

QUOTATIONS

14 He could boast that he inherited it brick and left it marble.
referring to the city of Rome
Augustus 63 BC–AD 14: Suetonius *Lives of the Caesars* 'Divus Augustus'

15 Once did she hold the gorgeous East in fee, And was the safeguard of the West.
William Wordsworth 1770–1850: 'On the Extinction of the Venetian Republic' (1807)

16 Sun-girt city, thou hast been
Ocean's child, and then his queen;
Now is come a darker day,

And thou soon must be his prey.
of Venice
Percy Bysshe Shelley 1792–1822: 'Lines written amongst the Euganean Hills' (1818)

17 While stands the Coliseum, Rome shall stand;
When falls the Coliseum, Rome shall fall;
And when Rome falls—the World.
Lord Byron 1788–1824: *Childe Harold's Pilgrimage* (1812–18)

18 Let there be light! said Liberty,
And like sunrise from the sea,
Athens arose!
Percy Bysshe Shelley 1792–1822: *Hellas* (1822)

19 Moscow: those syllables can start
A tumult in the Russian heart.
Alexander Pushkin 1799–1837: *Eugene Onegin* (1833)

20 Match me such marvel, save in Eastern clime,—
A rose-red city—half as old as Time!
John William Burgon 1813–88: *Petra* (1845)

21 Petersburg, the most abstract and premeditated city on earth.
Fedor Dostoevsky 1821–81: *Notes from Underground* (1864)

22 God made the harbour, and that's all right, but Satan made Sydney.
Anonymous: unnamed Sydney citizen; Mark Twain *More Tramps Abroad* (1897)

23 The last time I saw Paris
Her heart was warm and gay,
I heard the laughter of her heart in ev'ry street café.
Oscar Hammerstein II 1895–1960: 'The Last Time I saw Paris' (1941 song)

24 STREETS FLOODED. PLEASE ADVISE.
telegraph message on arriving in Venice
Robert Benchley 1889–1945: R. E. Drennan (ed.) *Wits End* (1973)

25 No history much? Perhaps. Only this ominous
Dark beauty flowering under veils,
Trapped in the spectrum of a dying style:
A village like an instinct left to rust,
Composed around the echo of a pistol-shot.
Lawrence Durrell 1912–90: 'Sarajevo' (1951)

26 Paris is a movable feast.
Ernest Hemingway 1899–1961: *A Movable Feast* (1964) epigraph; see **Time** 13

27 Venice is like eating an entire box of chocolate liqueurs in one go.
Truman Capote 1924–84: in *Observer* 26 November 1961

28 Rome's just a city like anywhere else. A vastly overrated city, I'd say. It trades on belief just as Stratford trades on Shakespeare.
Anthony Burgess 1917–93: *Inside Mr Enderby* (1963)

29 Some say that no one ever leaves Montreal, for that city, like Canada itself, is designed to preserve the past, a past that happened somewhere else.
Leonard Cohen 1934– : *The Favourite Game* (1963) bk. 2, ch. 19

30 By God what a site! By man what a mess!
of Sydney
Clough Williams-Ellis 1883–1978: *Architect Errant* (1971)

31 Toronto is a kind of New York operated by the Swiss.
Peter Ustinov 1921–2004: in *Globe & Mail* 1 August 1987; attributed

32 Saigon is like all the other great modern cities of the world. It's the mess left over from people getting rich.
P. J. O'Rourke 1947– : *Give War a Chance* (1992)

⤙ Transience ⤚

see also **Opportunity**, **Time**

PROVERBS AND SAYINGS

1 **And this, too, shall pass away.**
traditional saying said to be true for all times and situations; the story is told by Edward Fitzgerald in *Polonius* (1852) 'The Sultan asked for a signet motto, that should hold good for Adversity or Prosperity. Solomon gave him—"This also shall pass away" '

2 **Sic transit gloria mundi**.
Latin = Thus passes the glory of the world; said during the coronation of a new Pope, while flax is burned (used at the coronation of Alexander V in Pisa, 7 July 1409, but earlier in origin)

3 **Time flies.**
English proverb, late 14th century, from Virgil: see **Time** 21

QUOTATIONS

4 Like that of leaves is a generation of men.
Homer: *The Iliad*

5 For a thousand years in thy sight are but as yesterday: seeing that is past as a watch in the night.
Bible: Psalm 90

6 *Eheu fugaces, Postume, Postume,*
Labuntur anni.
Ah me, Postumus, Postumus, the fleeting years are slipping by.
Horace 65–8 BC: *Odes*

7 All flesh is as grass, and all the glory of man as the flower of grass. The grass withereth, and the flower thereof falleth away.
Bible: I Peter; see **Life** 10

8 Gather ye rosebuds while ye may,
Old Time is still a-flying:
And this same flower that smiles to-day,
To-morrow will be dying.
Robert Herrick 1591–1674: 'To the Virgins, to Make Much of Time' (1648)

9 *Pourvu que ça dure!*
Let's hope it lasts!
on her son Napoleon becoming Emperor, 1804
Laetitia Bonaparte 1750–1836: attributed, possibly apocryphal

10 Though nothing can bring back the hour Of splendour in the grass, of glory in the flower;
We will grieve not, rather find Strength in what remains behind.
William Wordsworth 1770–1850: 'Ode. Intimations of Immortality' (1807)

11 I never nursed a dear gazelle,
To glad me with its soft black eye,
But when it came to know me well,
And love me, it was sure to die!
Thomas Moore 1779–1852: *Lalla Rookh* (1817) 'The Fire-Worshippers'; see **Value** 32

12 He who binds to himself a joy
Doth the winged life destroy
But he who kisses the joy as it flies

Lives in Eternity's sunrise.
William Blake 1757–1827: *MS Note-Book*

13 They are not long, the days of wine and roses.
Ernest Dowson 1867–1900: 'Vitae Summa Brevis' (1896)

14 Look thy last on all things lovely,
Every hour.
Walter de la Mare 1873–1956: 'Fare Well' (1918)

15 My candle burns at both ends;
It will not last the night;
But ah, my foes, and oh, my friends—
It gives a lovely light.
Edna St Vincent Millay 1892–1950: *A Few Figs From Thistles* (1920) 'First Fig'; see **Effort** 11

16 He will be just like the scent on a pocket handkerchief.
on being asked what place Arthur Balfour would have in history
David Lloyd George 1863–1945: Thomas Jones diary 9 June 1922

17 The sunlight on the garden
Hardens and grows cold,
We cannot cage the minute
Within its net of gold.
Louis MacNeice 1907–63: 'Sunlight on the Garden' (1938)

18 Treaties, you see, are like girls and roses: they last while they last.
Charles de Gaulle 1890–1970: speech at Elysée Palace, 2 July 1963

19 And it seems to me you lived your life
Like a candle in the wind.
of Marilyn Monroe, later revised for Diana Princess of Wales
Elton John 1947– and **Bernie Taupin** 1950– : 'Candle in the Wind' (song, 1973); see **Singing** 17

20 We are all of us balloons dancing in a world of pins.
Anthony Montague Browne 1923– : *Long Sunset* (1995)

⤞ Translation ⤝

PROVERBS AND SAYINGS

1 **Traduttore traditore.**
Italian, meaning 'translators, traitors'

PHRASES

2 Translator General
Philemon Holland (1552–1637); he translated the work of Livy, Pliny, Plutarch, Suetonius, and others; Thomas Fuller named him the 'translator general in his age' and said that 'these books alone of his turning into English will make a country gentleman a competent library'

QUOTATIONS

3 Such is our pride, our folly, or our fate,
That few, but such as cannot write, translate.
John Denham 1615–69: 'To Richard Fanshaw' (1648)

4 He is translation's thief that addeth more,
As much as he that taketh from the store
Of the first author.
Andrew Marvell 1621–78: 'To His Worthy Friend Dr Witty' (1651)

5 Some hold translations not unlike to be
The wrong side of a Turkey tapestry.
James Howell 1593–1666: *Familiar Letters* (1645–55)

6 It is a pretty poem, Mr Pope, but you must not call it Homer.
when pressed by Pope to comment on 'My Homer', i.e. his translation of Homer's *Iliad*
Richard Bentley 1662–1742: John Hawkins (ed.) *The Works of Samuel Johnson* (1787)

7 It appears to me that men are hired to run down men of genius under the mask of translators.
William Blake 1757–1827: *Annotations to Boyd's Dante* (written c.1800)

8 The vanity of translation; it were as wise to cast a violet into a crucible that you might discover the formal principle of its colour and odour, as seek to transfuse from one language to another the creations of a poet. The plant must spring again from its seed, or it will bear no flower.
Percy Bysshe Shelley 1792–1822: *A Defence of Poetry* (written 1821)

9 A translation is no translation unless it will give you the music of a poem along with the words of it.
John Millington Synge 1871–1909: *The Aran Islands* (1907)

10 The original Greek is of great use in elucidating Browning's translation of the *Agamemnon*.
Robert Yelverton Tyrrell 1844–1914: Ulick O'Connor *Oliver St John Gogarty* (1964)

11 Translations (like wives) are seldom strictly faithful if they are in the least attractive.
Roy Campbell 1901–57: in *Poetry Review* June–July 1949

12 It has never occurred to Anderson that one foreign language can be translated into another. He assumes that every strange tongue exists only by virtue of its not being English.
Tom Stoppard 1937– : *Where Are They Now?* (1973)

13 The original is unfaithful to the translation.
on Henley's translation of Beckford's *Vathek*
Jorge Luis Borges 1899–1986: *Sobre el 'Vathek' de William Beckford*; in *Obras Completas* (1974)

14 Like playing Beethoven on the kazoo.
on his translation of Shakespeare into text messages
John Sutherland 1938– : in *Mail on Sunday* 20 November 2005

➔➤ Transport ◄◄•

PROVERBS AND SAYINGS

1 Clunk, click, every trip.
road safety campaign promoting the use of seat-belts, 1971

2 Let the train take the strain.
British Rail slogan, 1970 onwards

3 Put a tiger in your tank.
advertising slogan for Esso petrol, 1964; see **Strength 14**

PHRASES

4 a magic carpet
a means of sudden and effortless travel; a mythical carpet able to transport a person on it to any desired place

5 seven-league boots
the ability to travel very fast on foot; boots enabling the wearer to go seven leagues at each stride, from the fairy story of Hop o' my Thumb.

➤◄➤

QUOTATIONS

6 The driving is like the driving of Jehu, the son of Nimshi; for he driveth furiously.
Bible: II Kings

7 There was a rocky valley between Buxton and Bakewell . . . You enterprised a railroad . . . you blasted its rocks away . . . And now, every fool in Buxton can be at Bakewell in half-an-hour, and every fool in Bakewell at Buxton.
John Ruskin 1819–1900: *Praeterita* vol. 3 (1889)

8 There is *nothing*—absolutely nothing—half so much worth doing as simply messing about in boats.
Kenneth Grahame 1859–1932: *The Wind in the Willows* (1908)

9 The poetry of motion! The *real* way to travel! The *only* way to travel! Here today—in next week tomorrow! Villages skipped, towns and cities jumped—always somebody else's horizon! O bliss! O poop-poop! O my! O my!
on the car
Kenneth Grahame 1859–1932: *The Wind in the Willows* (1908)

10 What good is speed if the brain has oozed out on the way?
Karl Kraus 1874–1936: in *Die Fackel* September 1909 'The Discovery of the North Pole'

11 Railway termini. They are our gates to the glorious and the unknown. Through them we pass out into adventure and sunshine, to them, alas! we return.
E. M. Forster 1879–1970: *Howards End* (1910)

12 Sir, Saturday morning, although recurring at regular and well-foreseen intervals, always seems to take this railway by surprise.
W. S. Gilbert 1836–1911: letter to the station-master at Baker Street, on the Metropolitan line; John Julius Norwich *Christmas Crackers* (1980)

13 Walk! Not bloody likely. I am going in a taxi.
George Bernard Shaw 1856–1950: *Pygmalion* (1916); see **Swearing** 3

14 Men travel faster now, but I do not know if they go to better things.
Willa Cather 1873–1947: *Death Comes for the Archbishop* (1927)

15 [There are] only two classes of pedestrians in these days of reckless motor traffic—the quick, and the dead.
Lord Dewar 1864–1930: George Robey *Looking Back on Life* (1933); see **Heaven** 12

16 Home James, and don't spare the horses.
Fred Hillebrand 1893– : title of song (1934)

17 This is the Night Mail crossing the Border, Bringing the cheque and the postal order,

Letters for the rich, letters for the poor, The shop at the corner, the girl next door.
W. H. Auden 1907–73: 'Night Mail' (1936)

18 Oh! I have slipped the surly bonds of earth And danced the skies on laughter-silvered wings; . . .
And, while with silent lifting mind I've trod The high, untrespassed sanctity of space, Put out my hand and touched the face of God.
quoted by Ronald Reagan following the explosion of the space shuttle *Challenger*, January 1986
John Gillespie Magee 1922–41: 'High Flight' (1943)

19 That life-quickening atmosphere of a big railway station where everything is something trembling on the brink of something else.
Vladimir Nabokov 1899–1977: *Spring in Fialta and other stories* (1956) 'Spring in Fialta'

20 The automobile changed our dress, manners, social customs, vacation habits, the shape of our cities, consumer purchasing patterns, common tastes and positions in intercourse.
John Keats 1920– : *The Insolent Chariots* (1958)

21 There is no class of person more moved by hatred than the motorist and the policeman is a convenient receptacle for his feeling.
C. W. Hewitt: speech to the Lawyers' Club of the London School of Economics, 22 October 1959

22 The car has become an article of dress without which we feel uncertain, unclad and incomplete in the urban compound.
Marshall McLuhan 1911–80: *Understanding Media* (1964)

23 I myself see the car crash as a tremendous sexual event really: a liberation of human and machine libido (if there is such a thing).
J. G. Ballard 1930– : in *Penthouse* September 1970

24 I was astonished at the effect my successful landing in France had on the nations of the world. To me, it was like a match lighting a bonfire.
of the first solo transatlantic flight
Charles Lindbergh 1902–74: *Autobiography of Values* (1978)

25 I have seldom heard a train go by and not wished I was on it. Those whistles sing bewitchment: railways are irresistible bazaars, snaking along perfectly level no matter what the landscape, improving your mood with speed, and never upsetting your drink.
Paul Theroux 1941– : *The Great Railway Bazaar* (1975)

26 We have now to plan no longer for soft little animals pottering about on their own two legs, but for hard steel canisters hurtling about with these same little animals inside them.

Hugh Casson 1910– : Clough Williams-Ellis *Around the World in 90 Years* (1978)

27 There are only two emotions in a plane: boredom and terror.

Orson Welles 1915–85: interview to celebrate his 70th birthday, in *The Times* 6 May 1985

28 Railways and the Church have their critics, but both are the best ways of getting a man to his ultimate destination.

Revd W. Awdry 1911–97: in *Daily Telegraph* 22 March 1997; obituary

⤚⤙ Travel ⤙⤚

see also **Countries and Peoples, Exploration**

PROVERBS AND SAYINGS

1 Been there, done that, got the T-shirt.
evoking a jaded tourist as the image of someone who is bored by too much sight-seeing; see **Boredom 1**

2 Every two miles the water changes, every twelve miles the speech.
commenting on the changes experienced by travellers (the number of miles varies); Indian proverb

3 Go abroad and you'll hear news of home.
information about one's immediate vicinity may have become more widely publicized; English proverb, late 17th century

4 If it's Tuesday, this must be Belgium.
late 20th century saying, from the title of a 1969 film written by David Shaw

5 Is your journey *really* necessary?
1939 slogan, coined to discourage Civil Servants from going home for Christmas

6 Thursday's child has far to go.
traditional rhyme, mid 19th century; see also **Beauty 7, Gifts 2, Pregnancy and Birth 1, Sorrow 2, Work 6**

7 Travel broadens the mind.
English proverb, early 20th century

8 Travelling is learning.
African proverb

9 Travelling is one way of lengthening life, at least in appearance.
American proverb, mid 20th century

10 A wise man will climb Mount Fuji once, but only a fool will climb it twice.
Japanese proverb

PHRASES

11 curse of Cain
the fate of someone compelled to lead a wandering life; after the Bible (Genesis) 'a fugitive . . . shalt thou [Cain] be in the earth'; see also **Canada 3, Murder 7, Order 8**

12 genius loci
the presiding god or spirit of a particular place; originally with reference to Virgil *Aeneid* 'He prays to the spirit of the place and to Earth'; later with *genius* taken as referring to the body of associations connected with or inspirations derived from a place, rather than to a tutelary deity

13 port out, starboard home
according to folk etymology, for which there is no supporting evidence, the adjective *posh* was formed from the initials of these words, referring to the more comfortable accommodation, out of the heat of the sun, on ships between England and India (in fact, it seems most likely that the origin is the earlier slang *posh*, denoting a dandy)

14 round Robin Hood's barn
by a circuitous route; *Robin Hood* = a popular English outlaw traditionally famous from medieval times, *Robin Hood's barn* = an out-of-the-way place

15 Sabbath day's journey
an easy journey; the distance a Jew might travel on the Sabbath (approximately two-thirds of a mile); in the Bible (Acts) the distance from Mount Olivet to Jerusalem is described as being 'a Sabbath day's journey'

16 traveller's tale
a story about the unusual characteristics or customs of a foreign country, regarded as typically exaggerated or untrue

17 wild blue yonder
the far distance; a remote place; from R. Crawford *Army Air Corps* (song, 1939) 'Off we go into the wild blue yonder, Climbing high into the sun'

QUOTATIONS

18 And the Lord said unto Satan, Whence comest thou? Then Satan answered the Lord, and said, From going to and fro in the earth, and from walking up and down in it.
Bible: Job

19 They change their clime, not their frame of mind, who rush across the sea.
Horace 65–8 BC: *Epistles*

20 I have not told even half of the things that I have seen.
when asked if he wished to deny any of his stories of his travels
Marco Polo c.1254–c.1324:attributed, but probably apocryphal

21 Ay, now am I in Arden; the more fool I. When I was at home I was in a better place; but travellers must be content.
William Shakespeare 1564–1616: *As You Like It* (1599)

22 He disdains all things above his reach, and preferreth all countries before his own.
Thomas Overbury 1581–1613: *Miscellaneous Works* (1632) 'An Affected Traveller'

23 Travel, in the younger sort, is a part of education; in the elder, a part of experience. He that travelleth into a country before he hath some entrance into the language, goeth to school, and not to travel.
Francis Bacon 1561–1626: *Essays* (1625) 'Of Travel'

24 See one promontory (said Socrates of old), one mountain, one sea, one river, and see all.
Robert Burton 1577–1640: *The Anatomy of Melancholy* (1621–51)

25 I always love to begin a journey on Sundays, because I shall have the prayers of the church, to preserve all that travel by land, or by water.
Jonathan Swift 1667–1745: *Polite Conversation* (1738)

26 So it is in travelling; a man must carry knowledge with him, if he would bring home knowledge.
Samuel Johnson 1709–84: James Boswell *Life of Samuel Johnson* (1791) 17 April 1778

27 Worth seeing, yes; but not worth going to see.
on the Giant's Causeway
Samuel Johnson 1709–84: James Boswell *Life of Samuel Johnson* (1791) 12 October 1779

28 Travelling is the ruin of all happiness! There's no looking at a building here after seeing Italy.
Fanny Burney 1752–1840: *Cecilia* (1782)

29   I am become a name;
For always roaming with a hungry heart.
Alfred, Lord Tennyson 1809–92: 'Ulysses' (1842)

30 Some minds improve by travel, others, rather
Resemble copper wire, or brass,
Which gets the narrower by going farther!
Thomas Hood 1799–1845: 'Ode to Rae Wilson, Esq.'

31 It is not worthwhile to go around the world to count the cats in Zanzibar.
Henry David Thoreau 1817–62: *Walden* (1854) 'Conclusion'

32 Of all noxious animals, too, the most noxious is a tourist. And of all tourists the most vulgar, ill-bred, offensive and loathsome is the British tourist.
Francis Kilvert 1840–79: diary 5 April 1870

33 To travel hopefully is a better thing than to arrive, and the true success is to labour.
Robert Louis Stevenson 1850–94: *Virginibus Puerisque* (1881); see **Hope 8**

34 A man travels the world in search of what he needs and returns home to find it.
George Moore 1852–1933: *The Brook Kerith* (1916)

35 How 'ya gonna keep 'em down on the farm (after they've seen Paree)?
Sam M. Lewis 1885–1959 and **Joe Young** 1889–1939: title of song (1919)

36 In America there are two classes of travel—first class, and with children.
Robert Benchley 1889–1945: *Pluck and Luck* (1925)

37 São Paulo is like Reading, only much farther away.
Peter Fleming 1907–71: *Brazilian Adventure* (1933)

38 A good traveller is one who does not know where he is going to, and a perfect traveller does not know where he came from.
Lin Yutang 1895–1976: *The Importance of Living* (1938)

39 Why do the wrong people travel, travel, travel,
When the right people stay back home?
Noël Coward 1899–1973: 'Why do the Wrong People Travel?' (1961 song)

40 I did not fully understand the dread term 'terminal illness' until I saw Heathrow for myself.
Dennis Potter 1935–94: in *Sunday Times* 4 June 1978

41 I wouldn't mind seeing China if I could come back the same day.
Philip Larkin 1922–85: interview with *Observer*, 1979, in *Required Writing* (1983)

42 The Devil himself had probably re-designed Hell in the light of information he had gained from observing airport layouts.
Anthony Price 1928– : *The Memory Trap* (1989)

43 To infinity and beyond.
Joel Cohen et al.: *Toy Story* (1995 film); spoken by Buzz Lightyear

44 Tourists look at themselves as the be all and end all, but they are not. They are just another crop, like cotton was in the past.
Lord Glenconner 1926– : in *Sunday Times* 7 January 2001

Treachery see **Trust and Treachery**

Trees

PROVERBS AND SAYINGS

1 **Beware of an oak, it draws the stroke; avoid an ash, it counts the flash; creep under the thorn, it can save you from harm.**
recording traditional beliefs on where to shelter from lightning during a thunderstorm; English proverb, late 19th century

2 **Every elm has its man.**
perhaps referring to the readiness of the tree to drop its branches on the unwary. Elm wood was also

traditionally used for coffins; English proverb, early 20th century

3 **A seed hidden in the heart of an apple is an orchard invisible.**
Welsh proverb; see **Gardens** 1

4 **Trees planted by the ancestors provide shade for their descendants.**
Chinese proverb; see 7 below

PHRASES

5 **upas tree**
in folklore, a Javanese tree alleged to poison its surroundings and said to be fatal to approach; an account of the tree given in the *London Magazine* of

1783 was said to be translated from one written in Dutch by Mr Foersch, a surgeon at Samarang in 1773, but was in fact invented by the writer and critic George Steevens (1736–1800)

QUOTATIONS

6 Something sweet is the whisper of the pine, O goatherd, that makes her music by yonder springs.
Theocritus *c.*300–260 BC: *Idylls*

7 He plants the trees to serve another age.
Caecilius Statius d. after 166 BC: *Synephebi*; quoted in Cicero 'De Senectute'; see 4 above

8 Generations pass while some trees stand, and old families last not three oaks.
Thomas Browne 1605–82: *Hydriotaphia* (Urn Burial, 1658)

9 Under the cherry—
blossom soup,
blossom salad.
Matsuo Basho 1644–94: translated by Lucien Stryk

10 He that plants trees loves others beside himself.
Thomas Fuller 1654–1734: *Gnomologia* (1732)

11 The poplars are felled, farewell to the shade And the whispering sound of the cool colonnade.
William Cowper 1731–1800: 'The Poplar-Field' (written 1784)

12 O leave this barren spot to me!
Spare, woodman, spare the beechen tree.
Thomas Campbell 1777–1844: 'The Beech-Tree's Petition' (1800)

13 And since to look at things in bloom
Fifty springs are little room,
About the woodlands I will go
To see the cherry hung with snow.
A. E. Housman 1859–1936: *A Shropshire Lad* (1896)

14 Of all the trees that grow so fair,
Old England to adorn,
Greater are none beneath the Sun,
Than Oak, and Ash, and Thorn.
Rudyard Kipling 1865–1936: *Puck of Pook's Hill* (1906) 'A Tree Song'

15 For pines are gossip pines the wide world through
And full of runic tales to sigh or sing.
James Elroy Flecker 1884–1915: *Golden Journey to Samarkand* (1913) 'Brumana'

16 I like trees because they seem more resigned to the way they have to live than other things do.
Willa Cather 1873–1947: *O Pioneers!* (1913)

17 I think that I shall never see
A poem lovely as a tree.
Joyce Kilmer 1886–1918: 'Trees' (1914); see
Pollution 16

18 O chestnut-tree, great-rooted blossomer,
Are you the leaf, the blossom or the bole?
W. B. Yeats 1865–1939: 'Among School Children'
(1928)

19 I am for the woods against the world,
But are the woods for me?
Edmund Blunden 1896–1974: 'The Kiss' (1931)

20 In every wood, in every spring,
there is a different green.
J. R. R. Tolkien 1892–1973: *The Fellowship of the
Ring* (1954)

21 As a tree in a beautiful forest.
on how she would like to return in her next life
Olivia Newton-John 1948– : in *Observer* 17
April 2005

Trust and Treachery

PROVERBS AND SAYINGS

1 **Fear the Greeks bearing gifts.**
English proverb, late 19th century; originally from
Virgil: see 19 below; see also 16 below, **Gifts** 8

2 **Please to remember the Fifth of
November,
Gunpowder Treason and Plot.
We know no reason why gunpowder
treason
Should ever be forgot.**
traditional rhyme on the Gunpowder Plot (1605); see
Festivals 24

3 **Promises, like pie-crust, are made to
be broken.**
English proverb, late 17th century

4 **Test before you trust.**
Russian proverb; see 42 below

5 **Would you buy a used car from
this man?**
campaign slogan directed against Richard
Nixon, 1968

6 **You cannot run with the hare and
hunt with the hounds.**
you must take one of two opposing sides; English
proverb, mid 15th century; see 12 below

PHRASES

7 **drop the pilot**
abandon a trustworthy adviser; from *dropping the
pilot*, caption to Tenniel's cartoon, and title of poem,
on Bismarck's dismissal as German Chancellor by the
young Kaiser; in *Punch* 29 March 1890

8 **fifth column**
an organized body sympathizing with and working
for the enemy within a country at war or otherwise
under attack; translating Spanish *quinta columna*, an
extra body of supporters claimed by General Mola as
being within Madrid when he besieged the city with
four columns of Nationalist forces in 1936

9 **Judas kiss**
an act of betrayal; *Judas* Iscariot, the disciple who
betrayed Jesus, after the Bible (Matthew), 'And he
that betrayed him gave them a sign, saying,
Whomsoever I shall kiss, that same is he: hold him
fast'; see 39 below

10 **night of the long knives**
a ruthless or decisive action held to resemble a
treacherous massacre; after the massacre (according
to legend) of the Britons by Hengist in 472, or of
Ernst Roehm and his associates by Hitler on 29–30
June 1934

11 **Punic faith**
treachery; from Latin *Punica fide* 'with Carthaginian
trustworthiness' (Sallust *Jugurtha*), reflecting the
traditional hostility of Rome to Carthage

12 **run with the hare and hunt with the
hounds**
try to remain on good terms with both sides in a
quarrel; play a double role; see 6 above

13 **a scrap of paper**
a treaty or pledge which one does not intend to
honour; said to have been used by the German
Chancellor, Bethmann-Hollweg (1856–1921) in
connection with German violation of Belgian
neutrality in August 1914; see **International
Relations** 24

14 **sell down the river**
let down, betray; originally of selling a troublesome
slave to the owner of a sugar cane plantation on the
lower Mississippi, where conditions were harsher
than in the northern slave states

15 **thirty pieces of silver**
a material gain for which a principle has been
betrayed; from the price for which Judas betrayed
Jesus to the Jewish authorities, as told in the Bible
(Matthew): 'and they covenanted with him for thirty
pieces of silver'; see **Death** 18

16 **Trojan horse**

a person or device deliberately set to bring about an enemy's downfall or to undermine from within; a hollow wooden statue of a horse in which the Greeks are said to have concealed themselves to enter Troy: see 19 below; see also **Computers** 8

17 **true blue**

faithful, staunch, and unwavering; perhaps with regard to the blue of the sky, or to some specially fast dye; from the mid 17th century applied specifically to the Scottish Presbyterian or Whig party, and later (in the current sense), to the Tory, or Conservative, Party; see **Political Parties** 16

QUOTATIONS

18 O put not your trust in princes, nor in any child of man: for there is no help in them.
Bible: Psalm 146

19   *Equo ne credite, Teucri.*
Quidquid id est, timeo Danaos et dona ferentes.
Do not trust the horse, Trojans. Whatever it is, I fear the Greeks even when they bring gifts.
Virgil 70–19 BC: *Aeneid*; see 1, 16 above, see also **Gifts** 8

20 *Et tu, Brute?*
You too, Brutus?
said to his friend Brutus as he was assassinated by him
Julius Caesar 100–44 BC: traditional rendering of Suetonius *Lives of the Caesars* 'Divus Julius'

21 This night, before the cock crow, thou shalt deny me thrice.
Bible: St Matthew

22 *Quis custodiet ipsos custodes?*
Who is to guard the guards themselves?
Juvenal c.AD 60–c.130: *Satires*

23 The smylere with the knyf under the cloke.
Geoffrey Chaucer 1343–1400: *The Canterbury Tales* 'The Knight's Tale'

24 I know what it is to be a subject, what to be a Sovereign, what to have good neighbours, and sometimes meet evil-willers.
the traditional version concludes: 'and in trust I have found treason'
Elizabeth I 1533–1603: speech to a Parliamentary deputation at Richmond, 12 November 1586; John Neale *Elizabeth I and her Parliaments 1584–1601* (1957), from a report 'which the Queen herself heavily amended in her own hand'

25 Treason doth never prosper, what's the reason?
For if it prosper, none dare call it treason.
John Harington 1561–1612: *Epigrams* (1618)

26 There is nothing makes a man suspect much, more than to know little.
Francis Bacon 1561–1626: *Essays* (1625) 'Of Suspicion'

27 A man who does not trust himself will never really trust anybody.
Cardinal de Retz 1613–79: *Mémoires* (1717)

28 It is better to suffer wrong than to do it, and happier to be sometimes cheated than not to trust.
Samuel Johnson 1709–84: in *Rambler* 18 December 1750

29 Caesar had his Brutus—Charles the First, his Cromwell—and George the Third—('Treason,' cried the Speaker) . . . *may profit by their example. If this* be treason, make the most of it.
Patrick Henry 1736–99: speech in the Virginia assembly, May 1765

30 *to the Emperor of Russia, who had spoken bitterly of those who had betrayed the cause of Europe:*
That, Sire, is a question of dates.
often quoted as, 'treason is a matter of dates'
Charles-Maurice de Talleyrand 1754–1838: Duff Cooper *Talleyrand* (1932)

31 Just for a handful of silver he left us,
Just for a riband to stick in his coat.
of Wordsworth's apparent betrayal of his radical principles by accepting the position of poet laureate
Robert Browning 1812–89: 'The Lost Leader' (1845)

32 And trust me not at all or all in all.
Alfred, Lord Tennyson 1809–92: *Idylls of the King* 'Merlin and Vivien' (1859)

33 A promise made is a debt unpaid, and the trail has its own stern code.
Robert W. Service 1874–1958: 'The Cremation of Sam McGee' (1907)

34 To trust people is a luxury in which only the wealthy can indulge; the poor cannot afford it.
E. M. Forster 1879–1970: *Howards End* (1910)

35 Anyone can rat, but it takes a certain amount of ingenuity to re-rat.
on rejoining the Conservatives twenty years after leaving them for the Liberals, c.1924
Winston Churchill 1874–1965: Kay Halle *Irrepressible Churchill* (1966)

36 He trusted neither of them as far as he could spit, and he was a poor spitter, lacking both distance and control.
P. G. Wodehouse 1881–1975: *Money in the Bank* (1946)

37 Greater love hath no man than this, that he lay down his friends for his life.

on Harold Macmillan sacking seven of his Cabinet on 13 July 1962

Jeremy Thorpe 1929– : D. E. Butler and Anthony King *The General Election of 1964* (1965); see **Self-Sacrifice** 4

38 To betray, you must first belong.

Kim Philby 1912–88: in *Sunday Times* 17 December 1967

39 Judas was paid! I am sacrificing my whole political life.

response to a heckler's call of 'Judas', having advised Conservatives to vote Labour at the coming general election

Enoch Powell 1912–98: speech at Bull Ring, Birmingham, 23 February 1974; see 9 above

40 Frankly speaking it is difficult to trust the Chinese. Once bitten by a snake you feel suspicious even when you see a piece of rope.

Dalai Lama 1935– : attributed, 1981; see **Caution** 19

41 He who wields the knife never wears the crown.

Michael Heseltine 1933– : in *New Society* 14 February 1986

42 We have listened to the wisdom in an old Russian maxim. And I'm sure you're familiar with it, Mr General Secretary. The maxim is . . . 'trust, but verify'.

Ronald Reagan 1911–2004: at the signing of the INF treaty on arms limitation, 8 December 1987, and used frequently thereafter; see 4 above

43 It is rather like sending your opening batsmen to the crease only for them to find the moment that the first balls are bowled that their bats have been broken before the game by the team captain.

Geoffrey Howe 1926– : resignation speech as Deputy Prime Minister, House of Commons 13 November 1990

⤜⤜ Truth ⤚⤚

see also **Honesty, Lies**

PROVERBS AND SAYINGS

1 Believe it or not.

title of syndicated newspaper feature (from 1918), written by Robert L. Ripley

2 Many a true word is spoken in jest.

an apparent joke may often include a shrewd comment, or that what is spoken of as unlikely or improbable may in the future turn out to be true; English proverb, late 14th century

3 Se non è vero, è molto ben trovato.

Italian = If it is not true, it is a happy invention; common saying from the 16th century; see 11 below

4 Tell the truth and shame the devil.

by telling the truth one is taking the right course however embarrassing or difficult it may be; English proverb, mid 16th century; see 7 below

5 Truth is stranger than fiction.

implying that no invention can be as remarkable as what may actually happen; English proverb, early

19th century, from Byron: see 29 below; see also **Fiction** 1

6 Truth lies at the bottom of a well.

sometimes used to imply that the truth of a situation can be hard to find; English proverb, mid 16th century

7 Truth makes the Devil blush.

English proverb, mid 20th century; see 4 above

8 Truth will out.

in the end what has really happened will become apparent; English proverb, mid 15th century

9 What everybody says must be true.

sometimes used ironically to assert that popular gossip is often inaccurate; English proverb, late 14th century

10 When you shoot an arrow of truth, dip its point in honey.

advocating tact; Arab proverb

PHRASES

11 ben trovato

happily invented; appropriate though untrue; Italian, literally 'well found': see 3 above

12 the truth, the whole truth, and nothing but the truth

the absolute truth, without concealment or addition; part of the formula of the oath taken by witnesses in court

QUOTATIONS

13 Great is Truth, and mighty above all things.
Bible: I Esdras

14 But, my dearest Agathon, it is truth which you cannot contradict; you can without any difficulty contradict Socrates.
Socrates 469–399 BC: Plato *Symposium*

15 Plato is dear to me, but dearer still is truth.
Aristotle 384–322 BC: attributed

16 And ye shall know the truth, and the truth shall make you free.
Bible: St John; see 37 below

17 Truth will come to light; murder cannot be hid long.
William Shakespeare 1564–1616: *The Merchant of Venice* (1596–8)

18 What is truth? said jesting Pilate; and would not stay for an answer.
Francis Bacon 1561–1626: *Essays* (1625) 'Of Truth'

19 Many from . . . an inconsiderate zeal unto truth, have too rashly charged the troops of error, and remain as trophies unto the enemies of truth.
Thomas Browne 1605–82: *Religio Medici* (1643)

20 Though all the winds of doctrine were let loose to play upon the earth, so Truth be in the field, we do injuriously by licensing and prohibiting to misdoubt her strength. Let her and Falsehood grapple; who ever knew Truth put to the worse, in a free and open encounter?
John Milton 1608–74: *Areopagitica* (1644)

21 True and False are attributes of speech, not of things. And where speech is not, there is neither Truth nor Falsehood.
Thomas Hobbes 1588–1679: *Leviathan* (1651)

22 It is one thing to show a man that he is in error, and another to put him in possession of truth.
John Locke 1632–1704: *An Essay concerning Human Understanding* (1690)

23 I design plain truth for plain people.
John Wesley 1703–91: *Sermons on Several Occasions* (1746)

24 It is commonly said, and more particularly by Lord Shaftesbury, that ridicule is the best test of truth.
Lord Chesterfield 1694–1773: *Letters to his Son* (1774) 6 February 1752

25 In lapidary inscriptions a man is not upon oath.
Samuel Johnson 1709–84: James Boswell *Life of Samuel Johnson* (1791) 1775

26 If God were to hold out enclosed in His right hand all Truth, and in His left hand just the active search for Truth, though with the condition that I should always err therein, and He should say to me: Choose! I should humbly take His left hand and say: Father! Give me this one; absolute Truth belongs to Thee alone.
G. E. Lessing 1729–81: *Eine Duplik* (1778)

27 A truth that's told with bad intent
Beats all the lies you can invent.
William Blake 1757–1827: 'Auguries of Innocence' (*c.*1803)

28 I am certain of nothing but the holiness of the heart's affections and the truth of imagination—what the imagination seizes as beauty must be truth—whether it existed before or not.
John Keats 1795–1821: letter to Benjamin Bailey, 22 November 1817; see **Beauty** 22

29 'Tis strange—but true; for truth is always strange;
Stranger than fiction.
Lord Byron 1788–1824: *Don Juan* (1819–24); see 5 above

30 What I tell you three times is true.
Lewis Carroll 1832–98: *The Hunting of the Snark* (1876)

31 It is the customary fate of new truths to begin as heresies and to end as superstitions.
T. H. Huxley 1825–95: *Science and Culture and Other Essays* (1881) 'The Coming of Age of the Origin of Species'

32 The truth is rarely pure, and never simple.
Oscar Wilde 1854–1900: *The Importance of Being Earnest* (1895)

33 Truth is the most valuable thing we have. Let us economize it.
Mark Twain 1835–1910: *Following the Equator* (1897); see 42 below

34 A platitude is simply a truth repeated until people get tired of hearing it.
Stanley Baldwin 1867–1947: speech, House of Commons, 29 May 1924

35 An exaggeration is a truth that has lost its temper.
Kahlil Gibran 1883–1931: *Sand and Foam* (1926)

36 The truth is often a terrible weapon of aggression. It is possible to lie, and even to murder, for the truth.
Alfred Adler 1870–1937: *The Problems of Neurosis* (1929)

37 The truth which makes men free is for the most part the truth which men prefer not to hear.
Herbert Agar 1897–1980: *A Time for Greatness* (1942); see 16 above

38 There are no whole truths; all truths are half-truths. It is trying to treat them as whole truths that plays the devil.
Alfred North Whitehead 1861–1947: *Dialogues* (1954)

39 Truth exists; only lies are invented.
Georges Braque 1882–1963: *Le Jour et la nuit: Cahiers 1917–52*

40 One of the favourite maxims of my father was the distinction between the two sorts of truths, profound truths recognized by the fact that the opposite is also a profound truth, in contrast to trivialities where opposites are obviously absurd.
Niels Bohr 1885–1962: S. Rozental *Niels Bohr* (1967)

41 Truth is not merely what we are thinking, but also why, to whom and under what circumstances we say it.
Václav Havel 1936– : *Temptation* (1985)

42 It contains a misleading impression, not a lie. It was being economical with the truth.
the phrase 'economy of truth' was earlier used by Edmund Burke (1729–97)
Robert Armstrong 1927– : referring to a letter during the 'Spycatcher' trial, Supreme Court, New South Wales, in *Daily Telegraph* 19 November 1986; see 33 above, **Lies** 8

43 In exceptional circumstances it is necessary to say something that is untrue in the House of Commons.
William Waldegrave 1946– : in *Guardian* 9 March 1994

⤜ The Universe ⤛

see also **The Earth, The Skies**

PHRASES

1 big bang
the explosion of dense matter which according to current cosmological theories marked the origin of the universe; see 15 below

2 the four elements
earth, air, fire, and water; collectively regarded as constituents of the material world by ancient and medieval philosophers

3 Ptolemaic system
the theory that the earth is the stationary centre of the universe, with the planets moving in epicyclic orbits within surrounding concentric spheres; after Ptolemy (2nd century), Greek astronomer and geographer; see 6 below, see also **Music** 4

QUOTATIONS

4 Is it not worthy of tears that, when the number of worlds is infinite, we have not yet become lords of a single one?
when asked why he wept on hearing from Anaxarchus that there was an infinite number of worlds
Alexander the Great 356–323 BC: Plutarch *Moralia*

5 The universe and I exist together, and all things and I are one.
Zhuangzi c.369–286 BC: *Chuang Tzu* ch. 2

6 Had I been present at the Creation, I would have given some useful hints for the better ordering of the universe.
on studying the Ptolemaic system
Alfonso 'the Wise' of Castile 1221–84: attributed; see 3 above

7 The eternal silence of these infinite spaces [the heavens] terrifies me.
Blaise Pascal 1623–62: *Pensées* (1670)

8 *on hearing that Margaret Fuller 'accepted the universe':*
'Gad! she'd better!'
Thomas Carlyle 1795–1881: William James *Varieties of Religious Experience* (1902)

9 The world is everything that is the case.
Ludwig Wittgenstein 1889–1951: *Tractatus Logico-Philosophicus* (1922)

10 Now, my own suspicion is that the universe is not only queerer than we suppose, but queerer than we *can* suppose . . . I suspect that there are more things in heaven and earth than are dreamed of, or can be dreamed of, in any philosophy.
J. B. S. Haldane 1892–1964: *Possible Worlds and Other Essays* (1927) 'Possible Worlds'; see **The Supernatural** 11

11 From the intrinsic evidence of his creation, the Great Architect of the Universe now begins to appear as a pure mathematician.
James Jeans 1877–1946: *The Mysterious Universe* (1930)

12 This, now, is the judgement of our scientific age—the third reaction of man upon the universe! This universe is not hostile, nor yet is it friendly. It is simply indifferent.
John H. Holmes 1879–1964: *The Sensible Man's View of Religion* (1932)

13 The eternal mystery of the world is its comprehensibility . . . The fact that it is comprehensible is a miracle.
usually quoted as 'The most incomprehensible fact about the universe is that it is comprehensible'
Albert Einstein 1879–1955: in *Franklin Institute Journal* March 1936 'Physics and Reality'

14 Ptolemy made a universe, which lasted 1400 years. Newton, also, made a universe, which lasted 300 years. Einstein has made a universe, and I can't tell you how long that will last.
George Bernard Shaw 1856–1950: David Cassidy *Einstein and Our World* (1995)

15 One [idea] was that the Universe started its life a finite time ago in a single huge explosion. . . . This big bang idea seemed to me to be unsatisfactory.
Fred Hoyle 1915–2001: *The Nature of the Universe* (1950); see 1 above

16 The Greeks said God was always doing geometry, modern physicists say he's playing roulette, everything depends on the observer, the universe is a totality of observations, it's a work of art created by us.
Iris Murdoch 1919–99: *The Good Apprentice* (1985); see **God** 8

17 What is it that breathes fire into the equations and makes a universe for them to describe . . . Why does the universe go to all the bother of existing?
Stephen Hawking 1942– : *A Brief History of Time* (1988)

18 Space is almost infinite. As a matter of fact, we think it is infinite.
Dan Quayle 1947– : in *Daily Telegraph* 8 March 1989

19 It is often said that there is no such thing as a free lunch. The Universe, however, is a free lunch.
Alan Guth 1947– : in *Harpers* November 1994; see **Economics** 3

⤜ Universities ⤛

see also **Education, Teaching**

PROVERBS AND SAYINGS

1 **Lady Margaret Hall for ladies,
St Hugh's for girls,
St Hilda's for wenches,**

Somerville for women.
Oxford saying, *c.* 1930s

PHRASES

2 **the Ivy League**
a group of long-established eastern US universities of high academic and social prestige, including Harvard, Yale, Princeton, and Columbia

3 **redbrick university**
a British university founded in the late 19th or early 20th century, usually in a large industrial city, and

especially as contrasted with Oxford and Cambridge; see 22 below

4 **town and gown**
non-members and members of a university in a particular place; *gown* as worn by members of a university

QUOTATIONS

5 A Clerk there was of Oxenford also,
That unto logyk hadde longe ygo.
As leene was his hors as is a rake,
And he was nat right fat, I undertake,
But looked holwe, and therto sobrely.
Geoffrey Chaucer 1343–1400: *The Canterbury Tales* 'The General Prologue'

6 Universities incline wits to sophistry and affectation.
Francis Bacon 1561–1626: *Valerius Terminus of the Interpretation of Nature*

7 Aye, 'tis well enough for a servant to be bred at an University. But the education is a little too pedantic for a gentleman.
William Congreve 1670–1729: *Love for Love* (1695)

8 The discipline of colleges and universities is in general contrived, not for the benefit of the students, but for the interest, or more properly speaking, for the ease of the masters.
Adam Smith 1723–90: *Wealth of Nations* (1776)

9 To the University of Oxford I acknowledge no obligation; and she will as cheerfully renounce me for a son, as I am willing to disclaim her for a mother. I spent fourteen months at Magdalen College: they proved the fourteen months the most idle and unprofitable of my whole life.
Edward Gibbon 1737–94: *Memoirs of My Life* (1796)

10 The most prominent requisite to a lecturer, though perhaps not really the most important, is a good delivery; for though to all true philosophers science and nature will have charms innumerable in every dress, yet I am sorry to say that the generality of mankind cannot accompany us one short hour unless the path is strewed with flowers.
Michael Faraday 1791–1867: *Advice to a Lecturer* (1960); from his letters and notebook written at age 21

11 Universities never reform themselves; everyone knows that.
Lord Melbourne 1779–1848: speech, House of Lords, 11 April 1837

12 The true University of these days is a collection of books.
Thomas Carlyle 1795–1881: *On Heroes, Hero-Worship, and the Heroic* (1841)

13 A classic lecture, rich in sentiment,
With scraps of thundrous epic lilted out
By violet-hooded Doctors, elegies
And quoted odes, and jewels five-words-long,
That on the stretched forefinger of all Time
Sparkle for ever.
Alfred, Lord Tennyson 1809–92: *The Princess* (1847)

14 A whaleship was my Yale College and my Harvard.
Herman Melville 1819–91: *Moby Dick* (1851)

15 Nor can I do better, in conclusion, than impress upon you the study of Greek literature, which not only elevates above the vulgar herd, but leads not infrequently to positions of considerable emolument.
Thomas Gaisford 1779–1855: Christmas Day Sermon in the Cathedral, Oxford; W. Tuckwell *Reminiscences of Oxford* (2nd ed., 1907)

16 Home of lost causes, and forsaken beliefs, and unpopular names, and impossible loyalties!
of Oxford
Matthew Arnold 1822–88: *Essays in Criticism* First Series (1865)

17 A University should be a place of light, of liberty, and of learning.
Benjamin Disraeli 1804–81: speech, House of Commons, 11 March 1873

18 Undergraduates owe their happiness chiefly to the consciousness that they are no longer at school. The nonsense which was knocked out of them at school is all put gently back at Oxford or Cambridge.
Max Beerbohm 1872–1956: *More* (1899)

19 Gentlemen: I have not had your advantages. What poor education I have received has been gained in the University of Life.
Horatio Bottomley 1860–1933: speech at the Oxford Union, 2 December 1920

20 Our American professors like their literature clear and cold and pure and very dead.
Sinclair Lewis 1885–1951: Nobel Prize Address, 12 December 1930

21 Princeton is a wonderful little spot. A quaint and ceremonious village of puny demigods on stilts.
Albert Einstein 1879–1955: letter to Queen Elisabeth of Belgium, 20 November 1933

22 I don't think one 'comes down' from Jimmy's university. According to him, it's not even red brick, but white tile.
John Osborne 1929–94: *Look Back in Anger* (1956); see 3 above

23 The delusion that there are thousands of young people about who are capable of benefiting from university training, but have somehow failed to find their way there, is . . . a necessary component of the expansionist case . . . More will mean worse.
Kingsley Amis 1922–95: in *Encounter* July 1960

24 Four times, under our educational rules, the human pack is shuffled and cut—at eleven-plus, sixteen-plus, eighteen-plus and twenty-plus—and happy is he who comes top of the deck on each occasion, but especially the last. This is called Finals, the very name of which implies that nothing of importance can happen after it.
David Lodge 1935– : *Changing Places* (1975)

25 City of perspiring dreams.
of Cambridge
Frederic Raphael 1931– : *The Glittering Prizes* (1976); see **British Towns** 18

26 There is one thing that a professor can be absolutely certain of: almost every student entering the university believes, or says he believes, that truth is relative.
Allan Bloom 1930–92: *The Closing of the American Mind* (1987)

27 Why am I the first Kinnock in a thousand generations to be able to get to a university?
later plagiarized by the American politician Joe Biden
Neil Kinnock 1942– : speech in party political broadcast, 21 May 1987

28 As to our universities, I've come to the conclusion that they are élitist where they should be egalitarian and egalitarian where they should be élitist.
David Lodge 1935– : *Nice Work* (1989)

⤚ Value ⤙

PROVERBS AND SAYINGS

1 Everything has a price, but jade is priceless.
modern saying, said to derive from a Chinese proverb extolling the value of jade

2 Gold may be bought too dear.
wealth may be acquired at too great a price; English proverb, mid 16th century

3 If you pay peanuts, you get monkeys.
a poor rate of pay will attract only poorly qualified and incompetent staff (*peanuts* here means 'a small sum of money'); English proverb, mid 20th century

4 It is a poor dog that's not worth whistling for.
a dog is of no value if the owner will not even go to the trouble of whistling for it; English proverb, mid 16th century

5 Little things please little minds.
English proverb, late 16th century

6 Nothing comes of nothing.
English proverb, late 14th century

7 Nothing for nothing.
summarizing the attitude that nothing will be offered unless a return is assured; English proverb, early 18th century

8 What can a monkey know of the taste of ginger?
ginger was a rare and expensive delicacy; Indian proverb

9 Worth a guinea a box.
advertising slogan for Beecham's pills, from *c.*1859, from the chance remark of a lady purchaser

10 The worth of a thing is what it will bring.
the real value of something can only be measured by what another person is willing to pay for it; English proverb, mid 16th century

PHRASES

11 bang for one's buck
an informal US expression meaning value for money; the phrase was notably used in 1954 by Charles E. Wilson: see **Warfare** 2

12 elephants' graveyard
a repository for unwanted goods, from the belief (recorded from the early 20th century) that elephants in the wild seek out a particular spot in which to die, where their remains then lie

13 the end of the rainbow
the place where something precious is found at last; with allusion to the proverbial belief in the existence of a crock of gold (or something else of great value) at the end of a rainbow; see **18** below

14 golden calf
something, especially wealth, as an object of excessive or unworthy worship; from the story in the Bible (Exodus) of the idol made and worshipped by the Israelites in disobedience to Moses

15 holy of holies
a thing regarded as sacrosanct; the inner chamber of the sanctuary in the Jewish Temple, separated by a veil from the outer chamber

16 make a mountain out of a molehill
laying unnecessary stress on a small matter; see **Optimism** 36

17 mess of pottage
a material or trivial comfort gained at the expense of something more important; the price, according to the Bible (Genesis), for which Esau sold his birthright to his brother Jacob; see **Theatre** 2

18 pot of gold
an imaginary reward; a jackpot; an ideal; supposedly to be found at *the end of the rainbow*: see **13** above

19 pride of place
the most prominent or important position among a group of things; in falconry, the high position from which a falcon or similar bird swoops down on its prey; first recorded in Shakespeare's *Macbeth*

QUOTATIONS

20 Thirty spokes share the wheel's hub;
It is the centre hole that makes it useful.
Shape clay into a vessel;
It is the space within that makes it useful.
Cut doors and windows for a room;
It is the holes which make it useful.
Therefore profit comes from what is there;
Usefulness from what is not there.
Lao Tzu c.604–c.531 BC: *Tao-Te Ching*

21 A living dog is better than a dead lion.
Bible: Ecclesiastes; see **Life** 7

22 Neither cast ye your pearls before swine.
Bible: St Matthew; see **Futility** 8

23 Men do not weigh the stalk for that it was,
When once they find her flower, her glory,
pass.
Samuel Daniel 1563–1619: *Delia* (1592) sonnet 32

24 O monstrous! but one half-pennyworth of
bread to this intolerable deal of sack!
William Shakespeare 1564–1616: *Henry IV, Part 1*
(1597)

25　　　Of one whose hand,
Like the base Indian, threw a pearl away
Richer than all his tribe.
William Shakespeare 1564–1616: *Othello*
(1602–4)

26　　　Then on the shore
Of the wide world I stand alone and think
Till love and fame to nothingness do sink.
John Keats 1795–1821: 'When I have fears that I
may cease to be' (written 1818)

27 It is not that pearls fetch a high price *because*
men have dived for them; but on the
contrary, men dive for them because they
fetch a high price.
Richard Whately 1787–1863: *Introductory Lectures
on Political Economy* (1832)

28 An acre in Middlesex is better than a
principality in Utopia.
Lord Macaulay 1800–59: *Essays Contributed to the
Edinburgh Review* (1843) 'Lord Bacon'

29 Every man is wanted, and no man is wanted
much.
Ralph Waldo Emerson 1803–82: *Essays. Second
Series* (1844) 'Nominalist and Realist'

30 You can calculate the worth of a man by the
number of his enemies, and the importance
of a work of art by the harm that is spoken
of it.
Gustave Flaubert 1821–80: letter to Louise Colet,
14 June 1853

31 Nothink for nothink 'ere, and precious little
for sixpence.
Punch: in 1869

32 I never loved a dear Gazelle—
Nor anything that cost me much:
High prices profit those who sell,
But why should I be fond of such?
Lewis Carroll 1832–98: *Phantasmagoria* (1869)
'Theme with Variations'; see **Transience** 11

33 It is the peculiar beauty of this method,
gentlemen, and the one that endears it to
the really scientific mind that under no
circumstances can it possibly be of the
smallest possible utility to anyone.
H. J. A. Smith 1826–83: C. H. Pearson *Biographical
Sketches and Recollections of Henry John Skipton Scott*
(1894)

34 I cannot help it that my pictures do not sell.
Nevertheless the time will come when
people will see that they are worth more
than the price of the paint.
Vincent Van Gogh 1853–90: letter to his brother
Theo, 20 October 1888

35 It has long been an axiom of mine that the
little things are infinitely the most
important.
Arthur Conan Doyle 1859–1930: *Adventures of
Sherlock Holmes* (1892)

36 No more impressive warning can be given to
those who would confine knowledge and
research to what is apparently useful, than
the reflection that conic sections were
studied for eighteen hundred years merely
as an abstract science, without regard to any
utility other than to satisfy the craving for
knowledge on the part of mathematicians,
and that then at the end of this long period
of abstract study, they were found to be the
necessary key with which to attain the
knowledge of the most important laws of
nature.
Alfred North Whitehead 1861–1947: *Introduction
to Mathematics* (1911)

37 Precious . . . My Precious!
Gollum, referring to the Ring
J. R. R. Tolkien 1892–1973: *The Lord of the Rings* pt.
3 *The Return of the King* (1955)

38 Nothing that costs only a dollar is worth
having.
Elizabeth Arden 1876–1966: attributed; in *Fortune*
October 1973

⤛Violence⤜

1 **Burn, baby, burn.**
black extremist slogan in use during the Los Angeles riots, August 1965

PHRASES

2 **blood and thunder**
violence and bloodshed, especially in fiction

QUOTATIONS

3 Force, unaided by judgement, collapses through its own weight.
Horace 65–8 BC: *Odes*

4 Resist not evil: but whosoever shall smite thee on thy right cheek, turn to him the other also.
Bible: St Matthew; see 7 below, **Forgiveness** 9

5 All they that take the sword shall perish with the sword.
Bible: St Matthew

6 Who overcomes
By force, hath overcome but half his foe.
John Milton 1608–74: *Paradise Lost* (1667)

7 Wisdom has taught us to be calm and meek,
To take one blow, and turn the other cheek;
It is not written what a man shall do
If the rude caitiff smite the other too!
Oliver Wendell Holmes 1809–94: 'Non-Resistance' (1861); see 4 above

8 If you strike a child take care that you strike it in anger, even at the risk of maiming it for life. A blow in cold blood neither can nor should be forgiven.
George Bernard Shaw 1856–1950: *Man and Superman* (1903) 'Maxims: How to Beat Children'; see **Emotions** 4

9 Non-violence is the first article of my faith. It is also the last article of my creed.
Mahatma Gandhi 1869–1948: speech at Shahi Bag, 18 March 1922, on a charge of sedition

10 A man may build himself a throne of bayonets, but he cannot sit on it.
quoted by Boris Yeltsin at the time of the failed military coup in Russia, August 1991
William Ralph Inge 1860–1954: *Philosophy of Plotinus* (1923)

11 Where force is necessary, there it must be applied boldly, decisively and completely. But one must know the limitations of force; one must know when to blend force with a manoeuvre, a blow with an agreement.
Leon Trotsky 1879–1940: *What Next?* (1932)

12 Pale Ebenezer thought it wrong to fight,
But Roaring Bill (who killed him) thought it right.
Hilaire Belloc 1870–1953: 'The Pacifist' (1938)

13 In violence, we forget who we are.
Mary McCarthy 1912–89: *On the Contrary* (1961) 'Characters in Fiction'

14 I don't think there is anything particularly wrong about hitting a woman—although I don't recommend doing it in the same way that you'd hit a man.
Sean Connery 1930– : in *Playboy* November 1965

15 A riot is at bottom the language of the unheard.
Martin Luther King 1929–68: *Where Do We Go From Here?* (1967)

16 I say violence is necessary. It is as American as cherry pie.
H. Rap Brown 1943– : speech at Washington, 27 July 1967

17 Keep violence in the mind
Where it belongs.
Brian Aldiss 1925– : *Barefoot in the Head* (1969) 'Charteris'

18 The only thing that's been a worse flop than the organization of non-violence has been the organization of violence.
Joan Baez 1941– : *Daybreak* (1970)

19 The quietly pacifist peaceful
always die
to make room for men
who shout.
Alice Walker 1944– : 'The QPP' (1973)

20 The terrible thing about terrorism is that ultimately it destroys those who practise it. Slowly but surely, as they try to extinguish life in others, the light within them dies.
Terry Waite 1939– : in *Guardian* 20 February 1992

⤙ Virtue ⤚

see also **Good and Evil, Sin**

PROVERBS AND SAYINGS

1 The good die young.
English proverb, late 17th century, often used ironically; see **Youth** 3

2 Good men are scarce.
English proverb, early 17th century

3 He lives long who lives well.
the reputation derived from living a good and moral life will mean that one's name will last; English proverb, mid 16th century

4 No good deed goes unpunished.
modern humorous saying, sometimes attributed to Oscar Wilde but not traced in his writings

5 See no evil, hear no evil, speak no evil.
conventionally represented by 'the three wise monkeys' covering their eyes, ears, and mouth respectively with their hands, and used particularly to imply a deliberate refusal to notice something that is wrong; English proverb, early 20th century; see **Good and Evil** 13

6 Virtue is its own reward.
the satisfaction of knowing that one has observed appropriate moral standards should be all that is sought; English proverb, early 16th century

PHRASES

7 the book of life
the record of those achieving salvation; after the Bible (Revelation) 'I will not blot out his name out of the book of life'

8 a cardinal virtue
a particular strength or attribute; each of the chief moral attributes (originally of scholastic philosophy), justice, prudence, temperance, and fortitude, which with the three theological virtues of faith, hope, and charity, comprise the seven virtues; *cardinal* meaning 'a hinge'

9 odour of sanctity
a state of holiness or saintliness; translation of French *odeur de sainteté* a sweet or balsamic odour reputedly emitted by the bodies of saints at or after death

10 pure as the driven snow
completely pure; *driven* of snow that has been piled into drifts or made smooth by the wind; see **46** below

11 salt of the earth
of complete kindness, honesty, and reliability; after the Bible (Matthew) 'Ye are the salt of the earth'

12 sans peur et sans reproche
without fear and without blame, fearless and blameless; French; *Chevalier sans peur et sans reproche* 'Fearless, blameless knight' was the description in contemporary chronicles of Pierre Bayard (1476–1524)

13 the unco guid
those who are professedly strict in matters of morals and religion; originally alluding to Robert Burns 'Address to the Unco Guid, or the Rigidly Righteous': see **Temptation** 11

14 Victorian values
values based on high standards of self-reliance and personal morality supposedly typical of the reign of Queen Victoria (1819–1901), but alternatively regarded as representing a restrictive moral earnestness; associated particularly with Margaret Thatcher as Conservative Prime Minister: see **49** below

15 without any spot or wrinkle
without any moral stain or blemish; originally in Tyndale's translation of the Bible (Ephesians)

QUOTATIONS

16 Strait is the gate, and narrow is the way, which leadeth unto life, and few there be that find it.
Bible: St Matthew

17 *Puro e disposto a salire alle stelle.*
Pure and ready to mount to the stars.
Dante Alighieri 1265–1321: *Divina Commedia* 'Purgatorio'

18 Would that we had spent one whole day well in this world!
Thomas à Kempis 1380–1471: *The Imitation of Christ*

19 We may not look at our pleasure to go to heaven in feather-beds; it is not the way.
Thomas More 1478–1535: William Roper *Life of Sir Thomas More*

20 Our goodness derives not from our capacity to think but to love.
St Teresa of Ávila 1512–82: *Book of the Foundations* (1610)

21 How far that little candle throws his beams! So shines a good deed in a naughty world.
William Shakespeare 1564–1616: *The Merchant of Venice* (1596–8)

22 Dost thou think, because thou art virtuous, there shall be no more cakes and ale?
William Shakespeare 1564–1616: *Twelfth Night* (1601); see Pleasure 3

23 Virtue is like a rich stone, best plain set.
Francis Bacon 1561–1626: *Essays* (1625) 'Of Beauty'

24 I cannot praise a fugitive and cloistered virtue, unexercised and unbreathed, that never sallies out and sees her adversary, but slinks out of the race, where that immortal garland is to be run for, not without dust and heat.
John Milton 1608–74: *Areopagitica* (1644)

25 Instead of dirt and poison we have rather chosen to fill our hives with honey and wax; thus furnishing mankind with the two noblest of things, which are sweetness and light.
Jonathan Swift 1667–1745: *The Battle of the Books* (1704); see Behaviour 16

26 When men grow virtuous in their old age, they only make a sacrifice to God of the devil's leavings.
Alexander Pope 1688–1744: *Miscellanies* (1727) 'Thoughts on Various Subjects'

27 Virtue she finds too painful an endeavour, Content to dwell in decencies for ever.
Alexander Pope 1688–1744: *Epistles to Several Persons* 'To a Lady' (1735)

28 Let humble Allen, with an awkward shame, Do good by stealth, and blush to find it fame.
Alexander Pope 1688–1744: *Imitations of Horace* (1738)

29 The virtue which requires to be ever guarded is scarce worth the sentinel.
Oliver Goldsmith 1728–74: *The Vicar of Wakefield* (1766)

30 Tell me, ye divines, which is the most virtuous man, he who begets twenty bastards, or he who sacrifices an hundred thousand lives?
Horace Walpole 1717–97: letter to Sir Horace Mann, 7 July 1778

31 Minute attention to propriety stops the growth of virtue.
Mary Wollstonecraft 1759–97: letter to Everina Wollstonecraft, 4 March 1787

32 Virtue knows to a farthing what it has lost by not having been vice.
Horace Walpole 1717–97: L. Kronenberger *The Extraordinary Mr Wilkes* (1974)

33   That best portion of a good man's life,
His little, nameless, unremembered, acts
Of kindness and of love.
William Wordsworth 1770–1850: 'Lines composed a few miles above Tintern Abbey' (1798)

34 The greatest offence against virtue is to speak ill of it.
William Hazlitt 1778–1830: *Sketches and Essays* (1839) 'On Cant and Hypocrisy'

35 My strength is as the strength of ten, Because my heart is pure.
Alfred, Lord Tennyson 1809–92: 'Sir Galahad' (1842)

36 More people are flattered into virtue than bullied out of vice.
R. S. Surtees 1805–64: *The Analysis of the Hunting Field* (1846)

37 I expect to pass through this world but once; any good thing therefore that I can do, or any kindness that I can show to any fellow-creature, let me do it now; let me not defer or neglect it, for I shall not pass this way again.
Stephen Grellet 1773–1855: attributed; see John o' London *Treasure Trove* (1925) for some of the many other claimants to authorship

38 Be good, sweet maid, and let who will be clever.
Charles Kingsley 1819–75: 'A Farewell' (1858)

39 If some great Power would agree to make me always think what is true and do what is right, on condition of being turned into a sort of clock and wound up every morning before I got out of bed, I should instantly close with the offer.
T. H. Huxley 1825–95: 'On Descartes' *Discourse on Method*' (written 1870)

40 Few things are harder to put up with than the annoyance of a good example.
Mark Twain 1835–1910: *Pudd'nhead Wilson* (1894)

41 No people do so much harm as those who go about doing good.
Mandell Creighton 1843–1901: *The Life and Letters of Mandell Creighton* by his wife (1904)

42 She was poor but she was honest
Victim of a rich man's game.
First he loved her, then he left her,
And she lost her maiden name . . .
Anonymous: 'She was Poor but she was Honest'; sung by British soldiers in the First World War

43 'Goodness, what beautiful diamonds!'
'Goodness had nothing to do with it.'
Mae West 1892–1980: *Night After Night* (1932 film)

44 If all the good people were clever,
And all clever people were good,
The world would be nicer than ever
We thought that it possibly could.
But somehow, 'tis seldom or never
The two hit it off as they should;
The good are so harsh to the clever,
The clever so rude to the good!
Elizabeth Wordsworth 1840–1932: 'Good and Clever'

45 Courage is not simply *one* of the virtues but the form of every virtue at the testing point.
C. S. Lewis 1898–1963: Cyril Connolly *The Unquiet Grave* (1944)

46 I'm as pure as the driven slush.
Tallulah Bankhead 1903–68: in *Saturday Evening Post* 12 April 1947; see 10 above

47 Terrible is the temptation to be good.
Bertolt Brecht 1898–1956: *The Caucasian Chalk Circle* (1948)

48   What after all
Is a halo? It's only one more thing to keep clean.
Christopher Fry 1907– : *The Lady's not for Burning* (1949)

49 I was asked whether I was trying to restore Victorian values. I said straight out I was. And I am.
Margaret Thatcher 1925– : speech to the British Jewish Community, 21 July 1983, referring to an interview with Brian Walden on 17 January 1983; see 14 above

⇥ Wales ⇤

PHRASES

1 Land of my Fathers
Wales; from the opening words of the first verse of the Welsh national anthem by Evan James; see 5, 8 below

2 Little England beyond Wales
the English-speaking area of Pembrokeshire (Dyfed); a name first recorded in Camden's *Britannia* (1586)

QUOTATIONS

3 Who dare compare the English, the most degraded of all the races under heaven, with the Welsh?
Giraldus Cambrensis 1146–?1220?: attributed

4 Though it appear a little out of fashion,
There is much care and valour in this Welshman.
William Shakespeare 1564–1616: *Henry V* (1599)

5 Wales, Wales, sweet are thy hills and vales,
Thy speech, thy song,
To thee belong,
O may they live ever in Wales.
Evan James: 'Land of My Fathers' (1856); see 1 above

6 Among our ancient mountains,
And from our lovely vales,
Oh, let the prayer re-echo:
'God bless the Prince of Wales!'
George Linley 1798–1865: 'God Bless the Prince of Wales' (1862 song); translated from the Welsh original by J. C. Hughes (1837–87)

7 'I often think,' he continued, 'that we can trace almost all the disasters of English history to the influence of Wales!'
Evelyn Waugh 1903–66: *Decline and Fall* (1928)

8 The land of my fathers. My fathers can have it.
Dylan Thomas 1914–53: in *Adam* December 1953; see 1 above

9 It profits a man nothing to give his soul for the whole world . . . But for Wales—!
Robert Bolt 1924–95: *A Man for All Seasons* (1960); see **Success** 24

10 I wanted a play that would paint the full face of sensuality, rebellion and revivalism. In South Wales these three phenomena have played second fiddle only to Rugby Union which is a distillation of all three.
Gwyn Thomas 1913–81: introduction to *Jackie the Jumper* (1962)

11 Everyday when I wake up, I thank the Lord I'm Welsh.
Cerys Matthews 1969– : 'International Velvet' (1998 song)

12 What are they for? They are always so
pleased with themselves.
of the Welsh; comment made on BBC2's *Room 101*
programme
Anne Robinson 1944– : in *Daily Telegraph* 7
March 2001

⊁⊱ Warfare ⊰⊱

see also **The Armed Forces, Peace, Wars**

PROVERBS AND SAYINGS

1 **A bayonet is a weapon with a worker
at each end.**
British pacifist slogan (1940)

2 **A bigger bang for a buck.**
Charles E. Wilson's defence policy, in *Newsweek* 22
March 1954; see **Value** 11

3 **War will cease when men refuse to
fight.**
pacifist slogan, from *c.*1936; often quoted as 'Wars
will cease . . . '

PHRASES

5 **blood and iron**
military force as distinguished from diplomacy;
translation of German *Blut und Eisen*: see
International Relations 22

6 **dogs of war**
the havoc accompanying war; from Shakespeare
Julius Caesar: see **Revenge** 13

7 **draw one's sword against**
take up arms against, attack; see **Revolution** 4

8 **fog of war**
used to describe the complexity of military conflicts.
Fog of war is often attributed to the Prussian military
theorist Karl von Clausewitz (1780–1831), but is in
fact a paraphrase of what he said: 'War is the realm
of uncertainty; three quarters of the factors on which
action in war is based are wrapped in a fog of greater
or lesser uncertainty.'

4 **When war is declared, Truth is the
first casualty.**
epigraph to Arthur Ponsonby's *Falsehood in Wartime*
(1928), perhaps deriving from Johnson: see 21
below; attributed also to Hiram Johnson, speaking in
the US Senate, 1918, but not recorded in his speech

9 **just war**
a war which is deemed to be morally or theologically
justifiable; in the Middle Ages, St Thomas Aquinas
laid down three conditions which a *just war* must
meet: it had to be authorized by the sovereign, the
cause must be just, and those engaging in it must
have the intention of advancing good or avoiding
evil; see **34** below

10 **shock and awe**
term for a military strategy based on achieving rapid
dominance over an adversary by the initial
imposition of overwhelming force and firepower.
The concept was formulated by the American
strategic analysts Harlan K. Ullman and James P.
Wade in a Pentagon briefing document of 1996, and
came to wider prominence during the campaign in
Iraq in 2003

11 **throw away the scabbard**
abandon all thought of making peace; from the
proverb: see **Revolution** 4

QUOTATIONS

12 We make war that we may live in peace.
Aristotle 384–322 BC: *Nicomachean Ethics*; see
Preparation 9

13 Laws are silent in time of war.
Cicero 106–43 BC: *Pro Milone*

14 The sinews of war, unlimited money.
Cicero 106–43 BC: *Fifth Philippic*; see **Money** 30

15 I see wars, horrible wars, and the Tiber
foaming with much blood.
Virgil 70–19 BC: *Aeneid*; see **Race** 27

16 Wars begin when you will, but they do not
end when you please.
Niccolò Machiavelli 1469–1527: *History of Florence*
(1521–4)

17 Once more unto the breach, dear friends,
     once more;
Or close the wall up with our English dead!
In peace there's nothing so becomes a man
As modest stillness and humility:
But when the blast of war blows in our ears,
Then imitate the action of the tiger;
Stiffen the sinews, summon up the blood,

Disguise fair nature with hard-favoured rage.
William Shakespeare 1564–1616: *Henry V* (1599)

18 For what can war, but endless war still
breed?
John Milton 1608–74: 'On the Lord General Fairfax
at the Siege of Colchester' (written 1648)

19 Force, and fraud, are in war the two cardinal
virtues.
Thomas Hobbes 1588–1679: *Leviathan* (1651)

20 God is on the side not of the heavy
battalions, but of the best shots.
Voltaire 1694–1778: 'The Piccini Notebooks'
(*c*.1735–50); see **The Armed Forces 8, God 23**

21 Among the calamities of war may be jointly
numbered the diminution of the love of
truth, by the falsehoods which interest
dictates and credulity encourages.
Samuel Johnson 1709–84: in *The Idler* 11
November 1758; see 4 above

22 There never was a good war, or a bad peace.
Benjamin Franklin 1706–90: letter to Josiah
Quincy, 11 September 1783

23 In war, three-quarters turns on personal
character and relations; the balance of
manpower and materials counts only for the
remaining quarter.
Napoléon I 1769–1821: 'Observations sur les
affaires d'Espagne, Saint-Cloud, 27 août 1808'

24 Next to a battle lost, the greatest misery is a
battle gained.
Duke of Wellington 1769–1852: in *Diary of
Frances, Lady Shelley 1787–1817* (ed. R. Edgcumbe)

25 Everything is very simple in war, but the
simplest thing is difficult. These difficulties
accumulate and produce a friction which no
man can imagine exactly who has not
seen war.
Karl von Clausewitz 1780–1831: *On War* (1832–4)

26 War is nothing but a continuation of
politics with the admixture of other means.
commonly rendered as 'War is the continuation of
politics by other means'
Karl von Clausewitz 1780–1831: *On War* (1832–4)

27 He knew that the essence of war is violence,
and that moderation in war is imbecility.
Lord Macaulay 1800–59: *Essays Contributed to the
Edinburgh Review* (1843) 'John Hampden'

28 All the business of war, and indeed all the
business of life, is to endeavour to find out
what you don't know by what you do; that's
what I called 'guessing what was at the other
side of the hill'.
Duke of Wellington 1769–1852: in *The Croker
Papers* (1885)

29 It is well that war is so terrible. We should
grow too fond of it.
Robert E. Lee 1807–70: after the battle of
Fredericksburg, December 1862; attributed

30 Always mystify, mislead, and surprise the
enemy, if possible.
his strategic motto during the Civil War
Thomas Jonathan 'Stonewall' Jackson
1824–63: M. Miner and H. Rawson *American Heritage
Dictionary of American Quotations* (1997)

31 There is many a boy here to-day who looks
on war as all glory, but, boys, it is all hell.
William Sherman 1820–91: speech at Columbus,
Ohio, 11 August 1880

32 War is a necessary part of God's
arrangement of the world . . . Without war
the world would deteriorate into
materialism.
Helmuth von Moltke 1800–91: letter to Dr J. K.
Bluntschli, 11 December 1880

33 *of possible German involvement in the Balkans:*
Not worth the healthy bones of a single
Pomeranian grenadier.
Otto von Bismarck 1815–98: George O. Kent
Bismarck and his Times (1978); see **World War II 23**

34 I do wish people would not deceive
themselves by talk of a just war. There is no
such thing as a just war. What we are doing
is casting out Satan by Satan.
Charles Hamilton Sorley 1895–1915: letter to his
mother from Aldershot, March 1915; see 9 above,
Good and Evil 18

35 War is hell, and all that, but it has a good
deal to recommend it. It wipes out all the
small nuisances of peace-time.
Ian Hay 1876–1952: *The First Hundred Thousand*
(1915)

36 Once lead this people into war and they will
forget there ever was such a thing as
tolerance.
Woodrow Wilson 1856–1924: John Dos Passos *Mr
Wilson's War* (1917)

37 My subject is War, and the pity of War.
The Poetry is in the pity.
Wilfred Owen 1893–1918: preface (written 1918)
in *Poems* (1963)

38 If you could hear, at every jolt, the blood
Come gargling from the froth-corrupted
lungs,
Obscene as cancer, bitter as the cud
Of vile, incurable sores on innocent
tongues,—
My friend, you would not tell with such
high zest
To children ardent for some desperate glory,
The old Lie: Dulce et decorum est

Pro patria mori.
Wilfred Owen 1893–1918: 'Dulce et Decorum Est';
see **Patriotism** 7

39 Waste of Blood, and waste of Tears,
Waste of youth's most precious years,
Waste of ways the saints have trod,
Waste of Glory, waste of God,
War!
G. A. Studdert Kennedy 1883–1929: 'Waste'
(1919)

40 War is too serious a matter to entrust to
military men.
Georges Clemenceau 1841–1929: attributed to
Clemenceau, e.g. in Hampden Jackson *Clemenceau
and the Third Republic* (1946); but also to Briand and
Talleyrand; see **Politics** 26

41 The bomber will always get through. The
only defence is in offence, which means
that you have to kill more women and
children more quickly than the enemy if
you want to save yourselves.
Stanley Baldwin 1867–1947: speech, House of
Commons, 10 November 1932

42 Wars may be fought with weapons, but they
are won by men.
George S. Patton 1885–1945: in *Cavalry Journal*
September 1933

43 We can manage without butter but not, for
example, without guns. If we are attacked
we can only defend ourselves with guns not
with butter.
Joseph Goebbels 1897–1945: speech in Berlin, 17
January 1936; see 44 below

44 We have no butter . . . but I ask you—would
you rather have butter or guns? . . .
preparedness makes us powerful. Butter
merely makes us fat.
Hermann Goering 1893–1946: speech at
Hamburg, 1936; W. Frischauer *Goering* (1951); see
43 above

45 Little girl . . . Sometime they'll give a war
and nobody will come.
Carl Sandburg 1878–1967: *The People, Yes* (1936);
'Suppose They Gave a War and Nobody Came?' was
the title of a 1970 film

46 In war, whichever side may call itself the
victor, there are no winners, but all are
losers.
Neville Chamberlain 1869–1940: speech at
Kettering, 3 July 1938

47 War always finds a way.
Bertolt Brecht 1898–1956: *Mother Courage* (1939)

48 War will be won by Blood and Guts alone.
George Patton 1885–1945: address to fellow
officers, Fort Benning, Georgia, 1940; see **World
War II** 7

49 Probably the battle of Waterloo *was* won on
the playing-fields of Eton, but the opening
battles of all subsequent wars have been lost
there.
George Orwell 1903–50: *The Lion and the Unicorn*
(1941) 'England Your England'; see **Wars** 13

50 What difference does it make to the dead,
the orphans and the homeless, whether the
mad destruction is wrought under the name
of totalitarianism or the holy name of
liberty or democracy?
Mahatma Gandhi 1869–1948: *Non-Violence in
Peace and War* (1942)

51 Older men declare war. But it is youth who
must fight and die.
Herbert Hoover 1874–1964: speech at the
Republican National Convention, Chicago, 27
June 1944

52 I have never met anyone who wasn't against
war. Even Hitler and Mussolini were,
according to themselves.
David Low 1891–1963: in *New York Times Magazine*
10 February 1946

53 The quickest way of ending a war is to
lose it.
George Orwell 1903–50: in *Polemic* May 1946

54 In war: resolution. In defeat: defiance. In
victory: magnanimity. In peace: goodwill.
Winston Churchill 1874–1965: *The Second World
War* vol. 1 (1948)

55 Every gun that is made, every warship
launched, every rocket fired signifies, in the
final sense, a theft from those who hunger
and are not fed, those who are cold and are
not clothed. This world in arms is not
spending money alone. It is spending the
sweat of its labourers, the genius of its
scientists, the hopes of its children.
Dwight D. Eisenhower 1890–1969: speech in
Washington, 16 April 1953

56 Mankind must put an end to war or war will
put an end to mankind.
John F. Kennedy 1917–63: speech to United
Nations General Assembly, 25 September 1961

57 Rule 1, on page 1 of the book of war, is: 'Do
not march on Moscow' . . . [Rule 2] is: 'Do
not go fighting with your land armies in
China.'
Lord Montgomery 1887–1976: speech, House of
Lords, 30 May 1962

58 History is littered with the wars which
everybody knew would never happen.
Enoch Powell 1912–98: speech to the Conservative
Party Conference, 19 October 1967

59 The conventional army loses if it does not
win. The guerrilla wins if he does not lose.
Henry Kissinger 1923– : in *Foreign Affairs*
January 1969

60 War is the most exciting and dramatic thing in life. In fighting to the death you feel terribly relaxed when you manage to come through.
Moshe Dayan 1915–81: in *Observer* 13 February 1972

61 I love the smell of napalm in the morning. It smells like victory.
John Milius and **Francis Ford Coppola** 1939– : *Apocalypse Now* (1979 film)

62 Once you're committed to war, then be ferocious enough to do whatever is necessary to get it over with as quickly as possible in victory.
H. Norman Schwarzkopf III 1934– : in *New York Times* 28 January 1991

➵➵ Wars ➴➴

see also **World War I, World War II**

PROVERBS AND SAYINGS

1 **Hey, hey, LBJ, how many kids have you killed today?**
anti-Vietnam marching slogan

2 **Remember the Alamo!**
Texan battle-cry at the battle of San Jacinto, 1836, referring to the defence of a Franciscan mission in the Texan War of Independence, in which all the defenders were killed

PHRASES

3 **the late unpleasantness**
the war that took place recently; originally the American Civil War

QUOTATIONS

4 Men said openly that Christ and His saints slept.
of twelfth-century England during the civil war between Stephen and Matilda
Anonymous: *Anglo-Saxon Chronicle* for 1137

5 The singeing of the King of Spain's Beard.
on the expedition to Cadiz, 1587
Francis Drake 1540–96: Francis Bacon *Considerations touching a War with Spain* (1629)

6 The dimensions of this mercy are above my thoughts. It is, for aught I know, a crowning mercy.
on the battle of Worcester, 1651
Oliver Cromwell 1599–1658: letter to William Lenthall, Speaker of the Parliament of England, 4 September 1651

7 They now *ring* the bells, but they will soon *wring* their hands.
on the declaration of war with Spain, 1739
Robert Walpole 1676–1745: W. Coxe *Memoirs of Sir Robert Walpole* (1798)

8 What a glorious morning is this.
on hearing gunfire at Lexington, 19 April 1775; traditionally quoted 'What a glorious morning for America'
Samuel Adams 1722–1803: J. K. Hosmer *Samuel Adams* (1886)

9 Men, you are all marksmen—don't one of you fire until you see the white of their eyes.
at Bunker Hill, 1775
Israel Putnam 1718–90: R. Frothingham *History of the Siege of Boston* (1873) ; also attributed to William Prescott, 1726–95

10 *Guerra a cuchillo.*
War to the knife.
at the siege of Saragossa, 4 August 1808, replying to the suggestion that he should surrender
José de Palafox 1780–1847: as reported; he actually said: '*Guerra y cuchillo* [War and the knife]'; José Gòmez de Arteche y Moro *Guerra de la Independencia* (1875)

11 Up Guards and at them!
Duke of Wellington 1769–1852: in *The Battle of Waterloo* by a Near Observer [J. Booth] (1815); later denied by Wellington

12 Hard pounding this, gentlemen; let's see
who will pound longest.
at the battle of Waterloo
Duke of Wellington 1769–1852: Sir Walter Scott
Paul's Letters (1816)

13 The battle of Waterloo was won on the
playing fields of Eton.
Duke of Wellington 1769–1852: oral tradition, but
not found in this form of words; C. F. R.
Montalembert *De l'avenir politique de l'Angleterre*
(1856); see **Warfare 49**

14 Half a league, half a league,
Half a league onward,
All in the valley of Death
Rode the six hundred . . .
Cannon to right of them,
Cannon to left of them,
Cannon in front of them
Volleyed and thundered.
Alfred, Lord Tennyson 1809–92: 'The Charge of
the Light Brigade' (1854)

15 *J'y suis, j'y reste.*
Here I am, and here I stay.
at the taking of the Malakoff fortress during the
Crimean War, 8 September 1855
Comte de Macmahon 1808–93: G. Hanotaux
Histoire de la France Contemporaine (1903–8)

16 There is Jackson with his Virginians,
standing like a stone wall. Let us determine
to die here, and we will conquer.
referring to General T. J. ('Stonewall') Jackson at the
battle of Bull Run, 21 July, 1861 (in which Bee
himself was killed)
Barnard Elliott Bee 1823–61: B. Perley Poore
Perley's Reminiscences (1886)

17 All quiet along the Potomac to-night,
No sound save the rush of the river,
While soft falls the dew on the face of the
dead—
The picket's off duty forever.
Ethel Lynn Beers 1827–79: 'The Picket Guard'
(1861); the first line is also attributed to George B.
McClellan (1826–85)

18 Give them the cold steel, boys!
Lewis Addison Armistead 1817–63: attributed
during the American Civil War, 1863

19 Hold out. Relief is coming.
usually quoted as 'Hold the fort! I am coming!'
William Tecumsah Sherman 1820–91: flag signal
from Kennesaw Mountain to General John Murray
Corse at Allatoona Pass, 5 October 1864

20 Don't cheer, men; those poor devils are
dying.
John Woodward ('Jack') Philip 1840–1900: at
the battle of Santiago, 4 July 1898; in *Dictionary of
American Biography* vol. 14 (1934)

21 The Cavaliers (Wrong but Wromantic) and
the Roundheads (Right but Repulsive).
of the two sides in the English Civil War
W. C. Sellar 1898–1951 and **R. J. Yeatman**
1898–1968: *1066 and All That* (1930)

22 We are not about to send American boys 9
or 10,000 miles away from home to do what
Asian boys ought to be doing for
themselves.
Lyndon Baines Johnson 1908–73: speech at
Akron University, 21 October 1964

23 They've got to draw in their horns and stop
their aggression, or we're going to bomb
them back into the Stone Age.
on the North Vietnamese
Curtis E. LeMay 1906–90: *Mission with LeMay*
(1965)

24 It became necessary to destroy the town to
save it.
statement by unidentified US Army Major, referring
to Ben Tre in Vietnam
Anonymous: Associated Press Report, *New York
Times* 8 February 1968

25 Just rejoice at that news and congratulate
our forces and the Marines . . . Rejoice!
on the recapture of South Georgia; usually quoted as
'Rejoice, rejoice'
Margaret Thatcher 1925– : to newsmen outside
Downing Street, 25 April 1982

26 I counted them all out and I counted them
all back.
on the number of British aeroplanes (which he was
not permitted to disclose) joining the raid on Port
Stanley in the Falkland Islands
Brian Hanrahan 1949– : BBC broadcast report, 1
May 1982

27 Gotcha!
Anonymous: headline on the sinking of the *General
Belgrano*, in *Sun* 4 May 1982

28 The Falklands thing was a fight between two
bald men over a comb.
Jorge Luis Borges 1899–1986: in *Time* 14 February
1983; see **Experience 3**

29 The mother of battles.
popular interpretation of his description of the
approaching Gulf War
Saddam Hussein 1937– : speech in Baghdad, 6
January 1991; *The Times*, 7 January 1991, reported
that Saddam had no intention of relinquishing
Kuwait and was ready for the 'mother of all wars'

30 It is time for us to win the first war of the
21st century.
of the 'war on terrorism'
George W. Bush 1946– : at a White House press
conference, 16 September 2001

➤➤ Ways and Means ◄◄

PROVERBS AND SAYINGS

1 **Catching's before hanging.**
an essential step must be taken before the consequence can ensue; English proverb, early 19th century

2 **Eat the mangoes. Do not count the trees.**
concentrate on the task in hand; Indian proverb

3 **The end justifies the means.**
English proverb, late 16th century; see **Morality** 5

4 **Fight fire with fire.**
one should counter like with like; English proverb, mid 19th century

5 **Fire is a good servant but a bad master.**
acknowledging that fire is both essential for living and potentially destructive; English proverb, early 17th century

6 **First catch your hare.**
referring to the first essential step that must be taken before a process can begin; English proverb, early 19th century, often attributed to the English cook Hannah Glasse (fl. 1747), but her directions for making hare soup are, 'Take your hare when it is cased' (*cased* here meaning 'skinned')

7 **Give a man enough rope and he will hang himself.**
often used to mean that someone given enough licence or freedom will defeat themselves through their own mistakes; English proverb, mid 17th century

8 **The hammer shatters glass but forges steel.**
modern saying, said to be of Russian origin

9 **Honey catches more flies than vinegar.**
soft or ingratiating words achieve more than sharpness; English proverb, mid 17th century

10 **If you can't beat them, join them.**
often used in consolation or resignation; English proverb, mid 20th century

11 **It hardly matters if it is a white cat or a black cat that catches the mice.**
Chinese proverb; see 31 below

12 **It is good to make a bridge of gold to a flying enemy.**
it is wiser to give passage to an enemy in flight, who may be desperate; English proverb, late 16th century

13 **An old poacher makes the best gamekeeper.**
someone who has formerly taken part in wrongdoing knows best how to counter it in others; English proverb, late 14th century

14 **One size does not fit all.**
an assertion of individual requirements; earlier versions are based on the metaphor of different size shoes for different feet; English proverb, early 17th century

15 **The paths are many, but the goal is the same.**
Indian proverb, deriving from Sanskrit

16 **The pen is mightier than the sword.**
written words may often have more lasting force than military strength; English proverb, late 16th century; see **Technology** 12, **Writing** 4, **Writing** 29

17 **Set a thief to catch a thief.**
used to imply that the person best placed to catch someone out in dishonest practices is one whose own nature tends that way; English proverb, mid 17th century

18 **There are more ways of killing a cat than choking it with cream.**
there are more ways of achieving an end than giving an opponent a glut of what they most want; English proverb, mid 19th century

19 **There are more ways of killing a dog than choking it with butter.**
there are more ways of achieving an end than giving an opponent a glut of what they most want; English proverb, mid 19th century

20 **There are more ways of killing a dog than hanging it.**
there are more ways than one of achieving an end; English proverb, late 17th century

21 **There is more than one way to skin a cat.**
English proverb, mid 19th century

22 **There is nothing like leather.**
referring to the toughness and durability of leather. The saying comes from one of Aesop's fables, in which a leatherworker contributed this opinion to a discussion on how to fortify a city; English proverb, late 17th century

23 **What matters is what works.**
late 20th century saying

PHRASES

24 drive a coach and six through
make useless by the disregard of law or custom; from
Stephen Rice (1637–1715) 'I will drive a coach and
six horses through the Act of Settlement'

25 play the — card
introduce a specified (advantageous) factor; from
Lord Randolph Churchill: see **Ireland** 12; see also
The Law 43

QUOTATIONS

26 It is in life as it is in ways, the shortest way is
commonly the foulest, and surely the fairer
way is not much about.
Francis Bacon 1561–1626: *The Advancement of
Learning* (1605)

27 There are no small steps in great affairs.
Cardinal de Retz 1613–79: *Mémoires* (1717) bk. 2

28 *Dans ce pays-ci il est bon de tuer de temps en
temps un amiral pour encourager les autres.*
In this country [England] it is thought well
to kill an admiral from time to time to
encourage the others.
referring to the execution of Admiral John Byng, 1757
Voltaire 1694–1778: *Candide* (1759); see
Management 5

29 A servant's too often a negligent elf;
—If it's business of consequence, DO IT
YOURSELF!
R. H. Barham 1788–1845: 'The Ingoldsby
Penance!—Moral' (1842)

30 They sought it with thimbles, they sought it
with care;
They pursued it with forks and hope;
They threatened its life with a railway-share;
They charmed it with smiles and soap.
Lewis Carroll 1832–98: *The Hunting of the Snark*
(1876)

31 The colour of the cat doesn't matter as long
as it catches the mice.
Deng Xiaoping 1904–97: in *Financial Times* 18
December 1986; see 11 above

Weakness see Strength and Weakness

⤗ Wealth and Luxury ⤖

see also Money, Thrift and Extravagance

PROVERBS AND SAYINGS

1 A diamond is forever.
advertising slogan for De Beers Consolidated Mines,
1940s onwards

**2 If you really want to make a million
. . . the quickest way is to start your
own religion.**
previously attributed to L. Ron Hubbard 1911–86 in
B. Corydon and L. Ron Hubbard Jr. *L. Ron Hubbard*
(1987), but attribution subsequently rejected by L.
Ron Hubbard Jr., who also dissociated himself from
the book

3 Money makes a man.
possession of wealth confers status; English proverb,
early 16th century

4 Money makes money.
implying that those who are already wealthy are
likely to become more so; English proverb, late 16th
century

**5 The rich man has his ice in the
summer and the poor man gets his in
the winter.**
contrasting luxury with hardship through apparent
equality; English proverb, early 20th century

PHRASES

6 the affluent society
a society in which material wealth is widely
distributed, a rich society; usually in allusion to the
book *The Affluent Society* (1958) by the Canadian-
born economist John Kenneth Galbraith

7 Aladdin's cave
a place of great riches; in the *Arabian Nights*, the
cave in which Aladdin found an old lamp which,
when rubbed, brought a genie to obey his will; see
Chance 16

**8 born with a silver spoon in one's
mouth**
born in affluence; see **Class** 31, **Presidency** 20

9 gilded cage
a luxurious but restrictive environment; see
Creativity 8

10 the Mammon of unrighteousness
wealth ill-used or ill-gained; *Mammon* (ultimately
from Hebrew *māmōn* money, wealth), in early use,

(the proper name of) the devil of covetousness, later with personification, wealth regarded as an idol or an evil influence; see **Money** 26

11 **the Midas touch**
the ability to turn one's actions to financial advantage; *Midas*, in classical legend a king of Phrygia whose touch was said to turn all things to gold

12 **milk and honey**
abundance, comfort, prosperity; with allusion to the biblical description of the promised land: see 15 below

13 **poor little rich girl**
a wealthy girl or woman whose money brings her no happiness; title of a 1925 song by Noël Coward

14 **Tom Tiddler's ground**
a place where money or profit is readily made; a children's game in which one player tries to catch the others who run on to his or her territory crying 'We're on Tom Tiddler's ground, picking up gold and silver'

QUOTATIONS

15 A land flowing with milk and honey.
Bible: Exodus; see 12 above

16 It is easier for a camel to go through the eye of a needle, than for a rich man to enter into the kingdom of God.
Bible: St Matthew; see **Quantities** 14

17   I glory
More in the cunning purchase of my wealth
Than in the glad possession.
Ben Jonson 1573–1637: *Volpone* (1606)

18 Riches are for spending.
Francis Bacon 1561–1626: *Essays* (1625) 'Of Expense'

19   Let none admire
That riches grow in hell; that soil may best
Deserve the precious bane.
John Milton 1608–74: *Paradise Lost* (1667)

20 It was very prettily said, that we may learn the little value of fortune by the persons on whom heaven is pleased to bestow it.
Richard Steele 1672–1729: in *The Tatler* 27 July 1710

21 We are all Adam's children but silk makes the difference.
Thomas Fuller 1654–1734: *Gnomologia* (1732)

22 Get place and wealth, if possible, with grace; If not, by any means get wealth and place.
Alexander Pope 1688–1744: *Imitations of Horace* (1738); see **Money** 25

23 The chief enjoyment of riches consists in the parade of riches.
Adam Smith 1723–90: *Wealth of Nations* (1776)

24 We are not here to sell a parcel of boilers and vats, but the potentiality of growing rich, beyond the dreams of avarice.
at the sale of Thrale's brewery
Samuel Johnson 1709–84: James Boswell *Life of Samuel Johnson* (1791) 6 April 1781

25 'Two nations; between whom there is no intercourse and no sympathy; who are as ignorant of each other's habits, thoughts, and feelings, as if they were dwellers in different zones, or inhabitants of different planets . . . ' 'You speak of—' said Egremont, hesitatingly, 'THE RICH AND THE POOR.'
Benjamin Disraeli 1804–81: *Sybil* (1845); see **Politics** 9

26 I spend my life ministering to the swinish luxury of the rich.
William Morris 1834–96: attributed, *c.*1877; W. R. Lethaby *Philip Webb* (1935)

27 The man who dies . . . rich dies disgraced.
Andrew Carnegie 1835–1919: in *North American Review* June 1889 'Wealth'

28 In every well-governed state, wealth is a sacred thing; in democracies it is the only sacred thing.
Anatole France 1844–1924: *L'Île des pingouins* (1908)

29 To be clever enough to get all that money, one must be stupid enough to want it.
G. K. Chesterton 1874–1936: *Wisdom of Father Brown* (1914)

30 Her voice is full of money.
F. Scott Fitzgerald 1896–1940: *The Great Gatsby* (1925)

31 Let me tell you about the very rich. They are different from you and me.
F. Scott Fitzgerald 1896–1940: *All the Sad Young Men* (1926) 'Rich Boy'; to which Ernest Hemingway replied, 'Yes, they have more money', in *Esquire* August 1936 'The Snows of Kilimanjaro'

32 I am absolutely convinced that no wealth in the world can help humanity forward, even in the hands of the most devoted worker in this cause . . . Can anyone imagine Moses, Jesus, or Gandhi with the moneybags of Carnegie?
Albert Einstein 1879–1955: *Mein Weltbild* (1934)

33 The necessities were going by default to save the luxuries until I hardly knew which were necessities and which luxuries.
Frank Lloyd Wright 1867–1959: *Autobiography* (1945)

34 A kiss on the hand may be quite
    continental,

But diamonds are a girl's best friend.
Leo Robin 1900–84: 'Diamonds are a Girl's Best Friend' (1949 song)

35 If you can actually count your money, then you are not really a rich man.
J. Paul Getty 1892–1976: in *Observer* 3 November 1957

36 The greater the wealth, the thicker will be the dirt.
J. K. Galbraith 1908– : *The Affluent Society* (1958)

37 I want to spend, and spend, and spend.
said to reporters on arriving to collect her husband's football pools winnings of £152,000
Vivian Nicholson 1936– : in *Daily Herald* 28 September 1961

38 The saddest thing I can imagine is to get used to luxury.
Charlie Chaplin 1889–1977: *My Autobiography* (1964)

39 I've been rich and I've been poor: rich is better.
Sophie Tucker 1884–1966: attributed

40 The minute you walked in the joint,
I could see you were a man of distinction,
A real big spender . . .
Hey! big spender, spend a little time with me.
Dorothy Fields 1905–74: 'Big Spender' (1966 song)

41 Having money is rather like being a blonde.
It is more fun but not vital.
Mary Quant 1934– : in *Observer* 2 November 1986

⤜ Weather ⤛

PROVERBS AND SAYINGS

1 **April showers bring forth May flowers.**
referring to the value of rain during April to early growth; English proverb, mid 16th century

2 **As the day lengthens, so the cold strengthens.**
recording the tradition that the coldest weather arrives when days begin to grow lighter; English proverb, early 17th century

3 **A dripping June sets all in tune.**
rain in June is beneficial to all crops and plants; English proverb, mid 18th century

4 **February fill dyke, be it black or be it white.**
February is a month likely to bring heavy rain (black) or snow (white); English proverb, mid 16th century; see **Seasons** 10

5 **If Candlemas day be sunny and bright, winter will have another flight; if Candlemas day be cloudy with rain, winter is gone and won't come again.**
in the Church calendar 2 February is the date of the feast of the Purification of the Virgin Mary and the Presentation of Christ in the Temple. This is known as *Candlemas Day* because candles are blessed at services on that day; English proverb, late 17th century

6 **If in February there be no rain, 'tis neither good for hay nor grain.**
a drought in February will be damaging to crops later in the year; English proverb, early 18th century

7 **Long foretold, long last; short notice, soon past.**
if there is a long gap between the signs that the weather will change and the change itself, then the predicted weather will last a long time. If the intervening period is a short one, then the predicted weather will be of correspondingly short duration; English proverb, mid 19th century

8 **March borrowed from April three days, and they were ill.**
traditional saying, implying that bad weather in early April reflects the influence of March; English proverb, mid 17th century; see 22 below

9 **March comes in like a lion, and goes out like a lamb.**
weather is traditionally stormy at the beginning of March, but calm at the end; English proverb, early 17th century

10 **North wind doth blow, we shall have snow.**
traditional weather rhyme, deriving from a nursery rhyme of the early 19th century

11 **A peck of March dust is worth a king's ransom.**
March is traditionally a wet month, and dust is rare (a *peck* was a dry measure of two gallons); English proverb, early 16th century

12 **Rain before seven, fine before eleven.**
English proverb, mid 19th century

13 **Rain, rain, go away,
Come again another day.**
traditional rhyme, mid 17th century

14 **Red sky at night, shepherd's delight; red sky in the morning, shepherd's warning.**
good and bad weather respectively is presaged by a red sky at sunset and dawn; English proverb, late 14th century

15 **Robin Hood could brave all weathers but a thaw wind.**
a *thaw wind* is a cold wind which accompanies the breaking up of frost; English proverb, mid 19th century

16 **Saint Swithin's day, if thou be fair, for forty days it will remain; Saint Swithin's day, if thou bring rain, for forty days it will remain.**
St Swithin's day is 15 July, and the tradition may have its origin in the heavy rain said to have occurred when his relics were to be transferred to a shrine in Winchester cathedral; English proverb, early 17th century

17 **September blow soft till the fruit's in the loft.**
expressing the hope that fine weather often traditional in September will hold until a crop of apples or other fruit has been picked and stored; English proverb, late 16th century

18 **So many mists in March, so many frosts in May.**
mist or fog in March presages frost in May; English proverb, early 17th century

19 **There is no such thing as bad weather, only the wrong clothes.**
late 20th century saying

20 **When the oak is before the ash, then you will only get a splash; when the ash is before the oak, then you may expect a soak.**
a traditional way of predicting whether the summer will be wet or dry on the basis of whether the oak or the ash is first to come into leaf in the spring; English proverb, mid 19th century

21 **When the wind is in the east, 'tis neither good for man nor beast.**
referring to the traditional bitterness of the east wind; English proverb, early 17th century

PHRASES

22 **borrowed days**
in Scottish tradition, the last three days of March (Old Style), said to have been borrowed from April and to be particularly stormy; see 8 above

23 **the bow of promise**
a rainbow; after the Bible (Genesis) 'I do set my bow in the cloud, and it shall be for a token of a covenant between me and the earth'

24 **Groundhog Day**
in North American usage, a day (in most areas 2 February) which, if sunny, is believed to indicate wintry weather to come; from the story that, if there is enough sun for the *groundhog* (a woodchuck) to see its shadow, it retires underground for further hibernation

25 **Indian summer**
a period of calm dry warm weather in late autumn in the northern US or elsewhere; see **Old Age 8**

26 **London particular**
a dense fog affecting London; see **41** below

27 **queen's weather**
fine weather; of the kind supposedly associated with public appearances by Queen Victoria

28 **St Luke's summer**
a period of fine weather occurring about the feast of St Luke (18 October)

29 **St Martin's summer**
a period of fine weather occurring about Martinmas (11 November)

QUOTATIONS

30 'After sharpest shoures,' quath Pees 'most shene is the sonne;
Is no weder warmer than after watry cloudes.'
Pees Peace
William Langland c.1330–c.1400: *The Vision of Piers Plowman*

31 For I have seyn of a ful misty morwe
Folowen ful ofte a myrie someris day.
Geoffrey Chaucer 1343–1400: *Troilus and Criseyde*

32 There is no such thing as bad weather. All weather is good because it is God's.
St Teresa of Ávila 1512–82: attributed; H. Ward and J. Wild (eds.) *The Lion Christian Quotation Collection* (1997)

33 The uncertain glory of an April day.
William Shakespeare 1564–1616: *The Two Gentlemen of Verona* (1592–3)

34 So foul and fair a day I have not seen.
William Shakespeare 1564–1616: *Macbeth* (1606)

35 Rainy days—
silkworms droop
on mulberries.
Matsuo Basho 1644–94: translated by Lucien Stryk

36 When two Englishmen meet, their first talk is of the weather.
Samuel Johnson 1709–84: in *The Idler* 24 June 1758

37 The best sun we have is made of Newcastle coal.
Horace Walpole 1717–97: letter to George Montagu, 15 June 1768

38 The frost performs its secret ministry,
Unhelped by any wind.
Samuel Taylor Coleridge 1772–1834: 'Frost at Midnight' (1798)

39 It is impossible to live in a country which is continually under hatches . . . Rain! Rain! Rain!
John Keats 1795–1821: letter to J. H. Reynolds from Devon, 10 April 1818

40 O wild West Wind, thou breath of Autumn's being,
Thou, from whose unseen presence the leaves dead
Are driven, like ghosts from an enchanter fleeing.
Percy Bysshe Shelley 1792–1822: 'Ode to the West Wind' (1819)

41 This is a London particular . . . A fog, miss.
Charles Dickens 1812–70: *Bleak House* (1853); see 26 above

42 They say a green Yule makes a fat churchyard; but so does a white Yule too.
George Eliot 1819–80: *The Sad Fortunes of the Reverend Amos Barton* (1858); see **Christmas** 1

43 Welcome, wild North-easter!
Shame it is to see
Odes to every zephyr;
Ne'er a verse to thee.
Charles Kingsley 1819–75: 'Ode to the North-East Wind' (1858)

44 There is a sumptuous variety about the New England weather that compels the stranger's admiration—and regret. The weather is always doing something there; always attending strictly to business; always getting up new designs and trying them on the people to see how they will go.
Mark Twain 1835–1910: speech to New England Society, 22 December 1876

45 The weather is like the Government, always in the wrong.
Jerome K. Jerome 1859–1927: *Idle Thoughts of an Idle Fellow* (1889)

46 The rain, it raineth on the just
And also on the unjust fella:
But chiefly on the just, because

The unjust steals the just's umbrella.
Lord Bowen 1835–94: Walter Sichel *Sands of Time* (1923); see **Equality** 4

47 The yellow fog that rubs its back upon the window-panes.
T. S. Eliot 1888–1965: 'The Love Song of J. Alfred Prufrock' (1917)

48 No one can tell me,
Nobody knows,
Where the wind comes from,
Where the wind goes.
A. A. Milne 1882–1956: 'Wind on the Hill' (1927)

49 The first fall of snow is not only an event, but it is a magical event. You go to bed in one kind of world and wake up to find yourself in another quite different, and if this is not enchantment, then where is it to be found?
J. B. Priestley 1894–1984: *Apes and Angels* (1928) 'First Snow'

50 Thank heavens, the sun has gone in, and I don't have to go out and enjoy it.
Logan Pearsall Smith 1865–1946: *Afterthoughts* (1931)

51 It ain't a fit night out for man or beast.
W. C. Fields 1880–1946: adopted by Fields but claimed by him not to be original; letter, 8 February 1944

52 I believe we should all behave quite differently if we lived in a warm, sunny climate all the time.
Noël Coward 1899–1973: *Brief Encounter* (1945)

53 You can call this rain bad weather, but it is not. It is simply weather, and weather means rough weather. It reminds us forcibly that its element is water, falling water. And water is hard.
Heinrich Böll 1917–85: *Irish Journal* (1957, translated Leila Vennewitz)

54 A woman rang to say she heard there was a hurricane on the way. Well don't worry, there isn't.
weather forecast on the night before serious gales in southern England
Michael Fish 1944– : BBC TV, 15 October 1987

55 It was the wrong kind of snow.
explaining disruption on British Rail
Terry Worrall: in *The Independent* 16 February 1991

➤► Weddings ◄◄

see also **Marriage**

PROVERBS AND SAYINGS

1 **Always a bridesmaid, never a bride.**
recording the belief that to be a bridesmaid too often
is unlucky for one's own chances of marriage;
English proverb, late 19th century

2 **Happy is the bride that the sun
shines on.**
English proverb, mid 17th century

3 **Marry in May, rue for aye.**
English proverb, late 17th century; see **Seasons** 3

4 **Now you will feel no rain, for each of
you will be shelter for the other. Now
you will feel no cold, for each of you
will be warmth for the other.**
from the saying known as the 'Apache Blessing'

5 **One wedding brings another.**
English proverb, mid 17th century

QUOTATIONS

6 As the bridegroom rejoiceth over the bride.
Bible: Isaiah

7 With this Ring I thee wed, with my body I
thee worship, and with all my worldly goods
I thee endow.
The Book of Common Prayer 1662:
Solemnization of Matrimony Wedding

8 O! how short a time does it take to put an
end to a woman's liberty!
Fanny Burney 1752–1840: diary 20 July 1768

9 What woman, however old, has not the
bridal-favours and raiment stowed away, and
packed in lavender, in the inmost cupboards
of her heart?
William Makepeace Thackeray 1811–63: *The
Virginians* (1857–9)

10 The flowers in the bride's hand are sadly like
the garland which decked the heifers of
sacrifice in old times.
Thomas Hardy 1840–1928: *Jude the Obscure*
(1896)

11 If it were not for the presents, an elopement
would be preferable.
George Ade 1866–1944: *Forty Modern Fables*
(1901)

12 Why am I always the bridesmaid,
Never the blushing bride?
Fred W. Leigh d. 1924: 'Why Am I Always the
Bridesmaid?' (1917 song, with Charles Collins and
Lily Morris)

13 I'm getting married in the morning,
Ding dong! The bells are gonna chime.
Pull out the stopper;
Let's have a whopper;
But get me to the church on time!
Alan Jay Lerner 1918–86: 'Get Me to the Church
on Time' (1956 song)

14 I think weddings is sadder than funerals,
because they remind you of your own
wedding. You can't be reminded of your
own funeral because it hasn't happened. But
weddings always make me cry.
Brendan Behan 1923–64: *Richard's Cork Leg*

15 I love to cry at weddings, anybody's
weddings anytime!
. . . anybody's weddings just so long as it's
not mine!
Dorothy Fields 1905–74: 'I Love to Cry at
Weddings' (1966)

16   The trouble
with being best man is, you don't get a
chance to prove it.
Les A. Murray 1938– : *The Boys Who Stole the
Funeral* (1989)

17 It's pretty easy. Just say 'I do' whenever
anyone asks you a question.
Richard Curtis 1956– : *Four Weddings and a
Funeral* (1994 film)

➤➤ Winning and Losing ◆◆

see also **Success and Failure**

PROVERBS AND SAYINGS

1 **All your base are belong to us.**
deriving from the poor English translation of the Japanese video game Zero Wing, released 1989; late 20th century saying

2 **Heads I win, tails you lose.**
I win in any event; *heads* and *tails* the obverse and reverse images on a coin; English proverb, late 17th century

3 **What you lose on the swings you gain on the roundabouts.**
ones losses and gains tend to cancel one another out; English proverb, early 20th century; see 18 below, **Circumstance 20**

4 **You can't win them all.**
used as an expression of consolation or resignation; English proverb, mid 20th century

PHRASES

5 **Pyrrhic victory**
a victory gained at too great a cost, like that of Pyrrhus over the Romans at Asculum in 279 BC: see 6 below

QUOTATIONS

6 One more such victory and we are lost.
on defeating the Romans at Asculum, 279 BC
Pyrrhus 319–272 BC: Plutarch *Parallel Lives* 'Pyrrhus'; see 5 above

7 The only safe course for the defeated is to expect no safety.
Virgil 70–19 BC: *Aeneid*

8 The happy state of winning the palm without the dust of racing.
Horace 65–8 BC: *Epistles*

9 Know ye not that they which run in a race run all, but one receiveth the prize.
Bible: I Corinthians

10 *Vae victis.*
Down with the defeated!
cry (already proverbial) of the Gallic King, Brennus, on capturing Rome (390 BC)
Livy 59 BC–AD 17: *Ab Urbe Condita*

11 Eclipse first, the rest nowhere.
comment on a horse-race at Epsom, 3 May 1769; *Eclipse* was the most famous racehorse of the 18th century, one of the ancestors in the direct male line of all thoroughbred racehorses throughout the world
Dennis O'Kelly 1720–87: in *Annals of Sporting* (1822); *Dictionary of National Biography* gives the occasion as the Queen's Plate at Winchester, 1769

12 When in doubt, win the trick.
Edmond Hoyle 1672–1769: *Hoyle's Games Improved* (ed. Charles Jones, 1790) 'Twenty-four Short Rules for Learners' (though attributed to Hoyle, this may well have been an editorial addition by Jones, since it is not found in earlier editions)

13 'The game,' said he, 'is never lost till won.'
George Crabbe 1754–1832: *Tales of the Hall* (1819) 'Gretna Green'

14 The politicians of New York . . . see nothing wrong in the rule, that to the victor belong the spoils of the enemy.
William Learned Marcy 1786–1857: speech to the Senate, 25 January 1832

15 EVERYBODY has won, and all must have prizes.
Lewis Carroll 1832–98: *Alice's Adventures in Wonderland* (1865)

16 We are not interested in the possibilities of defeat; they do not exist.
on the Boer War during 'Black Week', December 1899
Queen Victoria 1819–1901: Lady Gwendolen Cecil *Life of Robert, Marquis of Salisbury* (1931)

17 The important thing in life is not the victory but the contest; the essential thing is not to have won but to have fought well.
Baron Pierre de Coubertin 1863–1937: speech on the Olympic Games, London, 24 July 1908

18 What's lost upon the roundabouts we pulls up on the swings!
Patrick Reginald Chalmers 1872–1942: 'Roundabouts and Swings' (1912); see 3 above

19 Honey, I just forgot to duck.
to his wife, on losing the World Heavyweight title, 23 September 1926
Jack Dempsey 1895–1983: J. and B. P. Dempsey *Dempsey* (1977); after a failed attempt on his life in 1981, Ronald Reagan quipped to his wife 'Honey, I forgot to duck'

20 What is our aim? . . . Victory, victory at all costs, victory in spite of all terror; victory, however long and hard the road may be; for without victory, there is no survival.
Winston Churchill 1874–1965: speech, House of Commons, 13 May 1940

21 The war situation has developed not necessarily to Japan's advantage.
announcing Japan's surrender, in a broadcast to his people after atom bombs had destroyed Hiroshima and Nagasaki
Emperor Hirohito 1901–89: on 15 August 1945

22 Man is not made for defeat. A man can be destroyed but not defeated.
Ernest Hemingway 1899–1961: *The Old Man and the Sea* (1952)

23 Sure, winning isn't everything. It's the only thing.
Henry 'Red' Sanders: in *Sports Illustrated* 26 December 1955; often attributed to Vince Lombardi

24 Defeat doesn't finish a man—quit does. A man is not finished when he's defeated. He's finished when he quits.
Richard Nixon 1913–94: William Safire *Before the Fall* (1975)

25 A man able to think isn't defeated—even when he is defeated.
Milan Kundera 1929– : in *Sunday Times* 20 May 1984

26 The moment of victory is much too short to live for that and nothing else.
Martina Navratilova 1956– : in *Independent* 21 June 1989

27 Winning is everything. The only ones who remember you when you come second are your wife and your dog.
Damon Hill 1960– : in *Sunday Times* 18 December 1994

28 Sometimes it's better to lose and do the right thing than win and do the wrong thing.
Tony Blair 1953– : on losing the vote on the Terrorism Bill, 9 November 2005

⇢⇢ Wit and Wordplay ⇠⇠

see also **Humour**

PROVERBS AND SAYINGS

1 **Brevity is the soul of wit.**
English proverb, early 17th century, from Shakespeare: see 5 below

PHRASES

2 **Attic salt**
refined, delicate, poignant wit; *Attic* of Attica, district of ancient Greece, or Athens, its chief city

3 **esprit de l'escalier**
a clever remark that occurs to one after the opportunity to make it is lost; French = staircase wit,

from Denis Diderot (1713–84) *Paradoxe sur le Comédien* (written 1773–8) 'The witty riposte one thinks of only when one has left the drawing-room and is already on the way downstairs'

QUOTATIONS

4 I am not only witty in myself, but the cause that wit is in other men.
William Shakespeare 1564–1616: *Henry IV, Part 2* (1597)

5 Brevity is the soul of wit.
William Shakespeare 1564–1616: *Hamlet* (1601); see 1 above, 18 below

6 I do utter as good things every hour, if they were collected and observed, as either of 'em.
Ben Jonson 1573–1637: *Epicene* (1609)

7 A thing well said will be wit in all languages.
John Dryden 1631–1700: *An Essay of Dramatic Poesy* (1668)

8   Wit will shine
Through the harsh cadence of a rugged line.
John Dryden 1631–1700: 'To the Memory of Mr Oldham' (1684)

9 A man who could make so vile a pun would not scruple to pick a pocket.
John Dennis 1657–1734: editorial note in *The Gentleman's Magazine* (1781)

10 Apt Alliteration's artful aid.
   Charles Churchill 1731–64: *The Prophecy of Famine* (1763)

11 If I reprehend any thing in this world, it is the use of my oracular tongue, and a nice derangement of epitaphs!
   Richard Brinsley Sheridan 1751–1816: *The Rivals* (1775)

12 There's no possibility of being witty without a little ill-nature; the malice of a good thing is the barb that makes it stick.
   Richard Brinsley Sheridan 1751–1816: *The School for Scandal* (1777)

13 His wit invites you by his looks to come, But when you knock it never is at home.
   William Cowper 1731–1800: 'Conversation' (1782)

14 What is an Epigram? a dwarfish whole, Its body brevity, and wit its soul.
   Samuel Taylor Coleridge 1772–1834: 'Epigram' (1809)

15 Those who cannot miss an opportunity of saying a good thing . . . are not to be trusted with the management of any great question.
   William Hazlitt 1778–1830: *Characteristics* (1823)

16 [A pun] is a pistol let off at the ear; not a feather to tickle the intellect.
   Charles Lamb 1775–1834: *Last Essays of Elia* (1833) 'Popular Fallacies'

17 Wit is the epitaph of an emotion.
   Friedrich Nietzsche 1844–1900: *Menschliches, Allzumenschliches* (1867–80)

18 Impropriety is the soul of wit.
   W. Somerset Maugham 1874–1965: *The Moon and Sixpence* (1919); see 5 above

19 If, with the literate, I am
   Impelled to try an epigram,
   I never seek to take the credit;
   We all assume that Oscar said it.
   Dorothy Parker 1893–1967: 'A Pig's-Eye View of Literature' (1937)

20 There's a hell of a distance between wise-cracking and wit. Wit has truth in it; wise-cracking is simply callisthenics with words.
   Dorothy Parker 1893–1967: in *Paris Review* Summer 1956

21 Satire is a lesson, parody is a game.
   Vladimir Nabokov 1899–1977: *Strong Opinions* (1974)

22 Satire is dependent on strong beliefs, and on strong beliefs wounded.
   Anita Brookner 1928– : in *Spectator* 23 March 1989

⇥ Woman's Role ⇤

see also **Men and Women**

PROVERBS AND SAYINGS

1 **Burn your bra.**
   feminist slogan, 1970s

2 **Silence is a woman's best garment.**
   often used as recommending a traditionally submissive and discreet role for women; English proverb, mid 16th century

3 **Votes for women.**
   slogan of the women's suffrage movement, adopted when it proved impossible to use a banner with the longer slogan 'Will the Liberal Party Give Votes for Women?' made by Emmeline Pankhurst, Christabel Pankhurst, and Annie Kenney

4 **A woman's place is in the home.**
   reflecting the traditional view of a woman's role; English proverb, mid 19th century

PHRASES

5 **the angel in the house**
   a woman who is completely devoted to her husband and family; from the title of a poem (1854–62) by Coventry Patmore; now often used ironically

QUOTATIONS

6 Men are the managers of the affairs of
women.
The Koran: sura 4

7 The First Blast of the Trumpet Against the
Monstrous Regiment of Women.
regiment = rule or government over a country,
directed against the rule of Mary Tudor in England
and Mary of Lorraine in Scotland (as regent for her
daughter Mary Queen of Scots)
John Knox 1505–72: title of pamphlet (1558)

8 I am obnoxious to each carping tongue,
Who says my hand a needle better fits,
A poet's pen, all scorn, I should thus wrong.
Anne Bradstreet 1612–72: 'The Prologue' (1650)

9 Why then should women be denied the
benefits of instruction? If knowledge and
understanding had been useless additions to
the sex, God almighty would never have
given them capacities.
Daniel Defoe 1660–1731: *An Essay Upon Projects*
(1697) 'Of Academies: An Academy for Women'

10 If all men are born free, how is it that all
women are born slaves?
Mary Astell 1668–1731: *Some Reflections upon
Marriage* (1706 ed.)

11 A woman's preaching is like a dog's walking
on his hinder legs. It is not done well; but
you are surprised to find it done at all.
Samuel Johnson 1709–84: James Boswell *Life of
Samuel Johnson* (1791) 31 July 1763

12 In the new code of laws which I suppose it
will be necessary for you to make I desire
you would remember the ladies, and be
more generous and favourable to them than
your ancestors. Do not put such unlimited
power into the hands of the husbands.
Remember all men would be tyrants if they
could.
Abigail Adams 1744–1818: letter to John Adams,
31 March 1776

13 A man is in general better pleased when he
has a good dinner upon his table, than
when his wife talks Greek.
Samuel Johnson 1709–84: John Hawkins (ed.) *The
Works of Samuel Johnson* (1787) 'Apophthegms,
Sentiments, Opinions, etc.'

14 Can anything be more absurd than keeping
women in a state of ignorance, and yet so
vehemently to insist on their resisting
temptation?
Vicesimus Knox 1752–1821: Mary Wollstonecraft *A
Vindication of the Rights of Woman* (1792)

15 I do not wish them [women] to have power
over men; but over themselves.
Mary Wollstonecraft 1759–97: *A Vindication of the
Rights of Woman* (1792)

16 Religion is an all-important matter in a
public school for girls. Whatever people say,
it is the mother's safeguard, and the
husband's. What we ask of education is not
that girls should think, but that they should
believe.
Napoleon I 1769–1821: 'Note sur L'Établissement
D'Écouen' 15 May 1807

17 That little man . . . he says women can't
have as much rights as men, cause Christ
wasn't a woman. Where did your Christ
come from? From God and a woman. Man
had nothing to do with Him.
Sojourner Truth 1797–1883: speech at Women's
Rights Convention, Akron, Ohio, 1851

18 Woman stock is rising in the market. I shall
not live to see women vote, but I'll come
and rap at the ballot box.
Lydia Maria Child 1802–80: letter to Sarah Shaw, 3
August 1856

19 I should like to know what is the proper
function of women, if it is not to make
reasons for husbands to stay at home, and
still stronger reasons for bachelors to go out.
George Eliot 1819–80: *The Mill on the Floss* (1860)

20 I want to be something so much worthier
than the doll in the doll's house.
Charles Dickens 1812–70: *Our Mutual Friend*
(1865)

21 The Queen is most anxious to enlist every
one who can speak or write to join in
checking this mad, wicked folly of
'Woman's Rights', with all its attendant
horrors, on which her poor feeble sex is
bent, forgetting every sense of womanly
feeling and propriety.
Queen Victoria 1819–1901: letter to Theodore
Martin, 29 May 1870

22 Inferior to us God made you, and inferior to
the end of time you will remain.
on the admission of women to university
John William Burgon 1813–88: University
Sermon, New College, Oxford, 8 June 1884

23 The one point on which all women are in
furious secret rebellion against the existing
law is the saddling of the right to a child
with the obligation to become the servant
of a man.
George Bernard Shaw 1856–1950: *Getting
Married* (1911)

24 We are here to claim our right as women,
not only to be free, but to fight for freedom.
That is our right as well as our duty.
Christabel Pankhurst 1880–1958: in *Votes for
Women* 31 March 1911

25 I myself have never been able to find out precisely what feminism is: I only know that people call me a feminist whenever I express sentiments that differentiate me from a doormat or a prostitute.
Rebecca West 1892–1983: in *The Clarion* 14 November 1913

26 Woman is the nigger of the world.
Yoko Ono 1933– : remark made in a 1968 interview for *Nova* magazine and adopted by John Lennon as the title of a song (1972)

27 But if God had wanted us to think just with our wombs, why did He give us a brain?
Clare Booth Luce 1903–87: in *Life* 16 October 1970

28 Women's Liberation is just a lot of foolishness. It's the men who are discriminated against. They can't bear children. And no-one's likely to do anything about that.
Golda Meir 1898–1978: in *Newsweek* 23 October 1972

29 We are becoming the men we wanted to marry.
Gloria Steinem 1934– : in *Ms* July/August 1982

30 The freedom women were supposed to have found in the Sixties largely boiled down to easy contraception and abortion: things to make life easier for men, in fact.
Julie Burchill 1960– : *Damaged Goods* (1986)

31 I didn't fight to get women out from behind the vacuum cleaner to get them onto the board of Hoover.
Germaine Greer 1939– : in *Guardian* 27 October 1986

32 Today the problem that has no name is how to juggle work, love, home and children.
Betty Friedan 1921– : *The Second Stage* (1987)

33 I could have stayed home and baked cookies and had teas. But what I decided was to fulfil my profession, which I entered before my husband was in public life.
Hillary Rodham Clinton 1947– : comment on questions raised by rival Democratic contender Edmund G. Brown Jr.; in *Albany Times-Union* 17 March 1992

34 Women have been trained to speak softly and carry lipstick. Those days are over.
Bella Abzug 1920–98: attributed; in *Times* 2 April 1998; see **Diplomacy** 11

35 I want to deal with women's issues because I just don't think they clean behind the fridge enough.
view of a UKIP MEP
Godfrey Bloom 1949– : in *Guardian* 21 July 2004

⤜ Women ⤛

see also **Men and Women**

PROVERBS AND SAYINGS

1 **Far-fetched and dear-bought is good for ladies.**
expensive or exotic articles are suitable for women; English proverb, mid 14th century

2 **The female of the species is more deadly than the male.**
English proverb, early 20th century; from Kipling: see 41 below

3 **The hand that rocks the cradle rules the world.**
referring to the strength of a woman's indirect influence on the male world; English proverb, mid 19th century; see **Elections** 19, **Parents** 14

4 **Hell hath no fury like a woman scorned.**
a woman whose love has turned to hate is the most savage of creatures; a *fury* here may be either one of the avenging deities of classical mythology, or more generally someone in a state of frenzied rage; English proverb, late 17th century, see **Revenge** 16

5 **Long and lazy, little and loud; fat and fulsome, pretty and proud.**
categorizing supposed physical and temperamental characteristics in women; English proverb, late 16th century

6 **A whistling woman and a crowing hen are neither fit for God nor men.**
both the woman and the hen are considered unnatural, and therefore unlucky; English proverb, early 18th century

7 **A woman, a dog, and a walnut tree, the more you beat them the better they be.**
the walnut tree was beaten firstly to bring down the fruit, and then to break down long shoots and encourage short fruit-bearing ones; English proverb, late 16th century

8 **A woman and a ship ever want mending.**
both women and ships require constant attention and expenditure; English proverb, late 16th century

9 **Women hold up half the sky.**
women should be considered equal in status to men; Chinese proverb

PHRASES

10 **daughter of Eve**
a woman, especially one regarded as showing a typically feminine trait

11 **Essex girl**
a derogatory term applied to a type of young woman, supposedly to be found in and around Essex, and variously characterized as unintelligent, promiscuous, and materialistic; she is typically the butt of politically incorrect jokes; see also **Class** 4

12 **the fair sex**
the female sex, women collectively; see 35 below

13 **It girl**
an actress or model, usually vivacious and outgoing, considered to have particular sex appeal. In later use, also a young woman who has achieved celebrity

because of her socialite lifestyle; coined by the screenwriter Elinor Glyn (1864–1943) and personified by the actress Clara Bow (1905–65). The use of *it* meaning sex appeal is first recorded in Kipling: see **Sex** 19

14 **page three girl**
a model whose nude or semi-nude photograph appears as part of a regular series in a tabloid newspaper; after the standard page position in the *Sun*, a British newspaper

QUOTATIONS

15 This is now bone of my bones, and flesh of my flesh: she shall be called Woman, because she was taken out of Man.
Bible: Genesis

16 Who can find a virtuous woman? for her price is far above rubies.
Bible: Proverbs

17 The greatest glory of a woman is to be least talked about by men.
Pericles c.495–429 BC: Thucydides *History of the Peloponnesian War*

18 Men say of us that we live a life free from danger at home while they fight wars. How wrong they are! I would rather stand three times in the battle line than bear one child.
Euripides c.485–c.406 BC: *Medea*

19 *Varium et mutabile semper Femina.*
Fickle and changeable always is woman.
Virgil 70–19 BC: *Aeneid*

20 Whoever has a daughter and does not bury her alive, nor insult her nor favour his son over her, Allah will enter him into Paradise.
Ahmad ibn Hanbal 780–855: *Musnad* no. 1957

21 Frailty, thy name is woman!
William Shakespeare 1564–1616: *Hamlet* (1601)

22 The weaker sex, to piety more prone.
William Alexander, Earl of Stirling 1567–1640: 'Doomsday' 5th Hour (1637)

23 She floats, she hesitates; in a word, she's a woman.
Jean Racine 1639–99: *Athalie* (1691)

24 She knows her man, and when you rant and swear,
Can draw you to her *with a single hair.*
John Dryden 1631–1700: translation of Persius *Satires*

25 I have never had any great esteem for the generality of the fair sex, and my only consolation for being of that gender has been the assurance it gave me of never being married to anyone amongst them.
Lady Mary Wortley Montagu 1689–1762: letter to Mrs Calthorpe, 7 December 1723

26 Woman's at best a contradiction still.
Alexander Pope 1688–1744: *Epistles to Several Persons* 'To a Lady' (1735)

27 Women, then, are only children of a larger growth.
Lord Chesterfield 1694–1773: *Letters to his Son* (1774) 5 September 1748

28 Here's to the maiden of bashful fifteen
Here's to the widow of fifty
Here's to the flaunting, extravagant quean;
And here's to the housewife that's thrifty.
Richard Brinsley Sheridan 1751–1816: *The School for Scandal* (1777)

29 Auld nature swears, the lovely dears
Her noblest work she classes, O;
Her prentice han' she tried on man,
An' then she made the lasses, O.
Robert Burns 1759–96: 'Green Grow the Rashes' (1787)

30 O Woman! in our hours of ease,
Uncertain, coy, and hard to please,
And variable as the shade
By the light quivering aspen made;

When pain and anguish wring the brow,
A ministering angel thou!
Sir Walter Scott 1771–1832: *Marmion* (1808); see
Charity 10

31 All the privilege I claim for my own sex . . .
is that of loving longest, when existence or
when hope is gone.
Jane Austen 1775–1817: *Persuasion* (1818)

32 In her first passion woman loves her lover,
In all the others all she loves is love.
Lord Byron 1788–1824: *Don Juan* (1819–24)

33 Eternal Woman draws us upward.
Johann Wolfgang von Goethe 1749–1832: *Faust*
pt. 2 (1832) 'Hochgebirg'

34   The woman is so hard
Upon the woman.
Alfred, Lord Tennyson 1809–92: *The Princess*
(1847)

35 Only the male intellect, clouded by sexual
impulse, could call the undersized, narrow-
shouldered, broad-hipped, and short-legged
sex the fair sex.
Arthur Schopenhauer 1788–1860: 'On Women'
(1851); see 12 above

36 The happiest women, like the happiest
nations, have no history.
George Eliot 1819–80: *The Mill on the Floss* (1860)

37 Women—one half the human race at
least—care fifty times more for a marriage
than a ministry.
Walter Bagehot 1826–77: *The English Constitution*
(1867) 'The Monarchy'

38 Woman was God's second blunder.
Friedrich Nietzsche 1844–1900: *Der Antichrist*
(1888)

39 When you get to a man in the case,
They're like as a row of pins—
For the Colonel's Lady an' Judy O'Grady
Are sisters under their skins!
Rudyard Kipling 1865–1936: 'The Ladies' (1896)

40 The prime truth of woman, the universal
mother . . . that if a thing is worth doing, it
is worth doing badly.
G. K. Chesterton 1874–1936: *What's Wrong with
the World* (1910) 'Folly and Female Education'; see
Effort 5

41 The female of the species is more deadly
than the male.
Rudyard Kipling 1865–1936: 'The Female of the
Species' (1919); see 2 above

42 The perpetual hunger to be beautiful and
that thirst to be loved which is the real curse
of Eve.
Jean Rhys 1890–1979: *The Left Bank* (1927)
'Illusion'

43 Certain women should be struck regularly,
like gongs.
Noël Coward 1899–1973: *Private Lives* (1930)

44 The great and almost only comfort about
being a woman is that one can always
pretend to be more stupid than one is and
no one is surprised.
Freya Stark 1893–1993: *The Valleys of the Assassins*
(1934)

45 Woman may born you, love you, an'
        mourn you,
But a woman is a sometime thing.
Du Bose Heyward 1885–1940 and **Ira Gershwin**
1896–1983: 'A Woman is a Sometime Thing' (1935
song)

46 The great question that has never been
answered and which I have not yet been
able to answer, despite my thirty years of
research into the feminine soul, is 'What
does a woman want?'
Sigmund Freud 1856–1939: to Marie Bonaparte;
Ernest Jones *Sigmund Freud: Life and Work* (1955)

47 Women would rather be right than be
        reasonable.
Ogden Nash 1902–71: 'Frailty, Thy Name is a
Misnomer' (1942)

48 One is not born a woman: one becomes one.
Simone de Beauvoir 1908–86: *Le deuxième sexe*
(1949)

49 There is nothin' like a dame.
Oscar Hammerstein II 1895–1960: title of song
(1949)

50 Thank heaven for little girls!
For little girls get bigger every day.
Alan Jay Lerner 1918–86: 'Thank Heaven for Little
Girls' (1958 song)

51 Women never have young minds. They are
born three thousand years old.
Shelagh Delaney 1939– : *A Taste of Honey* (1959)

52 I got a twenty dollar piece says
There ain't nothin' I can't do.
I can make a dress out of a feed bag an' I can
        make a man out of you.
'Cause I'm a woman
W-O-M-A-N
I'll say it again.
Jerry Leiber 1933– : 'I'm a Woman' (1962 song)

53 From birth to 18 a girl needs good parents.
From 18 to 35, she needs good looks. From
35 to 55, good personality. From 55 on, she
needs good cash.
Sophie Tucker 1884–1966: Michael Freedland
Sophie (1978)

54 She takes just like a woman, yes, she does
She makes love just like a woman, yes,
        she does
And she aches just like a woman

But she breaks like a little girl.
Bob Dylan 1941– : 'Just Like a Woman' (1966 song)

55 Sisterhood is powerful.
Robin Morgan 1941– : title of book (1970)

56 Being a woman is of special interest only to aspiring male transsexuals. To actual women, it is merely a good excuse not to play football.
Fran Lebowitz 1946– : *Metropolitan Life* (1978)

57 a woman is not
a potted plant
her leaves trimmed

to the contours
of her sex.
Alice Walker 1944– : 'A woman is not a potted plant'

58 You can now see the Female Eunuch the world over . . . spreading herself wherever blue jeans and Coca-Cola may go. Wherever you see nail varnish, lipstick, brassieres, and high heels, the Eunuch has set up her camp.
Germaine Greer 1939– : *The Female Eunuch* (20th anniversary ed., 1991)

59 You can have it all, but you can't do it all.
Michelle Pfeiffer 1959– : attributed; in *Guardian* 4 January 1996

Wordplay see Wit and Wordplay

⤞ Words ⤝

see also **Language, Meaning, Names, Words and Deeds**

PROVERBS AND SAYINGS

1 **All words are pegs to hang ideas on.**
American proverb, late 19th century

2 **Hard words break no bones.**
the damage done by verbal attack is limited; English proverb, late 17th century

3 **I before e, except after c.**
traditional spelling rule, 19th century

4 **If you take hyphens seriously you will surely go mad.**
said to be from a style book in use with Oxford University Press, New York; perhaps apocryphal

5 **The swiftest horse cannot overtake the word once spoken.**
Chinese proverb; see 7 below

6 **Sticks and stones may break my bones, but words will never hurt me.**
verbal attack does no real injury; English proverb, late 19th century

QUOTATIONS

7 And once sent out a word takes wing beyond recall.
Horace 65–8 BC: *Epistles*; see 5 above

8 But words are words; I never yet did hear
That the bruisèd heart was piercèd through the ear.
William Shakespeare 1564–1616: *Othello* (1602–4)

9 Words are the tokens current and accepted for conceits, as moneys are for values.
Francis Bacon 1561–1626: *The Advancement of Learning* (1605)

10 Words are wise men's counters, they do but reckon by them: but they are the money of fools, that value them by the authority of an Aristotle, a Cicero, or a Thomas, or any other doctor whatsoever, if but a man.
Thomas Hobbes 1588–1679: *Leviathan* (1651)

11 Words easy to be understood do often hit the mark; when high and learned ones do only pierce the air.
John Bunyan 1628–88: *The Holy City* (1665)

12 Words are like leaves; and where they most abound,
Much fruit of sense beneath is rarely found.
Alexander Pope 1688–1744: *An Essay on Criticism* (1711)

13 I am not yet so lost in lexicography as to forget that words are the daughters of earth, and that things are the sons of heaven. Language is only the instrument of science, and words are but the signs of ideas: I wish, however, that the instrument might be less apt to decay, and that signs might be permanent, like the things which they denote.
Samuel Johnson 1709–84: *A Dictionary of the English Language* (1755)

14 It's exactly where a thought is lacking
That, just in time, a word shows up instead.
Goethe 1749–1832: *Faust* (1808)

15 With words we govern men.
Benjamin Disraeli 1804–81: *Contarini Fleming* (1832) pt. 1, ch. 21

16 'Do you spell it with a "V" or a "W"?' inquired the judge. 'That depends upon the taste and fancy of the speller, my Lord,' replied Sam [Weller].
Charles Dickens 1812–70: *Pickwick Papers* (1837)

17 'When *I* use a word,' Humpty Dumpty said in a rather scornful tone, 'it means just what I choose it to mean—neither more nor less.'
Lewis Carroll 1832–98: *Through the Looking-Glass* (1872)

18 Some word that teems with hidden meaning—like Basingstoke.
W. S. Gilbert 1836–1911: *Ruddigore* (1887)

19 Only those ideas which least belong to us can be adequately expressed in words.
Henri Bergson 1859–1941:*Time and Free Will* (1910)

20 I fear those big words, Stephen said, which make us so unhappy.
James Joyce 1882–1941: *Ulysses* (1922)

21 Words are, of course, the most powerful drug used by mankind.
Rudyard Kipling 1865–1936: speech, 14 February 1923

22 My spelling is Wobbly. It's good spelling but it Wobbles, and the letters get in the wrong places.
A. A. Milne 1882–1956: *Winnie-the-Pooh* (1926)

23 The Greeks had a word for it.
Zoë Akins 1886–1958: title of play (1930)

24 I gotta use words when I talk to you.
T. S. Eliot 1888–1965: *Sweeney Agonistes* (1932)

25   Words strain,
Crack and sometimes break, under the burden,

Under the tension, slip, slide, perish,
Decay with imprecision, will not stay in place,
Will not stay still.
T. S. Eliot 1888–1965: *Four Quartets* 'Burnt Norton' (1936)

26 Today words have become battles. The right words, battles won; the wrong words, battles lost.
Erich von Ludendorff 1865–1937: George C. Bruntz *Allied Propaganda and the Collapse of the German Empire in 1918* (1938)

27 Words are chameleons, which reflect the colour of their environment.
Learned Hand 1872–1961: in *Commissioner v. National Carbide Corp.* (1948)

28 There is no use indicting words, they are no shoddier than what they peddle.
Samuel Beckett 1906–89: *Malone Dies* (1958)

29 Man does not live by words alone, despite the fact that he sometimes has to eat them.
Adlai Stevenson 1900–65: *The Wit and Wisdom of Adlai Stevenson* (1965)

30 MIKE: There's no word in the Irish language for what you were doing.
WILSON: In Lapland they have no word for snow.
Joe Orton 1933–67: *The Ruffian on the Stair* (rev. ed. 1967)

31 If *Miss* means respectably unmarried, and *Mrs* respectably married, then *Ms* means nudge, nudge, wink, wink.
Angela Carter 1940–92: 'The Language of Sisterhood' in Christopher Ricks (ed.) *The State of the Language* (1980); see **Sex** 6

32 In my youth there were words you couldn't say in front of a girl; now you can't say 'girl'.
Tom Lehrer 1928– : interview in *The Oldie* 1996; in *Sunday Telegraph* 10 March 1996

⤙⤚ Words and Deeds ⤙⤚

PROVERBS AND SAYINGS

1 **Actions speak louder than words.**
real feeling is expressed not by what someone says but by what they do; English proverb, early 17th century

2 **Brag is a good dog, but Holdfast is better.**
perseverance is a better quality than ostentation; English proverb, early 18th century

3 **Example is better than precept.**
English proverb, early 15th century

4 **Fine words butter no parsnips.**
nothing is ever achieved by fine words alone (*butter* was the traditional garnish for parsnips); English proverb, mid 17th century

5 **One picture is worth ten thousand words.**
English proverb, early 20th century; see Language 20

6 **An ounce of practice is worth a pound of precept.**
a small amount of practical assistance is worth more than a great deal of advice; English proverb, late 16th century

7 **Practise what you preach.**
you should follow the advice you give to others; English proverb, late 14th century

QUOTATIONS

10 But be ye doers of the word, and not hearers only.
Bible: James

11 Woord is but wynd; leff woord and tak the dede.
John Lydgate c.1370–c.1451: *Secrets of Old Philosophers*

12 Do not, as some ungracious pastors do,
Show me the steep and thorny way to heaven,
Whiles, like a puffed and reckless libertine,
Himself the primrose path of dalliance treads,
And recks not his own rede.
William Shakespeare 1564–1616: *Hamlet* (1601); see Pleasure 6

13 Oh that thou hadst like others been all words,
And no performance.
Philip Massinger 1583–1640: *The Parliament of Love* (1624)

14 Here lies a great and mighty king
Whose promise none relies on;
He never said a foolish thing,
Nor ever did a wise one.
on Charles II
John Wilmot, Lord Rochester 1647–80: 'The King's Epitaph' (alternatively 'Here lies our sovereign lord the King'); in C. E. Doble et al. *Thomas Hearne: Remarks and Collections* (1885–1921) 17 November 1706; see 15 below

8 **Talk is cheap.**
it is easier to say than to do something; English proverb, mid 19th century

9 **Threatened men live long.**
threats are often not put into effect, and those who express resentment are actually much less dangerous than those who conceal animosity; English proverb, mid 16th century

15 This is very true: for my words are my own, and my actions are my ministers'.
reply to Lord Rochester's epitaph
Charles II 1630–85: in *Thomas Hearne: Remarks and Collections* (1885–1921) 17 November 1706; see 14 above

16 Because half a dozen grasshoppers under a fern make the field ring with their importunate chink, whilst thousands of great cattle, reposed beneath the shadow of the British oak, chew the cud and are silent, pray do not imagine that those who make the noise are the only inhabitants of the field.
Edmund Burke 1729–97: *Reflections on the Revolution in France* (1790)

17 I prefer the talents of action—of war—of the senate—or even of science—to all the speculations of those mere dreamers of another existence.
Lord Byron 1788–1824: letter to Annabella Milbanke, 29 November 1813

18 The end of man is an action and not a thought, though it were the noblest.
Thomas Carlyle 1795–1881: *Sartor Resartus* (1834)

19 Considering how foolishly people act and how pleasantly they prattle, perhaps it would be better for the world if they talked more and did less.
W. Somerset Maugham 1874–1965: *A Writer's Notebook* (1949) written in 1892

20 Enough of talking—it is time now to do.
Tony Blair 1953– : on taking office as Prime Minister; Downing Street, 2 May 1997

→→ Work ←←

see also **Employment, Idleness, Leisure**

PROVERBS AND SAYINGS

1 Arbeit macht frei.

German, *Work liberates*, words inscribed on the gates of Dachau concentration camp, 1933, and subsequently on those of Auschwitz

2 Every man to his trade.

one should operate within one's own area of expertise; English proverb, late 16th century

3 Fools and bairns should never see half-done work.

the unwise and the inexperienced may judge the quality of a finished article from its rough unfinished state; English proverb, early 18th century

4 One volunteer is worth two pressed men.

a *pressed man* was someone forcibly enlisted by the press gang, a body of men which in the 18th and 19th centuries was employed to enlist men forcibly into service in the army or navy; English proverb, early 18th century

5 Practice makes perfect.

often used as an encouragement; English proverb, mid 16th century

6 Saturday's child works hard for its living.

traditional rhyme, mid 19th century; see also **Beauty 7, Gifts 2, Pregnancy 1, Sorrow 2, Travel 6**

7 A short horse is soon curried.

a slight task is soon completed (literally, that it does not take long to rub down a short horse with a curry-comb); English proverb, mid 14th century

8 Too many cooks spoil the broth.

the involvement of too many people is likely to mean that something is done badly; English proverb, late 16th century

9 Two boys are half a boy, and three boys are no boy at all.

the more boys there are present, the less work will be done; English proverb, mid 20th century

10 Where bees are, there is honey.

industrious work is necessary to create riches; English proverb, early 17th century

11 Work expands so as to fill the time available.

English proverb, mid 20th century, from Parkinson: see 39 below

PHRASES

12 the bread of idleness

food or sustenance for which one has not worked; after the Bible (Proverbs) 'She . . . eateth not the bread of idleness'

13 burn the midnight oil

study late into the night; see 25 below

14 by the sweat of one's brow

by one's own hard work; from the Bible: see 19 below

15 daily bread

a livelihood; after the Bible (Matthew) 'Give us this day our daily bread' (part of the Lord's Prayer)

16 a glutton for punishment

a person who is always eager to undertake hard or unpleasant tasks. *Glutton of —* was used figuratively

from the early 18th century for someone who is inordinately fond of the thing specified, especially translating the Latin phrase *helluo librorum* 'a glutton of books'. The current usage may originate with early 19th-century sporting slang

17 ply the labouring oar

do much of the work; *labouring oar* = the hardest to pull, originally with allusion to Dryden *Aeneid* 'three Trojans tug at ev'ry lab'ring oar'

18 sing for one's supper

provide a service in order to earn a benefit; after the nursery rhyme *Little Tommy Tucker*

QUOTATIONS

19 In the sweat of thy face shalt thou eat bread.
Bible: Genesis; see 14 above

20 For it is commonly said: completed labours are pleasant.
Cicero 106–43 BC: *De Finibus*

21 Come unto me, all ye that labour and are heavy laden, and I will give you rest . . .
For my yoke is easy, and my burden is light.
Bible: St Matthew

22 If any would not work, neither should
he eat.
Bible: II Thessalonians; see **Idleness** 8

23 Set thy heart upon thy work but never upon
its reward. Work not for a reward: but never
cease to do thy work.
Bhagavadgita: ch. 2, v. 47

24 The labour we delight in physics pain.
William Shakespeare 1564–1616: *Macbeth* (1606)

25 We spend our midday sweat, our
midnight oil;
We tire the night in thought, the day in toil.
Francis Quarles 1592–1644: *Emblems* (1635); see
13 above

26 How doth the little busy bee
Improve each shining hour,
And gather honey all the day
From every opening flower!
Isaac Watts 1674–1748: 'Against Idleness and
Mischief' (1715); see **Effort** 12

27 If you have great talents, industry will
improve them: if you have but moderate
abilities, industry will supply their
deficiency.
Joshua Reynolds 1723–92: *Discourses on Art* 11
December 1769

28 The world is too much with us; late and
soon,
Getting and spending, we lay waste our
powers.
William Wordsworth 1770–1850: 'The world is
too much with us' (1807)

29 Who first invented work—and tied the free
And holy-day rejoicing spirit down
To the ever-haunting importunity
Of business?
Charles Lamb 1775–1834: letter to Bernard Barton,
11 September 1822

30 My life is one demd horrid grind!
Charles Dickens 1812–70: *Nicholas Nickleby* (1839)

31 Blessèd are the horny hands of toil!
James Russell Lowell 1819–91: 'A Glance Behind
the Curtain' (1844)

32 For men must work, and women must weep,
And there's little to earn, and many to keep,
Though the harbour bar be moaning.
Charles Kingsley 1819–75: 'The Three Fishers'
(1858)

33 Labour without joy is base. Labour without
sorrow is base. Sorrow without labour is
base. Joy without labour is base.
John Ruskin 1819–1900: *Time and Tide* (1867)

34 Generations have trod, have trod, have trod;
And all is seared with trade; bleared,
smeared with toil.
Gerard Manley Hopkins 1844–89: 'God's
Grandeur' (written 1877)

35 I like work: it fascinates me. I can sit and
look at it for hours. I love to keep it by me:
the idea of getting rid of it nearly breaks my
heart.
Jerome K. Jerome 1859–1927: *Three Men in a Boat*
(1889)

36 Work is love made visible.
Kahlil Gibran 1883–1931: *The Prophet* (1923)

37 Who built Thebes of the seven gates?
In the books you will find the names of
kings.
Did the kings haul up the lumps of rock? . . .
Where, the evening that the wall of China
was finished
Did the masons go?
Bertolt Brecht 1898–1956: 'Questions From A
Worker Who Reads' (1935)

38 Why should I let the toad *work*
Squat on my life?
Philip Larkin 1922–85: 'Toads' (1955)

39 Work expands so as to fill the time available
for its completion.
C. Northcote Parkinson 1909–93: *Parkinson's
Law* (1958); see 11 above

40 Without work, all life goes rotten, but when
work is soulless, life stifles and dies.
Albert Camus 1913–60: attributed; E. F.
Schumacher *Good Work* (1979)

41 It has been my experience that one cannot,
in any shape or form, depend on human
relations for lasting reward. It is only work
that truly satisfies.
Bette Davis 1908–89: *The Lonely Life* (1962)

42 Work was like a stick. It had two ends. When
you worked for the knowing you gave them
quality; when you worked for a fool you
simply gave him eye-wash.
Alexander Solzhenitsyn 1918– : *One Day in the
Life of Ivan Denisovich* (1962)

43 It's true hard work never killed anybody, but
I figure why take the chance?
Ronald Reagan 1911–2004: interview, *Guardian* 31
March 1987

44 I have long been of the opinion that if work
were such a splendid thing the rich would
have kept more of it for themselves.
Bruce Grocott 1940– : in *Observer* 22 May 1988

World War I

see also **The Armed Forces, Warfare**

PROVERBS AND SAYINGS

1 Ils ne passeront pas.
French, *They shall not pass*, slogan used by the
French army at the defence of Verdun in 1916;
variously attributed to Marshal Pétain and to General
Robert Nivelle, and taken up by the Republicans in
the Spanish Civil War in the form '*No pasarán!*'; see
Defiance 17

PHRASES

2 the Angels of Mons
protective spirits supposedly seen over the First
World War battlefield. The origin was in fact a short
story, 'The Angel of Mons' (1915) by Arthur Machen
(1843–1947), which circulated widely by word of
mouth as a factual account

3 Flanders poppy
a red poppy used as an emblem of the soldiers of the
Allies who fell in the First World War; chosen as a
flower which grew on the battlefields: see 15 below

4 lions led by donkeys
associated with British soldiers during the First World
War; attributed to Max Hoffman (1869–1927) in Alan
Clark *The Donkeys* (1961); this attribution has not
been traced elsewhere, and the phrase is of much
earlier origin

5 the Old Contemptibles
the British army in France in 1914; referring to the
German Emperor's alleged mention of a
'contemptible little army'

6 the war to end wars
the war of 1914–18, as a war intended to make
further wars impossible; after the title of book by H.
G. Wells in 1914, *The War That Will End War*

QUOTATIONS

7 If there is ever another war in Europe, it will
come out of some damned silly thing in the
Balkans.
Otto von Bismarck 1815–98: quoted in speech,
House of Commons, 16 August 1945

8 The lamps are going out all over Europe; we
shall not see them lit again in our lifetime.
on the eve of the First World War
Edward Grey 1862–1933: *25 Years* (1925)

9 Do your duty bravely. Fear God. Honour the
King.
Lord Kitchener 1850–1916: message to soldiers of
the British Expeditionary Force, August 1914

10 *Gott strafe England!*
God punish England!
Alfred Funke 1869–1941: *Schwert und Myrte* (1914)

11 Belgium put the kibosh on the Kaiser.
Alf Ellerton: title of song (1914)

12 Now, God be thanked Who has matched us
with His hour.
Rupert Brooke 1887–1915: 'Peace' (1914)

13 Oh! we don't want to lose you but we think
you ought to go
For your King and your Country both need
you so.
Paul Alfred Rubens 1875–1917: 'Your King and
Country Want You' (1914 song)

14 My centre is giving way, my right is
retreating, situation excellent, I am
attacking.
Ferdinand Foch 1851–1929: message sent during
the first Battle of the Marne, September 1914; R.
Recouly *Foch* (1919)

15 In Flanders fields the poppies blow
Between the crosses, row on row.
John McCrae 1872–1918: 'In Flanders Fields'
(1915); see 3 above

16 What passing-bells for these who die as
cattle?
Only the monstrous anger of the guns.
Only the stuttering rifles' rapid rattle
Can patter out their hasty orisons.
Wilfred Owen 1893–1918: 'Anthem for Doomed
Youth' (written 1917)

17 *Lafayette, nous voilà!*
Lafayette, we are here.
Charles E. Stanton 1859–1933: at the tomb of
Lafayette in Paris, 4 July 1917

18 Over there, over there,
Send the word, send the word over there
That the Yanks are coming, the Yanks are
coming . . .
We'll be over, we're coming over

And we won't come back till it's over, over there.
George M. Cohan 1878–1942: 'Over There' (1917 song); see **World War II** 1

19 If I were fierce, and bald, and short of breath,
I'd live with scarlet Majors at the Base,
And speed glum heroes up the line to death.
Siegfried Sassoon 1886–1967: 'Base Details' (1918)

20 O Death, where is thy sting-a-ling-a-ling,
O grave, thy victory?
The bells of Hell go ting-a-ling-a-ling
For you but not for me.
Anonymous: 'For You But Not For Me' (First World War song); see **Death** 27

21 My home policy: I wage war; my foreign policy: I wage war. All the time I wage war.
Georges Clemenceau 1841–1929: speech to French Chamber of Deputies, 8 March 1918

22 At eleven o'clock this morning came to an end the cruellest and most terrible war that has ever scourged mankind. I hope we may say that thus, this fateful morning, came to an end all wars.
David Lloyd George 1863–1945: speech, House of Commons, 11 November 1918

23 This is not a peace treaty, it is an armistice for twenty years.
Ferdinand Foch 1851–1929: at the signing of the Treaty of Versailles, 1919; Paul Reynaud *Mémoires* (1963)

24 You are all a lost generation.
of the young who served in the First World War; phrase borrowed (in translation) from a French

garage mechanic, whom Stein heard address it disparagingly to an incompetent apprentice
Gertrude Stein 1874–1946: Ernest Hemingway subsequently took it as his epigraph to *The Sun Also Rises* (1926)

25 All quiet on the western front.
Erich Maria Remarque 1898–1970: English title of *Im Westen nichts Neues* (1929 novel)

26 See that little stream—we could walk to it in two minutes. It took the British a month to walk it—a whole empire walking very slowly, dying in front and pushing forward behind. And another empire walked very slowly backward a few inches a day, leaving the dead like a million bloody rugs.
F. Scott Fitzgerald 1896–1940: *Tender is the Night* (1934)

27 Oh what a lovely war.
Joan Littlewood 1914–2002 and **Charles Chilton** 1914– : title of stage show (1963)

28 The First World War had begun—imposed on the statesmen of Europe by railway timetables.
A. J. P. Taylor 1906–90: *The First World War* (1963)

29 The Somme is like the Holocaust. It revealed things about mankind that we cannot come to terms with and cannot forget. It can never become the past.
Pat Barker 1943– : on winning the Booker Prize, November 1995

⇥ World War II ⇤

see also **Warfare**

PROVERBS AND SAYINGS
1 **Overpaid, overfed, oversexed, and over here.**
of American troops in Britain during the Second World War; associated with Tommy Trinder, but probably not his invention; see **World War I** 18

PHRASES
2 **the Baedeker raids**
a series of German reprisal air raids in 1942 on places in Britain of cultural and historical importance; after the series of guidebooks published by Karl *Baedeker* (1801–59), German publisher

3 **the Battle of Britain**
a series of air battles fought over Britain (August–October 1940), in which the RAF successfully resisted raids by the numerically superior German air force; from Winston Churchill, 18 June 1940, 'What General Weygand called the Battle of France is over. I expect that the Battle of Britain is about to begin'; the words 'The Battle of

Britain is about to begin' appeared in the order of the day for pilots on 10 July

4 the Desert Fox
Erwin Rommel (1891–1944), German Field Marshal, from his early successes in the North African campaign, 1941–2

5 the desert rats
soldiers of the 7th British armoured division in the North African desert campaign of 1941–2; the badge of the division was a jerboa

6 the forgotten army
the British army in Burma after the fall of Rangoon in 1942 and the evacuation west, and the subsequent cutting by the Japanese of the supply link from India to Nationalist China; said to derive from Lord Louis Mountbatten's encouragement to his troops after taking over as supreme Allied commander in South-East Asia, 'You are not the Forgotten Army—no one's even heard of you'

7 Old Blood and Guts
George Patton (1885–1945); name given to General Patton by his men; see **Warfare** 48

QUOTATIONS

8 How horrible, fantastic, incredible it is that we should be digging trenches and trying on gas-masks here because of a quarrel in a far away country between people of whom we know nothing.
on Germany's annexation of the Sudetenland
Neville Chamberlain 1869–1940: radio broadcast, 27 September 1938

9 We're gonna hang out the washing on the Siegfried Line.
Jimmy Kennedy and **Michael Carr**: title of song (1939)

10 We shall not flag or fail. We shall go on to the end. We shall fight in France, we shall fight on the seas and oceans, we shall fight with growing confidence and growing strength in the air, we shall defend our island, whatever the cost may be. We shall fight on the beaches, we shall fight on the landing grounds, we shall fight in the fields and in the streets, we shall fight in the hills; we shall never surrender.
Winston Churchill 1874–1965: speech, House of Commons, 4 June 1940

11 This little steamer, like all her brave and battered sisters, is immortal. She'll go sailing proudly down the years in the epic of Dunkirk. And our great-grand-children, when they learn how we began this war by snatching glory out of defeat, and then swept on to victory, may also learn how the little holiday steamers made an excursion to hell and came back glorious.
J. B. Priestley 1894–1984: radio broadcast, 5 June 1940; see **Crises** 6

12 France has lost a battle. But France has not lost the war!
Charles de Gaulle 1890–1970: proclamation, 18 June 1940

13 Let us therefore brace ourselves to our duty, and so bear ourselves that, if the British Empire and its Commonwealth lasts for a thousand years, men will still say, 'This was their finest hour.'
Winston Churchill 1874–1965: speech, House of Commons, 18 June 1940; see **Success** 17

14 I'm glad we've been bombed. It makes me feel I can look the East End in the face.
Queen Elizabeth, the Queen Mother 1900–2002: to a London policeman, 13 September 1940

15 We have the men—the skill—the wealth—and above all, the will . . . We must be the great arsenal of democracy.
Franklin D. Roosevelt 1882–1945: 'Fireside Chat' radio broadcast, 29 December 1940

16 Yesterday, December 7, 1941—a date which will live in infamy—the United States of America was suddenly and deliberately attacked by naval and air forces of the Empire of Japan.
Franklin D. Roosevelt 1882–1945: address to Congress, 8 December 1941

17 Sighted sub, sank same.
on sinking a Japanese submarine in the Atlantic region (the first US naval success in the war)
Donald Mason 1913– : radio message, 28 January 1942

18 I came through and I shall return.
on reaching Australia, having broken through Japanese lines en route from Corregidor
Douglas MacArthur 1880–1964: statement in Adelaide, 20 March 1942

19 Don't let's be beastly to the Germans When our Victory is ultimately won.
Noël Coward 1899–1973: 'Don't Let's Be Beastly to the Germans' (1943 song)

20 I think we might be going a bridge too far.
expressing reservations about the Arnhem 'Market Garden' operation
Frederick ('Boy') Browning 1896–1965: to Field Marshal Montgomery on 10 September 1944

21 The Third Fleet's sunken and damaged ships have been salvaged and are retiring at high speed toward the enemy.
on hearing claims that the Japanese had virtually annihilated the US fleet
W. F. ('Bull') Halsey 1882–1959: report, 14 October 1944

22 Nuts!
Anthony McAuliffe 1898–1975: replying to the German demand for surrender at Bastogne, Belgium, 22 December 1944

23 I would not regard the whole of the remaining cities of Germany as worth the bones of one British Grenadier.
supporting the continued strategic bombing of German cities
Arthur Harris 1892–1984: letter to Norman Bottomley, deputy Chief of Air Staff, 29 March 1945;

Max Hastings *Bomber Command* (1979); see **Warfare** 33

24 Who do you think you are kidding, Mister Hitler?
If you think we're on the run?
We are the boys who will stop your little game
We are the boys who will make you think again.
Jimmy Perry: 'Who do you think you are kidding, Mister Hitler' (theme song of *Dad's Army*, BBC television, 1968–77)

25 This happened near the core
Of a world's culture. This
Occurred among higher things.
This was a philosophical conclusion.
Everybody gets what he deserves.
Alan Bold 1943– : 'June 1967 at Buchenwald' (1969); see **Justice** 15

⤙ Worry ⤚

PROVERBS AND SAYINGS

1 **Care killed the cat.**
the meaning of *care* has shifted somewhat from 'worry, grief' to 'care, caution'; English proverb, late 16th century; see 8 below

2 **Do not meet troubles half-way.**
warning against anxiety about something that has not yet happened; English proverb, late 19th century

3 **It is not work that kills, but worry.**
direct effort is less stressful than constant concern; English proverb, late 19th century

4 **Sufficient unto the day is the evil thereof.**
dealing with unpleasant matters should be left until it becomes necessary; English proverb, mid 18th century, from the Bible: see **The Present** 6

5 **Worry is interest paid on trouble before it falls due.**
American proverb, early 20th century

6 **Worry is like a rocking chair: both give you something to do, but neither gets you anywhere.**
American proverb, mid 20th century

QUOTATIONS

7 O polished perturbation! golden care!
That keep'st the ports of slumber open wide
To many a watchful night!
William Shakespeare 1564–1616: *Henry IV, Part 2* (1597)

8 What though care killed a cat, thou hast mettle enough in thee to kill care.
William Shakespeare 1564–1616: *Much Ado About Nothing* (1598–9); see 1 above

9 In trouble to be troubled
Is to have your trouble doubled.
Daniel Defoe 1660–1731: *The Farther Adventures of Robinson Crusoe* (1719)

10 Nothing puzzles me more than time and space; and yet nothing troubles me less, as I never think about them.
Charles Lamb 1775–1834: letter to Thomas Manning, 2 January 1810

11 What's the use of worrying?
It never was worth while,
So, pack up your troubles in your old kit-bag,
And smile, smile, smile.
George Asaf 1880–1951: 'Pack up your Troubles' (1915 song)

12 Neurosis is the way of avoiding non-being by avoiding being.
Paul Tillich 1886–1965: *The Courage To Be* (1952)

13 I'm not [biting my fingernails]. I'm biting my knuckles. I finished the fingernails months ago.
while directing *Cleopatra* (1963)
Joseph L. Mankiewicz 1909– : Dick Sheppard *Elizabeth* (1975)

14 A neurosis is a secret you don't know you're keeping.
Kenneth Tynan 1927–80: Kathleen Tynan *Life of Kenneth Tynan* (1987)

 Writers

see also **Poets**

PHRASES

1 **Aesthetic Movement**
a literary and artistic movement which flourished in England in the 1880s; devoted to 'art for art's sake' and rejecting the notion that art should have a social or moral purpose, its chief exponents included Oscar Wilde, Max Beerbohm, and others associated with the journal the *Yellow Book*; see **The Arts** 5, 15

2 **angry young men**
a group of socially conscious writers in the 1950s, including particularly the playwright John Osborne; see **The Generation Gap** 2

3 **Bloomsbury Group**
a group of writers, artists, and philosophers living in or associated with Bloomsbury in the early 20th century; the group included Virginia Woolf, Lytton Strachey, Vanessa Bell, Duncan Grant, and Roger Fry

4 **Kaleyard School**
a group of late 19th-century fiction writers, including J. M. Barrie; they described local town life in Scotland in a romantic vein and with much use of the vernacular; *kaleyard* in Scots means literally 'kitchen garden'

5 **the Swan of Avon**
Shakespeare, after Ben Jonson's line 'Sweet Swan of Avon' (1623)

QUOTATIONS

6 Will you have all in all for prose and verse? Take the miracle of our age, Sir Philip Sidney.
Richard Carew 1555–1620: William Camden *Remains concerning Britain* (1614) 'The Excellency of the English Tongue'

7 He was not of an age, but for all time!
Ben Jonson 1573–1637: 'To the Memory of My Beloved, the Author, Mr William Shakespeare' (1623)

8 That great Cham of literature, Samuel Johnson.
Tobias Smollett 1721–71: letter to John Wilkes, 16 March 1759

9 Why, Sir, if you were to read Richardson for the story, your impatience would be so much fretted that you would hang yourself.
Samuel Johnson 1709–84: James Boswell *Life of Samuel Johnson* (1791) 6 April 1772

10 What should I do with your strong, manly, spirited sketches, full of variety and glow?—How could I possibly join them on to the little bit (two inches wide) of ivory on which I work with so fine a brush, as produces little effect after much labour?
Jane Austen 1775–1817: letter to J. Edward Austen, 16 December 1816

11 The Big Bow-Wow strain I can do myself like any now going; but the exquisite touch, which renders ordinary commonplace things and characters interesting, from the truth of the description and the sentiment, is denied to me.
of Jane Austen
Sir Walter Scott 1771–1832: diary 14 March 1826

12 Swift was *anima Rabelaisii habitans in sicco*—the soul of Rabelais dwelling in a dry place.
Samuel Taylor Coleridge 1772–1834: *Table Talk* (1835) 15 June 1830

13 Johnson hewed passages through the Alps, while Gibbon levelled walks through parks and gardens.
George Colman, the Younger 1762–1836: *Random Records* (1830)

14 Voltaire speaks to a party, Molière speaks to society, Shakespeare speaks to mankind.
Victor Hugo 1802–85: *Littérature et philosophie mêlées* (1834)

15 Thou large-brained woman and large-hearted man.
Elizabeth Barrett Browning 1806–61: 'To George Sand—A Desire' (1844)

16 A rake among scholars, and a scholar among rakes.
of Richard Steele
Lord Macaulay 1800–59: *Essays Contributed to the Edinburgh Review* (1850) 'The Life and Writings of Addison'

17 He describes London like a special correspondent for posterity.
Walter Bagehot 1826–77: *National Review* 7 October 1858 'Charles Dickens'

18 With the single exception of Homer, there is no eminent writer, not even Sir Walter Scott, whom I can despise so entirely as I despise Shakespeare when I measure my mind against his.
George Bernard Shaw 1856–1950: in *Saturday Review* 26 September 1896

19 It is leviathan retrieving pebbles. It is a magnificent but painful hippopotamus resolved at any cost, even at the cost of its dignity, upon picking up a pea which has got into a corner of its den.
of Henry James
H. G. Wells 1866–1946: *Boon* (1915)

20 E. M. Forster never gets any further than warming the teapot. He's a rare fine hand at that. Feel this teapot. Is it not beautifully warm? Yes, but there ain't going to be no tea.
Katherine Mansfield 1888–1923: diary, May 1917

21 The humour of Dostoievsky is the humour of a bar-loafer who ties a kettle to a dog's tail.
W. Somerset Maugham 1874–1965: *A Writer's Notebook* (1949) written in 1917

22 The work of Henry James has always seemed divisible by a simple dynastic arrangement into three reigns: James I, James II, and the Old Pretender.
Philip Guedalla 1889–1944: *Supers and Supermen* (1920); see **Royalty** 12

23 A dogged attempt to cover the universe with mud, an inverted Victorianism, an attempt to make crossness and dirt succeed where sweetness and light failed.
of James Joyce's *Ulysses*
E. M. Forster 1879–1970: *Aspects of the Novel* (1927); see **Behaviour** 16

24 Shaw's plays are the price we pay for Shaw's prefaces.
James Agate 1877–1947: diary 10 March 1933

25 English literature's performing flea.
of P. G. Wodehouse
Sean O'Casey 1880–1964: P. G. Wodehouse *Performing Flea* (1953)

26 For years a secret shame destroyed my
    peace—
I'd not read Eliot, Auden or MacNeice.
But then I had a thought that brought me
    hope—
Neither had Chaucer, Shakespeare, Milton,
    Pope.
Justin Richardson: 'Take Heart, Illiterates' (1966)

27 He could not blow his nose without moralising on the state of the handkerchief industry.
of George Orwell
Cyril Connolly 1903–74: in *Sunday Times* 29 September 1968

28 Shakespeare—the nearest thing in incarnation to the eye of God.
Laurence Olivier 1907–89: in *Kenneth Harris Talking To* (1971) 'Sir Laurence Olivier'

29 We were put to Dickens as children but it never quite took. That unremitting humanity soon had me cheesed off.
Alan Bennett 1934– : *The Old Country* (1978)

➤➤ Writing ◄◄

see also **Books, Fiction and Story-telling, Originality, Poetry, Style, Words**

PROVERBS AND SAYINGS

1 **The art of writing is the art of applying the seat of the pants to the seat of the chair.**
American proverb, mid 20th century

2 **He who would write and can't write can surely review.**
American proverb, mid 19th century

3 **What is written with a pen cannot be cut out with an axe.**
words are more powerful than violence; Russian proverb; see **Ways and Means** 16

4 **Writing is a picture of the writer's heart.**
Chinese proverb

PHRASES

5 cacoethes scribendi
an irresistible desire to write; from Juvenal (see 9 below); Latin from Greek *kakoēthes* use as noun of adjective *kakoēthes* ill-disposed

6 disjecta membra
scattered fragments, especially of a written work; Latin, an alteration of *disjecti membra poetae*, as used

by the poet Horace, 'in our case you would not recognize, as you would in the case of Ennius, the limbs, even though you had dismembered him, of a poet'

QUOTATIONS

7 It is a foolish thing to make a long prologue, and to be short in the story itself.
Bible: II Maccabees

8 You will have written exceptionally well if, by skilful arrangement of your words, you have made an ordinary one seem original.
Horace 65–8 BC: *Ars Poetica*

9　　　*Tenet insanabile multos*
Scribendi cacoethes et aegro in corde senescit.
Many suffer from the incurable disease of writing, and it becomes chronic in their sick minds.
Juvenal c.AD 60–c.130: *Satires*; see 5 above

10 If writing did not exist, what terrible depressions we should suffer from.
Sei Shōnagon c.966–c.1013: *The Pillow Book of Sei Shōnagon*

11 Go, litel bok, go, litel myn tragedye,
Ther God thi makere yet, er that he dye,
So sende mygth to make in som comedye!
Geoffrey Chaucer 1343–1400: *Troilus and Criseyde*

12 In the mind, as in the body, there is the necessity of getting rid of waste, and a man of active literary habits will write for the fire as well as for the press.
Jerome Cardan 1501–76: William Osler *Aequanimites* (1904); epigraph

13 And, as imagination bodies forth
The forms of things unknown, the poet's pen
Turns them to shapes, and gives to airy nothing
A local habitation and a name.
William Shakespeare 1564–1616: *A Midsummer Night's Dream* (1595–6)

14 If all the earth were paper white
And all the sea were ink
'Twere not enough for me to write
As my poor heart doth think.
John Lyly 1554–1606: 'If all the earth were paper white'

15 The last thing one knows in constructing a work is what to put first.
Blaise Pascal 1623–62: *Pensées* (1670)

16 Of every four words I write, I strike out three.
Nicolas Boileau 1636–1711: *Satire* (2). *A M. Molière* (1665)

17　　　What in me is dark
Illumine, what is low raise and support;
That to the height of this great argument
I may assert eternal providence,
And justify the ways of God to men.
John Milton 1608–74: *Paradise Lost* (1667); see **Alcohol 20**

18 Learn to write well, or not to write at all.
John Sheffield, Duke of Buckingham and Normanby 1648–1721: 'An Essay upon Satire' (1689)

19 Writing, when properly managed (as you may be sure I think mine is) is but a different name for conversation.
Laurence Sterne 1713–68: *Tristram Shandy* (1759–67)

20 Any fool may write a most valuable book by chance, if he will only tell us what he heard and saw with veracity.
Thomas Gray 1716–71: letter to Horace Walpole, 25 February 1768

21 You write with ease, to show your breeding, But easy writing's vile hard reading.
Richard Brinsley Sheridan 1751–1816: 'Clio's Protest' (written 1771, published 1819)

22 Read over your compositions, and where ever you meet with a passage which you think is particularly fine, strike it out.
Samuel Johnson 1709–84: quoting a college tutor; James Boswell *Life of Samuel Johnson* (1791) 30 April 1773

23 No man but a blockhead ever wrote, except for money.
Samuel Johnson 1709–84: James Boswell *Life of Samuel Johnson* (1791) 5 April 1776

24 Another damned, thick, square book! Always scribble, scribble, scribble! Eh! Mr Gibbon?
William Henry, Duke of Gloucester 1743–1805: Henry Best *Personal and Literary Memorials* (1829); also attributed to the Duke of Cumberland and King George III; D. M. Low *Edward Gibbon* (1937)

25 Let other pens dwell on guilt and misery. I quit such odious subjects as soon as I can.
Jane Austen 1775–1817: *Mansfield Park* (1814)

26 Until you understand a writer's ignorance, presume yourself ignorant of his understanding.
Samuel Taylor Coleridge 1772–1834: *Biographia Literaria* (1817)

27 I am convinced more and more day by day that fine writing is next to fine doing the top thing in the world.
John Keats 1795–1821: letter to J. H. Reynolds, 24 August 1819

28 When my sonnet was rejected, I exclaimed, 'Damn the age; I will write for Antiquity!'
Charles Lamb 1775–1834: letter to B. W. Proctor 22 January 1829

29 Beneath the rule of men entirely great
The pen is mightier than the sword.
Edward George Bulwer-Lytton 1803–73: *Richelieu* (1839); see **Ways and Means** 16

30 A losing trade, I assure you, sir: literature is a drug.
George Borrow 1803–81: *Lavengro* (1851)

31 Writers, like teeth, are divided into incisors and grinders.
Walter Bagehot 1826–77: *Estimates of some Englishmen and Scotchmen* (1858) 'The First Edinburgh Reviewers'

32 The business of the poet and novelist is to show the sorriness underlying the grandest things, and the grandeur underlying the sorriest things.
Thomas Hardy 1840–1928: notebook entry for 19 April 1885

33 A writer must be as objective as a chemist: he must abandon the subjective line; he must know that dung-heaps play a very reasonable part in a landscape, and that evil passions are as inherent in life as good ones.
Anton Chekhov 1860–1904: letter to M. V. Kiselev, 14 January 1887

34 Only connect! . . . Only connect the prose and the passion, and both will be exalted, and human love will be seen at its height.
E. M. Forster 1879–1970: *Howards End* (1910)

35 My theory of writing I can sum up in one sentence. An author ought to write for the youth of his own generation, the critics of the next, and the schoolmasters of ever after.
F. Scott Fitzgerald 1896–1940: letter to the Booksellers' Convention, April 1920

36 This writing business. Pencils and what-not. Over-rated, if you ask me. Silly stuff. Nothing in it.
A. A. Milne 1882–1956: *Winnie-the-Pooh* (1926)

37 A woman must have money and a room of her own if she is to write fiction.
Virginia Woolf 1882–1941: *A Room of One's Own* (1929)

38 I am a camera with its shutter open, quite passive, recording, not thinking.
Christopher Isherwood 1904–86: *Goodbye to Berlin* (1939) 'Berlin Diary' Autumn 1930

39 Remarks are not literature.
Gertrude Stein 1874–1946: *Autobiography of Alice B. Toklas* (1933)

40 Literature is news that STAYS news.
Ezra Pound 1885–1972: *The ABC of Reading* (1934)

41 Manuscripts don't burn.
Mikhail Bulgakov 1891–1940: *The Master and Margarita* (1966–67)

42 There is no need for the writer to eat a whole sheep to be able to tell you what mutton tastes like. It is enough if he eats a cutlet. But he should do that.
W. Somerset Maugham 1874–1965: *A Writer's Notebook* (1949) written in 1941

43 A writer's ambition should be . . . to trade a hundred contemporary readers for ten readers in ten years' time and for one reader in a hundred years.
Arthur Koestler 1905–83: in *New York Times Book Review* 1 April 1951

44 Writing is not a profession but a vocation of unhappiness.
Georges Simenon 1903–89: interview in *Paris Review* Summer 1955

45 The writer's only responsibility is to his art. He will be completely ruthless if he is a good one. . . . If a writer has to rob his mother, he will not hesitate; the *Ode on a Grecian Urn* is worth any number of old ladies.
William Faulkner 1897–1962: in *Paris Review* Spring 1956

46 The most essential gift for a good writer is a built-in, shock-proof shit detector. This is the writer's radar and all great writers have had it.
Ernest Hemingway 1899–1961: in *Paris Review* Spring 1958

47 A writer must refuse, therefore, to allow himself to be transformed into an institution.
Jean-Paul Sartre 1905–80: refusing the Nobel Prize at Stockholm, 22 October 1964

48 Good prose is like a window-pane.
George Orwell 1903–50: *Collected Essays* (1968) vol. 1 'Why I Write'

49 Nothing I wrote in the thirties saved one Jew from Auschwitz.
W. H. Auden 1907–73: attributed

50 The shelf life of the modern hardback writer is somewhere between the milk and the yoghurt.
Calvin Trillin: in *Sunday Times* 9 June 1991; attributed

51 One of the things a writer is for is to say the unsayable, speak the unspeakable and ask difficult questions.
Salman Rushdie 1947– : in *Independent on Sunday* 10 September 1995

52 I come from a backward place: your duty is supplied by life around you. One guy plants bananas; another plants cocoa; I'm a writer, I plant lines. There's the same clarity of occupation, and the sense of devotion.
Derek Walcott 1930– : in *Guardian* 12 July 1997

⇥ Youth ⇤

see also **Children, Generation Gap**

PROVERBS AND SAYINGS

1 **The old net is cast aside while the new net goes fishing.**
the future belongs to the young; Maori proverb

2 **Wanton kittens make sober cats.**
someone who in youth is light-minded and lascivious may be soberly behaved in later life; English proverb, early 18th century

3 **Whom the gods love die young.**
the happiest fate is to die before health and strength are lost; English proverb, mid 16th century; see 7 below, **Virtue** 1

4 **Youth must be served.**
some indulgence should be given to the wishes and enthusiasms of youth; English proverb, early 19th century

PHRASES

5 **salad days**
the period when one is young and inexperienced, one's time of youth; from Shakespeare's *Antony and Cleopatra* (1606–7) 'My salad days, When I was green in judgment'

6 **an ugly duckling**
a young person who shows no promise at all of the beauty and success that will eventually come with maturity; in allusion to a tale by Hans Andersen of a cygnet in a brood of ducks

QUOTATIONS

7 Whom the gods love dies young.
Menander 342–c.292 BC: *Dis Exapaton*; see 3 above, **Virtue** 1

8 In delay there lies no plenty;
Then come kiss me, sweet and twenty,
Youth's a stuff will not endure.
William Shakespeare 1564–1616: *Twelfth Night* (1601)

9 Young men are fitter to invent than to judge, fitter for execution than for counsel, and fitter for new projects than for settled business.
Francis Bacon 1561–1626: *Essays* (1625) 'Of Youth and Age'

10 To find a young fellow that is neither a wit in his own eye, nor a fool in the eye of the world, is a very hard task.
William Congreve 1670–1729: *Love for Love* (1695)

11 The atrocious crime of being a young man . . . I shall neither attempt to palliate nor deny.
William Pitt, Earl of Chatham 1708–78: speech, House of Commons, 2 March 1741

12 In gallant trim the gilded vessel goes;
Youth on the prow, and Pleasure at the helm.
Thomas Gray 1716–71: 'The Bard' (1757)

13 Heaven lies about us in our infancy!
Shades of the prison-house begin to close
Upon the growing boy,
William Wordsworth 1770–1850: 'Ode. Intimations of Immortality' (1807)

14 Live as long as you may, the first twenty years are the longest half of your life.
Robert Southey 1774–1843: *The Doctor* (1812)

15 Oh, talk not to me of a name great in story;
The days of our youth are the days of our glory;
And the myrtle and ivy of sweet two-and-twenty

Are worth all your laurels, though ever so
plenty.
Lord Byron 1788–1824: 'Stanzas Written on the
Road between Florence and Pisa, November 1821';
see **Success** 20

16 The Youth of a Nation are the trustees of
Posterity.
Benjamin Disraeli 1804–81: *Sybil* (1845)

17 I'm not young enough to know everything.
J. M. Barrie 1860–1937: *The Admirable Crichton*
(performed 1902, published 1914)

18 Youth would be an ideal state if it came a
little later in life.
Herbert Henry Asquith 1852–1928: in *Observer*
15 April 1923

19 It is better to waste one's youth than to do
nothing with it at all.
Georges Courteline 1858–1929: *La Philosophie de
Georges Courteline* (1948)

20 The force that through the green fuse drives
the flower
Drives my green age.
Dylan Thomas 1914–53: 'The force that through
the green fuse drives the flower' (1934)

21 It's that second time you hear your love
song sung,
Makes you think perhaps, that
Love like youth is wasted on the young.
Sammy Cahn 1913–93: 'The Second Time Around'
(1960 song)

22 It is thinking about themselves that is really
the curse of the younger generation—they
appear to have no other subject which
interests them at all.
Harold Macmillan 1894–1986: the 'Tuesday
memorandum', a draft of a letter to the Queen,

advising on his successor but not sent, 1963; D. R.
Thorpe *Alec Douglas-Home* (1996)

23 Being young is not having any money;
being young is not minding not having any
money.
Katharine Whitehorn 1928– : *Observations*
(1970)

24 Youth is something very new: twenty years
ago no one mentioned it.
Coco Chanel 1883–1971: Marcel Haedrich *Coco
Chanel, Her Life, Her Secrets* (1971)

25 Make me young, make me young, make me
young!
Kurt Vonnegut 1922– : *Breakfast of Champions*
(1973)

26 Remember that as a teenager you are at the
last stage in your life when you will be
happy to hear that the phone is for you.
Fran Lebowitz 1946– : *Social Studies* (1981)

27 Youth is vivid rather than happy, but
memory always remembers the happy
things.
Bernard Lovell 1913– : in *The Times* 20
August 1993

28 Being young is greatly overestimated . . . Any
failure seems so total. Later on you realize
you can have another go.
Mary Quant 1934— : interview in *Observer* 5
May 1996

29 The only way to stay young is to avoid old
people.
James D. Watson 1928– : in *The Times* 9
March 2002

⤞ Keyword Index ⤝

bitten b. in half by a shark	CHOICE 31	b. lead the blind	IGNORANCE 10
fear it will be b.	RELATIONSHIPS 26	b. lead the blind	LEADERSHIP 9
Once b.	EXPERIENCE 8	b. man in a dark room	JUSTICE 31
bitterness fuelled by b.	REVENGE 24	b. man's wife	APPEARANCE 2
black beyond the b. stump	AUSTRALIA 4	b. watchmaker	LIFE SCI 26
b. and grey	HUMAN NATURE 19	b. wife	MARRIAGE 4
b. as he is painted	REPUTATION 4	bold as a b. mare	IGNORANCE 6
B. Death	SICKNESS 4	Booth died b.	FAITH 15
b. dog	DESPAIR 1	country of the b.	ABILITY 5
b. dog I hope	DESPAIR 6	I have a right to be b.	DETERMINATION 36
b. face and a different religion	RACE 10	knowledge e'er accompany the b.	KNOWLEDGE 25
B. is beautiful	RACE 2	Love is b.	LOVE 6
B. Prince	ROYALTY 4	none so b.	PREJUDICE 4
b. sheep	FAMILY 12	splendid work for the b.	SENSES 15
Black's not so b.	DISILLUSION 13	whole world b.	REVENGE 3
creeping through the b.	RIVERS 13	without science is b.	SCIENCE AND RELIG 14
devil damn thee, b.	INSULTS 3	**blindness** heathen in his b.	RELIGION 18
looking for a b. hat	JUSTICE 31	**blinds** Truth, like the light, b.	LIES 24
neutralize the b.	CHOICE 20	**blinked** other fellow just b.	CRISES 22
new b.	FASHION 3	**bliss** B. was it in that dawn	REVOLUTION 13
pot calling the kettle b.	CRITICISM 5	everlasting b.	HEAVEN 10
rainbow which includes b.	LIFE 53	Everywhere I see b.	DESPAIR 7
so long as it is b.	CHOICE 21	Ignorance is b.	IGNORANCE 2
some b. people about me	RACE 7	ignorance is b.	IGNORANCE 18
white cat or a b. cat	WAYS 11	**blithe** b. Spirit	BIRDS 11
Why do you wear b.	SORROW 20	**block** big black b.	CRIME 37
young, gifted and b.	RACE 26	chip off the old b.	FAMILY 13
blackberries plentiful as b.	ARGUMENT 10	chip of the old 'b.'	SPEECHES 11
blackbird B. has spoken	DAY 17	**blockhead** bookful b.	READING 9
blackbirds B. are the cellos	BIRDS 19	No man but a b.	WRITING 23
blackens b. the water	ARGUMENT 11	**blocks** hew b. with a razor	FUTILITY 20
blacks b. don't make a white	GOOD 6	**blonde** artifice of being b.	APPEARANCE 33
poor are Europe's b.	POVERTY 23	rather like being a b.	WEALTH 41
blackthorn b. winter	SEASONS 8	**blood** Africa in our b.	HUMAN RACE 34
Black Widow B., death	DEATH 72	belong by b. relationship	FAMILY 7
blame as is the b.	CONSTANCY 7	b. and iron	INTERNAT REL 22
attaches blame to its 'victims'	SICKNESS 22	b. and iron	WARFARE 5
lay the b. on men	PARENTS 24	b. and love	THEATRE 24
manager who gets the b.	FOOTBALL 11	b. and tears	PEACE 29
quick to b. the alien	GUILT 5	b. and thunder	VIOLENCE 2
seldom to b.	REPUTATION 2	b. from a stone	FUTILITY 5
what they b. at night	OPINION 16	b. has been cleaned up	GENIUS 16
women never take the b.	GUILT 20	B. is thicker	FAMILY 2
wrong to b. Marx	CAPITALISM 29	b. may be thicker	EMOTIONS 10
blamed mothers go on getting b.	PARENTS 26	B. may be thicker	FAMILY 21
blameless bishop then must be b.	CLERGY 7	b. of a martyr	EDUCATION 4
blames b. his tools	APOLOGY 3	b. of Christians	CHRISTIAN CH 16
cannot dance b. the uneven floor	APOLOGY 7	b. of patriots	LIBERTY 14
blaming b. on his boots	HUMAN NATURE 20	b. of the martyrs	CHRISTIAN CH 1
blancmange b. and rhubarb tart	HOSPITALITY 22	b. on my hands	INDIFFERENCE 13
bland bland lead the b.	CONFORMITY 14	b. out of a stone	CHARITY 7
blank b., my lord	SECRECY 26	B. sport is brought	GOSSIP 27
not as a b. tablet	MIND 29	b., toil, tears	SELF-SACRIFICE 16
blankets male kiss Of b.	SLEEP 17	B. will have blood	MURDER 1
Blarney kissed the B. stone	SPEECH 4	B. will tell	FAMILY 3
blasphemy b. against the Holy Ghost	SIN 8	flesh and b. so cheap	POVERTY 24
soldier is flat b.	CLASS 11	flow of human b.	RIVERS 14
blasted b. with excess	POETS 12	freeze one's b.	FEAR 5
bleating b. of the kid excites	HUNTING 1	hawser of the b.-tie	RELATIONSHIPS 24
b. sheep loses	OPPORTUNITY 3	in cold b.	EMOTIONS 4
bleed prick us, do we not b.	EQUALITY 5	innocent of the b.	GUILT 6
bleeds 'til it b. daylight	DETERMINATION 51	make someone's b. boil	ANGER 5
bless B. 'em all	ARMED FORCES 44	never run with b.	BRITAIN 18
God b. America	AMERICA 34	Old B. and Guts	WORLD W II 7
blessed B. are the meek	PRIDE 5	River Tiber foaming with blood	RACE 27
b. be the name	PATIENCE 23	salt in our b.	SEA 24
b. to give	GIFTS 13	show business with b.	SPORTS 35
blessing b. that money cannot buy	HEALTH 16	summon up the b.	WARFARE 17
national b.	DEBT 6	Tiber foaming with much b.	WARFARE 15
unmixed b.	PERFECTION 3	trading on the b.	BIOGRAPHY 10
blessings B. brighten	HAPPINESS 1	won by B. and Guts alone	WARFARE 48
b. on the falling out	FORGIVENESS 21	**bloodshed** war without b.	POLITICS 20
recognized their b.	FARMING 8	**bloody** b. but unbowed	COURAGE 21
blest To be b.	HOPE 13	b. war and a sickly season	ARMED FORCES 2
blind Be not b.	NATURE 7	Not b. likely	TRANSPORT 13
B. chance	CHANCE 2	**bloom** furze is in b.	LOVE 15

Buckley B.'s chance   CHANCE 18
  two chances, B.'s and none   CHANCE 15
bud nip him in the b.   DECEPTION 20
  worm i' the b.   SECRECY 26
Buddha B., the Godhead   GOD 34
budget Balancing the b.   ECONOMICS 21
buds Hey, b. below   FLOWERS 12
bug not a b., it's a feature   COMPUTERS 3
bugger B. Bognor   BRITISH TOWNS 39
build Birds b.   CREATIVITY 9
  b. a church   CHRISTIAN CH 8
  b. a tower   FORESIGHT 9
  b. shopping malls   BUSINESS 52
  easier to b. two chimneys   ARCHITECTURE 2
  Fools b. houses   FOOLS 4
  I do not drink, I b.   ARCHITECTURE 10
building be able to read a b.   ARCHITECTURE 23
  beauty in b.   ARCHITECTURE 8
  b. hath three conditions   ARCHITECTURE 6
  first b. erected by   ARCHITECTURE 1
  it's a very old b.   THEATRE 19
  Modern body b. is ritual   BODY 32
  No good b. without   ARCHITECTURE 3
buildings architecture applies only to b.   ARCHITECTURE 16
  our b. shape us   ARCHITECTURE 15
builds b. on mud   DEMOCRACY 4
built b. in a day   PATIENCE 14
  b. on sand   STRENGTH 12
  b. Thebes of the seven gates   WORK 37
bulimia yuppie version of b.   HEALTH 23
bull b. market   BUSINESS 20
  milk the b.   BELIEF 18
  red rag to a b.   ANGER 6
  strong as a b. moose   STRENGTH 25
bullet Every b. has its billet   FATE 18
  stronger than the b.   ELECTIONS 7
bullied b. out of vice   VIRTUE 36
bully b. is always a coward   COURAGE 3
  b. pulpit   PRESIDENCY 1
  such a b. pulpit   PRESIDENCY 7
bump go b. in the night   SUPERNATURAL 1
  go b. in the night   SUPERNATURAL 4
bumping b. your head   EDUCATION 2
Bunbury invalid called B.   APOLOGY 15
Buncombe talking to B.   SPEECHES 4
bung-hole let out the b.   THRIFT 6
bungle b. raising your children   CHILD CARE 15
bungler good nature is a b.   POLITICS 11
  Man is a b.   PEACE 14
bunk Exercise is b.   HEALTH 19
  more or less b.   HISTORY 22
bunkers Give up and live in b.   ARCHITECTURE 25
burden bear any b.   LIBERTY 36
  heavy b. of responsibility   ROYALTY 41
  makes the back to the b.   SYMPATHY 1
  my b. is light   WORK 21
  White Man's b.   DUTY 19
  white man's b.   RACE 5
bureaucrats b. will care more   ADMINISTRATION 10
  Guidelines for b.   ADMINISTRATION 20
burglars fear of b. is not only   CRIME 45
burgundy naïve domestic B.   ALCOHOL 25
burials b., swindlings, affairs of state   FRANCE 16
buried b. in so sweet a place   DEATH 53
burn better to b. out   SUICIDE 11
  b. and I am ice   LOVE 28
  B., baby, burn   VIOLENCE 1
  b. the candle at both ends   EFFORT 11
  b. the midnight oil   WORK 13
  B. your bra   WOMAN'S ROLE 1
  Manuscripts don't b.   WRITING 41
  marry than to b.   MARRIAGE 21
burned in the end, are b.   CENSORSHIP 7
burning b. the rain forest   POLLUTION 25
  b. within my veins   LOVE 39

but by b. him   ENEMIES 22
Tyger, b. bright   ANIMALS 19
burns B. Night   FESTIVALS 11
  candle b. at both ends   TRANSIENCE 15
burnt b. at the stake   PAST 38
  b. child dreads   EXPERIENCE 2
  Christians have b. each other   CHRISTIAN CH 24
  never have been b.   FRANCE 15
bury b. bad news   DECEPTION 27
  b. his mistakes   ARCHITECTURE 18
  b. the dead   MOURNING 3
  does not b. her alive   WOMEN 20
  We will b. you   CAPITALISM 21
bus Anybody seen in a b.   SUCCESS 40
  front of a b.   FUTILITY 28
  good design for a b.   ARTS 33
  I'm not even a b.   FATE 21
  I never run for the b.   HASTE 23
buses red b.   ENGLAND 20
bush aims at a b.   AMBITION 8
  b. telegraph   GOSSIP 11
  copiousy branching b.   LIFE SCI 29
  good wine needs no b.   ADVERTISING 3
  Poke a b., a snake comes out   CAUTION 20
  thief doth fear each b.   GUILT 8
  two in the b.   CAUTION 2
  wine need no b.   ADVERTISING 16
bushel light under a b.   SELF-ESTEEM 8
bushes b. trimmed and trained   LANGUAGE 26
bushmen they were not b.   RACE 28
busiest b. men have the most   LEISURE 2
business American people is b.   AMERICA 30
  B. before pleasure   BUSINESS 1
  B. carried on as usual   CRISES 18
  B. goes where it is invited   BUSINESS 2
  b. in your heart   BUSINESS 40
  B. is becoming more and more   BUSINESS 55
  B. is like a car   BUSINESS 3
  b. is not   MUSIC 31
  B. is war   BUSINESS 4
  B. neglected   BUSINESS 5
  b. practices would improve   BUSINESS 53
  b. shall become wise   LEISURE 4
  b. that we love   LIKES 8
  b. to get him   SPORTS 19
  b. when the wall   CRISES 12
  ever-haunting importunity Of b.   WORK 29
  Everybody's b.   DUTY 2
  How to succeed in b.   BUSINESS 38
  If b. always made the right decisions   BUSINESS 43
  no b. like show business   THEATRE 16
  No praying, it spoils b.   PRAYER 18
  requisite in b.   BUSINESS 27
  sane b. management   MANAGEMENT 9
  soul of b.   PUNCTUALITY 6
  spring of b.   GOVERNMENT 29
  true b. precept   BUSINESS 32
  unfinished b.   LIBERTY 33
  well-placed b. men   BUSINESS 49
businessman toward making a b.   DRESS 20
buskin sock and b.   ACTING 3
  sock and b.   ACTING 5
bust urn or animated b.   DEATH 48
busting June is b. out   SEASONS 28
busy ask a b. person   ACTION 7
  b., and you will be safe   LOVE 25
  B. old fool   SKIES 13
  English are b.   ENGLAND 9
  get b. dying   DRUGS 15
  how b. I must be   PRAYER 15
  Nowher so b. a man   ACTION 16
butcher benevolence of the b.   SELF-INTEREST 27
  b. and know the joints   POLITICIANS 32
  b., the baker   EMPLOYMENT 3
  Hog B. for the World   AMERICAN CITIES 52
butchered B. to make a Roman holiday   CRUELTY 8

charmer t'other dear c. away	CHOICE 16	**cherry** as American as c. pie	VIOLENCE 16
charming c. is divine philosophy	PHILOSOPHY 7	c. hung with snow	TREES 13
charms Music has c.	MUSIC 8	c. year	SEASONS 1
chase c. the dragon	DRUGS 2	second bite at the c.	OPPORTUNITY 23
on the c. or on aiming	SPORTS 34	Under the c.	TREES 9
stern c.	DETERMINATION 15	**cherry-stones** carve heads upon c.	POETS 13
wild-goose c.	FUTILITY 15	**Cheshire** C. cat	CATS 3
chases man c. a girl	COURTSHIP 11	cosmic C. cat	GOD 31
chaste c. and fair	SKIES 11	face of the C. Cat	BRITAIN 15
c. whore	HUMOUR 20	**chess** C. is a sea	SPORTS 1
chastised c. you with whips	CRIME 20	**chestnut** c.-tree, great-rooted blossomer	TREES 18
chastity c. and continence	SEX 9	**chestnuts** c. out of the fire	DANGER 21
C.—the most unnatural	SEX 23	**chevalier** Young C.	ROYALTY 17
Eunuchs boasting of their c.	TEMPTATION 17	**chew** fart and c. gum	FOOLS 28
vice of c.	SINGLE 5	more than one can c.	ACHIEVEMENT 12
chat agreement kills a c.	CONVERSATION 20	**chewing gum** c. for the eyes	BROADCASTING 4
chateaux c. would never have been	FRANCE 15	**chic** radical c.	FASHION 4
chattels goods and c.	POSSESSIONS 10	Radical C.	FASHION 11
chatter idle c.	MEANING 10	**chicken** c.-and-egg problem	PROBLEMS 6
chattering c. classes	INTELLIGENCE 3	c. cross the road	PROBLEMS 5
Chatterley end of the C. ban	SEX 34	c. in his pot	POVERTY 17
Chaucer Master Geoffrey C.	POETS 8	C. Little	FEAR 4
cheap as c. sitting	ACTION 8	Left wing, c. wing	CAPITALISM 26
dressed in c. shoes	DRESS 23	man who has fed the c.	FORESIGHT 15
flesh and blood so c.	POVERTY 24	Mother Carey's c.	BIRDS 7
how potent cheap music is	MUSIC 19	rubber c. circuit	SPEECHES 2
sell it c.	BUSINESS 14	**chickens** all my pretty c.	MOURNING 10
Talk is c.	WORDS AND DEEDS 8	C. are counted in autumn	OPTIMISM 3
they call him c.	THRIFT 20	count one's c.	OPTIMISM 17
to look this c.	APPEARANCE 34	Curses, like c.	HATRED 2
whem milk is so c.	SINGLE 1	Don't count your c.	OPTIMISM 6
cheaper people in the c. seats	CLASS 28	May c. come	SEASONS 3
cheapest Buy in the c.	ECONOMICS 1	stealin' no c.	ANIMALS 3
cheat c. at cards genteelly	MANNERS 14	**chieftain** c. of the puddin'-race	FOOD 16
lucrative to c.	CRIME 34	**child** battle line than bear one c.	WOMEN 18
cheated c., as to cheat	DECEPTION 16	change in the c.	CHILD CARE 10
happier to be sometimes c.	TRUST 28	cherished c.	PARENTS 12
cheating c. of our friends	DECEPTION 19	c. becomes an adult	CHILDREN 22
cheats C. never prosper	DECEPTION 1	c. born therein	HUMAN RIGHTS 12
checks c. and balances	GOVERNMENT 7	C. is father of the Man	CHILDREN 14
cheek dancing c.-to-cheek	DANCE 13	c. is not a vase	CHILDREN 7
one who turns the c.	RELATIONSHIPS 4	c. is owed the greatest respect	CHILDREN 6
smite thee on thy right c.	VIOLENCE 4	c. is the father	CHARACTER 6
turn the other c.	FORGIVENESS 9	c. makes you a parent	FAMILY 30
turn the other c.	VIOLENCE 7	c. of a frog is a frog	FAMILY 4
cheeping chickens come c.	SEASONS 3	c. shall lead them	COOPERATION 22
cheer could scarce forbear to c.	PRAISE 16	c.'s strength	BELIEF 20
Don't c., men	WARS 20	c. who hasn't been handled	MUSICIANS 16
which side do they c. for	PATRIOTISM 31	first c. is made of glass	CHILD CARE 18
cheerful c. as any man	CRIME 23	Give me a c.	EDUCATION 3
c. countenance	APPEARANCE 13	have a thankless c.	GRATITUDE 9
c. giver	GIFTS 14	If you strike a c.	VIOLENCE 8
cheerfulness C. gives elasticity	HAPPINESS 21	knows his own c.	PARENTS 8
c. keeps up	HAPPINESS 13	like to be a c.	MATURITY 14
c. was always breaking in	PHILOSOPHY 11	Monday's c.	BEAUTY 7
cheeriness insistent c.	SICKNESS 24	my absent c.	MOURNING 2
cheers Two c. for Democracy	DEMOCRACY 21	never was a c. so lovely	CHILD CARE 7
cheese apple-pie without some c.	FOOD 1	Praise the c.	PARENTS 4
born i' the rotten c.	FAMILIARITY 20	right to a c. with the obligation	WOMAN'S ROLE 23
c.—toasted mostly	FOOD 18	Saturday's c. works hard	WORK 6
fill hup the chinks wi' c.	COOKING 22	shocks the mind of a c.	RELIGION 17
like some valley c.	POETRY 36	spoiled c. of art	FICTION 17
only free c.	ECONOMICS 2	spoil the c.	CHILD CARE 3
second mouse that gets the c.	PREPARATION 10	Thursday's c. has far to go	TRAVEL 6
varieties of c.	FRANCE 17	Train up a c.	CHILD CARE 4
chemical certain c. elements	HUMAN RACE 30	unto us a c. is born	CHRISTMAS 5
two c. substances	RELATIONSHIPS 17	use of a new-born c.	INVENTIONS 8
chemicals found more dangerous c.	DANGER 38	village to raise a c.	CHILD CARE 1
chemist as objective as a c.	WRITING 33	Wednesday's c.	SORROW 2
chemistry c. and machinery	DEATH 61	wise c. that knows	PARENTS 1
c. that works	LIFE SCI 30	**childbirth** Death and taxes and c.	PREGNANCY 10
cheque statement is like a c.	MEANING 13	Poverty is a lot like c.	POVERTY 37
Chernobyl cultural C.	CULTURE 28	**childhood** C. is the kingdom	CHILDREN 16
cultural C.	CULTURE 29	C. is the Last Chance	CHILDREN 23
cherries bowl of c.	LIFE 43	one moment in c.	CHILDREN 18
c., hops, and women	BRITISH TOWNS 31	what my lousy c. was like	BIOGRAPHY 18

cleansed c. everything would appear — INSIGHT 10
clear c. is not French — FRANCE 9
Paul's day be fair and c. — FESTIVALS 5
clearly more c. than you think — SPEECH 30
clearness merit of language is c. — LANGUAGE 5
cleave c. unto his wife — MARRIAGE 18
Cleopatra C.'s nose — APPEARANCE 16
clercs trahison des c. — INTELLIGENCE 7
clergy benefit of c. — CLERGY 6
c. were beloved — CLERGY 14
clergymen C.'s sons — CLERGY 1
clerk C. there was of Oxenford — UNIVERSITIES 5
'twixt the Priest and C. — EQUALITY 6
clever brains to be that c. — INTELLIGENCE 23
c. and lazy — ARMED FORCES 42
c., but is it Art — ARTS 17
c. men at Oxford — KNOWLEDGE 47
c. theft was praiseworthy — CRIME 31
If all the good people were c. — VIRTUE 44
let who will be c. — VIRTUE 38
manage a c. man — MEN AND WOMEN 14
To be c. enough to get — WEALTH 29
too c. by half — INTELLIGENCE 6
Too c. by half — INTELLIGENCE 21
cleverness height of c. — INTELLIGENCE 10
Mere c. is not wisdom — INTELLIGENCE 8
cliché c. and an indiscretion — POLITICIANS 28
clichés some new c. — ORIGINALITY 18
click c. with people — PHOTOGRAPHY 15
Clunk, c., every trip — TRANSPORT 1
client c. will crawl — DRUGS 8
fool for his c. — LAW 6
cliffs c. of Dover — INTERNAT REL 28
c. of fall — MIND 21
white c. of Dover — ENGLAND 5
climate in love with a cold c. — COUNTRIES 15
lived in a warm, sunny c. — WEATHER 52
climax c. of all human ills — DEBT 15
climb C. ev'ry mountain — THOROUGHNESS 13
c. not at all — AMBITION 10
Fain would I c. — AMBITION 10
climbers Hasty c. — AMBITION 1
climbing c. into the ditch — SYMPATHY 26
climbs None c. so high — ACHIEVEMENT 16
clime They change their c. — TRAVEL 19
cloak knyf under the c. — TRUST 23
clock c. is always slow — TIME 43
Stands the Church c. — PAST 31
turned into a sort of c. — VIRTUE 39
clog c. of his body — APPEARANCE 15
clogs From c. to clogs — SUCCESS 2
cloistered fugitive and c. virtue — VIRTUE 24
close C. Encounter — PARANORMAL 5
c. my eyes — SEX 20
Do not c. a letter — LETTERS 1
you aren't c. enough — PHOTOGRAPHY 9
closed but it was c. — AMERICAN CITIES 56
like a c. door — PHOTOGRAPHY 9
We never c. — THEATRE 17
closer than a brother — FRIENDSHIP 9
closes c. Saturday night — THEATRE 21
closest c. friends won't tell you — HEALTH 6
cloth according to your c. — PRACTICALITY 1
wearing a c. coat — DRESS 17
clothed c., fed and educated — HUMAN RIGHTS 12
clothes brushers of noblemen's c. — CRITICISM 7
c. do not make a statement — DRESS 25
C. don't make the man — DRESS 20
C. make the man — DRESS 1
c. to have adventures in — DRESS 21
Nothing to wear but c. — OPTIMISM 25
only the wrong c. — WEATHER 19
out of these wet c. — ALCOHOL 6
require new c. — DRESS 5
She wears her c. — DRESS 7
clothing sheep's c. — HYPOCRISY 9

wolf in sheep's c. — DECEPTION 11
cloud c. as a golden throne — IGNORANCE 20
c. cuckoo land — REALITY 3
c. has a silver lining — OPTIMISM 9
c. in trousers — MEN 13
lonely as a c. — FLOWERS 5
Long White C. — COUNTRIES 6
clouds trailing c. of glory — PREGNANCY 6
cloudy if Candlemas day be c. — WEATHER 5
clout Ne'er cast a c. — DRESS 4
cloven c. hoof — GOOD 9
out pops the c. hoof — FAMILY 27
club BELONG TO ANY C. — PREJUDICE 25
best c. in London — PARLIAMENT 6
that terrible football c. — FOOTBALL 6
clue invariably a c. — CRIME 39
clunk C., click, every trip — TRANSPORT 1
clutch c. at a straw — HOPE 1
c. of circumstance — COURAGE 27
coach c. and six — IDEALISM 7
drive a c. and six — WAYS 24
looking for a body in the c. — CINEMA 14
rattling of a c. — PRAYER 14
coal made mainly of c. — ADMINISTRATION 14
made of Newcastle c. — WEATHER 37
coalition c. of the willing — DIPLOMACY 3
rainbow c. — RACE 4
real rainbow c. — RACE 30
coals c. of fire — FORGIVENESS 7
c. of fire upon his head — ENEMIES 6
coarseness c., revealing something — MANNERS 19
coast Gold C. — AFRICA 4
Slave C. — AFRICA 5
coat c. so grey — HUNTING 10
Cut your c. — PRACTICALITY 1
riband to stick in his c. — TRUST 31
cobbler c. stick to his last — KNOWLEDGE 7
c. to his last — KNOWLEDGE 1
Cobley Uncle Tom C. — QUANTITIES 20
Coca-Cola blue jeans and C. — WOMEN 58
C.'s Dasani mineral water — DANGER 38
cocaine c. habit-forming — DRUGS 6
cock before the c. crow — TRUST 21
c. will crow — HOME 4
like a c. who thought — SELF-ESTEEM 18
many a good c. — CHARACTER 17
Nationalism is a silly c. — PATRIOTISM 25
cock and bull c. story — FICTION 4
cockney C. impudence — PAINTING 11
cockpit c. of Christendom — COUNTRIES 13
c. of Europe — EUROPE 1
cocksure c. of anything — CERTAINTY 14
stupid are c. — CERTAINTY 26
cocktail weasel under the c. cabinet — THEATRE 22
cock-up c. theory — GOVERNMENT 39
cocoa C. is a cad — FOOD 21
cod photographer is like the c. — PHOTOGRAPHY 6
code trail has its own stern c. — TRUST 33
coffee After a man has had his c. — DRUNKENNESS 13
c., I want tea — FOOD 20
C., which makes the politician — FOOD 14
C. without tobacco — SMOKING 1
life with c. spoons — LIFE 39
coffin In death we will share one c. — MARRIAGE 2
plate on a c. — APPEARANCE 11
coffins walking behind the c. — HEALTH 2
cogito C., ergo sum — THINKING 4
coil shuffled off this mortal c. — DEATH 3
this mortal c. — LIFE 3
coincidence Twice is c. — CHANCE 3
coins If you have two c. — LIFESTYLES
Proverbs are the c. of the people — QUOTATIONS
coition After c. — SEX
vulgar way of c. — SEX 1
cold as c. and lonely — SELF 2
called a c. a cold — SICKNESS

cooks (*cont.*)
c. who sport white caps	COOKING 3
count the c.	COOKING 14
Devil sends c.	COOKING 7
Too many c. spoil the broth	WORK 8

cool Be still and c. — PRAYER 17
C. Britannia — BRITAIN 1
cooler c. to a hotter — PHYSICAL 16
coolness produced is c. — ARGUMENT 4
cools Time c. — EMOTIONS 23
cooperation c. is unnecessary — COOPERATION 8
c. with good — GOOD 36
don't believe in c. — COOPERATION 7
Government and c. — COOPERATION 29
coot haunts of c. — RIVERS 9
copier c. of nature — PAINTING 8
copies Make c. — ORIGINALITY 12
many c. — HISTORY 18
Copperfield that David C. kind of crap — BIOGRAPHY 18
cops C. are like a doctor — CRIME 44
copulation Birth and c. — LIFE 44
copybook blot one's c. — REPUTATION 14
Gods of the C. Headings — CAUSES 26
cord threefold c. — STRENGTH 16
core ain't-a-going to be no c. — GRATITUDE 14
cork c. out of my lunch — ALCOHOL 26
corkscrews crooked as c. — EMOTIONS 25
corn c. in Egypt — EXCESS 14
make two ears of c. — PRACTICALITY 9
other men's c. — ROYALTY 3
corner c. of a foreign field — PATRIOTISM 20
just around the c. — OPTIMISM 34
coronets more than c. — RANK 13
corporation c. to have a conscience — BUSINESS 31
corporations [c.] cannot commit treason — BUSINESS 25
corpore *mens sana in c. sano* — HEALTH 15
corpse good wishes to the c. — HUMAN NATURE 18
He'd make a lovely c. — DEATH 54
one's father's c. — CUSTOM 21
corpus habeas c. — LAW 11
correct c. with those men — MISTAKES 12
correctness political c. — PREJUDICE 6
correspondences C. are like small-clothes — LETTERS 13
correspondent special c. for posterity — WRITERS 17
corridors c. of power — GOVERNMENT 8
corroborative c. detail — FICTION 14
corrupt appointment by the c. — DEMOCRACY 15
c. press will produce — JOURNALISM 14
more c. the state — LAW 18
corrupted c. by any manner of gift — POLITICIANS 9
hath not been c. — TIME 30
corruptio C. optimi pessima — EXCELLENCE 1
corruption C. of the best — EXCELLENCE 1
C. will find a dozen — CORRUPTION 1
corrupts absolute power c. — POWER 28
Power c. — POWER 6
corsets thirty-shilling c. — DRESS 14
Corsican C. ogre — FRANCE 3
Cortez like stout C. — INVENTIONS 9
cosh c. of the English — BRITAIN 17
cosiness c. and irritation — RELATIONSHIPS 19
cosmetics we make c. — BUSINESS 45
cosmos eyes within a c. — LIFE SCI 22
cost But at what c. — THRIFT 19
c. of setting him up — IDEALISM 13
counteth the c. — FORESIGHT 9
count the c. — GIFTS 15
costs Civility c. nothing — MANNERS 1
letter sometimes c. — LETTERS 2
Nothing that c. only a dollar — VALUE 38
costume thirty-guinea c. — DRESS 14
cottage Love and a c. — IDEALISM 7
love in a c. — MARRIAGE 15
cotton just another crop, like c. — TRAVEL 44
couch c. potato — BROADCASTING 5
cough Keep a c. by them — SPEECHES 10

Love and a c. — LOVE 4
coughs C. and sneezes — SICKNESS 1
could It c. be you — CHANCE 7
councils C. of war — INDECISION 3
counsel c. of perfection — ADVICE 7
c. which you think best — POLITICIANS 9
give a wise man c. — ADVICE 3
Night brings c. — ADVICE 4
counsellors when c. blanch — ADVICE 12
count can't stop to c. it — CHARITY 23
c. one's chickens — OPTIMISM 17
c. our spoons — GOOD 28
c. the cooks — COOKING 14
c. the cost — GIFTS 15
c. what counts — STATISTICS 16
c. your birthdays thankfully — FESTIVALS 61
Don't c. your chickens — OPTIMISM 6
happens *before* you c. to five — ANGER 18
If you can actually c. your money — WEALTH 35
I won the c. — ELECTIONS 16
Let me c. the ways — LOVE 52
only people who c. — MARRIAGE 56
When angry c. a hundred — ANGER 3
When angry, c. four — ANGER 14
When angry, c. ten before — ANGER 13
counted Chickens are c. in autumn — OPTIMISM 3
c. our spoons — HONESTY 12
I c. them all out — WARS 9
countenance cheerful c. — APPEARANCE 13
disinheriting c. — APPEARANCE 18
countercheck c. quarrelsome — LIES 11
counterpoints c. to hack post-horses — MUSIC 10
counters Words are wise men's c. — WORDS 10
counting C. counts only — STATISTICS 16
c. of the omer — FESTIVALS 13
it's the c. — DEMOCRACY 23
countries preferreth all c. before his — TRAVEL 22
country Australia is a lucky c. — AUSTRALIA 24
betraying my c. — PATRIOTISM 28
billion dollar c. — AMERICA 25
c. be always successful — PATRIOTISM 17
c. die for me — PATRIOTISM 30
c. is a piece of land — COUNTRIES 31
c. mouse — COUNTRY AND TOWN 5
c. of the blind — ABILITY 5
c. out of the boy — COUNTRY AND TOWN 3
c., right or wrong — PATRIOTISM 16
c. which has no c. — HISTORY 1
die for one's c. — PATRIOTISM 7
do for your c. — PATRIOTISM 29
dying for your c. — PATRIOTISM 24
every c. but his own — PATRIOTISM 18
God made the c. — COUNTRY AND TOWN 2
God made the c. — COUNTRY AND TOWN 10
go down into the c. — APOLOGY 15
good for our c. — BUSINESS 39
good in the c. — COUNTRY AND TOWN 16
good of his c. — DIPLOMACY 5
good to be had in the c. — COUNTRY AND TOWN 13
govern a c. — FRANCE 17
health of our c. — POLITICAL PART 46
King and C. — ARMED FORCES 12
King and C. — PATRIOTISM 4
King and C. — PATRIOTISM 26
lose for my c. — PATRIOTISM 13
Lucky C. — AUSTRALIA 7
My c. is not a country — CANADA 16
My c. is the world — RELIGION 16
my c. still — PATRIOTISM 11
no relish for the c. — COUNTRY AND TOWN 15
our c.'s good — AUSTRALIA 13
past is a foreign c. — PAST 36
playing at the c. club — SPORTS 37
pray for the c. — POLITICIANS 23
quarrel in a far away c. — WORLD W II 8
Queen and c. — PATRIOTISM 5

save in his own c.	FAMILIARITY 11	C. die many times	COURAGE 14
save in his own c.	FAMILIARITY 15	C. may die many times	FEAR 2
see much of the c.	CRISES 16	cowl c. does not make	APPEARANCE 4
serve our c.	PATRIOTISM 10	cows That's for the c.	SATISFACTION 38
story of c. folk	COUNTRY AND TOWN 1	coy be not c.	MARRIAGE 25
tied to their c.	FARMING 9	coyness c., lady, were no crime	COURTSHIP 5
Union, sir, is my c.	AMERICA 18	coyote c. ain't stealin'	ANIMALS 3
vow to thee, my c.	PATRIOTISM 22	crab never make a c. walk straight	FUTILITY 17
while there's a c. lane	ENGLAND 21	crabbed C. age	GENERATION GAP 7
your King and your C.	WORLD W I 13	crabs like wet c. in a basket	CIRCUMSTANCE 33
countryman c. must have praise	COUNTRY AND TOWN 24	crack c. between the worlds	SUPERNATURAL 23
countrymen Friends, Romans, c.	SPEECHES 8	c. of doom	ENDING 8
countryside smiling and beautiful c.		crackling c. of thorns	FOOLS 11
	COUNTRY AND TOWN 17	cradle c. of the deep	SEA 17
start of the c.	COUNTRY AND TOWN 22	c. to the grave	DRESS 15
courage blending of moral c.	PATIENCE 29	grown man in the c.	PROGRESS 11
But screw your c.	SUCCESS 27	hand that rocks the c.	WOMEN 3
C. in your own	LIFE 35	rocking the c.	ELECTIONS 19
C. is fear	COURAGE 4	rocks the c.	PARENTS 14
C. is not simply	VIRTUE 45	cradling evil c.	BELIEF 15
C. is the price that Life	COURAGE 30	craft c. so long	EDUCATION 17
C. is the thing	COURAGE 29	teach his son a c.	EMPLOYMENT 7
c. never to submit	DEFIANCE 13	cranks sages and c.	PHILOSOPHY 22
C. of Heart	MANNERS 27	crash car c. as a sexual event	TRANSPORT 19
c. of my companions	COURAGE 28	crave still do c.	SATISFACTION 19
c. the greater	DETERMINATION 28	craving c. for gold	GREED 7
C. without conduct	COURAGE 5	full as c.	MATURITY 6
c. without ferocity	DOGS 7	getting rid of c.	SATISFACTION 17
enough c.—or money	REPUTATION 28	no stronger c.	RANK 23
Moral c. is a rarer commodity	COURAGE 33	crazy c. to fly more missions	MADNESS 14
originality or moral c.	CHARACTER 41	he's football c.	FOOTBALL 4
resolution is real c.	COURAGE 20	when I was c.	FRIENDSHIP 20
solitary, existential c.	PREGNANCY 16	creaking c. door hangs longest	SICKNESS 2
two o'clock in the morning c.	COURAGE 24	cream choking it with c.	WAYS 18
courageous freedom depends on being c.	COURAGE 13	c.-faced loon	INSULTS 3
course c. of true love	LOVE 31	create c. the taste	ORIGINALITY 11
courses Horses for c.	ABILITY 2	What I cannot c.	PROBLEMS 31
coursework Life isn't like c.	SCHOOLS 17	created c. out of nothing	CREATIVITY 3
court C. of Session	LAW 4	just c. like mistakes	CIRCUMSTANCE 36
courtesy Grace of God is in C.	MANNERS 20	creates August c. as she slumbers	SEASONS 29
courtiers c. who surround him	EXPERIENCE 21	that c. the wants	BUSINESS 41
courtmartialled c. in my absence	ABSENCE 16	creation about the agony of c.	CREATIVITY 14
courts C. and camps	EXPERIENCE 20	as God is in creation	ARTS 12
courtship C. to marriage	COURTSHIP 6	before you think c.'s	CREATIVITY 12
marriage follows c.	MOURNING 20	c. science	SCIENCE AND RELIG 1
Ten years of c.	COURTSHIP 12	hold C. in my foot	BIRDS 18
cousin brother and I against my c.	FAMILY 10	niche in c.	SEX 22
cousins brothers or eight c.	LIFE SCI 23	present at the C.	UNIVERSE 6
couture Haute C. should be fun	DRESS 22	creative All men are c.	CREATIVITY 13
covenant c. with death	DIPLOMACY 8	c. hate	HATRED 9
Coventry send to C.	SOLITUDE 4	Deception is not as c.	DEATH 78
cover book by its c.	APPEARANCE 11	destruction is also a c.	CREATIVITY 6
Duck and c.	CRISES 1	creatures c. great and small	ANIMALS 21
covet Thou shalt not c.	ENVY 7	living, sentient c.	ANIMALS 14
Thou shalt not c.	ENVY 14	credit children to be a c.	PARENTS 21
coveted desire to be c.	LIFESTYLES 20	Conscience gets a lot of c.	CONSCIENCE 2
cow bellowing c. soon forgets	MOURNING 1	c. goes to the man	SCIENCE 16
Better a good c.	CHARACTER 3	c. where credit is due	PRAISE 3
c.'s horn	ANIMALS 2	don't borrow on c. cards	DEBT 26
How now, brown c.	SPEECH 1	people who get the c.	EFFORT 25
like a c. or a dog	PREGNANCY 7	credite Experto c.	EXPERIENCE 17
old c. died of	MUSIC 6	Crediton C. was a borough town	BRITISH TOWNS 4
swallow the c.	DETERMINATION 8	creditor trembling at a c.	THINKING 13
three acres and a c.	FARMING 4	credo C. quia impossibile	BELIEF 14
Truth, Sir, is a c.	BELIEF 18	credulities c. of mankind	AMBITION 18
Why buy a c.	SINGLE 1	credulity C. is the man's weakness	BELIEF 20
coward bully is always a c.	COURAGE 3	season of c.	BELIEF 19
c. does it with a kiss	LOVE 58	credulous Man is a c. animal	BELIEF 29
c. who deserts her	DUTY 16	creed last article of my c.	VIOLENCE 9
No c. soul is mine	COURAGE 26	reciting the Athanasian C.	BELIEF 34
sea hates a c.	SEA 23	creeds half the c.	CERTAINTY 15
cowardice C., as distinguished from	FEAR 21	so many c.	RELIGION 22
c. keeps us in peace	COURAGE 22	creep c. as well as soar	AMBITION 15
surest is c.	TEMPTATION 14	make one's flesh c.	FEAR 6
cowards all men would be c.	COURAGE 17	make your flesh c.	FEAR 13
conscience doth make c.	CONSCIENCE 13	creeping c. through the black	RIVERS 13

d. the whores are us	DEMOCRACY 24	d. so absolute	DESPAIR 11
d. unbearable	BROADCASTING 19	far side of d.	DESPAIR 15
empire or a d.	RUSSIA 11	In d. there are the most	DESPAIR 12
holy name of liberty or d.	WARFARE 50	Magnaminious D.	DESPAIR 5
justice makes d.	DEMOCRACY 18	Mighty, and d.	FUTILITY 22
little less d.	DEMOCRACY 20	Never d.	HOPE 11
no d. in physics	PHYSICAL 21	perish of d.	LIES 22
pollution of d.	CORRUPTION 19	pressure of d.	SCULPTURE 4
safe for d.	DEMOCRACY 16	sins of d.	SIN 30
Two cheers for D.	DEMOCRACY 22	some divine d.	SORROW 18
Under d. one party	POLITICAL PART 32	**desperandum** *Nil d.*	HOPE 11
voting that's d.	DEMOCRACY 23	**desperate** Beware of d. steps	CAUTION 28
Democrat yellow-dog D.	POLITICAL PART 12	D. diseases	NECESSITY 3
democrat Santa Claus is a D.	POLITICAL PART 44	Diseases d. grown	MEDICINE 14
Senator, and a D.	POLITICAL PART 33	**desperation** lives of quiet d.	LIFE 33
democratic d. health of our country	POLITICAL PART 46	**despise** can d. so entirely	WRITERS 18
democrats lies about the D.	POLITICAL PART 31	**despised** Dangers by being d.	DANGER 32
demolition d. of a man	CRUELTY 14	**despotism** d. or unlimited sovereignty	POWER 24
demon Maxwell's d.	PHYSICAL 5	France was long a d.	FRANCE 12
denial d. of life	DANGER 37	**destination** could see our d.	EXPLORATION 15
denied justice d.	JUSTICE 7	**destiny** Anatomy is d.	BODY 20
deny d., or delay	JUSTICE 23	fabric of human d.	GOOD 34
D. self for self's sake	SELF 1	share a common d.	INTERNAT REL 39
thou shalt d. me thrice	TRUST 21	wiving go by d.	FATE 2
You must d. yourself	SELF-SACRIFICE 7	**destroy** d. the town to save it	WARS 24
denying they were d.	AUSTRALIA 32	Doth the winged life d.	TRANSIENCE 12
depart he will not d. from it	CHILD CARE 4	gods wish to d.	CRITICISM 22
departure d. is defined	LIBERTY 20	then they d. us	HUMAN RIGHTS 21
depends d. on what the meaning	MEANING 15	Whom the gods would d.	MADNESS 1
d. what you mean	MEANING 14	**destroyed** Carthage must be d.	ENEMIES 7
depraved suddenly became d.	SIN 10	d. but not defeated	WINNING 22
depravity sense of innate d.	SIN 21	ought to be d.	CENSORSHIP 3
depressed When you're d.	OPTIMISM 36	treated generously or d.	REVENGE 12
depression d. when you lose yours	ECONOMICS 13	**destroyer** d. of worlds	PHYSICAL 13
depressions what terrible d.	WRITING 10	only a d.	POLLUTION 14
deputy read by d.	BOOKS 6	**destroys** d. those who practise it	VIOLENCE 20
derangement nice d. of epitaphs	WIT 11	**destruction** d. of the whole world	SELF 13
descent d. from a monkey	LIFE SCI 14	Pride goeth before d.	PRIDE 4
desert D. Fox	WORLD W II 4	to his own d.	ARGUMENT 25
d. rats	WORLD W II 5	urge for d.	CREATIVITY 6
on the d. air	FAME 15	**detail** corroborative d.	FICTION 14
ship of the d.	ANIMALS 11	everything else is d.	LIFESTYLES 40
deserve have done nothing to d.	BEAUTY 37	frittered away by d.	EXCESS 30
we'll d. it	SUCCESS 28	**details** Devil is in the d.	ORDER 1
deserves criminal it d.	LAW 39	God is in the d.	ARCHITECTURE 1
Everybody gets what he d.	WORLD W II 25	suppresses idle d.	DAY 18
face he d.	APPEARANCE 28	**detect** moment you d.	LIFE SCI 11
good boy d. favour	MUSIC 1	**detector** shock-proof shit d.	WRITING 46
Stonehenge it d.	PAST 40	**determination** d. of a quiet man	CHARACTER 55
desiccated d. calculating machine	LEADERSHIP 18	Persistence and d.	DETERMINATION 44
design integrity in d.	FASHION 17	**determined** d. fellow can do more	DETERMINATION 2
intelligent d.	SCIENCE AND RELIG 3	**detest** d. at leisure	HATRED 6
not by a priori d.	LIFE SCI 21	**detrimental** d. to keep it	ANGER 17
desipere *d. in loco*	FOOLS 12	**Deutschland** master from D.	DEATH 71
desirable physically d.	APPEARANCE 30	**de Valera** Negotiating with D.	DIPLOMACY 15
desire by nature d. knowledge	KNOWLEDGE 22	**deviation** Without d. from the norm	SIMILARITY 28
d. accomplished is sweet	ACHIEVEMENT 14	Without hesitation, d.	SPEECH 6
d. for desires	BOREDOM 7	**devices** d. and desires	SIN 16
d. for their own happiness	SUFFERING 11	**devil** apology for the D.	BIBLE 16
d. is for the woman	MEN AND WOMEN 8	Better the d. you know	FAMILIARITY 1
d. should so many years	SEX 12	bid the D. good morrow	PROBLEMS 3
get your heart's d.	ACHIEVEMENT 25	covenant with the D.	MATHS 1
provokes the d.	DRUNKENNESS 5	d. can cite Scripture	BIBLE 8
strong as sexual d.	SEX 8	d. can quote Scripture	QUOTATIONS 1
Which of us has his d.	SATISFACTION 28	d. damn thee	INSULTS 3
desired d. so much	POETS 21	d. finds work	IDLENESS 3
desires d. but acts not	ACTION 24	d. have all the best	SINGING 1
d. of the heart	EMOTIONS 25	D. howling 'Ho'	SCIENCE 17
devices and d.	SIN 16	D. is in the details	ORDER 1
lopping off our d.	SATISFACTION 23	d. is not so black	REPUTATION 4
desiring d., of despair	HAPPINESS 6	d. looks after his own	CHANCE 3
desolation d. of war	PEACE 18	d. makes his Christmas pies	LAW 1
despair can never d.	HOPE 19	d.'s children	CHANCE 4
carrion comfort D.	DESPAIR 13	D. sends cooks	COOKING 7
D. is the price one pays	DESPAIR 16	d.'s gold ring	GIFTS 3
D. seeks its own	DESPAIR 17	D. should have right	JUSTICE 24

devil (cont.)

d.'s workshop	IDLENESS 4
D. take the hindmost	SELF-INTEREST 2
D. was sick	GRATITUDE 1
D. whoops	ARTS 17
D. will build a chapel	GOOD 8
d. would also build	GOOD 24
Drink and the d.	ALCOHOL 18
easier to raise the D.	BEGINNING 5
first Whig was the D.	POLITICAL PART 15
Give the D. his due	JUSTICE 6
good painter can draw a d.	PAINTING 1
Haste is from the D.	HASTE 4
home, as the D. said	LAW 4
nine times to the D.	GARDENS 7
of the D.'s party	POETS 14
old d.	HUMAN NATURE 4
over the D.'s back	SIN 2
Poetry is d.'s wine	POETRY 6
printer's d.	PUBLISHING 1
reference to the d.	INTERNAT REL 29
renounce the d.	SIN 15
ride to the D.	POWER 7
sacrifice to God of the d.'s leavings	VIRTUE 26
shame the d.	TRUTH 4
sups with the D.	CAUTION 11
Talk of the D.	MEETING 3
Truth makes the D. blush	TRUTH 7
very punctual with the D.	PUNCTUALITY 19
when the d. drives	NECESSITY 11
white man *was created* a d.	RACE 19
world, the flesh, and the d.	TEMPTATION 5
world, the flesh, and the d.	TEMPTATION 10

devilish d. thing is 8 times — MATHS 12

devils d. must print — PUBLISHING 8

d. to contest his vision	HEROES 20
d. would set on me	DEFIANCE 11

Devon glorious D. — BRITISH TOWNS 34

devour d. in turn each one — REVOLUTION 12

devourer Time the d. — TIME 22

dew as sunlight drinketh d. — KISSING 6

diagnostician makes a good d. — MEDICINE 26

dialect d. I understand — HUNTING 5

d. of the tribe	SPEECH 28
d. with an army	LANGUAGES 15

diamond D. cuts diamond — EQUALITY 2

d. is forever	WEALTH 1
D. State	AMERICAN CITIES 12
rough than polished d.	BRITAIN 7

diamonds d. are a girl's best friend — WEALTH 34

give him his d. back	HATRED 12
Goodness, what beautiful d.	VIRTUE 43

diaries keep d. to remember — MEMORY 20

dice God does not play d. — CHANCE 30

throw of the d. — CHANCE 28

Dickens put to D. as children — WRITERS 29

dictator Every d. uses religion — POWER 38

dictators d. may cultivate — IGNORANCE 26

dictatorship d. of the proletariat — CAPITALISM 3

made d. impossible — BROADCASTING 19

dictionary in a d. — SUCCESS 7

die afraid to d. — DEATH 77

Americans when they d.	AMERICA 2
as if you were to d. tomorrow	EDUCATION 15
asked this man to d.	ARMED FORCES 46
books never d.	BOOKS 19
Cowards d. many times	COURAGE 14
d. and know it	DEATH 72
d. before I get old	OLD AGE 30
d. beyond my means	MEDICINE 21
d. but once	PATRIOTISM 10
d. by famine	DEATH 47
d. for one's country	PATRIOTISM 2
d. for the industrialists	PATRIOTISM 24
d. in earnest	DEATH 38
d. in my week	SELF-INTEREST 32

d. in one's duty is life	DUTY 9
d. in the last ditch	DEFIANCE 5
d. in the last ditch	DEFIANCE 14
d. is cast	CRISES 11
d. like a true-blue rebel	REVOLUTION 20
d. many times	FEAR 2
D., my dear Doctor	DEATH 58
d. of the roar	INSIGHT 13
d. on your feet	LIBERTY 27
d. upon a kiss	KISSING 4
d. will be an awfully big	DEATH 66
Don't d. of ignorance	HEALTH 2
Eternal in man cannot d.	DEATH 24
Few d. and none resign	POLITICIANS 15
for tomorrow we d.	LIFESTYLES 3
frogs don't d. for 'fun'	CRUELTY 4
good d. young	VIRTUE 1
Guards d.	ARMED FORCES 28
How often are we to d.	MOURNING 12
ideal for which I am prepared to d.	AFRICA 13
I did not d.	MOURNING 18
If I should d.	PATRIOTISM 20
I'll d. young	DRUGS 10
I shall not altogether d.	DEATH 26
it was sure to d.	TRANSIENCE 11
last man to d. for a mistake	ARMED FORCES 49
let my country d.	PATRIOTISM 30
Let them d. of neglect	IDEAS 16
Let us determine to d. here	WARS 16
love one another or d.	SOCIETY 15
man can d. but once	DEATH 32
More d. of food	HEALTH 9
Old soldiers never d.	ARMED FORCES 41
rich to d.	DEATH 52
See Naples and d.	TOWNS 4
soldiers never d.	ARMED FORCES 6
something he will d. for	IDEALISM 14
something you d. for	FAITH 17
Theirs but to do and d.	ARMED FORCES 32
then you d.	LIFE 6
To d., to sleep	DEATH 33
To go away is to d.	ABSENCE 13
unfit to d.	CRIME 32
We shall d. alone	DEATH 42
will d. of strangeness	FICTION 20
You can only d. once	DEATH 11
you have to d. yourself	CAUSES 9
You'll d. facing the monument	CRIME 11
Young men may d.	DEATH 12
youth who must fight and d.	WARFARE 51

died d. last night — MEDICINE 18

liked it not, and d. — MOURNING 11

diem *Carpe d.* — PRESENT 5

dies As one fern frond d. — LEADERSHIP 1

d. pays all debts	DEATH 36
d. . . . . rich dies disgraced	WEALTH 27
Every moment d.	STATISTICS 5
every moment d.	STATISTICS 6
happy till he d.	HAPPINESS 2
how a man d.	DEATH 49
kingdom where nobody d.	CHILDREN 16
Music d.	MUSICIANS 3
Nobody d. from lack of sex	SINGLE 11
something in me d.	SUCCESS 48
soon as beauty, d.	BEAUTY 14
Whom the gods love d. young	YOUTH 7

diet d. unparalleled — SCHOOLS 6

Dr D. — MEDICINE 1

dietetics first law of d. — HEALTH 24

differ d. from others — SIMILARITY 22

difference d. of forty thousand — LEADERSHIP 12

d. within the sexes	MEN AND WOMEN 23
oh, The d. to me	MOURNING 13
that has made all the d.	CHOICE 22
What d. does it make	WARFARE 50

differences against small d. — PREJUDICE 20

dragons (*cont.*)

Dragons beget d.	FAMILY 6
Here be d.	EXPLORATION 1
drain From this foul d.	BRITISH TOWNS 30
drains Democracy and proper d.	ENGLAND 23
unblock your d.	PLEASURE 28
drakes play ducks and d. with	THRIFT 12
drama d. out of a crisis	CRISES 4
draw d. like these children	PAINTING 24
d. or hold so fast	LOVE 37
d. what I see	PAINTING 29
d. you to her *with a single hair*	WOMEN 24
drawbacks everything has its d.	ADVERSITY 18
drawing back to the d. board	BEGINNING 14
D. is the true test	PAINTING 10
inventor of the d. board	INVENTIONS 22
draws d. with a single hair	BEAUTY 1
dread d. nor hope attend	DEATH 69
d. of beatings	SCHOOLS 12
most men d. it	LIBERTY 22
dreaders evil d.	CONSCIENCE 4
dreadnoughts to keep up as two D.	RANK 18
dreads d. the fire	EXPERIENCE 2
dream American d.	AMERICA 4
D. of a funeral	DREAMS 1
d. of reason	DREAMS 9
d. of the soft look	OLD AGE 22
d. that we are dreaming	DREAMS 17
d. the impossible dream	IDEALISM 15
d. things that never were	IDEAS 9
d. within a dream	REALITY 13
d. yourself into a character	CHARACTER 21
European D. is worth living for	IDEALISM 19
glory and the d.	IMAGINATION 8
I have a d.	EQUALITY 16
love's young d.	LOVE 17
love's young d.	LOVE 45
salesman is got to d.	BUSINESS 37
sleep: perchance to d.	DEATH 33
vision, or a waking d.	DREAMS 10
dreamed d. of cheese	FOOD 18
d. that I dwelt	IMAGINATION 11
d. that life was beauty	LIFE 30
dreamer not a d.	IDEALISM 17
dreamers d. of dreams	MUSICIANS 6
mere d. of another existence	WORDS AND DEEDS 17
dreaming d. I was a butterfly	SELF-KNOWLEDGE 3
d. of a white Christmas	CHRISTMAS 13
d. spires	BRITISH TOWNS 18
dreams City of perspiring d.	UNIVERSITIES 25
D. go by contraries	DREAMS 2
d. is the royal road	DREAMS 5
D. retain the infirmities	DREAMS 3
I have bad d.	DREAMS 7
Morning d. come true	DREAMS 4
quick D.	DREAMS 11
rich, beyond the d. of avarice	WEALTH 24
scream for help in d.	DREAMS 16
see it in our d.	THEATRE 13
you tread on my d.	DREAMS 12
dreamt d. of in your philosophy	SUPERNATURAL 11
dreary If your morals make you d.	MORALITY 12
dregs d. are often filthy-tasting	REVENGE 14
dress article of d. without	TRANSPORT 22
changed our d., manners	TRANSPORT 20
d. of thought	LANGUAGE 10
d. of thought	STYLE 11
I d. sluts	FASHION 16
dressed d. up and no place to go	DRESS 13
drifting d. continent	AFRICA 9
drink d. and drive	ALCOHOL 2
D. and the devil	ALCOHOL 18
d., and to be merry	LIFESTYLES 12
D. deep, or taste not	KNOWLEDGE 32
D. is a great provoker	DRUNKENNESS 5
d. one another's healths	ALCOHOL 19

drunkard's cure is d.	DRUNKENNESS 1
Eat, d. and be merry	LIFESTYLES 3
I do not d., I build	ARCHITECTURE 10
little d. below	ALCOHOL 15
Nor any drop to d.	SEA 14
One more d.	DRUNKENNESS 16
reason why I don't d.	ALCOHOL 29
Refraining from strong d.	LIFESTYLES 14
still d. more	DRUNKENNESS 8
strong d. is raging	ALCOHOL 9
you can't make him d.	DEFIANCE 4
drinka D. Pinta Milka Day	HEALTH 3
drinking D. when we are not thirsty	HUMAN RACE 22
drinks d. as much as you	DRUNKENNESS 15
d. beer, thinks beer	DRUNKENNESS 2
dripping d. June sets all in tune	WEATHER 3
drive cannot d. you	REVENGE 24
can't d. the car	CRITICISM 25
difficult to d.	EDUCATION 23
drink and d.	ALCOHOL 2
d. a coach and six	WAYS 24
drives when the devil d.	NECESSITY 11
driving like the d. of Jehu	TRANSPORT 6
dromedary muse on d. trots	POETS 16
drop because of that missing d.	CHARITY 24
d. makes the cup run	EXCESS 7
d. out	LIFESTYLES 34
d. the pilot	TRUST 7
Nor any d. to drink	SEA 14
dropping Constant d. wears away	DETERMINATION 1
drops D. that gather one by one	QUANTITIES 1
penny d.	INSIGHT 2
drought d. is destroying his roots	FARMING 13
d. of March	SEASONS 13
drove Sussex won't be d.	BRITISH TOWNS 11
drown I d. twa	RIVERS 2
drowned BETTER D. THAN DUFFERS	ABILITY 13
d. now and again	SEA 20
you'll never be d.	FATE 3
drowning d. man will clutch	HOPE 1
like death by d.	SINGLE 10
not waving but d.	SOLITUDE 21
drudge his mother d.	ARTS 22
drug d. is neither moral or immoral	DRUGS 12
literature is a d.	WRITING 30
most powerful d. used	WORDS 21
drugs twenty d. for each disease	MEDICINE 25
drum marching to a different d.	CONFORMITY 4
drummer hears a different d.	CONFORMITY 9
drunk appeal from Philip d.	OPINION 6
art of getting d.	DRUNKENNESS 7
d. for about a week	LIBRARIES 11
genteel when he gets d.	MANNERS 14
inarticulate, and then d.	HOSPITALITY 14
Not d. is he	DRUNKENNESS 8
think as you d. I am	DRUNKENNESS 11
when he was d.	FRIENDSHIP 20
when they're d.	MEN 21
Winston, you're d.	INSULTS 11
you ain't still d. tomorrow	DRUNKENNESS 13
You're not d.	DRUNKENNESS 17
drunkard d.'s cure is drink	DRUNKENNESS 1
drunken d. man uses lampposts	STATISTICS 9
sailors and d. men	DANGER 3
drunkenness d. of things being	SIMILARITY 26
dry dwelling in a d. place	WRITERS 12
into a d. Martini	ALCOHOL 6
Sow d.	GARDENS 9
till the well runs d.	GRATITUDE 4
Dryden D. wanted, or forgot	POETS 11
poetry of D.	POETRY 23
duchess chambermaid as of a D.	IMAGINATION 7
duchesses D. are doing	GOSSIP 20
duck After that everything's a d.	BIRDS 20
break one's d.	CRICKET 2
D. and cover	CRISES 1

forgot to d. — WINNING 19
If it looks like a d. — HYPOTHESIS 25
seagull and says 'd.' — PARENTS 32
duckling ugly d. — YOUTH 6
ducks d. who float — MEMORY 6
play d. and drakes with — THRIFT 12
due Give the Devil his d. — JUSTICE 6
render everyone his d. — JUSTICE 22
duffers BETTER DROWNED THAN D. — ABILITY 13
dukes drawing room full of d. — ARTS AND SCI 12
d. are just as great — RANK 18
dulce D. et decorum est — PATRIOTISM 7
dull Clean. Christian. D. — CANADA 25
d. at whiles — DUTY 17
d. in himself — BOREDOM 5
d. it is to pause — IDLENESS 19
makes d. men witty — ANGER 10
makes Jack a d. boy — LEISURE 1
dullard d.'s envy — EXCELLENCE 15
dullness cardinal sin is d. — CINEMA 22
d. in others — BOREDOM 5
dumb deep are d. — EMOTIONS 11
d. year — SEASONS 1
So d. he can't fart — FOOLS 32
takes 40 d. animals — CRUELTY 1
dunces d. are all in confederacy — GENIUS 4
dungeon d. of self — SELF 20
dungfork d. in his hand — PRAYER 27
dunghill crowing on its own d. — PATRIOTISM 25
crow upon his own d. — HOME 4
Dunkirk appeals to the D. spirit — CRISES 21
D. spirit — CRISES 6
dupe d. of friendship — HATRED 7
duped than to be d. — FRIENDSHIP 14
dupes If hopes were d. — HOPE 18
duration for the d. — TIME 12
dure Pourvu que ça d. — TRANSIENCE 9
dusk d. with a light behind — APPEARANCE 22
falling of the d. — PHILOSOPHY 13
dust become like d. and ashes — ADVERSITY 12
d. and ashes — DISILLUSION 3
d. comes secretly — HOUSEWORK 10
d. of exploded beliefs — BELIEF 27
d. thou art — DEATH 23
D. thou art — LIFE 29
d. to dust — DEATH 44
D. yourself off — DETERMINATION 45
Grind them into the d. — CRICKET 12
handful of d. — FEAR 17
peck of March d. — WEATHER 11
raised a d. — KNOWLEDGE 31
This quiet D. — DEATH 57
To sweep the d. — PREPARATION 18
what a d. do I raise — SELF-ESTEEM 13
winning the palm without the d. — WINNING 8
with age and d. — TIME 29
dustbin d. of history — SUCCESS 41
d. upset — SLEEP 19
duster Rooster today, feather d. tomorrow — SUCCESS 10
dusty d. answer — CERTAINTY 16
d. answer — SATISFACTION 12
Dutch fault of the D. — INTERNAT REL 15
duties Property has its d. — POSSESSIONS 18
duty actor's d., to interpret — ACTING 12
citizen's first d. — SOCIETY 19
declares that it is his d. — DUTY 20
die in one's d. is life — DUTY 9
Do your d. — DUTY 12
Do your d. bravely — WORLD W I 9
d. bade me fight — ARMED FORCES 40
d. is the king's — CONSCIENCE 12
d. is to obey orders — CONFORMITY 10
d. is useful in work — DUTY 23
D. is what no-one else will do — DUTY 27
d. of an Opposition — PARLIAMENT 19
d. of a soldier — ARMED FORCES 4

d. to speak one's mind — DUTY 18
every man will do his d. — DUTY 14
from a sense of d. — DUTY 22
inattentive to his d. — DUTY 16
I've done my d. — GRATITUDE 12
life was d. — LIFE 30
voice of God! O D. — DUTY 15
We must do our d. — EUROPE 9
dwarfish What is an Epigram? a d. whole — WIT 14
dwarfs d. on the shoulders — PROGRESS 8
dyer like the d.'s hand — CIRCUMSTANCE 24
dying attend a d. animal — DEATH 69
distinguished from d. — DEATH 55
d. breath of Socrates — PHYSICAL 12
d. for four thousand years — THEATRE 20
d. is more the survivors' — DEATH 65
d. of a hundred — SICKNESS 8
d. of the light — OLD AGE 27
d. without having laughed — HUMOUR 7
feel that he is d. — CRUELTY 5
get busy d. — DRUGS 15
If this is d. — DEATH 68
indisposeth us for d. — DEATH 41
nothing new in d. — SUICIDE 8
prayers of the d. — PRAYER 33
those of the d. — LOVE 66
those poor devils are d. — WARS 20
tree without it d. — CUSTOM 4
words of a d. man — CENSORSHIP 5
dyke February fill-d. — SEASONS 10
February fill d. — WEATHER 4
dynamite barrel of d. — POETRY 28

e I before e, except after c — WORDS 3
each To e. his own — JUSTICE 15
eagle e. among blinking owls — POETS 17
E. has landed — SKIES 27
e. sees it — SENSES 1
Fate is not an e. — FATE 23
freethinker is an e. — BELIEF 24
Theban e. — POETS 7
eagles e. be gathered — GREED 4
E. don't catch flies — CHARACTER 7
ear cut his e. off — ARTS AND SCI 13
hearing of the e. — SENSES 4
heart was piercèd through the e. — WORDS 8
out of a sow's e. — FUTILITY 7
penetrates the e. — MUSIC 25
right sow by the e. — PRACTICALITY 5
sow by the e. — KNOWLEDGE 13
than meets the e. — MEANING 5
earlier one I made e. — PREPARATION 7
earls Flight of the E. — IRELAND 4
early always too late or too e. — TIME 46
e. bird catches — PREPARATION 3
E. Christian that gets the fattest — HASTE 18
e. man never borrows — PREPARATION 4
E. to bed — HEALTH 4
E. to rise — SLEEP 18
start e. — HASTE 3
think how e. I go — PUNCTUALITY 13
Vote e. — ELECTIONS 3
earned e. your wrinkles — MIDDLE AGE 17
penny saved is a penny e. — THRIFT 4
earnest die in e. — DEATH 38
Life is e. — LIFE 29
earrings e. for under £1 — BUSINESS 51
ears adder that stoppeth her e. — DEFIANCE 9
between the e. — POETRY 40
e., and hear not — INDIFFERENCE 3
keep both e. to the ground — POLITICIANS 2
lend me your e. — SPEECHES 8
pitchers have large e. — SECRECY 5
Too beautiful for our e. — MUSIC 9
two e. and only one mouth — SPEECH 9

ears *(cont.)*

Walls have e.	SECRECY 15
wolf by the e.	CRISES 14
wolf by the e.	DANGER 17
woods have e.	SECRECY 3

earth all e. to love — BRITISH TOWNS 35

begins with a heap of e.	BEGINNING 20
but He craves the e.	EARTH 14
call this planet E.	EARTH 16
daughter of E.	SKIES 18
Did the e. move	SEX 1
e.; for it is his footstool	SWEARING 4
E. has not anything	BRITISH TOWNS 26
e. is the Lord's	EARTH 8
e. to earth	DEATH 44
feel the e. move	SEX 26
girdle round the e.	HASTE 14
going to and fro in the e.	TRAVEL 18
heaven and a new e.	HEAVEN 8
heaven and the e.	BEGINNING 19
If all the e. were paper	WRITING 14
If there is a paradise on e.	COUNTRIES 12
inherit the e. from our parents	EARTH 2
I will move the e.	TECHNOLOGY 6
low as where this e.	EARTH 11
more things in heaven and e.	SUPERNATURAL 11
On e. there is nothing	MIND 17
salt of the e.	VIRTUE 11
Spaceship E.	EARTH 13
surly bonds of e.	TRANSPORT 18
they shall inherit the e.	PRIDE 5
thought the E. was flat	MISTAKES 28
Touch the e. lightly	EARTH 1
Which men call e.	EARTH 10
Yours is the E.	MATURITY 9

earthquake telegraph pole in an e. — SEA 27

ease inability to be at e. — MISFORTUNES 20

easier make life e. for men — WOMAN'S ROLE 30

east Britain calls the Far E. — AUSTRALIA 21

E. is East	EQUALITY 12
E. is east	SIMILARITY 4
E., west, home's best	HOME 2
e. wind made flesh	AMERICAN CITIES 50
hold the gorgeous E. in fee	TOWNS 15
neither from the e.	EMPLOYMENT 6
When the wind is in the e.	WEATHER 21

East End look the E. in the face — WORLD W II 14

Easter We are an E. people — CHRISTIAN CH 39

what they did for E. — FESTIVALS 73

eastward e. in Eden — GARDENS 11

easy Big E. — AMERICAN CITIES 5

e. as one's discourse	LETTERS 4
E. come, easy go	EFFORT 2
E. live	INDIFFERENCE 7
e. writing's vile hard reading	WRITING 21
Life is not meant to be e.	ADVERSITY 22
livin' is e.	SEASONS 26
No e. problems ever come	PRESIDENCY 11
resist the e. and preferred answers	EDUCATION 33
Words e. to be understood	WORDS 11

eat cake and e. it — ACHIEVEMENT 11

can e. you up	REVENGE 24
Dog does not e. dog	COOPERATION 2
e. and drunk and lived	BIOGRAPHY 5
e., and to drink	LIFESTYLES 12
e. a peck of dirt	COOKING 10
e. at a place called Mom's	LIFESTYLES 32
E., drink and be merry	LIFESTYLES 3
E. to live	COOKING 5
have meat and cannot e.	COOKING 16
He that would e. the fruit	EFFORT 3
neither should he e.	WORK 22
one should e. wisely	HOSPITALITY 18
see what I e.	MEANING 8
shalt thou e. bread	WORK 19
sometimes has to e. them	WORDS 29

Tell me what you e.	COOKING 19
won't work you shan't e.	IDLENESS 8
You are what you e.	COOKING 11

eaten can be e. cold — REVENGE 6

we've already e. — FORESIGHT 17

eater e. of beef — FOOD 12

eating Appetite comes with e. — EXPERIENCE 1

in the e.	HYPOTHESIS 5
someone else is e.	SUFFERING 31

ecclesiastic E. tyranny — CLERGY 11

éclair no more backbone than a chocolate é. — CHARACTER 42

eclipse at the sun's e. — NATURE 7

E. first, the rest nowhere — WINNING 11

economic e. experiment — ALCOHOL 23

read e. documents	ECONOMICS 16
vital e. interests	ECONOMICS 11
women are e. factors	EMPLOYMENT 14

economical e. with the truth — LIES 8

e. with the truth — TRUTH 42

economics it is bad e. — ECONOMICS 10

economists e., and calculators — EUROPE 5

economize Let us e. it — TRUTH 33

economy E. is going without something — THRIFT 16

E. was always elegant	POVERTY 25
general e.	ECONOMICS 12
Political E.	DEBT 21
There can be no e.	ECONOMICS 8
Yes to the market e.	CAPITALISM 32

eczema too often hides e. — STYLE 23

Eden eastward in E. — GARDENS 11

picnic in E. — GUILT 14

edge Come to the e. — INSIGHT 16

editing products of e. — LIFE SCI 21

edition read the wrong e. — PREGNANCY 2

editor e. did it — JOURNALISM 28

educate if you e. a woman — EDUCATION 30

schoolboys who e. him — SCHOOLS 8

educated fed and e. — HUMAN RIGHTS 12

education aim of e. — EDUCATION 26

cabbage with a college e.	FOOD 19
e. and catastrophe	HISTORY 23
E. doesn't come	EDUCATION 2
e., education	EDUCATION 34
E. has been theirs	MEN 9
E. is what survives	EDUCATION 32
E. is when you read	EXPERIENCE 36
E. makes a people easy	EDUCATION 23
e. of the heart	EMOTIONS 15
e. serves as a rattle	EDUCATION 13
e., taste	MANNERS 28
first part of politics? E.	POLITICS 15
Genius without e.	GENIUS 2
gets you an e.	CERTAINTY 22
In e. there should be	EDUCATION 12
never let your e.	EDUCATION 6
poor e. I have received	UNIVERSITIES 19
Soap and e.	EDUCATION 24
that is e.	CINEMA 7
Travel a part of e.	TRAVEL 23

eel e. out of a tub — HUMOUR 19

effect found in the e. — CAUSES 24

effective one e. advertisement — ADVERTISING 8

efficiency southern e. and northern charm — AMERICAN CITIES 62

where there is no e. — ECONOMICS 8

effort e. to write — LETTERS 16

redoubling your e.	EXCESS 32
Superhuman e. isn't worth	EFFORT 24

efforts e. made to solve — PROBLEMS 30

egalitarian e. where they should be — UNIVERSITIES 28

egg added e. — IDLENESS 1

chicken-and-e. problem	PROBLEMS 6
curate's e.	CHARACTER 22
e. boiled very soft	FOOD 17
e. is, quite simply	FOOD 30

encourager e. les autres	MANAGEMENT 5
pour e. les autres	WAYS 28
encyclopedia e. was the first book	COMPUTERS 22
encyclopedias E., centuries	LIBRARIES 12
end beginning is my e.	BEGINNING 23
beginning of the e.	ENDING 16
Better is the e.	ENDING 12
boys get at one e.	SCHOOLS 4
came to an e. all wars	WORLD W I 22
come to an e.	ENDING 1
continuing unto the e.	THOROUGHNESS 11
do not e. when you please	WARFARE 16
e. as superstitions	TRUTH 31
e. cannot justify	MORALITY 20
e. crowns the work	ENDING 4
e. for which	HOSPITALITY 11
e. in doubts	CERTAINTY 10
e. is my beginning	ENDING 6
e. justifies the means	MORALITY 5
e. justifies the means	WAYS 3
e. of ane old song	SCOTLAND 7
e. of a thousand years	EUROPE 16
e. of civilization	CULTURE 4
e. of history	HISTORY 26
e. of love	LOVE 25
e. of love	LOVE 32
e. of man is an action	WORDS AND DEEDS 18
e. of the beginning	ENDING 19
e. of the rainbow	VALUE 13
e. of the road	DETERMINATION 42
e. of the world	AMERICA 40
e. the sooner	HASTE 15
Everything has an e.	ENDING 5
make an e.	IDLENESS 19
Mankind must put an e. to war	WARFARE 56
middle and an e.	CINEMA 21
middle, and an e.	QUANTITIES 22
that it can ever e.	LOVE 47
this day to e. myself	SUICIDE 6
till you come to the e.	BEGINNING 22
Top E.	AUSTRALIA 10
where's it all going to e.	ENDING 22
wills the e.	CAUSES 22
wills the e.	DETERMINATION 5
world without e.	TIME 19
endears all the more e.	FORGIVENESS 21
ended Middle Ages e. suddenly	PROGRESS 25
ending makes a good e.	BEGINNING 4
quickest way of e. a war	WARFARE 53
Endor road to E.	SUPERNATURAL 20
witch of E.	SUPERNATURAL 6
endow all my worldly goods I thee e.	WEDDINGS 7
ends burn the candle at both e.	EFFORT 11
e. by our beginnings know	CHARACTER 33
on one's beam-e.	POVERTY 9
shapes our e.	FATE 16
similar sounds at their e.	POETRY 37
that e. well	ENDING 2
endurance e., and courage	COURAGE 28
patient e. is godlike	SUFFERING 21
endure Children's talent to e.	SUFFERING 34
e. their hard lot	SCIENCE AND RELIG 18
learn to e. adversity	ADVERSITY 19
nature itselfe cant e.	MATHS 12
endured e. with patient resignation	DUTY 23
must be e.	PATIENCE 20
Once you e. worse	SUFFERING 6
enemies against smiling e.	ENVY 16
by the number of his e.	VALUE 30
choice of his e.	ENEMIES 16
conciliates e.	RELATIONSHIPS 15
E.' gifts	GIFTS 11
e. of Freedom	LIBERTY 29
e. of liberty	CLERGY 13
e. of truth	TRUTH 19
e. will not believe you	APOLOGY 16

Happiness lies in conquering one's e.	HAPPINESS 8
Love your e.	ENEMIES 9
no perpetual e.	INTERNAT REL 18
time for making new e.	FORGIVENESS 18
we make our e.	HOME 22
wish their e. dead	ENEMIES 12
enemy at high speed toward the e.	WORLD W II 21
body of your e. float by	PATIENCE 7
bridge of gold to a flying e.	WAYS 12
e. and your friend	GOSSIP 24
e. be hungry	ENEMIES 6
e. of my enemy	ENEMIES 3
e. of the good	EXCELLENCE 12
e. that will run me through	INDIFFERENCE 6
first contact with the e.	PREPARATION 13
has one e.	RELATIONSHIPS 8
have upon the e.	ARMED FORCES 27
Love your e.	ENEMIES 4
met the e.	POLLUTION 21
my worst e.'s dog	TEACHING 23
no e. but the ignorant	SCIENCE 2
no e. but time	GUILT 13
no little e.	ENEMIES 5
quieten your e.	ENEMIES 22
sweet e.	FRANCE 6
third time it's e. action	CHANCE 34
with the e.'s main force	PREPARATION 22
worry's worst e.	ACTION 1
engine Analytical E. weaves	COMPUTERS 9
curious e.	BODY 11
e. of pollution	DOGS 15
e. that moves	FATE 21
engineer e. is a man who can do	TECHNOLOGY 15
engineering not social e.	SCHOOLS 14
engineers age of the e.	TECHNOLOGY 12
e. of the soul	ARTS 26
e. of the soul	ARTS 29
engines e. to play a little	PRACTICALITY 12
England always be an E.	ENGLAND 21
Be E. what she will	PATRIOTISM 11
deep sleep of E.	ENGLAND 20
defence of E.	INTERNAT REL 28
E. all is permitted	COUNTRIES 34
E. and America	LANGUAGES 16
E. expects	DUTY 14
E. forget her precedence	ENGLAND 8
E. is finished	ENGLAND 22
E. is the paradise	ENGLAND 1
E.'s difficulty	IRELAND 1
E.'s green and pleasant	ENGLAND 13
E. should be free	DRUNKENNESS 9
E.'s not a bad country	ENGLAND 26
E. to be the workshop	INTERNAT REL 16
E. was too pure an Air	LIBERTY 7
ensure summer in E.	SEASONS 16
garden of E.	BRITISH TOWNS 19
God punish E.	WORLD W I 10
Heart of E.	BRITISH TOWNS 24
keep your E.	INTERNAT REL 42
leads him to E.	SCOTLAND 8
Little E. beyond Wales	WALES 2
no harm to E.'s native people	AUSTRALIA 29
Oh, to be in E.	SEASONS 5
stately homes of E.	RANK 15
suspended in favour of E.	CAUSES 25
That is for ever E.	PATRIOTISM 20
think of E.	SEX 20
who only E. know	ENGLAND 16
English compare the E., the most degraded	WALES 3
cosh of the E.	BRITAIN 17
Cricket—a game which the E.	CRICKET 11
dominion of the E.	SCOTLAND 3
E. approach to ideas	IDEAS 16
E. are busy	ENGLAND 9
E. is the language	LANGUAGES 14
E. manners	MANNERS 25

f. are on expenses	JOURNALISM 25
f. are scared	JOURNALISM 16
F. are stubborn	HYPOTHESIS 2
F. do not cease to exist	HYPOTHESIS 22
Get your f. first	HYPOTHESIS 19
imagination for his f.	SPEECHES 12
knowledge not of f.	EDUCATION 26
faculty cramps every f.	PARENTS 11
fade simply f. away	ARMED FORCES 41
Than to f. away	SUICIDE 11
faded beauty f.	BEAUTY 18
faery f. lands forlorn	IMAGINATION 9
fail F. better	SUCCESS 50
People f. you	RANK 25
Those who f.	ECONOMICS 24
To f. to prepare	PREPARATION 14
failed f. in literature	CRITICISM 15
failure Any f. seems so total	YOUTH 28
end in f.	POLITICIANS 36
f. in life	SUCCESS 40
f. is an orphan	SUCCESS 11
F. of planning	COURAGE 34
only a delayed f.	SUCCESS 47
failures provided us for our f.	RUSSIA 9
fainéant f. government	GOVERNMENT 30
faint damn with f. praise	PRAISE 6
Damn with f. praise	PRAISE 13
F. heart never won	COURAGE 7
F. yet pursuing	DETERMINATION 25
fair brave deserves the f.	COURAGE 18
brave deserve the f.	COURAGE 9
British f. play	JUSTICE 40
f. as is the rose	BEAUTY 12
f. exchange is no robbery	JUSTICE 3
f. field and no favour	JUSTICE 14
f. in love and war	JUSTICE 1
f. of face	BEAUTY 7
f. play	JUSTICE 5
F. play's a jewel	JUSTICE 4
f. sex	WOMEN 12
If Saint Paul's day be f.	FESTIVALS 3
My f. lady	BRITISH TOWNS 6
Outward be f.	HYPOCRISY 14
right and f.	ARGUMENT 18
short-legged sex the f. sex	WOMEN 35
So foul and f. a day	WEATHER 34
to show more f.	BRITISH TOWNS 26
Turn about is f. play	JUSTICE 10
fairer f. way is not much about	WAYS 26
fairest Who is the f. of them all	BEAUTY 6
fairies f. at the bottom	SUPERNATURAL 19
f. left off dancing	PAST 22
I don't believe in f.	SUPERNATURAL 21
fairness not equality or f.	LIBERTY 35
fairy airy-f.	IDEALISM 2
He dug up a f.-mount	SUPERNATURAL 15
faith do very little with f.	FAITH 12
event which creates f.	FAITH 16
f. and morals hold	ENGLAND 12
f. in honest doubt	CERTAINTY 15
f. in the people	GOVERNMENT 31
f. is something you die	FAITH 17
f. of the heart	FAITH 5
f. shines equal	COURAGE 26
f. that stands on authority	FAITH 10
f. unfaithful	CONSTANCY 13
F. will move mountains	FAITH 1
f. without doubt	CERTAINTY 21
F. without works	FAITH 4
first article of my f.	VIOLENCE 9
great act of f.	FAITH 13
If ye have f.	FAITH 3
kept the f.	ACHIEVEMENT 15
now abideth f.	LOVE 23
Punic f.	TRUST 11
Sea of F.	FAITH 11

shake a man's f.	SELF-ESTEEM 23
still by f. he trod	FAITH 15
thou of little f.	CERTAINTY 9
faithful f. in love	HEROES 8
f. to himself	FAITH 9
f. to thee, Cynara	CONSTANCY 14
f. to the state	POLITICIANS 9
seldom strictly f.	TRANSLATION 11
fake yours is a f.	SYMPATHY 28
falcon dapple-dawn-drawn F.	BIRDS 15
Falklands F. thing was a fight	WARS 28
fall diggeth a pit shall f.	CAUSES 17
divided we f.	COOPERATION 19
dividing we f.	AMERICA 12
Even monkeys sometimes f.	MISTAKES 1
f. flat on your face	PREJUDICE 21
f. for anything	CHARACTER 50
f. of the leaf	SEASONS 9
f. out with those we love	FORGIVENESS 21
F. seven times, stand up eight	DETERMINATION 3
f. without shaking	EFFORT 19
fear I to f.	AMBITION 10
fear no f.	PRIDE 6
harder they f.	SUCCESS 1
haughty spirit before a f.	PRIDE 4
horizontal f.	LIFE 42
Pride goes before a f.	PRIDE 2
rise by other's f.	SELF-INTEREST 23
Spring forward, f. back	TIME 5
Things f. apart	ORDER 17
When thieves f. out	CRIME 10
fallacy pathetic f.	EMOTIONS 5
fallen anybody f. by the wayside	SYMPATHY 26
f. by the edge	GOSSIP 15
how are the mighty f.	GREATNESS 2
falling amidst a f. world	DEFIANCE 15
but by oft f.	DETERMINATION 30
f. domino	CAUSES 27
f. sickness	SICKNESS 5
sky is f.	CRISES 10
falls apple never f.	FAMILY 1
As a tree f.	DEATH 1
f. on top of you	MISFORTUNES 30
false Beware of f. prophets	HYPOCRISY 9
f. guilt is guilt	GUILT 16
f. report	DECEPTION 15
f. that I advance	FOOLS 20
Ring out the f.	FESTIVALS 65
True and F. are attributes	TRUTH 21
falsehood F. has a perennial spring	LIES 15
f. is like the cut of a sabre	LIES 7
Refraining from f.	LIFESTYLES 14
falsely kept him f. true	CONSTANCY 13
falseness proving their f.	HYPOTHESIS 15
falter moment that you f.	POLITICIANS 38
falters love that never f.	SELF-SACRIFICE 13
fame blush to find it f.	VIRTUE 28
Common f. is seldom	REPUTATION 2
F. is like a river	FAME 1
F. is the spur	FAME 12
F. vaporizes	CHARACTER 49
love and f. to nothingness do sink	VALUE 26
Man dreams of f.	MEN AND WOMEN 11
to get f.	MUSICIANS 17
famed f. in all great arts	FRANCE 13
fames *Auri sacra f.*	GREED 7
familiar more f. surroundings	LEISURE 12
old f. faces	MOURNING 14
familiarity F. breeds contempt	FAMILIARITY 5
F. breeds contempt	FAMILIARITY 2
families American f. more like	FAMILY 31
best-regulated f.	CHANCE 1
f. resemble one another	FAMILY 19
old f. last not three oaks	TREES 8
there are f.	SOCIETY 21
family f. firm	ROYALTY 43

halt How long h. ye	CERTAINTY 7
halved trouble h.	COOPERATION 17
halves not like doing things by h.	RUSSIA 3
hamburger polystyrene h. cartons	ENGLAND 26
Hamlet cigar called H.	SMOKING 2
had not written *H.*	ARTS AND SCI 16
H. is so much paper	FOOTBALL 5
H. without the Prince	ABSENCE 8
hammer all you have is a h.	PROBLEMS 4
carpenter's h.	MUSIC 11
h. shatters glass	WAYS 8
once the h. has been pried	GENIUS 16
hammered certain to be h. down	CONFORMITY 1
hammers worn out many h.	CHRISTIAN CH 5
hamsters children love h.	RELATIONSHIPS 25
hand bird in the h.	CAUTION 2
bird in the h.	CERTAINTY 4
biting the h.	GRATITUDE 15
bringing me up by h.	CHILD CARE 8
gladly shake your h.	RANK 9
God's almighty h.	FARMING 11
h. is the cutting edge	ACTION 31
h. of God	FOOTBALL 10
h. of Jean Jacques Rousseau	REVOLUTION 16
h. that feeds	GRATITUDE 5
h. that rocks	PARENTS 14
h. that rocks the cradle	WOMEN 3
h. to the plough	DETERMINATION 24
h. to the plough	DETERMINATION 26
h. will not reach	ACHIEVEMENT 3
made by the h.	SCULPTURE 5
man a free h.	SEX 25
never stretch out the h.	RELATIONSHIPS 26
One h. for oneself	SEA 3
One h. washes	COOPERATION 14
sound of the single h.	COOPERATION 24
steady h.	CAUTION 8
sweeten this little h.	GUILT 9
thinking h.	SENSES 18
thy h. findeth to do	THOROUGHNESS 10
what thy right h. doeth	CHARITY 12
whom you take by the h.	DANCE 1
written with mine own h.	LETTERS 4
your white h.	BODY 11
handbook constable's h.	BIBLE 14
handful h. of dust	FEAR 17
handicap My h. is your negative	BODY 30
handkerchief scent on a pocket h.	TRANSIENCE 16
state of the h. industry	WRITERS 27
handle h. of the basket	COOPERATION 3
him that can h. them	OPPORTUNITY 34
handles Every thing hath two h.	REALITY 9
hands Cold h.	BODY 1
h. across the sea	INTERNAT REL 5
H. across the sea	INTERNAT REL 19
h. across the sea	INTERNAT REL 25
h., and handle not	INDIFFERENCE 3
h. are a sort of feet	BODY 13
Holding h. at midnight	COURTSHIP 9
horny h. of toil	WORK 31
I think with my h.	BODY 31
leave a man's h. empty	CREATIVITY 15
Licence my roving h.	SEX 11
Many h. make light work	COOPERATION 12
more work than both his h.	MANAGEMENT 1
no h. but yours	CHRISTIAN CH 2
raise h. together	RELATIONSHIPS 16
spits on its h.	LANGUAGE 25
washed his h.	GUILT 6
wash one's h.	DUTY 8
work for idle h.	IDLENESS 3
handsaw hawk from a h.	INTELLIGENCE 4
hawk from a h.	MADNESS 1
handsome H. is	BEHAVIOUR 6
hang enough rope and he will h. himself	WAYS 7
H. a thief when he's young	CRIME 4

h. my hat	HOME 20
let him h. there	HASTE 22
We must h. together	COOPERATION 22
wretches h.	LAW 22
hanged born to be h.	FATE 3
Confess and be h.	GUILT 1
h., drawn, and quartered	CRIME 23
h. for a sheep	THOROUGHNESS 5
h. for stealing horses	CRIME 25
h. in a fortnight	DEATH 50
ill name is half h.	REPUTATION 6
Little thieves are h.	CRIME 7
hanging capacity women have for just h. on	DETERMINATION 46
Catching's before h.	WAYS 1
H. and wiving	FATE 2
H. is too good for him	CRIME 24
h. men an' women	IRELAND 8
killing a dog than h. it	WAYS 20
hanging-look h. to me	APPEARANCE 17
hangs thereby h. a tale	MATURITY 4
What h. people	GUILT 12
happen Accidents will h.	CHANCE 1
everybody knew would never h.	WARFARE 58
h. tomorrow, next week	POLITICIANS 31
may or may not h.	PREPARATION 27
people to whom things h.	MISFORTUNES 32
things can h.	MISFORTUNES 29
We make things h.	CHANCE 36
happened LSD? Nothing much h.	DRUGS 11
happens dependent on what h. to her	CHOICE 19
h. anywhere	BOREDOM 11
Nothing h.	BOREDOM 10
nothing h.	LIFE 55
there when it h.	DEATH 77
what h. to a man	EXPERIENCE 30
happenstance Once is h.	CHANCE 34
happier h. than we Europeans	AUSTRALIA 11
happiest h. and best minds	POETRY 18
h. days of your life	SCHOOLS 2
h. people in the world	SATISFACTION 21
h. women, like the happiest nations	WOMEN 36
happily h. ever after	ENDING 3
living h. ever after	OPTIMISM 39
happiness best recipe for h.	HAPPINESS 19
desire for their own h.	SUFFERING 11
fatal to true h.	CAUTION 34
great enemy to human h.	POVERTY 21
greatest h.	MORALITY 6
greatest h.	SOCIETY 10
h. alone is salutary	HAPPINESS 24
H. depends on being free	COURAGE 13
h. he feels	PLEASURE 17
H. is a cigar	SMOKING 2
H. is an imaginary condition	HAPPINESS 30
H. is a warm gun	HAPPINESS 29
H. is a warm puppy	DOGS 14
h. I seek	DANCE 13
H. is no laughing matter	HAPPINESS 20
H. is what you make of it	HAPPINESS 3
H. lies in conquering one's enemies	HAPPINESS 8
H. makes up in height	HAPPINESS 26
h. mankind can gain	HAPPINESS 12
h. of an individual	GOVERNMENT 19
h. of society	GOVERNMENT 21
h. of the next world	HEAVEN 11
H. washes away many things	HAPPINESS 28
In solitude, What h.	SOLITUDE 8
its own kind of h.	MIDDLE AGE 5
justice or human h.	LIBERTY 35
Last Chance Gulch for h.	CHILDREN 23
lifetime of h.	HAPPINESS 23
Money can't buy h.	MONEY 5
more for human h.	INVENTIONS 10
pursuit of h.	HUMAN RIGHTS 7
result h.	DEBT 17

hatter mad as a h. — MADNESS 2
haunted h. town it is to me — BRITISH TOWNS 33
haunts h. of coot — RIVERS 9
have h.-his-carcase, next to the perpetual — LAW 26
  h. to take you in — HOME 23
  I'll h. what she's having — SEX 42
  more we h. — GIFTS 22
  take away everything you h. — GOVERNMENT 37
  What you h., hold — POSSESSIONS 5
  What you spend, you h. — POSSESSIONS 6
  You can h. it all — WOMEN 59
have-nots haves and the h. — POSSESSIONS 16
haves h. and the have-nots — POSSESSIONS 16
havoc Cry, 'H.' — REVENGE 13
hawk h. from a handsaw — INTELLIGENCE 4
  h. from a handsaw — MADNESS 5
  his horse, his h., and his greyhound — RANK 4
hawkeye H. State — AMERICAN CITIES 23
hawks Clever h. conceal their claws — SELF-ESTEEM 2
  H. will not pick out — COOPERATION 6
haws welcome h. — NECESSITY 12
hay antic h. — DANCE 3
  antic h. — DANCE 5
  h. while the sun shines — OPPORTUNITY 7
  live on h. — FUTURE 19
  neither good for h. nor grain — WEATHER 6
  So *that's* what h. looks like — COUNTRY AND TOWN 19
  worth a load of h. — SEASONS 6
haze Purple h. — MIND 24
he H. would — SELF-INTEREST 30
  Who h. — FAME 2
head at the command—of his h. — POLITICAL PART 28
  bumping its h. — GOOD 37
  for you good h. — PRACTICALITY 7
  God be in my h. — PRAYER 11
  h. full of goblins — PRACTICALITY 17
  h. of Maradona — FOOTBALL 10
  h. on young shoulders — EXPERIENCE 13
  hit us over the h. — DIPLOMACY 17
  If you can keep your h. — CRISES 17
  keep your h. — CRISES 20
  King Charles's h. — IDEAS 4
  makes a wise h. — SILENCE 5
  proof of want of h. — POLITICAL PART 4
  stinks from the h. — LEADERSHIP 2
  Uneasy lies the h. — ROYALTY 23
  weak in the h. — BRITISH TOWNS 13
  where to lay his h. — HOME 14
headmasters H. have powers — SCHOOLS 10
headpiece H. filled with straw — FUTILITY 25
heads Assistant h. must roll — BROADCASTING 2
  H. I win — WINNING 2
  Two h. are better — THINKING 3
heal Physician, h. thyself — MEDICINE 11
healer Time is a great h. — TIME 7
healing H. is a matter of time — MEDICINE 10
  no h. has been necessary — TIME 47
health damage your h. — SMOKING 3
  drink one another's h. — ALCOHOL 19
  have both, it's h. — SATISFACTION 35
  h. and no wealth — BRITISH TOWNS 10
  in sickness and in h. — MARRIAGE 27
  Look to your h. — HEALTH 16
  no h. in us — ACTION 22
healthful most h. of beverages — ALCOHOL 17
healthier h. Western society becomes — MEDICINE 31
healthy generous and h. human being — HOSPITALITY 25
  Greed is h. — GREED 16
  h. and wealthy — SLEEP 18
  h. man does not torture — CRUELTY 12
  h., wealthy, and wise — HEALTH 4
  h., you don't need it — HEALTH 19
  in order to die h. — HEALTH 26
hear H. all, see all — SELF-INTEREST 3
  h. in my imagination — CREATIVITY 5
  h. it through their feet — JAZZ 2

h. no evil — VIRTUE 5
h. on the grapevine — GOSSIP 13
h. people smile — SENSES 19
H. the other side — PREJUDICE 8
men prefer not to h. — TRUTH 37
nothing of what you h. — BELIEF 1
one may h. — CONVERSATION 13
those who will not h. — PREJUDICE 5
heard ain't h. nuttin' yet — SINGING 11
  I will be h. — DETERMINATION 37
  seen and not h. — CHILDREN 1
hearers favourable h. — POLITICIANS 10
  not h. only — WORDS AND DEEDS 10
hearing h. of the ear — SENSES 1
  h. without listening — SILENCE 14
  our sense of h. — POLLUTION 15
heart anniversaries of the h. — FESTIVALS 67
  ás the h. grows older — SORROW 19
  Batter my h. — GOD 16
  beak from out my h. — DESPAIR 10
  Because my h. is pure — VIRTUE 35
  bigger the h. — BODY 3
  bone shop of the h. — EMOTIONS 26
  breaks the h. — FLOWERS 11
  committed adultery in my h. — TEMPTATION 18
  desires of the h. — EMOTIONS 25
  ease a h. — DRESS 16
  education of the h. — EMOTIONS 15
  Faint h. never won — COURAGE 7
  faith of the h. — FAITH 5
  Fourteen h. attacks — SELF-INTEREST 32
  fullness of the h. — EMOTIONS 1
  get your h.'s desire — ACHIEVEMENT 25
  giving your h. to a dog — DOGS 11
  Have patience, h. — SUFFERING 6
  h. and hand that once — LOVE 42
  h. and stomach — ROYALTY 21
  h. beats so that I can — DANCE 13
  h. does not long for — ACHIEVEMENT 3
  h. doesn't grieve over — IGNORANCE 8
  h. for any fate — DETERMINATION 38
  h. gets tired too — EMOTIONS 21
  h. grow fonder — ABSENCE 2
  h. has its reasons — EMOTIONS 12
  h. in the business — BUSINESS 40
  h. into his hand — PRAYER 8
  h. is a lonely hunter — SOLITUDE 14
  h. is an organ of fire — EMOTIONS 30
  h. is Highland — SCOTLAND 12
  H. of England — BRITISH TOWNS 24
  h. of man — BEAUTY 26
  h. of marriage is memories — MARRIAGE 53
  H. of oak — ARMED FORCES 23
  h. of oak — CHARACTER 24
  h. on one's sleeve — EMOTIONS 6
  h. *prefers* to move — ADVERSITY 21
  h. speaks to heart — SPEECH 12
  h. that has truly loved — CONSTANCY 10
  h. that never rejoices — HAPPINESS 4
  h. that one can see — INSIGHT 15
  h. the keener — DETERMINATION 28
  h. to a stey brae — DETERMINATION 11
  h. upon my sleeve — EMOTIONS 9
  h. upon paper — LETTERS 11
  h. was piercèd through the ear — WORDS 8
  h. was warm and gay — TOWNS 23
  h. would break — HOPE 6
  holiness of the h.'s affections — TRUTH 28
  hope in your h. — HOPE 21
  human h. likes a little disorder — EMOTIONS 31
  If thy h. fails thee — AMBITION 10
  imagination of a man's h. — IMAGINATION 4
  inmost cupboards of her h. — WEDDINGS 9
  left my h. in San Francisco — AMERICAN CITIES 60
  looketh on the h. — INSIGHT 5
  makes the h. sick — HOPE 3

ignorant (*cont.*)

that of which he is i.	IGNORANCE 5

ignore i. most poetry — POETRY 34

nothing to i.	PARENTS 22

ignored because they are i. — HYPOTHESIS 22

ill I. gotten goods — CRIME 6

I. met by moonlight	MEETING 9
i. name is half hanged	REPUTATION 6
I. news hath wings	NEWS 9
I. weeds grow apace	GOOD 33
It's an i. wind	OPTIMISM 13
Looking i. prevail	COURTSHIP 4
means to do i. deeds	OPPORTUNITY 28
rail at the i.	GOOD 33
speak i. of everybody	BIOGRAPHY 17
speak i. of the dead	REPUTATION 8

ill-bred illiberal and i. — MANNERS 12

illegal i., immoral — PLEASURE 27

means that it is not i.	PRESIDENCY 17
Nothing is i.	BUSINESS 49

illegitimate i. child of Karl Marx — RUSSIA 8

illiberal i. and ill-bred — MANNERS 12

illimitable i. was annihilated — EXPLORATION 8

illness conscious is an i. — MIND 19

dread term 'terminal i.'	TRAVEL 40
find time for i.	HEALTH 12
i. is his private	SICKNESS 20
I. is not something	SICKNESS 21
I. is the doctor	SICKNESS 15
i. which becomes identified	SICKNESS 22
makes i. worthwhile	SICKNESS 14

ills climax of all human i. — DEBT 15

cure for the i. of Democracy	DEMOCRACY 14

illusion all else an i. — PARANORMAL 7

I. even to the thinker	SUPERNATURAL 18

illusions friend of flattering i. — ACTION 27

It's life's i. I recall	EXPERIENCE 35

image graven i. — RELIGION 2

i. of death	MEETING 14
i. of myself	SELF 22
kills the i. of God	CENSORSHIP 2
live without any i.	SELF-KNOWLEDGE 16
make man in our i.	HUMAN RACE 8

imagery science for their i. — ARTS AND SCI 14

imaginary Happiness is an i. condition — HAPPINESS 30

indistinguishable from the i.	EMOTIONS 24
make i. evils	GOOD 29

imagination as i. bodies forth — WRITING 13

by i. that we can form	IMAGINATION 6
functioning of the i.	FEAR 21
i. all compact	IMAGINATION 5
i. for his facts	SPEECHES 12
i. is man's power	IMAGINATION 16
I. isn't merely a surplus	IMAGINATION 18
i. of a boy	MATURITY 4
i. of a man's heart	IMAGINATION 4
i. resembled the wings	IMAGINATION 10
i. there is no horror	IMAGINATION 13
i. to the proper pitch	FAITH 8
life in the i.	ARTS 34
poetic i.	IMAGINATION 12
reason but of i.	HAPPINESS 18
takes a lot of i.	PHOTOGRAPHY 12
Television contracts the i.	BROADCASTING 16
those that have no i.	IMAGINATION 14
twisted i.	SCULPTURE 10
Were it not for i.	IMAGINATION 7
Western i.	SKIES 29
When the i. sleeps	IMAGINATION 17

imaginative i. literature — FICTION 22

imaginings horrible i. — FEAR 9

imitate i. the action of the tiger — WARFARE 17

i. what is before him	ORIGINALITY 13
Immature poets i.	ORIGINALITY 14

imitated i. by none — ORIGINALITY 10

imitates Life i. Art — ARTS 16

imitation i. in lines — PAINTING 7

I. is the sincerest form	PRAISE 4
I. lies at the root	CONFORMITY 12
i. without benefit	FASHION 9

immature I. love says — MATURITY 11

I. poets imitate	ORIGINALITY 14

immaturity symptom of i. — ARTS 24

immemorial its i. work — TIME 50

time i.	TIME 17

immense error is i. — MISTAKES 17

immoral i. book — BOOKS 15

i., or fattening	PLEASURE 27

immorality i. of the lower classes — CLASS 17

immortal do not seek i. life — SATISFACTION 15

i. hand or eye	ANIMALS 19
i. with a kiss	BEAUTY 13

immortality i. can be assured — MISTAKES 29

Milk's leap toward i.	FOOD 26
millions long for i.	BOREDOM 9

impartial i. as between fire brigade — PREJUDICE 17

impartiality i. is bias — PREJUDICE 24

impatience one cardinal sin: i. — PATIENCE 31

your i. would be so much	WRITERS 9

impediments i.— in common times — CHARACTER 39

imperfect i. man — PRESIDENCY 5

imperialism I. is the monopoly — CAPITALISM 15

importance i. of the country — ADMINISTRATION 13

important being less i. — HOUSEWORK 7

i. thing in the world	MONEY 45
little things are the most i.	VALUE 35
most i. thing in life	HUMAN RACE 2
same as i.	SELF 25

importunate business is no less i. — HOUSEWORK 7

importunity ever-haunting i. Of business — WORK 29

impossibilities Probable i. — PROBLEMS 16

impossible art of the i. — POLITICS 32

because it is i.	BELIEF 14
eliminated the i.	PROBLEMS 18
i. aim	DESPAIR 16
i. dream	IDEALISM 15
i. takes a little longer	ACHIEVEMENT 2
i. to enjoy idling	IDLENESS 21
I wish it were i.	MUSICIANS 4
says that it is i.	HYPOTHESIS 29
six i. things	BELIEF 23
With men this is i.	GOD 9

imposture carry on the i. — OLD AGE 24

imprecision Decay with i. — WORDS 2

impressed Too easily i. — TASTE 8

impressions First i. — BEGINNING 2

imprint set it in i. — PUBLISHING 3

imprisoned I. in every fat man — BODY 23

i. or dispossessed	HUMAN RIGHTS 5

improbability statistical i. — LIFE SCI 27

improbable *however* i. — PROBLEMS 18

i. possibilities	PROBLEMS 16

impropriety I. is the soul of wit — WIT 18

It is an i.	MANNERS 18

improve I. each shining hour — WORK 26

i. the shining hour	EFFORT 12
want to i. on it	LIFE SCI 17
we i. them as far as	RELATIONSHIPS 11

improvement signs of i. — PARENTS 25

improves Anger i. nothing — ANGER 1

improvisation I. is too good — MUSIC 33

impudence Cockney i. — PAINTING 11

impudent called John a I. Bitch — INSULTS 6

impulse first i. — ACTION 20

i. from a vernal wood	GOOD 31
i. of the moment	BEHAVIOUR 25

impulses truck with first i. — CAUTION 30

impunity provokes me with i. — DEFIANCE 1

impure all things are i. — GOOD 38

in Garbage i. — COMPUTERS 2

inability i. to cross the street — FRIENDSHIP 22

inaccuracy i. sometimes saves — LIES 21

kaiser put the kibosh on the K.	WORLD W I 11
kaleyard K. School	WRITERS 4
kamikaze k. pilot	SUICIDE 2
Kansas not in K. any more	CHANGE 49
kazoo playing Beethoven on the k.	TRANSLATION 14
Keating you can call Paul K.	INSULTS 13
keep Ideas won't k.	IDEAS 14
If you can k. your head	CRISES 17
K. a thing seven years	POSSESSIONS 3
K. right on	DETERMINATION 42
k. up with the Joneses	ENVY 5
k. up with them	MORALITY 1
k. your England	INTERNAT REL 42
K. your own shop	BUSINESS 9
should k. who can	POWER 23
too good to k.	SECRECY 11
worth while to k. them	EMPLOYMENT 15
keeper Am I my brother's k.	RELATIONSHIPS 6
keepers Finders k.	POSSESSIONS 1
keepings Findings k.	POSSESSIONS 2
Kennedy K. was dead	MEMORY 27
Kent everybody knows K.	BRITISH TOWNS 31
Some places of K.	BRITISH TOWNS 10
Kentish K. miles	BRITISH TOWNS 1
kettle k. of fish	ORDER 7
pot calling the k. black	CRITICISM 5
ties a k. to a dog's tail	WRITERS 21
key k. can open any door	CORRUPTION 3
Turn the k. deftly	SLEEP 15
while I keep the k.	SUICIDE 4
keyboards people want k.	COMPUTERS 21
keystone K. State	AMERICAN CITIES 24
kibosh put the k. on the Kaiser	WORLD W I 11
kick first k. I took	POVERTY 33
Got to k. at the darkness	DETERMINATION 51
great k. at misery	SUFFERING 27
if you do, she'll k.	GRATITUDE 2
k. against the pricks	DEFIANCE 7
k. to come to the top	DESPAIR 8
kicking running fast and k. something	PROBLEMS 32
kicks how I get my k.	BUSINESS 48
kid bleating of the k. excites	HUNTING 1
dead-end k.	CRIME 13
kiddies k. have crumpled the serviettes	MANNERS 24
kidding you are k., Mister Hitler	WORLD W II 24
kids don't have any k.	DISILLUSION 22
how many k. have you killed today	WARS 1
Kilkenny fight like K. cats	CATS 4
kill as soon k. a pig	LETTERS 14
enough in thee to k. care	WORRY 8
Eternal in man cannot k.	DEATH 24
get out and k. something	HUNTING 16
Guns don't k. people	MURDER 2
k. a good book	CENSORSHIP 4
K. a man	MURDER 18
k. the fatted calf	FESTIVALS 29
K. them all	DISILLUSION 8
licensed to k.	MURDER 6
not going to k. too many	MURDER 22
right to k.	MURDER 21
something you k. for	FAITH 17
Thou shalt not k.	MURDER 8
Thou shalt not k.	MURDER 17
What does not k. me	SUFFERING 25
killed Better be k.	FEAR 14
Care k. the cat	WORRY 1
hard work never k. anybody	WORK 43
He must try and get k.	ARMED FORCES 33
how many kids have you k. today	WARS 1
If hate k. men	HATRED 8
k. myself long ago	SUICIDE 13
who k. him	VIOLENCE 12
killing If k. foxes is necessary	HUNTING 20
K. myself to die	KISSING 4
K. no murder	MURDER 3
K. no murder	MURDER 13
Men talk of k. time	TIME 37
more ways of k. a cat	WAYS 18
more ways of k. a dog	WAYS 19
more ways of k. a dog	WAYS 20
kills it k. me	HONESTY 18
k. all its pupils	TIME 40
K. all known germs	POLLUTION 1
k. the thing he loves	LOVE 58
not work that k.	WORRY 3
pace that k.	STRENGTH 4
pity k.	SYMPATHY 24
suicide k. two people	SUICIDE 10
that which k.	MEN AND WOMEN 22
Kim K.'s game	MEMORY 3
kin little more than k.	FAMILY 15
makes the whole world k.	HUMAN NATURE 9
one's own k. and kith	FAMILY 24
kind art of being k.	RELIGION 22
cruel only to be k.	CRUELTY 6
cruel to be k.	CRUELTY 11
k. as it is green	IRELAND 18
K. hearts are more than	RANK 13
k. parent to man	NATURE 6
k. to Belfast	BRITISH TOWNS 44
k. to your friends	FRIENDSHIP 1
less than k.	FAMILY 15
One k. word warms	SYMPATHY 5
people will always be k.	SENSES 15
kindle k. light in the darkness	LIFE 49
kindliness k. of sheets	SLEEP 17
kindling it only requires k.	MIND 7
kindness By a sweet tongue and k.	BEHAVIOUR 2
cup o' k.	MEMORY 9
generates k.	SPORTS 8
good human behaviour is k.	BEHAVIOUR 35
k. and lies are worth	RELATIONSHIPS 18
K. in another's trouble	LIFE 35
k. of strangers	CHARITY 22
milk of human k.	SYMPATHY 8
milk of human k.	SYMPATHY 16
remember your k. for three years	ANIMALS 1
soup of human k.	CHARITY 29
king cat may look at a k.	EQUALITY 1
consumer is the k.	BUYING 9
duty is the k.'s	CONSCIENCE 12
esteem of a k.	ROYALTY 26
fight for its K.	PATRIOTISM 26
from an anointed k.	ROYALTY 22
God save our gracious k.	ROYALTY 30
Here lies a great and mighty k.	WORDS AND DEEDS 14
K. and Country	ARMED FORCES 12
K. and country	PATRIOTISM 4
k. can do no wrong	ROYALTY 2
K. Charles's head	IDEAS 4
K. James Bible	BIBLE 3
K. of all these	DEATH 22
k. of beasts	ANIMALS 8
K. of Great Britain	CORRUPTION 13
k. of infinite space	DREAMS 7
K. over the Water	ROYALTY 9
k.'s chaff is worth	ROYALTY 3
k.'s evil	SICKNESS 6
one eyed man is k.	ABILITY 5
rightwise K. born	ROYALTY 19
smote the k. of Israel	CHANCE 21
stomach of a k.	ROYALTY 21
take the k.'s shilling	ARMED FORCES 15
unless you're a k.	ACTING 10
waltz k.	MUSICIANS 2
who is K.	ROYALTY 31
you, as their K.	SELF-SACRIFICE 15
your K. and your Country	WORLD W I 13
kingdom k. where nobody dies	CHILDREN 16
till k. come	TIME 16
to me a k. is	MIND 8
kingdom of God fit for the k.	DETERMINATION 26

land *(cont.)*

This l. is your land	AMERICA	36
we had the l.	CANADA	19
You buy l.	BUYING	3
landed Eagle has l.	SKIES	27
landing successful l. in France	TRANSPORT	24
landings l. on the Moon	SKIES	29
landscape gardening is l.-painting	GARDENS	15
to the great l.	SENSES	17
landscapes l. were sold	PAINTING	12
Land's End L. to John o'Groats	BRITAIN	2
landslide pay for a l.	ELECTIONS	14
lane down memory l.	MEMORY	2
l. that has no turning	PATIENCE	9
lang auld l. syne	PAST	10
L. may yer lum reek	HOME	9
language best chosen l.	FICTION	11
divided by a common l.	LANGUAGES	16
everything else in our l.	BIBLE	12
feelings in l.	LANGUAGE	14
foreign l. can be translated	TRANSLATION	12
hidden l. of the soul	DANCE	17
l. all nations understand	MONEY	29
l. is a dialect with	LANGUAGES	15
L. is fossil poetry	LANGUAGE	13
L. is the dress	LANGUAGE	10
l. of his poems	POETRY	31
l. of priorities	POLITICAL PART	30
l. of the unheard	VIOLENCE	15
l. only speaks	SPEECH	12
l., the ignorant	LANGUAGE	11
limits of my l.	LANGUAGE	19
mathematical l.	MATHS	10
merit of l. is clearness	LANGUAGE	5
mobilized the English l.	SPEECHES	19
mystery of l.	LANGUAGE	16
nation without a l.	LANGUAGES	1
no word in the Irish l.	WORDS	30
people without a l.	LANGUAGES	13
rich and delicate l.	POETS	26
some entrance into the l.	TRAVEL	23
You taught me l.	SWEARING	5
languages l. are the pedigree	LANGUAGES	11
wit in all l.	WIT	7
lantern l. on the stern	EXPERIENCE	23
lap l. of the gods	CHANCE	19
l. of the gods	FATE	11
lapidary In l. inscriptions	TRUTH	25
lard l. their lean books	ORIGINALITY	8
lares l. and penates	HOME	12
my own L. and Penates	HOME	16
large how l. a letter I have written	LETTERS	4
l. as life	APPEARANCE	21
large-hearted l. man	WRITERS	15
larger l. the body	BODY	3
largest Shout with the l.	CONFORMITY	6
lark holy l.	SIMILARITY	21
l.'s on the wing	OPTIMISM	22
larks we shall catch l.	EFFORT	6
Lascaux L. to Jackson Pollock	JAZZ	10
lascivious l. gloating	BODY	19
lash l. of scorpions	CRIME	14
prayers, and the l.	ARMED FORCES	45
lass It came with a l.	SCOTLAND	4
lasses then she made the l., O	WOMEN	29
last cobbler stick to his l.	KNOWLEDGE	7
cobbler to his l.	KNOWLEDGE	1
famous l. words	FORESIGHT	7
Finish l.	SPORTS	18
four l. things	ENDING	9
He who laughs l.	REVENGE	5
how long that will l.	UNIVERSE	14
in the l. chance saloon	OPPORTUNITY	21
Kissing don't l.	COOKING	24
l. day of an era	RUSSIA	12
l. my time	IDLENESS	18

l. of the Mohicans	ENDING	10
L. scene of all	OLD AGE	12
l. straw	EXCESS	5
l. thing I shall do	DEATH	58
l. thing one knows	WRITING	15
l. to know	IGNORANCE	1
Long foretold, long l.	WEATHER	7
Look thy l. on all things	TRANSIENCE	14
Nice guys finish l.	SPORTS	2
Seven L. Words	DEATH	19
who laughs l.	REVENGE	4
world's l. night	ENDING	15
lasts Lets hope it l.	TRANSIENCE	9
Love that l. longest	LOVE	55
late always too l. or too early	TIME	46
Better l. than never	PUNCTUALITY	1
Dread of being l.	SCHOOLS	12
guessing correctly how l.	PUNCTUALITY	4
human thought too l.	DISILLUSION	11
l. thanks are ever best	GRATITUDE	8
l. to shut the stable-door	FORESIGHT	3
l. unpleasantness	WARS	3
never come l.	BEHAVIOUR	34
never too l. to mend	CHANGE	3
people who are l.	PUNCTUALITY	15
surprise God because I'm l.	PUNCTUALITY	19
too l. to learn	EDUCATION	5
You were l.	MEMORY	24
later if it came a little l. in life	YOUTH	18
l. than you think	TIME	43
lateral l. thinking	THINKING	9
lath l. of wood	STRENGTH	23
Latin carve in L.	LANGUAGES	9
half Greek, half L.	BROADCASTING	6
No more L.	SCHOOLS	1
small L.	LANGUAGES	8
Latins L. are tenderly enthusiastic	COUNTRIES	30
laugh l. all the time	HUMOUR	16
L. and the world laughs	SORROW	21
L. and the world laughs	SYMPATHY	3
l. at everything	HUMOUR	10
l. at human actions	INSIGHT	9
l. at them in our turn	HUMOUR	12
Let them l.	SUCCESS	5
must l. before we are happy	HUMOUR	7
old man who will not l.	GENERATION GAP	11
why people l.	HUMOUR	19
laughable very l. things	POLITICS	12
laughed one has not l.	HUMOUR	11
laughing ever had without l.	SEX	39
no l. matter	HAPPINESS	20
laughs He who l. last	REVENGE	5
l. with a harvest	AUSTRALIA	16
Love l. at locksmiths	LOVE	7
who l. last	REVENGE	4
laughter audible l.	MANNERS	12
grail of l.	SKIES	24
Homeric l.	HUMOUR	2
L. hath only a scornful	HUMOUR	5
L. is pleasant	HUMOUR	13
L. is the best medicine	MEDICINE	4
l. of a fool	FOOLS	11
l. of her heart	TOWNS	23
L. would be bereaved	HUMOUR	21
more frightful than l.	ENVY	17
launched l. a thousand ships	BEAUTY	13
laureate Poet L.	POETS	6
laurels rest on one's l.	REPUTATION	17
want l. for ourselves most	ENVY	15
win one's l.	SUCCESS	20
worth all your l.	YOUTH	15
lava l. I still find most	MADNESS	13
lavender lay up in l.	HOUSEWORK	9
packed in l.	WEDDINGS	9
law before all l.	CUSTOM	12
chief l.	LAW	17

l. of the individual	LIBERTY 19	breath of l.	NECESSITY 14
L. to be saucy	POWER 19	cannot show The l. within	PHOTOGRAPHY 8
l. when of Devils	POETS 14	Chaos breeds l.	ORDER 16
life, l.	HUMAN RIGHTS 7	colours from my l.	SUFFERING 22
light! said L.	TOWNS 18	conditions of l.	FAMILIARITY 21
nation, conceived in l.	DEMOCRACY 13	content to manufacture l.	LIFE SCI 17
O l.	LIBERTY 17	crowd out real l.	GOSSIP 25
place of light, of l.	UNIVERSITIES 17	denial of l.	DANGER 37
success of l.	LIBERTY 36	die in one's duty is l.	DUTY 9
tree of l.	LIBERTY 14	discovered the secret of l.	LIFE SCI 20
wait for l.	LIBERTY 18	dog is for l.	DOGS 2
libraries out of circulating l.	LIBRARIES 9	elixir of l.	LIFE 12
library choice of all my l.	LIBRARIES 4	Get a l.	BROADCASTING 17
hopes than a public l.	LIBRARIES 6	give for his l.	LIFE 16
l., and be chained	LIBRARIES 5	gives l. to thee	FAME 10
l. is a repository	LIBRARIES 1	giving l. to an immortal soul	PREGNANCY 7
lumber room of his l.	LIBRARIES 10	God's opinion that l. should	CHILDREN 19
Majesty's l.	LIBRARIES 8	golden tree of actual l.	REALITY 11
more important in a l.	LIBRARIES 13	has bodily l.	LIFE 10
sober me up to sit in a l.	LIBRARIES 11	his l. for his friends	SELF-SACRIFICE 4
whole l. has burned down	OLD AGE 6	I'd lay down my l.	LIFE SCI 23
you have a public l.	LIBRARIES 14	if it came a little later in l.	YOUTH 18
licence L. my roving hands	SEX 11	If l. hands you lemons	ADVERSITY 4
l. to act like an asshole	DRUGS 12	in mourning for my l.	SORROW 20
l. to print your own money	BROADCASTING 10	in risking l.	MEN AND WOMEN 22
not freedom, but l.	LIBERTY 10	I tasted l.	SENSES 12
licensed l. to kill	MURDER 6	It's l., Jim	PARANORMAL 1
lie Anyone who tells a l.	COOKING 21	lay down his friends for his l.	TRUST 37
Art is a l.	ARTS 30	l. a terrible thing	LIFE 48
bodies never l.	DANCE 16	l. a thing apart	MEN AND WOMEN 7
can't pray a l.	PRAYER 28	L. begins at forty	MIDDLE AGE 2
Deceit is a l.	DECEPTION 2	L. exists in the universe	LIFE SCI 18
I can't tell a l.	LIES 16	L. for life	JUSTICE 18
In our country the l.	LIES 25	L., friends, is boring	BOREDOM 12
isn't told a l.	CAUTION 33	l. from both sides	EXPERIENCE 35
learns to l.	CRIME 36	L. imitates Art	ARTS 16
l., and even to murder	TRUTH 36	l. in my men	MEN 16
l. can go around the world	LIES 5	L. is a copiously branching	LIFE SCI 29
l. circumstantial	LIES 11	L. is a horizontal fall	LIFE 42
L. follows by post	APOLOGY 19	L. is a jest	HUMOUR 9
l. till seven	IDLENESS 13	L. is all a VARIORUM	LIFESTYLES 21
l. usefully	LIES 14	l. is a luminous halo	LIFE 40
l. will go round the world	LIES 17	L. is an incurable disease	LIFE 24
meets a lonely l.	LIES 6	L. is a rainbow	LIFE 53
mixture of a l.	LIES 12	L. is a sexually transmitted	LIFE 2
often a whole l.	LIES 2	L. is doubt	CERTAINTY 21
old L.: Dulce et decorum est	WARFARE 38	L. is first boredom	LIFE 50
sent to l. abroad	DIPLOMACY 5	l. is given to none	LIFE 18
sleeping dogs l.	CAUTION 14	L. is harder than crossing	LIFE 3
so you must l.	CAUSES 4	L. is just a bowl	LIFE 43
to their laws we l.	SELF-SACRIFICE 3	L. is just one damned thing	LIFE 38
victim to a big l.	LIES 13	L. is like a sewer	LIFE 44
Washington could not l.	LIES 18	L. is like playing	LIFE 37
lied Or being l. about	CHARACTER 43	L. is mostly froth	LIFE 35
lies beats all the l.	TRUTH 27	L. is not meant to be easy	ADVERSITY 22
bodyguard of l.	DECEPTION 25	L. isn't all beer	LIFE 4
camera never l.	PHOTOGRAPHY 1	L. isn't like coursework	SCHOOLS 17
damned l. and statistics	STATISTICS 7	L. is real	LIFE 29
kindness and l. are worth	RELATIONSHIPS 18	l. is short	ARTS 2
l. about the Democrats	POLITICAL PART 31	L. is short	MEDICINE 9
l. are often told	LIES 19	L. is the best gift	LIFE 5
L. are the mortar	SOCIETY 14	l. is the thing	READING 13
l. he has been telling	CONVERSATION 14	L. is too short to	PRACTICALITY 16
l. humanity would perish	LIES 22	l., liberty	HUMAN RIGHTS 7
l. sound truthful	POLITICS 24	L., like a dome	LIFE 28
only l. are invented	TRUTH 39	l. might be put on parade	ROYALTY 40
swaddled in l.	AFRICA 14	L. must be understood	LIFE 31
told such Dreadful L.	LIES 20	l., not for lunch	MEN 2
life afternoon of human l.	MIDDLE AGE 11	l. of man	LIFE 23
all human l.	LIFE 11	l. of men on earth	LIFE 19
all human l. is there	LIFE 36	l. of somebody else	BIOGRAPHY 20
all l. goes rotten	WORK 40	L.'s a bitch	LIFE 6
another person's l.	LIFESTYLES 38	L. says: she did this	BOOKS 26
As though to breathe were l.	IDLENESS 19	L.'s but a walking shadow	LIFE 22
best things in l.	MONEY 2	l.'s *mater*	LIFE SCI 25
book of l.	VIRTUE 7	L.'s not just being alive	HEALTH 14

-»->=<-|->»<-|->»<-|->»=<-|->»<-|->»<-|->»=<-|->»<-|->»<-|->»=<-|->»<-|->»<-|->»=<-|->»<-|->»<-|->»=<-|->»<-|->»<-|->»=<-|->»<-|->

Having m. is rather like	WEALTH 41	many-headed m.	CLASS 7
He had m. as well	CHARITY 25	many-headed m. of the pit	THEATRE 11
hired the m.	DEBT 22	memory is a m.	MEMORY 28
If you can actually count your m.	WEALTH 35	**monsters** reason produces m.	DREAMS 9
lend you m.	MONEY 39	**monstrous** m. carbuncle	ARCHITECTURE 21
Lend your m.	DEBT 4	M. Regiment of Women	WOMAN'S ROLE 7
love of m.	MONEY 27	**Monte Carlo** when they can go to M.	EXPLORATION 11
m. answereth all	MONEY 24	**montes** *Parturient m.*	EFFORT 15
m. cannot buy	HEALTH 16	**month** cruellest m.	SEASONS 24
M. can't buy happiness	MONEY 5	flavour of the m.	FASHION 2
M. doesn't talk	MONEY 42	if they wait for a m.	LETTERS 15
M. gives me pleasure	MONEY 36	R in the m.	FOOD 2
m. goes with the wind	CHARACTER 49	**months** mother of the m.	SKIES 4
M. has no smell	MONEY 6	**Montreal** no one ever leaves M.	TOWNS 29
M. has no smell	TAXES 5	O God! O M.	CANADA 9
M. is like a sixth sense	MONEY 35	**monument** seek a m.	ARCHITECTURE 4
M. is like muck	MONEY 28	You'll die facing the m.	CRIME 11
M. . . . is none of the wheels	MONEY 32	**monumental** M. City	AMERICAN CITIES 28
M. isn't everything	MONEY 7	**monumentum** *Si m. requiris*	ARCHITECTURE 4
m. I spend on advertising	ADVERTISING 10	**mood** no m. can be maintained	EMOTIONS 23
M. is power	MONEY 8	**moods** such extraordinary m.	SEA 26
M. is the root	MONEY 9	**moon** glimpses of the m.	EARTH 5
M. is the sinews	MONEY 30	hornèd m.	SKIES 16
M., it turned out	MONEY 40	landings on the M.	SKIES 29
M., like manure	MONEY 10	m. belongs to everyone	POSSESSIONS 24
M. makes a man	WEALTH 3	m. in lonely alleys	SKIES 24
M. makes money	WEALTH 4	m.'s an arrant thief	SKIES 12
M. makes the mare	MONEY 11	No m., no man	PREGNANCY 3
M. makes the world go around	MONEY 43	now the m.	SKIES 21
M. speaks sense	MONEY 29	once in a blue m.	TIME 15
M. talks	MONEY 12	**moonlight** Ill met by m.	MEETING 9
Never marry for m.	MARRIAGE 10	m. and music	DANCE 14
poor know that it is m.	MONEY 45	m. and roses	LOVE 18
print your own m.	BROADCASTING 10	**moonlit** Knocking on the m. door	MEETING 18
private parts, his m.	MEN 11	**moons** walked two m. in his moccasins	CRITICISM 3
put the m. in	PROBLEMS 29	**moonshine** every thing as m.	EMOTIONS 15
Remember that time is m.	TIME 35	**moor** mixen than the m.	FAMILIARITY 2
rub up against m.	MONEY 38	**Moore** M.'s law	COMPUTERS 7
sinews of war, unlimited m.	WARFARE 14	**moored** m. only lightly	IRELAND 21
somehow, make m.	MONEY 25	**moose** strong as a bull m.	STRENGTH 25
spends his m. foolishly	THRIFT 20	**moral** act on m. convictions	FICTION 22
taking m. from poor people	CHARITY 28	blending of m. courage	PATIENCE 29
Time is m.	MONEY 14	build up his m. power	SEX 8
to get all that m.	WEALTH 29	don't have a m. plan	CANADA 27
using its m.	CAPITALISM 25	drug is neither m. or immoral	DRUGS 12
voice is full of m.	WEALTH 30	m. act that has no hope	MORALITY 23
we can't eat m.	POLLUTION 4	M. courage is a rarer commodity	COURAGE 33
world in arms is not spending m. alone	WARFARE 55	m. evil and of good	GOOD 31
You pays your m.	CHOICE 10	m. indigestion	PLEASURE 23
moneybags with the m. of Carnegie	WEALTH 32	M. indignation is jealousy	MORALITY 15
moneyless m. man goes fast	POVERTY 4	m. law within me	THINKING 14
mongrels continent of energetic m.	EUROPE 11	m. or immoral book	BOOKS 15
monk make the m.	APPEARANCE 4	m. principles please	MORALITY 3
monkey attack the m.	POLITICIANS 29	m. virtues at the highest	RELIGION 14
descent from a m.	LIFE SCI 14	not just a m. category	LIES 25
higher the m. climbs	AMBITION 2	party is a m. crusade	POLITICAL PART 38
m. who misses his branch	OPPORTUNITY 13	stage in m. culture	MORALITY 10
nothing but a painted m.	MEDICINE 13	**moralist** problem for the m.	BOREDOM 8
softly, catchee m.	PATIENCE 16	**moralists** delight to m.	CRUELTY 10
What can a m. know	VALUE 8	**morality** cities for our best m.	COUNTRY AND TOWN 12
monkeys army of m.	CHANCE 31	fits of m.	MORALITY 8
Cats and m.	LIFE 36	M. is a private	MORALITY 13
Even m. sometimes fall	MISTAKES 1	M. is the herd-instinct	MORALITY 11
million m. banging	COMPUTERS 17	M.'s *not* practical	MORALITY 22
pay peanuts, you get m.	VALUE 3	some people talk of m.	POSSESSIONS 17
three wise m.	GOOD 13	surely about m.	SPORTS 23
three wise m.	VIRTUE 5	**morals** Food comes first, then m.	MORALITY 17
monogamist kind of serial m.	CONSTANCY 17	If your m. make you dreary	MORALITY 12
monologues intersecting m.	CONVERSATION 19	m. are like its teeth	MORALITY 14
monopoly m. profits	BUSINESS 36	m. of a whore	BEHAVIOUR 23
m. stage of capitalism	CAPITALISM 15	m. on a high plane	MORALITY 1
Monroe M. doctrine	INTERNAT REL 6	self-interest was bad m.	ECONOMICS 10
monster Frankenstein's m.	PROBLEMS 8	**more** days that are no m.	MEMORY 11
green-eyed m.	ENVY 4	I want some m.	GREED 11
green-eyed m.	ENVY 10	Less is m.	ARCHITECTURE 17
hopeful m.	LIFE SCI 3	Less is m.	EXCESS 8

net (*cont.*)

fish that comes to the n.	OPPORTUNITY 1
n. is spread	FUTILITY 2
old n. is cast aside	YOUTH 1
rush up to the n.	MIDDLE AGE 14
tennis with the n. down	POETRY 33
Netherlands N. have been	COUNTRIES 13
nettle grasp the n.	COURAGE 11
n. of danger	DANGER 28
stroke a n.	COURAGE 19
nettles overrun with n.	MIND 13
neurosis n. is a secret	WORRY 14
N. is the way of avoiding	WORRY 12
neutrality Armed n. is ineffectual	INTERNAT REL 26
Just for a word 'n.'	INTERNAT REL 24
neutralize n. the black	CHOICE 20
neutrinos N., they are very small	PHYSICAL 20
never Better late than n.	PUNCTUALITY 1
N. do today	IDLENESS 20
N. give a sucker	FOOLS 27
N. glad confident morning	DISILLUSION 14
n. had it so good	SATISFACTION 36
N. is a long time	TIME 4
N. Never Land	AUSTRALIA 8
N. say never	CHANGE 5
N. the time	OPPORTUNITY 35
n. to have been loved	LOVE 41
N. to have lived	LIFE 41
n. use a big, big D	SWEARING 7
This will n. do	CRITICISM 13
What, n.	CERTAINTY 18
What you've n. had	SATISFACTION 8
nevermore Quoth the Raven, 'N.'	DESPAIR 10
new acquired something n.	POSSESSIONS 27
brave n. world	PROGRESS 2
find something n.	CHANGE 35
I saw a n. heaven	HEAVEN 8
my n. found land	SEX 11
n. black	FASHION 3
n. deal	AMERICA 32
N. Jerusalem	HEAVEN 6
n. life	BEGINNING 18
N. lords, new laws	CHANGE 7
n. man may be raised	HUMAN NATURE 11
N. opinions are always	IDEAS 5
n. under the sun	FAMILIARITY 12
n. wine	CHANGE 25
n. wine in old bottles	CHANGE 17
n. world order	FUTURE 28
N. World Order	INTERNAT REL 7
N. Year's Day	FESTIVALS 43
no n. thing under the sun	PROGRESS 6
nothing n. in dying	SUICIDE 8
O brave n. world	HUMAN RACE 14
on with the n.	LOVE 2
quite n. a thing	SEX 21
ring in the n.	FESTIVALS 65
run over by 'N. Man'	PROGRESS 18
some n. clichés	ORIGINALITY 18
something n.	AFRICA 7
something n. out of Africa	AFRICA 1
time for making n. enemies	FORGIVENESS 18
to find out the n.	TEACHING 6
What is n. cannot be true	CUSTOM 3
Youth is something very n.	YOUTH 24
new-born use of a n. child	INVENTIONS 8
New England variety about the N. weather	WEATHER 44
newest n. kind of ways	SIN 13
n. works	ARTS AND SCI 5
New Holland natives of N.	AUSTRALIA 11
news bad n. infects	NEWS 10
Bad n. travels fast	NEWS 1
hear n. of home	TRAVEL 3
how much n. there is	LETTERS 15
Ill n. have wings	NEWS 9
love of n.	NEWS 11

n. that's fit to print	JOURNALISM 1
news that STAYS n.	WRITING 40
n. until he's read it	NEWS 13
No n. is good	NEWS 2
other to get the n.	GOSSIP 24
that ain't n.	NEWS 14
that is n.	NEWS 12
What n. on the Rialto	NEWS 8
New South Wales revive in N.	AUSTRALIA 14
newspaper n., I suppose, is a nation	JOURNALISM 20
seen in a n.	JOURNALISM 8
Third World never sold a n.	JOURNALISM 24
Newspeak aim of N.	CENSORSHIP 13
Newton *Let N. be*	SCIENCE 8
N., also, made a universe	UNIVERSE 14
Newtons many N. to make one Milton	ARTS AND SCI 4
New World N. into existence	AMERICA 17
New York gullet of N.	AMERICAN CITIES 61
kind of N.	TOWNS 31
N.,—a helluva town	AMERICAN CITIES 54
N. is a catastrophe	AMERICAN CITIES 57
N. makes one think of the collapse	AMERICAN CITIES 63
Xenophon at N.	FUTURE 16
New Zealanders When N. emigrate	AUSTRALIA 31
next forty-five, What n.	MIDDLE AGE 15
N. year in Jerusalem	TOWNS 3
NHS N. is quite like heaven	SICKNESS 17
nice If you can't say something n.	MANNERS 23
Mr N. Guy	CHANGE 9
Naughty but n.	TEMPTATION 1
N. guys	SPORTS 18
N. guys finish last	SPORTS 1
N. guys, when we turn nasty	CHARACTER 53
N. to see you	MEETING 2
n. work	ENVY 6
N. work if you can get it	COURTSHIP 9
not about being n.	LEADERSHIP 23
thoroughly n. people	RELATIONSHIPS 19
nicely That'll do n.	DEBT 2
niche n. in creation	SEX 22
nickname n. is the heaviest	NAMES 11
Nigeria daughter of N.	AFRICA 15
nigger Woman is the n. of the world	WOMAN'S ROLE 26
night acquainted with the n.	DAY 16
ain't a fit n. out	WEATHER 51
as a watch in the n.	TRANSIENCE 5
bowl of n.	DAY 12
By n. an atheist	BELIEF 17
dark and stormy n.	BEGINNING 7
dark n. of the soul	DESPAIR 2
dark n. of the soul	DESPAIR 14
days have melted into n.	CHILDREN 25
fearful of the n.	SKIES 22
firebell in the n.	DANGER 15
gentle into that good n.	OLD AGE 27
go bump in the n.	SUPERNATURAL 4
hard day's n.	DAY 20
I get up at n.	SEASONS 22
like the n.	BEAUTY 20
many a bad n.	SUICIDE 7
N. brings counsel	ADVICE 4
n. has a thousand eyes	SKIES 20
N. Mail crossing the Border	TRANSPORT 17
N. makes no difference	EQUALITY 6
n. of the long knives	TRUST 10
N.'s candles are burnt out	DAY 5
n. to do with sleep	SLEEP 12
on the previous n.	PHYSICAL 10
pass in the n.	MEETING 5
Red sky at n.	WEATHER 14
Ships that pass in the n.	RELATIONSHIPS 12
solitude of the n.	DAY 18
terror by n.	FEAR 7
things that go bump in the n.	SUPERNATURAL 1
This ae n.	DEATH 10
'Twas the n. before Christmas	CHRISTMAS 8

Twelfth N.	FESTIVALS 58
watches of the n.	DAY 3
when on a winter's n.	LIFE 19
witching time of n.	DAY 6
world's last n.	ENDING 15
night-light I was just a tiny n.	DEATH 76
nightmare Action without vision is a n.	IDEALISM 1
third act in a n.	DREAMS 15
weighs like a n.	CUSTOM 17
nightmares darken into n.	DREAMS 14
night-time dog in the n.	LOGIC 15
nihil Aut Caesar, aut n.	AMBITION 7
nil N. admirari	HAPPINESS 7
N. carborundum	DETERMINATION 10
N. desperandum	HOPE 11
nine cat has n. lives	CATS 1
N. Days' Queen	ROYALTY 11
n. days' wonder	FAME 6
n. Muses	ARTS AND SCI 1
n. points of the law	LAW 9
n. times to the Devil	GARDENS 7
nineties naughty n.	PAST 13
ninety-nine n. names of God	NAMES 5
nip n. him in the bud	DECEPTION 20
nipple behind the left n.	POETRY 40
nirvana called N. because	SATISFACTION 17
no Just say n.	DRUGS 1
leadership is saying n.	LEADERSHIP 2
man who says n.	REVOLUTION 23
N. fruits, no flowers	SEASONS 20
N. pain, no palm	SUFFERING 17
omnipotent n.	SCOTLAND 17
she said 'n.'	PREGNANCY 14
nobility n. and sacrifice	SCULPTURE 7
N. is a graceful ornament	RANK 10
n. without pride	ANIMALS 29
one and only n.	RANK 5
order of n.	RANK 16
noble n. acts of chivalry	PUBLISHING 3
n. in reason	HUMAN RACE 13
n. savage	CULTURE 6
n. savage ran	CULTURE 9
noblest n. work of man	GOD 27
nobody I care for n.	INDIFFERENCE 5
n. comes	BOREDOM 10
n. is sure about	CERTAINTY 20
n. tells me anything	IGNORANCE 23
n. will come	WARFARE 45
nod land of N.	SLEEP 6
n.'s as good as a wink	ADVICE 5
nods Homer n.	MISTAKES 13
Homer sometimes n.	MISTAKES 2
noise Go placidly amid the n.	PEACE 22
most sublime n.	MUSICIANS 9
n. is an effective means	ARGUMENT 23
Silence is a still n.	SILENCE 2
till they make a n.	SECRECY 30
noises squishing n.	SEX 41
noisy goes into the n. crowd	SOLITUDE 15
nomadic characterize n. traits as godly	
	COUNTRY AND TOWN 28
non-commissioned n. man	ARMED FORCES 34
nonconformist man must be a n.	CONFORMITY 7
non-cooperation n. with evil	GOOD 36
none malice toward n.	POLITICIANS 19
nones December's N. are gay	FESTIVALS 64
nonexistent obsolescent and the n.	COMPUTERS 13
nonsense firm anchor in n.	THINKING 25
music that is not n.	SINGING 5
n. upon stilts	HUMAN RIGHTS 10
n. which was knocked	UNIVERSITIES 18
non-violence N. is the first article	VIOLENCE 9
organization of n.	VIOLENCE 18
noon n. a purple glow	DAY 13
no-one Duty is what n. else will do	DUTY 27
n. left to speak up	INDIFFERENCE 14

nooses N. give	SUICIDE 9
Norfolk N. wiles	BRITISH TOWNS 1
Very flat, N.	BRITISH TOWNS 40
norm Without deviation from the n.	SIMILARITY 28
normal N. is the good smile	CONFORMITY 16
north Athens of the N.	BRITISH TOWNS 14
heart of the N. is dead	SEASONS 25
He was my N.	MOURNING 19
N. Star State	AMERICAN CITIES 30
N. wind doth blow	WEATHER 10
to us the near n.	AUSTRALIA 21
True N. strong and free	CANADA 12
Venice of the N.	TOWNS 13
Northamptonshire N. for squires	BRITISH TOWNS 8
north-easter Welcome, wild N.	WEATHER 43
northern constant as the n. star	CONSTANCY 6
n. lights	SKIES 5
N. reticence	IRELAND 20
north-north-west mad n.	MADNESS 5
nose Any n. May ravage	SENSES 11
Cleopatra's n.	APPEARANCE 16
cut off your n.	REVENGE 2
hateful to the n.	SMOKING 6
large n. is in fact	BODY 18
n. and cheeks stand out	INSULTS 4
not blow his n. without	WRITERS 27
what lies under one's n.	INTELLIGENCE 22
noses n. have they	INDIFFERENCE 3
Where do the n. go	KISSING 11
nostalgia N. isn't what it used to be	PAST 1
not said the thing which was n.	LIES 13
say what it is n.	POETRY 13
note living had no n.	BIRDS 8
same n. can be played	JAZZ 8
notes n. I handle no better	MUSIC 26
n. like little fishes	MUSIC 22
quantity of the n.	MUSICIANS 12
too many n.	MUSIC 9
nothing ain't heard n. yet	SINGING 11
avoid by saying n.	CRITICISM 2
better than n.	SATISFACTION 7
better to know n.	KNOWLEDGE 40
brought n. into this world	POSSESSIONS 14
Caesar or n.	AMBITION 7
Death is n.	DEATH 62
do n. with it at all	YOUTH 19
do n. without it	FAITH 12
Emperor has n. on	HONESTY 10
good man to do n.	GOOD 30
Goodness had n. to do with it	VIRTUE 43
I do n.	ACTION 34
I know n.	IGNORANCE 23
individually can do n.	ADMINISTRATION 17
learn to do n.	IDLENESS 23
marvel at n.	HAPPINESS 7
N. ain't worth nothin'	LIBERTY 37
n. but the truth	TRUTH 12
N. can be created	CREATIVITY 3
N. comes of nothing	VALUE 6
N. for nothing	VALUE 7
N. for nothink 'ere	VALUE 31
N. happens	BOREDOM 10
n. happens	LIFE 55
N. happens to anybody	SUFFERING 10
n. has to be better	SATISFACTION 37
n. has value	FUTILITY 24
N. have I found	NECESSITY 16
n. in excess	EXCESS 20
n. in respect of that	HUMAN RACE 17
N. is for ever	CHANGE 10
N. is here for tears	SORROW 14
N. is more dangerous	IDEAS 11
n. like a dame	WOMEN 49
N., like something	BOREDOM 11
n. should ever be done	CUSTOM 20
N. to be done	FUTILITY 26

painter (*cont.*)

I am a p.	PAINTING 22
scenes made me a p.	PAINTING 9
painters p. imitate nature	PAINTING 5
painting p. and punctuality	PUNCTUALITY 9
p. is not made to decorate	PAINTING 20
P. is saying 'Ta'	PAINTING 26
P. is silent poetry	ARTS 6
paintings p. can come to life	PAINTING 30
palace Love in a p.	LOVE 46
p. of wisdom	EXCESS 28
palaces p. of kings	GOVERNMENT 22
pleasures and p.	HOME 17
pale beyond the p.	BEHAVIOUR 11
her p. fire	SKIES 12
p. contented sort	SATISFACTION 27
pink pills for p. people	MEDICINE 2
Why so p. and wan	COURTSHIP 4
palm bear the p.	ACHIEVEMENT 4
cross a person's p.	FORESIGHT 6
itching p.	CORRUPTION 6
itching p.	CORRUPTION 10
P. Sunday	FESTIVALS 45
winning the p. without the dust	WINNING 8
palmetto P. State	AMERICAN CITIES 33
palmistry About astrology and p.	PARANORMAL 15
pamphleteers not the age of p.	TECHNOLOGY 12
pan Tin P. Alley	MUSIC 5
pancake P. Day	FESTIVALS 46
pancreas adorable p.	BEAUTY 32
Pandora open that P.'s Box	EUROPE 13
P.'s box	PROBLEMS 11
panic distinguished from p.	FEAR 21
Don't p.	CRISES 27
p.'s in thy breastie	FEAR 12
pans pots and p.	OPTIMISM 11
pants applying the seat of the p.	WRITING 1
limbs in p.	APPEARANCE 27
papa After God comes my P.	PARENTS 10
papacy corruption of the p.	COUNTRIES 24
p. is not other	CHRISTIAN CH 20
paper *Hamlet* is so much p.	FOOTBALL 5
heart upon p.	LETTERS 11
If all the earth were p.	WRITING 14
just for a scrap of p.	INTERNAT REL 24
kisses on p.	KISSING 5
p. government	ADMINISTRATION 6
p. it is written on	LAW 36
piece of tissue p.	SURPRISE 13
reactionaries are p. tigers	POLITICS 22
scrap of p.	TRUST 13
than a p. cup	AMERICAN CITIES 58
papers He's got my p.	OPPORTUNITY 36
P. are power	ADMINISTRATION 22
parachutes Minds are like p.	MIND 22
parade life might be put on p.	ROYALTY 40
p. of riches	WEALTH 23
paradise bowers of p.	GOVERNMENT 22
catch the bird of p.	CHOICE 26
driven out of P.	PATIENCE 31
If there is a p. on earth	COUNTRIES 12
keys of P.	DRUGS 5
p. of women	ENGLAND 1
rudiments of P.	SCIENCE AND RELIG 7
see John Knox in P.	HEAVEN 19
squeeze into P.	BODY 15
wilderness were p. enow	SATISFACTION 31
paradises true p.	HEAVEN 17
paradox Fermi p.	PARANORMAL 6
liar p.	LIES 9
what was a p.	LOGIC 16
parallel North of the 49th p.	CANADA 26
paralysed p. cyclops	PHOTOGRAPHY 13
parameters five free p.	HYPOTHESIS 28
paranoia God, guts and p.	AMERICA 41
paranoid Only the p. survive	BUSINESS 54

pardon God will p. me	FORGIVENESS 22
Offenders never p.	FORGIVENESS 5
sun for p.	GARDENS 19
parent art of being a p.	CHILD CARE 1
child makes you a p.	FAMILY 30
Dear P.	SCHOOLS 15
kind p. to man	NATURE 6
lose one p.	MISTAKES 22
p. of safety	CAUTION 4
parentage P. is a very important profession	
	CHILD CARE 13
parents bondage to p.	PARENTS 11
girl needs good p.	WOMEN 53
joys of p.	PARENTS 9
lives of their p.	PARENTS 23
loving their p.	PARENTS 16
P. are the bones	PARENTS 31
P. want their children	PARENTS 3
p. were created	PARENTS 22
sexual lives of their p.	PARENTS 2
stranger to one of your p.	CHOICE 17
tangled web do p. weave	CHILD CARE 11
To understand your p.' love	PARENTS 5
what their p. do not wish	CHILD CARE 2
parfit p. gentil knight	CHARACTER 30
Paris after they've seen P.	TRAVEL 35
go to P.	AMERICA 2
last time I saw P.	TOWNS 23
P. is a movable feast	TOWNS 26
P. is well worth a mass	DISILLUSION 9
parish it would be found in my p.	CHRISTIAN CH 27
p. of rich women	POETS 24
world as my p.	CLERGY 12
park p., a policeman	CINEMA 17
parking hunting for p. places	BRITISH TOWNS 45
Parkinson against P.'s disease	SICKNESS 25
parks p. are the lungs	POLLUTION 9
parliament in a 21st-century p.	PARLIAMENT 32
p. can do any thing	PARLIAMENT 13
p. of whores	DEMOCRACY 24
P. would not exist	PARLIAMENT 28
Scottish P. which adjourned	SCOTLAND 20
parliamentarian pleasure for a p.	PARLIAMENT 29
parliaments Mother of P.	BRITAIN 3
mother of P.	PARLIAMENT 21
Parnassus Mount P.	POETRY 2
parodies P. and caricatures	CRITICISM 20
parody p. is a game	WIT 21
parrot This p. is no more	DEATH 75
parsley P., sage, rosemary	COURTSHIP 1
P. seed goes nine times	GARDENS 7
parsnips Fine words butter no p.	WORDS AND DEEDS 4
parson P. left conjuring	PAST 22
P. lost his senses	ANIMALS 26
part friends must p.	MEETING 1
had but known one p.	KNOWLEDGE 25
kiss and p.	MEETING 11
p. of ourselves	HATRED 10
p. of ourselves	MOURNING 12
p. of the union	EMPLOYMENT 25
till death us do p.	MARRIAGE 27
partiality neither anger nor p.	PREJUDICE 7
particles names of all these p.	PHYSICAL 25
particular London p.	WEATHER 26
This is a London p.	WEATHER 41
particulars minute p.	GOOD 32
parties Bachelors know all about p.	HOSPITALITY 24
p. of the kind	HOSPITALITY 14
talk about at some p.	HOSPITALITY 7
parting P. is all we know	MEETING 17
p. is such sweet sorrow	MEETING 8
p. of the ways	CRISES 9
p. there is an image	MEETING 14
partir P. c'est mourir un peu	ABSENCE 13
partridge p. in pear tree	GIFTS 6
parts above its p.	CAUSES 19

P. of it are excellent	SATISFACTION 32	p. as a watch in the night	TRANSIENCE 5
p. other beers	ALCOHOL 4	p. at least is secure	PAST 4
plays many p.	LIFE 21	p. cannot be recalled	PAST 6
Points Have no p.	MATHS 25	p. is a bucket	PAST 32
save all the p.	TECHNOLOGY 22	p. is a foreign country	PAST 36
sum of the p.	QUANTITIES 12	p. is always ahead of us	PAST 5
parturient *P. montes*	EFFORT 15	p. is like a collection	PAST 42
party collapse of Stout P.	HUMOUR 1	p. is never dead	PAST 35
don't dream of giving a p.	HOSPITALITY 25	praising the p.	PAST 38
Grand Old P.	POLITICAL PART 8	record of the p.	REPUTATION 7
Heaven but with a p.	POLITICAL PART 17	remember the p.	PAST 30
leave the p.	HOSPITALITY 1	remember what is p.	FORESIGHT 10
more important than the p.	POLITICAL PART 46	remembrance of things p.	MEMORY 8
nasty p.	POLITICAL PART 47	Time is past	TIME 25
p. breaks up	HOSPITALITY 15	Time present and time p.	TIME 45
p. is a moral crusade	POLITICAL PART 38	water that is p.	OPPORTUNITY 8
p. is an old stage-coach	POLITICAL PART 41	**pastors** P. need to start where	CLERGY 19
P. is little less	POLITICAL PART 13	some ungracious p.	WORDS AND DEEDS 12
p. is unfit to rule	POLITICAL PART 32	**pasture** feed me in a green p.	GOD 7
p.'s over	ENDING 20	**pastures** p. new	CHANGE 21
save the P.	POLITICAL PART 35	p. new	CHANGE 32
speaks to a p.	WRITERS 14	**patch** purple p.	STYLE 4
spirit of the p.	POLITICAL PART 18	purple p. or two	STYLE 6
Stick to your p.	POLITICAL PART 21	**patches** shreds and p.	CHARACTER 28
there is no P. line	CONFORMITY 13	**pate** beat your p.	INTELLIGENCE 11
voted at my p.'s call	POLITICAL PART 20	**pâté de foie gras** eating *p.*	HEAVEN 14
party spirit P., which at best	POLITICAL PART 14	**Patent Office** P. is the gatekeeper	INVENTIONS 21
Pascal P.'s wager	GOD 6	**paternity** bond of p.	PARENTS 24
P.'s wager	GOD 19	**paternoster** No penny, no p.	BUSINESS 12
pass And this, too, shall p. away	TRANSIENCE 1	**path** primrose p.	PLEASURE 6
Horseman p. by	INDIFFERENCE 12	**pathetic** p. fallacy	EMOTIONS 5
I see the hours p.	ACTION 34	**pathless** pleasure in the p. woods	NATURE 12
p. on good advice	ADVICE 18	**paths** p. are many	WAYS 15
p. on the torch	CUSTOM 6	**patience** All commend p.	PATIENCE 1
p. the ammunition	PRACTICALITY 14	Have p., heart	SUFFERING 6
p. the buck	DUTY 7	p. have her perfect work	PATIENCE 24
p. through this world but once	VIRTUE 37	P. is a virtue	PATIENCE 13
Ships that p. in the night	RELATIONSHIPS 12	p. of Job	PATIENCE 22
They shall not p.	DEFIANCE 17	P., that blending	PATIENCE 29
They shall not p.	WORLD W I 1	p. will achieve more	PATIENCE 28
passage long black p.	SLEEP 16	**patient** fury of the p. man	PATIENCE 27
passed p. by on the other side	CHARITY 13	I am extraordinarily p.	PATIENCE 32
That p. the time	TIME 48	P. endurance attains all	PATIENCE 25
passes everything p.	LIFE 9	p. etherized	DAY 14
Free speech, free p.	ENGLAND 23	p. etherized upon a table	POETRY 32
Men seldom make p.	APPEARANCE 26	**patients** live their lives as p.	HEALTH 26
Thus p. the glory	TRANSIENCE 2	**patois** p. of Europe	LANGUAGES 14
passing-bells What p. for these	WORLD W I 16	**patria** *pro p. mori*	PATRIOTISM 7
passion all p. spent	EMOTIONS 13	**patriot** Never was p. yet	PATRIOTISM 9
held with p.	OPINION 25	p. of the world	PATRIOTISM 18
In her first p.	WOMEN 32	sunshine p.	PATRIOTISM 14
in such a p. about	POLITICIANS 14	**patriotism** knock the p. out	PATRIOTISM 23
p. is our task	ARTS 18	no Canadian p.	CANADA 11
p. or even sex	MARRIAGE 52	P. is a lively sense	PATRIOTISM 25
ruling p.	EMOTIONS 14	p. is not enough	PATRIOTISM 21
sentimental p.	ARTS 15	P. is the last refuge	PATRIOTISM 12
tender p.	LOVE 20	p. run amok	PATRIOTISM 32
passionate full of p. intensity	EXCELLENCE 16	**patriots** p. and tyrants	LIBERTY 14
passionless grief is p.	SORROW 17	True p. we	AUSTRALIA 13
passions inferno of his p.	EMOTIONS 28	**pattern** p. in most lives	LIFE 55
p. break not through	EMOTIONS 8	**patterns** taken all the p. away	MATHS 27
two primal p.	HUMAN NATURE 16	weaves algebraic p.	COMPUTERS 9
past controls the p.	POWER 32	**paucity** p. of human pleasures	HUNTING 9
day of an era p.	RUSSIA 12	**Paul** P.'s day be fair	FESTIVALS 3
designed to preserve the p.	TOWNS 29	pay P.	DEBT 11
distinction between p., present	TIME 49	**Pauli** P. [exclusion] principle	PHYSICAL 18
every saint has a p.	SIN 24	**pause** dull it is to p.	IDLENESS 19
forgetting the p.	FORGIVENESS 29	**pauses** p. between the notes	MUSIC 26
forward to the p.	FUTURE 25	**paved** p. with gold	OPPORTUNITY 24
funeral of the p.	PRESENT 9	**paw** cat's p.	DUTY 6
future by the p.	FORESIGHT 13	**pay** Can't p., won't pay	TAXES 1
God cannot alter the p.	HISTORY 20	Crime doesn't p.	CRIME 2
god cannot change the p.	PAST 18	dance must p. the fiddler	POWER 8
nothing more than the p.	CAUSES 24	for what p.	EMPLOYMENT 12
our p. is real	SUFFERING 36	He that cannot p.	MONEY 4
p. always looks better	PAST 3	made to p. for	GOVERNMENT 42

-▸-◂-▸-◂-▸-◂-▸-◂-▸-◂-▸-◂-▸-◂-▸-◂-▸-◂-▸-◂-▸-◂-▸-◂-▸-◂-▸-◂-▸-◂-▸-◂-▸-

left to the p.	POLITICS 26
p. and civil servants	CULTURE 25
P. are entitled	POLITICIANS 41
P. have no leisure	POLITICIANS 8
whole race of p.	PRACTICALITY 9
politics continuation of p. by other means	WARFARE 26
first part of p.	POLITICS 15
In p. if you want	POLITICIANS 33
in p. the middle way	POLITICS 14
Magnanimity in p.	POLITICS 13
no true friends in p.	POLITICIANS 40
p. and equations	MATHS 21
p. and religion don't mix	BIBLE 20
p. is a disease	CANADA 22
P. is a marathon	POLITICS 33
p. is present history	HISTORY 19
P. makes strange bedfellows	POLITICS 4
p. out of politics	POLITICAL PART 40
p. with bloodshed	POLITICS 20
some subjects in p.	SILENCE 15
to succeed in p.	POLITICIANS 26
poll p. tax	TAXES 3
science of p.-taking	STATISTICS 13
Pollock from Lascaux to Jackson P.	JAZZ 10
polluted filthy and p.	POLLUTION 5
pollution engine of p.	DOGS 15
p. of democracy	CORRUPTION 19
Pomeranian bones of a single P. grenadier	WARFARE 33
pomps p. and vanities	TEMPTATION 4
p. and vanity	SIN 15
pons p. asinorum	MATHS 5
poodle Balfour's p.	PARLIAMENT 11
hon. Gentleman's p.	PARLIAMENT 25
pooh p.-bah	SELF-ESTEEM 10
pool first fill a p.	CLERGY 9
poop-poop O p.	TRANSPORT 9
poor another for the p.	JUSTICE 8
cannot help one p. man	CHARITY 21
grind the faces of the p.	POVERTY 13
how expensive it is to be p.	POVERTY 32
Laws grind the p.	POVERTY 20
luxury to the p.	SELF-INTEREST 31
many who are p.	SOCIETY 17
murmuring p.	POVERTY 22
peasant in my kingdom so p.	POVERTY 17
Plenty has made me p.	THRIFT 13
p. always ye have	POVERTY 14
p. are Europe's blacks	POVERTY 23
p. as Job	POVERTY 11
p. but she was honest	VIRTUE 42
p. cannot always reach	POVERTY 28
p. get children	POVERTY 29
p. know that it is money	MONEY 45
p. little rich girl	WEALTH 13
p. man at his gate	CLASS 15
p. man had nothing	POSSESSIONS 12
p. people in rich countries	CHARITY 28
P. people's memory is less nourished	MEMORY 25
p. poorer	CAPITALISM 23
p. tread lightest	POLLUTION 26
propensity for being p.	SINGLE 8
use the money for the p.	CHARITY 23
why the p. have no food	POVERTY 35
your tired, your p.	AMERICA 24
poorer for richer for p.	MARRIAGE 27
pope Pole first, a p. second	CLERGY 18
P. afterwards	CONSCIENCE 14
P., and all their school	POETRY 23
poplars p. are felled	TREES 11
poppies In Flanders fields the p. blow	WORLD W I 15
poppy Flanders p.	WORLD W I 3
flushed print in a p.	FLOWERS 8
P. Day	FESTIVALS 47
tall p.	FAME 7
popular more p. than Jesus	CHRISTIAN CH 36
P. culture is a contradiction	CULTURE 30

p. politician	POLITICIANS 7
population P., when unchecked	LIFE SCI 12
populi Salus p.	LAW 17
vox p.	OPINION 9
porcupines couple of p.	REVENGE 22
pork p. please our mouths	MORALITY 3
pornography P. is the attempt	SEX 24
porridge sand in the p.	LEISURE 10
port p., for the men	ALCOHOL 12
p. in a storm	NECESSITY 1
p. one is sailing	IGNORANCE 15
p. out, starboard home	TRAVEL 13
portion Benjamin's p.	QUANTITIES 13
portmanteau like a p.	MEANING 9
portrait paint a p.	PAINTING 19
position p. of matter	EMPLOYMENT 21
p. ridiculous	SEX 17
positions put into p. slightly above	ACHIEVEMENT 32
positive ac-cent-tchu-ate the p.	OPTIMISM 33
p. thinking	THINKING 6
p. value has its price	CAUSES 29
such a p. role model	BEHAVIOUR 37
positivists logical p. capable of love	LOGIC 20
possess you can't p. it	GUILT 22
possessed p. by death	DEATH 64
possession Man's best p.	MARRIAGE 19
p. for all time	HISTORY 9
P. is nine points	LAW 9
p. of a book	BOOKS 23
Than in the glad p.	WEALTH 17
title and p.	CAPITALISM 9
possessions least of p.	AUSTRALIA 25
multitude of p.	CHARITY 18
other people's p.	POSSESSIONS 29
p. for a moment	POSSESSIONS 15
possessive p. of things we do	GIFTS 24
possibilities improbable p.	PROBLEMS 16
not interested in the p.	WINNING 4
possibility p. of anything	CERTAINTY 19
p. of suicide	SUICIDE 13
possible all p. worlds	OPTIMISM 1
all p. worlds	OPTIMISM 20
All things are p.	GOD 1
all things are p.	GOD 9
art of the p.	POLITICS 19
p. you may be mistaken	CERTAINTY 11
realm of the p.	SATISFACTION 15
something is p.	HYPOTHESIS 29
possumus p. omnes	ABILITY 9
post Lie follows by p.	APOLOGY 19
may not quit the p.	SUICIDE 6
p. of honour	DANGER 9
poster p. is a visual telegram	ADVERTISING 15
posterity forward to p.	FUTURE 17
go down to p.	LANGUAGE 15
something for P.	FUTURE 15
special correspondent for p.	WRITERS 17
trustees of P.	YOUTH 16
postern p. door makes a thief	OPPORTUNITY 14
post office go into a p.	SELF-ESTEEM 25
postscript material in the p.	LETTERS 7
mind but in her p.	LETTERS 10
pot chicken in his p.	POVERTY 17
Look at p.	ADVERTISING 16
p. calling the kettle black	CRITICISM 5
p. is soon hot	ANGER 2
p. never boils	PATIENCE 18
p. of gold	VALUE 18
potato couch p.	BROADCASTING 5
Where the p.-gatherers	IRELAND 19
You like p.	SPEECH 27
potatoes just to peel the p.	RELIGION 26
Potemkin P. village	DECEPTION 9
potent p. cheap music is	MUSIC 19
Potomac All quiet along the P. to-night	WARS 17
pots among the p. and pans	HOUSEWORK 8

refuge r. of a scoundrel — PATRIOTISM 12
r. of weak minds — IDLENESS 14
refuse offer he can't r. — CHOICE 29
sewage and r. — PROGRESS 21
when men r. to fight — WARFARE 3
refused practice in being r. — DISILLUSION 7
refute I r. it *thus* — REALITY 10
Who can r. a sneer — ARGUMENT 16
regardless r. of their doom — CHILDREN 13
régime ancien r. — PAST 9
regiment Monstrous R. of Women — WOMAN'S ROLE 7
register r. of crimes — HISTORY 14
regret Old Age a r. — LIFE 32
one r. in life — SELF 24
r. time not spent — ACHIEVEMENT 31
usually a quick r. — CHOICE 5
regular icily r. — PERFECTION 9
regulations R.—they're written for — LAW 34
reign r. in hell — AMBITION 12
reigned r. with your loves — GOVERNMENT 14
reigns he r. — ROYALTY 34
reinfection merry-go-round of r. — SICKNESS 19
reinvent r. the wheel — INVENTIONS 3
r. the world — REALITY 22
rejection crushing r. — PARENTS 29
rejoice R., rejoice — WARS 25
rejoices heart that never r. — HAPPINESS 4
relation cold r. — FAMILY 17
nobody like a r. — FAMILY 18
relations apology for r. — FRIENDSHIP 27
offensive in personal r. — DUTY 23
relationship human r. suffers — ADMINISTRATION 12
r. consisted — RELATIONSHIPS 28
special r. — INTERNAT REL 8
relationships Human r. grow — RELATIONSHIPS 20
R., relationships — RELATIONSHIPS 27
relative in a r. way — PHYSICAL 10
Success is r. — SUCCESS 44
truth is r. — UNIVERSITIES 26
relaxed you feel terribly r. — WARFARE 60
release called r. from bondage — SATISFACTION 16
relent make him once r. — DETERMINATION 33
relic r. of Empire — BRITAIN 15
relief After hardship comes r. — ADVERSITY 2
what a r. — SOLITUDE 19
religion Art and R. — CULTURE 24
become a popular r. — RELIGION 23
Belfast must be the most r.-conscious — BRITISH TOWNS 43
bring r. into it — RELIGION 24
concerned with r. — GOD 30
cultivation of r. — SCIENCE AND RELIG 4
Every dictator uses r. — POWER 38
for r. when in rags — RELIGION 10
in Quebec a r. — CANADA 22
much wrong could r. — RELIGION 5
no r. but social — CHRISTIAN CH 22
One r. is as true — RELIGION 9
politics and r. don't mix — BIBLE 20
really but of one r. — RELIGION 11
r. but a childish toy — RELIGION 8
r. into after-dinner toasts — CONSCIENCE 14
R. is an all-important matter — WOMAN'S ROLE 16
R. is by no means — CONVERSATION 10
r. is powerless — DRESS 10
R. is the frozen thought — RELIGION 25
R. . . . is the opium — RELIGION 19
r. is to do good — RELIGION 16
r. of Socialism — POLITICAL PART 30
r. to make us hate — RELIGION 12
r. weak — MEDICINE 29
Science without r. — SCIENCE AND RELIG 14
slovenliness is no part of r. — DRESS 8
some of r. — POSSESSIONS 17
start your own r. — WEALTH 2
wisest r. — POLITICAL PART 29
religions sixty different r. — ENGLAND 11

religious r. opinions — MEN 11
remain place where he wanted to 'r.' — EXPLORATION 9
things r. — EFFORT 22
remains aught r. to do — ACTION 25
Strength in what r. behind — TRANSIENCE 10
remark R. all these roughnesses — PAINTING 6
remarks R. are not literature — WRITING 39
said our r. before us — QUOTATIONS 6
remedies apply new r. — CHANGE 31
desperate r. — NECESSITY 3
encumbering it with r. — BODY 17
remedy dangerous r. — REVOLUTION 5
r. for everything — DEATH 9
r. for the sorrows — SYMPATHY 28
r. is worse — MEDICINE 16
r. of so universal — DRUGS 4
what r. remains — DOGS 6
remember cheering to r. — MEMORY 5
I r. it well — MEMORY 24
It is what you can r. — HISTORY 24
keep diaries to r. — MEMORY 20
r. a happy time — SORROW 9
r. and be sad — MEMORY 13
r. more than seven — QUANTITIES 24
R. the Alamo — WARS 2
r. the Fifth of November — TRUST 2
r. what is past — FORESIGHT 10
r. with advantages — MEMORY 7
r. with great clarity — MEMORY 27
Those who cannot r. — PAST 30
We will r. them — ARMED FORCES 37
who I r. he was — PARENTS 28
You must r. this — KISSING 9
remembered blue r. hills — PAST 29
undeservedly r. — BOOKS 22
remembering r. my good friends — FRIENDSHIP 12
remembers always r. the happy things — YOUTH 27
r. today the extermination — RACE 16
remembrance R. Day — FESTIVALS 49
r. of things past — MEMORY 8
remind r. me of you — MEMORY 21
reminded day upon which we are r. — FESTIVALS 68
remorse R., the fatal egg — FORGIVENESS 19
remote Space isn't r. at all — SKIES 28
removals infidelity and household r. — CHANGE 43
Three r. are as bad — CHANGE 14
render R. therefore unto Caesar — RELIGION 6
renewal r. of love — LOVE 12
renounce r. the devil — SIN 15
rent r. we pay for our room — CHARITY 6
reorganized we would be r. — MANAGEMENT 2
repair friendship in constant r. — FRIENDSHIP 15
repartee always the best r. — DEMOCRACY 12
repay I will r. — REVENGE 10
repeal method to secure the r. — LAW 29
repeat begins to r. itself — EXPERIENCE 33
called on to r. it — SPEECHES 18
condemned to r. it — PAST 30
r. what we all know — ORIGINALITY 17
repeats History r. itself — HISTORY 5
History r. itself — HISTORY 21
repent r. at leisure — MARRIAGE 8
r. at leisure — MARRIAGE 28
repentance cool r. came — FORGIVENESS 20
R. is but want of power — FORGIVENESS 16
repetition deviation, or r. — SPEECH 6
housework, with its endless r. — HOUSEWORK 11
housework, with its endless r. — HOUSEWORK 12
Nagging is the r. — SPEECH 29
reply r. churlish — LIES 11
Theirs not to make r. — ARMED FORCES 32
report false r. — DECEPTION 15
reports R. of my death — MISTAKES 23
representation Taxation without r. — TAXES 9
representative r. owes you — PARLIAMENT 17
reproche sans peur et sans r. — VIRTUE 12

set his hand to a r.	CLASS 10
rose American beauty r.	BUSINESS 34
fayr as is the r.	BEAUTY 12
ghost of a r.	SENSES 7
He who wants a r.	PRACTICALITY 2
like a red, red r.	LOVE 43
No r. without a thorn	CIRCUMSTANCE 5
not the r. but near it	PERFECTION 2
One perfect r.	GIFTS 21
plant a r. in the best soil	CLASS 3
r. by any other name	NAMES 6
R. is a rose	SELF 17
r. of Scotland	FLOWERS 11
r.-red city	TOWNS 20
r. trees have thorns	SATISFACTION 4
Roves back the r.	FLOWERS 9
that which we call a r.	NAMES 8
under the r.	SECRECY 24
unofficial r.	FLOWERS 10
with impunity a r.	SENSES 11
rosebuds Gather ye r. while ye may	TRANSIENCE 8
roses bread and r.	HUMAN RIGHTS 2
coming up r.	OPTIMISM 35
days of wine and r.	TRANSIENCE 13
Flung r., roses	MEMORY 15
Give us Bread, but give us R.	HUMAN RIGHTS 14
like girls and r.	TRANSIENCE 18
moonlight and r.	LOVE 18
not a bed of r.	MARRIAGE 33
not expect to gather r.	CAUSES 8
r. in December	MEMORY 18
r., roses, all the way	SUCCESS 34
scent of the r.	MEMORY 10
soft words are like r.	HYPOCRISY 5
rosewater not made with r.	REVOLUTION 3
Rosh Hashana R.	FESTIVALS 51
rot one to r.	FARMING 2
r. and rot	MATURITY 4
rots Winter never r.	SEASONS 7
rotted simply r. early	MIDDLE AGE 13
rotten choice in r. apples	CHOICE 7
hypocrite is really r.	HYPOCRISY 19
r. apple	CORRUPTION 5
soon r.	MATURITY 2
rough R. in my pebbles	RIVERS 18
rough-hew R. them how we will	FATE 16
roughness r. breedeth hate	CRIME 22
roughnesses Remark all these r.	PAINTING 6
roulette say he's playing r.	UNIVERSE 16
round in a r. hole	CIRCUMSTANCE 19
makes the world go r.	LOVE 8
squeezed himself into the r. hole	CIRCUMSTANCE 27
roundabouts swings and r.	CIRCUMSTANCE 20
What's lost upon the r.	WINNING 18
you gain on the r.	WINNING 3
Roundheads R. (Right but Repulsive)	WARS 21
Rousseau hand of Jean Jacques R.	REVOLUTION 16
routine care more for r.	ADMINISTRATION 10
R., in an intelligent man	CUSTOM 24
royal needed no r. title	RANK 26
r. road	DREAMS 13
r. road to geometry	MATHS 8
r. road to learning	EDUCATION 8
r. throne of kings	ENGLAND 7
royalties entertain four r.	DIPLOMACY 10
royalty when you come to R.	ROYALTY 39
rub r. up against money	MONEY 38
there's the r.	PROBLEMS 15
rubber rest of r., steel, and granite	CHILD CARE 18
r. chicken circuit	SPEECHES 5
rubbers look out for r.	CAUTION 25
rubbish What r.	BRITISH TOWNS 27
Rubicon cross the R.	CRISES 5
rubies her price is far above r.	WOMEN 16
wisdom is above r.	KNOWLEDGE 20
rubs r. nor botches	MISTAKES 14

yellow fog that r. its back	WEATHER 47
rudder r. is of verses	POETRY 10
ruled by the r.	CAUSES 12
rudeness indistinguishable from r.	MANNERS 27
rugby second fiddle only to R. Union	WALES 10
we play r.	SPORTS 38
rugged harsh cadence of a r. line	WIT 8
r. individualism	AMERICA 31
rugs dead like a million bloody r.	WORLD W I 26
ruin r. of all happiness	TRAVEL 28
r. of the soul	KNOWLEDGE 27
r. upon ruin	ORDER 14
ruined r. at our own request	PRAYER 21
ruins mind in r.	MADNESS 10
r. of forgotten times	PAST 23
r. of St Paul's	FUTURE 16
with other's r. built	SELF-INTEREST 23
rule Divide and r.	GOVERNMENT 2
exception proves the r.	HYPOTHESIS 1
exception to every r.	HYPOTHESIS 6
golden r.	SUCCESS 16
golden r. of life	BEGINNING 3
greatest r. of all	PLEASURE 14
party is unfit to r.	POLITICAL PART 32
R. 1, on page 1	WARFARE 57
R., Britannia	BRITAIN 6
to r. the day	SKIES 8
ruled r. by the rudder	CAUSES 12
rulers r. of the darkness	SUPERNATURAL 9
rules artificial r.	MORALITY 7
break known r.	NECESSITY 20
Integrity has no need of r.	HONESTY 15
no r. in filmmaking	CINEMA 22
Queensberry R.	BEHAVIOUR 15
rocks the cradle r. the world	WOMEN 3
R. and models destroy	TASTE 7
R. are made to be broken	LAW 10
r. of art	GENIUS 5
r. the world	PARENTS 14
wouldn't obey the r.	SOCIETY 20
ruling hands of the r. class	CAPITALISM 18
r. passion	EMOTIONS 14
rum antecedents are r.	POLITICAL PART 22
bottle of r.	ALCOHOL 18
r., sodomy, prayers	ARMED FORCES 45
rumble r. in the jungle	SPORTS 4
rumour R., painted	GOSSIP 17
run cannot r. with the hare	TRUST 6
I never r. for the bus	HASTE 23
r. after two hares	INDECISION 6
R. and find out	KNOWLEDGE 44
r. at least twice as fast	EFFORT 23
r. down men of genius	TRANSLATION 7
r. it up the flagpole	ADVERTISING 5
r., though not to soar	IMAGINATION 10
r. with the hare	TRUST 12
they get r. down	EXCESS 34
they which r. in a race	WINNING 9
walk before we can r.	EXPERIENCE 16
walk before we can r.	PATIENCE 19
runaway r. Presidency	PRESIDENCY 14
running Avoid r. at all times	HEALTH 20
r. fast and kicking something	PROBLEMS 32
r. has given me a glimpse	HEALTH 21
r. over	GIFTS 12
R.'s like breathing	SPORTS 36
runs fights and r. away	CAUTION 5
guilty one always r.	GUILT 2
He that r. may read	READING 2
r. up and down the keyboard	MUSICIANS 14
Rupert R. of Debate	SPEECHES 3
rus r. in urbe	COUNTRY AND TOWN 6
rushed we have r. though life	TIME 44
Ruskin doubt that art needed R.	CRITICISM 27
russet-coated r. captain	ARMED FORCES 20
Russian R. autocracy	CAPITALISM 13

Russian (*cont.*)

R. scandal	GOSSIP 14
Scratch a R.	RUSSIA 1
tumult in the R. heart	TOWNS 19
Russians Some people . . . may be R.	COUNTRIES 21
rust If gold r.	CORRUPTION 9
wear out than to r. out	IDLENESS 2
rusts r. from disuse	ACTION 17
rye Comin' thro' the r.	MEETING 12

Sabaoth Lord of S.	GOD 5
sabbath born on the S. day	PREGNANCY 1
S. day's journey	TRAVEL 15
sabotage sagacious use of s.	MANAGEMENT 9
sack can't hide an awl in a s.	SECRECY 17
S. the lot	ADMINISTRATION 11
this intolerable deal of s.	VALUE 24
sackcloth s. and ashes	MOURNING 6
sacks Empty s. will never stand	POVERTY 2
sacraments minister the S.	LANGUAGES 6
sacred facts are s.	JOURNALISM 16
sense of the s. without	RELIGION 29
wealth is a s. thing	WEALTH 28
sacrifice always s. herself	SELF-SACRIFICE 14
decked the heifers of s.	WEDDINGS 10
final s.	SELF-SACRIFICE 13
refused a lesser s.	SELF-SACRIFICE 15
s. of praise	PRAYER 4
s. one's own happiness	SELF-SACRIFICE 9
s. other people	SELF-SACRIFICE 10
s. themselves completely	SELF-SACRIFICE 19
s. to God of the devil's leavings	VIRTUE 26
supreme s.	SELF-SACRIFICE 2
Too long a s.	SUFFERING 29
sacrificed it can always be s.	MORALITY 16
sacrifices forgive him for the s.	MEN AND WOMEN 19
s. an hundred thousand lives	VIRTUE 30
s. it to your opinion	PARLIAMENT 17
sad best thing for being s.	EDUCATION 27
every animal is s.	SEX 3
remember and be s.	MEMORY 13
s. words of tongue or pen	CIRCUMSTANCE 28
songs are s.	IRELAND 14
What a s. old age	SPORTS 9
sadder s. and a wiser man	EXPERIENCE 22
weddings is s. than funerals	WEDDINGS 14
saddest s. thing I can imagine	WEALTH 38
saddle Things are in the s.	POSSESSIONS 20
saddled s. and bridled	DEMOCRACY 6
sadistic brutality and s. conduct	BIBLE 18
safe feeling s. with a person	FRIENDSHIP 4
only s. course for the defeated	WINNING 7
S. bind	CAUTION 21
s. for democracy	DEMOCRACY 16
s. than sorry	CAUTION 1
s. to go back in	DANGER 6
s. to use	SLEEP 20
tries to keep truth s.	PREJUDICE 18
We are none of us s.	CHANCE 29
world s. for diversity	SIMILARITY 27
safeguard s. of the West	TOWNS 15
safer s. for a prince	GOVERNMENT 13
s. than a known way	FAITH 14
s. to be in subordinate position	DUTY 10
safety flower of s.	DANGER 28
parent of s.	CAUTION 4
s., honour, and welfare	ARMED FORCES 21
s. in numbers	QUANTITIES 11
s. is in our speed	DANGER 33
sage Parsley, s., rosemary	COURTSHIP 1
sages s. and cranks	PHILOSOPHY 22
than all the s.	GOOD 31
Sagittarius I'm a S.	PARANORMAL 21
said all assume that Oscar s. it	WIT 19
been s. before	ORIGINALITY 6

can be s. at all	SPEECH 25
Everything has been s.	DISILLUSION 11
if you want anything s.	POLITICIANS 33
Nothing that can be s.	MOURNING 25
s. on both sides	PREJUDICE 9
s. our remarks before us	QUOTATIONS 5
s. *the thing which was not*	LIES 13
that's as well s.	SPEECH 17
What the soldier s.	GOSSIP 10
wish I had s. that	QUOTATIONS 11
Saigon S. is like all the other	TOWNS 32
sailing to which port one is s.	IGNORANCE 15
sailor cannot become a good s.	EFFORT 9
sailors s. and drunken men	DANGER 3
s. won't believe it	BELIEF 21
saint call me a s.	POVERTY 35
Devil a s. would be	GRATITUDE 1
every s. has a past	SIN 24
greater the s.	GOOD 1
s. in crape	RANK 8
Young s.	HUMAN NATURE 4
saints All S.' Day	FESTIVALS 5
Christ and His s. slept	WARS 4
Land of S.	IRELAND 5
sais *Que s.-je*	KNOWLEDGE 28
sake art for art's s.	ARTS 5
Art for art's s.	ARTS 9
for love's s.	LOVE 51
salad s. days	YOUTH 5
salary s. depends on not understanding	EMPLOYMENT 24
s. of the chief executive	BUSINESS 47
sales halve the s.	MATHS 26
salesman s. is got to dream	BUSINESS 37
saloon in the last chance s.	OPPORTUNITY 21
salt Attic s.	WIT 2
Help you to s.	MISFORTUNES 3
s. in our blood	SEA 24
s. of the earth	VIRTUE 11
s. rubbed into their wounds	SUFFERING 30
with a pinch of s.	BELIEF 10
salty Those who eat s. fish	DUTY 5
salus S. *populi*	LAW 17
salute If it moves, s. it	ARMED FORCES 5
salutes s. of cannon	FESTIVALS 66
see if anyone s.	ADVERTISING 9
salvation Our s. can only come	FARMING 12
Sam Play it again, S.	CINEMA 3
Samaritan good S.	CHARITY 8
remember the Good S.	CHARITY 25
Samarkand Golden Road to S.	KNOWLEDGE 48
Samarra appointment in S.	FATE 9
tonight in S.	FATE 22
same come back the s. day	TRAVEL 41
Ever the s.	CHANGE 12
I should be the s.	CONSTANCY 7
more they are the s.	CHANGE 42
one and the s.	SIMILARITY 15
read the s. book	BOOKS 3
s. in a hundred years	MISTAKES 19
sana *mens s. in corpore sano*	HEALTH 15
sanctity odour of s.	VIRTUE 9
sand built on s.	STRENGTH 12
plough the s.	FUTILITY 11
s. in the porridge	LEISURE 10
sands s. of time	BIOGRAPHY 6
s. upon the Red Sea shore	SCIENCE AND RELIG 5
sandwich s. from Marks	BUSINESS 51
sane remain s.	MATHS 24
s. if he didn't	MADNESS 14
San Francisco left my heart in S.	AMERICAN CITIES 60
sank Sighted sub, s. same	WORLD W II 17
They s. my boat	HEROES 18
sans s. peur et sans reproche	VIRTUE 12
S. teeth, sans eyes	OLD AGE 12
Santa Claus S. is a Democrat	POLITICAL PART 44
there is a S.	CHRISTMAS 12

S. is the most perfect | INSULTS 8
S. means consent | SILENCE 3
s. of these infinite spaces | UNIVERSE 7
Sorrow and s. | SUFFERING 21
sound of s. | SILENCE 14
told in s. | LIES 19
wonderful, deep s. | THEATRE 18
silenced you have s. him | CENSORSHIP 9
silencing s. mankind | OPINION 20
silent gradual and s. encroachments | LIBERTY 15
great ones are s. | SORROW 8
Laws are s. in time of war | WARFARE 13
mornings are strangely s. | POLLUTION 19
one must be s. | SPEECH 25
S., upon a peak | INVENTIONS 9
s. witnesses | PEACE 18
unlocked her s. throat | BIRDS 8
silently Slowly, s. | SKIES 21
silk make a s. purse | FUTILITY 7
s. makes the difference | WEALTH 21
s. or scarlet | CHARACTER 1
s. stockings | SEX 16
soft as s. | COURAGE 19
style, like sheer s. | STYLE 23
silkworms s. droop | WEATHER 35
silliest s. woman can manage | MEN AND WOMEN 14
silly Ask a s. question | FOOLS 1
damned s. thing in the Balkans | WORLD W I 7
s. at the right moment | FOOLS 12
s. like us | POETS 24
s. season | JOURNALISM 6
silver About a s. lining | OPTIMISM 34
born with a s. spoon | WEALTH 8
cloud has a s. lining | OPTIMISM 9
Georgian s. goes | ECONOMICS 19
in her s. shoon | SKIES 21
Just for a handful of s. | TRUST 31
palm with s. | FORESIGHT 6
pictures of s. | LANGUAGE 4
s. becks me | GREED 8
s. foot in his mouth | PRESIDENCY 20
s. in the mine | GENIUS 2
s. or small change | CHARACTER 36
s. plate on a coffin | APPEARANCE 19
S. State | AMERICAN CITIES 40
s. tongue | SPEECH 5
Speech is s. | SILENCE 4
thirty pieces of s. | TRUST 15
similia S. similibus | MEDICINE 4
simple as complicated and as s. | THEATRE 14
Everything is very s. in war | WARFARE 25
hard question is s. | PHILOSOPHY 20
rarely pure, and never s. | TRUTH 32
simplicities intense s. emerge | SIMILARITY 25
simplicity but holy s. | STYLE 7
simplify S., simplify | EXCESS 30
Simpsons less like the S. | FAMILY 31
sin brother s. against me | FORGIVENESS 12
by making a s. of it | LOVE 56
cardinal s. is dullness | CINEMA 22
doing nothing was a s. | IDLENESS 23
dreadful record of s. | COUNTRY AND TOWN 17
hate the s. | GOOD 21
He that is without s. | GUILT 7
learns not to fear s. | CRIME 36
no s. but ignorance | RELIGION 8
Nothing emboldens s. | SIN 14
not innocence but s. | IGNORANCE 21
one single venial s. | SIN 22
only one cardinal s. | PATIENCE 31
original s. | SIN 4
physicists have known s. | PHYSICAL 14
Satan rebuking s. | SIN 1
s. against the Holy Ghost | SIN 6
s. fell the angels | AMBITION 11
S. is behovely | OPTIMISM 18

S. On Bible | BIBLE 4
s. tends to be addictive | SIN 29
s. to steal a pin | HONESTY 5
s. towards our fellow | INDIFFERENCE 9
s. will destroy a sinner | CAUSES 21
s. will find you out | SIN 7
s. ye do by two | SIN 23
sort of s. now | SILENCE 15
then in secret s. | HYPOCRISY 14
to s. in secret | SIN 17
wages of s. is death | SIN 9
want of power to s. | FORGIVENESS 16
what did he say about s. | SIN 26
sincere Always be s. | HONESTY 17
hopeless are starkly s. | SYMPATHY 25
s. ignorance | IGNORANCE 28
sincerely s. from the author's soul | BOOKS 17
s. want to be rich | AMBITION 20
sincerest s. form of flattery | PRAISE 4
sincerity s. is a dangerous thing | HONESTY 13
sinews s. of love | MONEY 30
s. of war, unlimited money | WARFARE 14
Stiffen the s. | WARFARE 17
sing Elected Silence, s. | SILENCE 13
If you can talk, you can s. | ABILITY 3
I, too, s. America | RACE 14
Little birds that can s. | COOPERATION 11
mothers no longer s. | CHILD CARE 19
s. at dawn | SIMILARITY 21
s. before breakfast | EMOTIONS 2
s. for one's supper | WORK 18
s. the body electric | BODY 16
singe That it do s. yourself | ENEMIES 11
singeing s. of the King of Spain's Beard | WARS 5
singing all-s. all dancing | ABILITY 7
burst out s. | SINGING 12
exercise of s. | SINGING 2
s. army | ARMED FORCES 9
single draw you to her *with a s. hair* | WOMEN 24
married to a s. life | SINGLE 3
not s. spies | SORROW 11
s. life doth well | CLERGY 9
s. man in possession | SINGLE 6
S. women have a dreadful | SINGLE 8
sound of the s. hand | COOPERATION 24
with but a s. thought | LOVE 49
single-handedly perhaps be won s. | PEACE 30
singly never come s. | MISFORTUNES 8
sings fat lady s. | ENDING 2
s. each song twice | BIRDS 13
song my paddle s. | RIVERS 12
singularity S. is invariably a clue | CRIME 39
sink how our birthdays slowly s. | FESTIVALS 72
sinking s. middle class | CLASS 25
sinned I have s. exceedingly | SIN 12
people s. against | SIN 28
sinner every s. has a future | SIN 24
greater the s. | GOOD 1
Love the s. | GOOD 21
one sin will destroy a s. | CAUSES 21
sinners soft spot for s. | HEAVEN 23
sins All s. are attempts | SIN 27
Commit The oldest s. | SIN 13
multitude of s. | FORGIVENESS 1
multitude of s. | FORGIVENESS 13
seven deadly s. | SIN 5
s. be scarlet | FORGIVENESS 11
s. cast long shadows | PAST 2
s. of despair | SIN 30
s. of mankind | BOREDOM 8
s. of the fathers | CRIME 18
s. of the fathers | FAMILY 29
s. we have committed | TEMPTATION 15
who s. most | TEMPTATION 9
sir all S. Garnet | SATISFACTION 10
sisterhood S. is powerful | WOMEN 55

stronger (*cont.*)
s. than all the armies   IDEAS 2
s. than Necessity   NECESSITY 16
strongest s. man in the world   STRENGTH 22
struck Diogenes s. the father   CHILD CARE 5
s. regularly, like gongs   WOMEN 43
struggle cease to s.   SINGLE 10
gods themselves s.   FOOLS 22
Manhood a s.   LIFE 32
s. naught availeth   EFFORT 22
s. of man against power   POWER 37
tired of the s.   EFFORT 20
today the s.   PRESENT 12
struggles skip his spiritual s.   MUSICIANS 14
stubborn Facts are s.   HYPOTHESIS 2
students benefit of the s.   UNIVERSITIES 8
S. accept astonishing   LIFE SCI 32
studies S. serve for delight   EDUCATION 18
study I must s. politics and war   CULTURE 10
leisure, I will s.   EDUCATION 14
result of previous s.   BEHAVIOUR 25
S. as if you were to live   EDUCATION 15
s. is a weariness   BOOKS 4
stuff made of sterner s.   AMBITION 9
s. a mushroom   PRACTICALITY 16
stuffed s. owl   POETRY 4
s. their mouths   CORRUPTION 18
We are the s. men   FUTILITY 25
stumbled we s. on gold   INVENTIONS 18
stumbling-blocks church with s.   CHRISTIAN CH 8
stump beyond the black s.   AUSTRALIA 4
stupid *all* questions were s.   IGNORANCE 30
mouth shut and appear s.   FOOLS 26
pretend to be more s.   WOMEN 44
s. and industrious   ARMED FORCES 42
s. are cocksure   CERTAINTY 26
s. enough to want it   WEALTH 29
s. man is doing something   DUTY 20
s. neither forgive   FORGIVENESS 27
stupidity conscientious s.   IGNORANCE 28
s. the gods themselves   FOOLS 22
stupor S. Mundi   ROYALTY 14
Sturm S. und drang   ORDER 10
style doing things in s.   FOOTBALL 7
Old S.   TIME 14
only secret of s.   STYLE 16
see a natural s.   STYLE 10
S. is life   STYLE 15
s. is one's signature   STYLE 17
S. is the dress   STYLE 11
s. is the man   STYLE 1
s. is the man   STYLE 13
s., like sheer silk   STYLE 23
taste, and s.   MANNERS 28
sub Sighted s., sank same   WORLD W II 17
subdued nature is s.   CIRCUMSTANCE 24
s. to what one works in   CHANGE 18
subject grasp the s.   SPEECHES 7
My s. is War   WARFARE 37
no other s. which interests them   YOUTH 22
shocked by this s.   PHYSICAL 19
s. and a sovereign   ROYALTY 25
s. of conversation   CONVERSATION 10
s.'s duty is the king's   CONSCIENCE 12
uninteresting s.   KNOWLEDGE 46
We know a s. ourselves   KNOWLEDGE 34
subjunctive hope to use the s.   LANGUAGE 29
s. mood   LANGUAGE 21
sublime from the s.   SUCCESS 4
most s. noise   MUSICIANS 9
object all s.   CRIME 38
step above the s.   SUCCESS 32
s. to the ridiculous   SUCCESS 33
submerged s. tenth   POVERTY 12
subordinate safer to be in s. position   DUTY 10
subsistence S. only increases   LIFE SCI 12

substitute s. for reading it   BOOKS 23
subtle God is s.   GOD 29
subtlety s. of nature   NATURE 10
subtopias ditch between S.   COUNTRY AND TOWN 22
suburbia I come from s.   COUNTRY AND TOWN 26
suburbs walk through the s.   DAY 18
subversive funny is s.   HUMOUR 18
succeed how long it takes to s.   SUCCESS 29
How to s. in business   BUSINESS 38
I didn't s.   INTELLIGENCE 16
If at first you don't s.   DETERMINATION 6
If at first you don't s.   DETERMINATION 47
possible to s. without   SUCCESS 49
they're not going to s.   CLASS 30
succeeds Nothing s. like   SUCCESS 6
Nothing s. like excess   EXCESS 31
Whenever a friend s.   SUCCESS 48
success after your technical s.   TECHNOLOGY 14
rudiments of s. in life   HOUSEWORK 16
succeeds like s.   SUCCESS 6
s. comes before work   SUCCESS 7
s. depends on   SUCCESS 29
S. has many fathers   SUCCESS 11
S. in journalism   JOURNALISM 23
s. in life   SUCCESS 46
S. is a science   SUCCESS 36
s. is only a delayed   SUCCESS 47
S. is relative   SUCCESS 44
to command s.   SUCCESS 28
You cannot be a s.   BUSINESS 40
successful country be always s.   PATRIOTISM 17
s. is good   SUCCESS 51
successively hear the parts s.   CREATIVITY 5
suck s. melancholy   SINGING 3
sucked s. into the brain   TEACHING 22
sucker s. an even break   FOOLS 27
s. born every minute   FOOLS 25
sudden splendour of a s. thought   THINKING 15
suddenly s. became depraved   SIN 10
sue S. a beggar   FUTILITY 3
suffer better to s. wrong   TRUST 28
can tell what I s.   SYMPATHY 22
Can they s.   ANIMALS 18
endure to s.   PATIENCE 1
prepared to s.   IDEALISM 11
s. fools (gladly)   FOOLS 6
s. fools gladly   FOOLS 13
S. the little children   CHILDREN 5
sufferance s. is the badge   PATIENCE 26
suffered not determined by the penalty s.
s. and be healed   SELF-SACRIFICE 5
   DESPAIR 11
suffering About s. they were   SUFFERING 31
comes at the price of s.   SUFFERING 9
not a hopeless s.   HEAVEN 16
put we to s.   SELF-SACRIFICE 4
s. makes men petty   SUFFERING 28
Today somebody is s.   CHARITY 27
sufferings s. of my fellow-creatures   SYMPATHY 23
s. which thou art spared   SUFFERING 13
suffers inform us of what he s.   IMAGINATION 6
suffices God alone s.   PATIENCE 25
sufficient s. to finish it   FORESIGHT 9
s. to keep him straight   CONSCIENCE 19
S. unto the day   PRESENT 6
S. unto the day   WORRY 4
suffocated s. in its own wax   DEATH 76
suicide assisted s.   SUICIDE 1
longest s. note   POLITICAL PART 43
s. kills two people   SUICIDE 10
s. to avoid assassination   CENSORSHIP 14
thought of s.   SUICIDE 7
suit come in a pinstripe s.   STRENGTH 30
suites get to the s.   POLITICS 34
suits men in s.   ADMINISTRATION 2
omelette all over our s.   FOOLS 29

swallow (*cont.*)

One s. does not make	SEASONS 4
s. a camel	BELIEF 9
s. the cow	DETERMINATION 7
swallowed compromise with being s.	CHOICE 31
smelled, not s.	PRAISE 2
swamp to drain the s.	MANAGEMENT 18
swan silver s., who living	BIRDS 8
S. of Avon	WRITERS 5
swans s. of others are geese	SELF-ESTEEM 16
turn geese into s.	PRAISE 7
swarm s. in May	SEASONS 6
S. over, Death	POLLUTION 18
swear Don't s., boy.	SWEARING 12
S. not at all	SWEARING 4
when very angry, s.	ANGER 16
swearing s. is very much part	SPORTS 3
swears doesn't talk, it s.	MONEY 42
swear words abused his fellows with s.	SWEARING 11
S. are neutral	SWEARING 15
sweat In the s. of thy face	WORK 19
placed the s. of our brows	EXCELLENCE 9
spend our midday s.	WORK 25
s. but for promotion	EMPLOYMENT 9
s. of one's brow	WORK 14
tears and s.	SELF-SACRIFICE 16
sweep s. his own doorstep	SOCIETY 1
To s. the dust	PREPARATION 18
sweeps beats as it s.	HOUSEWORK 2
sweet buried in so s. a place	DEATH 53
By a s. tongue and kindness	BEHAVIOUR 2
come kiss me, s. and twenty	YOUTH 8
Little fish are s.	QUANTITIES 3
Revenge is s.	REVENGE 7
smells sharp and s.	FLOWERS 11
Stolen fruit is s.	TEMPTATION 2
Stolen waters are s.	TEMPTATION 3
such s. sorrow	MEETING 8
s., soft, plenty rhythm	JAZZ 2
sweeten Children s. labours	CHILDREN 10
s. this little hand	GUILT 9
sweeteners s. of tea	GOSSIP 19
sweeter s. the meat	QUANTITIES 7
sweetest s. wine	SIMILARITY 6
sweetness speak of its own s.	SELF-ESTEEM 5
s. and light	BEHAVIOUR 8
s. and light	PERFECTION 11
s. and light	VIRTUE 25
s. of nature	APPEARANCE 24
waste its s.	FAME 15
sweet peas s. on tiptoe	FLOWERS 6
sweets bag of boiled s.	PARLIAMENT 29
sucking s.	POETRY 30
swift race is not to the s.	SUCCESS 8
race is not to the s.	SUCCESS 22
Too s. for those who fear	TIME 41
swimming S. for his life	CRISES 16
swindles all truly great s.	DECEPTION 23
swine cast ye your pearls before s.	VALUE 22
geese and s.	FARMING 3
pearls before s.	FUTILITY 8
swing If it ain't got that s.	JAZZ 3
swinging s. sixties	PAST 16
swings s. and roundabouts	CIRCUMSTANCE 20
we pulls up on the s.	WINNING 18
What you lose on the s.	WINNING 3
swinish s. luxury of the rich	WEALTH 26
Swiss operated by the S.	TOWNS 31
Swithin Saint S.'s day	WEATHER 2
Switzerland S. as an inferior sort	COUNTRIES 16
S. is proud of this	COUNTRIES 27
S. they had brotherly love	CULTURE 23
swoop At one fell s.	MOURNING 10
at one fell s.	THOROUGHNESS 6
sword brave man with a s.	LOVE 58

draw one's s. against	WARFARE 7
edge of the s.	GOSSIP 15
I gave them a s.	GUILT 18
pen is mightier than the s.	WAYS 16
pen is mightier than the s.	WRITING 29
perish with the s.	VIOLENCE 5
s. against the prince	REVOLUTION 4
s. of Damocles	DANGER 24
s. of truth	JUSTICE 40
s. out of this stone	ROYALTY 19
swords s. into plowshares	PEACE 7
Two s. do not fit	SIMILARITY 11
swore My tongue s.	HYPOCRISY 8
s. terribly in Flanders	SWEARING 6
when the son s.	CHILD CARE 5
sworn only need to be s. at	SWEARING 9
swots various s., bulies	SCHOOLS 11
Sydney of S.	TOWNS 30
Satan made S.	TOWNS 22
syllable last s. of recorded time	TIME 28
syllables S. govern the world	LANGUAGE 7
symbolic s. expression	SCIENCE 10
symmetry fearful s.	ANIMALS 19
sympathetic s. wife	MARRIAGE 19
sympathy give or take s.	SYMPATHY 25
s. is cold	SYMPATHY 19
tea and s.	SYMPATHY 9
symphony s. must be like the world	MUSIC 16
symptoms hundred good s.	SICKNESS 8
syne auld land s.	PAST 10
auld lang s.	MEMORY 9
Syrens song the S. sang	KNOWLEDGE 30
system Ptolemaic s.	UNIVERSE 3
rocked the s.	ELECTIONS 19

t cross the t's	HYPOTHESIS 8
ta saying 'T.' to God	PAINTING 26
table etherized upon a t.	DAY 14
head of the t.	RANK 3
made you a bad t.	CRITICISM 10
tablet keep taking The T.	PREGNANCY 19
tablets Keep taking the t.	MEDICINE 3
tabula rasa tablet (a *t.*)	MIND 29
tactful t. in audacity	BEHAVIOUR 32
taffeta changeable t.	INDECISION 9
tail choke on the t.	DETERMINATION 7
likerous t.	SEX 10
shows his t.	AMBITION 2
such a little t. behind	ANIMALS 24
ties a kettle to a dog's t.	WRITERS 21
tiger by the t.	DANGER 16
twist the lion's t.	BRITAIN 5
tailors Nine t. make a man	DRESS 5
tails t. you lose	WINNING 2
take Give and t.	JUSTICE 5
no longer anything to t. away	PERFECTION 14
t. a thing	GIFTS 3
t. away everything you have	GOVERNMENT 37
T. away these baubles	PARLIAMENT 16
T. me to your leader	LEADERSHIP 6
T. what you want	DUTY 4
t. who have the power	POWER 23
taken Lord hath t. away	PATIENCE 23
t. more out of alcohol	ALCOHOL 31
taking t. the tablets	MEDICINE 3
tale bodies must tell the t.	COURAGE 28
Canterbury t.	FICTION 3
t. never loses	GOSSIP 8
t. of a tub	FICTION 6
t. told by an idiot	LIFE 22
t. which holdeth children	FICTION 9
thereby hangs a t.	MATURITY 4
traveller's t.	TRAVEL 16
talent t. at twenty-five	GENIUS 13
T. develops in quiet places	CHARACTER 35

sleeps in t.	CONSCIENCE 7	no enemy but t.	GUILT 13
steal someone's t.	STRENGTH 13	No t. like the present	OPPORTUNITY 9
they steal my t.	THEATRE 10	No t. like the present	PREPARATION 19
Thursday Maundy T.	FESTIVALS 37	now doth t. waste me	TIME 26
T.'s child has far to go	TRAVEL 6	Old T. is still a-flying	TRANSIENCE 8
thyme where the wild t. blows	FLOWERS 3	once upon a t.	PAST 14
thyself Know t.	SELF-KNOWLEDGE 1	peace for our t.	PEACE 20
Tiber T.! father T.	RIVERS 8	peace in our t.	PEACE 12
T. foaming with much blood	WARFARE 15	possession for all t.	HISTORY 9
Tiberius Had T. been a cat	CATS 8	pyramids must fear t.	ARCHITECTURE 24
ticket t. to ride	OPPORTUNITY 37	rapid flight of t.	LEISURE 12
tickle t. her with a hoe	AUSTRALIA 16	regret t. not spent	ACHIEVEMENT 31
tickled t. with a straw	CHILDREN 12	Remember that t. is money	TIME 35
tickling scornful t.	HUMOUR 5	sands of t.	BIOGRAPHY 6
tiddler Tom T.'s ground	WEALTH 14	sell t.	DEBT 20
tide rising t. lifts all	SUCCESS 9	shallow as T.	SILENCE 11
t. in the affairs	OPPORTUNITY 29	shipwreck of t.	PAST 21
Time and t.	OPPORTUNITY 17	spend more t. with one's family	POLITICIANS 6
tides queen of t.	SKIES 6	stitch in t.	CAUTION 23
tidings bringeth good t.	NEWS 7	take t. by the forelock	OPPORTUNITY 25
tiger imitate the action of the t.	WARFARE 17	That passed the t.	TIME 48
kid excites the t.	HUNTING 1	thief of t.	HASTE 9
lived one day as a t.	HEROES 1	third t. pays	DETERMINATION 16
murder a t.	HUNTING 14	t. and place	BEGINNING 21
ride a t.	DANGER 22	t. and place for everything	CIRCUMSTANCE 8
rides a t.	DANGER 4	t. and season	CIRCUMSTANCE 21
t. by the tail	DANGER 16	t. and the place	OPPORTUNITY 35
t. dies it leaves its skin	REPUTATION 13	T. and tide	OPPORTUNITY 17
t. in one's tank	STRENGTH 14	T. cools	EMOTIONS 23
t. in your tank	TRANSPORT 3	T. fears the Pyramids	TIME 3
T., Tyger	ANIMALS 19	t. flies	TIME 21
two days like a t.	HEROES 7	T. flies	TRANSIENCE 3
tigers reactionaries are paper t.	POLITICS 22	T. for a little something	COOKING 29
tamed and shabby t.	ANIMALS 26	t. for everything	TIME 6
t. of wrath	ANGER 12	t. grown old to destroy	TIME 24
Tiggers T. don't like honey	LIKES 16	t. has come	CONVERSATION 15
tile but white t.	UNIVERSITIES 22	t. has come	IDEAS 2
tiles t. on the roofs	DEFIANCE 11	t. has no conscience	IDLENESS 16
tilling T. and grazing	FRANCE 7	T. has no divisions	FESTIVALS 70
tilt t. at windmills	FUTILITY 13	t. has shaken me	OLD AGE 17
We do not t. on either side	INTERNAT REL 37	T. hath, my lord, a wallet	TIME 27
timber crooked t. of humanity	HUMAN RACE 21	t. immemorial	TIME 17
Knowledge and t.	KNOWLEDGE 3	T. is a great healer	TIME 7
time always a first t.	BEGINNING 11	T. is a great teacher	TIME 40
As t. goes by	KISSING 9	T. is money	MONEY 14
bid t. return	PAST 20	T. is on our side	FUTURE 18
bourne of t. and place	DEATH 60	t. is out of joint	CIRCUMSTANCE 23
broad wing of t.	FESTIVALS 62	t. is running out	GOD 33
cannot buy an inch of t.	TIME 2	T. is that wherein	OPPORTUNITY 27
Cathedral t. is five minutes	PUNCTUALITY 2	t. is the greatest innovator	CHANGE 31
child of T.	PERFECTION 6	T. is . . . time was	TIME 25
devote more t.	POLITICIANS 39	T. is Too slow	TIME 41
Even such is T.	TIME 29	T., like an ever-rolling stream	TIME 33
fewer reference points in t.	MEMORY 25	t.'s arrow	TIME 18
fill the t. available	HOUSEWORK 14	T.'s eunuch	CREATIVITY 9
fill the t. available	WORK 11	T. spent on any item	ADMINISTRATION 18
fill the t. available	WORK 39	T.'s wingèd chariot	TIME 31
find t. for exercise	HEALTH 12	T. the devourer	TIME 22
for all t.	WRITERS 7	t. to call it a day	ENDING 20
get me to the church on t.	WEDDINGS 13	t. to every purpose	TIME 20
good t. was had	PLEASURE 1	t. to learn the technology	INVENTIONS 20
half as old as T.	TOWNS 20	t. to make it shorter	LETTERS 9
have t. to think	SPEECH 18	t. to stand	LEISURE 8
having a good t.	HOSPITALITY 1	t. to weep	TIME 20
How t. flies	CONVERSATION 21	t. to win this game	SPORTS 6
It saves t.	MANNERS 17	T. will tell	TIME 8
It will last my t.	IDLENESS 18	T. works wonders	TIME 9
I was on t.	MEMORY 24	T., you old gypsy man	TIME 42
last syllable of recorded t.	TIME 28	use your t.	MARRIAGE 25
leave exactly on t.	PUNCTUALITY 16	waste of t.	THRIFT 17
matter of t.	MEDICINE 10	week is a long t.	POLITICS 28
may be some t.	SELF-SACRIFICE 11	whips and scorns of t.	SUICIDE 3
Men talk of killing t.	TIME 37	world enough, and t.	COURTSHIP 5
moment of t.	POSSESSIONS 15	**timeo** t. Danaos	TRUST 19
more than t. and space	WORRY 10	**times** bad t. just around	OPTIMISM 34
Never is a long t.	TIME 4	best of t.	CIRCUMSTANCE 29

tub every t. must stand	STRENGTH 2
tale of a t.	FICTION 6
tube toothpaste is out of the t.	SECRECY 34
Tudor T. monarchy plus telephones	PRESIDENCY 16
Tuesday If it's T.	TRAVEL 4
Shrove T.	FESTIVALS 53
tug comes the t. of war	SIMILARITY 12
then was the t. of war	SIMILARITY 19
tumour aspirin for a brain t.	CRIME 44
confronts the t.	SICKNESS 17
tumult t. and the shouting	HOSPITALITY 22
t. and the shouting	PRIDE 10
tune America is a t.	AMERICA 1
calls the t.	POWER 2
call the t.	POWER 14
dances to an ill t.	HOPE 2
dripping June sets all in t.	WEATHER 3
Go in, stay in, t. in	CRISES 2
incapable of a t.	SINGING 7
love's in t.	LOVE 15
many a good t.	OLD AGE 4
t. in	LIFESTYLES 34
t. the old cow died of	MUSIC 6
tunes all the best t.	SINGING 1
tunnel end of the t.	ADVERSITY 7
end of the t.	OPTIMISM 37
turbulent this t. priest	MURDER 10
turd rymyng is nat worth a t.	POETRY 7
turf blue ribbon of the t.	SPORTS 3
turkey cold t.	DRUGS 3
myrtle and t.	HAPPINESS 19
T., heresy, hops	INVENTIONS 1
turkeys kill all t.	FARMING 3
t. known to vote	SELF-INTEREST 34
t. voting for Christmas	SELF-INTEREST 17
turn One good t.	COOPERATION 13
T. about is fair play	JUSTICE 10
T. on	LIFESTYLES 34
t. over the sheet	ADMINISTRATION 7
t. the radio on	BROADCASTING 1
worm will t.	NECESSITY 4
turned anything t. up	OPTIMISM 23
turning lady's not for t.	DETERMINATION 50
lane that has no t.	PATIENCE 9
turns Times go by t.	CHANGE 30
turpentine strong smell of t. prevails	INSIGHT 12
T. State	AMERICAN CITIES 45
Tuscany even the ranks of T.	PRAISE 16
twang t., and you've got music	MUSIC 30
tweed Says T. to Till	RIVERS 2
twelfth glorious T.	FESTIVALS 22
T. Night	FESTIVALS 58
twelve t. days of Christmas	CHRISTMAS 3
t. good men	LAW 14
twenties roaring t.	PAST 15
twentieth t. century belongs	CANADA 10
twenty first t. years are the longest	YOUTH 14
t. years of age	MATURITY 7
twenty-first first war of the t. century	WARS 30
twenty-five talent at t.	GENIUS 13
twenty-twenty hindsight is always t.	PAST 41
twice He gives t.	GIFTS 4
must do t. as well	MEN AND WOMEN 26
never knocks t.	OPPORTUNITY 11
strikes the same place t.	CHANCE 9
t. into the same river	CHANGE 29
twig t. is bent	EDUCATION 1
twilight beautiful t.	LIES 24
Celtic t.	IRELAND 11
t. grey	DAY 8
t. is the crack	SUPERNATURAL 23
twinkle T., twinkle	SKIES 17
twist t. in the wind	CERTAINTY 8
t. slowly	HASTE 22
t. the lion's tail	BRITAIN 5
two do by t. and two	SIN 23

Every thing hath t. handles	REALITY 9
If t. ride on a horse	RANK 2
only t. people miserable	MARRIAGE 34
suicide kills t. people	SUICIDE 10
twice t. be not four	PRAYER 26
t. and two	ANIMALS 12
T. boys are half a boy	WORK 9
t. can play	PHILOSOPHY 17
t. cultures	ARTS AND SCI 2
t. for mirth	BIRDS 2
T. is company	FRIENDSHIP 6
t. is fun	CHILDREN 2
t. nations	POLITICS 9
T. nations	WEALTH 25
t. o'clock in the morning	COURAGE 24
t. plus two makes four	LIBERTY 30
t. that are in it	MARRIAGE 56
t. to make a bargain	COOPERATION 9
t. to make a quarrel	ARGUMENT 2
t. to tango	COOPERATION 4
We're number t.	EFFORT 10
twopence t. coloured	PAINTING 12
Tyburn damned T.-face	APPEARANCE 17
type people couldn't t.	COMPUTERS 21
typewriters banging on a million t.	COMPUTERS 17
strumming on t.	CHANCE 31
tyrannis *Sic semper t.*	REVENGE 18
tyranny better than t.	DEMOCRACY 1
conditions of t.	ACTION 30
dark night of t.	SPEECHES 19
Ecclesiastic t.	CLERGY 11
thousand years of t.	ORDER 2
T. is better organized	LIBERTY 23
worst sort of t.	LAW 24
tyrants all men would be t.	POWER 20
all men would be t. if they could	WOMAN'S ROLE 12
argument of t.	NECESSITY 23
barbarity of t.	IRELAND 9
between t. and slaves	RELATIONSHIPS 10
Excessive dealings with t.	INTERNAT REL 11
Rebellion to t.	REVOLUTION 7

ugliest u. place on earth	AUSTRALIA 28
ugly Bessie, you're u.	INSULTS 11
only his u. foot	INSIGHT 6
There are no u. women	BEAUTY 33
There is nothing u.	BEAUTY 23
u. duckling	YOUTH 6
u. mathematics	MATHS 20
UK U. is three small nations	BRITAIN 17
Ulster U. will fight	IRELAND 13
Ulsterman when an U. says	CERTAINTY 28
ultra ne plus u.	EXCELLENCE 7
umbrella unjust steals the just's u.	WEATHER 46
umpire Chaos u. sits	SPORTS 7
unacceptable u. face of capitalism	CAPITALISM 28
unaccustomed U. as I am	SPEECHES 1
unaffected Affecting to seem u.	BEHAVIOUR 2
unalike alike than we are u.	HUMAN RACE 33
unbecoming conduct u.	BEHAVIOUR 12
unbelief help thou mine u.	BELIEF 12
unbelieving core of u.	BELIEF 3
un-birthday u. present	GIFTS 19
unbowed bloody but u.	COURAGE 27
unbribed what the man will do u.	JOURNALISM 3
uncertain I lived u.	CERTAINTY 8
U., coy, and hard to please	WOMEN 30
u. glory of an April day	WEATHER 33
uncertainty set by the u. principle	SCIENCE 27
u. principle	PHYSICAL 9
uncle U. Tom Cobley	QUANTITIES 20
Uncle Sam nephew of my U.	AMERICA 27
unco u. guid	VIRTUE 13
unconquerable u. will	DEFIANCE 13
unconscious knowledge of the u.	DREAMS 13

unreliable death is u. — DEATH 79
unremembered little, nameless, u., acts — VIRTUE 33
unrequited what u. affection is — LOVE 50
unrewarded Nothing went u., but desert — THRIFT 15
unrighteousness Mammon of u. — WEALTH 10
unruly u. evil — SPEECH 10
  u. member — BODY 8
  u. sun — SKIES 13
unsatisfied leaves one u. — SMOKING 10
unsayable say the u. — WRITING 51
unsettled as far as they are u. — CUSTOM 16
unsorted all the u. stuff — SLEEP 19
unspeakable speak the u. — WRITING 51
  u. in full pursuit — HUNTING 13
untalented product of the u. — PAINTING 28
unthought can never be u. — THINKING 26
untrue u. in the House of Commons — TRUTH 43
  u. to his wife — INTELLIGENCE 19
untruth one wilful u. — SIN 22
unturned leave no stone u. — EFFORT 13
untutored u. savage — FAMILY 22
unusual cruel and u. punishment — CRIME 12
  cruel and u. punishment — CRIME 27
  moved by what is not u. — EMOTIONS 20
unwearable foolish and almost u. — DRESS 22
unwholesome soft is not u. — FOOD 17
unwilling group of the u. — ADMINISTRATION 1
unwritten Custom, that u. law — CUSTOM 13
unwrung our withers are u. — EMOTIONS 7
up to be u. betimes — SLEEP 9
  U. Guards and at them — WARS 11
  u. is where to grow — FLOWERS 12
  What goes u. — FATE 7
upas u. tree — TREES 5
upper To prove the u. classes — RANK 20
  u. station of low life — CLASS 12
  You may tempt the u. classes — CLASS 21
upper hand get the u. — HOSPITALITY 21
upright made man u. — INVENTIONS 4
  we walk u. — INTERNAT REL 37
upward Eternal Woman draws us u. — WOMEN 33
upwards car could go straight u. — SKIES 28
urban incomplete in the u. compound — TRANSPORT 22
  u., squat, and packed with guile — BRITISH TOWNS 37
urbe rus in u. — COUNTRY AND TOWN 8
urge Always the procreant u. — CREATIVITY 7
  u. for destruction — CREATIVITY 6
urine wine of Shiraz into u. — HUMAN RACE 29
urn u. or animated bust — DEATH 48
urs those dreadful u. — SPEECH 20
us he is u. — POLLUTION 21
use always find a u. for it — POSSESSIONS 3
  let u. be preferred — ARCHITECTURE 7
  main thing is to u. it well — MIND 9
  make proper u. of it — ARMED FORCES 1
  u. alone that sanctifies — PRACTICALITY 10
  u. of a new-born child — INVENTIONS 8
  we make u. of you — PRACTICALITY 7
used ain't what it u. to be — FUTURE 27
  just get u. to them — MATHS 22
  what they u. to be — PAST 33
  Would you buy a u. car — TRUST 5
useful holes which make it u. — VALUE 20
  know to be u. — POSSESSIONS 21
  what is apparently u. — VALUE 36
usefully lie u. — LIES 14
useless plans are u. — PREPARATION 24
  u. and irrational — CRIME 35
  u. and need not be preserved — CENSORSHIP 3
  u.; peacocks and lilies — BEAUTY 24
  U.! useless — FUTILITY 23
usual Business carried on as u. — CRISES 18
  u. suspects — CRIME 43
usury u. is contrary to Scripture — DEBT 20
utilities outvalues all the u. — FLOWERS 7
utility of the smallest possible u. — VALUE 33

utopia better than a principality in U. — VALUE 28
U-turn catchphrase, the U. — DETERMINATION 50

v spell it with a "V" or a "W" — WORDS 16
vacancies v. to be obtained — POLITICIANS 15
vacant V. heart — INDIFFERENCE 7
vacations no v. — SCHOOLS 6
vacuum Nature abhors a v. — NATURE 1
  out from behind the v. cleaner — WOMAN'S ROLE 31
  v. is a hell of a lot — NATURE 20
vae V. victis — WINNING 10
vague Don't be v. — CERTAINTY 2
vagueness v., my two bêtes noires — MATHS 15
vain In v. the net is spread — FUTILITY 2
vale ave atque v. — MEETING 6
Valentine St V.'s day — FESTIVALS 52
vales sweet are thy hills and v. — WALES 5
valet hero to his v. — FAMILIARITY 10
  hero to his v. — HEROES 5
  v. seemed a hero — HEROES 9
valiant become v. and martial — TAXES 6
  v. never taste of death — COURAGE 14
valley All in the v. of Death — WARS 14
  bicker down a v. — RIVERS 5
  great things from the v. — INSIGHT 14
  v. of the shadow — DANGER 26
Vallombrosa strew the brooks in V. — QUANTITIES 25
valorous childish v. — MATURITY 3
valour better part of v. — CAUTION 6
  much care and v. in this Welshman — WALES 4
  v. is certainly going — COURAGE 21
valuable most v. thing we have — TRUTH 33
value little v. of fortune — WEALTH 20
  nothing has v. — FUTILITY 24
  v. depends on what is there — MEANING 13
  v. of nothing — DISILLUSION 16
valued not merely tolerated but v. — MEN AND WOMEN 33
values not of facts but of v. — EDUCATION 26
  V. are tapes — MORALITY 24
  Victorian v. — VIRTUE 14
  Victorian v. — VIRTUE 49
valuing v. myself according to the job — EMPLOYMENT 30
vampires stand against the v. — SUPERNATURAL 24
vanitas v. vanitatum — DISILLUSION 4
vanities pomps and v. — TEMPTATION 4
vanity beauty without v. — ANIMALS 29
  MP feeds your v. — PARLIAMENT 31
  pomps and v. — SIN 15
  v. of human hopes — LIBRARIES 6
  v. of vanities — DISILLUSION 6
  V. of vanities — FUTILITY 16
vapours congregation of v. — POLLUTION 7
variety it admits v. — DEMOCRACY 21
  v. about the New England weather — WEATHER 44
  V. is the spice — CHANGE 16
  V.'s the very spice — CHANGE 36
variorum Life is all a v. — LIFESTYLES 21
various things being v. — SIMILARITY 26
varlet v.'s a varlet — CHARACTER 1
vase child is not a v. — CHILDREN 7
  Sèvres v. in the hands — POETS 26
  shatter the v. — MEMORY 14
vat doing your V. return — PRACTICALITY 17
vegetable v., and mineral — LIFE SCI 2
  v. fashion — ARTS 15
vegetarianism in favour of v. — ARGUMENT 20
veil beyond the v. — DEATH 13
vein giving v. — GIFTS 16
velvet gentleman in black v. — ANIMALS 10
venal v. city — CORRUPTION 7
vengeance gods forbade v. — REVENGE 19
  V. is mine — REVENGE 10
veni V., vidi, vici — SUCCESS 23
Venice V. is like eating an entire — TOWNS 27
  V. of the North — TOWNS 13

w. in beauty	BEAUTY 20
wall Chinese w.	BUSINESS 21
turn one's face to the w.	DEATH 21
w. next door catches fire	CRISES 12
w. of China was finished	WORK 37
Watch the w., my darling	CAUTION 33
weakest go to the w.	STRENGTH 8
writing on the w.	FUTURE 11
Wallace wi' W. bled	SCOTLAND 10
wallet w. at his back	TIME 27
walls God between four w.	CHRISTIAN CH 4
w. do not a prison	LIBERTY 9
W. have ears	SECRECY 15
w. nor in ships empty	ARMED FORCES 18
wooden w.	ARMED FORCES 17
wooden w. are the best	SEA 12
walnut woman, a dog, and a w. tree	WOMEN 7
walnuts W. and pears	GARDENS 10
Waltons more like the W.	FAMILY 31
waltz dance a second w.	CANADA 25
w. king	MUSICIANS 2
waltzing a-w., Matilda, with me	AUSTRALIA 19
wander people so love to w.	EXPLORATION 10
will not w. more	IDLENESS 17
wandered w. lonely as a cloud	FLOWERS 5
wandering w. minstrel I	SINGING 10
w. voice	BIRDS 10
want do what you w.	ABILITY 12
For w. of a nail	PREPARATION 6
freedom from w.	HUMAN RIGHTS 16
get what you w. in life	LIFE 51
gittin all you w.	CIRCUMSTANCE 31
give you everything you w.	GOVERNMENT 37
I w. some more	GREED 11
more you w.	GREED 1
something you probably won't w.	THRIFT 16
W. is only one of five	PROGRESS 19
w. of decency	MANNERS 11
What does a woman w.	WOMEN 46
what I really really w.	AMBITION 21
Whose finger do you w.	CHOICE 9
Wilful waste makes woeful w.	THRIFT 11
wanted no man is w. much	VALUE 29
wanting found w.	SUCCESS 19
wanton W. kittens make sober cats	YOUTH 2
wants Man w. but little	LIFE 26
process of satisfying w.	BUSINESS 41
supplying our w.	SATISFACTION 23
w. that thing done	JUSTICE 21
what he thinks the public w.	BROADCASTING 7
wanwood worlds of w.	SORROW 19
war After each w.	DEMOCRACY 20
another w. in Europe	WORLD W I 9
bloody w. and a sickly season	ARMED FORCES 2
Business is w.	BUSINESS 4
cold w.	INTERNAT REL 3
comes the tug of w.	SIMILARITY 12
Councils of w.	INDECISION 3
desolation of w.	PEACE 18
dogs of w.	WARFARE 6
do in the Great W.	ARMED FORCES 3
Don't mention the w.	INTERNAT REL 36
easier to make w.	PEACE 16
enable it to make w.	ECONOMICS 11
fair in love and w.	JUSTICE 1
first w. fought without	CENSORSHIP 21
first w. of the 21st century	WARS 30
fog of w.	WARFARE 8
I'll furnish the w.	JOURNALISM 11
I must study politics and w.	CULTURE 10
In w.: resolution	WARFARE 54
it is not w.	ARMED FORCES 31
I wage w.	WORLD W I 21
just w.	WARFARE 9
Laws are silent in time of w.	WARFARE 13
learn w. anymore	PEACE 7
looks on w. as all glory	WARFARE 31
love as of w.	MONEY 30
Make love not w.	LIFESTYLES 5
make w. that we may live in peace	WARFARE 12
Mankind must put an end to w.	WARFARE 56
moderation in w. is imbecility	WARFARE 27
must prepare for w.	PREPARATION 9
no discharge in the w.	ARMED FORCES 36
Once lead this people into w.	WARFARE 36
question of w. and peace	EUROPE 19
sinews of w., unlimited money	WARFARE 14
slip the dogs of w.	REVENGE 13
Sometime they'll give a w.	WARFARE 45
There never was a good w.	WARFARE 22
thinks of w.	CAUTION 27
too long without a w.	PEACE 21
W. always finds a way	WARFARE 47
w. creates order	PEACE 21
w. in which everyone	GENERATION GAP 14
W. is a necessary part	WARFARE 32
W. is hell, and all that	WARFARE 35
W. is the continuation of politics	WARFARE 26
W. is too serious a matter	WARFARE 40
w. like precocious giants	PEACE 24
W. makes good history	PEACE 15
w. minus the shooting	SPORTS 20
w. situation has developed	WINNING 21
w. to end wars	WORLD W I 6
W. to the knife	WARS 10
W. will cease when men refuse	WARFARE 3
w. without bloodshed	POLITICS 20
w., without its guilt	HUNTING 7
w. without its guilt	HUNTING 12
well out of the w.	PARLIAMENT 26
well that w. is so terrible	WARFARE 29
what a lovely w.	WORLD W I 27
wardrobe open your w.	DRESS 24
warehouse by a Dutchman, a w.	ARCHITECTURE 1
warfare mother of arts, of w.	FRANCE 5
warm lived in a w., sunny climate	WEATHER 52
man who's w.	SUFFERING 33
w. heart	BODY 1
warming w. his five wits	BIRDS 12
warms One kind word w.	SYMPATHY 5
warmth w. for the other	WEDDINGS 4
warn All a poet can do is w.	POETRY 25
right to w.	ROYALTY 38
warning come without w.	HOSPITALITY 16
Scarborough w.	SURPRISE 7
warring two nations w.	CANADA 8
warrior This is the happy w.	ARMED FORCES 39
Who is the happy W.	ARMED FORCES 26
wars at home while they fight w.	WOMEN 18
beginning of all w.	PEACE 23
came to an end all w.	WORLD W I 22
w. are merry	IRELAND 14
W. begin when you will	WARFARE 16
W. may be fought with weapons	ARMED FORCES 43
w. which everybody knew would never	WARFARE 58
war to end w.	WORLD W I 6
wartime In w. . . . truth is so precious	DECEPTION 25
warts w. and all	PAINTING 4
w., and everything	PAINTING 6
war-war better than to w.	DIPLOMACY 16
wary w. walking	DANGER 29
was what ne'er w.	PERFECTION 7
wash They that w. on Monday	HOUSEWORK 4
w. one's dirty linen	SECRECY 9
w. one's hands	DUTY 8
w. the river Rhine	POLLUTION 11
w. the wind	POLLUTION 17
washed w. his hands	GUILT 6
washed-up w. has-been	REPUTATION 5
washes Happiness w. away many things	HAPPINESS 28
One hand w.	COOPERATION 14
Persil w. whiter	HOUSEWORK 3

washing always another load of w.	CHILD CARE 21	Still w. run deep	CHARACTER 14
w. on the Siegfried Line	WORLD W II 9	Stolen w. are sweet	TEMPTATION 3
Washington W. could not lie	LIES 18	w. cannot quench	LOVE 21
W. is a city of	AMERICAN CITIES 62	w. of Babylon	SORROW 6
waste better to w. one's youth	YOUTH 19	w. of comfort	GOD 7
getting rid of w.	WRITING 12	**Watson** Elementary, my dear W.	INTELLIGENCE 1
Haste makes w.	HASTE 5	**wave** grasped w. functions	ARTS AND SCI 14
how to w. space	ARCHITECTURE 19	**waves** When the w. turn the minutes	CRISES 25
more w. than there should be	POLLUTION 23	**waving** not w. but drowning	SOLITUDE 21
now doth time w. me	TIME 26	**wax** clay grows hard and w. melts	SIMILARITY 17
terrible thing to w.	MIND 2	suffocated in its own w.	DEATH 76
w. it is to lose	MIND 27	**way** best w. out	DETERMINATION 41
W. of Blood	WARFARE 39	Great White W.	AMERICAN CITIES 22
w. of time	THRIFT 17	I did it my w.	LIFESTYLES 35
Wilful w. makes woeful want	THRIFT 11	I get my own w.	PATIENCE 32
wasted advertising is w.	ADVERTISING 10	I'm on the w.	IDEALISM 10
day most surely w.	HUMOUR 11	lion in the w.	DANGER 18
it was all w. effort	FUTILITY 31	Love will find a w.	LOVE 10
w. his time	BOOKS 24	man must have his w.	DETERMINATION 20
wasteful w., blundering	NATURE 15	moves in a mysterious w.	GOD 23
waste-paper file your w. basket	LIBRARIES 14	Prepare ye the w.	PREPARATION 11
watch as a w. in the night	TRANSIENCE 5	*so* in the w.	MEN 10
If you w. a game	SPORTS 22	there's a w.	DETERMINATION 19
learning, like your w.	EDUCATION 19	War always finds a w.	WARFARE 47
like a fat gold w.	PREGNANCY 13	w. I do it	STYLE 24
w. between me and thee	ABSENCE 9	w. of all flesh	DEATH 14
w. must have had a maker	GOD 24	w., the truth, and the life	CHRISTIAN CH 15
W. therefore	PREPARATION 17	w. the world ends	ENDING 18
W. the wall, my darling	CAUTION 33	w. to skin a cat	WAYS 21
W. this space	JOURNALISM 3	**ways** justify the w. of God	WRITING 17
watched w. pot never boils	PATIENCE 18	Let me count the w.	LOVE 52
watcher w. of the skies	INVENTIONS 9	parting of the w.	CRISES 17
watches looking at their w.	SPEECHES 20	w. of making you talk	POWER 9
w. of the night	DAY 3	**we** w. are because I am	RELATIONSHIPS 1
whose mind w. itself	INTELLIGENCE 20	W. the people	AMERICA 13
woman w. her body uneasily	BODY 25	**weak** concessions of the w.	STRENGTH 21
watchful w. waiting	INTERNAT REL 10	flesh is w.	TEMPTATION 8
watching BIG BROTHER IS W. YOU	GOVERNMENT 36	refuge of w. minds	IDLENESS 14
watchmaker *blind* w.	LIFE SCI 26	those too w. to seek it	MORALITY 25
water blackens the w.	ARGUMENT 11	w. always have to decide	CHARACTER 45
bread and w.	FOOD 8	w. are strong	STRENGTH 24
bridge over troubled w.	SYMPATHY 29	w. by time and fate	DETERMINATION 39
clear blue w.	POLITICAL PART 7	w. have one weapon	MISTAKES 26
Dirty w. will quench	SEX 2	w. in the head	BRITISH TOWNS 13
Earth and W.	SKIES 18	w. overcomes the strong	STRENGTH 17
Every two miles the w. changes	TRAVEL 2	W. shall perish	STRENGTH 26
fish out of w.	CIRCUMSTANCE 15	**weaker** w. sex, to piety more prone	WOMEN 22
fish that are still in the w.	OPTIMISM 5	w. vessel	MARRIAGE 17
go back in the w.	DANGER 6	**weakest** stronger than its w. link	COOPERATION 1
horse to the w.	DEFIANCE 4	w. go to the wall	STRENGTH 8
if I were under w.	DESPAIR 8	You are the w. link	STRENGTH 9
its element is w., falling water	WEATHER 53	**weakling** seven-stone w.	HEALTH 8
King over the W.	ROYALTY 9	**weakness** credulity is the man's w.	BELIEF 20
movement of w. embodied	CATS 14	**weal** common w.	GOVERNMENT 15
need of gardens for w.	EARTH 9	**wealth** get w. and place	WEALTH 22
never miss the w.	GRATITUDE 4	greater the w.	WEALTH 36
sound of w.	PAINTING 9	health and no w.	BRITISH TOWNS 10
thicker than w.	FAMILY 2	In squandering w.	THRIFT 15
thicker than w.	FAMILY 21	men to produce more w.	EMPLOYMENT 14
to cup w. in our hands	DETERMINATION 48	prevents the rule of w.	RANK 16
w. and a crust	LOVE 46	w. is a sacred thing	WEALTH 28
w. finds its own level	DESPAIR 17	**wealthy** business of the w. man	EMPLOYMENT 16
W. is life's *mater*	LIFE SCI 25	w., and wise	HEALTH 4
w. like Pilate	INDIFFERENCE 13	**weapon** art is not a w.	ARTS 29
w. that is past	OPPORTUNITY 8	most potent w.	STRENGTH 29
w. the ground	CLERGY 9	terrible w. of aggression	TRUTH 36
W., water, everywhere	SEA 14	Tory's secret w.	POLITICAL PART 37
When drinking w.	OLD AGE 7	weak have one w.	MISTAKES 26
Where w. flows	PATIENCE 21	w. against the enemy	PAINTING 20
written by drinkers of w.	ALCOHOL 10	w. with a worker at each end	WARFARE 1
Waterloo battle of W. *was* won	WARFARE 49	**weapons** books are w.	BOOKS 19
battle of W. was won	WARS 13	Wars may be fought with w.	ARMED FORCES 43
waters bread upon the w.	CHANCE 22	Wars may be fought with w.	WARFARE 42
bread upon the w.	FUTURE 8	**wear** Better to w. out	IDLENESS 2
Father Of W.	RIVERS 3	qualities as would w. well	MARRIAGE 29
in the great w.	SEA 9	w. motley	FOOLS 7

w. the green willow	MOURNING 7	W., all wonders	CHRISTMAS 7
w. the purple	ROYALTY 15	W. the coming	HOSPITALITY 13
what you are going to w.	DRESS 24	W. to your gory bed	SCOTLAND 10
weariest Even the w. river	RIVERS 10	**welcomest** w. when they are gone	HOSPITALITY 10
weariness w. of the flesh	BOOKS 4	**welfare** w. of this realm	ARMED FORCES 21
wearing w. o' the Green	IRELAND 8	**well** alive, but being w.	HEALTH 14
weary Age shall not w. them	ARMED FORCES 37	all shall be w.	OPTIMISM 18
Be the day w.	DAY 1	All's w.	ENDING 2
w., stale, flat	FUTILITY 18	Didn't she do w.	ACHIEVEMENT 1
weasel w. took the cork	ALCOHOL 26	foolish thing w. done	ACHIEVEMENT 19
w. under the cocktail cabinet	THEATRE 22	frog in a w. knows nothing	SELF-ESTEEM 3
w. words	LANGUAGE 2	Let w. alone	CAUTION 15
w. words	LANGUAGE 18	lies at the bottom of a w.	TRUTH 6
weather call this rain bad w.	WEATHER 53	lies in acting w.	EXCELLENCE 11
first talk is of the w.	WEATHER 36	not wisely but too w.	LOVE 33
flew through miserable w.	EXPLORATION 15	pitcher will go to the w.	EXCESS 10
known in bad w.	SEA 1	something will turn out w.	HOPE 22
no such thing as bad w.	WEATHER 19	speak w. of you	REPUTATION 21
no such thing as bad w.	WEATHER 32	that's as w. said	SPEECH 17
queen's w.	WEATHER 27	thing done w.	SELF-INTEREST 4
variety about the New England w.	WEATHER 44	till the w. runs dry	GRATITUDE 4
w. is like the government	WEATHER 45	W. begun	BEGINNING 12
weave tangled web we w.	DECEPTION 21	w. but not too wisely	HOSPITALITY 18
web O what a tangled w.	DECEPTION 21	Will, when looking w.	COURTSHIP 4
tangled w. do parents weave	CHILD CARE 11	worth doing w.	EFFORT 5
W. is a grassroots revolution	COMPUTERS 19	**well-bred** Conscience is w.	CONSCIENCE 15
webs laws are like spider's w.	LAW 16	**well dressed** sense of being w.	DRESS 10
Webster W. was much possessed	DEATH 64	w. in cheap shoes	DRESS 23
wed w. over the mixen	FAMILIARITY 2	**wells** drunk from w. you did not dig	PAST 8
wedded w. to the truth	POLITICIANS 25	**well-spent** rare as a w. one	BIOGRAPHY 7
wedding as she did her w. gown	MARRIAGE 29	**well-treated** stays where it is w.	BUSINESS 2
One w. brings another	WEDDINGS 2	**well-written** w. Life	BIOGRAPHY 7
three for a w.	BIRDS 2	**Welsh** compare the English with the W.	WALES 3
wedding cake face looks like a w.	APPEARANCE 29	thank the Lord I'm W.	WALES 11
weddings love to cry at w.	WEDDINGS 15	**Welshman** much care and valour in this W.	WALES 4
W., christenings, duels	FRANCE 16	**wen** great w.	BRITISH TOWNS 21
w. is sadder than funerals	WEDDINGS 14	**wenches** St Hilda's for w.	UNIVERSITIES 1
wedlock W. is a padlock	MARRIAGE 12	**wept** sat down and w.	SORROW 6
Wednesday Ash W.	FESTIVALS 4	young man who has not w.	GENERATION GAP 11
W.'s child	SORROW 2	**west** down in the w.	BRITISH TOWNS 34
wee w. folk	SUPERNATURAL 5	Go W., young man	AMERICA 20
w. pretendy government	SCOTLAND 19	Go W., young man	EXPLORATION 7
W., sleekit	FEAR 12	O wild W. Wind	WEATHER 40
weed evil w.	IGNORANCE 26	Queen of the W.	AMERICAN CITIES 39
ought law to w. it	REVENGE 14	safeguard of the W.	TOWNS 15
precious w.	SMOKING 5	w. is west	SIMILARITY 4
w. their own minds	MIND 13	W. Lothian question	PARLIAMENT 12
What is a w.	GARDENS 17	**western** All quiet on the w. front	WORLD W I 25
weeding seven year's w.	GARDENS 5	delivered by W. Union	CINEMA 19
weeds he must also love w.	GARDENS 5	**westerners** W. have aggressive	AFRICA 16
w. and tares	ORIGINALITY 9	**Westminster** change at W.	PARLIAMENT 34
w. and the wilderness	POLLUTION 12	**Westminster Abbey** peerage or W.	AMBITION 14
W. are not supposed to grow	GARDENS 21	**westward** w., look	OPTIMISM 24
w. grow apace	GOOD 4	**wet** out of these w. clothes	ALCOHOL 6
week die in my w.	SELF-INTEREST 32	set w.	GARDENS 9
Holy W.	FESTIVALS 26	w. and wildness	POLLUTION 12
My working w.	MOURNING 19	w. her feet	INDECISION 4
next w. in Japan	COUNTRIES 36	w. sheet and a flowing sea	SEA 16
others can in a w.	HOSPITALITY 19	**whacks** gave her mother forty w.	MURDER 4
w. after next	HASTE 17	**whale** point of view of the w.	CANADA 20
w. for preparation	SPEECHES 17	Save the w.	POLLUTION 2
w. is a long time	POLITICS 28	screw the w.	LANGUAGE 27
weep fear of having to w.	HUMOUR 10	**whaleship** w. was my Yale College	UNIVERSITIES 4
If you want me to w.	SYMPATHY 12	**what** great united w.	BEGINNING 21
stand at my grave and w.	MOURNING 18	It's not w. you know	CORRUPTION 4
w. and know why	SORROW 19	not w. you know	OPPORTUNITY 6
W., and you weep alone	SORROW 21	W. and Why	KNOWLEDGE 45
w. and you weep alone	SYMPATHY 3	w., when and why	CRICKET 14
w. as a woman	SUCCESS 25	w. you do	LIBERTY 38
women must w.	WORK 32	**wheel** butterfly on a w.	EXCESS 13
weepers losers w.	POSSESSIONS 1	butterfly upon a w.	FUTILITY 21
weeping w. and gnashing of teeth	HEAVEN 7	fly on the w.	SELF-ESTEEM 7
weigh more people see than w.	KNOWLEDGE 33	he created the w.	INVENTIONS 13
weighed w. in the balance	SUCCESS 19	invented the w.	INVENTIONS 19
weight w. of the backside	BROADCASTING 12	reinvent the w.	INVENTIONS 3
welcome Advice is seldom w.	ADVICE 13	w. has come full circle	CIRCUMSTANCE 10

my neighbour's w.	LIFESTYLES 20	gone with the w.	ABSENCE 7
Petrarch's w.	FAMILIARITY 19	gone with the w.	MEMORY 15
she is your w.	ADVERTISING 14	how the w. doth ramm	SEASONS 23
so as to suit his w.	MARRIAGE 32	It's an ill w.	OPTIMISM 13
sympathetic w.	MARRIAGE 19	Like a candle in the w.	TRANSIENCE 19
take a w.	GARDENS 4	like the w., that shifts	REPUTATION 22
untrue to his w.	INTELLIGENCE 19	North w. doth blow	WEATHER 10
when his w. talks Greek	WOMAN'S ROLE 13	no w. is favourable	IGNORANCE 15
w. and children	FAMILY 16	O wild West W.	WEATHER 40
w., and my name	DEBT 16	reed before the w.	STRENGTH 6
w. or servants	CENSORSHIP 16	slowly in the w.	HASTE 22
w. shall be as the fruitful vine	FAMILY 14	solidity to pure w.	POLITICS 24
world and his w.	FASHION 1	sown the w.	CAUSES 18
wild Caledonia! stern and w.	SCOTLAND 11	sow the w.	CAUSES 11
sow one's w. oats	LIFESTYLES 9	straw in the w.	FUTURE 10
W. Geese	IRELAND 6	twist in the w.	CERTAINTY 6
w.-goose chase	FUTILITY 15	Unhelped by any w.	WEATHER 38
wilderness crieth in the w.	PREPARATION 16	upset in a high w.	SLEEP 19
make a w.	PEACE 9	wait for the w.	PATIENCE 8
voice in the w.	FUTILITY 14	When the w. is in the east	WEATHER 21
weeds and the w.	POLLUTION 12	when the w. is southerly	MADNESS 5
w. of idea	LANGUAGE 17	Where the w. comes from	WEATHER 48
w. were paradise enow	SATISFACTION 31	wherever the w. takes me	LIBERTY 6
wiles Norfolk w.	BRITISH TOWNS 7	which way the w. blows	MEANING 2
wilful w. man must have his way	DETERMINATION 20	w. extinguishes candles	ABSENCE 11
W. waste makes woeful want	THRIFT 11	w. of change	AFRICA 10
will common w.	GOVERNMENT 15	Woord is but w.	WORDS AND DEEDS 11
complies against his w.	OPINION 1	**windbags** W. can be right	QUOTATIONS 18
complies against his w.	OPINION 15	**winding** by a w. stair	POWER 18
general w. rules	SOCIETY 8	**windmills** tilt at w.	FUTILITY 13
let my w. replace	DETERMINATION 27	**window** argument of the broken w.	ARGUMENT 22
not because we w.	MEMORY 12	der, w., a casement	TEACHING 14
political w.	GOVERNMENT 40	Good prose is like a w.-pane	WRITING 48
Where there's a w.	DETERMINATION 19	love flies out of the w.	POVERTY 8
w. not when he may	OPPORTUNITY 5	return through the w.	PREJUDICE 11
w. of even common man	SELF 3	w. of opportunity	OPPORTUNITY 26
w. of the majority	DEMOCRACY 9	w. of the soul	BODY 2
w. reigns	MATURITY 7	**window-panes** its back upon the w.	WEATHER 47
w. to carry on	LEADERSHIP 16	**windows** w. into men's souls	SECRECY 27
w. to Cupar	DETERMINATION 4	w. of the Church	CHRISTIAN CH 34
W. you, won't you	DANCE 10	**winds** to the four w.	ORDER 11
You w., Oscar	QUOTATIONS 11	to the w.	ORDER 11
William People's W.	POLITICIANS 5	w. of March	FLOWERS 4
Willie holy W.	HYPOCRISY 4	W. of the World	ENGLAND 16
willing Barkis is w.	PREPARATION 20	**Windsor** Widow at W.	ROYALTY 16
coalition of the w.	DIPLOMACY 3	**windy** W. City	AMERICAN CITIES 47
spirit indeed is w.	TEMPTATION 8	**wine** buy a bottle of w.	SEX 37
willingness w. to be deceived	BELIEF 30	days of w. and roses	TRANSIENCE 13
willow wear the green w.	MOURNING 7	jug of w.	SATISFACTION 31
willows w., old rotten planks	PAINTING 9	keep poets and w. at home	AUSTRALIA 22
wills w. the end	DETERMINATION 5	Not given to w.	CLERGY 7
wilt Do what thou w.	LIFESTYLES 29	old w. wholesomest	MATURITY 5
wimps Lunch is for w.	COOKING 34	Poetry is devil's w.	POETRY 6
win arguments you w.	ARGUMENT 3	sweetest w.	SIMILARITY 6
Heads I w.	WINNING 2	true w. of the bottle	CHRISTIAN CH 37
How to w. friends	SUCCESS 42	truth in w.	DRUNKENNESS 3
if only you w.	HASTE 19	Vodka is an aunt of w.	ALCOHOL 7
laugh that w.	SUCCESS 5	w., and song	PLEASURE 12
When in doubt, w. the trick	WINNING 12	w. and women	PLEASURE 19
w. and do the wrong thing	WINNING 28	w. for thy stomach's sake	ALCOHOL 11
w. and lose	EXPERIENCE 35	w. in old bottles	CHANGE 17
w. his spurs	EFFORT 16	w. in old bottles	CHANGE 25
w. one's laurels	SUCCESS 20	W. is a mocker	ALCOHOL 9
w. one's spurs	SUCCESS 21	W. is for drinking and enjoying	ALCOHOL 33
w. or lose it all	COURAGE 16	w. is in	DRUNKENNESS 4
w. unless you hate them	HATRED 13	W. maketh merry	MONEY 24
You cannot w.	PHYSICAL 1	W. may well be considered	ALCOHOL 17
You can't w. them all	WINNING 4	w. need no bush	ADVERTISING 16
You w. a few	SUCCESS 14	w. needs no bush	ADVERTISING 3
wind all weathers but a thaw w.	WEATHER 15	w. of Shiraz	HUMAN RACE 29
available with an east w.	ARGUMENT 19	w., women, and song	PLEASURE 9
blowin' in the w.	MATURITY 13	with w. dispense	DRUNKENNESS 6
blow, thou winter w.	GRATITUDE 7	**wing** broad w. of time	FESTIVALS 62
candle in the w.	RELATIONSHIPS 22	flapped its tinsel w.	DESPAIR 5
east w. made flesh	AMERICAN CITIES 50	flew on one w.	GIFTS 1
God tempers the w.	SYMPATHY 2	joy is ever on the w.	HAPPINESS 10

throw someone to the w.	SELF-INTEREST 20	institution for comfortable w.	FAMILY 20
turn on you like w.	POLITICIANS 38	keeping w. in a state of ignorance	WOMAN'S ROLE 14
woman ask a w.	POLITICIANS 33	labour of w. in the house	EMPLOYMENT 14
born of a w.	LIFE 25	managers of affairs of w.	WOMAN'S ROLE 6
cause Christ wasn't a w.	WOMAN'S ROLE 17	Monstrous Regiment of W.	WOMAN'S ROLE 7
'Cause I'm a w.	WOMEN 52	more interesting than w.	INTELLIGENCE 17
end to a w.'s liberty	WEDDINGS 8	Music and w.	PLEASURE 15
Eternal W. draws us upward	WOMEN 33	paradise of w.	ENGLAND 1
Every w. adores a Fascist	MEN AND WOMEN 25	plain w. on television	BROADCASTING 14
excellent thing in w.	SPEECH 13	Somerville for w.	UNIVERSITIES 1
flattering a w.	PRAISE 19	Tenors get w. by the score	SINGING 13
Frailty, thy name is w.	WOMEN 21	There are no ugly w.	BEAUTY 33
greatest glory of a w.	WOMEN 17	Votes for w.	WOMAN'S ROLE 3
if you educate a w.	EDUCATION 30	whisky and wild, wild w.	LIFESTYLES 41
inconstant w.	CONSTANCY 9	wine and w.	PLEASURE 19
just like a w.	WOMEN 54	w. always think	GUILT 20
like a w. scorned	WOMEN 4	W. and children first	DANGER 12
not born a w.	WOMEN 48	w., and song	PLEASURE 9
One hair of a w.	STRENGTH 20	w. are not so young	APPEARANCE 23
play without a w. in it	THEATRE 5	W. are people who shop	BUYING 14
Prudence is the other w.	THRIFT 21	w. become like their mothers	MEN AND WOMEN 15
She is a w.	COURTSHIP 3	w. come to see the show	FASHION 5
she shall be called W.	WOMEN 15	w. have fewer teeth	HYPOTHESIS 24
Silence is a w.'s best garment	WOMAN'S ROLE 2	W. hold up half the sky	WOMEN 9
so hard Upon the w.	WOMEN 34	w., Italian	LANGUAGES 5
weak and feeble w.	ROYALTY 21	w. love children	RELATIONSHIPS 25
weep as a w.	SUCCESS 25	w. must weep	WORK 32
What does a w. want	WOMEN 46	w. or linen	APPEARANCE 9
whistling w. and a crowing hen	WOMEN 6	w. you will wow	QUOTATIONS 16
Who can find a virtuous w.	WOMEN 16	**won** game is never lost till w.	WINNING 13
wicked folly of 'W.'s Rights'	WOMAN'S ROLE 21	I w. the count	ELECTIONS 16
with a brawling w.	ARGUMENT 9	Let him who has w. it	ACHIEVEMENT 4
w., a dog, and a walnut tree	WOMEN 7	not to have w. but to have fought well	WINNING 17
w. a man	PARLIAMENT 13	therefore may be w.	COURTSHIP 3
w. and a ship ever want mending	WOMEN 8	they are w. by men	WARFARE 42
w. be more like a man	MEN AND WOMEN 24	Things w. are done	EFFORT 17
w. can hardly ever choose	CHOICE 19	we'd have w. the war	CINEMA 10
w. have long hair	BODY 10	w. or lost	SPORTS 16
w. is a sometime thing	WOMEN 45	**wonder** boneless w.	BODY 4
w. is his game	MEN AND WOMEN 9	boneless w.	POLITICIANS 27
w. is like a teabag	ADVERSITY 23	eighth w. of the world	EXCELLENCE 6
W. is the nigger of the world	WOMAN'S ROLE 26	nine days' w.	FAME 6
w. makes the statement	DRESS 25	shoreline of w.	KNOWLEDGE 5
w. must have money	WRITING 37	w. who's kissing her	KISSING 8
w. must submit	OPINION 19	**wonderful** more w. than man	HUMAN RACE 10
w. of Africa	AFRICA 15	most w. wonderful	SURPRISE 8
w. scorned	REVENGE 16	Nothing is too w.	HYPOTHESIS 13
w.'s desire	MEN AND WOMEN 8	w. things	INVENTIONS 14
w. seldom writes	LETTERS 10	**wonderfully** w. made	BODY 9
w.'s finest ornament	SILENCE 6	**wonders** all w. in one sight	CHRISTMAS 7
w.'s place is in the home	WOMAN'S ROLE 4	His w. to perform	GOD 23
w.'s preaching is like	WOMAN'S ROLE 11	Seven W. of the World	ARCHITECTURE 5
w.'s reason	LOGIC 7	signs and w.	BELIEF 13
w.'s whole existence	MEN AND WOMEN 7	Time works w.	TIME 9
w.'s workhouse	HOME 21	w. in the deep	SEA 9
w.'s work is never done	HOUSEWORK 5	w. we seek without us	HUMAN RACE 15
w. the happiness he gives	PLEASURE 17	W. will never cease	SURPRISE 4
w., the universal mother	WOMEN 40	**won't** administrative w.	GOVERNMENT 40
w. to define her feelings	LANGUAGE 14	**wood** babes in the w.	EXPERIENCE 15
w. wakes to love	MEN AND WOMEN 11	don't drag w. about	INTELLIGENCE 16
w. watches her body uneasily	BODY 25	In every w., in every spring	TREES 20
w. will always sacrifice	SELF-SACRIFICE 14	lath of w.	STRENGTH 23
w., wine, and song	PLEASURE 12	out of the w.	OPTIMISM 7
w. without a man	MEN AND WOMEN 31	wolf out of the w.	NECESSITY 5
w. yet think him an angel	MEN AND WOMEN 10	**woodbine** canopied with luscious w.	FLOWERS 3
wrong about hitting a w.	VIOLENCE 14	**wooden** Within this w. O	THEATRE 6
womb dark w. where I began	PREGNANCY 8	w. nutmeg	DECEPTION 12
wombs think just with our w.	WOMAN'S ROLE 27	w. walls	ARMED FORCES 17
women all the w. MPs	PARLIAMENT 33	w. walls are the best	SEA 12
all w. are born slaves	WOMAN'S ROLE 10	**woodman** w., spare the beechen tree	TREES 12
cherries, hops, and w.	BRITISH TOWNS 31	**woods** fresh w.	CHANGE 32
come to terms with w.	CHRISTIAN CH 40	in the pathless w.	NATURE 12
company of w.	MEN AND WOMEN 18	w. against the world	TREES 19
Few w., I fear	MIDDLE AGE 8	w. have ears	SECRECY 3
Half the sorrows of w.	SPEECH 23	**woodshed** something nasty in the w.	SECRECY 23
if all the w. were wise	FICTION 23	**wooed** therefore may be w.	COURTSHIP 3